Wolters Kluwer

Connect Online!

For your convenience, earn CPE credit and stay on top of **Federal Tax Issues** online.

Go to **CCHGroup.com/PrintCPE** for your digital CPE course in PDF format.

CCHGroup.com/PrintCPE

7

ook to

CALIFORNIA
TAXES

Includes Personal

Income Tax Return

Preparation Guide

Christopher A. Whitney

Contributing Editor

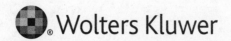 Wolters Kluwer

Wolters Kluwer Editorial Staff Publication

Editors . . . . Carol Kokinis-Graves, Carolyn Kwock, Rocky Mengle, Glenn Wesley

Production Coordinator . . . . Govardhan. L

Production . . . . Chandrasekhar T

This publication is designed to provide accurate and authoritative information in regard to the subject matter covered. It is sold with the understanding that the publisher is not engaged in rendering legal, accounting, or other professional service and that the authors are not offering such advice in this publication. If legal advice or other expert assistance is required, the services of a competent professional person should be sought.

ISBN 978-0-8080-4385-0

Printed in the United States of America

MIX
From responsible
sources
FSC® C099992

PREFACE

This *Guidebook* gives a general picture of the taxes imposed by the state of California and the general property tax levied by the local governments. All 2016 legislative amendments received as of press time are reflected, and references to California and federal laws are to the laws as of the date of publication of this book.

The emphasis is on the law applicable to the filing of income tax returns in 2017 for the 2016 tax year. However, if legislation has made changes effective after 2016, we have tried to note this also, with an indication of the effective date to avoid confusion.

The taxes of major interest—income and sales and use—are discussed in detail. Other California taxes, including estate taxes, are summarized, with particular emphasis on application, exemptions, returns, and payment.

Throughout the *Guidebook*, tax tips are highlighted to help practitioners avoid pitfalls and use the tax laws to their best advantage.

The *Guidebook* is designed as a quick reference work, describing the general provisions of the various tax laws, regulations, and administrative practices. It is useful to tax practitioners, business persons, and others who prepare or file California returns or who are required to deal with California taxes.

The *Guidebook* is not designed to eliminate the necessity of referring to the law and regulations for answers to complicated problems, nor is it intended to take the place of detailed reference works such as the CCH CALIFORNIA TAX REPORTS. With this in mind, specific references to the publisher's California tax product are inserted in most paragraphs. By assuming some knowledge of federal taxes, the *Guidebook* is able to provide a concise, readable treatment of California taxes that will supply a complete answer to most questions and will serve as a time-saving aid where it does not provide the complete answer.

With the 1987 edition, Mr. Russell S. Bock relinquished his role as primary author of the *Guidebook to California Taxes*, but continued in close association as a valued consultant for over 15 years thereafter.

In this edition, the *Guidebook* includes materials from Contributing Editor: Chris Whitney. Chris Whitney is a well-known practitioner who provides practitioner comments throughout the book providing key insights into complex and controversial areas of tax law.

SCOPE OF THE BOOK

This *Guidebook* is designed to do four things:

1. Provide a quick step-by-step guide to the preparation of individual resident, nonresident, and part-year resident income tax returns.

2. Give a general picture of the impact and pattern of all taxes levied by the state of California and the general property tax levied by local governmental units.

3. Provide a readable quick-reference work for the personal income tax and the tax on corporate income. As such, it explains briefly what the California law provides and indicates whether the California provision is the same as federal law.

4. Analyze and explain the differences, in most cases, between California and federal law.

HOW TO USE THE BOOK

1. If you know the section number of the comparable federal law on the point in which you are interested, consult the Federal-California Cross-Reference Table and Index at the beginning of the portion of the book devoted to the tax involved.

2. If you know the section number of the California law, consult the California-Federal Cross-Reference Table and Index.

HOW TO USE THE RETURN PREPARATION GUIDE

1. Information can easily be found by consulting the Table of Contents to the *Guidebook* for residents' returns at page 45, or for nonresidents' and part-year residents' returns at page 65.

2. Explanations relating to specific lines on the residents' return can be found by consulting the cross-reference chart at page 46.

HIGHLIGHTS OF 2016 CALIFORNIA TAX CHANGES

The most important 2016 California tax changes received by press time are noted in the "Highlights of 2016 California Tax Changes" section of the *Guidebook*, beginning on page 11. This useful reference gives the practitioner up-to-the-minute information on changes in tax legislation.

FINDERS

The practitioner may find the information wanted by consulting the general Table of Contents at the beginning of the *Guidebook*, the Table of Contents at the beginning of each chapter, the Topical Index, the Table of Cases Cited, the Table of Franchise Tax Board Legal Rulings, or the Summary of Principal Items of 2016 Legislation.

The Topical Index is a useful tool. Specific taxes and information on rates, allocations, credits, exemptions, returns, payments, collection, penalties, and remedies are thoroughly indexed and cross-referenced to paragraph numbers in the *Guidebook*.

November 2016

ABOUT THE EDITOR

Christopher A. Whitney

Christopher A. Whitney is a partner with PricewaterhouseCoopers LLP, based in Los Angeles, California. Mr. Whitney specializes in state and local tax, with a particular emphasis on California tax matters. Key areas of his practice include combined reporting and California water's edge issues as well as state tax implications of mergers and acquisitions. Mr. Whitney is a frequent speaker at local and national tax conferences, is an instructor at the Center for State and Local Taxation's Annual Summer Institute at the University of California Davis, and has authored several articles on a variety of state and local taxation issues. He is also an Author for the CCH Expert Treatise Library: State Taxation of Income and Other Business Taxes and an Editorial Consultant for CCH Incorporated's California Tax Analysis: Corporation Tax publication.

CONTENTS

HIGHLIGHTS OF 2016 CALIFORNIA TAX CHANGES

Highlights of the 2016 California tax changes are noted below.

Multiple Taxes

• *Partnership and C corporation return due dates*

Applicable to returns for taxable years beginning on or after January 1, 2016, the California partnership return and C corporation tax return due dates are modified to be similar to federal law. See ¶622, ¶625, ¶810. (Ch. 348 (A.B. 1775), Laws 2016)

• *California Competes credit online reporting requirements and criteria for written agreements*

Effective January 1, 2017, the online reporting requirements for the Governor's Office of Business and Economic Development (GO-Biz) with regarding to the "California Competes" credit against corporation franchise and income taxes and personal income taxes are expanded. In addition, additional factors are added for GO-Biz when it determines whether to enter into a written agreement with a taxpayer eligible for the credit. See ¶134, ¶818. (Ch. 31 (S.B. 836), Laws 2016; Ch. 582 (A.B. 2900), Laws 2016)

• *New donated fruits and vegetables credit*

For taxable years beginning on or after January 1, 2017, and before January 1, 2022, a new corporation franchise and income and personal income tax credit is allowed to qualified taxpayers who donate fresh fruits or vegetables to a food bank in California. See ¶141, ¶818. (Ch. 32 (S.B. 837), Laws 2016)

• *Low-income housing credit*

Provisions that allow a low-income housing credit for corporation franchise and income, personal income, and insurance gross premiums tax purposes are modified to continue to allow allocations of the credit among partners based upon the partnership agreement, and to allow elections to sell all or any portion of the credit. See ¶138, ¶818, ¶1902. (Ch. 32 (S.B. 837), Laws 2016)

• *Discriminatory practices by a club*

Effective January 1, 2017, the list of discriminatory practices that can result in the denial of a club's business expense deduction is expanded for California corporation franchise and income and personal income tax purposes. See ¶336. (Ch. 870 (S.B. 1442), Laws 2016)

• *Managed care organization provider tax*

For fiscal years 2016-17, 2017-18, and 2018-19, a new California managed care organization provider tax is imposed on licensed health care service plans, managed care plans contracted with the Department of Health Care Services to provide Medi-Cal services, and Alternate Health care Service Plans (AHCSPs), except for specifically excluded plans. Qualified health care service plan income that is accrued with respect to enrollment or services that occur on or after July 1, 2016, and on or before June 30, 2019, by a health care service plan that is subject to the managed care organization provider tax is excluded from gross income for California corporation franchise and income tax purposes. Also, a qualified health care service plan with no income other than qualified health care service plan income that is excluded from gross income pursuant to this provision will be exempt from the $800 minimum franchise tax. See ¶816, ¶929, ¶1902. (Ch. 2 (S.B. 2), Laws 2016, Second Extraordinary Session)

• *Electronic withholding returns, reports, and payments*

Beginning January 1, 2017, for employers with 10 or more employees, and January 1, 2018, for all employers, an employer must file all income tax withholding returns and reports electronically and remit all payments of withheld income taxes to the Employment Development Department (EDD) by electronic funds transfer (EFT). See ¶715. (Ch. 222 (A.B. 1245), Laws 2015)

Personal Income Taxes

• *Earned income credit for large families revised*

The earned income tax credit (EITC) percentage is permanently set at 45% for eligible individuals with three or more qualifying children. This change is consistent with recent federal tax law changes and applies to taxable years beginning on or after January 1, 2016. Ch. 722 (S.B. 1073), Laws 2016, effective January 1, 2017. See ¶158. (Ch. 722 (S.B. 1073), Laws 2016)

Corporation Franchise and Income Taxes

• *Gillette litigation concludes; FTB issues post-Gillette guidance*

The California Supreme Court reversed an earlier appellate court decision and held that multistate corporate taxpayers may no longer elect to use the Multistate Tax Compact's equally-weighted three-factor formula to apportion net income for California corporation franchise and income tax purposes. Instead, taxpayers must use the apportionment formula required under California law (i.e., a double-weighted sales factor formula for tax years beginning before 2013, or a single-sales factor formula for tax years beginning after 2012). The U.S. Supreme Court later denied a petition to review the California Supreme Court's decision, which ended the litigation. The Franchise Tax Board (FTB) has issued a notice on its intended courses of action on cases involving the Compact election issue following the U.S. Supreme Court's denial of review of the decision. See ¶1301. (*The Gillette Co. v. Franchise Tax Board*, California Supreme Court, S206587, December 31, 2015; U.S. Supreme Court, Dkt. 15-1442, petition for certiorari denied October 11, 2016; *FTB Notice 2016-03*, California Franchise Tax Board, November 1, 2016)

• *Summary judgment granted for FTB in challenge to combined reporting requirement*

On remand from a California court of appeal's decision, a California superior court granted the California Franchise Tax Board's motion for summary judgment on the issue of whether the state's differential treatment of intrastate and interstate unitary businesses for California corporation franchise and income tax purposes discriminated against interstate commerce in violation of the Commerce Clause. Summary judgment was proper on the issue of whether there was discriminatory differential treatment and whether such treatment passed strict scrutiny. See ¶1310. (*Harley-Davidson, Inc. & Subsidiaries v. California Franchise Tax Board*, Superior Court of California, County of San Diego, No. 37-2011-001008-CU-MC-CTL, October 31, 2016)

• *Filing extension period reduced*

For taxable years beginning on or after January 1, 2016, the automatic filing extension period allowed for corporations and exempt organizations is reduced from seven months to six months. See ¶810, ¶811. (*FTB Notice 2016-04*, California Franchise Tax Board, November 4, 2016)

• *Market-based sourcing rules amended*

Regulations concerning market-based sourcing for sales other than sales of tangible personal property are amended to address marketable securities, asset management fees, dividends, goodwill, and interest. The amended regulations also instruct multistate taxpayers on how to assign sales of intangible personal property based on the location of the taxpayer's market. The amendments are generally applicable for taxable years beginning on or after January 1, 2015; however, any taxpayer may elect to have the amendments apply retroactively to taxable years beginning on or after January 1, 2012, if those taxable years are open to adjustment under applicable statutes of limitation. See ¶1309. (Reg. 25136-2, 18 CCR)

- *Water's-edge elections and expanded nexus thresholds*

The FTB addressed the treatment of a water's-edge election when the addition of factor-based nexus standards results in a unitary foreign affiliate becoming subject to tax in California. See ¶1311. (*FTB Notice 2016-02*, California Franchise Tax Board, September 9, 2016)

- *Advanced strategic aircraft credit operative dates adjusted*

So that taxpayers can claim the advanced strategic aircraft credit for the entire 15 years of the project, the credit's specific operative date is changed from taxable years beginning on or after January 1, 2015, and before January 1, 2030, to taxable years beginning on or after January 1, 2016, and before January 1, 2031. See ¶818. (Ch. 31 (S.B. 836), Laws 2016)

Sales and Use Taxes

- *Rate drop in 2017*

Effective January 1, 2017, the 0.25% increase in the statewide sales and use tax rate approved by voters in 2012 and made effective January 1, 2013, will expire, and the general statewide rate will drop from 7.5% to 7.25%. See ¶1503. (*BOE Publication 542, News for Tax Practitioners*, California State Board of Equalization, September 2016)

- *California Supreme Court declines to review Lucent decision*

See ¶1504. (*Lucent Technologies, Inc. v. State Board of Equalization*, Court of Appeal of California, Second District, No. B257808, October 8, 2015; petition for review denied, California Supreme Court, No. S230657, January 20, 2016)

- *Lessee was liable for transient occupancy tax as motel operator*

The California Court of Appeal held that a lessee and operator of a motel was liable for California local transient occupancy taxes (TOT) since he was not denied the procedural due process right to notice and opportunity to be heard at the administrative level to contest the owner's appeal hearing regarding whether he was a lessee or property manager. See ¶1504. (*City of Los Angeles v. Ahir*, Court of Appeal of California, Second District, No. B259818, September 15, 2016)

Property Taxes

- *New construction in progress decision supersedes handbook provisions*

The California State Board of Equalization (BOE) has advised taxpayers that part of the Assessors' Handbook is superseded by a 2016 appellate court decision concerning base year value determination for construction in progress. The court found, in part, that each lien date value of construction work in progress is a base year value; thus, a new base year value is established every lien date during construction. The state supreme court has declined to hear an appeal of the decision.

The decision superseded guidance in the Assessors' Handbook Section 502, Advanced Appraisal, which states that partially completed new construction does not acquire a base year value. Rather, new construction in progress is assessed as a separate appraisal unit at its market value as of that date. The handbook also notes that, upon completion, the entire portion of the property that is newly constructed is reappraised at its market value and acquires its own base year value.

According to the BOE, the decision clarifies four principles in the valuation and appeal of new construction in progress:

(1) the value of construction in progress on the lien date is a base year value;

(2) construction in progress must be appraised at its full value each lien date until construction is complete;

(3) appeals of an assessor's valuation of construction in progress are appeals of base year value, and taxpayers may file appeals in the year of the assessment or in any of the three succeeding years; and

(4) a taxpayer who successfully appeals a base year value on construction in progress is entitled to a refund of taxes only if the appeal was filed in the same year the base year value was established and only for the year in which that base year value was established.

See ¶1707. (*Ellis v. County of Calaveras, Court of Appeal of California*, Third District, C078705, February 25, 2016; *Letter to County Assessors, No. 2016/042*, California State Board of Equalization, October 26, 2016)

• *Disabled "veteran" redefined for exemption purposes*

For purposes of the California property tax homestead exemption for disabled veterans, the term "veteran" has been redefined to include a person who has been discharged in other than dishonorable conditions from service under certain conditions and is eligible for federal veterans' health and medical benefits. Formerly, the definition was taken from a constitutional provision that specified a discharge from service "under honorable conditions." This amendment applies for property tax lien dates for the 2017-2018 fiscal year and thereafter.

Under a new provision, corrections to the roll that relate to the disabled veterans' exemption may be made within eight years after the making of the assessment being corrected. Another new provision specifies that any taxes paid before or after delinquency may be refunded within eight years after the date of payment if the amount paid exceeds the amount due on the property as a result of corrections to the roll that relate to the exemption. A current provision that allows for a refund within eight years for taxes relating to the disabled veterans' exemption is amended to allow a refund within the later of the eight years or 60 days after a certain notice. See ¶1704. (Ch. 871 (S.B. 1458), Laws 2016, effective September 30, 2016)

• *Counties allowing intercounty base year value transfers identified*

Eleven California counties have property tax ordinances implementing the intercounty base year value transfer provisions for persons who are at least age 55 or are severely and permanently disabled. The counties are Alameda, El Dorado, Los Angeles, Orange, Riverside, San Bernardino, San Diego, San Mateo, Santa Clara, Tuolomne, and Ventura. See ¶1706. (*Letter to County Assessors, No. 2016/034*, California State Board of Equalization, September 15, 2016)

Motor Fuel Taxes

• *Fuel tax rates set*

Motor fuel tax rate changes are effective for fiscal year 2016-2017. The motor vehicle fuel tax (gasoline) rate (exclusive of aviation fuel) will decrease from $0.30 (effective through June 30) to $0.278; the diesel fuel tax rate will increase from $0.13 (effective through June 30) to $0.16; and the International Fuel Tax Rate (IFTA) will decrease from $0.45 (effective through June 30) to $0.40. All rates are charged on a per-gallon basis. See ¶1907. (*Tax Rates—Special Taxes and Fees*, California State Board of Equalization, rates posted March 8, 2016)

Severance Tax

• *Oil, gas production assessment rate set for 2016-2017*

The Division of Oil, Gas, & Geothermal Resources (DOGGR) of the California Department of Conservation has published the oil and gas production assessment rate for fiscal year 2016-2017. The rate is set at 36.26051 cents per barrel of oil or 10 Mcf of natural gas produced (2015-2016 rate was 32.43123 cents). See ¶ 1907. (*DOGGR Announces New Assessment Rate*, California Department of Conservation, August 8, 2016)

Cigarettes and Tobacco Product Taxes

• *E-cigarettes subject to tobacco licensing laws*

Legislation in 2016 extended existing laws that relate to licensing of tobacco product retailers, distributors, and wholesalers to electronic cigarettes. The legislation broadened the definition of "tobacco product" to include any product containing, made, or derived from tobacco or nicotine that is intended for human consumption, whether smoked, heated, chewed, absorbed, dissolved, inhaled, snorted, sniffed, or ingested by any other means, including, but not limited to, cigarettes, cigars, little cigars, chewing tobacco, pipe tobacco, or snuff. The definition also specifically includes electronic devices that deliver nicotine or other vaporized liquids to the person inhaling from the device, including, but not limited to, an electronic cigarette, cigar, pipe, or hookah. The legislation also requires electronic cigarette retailers that are not subject to the California tobacco products tax to apply for a license and pay an annual license fee of $265 beginning January 1, 2017. See ¶ 1906. (Ch. 7 (S.B. 5), Laws 2016, Second Extraordinary Session, effective June 9, 2016)

• *Tax rates*

California cigarette and tobacco products tax rates for the period July 1, 2016, through June 30, 2017, are posted on the State Board of Equalization website. Cigarettes remain at their statutory level of $0.0435/cigarette ($0.87 per pack), and the rate for tobacco products decreased to 27.30% (formerly, 28.13%) of wholesale cost. See ¶ 1906. (Tax Rates—Special Taxes and Fees, California State Board of Equalization, April 2016)

Utility Taxes

• *Mobile telephony services surcharge imposed*

Beginning January 1, 2017, a new mobile telephony services (MTS) surcharge was imposed on consumers of postpaid or contract wireless services. At the point of sale, all consumers of prepaid wireless services will pay a statewide minimum of 5.9% (formerly, 9.26%) of the sales price. See ¶ 1907. (*Special Notice L-843*, California State Board of Equalization, November 28, 2016)

• *MTS sellers with de minimis sales need not register*

For purposes of the California mobile telephony services surcharge, sellers who qualify for the *de minimis* sales exemption from collecting the surcharge are not required to register with the State Board of Equalization (BOE). However, they may do so voluntarily. See ¶ 1907. (Ch. 89 (S.B. 1481), Laws 2016, effective January 1, 2017)

Unclaimed Property

• *Electronic transactions showing account activity defined*

Commencing on or before January 1, 2018, California unclaimed property holders must regard certain electronically initiated transactions that are reflected in the books and records of a banking or financial organization as evidence that the owner has increased or decreased the amount of the funds or deposit in an account. The electronically initiated transactions are:

— a single or recurring debit transaction authorized by the owner;

— a single or recurring credit transaction authorized by the owner;

— recurring transactions authorized by the owner that represent payroll deposits or deductions; or

— recurring transactions authorized by the owner that represent the deposit of any federal benefits, including social security benefits, veterans' benefits, and pension payments.

See ¶2201. (Ch. 463 (A.B. 2258), Laws 2016, effective January 1, 2017 and applicable as noted)

• *Notice of 2015 law changes issued*

The California State Controller's Office released two 2015 unclaimed property law change notices concerning safe deposit boxes and interest on Lawyers' Trust Accounts (IOLTA). Both laws were effective January 1, 2016.

Under A.B. 355, the Controller is authorized to mail a separate notice to an apparent owner of a United States saving bond or military award inside a safe deposit box or other safekeeping repository whose name is shown on or can be associated with the item. This law only affects the Controller's office.

S.B. 134 requires that funds held in IOLTAs that escheat to the state be deposited into a new Abandoned IOLTA Property Account within the unclaimed property fund. The dormancy period for property held in an IOLTA is three years. An IOLTA is an interest-bearing demand trust account, generally held by attorneys and law firms, established for all client deposits that are nominal in amount or are on deposit for a short period of time. See ¶2201. (*Notice to Holders* (2), California State Controller's Office, April 18, 2016)

• *Dismissal of class action will not be reviewed*

The U.S. Supreme Court will not review dismissal of a class action challenging the constitutionality of the California unclaimed property law. The class claimed that the law violated the Due Process Clause because it deprived owners of their property without affording constitutionally adequate notice, as reported. See ¶2201. (*Taylor v. Yee*, U.S. Supreme Court Dkt. 15-169, petition for certiorari denied February 29, 2016)

Miscellaneous Taxes and Fees

• *Quality assurance "fee" was a tax*

A quality assurance fee levied on all skilled nursing facilities (facilities) in California was a tax and not a fee because its purpose was to raise revenue to enhance federal financial participation in the state's Medi-Cal program, provide additional reimbursement, and facilitate quality improvement efforts in those facilities. The levy was enacted by a vote of more than 2/3 of the Legislature and had been reviewed and approved by the federal agency that oversees the Medi-Cal program. The taxpayers challenging the characteristics of the fee as a tax argued that the levy was not for general revenue purposes but targeted for the specific purpose of enhancing the quality of the facilities. However, the fee was:

(1) compulsory,

(2) imposed uniformly on all these facilities,

(3) beneficial to all Medicaid patients in nursing homes, and

(4) not part of a discrete service, and no permanent public improvement was involved.

While fees generally may not exceed the reasonable cost of providing services necessary to regulate the activity for which the fee is charged, the taxpayers, in this case, did not present any evidence that the fee's purpose was to create a regulatory program. Additionally, the fee fit the description of a tax and was not within any of the exceptions under Proposition 26, and the taxpayers who did not participate in the Medi-Cal program were not entitled to receive benefits or services in exchange for its payment. See ¶1907. (*The Rehabilitation Center of Beverly Hills v. Department of Health Care Services*, Court of Appeal of California, Third District, No. C070361, February 22, 2016)

SUMMARY OF PRINCIPAL ITEMS OF 2016 LEGISLATION
AFFECTING CALIFORNIA PERSONAL INCOME TAX
AND TAXES ON CORPORATE INCOME

Law Section	Comparable Federal	Summary of Change
PERSONAL INCOME TAX:		
17052	22	Permanently sets earned income tax credit percentage for individuals with three or more children
17053.88.5	...	Provides post-2016 donated fruits and vegetables tax credit
17058	42	Revises low-income housing tax credit provisions
17059.2	...	Expands online reporting requirements and criteria for written agreements with regarding to the California Competes Credit
ADMINISTRATION:		
18601	6072	Changes C corporation return due date
18633	6072	Changes partnership return due date
18633.5	6072	Changes LLC return due date
18706 - 18709	...	Enacts Special Olympics Fund checkoff provisions
18711 - 18714	...	Enacts California Domestic Violence Victims Fund checkoff provisions
18735 - 18738	...	Enacts Revive the Salton Sea Fund checkoff provisions
18781 - 18784	...	Enacts Type 1 Diabetes Research Fund checkoff provisions
18898	...	Extends sunset date for School Supplies for Homeless Children Fund checkoff
19853	...	Expands earned income tax credit notification requirements
19854	...	Updates required earned income tax credit notice language
TAXES ON CORPORATE INCOME:		
23610.5	42	Revises low-income housing tax credit provisions
23636	...	Operative dates for advanced strategic aircraft credit modified

Law Section	Comparable Federal	Summary of Change
23688.5	...	Provides post-2016 donated fruits and vegetables tax credit
23689	...	Expands online reporting requirements and criteria for written agreements with regarding to the California Competes Credit
24330	...	Provides an exclusion from gross income for qualified income accrued by a health care service plan subject to the managed care organization provider tax

TAX CALENDAR

The following table lists significant dates of interest to California taxpayers and tax practitioners.

ANNUAL DEADLINES
January
1st—Property tax assessment date; property tax liens attach

2nd—Property tax on race horses due

31st—Employers must furnish W-2 Form to each employee subject to withholding of personal income tax, state disability insurance, or voluntary disability insurance

Annual withholding reconciliation returns for annual household employers and for disability insurance elective coverage filers delinquent

Persons required to file information returns concerning patronage dividend, rebate, or refund payments; employee group life insurance costs; transfers of stock pursuant to a stock option plan; brokerage services; remuneration of fishing boat crew members; or dividends, interest, or distributions out of earnings or profits must furnish a statement to each person named in a return

February
1st—Second installment of real property tax due

Second installment of oil and gas producers' tax delinquent

15th—Property tax on race horses delinquent

Affidavits due for church, cemetery, college, exhibition, welfare, veterans', homeowners', veterans' organization, free public libraries, free museums, aircraft of historical significance, tribal housing, public schools, or documented vessel property tax exemptions

March
1st—Surplus line brokers annual return due

Property tax statements due

Oil and gas producers' annual reports due

15th—Calendar-year taxpayers' S corporation and partnership returns due

April
2nd—Insurers' (other than ocean marine insurers and surplus line brokers) returns and tax due

10th—Second installment of real property tax delinquent

15th—Calendar-year taxpayers' personal income tax returns and tax due

Calendar-year taxpayers' corporate income and franchise tax returns due

Use tax returns due

30th—Property tax reports on private railroad cars due

May
15th—Calendar-year exempt organizations' information returns due

May 31—Personal property statements due

June
15th—Ocean marine insurers' returns and tax due

Estimated LLC fee due

July

1st—Oil and gas producers' tax due

August

15th—First installment of oil and gas producers' tax delinquent

31st—Tax on unsecured property delinquent

November

1st—Personal property tax and first installment of real property tax due

December

10th—Personal property tax and first installment of real property tax delinquent

Property tax on private railroad cars due

MONTHLY DEADLINES

1st—Common carriers' distilled spirits monthly reports and tax due

15th—Beer and wine manufacturers', growers', importers', and sellers' monthly reports and tax due

Distilled spirits agents', manufacturers', rectifiers', wholesalers', and sellers' monthly reports and tax due

25th—Cigarette monthly reports or returns and tax due

Last day—Oil and gas producers' monthly reports due

Motor fuel distributors', producers', and brokers' monthly reports and tax due

Aircraft jet fuel monthly reports and tax due

QUARTERLY DEADLINES
Jan., April, July, and Oct.

Last day—Quarterly reports and payment of withheld personal income tax due

Quarterly unemployment insurance due

Quarterly disability insurance taxable wages and contributions returns due

Quarterly disability insurance voluntary plan filers returns due

Quarterly Employment training tax returns due

Use fuel vendors and users reports and tax due

Quarterly returns and payment of sales and use tax due

Quarterly returns and payment of timber yield tax due

April, June, Sept., and Jan.

15th—Estimated tax installments for personal income taxpayers due

Fourth, Sixth, Ninth, and 12th Month of Income Year

15th—Estimated tax installments exceeding $800 for corporate income taxpayers due

PART I

TAX RATE SCHEDULES AND TABLES

¶1 Personal Income Tax Tables for 2016

The Tax Tables for 2016 Personal Income Tax start on the following page.

2016 California Tax Table

To Find Your Tax:
- Read down the column labeled "If Your Taxable Income Is ..." to find the range that includes your taxable income from Form 540, line 19.
- Read across the columns labeled "The Tax For Filing Status" until you find the tax that applies for your taxable income and filing status.

Filing status: 1 or 3 (Single; Married/RDP Filing Separately)   2 or 5 (Married/RDP Filing Jointly; Qualifying Widow(er))   4 (Head of Household)

If Your Taxable Income Is ...		The Tax For Filing Status			If Your Taxable Income Is ...		The Tax For Filing Status			If Your Taxable Income Is ...		The Tax For Filing Status		
At Least	But Not Over	1 Or 3 Is	2 Or 5 Is	4 Is	At Least	But Not Over	1 Or 3 Is	2 Or 5 Is	4 Is	At Least	But Not Over	1 Or 3 Is	2 Or 5 Is	4 Is
$1	$50	$0	$0	$0	6,451	6,550	65	65	65	12,951	13,050	180	130	130
51	150	1	1	1	6,551	6,650	66	66	66	13,051	13,150	182	131	131
151	250	2	2	2	6,651	6,750	67	67	67	13,151	13,250	184	132	132
251	350	3	3	3	6,751	6,850	68	68	68	13,251	13,350	186	133	133
351	450	4	4	4	6,851	6,950	69	69	69	13,351	13,450	188	134	134
451	550	5	5	5	6,951	7,050	70	70	70	13,451	13,550	190	135	135
551	650	6	6	6	7,051	7,150	71	71	71	13,551	13,650	192	136	136
651	750	7	7	7	7,151	7,250	72	72	72	13,651	13,750	194	137	137
751	850	8	8	8	7,251	7,350	73	73	73	13,751	13,850	196	138	138
851	950	9	9	9	7,351	7,450	74	74	74	13,851	13,950	198	139	139
951	1,050	10	10	10	7,451	7,550	75	75	75	13,951	14,050	200	140	140
1,051	1,150	11	11	11	7,551	7,650	76	76	76	14,051	14,150	202	141	141
1,151	1,250	12	12	12	7,651	7,750	77	77	77	14,151	14,250	204	142	142
1,251	1,350	13	13	13	7,751	7,850	78	78	78	14,251	14,350	206	143	143
1,351	1,450	14	14	14	7,851	7,950	79	79	79	14,351	14,450	208	144	144
1,451	1,550	15	15	15	7,951	8,050	80	80	80	14,451	14,550	210	145	145
1,551	1,650	16	16	16	8,051	8,150	82	81	81	14,551	14,650	212	146	146
1,651	1,750	17	17	17	8,151	8,250	84	82	82	14,651	14,750	214	147	147
1,751	1,850	18	18	18	8,251	8,350	86	83	83	14,751	14,850	216	148	148
1,851	1,950	19	19	19	8,351	8,450	88	84	84	14,851	14,950	218	149	149
1,951	2,050	20	20	20	8,451	8,550	90	85	85	14,951	15,050	220	150	150
2,051	2,150	21	21	21	8,551	8,650	92	86	86	15,051	15,150	222	151	151
2,151	2,250	22	22	22	8,651	8,750	94	87	87	15,151	15,250	224	152	152
2,251	2,350	23	23	23	8,751	8,850	96	88	88	15,251	15,350	226	153	153
2,351	2,450	24	24	24	8,851	8,950	98	89	89	15,351	15,450	228	154	154
2,451	2,550	25	25	25	8,951	9,050	100	90	90	15,451	15,550	230	155	155
2,551	2,650	26	26	26	9,051	9,150	102	91	91	15,551	15,650	232	156	156
2,651	2,750	27	27	27	9,151	9,250	104	92	92	15,651	15,750	234	157	157
2,751	2,850	28	28	28	9,251	9,350	106	93	93	15,751	15,850	236	158	158
2,851	2,950	29	29	29	9,351	9,450	108	94	94	15,851	15,950	238	159	159
2,951	3,050	30	30	30	9,451	9,550	110	95	95	15,951	16,050	240	160	160
3,051	3,150	31	31	31	9,551	9,650	112	96	96	16,051	16,150	242	162	162
3,151	3,250	32	32	32	9,651	9,750	114	97	97	16,151	16,250	244	164	164
3,251	3,350	33	33	33	9,751	9,850	116	98	98	16,251	16,350	246	166	166
3,351	3,450	34	34	34	9,851	9,950	118	99	99	16,351	16,450	248	168	168
3,451	3,550	35	35	35	9,951	10,050	120	100	100	16,451	16,550	250	170	170
3,551	3,650	36	36	36	10,051	10,150	122	101	101	16,551	16,650	252	172	172
3,651	3,750	37	37	37	10,151	10,250	124	102	102	16,651	16,750	254	174	174
3,751	3,850	38	38	38	10,251	10,350	126	103	103	16,751	16,850	256	176	176
3,851	3,950	39	39	39	10,351	10,450	128	104	104	16,851	16,950	258	178	178
3,951	4,050	40	40	40	10,451	10,550	130	105	105	16,951	17,050	260	180	180
4,051	4,150	41	41	41	10,551	10,650	132	106	106	17,051	17,150	262	182	182
4,151	4,250	42	42	42	10,651	10,750	134	107	107	17,151	17,250	264	184	184
4,251	4,350	43	43	43	10,751	10,850	136	108	108	17,251	17,350	266	186	186
4,351	4,450	44	44	44	10,851	10,950	138	109	109	17,351	17,450	268	188	188
4,451	4,550	45	45	45	10,951	11,050	140	110	110	17,451	17,550	270	190	190
4,551	4,650	46	46	46	11,051	11,150	142	111	111	17,551	17,650	272	192	192
4,651	4,750	47	47	47	11,151	11,250	144	112	112	17,651	17,750	274	194	194
4,751	4,850	48	48	48	11,251	11,350	146	113	113	17,751	17,850	276	196	196
4,851	4,950	49	49	49	11,351	11,450	148	114	114	17,851	17,950	278	198	198
4,951	5,050	50	50	50	11,451	11,550	150	115	115	17,951	18,050	280	200	200
5,051	5,150	51	51	51	11,551	11,650	152	116	116	18,051	18,150	282	202	202
5,151	5,250	52	52	52	11,651	11,750	154	117	117	18,151	18,250	284	204	204
5,251	5,350	53	53	53	11,751	11,850	156	118	118	18,251	18,350	286	206	206
5,351	5,450	54	54	54	11,851	11,950	158	119	119	18,351	18,450	288	208	208
5,451	5,550	55	55	55	11,951	12,050	160	120	120	18,451	18,550	290	210	210
5,551	5,650	56	56	56	12,051	12,150	162	121	121	18,551	18,650	292	212	212
5,651	5,750	57	57	57	12,151	12,250	164	122	122	18,651	18,750	294	214	214
5,751	5,850	58	58	58	12,251	12,350	166	123	123	18,751	18,850	296	216	216
5,851	5,950	59	59	59	12,351	12,450	168	124	124	18,851	18,950	298	218	218
5,951	6,050	60	60	60	12,451	12,550	170	125	125	18,951	19,050	300	220	220
6,051	6,150	61	61	61	12,551	12,650	172	126	126	19,051	19,150	304	222	222
6,151	6,250	62	62	62	12,651	12,750	174	127	127	19,151	19,250	308	224	224
6,251	6,350	63	63	63	12,751	12,850	176	128	128	19,251	19,350	312	226	226
6,351	6,450	64	64	64	12,851	12,950	178	129	129	19,351	19,450	316	228	228

Continued on next page.

2016 California Tax Table – *Continued*

Filing status: 1 or 3 (Single; Married/RDP Filing Separately)   2 or 5 (Married/RDP Filing Jointly; Qualifying Widow(er))   4 (Head of Household)

If Your Taxable Income Is …		The Tax For Filing Status			If Your Taxable Income Is …		The Tax For Filing Status			If Your Taxable Income Is …		The Tax For Filing Status		
At Least	But Not Over	1 Or 3 Is	2 Or 5 Is	4 Is	At Least	But Not Over	1 Or 3 Is	2 Or 5 Is	4 Is	At Least	But Not Over	1 Or 3 Is	2 Or 5 Is	4 Is
19,451	19,550	320	230	230	26,451	26,550	600	370	370	33,451	33,550	950	510	510
19,551	19,650	324	232	232	26,551	26,650	604	372	372	33,551	33,650	956	512	512
19,651	19,750	328	234	234	26,651	26,750	608	374	374	33,651	33,750	962	514	514
19,751	19,850	332	236	236	26,751	26,850	612	376	376	33,751	33,850	968	516	516
19,851	19,950	336	238	238	26,851	26,950	616	378	378	33,851	33,950	974	518	518
19,951	20,050	340	240	240	26,951	27,050	620	380	380	33,951	34,050	980	520	520
20,051	20,150	344	242	242	27,051	27,150	624	382	382	34,051	34,150	986	522	522
20,151	20,250	348	244	244	27,151	27,250	628	384	384	34,151	34,250	992	524	524
20,251	20,350	352	246	246	27,251	27,350	632	386	386	34,251	34,350	998	526	526
20,351	20,450	356	248	248	27,351	27,450	636	388	388	34,351	34,450	1,004	528	528
20,451	20,550	360	250	250	27,451	27,550	640	390	390	34,451	34,550	1,010	530	530
20,551	20,650	364	252	252	27,551	27,650	644	392	392	34,551	34,650	1,016	532	532
20,651	20,750	368	254	254	27,651	27,750	648	394	394	34,651	34,750	1,022	534	534
20,751	20,850	372	256	256	27,751	27,850	652	396	396	34,751	34,850	1,028	536	536
20,851	20,950	376	258	258	27,851	27,950	656	398	398	34,851	34,950	1,034	538	538
20,951	21,050	380	260	260	27,951	28,050	660	400	400	34,951	35,050	1,040	540	540
21,051	21,150	384	262	262	28,051	28,150	664	402	402	35,051	35,150	1,046	542	542
21,151	21,250	388	264	264	28,151	28,250	668	404	404	35,151	35,250	1,052	544	544
21,251	21,350	392	266	266	28,251	28,350	672	406	406	35,251	35,350	1,058	546	546
21,351	21,450	396	268	268	28,351	28,450	676	408	408	35,351	35,450	1,064	548	548
21,451	21,550	400	270	270	28,451	28,550	680	410	410	35,451	35,550	1,070	550	550
21,551	21,650	404	272	272	28,551	28,650	684	412	412	35,551	35,650	1,076	552	552
21,651	21,750	408	274	274	28,651	28,750	688	414	414	35,651	35,750	1,082	554	554
21,751	21,850	412	276	276	28,751	28,850	692	416	416	35,751	35,850	1,088	556	556
21,851	21,950	416	278	278	28,851	28,950	696	418	418	35,851	35,950	1,094	558	558
21,951	22,050	420	280	280	28,951	29,050	700	420	420	35,951	36,050	1,100	560	560
22,051	22,150	424	282	282	29,051	29,150	704	422	422	36,051	36,150	1,106	562	562
22,151	22,250	428	284	284	29,151	29,250	708	424	424	36,151	36,250	1,112	564	564
22,251	22,350	432	286	286	29,251	29,350	712	426	426	36,251	36,350	1,118	566	566
22,351	22,450	436	288	288	29,351	29,450	716	428	428	36,351	36,450	1,124	568	568
22,451	22,550	440	290	290	29,451	29,550	720	430	430	36,451	36,550	1,130	570	570
22,551	22,650	444	292	292	29,551	29,650	724	432	432	36,551	36,650	1,136	572	572
22,651	22,750	448	294	294	29,651	29,750	728	434	434	36,651	36,750	1,142	574	574
22,751	22,850	452	296	296	29,751	29,850	732	436	436	36,751	36,850	1,148	576	576
22,851	22,950	456	298	298	29,851	29,950	736	438	438	36,851	36,950	1,154	578	578
22,951	23,050	460	300	300	29,951	30,050	740	440	440	36,951	37,050	1,160	580	580
23,051	23,150	464	302	302	30,051	30,150	746	442	442	37,051	37,150	1,166	582	582
23,151	23,250	468	304	304	30,151	30,250	752	444	444	37,151	37,250	1,172	584	584
23,251	23,350	472	306	306	30,251	30,350	758	446	446	37,251	37,350	1,178	586	586
23,351	23,450	476	308	308	30,351	30,450	764	448	448	37,351	37,450	1,184	588	588
23,451	23,550	480	310	310	30,451	30,550	770	450	450	37,451	37,550	1,190	590	590
23,551	23,650	484	312	312	30,551	30,650	776	452	452	37,551	37,650	1,196	592	592
23,651	23,750	488	314	314	30,651	30,750	782	454	454	37,651	37,750	1,202	594	594
23,751	23,850	492	316	316	30,751	30,850	788	456	456	37,751	37,850	1,208	596	596
23,851	23,950	496	318	318	30,851	30,950	794	458	458	37,851	37,950	1,214	598	598
23,951	24,050	500	320	320	30,951	31,050	800	460	460	37,951	38,050	1,220	600	600
24,051	24,150	504	322	322	31,051	31,150	806	462	462	38,051	38,150	1,226	604	604
24,151	24,250	508	324	324	31,151	31,250	812	464	464	38,151	38,250	1,232	608	608
24,251	24,350	512	326	326	31,251	31,350	818	466	466	38,251	38,350	1,238	612	612
24,351	24,450	516	328	328	31,351	31,450	824	468	468	38,351	38,450	1,244	616	616
24,451	24,550	520	330	330	31,451	31,550	830	470	470	38,451	38,550	1,250	620	620
24,551	24,650	524	332	332	31,551	31,650	836	472	472	38,551	38,650	1,256	624	624
24,651	24,750	528	334	334	31,651	31,750	842	474	474	38,651	38,750	1,262	628	628
24,751	24,850	532	336	336	31,751	31,850	848	476	476	38,751	38,850	1,268	632	632
24,851	24,950	536	338	338	31,851	31,950	854	478	478	38,851	38,950	1,274	636	636
24,951	25,050	540	340	340	31,951	32,050	860	480	480	38,951	39,050	1,280	640	640
25,051	25,150	544	342	342	32,051	32,150	866	482	482	39,051	39,150	1,286	644	644
25,151	25,250	548	344	344	32,151	32,250	872	484	484	39,151	39,250	1,292	648	648
25,251	25,350	552	346	346	32,251	32,350	878	486	486	39,251	39,350	1,298	652	652
25,351	25,450	556	348	348	32,351	32,450	884	488	488	39,351	39,450	1,304	656	656
25,451	25,550	560	350	350	32,451	32,550	890	490	490	39,451	39,550	1,310	660	660
25,551	25,650	564	352	352	32,551	32,650	896	492	492	39,551	39,650	1,316	664	664
25,651	25,750	568	354	354	32,651	32,750	902	494	494	39,651	39,750	1,322	668	668
25,751	25,850	572	356	356	32,751	32,850	908	496	496	39,751	39,850	1,328	672	672
25,851	25,950	576	358	358	32,851	32,950	914	498	498	39,851	39,950	1,334	676	676
25,951	26,050	580	360	360	32,951	33,050	920	500	500	39,951	40,050	1,340	680	680
26,051	26,150	584	362	362	33,051	33,150	926	502	502	40,051	40,150	1,346	684	684
26,151	26,250	588	364	364	33,151	33,250	932	504	504	40,151	40,250	1,352	688	688
26,251	26,350	592	366	366	33,251	33,350	938	506	506	40,251	40,350	1,358	692	692
26,351	26,450	596	368	368	33,351	33,450	944	508	508	40,351	40,450	1,364	696	696

Continued on next page.

2016 California Tax Table – *Continued*

Filing status:　1 or 3 (Single; Married/RDP Filing Separately)　　2 or 5 (Married/RDP Filing Jointly; Qualifying Widow(er))　　4 (Head of Household)

If Your Taxable Income Is ...		The Tax For Filing Status			If Your Taxable Income Is ...		The Tax For Filing Status			If Your Taxable Income Is ...		The Tax For Filing Status		
At Least	But Not Over	1 Or 3 Is	2 Or 5 Is	4 Is	At Least	But Not Over	1 Or 3 Is	2 Or 5 Is	4 Is	At Least	But Not Over	1 Or 3 Is	2 Or 5 Is	4 Is
40,451	40,550	1,370	700	700	47,451	47,550	1,907	980	980	54,451	54,550	2,492	1,260	1,370
40,551	40,650	1,376	704	704	47,551	47,650	1,915	984	984	54,551	54,650	2,501	1,264	1,376
40,651	40,750	1,382	708	708	47,651	47,750	1,923	988	988	54,651	54,750	2,511	1,268	1,382
40,751	40,850	1,388	712	712	47,751	47,850	1,931	992	992	54,751	54,850	2,520	1,272	1,388
40,851	40,950	1,394	716	716	47,851	47,950	1,939	996	996	54,851	54,950	2,529	1,276	1,394
40,951	41,050	1,400	720	720	47,951	48,050	1,947	1,000	1,000	54,951	55,050	2,539	1,280	1,400
41,051	41,150	1,406	724	724	48,051	48,150	1,955	1,004	1,004	55,051	55,150	2,548	1,284	1,406
41,151	41,250	1,412	728	728	48,151	48,250	1,963	1,008	1,008	55,151	55,250	2,557	1,288	1,412
41,251	41,350	1,418	732	732	48,251	48,350	1,971	1,012	1,012	55,251	55,350	2,566	1,292	1,418
41,351	41,450	1,424	736	736	48,351	48,450	1,979	1,016	1,016	55,351	55,450	2,576	1,296	1,424
41,451	41,550	1,430	740	740	48,451	48,550	1,987	1,020	1,020	55,451	55,550	2,585	1,300	1,430
41,551	41,650	1,436	744	744	48,551	48,650	1,995	1,024	1,024	55,551	55,650	2,594	1,304	1,436
41,651	41,750	1,443	748	748	48,651	48,750	2,003	1,028	1,028	55,651	55,750	2,604	1,308	1,442
41,751	41,850	1,451	752	752	48,751	48,850	2,011	1,032	1,032	55,751	55,850	2,613	1,312	1,448
41,851	41,950	1,459	756	756	48,851	48,950	2,019	1,036	1,036	55,851	55,950	2,622	1,316	1,454
41,951	42,050	1,467	760	760	48,951	49,050	2,027	1,040	1,040	55,951	56,050	2,632	1,320	1,460
42,051	42,150	1,475	764	764	49,051	49,150	2,035	1,044	1,046	56,051	56,150	2,641	1,324	1,466
42,151	42,250	1,483	768	768	49,151	49,250	2,043	1,048	1,052	56,151	56,250	2,650	1,328	1,472
42,251	42,350	1,491	772	772	49,251	49,350	2,051	1,052	1,058	56,251	56,350	2,659	1,332	1,478
42,351	42,450	1,499	776	776	49,351	49,450	2,059	1,056	1,064	56,351	56,450	2,669	1,336	1,484
42,451	42,550	1,507	780	780	49,451	49,550	2,067	1,060	1,070	56,451	56,550	2,678	1,340	1,490
42,551	42,650	1,515	784	784	49,551	49,650	2,075	1,064	1,076	56,551	56,650	2,687	1,344	1,496
42,651	42,750	1,523	788	788	49,651	49,750	2,083	1,068	1,082	56,651	56,750	2,697	1,348	1,502
42,751	42,850	1,531	792	792	49,751	49,850	2,091	1,072	1,088	56,751	56,850	2,706	1,352	1,508
42,851	42,950	1,539	796	796	49,851	49,950	2,099	1,076	1,094	56,851	56,950	2,715	1,356	1,514
42,951	43,050	1,547	800	800	49,951	50,050	2,107	1,080	1,100	56,951	57,050	2,725	1,360	1,520
43,051	43,150	1,555	804	804	50,051	50,150	2,115	1,084	1,106	57,051	57,150	2,734	1,364	1,526
43,151	43,250	1,563	808	808	50,151	50,250	2,123	1,088	1,112	57,151	57,250	2,743	1,368	1,532
43,251	43,350	1,571	812	812	50,251	50,350	2,131	1,092	1,118	57,251	57,350	2,752	1,372	1,538
43,351	43,450	1,579	816	816	50,351	50,450	2,139	1,096	1,124	57,351	57,450	2,762	1,376	1,544
43,451	43,550	1,587	820	820	50,451	50,550	2,147	1,100	1,130	57,451	57,550	2,771	1,380	1,550
43,551	43,650	1,595	824	824	50,551	50,650	2,155	1,104	1,136	57,551	57,650	2,780	1,384	1,556
43,651	43,750	1,603	828	828	50,651	50,750	2,163	1,108	1,142	57,651	57,750	2,790	1,388	1,562
43,751	43,850	1,611	832	832	50,751	50,850	2,171	1,112	1,148	57,751	57,850	2,799	1,392	1,568
43,851	43,950	1,619	836	836	50,851	50,950	2,179	1,116	1,154	57,851	57,950	2,808	1,396	1,574
43,951	44,050	1,627	840	840	50,951	51,050	2,187	1,120	1,160	57,951	58,050	2,818	1,400	1,580
44,051	44,150	1,635	844	844	51,051	51,150	2,195	1,124	1,166	58,051	58,150	2,827	1,404	1,586
44,151	44,250	1,643	848	848	51,151	51,250	2,203	1,128	1,172	58,151	58,250	2,836	1,408	1,592
44,251	44,350	1,651	852	852	51,251	51,350	2,211	1,132	1,178	58,251	58,350	2,845	1,412	1,598
44,351	44,450	1,659	856	856	51,351	51,450	2,219	1,136	1,184	58,351	58,450	2,855	1,416	1,604
44,451	44,550	1,667	860	860	51,451	51,550	2,227	1,140	1,190	58,451	58,550	2,864	1,420	1,610
44,551	44,650	1,675	864	864	51,551	51,650	2,235	1,144	1,196	58,551	58,650	2,873	1,424	1,616
44,651	44,750	1,683	868	868	51,651	51,750	2,243	1,148	1,202	58,651	58,750	2,883	1,428	1,622
44,751	44,850	1,691	872	872	51,751	51,850	2,251	1,152	1,208	58,751	58,850	2,892	1,432	1,628
44,851	44,950	1,699	876	876	51,851	51,950	2,259	1,156	1,214	58,851	58,950	2,901	1,436	1,634
44,951	45,050	1,707	880	880	51,951	52,050	2,267	1,160	1,220	58,951	59,050	2,911	1,440	1,640
45,051	45,150	1,715	884	884	52,051	52,150	2,275	1,164	1,226	59,051	59,150	2,920	1,444	1,646
45,151	45,250	1,723	888	888	52,151	52,250	2,283	1,168	1,232	59,151	59,250	2,929	1,448	1,652
45,251	45,350	1,731	892	892	52,251	52,350	2,291	1,172	1,238	59,251	59,350	2,938	1,452	1,658
45,351	45,450	1,739	896	896	52,351	52,450	2,299	1,176	1,244	59,351	59,450	2,948	1,456	1,664
45,451	45,550	1,747	900	900	52,451	52,550	2,307	1,180	1,250	59,451	59,550	2,957	1,460	1,670
45,551	45,650	1,755	904	904	52,551	52,650	2,315	1,184	1,256	59,551	59,650	2,966	1,464	1,676
45,651	45,750	1,763	908	908	52,651	52,750	2,325	1,188	1,262	59,651	59,750	2,976	1,468	1,682
45,751	45,850	1,771	912	912	52,751	52,850	2,334	1,192	1,268	59,751	59,850	2,985	1,472	1,688
45,851	45,950	1,779	916	916	52,851	52,950	2,343	1,196	1,274	59,851	59,950	2,994	1,476	1,694
45,951	46,050	1,787	920	920	52,951	53,050	2,353	1,200	1,280	59,951	60,050	3,004	1,480	1,700
46,051	46,150	1,795	924	924	53,051	53,150	2,362	1,204	1,286	60,051	60,150	3,013	1,486	1,706
46,151	46,250	1,803	928	928	53,151	53,250	2,371	1,208	1,292	60,151	60,250	3,022	1,492	1,712
46,251	46,350	1,811	932	932	53,251	53,350	2,380	1,212	1,298	60,251	60,350	3,031	1,498	1,718
46,351	46,450	1,819	936	936	53,351	53,450	2,390	1,216	1,304	60,351	60,450	3,041	1,504	1,724
46,451	46,550	1,827	940	940	53,451	53,550	2,399	1,220	1,310	60,451	60,550	3,050	1,510	1,730
46,551	46,650	1,835	944	944	53,551	53,650	2,408	1,224	1,316	60,551	60,650	3,059	1,516	1,736
46,651	46,750	1,843	948	948	53,651	53,750	2,418	1,228	1,322	60,651	60,750	3,069	1,522	1,743
46,751	46,850	1,851	952	952	53,751	53,850	2,427	1,232	1,328	60,751	60,850	3,078	1,528	1,751
46,851	46,950	1,859	956	956	53,851	53,950	2,436	1,236	1,334	60,851	60,950	3,087	1,534	1,759
46,951	47,050	1,867	960	960	53,951	54,050	2,446	1,240	1,340	60,951	61,050	3,097	1,540	1,767
47,051	47,150	1,875	964	964	54,051	54,150	2,455	1,244	1,346	61,051	61,150	3,106	1,546	1,775
47,151	47,250	1,883	968	968	54,151	54,250	2,464	1,248	1,352	61,151	61,250	3,115	1,552	1,783
47,251	47,350	1,891	972	972	54,251	54,350	2,473	1,252	1,358	61,251	61,350	3,124	1,558	1,791
47,351	47,450	1,899	976	976	54,351	54,450	2,483	1,256	1,364	61,351	61,450	3,134	1,564	1,799

Continued on next page.

2016 California Tax Table – Continued

Filing status: 1 or 3 (Single; Married/RDP Filing Separately)   2 or 5 (Married/RDP Filing Jointly; Qualifying Widow(er))   4 (Head of Household)

If Your Taxable Income Is ... At Least	But Not Over	1 Or 3 Is	2 Or 5 Is	4 Is
61,451	61,550	3,143	1,570	1,807
61,551	61,650	3,152	1,576	1,815
61,651	61,750	3,162	1,582	1,823
61,751	61,850	3,171	1,588	1,831
61,851	61,950	3,180	1,594	1,839
61,951	62,050	3,190	1,600	1,847
62,051	62,150	3,199	1,606	1,855
62,151	62,250	3,208	1,612	1,863
62,251	62,350	3,217	1,618	1,871
62,351	62,450	3,227	1,624	1,879
62,451	62,550	3,236	1,630	1,887
62,551	62,650	3,245	1,636	1,895
62,651	62,750	3,255	1,642	1,903
62,751	62,850	3,264	1,648	1,911
62,851	62,950	3,273	1,654	1,919
62,951	63,050	3,283	1,660	1,927
63,051	63,150	3,292	1,666	1,935
63,151	63,250	3,301	1,672	1,943
63,251	63,350	3,310	1,678	1,951
63,351	63,450	3,320	1,684	1,959
63,451	63,550	3,329	1,690	1,967
63,551	63,650	3,338	1,696	1,975
63,651	63,750	3,348	1,702	1,983
63,751	63,850	3,357	1,708	1,991
63,851	63,950	3,366	1,714	1,999
63,951	64,050	3,376	1,720	2,007
64,051	64,150	3,385	1,726	2,015
64,151	64,250	3,394	1,732	2,023
64,251	64,350	3,403	1,738	2,031
64,351	64,450	3,413	1,744	2,039
64,451	64,550	3,422	1,750	2,047
64,551	64,650	3,431	1,756	2,055
64,651	64,750	3,441	1,762	2,063
64,751	64,850	3,450	1,768	2,071
64,851	64,950	3,459	1,774	2,079
64,951	65,050	3,469	1,780	2,087
65,051	65,150	3,478	1,786	2,095
65,151	65,250	3,487	1,792	2,103
65,251	65,350	3,496	1,798	2,111
65,351	65,450	3,506	1,804	2,119
65,451	65,550	3,515	1,810	2,127
65,551	65,650	3,524	1,816	2,135
65,651	65,750	3,534	1,822	2,143
65,751	65,850	3,543	1,828	2,151
65,851	65,950	3,552	1,834	2,159
65,951	66,050	3,562	1,840	2,167
66,051	66,150	3,571	1,846	2,175
66,151	66,250	3,580	1,852	2,183
66,251	66,350	3,589	1,858	2,191
66,351	66,450	3,599	1,864	2,199
66,451	66,550	3,608	1,870	2,207
66,551	66,650	3,617	1,876	2,215
66,651	66,750	3,627	1,882	2,223
66,751	66,850	3,636	1,888	2,231
66,851	66,950	3,645	1,894	2,239
66,951	67,050	3,655	1,900	2,247
67,051	67,150	3,664	1,906	2,255
67,151	67,250	3,673	1,912	2,263
67,251	67,350	3,682	1,918	2,271
67,351	67,450	3,692	1,924	2,279
67,451	67,550	3,701	1,930	2,287
67,551	67,650	3,710	1,936	2,295
67,651	67,750	3,720	1,942	2,303
67,751	67,850	3,729	1,948	2,311
67,851	67,950	3,738	1,954	2,319
67,951	68,050	3,748	1,960	2,327
68,051	68,150	3,757	1,966	2,335
68,151	68,250	3,766	1,972	2,343
68,251	68,350	3,775	1,978	2,351
68,351	68,450	3,785	1,984	2,359

If Your Taxable Income Is ... At Least	But Not Over	1 Or 3 Is	2 Or 5 Is	4 Is
68,451	68,550	3,794	1,990	2,367
68,551	68,650	3,803	1,996	2,375
68,651	68,750	3,813	2,002	2,383
68,751	68,850	3,822	2,008	2,391
68,851	68,950	3,831	2,014	2,399
68,951	69,050	3,841	2,020	2,407
69,051	69,150	3,850	2,026	2,415
69,151	69,250	3,859	2,032	2,423
69,251	69,350	3,868	2,038	2,431
69,351	69,450	3,878	2,044	2,439
69,451	69,550	3,887	2,050	2,447
69,551	69,650	3,896	2,056	2,455
69,651	69,750	3,906	2,062	2,463
69,751	69,850	3,915	2,068	2,471
69,851	69,950	3,924	2,074	2,479
69,951	70,050	3,934	2,080	2,487
70,051	70,150	3,943	2,086	2,495
70,151	70,250	3,952	2,092	2,503
70,251	70,350	3,961	2,098	2,511
70,351	70,450	3,971	2,104	2,519
70,451	70,550	3,980	2,110	2,527
70,551	70,650	3,989	2,116	2,535
70,651	70,750	3,999	2,122	2,543
70,751	70,850	4,008	2,128	2,551
70,851	70,950	4,017	2,134	2,559
70,951	71,050	4,027	2,140	2,567
71,051	71,150	4,036	2,146	2,575
71,151	71,250	4,045	2,152	2,583
71,251	71,350	4,054	2,158	2,591
71,351	71,450	4,064	2,164	2,599
71,451	71,550	4,073	2,170	2,607
71,551	71,650	4,082	2,176	2,615
71,651	71,750	4,092	2,182	2,624
71,751	71,850	4,101	2,188	2,634
71,851	71,950	4,110	2,194	2,643
71,951	72,050	4,120	2,200	2,652
72,051	72,150	4,129	2,206	2,661
72,151	72,250	4,138	2,212	2,671
72,251	72,350	4,147	2,218	2,680
72,351	72,450	4,157	2,224	2,689
72,451	72,550	4,166	2,230	2,699
72,551	72,650	4,175	2,236	2,708
72,651	72,750	4,185	2,242	2,717
72,751	72,850	4,194	2,248	2,727
72,851	72,950	4,203	2,254	2,736
72,951	73,050	4,213	2,260	2,745
73,051	73,150	4,222	2,266	2,754
73,151	73,250	4,231	2,272	2,764
73,251	73,350	4,240	2,278	2,773
73,351	73,450	4,250	2,284	2,782
73,451	73,550	4,259	2,290	2,792
73,551	73,650	4,268	2,296	2,801
73,651	73,750	4,278	2,302	2,810
73,751	73,850	4,287	2,308	2,820
73,851	73,950	4,296	2,314	2,829
73,951	74,050	4,306	2,320	2,838
74,051	74,150	4,315	2,326	2,847
74,151	74,250	4,324	2,332	2,857
74,251	74,350	4,333	2,338	2,866
74,351	74,450	4,343	2,344	2,875
74,451	74,550	4,352	2,350	2,885
74,551	74,650	4,361	2,356	2,894
74,651	74,750	4,371	2,362	2,903
74,751	74,850	4,380	2,368	2,913
74,851	74,950	4,389	2,374	2,922
74,951	75,050	4,399	2,380	2,931
75,051	75,150	4,408	2,386	2,940
75,151	75,250	4,417	2,392	2,950
75,251	75,350	4,426	2,398	2,959
75,351	75,450	4,436	2,404	2,968

If Your Taxable Income Is ... At Least	But Not Over	1 Or 3 Is	2 Or 5 Is	4 Is
75,451	75,550	4,445	2,410	2,978
75,551	75,650	4,454	2,416	2,987
75,651	75,750	4,464	2,422	2,996
75,751	75,850	4,473	2,428	3,006
75,851	75,950	4,482	2,434	3,015
75,951	76,050	4,492	2,440	3,024
76,051	76,150	4,501	2,446	3,033
76,151	76,250	4,510	2,452	3,043
76,251	76,350	4,519	2,458	3,052
76,351	76,450	4,529	2,464	3,061
76,451	76,550	4,538	2,470	3,071
76,551	76,650	4,547	2,476	3,080
76,651	76,750	4,557	2,482	3,089
76,751	76,850	4,566	2,488	3,099
76,851	76,950	4,575	2,494	3,108
76,951	77,050	4,585	2,500	3,117
77,051	77,150	4,594	2,506	3,126
77,151	77,250	4,603	2,512	3,136
77,251	77,350	4,612	2,518	3,145
77,351	77,450	4,622	2,524	3,154
77,451	77,550	4,631	2,530	3,164
77,551	77,650	4,640	2,536	3,173
77,651	77,750	4,650	2,542	3,182
77,751	77,850	4,659	2,548	3,192
77,851	77,950	4,668	2,554	3,201
77,951	78,050	4,678	2,560	3,210
78,051	78,150	4,687	2,566	3,219
78,151	78,250	4,696	2,572	3,229
78,251	78,350	4,705	2,578	3,238
78,351	78,450	4,715	2,584	3,247
78,451	78,550	4,724	2,590	3,257
78,551	78,650	4,733	2,596	3,266
78,651	78,750	4,743	2,602	3,275
78,751	78,850	4,752	2,608	3,285
78,851	78,950	4,761	2,614	3,294
78,951	79,050	4,771	2,620	3,303
79,051	79,150	4,780	2,626	3,312
79,151	79,250	4,789	2,632	3,322
79,251	79,350	4,798	2,638	3,331
79,351	79,450	4,808	2,644	3,340
79,451	79,550	4,817	2,650	3,350
79,551	79,650	4,826	2,656	3,359
79,651	79,750	4,836	2,662	3,368
79,751	79,850	4,845	2,668	3,378
79,851	79,950	4,854	2,674	3,387
79,951	80,050	4,864	2,680	3,396
80,051	80,150	4,873	2,686	3,405
80,151	80,250	4,882	2,692	3,415
80,251	80,350	4,891	2,698	3,424
80,351	80,450	4,901	2,704	3,433
80,451	80,550	4,910	2,710	3,443
80,551	80,650	4,919	2,716	3,452
80,651	80,750	4,929	2,722	3,461
80,751	80,850	4,938	2,728	3,471
80,851	80,950	4,947	2,734	3,480
80,951	81,050	4,957	2,740	3,489
81,051	81,150	4,966	2,746	3,498
81,151	81,250	4,975	2,752	3,508
81,251	81,350	4,984	2,758	3,517
81,351	81,450	4,994	2,764	3,526
81,451	81,550	5,003	2,770	3,536
81,551	81,650	5,012	2,776	3,545
81,651	81,750	5,022	2,782	3,554
81,751	81,850	5,031	2,788	3,564
81,851	81,950	5,040	2,794	3,573
81,951	82,050	5,050	2,800	3,582
82,051	82,150	5,059	2,806	3,591
82,151	82,250	5,068	2,812	3,601
82,251	82,350	5,077	2,818	3,610
82,351	82,450	5,087	2,824	3,619

Continued on next page.

2016 California Tax Table — Continued

Filing status: 1 or 3 (Single; Married/RDP Filing Separately)   2 or 5 (Married/RDP Filing Jointly; Qualifying Widow(er))   4 (Head of Household)

If Your Taxable Income Is ...		The Tax For Filing Status		
At Least	But Not Over	1 Or 3 ls	2 Or 5 ls	4 ls
82,451	82,550	5,096	2,830	3,629
82,551	82,650	5,105	2,836	3,638
82,651	82,750	5,115	2,842	3,647
82,751	82,850	5,124	2,848	3,657
82,851	82,950	5,133	2,854	3,666
82,951	83,050	5,143	2,860	3,675
83,051	83,150	5,152	2,866	3,684
83,151	83,250	5,161	2,872	3,694
83,251	83,350	5,170	2,879	3,703
83,351	83,450	5,180	2,887	3,712
83,451	83,550	5,189	2,895	3,722
83,551	83,650	5,198	2,903	3,731
83,651	83,750	5,208	2,911	3,740
83,751	83,850	5,217	2,919	3,750
83,851	83,950	5,226	2,927	3,759
83,951	84,050	5,236	2,935	3,768
84,051	84,150	5,245	2,943	3,777
84,151	84,250	5,254	2,951	3,787
84,251	84,350	5,263	2,959	3,796
84,351	84,450	5,273	2,967	3,805
84,451	84,550	5,282	2,975	3,815
84,551	84,650	5,291	2,983	3,824
84,651	84,750	5,301	2,991	3,833
84,751	84,850	5,310	2,999	3,843
84,851	84,950	5,319	3,007	3,852
84,951	85,050	5,329	3,015	3,861
85,051	85,150	5,338	3,023	3,870
85,151	85,250	5,347	3,031	3,880
85,251	85,350	5,356	3,039	3,889
85,351	85,450	5,366	3,047	3,898
85,451	85,550	5,375	3,055	3,908
85,551	85,650	5,384	3,063	3,917
85,651	85,750	5,394	3,071	3,926
85,751	85,850	5,403	3,079	3,936
85,851	85,950	5,412	3,087	3,945
85,951	86,050	5,422	3,095	3,954
86,051	86,150	5,431	3,103	3,963
86,151	86,250	5,440	3,111	3,973
86,251	86,350	5,449	3,119	3,982
86,351	86,450	5,459	3,127	3,991
86,451	86,550	5,468	3,135	4,001
86,551	86,650	5,477	3,143	4,010
86,651	86,750	5,487	3,151	4,019
86,751	86,850	5,496	3,159	4,029
86,851	86,950	5,505	3,167	4,038
86,951	87,050	5,515	3,175	4,047
87,051	87,150	5,524	3,183	4,056
87,151	87,250	5,533	3,191	4,066
87,251	87,350	5,542	3,199	4,075
87,351	87,450	5,552	3,207	4,084
87,451	87,550	5,561	3,215	4,094
87,551	87,650	5,570	3,223	4,103
87,651	87,750	5,580	3,231	4,112
87,751	87,850	5,589	3,239	4,122
87,851	87,950	5,598	3,247	4,131
87,951	88,050	5,608	3,255	4,140
88,051	88,150	5,617	3,263	4,149
88,151	88,250	5,626	3,271	4,159
88,251	88,350	5,635	3,279	4,168
88,351	88,450	5,645	3,287	4,177
88,451	88,550	5,654	3,295	4,187
88,551	88,650	5,663	3,303	4,196
88,651	88,750	5,673	3,311	4,205
88,751	88,850	5,682	3,319	4,215
88,851	88,950	5,691	3,327	4,224

If Your Taxable Income Is ...		The Tax For Filing Status		
At Least	But Not Over	1 Or 3 ls	2 Or 5 ls	4 ls
88,951	89,050	5,701	3,335	4,233
89,051	89,150	5,710	3,343	4,242
89,151	89,250	5,719	3,351	4,252
89,251	89,350	5,728	3,359	4,261
89,351	89,450	5,738	3,367	4,270
89,451	89,550	5,747	3,375	4,280
89,551	89,650	5,756	3,383	4,289
89,651	89,750	5,766	3,391	4,298
89,751	89,850	5,775	3,399	4,308
89,851	89,950	5,784	3,407	4,317
89,951	90,050	5,794	3,415	4,326
90,051	90,150	5,803	3,423	4,335
90,151	90,250	5,812	3,431	4,345
90,251	90,350	5,821	3,439	4,354
90,351	90,450	5,831	3,447	4,363
90,451	90,550	5,840	3,455	4,373
90,551	90,650	5,849	3,463	4,382
90,651	90,750	5,859	3,471	4,391
90,751	90,850	5,868	3,479	4,401
90,851	90,950	5,877	3,487	4,410
90,951	91,050	5,887	3,495	4,419
91,051	91,150	5,896	3,503	4,428
91,151	91,250	5,905	3,511	4,438
91,251	91,350	5,914	3,519	4,447
91,351	91,450	5,924	3,527	4,456
91,451	91,550	5,933	3,535	4,466
91,551	91,650	5,942	3,543	4,475
91,651	91,750	5,952	3,551	4,484
91,751	91,850	5,961	3,559	4,494
91,851	91,950	5,970	3,567	4,503
91,951	92,050	5,980	3,575	4,512
92,051	92,150	5,989	3,583	4,521
92,151	92,250	5,998	3,591	4,531
92,251	92,350	6,007	3,599	4,540
92,351	92,450	6,017	3,607	4,549
92,451	92,550	6,026	3,615	4,559
92,551	92,650	6,035	3,623	4,568
92,651	92,750	6,045	3,631	4,577
92,751	92,850	6,054	3,639	4,587
92,851	92,950	6,063	3,647	4,596
92,951	93,050	6,073	3,655	4,605
93,051	93,150	6,082	3,663	4,614
93,151	93,250	6,091	3,671	4,624
93,251	93,350	6,100	3,679	4,633
93,351	93,450	6,110	3,687	4,642
93,451	93,550	6,119	3,695	4,652
93,551	93,650	6,128	3,703	4,661
93,651	93,750	6,138	3,711	4,670
93,751	93,850	6,147	3,719	4,680
93,851	93,950	6,156	3,727	4,689
93,951	94,050	6,166	3,735	4,698
94,051	94,150	6,175	3,743	4,707
94,151	94,250	6,184	3,751	4,717
94,251	94,350	6,193	3,759	4,726
94,351	94,450	6,203	3,767	4,735
94,451	94,550	6,212	3,775	4,745
94,551	94,650	6,221	3,783	4,754
94,651	94,750	6,231	3,791	4,763
94,751	94,850	6,240	3,799	4,773
94,851	94,950	6,249	3,807	4,782
94,951	95,050	6,259	3,815	4,791
95,051	95,150	6,268	3,823	4,800
95,151	95,250	6,277	3,831	4,810
95,251	95,350	6,286	3,839	4,819
95,351	95,450	6,296	3,847	4,828

If Your Taxable Income Is ...		The Tax For Filing Status		
At Least	But Not Over	1 Or 3 ls	2 Or 5 ls	4 ls
95,451	95,550	6,305	3,855	4,838
95,551	95,650	6,314	3,863	4,847
95,651	95,750	6,324	3,871	4,856
95,751	95,850	6,333	3,879	4,866
95,851	95,950	6,342	3,887	4,875
95,951	96,050	6,352	3,895	4,884
96,051	96,150	6,361	3,903	4,893
96,151	96,250	6,370	3,911	4,903
96,251	96,350	6,379	3,919	4,912
96,351	96,450	6,389	3,927	4,921
96,451	96,550	6,398	3,935	4,931
96,551	96,650	6,407	3,943	4,940
96,651	96,750	6,417	3,951	4,949
96,751	96,850	6,426	3,959	4,959
96,851	96,950	6,435	3,967	4,968
96,951	97,050	6,445	3,975	4,977
97,051	97,150	6,454	3,983	4,986
97,151	97,250	6,463	3,991	4,996
97,251	97,350	6,472	3,999	5,005
97,351	97,450	6,482	4,007	5,014
97,451	97,550	6,491	4,015	5,024
97,551	97,650	6,500	4,023	5,033
97,651	97,750	6,510	4,031	5,042
97,751	97,850	6,519	4,039	5,052
97,851	97,950	6,528	4,047	5,061
97,951	98,050	6,538	4,055	5,070
98,051	98,150	6,547	4,063	5,079
98,151	98,250	6,556	4,071	5,089
98,251	98,350	6,565	4,079	5,098
98,351	98,450	6,575	4,087	5,107
98,451	98,550	6,584	4,095	5,117
98,551	98,650	6,593	4,103	5,126
98,651	98,750	6,603	4,111	5,135
98,751	98,850	6,612	4,119	5,145
98,851	98,950	6,621	4,127	5,154
98,951	99,050	6,631	4,135	5,163
99,051	99,150	6,640	4,143	5,172
99,151	99,250	6,649	4,151	5,182
99,251	99,350	6,658	4,159	5,191
99,351	99,450	6,668	4,167	5,200
99,451	99,550	6,677	4,175	5,210
99,551	99,650	6,686	4,183	5,219
99,651	99,750	6,696	4,191	5,228
99,751	99,850	6,705	4,199	5,238
99,851	99,950	6,714	4,207	5,247
99,951	100,000	6,721	4,213	5,254

OVER $100,000 YOU MUST COMPUTE YOUR TAX USING THE TAX RATE SCHEDULES.

¶2 Alternative Minimum Tax

The tentative minimum tax rate is 7.0% (¶117).

¶3 Personal Income Tax Rate Schedules for 2016

These are the official rate schedules on which the tax tables that follow are based. These schedules *must* be used if taxable income is more than $100,000. For taxable income of $100,000 or less, the tax must be determined using the tax tables. Taxpayers filing Form 540 2EZ must use the tax tables in the 2016 California Form 540 2EZ Tax Booklet.

¶2

2016 CALIFORNIA TAX RATE SCHEDULES
SCHEDULE X
SINGLE, MARRIED/RDP FILING SEPARATE AND FIDUCIARY TAXPAYERS

IF THE TAXABLE INCOME IS		COMPUTED TAX IS			
OVER	BUT NOT OVER				OF THE AMOUNT OVER
$0	$8,015	$0.00	PLUS	1.0%	$0
$8,015	$19,001	$80.15	PLUS	2.0%	$8,015
$19,001	$29,989	$299.87	PLUS	4.0%	$19,001
$29,989	$41,629	$739.39	PLUS	6.0%	$29,989
$41,629	$52,612	$1,437.79	PLUS	8.0%	$41,629
$52,612	$268,750	$2,316.43	PLUS	9.3%	$52,612
$268,750	$322,499	$22,417.26	PLUS	10.3%	$268,750
$322,499	$537,498	$27,953.41	PLUS	11.3%	$322,499
$537,498	AND OVER	52,248.30	PLUS	12.3%	$537,498

SCHEDULE Y **MARRIED/RDP FILING JOINT / QUALIFYING WIDOW(ER) WITH DEPENDENT CHILD**

IF THE TAXABLE INCOME IS		COMPUTED TAX IS			
OVER	BUT NOT OVER				OF THE AMOUNT OVER
$0	$16,030	$0.00	PLUS	1.0%	$0
$16,030	$38,002	$160.30	PLUS	2.0%	$16,030
$38,002	$59,978	$599.74	PLUS	4.0%	$38,002
$59,978	$83,258	$1,478.78	PLUS	6.0%	$59,978
$83,258	$105,224	$2,875.58	PLUS	8.0%	$83,258
$105,224	$537,500	$4,632.86	PLUS	9.3%	$105,224
$537,500	$644,998	$44,834.53	PLUS	10.3%	$537,500
$644,998	$1,074,996	$55,906.82	PLUS	11.3%	$644,998
$1,074,996	AND OVER	$104,496.59	PLUS	12.3%	$1,074,996

SCHEDULE Z **HEAD OF HOUSEHOLD TAXPAYERS**

IF THE TAXABLE INCOME IS		COMPUTED TAX IS			
OVER	BUT NOT OVER				OF THE AMOUNT OVER
$0	$16,040	$0.00	PLUS	1.0%	$0
$16,040	$38,003	$160.40	PLUS	2.0%	$16,040
$38,003	$48,990	$599.66	PLUS	4.0%	$38,003
$48,990	$60,630	$1,039.14	PLUS	6.0%	$48,990
$60,630	$71,615	$1,737.54	PLUS	8.0%	$60,630
$71,615	$365,499	$2,616.34	PLUS	9.3%	$71,615
$365,499	$438,599	$29,947.55	PLUS	10.3%	$365,499
$438,599	$730,997	$37,476.85	PLUS	11.3%	$438,599
$730,997	AND OVER	$70,715.82	PLUS	12.3%	$730,997

Franchise Tax and Corporation Income Tax Rates

¶10 Bank and Corporation Franchise Tax

Corporations, other than banks and financial institutions, are taxed at the rate of 8.84% (¶816).

For the rate on banks and financial institutions, see ¶816.

For the rate on S corporations, see ¶806.

The minimum franchise tax is $800 for existing corporations (¶816).

Corporations are exempt from the minimum franchise tax for their first taxable year, see ¶816.

¶11 Corporation Income Tax

The rate is the same as the franchise tax on corporations other than banks and financial institutions (see above and ¶816).

¶12 Alternative Minimum Tax

The alternative minimum tax rate is 6.65% (¶817).

Federal/State Key Feature Comparisons

¶13 Personal Income Tax Comparison of Federal/State Key Features

The following is a comparison of key features of federal income tax laws that have been enacted as of December 18, 2015, and California personal income tax laws. California adjusted gross income (AGI) is based on federal AGI. The California personal income tax combines unique state provisions with subchapters and individual provisions of the Internal Revenue Code (IRC) that are incorporated by reference as amended through a specified date and modified for California purposes (¶101, ¶103, ¶201, ¶202). State modifications to federal adjusted gross income required by law differences are discussed beginning at ¶201. Special attention should be paid to adjustments required for same-sex married individuals and registered domestic partners (¶119) who are required to use the joint or married filing separately filing status.

Nonresidents and part-year residents.—California taxes its residents on their entire income, regardless of its source, while nonresidents are taxed only on income derived from California. A part-year resident must include in California AGI all income from any source for the part of the tax year when he or she resided in the state and income received from California sources during the portion of the year he or she was a nonresident (see ¶60, ¶61).

A nonresident's or part-year resident's tax liability is determined by first computing tax on total taxable income, as though the taxpayer were a full-year California resident for the taxable year and for all prior taxable years for any carryover items, deferred income, suspended losses, or suspended deductions, and dividing that tax by the income that the tax was calculated upon, to arrive at the tax rate. This rate is then applied to the California source taxable income of the nonresident or part-year resident to determine the nonresident's or part-year resident's tax liability (¶116).

• *Alternative minimum tax (IRC Sec. 55—IRC Sec. 59)*

California imposes an alternative minimum tax (AMT) that is a modified version of the federal AMT (IRC Sec. 55—IRC Sec. 59) (¶117).

• *Asset expense election (IRC Sec. 179)*

California allows an asset expense election (IRC Sec. 179) for personal income tax purposes that is limited to $25,000. California does not allow an IRC Sec. 179 deduction for qualified leasehold improvement property, qualified restaurant property, and qualified retail improvement property, nor does it allow a taxpayer's deduction for 2010 through 2015 tax years with respect to qualified real property that is limited by the taxpayer's active trade or business income to be carried over only to pre-2016 tax years and to be treated as property placed in service prior to 2016. California also does not allow the expensing of off-the-shelf computer software or of air conditioning and heating units (see ¶311).

• *Bad debts (IRC Sec. 166)*

California's treatment of bad debts is the same as federal because IRC Sec. 166 is incorporated by reference (see ¶308).

¶12

• *Capital gains and capital losses (IRC Sec. 1(h), IRC Sec. 1202, IRC Sec. 1211, IRC Sec. 1212, and IRC Sec. 1221)*

California generally determines capital gains and losses in the same manner as federal law (IRC Sec. 1(h), IRC Sec. 1211, IRC Sec. 1212, and IRC Sec. 1221). However, unlike federal law (1) California law treats capital gains as ordinary income and the amount of tax is not dependent on the holding period, (2) California does not permit capital loss carrybacks, and (3) California law does not provide for any special tax rates for capital gains (see ¶526). California no longer allows the deferral or exclusion of gain from the sale of qualified small business stock (see ¶525).

• *Charitable contributions (IRC Sec. 170)*

The California charitable contribution deduction is generally the same as the federal (IRC Sec. 170). However, California does not conform to federal provisions that provide an enhanced deduction for contributions of real property for conservation purposes and donations by businesses of food inventory, or disallow the deduction for contributions made to certain donor-advised funds (see ¶321).

In addition, California offers a credit for donations of real property for conservation purposes (see ¶143) and a credit for the costs of transporting donated agricultural products to nonprofit charitable organizations. However, California does not adopt amendments allowing individuals to claim a maximum 50% charitable deduction for contributions to certain agricultural research organizations applicable to contributions made on and after December 18, 2015 (see ¶141).

• *Child care credit (IRC Sec. 45F)*

California does not incorporate the federal child care credit (IRC Sec. 45F), but prior to the 2012 tax year California allowed an employer two separate credits for employee child care expenses: one for a portion of the costs of establishing a child care program or contributing to child care referral services and another for contributions to a qualified employee child care plan (see ¶125).

• *Civil rights deduction (IRC Sec. 62)*

California incorporates the federal civil rights deduction (IRC Sec. 62) (see ¶202).

• *Dependents (IRC Sec. 152)*

California conforms to the federal definition of "dependent" (IRC Sec. 152) (see ¶115).

• *Depreciation (IRC Sec. 167 and IRC Sec. 168 and IRC Sec. 1400N)*

California adopts federal depreciation provisions (IRC Sec. 167 and IRC Sec. 168) for personal income tax purposes. However, California does not adopt "bonus" depreciation allowed under IRC Sec. 168(k) or IRC Sec. 1400N. In addition, California does not incorporate the shortened recovery periods for leasehold improvements, restaurant, retail property, and motorsports entertainment complexes; the accelerated MACRS recovery periods for Indian reservation property; the special depreciation treatment for participations and residuals; the requirement that certain major integrated oil companies amortize geological and geophysical expenditures over a five-year period instead of a 24-month period; or the 50% additional depreciation allowance for qualified cellulosic biomass ethanol plant property. Also, because of California's conformity date, California has not yet conformed to the extension of the shortened recovery period for young racehorses placed in service after 2014 (see ¶310).

• *Earned income credit (IRC Sec. 32)*

For taxable years beginning on or after January 1, 2015, California provides an earned income tax credit in modified conformity with the federal earned income tax credit (IRC Sec. 32) (see ¶158).

• *Educational assistance benefits and deductions (IRC Sec. 62(a)(2)(D); IRC Sec. 127; IRC Sec. 221; IRC Sec. 222; IRC Sec. 529)*

California law is generally the same as federal law concerning employee educational assistance benefits (IRC Sec. 127) and the above-the-line deduction for interest on student loans (IRC Sec. 221) (see ¶242, ¶305). However, California does not allow the federal above-the-line deduction for qualified tuition and related expenses (IRC Sec. 222). Nor does California allow the above-the-line deduction for teacher's expenses (IRC Sec. 62(a)(2)(D)) (see ¶344, ¶202). Although California adopts the federal treatment of qualified tuition programs (IRC Sec. 529), California did not treat expenses for computer equipment and technology, or for Internet access and related services as qualified education expenses (see ¶250).

• *Foreign earned income (IRC Sec. 911 and IRC Sec. 912)*

The federal provision allowing an exemption for income earned by U.S. citizens living abroad (IRC Sec. 911) is not applicable in California; therefore, amounts excluded from federal AGI must be added back for California personal income tax purposes. Presumably, amounts excluded under IRC Sec. 912, providing an exemption for certain allowances paid to civilian employees of the U.S. working abroad, also have to be added back (see ¶231, ¶235).

• *Health insurance and medical expenses; Health savings accounts (HSAs) (IRC Sec. 105(b); IRC Sec. 106(e); IRC Sec. 139C; IRC Sec. 139D; IRC Sec. 162(l); IRC Sec. 213(a); IRC Sec. 223)*

California, like federal law (IRC Sec. 213(a)), allows taxpayers to claim an itemized deduction for unreimbursed medical expenses. However, unlike federal law, California has not increased the medical expense itemized deduction threshold from 7.5% to 10% for post-2012 tax years (see ¶325). California law is also the same as federal law concerning (1) the exclusion of reimbursements under an employer-provided accident or health insurance plan of medical expenses of an employee and an employee's spouse and dependents (IRC Sec. 105(b)) (see ¶219), and (2) the deduction of health insurance premiums for self-employed individuals (IRC Sec. 162(l)) (see ¶301). In addition, California incorporates the federal exclusion of qualified health care benefits provided to the member of an Indian tribe, the member's spouse, or the member's dependents (IRC Sec. 139D) (see ¶252), and the federal exclusion of the 65% premium reduction for COBRA continuation coverage (IRC Sec. 139C). Self-employed individuals may also claim a deduction for health insurance costs paid for a registered domestic partner and the domestic partner's dependents (see ¶301). However, California does not recognize health savings accounts (HSAs). Consequently, an addition adjustment is required for contributions to and earnings on HSAs. However, California personal income taxpayers may subtract any nonqualified distributions from an HSA included in federal taxable income (see ¶219, ¶247).

• *Indebtedness (IRC Sec. 108 and IRC Sec. 163)*

Generally, California incorporates IRC Sec. 108 by reference, with some modifications, including modifications for the discharge of student loans when the borrower is unable to complete a program of study because the school closes or did something wrong (applies to discharges from 2015 to 2019) (see ¶221). California only partially conforms to federal provisions allowing an exclusion from gross income for income from the discharge of an individual's qualified principal residence indebtedness, and only allows the exclusion through 2013. In addition, California does not adopt the federal provision allowing taxpayers to defer the recognition of discharge of indebtedness income arising from a qualified reacquisition of business debt instruments issued by the taxpayer or a related person. California's treatment of interest on indebtedness is generally the same as federal because IRC Sec. 163 is incorporated by reference; however, certain modifications regarding original issue discount (OID) instruments, mortgage interest, investment interest, and interest from loans made to enterprise zone businesses apply with the exception of certain OID instruments and investment interest. California has not adopted the repeal of the exception from the registration requirements for foreign targeted obligations under IRC Sec. 163(f) (see ¶217, ¶237, ¶305).

• *Interest on federal obligations (IRC Sec. 61)*

Generally, California does not tax interest received from obligations of the United States and its political subdivisions (IRC Sec. 61). The interest from these bonds is subtracted from federal AGI in computing California AGI (see ¶217). The FTB has ruled that interest from certain specified federal agency obligations is not taxable, whereas the interest from other federal agency obligations is taxable (see ¶217).

• *Interest on state and local obligations (IRC Sec. 103)*

Interest on obligations of state and local governments, other than from obligations of California and its political subdivisions, must be added to federal adjusted gross income in determining California taxable income (see ¶217).

• *Losses not otherwise compensated (IRC Sec. 165)*

The California deduction for business losses, casualty and disaster losses, and theft losses is generally the same as the federal deduction for such losses (IRC Sec. 165) (see ¶307). California, but not federal, law also allows 100% of any excess loss resulting from specified disasters to be carried forward to the next succeeding 15 years.

• *Net operating loss (IRC Sec. 172 and IRC Sec. 1400N)*

California allows a deduction for net operating losses (NOLs) that is patterned on the federal net operating loss (IRC Sec. 172), including the 20-year carryover for post-2007 NOLs, except that (1) California suspended NOL deductions for the 2008—2011 taxable years; (2) there is no carryback allowed prior to the 2013 taxable year and post-2012 carrybacks are limited to two years; (3) for pre-2008 taxable years, the carryforward period was limited to 10 years; (4) California does not follow the federal expanded NOL (IRC Sec. 1400N) for qualified hurricane and tornado disaster victims or federal disaster victims; and (5) only a specified percentage of pre-2004 NOLs could be carried over (an exception was provided for losses of businesses located in economic incentive areas and certain new businesses and small businesses) (see ¶309). Special rules apply to taxpayers residing in California for less than the entire tax year in which a net operating loss is incurred.

• *Personal residence (IRC Sec. 121, IRC Sec. 132(n), IRC Sec. 163(h)(3), and IRC Sec. 1033)*

California incorporates, with modifications, the federal provision regarding the gross income exclusion of income from the sale of a personal residence (IRC Sec. 121) (see ¶229) and the federal provision regarding nonrecognition of gain when property is involuntarily converted (IRC Sec. 1033) (see ¶229, ¶503).

California does not allow a deduction for mortgage insurance premiums (see ¶305).

• *Retirement plans (IRC Sec. 401—IRC Sec. 424, and IRC Sec. 1400Q)*

California generally conforms to federal provisions, as amended to date, regarding retirement plans (IRC Sec. 401—IRC Sec. 424) (see ¶206, ¶330, ¶607). The favorable treatment provided by federal law applies for California purposes to incentive and employee stock options to California qualified stock options (see ¶207). Although California generally conforms to federal deferred compensation provisions as amended to date, because California does not recognize health savings accounts (HSAs) it does not conform to an amendment made to IRC Sec. 408 that authorizes a one-time tax-free distribution from an IRA to an HSA (see ¶206). Consequently, a

¶13

California taxpayer who makes such a distribution is required to include the distribution in his or her gross income and is subject to California's penalty on premature withdrawals.

• *Start-up expenses (IRC Sec. 195)*

California's treatment of start-up expenditures is the same as IRC Sec. 195, because IRC Sec. 195 is incorporated by reference (see ¶334).

• *Taxes paid (IRC Sec. 164)*

Although California incorporates IRC Sec. 164, California does not allow the federal deductions for state, local, and foreign income taxes; state disability insurance; foreign real property taxes; or sales and use taxes. These disallowed federal tax deductions must be subtracted from federal itemized deductions in computing California itemized deductions (see ¶303, ¶306). California permits credits for net income taxes paid to other states, the District of Columbia, or U.S. possessions (but not to the United States or to foreign countries) on income that is also taxed by California (see ¶127). Such credits are available to residents (see ¶128), nonresidents (see ¶129), estates and trusts (see ¶130), partners (see ¶131), S corporation shareholders (see ¶131), limited liability company members (see ¶131), and estate and trust beneficiaries (see ¶130).

• *Unemployment compensation (IRC Sec. 85)*

California does not tax unemployment compensation (see ¶201).

¶14 Corporate Income Tax Comparison of Federal/State Key Features

The following is a comparison of key features of federal income tax laws that have been enacted as of December 18, 2015, and California corporation income tax laws. California incorporates by reference numerous Internal Revenue Code (IRC) provisions as of a specified date (see ¶803, ¶901). Some federal provisions are incorporated by reference with specific modifications, others are incorporated without any modifications, and some are not incorporated at all. State modifications to federal taxable income required by law differences are discussed beginning at ¶901.

• *IRC Sec. 27 foreign tax credit*

California has no equivalent to the federal foreign tax credit (IRC Sec. 27).

• *IRC Sec. 40 alcohol fuels credit*

California has no equivalent to the federal alcohol fuels credit (IRC Sec. 40).

• *IRC Sec. 41 incremental research expenditures credit*

California allows a credit for research expenditures that is generally based on the federal credit (IRC Sec. 41). However, California does not adopt federal changes that (1) increase the credit for amounts paid to eligible small businesses, universities, and federal laboratories; (2) allow a credit for amounts paid to a research consortium for energy research; (3) increase the rates used to compute the alternative incremental credit and allow taxpayers to elect to compute the credit under a third method, the alternative simplified credit; (4) repeal the alternative incremental credit election or the 14% alternative simplified credit calculation; (5) specify how qualified research expenses are allocated in transactions involving acquisitions or between members of a controlled group of businesses; (6) allow qualifying small businesses to apply a specified amount of the credit against payroll taxes; or (7) allow the credit to be applied against alternative minimum tax liability (see ¶818). California incorporates the IRC Sec. 280C provision that disallows a deduction for that portion of qualified research expenses or basic research expenses that equals the credit amount allowed for such expenses under IRC Sec. 41 (see ¶1023).

¶14

• *IRC Sec. 42 low-income housing*

California allows a low-income housing credit that is generally based on the federal credit (IRC Sec. 42) (see ¶818).

• *IRC Sec. 44 disabled access credit*

California allows a disabled access expenditures credit that is generally based on the federal credit (IRC Sec. 44) (see ¶818).

• *IRC Sec. 45A Indian employment credit*

California has no equivalent to the Indian employment credit (IRC Sec. 45A). Taxpayers may deduct expenses for which a federal Indian employment credit was claimed, as California does not incorporate the applicable IRC Sec. 280C provision (see ¶1023). California previously allowed credits to employers in certain areas for wages paid to qualified employees, among whom are members of a federally recognized Indian tribe, band, or other group of Native American descent (see ¶818).

• *IRC Sec. 45B employer social security credit*

California has no equivalent to the employer social security credit (IRC Sec. 45B).

• *IRC Sec. 45C orphan drug credit*

California has no equivalent to the orphan drug credit (IRC Sec. 45C). California incorporates the IRC Sec. 280C provision that disallows a deduction for the portion of qualified clinical testing expenses for which a credit is claimed under IRC Sec. 45C (see ¶1023).

• *IRC Sec. 45D new markets credit*

California has no equivalent to the new markets credit (IRC Sec. 45D). However, California does provide a credit for deposits made to certain community development financial institutions (see ¶818).

• *IRC Sec. 45E small business pension start-up costs credit*

California has no equivalent to the small employer pension plan start-up costs credit (IRC Sec. 45E).

• *IRC Sec. 45F employer-provided child care credit*

California has no equivalent to the federal employer-provide child care credit (IRC Sec. 45F).

• *IRC Sec. 45K fuel from nonconventional source credit*

California has no equivalent to the federal fuel-from-nonconventional-source credit (IRC Sec. 45K).

• *IRC Sec. 45L new energy-efficient homes credit*

California has no equivalent to the federal new energy-efficient homes credit (IRC Sec. 45L).

• *IRC Sec. 45M energy efficient appliance credit*

California has no equivalent to the federal new energy-efficient appliance credit (IRC Sec. 45M).

• *IRC Sec. 46—IRC Sec. 49 investment credit (former law)*

California has no equivalent to the former federal investment credit (repealed effective for property placed in service after 1985) or to the current federal investment credits (IRC Sec. 47, IRC Sec. 48, IRC Sec. 48A, IRC Sec. 48B, and IRC Sec. 48C). California does not provide an exclusion for grants received in lieu of the IRC Sec. 48 credit.

- *IRC Sec. 51—IRC Sec. 52 (and IRC Sec. 1396) wage credits*

California has no equivalent to the federal work opportunity credit (IRC Sec. 51—IRC Sec. 52) or the empowerment zone employment credit (IRC Sec. 1396). However, California allows a deduction for wages disallowed under IRC Sec. 280C when the credits are claimed (see ¶1023). California also allows credits to employers in certain areas for wages paid to qualified employees (see ¶818).

- *IRC Sec. 55—IRC Sec. 59 alternative minimum tax*

California imposes an alternative minimum tax (AMT) that is a modified version of the federal AMT (IRC Sec. 55—IRC Sec. 59). However, California has not adopted the federal provision allowing an alternative maximum capital gains tax rate for qualified timber gain of a C corporation for a tax year beginning in 2016 (see ¶817).

- *IRC Sec. 78 deemed dividends*

California allows a deduction from gross income for the amount of dividend gross-up included in federal gross income (IRC Sec. 78) when a corporation claims a federal foreign tax credit (see ¶909).

- *Interest on federal obligations*

Interest on federal obligations is taxable under the California franchise tax, but exempt under the corporate income tax (see ¶910).

- *IRC Sec. 103 interest on state obligations*

Under California's franchise tax, all state and municipal bond interest, including California's, is taxable and must be added back to federal taxable income. California bond interest is exempt under the corporate income tax and may be subtracted from federal taxable income (see ¶910).

- *IRC Sec. 108 discharge of indebtedness*

California generally follows the federal treatment of discharge of indebtedness (IRC Sec. 108), with modifications concerning the reduction of tax attributes. California does not adopt the federal provision allowing taxpayers to defer the recognition of discharge of indebtedness income arising from a qualified reacquisition of corporate or business debt instruments issued by the taxpayer or a related person (see ¶908).

- *IRC Sec. 163 interest on indebtedness*

California's treatment of interest on indebtedness is the same as federal because IRC Sec. 163 is incorporated by reference. California has not adopted the repeal of the exception from the registration requirements for foreign targeted obligations under IRC Sec. 163(f) (see ¶1004).

- *IRC Sec. 164 income and franchise tax deductions*

California does not allow a subtraction for state, federal, or foreign taxes on or measured by income (see ¶1006).

- *IRC Sec. 165 losses*

Generally, California's treatment of losses is the same as federal because IRC Sec. 165 is incorporated by reference. California, but not federal, law also allows 100% of any excess loss resulting from specified disasters to be carried forward to the next succeeding 15 years (see ¶1007, ¶1010).

- *IRC Sec. 166 bad debts*

California's treatment of bad debts is the same as federal because IRC Sec. 166 is incorporated by reference (see ¶1009).

¶14

• *IRC Sec. 167 and IRC Sec. 168 (and IRC Sec. 1400N) depreciation*

California does not follow federal ACRS or MACRS depreciation with respect to corporate taxpayers (IRC Sec. 167 and IRC Sec. 168). The pre-ACRS federal Asset Depreciation Range System (ADR) is applicable in California. Consequently, neither federal bonus depreciation nor the limits placed on sales-in, lease out (SILO) transactions or the shortened recovery periods for leasehold improvements, restaurant property, or retail improvement property apply in California. Although California does allow the income forecast method of depreciation, it has not incorporated the special federal treatment provided to distribution costs and participations and residuals. California also does not adopt various federal provisions, including those relating to (1) amortization of geological and geophysical expenses, electric transmission property, and natural gas lines; (2) the shortening of the recovery period for young racehorses, electric meter systems, and electric grid systems; and (3) the accelerated write-offs for biomass ethanol plant property, reuse and recycling property, and qualified disaster assistance property (see ¶1011).

• *IRC Sec. 168(f) safe harbor leasing (pre-1984 leases)*

California recognizes safe harbor leases under former IRC Sec. 168(f) (see ¶1011).

• *IRC Sec. 169 pollution control facilities amortization*

California's treatment of pollution control facilities is the same as federal (IRC Sec. 169) because the IRC is incorporated by reference, except that the facility must be located in California (see ¶1011).

• *IRC Sec. 170 charitable contributions*

California and federal laws are generally parallel. However, there are differences in the (1) income from which the contributions are deducted, (2) types of contributions eligible for the deduction, and (3) treatment of appreciated property. For example, California does not follow the special rules for deductions of charitable contributions of real property for conservation purposes (which were made available to native corporations under the Alaska Native Claims Settlement Act after 2015). However, California does offer a credit for donations of real property for conservation purposes. In addition, California does not follow federal provisions that limit the charitable contribution deduction for patents and most other intellectual property, increase the substantiation requirements for donations of $500 or more, and limit the deductions for donations of vehicles, boats, and aircraft while simultaneously increasing the substantiation requirements. California has also not conformed to federal provisions that allow enhanced deductions for donations of food inventory (see ¶818, ¶1014, ¶1312). California allows a credit for the costs of transporting donated agricultural products to nonprofit charitable organizations (see ¶818).

• *IRC Sec. 171 amortizable bond premium*

The California provisions are generally the same as federal law (IRC Sec. 171). However, a rule in the California provision for computing the amount of amortizable bond premium for the year in which a bond having a call date is actually called differs from the federal rule (see ¶1015).

• *IRC Sec. 172 (and IRC Sec. 1400N) net operating loss*

California permits the deduction of an apportioned and allocated NOL, generally in accord with the federal provisions (IRC Sec. 172), except that (1) California suspended NOL deductions for the 2008—2011 taxable years, (2) there was no carryback allowed prior to the 2013 taxable year and post-2012 carrybacks are limited to two years, (3) for pre-2008 taxable years, the carryforward period was limited to 10 years, (4) California does not follow the federal expanded NOL (IRC Sec. 1400N) for qualified hurricane and tornado disaster victims or federal disaster victims, and (5) only a specified percentage of pre-2004 NOLs could be carried over (an exception was

¶14

provided for losses of businesses located in economic incentive areas and certain new businesses and small businesses). NOLs incurred after 2011 may be carried forward for 20 years (see ¶ 1024).

• *IRC Sec. 174 research and experimental expenditures*

California's treatment of research and experimental expenditures is the same as federal because IRC Sec. 174 is incorporated by reference (see ¶ 1011).

• *IRC Sec. 179 asset expense election*

California allows a limited asset expense election (IRC Sec. 179) for corporation franchise and income tax purposes that is limited to $25,000, and reduced if the cost of all IRC Sec. 179 property placed in service during the taxable year is more than $200,000. California does not allow an expanded asset expense election for disaster assistance property (IRC Sec. 179(e)), nor does it permit revocation of an election without approval after 2014 (IRC Sec. 179(c)(2)). California also does not allow the expensing of off-the-shelf computer software, air conditioning units, or heating units. In addition, California does not conform to federal changes that repealed the limitation on the amount of Sec. 179 property that can be attributable to qualified real property and the corresponding provision on carryforwards of disallowed amounts attributable to qualified real property (IRC Sec. 179(f)) (see ¶ 1011).

• *IRC Sec. 179D energy efficient commercial building deduction*

California does not incorporate the federal provisions allowing qualified taxpayers to claim a deduction for energy efficiency improvements installed on U.S. commercial property (IRC Sec. 179D) (see ¶ 1027).

• *IRC Sec. 190 deduction for barriers removal*

The California provision is generally the same as the federal provision (IRC Sec. 190), except that under California law, but not federal law, the deduction is extended to cover the costs of installing a qualified emergency exit/safe area refuge system (see ¶ 1001).

• *IRC Sec. 195 start-up expenses*

California's treatment of start-up expenditures is the same as federal because IRC Sec. 195 is incorporated by reference. However, California does not allow the increased deduction and threshold amounts for the 2010 tax year (see ¶ 1018).

• *IRC Sec. 197 amortization of intangibles*

California's treatment of amortization of intangibles is the same as federal because IRC Sec. 197 is incorporated by reference (see ¶ 1011).

• *IRC Sec. 199 domestic production activities deduction*

California does not allow the domestic production activities deduction (IRC Sec. 199) (see ¶ 925).

• *IRC Sec. 243—IRC Sec. 245 dividends received deduction*

California does not incorporate the federal dividends received deduction (IRC Sec. 243—IRC Sec. 245), but does allow a deduction for intercompany dividends and a deduction for dividends received from an insurance company subsidiary (see ¶ 909).

• *IRC Sec. 248 organizational expenditures*

California law is similar, but not identical to the federal provision (IRC Sec. 248) regarding the treatment of organizational expenditures (see ¶ 1011).

¶14

- *IRC Sec. 301—IRC Sec. 385 corporate distributions and adjustments*

Generally, California's treatment of corporate distributions and adjustments is the same as federal (IRC Sec. 301—IRC Sec. 385) with minor modifications (see ¶1211 et seq.). However, California has not incorporated amendments made to IRC Sec. 382 that provide an exception to the rule that limits the offset of taxable income post-change tax years by pre-change net operating losses, certain built-in gains, and deductions for a loss corporation that experiences an ownership change as a result of specified restructuring plans required by the Treasury Department (see ¶1024). In addition, while California incorporates IRC Sec. 355 as of its conformity date, California has not adopted amendments effective generally for distributions on or after December 7, 2015, providing that IRC Sec. 355 will not apply to any distribution if either the distributing corporation or the controlled corporation is a real estate investment trust (REIT) (see ¶1215).

- *IRC Sec. 441—IRC Sec. 483 accounting periods and methods*

Generally, California's accounting periods and methods are the same as federal because California automatically incorporates most federal changes made to IRC Sec. 457 (see ¶1100 et seq.).

The incorporation of IRC Sec. 482 gives the state tax agency the authority to allocate income and deductions among related taxpayers to avoid evasion of tax or to clearly reflect income (see ¶1110).

California does not incorporate IRC Sec. 457A, which provides rules for compensation from nonqualified deferred compensation plans maintained by foreign corporations (see ¶1100). California also has not conformed to the provision of IRC Sec. 451(i) that allows a taxpayer to elect to recognize qualified gain from a qualifying electric transmission transaction over an eight-year period (see ¶1106). In addition, California differs from IRC Sec. 469 for personal holding companies and closely held corporations with regard to special rules for rental real estate activities engaged in by real estate businesses, passive activity credits that are eligible to be carried over, the disposition of a passive activity in a taxable transaction, and the offset for rental real estate activities (see ¶1005).

- *IRC Sec. 501—IRC Sec. 530 exempt organizations*

The California provisions are similar, but not identical to the federal provisions (IRC Sec. 501—IRC Sec. 530). California incorporates the federal provisions regarding taxation of unrelated business income (IRC Sec. 512—IRC Sec. 514) with modifications (see ¶808, ¶809).

- *IRC Sec. 531—IRC Sec. 547 corporations used to avoid shareholder taxation*

California has no provisions comparable to the federal provisions regarding corporations used to avoid shareholder taxation (IRC Sec. 531—IRC Sec. 547). California does not impose a tax on accumulated earnings or on personal holding companies.

- *IRC Sec. 581—IRC Sec. 597 banking institutions*

California incorporates IRC Sec. 582, regarding bad debts, gains and losses involving securities or bonds. California has some provisions regarding financial institutions that are similar to the federal provisions but, in some instances, California has no comparable provisions (see ¶1009).

- *IRC Sec. 611—IRC Sec. 638 natural resources*

California's treatment of natural resources is generally the same as federal because IRC Sec. 611—IRC Sec. 638 are incorporated by reference. However, California did not incorporate the IRC Sec. 613A suspension of the 100% taxable income limit on percentage depletion deductions for oil and gas production from marginal properties or the modifications to the depletion deduction refinery exemption for independent producers that applied prior to 2012 (see ¶1012, ¶1013, ¶1250).

• *IRC Sec. 801—IRC Sec. 848 insurance companies*

There is no equivalent to the federal provisions relating to insurance companies (IRC Sec. 801—IRC Sec. 848). A gross premiums tax is imposed on foreign and domestic insurers in lieu of the corporation income tax (see ¶1902).

• *IRC Sec. 851—IRC Sec. 860L RICs, REITs, REMICs, and FASITs*

California incorporates, with certain exceptions, the federal provisions on RICs, REITs, REMICs, and former FASITs (see ¶805).

• *IRC Sec. 861—IRC Sec. 865 foreign source income*

California does not follow the foreign sourcing rules (IRC Sec. 861—IRC Sec. 865). Multistate and international businesses that conduct business both inside and outside California utilize the state's allocation (see ¶1303) and apportionment rules (see ¶1302) for determining whether income is attributable to state sources. California allows a subtraction from taxable income for income derived from the operation of aircraft or ships by a foreign corporation. (see ¶916)

• *IRC Sec. 901—IRC Sec. 908 foreign tax credit*

California has no provisions comparable to those relating to the foreign tax credit (IRC Sec. 901—IRC Sec. 908).

• *IRC Sec. 1001—IRC Sec. 1092 gain or loss on disposition of property*

California specifically incorporates several federal provisions; has some provisions that are similar to the federal provisions; and, in some cases, has no comparable provisions (see ¶1201 et seq.). For corporate income tax purposes, California has no comparable provision to IRC Sec. 1014, concerning the basis of property acquired from a decedent. California has not incorporated federal amendments that (1) extend the IRC Sec. 1033 replacement period for nonrecognition of gain as a result of an involuntary conversion of business property from two years to five years for property converted by Hurricane Katrina or by the 2007 Kansas tornadoes (¶1202); (2) provide for the nonrecognition of gain from the exchange of certain long-term care contracts (¶1207); and (3) amend IRC Sec. 1031 to preclude certain exchanges of mutual ditch, reservoir or irrigation company stock.

• *IRC Sec. 1201 alternative capital gains tax*

California does not provide for an alternative tax rate on capital gains.

• *IRC Sec. 1211 and IRC Sec. 1212 capital losses*

California's treatment of capital loss carryovers is the same as federal because IRC Sec. 1211 and IRC Sec. 1212 are incorporated by reference. However, California does not allow capital loss carrybacks (see ¶1222).

• *IRC Sec. 1221—IRC Sec. 1260 determining capital gains and losses*

Generally, California's determination of capital gains and losses is the same as federal because IRC Sec. 1221—IRC Sec. 1260 are incorporated by reference (see ¶1222 et seq.).

• *IRC Sec. 1361—IRC Sec. 1379 S corporations*

California adopts federal treatment of S corporations and their shareholders (IRC Sec. 1361—IRC Sec. 1379), but imposes a 1.5% tax on S corporation net income prior to its pass-through to shareholders. California did not adopt the amendment to IRC Sec. 1367, regarding the basis reduction in stock of a shareholder as the result of a charitable contribution or amendments that changed this rule so that the basis reduction does not apply to a charitable contribution of appreciated property to the extent that the shareholder's pro rata share of the contribution exceeds the shareholder's pro rata share of the adjusted basis of the property. Nor does California conform to the seven-year recognition period under IRC Sec. 1374 for imposition of the built-in gains tax applicable to the 2009 and 2010 tax years, or the five-year recognition period for tax years after 2010. California conforms to IRC Sec. 1361 and IRC Sec. 1362 that impact eligibility, elections, and terminations, as those provisions are currently in effect for federal purposes, but does not conform to other amendments made to those IRC sections (see ¶806).

• *Sec. 1391--IRC Sec. 1397F and IRC Sec. 1400E—IRC Sec. 1400J empowerment zones and renewal communities*

California has no provisions directly comparable to the federal provisions regarding empowerment zones and renewal communities (IRC Sec. 1391—IRC Sec. 1400J). However, prior to the 2014 tax year, California provided its own tax incentives for taxpayers conducting business activities within geographically targeted economic development areas (EDAs), including enterprise zones, manufacturing enhancement areas, targeted tax areas, and local agency military base recovery areas. The California EDA hiring credits are generally not operative for tax years beginning after 2013; however, the credits continue to apply for tax years beginning on or after January 1, 2014, with respect to qualified employees who are employed by qualified taxpayers within the 60-month period immediately preceding that date. Beginning with the 2014 tax year, a hiring credit is available to businesses hiring full-time employees for work in a designated census tract area or an economic development area (see ¶818). Taxpayers may deduct expenses for which a federal empowerment zone employment credit was claimed, as California does not incorporate the applicable IRC Sec. 280C provision (see ¶1023).

• *IRC Sec. 1501—IRC Sec. 1504 consolidated returns*

Except for certain affiliated groups of railroad corporations, California does not incorporate the federal provisions allowing affiliated corporations to file consolidated returns (see ¶812).

Business Incentives and Credits

¶15 Introduction

California has created a number of tax incentives designed to attract business to the state, stimulate expansion, and/or encourage certain economic activity. These incentives are listed below, by tax, with a brief description and a cross-reference to the paragraph at which they are discussed in greater detail. Most exemptions and deductions, which are too numerous to be fully included below, are discussed under the taxes to which they apply (see the Table of Contents or the Topical Index).

¶16 Corporate Franchise and Income Taxes

• *California competes credit*

Employers may negotiate with the Governor's Office of Business and Economic Development (GO-Biz) to receive credits for increased employment, investments, etc. (¶818).

• *College access credit*

For taxable years beginning after 2013 and before 2017, a credit is allowed for cash contributions made to the College Access Tax Credit Fund. Also, for taxable years beginning on or after January 1, 2017, and before January 1, 2018, a new college access tax credit is allowed in an amount equal to 50% of the amount contributed by the taxpayer to the College Access Tax Credit Fund, as allocated and certified by the California Educational Facilities Authority (CEFA) (¶818).

• *Community development financial institutions investment credit*

For taxable years beginning before 2017, California allows a credit equal to 20% of each qualified investment made into a community development financial institution. However, only investments certified by the California Organized Investment Network prior to January 1, 2017, qualify for the credit (¶818).

• *Disabled access expenditures credit*

California allows eligible small businesses a credit for 50% of up to $250 of the disabled access expenditures paid or incurred by those businesses to comply with the federal Americans with Disabilities Act (¶818).

• *Donated agricultural products credits*

California allows a credit against net tax for 50% of the costs paid or incurred in connection with the transportation of agricultural products donated to nonprofit charitable organizations and a credit for farmers who donate fresh fruit and/or vegetables to California food banks (¶818).

• *Enhanced oil recovery credit*

California allows certain independent oil producers an enhanced oil recovery credit equal to one third of the federal credit allowed under IRC Sec. 43, provided the costs for which the credit is claimed are attributable to projects located within California (¶818).

• *Enterprise zone hiring credit*

Employers operating in enterprise zones are allowed a credit for wages paid or incurred with respect to qualified employees hired before 2014 (¶818).

• *LAMBRA credit*

Employers operating in areas designated as local agency military base recovery areas (LAMBRAs) are allowed a credit for wages paid or incurred with respect to qualified disadvantaged individuals or displaced employees hired prior to 2014 (¶818).

• *Low-income housing credit*

Corporations may qualify for a low-income housing credit, generally based upon federal law (IRC Sec. 42) (¶818).

• *Manufacturing enhancement area hiring credit*

Employers operating in a manufacturing enhancement area are allowed a credit for wages paid or incurred with respect to qualified disadvantaged individuals hired prior to 2013 (¶818).

• *Motion picture and television production credit*

A credit is available for qualified motion picture and television production expenses. Also, for taxable years beginning on or after January 1, 2016, a new credit is available for motion picture production expenditures paid or incurred, which is provided in addition to the previously existing (original) motion picture production credit. However, the new credit will not be allowed for any expenditures for which the original credit has been claimed (¶818).

• *Natural heritage preservation credit*

A taxpayer may claim a credit equal to 55% of the fair market value of qualified real property donated after 2009 and before July 1, 2020, and before July 1, 2008, for conservation to the California Resources Agency (CRA), a local government, or a nonprofit land and water conservation organization designated by the CRA or local government to accept donations (¶818).

¶16

• *New advanced strategic aircraft program employment credit*

For taxable years beginning after 2014 and before 2030, qualified taxpayers who manufacture property for a new advanced strategic aircraft for the U.S. Air Force are allowed a nonrefundable credit for qualified wages paid to qualified full-time employees (¶818).

• *New employment credit*

Qualified employers may claim a new jobs credit for a percentage of qualified wages paid to qualified employees, provided the employer has a net increase in the number of statewide jobs (¶818).

• *Prison inmate job credit*

Employers may claim a credit equal to 10% of the wages paid to each prison inmate hired under a program established by the Director of Corrections (¶818).

• *Research and development credit*

California provides a credit for research and development expenditures that is generally the same as that allowed under federal law (Sec. 41), with some differences in the areas of rates and percentages. The qualifying research must be conducted in California (¶818).

• *Targeted tax area hiring credit*

Employers operating in a targeted tax area are allowed a credit for wages paid or incurred with respect to qualified employees hired before 2013 (¶818).

• *Ultra-low sulfur diesel fuel production credit*

A credit is available for ultra low-sulfur diesel fuel produced by a qualified small refiner at a California facility (¶818).

¶17 Sales and Use Taxes

See ¶1509 et seq. for a listing of the major exemptions from sales and use taxes.

¶18 Property Taxes

• *Solar energy construction*

Through the 2015-2016 fiscal year property tax lien dates, active solar energy system construction or additions do not constitute new construction for purposes of required valuation reassessment (¶1702).

• *Economic revitalization rebate*

Any city, county, or special district (except for school districts) is authorized to rebate property tax revenues derived from economic revitalization manufacturing property. In addition to a property component, the use of the property must also create new jobs in the taxing jurisdiction (¶1711).

• *Capital investment rebate*

The governing body of any city, city and county, or county may implement a capital investment incentive program and rebate certain tax revenues derived from taxation of an assessed value in excess of $150 million for any qualified manufacturing facility (¶1711).

PART II

RETURN PREPARATION GUIDE

RESIDENTS: PREPARING INDIVIDUAL FORM 540

¶25 How Residents Are Taxed

The computation of tax on a resident return (Form 540) begins with federal adjusted gross income. Modifications (¶30) are made for law differences, then modified itemized deductions (¶31) or the standard deduction (¶29) are subtracted to arrive at "taxable income." Special rules apply to registered domestic partners (¶119).

After the tax liability is determined, personal exemption and dependent exemption credits (¶28) are subtracted. Various other special credits are also allowed (¶33).

Special California rate provisions (¶32) deal with (1) the alternative minimum tax, (2) the penalty or recapture tax on premature distributions of IRAs, Keogh plans, or other qualified retirement plans, (3) the penalty on nonqualified distributions from Coverdell education savings accounts and qualified tuition programs, (4) the penalty tax on nonexempt withdrawals from medical savings accounts, (5) the separate tax on lump-sum distributions, and (6) the tax on certain children's unearned income ("kiddie tax").

The deadline for filing the 2016 Form 540 and paying the tax is the same as the federal deadline—April 18, 2017, for calendar-year taxpayers (¶34). California grants an automatic extension of time to file to October 16, 2017.

Paragraph references throughout this discussion are to explanations in the *Guidebook*. The CCH CALIFORNIA STATE TAX REPORTER, should also be consulted for further details on any point.

¶26 Return Filing Requirements

California Forms: Forms 540 (California Resident Income Tax Return), 540 2EZ (California Resident Income Tax Return).

The following filing levels apply in 2016 (¶106):

2016 Filing Thresholds

On 12/31/16, the taxpayer's filing status was:	and on 12/31/16, the taxpayer's age was[6]:	California Gross Income[1]			California Adjusted Gross Income[2]		
		Dependents			Dependents		
		0	1	2 or more	0	1	2 or more
Single or Head of household[3]	Under 65	16,597	28,064	36,664	13,278	24,745	33,345
	65 or older	22,147	30,747	37,627	18,828	27,428	34,308
Married/RDP filing jointly or filing separately[4]	Under 65 (both spouses/RDPs)	33,197	44,664	53,264	26,558	38,025	46,625
	65 or older (one spouse/RDP)	38,747	47,347	54,227	32,108	40,708	47,588
	65 or older (both spouses/RDPs)	44,297	52,897	59,777	37,658	46,258	53,138
Qualifying widow(er)[3]	Under 65	N/A	28,064	36,664	N/A	24,745	33,345
	65 or older	N/A	30,747	37,627	N/A	27,428	34,308
Dependent of another person Any filing status	Any age	More than your standard deduction[5]					

[1] **California gross income** is all income received from all sources in the form of money, goods, property, and services that are not exempt from tax. Gross income does not include any adjustments or deductions.
[2] **California adjusted gross income** is federal adjusted gross income from all sources reduced or increased by all California income adjustments.
[3] See ¶15-320.
[4] The income of both spouses or registered domestic partners (RDPs) must be combined; both spouses or RDPs may be required to file a return even if only one spouse or RDP had income over the amounts listed.
[5] Use the California Standard Deduction Worksheet for Dependents in the 2016 California Resident Booklet to compute the standard deduction.
[6] If the taxpayer's 65th birthday is on January 1, 2017, she or he is considered to be age 65 on December 31, 2016.

Income filing levels are determined by reference to federal gross and adjusted gross income.

For purposes of the filing thresholds (1) single persons include taxpayers filing as heads of households and qualifying widowers; and (2) married couples and RDPs include taxpayers filing either jointly or separately.

Special filing levels apply for the filing of a separate return by a dependent (¶106).

For information regarding which taxpayers may file Form 540 2EZ, see ¶106.

See ¶105 for a discussion as to who is considered a "resident" of the state.

• *Military personnel*

Members of the U.S. Armed Forces who are residents stationed in California are subject to the same return filing requirement amounts as other taxpayers (¶105).

¶27 Filing Status

With the exceptions noted below, a taxpayer's filing status on the California return is generally the same as his or her filing status on the federal Form 1040 (¶114).

Military: Spouses who file a joint federal return and who had different states of residence at any time during the year have the option of filing separate California returns if one spouse was an active member of the Armed Forces (Form 540). The tax should be figured both jointly and separately in order to determine the more favorable filing status.

Part-year residents and nonresidents: This exception is discussed at ¶63.

Registered domestic partners: Registered domestic partners must file California personal income tax returns jointly or separately by applying the same standards as are applied to married taxpayers under federal income tax law, see ¶ 114.

Same-sex married couples: See ¶ 114 for a discussion of the filing status for same-sex married couples.

Factors in determining which filing status is advantageous are discussed at ¶ 114.

¶28 Personal and Dependent Exemptions

California provides credits against the tax for personal and dependent exemptions in lieu of deductions from income (¶ 113).

The 2016 tax credit amounts are as follows:

Single	$111
Married/registered domestic partnership (RDP), separate return	111
Married/RDP, joint return	222
Head of household	111
Surviving spouse	222
Dependent	344
Visually impaired person (additional)	111
Elderly person aged 65 and over (additional)	111

A physician's statement must be filed with the first return on which the visually impaired exemption credit is claimed (Instructions to Form 540).

The exemption dependent credits must be reduced for taxpayers whose federal adjusted gross income exceeds the threshold amounts specified for the taxpayer's filing status (¶ 113).

¶29 Standard Deduction

The election of a California taxpayer to itemize or to claim a standard deduction is independent of the federal election (¶ 303). Taxpayers may choose the more favorable tax treatment. California does not adopt the additional standard deductions available for specified items allowed under federal law (¶ 203).

The California standard deduction amounts for 2016 are as follows:

Filing status	*Amount*
Single	$4,129
Married/RDP filing jointly	8,258
Married/RDP filing separately	4,129
Head of household	8,258
Qualifying widow(er)	8,258

The above amounts are not increased (as under federal law) if the taxpayer is elderly or blind.

The standard deduction amount for dependents is limited to the greater of (1) $1,050 (for 2016), or (2) the individual's earned income plus $350 (for 2016).

See ¶ 335 for more details.

¶30 Modifications to Federal Adjusted Gross Income

California Forms: Sch. CA (540) (California Adjustments - Residents), Sch. D (California Capital Gain or Loss Adjustment), Sch. D-1 (Sales of Business Property), FTB 3801 (Passive Activity Loss Limitations), FTB 3805V (Net Operating Loss (NOL) Computation and NOL and Disaster Loss Limitations - Individuals, Estates, and Trusts), FTB 3805Z (Enterprise Zone Deduction and Credit Summary), FTB 3806 (Los Angeles Revitalization Zone Deduction and Credit Summary), FTB 3807 (Local Agency Military Base Recovery Area Deduction and Credit Summary), FTB 3809 (Targeted Tax Area Deduction and Credit Summary), FTB 3885A (Depreciation and Amortization Adjustments).

The computation on Form 540 starts with federal adjusted gross income (AGI); modification adjustments are listed to reflect federal/state law differences. The adjustments are grouped as subtractions and as additions on California Schedule CA (540). They are aggregated and then netted before entry on Form 540.

The California Schedule CA (540) has two parts. Part I reports the subtractions and additions to federal adjusted gross income. Part II reports the modified federal itemized deductions. Part II adjustments are explained at ¶31.

Practice Note: Registered Domestic Partners

Registered domestic partners (RDPs) must make additional adjustments to reconcile the differences that arise from using a different filing status on their California tax returns than their federal income tax returns. These adjustments may be made by completing a pro forma federal return or by utilizing the worksheets provided in FTB Pub. 737, Tax Information for Registered Domestic Partnerships. For more information concerning RDPs, see the discussion at ¶119.

The most commonly made modifications to adjusted gross income (AGI) are discussed in the following paragraphs. Other modifications are discussed in FTB Pub. 1001, Supplemental Guidelines to California Adjustments.

Interest on state obligations (¶217): Interest on bonds of states other than California or on obligations issued by municipalities of other states is added back to federal adjusted gross income.

Notes:

— Interest received prior to 2014 from investment in an enterprise zone is deductible under California, but not federal, law (¶240).

— Interest on Community Energy Authority bonds issued in California is deductible under California, but not federal, law (¶201).

Interest on federal obligations (¶217): Interest on federal obligations is exempt and, consequently, is subtracted from federal AGI. See also ¶217 for the pass-through of tax-exempt interest from a mutual fund.

Interest income from Federal Farm Credit banks, Federal Home Loan banks, the Student Loan Marketing Association (SLMA), the Resolution Funding Corporation, the Production Credit Association, the Commodity Credit Corporation, Certificates of Accrual on Treasury Securities (CATS), and Treasury Investment Growth Receipts (TIGRS) is also exempt interest that is subtracted from federal adjusted gross income; however, interest from Fannie Maes, Ginnie Maes, or FHLMC securities is taxable in California and, therefore, no modification is made to federal AGI for interest from these instruments.

Depreciation (¶310, ¶311): California depreciation is generally the same as federal depreciation (the "modified accelerated cost recovery system" under IRC Sec. 168) for assets placed in service after 1986. However, California does not incorporate the additional IRC Sec. 168(k) bonus depreciation for property placed in service in 2008—2019, and did not incorporate the additional 30%/50% first-year bonus depreciation available for qualified property purchased after September 10, 2001, and before 2005. Nor has California incorporated the additional first-year bonus depreciation deduction allowed for qualified New York Liberty Zone property or the accelerated write-off for qualified property located in a renewal community.

For taxable years beginning after 2002, federal law allows taxpayers to currently expense higher amounts under IRC Sec. 179 than is allowed under California law. Also, if the maximum IRC Sec. 179 deduction was taken, the federal and California amounts may differ; see ¶311 for a detailed discussion. In addition, California has not conformed to additional federal amendments that increase the amount at which the phase-out of the IRC Sec. 179 deduction begins and that allow the deduction to be claimed for off-the-shelf computer software, qualified real property, air conditioning units, or heating units.

¶30

California adopts the federal 39-year depreciation recovery period for nonresidential real property acquired after May 12, 1993, but only for property placed in service after 1996 in taxable years beginning after 1996. Thus, for California purposes, nonresidential real property placed in service before 1997 in taxable years beginning before 1997 continues to be depreciated over a 31.5-year recovery period.

California has also not conformed to federal amendments that include:

— classifying qualified leasehold improvements, qualified restaurant property, and qualified retail improvement property as 15-year recovery property and require the use of the straight-line method;

— providing special depreciation treatment for participations and residuals;

— allowing a 50% additional depreciation allowance for qualified cellulosic biomass ethanol and qualified cellulosic biofuel plant property, qualified reuse and recycling property, and qualified disaster assistance property;

— extending the shortened MACRS recovery periods for qualified Indian reservation property to apply to qualified property placed in service prior to 2017;

— providing shortened recovery periods for qualified farming machinery and equipment, motorsports entertainment complexes, and young race horses; and

— easing the current expense allowance qualifying criteria for film production expenses.

Further differences in the amount of depreciation claimed for federal and California purposes may arise due to California provisions that allow taxpayers operating in specified depressed areas to claim accelerated write-offs for certain property (¶316) and federal provisions that allow accelerated writeoffs for small film production costs (¶311) and reforestation expenditures (¶315).

ACRS is allowed federally for assets placed in service after 1980 and before 1987. However, for California purposes, assets placed in service before 1987 are depreciated over the period of useful life, or guideline periods established in the appropriate federal Revenue Procedure, using sum-of-the-years digits, declining balance, straight-line, or other pre-ACRS federal method.

Note: The differences between federal and California deductions are adjusted on FTB 3885A. The net adjustment may be an addition or a subtraction.

Capital gains and losses (¶523): California law, unlike federal law, treats all capital gains realized after 1986 as ordinary income. Federal law subjects long-term capital gains to a lower tax rate.

Differences between the amount of capital gain or loss recognized for California and federal purposes can occur both in the year a gain or loss is recognized and also in loss carryover years. For the 2016 taxable year, differences can occur between the gain or loss allowed for federal and California purposes because of the following:

— California does not permit capital loss carrybacks (¶526);

— California, but not federal, law excludes gain on the sale or disposition of qualified assisted housing developments (¶505);

— California requires certain adjustments to basis not required by federal law and makes certain federal adjustments inapplicable (¶559);

— California has not incorporated federal law that limits the amount of long-term capital gain that a taxpayer can recognize from constructive ownership contracts involving pass-through entities (¶525);

¶30

— California did not incorporate federal amendments that increase the exclusion of gain on small business stock for stock acquired after February 17, 2009 and before January 1, 2014. Further, California's exclusion is repealed beginning with the 2013 tax year (¶525);

— different basis may apply to property for which an additional first-year bonus depreciation was claimed for federal, but not California, purposes (¶310); and

— different basis may apply as a result of the different amounts that may be claimed as an IRC Sec. 179 deduction (¶311).

Differences between pre-1987 California and federal laws that can affect the reporting of capital gain and loss include the following:

— A difference in capital loss carryover (¶526).

— The pre-1987 holding periods and taxable percentages of capital gains for California were different from the federal.

— The California adjustment to capital gains computed for purposes of the investment interest expense deduction was different from the federal adjustment.

— Dividends from mutual funds were treated as ordinary income for California purposes.

— Because of the various differences between California and federal law mentioned above, the California basis may not always be the same as the federal basis of the property. Examples of such situations are as follows:

(a) valuation of property acquired by inheritance (¶546);

(b) depreciation of business property (¶310, ¶311);

(c) basis adjustment of property for moves into California (¶504);

(d) basis adjustments for California and federal credits (¶142, ¶151); and

(e) basis in the stock of an S corporation (¶233).

Schedule D, Form 540, is used to calculate the differences, and the appropriate modification is carried to California Schedule CA (540).

See ¶523—541 for further details.

State income tax refund (¶201): Any California income tax refunds included in federal AGI are subtracted.

Unemployment compensation (¶201): Unemployment compensation included on the federal return is not taxed by California and is subtracted from federal AGI.

Paid family leave (¶201): Paid family leave included on the federal return is not taxed by California and is subtracted from federal AGI.

Social Security benefits (¶201): California does not tax Social Security benefits. Any Social Security benefits included in federal AGI are subtracted.

Railroad retirement benefits (¶201, ¶205): Both tier 1 and tier 2 railroad retirement benefits, including ridesharing benefits and sick pay, received under the Federal Insurance Contributions and Railroad Retirement Act are subtracted from federal AGI.

In-home supportive services supplemental payments: Unlike federal law, California excludes in-home supportive services supplemental payments from gross income (¶201).

California lottery winnings (¶201): Any California lottery winnings included in federal AGI, including amounts received pursuant to an assignment, are subtracted.

¶30

IRA and Keogh distributions (¶330): The California and federal deductible dollar limits are generally the same for post-1986 tax years. For pre-1987 tax years, the amounts differed; consequently, the amount taxable on a distribution will differ. Differences may also arise if the taxpayer changed residence during the time he or she made contributions to the IRA or Keogh plan.

A worksheet to compute differences in the tax treatment of distributions for federal and California purposes is included in FTB Pub. 1005, Pension and Annuity Guidelines.

Net operating loss (NOL) (¶309): With the exception of the suspension of the NOL deduction for losses incurred or carried over in the 2008—2011 and 2002 and 2003 taxable years, the California NOL is determined under the same rules as the federal NOL except that prior to 2013, no carrybacks are allowed (including the extended NOL carrybacks) and for pre-2004 losses the amount of loss eligible for carryover to future years is generally limited to a specified percentage of the California net operating loss dependent on the year the loss was incurred. In addition, California limits NOL carrybacks for 2013 to 50% of the NOL and for 2014 to 75% of the NOL. Furthermore, applicable to NOLs incurred prior to the 2008 taxable year, an NOL may be carried forward for California purposes for only 10 years (five years for losses incurred in taxable years prior to 2000) rather than the 20 years permitted under federal law (15 years for losses incurred in tax years beginning before August 6, 1997). Commencing with the 2008 taxable year, California NOLs may be carried over for 20 years. The NOL carryover period is extended for losses suspended during the 2008—2011, 2002 and 2003 taxable years as a result of the suspension provisions.

Special rules apply for taxpayers operating in enterprise zones, the former Los Angeles Revitalization Zone (LARZ), local agency military base recovery areas (LAMBRAs), or former targeted tax areas. For taxable years beginning after 2000 and before 2003, special provisions also applied to farming businesses directly impacted by Pierce's disease.

Calculation of the California NOL is made on FTB 3805V and the appropriate adjustment is entered on California Schedule CA (540). The order in which net operating losses are absorbed is computed on a separate worksheet (which is not filed with the return). Calculation of the NOL for enterprise zone businesses is made on FTB 3805Z. FTB 3806 is used to calculate the NOL for taxpayers who operated in the former LARZ, FTB 3807 is used to calculate the NOL for taxpayers operating in LAMBRAs, and FTB 3809 is used to calculate the NOL for taxpayers who operated in the former targeted tax areas.

Recycling revenues (¶201): The income received by a taxpayer for recycling empty beverage containers is exempt for California purposes and is subtracted if included in federal AGI.

Expenses related to tax-exempt income (¶305): Expenses related to federally tax-exempt income that were disallowed as a deduction in computing federal AGI are subtracted for California purposes. Expenses incurred to purchase or carry obligations that are tax-exempt under California but not federal law are added to federal AGI.

Note: These modifications, to the extent not business-related, are made to federal itemized deductions.

Income from exercising California qualified stock options (¶207): Compensation received from exercising a California qualified stock option is excluded from California gross income and may be subtracted if the compensation was included in federal AGI.

Ridesharing and employee commuter deductions (¶241): An exclusion from gross income is available to an employee for amounts received from his or her employer for certain ridesharing or commuting arrangements. Because California does not place a limit on the monthly benefits that may be excluded and allows for more excludable ridesharing/commuter options, a subtraction from federal AGI may be allowed.

Pensions and annuities (¶205, ¶206): California rules for taxing pensions and annuities are basically the same as federal; however, the taxable amount may differ because of federal/California differences in the years when contributions were made. For further information see FTB Pub. 1005, Pension and Annuity Guidelines.

Passive activity loss (¶340): California generally adopts federal rules for computing the limitation on deducting passive activity losses. However, California does not conform to the federal passive activity loss rules relating to rental real estate losses suffered by certain taxpayers who materially participate in real property trades or businesses. Differences may also exist because the amount of passive income and loss may differ. Taxpayers must segregate California adjustments that relate to passive activities from California adjustments that relate to nonpassive items (¶340). This calculation is made on FTB 3801, Passive Activity Loss Limitations.

Other gains or losses (¶503, ¶537): Although California law on the computation of gain from sales of business property and certain involuntary conversions is generally the same as federal, the amount of gain or loss may differ because of federal/California basis differences. These amounts are reported on Schedule D-1.

Other adjustments may arise as a result of transfers between same-sex spouses and registered domestic partners, in which no gain is recognized for California purposes (see ¶119). Federal law requires that gain or loss be recognized in such transactions, see ¶502.

Alimony (¶204): Alimony received by a nonresident alien that was not included in the taxpayer's federal gross income is treated as an addition on Schedule CA (540).

Income from specially treated sources: See the indicated paragraphs for possible federal/California differences in the taxation of the following items: (1) noncash patronage dividends from farmers' cooperatives or mutual associations (¶232), and (2) interest income from investment in enterprise zones (¶240).

Claim of right adjustment (¶415): A claim of right adjustment may be claimed as either a deduction or a credit. A taxpayer that claims a credit for repayment amount on his or her federal return may claim a deduction on his or her California personal income tax return. Deductions of $3,000 or less are subject to the 2% floor for miscellaneous itemized deductions. A taxpayer that claims a deduction on his or her federal return, may claim a credit for the repayment amount on his or her California personal income tax return.

Income from S corporations (¶233): Shareholders of California S corporations add or subtract, as appropriate, the difference between their distributive shares of federal and California S corporation income or loss.

Income from partnerships and limited liability partnerships (¶616, ¶623): Partners add or subtract, as appropriate, the difference between their distributive shares of federal and California partnership income or loss.

Income from limited liability companies (¶625): Members and persons with economic interests in an LLC add or subtract, as appropriate, the difference between their shares of federal and California LLC income in the same manner as partners must include their distributive shares of partnership income in their taxable income.

Income from trusts and estates (¶605): Trust or estate beneficiaries add or subtract, as appropriate, the difference between their shares of federal and California trust or estate income or loss.

Business expenses incurred in discriminatory clubs (¶301, ¶336): California prohibits a business expense deduction for expenditures at a club that restricts membership or use on the basis of sex, race, color, religion, ancestry, national origin, ethnic group identification, age, mental disability, physical disability, medical condition, genetic information, marital status, or sexual orientation. There is no similar federal prohibition.

Penalty assessed by professional sports league (¶336): California does not allow a business expense deduction for any fine or penalty paid or incurred by an owner of a professional sports franchise if assessed or imposed by the professional sports league that includes that franchise. There is no similar federal prohibition.

Wages (¶201): If there is a difference in wages because of an employee's fringe benefits, also reported on the W-2, an adjustment must be made because California does not adopt the federal rules; the amount of federal wages reported on the W-2 is subtracted and the amount reported as California wages is added.

Crime hotline rewards (¶246): Any rewards received from a government authorized crime hotline are excluded from gross income.

Water conservation rebates/vouchers (¶244): California excludes from gross income specified water conservation rebates/vouchers received from local water and energy agencies or suppliers.

Financial incentive for turf removal (¶244): California allows an income exclusion for rebates, vouchers, or other financial incentive issued by a local water agency or supplier in a turf removal water conservation program.

Conservation and environmental cost-share payments (¶243): Certain cost-share payments received by forest landowners from the Department of Forestry and Fire Protection are subtracted from federal gross income.

Reparation payments (¶248): An exclusion from gross income is provided for amounts received as reparation payments for individuals who were required to perform forced or slave labor during World War II, Canadian government reparation payments paid to persons of Japanese ancestry interned in Canada during World War II, and Armenian genocide settlement payments.

Wrongful conviction compensation (¶201): Amounts paid by the state of California to compensate an individual for wrongful conviction and incarceration are subtracted from federal AGI.

Energy-efficient home improvement grants (¶245): Energy-efficient home improvement grants awarded by the State Energy Resources Conservation and Development Commission to low-income individuals are subtracted from federal AGI (¶245).

Medical expenses (¶219, ¶301, ¶325): California taxpayers may subtract from federal AGI amounts received from employer-provided accident, health insurance, and medical expense reimbursements and self-employed health insurance payments associated with expenses for the taxpayer's registered domestic partner and the domestic partner's dependents (see ¶119).

Medical benefits (¶252): Unlike federal law, California law does not exclude prescription drug subsidies. Such amounts must be added back to federal AGI.

Health savings accounts (¶247): California does not allow an above-the-line deduction for contributions to a health savings account. Amounts deducted on a taxpayer's federal return should be added back to federal AGI.

Mortgage debt forgiveness (¶221): California currently does not conform to federal law allowing an exclusion for mortgage debt forgiveness.

Teacher expenses (¶201): Unreimbursed expenses incurred by eligible elementary and secondary school educators for books, supplies, equipment, and material used in the classroom, to the extent deductible under federal law, but not California law, are added back to federal AGI.

Tuition and education expenses (¶344): California requires an addition adjustment for qualified tuition and related expenses for which an above-the-line deduction was claimed on a taxpayer's federal return.

Energy efficient commercial building costs (¶345): California does not incorporate federal law allowing taxpayers to currently deduct a portion of the costs of installing energy efficient systems in commercial buildings. Such amounts must be added back to federal AGI and an increased California depreciation deduction may be claimed.

Environmental remediation expenses (¶346): California requires an addition adjustment and depreciation adjustment for environmental remediation costs currently expensed on a taxpayer's federal return.

Earthquake loss mitigation incentives (¶256): California excludes from gross income amounts received as a loan forgiveness, grant, credit, rebate, voucher, or other financial incentive issued by the California Residential Mitigation Program or the California Earthquake Authority to assist a residential property owner or occupant with expenses paid, or obligations incurred, for earthquake loss mitigation.

¶31 Itemized Deductions

California Form: Sch. CA (540) (California Adjustments - Residents).

California itemized deductions are based on federal itemized deductions, with the modifications discussed below. These modifications are independent of the adjustments to federal adjusted gross income (AGI) discussed at ¶30, even though both are calculated on Schedule CA (540).

Taxpayers may elect either the standard deduction or itemized deductions for California purposes, regardless of which was elected for federal purposes (¶29). A federal Schedule A must be completed if the taxpayer did not itemize federally but chooses to itemize on the California return. A copy of the federal Form 1040 and all supporting federal forms and schedules must be attached to Form 540 if the taxpayer filed federal schedules other than Schedules A and B.

Practice Note: Registered Domestic Partners

Registered domestic partners (RDPs) must make additional adjustments to itemized deductions to reconcile the differences that arise as a result of using a different filing status on their California tax returns than on their federal income tax returns. These adjustments may be made by (1) completing a pro forma federal return, or (2) by utilizing the worksheets provided in FTB Pub. 737, Tax Information for Registered Domestic Partnerships. For more information concerning RDPs, see the discussion at ¶119.

The adjustments are as follows:

— *Taxes* (¶306): State, local, and foreign income taxes (including state disability insurance—SDI) and sales and use taxes claimed on federal Schedule A are not allowable deductions for California purposes and are subtracted from federal itemized deductions.

— *California Lottery losses* (¶336): California Lottery losses are not deductible for California purposes. The amount of such losses, as shown on federal Schedule A, must be subtracted from federal itemized deductions.

— *Federal obligation expense* (¶305): Because California does not tax interest from federal obligations, any expenses relating to such interest that have been deducted for federal purposes on Schedule A should be subtracted from federal itemized deductions.

— *State obligation expense* (¶305): Because California taxes interest from state or local obligations of states other than California, which is exempt for federal purposes, any expenses related to this interest that were not entered on federal Schedule A may be added to federal itemized deductions.

— *Employee business expense deduction for depreciation* (¶310): If the employee business expense deduction claimed federally included depreciation of assets placed in service prior to 1987, the depreciation component is recomputed for California purposes because business property was depreciated under a different method for California and federal purposes prior to 1987. For taxable years beginning after 2002, federal law allows taxpayers to currently expense higher amounts under IRC Sec. 179 than is allowed under California law. Also, if the maximum IRC Sec. 179 deduction was taken for property placed in service in tax years beginning after 1992 and before 1999, the federal and California amounts will differ (¶311). Finally, differences will result if a taxpayer claimed the additional 168(k) first-year bonus depreciation deduction that was available for federal, but not California, purposes for qualified property purchased in 2008 through 2014 or after September 10, 2001, but before 2005, or for purchases of qualified New York Liberty Zone property (¶310). Additional differences may arise as a result of the shortened federal recovery periods for leasehold, restaurant property, and retail improvement property and the accelerated write-off allowed on the federal return for qualified property located in a renewal community. All these differences must be accounted for in computing California's deduction.

— *Adoption-related expenses* (¶139): California allows a credit for specified adoption-related expenses. If the taxpayer claims the California adoption costs credit for the same amounts deducted on the federal Schedule A, these amounts must be subtracted on California Schedule CA (540).

— *Investment interest expense* (¶305): This item is generally treated the same for California as for federal purposes. However, taxpayers filing federal Form 4952 must file the corresponding California FTB 3526. Differences, if any, are reported on Schedule CA (540). Differences may occur because of the capital gain component in computing pre-1987 investment interest expense; the pre-1987 holding period and taxable percentages of capital gains were different under California law.

— *Federal mortgage interest credit:* California does not have a credit comparable to the federal mortgage interest credit. If federal miscellaneous itemized deductions on Schedule A were reduced by the amount of this credit, California itemized deductions may be increased by the same amount on Schedule CA (540).

— *Limitation for high-income taxpayers* (¶303): The itemized deductions of taxpayers with adjusted gross incomes over a threshold amount must be reduced by the lesser of (1) 6% (3% under federal law) of the excess of adjusted gross income over the threshold amount, or (2) 80% of the amount of the itemized deductions otherwise allowable for the tax year. A worksheet is provided in the Schedule CA (540) Instructions for calculation of the adjustment.

— *Federal estate and generation-skipping transfer taxes:* California does not allow deductions for federal tax paid on income with respect to a decedent or for tax paid on generation-skipping transfers. Accordingly, amounts deducted on federal Schedule A for these items must be subtracted on California Schedule CA (540).

¶31

— *Legislators' travel expenses* (¶301): California does not follow the federal rule allowing legislators to deduct expenses for every legislative day. California allows legislators to deduct only those expenses incurred on days that the legislators are actually away from their districts overnight. Amounts deducted for federal purposes on Schedule A that do not qualify for California purposes must be subtracted from federal itemized deductions.

— *Interest on public utility-financed loans for energy conservation* (¶305): California allows taxpayers to claim a deduction, not subject to the 2% floor limit, for interest on public utility-financed loans used to obtain energy efficient equipment for California residences.

— *Charitable contributions* (¶321): Differences may arise in the treatment of contributions on the federal and state returns. For instance, if a charitable contribution deduction was claimed for federal purposes for the same amount for which the college access credit is claimed for California purposes, no deduction for that amount is allowed on the California return.

¶32 Tax Rates

California Forms: Sch. P (540) (Alternative Minimum Tax and Credit Limitations - Residents), Sch. G-1 (Tax on Lump-Sum Distributions), FTB 3800 (Tax Computation for Children Under Age 14 with Investment Income), FTB 3803 (Parents' Election to Report Child's Interest and Dividends), FTB 3805P (Additional Taxes on Qualified Plans (Including IRAs) and Other Tax-Favored Accounts).

The tax rates are progressive, ranging from 1% to 12.3% of taxable income (¶116). The tax tables are reproduced at ¶3. The tax rate schedules are reproduced at ¶1. An additional tax is also imposed on the portion of a taxpayer's income in excess of $1 million (¶116).

• *Alternative minimum tax*

The California alternative minimum tax is imposed at the rate of 7.0%. It is generally calculated in the same manner as for federal purposes, but there are differences (¶117).

The California AMT is computed on Schedule P (540).

California incorporates the IRC Sec. 53 credit for "prior year minimum tax" (¶33).

• *Tax on premature distributions of IRAs, Keogh plans, annuities, and life insurance contracts*

Both California and federal law impose a penalty tax on premature distributions from IRAs, Keogh plans, other self-employed plans, annuity plans, and "modified endowment contracts," to the extent the distribution is included in income (¶206). The amount of the premature distribution includible in income for California purposes may differ from that allowed federally because of differences in deductibility of contributions in pre-1987 tax years and because California, but not federal law, treats rollovers from an IRA to a health savings account as a premature distribution (¶206, ¶330).

The California penalty is 2.5%.

The tax is computed on form FTB 3805P and reported on the Other Taxes line of the Form 540.

• *Tax on income received under nonqualified deferred compensation plan*

Both California and federal law impose an additional tax on income received under IRC Sec. 409A on a nonqualified deferred compensation plan (¶206). Beginning in 2013, the rate of additional California tax is 5% of the amount required to be included in income, plus interest. The tax is reported on the Other Taxes line of the Form 540.

• *Tax on nonqualified distributions from educational savings accounts*

Both California and federal law impose a penalty tax on distributions from Coverdell education savings accounts and qualified tuition programs that are not used for qualified educational expenses (¶206, ¶250). The California penalty is 2.5% and is reported on FTB 3805P.

• *Tax on nonexempt withdrawals from medical savings accounts*

Distributions from a medical savings account for nonmedical purposes are subject to a 10% penalty tax (increased to 12.5% for disbursements made during taxable years beginning on or after January 1, 2016) for California purposes, rather than the 20% imposed under federal law. California law, unlike federal law, imposes the penalty on rollovers from medical savings accounts to health savings accounts. For further information see ¶247. Form FTB 3805P is used to make the computation.

• *Separate tax on lump-sum distributions*

Taxpayers with lump-sum distributions of retirement income compute and pay a separate tax on these distributions if they elected to pay the separate federal tax (¶206). The California tax, which is computed on Schedule G-1, is determined under the same rules as the federal tax. The tax is transferred from Schedule G-1 to Form 540 and is added to the regular tax.

• *Tax on certain child's unearned income ("kiddie tax")*

California conforms to the federal "kiddie tax" provisions for calculating the amount of income tax for a child who has unearned income in excess of $2,100 (for 2016) and who is (1) under age 18 at the end of the taxable year; (2) under 19 years old and does not provide half of his or her own support costs with earned income; or (3) 19 to 23 years old and is a full-time student who does not provide half of his or her own support costs with earned income (¶118). The tax is computed on FTB 3800, which parallels federal Form 8615.

Under certain circumstances, a parent may elect to include the unearned income of a child on the parent's return. If the parent elects to exercise this option, FTB 3803 must accompany the parent's return.

• *Tax rates for servicemembers domiciled outside California*

Military compensation of servicemembers domiciled outside California, and their spouses, may not be included in gross income for purposes of determining the tax rate on nonmilitary income (see ¶225).

¶33 Credits Against the Tax

California Forms: Form 540 (California Resident Income Tax Return), Sch. P (540) (Alternative Minimum Tax and Credit Limitations - Residents), Sch. S (Other State Tax Credit), FTB 3503 (Natural Heritage Preservation Credit), FTB 3506 (Child and Dependent Care Expenses Credit), FTB 3507 (Prison Inmate Labor Credit), FTB 3508 (Solar Energy System Credit), FTB 3510 (Credit for Prior Year Alternative Minimum Tax - Individuals or Fiduciaries), FTB 3511 (Environmental Tax Credit), FTB 3514 (Earned Income Tax Credit), FTB 3521 (Low Income Housing Credit), FTB 3523 (Research Credit), FTB 3527 (New Jobs Credit), FTB 3531 (California Competes Tax Credit), FTB 3540 (Credit Carryover Summary), FTB 3541 (California Motion Picture and Television Production Credit), FTB 3546 (Enhanced Oil Recovery Credit), FTB 3547 (Donated Agricultural Products Transportation Credit), FTB 3548 (Disabled Access Credit for Eligible Small Businesses), FTB 3551 (Sale of Credit Attributable to an Independent Film), FTB 3553 (Enterprise Zone Employee Credit), FTB 3554 (New Employment Credit), FTB 3592 (College Access Tax Credit), FTB 3596 (Paid Preparer's California Earned Income Tax Credit Checklist), FTB 3805Z (Enterprise Zone Deduction and Credit

Summary), FTB 3807 (Local Agency Military Base Recovery Area Deduction and Credit Summary), FTB 3808 (Manufacturing Enhancement Area Credit Summary), FTB 3809 (Targeted Tax Area Deduction and Credit Summary), FTB 3811 (Donated Fresh Fruit or Vegetables Credit).

The order of using the various tax credits is specified in the instructions to the California 540 return, with each credit identified by a code number. If there are more than three credits claimed, the taxpayer must attach the appropriate credit form and summarize each credit on California Schedule P (540).

The following is a brief description of the allowable credits:

1. **Renter's credit** (¶133): A nonrefundable credit is available to qualified renters. For the 2016 taxable year, the amount of the credit is (1) $120 for married couples and registered domestic partners filing joint returns, heads of households, and surviving spouses, provided adjusted gross income is $78,125 or less, and (2) $60 for other individuals, provided adjusted gross income is $39,062 or less. Unused credits may not be carried over.

2. **Joint custody head-of-household, dependent parent credits** (¶136): For the 2016 taxable year, these credits, which cover both dependent children and dependent parents, equal the lesser of 30% of the California tax liability or $440. A worksheet is provided in the Instructions to Form 540 for computation purposes. Qualifications that must be met in order to claim the credits are discussed at ¶136. Unused credit may not be carried over.

3. **Research and development credit** (¶150): California generally allows the federal credit for increasing research activities with the following changes:

— research must be conducted within California to qualify;

— the applicable California credit percentage is 15% of the excess of qualified research expenses for the tax year over the "base amount";

— California retains and modifies the formula used by those taxpayers that elect to compute the amount of the credit using an alternative incremental method;

— California does not authorize the use of the alternative simplified credit and does not recognize that repeal the alternative incremental method for tax years beginning after 2008;

— California does not allow a credit against personal income tax for basic research payments;

— California limits the "gross receipts" that may be taken into account for purposes of calculating the base amount;

— the California credit may be carried over while the federal credit is part of the general business credit subject to the limitations of IRC Sec. 38;

— California law disallows the credit for expenses incurred to purchase property for which a sales and use tax exemption for teleproduction or other postproduction property is claimed;

— California does not incorporate post-2004 federal amendments that allow a taxpayer to claim 20% of amounts paid or incurred by the taxpayer during the tax year to an energy research consortium and that repeal the limitation on contract research expenses paid to eligible small businesses, universities and federal laboratories for qualified energy research; and

— California did not incorporate the federal suspension periods of July 1, 1999—September 30, 2000, and October 1, 2000—September 30, 2001, that were enacted by the Tax Relief Extension Act of 1999.

A married couple or registered domestic partnership filing separately has the option of one spouse or partner taking the full credit or of dividing it equally between them.

FTB 3523 is used to compute the credit. Unused credit from nonpassive activities may be carried over until exhausted.

4. **Credit for income taxes paid to other states** (¶128): A credit is allowed for income taxes paid to certain states and possessions, but no credit is allowed for income taxes paid to any city, the federal government, or a foreign country. A list of the states and possessions for which the credit is allowed appears at ¶128.

The credit for income taxes paid to other states is available only for net income taxes (excluding any kind of alternative minimum tax or other tax on preference items) paid to another state on income with its source in the other state that is also taxed by California. The latter requirement rules out the credit for tax paid on income from intangible property because such income is deemed under California law to be attributable to California as the state of residence. The amount of the credit is limited to that proportion of the total California tax payable as the double-taxed income bears to the total income taxed by California.

Schedule S, showing computation of the credit, must be attached to the California return along with a copy of the other state's tax return.

There is no carryover of this credit.

5. **Excess state disability insurance credit** (¶132): Excess employee contributions for California disability insurance are treated as a refundable income tax credit. For 2016, the credit amount is the amount contributed in excess of $960.68. Excess contributions may occur when a taxpayer works for more than one employer during the tax year. The amount of the credit is calculated on a worksheet included in the Instructions to Form 540.

Note: If more than the maximum was withheld by a single employer, or at a higher rate, the excess amount must be claimed as a refund from the employer rather than as a tax credit.

6. **Personal exemption credits** (¶113): Credits are allowed for personal and dependency exemptions (¶28).

7. **Disabled access expenditures credit** (¶140): California allows eligible small businesses a credit for 50% of up to $250 of the disabled access expenditures paid or incurred by those businesses to comply with the federal Americans with Disabilities Act. Except for the amount, the credit is similar to the federal credit allowed under IRC Sec. 44. The credit is computed on FTB 3548. Unused credit may be carried over until exhausted.

8. **Motion picture production credit** (¶137): A credit is available for 20% (25% for independent films) of qualified motion picture and television production expenses. Also, a new motion picture production credit is added for taxable years beginning after 2015 (¶137a).

9. **Low-income housing credit** (¶138): California allows a low-income housing credit for owners of residential rental projects that provide low-income housing located in California. The credit is similar to the federal credit computed under IRC Sec. 42, but also provides a set-aside for promotion of farmworker housing projects. The California Tax Credit Allocation Committee certifies to the taxpayer on Form 3521A the amount of the credit for each year in the credit period.

The credit is computed on FTB 3521. A copy of Form 3521A must be provided to the FTB upon request. Unused credit may be carried over until exhausted.

10. **Credit for prior year minimum tax** (¶152): California incorporates the IRC Sec. 53 credit for alternative minimum tax paid in a prior year by a taxpayer who is

¶33

not liable for the AMT in the current year. The credit is based on preference items that defer tax liability rather than permanently reduce the tax. The amount allowable as a credit in any tax year is limited to the regular California personal income tax for the year, less (a) the refundable credits that have no carryover provisions and (b) the credit for taxes paid to other states. Unused credit may be carried over. The credit is computed on FTB 3510.

11. **Enhanced oil recovery credit** (¶153): California allows certain independent oil producers an enhanced oil recovery credit equal to $^1/_3$ of the federal credit allowed under IRC Sec. 43, provided the costs for which the credit is claimed are attributable to projects located within California. FTB 3546 is used to compute the credit. Unused credit may be carried forward for up to 15 years. Only a credit carryover from a prior year is allowed for the 2016 taxable year.

12. **Senior head-of-household credit** (¶135): A credit is available to qualified seniors. A worksheet to compute the credit is included in the Instructions to Form 540.

13. **Prison inmate labor credit** (¶154): A credit is available to employers for 10% of the wages paid to certain prison inmates. FTB 3507 is used to calculate the credit. There is no carryover of this credit.

14. **Adoption costs credit** (¶139): A credit is available for up to 50% of the costs directly related to the adoption of a U.S. citizen or legal resident minor child who was in the custody of a state or county public agency. A worksheet is provided in the Form 540 Instructions to compute the credit. Unused credit may be carried over until exhausted. The credit is similar to the federal credit.

15. **Donated agricultural products credits** (¶141): California allows a credit against net tax for 50% of the costs paid or incurred in connection with the transportation of agricultural products donated to nonprofit charitable organizations. FTB 3547 is used to compute the credit. Unused credit may be carried over until exhausted. Farmers may also claim a credit for specified agricultural products donated to California food banks. For tax years beginning before 2017, the credit is equal to 10% of the food's inventory costs. For tax years beginning after 2016, a credit is allowed equal to 15% of the qualified value of the fresh fruits and vegetables donated. The credit is claimed on FTB 3811.

16. **Credit for community development investments** (¶156): For taxable years beginning before 2017, California allows a credit equal to 20% of each qualified deposit that is made into a community development financial institution and certified by the California Organized Investment Network prior to January 1, 2017.

17. **Natural heritage preservation credit** (¶143): Taxpayers may claim a nonrefundable credit equal to 55% of the fair market value of real property donated before July 1, 2020, for qualified conservation purposes to the California Resources Agency (CRA), a local government, or an exempt nonprofit land and water conservation organization designated by the CRA or a local government to accept donations.

18. **Household and dependent care expense credit** (¶142): A nonrefundable credit for employment-related household and dependent care expenses is allowed in an amount that is a percentage of the allowable federal credit. Unused credits may not be carried over.

19. **Ultra-low sulfur diesel fuel production credit** (¶151): An environmental tax credit may be claimed for ultra-low sulfur diesel fuel produced by a qualified small refiner at a California facility. The credit is computed on FTB 3511.

20. **New employment credit** (¶157): Qualified employers may claim a new employment credit for a percentage of qualified wages paid to qualified employees, provided the employer has a net increase in the number statewide jobs.

21. **California competes credit** (¶134): Employers may negotiate with the Governor's Office of Business and Economic Development (GO-Biz) to receive credits for increased employment, investments, etc.

22. **College access credit** (¶156): A credit is allowed for cash contributions made to the College Access Tax Credit Fund.

23. **Earned income tax credit** (¶158): A refundable earned income tax credit is allowed to certain low-income taxpayers.

• *Carryover credits*

Other credits for which carryovers may still exist (and the years for which they were available) include the following:

1. water conservation credit (1980—1982);
2. solar pump (agricultural) credit (1981—1983);
3. solar energy installation credit (1985—1988);
4. energy conservation credit (1981—1986);
5. ridesharing credits (1981—1986 and 1989—1995);
6. commercial solar energy credit (1987—1988);
7. political contributions credit (1987—1991);
8. residential rental and farm sales credit (1987—1991);
9. orphan drug research credit (1987—1992);
10. qualified parent's infant care credit (1991—1993);
11. commercial solar electric system credit (1990—1993);
12. recycling equipment credit (1989—1995);
13. low-emission vehicle credit (1991—1995);
14. salmon and steelhead trout habitat credit (1995—1999);
15. rice straw credit (1997-2007);
16. farmworkers housing credit (1997-2008);
17. employer child care program credit (1994-2011);
18. employer child care contribution credit (1994-2012);
19. targeted tax area sales or use tax credit (1998-2012);
20. local agency military base recovery area credit (1996—2013); and
21. new jobs credit (2009—2013).

All of the above credit carryovers may be claimed on FTB 3540, except for the targeted tax area sales and use tax credit and LAMBRA sales and use tax credit. See prior editions of the *Guidebook* for details about these credits.

¶34 When and Where to File and Pay Tax

The due date for filing California Form 540 and paying the tax is the same as the federal due date—April 18, 2017, for calendar-year taxpayers (¶108, ¶110). Returns made by fiscal year taxpayers are due on or before the 15th day of the fourth month after the close of the fiscal year. Returns made by mail are considered timely if properly addressed and postmarked on or before the due date.

Returns are filed with the Franchise Tax Board (FTB). However, the address to which they are sent differs depending on (1) whether an amount is due or a refund is expected, and (2) the type of form used.

Refund requests made on Forms 540, 540 2EZ, 540NR (Long and Short), 540X, 541, and scannable Form 540 are sent to P.O. Box 942840, Sacramento, CA 94240-0001.

Regular returns for which an amount is due are sent to P.O. Box 942867, Sacramento, CA 94267-0001.

Checks or money orders should be made payable to the "Franchise Tax Board" with the taxpayer's Social Security number written on the check or money order.

• *E-file*

The FTB also accepts electronic filing of returns through the e-file program. Tax return preparers who prepare and file more than 100 timely original California personal income tax returns during any calendar year and who prepare at least one personal income tax return using tax preparation software in the current calendar year must file all personal income tax returns for the current calendar year and subsequent calendar years using electronic technology (unless the taxpayer elects to file a paper return). Detailed information concerning the mandatory e-file program is available at the FTB's Web site at http://www.ftb.ca.gov/professionals/efile/m_e_file.shtml.

• *Electronic payments*

Personal income taxpayers must make their tax payments electronically if their estimated personal income tax installment payment or extension request payment exceeds $20,000 or if their total annual tax liability exceeds $80,000 (see ¶110).

• *Military personnel*

The due date for returns by members of the armed forces is the same as for other taxpayers, except that it may be postponed in certain cases (*i.e.*, duty outside the United States, service in a combat zone) (¶109).

¶35 Extensions

California Forms: FTB 3519 (Payment Voucher for Automatic Extension for Individuals), FTB 3537 (Payment Voucher for Automatic Extension for Limited Liability Companies), FTB 3538 (Payment Voucher for Automatic Extension for Limited Liability Partnerships, LLPs, and REMICs), FTB 3563 (Payment Voucher for Automatic Extension for Fiduciaries).

The Franchise Tax Board (FTB) will allow an automatic six-month extension to file if the return is filed within six months of the original due date. No written request is required. The automatic extension does not extend the time for paying the tax. Tax payments must be accompanied by the appropriate form: FTB 3519 (Payment Voucher for Automatic Extension for Individuals); FTB 3537 (Payment Voucher for Automatic Extension for Limited Liability Companies); FTB 3538 (Payment Voucher for Automatic Extension for Limited Partnerships, LLPs, and REMICS); or FTB 3563 (Payment Voucher for Automatic Extension for Fiduciaries).

Taxpayers should send FTB 3519 or FTB 3563 to the FTB at P.O. Box 942867, Sacramento, CA 94267-0008. FTB 3537 and FTB 3538 are sent to the FTB at P.O. Box 942857, Sacramento, CA 94257-0531.

Payment extensions may be granted for a reasonable period by the FTB (¶110). There is no prescribed form. Extensions of up to one year are also available to disaster victims or victims of terroristic or militaristic actions (¶110).

Taxpayers abroad: Taxpayers who are outside the United States on the return due date are automatically granted an additional two-month extension of time to file (¶109). Consequently, the extended due date for such taxpayers is December 15. However, interest accrues on any unpaid tax from the original due date of the return. Any additional extensions must be applied for in writing with a letter of explanation.

¶36 Estimated Tax

California Forms: 540-ES (Estimated Tax for Individuals).

For the 2016 taxable year, estimated tax payments are generally due if (1) the 2015 or 2016 California tax (less withholding and allowable credits) exceeds $500 ($250 for married persons filing separately), or (2) more than 10% of the taxpayer's 2015 or 2016 tax will not be paid by withholding.

The California alternative minimum tax (¶32) is included in determining any required estimated tax payments.

Estimated tax is paid in quarterly installments on the same dates as federal payments: April 15, June 15, September 15, and January 15. The January 15 installment need not be made if the taxpayer files a tax return and pays the balance of tax due by February 1. When a due date falls on a Saturday, Sunday, or other legal holiday, payments are due on the next business day.

The amount of estimated tax is equal to 30% of the estimated tax due for the tax year for the first installment, 40% for the second installment, 0% for the third installment, and 30% for the fourth installment (see ¶111).

Married couples and registered domestic partners (RDPs) may file separate or joint estimated tax payment vouchers, but no joint Form 540-ES can be made if the spouses/RDPs have different tax years or are legally separated.

Form 540-ES is used for paying estimated tax.

¶37 State Tax Assistance

The Franchise Tax Board (FTB) offers various taxpayer assistance programs ranging from providing trained volunteers to assist taxpayers at no cost in completing their tax returns to in-state toll-free telephone assistance. The toll-free numbers are included in the Instructions to Form 540.

In addition, the FTB has several district offices located in principal cities throughout the state. These offices and their addresses are printed in the 540 Instruction booklet.

¶38 Forms

Forms are available from the FTB's Web site at: http://www.ftb.ca.gov/forms/index.shtml or may be ordered directly from the state at the following address:

Franchise Tax Board
Tax Forms Request Unit
P.O. Box 307
Rancho Cordova, CA 95741-0307

California income tax forms and publications may also be obtained through automated telephones. The Internet address and telephone numbers are listed in the Form 540 Instruction booklet.

¶39 Interest

The California rate of interest on underpayments and overpayments of tax is based on the federal underpayment rate (¶711). The interest rate is redetermined semiannually and is as follows:

January 1, 2013—December 31, 2013	3%
January 1, 2014—December 31, 2014	3%
January 1, 2015—December 31, 2015	3%
January 1, 2016—December 31, 2016	3%
January 1, 2017—June 30, 2017	4%

¶40 Penalties

A penalty of 5% per month, up to a maximum of 25%, is imposed for failure without reasonable cause to file a return. If the failure to file is fraudulent, the penalty is 15% per month, up to a maximum of 75%.

The penalty for failure to pay income tax when it is due is 5% of the unpaid amount plus $1/2$% per month. If the penalties for failure to file and failure to pay are both applicable, the penalty imposed is the higher of (1) the penalty for failure to pay, or (2) the total of the penalty for failure to file and the penalty for failure to furnish information.

A minimum penalty of the lesser of $135 or 100% of the tax liability is imposed if the return is not filed within 60 days of the due date.

Other penalties are discussed at ¶712.

NONRESIDENTS AND PART-YEAR RESIDENTS:

PREPARING RETURN FORM 540NR

¶60 How Nonresidents Are Taxed

Nonresidents compute California tax as if they were California residents, then the applicable tax rate is applied to the nonresident's California-source taxable income (¶116).

The computation of taxable income on a nonresident return (Form 540NR) begins with federal adjusted gross income (AGI). Modifications (¶67) are made for law differences, then modified itemized deductions (¶68) or the standard deduction (¶65) are subtracted to arrive at "taxable income." Special rules apply to registered domestic partners (¶119).

After tax liability is determined, personal exemption and dependent exemption credits (¶64) are subtracted. The resulting amount is prorated to determine California tax liability. A nonresident's taxable income is multiplied by the ratio of (1) the tax on the nonresident's entire taxable income, computed as if the nonresident was a California resident for the taxable year and for all prior taxable years for purposes of any carryover items, deferred income, suspended losses, or suspended deductions, over (2) the nonresident's total taxable income (¶116). Special rules apply to military compensation (¶225) and income earned or received by Native Americans (¶254).

Further reduction to California tax is available by way of various other special credits (¶70).

Special California rate provisions (¶32) deal with

— the alternative minimum tax,

— the penalty or recapture tax on premature distributions of IRAs, Keogh plans, or other qualified retirement plans,

— the penalty on nonqualified distributions from Coverdell education savings accounts and qualified tuition programs,

— the penalty tax on nonexempt withdrawals from medical savings accounts,

— the separate tax on lump-sum distributions, and

— the tax on certain children's unearned income ("kiddie tax").

Paragraph references throughout are to explanations in the *Guidebook*. The CCH CALIFORNIA STATE TAX REPORTER should also be consulted for further details on any point.

¶61 How Part-Year Residents Are Taxed

A part-year resident is taxed on income received while residing in California and, except for retirement income received for services performed while residing in California (¶405), on income derived from sources in California during any period of nonresidency.

Computation of income for part-year residents, as for nonresidents, begins with federal adjusted gross income (AGI). Part-year residents use the same form (Form 540NR) as nonresidents and execute the same computational steps, as follows: California adjustments to federal AGI are made (¶67), followed by subtraction of modified itemized deductions (¶68) or the standard deduction (¶65). After tax liability is determined, personal exemption and dependent exemption credits are subtracted (¶64) and the result is prorated to determine California tax.

A part-year resident's taxable income is multiplied by the ratio of (1) the part-year resident's entire taxable income computed as if the part-year resident was a California resident for the taxable year and for all prior taxable years for purposes of any carryover items, deferred income, suspended losses, or suspended deductions, over (2) the part-year resident's total taxable income; see ¶116. Different rules apply to military compensation.

Various other "special" credits reduce the California tax base. These special credits include prorated credits, credits that are taken in full, and carryover credits (¶70).

Special California rate provisions (¶32) deal with

— the alternative minimum tax,

— the penalty or recapture tax on premature distributions of IRAs, Keogh plans, or other qualified retirement plans,

— the penalty on nonqualified distributions from Coverdell education savings accounts and qualified tuition programs,

— the penalty tax on nonexempt withdrawals from medical savings accounts,

— the separate tax on lump-sum distributions, and

— the tax on certain children's unearned income ("kiddie tax").

Paragraph references throughout are to explanations in the *Guidebook*. The CCH CALIFORNIA STATE TAX REPORTER should also be consulted for further details on any tax point.

¶62 Return Filing Requirements

California Form: Form 540NR (California Nonresident or Part-Year Resident Income).

Nonresidents: Nonresident taxpayers must file California returns if they have income from California sources and at least the following federal gross or adjusted gross income amounts, which are the same as for residents (¶106):

2016 Filing Thresholds

On 12/31/16, the taxpayer's filing status was:	and on 12/31/16, the taxpayer's age was[6]:	California Gross Income[1]			California Adjusted Gross Income[2]		
		Dependents			Dependents		
		0	1	2 or more	0	1	2 or more
Single or Head of household[3]	Under 65	16,597	28,064	36,664	13,278	24,745	33,345
	65 or older	22,147	30,747	37,627	18,828	27,428	34,308
Married/RDP filing jointly or filing separately[4]	Under 65 (both spouses/RDPs)	33,197	44,664	53,264	26,558	38,025	46,625
	65 or older (one spouse/RDP)	38,747	47,347	54,227	32,108	40,708	47,588
	65 or older (both spouses/RDPs)	44,297	52,897	59,777	37,658	46,258	53,138
Qualifying widow(er)[3]	Under 65	N/A	28,064	36,664	N/A	24,745	33,345
	65 or older	N/A	30,747	37,627	N/A	27,428	34,308
Dependent of another person Any filing status	Any age	More than your standard deduction[5]					

[1] **California gross income** is all income received from all sources in the form of money, goods, property, and services that are not exempt from tax. Gross income does not include any adjustments or deductions.

[2] **California adjusted gross income** is federal adjusted gross income from all sources reduced or increased by all California income adjustments.

[3] See ¶ 15-320.

[4] The income of both spouses or registered domestic partners (RDPs) must be combined; both spouses or RDPs may be required to file a return even if only one spouse or RDP had income over the amounts listed.

[5] Use the California Standard Deduction Worksheet for Dependents in the 2016 California Resident Booklet to compute the standard deduction.

[6] If the taxpayer's 65th birthday is on January 1, 2017, she or he is considered to be age 65 on December 31, 2016.

Regardless of the above threshold amounts, a return must be filed for any tax liability of $1 or more. This may occur, for example, if California adjustments to federal income (*e.g.*, non-California municipal bond interest) cause California taxable income to be higher than federal.

For purposes of the filing thresholds (1) single persons include taxpayers filing as heads of households and qualifying widowers; and (2) married couples or registered domestic partners include taxpayers filing either jointly or separately.

A "nonresident" is an individual who is not a resident. Case law dealing with the question of residency is found at ¶ 105.

Part-year residents: Part-year residents are subject to the same income filing-level requirements as nonresidents.

A "part-year resident" is informally defined as an individual who moves into or out of California during the taxable year.

• *Military personnel*

Nonresidents stationed in California under military orders are not considered residents. Consequently, their military pay is not subject to California taxation (¶ 105). However, servicepersons are taxed on all other income derived from California sources.

A California resident stationed outside California under permanent military orders is considered a nonresident.

The spouses of military personnel who come to California neither lose or acquire residence or domicile if they come to California solely to be with their spouse in compliance with the servicemember's military orders.

¶62

• Attachment of federal return

A copy of the taxpayer's federal return and all supporting documents must be attached to the Form 540NR.

¶63 Filing Status

Unmarried taxpayers: Single taxpayers are generally required to use their federal filing status. However, registered domestic partners must file California personal income tax returns jointly or separately by applying the same standards as are applied to married taxpayers under federal income tax law (see ¶114).

Married taxpayers: If spouses file a joint federal income tax return, one of the spouses was a California resident for the entire year, and the other spouse was a nonresident for all or any portion of the taxable year, a joint nonresident return (Form 540NR) must be filed. There are two exceptions to this rule. A couple filing a joint federal income tax return may file either separate returns or a single joint return in California if:

— either spouse was an active member of the military during the taxable year; or

— either spouse was a nonresident of California for the entire taxable year and had no income from a California source during the taxable year.

If one of these exceptions applies, the tax should be figured both jointly and separately to determine the more favorable status.

¶64 Personal and Dependent Exemptions

California provides tax credits for personal and dependent exemptions in lieu of deductions from income as provided under federal law (¶113).

The 2016 credit amounts are:

Single	$111
Married/registered domestic partner (RDP), separate return	111
Married/RDP, joint return	222
Head of household	111
Surviving spouse	222
Dependent	344
Visually impaired person (additional)	111
Elderly aged 65 and over (additional)	111

A doctor's statement verifying a visual impairment must be attached to the first 540NR return on which the exemption credit is claimed (Instructions to Form 540NR).

The exemption credits must be reduced for taxpayers whose federal adjusted gross income exceeds the threshold amounts specified for the taxpayer's filing status (¶113).

¶65 Standard Deduction

The election of a nonresident or part-year resident to itemize or to claim a standard deduction is independent of the federal election (¶303). Taxpayers may choose the more favorable tax treatment. California does not adopt the additional standard deductions available for specified items allowed under federal law (¶203).

The California standard deduction amounts for 2016 are:

Filing status	Amount
Single	$4,129
Married/RDP, joint return	8,258
Married/RDP, separate return	4,129
Head of household	8,258
Surviving spouse	8,258

The above amounts are not increased (as under federal law) if the taxpayer is elderly or blind.

Individuals who can be claimed on another's tax return are limited to the greater of (1) $1,050 (for 2016), or (2) the amount of earned income plus $350 (for 2016).

See ¶ 335 for more details.

¶66 Income Attributable to California

California Form: Sch. CA (540NR) (California Adjustments - Nonresidents or Part-Year Residents).

Nonresidents: Nonresidents are generally taxed on California-source adjusted gross income (¶ 231).

Part-year residents: Generally, part-year residents must include in adjusted gross income (AGI) for California purposes income from all sources attributable to any part of the tax year during which they resided in California, and income from California sources for that portion of the year during which they resided elsewhere (¶ 231).

• *Attribution rules*

The rules of attribution for various types of income are discussed in the following paragraphs (see also ¶ 231). The details are reported on Schedule CA (540NR).

• *Income from trade or business*

Business income of a nonresident is attributed in full to California if the nonresident's trade or business is carried on entirely in California (¶ 231). On the other hand, if the nonresident's trade or business is conducted entirely outside of California, none of the income is attributed to California.

Where a trade or business is partly within California and partly in other states, the manner in which the income is attributed depends on the relationship of the segments of the taxpayer's business. If the California business activity is separate and distinct from that carried on elsewhere (*e.g.,* a California hotel but an out-of-state manufacturing activity), only the income from the California portion is reported to California. On the other hand, if the in-state and out-of-state portions are integral parts of a single trade or business (*i.e.,* "unitary"), business income is apportioned by a formula as discussed below.

The term "business income" means all income that arises from the conduct of the business operations of a taxpayer. Typically it includes those items reported on federal Schedules C or C-EZ. "Nonbusiness income" is all other income. Nonbusiness income is allocated, rather than apportioned, by rules described in the following paragraphs.

Formula: The apportionment formula prescribed is the same as the one generally used for the California corporation franchise tax: the single sales factor formula. For a discussion of formula apportionment and rules regarding its application, see Chapter 13 of the *Guidebook.*

• *Compensation for personal services*

Nonresidents: Nonresidents are taxed on compensation for personal services performed in California (¶ 231). The attribution rules for a number of specific occupations are as follows:

Salespersons: Nonresident salespersons determine the portion of commission income attributable to California by the ratio of sales volume in California to total sales volume.

Performers/athletes: Nonresident performers or athletes include gross amounts received for performances or athletic events in California.

Professionals: Fees received by nonresident professionals (*e.g.,* doctors, lawyers, accountants) for services performed in California are taxable.

Employees: Nonresident employees, excluding sales personnel, include total compensation for any period during which they are continuously employed in California.

Transportation workers: Nonresident transportation employees may prorate compensation on whatever basis is used by their employers to measure services. For example, proration may be based on the number of days worked or the number of miles traveled in California compared to days or miles everywhere. Federal law, incorporated by California, prohibits California from taxing income of certain interstate transportation workers; see ¶231 for details.

Part-year residents: All compensation received by part-year residents during the period of residency is taxable and attributed in full to California. Such income received during nonresidency is attributed under the rules applicable to nonresidents.

Military personnel: Federal law prohibits the taxation of military pay of nonresident servicemen while they are stationed in California, even though such income would be considered taxable to a nonresident under the regular rules (¶225). Also exempt from tax is pay of a nonresident military person that is attributed to a resident spouse by the community property laws.

Native Americans: Federal law prohibits the taxation of specified income received by Native Americans that is earned on tribal lands (¶254).

• *Interest, dividend, rent, and royalty income*

Nonresidents: A nonresident's income from interest or dividends that is not related to a trade or business is not taxed by California unless the nonresident buys the stock or obligations in California or places orders with brokers in California so regularly as to constitute doing business, in which case the income is California-source AGI and must be reported in full (¶231). Special rules apply for purposes of determining whether a nonresident's interest and dividends from qualifying investment securities are California-source income (¶231).

Royalty income from intangibles such as patents or franchises is taxable only if the intangible has a business situs in California. A business situs in California is established when (1) the property is employed as capital or (2) control of the property is localized in connection with a business in California so that its use becomes an asset of the business.

Rental income received by a nonresident from real estate or from tangible personal property located in California is California-source AGI regardless of whether it is related to a trade or business.

The source of gains and losses from the sale or other disposition of intangible personal property is determined at the time of the sale or disposition of that property.

Part-year residents: All income, of whatever kind, received by part-year residents during the period of residency is taxable and allocable to California. Such income received during nonresidency is attributed under the rules applicable to nonresidents.

• *Pensions and annuities*

Nonresidents: Nonresidents' retirement income is not subject to California income tax even if the income is received for services performed in California (¶231, ¶405).

Part-year residents: Part-year residents who move into California are taxed on pension income from non-California sources received after the taxpayer becomes a California resident. Part-year residents who move out of California are subject to California income tax only on their retirement income received during the period of their California residency (¶405).

• *Gains or losses from disposition of property*

Nonresidents: Gain or loss from the sale of real or tangible personal property in California is California-source income whether or not related to business activities (¶231).

Gain or loss from stock and bond sales made by a nonresident is not attributable to California unless the nonresident buys such property in California or places orders in California so regularly so as to constitute doing business in California, in which case the profits from such transactions would be considered California-source income. Special rules apply for purposes of determining whether gain or loss from the sale of qualifying investment securities by a nonresident is California-source income (¶231).

Part-year residents: Gains and losses derived from any source during the period of residency are California-source income to part-year residents. Such income received during nonresidency is attributed under the rules applicable to nonresidents.

• *Income from trusts and estates*

Nonresidents: The information needed to complete the beneficiary's 540NR return, including the portion attributable to California and the character of each item, is shown on Schedule K-1 (Form 541).

A nonresident beneficiary is taxed on the portion of the beneficiary's distributive share of the trust's or estate's modified federal taxable income from sources in California (¶605). Income or loss has the same character when passed through to a beneficiary as it had to the trust or estate. Dividends and interest from estate or trust stocks and bonds is not income from sources within the state and is not taxable to a nonresident unless the property is used by the estate or trust so as to acquire a business situs in California. The source of a nonresident's income from other trust or estate property that has not acquired a business situs in the state is determined by the fiduciaries under the general rules for allocation and apportionment (see Chapter 13).

Part-year residents: The information needed to complete the beneficiary's 540NR return, including the portion attributable to California and the character of each item, is shown on Schedule K-1 (Form 541).

A part-year resident beneficiary's distributive share of certain trust income is taxed based on the beneficiary's period of residency and nonresidency during the trust's taxable year (¶605). The allocation of income between the period of residency and the period of nonresidency must be made in a manner that reflects the actual date of realization. In the absence of information that reflects the actual date of realization, the annual amount of trust income must be allocated on a proportional basis between the two periods, using a daily pro rata method. Income or loss has the same character when passed through to the beneficiaries as it had to the trust or estate.

Part-year residents qualify for a credit for tax paid to other states on their income from trusts or estates that is also taxed by California (¶130).

• *Income from partnerships and limited liability partnerships*

Nonresidents: The information needed to complete the partner's 540NR return is shown on Schedule K-1 (Form 565). Amounts allocated outside California are shown as differences between California income and income reported on the federal return.

Nonresident partners are taxed on the part of their distributive shares of partnership income or loss derived from California sources (¶619).

Nonresident partners qualify for a credit for tax paid to certain states of residence on partnership income that is also taxed by California (¶131).

Part-year residents: A part-year resident partner's distributive share of partnership income is taxed based on the partner's period of residency and nonresidency during the partnership's taxable year (¶619). The allocation of income between the period of residency and the period of nonresidency must be made in a manner that reflects the actual date of realization. In the absence of information that reflects the actual date of realization, the annual amount of partnership income must be allocated on a proportional basis between the two periods, using a daily pro rata method.

Part-year resident partners qualify for a credit for tax paid to other states on partnership income taxed by California (¶131).

• *Income from S corporations*

Nonresidents: Nonresidents apply the S corporation apportionment percentage to their distributive shares of S corporation income to determine their portion taxable to California. The percentage is reported on Schedule K-1 (Form 100S), which is sent to the shareholders by the S corporation.

Nonresidents qualify for a credit for taxes paid to certain states of residence on their S corporation income taxed by California (¶131).

Part-year residents: A part-year resident shareholder's distributive share of S corporation income is taxed based on the shareholder's period of residency and nonresidency during the S corporation's taxable year (¶233). The allocation of income between the period of residency and the period of nonresidency must be made in a manner that reflects the actual date of realization. In the absence of information that reflects the actual date of realization, the annual amount of S corporation income must be on a proportional basis between the two periods, using a daily pro rata method.

Part-year resident shareholders qualify for a credit for taxes paid to other states on S corporation income taxed by California (¶131).

• *Alimony income*

Alimony received by a part-year resident during the period of California residence is attributed to California.

Alimony paid by a California resident to a nonresident is not taxable to the recipient (¶204, ¶323). Alimony paid either by a nonresident or part-year resident during a period of nonresidency is deductible on a prorated basis equal to the ratio that California adjusted gross income for the entire year bears to the total adjusted gross income (computed without regard to the alimony deduction).

¶67 Modifications to Federal Adjusted Gross Income

California Forms: Sch. CA (540NR) (California Adjustments - Nonresidents or Part-Year Residents), Sch. D (Capital Gain and Loss), Sch. D-1 (Sales of Business Property), FTB 3801 (Passive Activity Loss Limitations), FTB 3805V (Net Operating Loss (NOL) Computation and NOL and Disaster Loss Limitations - Individuals, Estates, and Trusts), FTB 3805Z (Enterprise Zone Deduction and Credit Summary), FTB 3806 (Los Angeles Revitalization Zone Deduction and Credit Summary), FTB 3807 (Local Agency Military Base Recovery Area Deduction and Credit Summary), FTB 3808 (Manufacturing Enhancement Area Business Booklet), FTB 3809 (Targeted Tax Area Deduction and Credit Summary), FTB 3885A (Corporation Depreciation and Amortization).

Nonresidents and part-year residents make the following three kinds of California modification adjustments on Schedule CA (540NR):

(1) addition and subtraction modifications to federal adjusted gross income (AGI) to arrive at total adjusted gross income (AGI) from all sources using California law;

(2) adjustments to determine the portion of total AGI that is subject to California tax (either because it is California source income or because it is attributable to the taxpayer's period of residency); and

(3) adjustments to federal itemized deductions, should the taxpayer itemize for California purposes (¶68 for such adjustments).

The adjustments under (2), above, are computed in accordance with the rules for attributing income to California (¶66).

Practice Note: Registered Domestic Partners

Registered domestic partners (RDPs) must make additional adjustments to reconcile the differences that arise from using a different filing status on their California tax returns than their federal income tax returns. These adjustments may be made by completing a pro forma federal return or by utilizing the worksheets provided in FTB Pub. 737, Tax Information for Registered Domestic Partnerships. For more information concerning RDPs, see the discussion at ¶119.

The most common adjustments under (1), above, are discussed in the following paragraphs. Other adjustments are discussed in FTB Pub. 1001, Supplemental Guidelines to California Adjustments.

Interest on state obligations (¶217): Interest earned on bonds issued by states other than California or on obligations issued by municipalities of other states is taxed by California and is added back to federal AGI. State bond interest (other than from California obligations) that passes through from S corporations, trusts, partnerships, limited liability companies, and limited and mutual funds is also treated as an addition.

Interest paid by California in conjunction with the refund of the smog impact fee is deductible under California, but not federal, law if the taxpayer was not allowed to deduct the fee when it was paid (¶201).

Interest on federal obligations (¶217): Interest on federal obligations is tax-exempt and, consequently, is subtracted from federal AGI. See also ¶217 for the pass-through of tax-exempt interest from a mutual fund.

Interest income from Federal Farm Credit banks, Federal Home Loan banks, the Student Loan Marketing Association (SLMA), the Resolution Funding Corporation, the Production Credit Association, the Commodity Credit Corporation, Certificates of Accrual on Treasury Securities (CATS), and Treasury Investment Growth Receipts (TIGRS) is also exempt and is subtracted from federal adjusted gross income. However, interest from Fannie Maes, Ginnie Maes, or FHLMC securities is taxable by California and, therefore, no modification is made to federal adjusted gross income for interest from these instruments.

Depreciation (¶310): Because nonresidents and part-year residents, in computing their California tax liability on Form 540NR, first compute a taxable income figure in the same manner as full-year residents, they must make the same California depreciation modifications required of resident taxpayers, even for assets not located in California (¶310).

California depreciation is generally the same as federal (the "modified accelerated cost recovery system" under IRC Sec. 168) for assets placed in service after 1986. However, California does not conform to the IRC Sec. 168(k) bonus depreciation deduction for qualified property placed in service in 2008—2019 and did not incorporate the additional 30%/50% first-year bonus depreciation for qualified property purchased after September 10, 2001, and before 2005. Nor does California incorporate the additional first-year bonus depreciation deduction allowed for qualified New York Liberty Zone property or the accelerated write-off for qualified property utilized in a renewal community.

The maximum allowable IRC Sec. 179 deduction for California purposes is lower than that allowed under federal law; see ¶311 for a detailed discussion. In addition, California does not conform to federal amendments that increase the amount at which the phase-out of the IRC Sec. 179 deduction begins and that allow the deduction to be claimed for off-the-shelf computer software, qualified real property, air conditioning units, or heating units.

California adopts the federal 39-year depreciation recovery period for nonresidential real property acquired after May 12, 1993, but only for property placed in service after 1996 in taxable years beginning after 1996. Thus, for California purposes, nonresidential real property placed in service before 1997 in taxable years beginning before 1997 continues to be depreciated over a 31.5-year recovery period.

California has also not conformed to numerous federal depreciation provisions, including those that

— classify qualified leasehold improvements, qualified restaurant property, and qualified retail improvement property as 15-year recovery property and require the use of the straight-line method;

— provide special depreciation treatment for participations and residuals;

— extend the shortened MACRS recovery periods for qualified Indian reservation property to apply to qualified property placed in service prior to 2017; and

— ease the current expense allowance qualifying criteria for film production expenses.

Further differences in the amount of depreciation claimed for federal and California purposes may arise due to California provisions that allow taxpayers operating in specified depressed areas to claim accelerated write-offs for certain property (¶316) and federal provisions that allow accelerated write-offs for small film production costs (¶310) and allow current deductions for reforestation expenditures (¶315).

Note: The differences between federal and California deductions are adjusted on FTB 3885A. The net adjustment may be an addition or a subtraction.

Capital gains and losses (¶523): California law, unlike federal law, treats all capital gains as ordinary income after 1986. Federal law subjects long-term capital gains to a lower tax rate.

Differences between the amount of capital gain or loss recognized for California and federal purposes can occur both in the year a gain or loss is recognized and in carryover years.

The following differences may occur for 2016 between the gain or loss recognized for federal and California purposes because

— California does not permit capital loss carrybacks (¶526);

— California, but not federal, law excludes gain on the sale or disposition of qualified assisted housing developments (¶505);

— California requires certain adjustments to basis not required by federal law and makes certain federal adjustments inapplicable (¶559);

— California has not incorporated federal law that limits the amount of long-term capital gain that a taxpayer can recognize from constructive ownership contracts involving pass-through entities (¶525);

— California has not incorporated federal amendments that increase the exclusion of gain on small business stock for stock acquired after February 17, 2009 and before January 1, 2013. In addition, California's exclusion is repealed beginning with the 2013 tax year (¶525); and

— the basis may be different due to different depreciation deductions (¶310) or asset expense deductions (¶311).

Differences between pre-1987 California and federal laws that can affect the reporting of capital gain and loss include the following:

— A capital loss carryover may be different for California purposes than for federal purposes.

— The pre-1987 holding periods and taxable percentages of capital gains for California were different than federal.

— The California adjustment to capital gains computed for purposes of the investment interest expense deduction was different from the federal adjustment.

— For years prior to 1987, the federal 50% limitation on long-term capital loss deductions did not apply for California.

— Dividends from mutual funds were treated as ordinary income for California.

— Gain or loss may be reported in different tax years for California purposes because changes to the federal law affecting the computation of gain or loss were not generally adopted by California until subsequent years.

— California Schedule D is used to calculate the differences, and the appropriate modification is carried to California Schedule CA (540NR).

— The California and federal basis of certain assets may be different at the time of disposition because of prior and current differences between California and federal law (¶542 and following). Examples of such situations are

(a) valuation of property acquired by inheritance (¶546),

(b) depreciation of business property (¶310, ¶311),

(c) basis adjustments for California and federal credits (¶144),

(d) basis of the stock of an S corporation (¶233), and

(e) basis adjustment of property for moves into California (¶504).

Calculation of capital gain and loss adjustments is made on California FTB 3885A.

State income tax refunds (¶201): Any California income tax refunds included in federal AGI are subtracted.

Unemployment compensation (¶201): The amount of unemployment compensation included on the federal return is subtracted from federal AGI.

Paid family leave (¶201): Paid family leave included on the federal return is not taxed by California and is subtracted from federal AGI.

Social Security benefits (¶201): The amount of Social Security benefits included in federal AGI is subtracted because California does not tax social security benefits.

Railroad retirement benefits, ridesharing benefits, and sick pay (¶205): Tier 1 and tier 2 railroad retirement benefits, including ridesharing benefits and sick pay, received under the Federal Insurance Contributions and Railroad Retirement Act are subtracted from federal AGI.

In-home supportive services supplemental payments: Unlike federal law, California excludes in-home supportive services supplemental payments from gross income (¶201).

California lottery winnings (¶201): Any California lottery winnings included in federal AGI are subtracted.

IRA and Keogh distributions (¶330): The California and federal deductible dollar amounts are generally the same for post-1986 tax years. However, for pre-1987 tax years, the amounts differed; consequently, the amount taxable on a distribution will differ. Differences may also arise if the taxpayer changed residence during the time he or she made contributions to the IRA or Keogh plan.

A worksheet to compute differences in the tax treatment of distributions for federal and California purposes is included in FTB Pub. 1005, Pension and Annuity Guidelines.

Net operating loss (NOL) (¶309): With the exception of the suspension of the NOL deduction for California income tax purposes for losses incurred or carried over in 2008—2011 and the 2002 and 2003 taxable years, California's treatment of NOLs is like federal treatment except that prior to 2013 no carrybacks are allowed, and for losses incurred prior to 2004 the amount of loss eligible for carryover to future years is generally limited to a specified percentage of the net operating loss dependent on the year the loss was incurred. In addition, California limits NOL carrybacks for 2013 to 50% of the NOL and for 2014 to 75% of the NOL. Furthermore, applicable to NOLs incurred prior to the 2008 taxable year, a California NOL may be carried forward for only 10 years (five years for losses incurred prior to the 2000 taxable year) rather than the 20 years permitted under federal law (15 years for losses incurred in tax years beginning before August 6, 1997). Commencing with the 2008 taxable year, California NOLs may be carried over for 20 years. The NOL carryover period is extended for NOLs suspended during the 2008—2011, 2002 and 2003 taxable years as a result of the suspension provisions.

Special rules apply to taxpayers operating in enterprise zones, the former Los Angeles Revitalization Zone (LARZ), local agency military base recovery areas (LAMBRAs), or the former targeted tax areas. For taxable years beginning after 2000 and before 2003, special provisions also applied to farming businesses directly impacted by Pierce's disease.

Calculation of the California NOL is on FTB 3805V and the appropriate adjustment entered on California Schedule CA (540NR). The NOL for enterprise zone businesses is calculated on FTB 3805Z, for former LARZ businesses is calculated on FTB 3806, for LAMBRA businesses is calculated on FTB 3807, and for targeted tax area businesses is calculated on FTB 3809.

Recycling revenues (¶201): The income received by a taxpayer for recycling empty beverage containers is exempt for California purposes and is subtracted if included in federal adjusted gross income.

Expenses related to tax-exempt income (¶305): Expenses related to federally tax-exempt income that were disallowed as a deduction in computing federal AGI are subtracted for California. Expenses incurred to purchase or carry obligations that are tax-exempt under California but not federal law are added to federal AGI.

Note: These modifications, to the extent not business-related, are made to federal itemized deductions (¶68).

Income from exercising California qualified stock option (¶207): Compensation received from exercising a California qualified stock option is excluded from California gross income and may be subtracted if the compensation was included in federal AGI.

Ridesharing and employee commuter deductions (¶241): An exclusion from gross income is available to an employee for amounts received from his or her employer for qualifying ridesharing or commuter arrangements. Because California does not place a limit on the monthly benefits that may be excluded and allows for more excludable ridesharing/commuter options, a subtraction from federal AGI may be allowed.

Pensions and annuities (¶206): California rules for taxing pensions and annuities are the same as federal; however, the taxable amount may differ because of federal/California differences in the years when contributions were made. For further information see FTB Pub. 1005, Pension and Annuity Guidelines.

Passive activity loss (¶340): California generally adopts federal rules for computing the limitation on deducting passive activity losses. However, California does not conform to the passive activity loss rules relating to rental real estate losses suffered by certain taxpayers who materially participate in a real property trade or business. Differences may also exist because the amount of passive income and loss may differ. Taxpayers must segregate California adjustments that relate to passive-activity items from California adjustments that relate to nonpassive items. This calculation is made on FTB 3801, Passive Activity Loss Limitations.

Other gains or losses (¶537): Although California law on the computation of gain from sales of business property and certain involuntary conversions is the same as federal, the amount of gain or loss may differ because of federal/California basis differences. These amounts are reported on Schedule D-1.

Other adjustments may arise as a result of transfers between registered domestic partners, in which no gain is recognized for California purposes. Federal law requires that gain or loss be recognized in such transactions, see ¶502.

Alimony (¶204): Alimony received by a nonresident alien that was not included in the taxpayer's federal gross income is treated as an addition on Schedule CA (540).

Income from specially treated sources: See the indicated paragraphs for possible federal/California differences in the taxation of the following items: (1) noncash patronage dividends from farmers' cooperatives or mutual associations (¶232); and (2) interest income from investment in enterprise zones (¶240).

Claim of right adjustment (¶415): A claim of right adjustment may be claimed as either a deduction or a credit. A taxpayer that claims a credit for repayment amount on his or her federal return may claim a deduction on his or her California personal income tax return. Deductions of $3,000 or less are subject to the 2% floor for miscellaneous itemized deductions. A taxpayer that claims a deduction on his or her federal return, may claim a credit for the repayment amount on his or her California personal income tax return. Nonresidents may only claim an adjustment for income that was attributable to California sources.

Income from S corporations (¶66, ¶233): Nonresident shareholders of California S corporations add or subtract, as appropriate, the difference between their distributive shares of federal and California S corporation income or loss.

Income from partnerships and limited liability partnerships (¶66, ¶616, ¶623): Partners add or subtract, as appropriate, the difference between their distributive shares of federal and California partnership income or loss.

Income from limited liability companies (¶625): Members and persons with economic interests in an LLC add or subtract, as appropriate, the difference between their shares of federal and California LLC income in the same manner as partners must include their distributive shares of partnership income in their taxable income.

Income from trusts and estates (¶66, ¶605): Trust or estate beneficiaries add or subtract, as appropriate, the difference between their shares of federal and California trust or estate income or loss.

Business expenses incurred in discriminatory clubs (¶301, ¶336): California prohibits a business expense deduction for expenditures at a club which restricts membership or use on the basis of sex, race, color, religion, ancestry, national origin, ethnic group identification, age, mental disability, physical disability, medical condition, genetic information, marital status, or sexual orientation. There is no similar federal prohibition.

Penalty assessed by professional sports league (¶336): California does not allow a business expense deduction for any fine or penalty paid or incurred by an owner of a professional sports franchise if assessed or imposed by the professional sports league that includes that franchise. There is no similar federal prohibition.

Wages (¶201): If there is a difference in wages because of an employee's fringe benefits, also reported on the W-2, an adjustment must be made because California does not adopt the federal rules; the amount of federal wages reported on the W-2 is subtracted and the amount reported as California wages is added.

Crime hotline rewards (¶246): Any rewards received from a government authorized crime hotline are excluded from gross income.

Water conservation rebates/vouchers (¶244): California excludes from gross income specified water conservation rebates/vouchers received from local water and energy agencies or suppliers.

Financial incentive for turf removal (¶244): California allows an income exclusion for rebates, vouchers, or other financial incentive issued by a local water agency or supplier in a turf removal water conservation program.

Conservation and environmental cost-share payments (¶243): Certain cost-share payments received by forest landowners from the Department of Forestry and Fire Protection are subtracted from federal gross income.

Reparation payments (¶248): An exclusion is available for amounts received as reparation payments for individuals who were required to perform forced or slave labor during World War II, Canadian reparation payments made to individuals of Japanese ancestry interned during World War II, and Armenian genocide settlement payments.

Wrongful conviction compensation (¶201): Amounts paid by the state of California to compensate an individual for wrongful conviction and incarceration are subtracted from federal AGI.

Energy-efficient home improvement grants (¶245): Energy-efficient home improvement grants awarded by the State Energy Resources Conservation and Development Commission to low-income individuals are subtracted from federal AGI.

Medical expenses (¶219, ¶301, ¶325): California taxpayers may subtract from federal AGI amounts received from employer-provided accident, health insurance, and medical expense reimbursements and self-employed health insurance payments associated with expenses for the taxpayer's registered domestic partner (RDP) and the RDP's dependents (see ¶219).

Medical benefits (¶252): Unlike federal law, California law does not exclude prescription drug subsidies.

Health savings accounts (¶246, ¶326): California does not recognize health savings accounts. Amounts deducted on a taxpayer's federal return should be added back to federal AGI.

Mortgage debt forgiveness (¶221): California currently does not conform to federal law allowing an exclusion for mortgage debt forgiveness.

Teacher expenses (¶201): Unreimbursed expenses incurred by eligible elementary and secondary school educators for books, supplies, equipment, and material used in the classroom, to the extent deductible under federal law, but not California law, are added back to federal AGI.

Tuition and education expenses (¶344): California requires an addition adjustment for qualified tuition and related expenses for which an above-the-line deduction was claimed on a taxpayer's federal return.

Energy efficient commercial building costs (¶345): California does not incorporate federal law allowing taxpayers to currently deduct a portion of the costs of installing energy efficient systems in commercial buildings. Such amounts must be added back to federal AGI and an increased California depreciation deduction may be claimed.

Environmental remediation expenses (¶346): California requires an addition adjustment and depreciation adjustment for environmental remediation costs currently expensed on a taxpayer's federal return.

Earthquake loss mitigation incentives (¶256): California excludes from gross income amounts received as a loan forgiveness, grant, credit, rebate, voucher, or other financial incentive issued by the California Residential Mitigation Program or the California Earthquake Authority to assist a residential property owner or occupant with expenses paid, or obligations incurred, for earthquake loss mitigation.

¶68 Itemized Deductions

California Forms: Sch. CA (540NR) (California Adjustments - Nonresidents or Part-Year Residents), FTB 3526 (Investment Interest Expense Deduction), FTB 3885A (540NR) (Depreciation and Amortization).

California itemized deductions are based on federal itemized deductions shown on federal Schedule A, with the modifications discussed below. These modifications are independent of the adjustments to federal adjusted gross income (AGI) discussed at ¶67.

Practice Note: Registered Domestic Partners

Registered domestic partners (RDPs) must make additional adjustments to itemized deductions to reconcile the differences that arise as a result of using a different filing status on their California tax returns than on their federal income tax returns. These adjustments may be made by (1) completing a pro forma federal return, or (2) by utilizing the worksheets provided in FTB Pub. 737, Tax Information for Registered Domestic Partnerships. For more information concerning RDPs, see the discussion at ¶119.

Taxpayers may elect either the standard deduction or itemized deductions for California purposes, regardless of which was elected for federal purposes (¶65). However, if itemized deductions are elected for California purposes, federal Schedule A must be attached to the California Form 540NR. The adjustments to federal itemized deductions are computed in Part III of California Schedule CA (540NR) ("California Adjustments—Nonresidents or Part-Year Residents").

The adjustments are as follows:

— *Taxes* (¶306): State, local, and foreign income taxes (including state disability insurance—"SDI"), sales and use taxes, federal estate tax, and generation-skipping transfer taxes claimed on federal Schedule A are not allowable deductions for California purposes and are subtracted from federal itemized deductions.

— *California Lottery losses* (¶336): California Lottery losses are not deductible for California purposes. The amount of such losses, as shown on federal Schedule A, must be subtracted from federal itemized deductions.

— *Federal obligation expense* (¶305): Because California does not tax interest from federal obligations, any expenses relating to such interest that have been deducted for federal purposes on Schedule A are subtracted from federal itemized deductions for California purposes.

— *State obligation expense* (¶305): Because, unlike federal law, California taxes interest from state or local obligations of states, other than California, any expenses related to this interest that were not entered on federal Schedule A should be added to federal itemized deductions for California purposes.

— *Employee business expense deduction for depreciation* (¶310): If the employee business expense deduction claimed federally included depreciation of assets placed in service prior to 1987, the depreciation component is recomputed for California purposes because of California/federal differences in depreciation methods prior to 1987. For taxable years beginning after 2002, federal law allows taxpayers to currently expense higher amounts under IRC Sec. 179 than is allowed under California law (¶311). Finally, adjustments may be required if the taxpayer claimed the IRC Sec. 168(k) first-year bonus depreciation deduction on his or her tax return for property purchased during 2008—2014 or after September 10, 2001, but before 2005, or for purchases of qualified New York Liberty Zone property. Additional differences may arise as a result of the shortened recovery periods for leasehold, restaurant property, and retail improvement property and the accelerated write-off for qualified property used in a renewal community that are allowed under federal law. Use FTB 3885A for computing the differences.

— *Adoption-related expenses* (¶139): California allows a credit for specified adoption-related expenses. If the taxpayer claims the California adoption costs credit for amounts deducted on the federal Schedule A, these amounts must be subtracted on California Schedule CA (540NR).

— *Investment expense* (¶305): This item is generally treated the same as under federal law. Taxpayers filing federal form 4952 must file the corresponding California FTB 3526. Differences, if any, are reported on Schedule CA (540NR). Differences may occur because of the capital gain component in computing pre-1987 investment interest expense; the pre-1987 holding period and taxable percentages of capital gains were different under California law (¶525).

— *Limitation for high-income taxpayers* (¶303): The itemized deductions of taxpayers with adjusted gross incomes over a threshold amount must be reduced by the lesser of (1) 6% (3% under federal law) of the excess of adjusted gross income over the threshold amount, or (2) 80% of the amount of the itemized deductions otherwise allowable for the tax year. A worksheet is provided in the Schedule CA (540NR) Instructions to calculate the adjustment.

— *Federal mortgage interest credit:* California does not have a credit comparable to the federal mortgage interest credit. If federal miscellaneous itemized deductions on Schedule A were reduced by the amount of this credit, California itemized deductions may be increased by the same amount on Schedule CA (540NR).

— *Legislators' travel expenses* (¶301): California does not follow the federal rule allowing legislators to deduct expenses for every legislative day. California allows legislators to deduct only those expenses incurred on days that they are actually away from their districts overnight. Amounts deducted for federal purposes on Schedule A that do not qualify for California purposes must be subtracted from federal itemized deductions.

¶68

— *Interest on public utility-financed loans for energy conservation* (¶ 305): California allows taxpayers to claim a deduction, not subject to the 2% floor limit, for interest on public utility-financed loans used to obtain energy-efficient equipment for California residences.

— *Charitable contributions* (¶ 321): Differences may arise in the treatment of contributions on the federal and state returns. For instance, if a charitable contribution deduction was claimed for federal purposes for the same amount for which the college access credit is claimed for California purposes, no deduction for that amount is allowed on the California return.

¶69 Tax Rates

California Forms: Sch. G-1 (Tax on Lump-Sum Distributions), Sch. P (540NR) (Alternative Minimum Tax and Credit Limitations - Nonresidents or Part-Year Residents), FTB 3800 (Tax Computation for Children Under Age 14 with Investment Income), FTB 3803 (Parents' Election to Report Child's Interest and Dividends), FTB 3805P (Additional Taxes on Qualified Plans (Including IRAs) and Other Tax-Favored Accounts).

Nonresidents and part-year residents pay tax at rates applied to their total income (California income plus other income) of the taxpayer. The rates are progressive, ranging from 1% to 12.3% of taxable income. An additional 1% tax is also imposed on taxable income in excess of $1 million. Total tax is then prorated, for nonresidents and part-year residents, on the basis of California taxable income (¶ 116).

The tax tables are reproduced at ¶ 3. The tax rate schedules are reproduced at ¶ 1.

• *Alternative minimum tax*

Nonresidents and part-year residents are subject to the alternative minimum tax in the same manner as residents, except that the tax is computed on the basis of prorated taxable income (¶ 117).

The California alternative minimum tax is imposed at the rate of 7.0%. It is generally computed the same as for federal purposes, but there are differences (¶ 117). The alternative minimum tax is computed on Schedule P (540NR).

California incorporates the IRC Sec. 53 "credit for prior year minimum tax" (¶ 70).

• *Tax on premature distributions of retirement plans and life insurance plans*

Nonresidents and part-year residents are liable in the same manner as residents for the penalty or recapture tax on premature distributions from IRAs, Keogh plans, annuities, and "modified endowment contracts," to the extent the distribution is included in California-source income (¶ 206, ¶ 405). The amount included for California purposes may differ from that required to be included federally because California, but not federal law, treats rollovers from an IRA to a health savings account as a premature distribution and because of differences in the deductibility of contributions in years prior to 1987.

The California penalty is 2.5%.

The tax is computed on form FTB 3805P and reported on the Other Taxes line of the Form 540.

• *Tax on income received under nonqualified deferred compensation plan*

Both California and federal law impose an additional tax on income received under IRC Sec. 409A on a nonqualified deferred compensation plan (¶ 206). Beginning in 2013, the rate of additional California tax is 5% of the amount required to be included in income, plus interest. The tax is reported on the Other Taxes line of the Form 540NR.

• *Tax on nonqualified distributions from educational savings accounts*

Both California and federal law impose a penalty tax on distributions from Coverdell education savings accounts and qualified tuition programs that are not used for qualified educational expenses (¶206, ¶250). The California penalty is 2.5% and is reported on FTB 3805P.

• *Tax on nonexempt withdrawals from medical savings accounts*

Distributions from a medical savings account for nonmedical purposes are subject to a 10% penalty tax (increased to 12.5% for disbursements made during taxable years beginning on or after January 1, 2016) for California purposes, rather than the 20% imposed under federal law. California law, unlike federal law, imposes the penalty on rollovers from medical savings accounts to health savings accounts. For further information see ¶247. Form FTB 3805P is used to make the computation.

• *Separate tax on lump-sum distributions*

Nonresidents and part-year residents with lump-sum distributions of retirement income attributable to California sources compute and pay a separate tax on these distributions if they elected to pay the separate federal tax (¶206, ¶405). The California tax, which is computed on Schedule G-1, is determined under the same rules as the federal tax. The tax is transferred from Schedule G-1 to Form 540NR and is added to the prorated tax on total taxable income.

• *Tax on certain children's unearned income ("kiddie tax")*

California conforms to the federal "kiddie tax" provisions for calculating the amount of income tax for a child who has unearned income in excess of $2,100 (for 2016) and who is (1) under age 18 at the end of the taxable year; (2) under 19 years old and does not provide half of his or her own support costs with earned income; or (3) 19 to 23 years old and is a full-time student who does not provide half of his or her own support costs with earned income (¶118). The tax is computed on FTB 3800, which parallels federal Form 8615. For nonresidents and part-year residents, the amounts needed to complete FTB 3800 come from the corresponding federal Form 8615 and from both the parent's and the child's Form 540NR (including California adjusted gross income amounts from Schedule CA (540NR)). The tax is subject to proration.

Under certain circumstances, a parent may elect to include the unearned income of a child on the parent's return. If the parent elects to exercise this option, FTB 3803 must accompany the parent's return.

• *Tax rates for servicemembers domiciled outside California*

Military compensation of servicemembers domiciled outside California, and their spouses, may not be included in gross income for purposes of determining the tax rate on nonmilitary income; see ¶225.

¶70 Credits Against Tax

California Forms: Form 540NR (California Nonresident or Part-Year Resident Income Tax Return), Sch. P (540NR) (Alternative Minimum Tax and Credit Limitations - Nonresidents or Part-Year Residents), Sch. S (Other State Tax Credit), FTB 3503 (Natural Heritage Preservation Credit), FTB 3507 (Prison Inmate Labor Credit), FTB 3508 (Solar Energy System Credit), FTB 3510 (Credit for Prior Year Alternative Minimum Tax - Individuals or Fiduciaries), FTB 3511 (Environmental Tax Credit), FTB 3514 (Earned Income Tax Credit), FTB 3521 (Low Income Housing Credit), FTB 3523 (Research Credit), FTB 3527 (New Jobs Credit), FTB 3531 (California Competes Tax Credit), FTB 3540 (Credit Carryover Summary), FTB 3541 (California Motion Picture and Television Production Credit), FTB 3546 (Enhanced Oil Recovery Credit), FTB 3547 (Donated Agricultural Products Transportation Credit), FTB 3548 (Disabled Access Credit for Eligible Small Businesses), FTB 3551 (Sale of Credit Attributable to an Independent

Film), FTB 3553 (Enterprise Zone Employee Credit), FTB 3554 (New Employment Credit), FTB 3592 (College Access Tax Credit), FTB 3596 (Paid Preparer's California Earned Income Tax Credit Checklist), FTB 3805Z (Enterprise Zone Deduction and Credit Summary), FTB 3807 (Local Agency Military Base Recovery Area Deduction and Credit Summary), FTB 3808 (Manufacturing Enhancement Area Credit Summary), FTB 3809 (Targeted Tax Area Deduction and Credit Summary), FTB 3811 (Donations of Fresh Fruit or Vegetables Credit).

Credits available to nonresidents and part-year residents are generally divided into the following two categories: (1) those that are prorated by the percentage of California taxable income to total taxable income; and (2) those that are taken in full because they are based upon a California transaction.

If there are more than three credits claimed, the taxpayer must attach the appropriate credit form and summarize them on California Schedule P (540NR).

Major credits are treated individually in the following paragraphs, and those credits that affect only a few taxpayers are treated together at the end of ¶70.

1. Exemption credits (¶113): Nonresidents and part-year residents are entitled to the same credits for personal or dependent exemptions as are residents. The amounts of these credits are at ¶64.

2. Renter's credit (¶133): Nonresidents cannot claim this credit.

Part-year residents who qualify for the credit are allowed a $1/12$ credit for each full month of California residence during the year.

3. Joint custody head-of-household, dependent parent credits (¶136): For the 2016 tax year, these credits, which cover both dependent children and dependent parents, equal the lesser of 30% of the California liability or $440. Qualifications that must be met in order to claim the credit are discussed at ¶136. A worksheet is provided in the Instructions to Form 540NR to compute the credit. There is no carryover of this credit.

4. Research and development credit (¶150): Nonresidents and part-year residents may generally take the same research and development credit as that provided by federal law, except the following:

— research must be conducted in California to qualify;

— the applicable California credit percentage is 15% of the excess of qualified research expenses for the tax year over the "base amount";

— California retains and modifies the formula used by those taxpayers that elect to compute the amount of the credit using an alternative incremental method and has not conformed to the federal repeal of the alternative incremental method for taxable years beginning after 2008;

— California law, unlike federal law, does not authorize the use of a the alternative simplified credit, generally effective for federal purposes in tax years ending after 2006;

— California does not allow a credit against personal income tax for basic research payments;

— California limits the "gross receipts" that may be taken into account for purposes of calculating the base amount;

— the California credit may be carried over, while the federal credit is part of the general business credit subject to the limitations of IRC Sec. 38;

— California disallows the credit for expenses incurred to purchase property for which a sales and use exemption for teleproduction or other postproduction property is claimed;

— California does not allow a taxpayer to claim 20% of amounts paid or incurred by the taxpayer during the tax year to an energy research consortium and repeal the limitation on contract research expenses paid to eligible small businesses, universities and federal laboratories for qualified energy research; and

— California did not incorporate the federal suspension periods of July 1, 1999—September 30, 2000, and October 1, 2000—September 30, 2001, that were enacted by the Tax Relief Extension Act of 1999.

A married couple or registered domestic partners filing separately may take the full credit or divide it equally between the spouses or partners.

FTB 3523 is used to compute the credit.

5. Credit for prior-year minimum tax (¶152): California incorporates the IRC Sec. 53 credit for alternative minimum tax paid in a prior year by a taxpayer who is not liable for the AMT in the current year. The credit is based on preference items that defer tax liability rather than permanently reduce the tax. The amount allowable as a credit in any tax year is limited to the regular California personal income tax for the year less the refundable credits that have no carryover provisions and the credit for taxes paid to other states. The credit is computed on FTB 3510.

6. Credit for income taxes paid other states (nonresidents) (¶129): The credit for income taxes paid other states is available for net income taxes paid to another state or possession on income also taxed by California when the state or possession of residence is one of the following: Arizona, Guam, Indiana, Oregon, and Virginia. Net tax does not include any tax comparable to the California AMT or preference tax (¶69) or any tax not based on net income.

There are the following two limitations: (1) the credit is limited to the same proportion of the total tax paid to the state of residence as the income taxed in both states bears to the total income taxed by the state of residence; and (2) it is similarly limited to the same proportion of the total California tax as the income taxed in both states bears to the total income taxed by California.

Schedule S is used to compute the credit.

7. Credit for income taxes paid other states (part-year residents) (¶128): For the period of time that part-year residents are residents of California, they are entitled to credit for net income taxes paid to other states. A listing of the states and possessions for which credit is allowed appears at ¶128. The amount of the credit is limited to the same proportion of the total California tax as the income taxed in both states bears to the total income taxed by California. See ¶128 for a discussion of the credit and an example of the credit calculation.

For the period of time that the part-year resident is a nonresident of California, he/she is entitled to the credit available to nonresidents as discussed above. Because the states for which credit is allowed are mutually exclusive as to treatment of residents or nonresidents, a two-step computation is required only when California-source adjusted gross income is received while a nonresident.

Schedule S is used to compute the credit. There is no carryover of this credit.

8. Excess state disability insurance credit (¶132): Excess employee contributions for California disability insurance are treated as a refundable credit against the income tax. For 2016, the credit amount is the excess of the amount contributed over $960.68. Excess contributions may occur when a taxpayer works for more than one employer during the tax year. The amount of the credit can be calculated on a worksheet included in the Instructions to Form 540NR.

9. Earned income tax credit (¶158): A refundable earned income tax credit is allowed to certain low-income taxpayers.

Note: If more than the maximum was withheld by a single employer, or at a higher rate, the excess amount must be claimed as a refund from the employer rather than as a tax credit.

• *Other credits*

Low-income housing credit (¶138): California allows a credit to owners of residential rental projects that provide low-income housing located in California. The credit is similar to the federal credit computed under IRC Sec. 42, however the California credit allocates a specified set-aside of funds to support farmworker housing projects. The California Tax Credit Allocation Committee certifies to the taxpayer on FTB 3521A the amount of the credit for each year in the credit period.

The credit is computed on FTB 3521. A copy of FTB 3521A must be provided to the FTB upon request. Unused credit may be carried over until exhausted.

Senior head-of-household credit (¶135): A credit is available to qualified seniors. A worksheet to compute the credit is included in the Instructions to Form 540NR.

Prison inmate labor credit (¶154): A credit is available to employers for 10% of the wages paid to certain prison inmates (FTB 3507). There is no carryover of this credit.

Adoption costs credit (¶139): A credit is available for costs directly related to the adoption of a U.S. citizen or legal resident minor child who was in the custody of a state or county public agency. A worksheet is provided in the Form 540NR Instructions to compute the credit. Unused credit may be carried over until exhausted.

Disabled access expenditures credit (¶140): California allows eligible small businesses a credit for 50% of up to $250 of the disabled access expenditures paid or incurred by those businesses to comply with the federal Americans with Disabilities Act. Except for the amount of the credit, the credit is similar to the federal credit allowed under IRC Sec. 44. The credit is computed on FTB 3548. Unused credit may be carried over until exhausted.

Enhanced oil recovery credit (¶153): California allows certain independent oil producers an enhanced oil recovery credit equal to $1/3$ of the federal credit allowed under IRC Sec. 43, provided the costs for which the credit is claimed are attributable to projects located within California. FTB 3546 is used to compute the credit. Unused credit may be carried forward for up to 15 years. Only a credit carryover from a prior year is allowed for the 2016 taxable year.

Donated agricultural products credits (¶141): California allows a credit against net tax for 50% of the costs paid or incurred in connection with the transportation of agricultural products donated to nonprofit charitable organizations. FTB 3547 is used to compute the credit. Unused credit may be carried over until exhausted. Farmers may also claim a credit for specified agricultural products donated to California food banks. For tax years beginning before 2017, the credit is equal to 10% of the food's inventory costs. For tax years beginning after 2016, a credit is allowed equal to 15% of the qualified value of the fresh fruits and vegetables donated. The credit is computed on FTB 3811.

Credit for community development investments (¶156): For taxable years beginning before 2017, California allows a credit equal to 20% of each qualified deposit that is made into a community development financial institution and certified by the California Organized Investment Network prior to January 1, 2017.

Natural heritage preservation credit (¶143): Taxpayers may claim a nonrefundable credit equal to 55% of the fair market value of real property donated before July 1, 2020, for qualified conservation purposes to the California Resources Agency

¶70

(CRA), a local government, or an exempt nonprofit land and water conservation organization designated by the CRA or a local government to accept donations.

Household and dependent care expense credit (¶142): A nonrefundable credit for employment-related household and dependent care expenses is allowed against California personal income tax in an amount that is a percentage of the allowable federal credit. Unused credit may not be carried over.

Ultra-low sulfur diesel fuel production credit (¶151): An environmental tax credit may be claimed for ultra-low sulfur diesel fuel produced by a qualified small refiner at a California facility. The credit is computed on FTB 3511.

Motion picture production credit (¶137): A credit is available for 20% (25% for independent films) of qualified motion picture and television production expenses. Also, a new motion picture production credit is added for taxable years beginning after 2015 (¶137a).

New employment credit (¶157): A new employment credit is available to qualified taxpayers that pay qualified wages to qualified employees hired to work in designated geographic areas provided that the taxpayer has a net-increase in California jobs.

California competes credit (¶134): Businesses may negotiate an agreement with the Governor's Business Office of Economic Development (GO-Biz) for jobs created or investments made, with emphasis on employers locating in low-income areas.

College access credit (¶156): A credit is allowed for cash contributions made to the College Access Tax Credit Fund.

• *Carryover credits*

Nonresidents and part-year residents may apply carryovers of certain credits that are no longer available. The credits for which such carryovers may still exist (and the years for which the credits were available) are as follows:

1. water conservation credit (1980—1982);
2. solar pump (agricultural) credit (1981—1983);
3. solar energy installation credit (1985—1988);
4. energy conservation credit (1981—1986);
5. ridesharing credits (1981—1986 and 1989—1995);
6. political contributions credit (1987—1991);
7. commercial solar energy credit (1987—1988);
8. residential rental and farm sales credit (1987—1991);
9. orphan drug research credit (1987—1992);
10. qualified parent's infant care credit (1991—1993);
11. commercial solar electric system credit (1990—1993);
12. recycling equipment credit (1989—1995);
13. low emission vehicle credit (1991—1995);
14. salmon and steelhead trout habitat credit (1995—1999);
15. rice straw credit (1997—2007);
16. farmworker housing credit (1997—2008);
17. employer childcare program (1994-2011);
18. employer childcare contribution credit (1994-2011);
19. targeted tax area sales or use tax credit (1998-2012);

20. local agency military base recovery area (LAMBRA) sales and use tax credit (1996—2013); and

21. new jobs credit (2009—2013).

All of the above credit carryovers may be claimed on FTB 3540, except for the targeted tax area sales and use tax credit and LAMBRA sales and use tax credit. See prior editions of the *Guidebook* for details about these credits.

¶71 When and Where to File and Pay Tax

The due date for filing Form 540NR and payment of the tax is April 18, 2017, for calendar-year taxpayers (¶108, ¶110). Returns made by fiscal-year taxpayers are due on or before the 15th day of the fourth month after the close of the fiscal year. Returns made by mail are considered timely if properly addressed and postmarked on or before the due date.

Returns are filed with the Franchise Tax Board (FTB). However, the address to which they are sent differs depending upon whether an amount is due or a refund is expected. Refund requests are sent to P.O. Box 942840, Sacramento, CA 94240-0001. Returns for which an amount is due are sent to P.O. Box 942867, Sacramento, CA 94267-0001.

Checks or money orders are payable to the "Franchise Tax Board" with the social security number written on the check or money order.

• *E-file*

The FTB also accepts electronic filing of returns through the e-file program. Tax return preparers who prepare and file more than 100 timely original California personal income tax returns during any calendar year and who prepare at least one personal income tax return using tax preparation software in the current calendar year must file all personal income tax returns for the current calendar year and subsequent calendar years using electronic technology (unless the taxpayer elects to file a paper return). Detailed information concerning the mandatory e-file program is available at the FTB's Web site at http://www.ftb.ca.gov/professionals/efile/m_e_file.shtml.

• *Electronic payments*

Personal income taxpayers must make their tax payments electronically, including utilizing a pay by phone option, if their estimated personal income tax installment payment or extension request payment exceeds $20,000 or if their total annual tax liability exceeds $80,000 (see ¶110).

• *Military personnel*

The due date for returns by members of the Armed Forces is the same as for civilians except that it may be postponed in certain cases, such as duty outside the U.S. or service in a combat zone (¶109).

¶72 Extensions

California Forms: FTB 3519 (Payment Voucher for Automatic Extension for Individuals), FTB 3537 (Payment Voucher for Automatic Extension for Limited Liability Companies), FTB 3538 (Payment Voucher for Automatic Extension for Limited Partnerships, LLPs and REMICs), or FTB 3563 (Payment Voucher for Automatic Extension for Fiduciaries).

The Franchise Tax Board (FTB) will allow an automatic six-month extension to file if the return is filed within six months of the original due date. No written request is required. The automatic extension does not extend the time for paying the tax. Tax payments must be accompanied by the appropriate form: FTB 3519 (Payment Voucher for Automatic Extension for Individuals); FTB 3537 (Payment Voucher for

Automatic Extension for Limited Liability Companies); FTB 3538 (Payment Voucher for Automatic Extension for Limited Partnerships, LLPs and REMICs); or FTB 3563 (Payment Voucher for Automatic Extension for Fiduciaries). Taxpayers should send FTB 3519 or FTB 3563 to the FTB at P.O. Box 942867, Sacramento, CA 94267-0008. FTB 3537 and FTB 3538 are sent to the FTB at P.O. Box 942857, Sacramento, CA 94257-0531.

Payment extensions may be granted for a reasonable period by the FTB. There is no prescribed form; presumably a letter of explanation may be used for this purpose. Extensions of up to one year are also available to disaster victims and victims of terroristic or militaristic actions (¶110).

Taxpayers abroad: An additional automatic two-month extension of time to file a return is granted to a taxpayer traveling or residing abroad on the due date (¶109). Consequently, the extended due date for such taxpayers is December 15. However, interest accrues on any unpaid tax from the original due date of the return. Any additional extensions must be applied for in writing with a letter of explanation.

¶73 Estimated Tax

California Form: 540-ES (Estimated Tax for Individuals).

Nonresidents or part-year residents are required to pay estimated taxes in the same manner as residents (¶36, ¶111).

The California alternative minimum tax (¶117) is included in determining any required estimated tax payments.

The estimated tax is paid in quarterly installments on the same dates as federal payments: April 15, June 15, September 15, and January 15. The January 15 installment need not be made if the taxpayer files the tax return and pays the balance of tax before February 1. When the due date falls on a Saturday, Sunday, or other legal holiday, payment may be made on the next business day.

Married couples may file separate or joint estimated tax payment vouchers, but no joint payments can be made if the spouses have different tax years, or if the spouses are legally separated.

Form 540-ES is used for paying estimated tax. This form consists of a four-part payment voucher, with the due date on each voucher.

¶74 State Tax Assistance

The Franchise Tax Board (FTB) offers various taxpayer assistance programs ranging from providing trained volunteers to assist taxpayers at no cost in completing their tax returns to toll-free telephone assistance. The toll-free telephone numbers are included in the instruction booklet for Form 540NR.

In addition, the FTB has several district offices located in principal cities throughout the state. These offices and their addresses are printed in the 540NR Instruction booklet.

¶75 Forms

Forms are available from the FTB's Web site at: http://www.ftb.ca.gov/forms/index.shtml or may be ordered directly from the state at the following address:

Franchise Tax Board
Tax Forms Request Unit
P.O. Box 307
Rancho Cordova, CA 95741-0307

California income tax forms and publications may also be obtained through automated telephones. The Internet address and telephone numbers are listed in the Form 540NR Instruction booklet.

¶76 Interest

The California rate of interest on underpayments and overpayments of tax is based on the federal underpayment rate (¶711). The interest rate is redetermined semiannually and is as follows:

January 1, 2013—December 31, 2013	3%
January 1, 2014—December 31, 2014	3%
January 1, 2015—December 31, 2015 . . . . :	3%
January 1, 2016—December 31, 2016	3%
January 1, 2017—June 30, 2017	4%

¶77 Penalties

A penalty of 5% per month, up to a maximum of 25%, is imposed for failure without reasonable cause to file a return. If the failure to file is fraudulent, the penalty is 15% per month, up to a maximum of 75%.

The penalty for failure to pay the income tax when it is due is 5% of the unpaid amount plus ½% per month. If the penalties for failure to file and failure to pay are both applicable, the penalty imposed is the higher of (1) the penalty for failure to pay, or (2) the total of the penalty for failure to file and the penalty for failure to furnish information.

A minimum penalty of the lesser of $135 or 100% of the tax liability is imposed if the return is not filed within 60 days of the due date.

Other penalties are discussed at ¶712.

PART III

PERSONAL INCOME TAX

FEDERAL-CALIFORNIA CROSS-REFERENCE TABLE AND INDEX

Showing Sections of California Personal Income Tax Law (Revenue and Taxation Code) Comparable to Sections of Federal Law (1986 Internal Revenue Code).

Federal	California	Subject	Paragraph
IRC Sec. 1	Secs. 17041, 17048	Tax Rates and Tables	¶116, ¶118
IRC Sec. 2(a)	Secs. 17046, 17142.5	"Surviving Spouse" Defined	¶107
IRC Secs. 2(b), 2(c)	Sec. 17042	"Head of Household" Defined	¶114
IRC Sec. 15	Sec. 17034	Effect of Changes	¶406
IRC Sec. 21	Sec. 17052.6	Credit—Child Care	¶142
IRC Sec. 23	...	Adoption Costs Credit	¶139
IRC Secs. 25-30A	Sec. 17039	Credits—Various	...
IRC Sec. 31	Sec. 19002	Credit—Tax Withheld	¶715
IRC Sec. 32	Sec. 17052	Earned Income Tax Credit	¶158
IRC Secs. 33-36	...	Credits—Various	...
IRC Sec. 36C	Sec. 17052.25	Adoption Costs Credit	¶139
IRC Sec. 38	Sec. 17053.57	Community Development Investment Credit	¶155
IRC Secs. 39-40	...	Credits—Various	...
IRC Sec. 41	Sec. 17052.12	Research Expenditures Credit	¶150
IRC Sec. 42	Secs. 17057.5, 17058	Low-income Housing Credit	¶138
IRC Sec. 43	Sec. 17052.8	Enhanced Oil Recovery Credit	¶153
IRC Sec. 44	Sec. 17053.42	Disabled Access Credit	¶140
IRC Sec. 45	...	Solar and Wind Energy Systems Credits	...
IRC Sec. 45C	...	Clinical Testing Credit	...
IRC Sec. 45D	...	New Markets Tax Credit	...
IRC Sec. 45E	...	Credit for Small Employer Pension Plan Startup Costs	...
IRC Sec. 45F	...	Employer-Provided Child Care Credit	...
IRC Sec. 45G	...	Railroad Track Maintenance Credit	...
IRC Sec. 45H	Sec. 17053.62	Low Sulfur Diesel Fuel Production Credit	151
IRC Sec. 45I	...	Marginal Well Production Credit	...
IRC Sec. 48	...	Energy Credit; Reforestation Credit	...
IRC Secs. 51-52	Sec. 17053.7	Work Opportunity Credit	...
IRC Sec. 53	Sec. 17063	Minimum Tax Credit	¶152
IRC Secs. 55-59	Secs. 17062, 17062.3, 17062.5	Alternative Minimum Tax	¶117, ¶331
IRC Sec. 61	Secs. 17071, 17087.6, 17090, 17131, 17133, 17133.5, 17135, 17136, 17138, 17140.5, 17147.7, 17149, 17153.5, 17555	"Gross Income" defined	¶201
IRC Sec. 62	Sec. 17072	"Adjusted Gross Income" defined	¶201, ¶202, ¶329
IRC Sec. 63	Secs. 17073, 17073.5, 17301, 17304	Standard Deduction	¶112, ¶203, ¶303, ¶335
IRC Sec. 64	Sec. 17074	"Ordinary Income" defined	...
IRC Sec. 65	Sec. 17075	"Ordinary Loss" defined	...
IRC Sec. 66	Sec. 18534	Income Where Spouses Living Apart	¶107, ¶239
IRC Sec. 67	Sec. 17076	2% Floor on Itemized Deductions	¶303, ¶329, ¶604
IRC Sec. 68	Sec. 17077	6% Floor on Itemized Deductions	¶303, ¶329
IRC Sec. 71	Sec. 17081	Spousal and Child Support Payments	Various
IRC Sec. 72	Secs. 17081, 17085, 17085.7, 17087	Annuities	¶205, ¶206, ¶214, ¶215
IRC Sec. 73	Sec. 17081	Services of Child	¶208
IRC Sec. 74	Sec. 17081	Prizes and Awards	¶209
IRC Sec. 75	Sec. 17081	Dealers in Tax-Exempt Securities	¶210
IRC Sec. 77	Sec. 17081	Commodity Credit Corp. Loans	¶211
IRC Sec. 79	Sec. 17081	Group Term Life Insurance	¶212
IRC Sec. 80	Sec. 17081	Restoration of Value of Certain Securities	...
IRC Sec. 82	Sec. 17081	Moving Expense Reimbursement	¶238
IRC Sec. 83	Sec. 17081	Property Transferred to Employee	¶207
IRC Sec. 84	Sec. 17081	Transfers to Political Organizations	¶201, ¶544
IRC Sec. 85	Secs. 17081, 17083	Unemployment Compensation	¶201
IRC Sec. 86	Secs. 17081, 17087	Social Security Benefits, etc.	¶201
IRC Sec. 88	Sec. 17081	Nuclear Plant Expenses	¶201
IRC Sec. 90	Sec. 17081	Illegal Irrigation Subsidies	¶201

Federal	California	Subject	Paragraph
IRC Sec. 101	Secs. 17131, 17132.5	Death Benefits	¶213, ¶215
IRC Sec. 102	Sec. 17131	Gifts and Inheritances	¶216
IRC Sec. 103	Secs. 17131, 17133, 17143	Interest on Government Bonds	¶217
IRC Sec. 104	Secs. 17131, 17132.7	Compensation—Injury or Sickness	¶218
IRC Sec. 105	Secs. 17131, 17087	Accident and Health Plans—Amounts Received	¶219
IRC Sec. 106	Secs. 17131, 17131.4	Accident and Health Plans—Employer Contributions	¶219, ¶247
IRC Sec. 107	Secs. 17131, 17131.6	Rental Value of Parsonages	¶220, ¶247
IRC Sec. 108	Secs. 17131, 17134, 17144, 17144.5, 17144.7	Income from Discharge of Indebtedness	¶221
IRC Sec. 109	Sec. 17131	Improvements by Lessee	¶222
IRC Sec. 110	Sec. 17131	Short-Term Lease Construction Allowances	¶223
IRC Sec. 111	Secs. 17131, 17142	Recovery of Bad Debts and Prior Taxes	¶224
IRC Sec. 112	Secs. 17131, 17142.5	Combat Pay of Members of Armed Forces	¶225
IRC Sec. 114	Sec. 17132	Extraterritorial Income	¶201
IRC Sec. 115	Sec. 17131	Income of States and Municipalities	. . .
IRC Sec. 117	Sec. 17131	Scholarship and Fellowship Grants	¶227
IRC Sec. 119	Sec. 17131	Employer-Furnished Meals and Lodging	¶228
IRC Sec. 120	Sec. 17131	Employer Contributions to Legal Services Plan	¶201, ¶244
IRC Sec. 121	Secs. 17131, 17152	Exclusion for Primary Residence Sale	¶229, ¶504
IRC Sec. 122	Sec. 17131	Reduced Uniformed Services Retirement Pay	¶205, ¶225
IRC Sec. 123	Sec. 17131	Living Expenses Paid by Insurance	¶238
IRC Sec. 125	Secs. 17131, 17131.5, 17131.10	Employer Contributions to "Cafeteria" Plans	¶201, ¶346
IRC Sec. 126	Secs. 17131, 17135.5	Government Payments for Environmental Conservation	¶201, ¶243
IRC Sec. 127	Secs. 17131, 17151	Educational Assistance Programs	¶242
IRC Sec. 129	Sec. 17131	Dependent Care Assistance Programs	¶201
IRC Sec. 130	Sec. 17131	Personal Injury Assignments	¶201
IRC Sec. 131	Sec. 17131	Foster Care Payments	¶201
IRC Sec. 132	Secs. 17131, 17154	Fringe Benefits	¶201, ¶238, ¶241
IRC Sec. 134	Sec. 17131	Military Benefits	¶201, ¶225
IRC Sec. 135	Sec. 17151	Bond Income Used for Higher Education	. . .
IRC Sec. 136	Sec. 17131	Energy Conservation Subsidies	¶201, ¶245
IRC Sec. 137	Sec. 17131	Adoption Assistance Programs	¶249
IRC Sec. 138	Sec. 17201	Medicare Advantage MSA	¶247
IRC Sec. 139	Sec. 17131, 17131.10	Disaster Relief Payments	¶201, ¶251
IRC Sec. 139A	Sec. 17139.6	Federal Subsidies for Prescription Drug Plans	¶252
IRC Sec. 139B	Sec. 17131	Exclusion of volunteer firefighter benefits	¶251
IRC Sec. 139C	. . .	Exclusion of COBRA premium assistance payments	. . .
IRC Sec. 139D	Sec. 17131	Indian health care benefits	¶252
IRC Sec. 140	Sec. 17131	Miscellaneous Non-IRC Federal Exemptions	. . .
IRC Secs. 141-50	Sec. 17143	Private Activity Bonds	¶217
IRC Sec. 151	Secs. 17054, 17054.1	Deductions for Personal and Dependent Exemptions	¶113
IRC Sec. 152	Sec. 17056	Dependents	¶115
IRC Sec. 161	Secs. 17201, 17202.5, 17274, 17275, 17278, 17299.8, 17299.9	Allowance of Deductions	¶300
IRC Sec. 162	Secs. 17201, 17202, 17269, 17270, 17273, 17273.1, 17286	Trade or Business Expense	Various
IRC Sec. 163	Secs. 17201, 17224, 17225, 17230, 17235	Interest	¶237, ¶303, ¶305
IRC Sec. 164	Secs. 17201, 17220, 17222	Taxes—Deductions	¶303, ¶306
IRC Sec. 165	Secs. 17201, 17204, 17207-07.14	Losses—Deductions	¶303, ¶307, ¶407
IRC Sec. 166	Sec. 17201	Bad Debts—Deductions	¶308
IRC Sec. 167	Secs. 17201, 17250.5	Depreciation	¶310, ¶332, ¶562
IRC Sec. 168	Secs. 17201, 17250	Accelerated Cost Recovery System	¶310
IRC Sec. 169	Secs. 17201, 17250	Amortization of Pollution Control Facilities	¶314
IRC Sec. 170	Secs. 17201, 17206.5, 17275.2-75.5	Charitable Contributions	¶302, ¶321
IRC Sec. 171	Sec. 17201	Amortization of Bond Premium	¶324
IRC Sec. 172	Secs. 17201, 17276-76.22	Net Operating Loss Carryover	¶309
IRC Sec. 173	Sec. 17201	Circulation Expenditures	¶303, ¶342
IRC Sec. 174	Sec. 17201	Research and Experimental Expenditures	¶331
IRC Sec. 175	Sec. 17201	Soil and Water Conservation Expenditures	¶302, ¶341
IRC Sec. 178	Sec. 17201	Depreciation or Amortization of Cost of Acquiring a Lease	¶313
IRC Sec. 179	Secs. 17201, 17255, 17268	Election to Expense Depreciable Assets	¶311

Federal	California	Subject	Paragraph
IRC Sec. 179B	Secs. 17201.4, 17255.5	Refiners' Sulfur Rules Compliance Costs	¶318
IRC Sec. 179C	Sec. 17257	Expensing of Qualified Refinery Property	¶311
IRC Sec. 179D	Sec. 17257.2	Energy Efficient Commercial Building Costs	¶345
IRC Sec. 179E	17257.4	Election to Expense Mining Safety Equipment	¶311
IRC Sec. 180	Sec. 17201	Farm Fertilizer Expenses	¶302, ¶341
IRC Sec. 181	Sec. 17201.5	Qualified Film and Television Productions	¶310
IRC Sec. 183	Sec. 17201	Hobby Losses	¶336, ¶338
IRC Sec. 186	Sec. 17201	Recovery of Antitrust Damages	. . .
IRC Sec. 190	Sec. 17201	Facilities for Handicapped	¶301
IRC Sec. 192	Sec. 17201	Contributions to Black Lung Benefit Trust	. . .
IRC Sec. 193	Secs. 17201, 17260	Tertiary Injectants	¶320
IRC Sec. 194	Secs. 17201, 17278.5	Amortization of Reforestation Expenses	¶315
IRC Sec. 194A	Sec. 17201	Contributions to Employer Liability Trusts	¶330
IRC Sec. 195	Sec. 17201	Start-Up Expenditures	¶334
IRC Sec. 196	Sec. 17024.5	Unused Business Credits—Deduction	. . .
IRC Sec. 197	Sec. 17279	Amortization of Goodwill	¶310, ¶333
IRC Sec. 198	Sec. 17279.4	Environmental Remediation Costs	¶346
IRC Sec. 198A	Sec. 17279.6	Expensing of qualified disaster costs	¶310
IRC Sec. 199	Sec. 17201.6	Domestic Production Deduction	¶317
IRC Sec. 211	Sec. 17201	Additional Allowance of Deductions	. . .
IRC Sec. 212	Sec. 17201	Expenses for Production of Income	¶304
IRC Sec. 213	Secs. 17201, 17241	Medical Expenses	¶325
IRC Sec. 215	Secs. 17201, 17302	Spousal Support	¶323
IRC Sec. 216	Sec. 17201	Taxes and Interest Paid to Cooperative Housing Corporation	¶327
IRC Sec. 217	Sec. 17201	Moving Expenses	¶328
IRC Sec. 219	Sec. 17201, 17501	Retirement Savings	¶330
IRC Sec. 220	Secs. 17201, 17215, 17215.1	Archer MSAs	¶247, ¶326
IRC Sec. 221	Secs. 17201, 17204	Interest on Education Loans	¶305
IRC Sec. 222	Secs. 17204.7	Qualified Tuition and Related Expenses Deduction	¶344
IRC Sec. 223	Sec. 17215.4	Health Savings Accounts	¶326
IRC Sec. 224	. . .	Cross Reference	. . .
IRC Sec. 261	Sec. 17201	Disallowance of Deductions	¶300, ¶336
IRC Sec. 262	Sec. 17201	Personal Living and Family Expenses	¶336
IRC Sec. 263	Secs. 17201, 17260	Capital Expenditures	¶320, ¶336
IRC Sec. 263A	Sec. 17201	Inventory Capitalization Rules	¶336, ¶407, ¶409, ¶416
IRC Sec. 264	Sec. 17201	Amounts Paid in Connection with Insurance Contracts	¶305, ¶336
IRC Sec. 265	Sec. 17280	Tax Exempt Income—Interest and Expenses	¶305, ¶336
IRC Sec. 266	Sec. 17201	Carrying Charges	¶336
IRC Sec. 267	Secs. 17201	Transactions Between Related Individuals	¶336
IRC Sec. 268	Sec. 17201	Sale of Land with Unharvested Crop	¶336
IRC Sec. 269	Sec. 17201	Acquisition Made to Avoid Income Tax	. . .
IRC Sec. 269A	Secs. 17201, 17287	Personal Service Corporations	¶412
IRC Sec. 269B	Sec. 17201	Stapled Stock	¶412
IRC Sec. 271	Sec. 17201	Debts Owed by Political Parties	¶308
IRC Sec. 272	Sec. 17201	Disposal of Coal or Domestic Iron Ore	. . .
IRC Sec. 273	Sec. 17201	Holders of Terminable Interest	¶336
IRC Sec. 274	Sec. 17201	Entertainment, Travel and Gift Expenses	¶302, ¶329, ¶336
IRC Sec. 275	Sec. 17222, 17240	Nondeductible Taxes	¶306
IRC Sec. 276	Sec. 17201	Indirect Political Contributions	¶336
IRC Sec. 277	Sec. 17201	Expenses by Membership Organizations	. . .
IRC Sec. 280A	Sec. 17201	Disallowance of Business Expenses of Home, Vacation Rentals	¶301, ¶336
IRC Sec. 280B	Sec. 17201	Demolition of Historic Structures	¶336
IRC Sec. 280C	Secs. 17201, 17270	Federal Credits	¶336
IRC Sec. 280E	Secs. 17201, 17282	Illegal Drug Sales	¶336
IRC Sec. 280F	Sec. 17201	Luxury Cars, etc.	¶310
IRC Sec. 280G	Sec. 17201	"Golden Parachute" Payments	¶336
IRC Sec. 280H	Sec. 17201	Salaries of Shareholder/Owners of Personal Service Corp.	. . .
IRC Sec. 301	Sec. 17321	Corporate Distributions of Property	¶226
IRC Sec. 302	Secs. 17321-22.1	Distributions in Redemption of Stock	¶226
IRC Sec. 303	Sec. 17321	Distributions in Redemption of Stock to Pay Death Taxes	¶226
IRC Sec. 304	Sec. 17321	Redemption Through Use of Related Corporations	¶226
IRC Sec. 305	Sec. 17321	Distributions of Stock and Rights	¶226
IRC Sec. 306	Sec. 17321	Dispositions of "306" Stock	¶226
IRC Sec. 307	Sec. 17321	Basis of Stock and Rights of Distribution	¶226, ¶558

Federal	California	Subject	Paragraph
IRC Sec. 312	Sec. 17321	Effect on Earnings and Profits	¶226
IRC Sec. 316	Secs. 17321	"Dividend" Defined	¶226
IRC Sec. 317	Sec. 17321	"Property," "Redemption" Defined	¶226
IRC Sec. 318	Sec. 17321	Constructive Ownership of Stock	¶226
IRC Sec. 331	Sec. 17321	Gain or Loss in Corporate Liquidations	¶226, ¶522
IRC Sec. 334	Sec. 17321	Basis of Property Received in Liquidation	¶226, ¶522, ¶548
IRC Sec. 346	Sec. 17321	"Partial Liquidation" Defined	¶226, ¶522
IRC Sec. 351	Sec. 17321	Corporate Organizations—Transfer to Controlled Corporation	¶512
IRC Sec. 354	Sec. 17321	Exchange of Stock in Reorganization	¶516
IRC Sec. 355	Sec. 17321	Reorganizations—Distributions by Controlled Corporation	¶517
IRC Sec. 356	Sec. 17321	Receipt of Additional Consideration	¶518
IRC Sec. 357	Sec. 17321	Assumption of Liability	. . .
IRC Sec. 358	Sec. 17321	Basis to Distributees	¶547, ¶549
IRC Sec. 367	Sec. 17321	Transfers to Foreign Corporations	¶519
IRC Sec. 368	Sec. 17321	Corporate Reorganizations—Definitions	¶516
IRC Sec. 382	Sec. 17321	Discharge of Indebtedness	¶221
IRC Sec. 385	Sec. 17321	Treatment of Corporate Interests as Stock or Indebtedness	. . .
IRC Sec. 401	Sec. 17501	Pension, Profit-Sharing, Stock Bonus Plans	¶206, ¶607
IRC Sec. 402	Secs. 17501, 17504	Taxability of Beneficiary of Employees' Trust	¶206, ¶330, ¶607
IRC Sec. 402A	Secs. 17501	Optional Treatment of Elective Deferrals as Roth Contributions	¶206, ¶607
IRC Sec. 403	Secs. 17501, 17506	Taxability of Employee Annuities	¶206, ¶607
IRC Sec. 404	Secs. 17203, 17501	Deduction for Employer's Contributions to Employee Pension, Profit-Sharing, and Stock Bonus Plans	¶330, ¶607
IRC Sec. 404A	Secs. 17501, 17563.5	Foreign Deferred Compensation Plans	¶330, ¶607
IRC Sec. 406	Sec. 17501	Employees of Foreign Subsidiaries	¶330, ¶607
IRC Sec. 407	Sec. 17501	Employees of Domestic Subsidiaries	¶330, ¶607
IRC Sec. 408	Secs. 17507, 17508	Individual Retirement Accounts	¶206, ¶330
IRC Sec. 408A	Sec. 17501	Roth IRAs	¶206, ¶330
IRC Sec. 409	Sec. 17501	Employee Stock Ownership Plans	¶330
IRC Sec. 409A	Sec. 17501	Treatment of Nonqualified Deferred Compensation Plans	¶206
IRC Sec. 410	Sec. 17501	Minimum Participation Standards	¶330
IRC Sec. 411	Sec. 17501	Minimum Vesting Standards	¶330
IRC Sec. 412	Sec. 17501	Minimum Funding Standards	¶330
IRC Sec. 413	Secs. 17501, 17509	Collectively Bargained Plans	¶330
IRC Sec. 414	Sec. 17501	Definitions and Special Rules—Plans	¶206, ¶330
IRC Sec. 415	Sec. 17501	Limitations on Benefits and Contributions	¶206, ¶330
IRC Sec. 416	Sec. 17501	Top-Heavy Plans	¶330
IRC Sec. 417	Sec. 17501	Minimum Survivor Annuity Requirements	¶330
IRC Secs. 418-18E	Sec. 17501	Pension Plan Reorganizations	¶330
IRC Sec. 419	Sec. 17501	Welfare Benefit Plans	¶330
IRC Sec. 419A	Sec. 17501	Qualified Asset Account; Limitation on Additions to Account	¶330
IRC Sec. 420	Sec. 17501	Transfers of Excess Pension Assets to Retiree Health Accounts	¶206
IRC Sec. 421	Secs. 17501, 17502	Employee Stock Options—Employer Deductions	¶207
IRC Sec. 422	Sec. 17501	Incentive Stock Options	¶207
IRC Sec. 423	Sec. 17501	Employee Stock Purchase Plan	¶207
IRC Sec. 424	Sec. 17501	Stock Options—Definitions and Special Rules	¶207
IRC Sec. 441	Secs. 17551, 17656	Accounting Periods—Generally	¶400, ¶401
IRC Sec. 442	Secs. 17551, 17556	Accounting—Change of Period	¶400, ¶402
IRC Sec. 443	Secs. 17551-52	Accounting—Short Period Returns	¶400, ¶403, ¶404
IRC Sec. 444	Sec. 17551	Election to Keep Same Tax Year—Partnerships	¶400, ¶401, ¶616
IRC Sec. 446	Sec. 17551	Methods of Accounting—General Rule	¶400, ¶407
IRC Sec. 447	Sec. 17551	Accounting—Corporations Engaged in Farming	¶400, ¶407
IRC Sec. 448	Sec. 17551	Restriction on Use of Cash Method	¶400, ¶407
IRC Sec. 451	Secs. 17551, 17552.3	Taxable Year of Inclusion	¶400, ¶407
IRC Sec. 453	Secs. 17551, 17560	Installment Method	¶400, ¶411
IRC Sec. 453A	Secs. 17551, 17560	Installment Method—Dealers in Personal Property	¶400, ¶411
IRC Sec. 453B	Sec. 17551	Gain or Loss Disposition of Installment Obligations	¶400, ¶411
IRC Sec. 454	Secs. 17551, 17553	Obligations Issued at Discount	¶400, ¶408

Federal	California	Subject	Paragraph
IRC Sec. 455	Sec. 17551	Prepaid Subscription Income	¶400, ¶407
IRC Sec. 456	Sec. 17551	Prepaid Dues Income	¶400, ¶407
IRC Sec. 457	Secs. 17501.5, 17501.7, 17551	State Deferred Compensation Plans	¶206, ¶330, ¶400
IRC Sec. 457A	Sec. 17551(g)	Nonqualified Deferred Compensation From Certain Tax Indifferent Parties	¶206
IRC Sec. 458	Sec. 17551	Returned Magazines	¶400, ¶407
IRC Sec. 460	Secs. 17551, 17564	Long-Term Contracts	¶400, ¶407
IRC Sec. 461	Sec. 17551, 17560.5	Taxable Year of Deduction	¶400, ¶407
IRC Sec. 464	Sec. 17551	Deduction Limitation—Farming Syndicates	¶400, ¶407
IRC Sec. 465	Sec. 17551	At-Risk Limitation	¶339, ¶400
IRC Sec. 467	Sec. 17551	Deferred Rental Payments	¶400, ¶407
IRC Sec. 468	Sec. 17551	Waste Disposal Costs	¶400, ¶407
IRC Sec. 468A	Sec. 17551	Nuclear Plant Expenses	¶400, ¶407
IRC Sec. 468B	Sec. 17551	Settlement Funds	¶400, ¶407
IRC Sec. 469	Secs. 17551, 17561	Passive Loss Limits	¶340, ¶400
IRC Sec. 470	Secs. 17551	Limitations on Deductions Allocable to Tax-Exempt Property	¶307
IRC Sec. 471	Sec. 17551	Inventories	¶400, ¶409
IRC Sec. 472	Sec. 17551	LIFO Inventories	¶400, ¶410
IRC Sec. 473	Sec. 17551	Liquidation of LIFO Inventories	¶400, ¶410
IRC Sec. 474	Sec. 17551	Dollar-Value LIFO Method	¶400, ¶410
IRC Sec. 475	Secs. 17551, 17570	Mark-to-Market Accounting	¶400, ¶409, ¶533
IRC Sec. 481	Sec. 17551	Adjustments	¶400, ¶407
IRC Sec. 482	Sec. 17551	Allocation of Income Among Taxpayers	¶400, ¶412
IRC Sec. 483	Sec. 17551	Imputed Interest	¶400, ¶414
IRC Sec. 501	Secs. 17631, 17632	Exempt Organizations and Trusts	¶321, ¶606, ¶607
IRC Sec. 503	Secs. 17635-40	Requirements for Exemption	¶607
IRC Secs. 511-14	Sec. 17651	Unrelated Business Income	¶607
IRC Sec. 529	Secs. 17140, 17140.3	Qualified Tuition Programs	¶250
IRC Sec. 529A	Sec. 17140.4	ABLE Accounts	¶255
IRC Secs. 530, 531	Sec. 23712	Coverdell Education Savings Accounts	¶206, ¶250, ¶330
IRC Secs. 541-58	Sec. 17024.5	Personal Holding Companies	. . .
IRC Sec. 584	Sec. 17671	Common Trust Funds	¶614
IRC Sec. 611	Sec. 17681	Depletion—Deduction	¶319
IRC Sec. 612	Sec. 17681	Basis for Cost Depletion	¶319, ¶562
IRC Sec. 613	Sec. 17681	Percentage Depletion	¶319
IRC Sec. 613A	Secs. 17681, 17734.6	Limitations on Depletion—Oil, Gas and Geothermal Wells	¶319, ¶562
IRC Sec. 614	Sec. 17681	"Property" Defined	¶319
IRC Sec. 616	Sec. 17681	Mine Development Expenses	¶320
IRC Sec. 617	Sec. 17681	Mine Exploration Expenses	¶320
IRC Sec. 631	Sec. 17681	Gain or Loss in Case of Timber, Coal or Iron	¶540
IRC Sec. 636	Sec. 17681	Mineral Production Payments	¶319
IRC Sec. 638	Sec. 17681	Continental Shelf Areas	¶319
IRC Sec. 641	Secs. 17731, 17731.5, 17734, 17742-45.1	Estates and Trusts—Imposition of Tax	¶601, ¶604, ¶606
IRC Sec. 642	Secs. 17731-33, 17736	Special Rules for Credits and Deductions	¶604, ¶605, ¶606
IRC Sec. 643	Secs. 17731, 17750	Estates and Trusts—Definitions	¶601, ¶604
IRC Sec. 644	Sec. 17731	Taxable Year of Trusts	¶601, ¶604
IRC Sec. 645	Secs. 17731, 17751	Certain Revocable Trusts Treated as Part of Estate	¶401, ¶604
IRC Sec. 646	. . .	Alaska Native Settlement Trusts	¶601
IRC Sec. 651	Sec. 17731	Simple Trusts	¶604
IRC Sec. 652	Sec. 17731	Beneficiaries of Simple Trusts	¶605
IRC Sec. 661	Secs. 17731, 17735	Complex Trusts—Deductions	¶604
IRC Sec. 662	Sec. 17731	Beneficiaries of Complex Trusts	¶605
IRC Sec. 663	Secs. 17731, 17752	Special Rules Applicable to §§ 661 and 662	¶605
IRC Sec. 664	Sec. 17731, 17755	Charitable Remainder Trusts	¶605, ¶606
IRC Sec. 665	Secs. 17731, 17779	Excess Distributions by Trusts—Definitions	¶601, ¶605
IRC Sec. 666	Secs. 17731, 17779	Accumulation Distribution Allocation	¶605
IRC Sec. 667	Secs. 17731, 17779	Amounts Distributed in Preceding Years	¶605
IRC Sec. 668	Secs. 17731, 17779	Interest on Accumulation from Foreign Trusts	¶605
IRC Sec. 671	Sec. 17731	Grantor Trusts—Trust Income	¶608
IRC Sec. 672	Sec. 17731	Grantor Trusts—Definitions	¶608
IRC Sec. 673	Sec. 17731	Reversionary Interests	¶608
IRC Sec. 674	Sec. 17731	Power to Control Beneficial Enjoyment	¶608
IRC Sec. 675	Sec. 17731	Administrative Powers	¶608
IRC Sec. 676	Sec. 17731	Power to Revoke	¶608
IRC Sec. 677	Sec. 17731	Income for Benefit of Grantor	¶608

Federal	California	Subject	Paragraph
IRC Sec. 678	Sec. 17731	Person Other Than Grantor Treated as Owner	¶608
IRC Sec. 679	Secs. 17024.5, 17731	Foreign Trusts with U.S. Beneficiaries	¶608
IRC Sec. 681	Sec. 17731	Limitation on Charitable Deduction—Unrelated Business Income	¶606
IRC Sec. 682	Secs. 17731, 17737	Income in Case of Divorce	¶611
IRC Sec. 683	Sec. 17731	Use of Trust as Exchange Fund	¶516
IRC Sec. 684	Secs. 17731, 17760	Gain on Transfers to Foreign Trusts and Estates	¶520
IRC Sec. 685	Secs. 17731, 17760.5	Funeral Trusts	¶608
IRC Sec. 691	Sec. 17731	Income in Respect of Decedents	¶413
IRC Sec. 692	Secs. 17731, 17142.5	Income Taxes of Armed Forces Members on Death	¶225
IRC Sec. 701	Secs. 17851, 17851.5	Partners, Not Partnership, Subject to Tax	¶616
IRC Sec. 702	Sec. 17851	Income and Credits of Partner	¶620
IRC Sec. 703	Secs. 17851, 17853	Partnership Computations	¶620
IRC Sec. 704	Secs. 17851, 17858	Partner's Distributive Share	¶617, ¶620
IRC Sec. 705	Sec. 17851	Determination of Basis of Partner's Interest	¶555, ¶618
IRC Sec. 706	Sec. 17851	Taxable Years of Partner and Partnership	¶621
IRC Sec. 707	Secs. 17851, 17854	Transactions Between Partner and Partnership	¶617, ¶620
IRC Sec. 708	Sec. 17851	Continuation of Partnership	¶621
IRC Sec. 709	Sec. 17851	Organization and Syndication Fees	¶620
IRC Sec. 721	Sec. 17851	Recognition of Gain or Loss Contribution	¶617
IRC Sec. 722	Sec. 17851	Basis of Contributing Partner's Interest	¶555, ¶617
IRC Sec. 723	Sec. 17851	Basis of Property Contributed to Partnership	¶555, ¶617
IRC Sec. 724	Sec. 17851	Disposition of Contributed Property	¶617
IRC Sec. 731	Sec. 17851	Recognition of Gain or Loss on Distribution	¶617
IRC Sec. 732	Sec. 17851	Basis of Distributed Property	¶555
IRC Sec. 733	Sec. 17851	Basis of Distributee Partner's Interest	¶555
IRC Sec. 734	Sec. 17851	Optional Adjustment to Basis of Undistributed Property	¶555
IRC Sec. 735	Sec. 17851	Character of Gain or Loss on Disposition of Distributed Property	¶617
IRC Sec. 736	Sec. 17851	Payments to Retiring Partner or Deceased Partner's Successor	¶617, ¶618
IRC Sec. 737	Sec. 17851	Precontribution Gain From Partnership Distributions	¶618
IRC Sec. 741	Sec. 17851	Gain or Loss on Sale or Exchange	¶618
IRC Sec. 742	Sec. 17851	Basis of Transferee Partner's Interest	¶555
IRC Sec. 743	Sec. 17851	Optional Adjustment to Basis of Property	¶555
IRC Sec. 751	Secs. 17851, 17855-57	Unrealized Receivables and Inventory Items	¶618
IRC Sec. 752	Sec. 17851	Treatment of Certain Liabilities	¶618
IRC Sec. 753	Sec. 17851	Partner Receiving Income in Respect of Decedent	¶618
IRC Sec. 754	Sec. 17851	Electing Optional Adjustment to Basis of Partnership Property	¶555, ¶618
IRC Sec. 755	Sec. 17851	Rules for Allocation of Basis	¶555, ¶618
IRC Sec. 761	Sec. 17851	Terms Defined	¶616
IRC Secs. 771-77	Secs. 17851, 17865	Special Rules for Electing Large Partnerships	¶624
IRC Sec. 851	Sec. 17088	Regulated Investment Company	¶226
IRC Sec. 852	Secs. 17088, 17145	Dividends to Shareholders of Certain Mutual Funds	¶217
IRC Sec. 853	Sec. 17024.5	Foreign Tax Credit for Shareholders	¶226
IRC Secs. 854-55	Sec. 17088	Dividends of Regulated Investment Company	¶217, ¶226, ¶559
IRC Secs. 856-60	Sec. 17088	Real Estate Investment Trusts	¶226, ¶609
IRC Secs. 860A-860G	Sec. 17088	Real Estate Mortgage Investment Conduits	¶615
IRC Secs. 860H-860L	Sec. 17088	Financial Asset Securatization Trusts	¶610
IRC Secs. 861-65	Secs. 17951-54	Sources of Income	¶201, ¶231
IRC Secs. 871-79	. . .	Nonresident Aliens	¶239
IRC Sec. 893	Sec. 17146	Employees of Foreign Country	¶230
IRC Secs. 901-05	. . .	Income from Sources Outside U.S.	¶127, Various
IRC Sec. 911	Sec. 17024.5	Foreign Income Exclusion	¶231, ¶235
IRC Sec. 912	. . .	Income from Sources Within U.S. Possessions	¶231, ¶235
IRC Sec. 941	. . .	Qualifying Foreign Trade Income	. . .
IRC Sec. 942	. . .	Foreign Trading Gross Receipts	. . .
IRC Sec. 943	. . .	Other Foreign Property	. . .
IRC Secs. 951-52	. . .	Controlled Foreign Corporations—Shareholders	¶226
IRC Sec. 988	Sec. 17078	Foreign Currency Transactions	¶521
IRC Secs. 991-99	Sec. 17024.5	Domestic International Sales Corp. (DISC)	. . .
IRC Sec. 995	. . .	Taxation of DISC Income to Shareholders	¶226
IRC Sec. 1001	Secs. 18031, 18041.5	Determination of Gain or Loss	¶501
IRC Sec. 1011	Sec. 18031	Adjusted Basis for Determining Gain or Loss	¶559

Federal	California	Subject	Paragraph
IRC Sec. 1012	Sec. 18031	Basis of Property	¶542
IRC Sec. 1013	Sec. 18031	Basis of Property Included in Inventory	¶543
IRC Sec. 1014	Secs. 18031, 18035.6	Basis of Property Acquired from Decedent	¶546
IRC Sec. 1015	Sec. 18031	Basis of Property Acquired by Gift and Transfers in Trust	¶544, ¶545
IRC Sec. 1016	Secs. 18031, 18036, 18036.5	Adjustments to Basis	¶559, ¶560
IRC Sec. 1017	Sec. 18031	Discharge of Indebtedness	¶221, ¶559
IRC Sec. 1019	Sec. 18031	Property on Which Lessee Has Made Improvements	¶559, 561
IRC Sec. 1021	Sec. 18031	Sale of Annuity Contract	¶559
IRC Sec. 1022	Sec. 18036.6	Basis of Property Acquired from Post-2009 Decedent	¶546
IRC Sec. 1031	Sec. 18031, 18031.5	Exchange of Property Held for Productive Use or Investment	¶507
IRC Sec. 1033	Secs. 18031, 18037, 18154	Involuntary Conversions	¶503, ¶550
IRC Sec. 1035	Sec. 18031	Exchange of Insurance Policies	¶508
IRC Sec. 1036	Sec. 18031	Exchange of Stock	¶509
IRC Sec. 1037	Sec. 18031	Exchanges of U.S. Obligations	¶510
IRC Sec. 1038	Sec. 18031	Reacquisition of Real Property	¶511
IRC Sec. 1040	Secs. 18031, 18038	Transfer of Certain Real Property	¶604
IRC Sec. 1041	Sec. 18031	Inter-Spousal Transfers	¶502
IRC Sec. 1042	Secs. 18031, 18042	Securities Sales to ESOPs	¶501, ¶514
IRC Sec. 1043	Sec. 18031	Sale of Property to Comply with Conflict of Interest Requirements	...
IRC Sec. 1044	Secs. 18031, 18049	Rollover of Publicly Traded Securities	¶501
IRC Sec. 1045	Secs. 18038.4, 18038.5	Rollover of Gain from Small Business Stock	¶515
IRC Sec. 1052	Secs. 18031, 18039	Basis Provisions from Prior Codes	¶554
IRC Sec. 1053	Sec. 18031	Basis of Property Acquired Before March 1913	¶556
IRC Sec. 1054	Sec. 18031	Basis of Stock Issued by FNMA	¶551
IRC Sec. 1055	Sec. 18031	Redeemable Ground Rents	¶552
IRC Sec. 1058	Sec. 18031	Transfer of Securities Under Loan Agreement	...
IRC Sec. 1059A	Sec. 18031	Basis or Inventor Costs on Imports	¶542
IRC Sec. 1060	Sec. 18031	Allocation of Transferred Business Assets	¶563
IRC Sec. 1081	Sec. 18031	Exchanges in Obedience to Orders of S.E.C.	¶506
IRC Sec. 1082	Sec. 18031	Basis for Determining Gain or Loss	¶557
IRC Sec. 1083	Sec. 18031	Definitions	...
IRC Sec. 1091	Sec. 18031	Wash Sales of Stock or Securities	¶527, ¶553
IRC Sec. 1092	Sec. 18031	Straddle Losses	¶532
IRC Sec. 1202	Secs. 18152, 18152.5	Small Business Stock	¶525
IRC Secs. 1211-12	Secs. 18151, 18155	Limitation on Capital Losses	¶523, ¶526
IRC Sec. 1221	Sec. 18151	"Capital Asset" Defined	¶504, ¶524
IRC Sec. 1222	Sec. 18151	Other Terms Relating to Capital Gains and Losses	¶525
IRC Sec. 1223	Secs. 18151, 18155.5, 18155.6	Holding Period of Property	¶528
IRC Sec. 1231	Sec. 18151	Sale of Business Property and Involuntary Conversions	¶537
IRC Sec. 1233	Sec. 18151	Gains and Losses from Short Sales	¶529
IRC Sec. 1234	Sec. 18151	Options to Buy and Sell	¶532
IRC Sec. 1234A	Sec. 18151	Gain or Loss from Certain Terminations	¶523
IRC Sec. 1234B	Sec. 18151	Gain or Loss from Securities Futures Contracts	¶523
IRC Sec. 1235	Sec. 18151	Sale or Exchange of Patents	¶530
IRC Sec. 1236	Sec. 18151	Dealers in Securities	¶533
IRC Sec. 1237	Sec. 18151	Real Property Subdivided for Sale	¶536
IRC Sec. 1239	Sec. 18151	Gain on Depreciable Property Transferred Between Related Taxpayers	¶537, ¶539
IRC Sec. 1241	Sec. 18151	Cancellation of Lease or Distributor's Agreement	¶541
IRC Sec. 1242	Sec. 18151	Losses on Small Business Investment Company Stock	¶307
IRC Sec. 1243	Sec. 18151	Stock Received Pursuant to Conversion Privilege	¶307
IRC Sec. 1244	Sec. 18151	Losses on Small Business Stock	¶307
IRC Sec. 1245	Secs. 18151, 18165	Recapture of Depreciation on Personal Property	¶539
IRC Sec. 1246	Sec. 17024.5	Gain on Foreign Investment Company Stock	¶538
IRC Secs. 1247-48	Secs. 17024.5, 18151	Special Rules on Foreign Investment Company Stock	¶538
IRC Sec. 1249	Secs. 17024.5, 18151	Patents Sold to Foreign Corporation	¶530, 538
IRC Sec. 1250	Secs. 18151, 18171, 18171.5	Recapture of Depreciation on Real Property	¶539
IRC Sec. 1252	Sec. 18151	Recapture of Soil and Water Conservation Expenditures	¶539
IRC Sec. 1253	Sec. 18151	Transfers of Franchises, Trademarks and Trade Names	¶332, ¶531, ¶539

Federal	California	Subject	Paragraph
IRC Sec. 1254	Sec. 18151	Recapture of Intangible Drilling Costs	¶539
IRC Sec. 1255	Sec. 18151	Certain Cost-Sharing Payments	¶539
IRC Sec. 1256	Sec. 18151	Regulated Futures Contracts	¶532
IRC Sec. 1257	Sec. 18151	Wetlands or Erodible Croplands	¶523
IRC Sec. 1258	Sec. 18151	Recharacterization of Gain from Certain Financial Transactions	. . .
IRC Sec. 1259	Sec. 18151	Constructive Sales Treatment for Appreciated Financial Positions	¶534
IRC Sec. 1260	. . .	Recharacterization of Derivative Contract Gains	¶523, 525
IRC Secs. 1271-88	Secs. 18151, 18177, 18178	Income from Discount Bonds, etc.	¶217, ¶237, ¶535
IRC Secs. 1291-1298	Sec. 18181	Treatment of Passive Investment Companies	¶523
IRC Secs. 1311-14	Secs. 19057-67	Mitigation of Effect of Limitations	¶710, ¶719
IRC Sec. 1341	Sec. 17049	Repayment of Amounts Received Under Claim of Right	¶415
IRC Secs. 1361-79	Secs. 17087.5, 18006	Subchapter S Corporations	¶233
IRC Secs. 1381-83	. . .	Tax Treatment of Cooperatives	¶232
IRC Sec. 1385	Sec. 17086	Amounts Includible in Patron's Gross Income	¶232
IRC Sec. 1396	Sec. 17053.74	Empowerment Zone Employment Credit	¶145
IRC Sec. 1445	Secs. 18662, 18668	Withholding—Disposition of Real Estate	¶714, ¶716
IRC Sec. 1446	Sec. 18666	Withholding—Amounts Paid to Foreign Partners	¶714
IRC Secs. 1491-94	. . .	Transfers of Property to Avoid Tax	. . .
IRC Secs. 3401-05	Secs. 18551, 18661-63, 18667, 18668	Withholding	¶715
IRC Sec. 3406	Sec. 18664	Backup Withholding	¶714
IRC Secs. 3501-05	Sec. 18677	Collection of Withholding Tax	¶715
IRC Secs. 4940-48	. . .	Private Foundations	¶606
IRC Secs. 4971-75	. . .	Pension Plans, etc.	¶206, ¶607
IRC Sec. 4980A	. . .	Excess Distributions from Qualified Plans	¶206
IRC Sec. 4980B	. . .	Excise Tax on Failure to Meet Health Care Continuous Coverage	. . .
IRC Sec. 6011	Secs. 18407, 18408, 18409	General Return Requirements/Abusive Tax Shelters	¶622, ¶715, ¶727
IRC Sec. 6012	Secs. 18501, 18503-9, 18601	Returns Required	¶106
IRC Sec. 6013	Secs. 18521-33, 19006	Joint Returns	¶106, ¶107, ¶709, ¶712
IRC Sec. 6014	..	Tax Not Computed by Taxpayer	¶106
IRC Sec. 6015	Sec. 18533	Innocent Spouse Relief	¶107
IRC Sec. 6031	Secs. 18535, 18633-33.5	Return of Partnership Income	¶622
IRC Sec. 6034	Sec. 18635	Information from Charitable Trust	¶606
IRC Sec. 6034A	Secs. 18505, 18631, 18635.5	Information to Beneficiaries	¶106, ¶601
IRC Sec. 6036	Sec. 19089	Notice of Executor's Qualification	. . .
IRC Sec. 6039	Sec. 18631	Returns for Stock Transfers	¶713
IRC Sec. 6039C	Sec. 18631	Returns by Foreign Persons	¶713
IRC Sec. 6039D	. . .	Fringe Benefit Plans Return	¶713
IRC Sec. 6039J	Sec. 18631	Commodity Credit Corporation Transactions	¶713
IRC Sec. 6039I	Sec. 18631	Employer-Owned Life Insurance Contracts	¶713
IRC Sec. 6041	Secs. 18631, 18661	Reporting Requirements	¶713
IRC Sec. 6041A	Sec. 18631	Reporting Certain Payments	¶713
IRC Sec. 6042	Secs. 18631, 18639	Returns for Dividends	¶713
IRC Sec. 6043	. . .	Returns for Dividends on Liquidation	¶713
IRC Sec. 6044	Sec. 18640	Returns by Cooperatives	¶713
IRC Sec. 6045	Sec. 18631	Reporting by Brokers	¶713
IRC Sec. 6046A	. . .	Foreign Partnership Return	¶713
IRC Sec. 6047	Sec. 19518	Information Returns	¶607, ¶713
IRC Sec. 6048	Sec. 18505	Consistency Rule	¶601, ¶711
IRC Sec. 6049	Secs. 18631, 18639	Returns for Interest	¶713
IRC Sec. 6050A	Sec. 18644	Fishing Boat Operators—Reporting Requirements	¶713
IRC Sec. 6050B	. . .	Reporting Unemployment Compensation	. . .
IRC Sec. 6050E	. . .	Reporting Tax Refunds	¶713
IRC Sec. 6050H-W	Sec. 18631	Information Returns	¶713
IRC Sec. 6051	. . .	Receipts for Employees	¶715
IRC Sec. 6052	Sec. 18631	Returns for Group-Term Life Insurance	¶713
IRC Sec. 6053	UI Code	Reporting Tips	¶713, ¶715
IRC Sec. 6060	. . .	Tax Preparer Information Returns	¶701
IRC Sec. 6072	Secs. 18566, 18601	Time for Filing Returns	¶108
IRC Sec. 6081	Secs. 18567, 18604	Extension of Time	¶108, ¶109
IRC Sec. 6091	Sec. 18621	Form of Return	¶108
IRC Sec. 6102	Sec. 18623	Fractional Dollar Calculations	¶106
IRC Secs. 6103-10	Secs. 19542-64	Secrecy and Disclosure of Returns	¶701, ¶704, ¶721
IRC Secs. 6111-12	Secs. 18628, 18648, 19182	Reportable and Listed Transactions	¶712, ¶713

Federal	California	Subject	Paragraph
IRC Sec. 6115	Sec. 18648.5	Disclosure Related to Quid Pro Quo Contributions	. . .
IRC Sec. 6151	Secs. 19001-06	Payment of Tax	¶107
IRC Sec. 6161	. . .	Extensions of Time for Payment	¶107
IRC Sec. 6201	Secs. 19054, 21024	Assessment Authority	¶208, ¶704
IRC Sec. 6211	Sec. 19043	"Deficiency" Defined	¶704, ¶705
IRC Sec. 6212	Secs. 19031-36, 19049, 19050	Notice of Deficiency	¶704
IRC Sec. 6213	Secs. 19041-48, 19051, 19332-34	Restrictions Applicable to Deficiencies	¶704-06
IRC Sec. 6225	Sec. 19063	SOL for Partnership Related Deficiencies	¶710
IRC Sec. 6233	. . .	Partnership Audits	. . .
IRC Sec. 6302	Sec. 19011	Electronic Funds Transfer	¶110
IRC Sec. 6311	Sec. 19222	Payment by Check or Money Order	¶110
IRC Sec. 6313	. . .	Fractional Dollar Calculations	¶110
IRC Sec. 6315	Sec. 19007	Payments of Estimated Taxes	¶111
IRC Sec. 6321	Sec. 19221	Lien on Tax	¶612
IRC Sec. 6322	Sec. 19221	Period of Lien	. . .
IRC Sec. 6323	Secs. 19253, 21016	Priority of Lien	. . .
IRC Sec. 6325	Secs. 19206-09, 19226	Release of Lien	. . .
IRC Sec. 6331	Secs. 19231, 19236, 19262, 21019	Levy to Collect Tax	. . .
IRC Sec. 6343	Sec. 21016	Release of Levy	¶702
IRC Sec. 6401	Secs. 19107, 19349, 19354	Excess of Tax Withheld	¶717, ¶718
IRC Sec. 6402	Secs. 19301, 19323, 19362, 19363	Credits and Refunds	¶706, ¶717, ¶718
IRC Sec. 6403	. . .	Overpayment of Installment	¶110
IRC Sec. 6404	Secs. 19104, 19109, 19116, 19431	Abatements	¶703, ¶711, ¶712
IRC Sec. 6428	. . .	Acceleration of 2001 10% Income Tax Bracket	. . .
IRC Secs. 6501-04	Secs. 19057, 19058, 19065-67, 19087, 19371	Limitations on Assessment	¶613, ¶710
IRC Sec. 6511	Secs. 19306-16	Limitation on Refunds	¶719
IRC Sec. 6513	Sec. 19002	Time Return Filed and Tax Paid	¶108
IRC Sec. 6531	Sec. 19704	Statute of Limitations—Criminal Actions	
IRC Sec. 6532	Secs. 19381-85, 19388-89	Suits for Refund	¶720, ¶726
IRC Sec. 6601	Secs. 19101-14	Interest on Tax Due	¶110, ¶711
IRC Sec. 6602	Sec. 19411	Interest on Erroneous Refund	¶726
IRC Sec. 6603	Secs. 19041.5	Deposits to Stop the Running of Interest	¶719, ¶720
IRC Sec. 6611	Secs. 19325, 19340-51	Interest on Overpayments	¶722
IRC Sec. 6621	Sec. 19521	Interest Rate	¶711
IRC Sec. 6622	Sec. 19521	Compounding of Interest	¶711
IRC Sec. 6631	Sec. 19117	Notice of Interest Charges	¶711
IRC Sec. 6651	Secs. 19131-32.5	Penalty—Failure to Make Return	¶712
IRC Sec. 6652	Sec. 19133.5	Penalty—Certain Information Returns	¶712
IRC Sec. 6653	. . .	Penalty—Failure to Pay Stamp Tax	¶712
IRC Sec. 6654	Secs. 19136-36.6	Underpayment of Estimated Tax	¶111
IRC Sec. 6657	Secs. 19005, 19134	Bad Checks	¶712
IRC Sec. 6658	Sec. 19161	Timely Payment During Bankruptcy	¶712
IRC Secs. 6662-65	Secs. 19164, 19164.5, 19772-74	Penalty for Substantial Understatement	¶712, ¶727
IRC Sec. 6672	Sec. 19708	Penalty—Failure to Collect and Pay Tax	¶712
IRC Sec. 6673	Sec. 19714	Penalty for Delay	¶712
IRC Sec. 6674	UI Code	Penalty—Fraudulent Statement	¶712
IRC Sec. 6682	Sec. 19176	Penalty—False Withholding Information	¶712
IRC Sec. 6690	. . .	Penalty—Fraudulent Statement to Pension Plan Participant	. . .
IRC Sec. 6693	Sec. 19184	Penalty—Failure to Properly Report IRA	¶712
IRC Sec. 6694	Sec. 19166	Understatement by Preparer	¶701, ¶712
IRC Secs. 6695-96	Secs. 19166-69, 19712, 19185	Penalties—Tax Preparers	¶701, ¶712
IRC Sec. 6698	Sec. 19172	Penalty—Partnership Returns	¶622, ¶712
IRC Sec. 6700	Secs. 19174, 19177	Penalty for Promoting Abusive Tax Shelters	¶727
IRC Sec. 6701	Sec. 19178	Penalty for Aiding and Abetting Understatement	¶712
IRC Sec. 6702	Sec. 19179	Penalty for Frivolous Returns	¶712
IRC Sec. 6702B	Sec. 19186	Fraudulent Identification of Exempt-Use Property Penalty	¶712
IRC Sec. 6703	Sec. 19180	Rules for Penalties	¶712
IRC Sec. 6704	. . .	Penalty—Failure to Keep Records	. . .
IRC Sec. 6705	. . .	Penalty—Broker's Failure to Notify Payors	. . .
IRC Sec. 6706	Secs. 18649, 19181	OID Information	¶237, ¶712
IRC Sec. 6707	Sec. 19182	Penalty—Tax Shelters	¶727
IRC Sec. 6707A	Sec. 19772	Reportable Transaction Nonreporting Penalty	¶727
IRC Sec. 6708	Sec. 19173	Tax Shelters	. . .
IRC Sec. 6714	Sec. 19182.5	Penalty; Failure to Disclose Quid Pro Quo Information	. . .
IRC Secs. 6721-24	Sec. 19183	Penalty—Failure to File Information Returns	¶712

Federal	California	Subject	Paragraph
IRC Sec. 6751	Sec. 19187	Procedures for Penalties	¶712
IRC Sec. 6861	Secs. 19081, 19086, 19092	Jeopardy Assessments	¶707
IRC Sec. 6863	Secs. 19083-85	Jeopardy Assessments—Stay of Collection	¶707
IRC Sec. 6867	Sec. 19093	Unexplained Cash	¶707
IRC Sec. 6871	Secs. 19088-90	Assessment in Receivership	¶708
IRC Sec. 6872	Sec. 19089	Suspension of Period of Assessment	¶708
IRC Sec. 6873	Sec. 19091	Unpaid Claims	¶708
IRC Sec. 6901	Secs. 19071-74	Liability of Transferees and Fiduciaries	¶613, ¶709
IRC Sec. 6903	Sec. 19512	Notice of Fiduciary Relationship	¶613, ¶709
IRC Sec. 6905	Sec. 19516	Discharge of Liability for Decedent's Taxes	¶613
IRC Sec. 7121	Sec. 19441	Closing Agreements	¶723
IRC Sec. 7122	Sec. 19702	Compromises	¶724
IRC Sec. 7201	Secs. 19701, 19708	Evasion of Tax	¶712
IRC Sec. 7202	Secs. 19708-09	Failure to Remit Withheld Tax	¶712
IRC Sec. 7203	Secs. 19701, 19706	Violation—Failure to File Return	¶712
IRC Sec. 7206	Secs. 19701, 19705	False Statements—Fraud	¶712
IRC Sec. 7207	Secs. 19701, 19706	Violation—Fraudulent Returns, Statements, or Other Documents	¶712
IRC Secs. 7213-16	Secs. 19542, 19542.3, 19552, 19713	Unauthorized Disclosure of Information	¶721
IRC Sec. 7403	Sec. 19371	Suit for Tax	. . .
IRC Sec. 7405	Sec. 19411	Recovery of Erroneous Refunds	¶726
IRC Sec. 7408	Sec. 19715	Injunctive Relief	¶712
IRC Sec. 7421	Sec. 19381	Suits to Restrain Collection Prohibited	¶701, ¶720
IRC Sec. 7422	Secs. 19381-83, 19387-89	Actions for Refunds	¶720
IRC Sec. 7429	Sec. 19084	Jeopardy Assessment Review	¶707
IRC Sec. 7430	Secs. 19717, 21013	Recovery of Litigation Costs	¶701
IRC Sec. 7502	Sec. 21027	Mailing	¶108
IRC Sec. 7503	Gov. Code	Due Date—Holiday	¶108
IRC Sec. 7508	Secs. 17142.5, 18570, 18571	Extension—Members of Armed Forces	¶109
IRC Sec. 7508A	Sec. 18572	Extensions for Disaster Victims	¶108, ¶110, ¶710, ¶719
IRC Sec. 7512	Sec. 19009	Separate Accounting for Certain Collected Taxes, etc.	¶715
IRC Sec. 7518	Sec. 17088.3	Capital Construction Funds for Vessels	¶234
IRC Sec. 7602	Sec. 19504.7	Notice of Contact of Third Parties	¶701
IRC Sec. 7612	Sec. 19504.5	Software Trade Secrets	¶720
IRC Sec. 7701	Various	Definitions	¶212, ¶607, ¶616
IRC Sec. 7702B	Sec. 17020.6	Qualified Long-Term Care Insurance	¶219
IRC Sec. 7703	Sec. 17021.5	Marital Status	¶114
IRC Sec. 7704	Sec. 17008.5	Publicly Traded Partnerships	¶616
IRC Sec. 7811	Secs. 21001-26	Taxpayers' Bill of Rights	¶701, ¶702, ¶703
IRC Sec. 7872	Sec. 18180	Loans with Below-Market Interest Rates	¶414

CALIFORNIA-FEDERAL CROSS-REFERENCE TABLE AND INDEX

Showing Sections of Federal Law (1986 Internal Revenue Code) Comparable to Sections of California Personal Income Tax Law (Revenue and Taxation Code)

California	Federal	Subject	Paragraph
Sec. 17002	IRC Sec. 7806	Definitions	. . .
Sec. 17003	IRC Sec. 7701(a)(11)	"Franchise Tax Board" defined	. . .
Sec. 17004	IRC Sec. 7701(a)(1), (14)	"Taxpayer" defined	. . .
Sec. 17005	. . .	"Individual" defined	. . .
Sec. 17006	IRC Sec. 7701(a)(6)	"Fiduciary" defined	. . .
Sec. 17007	IRC Sec. 7701(a)(1)	"Person" defined	. . .
Sec. 17008	IRC Sec. 7701(a)(2)	"Partnership" defined	¶616
Sec. 17008.5	IRC Sec. 7704	Publicly-traded partnerships	¶616
Sec. 17009	IRC Sec. 7701(a)(3)	"Corporation" defined	¶606
Sec. 17010	IRC Sec. 7701(a)(23)	"Taxable year" defined	. . .
Sec. 17011	IRC Sec. 7701(a)(24)	"Fiscal year" defined	. . .
Sec. 17012	IRC Sec. 7701(a)(25)	"Paid or incurred" defined	. . .
Sec. 17014	. . .	"Resident" defined	¶105
Sec. 17015	. . .	"Nonresident" defined	¶105
Sec. 17015.5	. . .	"Part-year resident" defined	¶105
Sec. 17016	. . .	Presumption of residence	¶105
Sec. 17017	IRC Sec. 7701(a)(9)	"United States" defined	. . .
Sec. 17018	IRC Sec. 7701(a)(10)	"State" defined	. . .
Sec. 17019	. . .	"Foreign country" defined	. . .
Sec. 17020	IRC Sec. 7701(a)(26)	"Trade or business" defined	. . .
Sec. 17020.1	IRC Sec. 7701(a)(42)	Substituted basis property	. . .
Sec. 17020.2	IRC Sec. 7701(a)(43)	Transferred basis property	. . .
Sec. 17020.3	IRC Sec. 7701(a)(44)	Exchanged basis property	. . .
Sec. 17020.4	IRC Sec. 7701(a)(45)	Nonrecognition transaction	. . .
Sec. 17020.5	IRC Sec. 7701(g)	Determination of gain or loss	. . .
Sec. 17020.6	IRC Sec. 7702-02B	"Life insurance contract" defined	. . .
Sec. 17020.7	IRC Sec. 7701(a)(46)	Collective bargaining agreement	. . .
Sec. 17020.8	IRC Sec. 7701(e)	Contracts for services	. . .
Sec. 17020.9	IRC Sec. 7701(a)(19)	Domestic building & loan association	. . .
Sec. 17020.11	IRC Sec. 7701(h)	Motor vehicle operating leases	. . .
Sec. 17020.12	IRC Sec. 7701(a)(20)	"Employee" defined	¶212
Sec. 17020.13	IRC Sec. 7701(k)	Treatment of amounts paid to charity	. . .
Sec. 17021	IRC Sec. 7701(a)(17)	"Spouse" defined	. . .
Sec. 17021.5	IRC Sec. 7703	Marital status	¶114
Sec. 17021.7	. . .	Treatment of domestic parnter	¶119, ¶206, ¶219, ¶247, ¶253, ¶301, ¶325
Sec. 17022	IRC Sec. 7701(a)(15)	"Armed Forces" defined	. . .
Sec. 17023	IRC Sec. 7801	"Franchise Tax Board" defined	. . .
Sec. 17024	IRC Sec. 7701(a)(29)	"Personal Income Tax Law of 1954" defined	. . .
Sec. 17024.5	IRC Secs. 196, 541-47, 551-58, 679, 853, 911, 991-99, 1246, 1551-3322, 7806	Federal conformity program	Various
Sec. 17024.7	IRC Sec. 222	Tuition and related expenses deduction	¶344
Sec. 17026	IRC Sec. 7851	Application of act	. . .
Sec. 17028	IRC Sec. 7807	Construction of code	. . .
Sec. 17029	IRC Sec. 7807	Rights and liabilities under prior code	. . .
Sec. 17029.5	. . .	Basis adjustments and carryovers	. . .
Sec. 17030	IRC Sec. 7807	Reference to corresponding law	. . .
Sec. 17031	IRC Sec. 7807	Reference to prior period	. . .
Sec. 17033	IRC Sec. 7852	Severability of law	. . .
Sec. 17034	IRC Sec. 15	Effect of law changes	¶406
Sec. 17035	IRC Sec. 7701(a)(16)	"Withholding agent" defined	. . .
Sec. 17036	. . .	Service of notice	. . .
Sec. 17038	. . .	"Consumer price index" defined	. . .
Sec. 17039	IRC Sec. 26	"Net tax" defined	¶117, ¶125, ¶126, ¶132
Sec. 17039.1	. . .	Natural heritage preservation credit	¶117
Sec. 17039.2	. . .	Temporary limits on business credits	¶125
Sec. 17041	IRC Sec. 1(g)	Rate of tax	¶60, ¶61, ¶116, ¶118, ¶309

California	Federal	Subject	Paragraph
Sec. 17041.5	. . .	Local income tax	¶ 101
Sec. 17042	IRC Sec. 2(b), (c)	"Head of household" defined	¶ 114
Sec. 17043	. . .	Additional tax on millionaires	¶ 116, ¶ 125
Sec. 17045	. . .	Joint return tax rate	¶ 107
Sec. 17046	IRC Sec. 2(a)	"Surviving spouse" defined	¶ 107
Sec. 17048	IRC Sec. 3	Tax table	¶ 116
Sec. 17049	IRC Sec. 1341	Claim of right adjustment	¶ 415
Sec. 17052	IRC Sec. 32	Earned income tax credit	¶ 158
Sec. 17052.6	IRC Sec. 21	Household and dependent care expense credit	¶ 142
Sec. 17052.8	IRC Sec. 43	Enhanced oil recovery credit	¶ 153
Sec. 17052.10	. . .	Rice straw credit	¶ 125
Sec. 17052.12	IRC Sec. 41	Research & development credit	¶ 150
Sec. 17052.25	IRC Sec. 36C	Adoption costs credit	¶ 139
Sec. 17053.5	. . .	Renter's credit	¶ 133
Sec. 17053.6	. . .	Prison inmate labor credit	¶ 154
Sec. 17053.7	IRC Sec. 51	Jobs tax credit	¶ 154
Sec. 17053.12	. . .	Credit for transportation of donated agricultural products	¶ 141
Sec. 17053.14	. . .	Farmworker Housing Credit	¶ 125
Sec. 17053.30	. . .	Natural heritage preservation credit	¶ 143
Sec. 17053.33	. . .	Sales tax credit	¶ 144
Sec. 17053.34	. . .	Targeted tax area employers'credit	¶ 148
Sec. 17053.42	IRC Sec. 44	Disabled access credit	¶ 140
Sec. 17053.45	. . .	LAMBRA credit, sales tax equivalent	¶ 144
Sec. 17053.46	. . .	LAMBRA credit, employers	¶ 147
Sec. 17053.47	. . .	Manufacturing enhancement area employers' credit	¶ 149
Sec. 17053.57	IRC Sec. 38	Community development investment credit	¶ 155
Sec. 17053.62	IRC Sec. 45H	Low-Sulfur Diesel Fuel Production Credit	¶ 160
Sec. 17053.70	. . .	Enterprise zone sales taxcredit	¶ 144
Sec. 17053.73	...	New employment credit	¶ 157
Sec. 17053.74	IRC Sec. 1396	Enterprise zone employer'scredit	¶ 145
Sec. 17053.75	. . .	Enterprise zone employee's credit	¶ 146
Sec. 17053.85	. . .	Motion picture production credit	¶ 137
Secs. 17053.86, 17053.87	. . .	College access tax credit	¶ 156
Secs. 17053.88, 17053.88.5	. . .	Credit for fresh produce donations to California food banks	¶ 141
Sec. 17053.95	. . .	New otion picture production credit	¶ 137a
Sec. 17054	IRC Sec. 151(c)	Credits for personal and dependent exemptions	¶ 113
Sec. 17054.1	IRC Sec. 151(d)	Credit reduction for high-income taxpayers	¶ 113
Sec. 17054.5	. . .	Joint custody head of household, dependent parent credits	¶ 136
Sec. 17054.7	. . .	Senior head of household credit	¶ 135
Sec. 17055	. . .	Credits for nonresidents, part-year residents	¶ 125
Sec. 17056	IRC Sec. 152(a)	"Dependent" defined	¶ 113, ¶ 115
Sec. 17057.5	IRC Sec. 42	Low-income housing credit	¶ 138
Sec. 17058	IRC Sec. 42	Low-income housing credit	¶ 138
Sec. 17059.2	...	California competes credit	¶ 134
Sec. 17061	. . .	Credit for excess SDI contributions	¶ 132
Sec. 17062	IRC Secs. 55-59	Alternative minimum tax	¶ 117
Sec. 17062.3	IRC Sec. 56(g)	Extraterritorial income AMT modification inapplicable	¶ 117
Sec. 17062.5	IRC Sec. 55(b)	Federal noncorporate AMT tax rate inapplicable	¶ 117
Sec. 17063	IRC Sec. 53	Minimum tax credit	¶ 152
Sec. 17071	IRC Sec. 61	"Gross income" defined	¶ 201
Sec. 17072	IRC Sec. 62	"Adjusted gross income" defined	¶ 202, ¶ 305, ¶ 328, ¶ 329
Sec. 17072.5	IRC Sec. 62(a)(2)(E)	National guard/reservists travel expenses	¶ 201
Sec. 17073	IRC Sec. 63	"Taxable income" defined	¶ 112, ¶ 203, ¶ 303
Sec. 17073.5	IRC Sec. 63	Standard deduction	¶ 203, ¶ 335
Sec. 17074	IRC Sec. 64	"Ordinary income" defined	. . .

California	Federal	Subject	Paragraph
Sec. 17075	IRC Sec. 65	"Ordinary loss" defined	...
Sec. 17076	IRC Sec. 67	2% floor on miscellaneous itemized deductions	¶303, ¶328, ¶329, ¶604
Sec. 17077	IRC Sec. 68	6% limit on itemized deductions	¶303
Sec. 17078	IRC Sec. 988	Foreign currency transactions	¶521
Sec. 17081	IRC Secs. 71-90	Items in gross income	Various
Sec. 17081	IRC Sec. 72	Annuities, endowments, and life insurance proceeds	¶205
Sec. 17081	IRC Sec. 83	Property transfers in connection with services	¶207
Sec. 17083	IRC Sec. 85	Unemployment compensation	¶201
Sec. 17085	IRC Sec. 72	Lump-sum distributions	¶205, ¶206, ¶214
Sec. 17085.7	IRC Sec. 72	Levies on retirement plans and IRAs	¶206
Sec. 17086	IRC Sec. 1385	Patronage allocations	¶232
Sec. 17087	IRC Secs. 72(r), 86, 105(i)	Social security benefits, etc.	¶201, ¶219
Sec. 17087.5	IRC Secs. 1361-79	S corporation shareholders	¶233
Sec. 17087.6	IRC Sec. 61	Limited liability companies	¶625
Sec. 17088	IRC Secs. 851-60L	RICs, REITs, REMICs, and FASITs	¶217, ¶226, ¶559, ¶609, ¶610, ¶615
Sec. 17088.3	IRC Sec. 7518	Capital construction funds for vessels	¶234
Sec. 17090	IRC Sec. 61	Subsidized employee parking	¶241
Sec. 17131	IRC Secs. 101-40	Exclusions—gross income	Various
Sec. 17131.1	Act Sec. 803 (P.L. 107-16)	Holocaust reparation exclusion	¶248
Sec. 17131.2	...	Armenian genocide settlement payments	¶248
Sec. 17131.3	...	Renewable energy grant exclusion	¶245
Sec. 17131.4	IRC Sec. 106(d)	Employer contributions to health savings accounts	¶219, ¶247
Sec. 17131.5	IRC Sec. 125(d)	Employer contributions to health savings accounts	¶223, ¶247
Sec. 17131.6	IRC Sec. 107	Rental value of parsonage	¶220
Sec. 17131.9	...	In-home supportive services supplemental payment exclusion	¶201
Sec. 17131.10	125	Cafeteria plans	¶201
Sec. 17131.10	139	Disaster relief for San Bruno explosion	¶251
Sec. 17132	IRC Sec. 114	Extraterritorial income exclusion	...
Sec. 17132.4	...	California national guard/reservists death benefit exclusion	¶225
Sec. 17132.5	IRC Sec. 101	Certain death benefits	¶213
Sec. 17132.7	IRC Sec. 104(a)	Exempt damages	¶218
Sec. 17132.8	...	Virginia Tech victim compensation exclusion	¶201
Sec. 17132.11	...	Discharged student loan debt exclusion	¶221
Sec. 17133	IRC Sec. 61	Constitutional prohibition	¶201, ¶217, ¶324
Sec. 17133.5	IRC Sec. 61	Gain or loss from exempt bonds	¶201, ¶513
Sec. 17134	IRC Sec. 108	Discharge of student loans	¶221
Sec. 17135	IRC Secs. 61, 132, 274	Automobile expenses of federal or state taxing authority agents	¶201
Sec. 17135.5	IRC Sec. 126	Cost-share payments received by forest landowners	¶201, ¶243
Sec. 17136	IRC Sec. 61	Forest Service payments	¶201
Sec. 17138	IRC Sec. 61	Water conservation rebates	¶244
Sec. 17138.1	IRC Sec. 136	Energy conservation subsidy exclusion	¶245
Sec. 17138.1	...	Turf removal water conservation program incentive exclusion	¶244
Sec. 17138.3	...	Earthquake loss mitigation incentive exclusion	¶256
Sec. 17139.5	...	Interest on smog impact fee refund	...
Sec. 17139.6	IRC Sec. 139A	Federal subsidies for prescription drugs	¶252
Sec. 17140	IRC Sec. 529	Golden State Scholarshare Trust	¶250
Sec. 17140.3	IRC Sec. 529	Qualified tuition programs	¶250
Sec. 17140.4	IRC Sec. 529A	ABLE accounts	¶255
Sec. 17140.5	IRC Sec. 61	Military compensation	¶225
Sec. 17141	...	Community Energy Authority	¶201
Sec. 17141.3	IRC Secs. 105, 106	Health care compensation reimbursement exclusion	¶219
Sec. 17142	IRC Sec. 111	Credits, credit carryovers	¶224
Sec. 17142.5	IRC Secs. 112, 692, 7508	Military combat pay	¶109, ¶225
Sec. 17143	IRC Secs. 103, 141-50	Exempt interest	¶217

California	Federal	Subject	Paragraph
Sec. 17144	IRC Sec. 108	Exclusion for income from discharge of indebtedness	¶221
Sec. 17144.5	IRC Sec. 108	Discharge of qualified residential property indebtedness	¶221
Sec. 17144.7	IRC Sec. 108	Discharge of student loan indebtedness	¶221
Sec. 17145	IRC Sec. 852	Exempt distributions from RICs	¶217
Sec. 17146	IRC Sec. 893	Employees of foreign countries	¶230
Sec. 17147.7	IRC Sec. 61	Crime hotline rewards	¶201, ¶246
Sec. 17149	IRC Secs. 61, 132	Subsidized commuter expense	¶241
Sec. 17151	IRC Sec. 127	Educational assistance	¶201, ¶242
Sec. 17152	IRC Sec. 121	Exclusion of gain from primary residence sale	¶229
Sec. 17153.5	IRC Sec. 61	Recycling income	¶201
Sec. 17154	IRC Sec. 132	Taxable education or training benefits	¶201
Sec. 17155	U.S.-Federal Republic of Germany Income Tax Convention	Holocaust victim compensation	¶248
Sec. 17155.5	...	WWII slave labor reparations	¶248
Sec. 17156.5	...	Japanese internment reparations	¶248
Sec. 17157	...	Wrongful conviction compensation	¶201
Sec. 17201	IRC Secs. 161-222, 261-280H	Allowance of deductions	Various
Sec. 17201	IRC Sec. 215	Alimony payments	¶323
Sec. 17201	IRC Sec. 280G	"Golden parachute" payments	¶336
Sec. 17201	IRC Sec. 179	Asset expense election	¶311
Sec. 17201.4	IRC Sec. 179B	EPA sulfur compliance costs	¶318
Sec. 17201.5	IRC Sec. 181	Film and production expenses	¶301, ¶310
Sec. 17201.6	IRC Sec. 199	Domestic production activities deduction	¶317
Sec. 17202	IRC Sec. 162	Employee parking cash-out programs	¶343
Sec. 17202.5	IRC Sec. 161(a)(2)	National guard/reservists travel expenses	¶202
Sec. 17203	IRC Secs. 162, 219, 404	"Compensation" or "earned income"	¶301, ¶330
Sec. 17204	IRC Sec. 165(h)(3)	Disaster losses	¶307
Sec. 17204.7	IRC Sec. 222	Tuition and related expenses	¶344
Sec. 17206	IRC Sec. 170	Tsunami relief donations	¶321
Sec. 17206.5	IRC Sec. 170	Haiti earthquake relief donations	¶321
Secs. 17207-07.14	IRC Sec. 165	Disaster losses	¶303, ¶307, ¶407
Sec. 17208.1	...	Energy-efficient equipment loan interest	¶305
Sec. 17215	IRC Sec. 220	Archer MSAs	¶247, ¶326
Sec. 17215.1	IRC Sec. 220	Rollover from MSA to HSA	¶247
Sec. 17215.4	IRC Sec. 223	Health savings accounts	¶247, ¶326
Sec. 17220	IRC Sec. 164	Deduction for taxes	¶303, ¶306
Sec. 17222	IRC Sec. 275	Withheld taxes	¶306
Sec. 17224	IRC Sec. 163(e)	Income from OIDs	¶237, ¶305
Sec. 17225	IRC Sec. 163(h)(3)(E)	Mortgage interest insurance premiums	¶305
Sec. 17228	...	Professional sports league-imposed fines or penalties	¶336
Sec. 17230	IRC Sec. 163	Buy-down mortgage fees	¶305
Sec. 17235	IRC Sec. 163	Interest deduction—depressed areas	¶240
Sec. 17240	IRC Sec. 275	Fee on branded prescription manufacturers and importers	¶306
Sec. 17241	IRC Sec. 213	Medical expenses—AGI floor	¶325
Sec. 17250	IRC Secs. 168, 169	ACRS depreciation	¶310, ¶314
Sec. 17250.5	IRC Secs. 167(g), 168	Depreciation under income forecast method	¶310
Sec. 17255	IRC Sec. 179	Expense election dollar limitation	¶311
Sec. 17255.5	IRC Sec. 179B	Sulfur regulation compliance costs	¶318
Sec. 17256	IRC Sec. 179A	Clean fuel vehicles deduction	...
Sec. 17257	IRC Sec. 179C	Expensing of qualified refinery property	¶311
Sec. 17257.2	IRC Sec. 179D	Energy efficient commercial building costs	¶345
Sec. 17257.4	IRC Sec. 179E	Expensing of advanced mine safety equipment	¶311
Sec. 17260(a)	IRC Sec. 193	Tertiary injectant expenses	¶320
Sec. 17260(b)	IRC Sec. 263	Capital expenditures	¶201, ¶322
Sec. 17267.6	...	Election to expense targeted tax area property	¶316
Sec. 17268	IRC Sec. 179	Accelerated write-off	¶316

California	Federal	Subject	Paragraph
Sec. 17269	IRC Sec. 162	No deductions for expenditures at discriminatory clubs	¶301, ¶336
Sec. 17270(a)	IRC Sec. 162	Trade and business expenses	¶301, ¶322
Sec. 17270(b)	IRC Sec. 280C(c)	Targeted employment credit(s)	¶336
Sec. 17270(c)	IRC Sec. 280C(a)	Legislators' expenses	¶301
Sec. 17273	IRC Sec. 162(l)	Trade or business expense	¶301
Sec. 17274	IRC Sec. 161	Expenses of substandard housing	¶336
Sec. 17275	IRC Sec. 161	Abandonment and recoupment fees	¶336
Sec. 17275.2-75.5	IRC Sec. 170	Charitable contributions	¶321
Secs. 17276-76.22	IRC Sec. 172	Net operating loss	¶309
Sec. 17278	IRC Secs. 161, 1031	Interindemnity payments	¶301
Sec. 17278.5	IRC Sec. 194	Amortization of forestation expenditures	¶315
Sec. 17279	IRC Sec. 197	Amortization of goodwill	¶333
Sec. 17279.4	IRC Sec. 198	Amortization of goodwill	¶346
Sec. 17279.6	IRC Sec. 198A	Expensing of qualified disaster payments	¶347
Sec. 17280	IRC Sec. 265	Expenses of tax-exempt income	¶305, ¶336
Secs. 17282	IRC Sec. 280E	Expenses of illegal activities	¶336
Sec. 17286	IRC Sec. 162	Illegal payments to foreign officials, etc.	¶336
Sec. 17287	IRC Sec. 269A	Personal service corporation formed to avoid/evade income tax	¶412
Secs. 17299.8-99.9	IRC Sec. 161	Deductions disallowed	¶336, ¶712
Secs. 17301-02	IRC Sec. 63	Deductions of nonresidents	¶323, ¶337
Secs. 17302	IRC Sec. 215	Alimony deduction for nonresidents	¶323
Sec. 17304	IRC Sec. 63	Itemized deductions for nonresidents/part-year residents	¶337
Secs. 17306-07	. . .	Nonresident deductions	¶337
Sec. 17321	IRC Secs. 301-85	Corporate distributions, etc.	Various
Sec. 17322	IRC Sec. 302	Limitation periods	¶226
Sec. 17501	IRC Secs. 401-24	Deferred compensation	Various
Sec. 17501.5	Various	Government pension plan rollovers	¶206
Sec. 17501.7	IRC Secs. 403, 457	Purchases of service credits	¶206
Sec. 17502	IRC Sec. 421	California qualified stock options	¶207
Sec. 17504	IRC Sec. 402(a)	Lump-sum distributions	¶206, ¶330, ¶607
		Beneficiaries of exempt trusts	¶206, ¶330, ¶607
Sec. 17506	IRC Sec. 403(a)	Employee annuities	¶206, ¶330
Sec. 17507	IRC Sec. 408	Individual retirement accounts	¶330
Sec. 17501	IRC Secs. 219, 408A	Roth IRAs	¶206, ¶330
Sec. 17508	IRC Sec. 408(o)	Nondeductible contributions to IRAs	¶318
Sec. 17508.2	IRC Sec. 409A	Nonqualified compensation additional tax	¶318
Sec. 17509	IRC Sec. 413	Liability for funding tax	¶330
Sec. 17510	IRC Sec. 7701(j)	Federal thrift savings funds	¶607
Sec. 17551	IRC Secs. 280H, 441-83	Accounting periods and methods	Various
Sec. 17552	IRC Sec. 443	Short-period returns	¶403
Sec. 17552.3	IRC Sec. 451	Farm production flexibility contract	¶407
Sec. 17553	IRC Sec. 454	Obligations issued at discount	¶408
Sec. 17555	IRC Sec. 61	Allocation of income—spouses	¶412
Sec. 17556	IRC Sec. 442	Change accounting period—estates	¶402
Sec. 17560	IRC Secs. 453, 453A	Allocable installment indebtedness	¶411
Sec. 17560.5	IRC Secs. 461(j)	Limitation on excess farm losses	¶401
Sec. 17561	IRC Sec. 469	Passive activity losses and credits	¶340
Sec. 17563.5	IRC Sec. 404(a)(11)	Accrued vacation	¶330
Sec. 17564	IRC Sec. 460	Long-term contracts	¶407
Sec. 17565	IRC Sec. 441	Taxable year	¶401
Sec. 17570	IRC Sec. 475	Mark-to-market accounting	¶400, ¶409
Sec. 17631	IRC Sec. 501(a)	Exemption for employee trusts	¶607
Sec. 17632	IRC Sec. 501(b)	Exempt organizations—unrelated income	¶607
Sec. 17635	IRC Sec. 503(a)	Prohibited transactions	¶607
Sec. 17636	IRC Sec. 503(a)	Application to Sec. 17501	¶607
Sec. 17637	IRC Sec. 503(b)	"Prohibited transactions" defined	¶607
Sec. 17638	IRC Sec. 503(c)	Claim for exemption	¶607
Sec. 17639	IRC Sec. 503(e)	Security for loan	¶607
Sec. 17640	IRC Sec. 503(f)	Trust loan to employer	¶607
Sec. 17651	IRC Secs. 511, 512	Unrelated business income	¶607
Sec. 17671	IRC Sec. 584	Common trust funds	¶614

California	Federal	Subject	Paragraph
Sec. 17677	IRC Secs. 584, 6032	Return for common trust	¶614
Sec. 17681	IRC Secs. 611-38	Taxation of natural resources	¶319, ¶320, ¶540
Sec. 17681.3	IRC Secs. 613A	Limitations on depletion	¶319
Sec. 17681.6	IRC Secs. 613A	Depletion limitation for marginal properties	¶319
		Basis for cost depletion	¶562
Sec. 17731	IRC Secs. 641-92	Taxation of estates and trusts	Various
Sec. 17731.5	IRC Sec. 641	Determining rates and special credits	¶604
Sec. 17732	IRC Sec. 642	No deduction personal exemptions	...
Sec. 17733	IRC Sec. 642	Exemption credits	¶113
Sec. 17734	IRC Sec. 641	Nonresident beneficiaries	¶605
Sec. 17734.6	IRC Sec. 646	Alaska Native Settlement trusts	¶601
Sec. 17735	IRC Sec. 661	Distributions to nonresidents	¶604
Sec. 17736	IRC Sec. 642	Modification I.R.C. Sec. 642	¶604
Sec. 17737	IRC Sec. 682	Alimony trusts	¶611
Secs. 17742-45.1	IRC Sec. 641	Effect of residence upon taxability	¶105, ¶602, ¶603
Sec. 17750	IRC Sec. 643	Estates and trusts—election	¶604
Sec. 17751	IRC Sec. 645	Certain revocable trusts treated as part of estate	¶604
Sec. 17752	IRC Sec. 663	Special rules applicable to IRC Secs. 661 and 662	¶605
Sec. 17755	IRC Secs. 664	Charitable remainder annuity trusts and unitrusts	¶606
Sec. 17760	IRC Sec. 684	Gain on transfers to foreign trusts	...
Sec. 17760.5	IRC Sec. 685	Funeral trusts	¶608
Sec. 17779	IRC Secs. 665-68	Accumulation distributions	¶605
Sec. 17851	IRC Secs. 701-61	Partners and partnerships	Various
Sec. 17851.5		Taxation of partnerships	¶620
Sec. 17853	IRC Sec. 703	Deductions not allowed	¶620
Sec. 17854	IRC Sec. 707	Guaranteed payments	¶620
Secs. 17855-57	IRC Sec. 751	Transfer of partnership interest	¶618
Sec. 17858	IRC Sec. 704	Depreciation election by partnership	¶620
Sec. 17865	IRC Secs. 771—777	Electing large partnerships	¶624
Secs. 17935—37	...	Tax on limited partnerships	¶116, ¶616
Secs. 17941—46	...	LLC taxes and fees	¶116, ¶625
Secs. 17948-48.3	...	LLP minimum tax	¶623
Sec. 17951	...	Income of nonresidents	¶231, ¶233, ¶619
Sec. 17952	...	Income of nonresidents from intangibles	¶231
Sec. 17952.5	...	California source retirement income	...
Sec. 17953	...	Income to nonresident beneficiaries	¶231
Sec. 17954	...	Allocation of income of nonresidents	¶231
Sec. 17955	...	Nonresident income from qualifying investment securities	¶231
Sec. 18001	...	Taxes paid by resident to other state—credit	¶127, ¶128
Sec. 18002	...	Taxes paid by nonresident to other state—credit	¶127, ¶129
Sec. 18003	...	Residence of estate or trust	¶127, ¶130
Sec. 18004	...	Estate or trust—credit for taxes paid another state	¶127, ¶130
Sec. 18005	...	Resident beneficiary credit	¶127, ¶130
Sec. 18006	...	Resident and nonresident S corporation shareholders and partners—credit for taxes paid another state by entity	¶127, ¶128, ¶129, ¶131, ¶233
Sec. 18007	...	Report of other state tax credit	¶127
Sec. 18008	...	Tax due on other state credit	¶127
Sec. 18009	...	Interest on credit	¶127
Sec. 18011	...	Discrimination resulting from taxes paid to other state	¶127
Sec. 18031	IRC Sec. 1041	Inter-spousal transfers	¶502
Sec. 18032	IRC Sec. 1031	Like-kind exchange annual reporting requirement	¶507
Sec. 18031	IRC Sec. 1001-92	Determination of gain or loss	¶501
Sec. 18031	IRC Sec. 1014	Basis of property acquired from decedent	Various
Sec. 18031	IRC Sec. 1015	Basis of property acquired by transfer in trust	¶546
Sec. 18031	IRC Sec. 1060	Allocation of transferred business assets	¶563

California	Federal	Subject	Paragraph
Sec. 18031.5	IRC Sec. 1031(i)	Special rules for exchange of mutual ditch, reservoir, or irrigation company stock	¶507
Sec. 18035.6	IRC Sec. 1014	Basis of property acquired from a decedent	¶546
Sec. 18036	IRC Sec. 1016	Adjustments to basis	¶316, ¶559
Sec. 18036.5	IRC Sec. 1016	Basis adjustment for sale of small business stock	¶559
Sec. 18036.6	IRC Sec. 1022	Basis of property acquired from a decedent	¶546
Sec. 18037, 18037.5	IRC Sec. 1033	Certain involuntary conversions	¶503, ¶550
Sec. 18038	IRC Sec. 1040	Transfer of certain real property	¶604
Sec. 18038.4	IRC Sec. 1045	Rollover of gain from small business stock	¶515
Sec. 18038.5	IRC Sec. 1045	Rollover of gain from small business stock	¶515
Sec. 18039	IRC Sec. 1052	Basis established by prior law	¶554
Sec. 18041.5	IRC Sec. 1001	Gain from sale of assisted housing	¶505
Sec. 18042	IRC Sec. 1042	Sales to ESOP's	¶501, ¶514
Sec. 18044	IRC Sec. 1044	Rollover of publicly traded securities	¶501
Sec. 18151, 18151.5	IRC Secs. 1201-98	Capital gains and losses	Various
Sec. 18152	IRC Sec. 1202	Small business stock	¶525
Sec. 18152.5	IRC Sec. 1202	Small business stock	¶523, ¶525
Sec. 18153	...	Abatement of penalties and interest related to qualified small business stock	¶525
Sec. 18154	IRC Sec. 1033	Involuntary conversions for San Bruno explosion victims	¶503
Sec. 18155	IRC Sec. 1212	Carryovers and carrybacks	¶523, ¶526
Secs. 18155.5, 18155.6	IRC Sec. 1223	Holding period for small business stock	¶528
Sec. 18165	IRC Sec. 1245	Recapture of depreciation on personal property	¶539
Sec. 18171	IRC Sec. 1250	Depreciation adjustments	¶523, ¶539
Sec. 18171.5	IRC Sec. 1250	IRC Sec. 1250(a) modified	¶539
Sec. 18177	IRC Sec. 1275	Tax-exempt obligations	...
Sec. 18178	IRC Sec. 1272	Original issue discount	¶236, ¶237, ¶512
Sec. 18180	IRC Sec. 7872	Loans with below-market interest rates	¶414
Sec. 18181	IRC Secs. 1291-98	Treatment of passive foreign investment companies	¶523
Secs. 18401-03	...	General application of administrative provisions	...
Sec. 18405	...	Relief upon noncompliance with new provisions	...
Sec. 18407	IRC Sec. 6011	Reporting abusive tax shelters	¶727
Sec. 18408	IRC Sec. 6011(b)	Information, i.e. taxpayer	¶715
Sec. 18409	IRC Sec. 6011	Returns on magnetic media	¶622
Sec. 18410	...	Federal holidays	¶108, ¶111
Sec. 18410.2	...	California competes tax credit committee	¶134
Secs. 18412-17	IRC Sec. 7807	Continuity of provisions with prior law	...
Secs. 18416	...	Last known address	¶704
Secs. 18416.5	...	Electronic communications with FTB	...
Sec. 18501	IRC Sec. 6012(a)	Returns required	¶106
Sec. 18505	IRC Sec. 6012(b)	Returns filed by fiduciary	¶106, ¶601
Sec. 18505.3	IRC Sec. 6012(b)(1)	Return of deceased individual	¶106
Sec. 18505.6	IRC Sec. 6012(b)	Agent for making return	¶106
Sec. 18506	IRC Sec. 6012(b)	Exempt trust—unrelated business income	¶106, ¶607
Sec. 18508	IRC Sec. 6012	Returns filed by joint fiduciaries	¶106
Sec. 18509	IRC Sec. 6012	Fiduciary as individual	¶106
Sec. 18510	...	Payment of qualified use taxes	¶108
Sec. 18521	IRC Sec. 6013	Filing of returns	¶106, ¶107, ¶114, ¶601
Sec. 18522	IRC Sec. 6013(b)	Joint return after filing separate return	¶107
Sec. 18523	IRC Sec. 6013(b)(1)	Elections made in separate returns	¶106, ¶107
Sec. 18524	IRC Sec. 6013(b)(1)	Death of spouse	¶106, ¶107
Sec. 18526	IRC Sec. 6013(b)(2)	Time limitation	¶106, ¶107
Sec. 18527	IRC Sec. 6013(b)(3)	Credit or refund periods	¶106, ¶107
Sec. 18528	IRC Sec. 6013(b)(3)	When return deemed filed	¶106, ¶107

California	Federal	Subject	Paragraph
Sec. 18529	IRC Sec. 6013(b)(4)	Assessment period extended	¶106, ¶107, ¶710
Sec. 18530	IRC Sec. 6013(b)(5)	Additions to tax, penalties	¶106, ¶107, ¶712
Sec. 18531	IRC Sec. 6013(b)(5)	Returns, criminal penalty	¶106
Sec. 18531.5	IRC Sec. 6013(c)	Death of one spouse	¶107
Sec. 18532	IRC Sec. 6013(d)	Marital status determined	¶106, ¶114
Sec. 18533	IRC Secs. 6013(e), 6015	Liability of spouse	¶107
Sec. 18534	IRC Sec. 66	Liability for community income	¶106, ¶107
Sec. 18535	IRC Sec. 6031	Returns by pass-through entities	¶233, ¶619, ¶622, ¶625
Sec. 18536	...	Group returns for nonresident corporate directors	¶714
Sec. 18542	...	Reporting of charitable contributions	...
Sec. 18551	IRC Sec. 3402(a)	Filing withholding return	¶715
Sec. 18566	IRC Sec. 6072	Time for filing returns	¶108
Sec. 18567	IRC Sec. 6081(a)	Extension of time	¶108, ¶109, ¶110
Sec. 18570	IRC Sec. 7508	Members of armed forces	¶109
Sec. 18571	IRC Sec. 7508	Extension—service in combat zone	¶109
Sec. 18572	IRC Sec. 7508A	Extensions for disaster victims	¶108, ¶110, ¶710, ¶719
Sec. 18601	IRC Secs. 6012(a), 6037, 6072	Filing of returns; due dates	...
Sec. 18604	IRC Sec. 6081	Extension of time for filing returns	...
Sec. 18606	IRC Secs. 6012(a), 6065	Filing of returns by receiver, trustee, or assignee of bankrupt taxpayer	...
Sec. 18621	IRC Secs. 6065, 6091	Form of return	¶105
Sec. 18621.5	...	Electronic filing	¶108
Sec. 18621.7	...	Electronic proprietary software	...
Sec. 18621.9	...	Mandatory electronic filing	¶108
Sec. 18622	...	Amendment of return after federal changes	¶106
Sec. 18623	IRC Sec. 6102(a)	Fractional dollar calculations	¶106
Sec. 18624	IRC Sec. 6109	Identifying numbers	¶701
Sec. 18625	IRC Sec. 6107	Copy to taxpayer	¶701
Sec. 18626	...	Return defined	...
Sec. 18628	IRC Sec. 6111	Reportable transactions	¶727
Sec. 18631	IRC Secs. 6034A, 6039, 6039C, 6041, 6041A, 6042, 6045, 6049, 6050H-S, 6052	Information returns	¶713
Sec. 18631.7	...	Check cashing business information return	¶712, ¶713
Sec. 18632	...	Administration of withholding	¶713
Sec. 18633	IRC Sec. 6031	Returns by partnerships	¶622
Sec. 18633.5	IRC Sec. 6031	Returns by LLCs	¶625
Sec. 18635	IRC Sec. 6013(a), 6034	Information from charitable trust	¶606
Sec. 18635.5	IRC Sec. 6034A	Information to beneficiaries	¶106
Sec. 18639	IRC Secs. 6042, 6049	Returns for interest, dividends, collections	¶713
Sec. 18640	IRC Sec. 6044	Returns by cooperatives	¶713
Sec. 18642	IRC Sec. 6045	Reporting—property owners	¶713
Sec. 18644	IRC Sec. 6050A	Fishing boat operators—reporting requirements	¶713
Sec. 18646	IRC Sec. 6050M	State agency head—reporting requirements	¶713
Sec. 18648	IRC Sec. 6112	Listed transactions	¶713
Sec. 18648.5	IRC Sec. 6115	Disclosure related to quid pro quo contributions	...
Sec. 18649	IRC Sec. 1275	Original issue discount reporting	¶713
Sec. 18661	IRC Secs. 3402, 6041(c)	Recipient of income	¶713
Sec. 18662	IRC Secs. 1445, 3402	Withholding of tax—nonresidents	¶625, ¶714, ¶715, ¶716
Sec. 18663	IRC Sec. 3402(a)	Withholding	¶715
Sec. 18664	IRC Sec. 3406	Withholding	¶714
Sec. 18665	...	Change in withholding due to legislative enactments	¶714, ¶715
Sec. 18666	IRC Sec. 1446	Withholding exemption certificates	¶625, ¶714, ¶715
Sec. 18667	IRC Sec. 3402	Withholding—foreign partners	¶714, ¶715
Sec. 18668	IRC Sec. 3403	Withholding penalties	¶714, ¶716
Sec. 18669	...	Sale, transfer, or disposition of business	¶709, ¶714
Sec. 18670	...	Withholding notice—delinquency	¶714
Sec. 18670.5	...	Electronic notice to withhold	...

California	Federal	Subject	Paragraph
Sec. 18671	...	Withholding—state agencies	¶714
Sec. 18672	...	Liability for failure to withhold	¶714
Sec. 18673	...	Employee relief from liability	¶715
Sec. 18674	...	Person required to withhold—compliance	¶714
Sec. 18675	IRC Sec. 6414	Remedies on taxes withheld	¶714
Sec. 18676	...	Withholding notice to state agencies	¶712
Sec. 18677	IRC Sec. 3505	Lender, surety or other person liable	¶714
Secs. 18711-18900.26	...	Designated contributions	¶322
Sec. 19001	IRC Sec. 6151	Date tax due	¶110
Sec. 19002	IRC Secs. 31(a), 6513	Credit for tax withheld	¶714, ¶715
Sec. 19004	IRC Secs. 6151, 6655	Payment prior to due date	¶110
Sec. 19005	IRC Sec. 6151	Remittance to FTB	¶110, ¶712
Sec. 19006	IRC Sec. 6151	Joint return liability	¶107, ¶709
Sec. 19007	IRC Sec. 6315	Payments of estimated taxes	¶111
Sec. 19008	IRC Sec. 6159	Installment payment of tax	¶110
Sec. 19009	IRC Sec. 7512	Failure to pay collected taxes	¶715
Sec. 19010	IRC Sec. 6655	Assessing delinquent estimated taxes	¶110
Sec. 19011	IRC Sec. 6302	Electronic funds transfer	¶110, ¶712
Sec. 19011.5	...	Electronic payment requirements	¶110, ¶111
Sec. 19031	IRC Sec. 6212	Deficiency assessments—FTB authority	¶704
Sec. 19032	IRC Sec. 6212	Examination of return	¶704
Sec. 19033	IRC Sec. 6212(a)	Notice of deficiency	¶704
Sec. 19034	...	Details of notice	¶704
Sec. 19035	IRC Sec. 6212	Joint return notice	¶704
Sec. 19036	IRC Sec. 6212	Addition to tax as deficiency	¶704
Sec. 19041	IRC Sec. 6213	Protest to assessment	¶704
Sec. 19041.5	6603	Treatment of deposits	¶719, ¶720
Sec. 19042	IRC Sec. 6213	Final decision if no protest	¶704, ¶706
Sec. 19043	IRC Sec. 6211	"Deficiency and rebate" defined	¶704
Sec. 19043.5	...	Carryforward adjustments	¶704
Sec. 19044	IRC Sec. 6213	Reconsideration of assessment	¶702
Sec. 19045	...	Appeal from FTB's action	¶705
Sec. 19046	IRC Sec. 6213	Mailing of appeal	¶705
Sec. 19047	IRC Sec. 6213	Notice of SBE's determination	¶705
Sec. 19048	IRC Sec. 6213	Petition for rehearing	¶705
Sec. 19049	IRC Sec. 6212	Notice and demand for payment	¶706
Sec. 19050	IRC Sec. 6212	Evidence of assessment	¶704
Sec. 19051	IRC Sec. 6213	Mathematical error in return	¶704
Sec. 19052	...	Limitations period for refund adjustments	¶719
Sec. 19054	IRC Sec. 6201	Overstatement of credit	¶726
Sec. 19057	IRC Sec. 6501	Limitation period on assessment	¶710
Sec. 19058	IRC Sec. 6501(e)	Limitation period extended	¶710
Sec. 19059	...	Limitation period after amended return	¶710
Sec. 19060	...	Limitation period following federal adjustment	¶710
Sec. 19061	IRC Secs. 1032, 1033(a)(2)(A)-(D)	Limitation period—involuntary conversion	¶710
Sec. 19063	IRC Secs. 6225, 6501(a)	Items of federally registered partnership	¶710
Sec. 19064	IRC Sec. 7609	Motion to quash subpoena	¶710
Sec. 19065	IRC Sec. 6501(c)	Agreement to extend period	¶710
Sec. 19066	IRC Sec. 6501(b)	Time return deemed filed	¶710, ¶719
Sec. 19067	IRC Sec. 6501(c)	Extension by agreement	¶710
Sec. 19071	IRC Sec. 6901	Assessments against persons secondarily liable	¶613, ¶709
Sec. 19072	IRC Sec. 6901	Collection from person secondarily liable	¶613, ¶709
Sec. 19073	IRC Sec. 6901	Assessment and collection from transferees and fiduciaries	¶613, ¶709
Sec. 19074	IRC Sec. 6901	Limitations period for assessment of transferee or fiduciary	¶613, ¶709
Sec. 19081	IRC Sec. 6861	Jeopardy assessment	¶707
Sec. 19082	IRC Sec. 6862	Taxable period terminated	¶707
Sec. 19083	IRC Secs. 6861, 6863	Collection of jeopardy assessment; bond	¶707
Sec. 19084	IRC Secs. 6213, 6863	Hearing	¶707
Sec. 19085	IRC Sec. 6863	Appeal	¶707
Sec. 19086	IRC Sec. 6861	Evidence of jeopardy	¶707

California	Federal	Subject	Paragraph
Sec. 19087	IRC Sec. 6501(c)	Fraudulent or no return	¶710
Sec. 19088	IRC Sec. 6871	Assessments in bankruptcy or receivership	¶708
Sec. 19089	IRC Secs. 6036, 6872	Notice; suspension of period	¶708
Sec. 19090	IRC Sec. 6871	Deficiency claims	¶708
Sec. 19091	IRC Sec. 6873	Unpaid claim	¶708
Sec. 19092	IRC Sec. 6861	Regulations	. . .
Sec. 19093	IRC Sec. 6867	Unexplained cash	¶707
Sec. 19101	IRC Sec. 6601	Interest on tax due	¶711
Sec. 19104	IRC Sec. 6404	Interest on deficiency	¶711
Sec. 19105	IRC Sec. 6601	No interest period	¶711
Sec. 19107	. . .	Overpayment applied to spouse's deficiency	¶711
Sec. 19108	. . .	Overpayment applied to another year's deficiency	¶709
Sec. 19109	. . .	Abatement of interest	¶710
Sec. 19110	. . .	Overpayment—estate or trust	¶110, ¶710
Sec. 19112	. . .	Interest waived	¶711
Sec. 19113	IRC Sec. 6601(f)	Satisfaction by credit	¶711
Sec. 19114	IRC Sec. 6601(g)	When interest may be collected	¶711
Sec. 19116	IRC Sec. 6404(g)	Suspension of interest and penalties	¶711, ¶712
Sec. 19117	IRC Sec. 6631	Notice of interest charges	¶711
Sec. 19120	. . .	Interest on erroneous refund	¶711
Sec. 19131	IRC Sec. 6651	Penalty—failure to make return	¶712
Sec. 19132	IRC Sec. 6651	Penalty for tax not paid	¶712
Sec. 19132.5	IRC Sec. 6651	Waiver of penalties for victims of Northridge earthquake	. . .
Sec. 19133	. . .	Penalty—failure to furnish information	¶704, ¶712
Sec. 19133.5	IRC Sec. 6652	Penalty—failure to report small business stock gain	¶712
Sec. 19134	IRC Sec. 6657	Bad check penalty	¶712
Sec. 19136	IRC Sec. 6654	Penalty—payments estimated tax	¶111
Sec. 19136.1	IRC Sec. 6654	Estimated payment installment percentages	¶111
Sec. 19136.2-36.13	. . .	Estimated tax penalty abatement	¶111
Sec. 19161	IRC Sec. 6658	Timely payment during bankruptcy	¶712
Sec. 19164	IRC Secs. 6662-65	Accuracy-related penalty	¶712
Sec. 19164.5	IRC Secs. 6662A	Accuracy-related penalty on reportable transactions	¶727
Sec. 19166	IRC Sec. 6694	Penalty—preparer understatement	¶712
Sec. 19167	IRC Sec. 6695	Penalties—tax preparers	¶712
Sec. 19168	IRC Sec. 6696	Penalties—tax preparers	¶712
Sec. 19169	IRC Sec. 6695(f)	Penalty—negotiating client's refund check	¶712
Sec. 19170	. . .	Penalty—electronic returns	¶712
Sec. 19172	IRC Sec. 6698	Penalty—partnership returns	¶622, ¶625, ¶712
Sec. 19173	IRC Sec. 6708	Penalty—tax shelters	¶712
Sec. 19174	IRC Sec. 6700	Penalty—tax shelters	¶712
Sec. 19175	. . .	Penalty—information returns	¶712, ¶713
Sec. 19176	IRC Sec. 6682	Penalty—false withholding information	¶712
Sec. 19177	IRC Sec. 6700	Penalty—abusive tax shelters	¶712
Sec. 19178	IRC Sec. 6701	Penalty—aiding and abetting tax understatement	¶712
Sec. 19179	IRC Sec. 6702	Penalty—frivolous return	¶710
Sec. 19180	IRC Sec. 6703	Penalty—burden of proof	. . .
Sec. 19181	IRC Sec. 6706	Penalty—original issue discount reporting	¶710
Sec. 19182	IRC Secs. 6111, 6707	Penalty—tax shelters	¶712, ¶713
Sec. 19182.5	IRC Sec. 6174	Penalty—failure to disclose quid pro quo information	. . .
Sec. 19183	IRC Secs. 6652, 6721-24	Penalty—certain information returns	¶712
Sec. 19184	IRC Sec. 6693	Penalty—failure to properly report IRA	¶712
Sec. 19185	IRC Sec. 6695A	Penalty—substantial and gross valuation misstatements attributable to incorrect appraisals	¶712
Sec. 19186	IRC Sec. 6702B	Penalty—fraudulent identification of exempt-use property	¶712

California	Federal	Subject	Paragraph
Sec. 19187	IRC Sec. 6751	Procedures for penalties	¶712
Secs. 19191-94	...	Voluntary disclosure agreements	¶725
Secs. 19195	...	Public disclosure of large delinquent taxpayers	¶721
Sec. 19201	...	Judgment for tax	...
Sec. 19202	...	Entry of judgment	...
Sec. 19203	...	Abstract as lien	...
Sec. 19204	...	Extension of lien	...
Sec. 19205	...	Execution of judgment	...
Sec. 19206	IRC Sec. 6325	Release of lien	...
Sec. 19207	IRC Sec. 6325	Release of unenforceable lien	...
Sec. 19208	IRC Sec. 6325	Certificate of release	...
Sec. 19209	IRC Sec. 6325	Cost for certificate	...
Sec. 19221	IRC Sec. 6321	Lien on tax	¶612
Sec. 19222	IRC Sec. 6311	Lien for dishonored checks	...
Sec. 19223	...	Lien against trust	¶612
Sec. 19224	...	Service of notice of fiduciary	¶612
Sec. 19225	...	Administrative review	¶702
Sec. 19226	IRC Sec. 6325	Release of third-party liens	...
Sec. 19231	IRC Sec. 6331	Warrant to collect tax	...
Sec. 19232	...	Warrant as writ of execution	...
Sec. 19233	...	Fees for warrant	...
Secs. 19234-35	...	Fees as obligation of taxpayer	...
Sec. 19236	IRC Sec. 6331	Seizure of property	...
Sec. 19251	...	Remedies are cumulative	...
Sec. 19252	...	FTB as representative	...
Sec. 19253	IRC Sec. 6323	Priority of lien	...
Sec. 19254	...	Collection and filing enforcement fees	¶712
Sec. 19255	IRC Sec. 6502	Limitations period for collections	¶710
Sec. 19256	IRC Sec. 7504	Fractional dollar amount	...
Sec. 19262	IRC Secs. 6331, 6335	Seizure and sale of personal property	...
Sec. 19263	IRC Secs. 6338, 6342	Bill of sale; disposition of excess	...
Sec. 19264	...	Earnings withholding tax order	...
Sec. 19266	...	Financial institutions record match (FIRM) system	¶721
Sec. 19271	...	Child support delinquency	...
Sec. 19271.6	...	Financial Institution Match System	...
Sec. 19291	...	Reciprocal collection agreements	¶721
Sec. 19301	IRC Sec. 6402	Credit for overpayment	¶717
Sec. 19302	...	Credit and refund approval	¶717
Sec. 19304	...	Direct deposit into Golden State Scholarshare Trust	...
Sec. 19306	IRC Sec. 6511(a)	Time limit for refund	¶719
Sec. 19307	...	Return as claim for refund	¶717, ¶719
Sec. 19308	IRC Sec. 6511(c)	Effect of assessment extension	¶717
Sec. 19309	IRC Sec. 6511(c)	Claims filed before assessment extension	¶719
Sec. 19311	IRC Sec. 6511	Time limit following federal adjusted return	¶719
Sec. 19311.5	...	Limitations period for refund of taxes paid to other state	¶719
Sec. 19312	IRC Sec. 6511(d)	Time limit where bad debts or worthless securities	¶719
Sec. 19313	IRC Sec. 6511(g)	Federally registered partnerships	¶719
Sec. 19314	...	Overpayment used as offset	¶719
Sec. 19316	IRC Sec. 6511(h)	Financially disabled individuals	¶719
Sec. 19321	...	Final action	¶717
Sec. 19322	...	Claim for refund	¶717
Sec. 19322.1	...	Informal refund claims	¶719
Sec. 19323	IRC Sec. 6402	Disallowance of claim	¶717
Sec. 19324	...	Appeal from FTB's action	¶718
Sec. 19325	...	Refunds resulting from federal law	¶718, ¶722
Sec. 19331	...	Failure to mail notice	¶718
Sec. 19332	IRC Sec. 6213	Mailing of appeals	¶718
Sec. 19333	IRC Sec. 6213	SBE determination	¶718
Sec. 19334	IRC Sec. 6213	Petition for rehearing	¶718
Sec. 19335	...	Payment of tax protested	¶718
Sec. 19340	IRC Sec. 6611(b)	Interest on overpayments	¶722
Sec. 19341	IRC Sec. 6611(e)	Refunds made within certain time	¶722
Sec. 19342	...	Notice of disallowance	¶722
Sec. 19343	...	Finality of notice	¶722

California	Federal	Subject	Paragraph
Sec. 19344	...	Appeal to SBE	¶722
Sec. 19345	...	Hearing	¶722
Sec. 19346	...	Finality of determination	¶722
Sec. 19347	...	Suit to recover interest	¶722
Sec. 19348	...	Failure of FTB to give notice	¶722
Sec. 19349	IRC Sec. 6401	Payments not entitled to interest	¶722
Sec. 19350	...	No interest on barred claim	¶722
Sec. 19351	IRC Sec. 6611(b)	Payment deemed made on due date	¶722
Sec. 19354	IRC Sec. 6401(b)	Excess of tax withheld	...
Sec. 19355	...	Refunding excess	...
Sec. 19361	IRC Sec. 6414	Employer's overpayment	...
Sec. 19362	IRC Sec. 6402	Credits against estimated tax	...
Sec. 19363	IRC Sec. 6402	Interest on overpayments of estimated tax	¶722
Sec. 19364	...	Estimated tax overpayment carryover	...
Sec. 19365	...	Transfers of S corporation tax payments	¶806
Sec. 19368	...	Erroneous refund	¶726
Sec. 19371	IRC Secs. 6502, 7403	Suit for tax	¶710
Sec. 19372	...	Prosecution of suit	...
Sec. 19373	...	Writ of attachment	...
Sec. 19374	...	Evidence of delinquency	...
Sec. 19375	...	Suit in any court	...
Sec. 19376	...	Collection of tax	...
Sec. 19377	IRC Sec. 6301	Agreements with collection agencies	...
Sec. 19377.5	...	Reciprocal collection agreements	¶721
Sec. 19378	IRC Sec. 6301	Collection and transfer of funds	...
Sec. 19381	IRC Sec. 7421	Injunction actions prohibited	¶720
Sec. 19382	IRC Sec. 7422	Action to recover void tax	¶720
Sec. 19383	IRC Sec. 7422	Credit for overpayment	¶720
Sec. 19384	IRC Sec. 6532	Time for filing	¶720
Sec. 19385	IRC Sec. 6532	No FTB notice of action	¶720
Sec. 19387	IRC Sec. 7422	Service of summons and complaint	¶720
Sec. 19388	IRC Secs. 6532, 7422(f)	Location of trial	¶720
Sec. 19389	IRC Sec. 6532	Defense of action	¶720
Sec. 19390	...	Failure to sue within time limit	¶720
Sec. 19391	IRC Sec. 6612	Interest on judgment	¶720
Sec. 19392	...	Judgment against FTB	¶720
Sec. 19394	...	Refund of unconstitutional LLC fee	¶625
Sec. 19411	IRC Secs. 6602, 7405	Recovery of erroneous refunds	¶726
Sec. 19412	...	Court of trial	¶726
Sec. 19413	...	Prosecution of suit	¶726
Sec. 19431	IRC Sec. 6404	Illegal levy	...
Sec. 19441	IRC Secs. 7121-23	Closing agreements	¶723
Sec. 19442	...	Settlement of tax disputes	¶723
Sec. 19443	...	Offers in compromise	¶724
Sec. 19444	...	Amnesty	¶710, ¶712
Sec. 19501	IRC Sec. 7621(a)	FTB—administering the law	¶701
Sec. 19502	IRC Sec. 7621(b)	FTB—establishment of districts	¶701
Sec. 19503	IRC Sec. 7805	FTB regulations	¶701
Sec. 19504	IRC Sec. 7602	FTB's powers	¶701
Sec. 19504.5	IRC Sec. 7612	Software trade secrets	¶701, ¶721
Sec. 19504.7	IRC Sec. 7602	Notice of contact of third parties	¶701
Sec. 19505	IRC Sec. 7803	FTB—appointment and removal	¶701
Sec. 19506	...	FTB deputies	¶701
Sec. 19507	...	FTB—temporary appointments	¶701
Sec. 19508	...	FTB—salaries	¶701
Sec. 19509	...	FTB—bond	¶701
Sec. 19511	IRC Sec. 7622	FTB—oath	¶701
Sec. 19512	IRC Sec. 6903	Fiduciary assuming taxpayer's duties	¶613
Sec. 19516	IRC Sec. 6905	Fiduciary personally liable	¶613
Sec. 19517	...	FTB assessment of tax	¶613
Sec. 19518	IRC Sec. 6047	Information returns—self-employed retirement trusts	¶607
Sec. 19519	...	Disability insurance—refund or credit	...
Sec. 19520	...	Tax enforcement definition	...
Sec. 19521	IRC Secs. 6621-22	Current interest rate for deficiencies and refunds	¶711

California	Federal	Subject	Paragraph
Sec. 19522	...	Federal tax changes	¶103
Sec. 19523	...	Disqualification of appraiser	¶712
Sec. 19523.5	...	Tax practitioner disbarment/ suspension	...
Sec. 19525	IRC Sec. 7623	Rewards for informers	¶701
Sec. 19526	...	Taxpayer cross-reference file	...
Sec. 19528	...	Information on state licensees	...
Sec. 19530	...	Preserving tax returns	¶721
Sec. 19532	...	Priority for application of collected amounts	...
Sec. 19533	...	Priority of payments	...
Sec. 19542	IRC Secs. 6103, 7213	Secrecy of returns	¶717
Secs. 19542.1-42.3	IRC Sec. 7213	Illegal disclosures	...
Sec. 19543	IRC Sec. 6103(b)	"Business affairs" defined	...
Sec. 19544	IRC Sec. 6103(b)	Nondisclosure of audit methods	¶721
Sec. 19545	IRC Sec. 6103(h)	Disclosure—judicial order	¶721
Secs. 19546-46.5	IRC Sec. 6103(f)	Disclosure to legislative committee	¶717
Sec. 19547	IRC Sec. 6103(h)	Disclosure to Attorney General	¶721
Sec. 19548	...	Disclosure to Calif. Parent Locator Service	¶721
Sec. 19548.2	...	Disclosure to Department of Public Health	¶721
Sec. 19548.5	...	Disclosure to state health care organizations	¶721
Sec. 19549	IRC Sec. 6103(b)	"Return" defined	¶721
Sec. 19550	...	Address of people from whome there is an outstanding warrant	...
Sec. 19551	IRC Sec. 6103(d)	Disclosure to proper authorities	¶721
Sec. 19551.5	...	Reciprocal information exchange program with cities	¶721
Sec. 19552	IRC Secs. 6103, 7213	Unwarranted disclosure	¶721
Sec. 19553	IRC Sec. 6103	Disclosure to Director of Social Services	¶721
Sec. 19554	IRC Sec. 6103	Locating owners of unclaimed property	¶721
Sec. 19555	IRC Sec. 6103	Unearned income information	¶721
Sec. 19556	...	Disclosure in FTB proceedings	¶721
Sec. 19557	IRC Sec. 6103	Student loan applicants	¶721
Sec. 19558	...	Disclosure to Public Employees' Retirement System	¶721
Sec. 19559	...	Disclosure for national security purposes	¶721
Sec. 19561	...	Fee for copies of returns	¶721
Sec. 19562	IRC Sec. 6103	Charge for reasonable cost	¶721
Sec. 19563	IRC Sec. 6108	Publication of statistics	¶721
Sec. 19564	IRC Sec. 6108	High income taxpayer report	¶721
Sec. 19565	IRC Sec. 6104	Disclosure of information	¶721
Sec. 19566	...	Information obtained by FTB	...
Sec. 19571-72	...	Disclosures to state agencies	...
Sec. 19581	...	Use of federal forms	Specimen return
Sec. 19582	...	Simplification of tax forms	...
Sec. 19582.5	...	Form 540 2EZ income limits	¶106
Sec. 19583	...	Forging spouse's signature	¶712
Secs. 19590-92	...	Tax service fees	...
Sec. 19701	IRC Secs. 7203, 7206	Violation—failure to file return	¶712
Sec. 19701.5	...	Forging spouse's signature	¶712
Sec. 19702	...	Prosecutor's compromise	¶712
Sec. 19703	...	Evidence of failure to file	¶712
Sec. 19704	IRC Sec. 6531	Statute of limitations—violations	¶712
Sec. 19705	IRC Sec. 7206	False statements—fraud	¶712
Sec. 19706	IRC Sec. 7203	Failure to file return	¶712
Sec. 19707	...	Venue	
Sec. 19708	IRC Sec. 7202	Failure to remit withheld tax	¶712
Sec. 19709	IRC Sec. 7202	Failure to withhold tax as misdemeanor	¶712
Sec. 19710	...	Writ of mandate	
Sec. 19711	IRC Sec. 7205	Penalties—employees	¶712
Sec. 19712	IRC Sec. 6695	Misdemeanor conviction for endorsing client's refund check	¶712
Sec. 19713	IRC Sec. 7215	Failure to set up withholding account	¶712
Sec. 19714	IRC Sec. 6673	Delay tactics	¶712
Sec. 19715	IRC Sec. 7408	Penalties—injunctive relief	¶712
Sec. 19717	IRC Sec. 7430	Recovery of litigation costs	¶701
Sec. 19718	...	Wage statements for immigrants	...

California	Federal	Subject	Paragraph
Secs. 19720-21	. . .	Penalty for fraudulently obtaining refunds	¶712
Secs. 19722	. . .	Restitution orders and other amounts collection	. . .
Secs. 19730-38	. . .	Amnesty	¶712
Secs. 19751-54	. . .	Abusive tax shelter voluntary compliance	¶727
Sec. 19755	. . .	Abusive tax shelter limitations period	¶710
Sec. 19761-62	. . .	Voluntary Compliance Initiative Two	¶727
Sec. 19772	IRC Sec. 6707A	Penalty—reportable transaction omission	¶727
Sec. 19774	IRC Secs. 6662, 6663	Penalty—noneconomic substance transaction understatement	¶712, ¶727
Sec. 19777	. . .	Interest-based penalty—abusive tax shelter deficiency	¶727
Sec. 19777.5	. . .	Amnesty enhanced interest penalty	¶711, ¶712
Sec. 19778	. . .	Interest—reportable transaction understatement	¶712
Sec. 19850-19854	. . .	EITC information provided by employer	¶158, ¶715
Secs. 21001-14	IRC Secs. 6404(f), 7430, 7521, 7811	Taxpayers' bill of rights	¶701, ¶702, ¶703
Sec. 21015	. . .	Relief from penalties	¶701, ¶712
Sec. 21015.5	. . .	Tax lien and levy protections	¶702
Secs. 21016-28	IRC Secs. 6103(e)(8), 6201(d)(4), 6331, 7433, 7435, 7502, 7524, 7811	Taxpayer's bill of rights	¶108, ¶702, ¶703

PERSONAL INCOME TAX

CHAPTER 1
IMPOSITION OF TAX, RATES, EXEMPTIONS, RETURNS

¶101 Overview of Personal Income Tax

The California personal income tax was first enacted in 1935 and has been amended on numerous occasions since then. It constitutes Part 10 of Division 2 of the Revenue and Taxation Code. Administrative provisions applicable to both personal income and corporate franchise and income taxpayers are encompassed by Part 10.2 of Division 2 of the Revenue and Taxation Code.

The law is administered by the Franchise Tax Board, composed of the State Controller, the Director of the Department of Finance, and the Chair of the State Board of Equalization.

California's personal income tax is generally patterned after the federal income tax. Moreover, interpretations of federal income tax law by the Internal Revenue Service and the courts have typically been followed in the administration of analogous provisions of California law. However, there remain significant differences between federal and California income tax laws. See ¶ 103 for an explanation of the federal conformity program established in 1983.

Personal income tax is imposed on the entire taxable income of California residents and on the taxable income of nonresidents derived from sources within California. It applies to individuals, estates, and trusts. Tax is computed on a graduated scale, at rates ranging from 1% to 13.3% (¶ 116). Under certain circumstances, tax is reduced by a credit for tax paid to another state or by various other credits (¶ 125 et seq.).

• *No local income tax*

California law specifically prohibits the imposition of an income tax by any city, county, or other local jurisdiction, and also prohibits local jurisdictions from imposing a tax on the earnings of nonresident employees unless the same tax is imposed on resident employees.

In *County of Alameda, County of Contra Costa, County of Santa Clara v. City and County of San Francisco* (1971) (CCH CALIFORNIA TAX REPORTS, ¶ 204-550), the California Court of Appeal held that a San Francisco nonresident commuter tax was unconstitutional. However, in *Weekes, et al. v. City of Oakland, et al.* (1978) (CCH CALIFORNIA TAX REPORTS, ¶ 205-861), the California Supreme Court upheld the validity of a 1% tax imposed on employee compensation by the City of Oakland. The Court held that the tax was a license tax rather than an income tax.

¶102 Scope of Chapter

This chapter discusses the questions of who is subject to the tax and who qualifies as a "resident," requirements for filing returns and payment of tax, the base upon which tax is imposed, and the rates of tax.

¶103 Federal Conformity Program

Law: Secs. 17024.5, 19522 (CCH CALIFORNIA TAX REPORTS, ¶ 15-515).

Prior to 1983, California personal income tax law was wholly self-contained. However, California statutes duplicated many provisions of federal law. This situation was remedied in 1983 when California law was completely restructured to incorporate much of the federal law by reference to Internal Revenue Code subchapters and provisions and to concentrate primarily on the *differences* between California and federal law.

Beginning with the 2015 taxable year, California conforms to the IRC provisions it incorporates as the provisions were amended on January 1, 2015. (Sec. 17024.5, Rev. & Tax. Code) Consequently, California has not conformed to amendments made by the following federal laws:

— Slain Officer Family Support Act of 2015 (P.L. 114-7);

— Medicare Access and CHIP Reauthorization Act of 2015 (P.L. 114-10);

— Don't Tax Our Fallen Public Safety Heroes Act (P.L. 114-14);

— Highway and Transportation Funding Act of 2015 (P.L. 114-21);

— Defending Public Safety Employees' Retirement Act (P.L. 114-26);

— Trade Preferences Extension Act of 2015 (P.L. 114-27);

— Surface Transportation and Veterans Health Care Choice Improvement Act of 2015 (P.L. 114-41);

— Protecting Americans From Tax Hikes Act of 2015 (P.L. 114-113); and

— United States Appreciation for Olympians and Paralympians Act of 2016 (P.L. 114-239).

Practitioner Comment: California Updates IRC Conformity Reference Date

Governor Jerry Brown signed A.B. 154 into law on September 30, 2015. A.B. 154 updates the conformity date with respect to adopted sections of the Internal Revenue Code to January 1, 2015, and also makes changes to the large corporate understatement penalty (LCUP). See Practitioner Comment: Limited Safe Harbors Exist with Respect to 20% Penalty for Large Corporate Understatements (LCUP) in ¶ 1411 Penalties regarding the changes to the LCUP under A.B. 154. A.B. 154 was approved by more than a two-thirds majority of the state Legislature and generally becomes operative for taxable years beginning on or after January 1, 2015, unless otherwise noted.

A.B. 154 is California's most recent conformity update since S.B. 401 was signed on April 12, 2010. Subsequently, California voters, on November 2, 2010, passed Proposition 26 (Prop 26), which was incorporated into Section 3 of Article XIII of the California Constitution and requires a two-thirds super majority vote from the Senate and Assembly for legislation that results in any taxpayer paying higher taxes in California. Prop 26 also voided measures adopted without a two-thirds vote between January 1, 2010, and

November 3, 2010, unless reenacted by the Legislature by a two-thirds vote. Because S.B. 401 was passed by only a simple majority vote and the Legislature did not reenact it by a two-thirds super majority vote, it was questionable whether changes made by S.B. 401 applied. The FTB issued Legal Division Guidance 2011-01-01 indicating that it would continue to apply the January 1, 2009 conformity date per S.B. 401 until such time as a California court of appeal holds that S.B. 401 is void.

In an attempt to resolve any ambiguities created by S.B. 401 passing by a simple majority, A.B. 154 explicitly states that "[i]t is the intent of the Legislature to confirm the validity and ongoing effect of Senate Bill No. 401 of the 2009-10 Regular Session." The impact of the Legislature's declaration that S.B. 401 is valid remains unclear because it is questionable whether that statement in A.B. 154 is sufficient to deem S.B. 104 reenacted as required under the terms of Prop 26.

Since California does not provide general conformity to the IRC, as with prior conformity bills, A.B. 154 updates references to the IRC contained within California statutes and has no impact on IRC provisions not adopted under California law. So while A.B. 154 provides certainty with respect to the conformity date relating to adopted IRC provisions such as IRC Sec. 355 (relating to tax-free spin off and similar transactions) it has no impact on provisions which are not adopted by reference under California law.

Chris Whitney, Contributing Editor

Planning Note: EGTRRA Sunset Provisions Incorporated

California incorporates the federal provision of the Economic Growth and Tax Relief Reconciliation Act of 2001 that provides that all provisions of, and amendments made by, the 2001 Act will not apply to taxable, plan, or limitation years beginning after 2010. However, to the extent that any of these provisions are extended or the sunset date repealed, California will incorporate the extension, whether the extension is temporary or permanent. (Sec. 17024.5(a)(2)(B), Rev. & Tax. Code) The sunset dates for all of these federal provisions were extended an additional one to two years by the federal Jobs Creation Act of 2010 and eliminated by the Taxpayer Relief Act of 2012, thus making the EGTRRA provisions permanent.

Any federal provisions that have not been incorporated—with the corresponding impact on the filing of the California personal income tax return—are discussed at appropriate paragraphs in the *Guidebook*.

Because of the extent of the state conformity to federal law, the state income tax return has been designed to reflect a modification format. The computation of income begins with federal adjusted gross income, to which state modifications are then made. Accordingly, the *Guidebook* includes a guide to aid in the preparation of California individual income tax returns (¶25 et seq.).

• *Federal regulations and guidance apply to California tax law*

When federal law has been incorporated into California law, as explained above, federal regulations issued under the law in both temporary and final form are applicable for California purposes unless they conflict with California law or California regulations. (Sec. 17024.5(h), Rev. & Tax. Code)

Similarly, federal rulings and administrative guidance dealing with the Internal Revenue Code (IRC) are persuasive authority in interpreting the California statutes. General administrative guidance applicable to the IRC also applies to California tax statutes that conform to the IRC, with due account for state terminology, state effective dates, and other obvious differences between state and federal law. However, private letter rulings will only be considered federal administrative guidance with respect to the particular taxpayer for whom the ruling was issued. (*Information Letter 2010-5*, California Franchise Tax Board, August 17, 2010)

• *Federal elections apply to California*

In most cases, federal conformity relieves a taxpayer from making a separate election for California purposes when an election is required. California law provides that a proper federal election is deemed to be a proper election for California purposes unless otherwise provided in California law or regulations. A copy of the federal election must be furnished to the Franchise Tax Board (FTB) upon request. (Sec. 17024.5(e), Rev. & Tax. Code)

A taxpayer may make an election for federal purposes and not for California purposes, or vice versa, when the law permits a choice. In such cases, the taxpayer must file a proper election or timely statement with the FTB setting forth relevant information and clearly expressing an intent to make a different election for California purposes. This rule does not apply where a California regulation has requirements that are substantially different from the federal requirements. (Sec. 17024.5(e), Rev. & Tax. Code)

Federal income tax elections, or lack thereof, made before becoming a California taxpayer are binding for California personal income tax purposes, unless a separate election is specifically authorized by a California law or regulation. (Sec. 17024.5(e), Rev. & Tax. Code)

See ¶ 400 for a discussion of the "doctrine of elections."

• *Federal approval applies to California*

Federal conformity also simplifies the requirement of obtaining approval from taxing authorities when such approval is required. Whenever a taxpayer is required to file an application or seek consent, proper action taken for federal purposes is deemed to be effective for California purposes, unless otherwise provided by California law or regulations. A copy of any such application must be furnished to the FTB upon request. (Sec. 17024.5(h), Rev. & Tax. Code)

A taxpayer may take certain actions for federal purposes and not for California purposes, or vice versa, when the law permits a choice and approval or consent is required. The rules discussed above, relating to elections, apply with equal force to these situations.

¶104 Special Programs for Economic Incentives

> *California Forms:* FTB 3805Z (Enterprise Zone Deduction and Credit Summary), FTB 3806 (Los Angeles Revitalization Zone Deduction and Credit Summary), FTB 3807 (Local Agency Military Base Recovery Area Deduction and Credit Summary), FTB 3808 (Manufacturing Enhancement Area Credit Summary), FTB 3809 (Target Tax Area Deduction and Credit Summary).

A geographically-targeted economic development area (G-TEDA) is an area designated as an enterprise zone, a manufacturing enhancement area, a targeted tax area, or a local agency military base recovery area. (Sec. 7072, Govt. Code)

Planning Note: *G-TEDA Programs Repealed*

The G-TEDA programs are repealed, generally effective January, 1, 2014. However, various incentives may still continue to be carried over. See the discussions noted below for more details.

The G-TEDA programs are administered by the California Department of Housing and Community Development (HCD). G-TEDAs were subject to audit at least once every five years. If a G-TEDA failed to successfully comply with a corrective plan after receiving a failing grade, the zone lost its designation. However, businesses located in a zone that lost its designation could continue to receive tax incentives for the remaining life of the zone. (Sec. 7076.1, Govt. Code)

Practitioner Comment: *Overview of Enterprise Zone Credit Repeal*

With A.B. 93 and S.B. 90, signed into law on July 11, 2013, the California legislature phases out California's Enterprise Zone ("EZ") Credit Program and replaces it with a new, temporary regime that goes into effect on January 1, 2014 and sunsets December

31, 2020. The new program consists of a hiring tax credit (¶157), a partial sales and use tax manufacturing exemption (¶1509), and an incentive fund (¶134) (the latter two features are discussed in separate Practitioner's Comments).

The new regime creates a credit for hiring qualified full-time employees in (i) designated census tracts with high unemployment and poverty rates, (ii) certain former Enterprise Zones, or (iii) local agency military base recovery areas ("LAMBRAs"). This hiring credit can offset California personal and corporate income taxes from January 1, 2014 until December 31, 2020. The EZ reform also eliminates the retroactive vouchering process. Previously employers were permitted to voucher qualified employees and claim the EZ credit in tax years after hiring to the extent the income tax statute of limitations period was still open. Under the new regime, taxpayers must request a tentative credit reservation ("TCR") from the FTB within 50 days of the hire date, claim the credit on the original tax return, and provide certification to the FTB annually that the qualified employee remains employed.

Subsequent legislation, A.B. 106, extended the time frame to voucher employees hired before December 31, 2013, to January 1, 2015. The bill also allayed concerns raised by the announcement of certain zone coordinators that they would discontinue vouchering prior to 2014.

Among other restrictions and requirements, the new hiring tax credit is only available to employers that create a net increase in jobs state-wide, which was not required under the EZ hiring credit. Also, taxpayers that terminate a qualified employee within 36 months of hire may be subject to certain recapture provisions. Moreover, this new hiring credit is not available to some businesses, such as retailers, food service and temporary employment agencies. Interestingly, the legislation states that the credit is not available to taxpayers "primarily engaged in" providing food services. Yet, taxpayers that simply "provide" temporary help services and retail trade services are similarly barred from the credit. It is unclear why the modifier "primarily" was omitted for temporary help and retail trade services and whether this omission carries any significance or was an unintentional oversight.

Additionally, A.B. 93 cuts the previously unlimited EZ credit carry-forward period for credits earned prior to January 1, 2014 to 10 years. A.B. 106 clarified that the 10 year carry-forward period commences January 1, 2014, and not from the date the credit was originally generated.

Chris Whitney, Contributing Editor

• *Enterprise zones*

The enterprise zone program in effect prior to January 1, 2014, provides special tax incentives and other benefits for businesses established in designated depressed areas. The tax incentives are as follows:

— Income tax credits for sales or use tax paid on purchases of certain machinery and equipment (¶144).

— Income tax credits to employers for certain wages paid to disadvantaged individuals (¶145).

— Income tax credits to employees who are disadvantaged individuals (¶146).

— Tax-exemption of income from investments in enterprise zones (¶240).

— Accelerated write-off of certain machinery and equipment costs (¶316).

— Carryover of 100% of net operating losses for up to 15 years (¶309).

The special tax incentives available to businesses operating within enterprise zones could be claimed only for costs paid or incurred after the zone was designated and before the designation expired or was repealed. (Instructions to Form 3805Z).

The various enterprise zone deductions and credits are reported on FTB 3805Z.

Below are the enterprise zones that were repealed effective January, 1, 2014. As noted at ¶157, businesses located in many of these zones will be eligible to claim the new employment credit that went into effect on January 1, 2014.

— Anaheim
— Arvin
— Barstow
— Calexico - Imperial County
— Coachella Valley
— Compton
— Delano
— Eureka
— Fresno, City of
— Fresno County
— Hesperia
— Imperial Valley
— Kings County
— Long Beach
— Los Angeles, East
— Los Angeles, Harbor Gateway Communities
— Los Angeles, Hollywood
— Merced Regional
— Oakland
— Oroville
— Pasadena
— Pittsburg
— Richmond
— Sacramento
— Salinas Valley
— San Bernardino
— San Diego
— San Francisco
— San Joaquin
— San Jose
— Santa Ana
— Santa Clarita Valley
— Sequoia Valley
— Shasta Metro
— Siskiyou County
— Southgate-Lynwood
— Stanislaus
— Taft
— West Sacramento
— Yuba-Sutter

(FTB Pub. 3805Z, Enterprise Zone Deduction and Credit Summary)

Numerous zones also expired. However, credits or deductions accrued prior to the expiration date may still be carried over. The following zones have expired, with the zone expiration dates indicated:

— Altadena/Pasadena (April 9, 2007)
— Antelope Valley (January 31, 2012)

- Bakersfield/Kern (SE Bakersfield) (October 14, 2006)
- Lindsay (October 5, 2010)
- Los Angeles (Central City) (October 14, 2006)
- Los Angeles (Harbor Area) (March 3, 2009)
- Los Angeles (Mid-Alameda Corridor) (October 14, 2006)
- Los Angeles (Northeast Valley) (October 14, 2006)
- Madera (March 3, 2009)
- Pittsburgh (January 10, 2008)
- Porterville (October 14, 2006)
- Richmond (March 1, 2007)
- Sacramento (Army Depot) (October 3, 2009)
- Sacramento (Flora Perkins) (April 4, 2009)
- San Diego (South Bay) (January 27, 2007)
- San Diego (Metro) (October 14, 2006)
- San Francisco (May 27, 2007)
- Shafter (October 3, 2010)
- Taft
- Watsonville (April 30, 2012)

(FTB Pub. 3805Z, Enterprise Zone Deduction and Credit Summary)

• *Local agency military base recovery areas*

As a means of stimulating business and industrial growth to offset revenue losses occasioned by military base closures, a number of income tax incentives are available to businesses conducted within designated local agency military base recovery areas (LAMBRAs), provided those businesses increase their number of employees by one or more during the first two taxable years after commencing business within the LAMBRA. Deductions and credits applicable to LAMBRAs are reported on FTB 3807.

The following LAMBRAs have been designated, but are repealed effective January 1, 2014. However, similar to the enterprise zones discussed above, as noted at ¶157, businesses located in these LAMBRAs will be eligible to claim the new jobs credit that goes into effect on January 1, 2014: Alameda Point, Castle Airport, Mare Island, Mather Field/McClellan Park, San Bernardino International Airport, San Diego Naval Training Center, Southern California Logistics Airport, and Tustin Legacy.

Income tax incentives provided for businesses conducted within a designated LAMBRA include the following:

— Income tax credits for sales and use tax paid or incurred for certain equipment, components, and depreciable property (¶144).

— Income tax credits for wages paid to disadvantaged individuals or displaced employees (¶147).

— Accelerated write-off of the cost of certain depreciable business assets (¶316).

— Carryover of 100% of net operating losses for up to 15 years (¶309).

• *Targeted tax area*

To encourage private investment and employment within a targeted tax area, special tax incentives were available to eligible businesses located in the area. Prior to 2013, when the fifteen-year designation period expired, all of the incorporated cities and portions of the unincorporated areas of Tulare County were designated as the targeted tax area. However, as noted in the discussions referenced below, all of the incentives, other than the accelerated bonus depreciation deduction, are eligible for carryover. Deductions and credits applicable to the targeted tax area are reported on FTB 3809.

Income tax incentives provided for businesses conducted within a targeted tax area include the following:

— Income tax credits for sales and use tax paid or incurred for certain equipment, machinery, and parts (¶144).

— Income tax credits for wages paid to disadvantaged individuals (¶148).

— Accelerated write-off of the cost of certain depreciable business assets (¶316).

— Carryover of 100% of net operating losses for up to 15 years (¶309).

• *Manufacturing enhancement area*

Finally, businesses conducted within manufacturing enhancement areas were eligible for an employer's credit for certain wages paid to disadvantaged individuals hired prior to 2013. The cities of Brawley and Calexico in Imperial County were designated as manufacturing enhancement areas prior to 2013. However unused credit may be carried over as discussed at ¶148. The credit is reported on FTB 3808.

¶105 Who Is a Resident

Law: Secs. 17014-16, 17745 (CCH CALIFORNIA TAX REPORTS, ¶15-110).

Comparable Federal: None.

California law defines "resident" to include the following:

— Every individual who is in the state for other than a temporary or transitory purpose. (As explained below, it does not matter whether such an individual's domicile, or permanent home, is in California or elsewhere.)

— Every individual who is domiciled in the state but who is outside the state for a temporary or transitory purpose. (Sec. 17014, Rev. & Tax. Code)

All individuals who are not "residents," as defined above, are "nonresidents." (Sec. 17015, Rev. & Tax. Code)

• *Temporary or transitory purpose*

A regulation (Reg. 17014) containing several examples of "temporary or transitory purpose" indicates: "the underlying theory . . . is that the state with which a person has the closest connection during the taxable year is the state of his residence."

California law specifically provides that an individual whose permanent home is in California, but who is absent from the state for an uninterrupted period of at least 546 days under an employment-related contract, will generally be considered to be outside the state for other than a temporary or transitory purpose and, therefore, will not be treated as a resident subject to California tax. A return to California for not more than 45 days during a taxable year will not affect the nonresident status of such an individual. However, the individual will be considered a resident if:

— the individual has intangible income exceeding $200,000 in any taxable year during which the employment-related contract is in effect, or

— the principal purpose of the individual's absence from the state is to avoid California personal income tax.

The same rules will apply to a spouse who accompanies such an individual. (Sec. 17014, Rev. & Tax. Code)

• *Effect of domicile*

"Residency" is not the same as "domicile," which is an individual's permanent home, the place to which the individual, whenever absent, intends to return. One may be domiciled outside California, and still be considered a California resident by remaining in the state for other than temporary or transitory purposes. Conversely, California domiciliaries may be considered nonresidents if they remain outside the state for purposes that are neither temporary nor transitory. (Reg. 17014, 18 CCR) It is not necessary to demonstrate residency in any particular foreign state or country to avoid being considered a California resident—see the *Vohs* case, discussed below under "Seamen not California residents."

Certain U.S. officials who are domiciled in California are classified as "residents" for income tax purposes. This applies to elected officials, congressional staff members, and presidential appointees subject to Senate confirmation, other than military and foreign service career appointees. (Sec. 17014(b), Rev. & Tax. Code)

• *Nine-month presumption*

California law provides that "every individual who spends in the aggregate more than nine months of the taxable year within this state shall be presumed to be a resident." The nine-month presumption is not conclusive and may be overcome by satisfactory evidence. (Sec. 17016, Rev. & Tax. Code)

Conversely, presence within the state for less than nine months does not necessarily mean that the individual is not a resident. This point was made in *Appeal of Raymond T. and Ann B. Stefani* (1984) (CCH CALIFORNIA TAX REPORTS, ¶ 15-110.782), involving a California professor who taught at a school in Switzerland while on sabbatical leave from his California position. Additionally, a regulation (Reg. 17016, 18 CCR) provides that "a person may be a resident even though not in the state during any portion of the year."

• *Nine-month presumption overcome*

The presumption based on nine-months' residence, described above, was overcome by the taxpayer in *Appeal of Edgar Montillion Woolley* (1951) (CCH CALIFORNIA TAX REPORTS, ¶ 200-134). The taxpayer, a well-known actor, maintained his permanent home in New York State. He was in California continuously for a period of a little over a year in 1944 and 1945, including over nine months in 1945. During that time he made two motion pictures and appeared in radio broadcasts. While in California, he lived in a hotel on a weekly basis. His departure was delayed because of illness and a studio strike. The State Board of Equalization (BOE) held that he was in California only for a temporary or transitory purpose and, therefore, was not a resident.

Another case in which the nine-month presumption was overcome is *Appeal of Joseph and Rebecca Peskin* (1962) (CCH CALIFORNIA TAX REPORTS, ¶ 15-110.734). Over a period of several years the taxpayer spent from six to ten months in California each year. He engaged in extensive business activities and owned property in California. He overcame the presumption of residence by showing that he was more closely connected with Illinois than with California.

• *Nine-month presumption upheld*

The presumption based on nine-months' residence was upheld in *Appeal of Ralph V. and Marvelle J. Currier* (1969) (CCH CALIFORNIA TAX REPORTS, ¶ 15-110.262). The taxpayer was employed in a job that required him to move frequently in the course of his employment, but he lived with his family in California for 2½ years. The BOE decided that the taxpayer was domiciled in Arizona but that, because his stay in California was for an indefinite period, he was a California resident.

• *Less than nine months in California*

In *Appeal of Morgan C. and Ann M. Jones* (1972) (CCH CALIFORNIA TAX REPORTS, ¶ 15-110.736), the taxpayers argued unsuccessfully that a presumption of nonresidency arises from living in California for a period of less than nine months. However, although the taxpayers were registered to vote in Texas, had Texas drivers' licenses, and Texas automobile registration plates, the BOE held that the taxpayers were California residents in 1961, when they lived in the state for eight months, and in 1962, when they lived in the state for only five months.

• *Military personnel—In general*

Military personnel are subject to special treatment with respect to residency. Under Legal Ruling No. 300 (CCH CALIFORNIA TAX REPORTS, ¶ 15-175.30), issued by the Franchise Tax Board (FTB) in 1965, California military personnel are treated as nonresidents when they leave the state under permanent military orders to serve at out-of-state posts of duty. If the service person retains a California domicile and has a spouse who remains a California resident, the resident spouse is taxable on one-half of their community income. Out-of-state military personnel serving at posts of duty in California are treated as nonresidents unless California domicile is adopted. If California domicile is adopted, California will tax the entire income received during the period of residence. Declarations filed with military service branches showing California as the state of legal residence are treated as presumptive evidence of California residence. The 1965 ruling resulted from a 1963 decision of the BOE: *Appeal of Harold L. and Miriam J. Naylor* (CCH CALIFORNIA TAX REPORTS, ¶ 15-175.25). See also ¶ 225.

FTB Pub. 1032 (Tax Information For Military Personnel) also provides information on determining resident status for military personnel.

• *Military personnel—Spouses*

The federal Military Residency Relief Act of 2009 (P.L. 111-97) prohibits a servicemember's spouse from either losing or acquiring a residence or domicile for purposes of taxation because he or she is absent or present in any U.S. tax jurisdiction solely to be with the servicemember in compliance with the servicemember's military orders, if the residence or domicile is the same for the servicemember and the spouse. P.L. 111-97 also prohibits a spouse's income from being considered income earned in a tax jurisdiction if the spouse is not a resident or domiciliary of such jurisdiction when the spouse is in that jurisdiction solely to be with a servicemember serving under military orders.

• *Effect of temporary military assignment*

In *Appeal of Cecil L. and Bonai G. Sanders* (1971) (CCH CALIFORNIA TAX REPORTS, ¶ 15-175.301), the BOE declined to follow the *Naylor* case, discussed above, where a serviceman spent most of the year outside California under military orders designating a "permanent change of station." Instead, the BOE held that the taxpayer's out-of-state duty was clearly "temporary rather than permanent or indefinite."

• *Civil employees of military*

The special rules for military personnel do not apply to civilian employees of the military. See *Appeal of Ronald L. and Joyce E. Surette* (1983) (CCH CALIFORNIA TAX REPORTS, ¶ 15-110.3312), where a civilian employee of the U.S. Army and his wife spent three years in West Germany on an Army assignment. They continued to own a California home and maintained California driver's licenses and voter registrations in California. The BOE held that they were California residents throughout the three-year period.

In *Appeal of Dennis W. and Emiko Leggett* (1984) (CCH CALIFORNIA TAX REPORTS, ¶ 400-671), the taxpayer, a civilian employee of the U.S. Navy, spent at least ten months a year aboard ships. His wife lived in California and reported one-half of his income as her share of community income. The BOE held that he was a California resident and that his entire income was taxable.

• *Business assignments outside California—In general*

Several decisions of the BOE have involved taxpayers whose domicile admittedly was California, but who claimed nonresident status when they were out of the state on business assignments or projects for varying periods. The cases turn largely on the extent to which the taxpayers sever their ties to California and establish connections elsewhere, and the extent to which out-of-state activities appear to require long or indefinite periods of time to accomplish.

¶105

• *Business assignment cases favorable to taxpayer*

In *Appeal of Richard H. and Doris J. May* (1987) (CCH CALIFORNIA TAX REPORTS, ¶ 15-115.751), the taxpayer was employed by a Washington wholesaler to service sales areas in Washington and Oregon. The taxpayer and his wife had all of their business interests in Washington, maintained most bank accounts in Washington and Oregon, were registered Washington voters, had Washington drivers' licenses, and had all their legal, accounting, and medical needs met by Washington and Oregon professionals. In holding that the taxpayer and his wife were Washington residents, the BOE held that the fact that they erroneously claimed residency for purposes of the California homeowners property tax exemption on their California condominium and for the federal exclusion of gain from the sale of a personal residence were factors to consider but were not conclusive with respect to residence.

In *Appeal of Berry Gordy, Jr.* (1986) (CCH CALIFORNIA TAX REPORTS, ¶ 15-110.42), where the taxpayer filed a 1969 California part-year resident return, the BOE held that the state with which a person has the closest connections is the state of residence, and that the taxpayer had the closest connections with Michigan, where he owned several houses, had the majority of his business interests, registered and licensed his cars, and voted, and where his attorney, accountant, physician, dentist, and insurance agent were all located.

In *Appeal of Jeffrey L. and Donna S. Egeberg* (1985) (CCH CALIFORNIA TAX REPORTS, ¶ 15-110.3381), the taxpayer was an engineer employed by a nuclear engineering firm in California. He spent 17 months in Europe on an assignment that was expected to last at least three years. The family and household goods were moved to Europe, memberships in California were terminated, and other ties with California were severed. Despite retention of some important California relationships, the BOE held that the taxpayer and his wife were not California residents during their absence from the state.

In *Appeal of Robert C. and Grace L. Weaver* (1985) (CCH CALIFORNIA TAX REPORTS, ¶ 15-110.88), the taxpayer was an engineer employed by an aircraft manufacturer in California. He spent two years on Kwajalein Island on a "long-term foreign assignment" that was described as "more than one year and indefinite in nature." The taxpayer and his wife took an active part in social activities on Kwajalein, their minor daughter attended school there, and they established other connections there. However, they retained ownership of a home, stored an automobile and other possessions, and maintained some financial connections in California. The BOE held that their absence from California was for other than a temporary or transitory purpose, and concluded that they were not California residents during their absence from the state.

In *Appeal of Tommy H. and Leila J. Thomas* (1983) (CCH CALIFORNIA TAX REPORTS, ¶ 15-110.338), the taxpayer made a commitment in 1977 to move to Iran for two or three years. He kept his home in California, maintained some other connections with the state, and left two daughters in school in California, but severed other connections. Due to the political unrest in Iran, the taxpayer's commitment was canceled and he returned to California after about a year overseas. The BOE held that he was not a California resident during his absence from the state.

In *Appeal of James E. Duncan* (1982) (CCH CALIFORNIA TAX REPORTS, ¶ 15-110.507), the taxpayer moved to Texas to accept an executive position with the intention of remaining indefinitely. Although he left the Texas position and returned to California after only seven months, the BOE held that he acquired a new domicile in Texas during his employment there and that, therefore, he was not a California resident during the relevant period.

In *Appeal of David A. and Frances W. Stevenson* (1977) (CCH CALIFORNIA TAX REPORTS, ¶ 15-110.506), the taxpayer was an untenured professor at a California university. He spent a period of 14 months in Europe working for most of that time under a research grant from the Fulbright Commission. The BOE accepted the taxpayer's contention that he intended to remain in Europe for at least two years and, consequently, held that he was not a California resident while he was absent from the state.

In *Appeal of Christopher T. and Hoda A. Rand* (1976) (CCH CALIFORNIA TAX REPORTS, ¶ 15-110.482), the taxpayer was a specialist in Near Eastern affairs and was fluent in Arabic and Persian. He had traveled widely in the Near East and elsewhere, and was married to an Egyptian national. He lived in California for several years, beginning in 1966, and was assumed to be domiciled in California. He moved to Libya in July 1970 to take a job there, but moved back to California four months later because he lost the job. The BOE held that the taxpayer was a nonresident for the four months that he was in Libya because he "intended and expected to remain in the Near East either permanently or indefinitely."

In *Appeal of Richards L. and Kathleen K. Hardman* (1975) (CCH CALIFORNIA TAX REPORTS, ¶ 15-110.481), a professional writer was held to be a nonresident in 1969 when he spent most of the year in England, even though his absence from the state in 1969 and 1970 lasted only 13 months. The taxpayer and his wife severed most of their connections with California before their departure, and it appeared that they originally expected to stay in England for several years.

• *Business assignment cases unfavorable to taxpayer*

In *Appeal of David A. Abbott* (1986) (CCH CALIFORNIA TAX REPORTS, ¶ 15-110.3143), the taxpayer was held by the BOE to be a California resident during his seven-month employment in Maryland because his absence was for a temporary or transitory purpose. His wife and two children remained in their California home while he lived in a hotel for his entire stay outside the state. He owned other property in California and also retained his driver's license, automobile registration, and bank accounts in California.

In *Appeal of Frank J. Milos* (1984) (CCH CALIFORNIA TAX REPORTS, ¶ 15-110.317), the taxpayer spent four years working as an engineer on Johnson Island. His wife and children remained in California and he retained other connections with California. He contended that he was no longer domiciled in California because he could not find employment in the state. The BOE held that he retained his California domicile and was a California resident during the entire period. For another case involving employment on Johnson Island, with somewhat similar facts and the same result, see *Appeal of John A. Purkins* (1984) (CCH CALIFORNIA TAX REPORTS, ¶ 15-110.331).

In *Appeal of Albert L. and Anna D. Tambini* (1984) (CCH CALIFORNIA TAX REPORTS, ¶ 15-110.339), the taxpayer spent about a year on an assignment of "indefinite" duration in Spain, with an agreement that his employer would transfer him back to California upon completion of the assignment. The BOE held that he was a California resident during the period involved.

In *Appeal of Harold L. and Wanda G. Benedict* (1982) (CCH CALIFORNIA TAX REPORTS, ¶ 15-110.339), the taxpayer was an airline flight engineer. He was transferred by his employer to an Australian base station, where he remained for about ten months and then returned to California. Although he retained close connections with California, he contended that he was no longer a California resident because he did not intend to return to California. The BOE held that he was a California resident throughout the period involved.

In *Appeal of Nelson and Doris DeAmicis* (1982) (CCH CALIFORNIA TAX REPORTS, ¶ 15-110.89), the taxpayer worked on Ascension Island for a year in 1976 and 1977. He argued that he had established residence there after he and his wife had agreed to a trial separation. However, he did not sever his principal personal and family California connections and he did not establish connections with Ascension Island. The BOE held that he was a California resident during the period involved.

In *Appeal of Pierre E.G. and Nicole Salinger* (1980) (CCH CALIFORNIA TAX REPORTS, ¶ 15-110.333), the taxpayer spent about a year on a business assignment in Europe, but maintained many close connections with California. The BOE cited some of the cases discussed above, and held that the taxpayer remained a California resident during the period involved. Also, to the same effect, see *Appeal of David C. and Livia P. Wensley* (1981) (CCH CALIFORNIA TAX REPORTS, ¶15-110.864); in this case the taxpayer spent 18 months on a business assignment in Germany, in a situation generally similar to the *Salinger* case. See also *Appeal of Robert J. Addington, Jr.* (1982) (CCH CALIFORNIA TAX REPORTS, ¶15-110.867), involving a one-year stay in England on an assignment that was expected to last for two or three years. Also, see *Appeal of Russell R. Stephens, Jr.* (1985) (CCH CALIFORNIA TAX REPORTS, ¶15-110.3351), where the tax-payer spent 18 months on a work assignment in Saudi Arabia.

In *Appeal of Robert J. and Kyung Y. Olsen* (1980) (CCH CALIFORNIA TAX REPORTS, ¶15-110.382), the taxpayer had a work assignment in Iran from December 1974 to December 1976. His wife and five children stayed in their California home while he was away. Although he spent 90% of the year 1976 in Iran, the BOE held that he was outside the state for temporary or transitory purposes and was a California resident throughout the period.

In *Appeal of Alexander B. and Margaret E. Salton* (1977) (CCH CALIFORNIA TAX REPORTS, ¶15-110.336), the taxpayer spent about two years on a job assignment in Japan. The BOE cited the *Broadhurst* case, discussed below, at some length, and held that the taxpayer was a California resident throughout the period involved.

In *Appeal of William and Mary Louise Oberholtzer* (1976) (CCH CALIFORNIA TAX REPORTS, ¶15-110.38), the taxpayer was a California engineer who worked in France for approximately eighteen months under a contract with his employer for that period. He kept a home and a car in California, and left a daughter there to finish her schooling. Although he was treated as a resident of France under French law, the BOE held that he was a California resident during the years in question.

In *Appeal of David J. and Amanda Broadhurst* (1976) (CCH CALIFORNIA TAX REPORTS, ¶15-110.335), the taxpayer worked for the United Nations in Argentina from April 1971 to December 1972. His family stayed in the house they owned in California. The BOE cited some of the cases discussed above and held that he remained a California resident in 1971. To the same effect, see *Appeal of Wilbert L. and Doris Penfold* (1986) (CCH CALIFORNIA TAX REPORTS, ¶15-110.318); in this case the taxpayer worked at numerous locations outside California for 30 years, usually remaining at each site for approximately one year.

In *Appeal of Malcolm A. Coffman* (1976) (CCH CALIFORNIA TAX REPORTS, ¶15-110.381), the taxpayer spent five months in Australia in 1970 on a short-term assignment with the idea of possibly returning later for a long-term assignment. He arranged for a long-term assignment shortly after his return to California, and went to Australia again early in 1971. The BOE held that he was a California resident throughout 1970.

In *Appeal of Anthony V. and Beverly Zupanovich* (1976) (CCH CALIFORNIA TAX REPORTS, ¶15-110.334), the taxpayer worked from December 1967 to February 1971 as a tugboat seaman in the Vietnam war zone. The BOE held that he was a California resident in 1968 and 1969, noting that, "although appellant's absence turned out to be rather lengthy, his family life, his social life, and much of his financial life remained centered in California throughout the years in question." The BOE's opinion dis-cusses the significance of "connections," and indicates that the connections main-tained by a taxpayer "are important both as a measure of the benefits and protection that the taxpayer has received from the laws and government of California, and also as an objective indication of whether the taxpayer entered or left this state for temporary or transitory purposes."

In *Appeal of John B. and Beverly A. Simpson* (1975) (California Tax Reports, CALIFORNIA TAX REPORTS, ¶15-110.332), an engineer was held to be a resident in 1971 although he spent the period from October 1970 to May 1972 on an assignment in Australia. In this case, the taxpayer's family stayed in California, and his assignment was originally scheduled for only one year.

• *Mixed residence of spouses/registered domestic partners—Community income*

When one spouse/registered domestic partner (RDP) is domiciled in California, works outside the state, and establishes nonresident status, while the other spouse/RDP remains a California resident, the resident spouse/RDP may be taxable on one-half of the nonresident spouse's/RDP's income because it is deemed to be community income. See cases to this effect cited at ¶239. (However, as explained at ¶239, in case of a permanent separation of the spouses/RDPs, their earnings are separate income; in this event the resident spouse/RDP would not be required to report any of the nonresident spouse's/RDP's earnings.)

• *Seamen held to be California residents*

In *Appeal of Charles F. Varn* (1977) (CCH CALIFORNIA TAX REPORTS, ¶15-110.708), the taxpayer was a merchant seaman on a ship that never called at California ports. On June 8, 1971, he married a California resident who continued to live in California and who filed a separate California income tax return for 1971. The BOE held that the taxpayer acquired a California domicile when he married, and that he was a California resident for the remainder of the year.

In *Appeal of Olav Valderhaug* (1954) (CCH CALIFORNIA TAX REPORTS, ¶15-110.26), the BOE held that a seaman who was in a California port three months of the year was a resident because California was the state with which he had the closest connection during the year. The seaman's wife and children lived in California for the full year. See also cases involving similar situations of merchant seamen decided by the BOE in later years, particularly *Appeal of Fernandez* (1971) (CCH CALIFORNIA TAX REPORTS, ¶15-110.70), *Appeal of Haring* (1975) (CCH CALIFORNIA TAX REPORTS, ¶15-110.703), *Appeal of Miller* (1975) (CCH CALIFORNIA TAX REPORTS, ¶15-110.704), *Appeal of Laude* (1976) (CCH CALIFORNIA TAX REPORTS, ¶15-110.707), and *Appeal of Estill William Fairchild* (1983) (CCH CALIFORNIA TAX REPORTS, ¶15-110.7092); the BOE held in each case that the taxpayer was domiciled in California and was outside the state for only a temporary or transitory purpose.

• *Seamen not California residents*

In *Appeal of John Jacobs* (1985) (CCH CALIFORNIA TAX REPORTS, ¶15-115.653), the taxpayer was an unmarried sea captain who was assigned by his employer to operations in the Persian Gulf. Although he had a California driver's license and some other connections with California, he had no home or business interests in the state. The BOE held that he was not a California resident, because his connections with California were insignificant, even though he had closer connections with California than elsewhere.

Another case holding that a merchant seaman was *not* a California resident was *Appeal of Thomas J. Tuppein* (1976) (CCH CALIFORNIA TAX REPORTS, ¶15-115.652). The taxpayer worked exclusively for California shipping companies, and was assumed to be domiciled in California. Although he was in California frequently for a few days between voyages, he spent a total of less than one month a year in the state. On the other hand, he spent longer periods in foreign countries and in Hawaii, and he maintained bank accounts and owned real estate in such locations. The BOE concluded that his closest connections were not with California and that he did not receive "sufficient benefits from the laws and government of California to warrant his classification as a resident."

In *Appeal of Richard W. Vohs* (1973) (CCH CALIFORNIA TAX REPORTS, ¶15-115.651), the BOE held that a merchant seaman was *not* a California resident despite the fact that his closest connections were with California. The taxpayer had been born and raised in California, was domiciled in the state, voted in the state, had a California driver's license, and had other connections in the state. The BOE held that the taxpayer was outside California for other than a temporary or transitory purpose,

¶105

and commented that "a taxpayer need not establish that he became a resident of any particular state or country in order to sustain his position that he was not a resident of California."

• *Resident though domiciled elsewhere*

In *Appeal of German A. Posada* (1987) (CCH CALIFORNIA TAX REPORTS, ¶ 15-110.453), the taxpayer was apparently a Colombian domiciliary, but was found to be a California resident for jeopardy assessment purposes. The taxpayer spent considerable time in California during the years at issue, obtaining a California driver's license, registering a car and boat there, and, after living for a time with friends in the state, prepaying six months rent on a California apartment. The BOE conceded that the taxpayer had "few contacts" with California, and that many of the usual indicia of residency, such as voter registration and bank accounts, were lacking, but concluded that this was evidence of the taxpayer's "nomadic nature" rather than of nonresidency in California.

In *Appeal of George D. Yaron* (1976) (CCH CALIFORNIA TAX REPORTS, ¶ 205-567), the taxpayer had substantial business interests and other connections in both California and Vietnam. Although he was considered a resident of Vietnam under the laws of that country and was assumed not to be domiciled in California, the BOE held that he was a California resident.

In *Appeal of Mary G. Steiner* (1954) (CCH CALIFORNIA TAX REPORTS, ¶ 15-110.26), the BOE held that an individual who resided in California for a substantial portion of the year was a California resident although it appeared that her domicile was in Florida. The individual involved owned property in Utah, had bank accounts in Utah and Florida, voted in Florida, paid property taxes there under a "resident" classification, and contributed to a church there. She rented a furnished apartment in California on a month-to-month basis and spent about half her time in the state.

A somewhat similar situation was involved in *Appeal of Lucille F. Betts* (1954) (CCH CALIFORNIA TAX REPORTS, ¶ 15-110.26). The individual in this case was a widow who claimed residence in New Jersey, where she owned property, maintained bank accounts, voted, etc. She lived in a hotel in California and, because of transportation difficulties, did not return to New Jersey for a period of years during World War II. The BOE held that she was a California resident, relying on the nine-month presumption discussed above.

• *Substantial connections with California*

In *Appeal of Beldon R. and Mildred Katleman* (1980) (CCH CALIFORNIA TAX REPORTS, ¶ 15-110.401), the taxpayer owned and managed a Las Vegas hotel and casino for several years until it burned down in 1960. From 1960 to 1970 he was engaged in efforts to reconstruct or develop the property. In 1962 he purchased a large home in California. Thereafter he spent a considerable amount of time and developed substantial connections in California. Although he maintained important connections in Nevada throughout the years involved, the BOE held that he was a California resident in 1962 and subsequent years.

In *Appeal of Jerald L. and Joan Katleman* (1976) (CCH CALIFORNIA TAX REPORTS, ¶ 15-110.223), the taxpayer had important ties with Illinois, including voting and filing state income tax returns there. The BOE held that he was a California resident, on the basis of a closer connection with California and also upon the fact the he "enjoyed substantial benefits and protection from the laws and government of California."

In *George and Elia Whittell v. Franchise Tax Board* (1964) (CCH CALIFORNIA TAX REPORTS, ¶ 15-110.261), decided by the California Court of Appeal, it was held that the taxpayers were California residents, even though they had a large home in Nevada, voted there, filed federal tax returns there, and had many other connections with that state. The taxpayers spent most of their time in California and had important family and business connections in the state.

In *Appeal of Ada E. Wrigley* (1955) (CCH CALIFORNIA TAX REPORTS, ¶ 15-110.26), the BOE held that the taxpayer was a resident of California despite these factors: important business interests in Chicago; maintenance of a home and club membership there; exercise of her voting privilege there; principal banking activity there; and maintenance of three other large homes outside of California. The BOE indicated: "Long continued preference for (spending her time in) California, when coupled with her extensive and long continued financial interests within the state, the burial of her husband in California, the retention of two large homes within the state and the exchange of her large apartment in Chicago for smaller quarters there, convinces us that . . . California had become her principal place of abode."

• *Nonresidency found despite substantial California connections*

In *Appeal of Stephen D. Bragg* (2003) (CCH CALIFORNIA TAX REPORTS, ¶ 15-110.266) the taxpayer had homes and business activities in both California and Arizona, had personal bank accounts in California, had vehicles registered in California, and obtained all of his professional services in California. In spite of these substantial contacts with California, the BOE determined that the taxpayer was a resident of Arizona, as he spent the majority of his time during the taxable year at his residence in Arizona, conducted the majority of his business and full-time employment in Arizona, and had no real intent to return to California to reside.

In *Corbett v. Franchise Tax Board* (1985) (CCH CALIFORNIA TAX REPORTS, ¶ 15-110.607), the taxpayers maintained important business, social, and other connections with Illinois, including voter registration and drivers' licenses there. Nonetheless, the BOE held that they were California residents because in the years involved they spent 6$^1/_2$ to 8$^1/_2$ months of each year in California, owned a substantial California home, and had important social and family connections with the state. However, a court of appeal reversed the BOE's decision, and held that the taxpayers were not California residents.

In *Fred C. Klemp v. Franchise Tax Board* (1975) (CCH CALIFORNIA TAX REPORTS, ¶ 15-110.557), the California Court of Appeal overruled the BOE and held that the taxpayers were not California residents, despite the fact that they owned a home in California and spent more time in California than they spent in the state of their domicile, Illinois. The court mentioned several factors that showed a closer connection with Illinois than with California. These included: voter registration, automobile registration, drivers' licenses, business offices and accounting, investment counselor, doctor, dentist, church affiliation, safe deposit box, all in Illinois.

• *Importance of supporting evidence*

In *Appeal of Raymond H. and Margaret R. Berner* (2001) (CCH CALIFORNIA TAX REPORTS, ¶ 15-115.75), the BOE overturned an FTB determination that the taxpayers were California residents on the basis of affidavits and declarations of friends, family, and Nevada professionals stating that the taxpayers changed their domicile from California to Nevada. The taxpayers owned homes in both Nevada and California, and appeals in previous years had resulted in determinations that the taxpayers were California residents. The FTB determined that the taxpayers were California residents during the tax years at issue on the basis of the taxpayers' California country club memberships, credit card records, California doctors' office visits, weekly home maintenance service records for their California home, and bank records. However, the BOE determined that the affidavits and declarations from friends, family, and Nevada professionals (including the postmaster for the Nevada town of residence) were sufficient to overcome the FTB's evidence.

In *Appeal of C.I. Schermer* (1961) (CCH CALIFORNIA TAX REPORTS, ¶ 15-110.604), the BOE sustained the findings of the FTB that the taxpayer became a resident in 1952, on the basis of bank accounts opened, credit applications filed, and the renting of an apartment. Taxpayer offered oral argument in opposition, but failed to supply affidavits of business associates or relatives concerning the amount of time spent in

California. Since the taxpayer was an attorney, the BOE noted that it was reasonable to assume he would have maintained detailed records of his time as a basis for charging clients, and he failed to introduce these records in support of his position.

• *Indefinite intentions regarding California stay*

Appeal of George W. and Gertrude S. Davis (1964) (CCH CALIFORNIA TAX REPORTS, ¶ 15-110.505) involved the intent of the taxpayers as a factor in determining residence. When the taxpayers initially came to California, they were uncertain whether, or when, they would depart. Accordingly, they were considered to have come for an indefinite period and were held to be residents for purposes of the California income tax.

• *"Nonresident alien" was California resident*

In *Appeal of Riad Ghali* (1971) (CCH CALIFORNIA TAX REPORTS, ¶ 15-110.263), an Egyptian citizen was held to be a California resident despite the fact that he was classified as a nonresident alien for federal tax purposes. During the period in question, the taxpayer had no lawfully permanent status in the United States but was allowed to remain in this country because he was in disfavor with the Egyptian government and was afraid to return to that country. Nevertheless, he was held to be a California resident on the basis of his continued residence in the state over a period of years and, accordingly, was taxed on gain from sale of oil and gas leases in Mexico.

• *Professors on out-of-state assignments*

In *Appeal of Thomas K. and Gail G. Boehme* (1985) (CCH CALIFORNIA TAX REPORTS, ¶ 15-110.783), the BOE held that a California university professor and his wife remained California residents throughout a 22-month assignment to a university study center in Egypt. The taxpayers rented out their California home on a month-to-month rather than a long-term basis, continued to claim the California homeowner's property tax exemption for it, left their family car in California, kept various California bank and charge accounts, and maintained a number of other contacts with California during their stay in Egypt. To the same effect, see *Appeal of Mortimer and Catherine Chambers* (1987) (CCH CALIFORNIA TAX REPORTS, ¶ 15-110.783), involving a university professor who taught in Germany for two years.

Appeal of William F. and June A. Massy (1972) (CCH CALIFORNIA TAX REPORTS, ¶ 204-755) involved the residence status of a Stanford University professor who spent a year in Pennsylvania as a visiting professor. The taxpayer moved to Pennsylvania with the understanding that a permanent position would become available there. The BOE held that the taxpayer was not a California resident during the period in question.

• *Airline pilots transferred to California*

Appeal of Warren L. and Marlys A. Christianson (1972) (CCH CALIFORNIA TAX REPORTS, ¶ 15-110.20) involved the residence status of an airline pilot (and family) in 1967 and 1968. He was transferred in 1966 from Texas to California to fly on military charter flights from California to Southeast Asia. Although he bought a home in California, he maintained business interests in Texas and other ties to that state. He argued that his presence in California was temporary because it was related to the uncertain duration of the Vietnam conflict. The BOE held that the taxpayer was a resident of California, although still domiciled in Texas. The BOE's opinion discusses the distinction between "residence" and "domicile," and comments that, "oftentimes in our mobile society they are not the same." See also the 1972 and 1973 decisions of the BOE in *Appeal of Donald E. and Betty J. MacInnes* (CCH CALIFORNIA TAX REPORTS, ¶ 15-110.201) and *Appeal of Henry C. Berger* (CCH CALIFORNIA TAX REPORTS, ¶ 15-110.202), involving other pilots transferred to California during the same time period; these taxpayers were also held to be California residents, although they were registered voters in other states and had other ties to those states.

• *Federal civil service employees*

In *Appeal of Paul Peringer* (1980) (CCH CALIFORNIA TAX REPORTS, ¶15-110.265), the taxpayer was a federal civil service employee who had been transferred several times during his government career. Although he had been stationed in California for several years before and during the taxable years, he argued that his job location was not "permanent" and also challenged California's constitutional power to tax a federal employee domiciled in another state. The BOE's holding that he was a California resident, and this was affirmed by the California Court of Appeal. To the same effect, see *Appeal of George M. and Georgia M. Webster* (1977) (CCH CALIFORNIA TAX REPORTS, ¶15-110.264), involving a taxpayer who had been a federal employee in California for 16 years.

• *Professional sports*

In *Appeal of Jimmy J. Childs* (1983) (CCH CALIFORNIA TAX REPORTS, ¶15-110.211), the taxpayer was a professional football player with the St. Louis Cardinals. During the year in question (1979), he spent eight months in Missouri and four months in California, where he stayed with his parents during the off-season. He filed a nonresident Missouri return, in which he stated that his home address was in California. The BOE held that he was a resident of California.

Appeal of Richard and Carolyn Selma (1977) (CCH CALIFORNIA TAX REPORTS, ¶15-110.212) involved a native Californian, admittedly domiciled in California, who played baseball for the Philadelphia Phillies. During the off-season he worked in California as a part-time bartender. He filed nonresident Pennsylvania tax returns in which he stated that he was a California resident and had numerous connections with California. The BOE held that he was a California resident. To the same effect, see *Appeal of Robert D. and Susan Owchinko* (1985) (CCH CALIFORNIA TAX REPORTS, ¶15-110.213); in this case the taxpayer played for the Cleveland Indians in the year involved and also played winter baseball in Puerto Rico. See also *Appeal of Joe and Gloria Morgan* (1985) (CCH CALIFORNIA TAX REPORTS, ¶15-110.213), in which the taxpayer played for the Houston Astros and kept a house or apartment in Houston.

• *Effect of homeowner's property tax exemption*

In *Appeal of Robert and Nancy D. Hanley* (1981) (CCH CALIFORNIA TAX REPORTS, ¶15-110.863), the taxpayer-husband spent about eight months in Florida and only 137 days in California during the year involved. He owned a home in Florida and managed a business there. However, his wife remained in California, where the couple also had business and other interests and where they claimed a California home as their permanent residence for purposes of the homeowner's property tax exemption. The BOE held that they were California residents.

• *Factors affecting residency*

As the illustrative cases summarized above indicate, there is no easy rule of thumb for determining when an individual is a California resident. All of the surrounding circumstances must be considered in making a residency determination. An FTB publication entitled "Guidelines for Determining Resident Status" (FTB Pub. 1031) provides the following list of some factors that should be considered, with a cautionary note that the list is only a partial one:

— the amount of time you spend in California versus amount of time you spend outside California;

— the location(s) of your spouse and children;

— the location of your principal residence;

— where you were issued your driver's license;

— where your vehicles are registered;

— where you maintain your professional licenses;

— where you are registered to vote;

¶105

— the locations of banks where you maintain accounts;

— the locations of your doctors, dentists, accountants, and attorneys;

— the locations of the church, temple, or mosque, professional associations, and social and country clubs of which you are a member;

— the locations of your real property and investments;

— the permanence of your work assignments in California; and

— the location of your social ties.

The State Board of Equalization has provided an even more extensive list of factors in *Appeal of Stephen D. Bragg* (2003) (CCH CALIFORNIA TAX REPORTS, ¶ 15-110.266).

• *Court action to determine residence status*

A person who is alleged to be a California resident can obtain a determination of the fact of his or her residence by the Superior Court by first protesting a notice of proposed deficiency issued by the FTB (¶ 704). If the action of the FTB is unfavorable, he or she must then appeal to the BOE (¶ 705). If the BOE also rules unfavorably, an action must then be brought in the Superior Court to determine the issue of residency. All of this can be done without first paying the underlying tax.

• *Special rule for trust beneficiaries*

A resident beneficiary of a trust is presumed to continue to be a resident when he or she receives an accumulation distribution from the trust within 12 months after leaving the state and returns to the state within 12 months after receiving the distribution (¶ 605). (Sec. 17745, Rev. & Tax. Code)

• *California-federal comparison*

Although in some respects the California rules relating to residence are similar to federal provisions regarding resident aliens, the two laws deal with quite different situations. Therefore, no attempt is made here to compare them.

¶106 Returns—Who Required to File—Forms

Law: Secs. 18409, 18501-34, 18622-23, 18635.5, 19582.5; Reg. 19524, 18 CCR (CCH CALIFORNIA TAX REPORTS, ¶ 15-260, 15-265, 15-270, 15-275, 89-102, 89-112).

Comparable Federal: Secs. 6011-14, 6034A, 6102 (CCH U.S. MASTER TAX GUIDE ¶ 510, 2501).

California Forms: Form 540 (California Resident Income Tax Return), Form 540 2EZ (California Resident Income Tax Return), Form 540NR (California Nonresident or Part-Year Resident Income Tax Return), Form 540X (Amended Individual Income Tax Return), Form 541 (California Fiduciary Income Tax Return), Form 565 (Partnership Return of Income), Form 568 (Limited Liability Company Return of Income).

For the 2016 tax year, California law requires that an income tax return be filed for every individual who has income in excess of the following amounts (Sec. 18501, Rev. & Tax. Code):

2016 Filing Thresholds

On 12/31/16, the taxpayer's filing status was:	and on 12/31/16, the taxpayer's age was[6]:	California Gross Income[1]			California Adjusted Gross Income[2]		
		Dependents			Dependents		
		0	1	2 or more	0	1	2 or more
Single or Head of household[3]	Under 65	16,597	28,064	36,664	13,278	24,745	33,345
	65 or older	22,147	30,747	37,627	18,828	27,428	34,308
Married/RDP filing jointly or filing separately[4]	Under 65 (both spouses/RDPs)	33,197	44,664	53,264	26,558	38,025	46,625
	65 or older (one spouse/RDP)	38,747	47,347	54,227	32,108	40,708	47,588
	65 or older (both spouses/RDPs)	44,297	52,897	59,777	37,658	46,258	53,138

Qualifying widow(er)[3]	Under 65	N/A	28,064	36,664	N/A	24,745	33,345
	65 or older	N/A	30,747	37,627	N/A	27,428	34,308
Dependent of another person Any filing status	Any age	More than your standard deduction[5]					

[1] **California gross income** is all income received from all sources in the form of money, goods, property, and services that are not exempt from tax. Gross income does not include any adjustments or deductions.

[2] **California adjusted gross income** is federal adjusted gross income from all sources reduced or increased by all California income adjustments.

[3] See ¶114.

[4] The income of both spouses or registered domestic partners (RDPs) must be combined; both spouses or RDPs may be required to file a return even if only one spouse or RDP had income over the amounts listed.

[5] Use the California Standard Deduction Worksheet for Dependents in the 2016California Resident Booklet to compute the standard deduction.

[6] If the taxpayer's 65th birthday is on January 1, 2017, she or he is considered to be age 65 on December 31, 2016.

For filing threshold purposes (1) single persons include taxpayers filing as heads of households and qualifying widowers and (2) married couples/registered domestic partners (RDPs) include couples and RDPs filing either jointly or separately. (Sec. 18501, Rev. & Tax. Code)

CCH Caution Note: Filing Thresholds Not Sole Criteria for Filing Requirement

The Franchise Tax Board (FTB) has taken the position that a taxpayer must file a personal income tax return and pay tax if a tax is due under the tax rate tables or under another code section even if the taxpayer's gross income and adjusted gross income (AGI) are both below the filing threshold amounts listed above. Although California law establishes thresholds that require an individual taxpayer to file a return, it does not state that an individual taxpayer does not have to file a return if the taxpayer's gross income or adjusted gross income is below those thresholds.

Instances in which this issue may arise involve married and registered domestic partner (RDP) taxpayers using the married filing separately filing status, when one spouse/RDP has primarily noncommunity property separate income and the other spouse/RDP has little or no taxable income. Additionally, there are other situations, such as those involving the 2.5% tax on early distributions from a retirement plan, where FTB forms and instructions currently require that a return be filed, even though the filing thresholds are not met. (*Technical Advice Memorandum 2008-1*, California Franchise Tax Board, November 20, 2008, CCH CALIFORNIA TAX REPORTS, ¶404-998)

Form 540 must also be filed if any of the following taxes are due:

— a tax on lump-sum distributions (¶206);

— a tax on a qualified retirement plan, including IRAs (¶206) or Archer MSAs (¶247);

— a tax for certain children with investment income in excess of $1,900 (¶118);

— alternative minimum tax (¶117);

— recapture taxes;

— deferred tax on certain installment obligations; and

— a tax on an accumulation distribution from a trust (¶605). (Instructions, Form 540)

Certain fiduciaries (except for fiduciaries acting on behalf of certain grantor trusts—see ¶608) must file a California return. A fiduciary acting on behalf of an individual must file if:

— the individual is single and has adjusted gross income over $8,000,

— the individual is married and has adjusted gross income over $16,000, or

— the gross income of the individual exceeds $10,000 ($20,000, if married). (Sec. 18505, Rev. & Tax. Code)

¶106

A fiduciary acting on behalf of an estate or trust must file if:
— the estate or trust owes alternative minimum tax,
— the estate has net income from all sources over $1,000,
— the trust has net income from all sources over $100, or
— the gross income from all sources of the estate or trust exceeds $10,000.
(Sec. 18506, Rev. & Tax. Code)

A fiduciary must also file a California return for *every* decedent for the year of death, and for all prior years in which the decedent should have filed returns but failed to do so. (Reg. 18505-4, 18 CCR) The return must be made by the decedent's executor, administrator, or other person charged with the property of the decedent. (Sec. 18505.3, Rev. & Tax. Code)

An individual for whom a federal dependent exemption may be claimed must file a separate state income tax return if the individual's gross income from all sources exceeds the amount of the basic standard deduction allowed to the individual under federal law. (Sec. 18501, Rev. & Tax. Code)

Married couples, and registered domestic partners (RDPs) (see ¶114, ¶119) may elect to file separate returns or a joint return. (Sec. 18521, Rev. & Tax. Code) For a discussion of joint returns, see ¶107.

Although partnerships are not taxed as such, they are required to file returns in some cases (¶622). A charitable trust is subject to special reporting requirements (¶606). See ¶607 regarding returns of employees' trusts.

Every common trust fund for which a trust company acts must file a return, regardless of the amount of gross or net income. (Sec. 17677, Rev. & Tax. Code) The fiduciary return form (Form 541) is used for this purpose.

• *Return forms*

The principal return forms are as follows:

Resident individuals	540, 540 2EZ
Nonresident and part-year residents	540NR, 540NR Short
Amended individual return	540X
Estates and trusts	541
Partnerships	565
Limited liability companies (LLCs) classified as partnerships and single member LLCs that are disregarded and treated as a sole proprietorship	568

A copy of the federal return and schedules must accompany the 540NR. It must also accompany the 540 if the taxpayer attached any federal schedules other than Schedule A or B to the federal return.

CCH Practice Tip: Protective Claims for Refund

Taxpayers filing a claim for refund on Form 540X for a tax year for which litigation or a final determination by the IRS is pending must write "PROTECTIVE CLAIM" in red ink at the top of their Form 540X. In addition, they must specify the pending litigation or reference the federal determination on Side 2, Part II, of Form 540X, so that the Franchise Tax Board can properly process their claims.

Caution Note: Attaching Letters to Forms Inadvisable

The FTB advises tax practitioners against attaching letters to their clients' income tax returns, stating that in most cases tax practitioners will get faster results by calling the FTB's Tax Practitioner Hotline at (916) 845-7057 to ask specific questions regarding their clients' tax returns or other issues requiring timely action. The Tax Practitioner Hotline is open from 8 a.m. to 5 p.m., Monday through Friday. Questions may also be sent by fax to (916) 845-9300, 24 hours a day, seven days a week.

Often letters attached to returns are not answered until they have traveled through the FTB's entire return processing system and are ultimately rerouted to the FTB's Taxpayer Service Center for a reply, which may take many weeks. Also, letters are sometimes inadvertently filed without a reply. (*Tax News*, California Franchise Tax Board, July/ August 2005)

• *Use of Form 540 2EZ*

Taxpayers who are single, married/registered domestic partner (RDP) joint filers, heads of household, or qualifying widow(er)s and who are not blind may use Form 540 2EZ if, for the taxable year to be reflected in the return, the taxpayer:

— was a full-year resident;

— had income only from wages, salaries, tips, interest, dividends, pensions, taxable scholarships and fellowship grants (only if reported on Form W-2), capital gains from mutual funds (reported on Form 1099-DIV, box 2a only), unemployment compensation reported on Form 1099-G, paid family leave, U.S. Social Security benefits, and tier 1 and tier 2 railroad retirement benefits;

— does not claim any itemized deductions, is not required to use a modified standard deduction for dependents, and does not make any adjustments to income;

— does not claim any tax credits other than the California earned income tax credit, the personal exemption credit, the senior exemption credit, up to three dependent exemption credits, and the nonrefundable renter's credit;

— does not pay any tax other than withholding shown on Form W-2 or Form 1099-R; and

— had total income consisting of items listed above of $100,000 or less if using the single or head of household filing status or $200,000 or less if using the married/RDP filing joint or qualifying widow(er) filing status.

Taxpayers who can be claimed as a dependent by another taxpayer cannot file Form 540 2EZ if they have dependents of their own or if their total income is $13,679 or less if single, $27,408 if married/RDP filing jointly or qualifying widow(er), or $19,408 if head of household.

• *Form for nonresidents—Full or part year*

A person who was a nonresident for any part of the year must file a return on Form 540NR or 540NR Short, regardless of status at the end of the year. Any change in residence status should be fully explained on the return or in an attached statement.

A nonresident or part-year resident taxpayer who is a single or joint filer, head of household, or qualifying widower may qualify to file Form 540NR Short as long as none of the following apply:

— the taxpayer or the taxpayer's spouse/RDP is 65 or older;

— the taxpayer claims for than five dependents;

— the taxpayer's total income is more than $100,000;

— the taxpayer has interest income from U.S. obligations, U.S. treasury bills, notes, bonds, or other sources that are taxable for federal purposes and exempt for state purposes;

— the taxpayer qualifies for the California nonrefundable child and dependent care expenses credit;

— the taxpayer has withholding from Form 592-B, *Resident and Nonresident Withholding Tax Statement*, or Form 593, *Real Estate Withholding Tax Statement*; or

— the taxpayer made estimated tax payments or has an estimated tax transfer available from 2015.

• *Reproduction of forms*

Most Franchise Tax Board (FTB) forms may be reproduced, along with their supplemental schedules, and the reproductions filed in lieu of the corresponding official forms. Details of specifications and conditions for reproducing forms, and for computer-prepared forms, are outlined in the FTB's publication *Annual Requirements and Specifications for the Development and Use of Substitute, Scannable, and Reproduced Tax Forms*, which may be obtained on the FTB's website.

• *Whole-dollar reporting*

California law is the same as federal law with respect to whole-dollar reporting (sometimes referred to as "cents-less" reporting). If any amount required to be shown on a return, statement, or other document is other than a whole dollar, the fractional part of a dollar may be rounded to the nearest dollar; that is, amounts under 50¢ are dropped and amounts from 50¢ to 99¢ are increased to the next dollar. (Sec. 18623, Rev. & Tax. Code)

• *Reporting federal changes*

A California taxpayer filing an amended federal return is required to file an amended California return within six months after filing the federal return if the change increases the amount of California tax due. Also, if any change or correction is made in gross income or deductions by federal authorities, or if gross income or deductions are changed by renegotiation of government contracts or subcontracts, such changes must be reported to the FTB within six months after the final determination of the federal change or correction or renegotiation if any such change increases the amount of California tax due. The "date of a final federal determination" is defined as the date that each adjustment or resolution resulting from an IRS examination is assessed pursuant to IRC Sec. 6203. (Sec. 18622, Rev. & Tax. Code)

The federal determination is presumed to be correct unless the taxpayer overcomes the burden of establishing that the determination is erroneous. This principle has been approved in many appeals decided by the State Board of Equalization (BOE) over the years.

• *Effect of failure to report federal changes*

Failure to comply with the requirements for reporting federal changes may result in extending the statute of limitations on deficiency assessments (¶710).

• *Effect of presumed correctness of federal report*

In *Norman P. Calhoun et al. v. Franchise Tax Board* (1978) (CCH CALIFORNIA TAX REPORTS, ¶89-066.20), the FTB assessed California tax on the basis of a federal audit report that showed an understatement of gross income. The federal tax was approved in a U.S. District Court case. Subsequently, the California Supreme Court applied the legal theory of "collateral estoppel" to justify the imposition of the California tax, based on the similarity of California and federal definitions of "gross income."

In *Appeal of M. Hunter and Martha J. Brown* (1974) (CCH CALIFORNIA TAX REPORTS, ¶89-206.6792), the BOE held that the FTB—not the taxpayer—must bear the burden of proof where a fraud penalty is proposed based on a federal audit report. The BOE upheld the assessment of California tax because of the presumed correctness of the federal determination, but held that the same presumption does not apply to a fraud penalty. However, the BOE has held in several cases that the presumption of federal correctness does apply to the 5% negligence penalty (¶712); that is, the burden of proof with respect to the negligence penalty is on the taxpayer. See *Appeal of Casper W. and Svea Smith* (1976) (CCH CALIFORNIA TAX REPORTS, ¶89-168.25).

¶107 Joint Returns

Law: Secs. 17045-46, 18521-22, 18531.5, 18533-34, 19006 (CCH CALIFORNIA TAX REPORTS, ¶15-310, 89-102, 89-210).

Comparable Federal: Secs. 2, 66, 6013, 6015 (CCH U.S. MASTER TAX GUIDE ¶152, 156, 162).

Individuals, including spouses in same-sex married couples, must generally use the same filing status for California purposes as they use federally. However, registered domestic partners also have the option of filing California joint returns (¶114). (Sec. 18521, Rev. & Tax. Code) See ¶119 for details.

• *Joint and several liability of spouses*

Although generally spouses are jointly and severally liable for taxes (including penalties and interest) resulting from filing a joint return, a spouse's liability may be limited as a result of a court decree, an election approved by the FTB for separate liability, the granting of innocent spouse relief by the FTB, or other equitable relief granted by the FTB. (Sec. 19006, Rev. & Tax. Code) (*Innocent Joint Filer Law Summary*, California Franchise Tax Board, March 25, 2010, CCH California Tax Reports, ¶405-147)

CCH Comment: Innocent Registered Domestic Partner Relief

As registered domestic partners (RDPs) and former RDPs must generally be treated as married taxpayers for California personal income tax purposes (see ¶119), the innocent spouse provisions discussed below apply equally to innocent RDPs. (FTB Pub. 737, Tax Information for Registered Domestic Partners)

Court decree: Subject to certain conditions and limitations, the joint and several liability for tax on the aggregate income in a joint return may be revised in a court proceeding for dissolution of the marriage. The court order becomes effective when the FTB is served with or acknowledges receipt of the order. A "tax revision clearance certificate" must be obtained from the FTB if the gross income exceeds $150,000 or the tax liability that a spouse is relieved of exceeds $7,500. (Sec. 19006, Rev. & Tax. Code)

Separate liability: An individual who filed a joint return may elect separate liability if the individual is no longer married to, is legally separated from, or for at least for the prior 12 months has been living apart from the person with whom the joint return was filed. This election must be made within two years after the FTB begins collection activities with respect to the individual. (Sec. 18533, Rev. & Tax. Code)

An individual making this election has the burden of proving his or her portion of any deficiency. An election may be partially or completely invalidated if (1) at the time of signing the return, the individual had actual knowledge of any item giving rise to a deficiency or portion thereof or (2) any assets were transferred between joint filers as part of a fraudulent scheme or to avoid tax. (Sec. 18533, Rev. & Tax. Code)

For separate liability purposes, an item giving rise to a deficiency must generally be allocated in the manner it would have been allocated if the taxpayers had filed separate returns. However, an item otherwise allocable to one individual may be allocated to the other individual to the extent the item gave rise to a tax benefit to the other individual. Also, the FTB may provide for a different manner of allocation in the case of fraud on the part of one or both of the individuals. (Sec. 18533, Rev. & Tax. Code)

Practice Tip: Credits and Refunds

A taxpayer seeking innocent spouse relief may not claim a credit or refund outside the general statute of limitations period as a result of his or her election to have his or her liability recomputed utilizing the separate income allocation method. (Sec. 18533(e), Rev. & Tax. Code)

The FTB must give notice to a joint filer of the other joint filer's election of separate liability, and the FTB must not make its determination with respect to the election earlier than 30 days after such notification. An individual who is denied a separate liability election may appeal that determination to the State Board of Equalization (BOE). (Sec. 18533, Rev. & Tax. Code)

Federal law contains comparable provisions for electing separate liability.

CCH Example: Separate Liability Election

Joe and Jennifer Jackson, who are separated, file a joint return reporting $60,000 of wage income earned by Joe, $60,000 of wage income earned by Jennifer, and $7,000 of investment income on the couple's jointly owned assets. The FTB assesses a $400 tax deficiency for $5,000 of unreported investment income from assets held in Joe's name. Jennifer knew about a bank account in Joe's name that generated $1,000 of interest income, but she had no actual knowledge of Joe's other separate investments.

If Jennifer properly elects separate liability, she will not be liable for $320 of the tax deficiency, which is the amount attributable to the $4,000 of unreported income of which she had no actual knowledge ($400 × [$4,000 ÷ $5,000]). However, she will be liable for $80 of the tax deficiency, which is the amount attributable to the $1,000 of unreported interest income from the bank account ($400 × [$1,000 ÷ $5,000]).

Innocent spouse relief: Under both California and federal law, an innocent spouse is relieved from tax liabilities (including penalties and interest) in certain cases of wrongdoing in joint return situations. Innocent spouse relief is available if an individual establishes that

— in signing a joint return, he or she did not know or have reason to know of any understatement on the return attributable to his or her spouse, and

— it would be inequitable to hold the individual liable.

Innocent spouse relief is also available on a partial basis if the individual establishes that he or she did not know or have reason to know of the *extent* of an understatement on the return attributable to his or her spouse. (Sec. 18533, Rev. & Tax. Code)

CCH Practice Pointer: Relief Unavailable if No Return Filed

In a nonprecedential opinion, the BOE has taken the position that a taxpayer is ineligible for innocent spouse relief under the rules discussed above if the deficiency arises as a result of the failure to file a timely return rather than as a result of an understatement of income (*Appeal of Clausen* (2001) (CCH CALIFORNIA TAX REPORTS, ¶89-226.369)).

An individual seeking innocent spouse relief must elect such relief within two years after the commencement of collection activities with respect to that individual. The FTB must give notice to a joint filer of the other joint filer's election of innocent spouse relief, and the FTB must not make its determination with respect to the election earlier than 30 days after such notification. An individual who is denied an innocent spouse election may appeal that determination to the BOE. (Sec. 18533, Rev. & Tax. Code)

Unless an individual's liability has been revised by a court in a divorce proceeding, an individual who filed a joint return will automatically be granted innocent spouse relief from California personal income tax liabilities if the individual was granted relief from federal income tax liabilities under the federal innocent spouse provisions provided that the following conditions are satisfied:

— the individual requests relief under the federal innocent spouse provisions;

— the facts and circumstances that apply to the understatement and liabilities for which relief is requested are the same facts and circumstances that applied to the understatement and liabilities for which the individual was granted federal income tax relief; and

— the individual provides the FTB with a copy of the federal determination and any other supporting documentation requested by the FTB. (18533, Rev. & Tax. Code)

Within 30 days of notification from the FTB, the non-requesting spouse may provide information to the FTB indicating why the requested relief should not be granted. If, prior to the date the FTB issues its determination with respect to a request for relief, the requesting individual demonstrates to the FTB that a request for federal relief involving the same facts and circumstances has been filed with the IRS, the FTB may not deny relief until there is a final action on the federal request for relief. (Sec. 18533, Rev. & Tax. Code)

CCH Practice Pointer: Separate Liability or Innocent Spouse Relief

The "actual knowledge" standard for separate liability is narrower than the "knew or should have known" standard for innocent spouse relief. This may make separate liability available under circumstances in which innocent spouse relief is not.

Equitable relief: Furthermore, if relief is not specifically available under the separate liability provisions or the innocent spouse provisions, equitable relief may still be provided if, taking into account all the facts and circumstances, it would be inequitable to hold the individual liable. The taxpayer must demonstrate that he or she did not benefit from the income at issue (*Appeal of Clausen* (2001) (CCH CALIFORNIA TAX REPORTS, ¶ 89-226.369)).

The FTB's denial of equitable relief may be appealed to the BOE so long as a taxpayer has requested relief under either the traditional innocent spouse relief or the separate liability election subsections of the innocent spouse relief statute (*Appeal of Tyler-Griffis*, 2006-SBE-004, CCH CALIFORNIA TAX REPORTS, ¶ 404-120).

• *Effect of mixed residence status*

A nonresident joint California return is required if one spouse/RDP was a resident for the entire taxable year and the other spouse/RDP was a nonresident for all or any portion of the taxable year. However, this rule does not apply to active military personnel and their spouses/RDPs. (Sec. 18521, Rev. & Tax. Code)

• *Returns by surviving spouse/RDP*

A joint return must be filed by a surviving spouse/RDP whose spouse/RDP dies during the taxable year if this status is elected federally. In instances in which spouses/RDPs have different taxable years because of the death of either spouse/RDP, the joint return will be treated as if the taxable years of both spouses/RDPs ended on the date of closing of the surviving spouse's/RDP's taxable year. (Sec. 18521, Rev. & Tax. Code)

• *Change from separate to joint return*

Spouses/RDPs who have filed separate California and federal returns may refile on a joint California return, provided they meet certain limitations as to the time for refiling and if they refile federally. This change may be made even if all previous separate liabilities of the individuals have not been paid. (Sec. 18522, Rev. & Tax. Code)

Under both California and federal laws, a change from a joint return to separate returns is permitted only if separate returns are filed on or before the due date. (Sec. 18522, Rev. & Tax. Code)

For statute of limitations and delinquency penalty purposes, both California and federal laws provide special rules for determining the date on which a joint return is deemed to be filed in situations where one or both of the spouses/RDPs previously filed a separate return. If only one spouse/RDP previously filed a separate return, the result depends on the amount of income of the spouse/RDP who did not file a separate return. (Sec. 18522, Rev. & Tax. Code)

¶108 Returns—Time and Place for Filing

Law: Secs. 6707, 11003, Government Code; Secs. 6452.1, 18510, 18566-67, 18410, 18572, 18621.5, 18621.9, 21027, Revenue and Taxation Code; Reg. 18567, 18 CCR (CCH CALIFORNIA TAX REPORTS, ¶ 89-102, 89-106, 89-110).

Comparable Federal: Secs. 6072, 6081, 6091, 7508A (CCH U.S. MASTER TAX GUIDE ¶ 118, 119, 122, 2537).

California Forms: Form 540 (California Resident Income Tax Return), Form 540 2EZ (California Resident Income Tax Return), FTB 3519 (Payment for Automatic Extension for Individuals), FTB 3537 (Payment for Automatic Extension for Limited Liability Companies), FTB 3538 (Payment for Automatic Extension for Limited Partnerships, LLPs, and REMICs), FTB 3563 (Payment for Automatic Extension for Fiduciaries), FTB 3582 (Payment Voucher for Individual e-filed Returns), FTB 3587 (Payment Voucher for LP, LLP, and REMIC e-filed Returns), FTB 3588 (Payment Voucher for LLC e-filed Returns), FTB 8453 (California e-file Return Authorization), FTB 8453-OL (California Online e-file Return Authorization), FTB 8454 (e-file Opt-Out Record), FTB 8455 (California e-file Payment Record), FTB 8633 (California Application to Participate in the e-file Program), FTB 8879 (California e-file Signature Authorization).

• *Due dates*

As is the case with the federal return, calendar-year income tax returns are due on April 15 following the close of the calendar year. Fiscal-year returns must be filed by the 15th day of the fourth month following the close of the fiscal year. (Sec. 18566, Rev. & Tax. Code; Sec. 19001, Rev. & Tax. Code) California returns of taxpayers residing or traveling abroad are due two months later than the regular due date; that is, calendar-year returns of such taxpayers are due on June 15 (¶ 109). (Sec. 18567, Rev. & Tax. Code)

CCH Practice Tip: Emancipation Day

Due to the federal Emancipation Day holiday observed on April 17, 2017, tax returns filed and payments mailed or submitted on April 18, 2017, will be considered timely. (Instructions, Form 540, California Resident Income Tax Return)

• *Final returns*

The final California return of a decedent is due on April 15 following the close of the calendar year in which death occurred or, in the case of a fiscal-year taxpayer, by the 15th day of the fourth month following the close of the decedent's fiscal year. (Reg. 18505-4, 18 CCR) This is the same as the federal rule.

As under federal law, the final California return of an estate or trust is due within $3^1/_2$ months after the close of the month in which the estate or trust is terminated.

• *Qualified use taxes*

Persons not required to hold a seller's permit or to register with the California State Board of Equalization (BOE) (see ¶ 1511) may self-report their qualified use tax liabilities on their timely filed original personal income tax returns. Persons electing to report such taxes are required to report and remit the tax on an income tax return that corresponds to the taxable year in which the use tax liability was incurred. A married individual filing a separate California personal income tax return may elect to report either one-half of the qualified use tax or the entire qualified use tax on his or her separate California personal income tax return. The non-electing spouse is not bound by the other spouse's election. (Sec. 6452.1, Rev. & Tax. Code)

CCH Practice Tip: Use Tax Look-Up Tables

Taxpayers that make one or more single nonbusiness purchases of individual items of tangible personal property, each with a sales price of less than $1,000, may determine their use tax liability to report on their personal income tax return by using a use tax table shown in the California personal income tax booklet instructions or by reporting the actual use tax due. Qualified taxpayers may not be assessed an underpayment for the proper use of these tables. (Sec. 6452.1, Rev. & Tax. Code)

Payments and credits on income tax returns of taxpayers that report use tax on those returns must be applied first to satisfy the use tax liability, with any excess amount then applied to the outstanding taxes, penalties, and interest owed to the Franchise Tax Board. See ¶1511 for details concerning the payment of use taxes.

Practice Pointer: Amended Use Tax Reporting

Taxpayers that want to revise their use tax previously reported on an income tax return should contact the BOE directly rather than filing an amended income tax return (California Personal Income Tax Booklet).

• *Extensions of time*

The Franchise Tax Board (FTB) may grant an extension or extensions of time for filing any return, declaration, statement, or other document for a period up to six months from the regular due date, or for a longer period in the case of a taxpayer who is abroad (¶109). (Sec. 18567, Rev. & Tax. Code) See ¶110 regarding extensions of time for payment of tax.

The FTB will allow an automatic six-month filing extension if the return is filed within six months of the original due date. No written request is required. The automatic extension does not extend the time for paying tax. Tax payments must accompany FTB 3519 (Payment Voucher for Automatic Extension for Individuals), FTB 3537 (Payment Voucher for Automatic Extension for Limited Liability Companies), FTB 3538 (Payment Voucher for Automatic Extension for Limited Partnerships, LLPs and REMICs), or FTB 3563 (Payment Voucher for Automatic Extension for Fiduciaries). See ¶712 for a discussion of the penalty for failure to pay an adequate amount of tax by the regular due date.

In addition, the FTB may postpone certain tax-related deadlines, including the deadline for filing a return, for a period of up to one year for taxpayers affected by a federally-declared disaster, a terroristic or militaristic action, or a state of emergency declared by the governor. (Sec. 18572, Rev. & Tax. Code) The deadlines that may be postponed are the same as those that may be postponed by reason of a taxpayer's service in a combat zone (¶109). See ¶711 for a discussion concerning the abatement of interest available to taxpayers granted such an extension.

An extension of time for filing the California return extends the statute of limitations on assessments to a date four years from the date the return is filed (¶710).

See ¶110 for interest charged during extension periods.

• *Filing by mail*

Returns and requests for extensions of time filed by mail are deemed to be filed on the date they are placed in the U.S. mail, provided they are properly addressed and the postage is prepaid. The date of the postmark is ordinarily deemed to be the date of mailing, although it may be possible to prove that the return was actually mailed on an earlier date. (Sec. 11003, Govt. Code) It is obviously desirable to mail early enough to be sure the postmark is timely. When the due date falls on a Saturday, Sunday, or other legal holiday (including IRS-recognized federal holidays), returns are due on the next business day. (Sec. 6707, Govt. Code; Sec. 18410, Rev. & Tax. Code) Federal law provides that the postmark date on a properly mailed return will be deemed to be the delivery date. (Note that a postage meter date is not a "postmark.")

CCH Caution: Returns Sent by Private Delivery Services

Returns sent by a private delivery service should be sent in time to be *received* by the due date.

Returns should be mailed to the FTB in Sacramento, or filed with any of the FTB's regional or district offices. The regular Sacramento address for filing personal income tax returns and the special address for returns that show a refund due, are indicated on the return form.

• *E-file*

The FTB also accepts electronic filing of returns by tax professionals through the e-file program. Detailed information concerning this program is available at the FTB's Web site at http://www.ftb.ca.gov/professionals/efile/proinfo.shtml.

Mandatory electronic filing: Tax return preparers who prepare and file more than 100 California personal income tax returns annually and who prepare at least one personal income tax return using tax preparation software in the current calendar year must file all personal income tax returns for the current calendar year and subsequent calendar years using electronic technology (see ¶712 for related penalties). The requirement ceases to apply to a tax return preparer if, during the previous calendar year, the tax return preparer prepared no more than 25 original personal income tax returns. A taxpayer may also elect to have his/her tax return preparer file a paper, rather than electronic, return by filing Form FTB 8454 (e-file Opt-Out Record for Individuals). (Sec. 18621.9, Rev. & Tax. Code) Although not included in the individual income tax return e-filing mandate, the FTB began accepting e-filed fiduciary returns on January 2, 2014, for tax years beginning on or after January 1, 2013. (*Public Service Bulletin 13-42*, California Franchise Tax Board, December 23, 2013)

E-signatures: The FTB accepts electronic signatures for individual e-filed returns and recognizes the same PIN methods available federally: the Self-Select PIN method, the Practitioner PIN method and the electronic return originator (ERO) PIN. All signature methods, including pen-on-paper using form FTB 8453, will be accepted for all California e-file return types (Forms 540, 540 2EZ, and 540NR Long and Short) throughout the duration of the e-file season. For more information see the FTB's Web site at: http://www.ftb.ca.gov/professionals/efile/esig.shtml

Filing procedures: Personal income tax returns and other documents that are filed using electronic technology must be in a form prescribed by the FTB and are not complete unless accompanied by an acceptable electronic signature. The FTB will accept electronic signatures using the Self-Select PIN and Practitioner PIN methods, in lieu of the California e-file Return Authorization for Individuals (FTB 8453). Tax payments made by check must be accompanied by FTB 3582 (Payment Voucher for Electronically Transmitted Returns).

EROs approved for the Internal Revenue Service (IRS) e-file program are automatically enrolled in the California e-file program. In addition, the FTB will automatically receive any updates made by approved EROs to their IRS accounts. (*Tax News*, California Franchise Tax Board, September 2007, CCH CALIFORNIA TAX REPORTS, ¶404-446)

California conforms to federal income tax provisions allowing electronic postmarks as proof of the date electronically filed returns are deemed filed.

CCH Practice Pointer: Identity Theft

If an electronically filed return is rejected because another return using the same Social Security number has already been filed for that tax year, the taxpayer should immediately contact the following:

Franchise Tax Board ID Theft Resolution Coordinator MS A462

P.O. Box 2952

Sacramento, CA 95812-2952

Telephone: (916) 845-3669

Fax: (916) 843-0561

The taxpayer will be asked to fill out FTB 3552PC, Identity Theft Affidavit. The electronically filed return that was rejected will need to be submitted on paper. The processing of the return will likely take several months. (*FTB Tax News*, February 2013, CCH CALIFORNIA TAX REPORTS, ¶ 405-816)

- *Magnetic media*

California generally adopts the federal standards in federal Reg. 301.6011-2 for determining which income tax returns must be filed on magnetic media or in other machine-readable form. (Reg. 18409, 18 CCR) The California standards must take into account the ability of the taxpayer to comply at reasonable cost with the filing requirements. The FTB may not require (1) that estates or trusts file any personal income tax returns in any manner other than on paper forms supplied by the FTB or (2) that returns filed on magnetic media contain more information than is required to be included under federal law. A copy of a magnetic media or other machine-readable return filed with the IRS may be filed with the FTB for state tax purposes instead of the return required under state law. (Sec. 18409, Rev. & Tax. Code)

California law, unlike federal law, does not require partnerships having more than 100 partners to file returns on magnetic media.

- *FTB offices*

The FTB has branch offices in principal cities throughout California and also in Chicago and New York.

¶109 Extensions of Time for Persons Outside the United States

Law: Secs. 17142.5, 18567-71 (CCH CALIFORNIA TAX REPORTS, ¶ 17-750).

Comparable Federal: Secs. 6081, 7508 (CCH U.S. MASTER TAX GUIDE ¶ 120, 2509, 2537).

California Form: FTB 3519 (Payment Voucher for Automatic Extension for Individuals).

- *Taxpayers abroad*

Taxpayers who are "abroad" can ordinarily obtain an unlimited extension of time for filing California returns, to cover the entire period of their absence from the country. A taxpayer who is outside the United States on the return due date is automatically granted a two-month extension of time; thus, the April 15 date for a calendar-year return is extended to June 15. This extension, combined with the automatic six-month paperless extension, extends the due date to December 15. However, interest accrues on any unpaid tax from the original due date of April 15 and late payment penalties may be imposed on any tax still unpaid as of June 15. (Sec. 18567, Rev. & Tax. Code) Payments made prior to filing the return should be accompanied by FTB 3519 (Payment Voucher for Automatic Extension for Individuals).

To obtain further extensions of time, the taxpayer must continue to file timely requests periodically during his or her sojourn abroad. California has not defined "abroad" by regulation. Under comparable federal regulations, "abroad" is defined as outside the United States and Puerto Rico, and taxpayers who are abroad are granted an automatic extension of time to June 15 for calendar-year federal returns.

- *Armed Forces and merchant marines*

California grants automatic extensions of time to members of the U.S. Armed Forces and merchant marines who serve outside the boundaries of the 50 states of the United States and the District of Columbia. The extension also applies to the spouses of such individuals. The extension runs to a date 180 days after a serviceperson or merchant marine returns to the United States, and applies to filing returns, paying taxes, filing protests, filing claims for refund, and filing appeals to the State Board of Equalization. (Sec. 18570, Rev. & Tax. Code)

California conforms to federal law as of the current IRC tie-in date (¶103), which allows members of the Armed Forces who serve in combat zones, overseas contingency operations, or who are hospitalized as a result of injuries received while serving in combat zones or hazardous duty areas to postpone the deadline for filing income tax returns and paying taxes (other than income taxes withheld at the source or employment taxes) by the following periods:

— the amount of time they served in a combat zone,

— the period of time they were hospitalized as a result of injuries sustained in the zone, or

— the period of time they were missing in action from the zone, plus

— 180 days following the end of their service, hospitalization, or missing status. (Sec. 18571, Rev. & Tax. Code)

Taxpayers serving in combat zones who are filing on extension should alert the FTB to this fact when they file by writing in red on the top of their return or payment the name of the specific combat zone served in. They must also indicate the dates they entered and left the combat zone (*News Release*, California Franchise Tax Board, March 27, 2003).

The combat zone/hazardous duty area/contingency operation extension also applies to deadlines for:

— tax assessments,

— tax collections,

— levies,

— the granting of a credit or refund of taxes,

— filing a claim for a refund or credit, and

— the filing of a suit for a refund or a credit.

¶110 Payment of Tax

Law: Secs. 18567, 18572, 19001-05, 19008, 19011, 19101; Sec. 415 of the Military and Veterans Code (CCH CALIFORNIA TAX REPORTS, ¶17-510, 89-102, 89-108, 89-188).

Comparable Federal: Secs. 6151, 7508A (CCH U.S. MASTER TAX GUIDE ¶2537).

California Form: FTB 3567BK (Installment Agreement Request), FTB 3567BK AMNESTY (Amnesty Installment Agreement Request).

The entire balance of tax due must be paid with the income tax return. Where tax has been withheld or a prepayment has been made during the year, the withholding or prepayment is deducted to arrive at the balance due with the return. See ¶111 regarding payment of estimated tax; see ¶714 and 715 regarding withholding.

• *Extension of time*

The Franchise Tax Board (FTB) may grant a reasonable extension of time for payment of tax whenever, in its judgment, good cause exists. Where an extension of time is granted, interest is charged from the regular due date to the date of payment. The interest rate is the rate charged on deficiencies, as explained at ¶711.

In addition, California incorporates federal law allowing the FTB to postpone certain tax-related deadlines, including the deadline for payment of tax, for a period of up to one year for taxpayers affected by a federally-declared disaster, a terroristic or militaristic action, or a state of emergency declared by the governor. (Sec. 18572, Rev. & Tax. Code) The deadlines that may be postponed are the same as those that may be postponed by reason of a taxpayer's service in a combat zone (¶109). See ¶711 for a discussion concerning the abatement of interest available to taxpayers granted such an extension.

• *Installment payments—Generally*

The FTB may allow taxpayers experiencing financial hardships to pay their tax in installment payments. Applicable interest (¶711) and penalties over the life of the installment period apply. The FTB must enter into an agreement to accept payment of an individual's liability in installments if, as of the date the individual offers to enter into the agreement, all of the following apply:

— the aggregate amount of the liability, excluding interest or penalties, does not exceed $10,000;

— the individual and, if the individual has filed a joint return, the individual's spouse or registered domestic partner has not during the preceding five years failed to file a return, failed to pay any tax required to be shown on the return, or entered into an installment agreement for payment of tax;

— the FTB determines that the individual is financially unable to pay the liability in full when due;

— the agreement requires full payment of the liability within three years; and

— the individual agrees to comply with the tax law for the period the agreement is in effect. (Sec. 19008, Rev. & Tax. Code)

CCH Practice Pointer: Installment Program Expanded

The FTB has expanded the statutory installment program to encompass taxpayers who have filed all required personal income tax returns if they (1) owe a balance of $25,000 or less and (2) can pay the outstanding balance within 60 months. A taxpayer is not required to submit a financial statement to enter into the agreement. The FTB reserves the right to file a lien as a condition of the installment agreement depending on a taxpayer's compliance history. For further information, taxpayers may contact the FTB's Collection Response and Resolution Section at 1-800-689-4776. (*News Release*, California Franchise Tax Board, January 2007)

A request for an independent administrative review submitted within 30 days of the date of rejection of an offer of an installment agreement or termination of an agreement will stay the collection of tax. (Sec. 19008, Rev. & Tax. Code)

Also, a levy may not be issued on the property or rights to property of any person with respect to any unpaid tax during any period for which an installment offer is pending, an installment agreement is in place, or a review of an installment agreement rejection or termination is pending. However, the levy restrictions do not apply to the following:

— any unpaid tax if the taxpayer waives the restrictions or if the FTB determines that the collection of tax is jeopardized;

— any levy that was first issued before the date that the proceeding commenced; and

— at the discretion of the FTB, any unpaid tax for which the taxpayer makes an offer of an installment agreement subsequent to a rejection of an offer of an installment agreement with respect to that unpaid tax. (Sec. 19008, Rev. & Tax. Code)

The period of limitations for the FTB to bring an action to recover unpaid tax is suspended for the period during which the FTB is prohibited under the above provisions from making a levy.

¶110

CCH Practice Pointer: Liens and Installment Agreements

If the balance owing exceeds $25,000 or will take longer than five years to resolve, the FTB will file a Notice of State Tax Lien to secure the state's interest in any real property held in the county where the lien is filed. In addition, if the account reflects a history of noncompliance, even though the balance due may be less than $25,000 or the repayment plan is within the five-year period, the FTB may file a lien as a condition of continuing the installment agreement. A history of noncompliance includes either a combination of three or more broken promises (nonpayment/dishonored payment) or three continuous accruals of additional liabilities during the life of the existing installment agreement. (*FTB Tax News*, May 2011, CCH CALIFORNIA TAX REPORTS, ¶ 405-410)

Taxpayers who owe less than $10,000 may enter into an electronic installment payment agreement on-line on the FTB's Web site at: http://www.ftb.ca.gov/online/eia/index.asp or by using the FTB's Interactive Voice Response system at (800) 689-4776. A taxpayer requesting an installment payment plan agrees to pay the income tax liability in monthly installments by electronic funds transfer. The taxpayer also agrees to

— ensure that adequate funds are available for the transfers;

— timely file all future returns;

— ensure that future tax liabilities are paid in full with the taxpayer's returns; and

— pay a $34 fee to the FTB for this service. (Sec. 19008, Rev. & Tax. Code)

Taxpayers who do not meet the above requirements may also request to enter into an installment agreement by submitting FTB 3567 (Installment Agreement Request).

Generally, any failure by the taxpayer to comply fully with the agreed-upon payment plan, other than for reasonable cause, ends the agreement, provided (1) the FTB notifies the taxpayer of the termination at least 30 days before the termination date and (2) such notice includes an explanation of the reason for the intended termination of the agreement. However, notice is not required if the FTB determines that collection of the tax is in jeopardy or there is mutual consent to terminate, alter, or modify the agreement. Taxpayers may seek administrative review by the Taxpayers' Advocate of any such termination. The administrative review will not stay the collection of tax. (Sec. 19008, Rev. & Tax. Code)

• *Provisional payment plan pilot program*

A provisional payment plan pilot program is available to taxpayers who do not qualify for an installment agreement because they have not yet filed tax returns for the last five years. Such taxpayers may participate in a provisional payment plan and avoid the commencement of involuntary collection actions while they are in the process of preparing their missing valid personal income tax returns. To qualify, taxpayers must:

— owe a balance of $25,000 or less;

— respond to billing notices prior to their account going into an involuntary collection state;

— file all their missing valid personal income tax returns within 30 days;

— agree to be compliant for all future tax years; and

— not have any legal actions in process or pending.

Involuntary collections will be brought against a taxpayer who fails to file the missing returns within 30 days. Taxpayers that file within 30 days, but who owe additional tax, will be placed in an installment agreement. (*Tax News*, FTB, December 2, 2009, CCH CALIFORNIA TAX REPORTS, ¶ 405-022)

• *Deferment for servicepersons*

The federal Servicemembers Civil Relief Act provides for the deferment of collection of state income taxes from servicepersons if their ability to pay is materially impaired by reason of their entering military service. (Sec. 409.6, Milit. & Vet. Code; Sec. 17140.5, Rev. & Tax. Code) Also, see ¶ 109 regarding automatic extension of time granted to certain individuals.

A member of the National Guard or an army reservist of the U.S. Military Reserve who is called up for active duty may be eligible for deferral of income tax payments for a period of up to six months after the termination of his or her period of military service if the person's ability to pay the tax is materially impaired by reason of the service. Interest and penalties may not be imposed during the deferment period. (FTB Pub. 1032, Tax Information for Military Personnel)

• *Payment by mail*

A payment is deemed to be made on the date it is mailed, provided it is properly addressed and the postage is prepaid. The federal rule is similar. (Sec. 11003, Govt. Code) See ¶ 108 for comment regarding the effect of a postmark date.

• *Payment by check*

Payment of personal income tax in the form of a check must be made payable in U.S. funds.

To expedite processing, payments for separate purposes (*e.g.*, balance due on return and estimate payment) should not be combined in one check. The taxpayer's social security number should be shown on each check. Also, returns and payments of estimated tax should be mailed in separate envelopes.

• *Payment by credit card*

Taxpayers may use Discover/NOVUS, MasterCard, Visa, or American Express cards to pay their personal income taxes, including any amounts past due.

• *Payment by Web Pay*

A taxpayer may pay the current amount owed and schedule future payments, such as estimated tax, up to one year in advance through a secure service offered on the FTB's website. The taxpayer dictates the amount paid and when he or she would like the payment made and the payment will be deducted from the taxpayer's account on the date indicated. (https://www.ftb.ca.gov/online/payment_choices.shtml)

• *Electronic payments*

Personal income taxpayers must make payments electronically if their estimated personal income tax installment payment or extension request payment exceeds $20,000 or if their total annual tax liability exceeds $80,000. Taxpayers may make a written election to not make their payments electronically if they did not meet the $20,000 or $80,000 threshold requirements for the preceding taxable year.

CCH Practice Pointer: Requests for Waiver or Discontinuance

Within a few days of receiving a payment or a posting to the FTB system that triggers the mandatory e-pay requirement, the FTB will send taxpayers an FTB Form 4106 MEO, Mandatory e-pay Program Participation Notice, that advises the taxpayers they must remit future payments electronically, and provides them with their options, including how to request a waiver from the requirement. The FTB attempts to process all Form 4107, Mandatory e-pay Election to Discontinue or Waiver Request, submissions within 30 days. To ensure the quick processing of the request, Form 4107 should be faxed to the FTB at (916) 843-0468. To have an e-pay penalty waived, practitioners should call the Tax Practitioner Hotline at (916) 845-7057 or fax a penalty waiver request to (916) 845-9300.

Individuals with a permanent physical or mental impairment that prevents them from using a computer may request a permanent waiver from the mandatory e-pay requirements by completing FTB 4107PC, Mandatory e-pay Election to Discontinue or Waiver Request, and have a physician complete and sign page 3 of the form. This signed affidavit must be attached to FTB 4107PC when it is submitted. Taxpayers may also check a box on the form to have the FTB review the taxpayer's account for possible waiver of a previously imposed mandatory e-pay penalty if all the following conditions exist:

> — the taxpayer received a mandatory e-pay penalty for payments made before receiving approval of his/her permanent physical or mental impairment request;

> — the date on the physician's affidavit of permanent physical or mental impairment pre-dates the assessment of the penalty; and

> — the statute of limitations for filing a claim for refund is still open.

The permanent waiver is not available to joint filers if one of the spouses/registered domestic partners does not have a physical or mental impairment. (Mandatory E-Pay for Individuals (2012), CCH CALIFORNIA TAX REPORTS, ¶ 405-615)

A penalty of 1% of the tax owed will be imposed against taxpayers who fail to make an electronic payment unless reasonable cause exists. In addition, the FTB may waive the electronic payment requirement if it determines that the particular amounts paid in excess of the threshold amounts were not representative of the taxpayer's tax liability. (Sec. 19011.5, Rev. & Tax. Code)

Electronic payments may be made using the following methods:

> — online with Web Pay (discussed above);

> — electronic funds withdrawal when e-filing a tax return;

> — credit card online at www.officialpayments.com or by calling toll free (800) 272-9829; or

> — pay-by-phone options by completing and submitting Form FTB 4073, Mandatory e-pay Pay-by-Phone Authorization Agreement for Individuals, available on the FTB's website at http://www.ftb.ca.gov.

CCH Practice Pointer: Banks' Online Bill Payment Systems

Making a payment using a bank's online bill payment system is not an electronic payment. The bank mails a paper check to the FTB, which does not meet the requirement to pay electronically.

The only option currently available to group nonresident/composite return filers is paying online with Web Pay.

Taxpayers not required to use e-pay may submit a request to the FTB to pay by electronic funds transfer. Once permission is granted, a 10% penalty is imposed if payments are not made in this manner (¶ 712).

¶111 Payment of Estimated Tax

Law: Secs. 18410, 19007, 19010, 19136–36.12 (CCH CALIFORNIA TAX REPORTS, ¶ 89-104, 89-204, 89-206, 89-210).

Comparable Federal: Secs. 6315, 6654 (CCH U.S. MASTER TAX GUIDE ¶ 2679— 2691).

California Forms: Form 540-ES (Estimated Tax for Individuals), FTB 5805 (Underpayment of Estimated Tax by Individuals and Fiduciaries), FTB 5805F (Underpayment of Estimated Tax by Farmers and Fisherman).

California law, including the special treatment for farmers and fishermen, is the same as federal law except that California, unlike federal law, imposes no penalty for underpayment, and therefore requires no estimated tax payments, if either the actual tax (after deduction of credits) for the preceding year or the estimated tax for the current year is under $500 for a single person or a married couple/registered domestic partnership (RDP) filing jointly, or $250 for a married person/RDP filing separately. (Sec. 19136, Rev. & Tax. Code) Federal law does not impose a penalty for underpayment of estimated tax if the actual tax is less than $1,000 after withholding.

• *Dates and amounts of payment*

For calendar-year taxpayers, estimated tax is payable in quarterly installments, on April 15, June 15, September 15, and January 15. If a due date for payment falls on a Saturday, Sunday, or legal holiday (including IRS-recognized federal holidays), it is extended to the next day that is not a Saturday, Sunday, or legal holiday. If the individual's tax situation changes during the year, payments for the remaining installments may be revised accordingly. (Sec. 18410, Rev. & Tax. Code; Sec. 19136, Rev. & Tax. Code)

For fiscal-year taxpayers, estimated tax payments are due by the 15th day of the fourth, sixth, and ninth months of the fiscal year and the first month of the following fiscal year.

Estimated tax installment payments must be paid as follows: 30% of the estimated amount due for the taxable year for the first installment, 40% for the second installment, 0% for the third installment, and 30% for the fourth installment. (Sec. 19136.1, Rev. & Tax. Code)

Practice Pointer: Application of Withholding Credits

The estimated tax underpayment penalty provision that credits the amount of withholding against the estimated tax payments due has been revised to reflect the applicable percentage of estimated tax payments required to be paid, as discussed above. Consequently, withholding payments are credited quarterly at percentages equal to 30%, 40%, 0%, and 30%. (Sec. 19136(e), Rev. & Tax. Code)

Practice Note: Safe Harbor

Except as discussed below, the required estimated tax amount is based on the lesser of (1) 90% of the current year's tax or (2) 100% (110% for taxpayers whose AGI for the current year exceeds $150,000) ($75,000 if married filing separately) of the preceding year's tax, provided the preceding taxable year was a 12-month taxable year. (Sec. 19136, Rev. & Tax. Code) However, individuals with annual adjusted gross incomes of $1 million ($500,000 if married filing separately) or more may not base their estimated tax payment on 110% of the preceding year's tax. (Sec. 19136.3, Rev. & Tax. Code)

• *Early return and full payment in place of fourth installment*

If a final return for the year is filed and the full amount of tax is paid by taxpayers generally before February 1, or by farmers or fishermen before March 2, it has the same effect as a payment of estimated tax on January 15. (Sec. 19136, Rev. & Tax. Code)

• *Account information*

To determine what payments a taxpayer has already made, and what payments the FTB has received, the FTB is posting secured tax information on its Web site. Taxpayers and tax preparers may access this information at http://www.ftb.ca.gov/online/myacct/index.html. This service allows taxpayers to view the following:

— estimated tax payments;
— recent payments applied to a balance due;
— a taxpayer's total current balance due; and
— a summary of each balance due by tax year on the taxpayer's account.

• *Penalty for underpayment*

A penalty is imposed for underpayment of estimated tax, computed as a percentage of the underpayment, for the period of the underpayment. The Instructions to Forms 5805 and 5805F state that for purposes of computing the amount of the underpayment, a taxpayer may use the figures listed on his or her amended return only if the amended return was filed on or prior to the due date for the original return. The penalty rate applied is the same as the interest rate on deficiencies and refunds, see ¶711. However, the penalty rate is not compounded. (Sec. 19136, Rev. & Tax. Code)

The amount of underpayment subject to penalty is based on 90% of tax for taxpayers generally and 66²/₃% for farmers and fishermen (for definition of "underpayment," see ¶813).

Waivers and abatements.—The underpayment penalty may be waived for newly retired or disabled individuals and in cases of casualties, disasters, or other unusual circumstances. (Sec. 19136, Rev. & Tax. Code) The waiver request is made on Form 5805 or 5805F. In instances where FTB 5805 is not submitted with the tax return or the taxpayer did not realize the penalty applied, the FTB will assess the penalty and send a bill. However, a taxpayer has the opportunity even after receiving a bill, and after the bill becomes final, to request a waiver of the estimated tax underpayment penalty by contacting the FTB and providing a completed FTB 5805. (*FTB Tax News*, June 2012, CCH CALIFORNIA TAX REPORTS, ¶405-680)

In addition, no penalty will be applied if the underpayment is attributable to any of the following:

— changes made to the laws of other states concerning the allowance of credits for taxes paid to another state (Sec. 19136.5, Rev. & Tax. Code);

— an erroneous levy, erroneous processing action, or erroneous collection action by the FTB (Sec. 19136.7, Rev. & Tax. Code);

— legislation chaptered and operative for the taxable year of the underpayment (Sec. 19136(g), Rev. & Tax. Code); and

— the earned income tax credit adjustment factor for the taxable year being less than the adjustment factor for the preceding taxable year (Sec. 19136(g), Rev. & Tax. Code).

Comment: Federal Legislation

The relief for underpayments resulting from legislation chaptered and operative for the taxable year of the underpayment does not apply to federal law changes that may create an underpayment of state tax, because federal law is enacted without being chaptered. (Bill Analysis, Ch. 242 (S.B. 14), Laws 2005, Senate Floor, August 23, 2005)

• *Reporting underpayment penalties*

Where the figures on a return indicate that there has been (or may have been) an underpayment of estimated tax, the taxpayer should attach FTB 5805 or FTB 5805F (for farmers and fishermen) to show computation of the penalty or to explain why no penalty is due. Federal Forms 2210 and 2210F should not be used with California returns.

• *Penalty for failure to pay*

Civil and criminal penalties are imposed for willful failure to make timely payments of estimated tax, see ¶712.

• *New residents, nonresidents, estates and trusts*

New residents and nonresidents are subject to the requirements for paying estimated tax as set forth above. The Instructions to FTB 5805 indicate that if the taxpayer had no California tax liability for the previous year, no estimated tax is due in the first taxable year of residence. Estates and trusts are subject to California estimated tax requirements, as they are under federal law.

¶112 Tax Base

Law: Sec. 17073 (CCH CALIFORNIA TAX REPORTS, ¶ 15-355, 15-505).

Comparable Federal: Sec. 63 (CCH U.S. MASTER TAX GUIDE ¶ 124, 126).

The income tax rates (except for the alternative minimum tax discussed at ¶ 117) are applied to the amount of taxable income, which is defined at ¶ 203.

¶113 Exemption Credits

Law: Secs. 17054, 17054.1, 17056, 17733 (CCH CALIFORNIA TAX REPORTS, ¶ 16-815).

Comparable Federal: Sec. 151 (CCH U.S. MASTER TAX GUIDE ¶ 133).

California Forms: Form 540 (California Resident Income Tax Return), Form 540 2EZ (California Resident Income Tax Return), Form 540NR (California Nonresident or Part-Year Resident Income Tax Return).

Tax credits are allowed for personal exemptions. (Sec. 17054, Rev. & Tax. Code) The credits are deducted from tax computed on taxable income without benefit of such exemptions. The credit applies to the separate tax on lump-sum distributions.

Following are the credits for the years shown:

	2012	2013	2014	2015	2016
Single person	$ 104	$ 106	$ 108	$ 109	$ 111
Married/RDP, separate return	104	106	108	109	111
Married/RDP, joint return	208	212	216	218	222
Head of household	104	106	108	109	111
Surviving spouse	208	212	216	218	222
Dependent	321	326	333	337	344
Blind person—additional	104	106	108	109	111
Estate	10	10	10	10	10
Trust	1	1	1	1	1
Elderly—additional	104	106	108	109	111

• *Disability trusts*

The exemption credit for disability trusts is equal to the personal exemption credit for single individuals and is subject to the limitations for high-income taxpayers discussed below. (Sec. 17733, Rev. & Tax. Code)

• *Dependents*

No dependent exemption credit will be allowed unless the dependent's taxpayer identification number (TIN) is included on the return on which the credit is claimed. A disallowance of the credit due to the omission of a TIN will be treated by the FTB as a mathematical error. A claimant will have the right to subsequently provide the TIN and claim a credit or refund prior to the expiration of the statute of limitations. (Sec. 17054, Rev. & Tax. Code) See ¶ 115 for a definition of "dependent."

In *Montoya v. Daniele* (2005), CCH CALIFORNIA TAX REPORTS, ¶ 403-793 (not to be cited as precedent), a California court of appeal held that a family law court properly exercised its discretion in a child support proceeding by allocating California personal income tax exemptions for two dependent children to their noncustodial parent so as to maximize the resources available to the children. It was reasonable for the court to make this allocation because the court had calculated that awarding the exemptions to the noncustodial parent would increase the amount of child support payable by the noncustodial parent to the custodial parent, thereby increasing the total resources available to the children, without adversely affecting the custodial parent's tax liability.

• *Reduction of credits for high-income taxpayers*

The exemption credits are reduced if a taxpayer's federal adjusted gross income exceeds a threshold amount. (Sec. 17054.1, Rev. & Tax. Code) For 2016, with respect to single taxpayers, each credit is reduced by $6 for each $2,500 or fraction thereof by which the taxpayer's federal adjusted gross income exceeds $182,459. For a married/RDP taxpayer filing a joint return or a surviving spouse, each credit is reduced by $12 for each $2,500 or fraction thereof by which the taxpayer's federal adjusted gross income exceeds $364,923. For married/RDP taxpayers filing separately, each credit is reduced by $6 for each $1,250 of federal adjusted gross income over $182,459. For heads of households, each credit is reduced by $6 for each $2,500 of federal adjusted gross income over $273,692.

A worksheet is provided in the Form 540 Instructions to assist taxpayers in determining the amount of the exemption credit reduction.

• *Nonresidents and part-year residents*

Nonresidents and part-year residents are allowed reduced credits for personal exemptions, on the basis of prorated taxable income. (Sec. 17055, Rev. & Tax. Code) The phase-out of exemption credits for high-income taxpayers (discussed above) must be applied before proration of the credits (¶ 132).

• *Missing children*

California follows federal law (TAM No. 200038059) allowing taxpayers to claim a dependent exemption for missing children.

• *California-federal differences*

California law, unlike federal law, has not repealed the additional exemption for blind individuals and the additional exemption for the elderly. (For 2016, California allows an additional $111 exemption credit for both blind and elderly taxpayers.)

Although California conforms in principle to federal law requiring a phase-out of the personal exemption, the reduction computation and the threshold amounts differ from federal law (see above).

¶114 Filing Status

> *Law:* Secs. 17021.5, 17042, 18521, 18532 (CCH CALIFORNIA TAX REPORTS, ¶ 15-305, 15-310, 15-315, 15-320, 15-325, 15-330).
>
> *Comparable Federal:* Secs. 2, 7703 (CCH U.S. MASTER TAX GUIDE ¶ 152, 173, 175).
>
> *California Forms:* FTB 3532 (Head of Household Filing Status Schedule).

For California purposes, with the exception of registered domestic partners (RDPs) discussed below, an individual must use the filing status used on his or her federal return for the same taxable year or, if no federal return was filed, the status that the individual would have used on a federal return. (Sec. 18521, Rev. & Tax. Code)

Married taxpayers are also required to use their federal filing status, except that married taxpayers who file a joint federal return may file either joint or separate California returns if (1) either spouse was an active member of the military or (2) one spouse was a nonresident for the entire year and had no California-source income. A joint nonresident income tax return is required of spouses who file a joint federal return if one of the spouses was a California resident for the entire taxable year and the other was a nonresident for all or any part of the tax year and had California-source income. (Sec. 18521, Rev. & Tax. Code)

The determination of whether an individual is married, a "surviving spouse," a "head of household," or blind is made as of the close of the taxable year. (Sec. 18532, Rev. & Tax. Code) A joint return may be filed if one spouse dies during the taxable year. (Sec. 18521, Rev. & Tax. Code) An individual who is legally separated from his or her spouse under a decree of divorce or of separate maintenance is not considered married. (Sec. 18532, Rev. & Tax. Code)

Planning Note: Registered Domestic Partners and Same-Sex Married Couples

Taxpayers who are registered as domestic partners by the close of the taxable year must file California personal income tax returns jointly or separately by applying the same standards as are applied to married taxpayers under federal income tax law. (Sec. 18521, Rev. & Tax. Code) For additional details concerning the tax treatment of RDPs, see ¶ 119.

Special rules apply for purposes of determining limitations based on adjusted gross income (¶202). Community property rules also apply (¶239).

In Revenue Ruling 2013-17, the U.S. Department of the Treasury and Internal Revenue Service (IRS) ruled that same-sex couples, legally married in jurisdictions that recognize their marriages, will be treated as married for federal tax purposes. The ruling applies regardless of whether the couple lives in a jurisdiction that recognizes same-sex marriage or a jurisdiction that does not recognize same-sex marriage.

This ruling aligns the federal and California filing status for same-sex married couples, and eliminates the need for same-sex couples to create a pro-forma federal income tax return prior to preparing their California joint income tax return.

In addition, for the period June 16, 2008, until November 4, 2008 when Proposition 8 was passed, California law recognized the right of same-sex individuals to enter into legal marriages. The FTB has taken the position that these same-sex married couples are to be treated as all other spouses for purposes of California taxation. (*Publication 776, Tax Information for Same-Sex Married Couples* (2012), California Franchise Tax Board) For additional details concerning the tax treatment of same-sex married couples, see ¶119.

The federal ruling does not apply to California RDPs, who must still claim married filing jointly or married filing separately filing status for California income tax purposes, but may not do so for federal income tax purposes. Consequently, the requirement that RDP couples create a pro-forma federal income tax return prior to preparing their California income tax return remains. (*Tax News*, California Franchise Tax Board, September 2013 (CCH CALIFORNIA TAX REPORTS, ¶405-969))

• *Head of household*

The federal law defining "head of household" is incorporated into California law by reference, as of the current IRC tie-in date (see ¶103). (Sec. 18521, Rev. & Tax. Code)

Head-of-household filing status is granted to unmarried taxpayers maintaining a household for qualifying persons, and to married persons and RDPs who are living apart from their spouse or RDP and who are maintaining a household for their child. (Sec. 17042, Rev. & Tax. Code)

In *Appeal of William Tierny* (1997) (CCH CALIFORNIA TAX REPORTS, ¶15-320.65), the State Board of Equalization (BOE) allowed a taxpayer who was not legally married at the end of the taxable year to include one-half of the time that he occupied the same household with his ex-wife and children to determine whether his household was his children's principal place of abode for more than one-half of the taxable year. The BOE reasoned that taxpayers who share their income with their children to the extent that they provide more than half of the children's support during the calendar year and pay for more than half of the expenses necessary to maintain a household are entitled to some relief. In *Appeal of Barbara Godek* (1999) (CCH CALIFORNIA TAX REPORTS, ¶15-320.552), the BOE extended the *Tierney* reasoning to a taxpayer who was legally married at the end of the taxable year before her divorce, but was "treated as not married" for the taxable year under the controlling statute.

CCH Example: Married Individual as Head of Household

Barbara and her daughter Monica lived in the same house with Barbara's spouse from January 1, 2016, through March 9, 2016 (68 days). During the period from March 10, 2016, through December 31, 2016, Barbara and Monica lived together for an additional 163 days without Barbara's spouse. Barbara and her spouse were still married at the end of 2016, but they qualified to be "treated as not married" for the year. Barbara may count 34 days ($^1/_2$ of the 68 days) plus 163 days in calculating the number of days that her household was the principal place of abode for Monica in 2016. Because the total of 197 days is more than $^1/_2$ of the year, Barbara qualifies for head of household filing status for the year.

In *Appeal of Patrick R. Lobo* (1999) (CCH California Tax Reports, ¶ 15-320.22), the BOE held that a taxpayer's unrelated 37-year old dependent was not a foster child and, thus, was not a qualifying individual for head of household filing purposes, because the foster relationship did not begin until after the dependent became an adult. The BOE noted that although there is no statutory definition of a "foster child" in the California tax laws, the term is intended to refer to an individual who was under the age of 18 at the time the foster child relationship began.

A checklist is included in the Instructions for Form 540 to assist taxpayers in determining whether they qualify for the head of household filing status.

CCH Practice Tip: Head of Household Filing Status Schedule

California requires taxpayers who use head of household filing status to file form FTB 3532 to report how the head of household filing status was determined.

Under federal law, a taxpayer is ineligible to claim head of household status if he or she fails to provide the correct taxpayer identification number for his or her dependent. California does not have a similar requirement.

• *Missing children*

Under both California and federal law, taxpayers are allowed to continue to claim surviving spouse or head of household filing status if their qualifying child has been kidnapped by a nonrelative. This special treatment ends with the first tax year of the taxpayer that begins after the year in which the kidnapped child is determined to be deceased or in which the child would have reached age 18, whichever occurs earlier. (Sec. 17042, Rev. & Tax. Code)

• *Unrelated individuals living together*

As indicated above, both California and federal laws require a specified relationship to qualify for "head of household" classification. This means that unrelated individuals living together do not qualify, even though one may furnish the chief support and be entitled to an exemption credit for a dependent. See *Appeal of Stephen M. Padwa* (1977) (CCH California Tax Reports, ¶ 15-320.40), cited in several later cases.

• *Married individuals treated as "unmarried"*

Certain married individuals may be treated as "unmarried" for purposes of determining their filing status. This applies where the individual lives apart from his or her spouse or RDP for the last six months of the year and maintains a home for a dependent child, under certain limited conditions. (Sec. 17021.5, Rev. & Tax. Code) The principal California advantage of the "unmarried" classification is that it puts the individual in a position where he or she may, under the rules discussed above, get the benefit of the lower rates that go with "head of household" classification. ("Head of household" classification is, of course, also advantageous on the federal return.)

• *Effect of interlocutory decree*

For both federal and California tax purposes, spouses are, by law, deemed *not* to be legally separated during the period between issuance of an interlocutory decree of divorce and issuance of the final decree. They are therefore considered to be married until issuance of the final decree.

¶115 Definition of Dependents

Law: Sec. 17056 (CCH California Tax Reports, ¶ 15-130).

Comparable Federal: Sec. 152 (CCH U.S. Master Tax Guide ¶ 137).

California law is the same as federal law as of the current IRC tie-in date (see ¶ 103). California incorporates the federal definition of a "dependent." (Sec. 17056, Rev. & Tax. Code)

• *Multiple-support agreements*

Under federal law, as incorporated by California, a taxpayer may satisfy the requirement of supporting a dependent even though he or she did not furnish over half the support, in certain "multiple support" situations. Under these rules, a taxpayer may claim a dependent for whom the taxpayer contributed less than one-half (but more than 10%) of the support, provided the taxpayer is a member of a group that contributed over one-half the support, and provided the other members of the group can meet the limitations imposed in these special provisions. (Sec. 17056, Rev. & Tax. Code)

• *Support paid from community income*

Where all of the income is community income neither spouse or registered domestic partner (RDP) contributes *over* half of their dependents' support, so technically neither is entitled to the credit for dependents on a separate return. However, as a practical matter, the credit is allowed under such circumstances to either spouse or RDP.

• *Divorced or separated parents*

The law provides detailed rules for determining which spouse or RDP is considered to have furnished over half the support of a child where the parents are divorced or separated. California law is the same as federal law. (Sec. 17056, Rev. & Tax. Code)

A California court of appeal has ruled that federal law did not preempt a family law court from alternating the California dependency exemption between two divorced parents who shared physical custody of their child, even though one parent received slightly more time with the child than the other parent. In the case at issue, the joint legal and custodial arrangement between the parents was, for all intents and purposes, equal, and allocation of the dependency exemption to both parents on an alternating basis was proper. (*Rios v. Pulido* (2002) (CCH California Tax Reports, ¶16-815.30))

In Legal Ruling No. 93-3 (1993) (CCH California Tax Reports, ¶402-643), the Franchise Tax Board indicated that a divorced, custodial parent who waives the federal dependent exemption deduction is precluded from claiming the corresponding state dependency credit.

• *Effect of classification as "dependent"*

The rules discussed above merely provide the *definition* of a "dependent." A taxpayer may or may not be allowed a *credit* for a person who qualifies as a "dependent," depending on the amount of the dependent's income and other conditions, see ¶113.

Regardless of whether or not a taxpayer is entitled to a credit, classification as a "dependent" may affect the deduction for medical expenses (¶325).

¶116 Tax Rates

Law: Secs. 17008.5, 17041, 17043, 17046, 17048, 17935, 17941, 17946, 17948, 23038 (CCH California Tax Reports, ¶10-235, 15-115, 15-355).

Comparable Federal: Sec. 1 (CCH U.S. Master Tax Guide ¶126).

California personal income tax is imposed on taxable income, as shown in the schedules and tables in Part I of this book. For purposes of determining the tax rate to be applied, taxable income is computed for the taxable year as if the resident were a California resident for the entire taxable year and for all prior taxable years for any carryover items, deferred income, suspended losses, or suspended deductions. For the definition of "taxable income," see ¶203.

The current progressive rates range from 1% to 12.3% (13.3% when the additional tax on millionaires discussed below is applied). For the 2011 tax year, the rates ranged from 1% to 9.3% (10.3% when the additional tax on millionaires tax was applied). Unlike federal law, California does not tax capital gains or dividend income at reduced rates. (Sec. 17041, Rev. & Tax. Code; Sec. 36, Article XIIIA, Cal. Const.)

Practice Pointer: Interplay of Proposition 30 Rate Increases With Estimated Taxes and Other Issues

An estimated tax underpayment penalty will not be imposed against taxpayers who underpaid their estimated personal income taxes to the extent that the underpayment was created or increased as a result of the personal income tax rate increases approved by the voters with the passage of Proposition 30, and applicable retroactively beginning with the 2012 tax year. California law contains a safe-harbor provision for underpayments resulting from any provision of law that is chaptered during and operative for the taxable year of the underpayment. (Sec. 19136(2)(g)(1), Rev. & Tax. Code) Consequently, taxpayers were not required to make any catch-up payments.

Taxpayers should be aware that the tax imposed on nonresident individuals participating in composite returns filed by corporations and pass-through entities is imposed at the highest marginal tax rate, which is currently 12.3%, see ¶619, ¶806, and ¶810. Similarly, sellers of California real property should note the impact of the increased tax rates on the alternative withholding rate, under which sellers may choose to compute the amount of withholding based on the reportable gain from the sale rather than on a percentage of the total sales price. Individuals and non-California partnerships making the election must compute the withholding on the reportable gain using the highest marginal personal income tax rate, see ¶716. Withholding on amounts paid by a partnership to its foreign partners, which is at the maximum personal income tax rate, is likewise affected, see ¶714.

Practitioner Comment: Entities' Final Year

A corporation, as well as other entities, is no longer required, prior to the dissolution of the entity, to obtain a tax clearance certificate from the FTB. Instead, the Secretary of State must notify the FTB of the dissolution.

In addition, a corporation will not be subject to the minimum tax in the year that a final return is filed if the corporation did not thereafter do business in California and dissolution, surrender or cancellation of the entity is completed before the end of the 12 month period following the date the final tax return was filed. Similar relief from the annual tax will be accorded to a limited partnership, limited liability company or limited liability partnership if these entities: 1) ceased doing business in California prior to the beginning of the taxable year; 2) filed a timely final tax return for the preceding taxable year; and 3) filed a certificate of cancellation with the Secretary of State before the end of the 12 month period beginning with the original due date of the tax return for the preceding taxable year.

Chris Whitney, Contributing Editor

• *Additional tax on millionaires*

An additional 1% tax, referred to as the Mental Health Services Tax, is imposed on the portion of a taxpayer's income in excess of $1 million. Personal income tax credits may not be applied against this additional tax. (Sec. 17043, Rev. & Tax. Code) The constitutionality of the tax was upheld in *Jensen v. Franchise Tax Board* (2009) (CCH CALIFORNIA TAX REPORTS, ¶404-994).

• *Annual tax on pass-through entities*

A minimum tax of $800 is imposed on limited partnerships, limited liability partnerships (LLPs), and limited liability companies (LLCs) that are treated as partnerships or that are disregarded and treated as sole proprietorships (¶625), unless a limited partnership, LLP, or LLC did no business in California during the taxable year and its taxable year was 15 days or less. (Secs. 17935, 17936, 17941, 17946, 17948, Sec. 17948.2, Rev. & Tax. Code) In addition, a domestic LLC that has not conducted any business in California and that has obtained a certificate of cancellation within 12 months from the date that the articles of organization were filed is exempt from the minimum tax. However, the LLC will not be entitled to a refund of any taxes or fees already paid. (Sec. 17946, Rev. & Tax. Code)

A limited partnership, LLP, or an LLC is relieved of liability from the minimum tax if it satisfies the following conditions:

— files a timely final annual tax return for a taxable year with the Franchise Tax Board (FTB);

— does not do business in this state after the end of the taxable year for which the final annual tax return was filed; and

— files a certificate of cancellation or notice of cessation or similar document with the Secretary of State's Office before the end of the 12-month period beginning with the date the final annual tax return was filed.

(Sec. 17937, Rev. & Tax. Code, Sec. 17947, Rev. & Tax. Code, Sec. 17948.3, Rev. & Tax. Code) Also see ¶625 for an additional exemption available to qualified LLCs owned by military personnel on deployment.

Practitioner Comment: Timely Filing of Certificates of Dissolution and Cancellation Certificates for Inactive Entities Can Save Minimum Tax

A limited partnership was found to be liable for the $800 minimum partnership tax for years after it had transferred all of its assets to a limited liability company and ceased operations because the limited partnership failed to file a cancellation certificate, the California State Board of Equalization (BOE) ruled. Under Cal. Sec. 17935, Rev. & Tax. Code, every limited partnership that has filed a certificate of limited partnership with the state must pay the annual tax until a certificate of cancellation is filed. As it was undisputed that the limited partnership failed to file a cancellation certificate, the BOE held that the minimum partnership tax was due, notwithstanding the fact that the transferee LLC filed and paid tax as an LLC for the same years [Uncitable Summary Decision, *Appeal of Cinema Plaza Partners, LP.*, Cal. State Bd. of Equal., No 207907, November 18, 2003, CCH St. Tax Rept., ¶10-225.30].

Similarly, a corporation was liable for the minimum tax for the year in which it surrendered its operations to another corporation because a certificate of dissolution was not timely filed with the Secretary of State. Despite the fact that the corporation had filed a "final" tax return and had clearly surrendered its business operations, state law provides that a corporation remains subject to the minimum tax until it files a certificate of dissolution with the Secretary of State. In the instant case, the certificate was not filed until more than two years after the "final" return was filed [Uncitable Summary Decision, *Red Bud Industries*, Cal. State Bd. of Equal., No. 224004, March 23, 2004, CCH St. Tax Rept., ¶10-215.35]

Chris Whitney, Contributing Editor

In a nonprecedential opinion, the BOE ruled in *Appeal of Wi LV #2* (2005) (CCH CALIFORNIA TAX REPORTS, ¶403-935) that the FTB was estopped from imposing the minimum tax against a limited partnership because the FTB failed to follow its mandate under Rev. & Tax. Code Sec. 17935(b)(2) to notify the partnership upon its filing of a "final" return that the minimum tax was due annually until a certificate of cancellation was filed with the Secretary of State.

Also, a special tax is imposed on the active conduct of any trade or business by certain grandfathered publicly traded partnerships that elect to continue to be treated as partnerships rather than corporations (¶616). (Secs. 17008.5, 23038.5(a), Rev. & Tax. Code)

• *Inflation adjustment*

Indexing of the rate brackets is based on the amount of inflation, or deflation, as measured by the change in the California Consumer Price Index from June of the prior year to June of the current year. The rate brackets for high-income taxpayers (discussed above) are indexed annually for inflation. (Sec. 17041, Rev. & Tax. Code)

- *Use of tax tables*

The tax rate *schedules* are shown in Part I. Also shown are the tax *tables* used to determine the amount of tax on the return. The tax schedules *must* be used for all California returns on which the taxpayer's taxable income is over $100,000.

Married couples filing joint returns receive "split-income" benefits that are built into the tax tables (Part I).

The rates for estates and trusts are the same as for single individuals.

- *Tax rates for nonresidents*

Tax is imposed on a nonresident's or part-year resident's taxable income as follows. A nonresident's or part-year resident's taxable income is all of the nonresident's or part-year resident's gross income and deductions for the portion of the taxable year that the taxpayer was a California resident and/or the gross income and deductions attributable to California during the period the taxpayer was a nonresident of California. Carryover items, deferred income, suspended losses, or suspended deductions are includible or allowable only to the extent that the carryover item, deferred income, suspended loss, or suspended deduction was derived from sources within this state.

The tax rate applied to the nonresident's or part-year resident's taxable income is computed by first determining the tax on the taxpayer's entire taxable income as if the nonresident or part-year resident were a California resident for the taxable year and for all prior taxable years for purposes of any carryover items, deferred income, suspended losses, or suspended deductions. This amount is divided by the taxpayer's total taxable income and the resultant amount is multiplied by the taxpayer's California-sourced taxable income to arrive at the taxpayer's California tax liability. (Sec. 17041, Rev. & Tax. Code) See FTB Pub. 1100, Taxation of Nonresidents and Individuals Who Change Residency, for more details.

- *Tax rates for servicemembers domiciled outside California*

Military compensation of servicemembers domiciled outside of California, and their spouses, may not be included in gross income for purposes of determining the tax rate on nonmilitary income; see ¶225.

¶117 Alternative Minimum Tax

Law: Secs. 17039, 17039.1, 17062, 17062.3, 17062.5 (CCH California Tax Reports, ¶15-405—15-440, 16-805).

Comparable Federal: Secs. 55-59 (CCH U.S. Master Tax Guide ¶1401—1480).

California Forms: Sch. P (540) (Alternative Minimum Tax and Credit Limitations - Residents), Sch. P (540NR) (Alternative Minimum Tax and Credit Limitations - Nonresidents or Part-Year Residents), Sch. P (541) (Alternative Minimum Tax and Credit Limitations - Fiduciaries).

The alternative minimum tax (AMT), which is in addition to regular tax, is imposed under both California and federal law in an amount equal to the excess (if any) of the tentative minimum tax for the taxable year over regular tax for the taxable year. (Sec. 17062, Rev. & Tax. Code)

- *"Regular tax" defined*

For California AMT purposes, "regular tax" is the personal income tax before reduction for any credits against tax. (Sec. 17062, Rev. & Tax. Code)

- *Federal-California differences*

The California tentative minimum tax rate is 7.0%. (Sec. 17062, Rev. & Tax. Code) For federal purposes, the tentative minimum tax rate is (1) 26% of the first $175,000 of a taxpayer's alternative minimum taxable income (AMTI) in excess of the exemption amount and (2) 28% of any additional AMTI in excess of the exemption amount.

However, the federal, but not California, minimum tax rate is lowered to reflect the reduction in the federal capital gains rate and the reduced rate applied to dividends.

A nonresident's or part-year resident's tentative minimum tax is determined by multiplying the nonresident's or part-year resident's AMTI by a ratio, the numerator of which is the tax determined as if the taxpayer were a California resident for the taxable year and for all prior taxable years for any carryover items, deferred income, suspended losses, or suspended deductions, and the denominator of which is the taxpayer's total AMTI. A nonresident or part-year resident's AMTI includes all items of AMTI during which the taxpayer was a California resident and only those items derived from California sources during any period that the taxpayer was a nonresident. Any carryover items, deferred income, suspended losses, or suspended deductions are allowable only to the extent that the carryover item, suspended loss, or suspended deduction was derived from California sources. There is no equivalent computation for federal purposes. (Sec. 17062(b)(3)(B), Rev. & Tax. Code) Consult FTB Pub. 1100, Taxation of Nonresidents and Individuals Who Change Residency, for detailed explanations and examples.

California, like federal law, includes as an item of tax preference (TPI) an amount equal to one-half of the amount of gain realized from the disposition of certain small business stock excluded from gross income. (Sec. 17062, Rev. & Tax. Code) Federal, but not California, law reduces the amount of tax preference from 50% to 7% of gain on the sale of small business stock excluded from gross income for dispositions of small business stock.

California modifies federal law disallowing the standard deduction and the deduction for personal exemptions for AMT computation purposes to disallow only the standard deduction. California also modifies federal law to exclude from AMTI the income, adjustments, or items of tax preference attributable to a trade or business of a taxpayer who (1) owns or has an ownership interest in a trade or business, and (2) has aggregate gross receipts, less returns and allowances, of less than $1 million during the taxable year from all trades or businesses owned by the taxpayer or in which the taxpayer has an ownership interest.

For purposes of computing the taxpayer's gross receipts, only the taxpayer's proportionate interest in a trade or business in which the taxpayer has an ownership interest is included. "Aggregate gross receipts, less returns and allowances" is the sum of (1) the gross receipts of the trades or businesses that the taxpayer owns, and (2) the proportionate interest of the gross receipts of the trades or businesses in which the taxpayer has an ownership interest and the pass-through entities in which the taxpayer holds an interest. The term includes gross income from the production of both business income and nonbusiness income. (Sec. 17062, Rev. & Tax. Code)

CCH Practice Tip: $1 Million Threshold

According to the Franchise Tax Board, the $1 million threshold applies regardless of the taxpayer's filing status. Thus, married taxpayers filing jointly are not allowed to increase the $1 million threshold to $2 million (Instructions to Sch. P (540)).

California specifically does not incorporate federal provisions (1) designating tax-exempt interest on specified private activity bonds as a TPI and (2) allowing an alternative minimum tax foreign tax credit. (Sec. 17062, Rev. & Tax. Code) However, California allows certain credits to reduce a taxpayer's regular tax below the tentative minimum tax, after an allowance for the minimum tax credit. The following are the credits that may reduce the regular tax below the tentative minimum tax:

— the former solar energy credits;

— the renter's credit;

— the research credit;

— the former manufacturer's investment credit;

— the former orphan drug research credit;

— the low-income housing credit;

— the credit for excess unemployment compensation contributions;

— the credits for taxes paid to other states;

— the credit for withheld tax;

— the personal, dependent, blind, and senior exemption credits;

— the credits for sales and use tax paid or incurred in connection with the purchase of qualified property used in an enterprise zone, a former program area, the former Los Angeles Revitalization Zone, or the former targeted tax area;

— the enterprise zone, former program area, former Los Angeles Revitalization Zone, and former targeted tax area hiring credits;

— the former teacher retention credit;

— the natural heritage preservation credit;

— the adoption costs credit;

— the credits for qualified joint custody head of household and a qualified taxpayer with a dependent parent;

— the senior head of household credit;

— the California Competes credit; and

— the college access tax credit. (Secs. 17039, 17039.1, Rev. & Tax. Code)

Finally, California (but not federal) law indexes the exemption amounts and the exemption phaseout amounts for inflation (see discussion below).

• *Computation of AMTI*

For both federal and California purposes, AMTI is regular taxable income after certain adjustments, increased by the amount of TPIs. However, as discussed above, for purposes of calculating AMTI, qualified taxpayers exclude income, adjustments, or items of tax preference from their trade or business. (Sec. 17062, Rev. & Tax. Code)

The following are the applicable adjustments and TPIs:

Adjustments: The following adjustments must be made to the deductions claimed or the methods used in calculating regular taxable income:

— *excess depreciation:* an AMT adjustment is required for depreciation claimed under the MACRS method if the taxpayer does not depreciate the property for regular tax purposes in the same manner prescribed for AMT purposes;

— *capitalizable expenses:* certain expenses that would ordinarily be treated as TPIs if deducted in the current year will not be treated as TPIs if the taxpayer elects to amortize them over a specified amortization period for regular tax purposes;

— *long-term contracts:* the percentage-of-completion method must be substituted for the completed-contract method to determine AMTI; for certain small construction contracts, simplified procedures for allocation of costs must be used;

— *alternative minimum tax NOL deduction:* NOL deductions must be recomputed on the same basis as AMTI (that is, reduced by TPIs and other adjustments); an alternative NOL may not offset more than 90% of the AMTI for a tax year without regard to the NOL deduction (100% for federal purposes only for NOLs attributable to qualified federal disasters and for NOLs generated or taken as carryovers in 2001 and 2002);

CCH Tip: Computation of AMTI NOL Deduction

The Franchise Tax Board's legal division has taken the position that AMTI NOL is computed without reference to the exclusion available to taxpayers involved in a trade or business with gross receipts of $1 million or less (Question and Answer No. 2, 1997, CPA/FTB Liaison Meeting, October 16, 1997).

— *certified pollution control facilities:* the five-year depreciation method must be replaced by the alternative depreciation system specified by federal law (straight-line method, without regard to salvage value); however, a facility placed in service after 1998 is depreciated using the IRC Sec. 168 straight-line method;

— *alternative tax itemized deductions:* in determining AMTI, no deduction is allowed for miscellaneous itemized deductions (including certain interest and medical expenses that are less than 10% of adjusted gross income (AGI)); state, local, and foreign real property taxes and state and local personal property taxes are not deductible for AMT purposes, nor are mortgage interest expenses associated with proceeds used for purposes other than buying, building, or improving the taxpayer's principal residence or qualified second home; the overall limitation on itemized deductions of 6% of AGI (3% of AGI for federal purposes) does not apply for AMT purposes;

— *adjusted gain or loss:* gain or loss from the sale or exchange of business property during the tax year or from a casualty to business or income-producing property must be recomputed for AMT purposes by using the AMT adjusted tax basis rather than the regular tax adjusted basis of the property;

— *passive farm tax shelter losses:* taxpayers who are not material participants in a farming business may not deduct passive farming losses from AMTI; however, a loss determined upon the disposition of the taxpayer's entire interest in a tax shelter farming activity is not considered a loss from a tax shelter farm activity and is deductible in computing AMTI;

— *passive nonfarm business activity losses:* the rules limiting deductibility of other passive activity losses for regular tax purposes are subject to the following adjustments: (1) the amount of passive loss denied is reduced by the amount of insolvency; (2) passive activity losses must be computed on the same basis as AMTI (that is, reduced by TPIs and other adjustments, including the adjustment for passive farm losses); and (3) qualified housing interests are not included in computing passive business activity losses;

— *incentive stock options:* a taxpayer must include in AMTI the excess (if any) of (1) the fair market value of an incentive stock option at the time the taxpayer's rights in the option are freely transferable or are no longer subject to a substantial risk of forfeiture over (2) the price paid for the option; the amount of income excluded for regular tax purposes from exercising a California incentive stock option (¶207) is added back for purposes of computing AMTI;

— *tax recoveries:* refunds of taxes that are included in computing AGI for regular tax purposes (*e.g.,* state and local personal property taxes and state, local, and foreign real property taxes) are not included in gross income for purposes of determining AMTI; and

— *depreciation of grapevines:* California (but not federal) law provides that if grapevines are replanted as a result of phylloxera infestation or Pierce's disease and are being depreciated over five years instead of 20 years for regular tax purposes, they must be depreciated over 10 years for AMT purposes.

Items of tax preference: The following TPIs must be added back in computing AMTI:

— *excess depreciation on property placed in service prior to 1987:* for nonrecovery real property, leased personal property, pollution control facilities, leased recovery property, 19-year real property, and low-income housing, the excess of accelerated depreciation deductions over normal depreciation is a TPI;

— *excess deductions from oil or mineral operations:* the excess of the depletion deduction claimed by a taxpayer (other than an independent oil and gas producer) for an interest in a mineral deposit over its adjusted basis at the end of the tax year must be added back, as must the amount by which an integrated oil company's excess intangible drilling costs exceed 65% of net income from oil, gas, and geothermal properties; and

— *excluded gain on sale of small business stock:* one-half of the amount of gain excluded from gross income on the sale or disposition of qualified small business stock (as calculated for California personal income tax purposes) is a TPI.

• *Exemption amount*

The California and federal alternative minimum tax is imposed on AMTI minus the exemption amount. For both California and federal purposes, the exemption amounts are reduced by 25¢ for each $1 that AMTI exceeds the beginning phase-out level, until the exemption is completely phased out. (Sec. 17062, Rev. & Tax. Code)

For the 2016 taxable year, the exemption amounts for California purposes are as follows:

	Exemption amount	Phaseout begins at	Phaseout ends at
Married/RDP filing jointly and surviving spouse	$89,467	$335,502	$693,370
Single and head of household	$67,101	$251,626	$520,030
Married/RDP filing separately and estates and trusts	$44,732	$167,749	$346,677

For married individuals filing separately, AMTI is adjusted so that the maximum amount of the exemption phase out is the same for married taxpayers filing jointly. California, but not federal, law requires the indexing for inflation of both the exemption amounts and the phase-out of exemption amounts.

In the case of certain children (see ¶118), the maximum exemption amount is the lesser of (1) the exemption available to an individual taxpayer ($67,101 for the 2016 tax year) for California purposes or (2) the sum of the child's earned income plus $7,400 (as adjusted for 2016).

CCH Practice Tip: Impact of NASSCO, Inc. Decision

The Franchise Tax Board has taken the position that the State Board of Equalization's (BOE) decision in *Appeal of NASSCO, Inc.*, in which the BOE held that taxpayers were entitled to claim corporation franchise and income tax manufacturing investment credits (MIC) and enterprise zone (EZ) credits against the alternative minimum tax (AMT), is inapplicable to the personal income alternative minimum tax. (*Notice 2011-02*, CCH California Tax Reports, ¶405-390)

¶118 Certain Children with Investment Income (Kiddie Tax)

Law: Sec. 17041(g) (CCH California Tax Reports, ¶15-360).

Comparable Federal: Sec. 1(g) (CCH U.S. Master Tax Guide ¶114, 706).

California Forms: FTB 3800 (Tax Computation for Certain Children With Investment Income), FTB 3803 (Parent's Election to Report Child's Interest and Dividends).

California conforms to federal law as of California's current federal conformity date (¶103) for purposes of calculating the amount of income tax for a child who has "investment income" in excess of a certain amount ($2,100 for 2016) who meets the following conditions: (Sec. 17041(g), Rev. & Tax. Code)

— is under age 18 at the end of the taxable year;

— is 18 years old and does not provide half of his or her own support costs with earned income; and

— is 19 to 23 years-old and is a full-time student who does not provide half of his or her own support costs with earned income.

In addition, either parent of the child must be living at the close of the taxable year and the parents must not have taken a special election (discussed below) to include the child's income on the parent's return.

The "kiddie" tax is computed on Form 3800 (Tax Computation for Certain Children With Investment Income), which parallels federal Form 8615.

The tax is designed to prevent parents from shifting investment income to a child in a lower bracket, and equals the greater of:

(1) the income tax on the child's taxable income figured at the child's rates without benefit of a personal exemption; or

(2) the total of:

(a) the "parental tax" (defined below); plus

(b) the income tax figured at the child's rates on the amount of the child's taxable income that remains after subtracting out the child's "net investment income" (defined below).

• *"Investment income," "net investment income," "parental tax" defined*

"Investment income" is all income other than wages, salaries, professional fees, and other amounts received as pay for work actually done.

"Net investment income" is investment income reduced by the greater of:

(1) $2,100 (for 2016); or

(2) $1,050 (for 2016) plus the child's itemized deductions that are directly connected with the production of his or her investment income.

"Parental tax" is the difference in tax on the parent's income figured with and without the child's net investment income.

• *Election to claim child's unearned income on parent's return*

A parent may elect to include on the parent's return the unearned income of a child whose income in 2016 is more than $1,050 but less than $10,500 and consists solely of interest, dividends, or Alaska Permanent Fund dividends. The child is treated as having no gross income and does not have to file a tax return if the child's parent makes the election. However, the election is not available if estimated tax payments were made in the child's name and taxpayer identification number for the tax year or if the child is subject to backup withholding. (Sec. 17041, Rev. & Tax. Code)

To report the unearned income of a child on the parent's return, FTB 3803 (comparable to federal Form 8814) must accompany the parent's return. In addition to the child's gross income in excess of $2,100 (for 2016) being taxed at the parent's highest marginal rate, additional tax liability must be reported equal to 1% (10% for federal purposes) of the lesser of $1,050 or the child's income exceeding $1,050. Special rules apply to unmarried taxpayers and married taxpayers filing separate returns, see Instructions to FTB 3803.

¶119 Registered Domestic Partners and Same-Sex Married Couples

Law: Sec. 17021.7 (CCH California Tax Reports, ¶15-165).

Comparable Federal: None.

California Forms: Form 540 (California Resident Income Tax Return), Sch. CA (540) (California Adjustments - Residents).

California, unlike federal law, recognizes registered domestic partners (RDPs) for tax purposes. With the issuance of federal Revenue Ruling 2013-17, same-sex married couples are now treated as spouses for both federal and California tax purposes.

- *Same-sex married couples*

Legally married same-sex couples generally must file their federal income tax return using either the married filing jointly or married filing separately filing status. California taxpayers are generally required to use the same filing status that they used for federal tax purposes. Because same-sex married couples (SSMCs) must file both federal and California income tax returns using the same filing status, no federal/California differences exist for SSMCs.

Practitioner Comment: California Employer Implications of Section 3 of DOMA Deemed Unconstitutional

The U.S. Supreme Court's decision in *United States v. Windsor*, 133 S. Ct. 2675 (2013), on June 26, 2013 deemed Section 3 of the Defense of Marriage Act ("DOMA") unconstitutional. DOMA is federal legislation which was enacted in 1996 which allowed states to effectively refuse to recognize same-sex marriages granted under the laws of other states. In addition, Section 3 of DOMA in defining marriage as between a man and a woman, permitted federal and state governments to deny same-sex spouses the benefits available to opposite-sex spouses.

The Department of the Treasury issued Revenue Ruling 2013-17 ("Ruling") to implement the federal tax aspects of the *Windsor* decision. The Ruling treats same-sex couples as married for all federal tax purposes, including income and gift and estate taxes. The ruling applies to all federal tax provisions where marriage is a factor, including filing status, claiming personal and dependency exemptions, taking the standard deduction, employee benefits, contributing to an IRA and claiming the earned income tax credit or child tax credit. California is following the ruling.

The Ruling aligns the federal and California filing status for same-sex married couples (but not domestic partnerships) because California already permitted certain same-sex married couples to file joint returns. As a result, the Treasury ruling eliminates the need for same-sex couples to create a pro-forma federal income tax return prior to preparing their California joint income tax return. In this regard it should be noted that on October 10, 2009, the Governor signed S.B. 54, which allowed same-sex spouses married in a state that permitted same-sex marriages to file joint returns effective 2010. FTB Publication 776 was created to assist these spouses with filing their California tax return.

California also passed AB 362, which states that beginning October 1, 2013 and until January 1, 2019, employee wages subject to withholding tax will not include any amounts received from an employer to compensate for additional federal income taxes incurred by the employee on employer provided health care benefits. Thus, similar to opposite-sex married couples, same-sex married couples will now have the value of employer-paid health care coverage, certain tuition benefits, or group-term life insurance premiums excluded from their gross income and wages. Previously under DOMA, married same-sex couples and their families could not qualify for certain tax benefits and protections, such as qualified benefits, that were available to married couples of the opposite sex.

Chris Whitney, Contributing Editor

- *Registered domestic partners*

Registered domestic partners (RDPs) or former RDPs who are qualified and are registered with the California Secretary of State's Office are required to be treated as married taxpayers or former spouses under California income and franchise tax laws, unless specified exceptions apply.

The statutory exceptions relate to business entity classifications, tax-favored accounts, and deferred compensation plans. Consequently, RDPs will not be treated as a single shareholder for purposes of determining whether an S corporation has exceeded the 100 shareholder limitation. In addition, an RDP will not be treated as a spouse if such treatment would result in disqualification of a federally qualified deferred compensation plan or disqualification of tax-favored accounts, such as individual retirement accounts, Archer medical savings accounts, qualified tuition programs, or Coverdell education savings accounts. (Sec. 17021.7, Rev. & Tax. Code)

Practice Tip: Other State Unions

The Franchise Tax Board has indicated that if individuals have entered into a same sex legal union, other than a marriage, in another state, and that union has been determined to be substantially equivalent to a California registered domestic partnership, the individuals are required to file using either the married/RDP filing jointly or married/RDP filing separately filing status. More information on what state unions are considered substantially equivalent to a California registered domestic partnership can be found on the FTB's Web site by searching for the term "RDP." (FTB Pub. 737, Tax Information for Registered Domestic Partners)

RDPs must use the same California filing status as required for married taxpayers (see ¶114). Special rules apply for purposes of determining limitations based on adjusted gross income (¶202). Community property rules also apply (¶239).

Comment: Federal Treatment of RDP's Community Property

The Internal Revenue Service (IRS) has concluded that a California registered domestic partner must report one-half of the RDP's community property income on his or her federal return. The federal advice is based on California law that treats the earned income of a RDP as community property for state income tax purposes. Previously, the IRS did not recognize this community property treatment.

For additional information on the federal and state treatment of RDPs, see IRS Pub. 555, Community Property, and the IRS's *Answers to Frequently Asked Questions for Registered Domestic Partners and Individuals in Civil Unions* located at http://www.irs.gov/uac/Answers-to-Frequently-Asked-Questions-for-Registered-Domestic-Partners-and-Individuals-in-Civil-Unions; FTB Publication 737, Tax Information for Registered Domestic Partners; and FTB Publication 1051A, Guidelines for Married/RDP Filing Separate Returns.

California allows an exclusion from gross income for employer-provided accident, health insurance, and medical expense reimbursements for an RDP and the RDP's dependents if the reimbursements were not previously excluded on the federal return. In contrast, under federal law, a company's contribution to a domestic partner's benefits is treated as taxable income to the employee partner. Self-employed individuals may also claim a deduction for health insurance costs paid for a RDP and the RDP's dependents. (Sec. 17021.7, Rev. & Tax. Code) (FTB Pub. 1001, Supplemental Guidelines to California Adjustments)

Additional adjustments are required to reconcile the differences that arise from RDPs using a different filing status on their California and federal personal income tax returns. These adjustments may be made by completing a pro forma federal return or by completing the worksheets provided in FTB Pub. 737, Tax Information for Registered Domestic Partners. RDP adjustments may include, but are not limited to:

— division of community property (¶239)
— capital losses (¶526)
— transactions between RDPs (¶502)
— sale of residence (¶229)
— dependent care assistance (¶253)
— investment interest (¶305)
— medical and dental expenses (¶325)
— job expenses and current miscellaneous deductions (¶303)
— qualified residence acquisition loan and equity loan interest (¶305)

¶119

— IRA income and deductions (¶206, ¶330)

— expense depreciation limitations (¶311)

— reforestation expenses (¶315)

— education loan interest (¶305)

— rental real estate passive loss (¶340)

— rollover of publicly traded securities gain into specialized small business investment companies (¶501).

Registered domestic partners are qualified to register with the Secretary of State's Office if all of the following requirements are met:

— both persons are of the same sex or one or both of the persons is/are over the age of 62 and is/are eligible for old-age insurance benefits under the Social Security program;

— both persons share a common residence;

— neither person is married to someone else or is a member of another RDP;

— the persons are not related by blood in a way that would prevent them from being legally married to each other in California;

— both persons are at least 18 years of age; and

— both persons are capable of consenting to the domestic partnership.

(Sec. 297, Family Code)

PERSONAL INCOME TAX

CHAPTER 1A
CREDITS

¶125 Credits—In General

Law: Secs. 17024.5(b)(10), 17039, 17039.2, 17043, 17055 (CCH CALIFORNIA TAX REPORTS, ¶ 16-805).

Comparable Federal: None.

California Forms: Form 540 (California Resident Income Tax Return), Form 540NR (California Nonresident or Part-Year Resident Income Tax Return), Sch. P (540) (Alternative Minimum Tax and Credit Limitations - Residents), Sch. P (540NR) (Alternative Minimum Tax and Credit Limitations - Nonresidents or Part-Year Residents), Sch. P (541) (Alternative Minimum Tax and Credit Limitations - Fiduciaries), FTB 3540 (Credit Carryover Summary), FTB 3801-CR (Passive Activity Credit Limitations).

In addition to the credits for personal and dependency exemptions (¶113), California law provides a variety of credits that may be used to reduce taxable income. However, as discussed at ¶117, certain credits may not be used to reduce the taxpayer's regular tax, plus the tax imposed on lump-sum distributions from employees' trusts, below the taxpayer's tentative minimum tax.

A taxpayer who claims more than three credits must complete the appropriate form for each credit and the credits must be summarized on Schedule P (Alternative Minimum Tax and Credit Limitations). Three or less credits may be claimed directly on Form 540.

Comment: Millionaire (Mental Health Services) Tax

Credits may not be applied against the mental health services additional tax on a taxpayer's taxable income in excess of $1 million (see ¶116). (Sec. 17043, Rev. & Tax. Code)

Also, some credits may be limited because they arise from passive activities (¶340). The taxpayer must file FTB 3801-CR (Passive Activity Credit Limitations) if the taxpayer claims any of the following credits and the credits arise from passive activities: low-income housing credit (¶138), research and development credit (¶139), orphan drug research credit carryover (see below), or targeted jobs credit generated prior to 1996.

Comment: Temporary Limitation on Credit Amounts Lifted

The amount of business credits and business credit carryovers that could be claimed by taxpayers during the 2008 and 2009 tax years was limited to 50% of a taxpayer's tax liability. Thereafter, the credits may be claimed in full. Any unused credit may be carried over and the carryover period is extended by the number of taxable years the credit, or any portion thereof, was not allowed as a result of the 50% limitation. A taxpayer with net business income of less than $500,000 for the taxable year was exempt from the 50% limitation. For purposes of determining the amount of business credits that may be claimed, nonbusiness credits were applied before any business credits.

The new jobs credit (¶157) and the credits for taxes paid to other states were not subject to the temporary 50% limitation. (Sec. 17039.2, Rev. & Tax. Code)

Although federal tax credits are not applicable under California law, certain California credits are similar to their federal counterparts. California also has many credits for which there are no comparable federal credits, and there are some federal credits that have no California counterparts.

• *Carryover credits*

Expired credits for which carryovers may be claimed (and the years for which the credits were available) include the following:

— water conservation credit (1980—1982);

— solar pump credit (1981—1983);

— solar energy credit (1985—1988);

— energy conservation credit (1981—1986);

— ridesharing credits (1981—1986 and 1989—1995);

— political contributions credit (1987—1991);

— commercial solar energy credit (1987—1988);

— residential rental and farm sales credit (1987—1991);

— orphan drug research credit (1987—1992);

— qualified parent's infant care credit (1991—1993);

— commercial solar electric system credit (1990—1993);

— recycling equipment credit (1989—1995);

— low-emission vehicle credit (1991—1995);

— salmon and steelhead trout habitat credit (1995—1999);

— rice straw credit (1997—2007);

— farmworker housing credit (1997—2008);

— employer childcare program credit (1994-2011);

— employer childcare contribution credit (1994-2011);

— targeted tax area sales and use tax credit (1998-2012);

— local agency military base recovery area (LAMBRA) sales and use tax credit (1996—2013); and

— new jobs credit (2009—2013).

All of the above credit carryovers may be claimed on FTB 3540, except for the targeted tax area sales and use tax credit and LAMBRA sales and use tax credit. See prior editions of the *Guidebook to California Taxes* for details about these credits.

Comment: Credit Carryover Amounts

When a taxpayer discovers that a credit carryover on a personal income tax return was understated or overstated due to the original credit not having been calculated properly, or additional credit amounts being found after the original (credit year) return was filed, questions arise as to whether the taxpayer must amend the prior year(s) return(s) or make the revisions to the carryover in the current year's tax return. When a credit carryover amount is revised, the tax return for the year the credit was generated does not need to be amended if the tax liability remains the same for that year. If the revision to the credit increases the tax liability for the credit year, an amended return should be filed reporting the increase in tax due for that year and for any subsequent tax years with an open statute of limitations where the eliminated credit carryover was used to reduce tax. Conversely, if there is no change in tax liability for the credit year and subsequent years, no amended return is required; instead, the change may be reflected on the current year's tax return. To correct a credit carryover amount on the current year's return, the taxpayer should provide the original credit form as filed; the amended credit form to show the revised credit generated; supporting schedules, if any; a revised credit carryover schedule; and a detailed statement explaining the changes. (*Tax News*, California Franchise Tax Board, December 2015, CCH CALIFORNIA TAX REPORTS, ¶406-447)

Comment: Recapture of Farmworker Housing Credit Claimed by Partnership

The current partners of a partnership that was allocated a former farmworker housing credit are liable for the recapture of the credit in the year of the disqualifying event even though they were not the partners that originally claimed the credit in the year that the credit was passed through from the partnership. (*Legal Ruling 2009-02*, California Franchise Tax Board, September 10, 2009, CCH CALIFORNIA TAX REPORTS, ¶404-982)

• *Credit sharing*

Unless a personal income tax credit provision specifies some other sharing arrangement, two or more taxpayers (other than spouses or registered domestic partners (RDPs)) may share a tax credit in proportion to their respective shares of the creditable costs. Partners may divide a credit in accordance with a written partnership agreement. In the case of spouses or RDPs filing separately, either may claim the whole of the credit or they may divide it equally between them. (Sec. 17021.7, Rev. & Tax. Code; Sec. 17039, Rev. & Tax. Code)

• *Pass-through entities*

Credits that become inoperative, and that are passed through (in the first tax year after they become inoperative) to a taxpayer who is a partner or shareholder of an eligible pass-through entity may be claimed in the year of the pass-through. An eligible pass-through entity is any partnership or S corporation that files a fiscal year return and is entitled to a credit in the last year that the credit is operative. (Sec. 17039(h), Rev. & Tax. Code)

• *Limitation on credit claimed by taxpayers with interest in a disregarded entity*

If a taxpayer owns an interest in a disregarded business entity, credits claimed for amounts paid or incurred by the business are limited to the difference between the taxpayer's regular tax figured with the income of the disregarded entity and the taxpayer's regular tax figured without the disregarded entity's income. If the disregarded entity reports a loss, the taxpayer may not claim the credit for the year of the loss, but can carry over the credit amount received from the disregarded entity. (Sec. 17039(g), Rev. & Tax. Code)

• *Reduced credits for nonresidents and part-year residents*

Nonresidents and part-year residents are allowed reduced tax credits, with some exceptions. Credits are allowed on the basis of a prorated taxable income formula (see ¶116). If California income is 50% of the total, allowable credits are 50% of total credits. However, different rules apply to the following credits:

— the renter's credit (¶133) is allowed in proportion to the period of residence;

— credits for taxes paid to other states (¶128, ¶129) are allowed in full; and

— credits that are conditional upon a transaction occurring wholly within California are allowed in full. (Sec. 17055, Rev. & Tax. Code)

¶126 Tax Credits—Priorities

Law: Sec. 17039 (CCH CALIFORNIA TAX REPORTS, ¶16-810).

Comparable Federal: None.

The law provides rules for the order in which various tax credits are to be applied. These rules are necessary because of the variety of provisions for carryovers, refundability, etc., in the various credits. Credits are allowed against "net tax" (the regular tax plus the tax on lump-sum distributions less exemption credits, but in no event less than the tax on lump-sum distributions) in the following order:

(1) credits, except the credits in categories 4 and 5, below, with no carryover or refundable provisions;

(2) credits with carryovers that are not refundable, except for those that are allowed to reduce "net tax" below the tentative minimum tax (see ¶117);

(3) credits with both carryover and refundable provisions;

(4) the minimum tax credit;

(5) credits that are allowed to reduce "net tax" below the tentative minimum tax (see ¶117);

(6) credits for taxes paid to other states; and

(7) credits with refundable provisions but no carryover (withholding, excess SDI). (Sec. 17039, Rev. & Tax. Code)

Also, see ¶125 for a discussion of the credit ordering as applied to the business credit limitations applicable to the 2008 and 2009 taxable years.

¶127 Credit for Taxes Paid Other States—General

Law: Secs. 18001-11 (CCH CALIFORNIA TAX REPORTS, ¶16-825).

Comparable Federal: Secs. 901-5 (CCH U.S. MASTER TAX GUIDE ¶1311).

California Form: Sch. S (Other State Tax Credit).

In an effort to relieve double taxation, California law allows in some cases a credit against California personal income tax for income tax paid to another state or to a U.S. territory or possession. (Sec. 18001, et. seq., Rev. & Tax. Code) (Note: Reference to territories or possessions is frequently omitted in the following discussion for the sake of simplicity; "other state" should be understood to include also territories or possessions.) Detailed rules for such credits in different situations are set forth below in ¶128—131, inclusive. General rules applicable to credits in all situations are included in this paragraph.

No credit is allowed for income taxes paid to cities or to foreign countries. However, some foreign taxes on gross receipts may be taken as a *deduction* (¶306).

Practice Tip: New Validation Rules

As a result of new validation rules, the Franchise Tax Board (FTB) has begun adjusting or disallowing the other state tax credit because of incomplete or missing information on the Schedule S. California residents included in other state composite (group) returns may claim a credit for their share of income taxes paid to the other state, as long as the state does not allow a credit for taxes paid to California for the group. Although the credit is not normally allowed for taxes paid to Arizona, Indiana, Oregon, and Virginia, the credit will be allowed for a California resident that is included in a group return filed in one of these states, unless any of these states allow a credit for taxes paid to California for the group. According to the Schedule S instructions, the taxpayer must attach a composite schedule or statement explaining that he/she is included in a group return. To avoid requests for additional information or an adjustment to a return during processing, taxpayers should fill out each Schedule S completely and attach all applicable Schedule S forms; should not lump all income or credits under "various," "see attached," or a particular state; and for California residents belonging to a group, should attach a composite schedule or statement explaining that they are in a group. (*Tax News*, California Franchise Tax Board, September 2016, CCH CALIFORNIA TAX REPORTS, ¶406-552)

Practitioner Comment: U.S. Supreme Court's Decision in Wynne May Raise Questions Concerning California's Credit for Taxes Paid to Other States

On May 18, 2015, the U.S Supreme Court issued its 5-4 decision in *Comptroller of the Treasury of Maryland v. Wynne*, 135 U.S. 1787 (2015), in which it held that while the application of Maryland statutes which provide a credit to residents for taxes paid to other states was consistent with the Due Process Clause, it violated the Commerce Clause of the U.S. Constitution.

Maryland subjects its residents to income tax on 100% of their income, including income sourced to and taxed in other states. In order to mitigate double taxation of income earned in other states, Maryland provides its residents with a credit for taxes paid to other states against the income tax imposed by Maryland on the same income. However, the income tax imposed by Maryland consists of a county income tax in addition to the state level income tax and provides that taxes paid to other states can only be taken as a credit against the state, but not the county, portion of the income tax.

The Wynnes were Maryland residents who received pass-through income from an S corporation which did business in multiple states. The Wynnes successfully argued that the inability to take a credit for taxes paid to other states against the local portion of the Maryland income tax effectively placed an additional burden on interstate business activity not born by businesses conducted wholly within Maryland. In reaching this conclusion, the Court utilized the "internal consistency" test under which a tax system is rejected as violating the Commerce Clause if its hypothetical imposition by every jurisdiction would inevitably result in interstate business bearing a higher tax burden than business conducted wholly within the state.

Like Maryland, California imposes personal income tax on 100% of the income earned by residents, including income which is sourced and which has been taxed by other state and local jurisdictions. However, California provides a credit only for state, but not local, taxes imposed on such double taxed income.

It is unclear what implications the Court's decision in *Wynne* might have in California. For example, California residents may own interests in pass through entities such as S corporations and partnerships which are subject to income taxes imposed by local jurisdictions located within other states which arguably creates a risk of double taxation. On the other hand, California, unlike Maryland, does not impose local income tax. Arguably under the "internal consistency" standard applied in *Wynne*, if all states imposed a similar tax system, there would be no local income taxes imposed on such income to begin with. Finally, it should be noted that the Court reached its conclusion in Wynne based upon the "internal consistency" standard and did not need to address the constitutionality of Maryland's provisions under the "external consistency" standard. Under the "external consistency" standard, the tax imposed must relate to activities actually conducted within the state. Application of this standard to the taxation of residents who hold interests in pass through entities engaged in multistate business operations could have much further reaching implications than the issue directly addressed in *Wynne*.

Chris Whitney, Contributing Editor

• *Tax based on net income*

The credit is allowed only for taxes of another state based on *net income* (excluding any tax comparable to the alternative minimum tax). It therefore does not apply to a tax imposed on *gross income*. In *Appeal of Jesson* (1957) (CCH California Tax Reports, ¶16-825.20), the State Board of Equalization held that the Alaska gross production tax on gold mining royalties was not based on net income and therefore is not eligible for credit against California personal income tax. Likewise, the revised Texas franchise (margin) tax is not a "net income tax" under California law because it is a tax on, or measured by, gross receipts. Therefore, payment of the Texas tax is not eligible for the credit for any taxable year. (*Technical Advice Memorandum 2016-01*, California Franchise Tax Board, January 12, 2016, CCH California Tax Reports, ¶406-469)

• *Credit to estates and trusts and pass-through entities*

Credit is allowed to estates or trusts as well as to individuals. (Sec. 18004, Rev. & Tax. Code) Credit may be allowed to an individual for taxes that were paid to another state by an estate or trust of which the individual is a beneficiary or by a partnership of which the individual is a partner, an S corporation for which the individual is a shareholder, or a limited liability company of which the individual is a member. (Sec. 18005, Rev. & Tax. Code; Sec. 18006, Rev. & Tax. Code) See ¶130—131 for details.

• *Timing of credit*

A taxpayer may not take credit for tax paid another state until the tax is actually paid. If the other-state tax has already been paid, the credit may be claimed at the time of filing the California return; if not, it may be claimed later by means of a refund claim. (Reg. 18001-1 (c), 18 CCR) See ¶719 for a discussion of the limitations period to claim a refund.

The claim for credit must be supported by filing Schedule S together with a copy of the return filed with the other state. A copy of the other state's return does not need to be filed with the California return if the taxpayer files electronically. However, the other state's return should be retained by the taxpayer for his or her records. (Instructions, Schedule S, Other State Tax Credit)

• *Effect of joint or separate returns*

In the case of spouses or registered domestic partners (RDPs) who file separate returns in California and a joint return in the other state, each spouse/RDP is allowed a credit based upon the portion of the other-state tax allocable to his or her own income. The total tax paid to the other state is prorated to each on the basis of the income that is included in the joint return and also taxed in the California separate returns. Where a joint return is filed in California, the entire amount of taxes paid by either spouse/RDP or both to the other state may be claimed as a credit, regardless of which spouse/RDP paid the other tax or whether a joint return or separate returns are filed in the other state. (Reg. 18001-1, 18 CCR) (Instructions, Schedule S, Other State Tax Credit)

• *Refunds must be reported*

A taxpayer who obtains a refund or a credit of any portion of tax paid to another state must report the refund or credit immediately to the FTB. The reduction in the credit against California personal income tax must be computed and the resulting increase in the net California personal income tax paid, with interest. (Instructions, Schedule S, Other State Tax Credit)

In *Appeal of Daniel W. Fessler* (1981) (CCH CALIFORNIA TAX REPORTS, ¶16-825.251), the taxpayer claimed credit based upon $726 withheld from his wages by the State of New York. The taxpayer's New York return showed a tax of only $130; he had claimed, but not yet received, a New York refund of $596. The State Board of Equalization held that the credit should be based upon the correct New York tax of $130, because the larger amount withheld was only an estimate of the anticipated tax liability.

• *California-federal differences*

There are many differences between the California credits for taxes paid to other states and the foreign tax credit in the federal law. The federal credit is allowed for income taxes generally; the California credit is allowed only for taxes based on *net income* (excluding any tax comparable to the alternative minimum tax). Federal credit is allowed only where the taxpayer elects to take the credit instead of using the foreign tax as a deduction; California requires no election, because it allows no deduction for income taxes under any circumstances.

¶128 Credit for Taxes Paid Other States—Residents

Law: Secs. 18001, 18006 (CCH CALIFORNIA TAX REPORTS, ¶16-825).

Comparable Federal: Secs. 901-5 (CCH U.S. MASTER TAX GUIDE ¶1311).

California Forms: Sch. R (Apportionment and Allocation of Income), Sch. S (Other State Tax Credit).

Credit is allowed California residents for *net income* taxes paid to another state (not including any tax comparable to California's alternative minimum tax) on income subject to the California income tax, subject to the conditions discussed below. (Sec. 18001, Rev. & Tax. Code)

Credit is allowed only if the other state does *not* allow California residents a credit for California taxes. The purpose is to prevent the allowance of credits by both states at the same time. Under this rule credit is allowable only for taxes paid to the following states and possessions:

Alabama	Mississippi
American Samoa	Missouri
Arkansas	Montana
Colorado	Nebraska
Connecticut	New Hampshire (business profits tax)
Delaware	New Jersey
District of Columbia (unincorporated business tax and	New Mexico
income tax, the latter for dual residents only—see	New York
below)	North Carolina
Georgia	North Dakota
Hawaii	Ohio
Idaho	Oklahoma
Illinois	Pennsylvania
Iowa	Puerto Rico
Kansas	Rhode Island
Kentucky	South Carolina
Louisiana	Utah
Maine	Vermont
Maryland	Virgin Islands
Massachusetts	Virginia (dual residents only—see below)
Michigan	West Virginia
Minnesota	Wisconsin

California will also generally allow a credit to its residents for income taxes paid to Oregon on "qualifying compensation."(*FTB Information Letter 2010-3*, July 29, 2010, CCH CALIFORNIA TAX REPORTS, ¶ 405-224)

Credit is allowed for District of Columbia and Virginia taxes paid by dual residents. A dual resident is any taxpayer who is defined as a resident under both California law and another jurisdiction's law. A taxpayer who is a dual resident is allowed to claim the other state tax credit for taxes paid to the other jurisdiction on income attributable to that other jurisdiction. Certain U.S. officials and staff are also treated as dual residents if, during their temporary absence from California, they are residents of another jurisdiction. (Instructions, Schedule S, Other State Tax Credit)

California residents who are included in a group nonresident return similar to the return described in Rev. & Tax. Code Sec. 18535 filed with any of the above-listed states or with Arizona, Indiana, Oregon, or Virginia may also claim a credit for their share of income taxes paid to these states, unless any of these states allow a credit for taxes paid to California on the group nonresident return. (Instructions, Schedule S, Other State Tax Credit) In *Appeal of Gregory K. Soukup and Mary Jo Carr* (1994) (CCH CALIFORNIA TAX REPORTS, ¶ 16-825.85), the State Board of Equalization (BOE) held that taxpayers who filed a composite Indiana return were entitled to credit on their California return for income taxes paid to Indiana because their election to file a composite return made them ineligible to claim the credit in Indiana.

Partners, S corporation shareholders, and limited liability company members are allowed a credit for their pro rata share of tax paid to other states (¶ 131). (Sec. 18006, Rev. & Tax. Code)

• *Nonresident of other state*

Credit is ordinarily allowed only for taxes (not including any tax comparable to California's alternative minimum tax) paid on net income that is taxable by the other state *irrespective* of residence or domicile of the recipient. See below for exceptions. In other words, the income taxed by the other state must be derived from sources within that state, under the California interpretation of what constitutes income from sources within that state. "Income from sources from within that state" is determined by applying the nonresident sourcing rules for determining income from sources within this state, see ¶ 231. (Sec. 18001, Rev. & Tax. Code)

The credit is intended to apply in a situation in which the California resident is taxed by the other state as a *nonresident* of that state, and not to a situation where the taxpayer is taxed as a resident by both states. The effect of this rule is to deny or limit the credit in cases where the taxpayer is treated as a resident of the other state as well as of California, and to deny credit in almost all cases for tax paid on income from intangible property. Such income (dividends, interest, etc.) is deemed under California law to be attributable to California as the state of residence and therefore not derived from sources in another state, on the theory that intangible property generally has its situs at the domicile of the owner. See below for discussion of cases to this effect. This rule would not apply in the rare case where an intangible asset has acquired a "business situs" outside of California; see ¶231 for explanation of "business situs."

The general requirement that the taxes paid to the other state be imposed without regard to the taxpayer's residence or domicile does not apply to certain U.S. governmental officials, who are considered to be California residents as explained at ¶105. The purpose of this exception presumably is to insure that such officials will not be denied credit if they are treated as residents by the other state as well as by California. (Sec. 18001, Rev. & Tax. Code)

• *"Alternative minimum taxes" do not qualify*

The credit does not apply to any preference, alternative, or minimum tax paid to other states that is comparable to California's alternative minimum tax (¶117). However, the credit may be applied against the taxpayer's alternative minimum tax, if the taxpayer is liable for that tax (¶117).

• *Limitation on amount*

The amount of the credit is limited to the same proportion of the total California tax as the income taxed by both states bears to the total income taxed by California. (Sec. 18001, Rev. & Tax. Code) The purpose of this rule is to ensure that the credit allowed will not be any greater than the California tax actually paid on the income that has been subjected to double taxation. In *Appeal of John and Olivia A. Poole* (1963) (CCH CALIFORNIA TAX REPORTS, ¶16-825.87), the BOE held that the word "income" for purposes of this limitation means the equivalent of "adjusted gross income" as defined in the California law.

A taxpayer who has income from a trade or business activity conducted both inside and outside California must use Schedule R for purposes of calculating the income apportionable to California for which the credit may be claimed.

Comment: Temporary Limitation on Credit Amounts Expires

See ¶125 for a discussion of the 50% limitation on the amount of business credits and credit carryovers that could be claimed during the 2008 and 2009 taxable years and the carryover of credits that could not be claimed. (Sec. 17039.2, Rev. & Tax. Code)

• *Procedure to determine credit*

A California resident (or part-year resident) should take the following steps to determine the credit:

— Find out from the list above whether the other state qualifies for the California credit.

— Determine what items of income are taxed to the resident/part-year resident as a *nonresident* by the other state and also taxed by California (called the "double-taxed income"). (As explained above, U.S. officials are not subject to the *nonresident* limitation; they should include at this point all income that is taxed by both states.)

¶128

— Determine the net amount of the "double-taxed income" that is actually subject to tax by California after deducting any expenses that apply specifically to that income (such as depreciation, etc.). This computation should be made by applying the California rules for determination of adjusted gross income to the "double-taxed income."

— Apply the limitation described under the heading *"Limitation on amount,"* above.

— The credit is the lower of two amounts: (1) the amount computed under step 4, below, or (2) the actual tax paid to the other state.

CCH Example: Computation of Credit

		California	State "X"
(a)	Total gross income	$25,000	$10,000
(b)	Gross income taxed in both states	10,000	10,000
(c)	Deductions directly attributable to income on line (b)	1,000	1,000
(d)	Other deductions, not directly attributable to any income	4,500	3,000
(e)	Taxable income	19,500	6,000
(f)	Tax paid (illustrative amounts)	1,205	285

Step 1—Assume that State "X" qualifies for California credit and that you are being taxed by "X" as a nonresident.

Step 2—"Double-taxed income" $10,000

Step 3—Net amount of "double-taxed income" taxed by both states 9,000

Step 4—Limitation:

$9,000/$24,000 × $1,205 = ... 452

Step 5—Credit = $3/4$ actual tax paid to "X" 285

• *Decisions of courts and State Board of Equalization*

In *Appeals of Michael A. DeBenedetti and Frances, Jr., and Joy Purcell* (1982) (CCH CALIFORNIA TAX REPORTS, ¶ 16-825.751), the taxpayers were California stockholders of a corporation that was taxed by Oregon as a "tax-option" (S) corporation. The taxpayers argued that the stock had acquired a "business situs" in Oregon, because it was pledged there to secure indebtedness of another corporation. The BOE held that the source of the dividend income was in California, and denied credit for the Oregon tax.

In *Appeal of Stanley K. and Beatrice L. Wong* (1978) (CCH CALIFORNIA TAX REPORTS, ¶ 16-825.751), the taxpayers were California residents who claimed credit for income tax paid to the state of Hawaii. The income taxed by Hawaii consisted of (1) interest on a note resulting from the sale of a Hawaii condominium and (2) dividends on stock of a family corporation located in Hawaii. The taxpayers argued that the note and the stock certificates were physically located in Hawaii and had acquired a "business situs" there. The BOE held that the source of the income was in California and denied the credit. To the same effect, see *Appeal of Marvin and Alice Bainbridge* (1981) (CCH CALIFORNIA TAX REPORTS, ¶ 16-825.703), involving interest received on a contract for sale of Hawaii land.

The case of *Theo Christman v. Franchise Tax Board* (1976) (CCH CALIFORNIA TAX REPORTS, ¶ 16-825.701) involved a taxpayer who was a California stockholder in a "tax-option" (S) corporation that operated in Georgia. His share of the corporation's income was taxed directly to him under Georgia's "tax-option" rules. He paid Georgia tax on the income and claimed credit against his California tax. A California court of appeal denied the credit on the grounds that the source of the income was California, despite the fact that the corporation was treated—in effect—as a partnership for purposes of federal and Georgia taxes. To the same effect, see *Appeal of Estate of Donald Durham* (1974) (CCH CALIFORNIA TAX REPORTS, ¶ 16-825.701), and *Appeal of Maude Peterson* (1978) (CCH CALIFORNIA TAX REPORTS, ¶ 16-825.25).

In *Appeal of Leland M. and June N. Wiscombe* (1975) (CCH CALIFORNIA TAX REPORTS, ¶ 16-825.98), a California resident received salary from an Alabama corporation for services rendered in California. The salary was taxed by Alabama, and the taxpayer claimed California tax credit for the tax paid to Alabama. The BOE denied the credit on the ground that the income was from a California source and was not properly taxed by Alabama to a nonresident, even though Alabama insisted on taxing it.

In *Appeal of Hugh Livie, et al.* (1964) (CCH CALIFORNIA TAX REPORTS, ¶ 16-825.751), a California resident paid Puerto Rico income tax on the gain realized upon liquidation of a Puerto Rico corporation. The BOE held that the Puerto Rico tax was not allowable as a credit against California tax, since the income was derived from a California source. See also *Appeal of Allan H. and Doris Rolfe* (1978) (CCH CALIFORNIA TAX REPORTS, ¶ 16-825.75), applying the same principle to disallow credit for Iowa tax.

¶129 Credit for Taxes Paid Other States—Nonresidents

> *Law:* Secs. 18002, 18006 (CCH CALIFORNIA TAX REPORTS, ¶ 16-825).
>
> *Comparable Federal:* Secs. 901-5 (CCH U.S. MASTER TAX GUIDE ¶ 1311).
>
> *California Forms:* Sch. R (Apportionment and Allocation of Income), Sch. S (Other State Tax Credit).

• *Conditions for credit*

Credit is allowed nonresidents for *net income* taxes (excluding minimum or preference taxes comparable to California's alternative minimum tax) paid to the taxpayer's state of residence on income that is also taxed by California, subject to the following conditions:

(1) Credit is allowed only where the state of residence either (a) does not tax income of California residents at all, or (b) allows California residents a credit for California taxes. In other words, California does not allow credit to a resident of another state unless the other state provides a similar credit to California residents. This is commonly referred to as the reciprocity requirement. The states that qualify under this rule are listed below.

(2) Credit is allowed only where the other state does *not* allow its residents a credit in the same situation. Where the other state would allow a credit *even though* California also allowed one, this rule prevents the allowance of the credit by California. The purpose is to keep a taxpayer from getting credits from both states at the same time. (Sec. 18002, Rev. & Tax. Code)

Because of above rules (1) and (2), credit is currently allowable to nonresidents only for taxes paid to the following states and territories (Instructions, Schedule S, Other State Tax Credit):

> Arizona
>
> Guam
>
> Indiana
>
> Oregon
>
> Virginia

However, in *Appeal of Daniel Q. and Janice R. Callister* (1999) (CCH CALIFORNIA TAX REPORTS, ¶ 16-825.353), the State Board of Equalization held that nonresidents were entitled to a credit for a portion of the local income tax surcharges they paid to another state because the other state required its counties to impose that portion of the surcharge. The portion of the local surcharges that the state required counties to impose was recognized as a state, rather than local, tax.

• *Limitations on amount*

The maximum credit amount is limited to the lesser of the following two amounts:

(1) the same proportion of the total tax paid to the state of residence as the income taxed in both states bears to the total income taxed by the state of residence; or

(2) the same proportion of the total California tax as the income taxed in both states bears to the total income taxed by California.

The total California tax for this purpose is the tax after deducting credit for personal exemptions. (Sec. 18002, Rev. & Tax. Code)

In computing limitations (1) and (2), follow the principles set forth in the example in ¶128. As with resident individuals, if the taxpayer has income from a trade or business activity conducted both inside and outside California, the taxpayer must use Schedule R for purposes of calculating the income apportionable to California for which the credit may be claimed.

• *Nonresident S corporation shareholders, partners, and LLC members*

Nonresident S corporation shareholders, nonresident partners, and nonresident limited liability company members are entitled to this credit for the pro rata share of taxes paid to another state (¶131). The taxes are treated as if paid by the individuals, and thus the conditions discussed above apply in determining this credit. (Sec. 18006, Rev. & Tax. Code) Nonresident beneficiaries are not entitled to this credit (FTB Information Letter No. 89-427, CCH CALIFORNIA TAX REPORTS, ¶401-748).

¶130 Credit for Taxes Paid Other States—Estates and Trusts

Law: Secs. 18003-05 (CCH CALIFORNIA TAX REPORTS, ¶16-825).

Comparable Federal: Secs. 901-5 (CCH U.S. MASTER TAX GUIDE ¶1311).

California Form: Sch. S (Other State Tax Credit).

Two types of credits are allowed in connection with estates and trusts: (1) credit may be allowed to the estate or trust itself where its income is taxed by two states; and (2) credit may be allowed to a resident beneficiary for taxes paid by the estate or trust to another state. (Sec. 18004, Rev. & Tax. Code; Sec. 18005, Rev. & Tax. Code)

• *Credit to estate or trust*

Credit is allowed to an estate or trust where it is treated as a "resident" of California and also of another state. (Sec. 18004, Rev. & Tax. Code) For this purpose, it is considered to be a "resident" of any state that taxes its income irrespective of whether the income is derived from sources within that state. (Sec. 18003, Rev. & Tax. Code) There are no reciprocal provisions for granting this credit as there are for resident and nonresident individuals as outlined above in ¶128 and ¶129, so the credit is allowable against net income taxes imposed by any state. The credit is subject to the following limitations:

— the amount of the credit may not exceed the same proportion of the total tax paid to the other state as the income taxed in both states bears to the total income taxed in the other state; and

— the amount of the credit is limited to the same proportion of the total California tax as the income taxed in both states bears to the total income taxed by California.

In *Appeal of Estate of Marilyn Monroe, Deceased* (1975) (CCH CALIFORNIA TAX REPORTS, ¶16-825.45), the estate was taxed on substantial income by both New York State and California. The State Board of Equalization denied the estate's claim for credit for the New York tax, on the ground that the estate was not a "resident" of both states, because Marilyn Monroe was not a California resident at the time of her death and "only estates of resident decedents are residents of California" for tax-credit purposes.

• *Credit to beneficiary*

Credit is also allowed to the *beneficiary* of an estate or trust where a beneficiary who is a California resident pays California tax on income that has been taxed to the estate or trust in another state. (Sec. 18005, Rev. & Tax. Code) The credit is subject to the following limitations:

— the amount of the credit may not exceed the same proportion of the total tax paid to the other state by the estate or trust as the income taxed to the *beneficiary* in California and also to the *estate* or *trust* in the other state bears to the total income taxed by the other state; and

— the amount of the credit is limited to the same proportion of the total California tax paid by the beneficiary as the income taxed to the *beneficiary* in California and also to the *estate* or *trust* in the other state bears to the beneficiary's total income taxed by California.

The purpose of these rules is to limit the credit to the amount of other-state tax and also to the amount of California tax actually paid on the net income that has been subjected to tax by both states. Computation of the limitations is similar in principle to that shown above in the example at ¶128, although it may become somewhat more complicated where credit to a beneficiary is involved.

• *Credit on distribution of accumulated income*

In Legal Ruling No. 375 (1974) (CCH CALIFORNIA TAX REPORTS, ¶16-825.375), the Franchise Tax Board discussed the tax credit for accumulated distributions made by a Minnesota trust to California beneficiaries. The ruling held that the beneficiaries were entitled to credit against their California tax for taxes paid to Minnesota by the trust. The credit was the amount that would have been allowed if the trust income had been distributed ratably in the year of distribution and the five preceding years, to conform to the method of taxing the distribution to the beneficiaries.

¶131 Credit for Taxes Paid Other States—Partners, S Corporation Shareholders, and LLC Members

Law: Sec. 18006 (CCH CALIFORNIA TAX REPORTS, ¶16-825).

Comparable Federal: Secs. 901-5 (CCH U.S. MASTER TAX GUIDE ¶1311).

California Form: Sch. S (Other State Tax Credit).

Resident partners, S corporation shareholders, and limited liability company (LLC) members are allowed a credit for their pro rata share of taxes paid another state by the partnership, S corporation, or LLC itself on income that is also taxed by California; the taxes are treated as if paid by the partners, shareholders, or members. (Sec. 18006, Rev. & Tax. Code) A resident S corporation shareholder may claim the credit only if (1) the other state imposing the taxes does not recognize S corporations or (2) the other state taxes S corporations and the California S corporation has elected to be an S corporation in the other state. The credit is computed using the same formula outlined at ¶128, above, under the heading "Procedure to determine credit."

Practitioner Comment: FTB Withdraws Guidance Regarding Whether Certain States' Taxes Qualify as Income-Based Taxes

The status of a tax as either an income tax or a non-income tax is important for California income and franchise tax purposes. For example, S corporation shareholders are generally permitted a credit against California tax for income taxes they pay on their pro rata share of income taxable in other states where the S corporation conducts business. In addition, such shareholders may claim a credit for their pro rata share of taxes paid by the S corporation to another state if the tax is on, according to, or measured by the S corporation's income or profits, paid or accrued. The credit is referred to as the "other state tax credit" or "OSTC." In addition, corporations may deduct only non-income taxes in determining their California corporate income and franchise tax liability. The determination of whether a tax is an income tax is also important in the sales factor throwback context. Under California's throwback rule, if tangible personal property is shipped from California to a state where the taxpayer is not taxable, that sale is thrown back into the taxpayer's California sale factor numerator. As a result, sales are generally thrown back from states where the taxpayer has P.L. 86-272 protection. The characterization of a tax as an income tax is important because that protection only applies to income based taxes.

The Texas Margin Tax (TMT), Michigan Business Tax (MBT), and Ohio Commercial Activity Tax (CAT) have historically given rise to the most uncertainty regarding whether each is an income tax or non-income tax. The FTB issued Notices and Technical Advice Memorandum (TAM) addressing this area but ultimately withdrew them in FTB Notice 2014-01 and TAM 2014-01, respectively.

The FTB did not provide any reasoning in FTB Notice 2014-01 except that it "has continued to receive questions as to the proper treatment of the [TMT]," and "is currently evaluating its position and exploring alternative methods to issue authoritative guidance." The FTB also did not provide any reasoning for TAM 2014-01 and instead cited its withdrawal of *FTB Notice 2010-02* via *FTB Notice 2014-01*.

In January of 2016, the FTB issued TAM 2016-01, which stated that the payment of the Revised Texas Franchise Tax (RTFT) is not eligible for the OSTC for any taxable year. The FTB reasoned that the RTFT is not a "net income tax" under California law because it is a tax on, or measured by, gross receipts. The TAM then stated that the FTB will issue a legal ruling with regard to applicability of the RTFT to credits and deductions for taxes paid to other states. As indicated in the TAM, the FTB intended to issue a comprehensive legal ruling discussing the RTFT before the end of the third quarter of 2016. However, at the time of this writing (November 2016), the FTB has yet to issue that ruling.

The series of TAMs and notices issued by the FTB on this subject to date has left many taxpayers justifiably confused. The earlier notices adopted a more flexible facts and circumstances based approach, which stands in stark contrast to the most recent TAM.

Additionally, it is not clear to what extent, if any, the FTB will ultimately be persuaded by authority in other jurisdictions. The status of these taxes is a critical part of the Multistate Tax Compact litigation nationwide, including, for example, the Michigan Supreme Court's decision in *International Business Machines Corp. v. Department of Treasury*, Docket No. 146440, July 14, 2014, and the Texas Court of Appeals' decision in *Graphic Packaging Corporation v. Hegar, et al.*, No. 03-13-00400-CV (Tex. App._Austin, July 28, 2015). Given the lack of guidance in California and ongoing litigation of this question in other states, treatment of these taxes from a California tax perspective continues to be uncertain.

Chris Whitney, Contributing Editor

A nonresident partner, S corporation shareholder, or LLC member is allowed a credit for his or her pro rata share of taxes paid by the partnership, S corporation, or LLC to the nonresident's state of residence on income also taxed by California. The taxes are treated as if paid by the nonresident partner, shareholder, or member. (Sec. 18006, Rev. & Tax. Code) For conditions governing determination of the credit, see ¶ 129, above.

Taxpayers are required to attach a copy of their Schedule K-1 (100S, 565, or 568) and a schedule showing their share of the net income tax paid to the other states. (Instructions, Schedule S, Other State Tax Credit)

¶132 Excess SDI Credit

Law: Sec. 17061, Revenue and Taxation Code; Sec. 1185 Unemployment Insurance Code (CCH CALIFORNIA TAX REPORTS, ¶ 16-826).

Comparable Federal: None.

California Forms: Form 540 (California Resident Income Tax Return).

An income tax credit is allowed for any excess employee contributions for disability insurance under the Unemployment Insurance Code. An employee who works for more than one employer during the year is entitled to recover any amounts withheld from wages in excess of the tax on the maximum wage limit (amount over $960.68 withheld in 2016), plus interest. An employee who files an income tax return recovers any such excess by claiming credit on the return. If the claim is disallowed, the employee may file a protest within 30 days with the Employment Development Department. Amounts withheld by a single employer that exceed the tax on the maximum wage limit must be recovered from the employer. (Sec. 17061, Rev. & Tax. Code; Sec. 1185, Unemp. Ins. Code)

¶133 Renter's Credit

> *Law:* Sec. 17053.5 (CCH CALIFORNIA TAX REPORTS, ¶ 16-907).
>
> *Comparable Federal:* None.
>
> *California Forms:* Form 540 (California Resident Income Tax Return).

A nonrefundable credit is allowed to anyone who is a "qualified renter," as explained below. The credit is not related in any way to the amount of rent paid. For the 2016 taxable year, the amount of the credit is $120 for married couples and registered domestic partners (RDPs) filing joint returns, heads of households, and surviving spouses, provided adjusted gross income is $78,125 or less, and $60 for other individuals, provided adjusted gross income is $39,062 or less. The adjusted gross income limits are adjusted annually for inflation. (Sec. 17053.5, Rev. & Tax. Code)

- *"Qualified renter" defined*

To be a "qualified renter" for purposes of claiming this credit, an individual must be a California "resident," as explained at ¶ 105, and have rented a principal residence in California for at least one-half of the year. (Sec. 17053.5, Rev. & Tax. Code)

An individual is *not* a "qualified renter"—and, therefore, gets no credit—if any of the following conditions described below exist:

— Someone living with the individual claims the individual as a dependent (¶ 115) for income tax purposes. (The Franchise Tax Board takes the position that this applies where the individual is claimed as a "dependent" for either California or federal income-tax purposes.)

— Either spouse or a RDP has been granted the homeowner's property-tax exemption (¶ 1704) during the taxable year. This does not apply to a spouse or RDP who is not granted the homeowner's exemption, if both maintain separate residences for the entire year.

— The property rented is exempt from property taxes (¶ 1704), unless the taxpayer, landlord, or owner pays possessory interest taxes or makes payments that are substantially equivalent to property taxes.

- *Special rules for married couples/RDPs*

The credit for a married couple or RDP that files separate returns may be taken by either spouse or RDP or divided equally between them, except as follows:

— if either spouse or RDP is not a California resident for part of the year, the credit is divided equally and prorated as described below for the period of nonresidency; or

— if both spouses or RDPs are California residents and maintain separate residences for the entire year, the credit must be divided equally between them; there is no option for one to take the full credit. (Sec. 17053.5, Rev. & Tax. Code)

- *Heads of household—Welfare recipients*

In *Appeals of Juanita A. Diaz and Constance B. Watts* (1989) (CCH CALIFORNIA TAX REPORTS, ¶ 16-907.55), the taxpayers were entitled to claim the head of household renter's credit rather than the individual renter's credit, even though more than half the expenses of maintaining their households were paid by Aid to Families with Dependent Children (AFDC).

• *Part-year residents*

A person who is a resident for only part of the year (provided he or she qualifies, as explained above) is allowed $1/12$ credit for each full month of California residence during the year. (Sec. 17053.5(e), Rev. & Tax. Code)

• *How to claim credit*

The credit should be claimed on the income tax return, with the appropriate supporting schedule.

¶134 California Competes Credit

Law: Sec. 17059.2 (CCH CALIFORNIA TAX REPORTS, ¶ 16-890c).

Comparable Federal: None.

California Form: FTB 3531 (California Competes Tax Credit).

A California competes credit (CCC) is available for the 2014 through 2024 taxable years. (Sec. 17059.2, Rev. & Tax. Code) Taxpayers locating or expanding their businesses in California that want to take advantage of this credit must apply to the Governor's Office of Business and Economic Development (GO-Biz). The credit is awarded on a competitive basis as discussed in more detail below.

Practitioner Comment: "California Competes" Incentives Credit Program

Under the California Competes Tax Credit (CCTC), enacted by A.B. 93 in 2013, GO-Biz will negotiate agreements for tax credits related to investments and employment expansion in California. The CCTC incentives under A.B. 93 range from $30 million to $200 million in each fiscal year starting in 2013 through 2018.

This fund is a discretionary fund without set guidelines for qualification. Taxpayers can negotiate agreements for tax credits under this program based on job creation and investment in California. GO-Biz will also consider factors such as the importance of the taxpayer's business to the state or region, the unemployment rate of the area where the business is/will locate, the taxpayer's commitment to remain in California, and other incentives available to the taxpayer in this state and in other states. The fund appears to be the California Legislature's attempt to compete with other states that have successfully lured companies to their states with negotiated credits and incentives packages. This marks the first time that California has offered negotiated credits.

The FTB is required to review the books and records of taxpayers allocated a CCTC, except for small businesses where the FTB has the discretion to conduct a review. The review is to ensure that taxpayers are complying with the contracts negotiated with GO-Biz and is not deemed an audit of tax returns. The FTB issued *Notice 2014-02*, November 7, 2014, CCH CALIFORNIA TAX REPORTS, ¶ 406-252, to inform taxpayers of the procedures it will use to review the books and records.

Chris Whitney, Contributing Editor

• *Credit amount*

The amount of the credit is determined on a case-by-case basis by the California Competes Tax Credit Committee (CTCC), which is comprised of the Treasurer, the Director of Finance, and the Director of GO-Biz, or their designated representatives, and one appointee each from the Assembly and the Senate. (Sec. 17059.2(a), Rev. & Tax. Code; Sec. 18410.2(a), Rev. & Tax. Code) The minimum credit amount that may be requested is $20,000. (Reg. 8010, 10 C.C.R.)

The credit may reduce a taxpayer's tax below the tentative minimum tax. (Sec. 17039(c), Rev. & Tax. Code)

• *Planning considerations*

Credit limitations.—Generally, the total amount of the credits that may be allocated may not exceed $200 million for each fiscal year from 2015-16 to 2017-18, plus the amount of any unallocated credits from the previous fiscal year and the amount of any previously allocated credits that have been recaptured. However, the total amount of the sales and use tax exemption for manufacturing equipment and research and development equipment (¶1509), hiring credits (¶158), and CCCs in aggregate may not exceed $750 million per year.

The aggregate amount of California Competes Credit that may be allocated for corporation franchise and income and personal income tax purposes must be reduced by the amount of corporation franchise and income tax credit allowed to all qualified taxpayers for wages paid or incurred with respect to qualified full-time employees that are allocable to property manufactured for use in or as a component of a new advanced strategic aircraft for the U.S. Air Force (see ¶818). (Sec. 17059.2(g)(1)(E), Rev. & Tax. Code)

To mitigate the effect of the reduction discussed above, the Director of Finance may increase the aggregate amount of California Competes Credits that may be allocated to taxpayers for California corporation franchise and income and personal income tax purposes by up to $25 million per fiscal year through the 2017-18 fiscal year. (Sec. 17059.2(g)(2), Rev. & Tax. Code)

Twenty-five percent of the CCCs must be reserved for small businesses, and no more than 20% of the amount available may be awarded to any one taxpayer. (Sec. 17059.2(g), Rev. & Tax. Code) A "small business" is a trade or business that has aggregate gross receipts, less returns and allowances reportable to California, of less than $2 million during the previous taxable year, but does not include a sexually-oriented business.

Credit application process.—Taxpayers must apply to GO-Biz for the credit, which will be awarded on a competitive basis based on the following criteria:

— The number of jobs to be created or retained.

— The compensation paid or proposed to be paid, including wages and benefits.

— The amount invested in California by the taxpayer.

— The unemployment or poverty level in the area where the business is located or proposed to be located.

— The incentives available to the taxpayer in California and also outside California.

— The duration of the project and how long the taxpayer commits to remaining in California.

— The overall economic impact in California of the taxpayer's project or business.

— The strategic importance of the taxpayer's project or business to the state, region, or locality.

— The opportunity for future growth and expansion in California by the taxpayer's business.

— The extent to which the anticipated benefit to California exceeds the projected benefit to the taxpayer from the tax credit.

All applications must be submitted online unless an applicant requests an alternative form as an accommodation. (*California Competes Tax Credit Application Guide*, California Governor's Office of Business and Economic Development, January 27, 2015)

Comment: Fiscal Year 2016-17 Application Periods and Amounts Available

GO-Biz announced that, for fiscal year 2016-17, it would accept applications during the following periods (with specified amounts available) for the credit: July 25, 2016, through August 22, 2016 ($75 million available); January 2, 2017, through January 23, 2017 ($100 million available); and March 6, 2017, through March, 27, 2017 ($68.3 million plus any remaining unallocated amounts from the previous application periods). (*Notice*, California Governor's Office of Business and Economic Development, June 29, 2016)

Practitioner Comment: California Trial Court Strikes Down Regulatory Ban on Contingent Fees

On January 7, 2016, a Sacramento Superior Court judge struck down a California regulation banning contingency fee arrangements for practitioners assisting companies in their applications for tax credits. The tax consulting firm, Ryan LLC, filed suit against GO-Biz alleging that California Code of Regulations ("CCR") title 10, section 8030(g)(2)(H), which put a cap on the contingent fee amount a practitioner can receive, was unconstitutional.

The court concluded that "limiting contingent fee arrangements to a 'reasonable hourly rate' is a de facto ban on contingent fee arrangements." Such a ban "is inconsistent with the purposes of the statute because it effectively disqualifies businesses with contingent fee arrangements from receiving the [California Competes] tax credit." The court further noted that GO-Biz's restriction of the use of a taxpayer's funds, made available by taking the credit instead of paying tax, gave rise to the logical conclusion that it could control or restrict any part of the taxpayer's business. This reach is clearly not supported by the statute.

The court found that there was no rational basis for banning contingent fee arrange-ments and that GO-Biz had "exceeded its regulatory authority by expanding the statutory factors on which the credit is required to be based and adding an additional factor -- the price applicants pay for outside site selection consultants. In addition, GO-Biz exceeded the scope of the statute by imposing a de facto ban on contingent fee arrangements." (*Ryan U.S. Tax Services, LLC v. State of California* (2016)) (CCH CALIFORNIA TAX REPORTS, ¶ 16-890c.23)

Chris Whitney, Contributing Editor

Written agreements.—Staff from the GO-Biz office will develop a proposed written agreement with the taxpayer, outlining the credit to be provided and the conditions that must be satisfied. The written agreement must be reviewed and approved by the CTCC at a public meeting. (Sec. 17059.2(a)(3), Rev. & Tax. Code; Sec. 18410.2(b), Rev. & Tax. Code)

When determining whether to enter into a written agreement with a taxpayer, GO-Biz may consider:

— the taxpayer's financial solvency and ability to finance its proposed expansion;

— the taxpayer's current and prior compliance with federal and state laws;

— current and prior litigation involving the taxpayer;

— the reasonableness of the fee arrangement between the taxpayer and any third party providing any services related to the credit; and

— any other factors GO-Biz deems necessary to ensure accountability and transparency in the credit's administration and that the effective use of the credit is maximized.

(Sec. 17059.2(c)(7), Rev. & Tax. Code)

Compliance review.—The FTB is responsible for reviewing the books and records of all taxpayers allocated a CCC to ensure compliance with the agreement's terms and conditions. However, if the taxpayer is a small business, the review will only be undertaken if the FTB determines it is appropriate or necessary in the best interest of the state. The FTB must notify GO-Biz of a possible breach of the agreement and must also provide information as to whether the taxpayer qualifies as a small business.

The credit review is separate from the FTB's normal tax return audits and does not preclude the FTB from auditing a taxpayer's tax return for other items. (*Frequently Asked Questions—California Competes Credit,* Franchise Tax Board (2015)) (CCH CALIFORNIA TAX REPORTS, ¶406-364; Reg. 8040, 10 C.C.R.)

Carryforward provisions.—Unused credits may be carried forward for up to six years. (Sec. 17059.2(e), Rev. & Tax. Code)

Recapture.—Credits are subject to recapture in accordance with the terms outlined in the written agreement. Any credit recapture must be reviewed and approved by the CTCC at a public meeting. Any recapture will be treated and assessed as a mathematical error appearing on the taxpayer's return and will be added to the tax otherwise due by the taxpayer for the taxable year in which the CTCC's recapture determination occurred. (Sec. 17059.2(c), Rev. & Tax. Code; Sec. 18410.2(b), Rev. & Tax. Code)

Sunset.—The credit is scheduled to be repealed on December 1, 2024. (Sec. 17059.2(k), Rev. & Tax. Code)

Public information.—GO-Biz is required to post on its website specified information concerning the credits allocated, including:

— the names of taxpayers receiving the credit;

— the estimated amount of each taxpayer's investment;

— the estimated number of jobs created or retained;

— the amount of credit allocated to each taxpayer;

— if applicable, the amount of credit recaptured from each taxpayer;

— the primary location where the taxpayer has committed to increasing the net number of jobs or making investments (listed by city or, in the case of unincorporated areas, by county);

— information that identifies each tax credit award that was given a priority for being located in a high unemployment or poverty area; and

— information that identifies each tax credit award that is being counted toward the 25% credit allocation requirement for small businesses.

(Sec. 17059.2(c)(6), Rev. & Tax. Code)

Practitioner Comment: Transparency, Structure, and Clarity Added to Credit Program

On September 29, 2016, Gov. Jerry Brown signed A.B. 2900, effective January 1, 2017. The new bill adds new types of information that GO-Biz must disclose about the companies that win the credit. GO-Biz already discloses information such as the names of companies that win the credit, the number of jobs, and the amount of income the company has agreed to make. A.B. 2900 further requires that GO-Biz disclose the location of facilities for which the company is asking for a credit. The legislative intent behind the new requirement is to increase oversight and transparency of the credit.

Additionally, on August 5, 2016, GO-Biz proposed amendments to the regulations on the California Competes Tax Credit program to standardize definitions, ensure accuracy in evaluating applicants, and clarify the information that applicants will need to submit as part of the application and evaluation process. In response to *Ryan U.S. Tax Serv. LLC v. California* (discussed above), the amendments remove the regulatory requirement that any contingency fee arrangement must result in a fee that is less than or equal to the product of the number of hours of service provided to the applicant and a reasonable hourly rate for such services.

Chris Whitney, Contributing Editor

¶135 Senior Head of Household Credit

Law: Sec. 17054.7 (CCH CALIFORNIA TAX REPORTS, ¶ 16-912).

Comparable Federal: None.

California Form: Form 540 (California Resident Income Tax Return).

California allows a "senior head of household" to claim a credit equal to 2% of taxable income, up to a maximum of $1,345 (for 2016). To qualify, a taxpayer must (1) be at least 65 years old as of the end of the taxable year and (2) have qualified as the head of household (¶114) for either of the two taxable years preceding the current taxable year by maintaining a household for a qualifying individual who died during either of those preceding taxable years. Additionally, the credit is limited to taxpayers whose adjusted gross income does not exceed a statutory maximum that is adjusted annually for inflation. The maximum adjusted gross income for 2016 is $71,370. (Sec. 17054.7, Rev. & Tax. Code)

¶136 Credits for Joint Custody Head of Household, Dependent Parent

Law: Sec. 17054.5 (CCH CALIFORNIA TAX REPORTS, ¶ 16-914a, 16-914b).

Comparable Federal: None.

California Form: Form 540 (California Resident Income Tax Return).

For the 2016 taxable year, the California joint custody head of household credits equal the lesser of 30% of the net tax or $440. The credits cover both dependent children and dependent parents. The credits are subject to the same annual inflation adjustment as the exemption credits (¶113). However, neither may be claimed if the taxpayer used either the head of household or qualifying widow(er) filing status. (Sec. 17054.5, Rev. & Tax. Code)

• *Dependent child*

To claim the credit as "joint custody head of household" for purposes of a dependent child the taxpayer must satisfy the following conditions:

— be unmarried at the end of the year;

— maintain a home that is the principal place of abode of the taxpayer's dependent or descendant for no less than 146 days but no more than 219 days of the year, under a decree of dissolution or separate maintenance, or under a written custody agreement prior to the issuance of such a decree where proceedings have been initiated; and

— furnish over half the cost of household expenses. (Sec. 17054.5, Rev. & Tax. Code)

• *Dependent parent*

A "qualified taxpayer," for purposes of claiming the dependent parent credit, is one who satisfies the following conditions:

— is married but living apart from the spouse for the last half of the tax year,

— files separately,

— furnishes over half of the cost of maintaining the household that is the principal residence of the dependent parent, and

— does not qualify to file as a head of household or as a surviving spouse.

The dependent parent does not have to live in the taxpayer's home for purposes of claiming the dependent care credit. (Sec. 17054.5, Rev. & Tax. Code)

¶137 Motion Picture Production Credit (Original)

Law: Sec. 17053.85, Rev. & Tax. Code; Regs. 5500-5507, 10 C.C.R. (CCH CALIFORNIA TAX REPORTS, ¶16-890a).

Comparable Federal: None.

California Forms: FTB 3541 (California Motion Picture and Television Production Credit), FTB 3551 (Sale of Credit Attributable to an Independent Film).

A nonrefundable motion picture production credit is available against personal income tax and corporation franchise and income taxes. Alternatively, taxpayers may claim a refundable credit against state sales and use taxes.

The credit may be claimed by qualified taxpayers for a percentage of qualified expenditures, as defined by statute and regulation, that are paid or incurred by the taxpayer in California in the production of a qualified motion picture. The credit is claimed for all qualified expenditures incurred in all taxable years for the qualified motion picture, but may be claimed only in the taxable year that the California Film Commission issues a credit certificate. (Sec. 17053.85, Rev. & Tax. Code) Reg. 5503, 10 CCR, guidelines, and a California Film Commission fact sheet on using the credits provide detailed information for taxpayers interested in applying for the credit.

For purposes of this credit, a "qualified motion picture" means a motion picture that is produced for distribution to the general public that is:

— a feature film with a minimum production budget of $1 million and a maximum production budget of $75 million;

— a movie of the week or miniseries with a minimum production budget of $500,000;

— a new television series produced in California with a minimum production budget of $1 million;

— an independent film; or

— a television series that relocated to California.

These types of productions are further defined by regulation (Regs. 5500 and 5502, 10 C.C.R.).

Specified types of productions such as commercial advertising, music videos, motion pictures for noncommercial use, news and public events programs, talk shows, game shows, reality programming, documentaries, and pornographic films are ineligible for the credit. In addition, the picture must be copyrighted and must meet specified criteria concerning:

— the percentage of production days performed in California or expenditures incurred in California, and

— time lines concerning commencement of principal photography and project completion.

An "independent film" is a motion picture with a minimum budget of $1 million and a maximum budget of $10 million that is produced by a company that is not publicly traded and is not more than 25% owned, directly or indirectly, by publicly traded companies.

• *Credit amount*

The maximum credit is equal to 20% (25% if the qualified motion picture is a television series that relocated to California or an independent film) of the qualified expenditures attributable to the production of a qualified motion picture in California. However the credit is limited to the amount specified in the certificate issued by the California Film Commission.

• *Planning considerations*

The issues discussed below may affect taxpayers claiming the motion picture production credit.

Application, approval, certification, and reporting process.—Taxpayers must apply to the California Film Commission for a credit allocation based on a proposed project budget. If the Commission approves an allocation, the taxpayer must meet certain filming and production deadlines, and must provide detailed information upon completion of the film prior to receiving certification. Total credit allocations are capped at $100 million per fiscal year, with additional amounts allowed for prior year unused credits. Up to $10 million of the $100 million allocation must be set aside for independent films. Applications will only be approved through June 30, 2017.

The California Film & Television Tax Credit Program Application Form, CFC Form A, is accepted by the Commission on a first-come, first-serve basis, and is available on the Commission's Web site at http://film.ca.gov/Incentives.htm. Reg. 5501, 10 C.C.R. outlines what materials must be included in the application.

Completed applications must be submitted at least 30 calendar days prior to the start of principal photography in California. Any expenditures for services, wages, or goods incurred prior to application approval will not be considered "qualified expenditures." (Reg. 5501, 10 C.C.R.)

Practice Tip: Duplicate Applications Prohibited

Applicants may not submit duplicate applications for a project. Submittal of duplicate applications will result in the application being disqualified. (Reg. 5501, 10 C.C.R.).

The credit is reported on FTB 3541, California Motion Picture and Television Production Credit. Taxpayers attaching FTB 3541 to their returns should write "CFC Credit" in red ink at the top margin of their returns.

Practice Tip: Form FTB 3541 Requirements

Separate forms FTB 3541 must be completed when a taxpayer claims both the old motion picture production credit and the new post-2015 credit (see ¶137a) in the same year. Check boxes were added to the form, so taxpayers can indicate whether they are using the form to claim the old credit or the new credit. Certificate numbers (below 5000 under the old program, and starting at 5000 under the new program) should always be provided on Form 3541. Also, to claim the credits correctly, taxpayers should use credit code 233 for the old credit and credit code 237 for the new credit. (*Tax News*, California Franchise Tax Board, June 2016, CCH CALIFORNIA TAX REPORTS, ¶406-517)

Assignment and transfer of credits.—Taxpayers may elect to assign the credit to affiliated corporations.

In addition, taxpayers may sell credits that are attributable to an independent film. Form 3551 must be used to report the sale of a credit attributable to an independent film. The qualified taxpayer selling the credit is required to report the information related to the sale to the FTB no later than 30 days after the sale of the credit. The requirement to notify the FTB of the sale also applies to partners, members, or shareholders who will sell any portion of their distributive share of the credit. (Instructions, FTB 3551, Sale of Credit Attributable to an Independent Film)

Carryforward provisions.—Unused credit may be carried over for six taxable years.

Credit revocation.—A qualified motion picture that exceeds the maximum total production budget of $75 million after having received a credit allocation will be disqualified from claiming the credit and the tax credit allocation will be revoked. There is no recapture provision.

An independent film that exceeds the total production budget of $10 million after having received a credit allocation will be reclassified as a feature film. The independent film applicant will not be required to submit a new application, but the credit allocation percentage will be reduced from 25% to 20% of qualified expenditures, and the application will be placed at the end of the queue for any available tax credits in the non-independent film allocation category.

Revocation of the tax credit allocation is final and is not subject to administrative appeal or review.

¶ 137a Motion Picture Production Credit (Post-2015 Tax Years)

Law: Sec. 17053.95, Rev. & Tax. Code; Regs. 5508-5516, 10 C.C.R. (CCH CALIFORNIA TAX REPORTS, ¶ 16-890b).

Comparable Federal: FTB 3541 (California Motion Picture and Television Production Credit), FTB 3551 (Sale of Credit Attributable to an Independent Film).

For taxable years beginning on or after January 1, 2016, a new motion picture production credit is available against personal income tax and corporation franchise and income taxes, with the credit subject to allocation by the California Film Commission according to a computation and ranking, as discussed below. Alternatively, taxpayers may claim a refundable credit against state sales and use taxes. (Sec. 17053.95, Rev. & Tax. Code)

The credit may be claimed for a percentage of all qualified expenditures paid or incurred in all taxable years for the qualified motion picture, but may be claimed only in the taxable year in which the commission issues a credit certificate. The credit will not be allowed for any qualified expenditures for which the original motion picture production credit under Sec. 17053.85 (see ¶ 137) has been claimed.

For purposes of this credit, a "qualified motion picture" means a motion picture that is produced for distribution to the general public that is:

— a feature film with a minimum production budget of $1 million;

— a movie of the week or miniseries with a minimum production budget of $500,000;

— a new television series of episodes longer than 40 minutes each of running time, exclusive of commercials, that is produced in California, with a minimum production budget of $1 million per episode;

— an independent film;

— a television series that relocated to California; or

— a pilot for a new television series that is longer than 40 minutes of running time, exclusive of commercials, that is produced in California, with a minimum production budget of $1 million.

Specified types of productions such as commercial advertising, music videos, motion pictures for noncommercial use, news and public events programs, talk shows, game shows, sporting events, awards shows, telethons, reality programming, certain clip-based programming, documentaries, variety programs, daytime dramas, strip shows, one-half hour episodic television shows, and sexually explicit productions are ineligible for the credit. In addition, a "qualified motion picture" must be copyrighted and must meet specified criteria concerning:

— the percentage of principal photography days in California or production expenditures incurred in California, and

— the time frames for commencement of principal photography and project completion.

An "independent film" is a motion picture with a minimum budget of $1 million that is produced by a company that is not publicly traded and is not more than 25% owned, directly or indirectly, by publicly traded companies.

Comment: Pass-Through Entities

For pass-through entities, the determination of eligibility for the credit will be made at the entity level, and the credit will not be allowed to the pass-through entity, but will be passed through to the entity's partners or shareholders.

• *Credit amount*

The applicable credit percentages are:

— 20% of the qualified expenditures (for up to $100 million in expenditures) attributable to the production of a qualified motion picture in California, including, but not limited to, a feature;

— 20% of the qualified expenditures attributable to the production of a television series that relocated to California that is in its second or a subsequent year of receiving a tax credit allocation pursuant to the new credit provisions or Sec. 17053.85;

— if either of the credit percentages above is determined to apply, an additional amount not to exceed, in the aggregate, 5% of the qualified expenditures relating to original photography outside the Los Angeles zone, music scoring and music track recording by musicians attributable to the production of a qualified motion picture in California, or qualified visual effects attributable to the production of a qualified motion picture in California;

— 25% of the qualified expenditures attributable to the production of a television series that relocated to California that is in its first year of receiving a tax credit allocation; and

— 25% of qualified expenditures (for up to $10 million in expenditures) attributable to the production of an independent film.

The aggregate amount of new credits that may be allocated by the commission for any fiscal year is the sum of the following:

— $230 million for the 2015-16 fiscal year or $330 million for the 2016-17 fiscal year and each fiscal year thereafter through the 2019-20 fiscal year;

— any unused allocated credit amount from the preceding fiscal year;

— the amount of previously allocated credit not certified; and

— the amount by which any allocated credit was reduced based on a recomputation of the applicant's jobs ratio.

• *Planning considerations*

The issues discussed below may affect taxpayers claiming the credit.

Allocation procedure.—Generally, the commission must allocate the aggregate credit amount subject to the following categories:

— 5% to independent films;

— 35% to features;

— 20% to relocating television series; and

— 40% to new television series, pilots for new television series, movies of the week, miniseries, and recurring television series.

Within 60 days after the allocation period, any unused amount within a category or categories must be reallocated first to the category for new television series, pilots for new television series, movies of the week, miniseries, and recurring television series and, if any unused amount remains, then to another category or categories with a higher demand, as determined by the commission. The commission may increase or decrease the percentage of the aggregate credit amount allocated to any category by 5%, if necessary, due to the jobs ratio (generally, the amount of qualified wages paid divided by the amount of tax credit allowed, not including the additional credit for up to 5% certain qualified expenditures), number of applications, or allocation of credit amounts by category compared to demand.

The commission must allocate the credit to applicants in one or more allocation periods per fiscal year on or after July 1, 2015, and before July 1, 2016, and in two or more allocation periods per fiscal year on or after July 1, 2016, and before July 1, 2020. For each allocation period and category, the commission must rank the applicants from highest to lowest according to their jobs ratio and then allocate the credit according to the highest jobs ratio, working down the list, until the aggregate amount of credit available is exhausted. The jobs ratio may be increased by up to 25% for a qualified motion picture that increases economic activity in California. Notwithstanding any other provision, any television series, relocating television series, or new television series based on a pilot for a new television series that has been approved and been issued a credit allocation by the commission under the new provisions or under Sec. 17053.85 will be issued a credit for each subsequent year, for the life of the television series, whenever credits are allocated within a fiscal year.

If all tax credits have been allocated for any application period, qualified motion pictures will be placed in a prioritized waiting list according to their project type and in the order of their job ratio ranking until one of the following occurs:

— credits become available that allocation period;

— the production elects to be removed from the queue;

— the credit is revoked; or

— the allocation period ends.

(Reg. 5512, 10 C.C.R.)

If the applicant is producing a series of feature films that will be filmed concurrently and the series of films continues the narrative of the original work and financing is confirmed, then the commission has the authority to divide the allocation over multiple fiscal years if it is determined that the production schedule occurs over more than one fiscal year. (Reg. 5512(c), 10 CCR) In addition, a 5% augmentation to the credit allocation will be made when the production company:

— pays or incurs qualified expenditures relating to music track recording and/or music scoring in California;

— pays or incurs qualified expenditures relating to qualified visual effects work totaling a minimum of $10 million or at least 75% of the qualified expenditures for visual effects incurred in California;

— pays or incurs qualified wages for services performed outside the Los Angeles zone during the applicable period relating to original photography outside the Los Angeles zone;

— purchases or leases tangible personal property outside the Los Angeles zone during the applicable period and the personal property is used or consumed outside the Los Angeles zone (the tangible personal property must be purchased, rented, or leased from an outside of Los Angeles vendor through an office or other place of business outside the Los Angeles zone; rentals or purchases from a pass-through business do not qualify for the 5% augmentation).

The maximum amount of tax credits allowed for independent films and/or relocating television series for their initial season in California is 25% and, therefore, the 5% augmentation is not applicable to such productions. (Reg. 5512, 10 C.C.R.)

Application process.—There is a two-phase application process for tax credit allocation. The first phase requires applicants to complete an online application on the commission's website. Applicants are then selected for the second phase based on their jobs ratio ranking (additional information must be submitted during the second phase). Within 30 business days of receipt of all information, the commission will notify applicants of their acceptance or disqualification. Upon approval, CFC Form DD, Credit Allocation Letter, will be issued indicating the amount of tax credits allocated. Principal photography must commence no later than 180 calendar days after the credit allocation letter is issued.

An applicant that begins principal photography in California prior to receiving a credit allocation letter will be disqualified from receiving a letter for that particular production. In addition, an applicant that has been issued a credit allocation for a particular production that begins, but does not complete, principal photography of that production is not eligible to reapply for a credit reservation for that particular production.

Applicants may not submit a duplicate application for a project during any given allocation period. Doing so will disqualify an applicant from the tax credit program. However, an applicant may submit an additional application for the same project during any fiscal year if the qualified production did not receive or retain a tax credit allocation from a previous allocation period in the same fiscal year. (Reg. 5509, 10 C.C.R.)

Reporting process.—The credit is reported on FTB 3541, California Motion Picture and Television Production Credit. Taxpayers attaching FTB 3541 to their returns should write "CFC Credit" in red ink at the top margin of their returns.

Practice Tip: Form FTB 3541 Requirements

Separate forms FTB 3541 must be completed when a taxpayer claims both the old motion picture production credit (see¶137) and the new post-2015 credit in the same year. Check boxes were added to the form, so taxpayers can indicate whether they are using the form to claim the old credit or the new credit. Certificate numbers (below 5000 under the old program, and starting at 5000 under the new program) should always be provided on Form 3541. Also, to claim the credits correctly, taxpayers should use credit code 233 for the old credit and credit code 237 for the new credit. (*Tax News*, California Franchise Tax Board, June 2016, CCH CALIFORNIA TAX REPORTS, ¶406-517)

Assignment and transfer of credits.—If the credit allowed exceeds a corporate taxpayer's tax liability, the taxpayer may make an election to assign any portion of the credit to one or more affiliated corporations for each taxable year in which the credit is allowed. Once made, the election is irrevocable for that taxable year, but may be changed for a subsequent taxable year.

In addition, taxpayers may sell a credits that is attributable to an independent film to an unrelated party. However, the credit may not be sold to more than one party, nor may it be resold by the unrelated party to another party. Also, in no event may a taxpayer assign or sell a credit to the extent that the credit allowed is claimed on any tax return of the taxpayer.

Carryforward provisions.—Unused credit may be carried over for up to six taxable years.

Responsibilities of credit recipients.—An applicant issued a credit allocation letter must comply with various requirements during the production period, including submitting certain reports, participating in career based learning and training programs and public service opportunities, and providing certain screen credits and promotional items. (Reg. 5513, 10 C.C.R.; Reg. 5514, 10 C.C.R.; Reg. 5516, 10 C.C.R.)

¶138 Low-Income Housing Credit

Law: Sec. 17058, Reg. 10300 et. seq. (CCH CALIFORNIA TAX REPORTS, ¶16-905).

Comparable Federal: Sec. 42 (CCH U.S. MASTER TAX GUIDE ¶1334).

California Form: FTB 3521 (Low-Income Housing Credit).

California provides a credit computed under federal law (as modified) as of the tie-in date (¶103) for investors in qualified low-income housing projects in California. The credit is applied against the net tax, and may reduce tax liability to below the "tentative minimum tax." (Sec. 17058, Rev. & Tax. Code)

The California credit is claimed over a four-year period, rather than over a 10-year period as under federal law. Generally, the percentage of costs for which credit may be claimed in the first three years is the highest percentage allowed federally in the month the building is placed in service. For the fourth year, the percentage is the difference between 30% and the sum of the credit percentage for the first three years. However, for (1) new buildings that are federally subsidized, and (2) existing buildings that are at risk of conversion to market rental rates, the percentage of creditable costs in the first three years is the same as the federal percentage applicable to subsidized new buildings, while for the fourth year the percentage is the difference between 13% and the sum of the credit percentages for the first three years. (Sec. 17058, Rev. & Tax. Code) California conforms to federal law that provides a minimum applicable percentage of 9% for computing the credit for newly constructed non-federally subsidized buildings placed in service after July 30, 2008, for which allocations have been made before January 1, 2015. However, California has not conformed to federal law making permanent this minimum applicable percentage for newly-constructed non-federally subsidized buildings.

The California provisions require a "compliance period" of 30 consecutive tax years, rather than the 15-year federal period. However, unlike federal law, California has no recapture provision (see IRC Sec. 42(i)(1)). If the credit exceeds the taxpayer's net tax for the taxable year, the excess may be carried forward to succeeding years.

When the basis of a building that has been granted a low-income housing tax credit is increased and exceeds the basis at the end of the first year of the four-year credit period, the taxpayer is eligible for a credit on the excess basis. This additional credit is also taken over a four-year period beginning with the taxable year in which the increase in qualified basis occurs.

California does not incorporate a federal provision that allows low-income housing investors to elect to claim 150% of the low-income housing credit otherwise allowable and to accept a corresponding pro rata reduction in the low-income housing credit taken in subsequent tax years. California also does not incorporate the federal provision allowing a taxpayer to reduce the credit for the portion of the first year that the housing remains unoccupied and claim such an amount in the year following the allowable credit period.

Taxpayers should consult the California Tax Credit Allocation Committee's Web site (http://www.treasurer.ca.gov/ctcac/) for detailed information on eligibility requirements, applications, and allocations of the state low-income housing credit.

Comment: Partnership Allocations

During the 2009 through 2019 taxable years, the credit must be allocated to the partners of a partnership owning the project in accordance with the partnership agreement, regardless of how the federal low-income housing tax credit is allocated to the partners, or whether the partnership agreement's credit allocation has substantial economic effect. If the credit allocation lacks substantial economic effect, losses or deductions attributable to a partnership interest sale or disposition that is made prior to the federal credit's expiration may not be claimed in the taxable year in which the sale or other disposition occurs. The loss or deduction must be deferred until and treated as if it occurred in the first taxable year immediately following the taxable year in which the federal credit period expires.

These rules do not apply to state low-income housing credits allocated for farmworker housing projects that are financed through the farmworker housing set-aside provision (discussed below) unless the project also receives a preliminary reservation of federal low-income housing tax credits.

California, unlike federal law, limits the total amount of low-income housing credits that the California Tax Credit Allocation Committee (CTCAC) may allocate for corporation franchise and income tax, personal income tax, and gross premiums tax on insurers to $70 million per year (indexed for inflation) plus any amounts returned and unused for preceding years. The Committee must set aside at least $500,000 of the funds available for the low-income housing credit, plus any unallocated or returned farmworker housing credits that may still be available, for use in promoting farmworker housing projects. Projects applying for the low-income housing credit for farmworker housing under this set-aside provision do not have to have been allocated a federal low-income housing credit to qualify for the state low-income housing credit.

For a project that receives a preliminary reservation beginning on or after January 1, 2016, and before January 1, 2020, a taxpayer may make an irrevocable election in its application to the CTCAC to sell all or any portion of the credit allowed to one or more unrelated parties for each taxable year in which the credit is allowed. The credit must be sold for consideration that is not less than 80% of the amount of the credit. Also, the unrelated party purchasing the credit must be a taxpayer allowed the state or federal credit for the taxable year of the purchase or any prior taxable year in connection with a project located in the state. The credit generally may not be resold by the unrelated party to another taxpayer or other party. A taxpayer may not sell the credit if the taxpayer was allowed the credit on any tax return. A taxpayer, with the approval of the Executive Director of the CTCAC, may rescind the election to sell all or any portion of the credit if the consideration for the credit falls below 80% of the amount of the credit after the CTCAC reservation. (Sec. 17058(q), Rev. & Tax. Code)

The credit is computed on FTB 3521, which must be attached to the return. A Certificate of Final Award of California Low-Income Housing Tax Credits (FTB 3521A) issued by the California Tax Credit Allocation Committee must be provided to the FTB upon request.

Comment: Temporary Limitation on Credit Amounts Lifted

See ¶125 for a discussion of the 50% limitation on the amount of business credits and credit carryovers that could be claimed during the 2008 and 2009 taxable years and the impact of such limitations on subsequent carryovers. (Sec. 17039.2, Rev. & Tax. Code)

¶139 Adoption Costs Credit

Law: Sec. 17052.25 (CCH California Tax Reports, ¶16-913).

Comparable Federal: Sec. 23 (CCH U.S. Master Tax Guide ¶1306).

California Form: Form 540 (California Resident Income Tax Return).

California provides a credit for an amount equal to 50% of the specified costs paid or incurred by a taxpayer for the adoption of any U.S. citizen or legal resident minor child who was in the custody of a state or county public agency. The credit may not exceed $2,500 per child and may be claimed only for specified costs directly related to the adoption. (Sec. 17052.25, Rev. & Tax. Code)

The adoption cost credit may be claimed only for the taxable year in which the decree or order of adoption is entered; however, the costs that are included may have been incurred in previous taxable years. Taxpayers may treat a prior unsuccessful attempt to adopt a child and a later successful adoption of a different child as one effort when computing the cost of adopting the child. (Instructions, Form 540)

The credit may be carried over until the total credit of $2,500 is exhausted. Any personal income tax deduction for any amount paid or incurred by the taxpayer upon which the credit is based must be reduced by the amount of the adoption cost credit.

The California credit is similar to the federal tax, with the following major exceptions:

— the amount of the California credit is lower (50% of qualifying costs vs. the 100% allowed under the federal credit);

— California law, unlike federal law, does not limit the credit for taxpayers above a certain income limit;

— the dollar cap on the California credit is lower;

— unlike the federal credit, California's credit is not phased out on the basis of the taxpayer's adjusted gross income;

— the expenses that may be claimed for purposes of the federal credit include any reasonable and necessary adoption fees, court costs, attorney fees, and other expenses that are directly related to the adoption proceedings; whereas California specifies that expenses include adoption fees charged by the Department of Social Services or a licensed adoption agency, travel expenses related to adoption, and unreimbursed medical fees related to adoption;

— California's requirements concerning the adoptive child's citizenship, residency, and custodial status do not apply for purposes of claiming the federal credit;

— California's credit may be carried over until exhausted, whereas there is a five-year carryover limit on the federal credit; and

— the federal credit, but not the California credit, was refundable during the 2010 through 2012 tax years.

¶140 Disabled Access Expenditures Credit

Law: Sec. 17053.42 (CCH California Tax Reports, ¶16-954).

Comparable Federal: Sec. 44 (CCH U.S. Master Tax Guide ¶1338).

California Form: FTB 3548 (Disabled Access Credit for Eligible Small Businesses).

California allows eligible small businesses a credit in an amount equal to 50% of up to $250 of the eligible access expenditures paid or incurred by those businesses to comply with the federal Americans with Disabilities Act. Thus, a California credit of up to $125 is allowed. Except for the credit amount, the California credit is the same as the credit allowed under federal law. (Sec. 17053.42, Rev. & Tax. Code)

An "eligible small business" is a business that elects to claim the credit and either (1) had gross receipts (less returns and allowances) of $1 million or less for the preceding taxable year or (2) had no more than 30 full-time employees during the preceding taxable year.

"Eligible access expenditures" include all reasonable amounts paid or incurred to perform the following:

— remove architectural, communication, physical, or transportation barriers that prevent a business from being accessible to, or usable by, disabled individuals,

— provide qualified interpreters or other effective methods of making aurally delivered materials available to hearing impaired individuals,

— provide qualified readers, taped texts, or other effective methods of making visually delivered materials available to visually impaired individuals,

— acquire or modify equipment or devices for disabled individuals, or

— provide other similar services, modifications, materials, or equipment.

Amounts paid or incurred in connection with any new facility first placed in service after November 5, 1990, are not eligible access expenditures.

If the credit allowable exceeds "net tax" for the year, the excess may be carried over to succeeding years until exhausted.

Any deduction allowed for the same expenditures for which the credit is claimed must be reduced by the amount of the credit. In addition, amounts for which the credit is claimed may not be used to increase the basis of the property.

Comment: Temporary Limitation on Credit Amounts Lifted

See ¶ 125 for a discussion of the 50% limitation on the amount of business credits and credit carryovers that could be claimed during the 2008 and 2009 taxable years and the impact on credit carryovers. (Sec. 17039.2, Rev. & Tax. Code)

¶141 Agricultural Product Donation Credits

Law: Secs. 17053.12, 17053.88, 17053.88.5 (CCH California Tax Reports, ¶ 16-952, 16-955).

Comparable Federal: None.

California Form: FTB 3547 (Donated Agricultural Products Transportation Credit), Form 3881 (Donated Fresh Fruits or Vegetables Credit).

California allows taxpayers engaged in the business of processing, distributing, or selling agricultural products to claim a credit equal to 50% of the costs paid or incurred in connection with the transportation of agricultural products donated to nonprofit charitable organizations. Eligible transportation costs may be determined in either of the following ways: (1) 14¢ per mile or (2) actual transportation expenses, excluding depreciation and insurance (Instructions to FTB 3547). (Sec. 17053.12, Rev. & Tax. Code)

Upon the delivery of donated agricultural products by a taxpayer, the nonprofit charitable organization must provide a certificate to the taxpayer stating the following:

— that the products were donated in accordance with requirements specified in the Food and Agriculture Code;

— the type and quantity of products donated;

— the distance transported;

— the transporter's name;

— the taxpayer donor's name and address; and

— the donee's name and address.

The certification must be provided to the Franchise Tax Board upon request.

If the credit is claimed, any deduction allowed for the same costs must be reduced by the amount of the credit allowed. Unused credit may be carried over until exhausted.

Comment: Temporary Limitation on Credit Amounts Lifted

See ¶125 for a discussion of the 50% limitation on the amount of business credits and credit carryovers that could be claimed during the 2008 and 2009 taxable years and the impact on credit carryovers. (Sec. 17039.2, Rev. & Tax. Code)

• *Credit for donating agricultural produce to California food banks*

For the 2012 through 2016 tax years, a credit against personal income taxes is available to qualified taxpayers who donate fresh fruit and/or vegetables to California food banks. (Sec. 17053.88, Rev. & Tax. Code) For the 2017 through 2021 tax years, a new credit is available to qualified taxpayers who donate fresh fruit or vegetables to a food bank in California. (Sec. 17053.88.5, Rev. & Tax. Code) The credits may only be claimed by taxpayers who plant, manage, and harvest the crops. (Sec. 17053.88, Rev. & Tax. Code; Sec. 17053.88.5, Rev. & Tax. Code)

Through tax year 2016, the credit is equal to 10% of the food's inventory costs required to be included under IRC §263A, without the exception applicable to farming businesses. (Sec. 17053.88, Rev. & Tax. Code)

For tax years after 2016, the credit is equal to 15% of the qualified value of the fresh fruits and vegetables donated. The qualified value must be calculated by using the weighted average wholesale price, based on the taxpayer's total like grade wholesale sales of the donated item within the calendar month of the donation. If no wholesale sales of the donated item have occurred in the calendar month of the taxpayer's donation, the qualified value will be equal to the nearest regional wholesale market price for the calendar month of the donation, based upon the same grade products as published by the U.S. Department of Agriculture's Agricultural Marketing Service or its successor. (Sec. 17053.88.5, Rev. & Tax. Code)

Upon the delivery of donated agricultural products by a taxpayer, the food bank must provide a certificate to the taxpayer stating the following:

— the type and quantity of the products donated,

— the name of the donor or donors,

— the name and address of the donee nonprofit organization, and

— as initially provided by the taxpayer, the estimated value of the donated products and the location where the donated product was grown.

The certification must be provided to the Franchise Tax Board upon request. (Sec. 17053.88, Rev. & Tax. Code; Sec. 17053.88.5, Rev. & Tax. Code)

Any deductions allowed with respect to costs for which a donated agricultural products transportation credit is claimed must be reduced by the amount of the credit in the taxable year that it is claimed. Unused credit may be carried forward for up to seven years. (Sec. 17053.88, Rev. & Tax. Code; Sec. 17053.88.5, Rev. & Tax. Code)

¶142 Household and Dependent Care Expense Credit

Law: Sec. 17052.6, Reg. 17052.6 (CCH CALIFORNIA TAX REPORTS, ¶16-914).

Comparable Federal: Sec. 21 (CCH U.S. MASTER TAX GUIDE ¶1301).

California Form: FTB 3506 (Child and Dependent Care Expenses Credit).

A credit for employment-related household and dependent care expenses is allowed against California personal income tax in an amount determined in accordance with IRC Sec. 21 as of the current conformity date (¶103). (Sec. 17052.6, Rev. & Tax. Code)

Comment: Credit Nonrefundable

The credit is nonrefundable. There is no carryover of unused credit.

• *Credit amount*

The amount of the California credit is a percentage of the allowable federal credit determined on the basis of the amount of federal adjusted gross income earned as follows (Sec. 17052.6, Rev. & Tax. Code):

Adjusted gross income of $40,000 or less	50% of the federal credit
Adjusted gross income over $40,000 but not over $70,000	43% of the federal credit
Adjusted gross income over $70,000 but not over $100,000	34% of the federal credit
Adjusted gross income over $100,000	0%

The credit is allowed only for care provided in California, and only to the extent of earned income subject to California personal income taxation. Earned income includes compensation, other than pensions or retirement pay, received by a member of the Armed Forces for active services as a member of the Armed Forces, whether or not the member is domiciled in California.

For California purposes, registered domestic partners (RDPs) may claim the credit in the same manner as married persons. Generally, married persons and RDPs must file a joint return to claim the credit. However, a married person or RDP may claim the credit on a separate return if he or she

— lived apart from his or her spouse/RDP at all times during the last six months of the year,

— had a qualifying person(s) living in his or her home for more than half of the year,

— provided over half the cost of keeping up the home, and

— otherwise meets all of the criteria for claiming the credit.

The Instructions to FTB 3506, Child and Dependent Care Expenses Credit, provide useful charts outlining (1) tie-breaker rules in instances in which there is a qualifying child of more than one person and (2) rules for divorced, separated, RDP-terminated, and never married persons.

To substantiate entitlement to the credit, Reg. 17052.6 requires that a taxpayer retain records of the following:

— the qualifying child/dependent's birth certificate and Social Security account number card;

— medical records that demonstrate the physical or mental incapacity of the qualifying child/dependent, if applicable;

— if the care provider is an individual, certain documents to establish the identity and taxpayer identification number of the care provider; and/or

— documents that establish the physical location at which the care was provided; and

— proof of payment to substantiate the employment-related expenses.

If a taxpayer is unable to acquire or maintain the specific documentation described above, the taxpayer may produce other evidence to establish entitlement to the credit. Upon request by the FTB, a taxpayer must produce the records or evidence required by the regulation. If a taxpayer fails to comply with such a request, the credit will be denied.

¶142

However, in a nonprecedential letter decision, the BOE has held that taxpayers cannot be denied the credit if they have made reasonable efforts to obtain this documentation but are unable to do so as a result of the provider's noncooperation. (*Appeal of Hernandez* (2011), (CCH CALIFORNIA TAX REPORTS, ¶405-507))

CCH Comment: Prior Notice Not Required Prior to Adjustment

A denial of the credit or a refund is treated in the same manner as a mathematical error, except that taxpayers denied a credit or portion of the credit have the right of protest and appeal. Consequently, the Franchise Tax Board may adjust the credit/refund amount without providing any prior notice.

¶143 Natural Heritage Preservation Credit

Law: Sec. 17053.30, Rev. & Tax. Code; Secs. 37001–37022, Public Resources Code (CCH CALIFORNIA TAX REPORTS, ¶16-900).

Comparable Federal: None.

California Form: FTB 3503 (Natural Heritage Preservation Credit).

Taxpayers may claim a nonrefundable credit equal to 55% of the fair market value of real property donated before July 1, 2020, for qualified conservation purposes to the California Resources Agency (CRA), a local government, or an exempt nonprofit land and water conservation organization designated by the CRA or a local government to accept donations. (Sec. 17053.30, Rev. & Tax. Code; Sec. 37001, Pub. Res. Code; Sec. 37002, Pub. Res. Code; Sec. 37006, Pub. Res. Code)

A donation, which may include the donation of a perpetual interest in property, may consist of land, conservation easements, land that includes water rights, or water rights and must also meet the criteria for a federal charitable contribution deduction. The donated property must help preserve wildlife and wildlife habitat, open space, agricultural land, fish, plants, water, or endangered species as evidenced by meeting specific criteria. However, the credit may not be claimed for property donated as a condition for obtaining use of the property from a public agency through a lease, permit, license, certificate, or other form of entitlement to property use. For contributions made on or after January 1, 2015, if the credit allowed exceeds a taxpayer's tax liability, the excess may be carried over to reduce tax for up to 15 years, if necessary, until the credit is exhausted. For contributions made before January 1, 2015, unused credit may be carried forward for up to eight succeeding taxable years.

The California Wildlife Conservation Board must approve the donated real property for purposes of claiming the credit and may award credits if funds are available to refund the general fund for foregone revenues. (Instructions, Form 3503, Natural Heritage Preservation Credit)

Information regarding current funding, qualified contributions of property, and the awarding of credits may be obtained from the Wildlife Conservation Board by phone at (916) 445-8448 or on the Internet at http://www.wcb.ca.gov/.

CCH Practice Pointer: Relationship with Other Credits and Deductions

The credit is in lieu of any other credit or deduction to which the taxpayer may otherwise be allowed with respect to the donated property. (Sec. 17053.30, Rev. & Tax. Code)

Shareholders or partners may claim a partnership or other pass-through entity's credit in proportion to their interest in the pass-through entity as of the date of the qualified contribution.

Comment: Temporary Limitation on Credit Amounts Lifted

See ¶ 125 for a discussion of the 50% limitation on the amount of business credits and credit carryovers that could be claimed during the 2008 and 2009 taxable years and the impact on credit carryovers. (Sec. 17039.2, Rev. & Tax. Code)

¶144 Tax-Incentive Credit—Sales Tax Equivalent

Law: Secs. 17053.33, 17053.45, 17053.70 (CCH CALIFORNIA TAX REPORTS, ¶ 16-865, 16-866, 16-867).

Comparable Federal: None.

California Forms: FTB 3805Z (Enterprise Zone Deduction and Credit Summary), FTB 3807 (Local Agency Military Base Recovery Area Deduction and Credit Summary), FTB 3809 (Targeted Tax Area Deduction and Credit Summary).

Planning Note: G-TEDA Programs Repealed

The geographically targeted economic development area (G-TEDA) programs for businesses located in enterprise zones, local agency military base recovery areas (LAMBRAs), the targeted tax area, and manufacturing enhancement areas are repealed, generally effective January, 1, 2014. Unused credits may still be carried over as discussed below.

• *Enterprise zones*

For pre-2014 taxable years, an income tax credit is allowed for sales or use tax paid or incurred with respect to property used for specific purposes that is:

— purchased before the date the enterprise zone designation expires, is revoked, is no longer binding, becomes inoperative, or is repealed; and

— placed in service in the enterprise zone prior to January 1, 2015.

(Secs. 17053.70, Rev. & Tax. Code) Designated enterprise zones are listed at ¶ 104.

The credit applies to purchases up to a value of $1 million of machinery and parts used for the following:

— fabricating, processing, assembling, and manufacturing;

— production of renewable energy resources;

— pollution control mechanisms;

— data processing and communications equipment; and

— motion picture manufacturing equipment central to production and post-production work.

Practitioner Comment: Capitalization Requirement

The underlying statutes (Secs. 17053.70 and 23612.2) refer only to qualified property that is placed in service in an enterprise zone. Unlike the former California Manufacturers Investment Tax Credit (or "MIC" discussed at ¶ 818) the statutes do not explicitly state that the qualified costs must be capitalized for tax purposes. Nonetheless, the California Court of Appeal affirmed both the State Board of Equalization and the California Superior Court, and held on March 13, 2012 in the *Taiheiyo Cement, Inc. v. FTB* 204 Cal.App.4th 254 (2012) (CCH CALIFORNIA TAX REPORTS, ¶ 405-597) that only capitalized costs qualify for the EZ sales and use tax credit. The California Supreme Court denied the petition for review on June 13, 2012.

Chris Whitney, Contributing Editor

The total amount of both the enterprise zone sales and use tax credit and the enterprise zone hiring credit (¶145), including any carryover from prior years, is limited to the amount of income tax attributable to income from the enterprise zone. A taxpayer who also operates a business elsewhere must use a special apportionment formula to determine the amount of income attributable to the zone. The amount of the taxpayer's business income attributable to California is first determined by applying the apportionment formula discussed at ¶1305—1309. For purposes of apportioning income to the enterprise zone, however, the sales factor is eliminated from the standard apportionment formula and the business income used in the apportionment formula is limited to California-based income rather than worldwide income.

The sales and use tax credit may be used to reduce an enterprise zone taxpayer's regular tax below the tentative minimum tax (¶117).

A taxpayer may claim the credit for use tax paid on qualified property only if qualified property of a comparable quality and price is not timely available for purchase in California.

• *Local agency military base recovery areas*

A credit is also allowed prior to the 2014 taxable year for sales or use tax paid or incurred by a local agency military base recovery area (LAMBRA) business for certain property purchased prior to 2014 for exclusive use in a recovery area. The credit is substantially similar to the sales tax equivalent credit allowed for property purchased by enterprise zone businesses except that, for purposes of LAMBRA businesses, the credit applies to (1) high technology equipment; (2) aircraft maintenance equipment; (3) aircraft components; or (4) property that is depreciable under IRC Sec. 1245(a)(3). (Sec. 17053.45, Rev. & Tax. Code)

Practice Tip: Placed in Service Date Inapplicable

Although the LAMBRA provisions require that qualified property be purchased for use within the LAMBRA, they do not contain a requirement that the property be placed in service by a specified date. (*Repeal of Geographically Targeted Economic Development Area Tax Incentives*, Franchise Tax Board (2013)) (CCH CALIFORNIA TAX REPORTS, ¶405-974)

A taxpayer who is allowed a LAMBRA credit for qualified property is limited to only one credit under the Personal Income Tax Law with respect to that property. The credit is subject to recapture in the year of noncompliance if the qualified property is disposed of, or is no longer used by, the taxpayer within the LAMBRA at any time before the close of the second taxable year after the property is placed in service or if the taxpayer has not increased the number of employees by one or more during the first two taxable years after commencing business within a LAMBRA.

The amount claimed by a taxpayer for both of the LAMBRA credits the sales tax credit and the hiring credit (¶147) combined may not exceed the amount of tax attributable to income from the area. The special apportionment formula used for purposes of calculating the enterprise zone and targeted tax area sales and use tax credits is also used to calculate the LAMBRA credit.

• *Targeted tax area*

For pre-2013 tax years, a similar credit was allowed for sales or use tax paid on the purchase of machinery and parts purchased prior to January 1, 2013, and placed in service prior to January 1, 2015, and used for the following (see ¶104):

— fabricating, processing, assembling, and manufacturing;

— producing renewable energy resources;

— air or water pollution control mechanisms;

— data processing and communications; and

— motion picture production. (Sec. 17053.33, Rev. & Tax. Code)

Comment: Credit May be Claimed on Amended Return

There is no requirement that the credit be filed on an original return. Consequently, taxpayers may claim the credit on an amended return as long as the qualified property is purchased prior to 2013 and placed in service prior to January 1, 2015. (*Repeal of Geographically Targeted Economic Development Area Tax Incentives*, Franchise Tax Board (2013), CCH CALIFORNIA TAX REPORTS, ¶ 405-974)

The amount that may be claimed for all of a taxpayer's targeted tax area credits combined is limited to the amount of tax that would be imposed on the taxpayer's business income attributable to the area as if that attributable income represented all of the taxpayer's income that was subject to personal income tax. A taxpayer who also operates outside that area must use a special apportionment formula to determine the amount of income attributable to the targeted tax area. The amount of business income attributable to California is first determined by applying the apportionment formula discussed at ¶ 1305—1309. For purposes of determining the amount attributable to the targeted tax area, however, the sales factor is eliminated from the standard apportionment formula and the business income used in the formula is limited to California-based income rather than worldwide income.

A taxpayer who is allowed a targeted tax area credit for qualified property is limited to only one credit under the Personal Income Tax Law with respect to that property.

• *Credit carryovers*

Unused credit for any of the credits discussed above may be carried over and added to the credit in succeeding years until the credit is exhausted. However, the carryover period is limited to 10 years, commencing with the 2014 tax year, for the portion of any credit remaining for carryover to post-2013 taxable years.

CCH Practice Tip: Impact on Basis

The basis of the property for which these credits are claimed may not be increased for the sales and use taxes paid on the property.

¶ 145 Tax-Incentive Credit—Enterprise Zone Employers

Law: Sec. 17053.74 (CCH CALIFORNIA TAX REPORTS, ¶ 16-855).

Comparable Federal: Sec. 1396 (CCH U.S. MASTER TAX GUIDE ¶ 996C, 1339A).

California Form: FTB 3805Z (Enterprise Zone Deduction and Credit Summary).

Planning Note: G-TEDA Programs Repealed

The geographically targeted economic development area (G-TEDA) programs for businesses located in enterprise zones, local agency military base recovery areas (LAM-BRAs), the targeted tax area, and manufacturing enhancement areas are repealed, generally effective January, 1, 2014. Unused credits may still be carried over as discussed below. A new jobs credit for taxpayers located in designated geographic areas is available to businesses who create new jobs, see ¶ 158.

Practitioner Comment: Enterprise Zone Credit Repeal May be Challenged on Constitutional Grounds

Taxpayers adversely impacted by the Enterprise Zone (EZ) credit repeal may be able to assert the legislation violates the Due Process and Contracts Clause of the U.S. and

California Constitutions. The Contracts Clause of the U.S. and California Constitutions prohibit California from passing any law that impairs "the obligation of contracts." Contracts Clause jurisprudence would support a constitutional challenge to the extent that the EZ credit repeal substantially impairs an existing contractual obligation, and the state lacks a significant and legitimate public purpose for the legislation. An argument can be made that a contract existed because the state offered EZ credits and taxpayers accepted the offer and paid consideration by investing and hiring in EZs. Furthermore, the repeal of the EZ credit arguably substantially impairs an obligation under that contract because taxpayers may be deprived of a significant amount of credits, both credits previously generated as well as future credits they anticipated generating.

Although the courts have given states a lot of leeway in terms of what constitutes a "legitimate and reasonable" justification, the U.S. Supreme Court has found that budgetary needs are an illegitimate justification for a State's impairment of its contractual obligations. See *U.S. Trust Co. of New York v. New Jersey*, 431 U.S. 1 (1977); see also *Campbell v. Boston Housing Authority* 823 N.E. 2d 363 (2005). In the instant case, taxpayers may attempt to argue that the repeal disadvantages both workers and corporations who invested in enterprise zones such that the government's purpose for this repeal should be deemed "illegitimate and unreasonable."

Under the Due Process Clause of the U.S. Constitution, taxpayers, among other things, may claim that the repeal either failed to achieve a legitimate purpose by rational means, or that the State had an illegitimate purpose for passing the legislation. For example, taxpayers may argue that the Enterprise Zone program induced them to engage in specific transactions in anticipation of such benefits, only for the state to later revoke these benefits.

Chris Whitney, Contributing Editor

A tax credit is allowed to employers for a portion of "qualified wages" paid to certain "qualified employees" who are hired to work in an enterprise zone prior to January 1, 2014. General business deductions that are otherwise allowable for wages paid to such individuals must be reduced by the amount of any credit claimed. (Sec. 17053.74, Rev. & Tax. Code) Detailed rules are provided in the law. Designated enterprise zones are listed at ¶ 104.

Comment: In the Zone?

In a nonprecedential summary decision the State Board of Equalization (BOE) upheld a denial of an enterprise zone hiring credit because the taxpayer's business did not operate within an enterprise zone during the tax years at issue even though the taxpayer stated that it relied in good faith on private and public databases to confirm that it was operating within the Los Angeles - East Valley Enterprise Zone (LA EZ) during the years at issue. The taxpayer provided copies of voucher certificates that were approved by the LA EZ manager and e-mails from the City of Los Angeles Community Development Department (LACDD) stating that "the original address range that was published when the zone received final approval contained a lot of errors." The BOE held that equitable estoppel did not apply because the FTB did not provide any erroneous information. The FTB had no responsibility for administering the LA EZ or publishing the LA EZ boundary or address information. Also, the incorrect information published by the LACDD was, at most, an oversight that was acknowledged by the LACDD, and there was no showing that the error resulted from an affirmative misrepresentation or concealment of a material fact. (*Appeal of DF & RW, Inc.* (2012) CCH CALIFORNIA TAX REPORTS, ¶ 12-061.66)

• *Definitions*

"Qualified wages" are generally the amounts, not in excess of 150% of the California minimum wage, paid to qualified disadvantaged employees. However, with respect to up to 1,350 otherwise qualified disadvantaged individuals employed in the Long Beach enterprise zone in certain aircraft manufacturing activities, "qualified wages" is expanded to include that portion of hourly wages that does not exceed 202% of the minimum wage. (Sec. 17053.74, Rev. & Tax. Code)

An individual is a "qualified employee" if the following conditions are satisfied:

— 90% of the individual's services in an enterprise zone for the taxpayer during the taxable year are directly related to the conduct of the taxpayer's enterprise zone trade or business;

— the individual performs at least 50% of his or her services for the taxpayer during the taxable year in an enterprise zone;

— the individual was hired after designation of the area as an enterprise zone; and

— immediately preceding the qualified employee's employment with the taxpayer, he or she was a qualified disadvantaged individual, a resident of a targeted employment area, or an employee who qualified the employer for the enterprise zone or program area hiring credits in effect prior to 1997.

A "qualified disadvantaged individual" is an individual who, immediately preceding employment with the taxpayer, was one of the following:

— an individual who was eligible for services under the federal Job Training Partnership Act (JTPA) or its successor, who was receiving, or was eligible to receive, subsidized employment, training, or services funded by the JTPA or its successor;

— an individual who was eligible to be a voluntary or mandatory registrant under the Greater Avenues for Independence (GAIN) Act or its successor;

— an economically disadvantaged individual 14 years of age or older;

— a qualified dislocated worker;

— a disabled individual who was eligible for, enrolled in, or had completed a state rehabilitation plan or was a service-connected disabled veteran, veteran of the Vietnam era, or veteran who was recently separated from military service;

— an ex-offender, including an individual placed on probation without a finding of guilt;

— a person who was eligible for, or a recipient of, benefits from certain specified public assistance programs;

— a member of a federally recognized Indian tribe, band, or other group of Native American descent; a resident of a targeted employment area;

— an employee who qualified the employer for a hiring credit under a former enterprise zone or program area; or

— a member of a targeted group under IRC Sec. 51(d).

• *Amount of credit*

The amount of the credit is 50% of "qualified wages" in the first year of employment, 40% in the second year, 30% in the third year, 20% in the fourth year, and 10% in the fifth year. For purposes of computing the credit, seasonal workers are treated as continuously employed. (Sec. 17053.74, Rev. & Tax. Code)

Even though the credit may not be claimed for employees hired after 2013, the credit installments may be claimed for the full five-years as long as the employee was hired prior to January 1, 2014, and continues to be otherwise eligible and the taxpayer has income attributable to the zone. (*Repeal of Geographically Targeted Economic Development Area Tax Incentives*, Franchise Tax Board (2013), CCH CALIFORNIA TAX REPORTS, ¶ 405-974)

The hiring credit may be used to reduce an enterprise zone taxpayer's regular tax below the tentative minimum tax (¶ 117).

¶145

The total amount of the enterprise zone hiring credit and the enterprise zone sales and use tax credit (¶ 144), including any carryover from prior years, is limited to the tax attributable to income from the enterprise zone. A taxpayer who also operates outside the zone area must use a special apportionment formula to determine the amount of income attributable to the zone area. The amount of business income attributable to California is first determined by applying the standard apportionment formula discussed at ¶ 1305—1309. For purposes of determining the amount of income attributable to the enterprise zone, however, the sales factor is eliminated from the standard apportionment formula and the income used in the apportionment formula is limited to California-based income rather than worldwide income.

• *Certification*

A taxpayer must obtain certification on VoucherApp 10-07 that an individual meets the requirements for a "qualified employee" from the local agency responsible for verifying employee eligibility prior to January 1, 2015. (Sec. 17053.74, Rev. & Tax. Code; FTB 3805Z Booklet, Enterprise Zone Business Booklet)

Planning Note: Credit May Be Claimed on Amended Return

There is no requirement that the credit be filed on an original return. Consequently, taxpayers may claim the credit on an amended return as long as the qualified employee was hired prior to 2014 and a certificate was issued on behalf of that employee prior to January 1, 2015. (*Repeal of Geographically Targeted Economic Development Area Tax Incentives*, Franchise Tax Board (2013), CCH CALIFORNIA TAX REPORTS, ¶ 405-974)

Practitioner Comment: Additional Documentation Required

Although the statute only requires that a taxpayer obtain a certification from a local zone administrator in order to claim this credit, the FTB on audit has requested that taxpayers provide it with the underlying documentation that was originally given to the local zone administrator. In many cases, taxpayers may no longer have such records at the time of the audit.

In the *Appeal of Deluxe Corp*, 2006-SBE-003, December 12, 2006, CCH CALIFORNIA TAX REPORTS, ¶ 404-121, the State Board of Equalization (BOE) in a formal decision held that the FTB had the authority to request the underlying substantiation supporting the taxpayer's enterprise zone hiring credit vouchers and can deny the hiring credit for employees that it deems are not qualified or for which substantiation is not provided. However, on May 7, 2009, the California Court of Appeal, Second District, held in its published decision in *Dicon Fiberoptics, Inc. v. FTB* that while the FTB may audit the vouchers, the vouchers are prima facie evidence that the employees are qualified and that the FTB may not reject vouchers solely based upon the absence of underlying documentation to support qualification.

On April 26, 2012, the California Supreme Court reversed the Court of Appeals decision, in part. (*Dicon Fiberoptics v. FTB*, 53 Cal.4th 1227 (2012), CCH CALIFORNIA TAX REPORTS, ¶ 405-627) The California Supreme Court affirmed that the FTB may conduct an audit to determine whether a taxpayer is entitled to the enterprise zone hiring tax credit. During such an audit, the FTB may require the taxpayer to establish that the worker is a "qualified employee" within the meaning of the statute. However, the California Supreme Court reversed and held the FTB is not required to accept a certification or voucher as conclusive or prima facie proof that an employee is qualified, nor is the FTB required to establish that the worker is not a "qualified employee." Therefore, taxpayers should consider preserving the approved vouchers, voucher applications, and supporting documentation in the event the FTB audits the credit and requests supporting documentation. While the standard California statute of limitations is four years, the hiring credit is available for the first five years a qualified employee works for the taxpayer. Therefore, it is recommended that taxpayers preserve the supporting documentation for the credit for up to 10 years.

Chris Whitney, Contributing Editor

• *Limitations and recapture*

The credit is reduced by any credit allowed under the federal work opportunity credit, as in effect as of California's IRC conformity date (see ¶103). (Sec. 17053.74, Rev. & Tax. Code)

• *Credit recapture*

Unless specified exceptions apply, the credit is subject to recapture if an involved employee is terminated within a prescribed period (generally, roughly one year). (Sec. 17053.74, Rev. & Tax. Code)

• *Credit carryover*

Unused credit may be carried forward and added to the credit in succeeding years. However, the carryover period is limited to 10 years, commencing with the 2014 tax year, for the portion of any credit remaining for carryover to post-2013 taxable years.

¶146 Tax-Incentive Credit—Enterprise Zone Employees

Law: Sec. 17053.75 (CCH California Tax Reports, ¶16-850).

Comparable Federal: None.

California Form: FTB 3553 (Enterprise Zone Employee Credit).

Prior to the 2014 taxable year, a limited tax credit is allowed to "qualified employees" for wages received from an enterprise zone business prior to the zone designation's termination or expiration. The amount of the credit is 5% of "qualified wages," defined as wages subject to federal unemployment insurance, up to a maximum of $525 per employee. The maximum amount of qualified wages for 2013 is $10,500. For each dollar of income received by the taxpayer in excess of "qualified wages," the credit is reduced by nine cents. The credit is not refundable and cannot be carried forward. The amount of the credit is further limited to the amount of tax that would be imposed on income from employment in the enterprise zone, computed as though that income represented the taxpayer's entire taxable net income. (Sec. 17053.75, Rev. & Tax. Code)

An individual is a "qualified employee" if he or she meets the following criteria:

— the individual is not an employee of the federal government, the State of California, or any political subdivision of the State;

— 90% of the individual's services in an enterprise zone for the taxpayer during the taxable year are directly related to the conduct of the taxpayer's enterprise zone trade or business; and

— the individual performs at least 50% of his or her services for the taxpayer during the taxable year in an enterprise zone.

Designated enterprise zones are listed at ¶104.

¶147 Tax-Incentive Credit—Local Agency Military Base Recovery Area Employers

Law: Sec. 17053.46 (CCH California Tax Reports, ¶16-857).

Comparable Federal: None.

California Form: FTB 3807 (Local Agency Military Base Recovery Area Deduction and Credit Summary).

Planning Note: G-TEDA Programs Repealed

The geographically targeted economic development area (G-TEDA) programs for businesses located in enterprise zones, local agency military base recovery areas (LAMBRAs), the targeted tax area, and manufacturing enhancement areas are repealed, generally effective January, 1, 2014. Unused credits may still be carried over as discussed below. A new jobs credit for taxpayers located in designated geographic areas is available to businesses who create new jobs, see ¶ 158.

Local agency military base recovery area (LAMBRA) employers are allowed a credit for qualified wages paid to specified disadvantaged individuals or displaced employees hired prior to January 1, 2014. LAMBRAs are discussed at ¶ 104. (Sec. 17053.46, Rev. & Tax. Code)

Only those employers with a net increase of one or more employees during the first two taxable years after commencing business within a LAMBRA are eligible to claim the credit. A business must obtain certification prior to January 1, 2015, from either the California Employment Development Department, the local county or city Job Training Partnership Act administrative entity, or the local county Greater Avenues to Independence (GAIN) office or social services agency that the employee meets the qualifications necessary for the employer to claim the credit (see discussion below). The certification must be made available to the California Franchise Tax Board upon request.

Planning Note: Credit May Be Claimed on Amended Return

There is no requirement that the credit be filed on an original return. Consequently, taxpayers may claim the credit on an amended return as long as the qualified employee was hired prior to 2014 and a certificate was issued on behalf of that employee prior to January 1, 2015. (*Repeal of Geographically Targeted Economic Development Area Tax Incentives*, Franchise Tax Board (2013), CCH CALIFORNIA TAX REPORTS, ¶ 405-974)

The credit that may be claimed during the first year of business operations within a LAMBRA is 50% of "qualified wages," which is defined as that portion of hourly wages that does not exceed 150% of the minimum wage established by the California Industrial Welfare Commission. For the second, third, fourth, and fifth years of operation, the credit is reduced to 40%, 30%, 20%, and 10%, respectively. Even though the credit may not be claimed for employees hired after 2013, the credit installments may be claimed for the full five-years as long as the employee was hired prior to January 1, 2014, and continues to be otherwise eligible and the taxpayer has income attributable to the zone. (*Repeal of Geographically Targeted Economic Development Area Tax Incentives*, Franchise Tax Board (2013), CCH CALIFORNIA TAX REPORTS, ¶ 405-974)

For purposes of computing the credit, seasonal workers are considered continuously employed. The total amount of wages paid or incurred by a LAMBRA employer for which the credit may be claimed is limited to $2 million.

• *"Disadvantaged individual," "displaced employee" defined*

To qualify as a "displaced employee," a person must be a military base employee who was displaced as a result of a base closure. To qualify as a "disadvantaged individual" a person must be one of the following:

    — determined eligible for services under the federal Job Training Partnership Act;

    — a voluntary or mandatory registrant under California's Greater Avenues for Independence Act;

    — an economically disadvantaged individual age 16 years or older;

— a qualified dislocated worker;

— an individual who is enrolled in or has completed a state rehabilitation plan or is a service-connected disabled veteran, veteran of the Vietnam era, or veteran who is recently separated from military service;

— an ex-offender;

— a recipient of specified federal, state, or local public assistance programs; or

— a member of a federally recognized Indian tribe, band, or other group of Native American descent. (Sec. 17053.46, Rev. & Tax. Code)

A "displaced employee" or "disadvantaged individual" must also be a person hired after the area in which the person's services are performed was designated a LAMBRA, at least 90% of whose services for the employer during the taxable year were directly related to the conduct of the employer's LAMBRA business, and at least 50% of whose services for the employer during the taxable year were performed within the LAMBRA.

• *Limitations on credit*

A taxpayer who is allowed a LAMBRA credit for qualified wages is limited to only one credit under the Personal Income Tax Law with respect to those amounts paid. The employer's wage payment credit must be reduced by the federal work opportunity credit and by the former state jobs tax credit. (Sec. 17053.46, Rev. & Tax. Code)

The amount of credit claimed for both the LAMBRA sales tax credit (discussed at ¶144) and the LAMBRA credit for qualified wages may not exceed the tax that would be imposed on the income attributed to the taxpayer's business activities within a LAMBRA. A taxpayer whose business also operates outside of the LAMBRA must use a special apportionment formula to determine the amount of income attributable to the LAMBRA. The amount of business income attributable to California is first determined by applying the standard apportionment formula discussed at ¶1305—1309. For purposes of determining the amount of income attributable to the LAMBRA, however, the sales factor is eliminated from the standard apportionment formula and the income used in the apportionment formula is limited to California-based income rather than worldwide income.

The credit is subject to recapture if an employee is terminated within a prescribed period (generally, roughly one year). In addition, any credit claimed is recaptured in the second taxable year if the employer fails to increase its number of jobs by one or more after commencing business within the LAMBRA. The law provides several exceptions to the recapture rules.

• *Credit carryover*

Unused credit may be carried over and applied to tax on income from the area in succeeding tax years until the credit is exhausted. However, the carryover period is limited to 10 years, commencing with the 2014 tax year, for the portion of any credit remaining for carryover to post-2013 taxable years.

¶148 Tax-Incentive Credit—Targeted Tax Area Employers

Law: Sec. 17053.34 (CCH CALIFORNIA TAX REPORTS, ¶16-856).

Comparable Federal: None.

California Form: FTB 3809 (Targeted Tax Area Deduction and Credit Summary).

Targeted tax area employers are allowed a credit for qualified wages paid to qualified employees who were hired prior to the January 1, 2013 targeted tax area designation expiration date. (*Repeal of Geographically Targeted Economic Development*

Area Tax Incentives, Franchise Tax Board (2013), CCH CALIFORNIA TAX REPORTS, ¶ 405-974) The targeted tax area is discussed at ¶ 104. Only those employers involved in the following business activities described in the Standard Industrial Classification Manual (SIC Manual) are eligible to claim the targeted tax area credit: manufacturing; transportation; communications; electric, gas, and sanitary services; and wholesale trade.

The credit that may be claimed for the first year of employment is 50% of "qualified wages," which is defined as that portion of hourly wages that does not exceed 150% of the minimum wage established by the California Industrial Welfare Commission. For the second, third, fourth, and fifth years of operation, the credit is reduced to 40%, 30%, 20%, and 10%, respectively. For purposes of computing the credit, seasonal workers are considered continuously employed. (Sec. 17053.34, Rev. & Tax. Code)

Even though the credit may not be claimed for employees hired after 2012, the credit installments may be claimed for the full five-years as long as the employee was hired prior to January 1, 2013, and continues to be otherwise eligible and the taxpayer has income attributable to the targeted tax area. (*Repeal of Geographically Targeted Economic Development Area Tax Incentives*, Franchise Tax Board (2013), CCH CALIFORNIA TAX REPORTS, ¶ 405-974)

• *Qualified employee*

An individual is a "qualified employee" if (1) he or she was hired after designation of the area as a targeted tax area, (2) 90% of the individual's services for the employer during the taxable year are directly related to the conduct of the employer's trade or business located in the targeted tax area, (3) the individual performs at least 50% of his or her services for the taxpayer during the taxable year in a targeted tax area, and (4) the individual is, or immediately preceding employment with the taxpayer was, any of the following:

— eligible for services under the federal Job Training Partnership Act (JTPA) or its successor, who was receiving, or was eligible to receive, subsidized employment, training, or services funded by the JTPA or its successor;

— eligible to be a voluntary or mandatory registrant under the Greater Avenues for Independence (GAIN) Act or its successor;

— an economically disadvantaged individual 14 years of age or older;

— a qualifying dislocated worker;

— a disabled individual eligible for, enrolled in, or having completed a state rehabilitation plan, or a service-connected disabled veteran, a veteran of the Vietnam era, or a veteran recently separated from military service;

— an ex-offender, including an individual placed on probation without a finding of guilt;

— a person who was eligible for, or a recipient of, benefits from certain specified public assistance programs;

— a member of a federally recognized Indian tribe, band, or other group of Native American descent;

— a resident of a targeted tax area; or

— a member of a targeted tax group for purposes of the federal Work Opportunity Credit, or its successor. (Sec. 17053.34, Rev. & Tax. Code)

• *Limitations and carryovers*

The total amount of the targeted tax area hiring credit and the targeted tax area sales and use tax credit (¶ 144), including any carryover from prior years, is limited to the tax attributable to income from the area. A taxpayer whose business also operates outside the targeted tax area must use a special apportionment formula to determine the amount of income attributable to the area. The amount of business income attributable to California is first determined by applying the standard apportionment formula discussed at ¶1305—1309. For purposes of determining the amount of income attributable to the targeted tax area, however, the sales factor is eliminated from the standard apportionment formula and the income used in the apportionment formula is limited to California-based income rather than worldwide income. (Sec. 17053.34, Rev. & Tax. Code)

The tax is subject to recapture if an employee is terminated within a prescribed period (generally, roughly one year). The law provides several exceptions to the operation of this recapture rule.

Unused credit may be carried over to succeeding taxable years until exhausted. However, the carryover period is limited to 10 years, commencing with the 2014 tax year, for the portion of any credit remaining for carryover to post-2013 taxable years.

¶149 Tax-Incentive Credit—Manufacturing Enhancement Area Employers

Law: Sec. 17053.47 (CCH CALIFORNIA TAX REPORTS, ¶16-858).

Comparable Federal: None.

California Form: FTB 3808 (Manufacturing Enhancement Area Credit Summary).

Manufacturing enhancement area (MEA) employers are allowed a credit for qualified wages paid to specified disadvantaged individuals or displaced employees who were hired prior to the January 1, 2013, MEA designation expiration date. (*Repeal of Geographically Targeted Economic Development Area Tax Incentives*, Franchise Tax Board (2013), CCH CALIFORNIA TAX REPORTS, ¶405-974). MEAs are discussed at ¶104. Only those employers involved in the following activities are eligible to claim the credit: business activities as described in Codes 2011 to 3999 of the Standard Industrial Classification Manual (SIC Manual); agricultural production; and livestock, animal specialties, or crop preparation services. (Sec. 17053.47, Rev. & Tax. Code)

The credit that may be claimed for the first year of employment is 50% of "qualified wages," which is defined as that portion of hourly wages that does not exceed 150% of the minimum wage established by the California Industrial Welfare Commission. For the second, third, fourth, and fifth years of employment, the credit is reduced to 40%, 30%, 20%, and 10%, respectively. Even though the credit may not be claimed for employees hired after 2012, the credit installments may be claimed for the full five-years as long as the employee was hired prior to January 1, 2013, and continues to be otherwise eligible and the taxpayer has income attributable to the TTA. (*Repeal of Geographically Targeted Economic Development Area Tax Incentives*, Franchise Tax Board (2013), CCH CALIFORNIA TAX REPORTS, ¶405-974)

For purposes of computing the credit, seasonal workers are considered continuously employed. The total amount of wages that may be taken into account for purposes of claiming the credit may not exceed $2 million per taxable year.

- *"Qualified taxpayer" and "qualified disadvantaged individual" defined*

A "qualified taxpayer" is a taxpayer engaged in a manufacturing trade or business within the area that, once the area has been designated as a manufacturing enhancement area, hires at least 50% of the business' employees from the county in which the area is located, 30% of whom are qualified disadvantaged individuals. (Sec. 17053.47, Rev. & Tax. Code)

An individual is a "qualified disadvantaged individual" if (1) he or she was hired after designation of the area as a manufacturing enhancement area, (2) 90% of the individual's services for the employer during the taxable year are directly related to the conduct of the employer's trade or business located in the manufacturing enhancement area, (3) the individual performs at least 50% of his or her services for the taxpayer during the taxable year in a manufacturing enhancement area, and (4) immediately preceding employment with the taxpayer, the individual was any of the following:

— determined eligible for services under the federal Job Training Partnership Act (JTPA) or any successor program;

— a voluntary or mandatory registrant under the Greater Avenues for Independence (GAIN) Act or any successor program; or

— certified eligible by the Employment Development Department under the Targeted Jobs Tax Credit Program or any successor program, whether or not the program is in effect.

• *Limitations*

The total amount of the credit, including any carryover from prior years, is limited to the tax attributable to income from the manufacturing enhancement area. A taxpayer whose business also operates outside the area must use a special apportionment formula to determine the amount of income attributable to the area. The amount of business income attributable to California is first determined by applying the apportionment formula discussed at ¶1305—1309. For purposes of determining the amount of income attributable to the manufacturing enhancement area, however, the sales factor is eliminated from the standard apportionment formula and the income used in the apportionment formula is limited to California-based income rather than worldwide income. (Sec. 17053.47, Rev. & Tax. Code)

The credit is reduced by the amount of any federal work opportunity credit allowed for the same wages. Unless specified exceptions apply, the tax is subject to recapture if an employee is terminated within a prescribed period (generally, roughly one year).

• *Credit carryovers*

If the amount of the credit exceeds the employer's tax for the taxable year, the excess may be carried over and claimed against income attributable to the area to succeeding taxable years until exhausted. However, the carryover period is limited to 10 years, commencing with the 2014 tax year, for the portion of any credit remaining for carryover to post-2013 taxable years.

¶150 Research and Development Credit

Law: Sec. 17052.12 (CCH CALIFORNIA TAX REPORTS, ¶16-870).

Comparable Federal: Sec. 41 (CCH U.S. MASTER TAX GUIDE ¶1330).

California Form: FTB 3523 (Research Credit).

California provides a credit for increased research expenditures that is similar to that provided by federal law, with the following exceptions (Sec. 17052.12, Rev. & Tax. Code):

— The applicable California percentage is 15% of the excess of qualified research expenses for the tax year over a specified percentage of the taxpayer's average annual gross receipts for the four preceding taxable years (the "base amount"). The federal percentage is 20% of the excess of qualified expenses over the base amount.

— California uses 1.49%, 1.98%, and 2.48% for the three tiers used to compute the amount of the credit under the alternative incremental computation (AIC) method. California has not adopted the federal repeal of the alternative incremental credit effective beginning with the 2009 taxable year. Thus, taxpayers are still able to utilize the AIC method for purposes of calculating their California research and development credit.

— California has not conformed federal provisions that authorize the use of a third method, the alternative simplified credit.

— California does not allow a credit against personal income tax for basic research payments. Under federal law, a credit equal to 20% of basic research payments is allowed.

— Research must be conducted in California to qualify for the California credit. Federal law provides that research must be conducted in the United States, Puerto Rico, or other U.S. possessions.

— The California credit may be carried over until exhausted. The federal credit is part of the general business credit subject to the limitations imposed by IRC Sec. 38.

— For purposes of determining the base amount under California law, only the gross receipts from the sale of property that is held primarily for sale to customers in the ordinary course of the taxpayer's trade or business and delivered or shipped to a purchaser within California, regardless of F.O.B. point or other conditions of sale, may be taken into account.

— California law, but not federal law, disallows the credit for expenses incurred to purchase property for which a sales and use tax exemption for teleproduction or other postproduction property is claimed (¶1507).

— California has not adopted federal provisions that (1) allow a taxpayer to claim 20% of amounts paid or incurred by the taxpayer during the tax year to an energy research consortium and (2) repeal the limitation on contract research expenses paid to eligible small businesses, universities, and federal laboratories for qualified energy research.

For additional details concerning this credit, taxpayers should consult FTB Pub. 1082, *Research and Development Credit: Frequently Asked Questions.*

Comment: *Taxpayers With Zero California Gross Receipts Still Eligible for the Credit*

Taxpayers with California qualified research expenses (QREs) and no California gross receipts are still eligible to claim the credit by multiplying the applicable California credit rate for the taxable year (15% for post-1999 tax years) by the excess of the taxpayer's current year qualified research expenses over a "base amount." The base amount is the taxpayer's "fixed base percentage" times the taxpayer's average annual gross receipts for the four taxable years preceding the taxable year for which the credit is being determined, not to exceed 50% of the QREs for the credit year. If the computed base amount is less than the minimum base amount (50% of the QREs), then the credit is equal to 15% of QREs in excess of the "minimum base amount." In cases where there are no gross receipts, the California credit is equal to 7.5% of the QREs for the credit year, or the reduced credit under IRC § 280(c)(3).

The 7.5% rate or the reduced credit under IRC § 280(c)(3) applies in all instances when the computed base amount is less than the minimum base amount. However, if the computed base amount is greater than the minimum base amount, the credit is equal to the applicable California credit rate (15% for 2000 and later) of the QREs in excess of the computed base amount. The taxpayer earns the credit only for the portion of qualified spending that exceeds the computed base amount. The amount of QREs allowed in the credit calculation for such a taxpayer will range between 50% and zero, depending on the excess QREs over the base amount. The credit for a taxpayer with no excess QREs will be zero.

A taxpayer with California gross receipts that cannot substantiate the base amount and/or fixed base percentage calculations for any reason may not simply claim that the minimum base amount applies in lieu of calculating the fixed base percentage. Such a taxpayer is not entitled to the credit for lack of substantiation. (FTB Legal Division Guidance 2012-03-01, CCH CALIFORNIA TAX REPORTS, ¶405-603)

Comment: Substantiation of Qualified Activities

In a nonprecedential letter decision, the State Board of Equalization upheld a taxpayer's substantiation of its qualified activities even though the taxpayer did not provide complete documentation of each individual project. The FTB had denied 80% of the credit as a result of the taxpayer's lack of documentation. However, the taxpayers argued that the corporation's projects were too numerous to examine individually to determine whether each innovative project met the requirements of IRC § 41(d), so they identified categories of qualifying activities without tying them to specific projects and determined the amounts of time that personnel spent on those activities. (*Appeal of Pacific Southwest Container, Inc.* (2011) CCH CALIFORNIA TAX REPORTS, ¶ 405-451)

The FTB does not currently have a program similar to the IRS's research credit recordkeeping agreements (RCRAs) that outlines what records taxpayers should maintain. The FTB is considering whether to establish an RCRA program for state tax purposes.

• *Alternative incremental research credit election*

If a taxpayer's "base amount" is higher than the taxpayer's current qualified research expenses, the taxpayer may not qualify for the regular research credit, but may be eligible to receive the benefit of the alternative incremental credit (AIC); see third item above. The AIC is elected and claimed on the California return. Taxpayers may want to attach a statement to their California returns indicating that they are making the AIC election, although this is not required.

Once taxpayers make the AIC election, they are required to continue using the AIC for California purposes until they obtain permission from the FTB to revoke the election. They must receive permission from the FTB to revoke the California AIC election even if their federal AIC is revoked.

Revocation of an election can only be granted on a current or prospective basis. Federal Form 3115, Application for Change in Accounting Method, or federal Form 1128, Application to Adopt, Change, or Retain a Tax Year, can be used to request the change. Federal Form 3115 or Federal Form 1128 should be completed using the appropriate California tax information, including the taxpayer's California Corporate Number (CCN) at the top of page 1. Any reference on these forms, or their instructions, to the Internal Revenue Code should be read as referring to the corresponding Revenue and Taxation Code section, if it exists. A cover letter, with the taxpayer's name and CCN, should be attached to the front of Form 3115 or Form 1128, with an indication that a "Change in Accounting Period" or a "Change in Accounting Method" is being requested. Requests should be sent to the Franchise Tax Board, Change in Accounting Periods and Methods Coordinator, P.O. Box 1998, Sacramento, CA 95812. (*Tax News*, California Franchise Tax Board, September 2006)

• *Special rules for start-up companies*

California conforms to federal law providing special rules to determine the fixed-base percentage used in determining the amount of the credit that may be claimed by start-up companies. (Sec. 17052.12, Rev. & Tax. Code)

Comment: Temporary Limitation on Credit Amounts Lifted

See ¶ 125 for a discussion of the 50% limitation on the amount of business credits and credit carryovers that could be claimed during the 2008 and 2009 taxable years and the impact on credit carryovers. (Sec. 17039.2, Rev. & Tax. Code)

• *Interaction with research deduction*

For both California and federal purposes, taxpayers must reduce any research expense deduction claimed by the amount of the research expense credit claimed, unless they elect to take a reduced credit. (¶331, ¶336). (Sec. 17052.12, Rev. & Tax. Code) Form FTB 3523 provides instructions for calculating the reduced credit. If the election is not made, a schedule must be attached to the taxpayer's return listing the deduction amounts that were reduced and the lines on the return on which the reductions were made. (Instructions, FTB 3523, Research Credit)

¶151 Ultra-Low Sulfur Diesel Fuel Credit

Law: Sec. 17053.62 (CCH CALIFORNIA TAX REPORTS, ¶16-887).

Comparable Federal: Secs. 45H (CCH U.S. MASTER TAX GUIDE ¶1344E).

California Form: FTB 3511 (Environmental Tax Credit)

For taxable years beginning before 2018, an environmental tax credit is available for ultra-low sulfur diesel fuel produced by a qualified small refiner at a California facility. (Sec. 17053.62, Rev. & Tax. Code) The credit is similar to the federal credit allowed under IRC Sec. 45H, except for the following differences:

— the credit is limited to ultra-low sulfur diesel fuel produced at a California facility;

— California's definition of a "small refiner" is more restrictive;

— the period in which the costs must be incurred to qualify for the credit is different; and

— the certification procedures may be different (see below).

For purposes of the California credit, the qualified capital costs had to be incurred during the period beginning January 1, 2004, and ending on May 31, 2007. (Sec. 17053.62(c)(6), Rev. & Tax. Code) Costs qualify for the federal credit if incurred during the period beginning January 1, 2003, and ending on the earlier of (1) the date that is one year after the date by which the taxpayer must comply with the applicable Environmental Protection Agency (EPA) regulations or (2) December 31, 2009.

Both the California credit and the federal credit may be claimed for diesel fuel with a sulfur content of 15 parts per million or less. In addition, for purposes of the California credit, it may also be rebuttably presumed that ultra-low sulfur diesel fuel for which the credit may be claimed includes vehicular diesel fuel produced and sold by a small refiner (1) after May 31, 2006, and (2) before June 2006 if the refiner proves that the fuel meets applicable California Air Resources Board (CARB) regulations. The presumption that the fuel sold by a small refiner after May 31, 2006, qualifies for the credit may be rebutted by the CARB. (Sec. 17053.62(c)(7), Rev. & Tax. Code)

• *Credit amount*

The credit is equal to five cents for each gallon of ultra-low sulfur diesel fuel produced during the taxable year. (Sec. 17053.62(a), Rev. & Tax. Code) The credit may not exceed 25% of the qualified capital costs certified by the U.S. Treasury Secretary or the CARB that are incurred by the small refiner with respect to each facility, reduced by the aggregate ultra-low sulfur diesel fuel credits for all prior taxable years with respect to that facility. (Sec. 17053.62(b), Rev. & Tax. Code)

Comment: *Temporary Limitation on Credit Amounts Lifted*

See ¶125 for a discussion of the 50% limitation on the amount of business credits and credit carryovers that could be claimed during the 2008 and 2009 taxable years and the impact on credit carryovers. (Sec. 17039.2, Rev. & Tax. Code)

• *Planning considerations*

Certification.—Prior to claiming the credit, taxpayers must receive certification from the CARB or the U.S. Secretary of the Treasury, in consultation with the EPA, that the qualified capital costs for which the taxpayer is claiming the credit are in compliance with the applicable CARB or EPA regulations. However, certification by the U.S. Secretary of the Treasury may not be sufficient if the CARB demonstrates that the fuel produced does not meet CARB regulations. (Sec. 17053.62(c)(2), Rev. & Tax. Code) The Instructions to the FTB 3511, Environmental Tax Credit, state that the taxpayer must receive certification from the CARB.

Basis.—The increase in basis that results from expenditures for which the credit is claimed must be reduced by the amount of the credit taken. (Sec. 17053.62(d), Rev. & Tax. Code)

Exclusivity provision.—No other deduction may be claimed for the expenses for which the credit is taken. (Sec. 17053.62(e), Rev. & Tax. Code)

Carryforward provisions.—Unused credit may be carried over for up to 10 years. (Sec. 17053.62(f), Rev. & Tax. Code)

Recapture provisions.—The credit is subject to recapture if a small refiner sells, transfers, or otherwise disposes of a facility within five years of the taxable year during which it first claimed the credit. (Sec. 17053.62(g), Rev. & Tax. Code)

¶152 Credit for Prior Year Minimum Tax

Law: Sec. 17063 (CCH CALIFORNIA TAX REPORTS, ¶ 15-440).

Comparable Federal: Sec. 53 (CCH U.S. MASTER TAX GUIDE ¶ 1370).

California Form: FTB 3510 (Credit for Prior Year Alternative Minimum Tax - Individuals or Fiduciaries).

California allows a credit in the form of a carryover to taxpayers who have incurred California alternative minimum tax in prior years but not in the current tax year. (Sec. 17063, Rev. & Tax. Code)

The credit is computed in the same manner as the federal credit under IRC Sec. 53 ("credit for prior year minimum tax") with the substitution of certain California figures in place of the federal. In addition, California did not incorporate the federal provision that created a refundable AMT credit for individuals with a long-term unused minimum tax credit, applicable for federal purposes to tax years beginning after December 20, 2006, and beginning before January 1, 2013.

Both the federal and California credits are based on the amount of alternative minimum tax paid on "deferral preferences" (items that defer tax liability) as distinct from "exclusion items" (items that permanently reduce tax liability).

The credit is computed on FTB 3510, and for a taxpayer claiming this credit for the first time, most of the figures needed for the computation come from Schedule P (540) of the prior year's California personal income tax return. The credit is equivalent to the adjusted net minimum tax for all prior taxable years beginning after 1986, reduced by the minimum tax credit for all such prior taxable years. However, the credit may not exceed the excess of the following:

— the California regular tax reduced by all credits except (1) refundable credits without carryover provisions and (2) any credit that reduces the tax below the tentative minimum tax over

— the tentative minimum tax for the taxable year (¶ 117).

The adjusted net minimum tax for any taxable year is the taxpayer's minimum tax for that year, reduced by a theoretical minimum tax, assuming that only the adjustments and preferences specified in IRC Sec. 53(d)(1)(B)(ii) and, for California tax purposes only, the California items of tax preference relating to small business stock.

Unused credit may be carried forward indefinitely.

Comment: Temporary Limitation on Credit Amounts Lifted

See ¶ 125 for a discussion of the 50% limitation on the amount of business credits and credit carryovers that could be claimed during the 2008 and 2009 taxable years and the impact on credit carryovers. (Sec. 17039.2, Rev. & Tax. Code)

• *Nonresidents and part-year residents*

Nonresidents and part-year residents prorate the credit on the basis of California taxable income. (Sec. 17055, Rev. & Tax. Code) This ratio is computed on FTB 3510; see ¶ 116 for a more detailed discussion.

¶153 Enhanced Oil Recovery Credit

> *Law:* Sec. 17052.8 (CCH CALIFORNIA TAX REPORTS, ¶ 16-953).
>
> *Comparable Federal:* Sec. 43 (CCH U.S. MASTER TAX GUIDE ¶ 1336).
>
> *California Form:* FTB 3546 (Enhanced Oil Recovery Credit).

California allows certain independent oil producers a credit equal to $1/3$ of the enhanced oil recovery credit allowed under federal law. Thus, a California credit is allowed in an amount equal to up to 5% of the taxpayer's qualified costs attributable to qualified enhanced oil recovery projects. However, for the 2016 taxable year, only a credit carryover from a prior year is allowed. Also,"California modifies the federal definition of "qualified enhanced oil recovery project" to include only projects located within California. (Sec. 17052.8, Rev. & Tax. Code)

• *"Qualified costs" defined*

Qualified costs include the following:

— amounts paid or incurred for tangible property that is an integral part of a qualified enhanced oil recovery project and for which depreciation or amortization is allowed;

— intangible drilling and development costs that are paid or incurred in connection with a qualified enhanced oil recovery project and that a taxpayer may elect to capitalize and amortize under state law; and

— tertiary injectant expenses paid or incurred with respect to a qualified enhanced oil recovery project. (Sec. 17052.8, Rev. & Tax. Code)

CCH Comment: Current Deduction of Tertiary Injectant Costs

California does not conform to federal law (IRC Sec. 193) allowing taxpayers to currently deduct tertiary injectant costs. Consequently, such costs must be capitalized and deducted through depreciation for California personal income tax purposes (Instructions, FTB 3546, Enhanced Oil Recovery Credit).

• *Limitations*

The credit is not available to certain retailers, refiners, and related persons who are not eligible for the percentage depletion specifically allowed to independent producers and royalty owners. (Sec. 17052.8, Rev. & Tax. Code)

No deduction is allowed for costs for which the credit is allowed. Also, the basis of any property for which a credit is allowed must be reduced by the amount of the credit attributable to the property.

Comment: Temporary Limitation on Credit Amounts Lifted

See ¶125 for a discussion of the 50% limitation on the amount of business credits and credit carryovers that could be claimed during the 2008 and 2009 taxable years and the impact on credit carryovers. (Sec. 17039.2, Rev. & Tax. Code)

• *Federal election binding*

A federal election not to have the credit apply is binding and irrevocable for California purposes. Also, a taxpayer must make an election between credits if the taxpayer's costs qualify for another credit. (Sec. 17052.8, Rev. & Tax. Code)

• *Carryover*

Any amount of the credit exceeding "net tax" for the taxable year may be carried forward for up to 15 years. (Sec. 17052.8, Rev. & Tax. Code)

¶154 Prison Inmate Labor Credit

Law: Sec. 17053.6 (CCH CALIFORNIA TAX REPORTS, ¶16-875).

Comparable Federal: None.

California Form: FTB 3507 (Prison Inmate Labor Credit).

California allows a credit equal to 10% of the wages paid to prison inmates employed under a prisoner employment joint venture agreement with the Director of Corrections. The credit is in addition to any other deduction to which the employer is entitled. (Sec. 17053.6, Rev. & Tax. Code) According to the Instructions to FTB 3507, the credit may only be claimed for wages paid to an individual who was hired after the joint venture agreement was executed.

There is no carryover allowed for unused credits.

Comment: Temporary Limitation on Credit Amounts Lifted

See ¶125 for a discussion of the 50% limitation on the amount of business credits and credit carryovers that could be claimed during the 2008 and 2009 taxable years and the impact on credit carryovers. (Sec. 17039.2, Rev. & Tax. Code)

¶155 Community Development Investment Credit

Law: Sec. 17053.57, Rev. & Tax. Code; Sec. 32301, Financial Code (CCH CALIFORNIA TAX REPORTS, ¶16-831).

Comparable Federal: Sec. 38 (CCH U.S. MASTER TAX GUIDE ¶1325).

California Forms: Form 540 (California Resident Income Tax Return), Sch. P (540) (Alternative Minimum Tax and Credit Limitations - Residents).

For taxable years beginning before 2017, a nonrefundable credit is available in an amount equal to 20% of each qualified investment made into a community development financial institution. However, the amount that may be claimed by a taxpayer is limited to the amount certified by the California Organized Investment Network (COIN) prior to January 1, 2017. (Sec. 17053.57, Rev. & Tax. Code)

"Community development financial institution" defined.—A "community development financial institution" (CDFI) is a private financial institution located in California that

— is certified by COIN;

— has community development as its primary mission; and

— makes loans in California urban, rural, or reservation-based communities.

CDFIs may include community development banks, community development loan funds, community development credit unions, microenterprise funds, community development corporation-based lenders, community development venture funds, and the State Assistance Fund for Enterprises, Business, and Industrial Development Corporation (SAFE-BIDCO).

A list of the currently certified CDFIs is available on the COIN's website at: http://www.insurance.ca.gov/0250-insurers/0700-coin/CDFITaxCredit.cfm.

Qualified investment defined.—A "qualified investment" is an investment of at least $50,000 in either of the following:

— a deposit or loan that does not earn interest; or

— an equity investment; or

— an equity-like debt instrument that meets the specifications of the U.S. Department of the Treasury, Community Development Financial Institution Fund, or its successor.

The investment must be made for at least 60 months. The entire credit previously claimed is subject to recapture if the qualified investment is withdrawn before the end of the 60-month period and not reinvested in another CDFI within 60 days. If a qualified investment is reduced before the end of the 60-month period, but not below $50,000, an amount equal to 20% of the total reduction will be recaptured.

Limitations.—The aggregate credits against personal income tax, corporation franchise or income tax, and insurance gross premiums tax may not exceed $50 million annually. However, unallowed credits from previous years may be added to the $50 million limit.

The total amount of qualified investments certified by COIN in any calendar year to any one CDFI, together with its affiliates, is limited to 30% of the annual aggregate amount of qualified investments certified. If, after October 1, COIN determines that the availability of tax credits exceeds the demand for the credits, then a CDFI that has been allocated 30% of the annual aggregate amount of qualified investments may apply to be certified for any remaining credits in that calendar year. COIN also must reserve 10% of the annual aggregate amount of qualified investments for investment amounts of less than or equal to $200,000. If, after October 1, there remains an unallocated portion of that reserved amount, then qualified investments in excess of $200,000 may be eligible for the remaining unallocated portion.

Application process.—A financial institution into which qualified investments are made must apply to COIN for certification of its status as a CDFI and apply on behalf of the taxpayer for certification of the amount of the investment and the credit amount allocated. The application process for both certification as a CDFI and for the investment certification is explained in detail on the COIN website at: http://www.insurance.ca.gov/0250-insurers/0700-coin/CDFITaxCredit.cfm.

Credit carryforward.—Unused credit may be carried forward for the next four taxable years.

Comment: Temporary Limitation on Credit Amounts Lifted

See ¶125 for a discussion of the 50% limitation on the amount of business credits and credit carryovers that could be claimed during the 2008 and 2009 taxable years and the impact on credit carryovers. (Sec. 17039.2, Rev. & Tax. Code)

¶156 College Access Credit

Law: Secs. 17053.86, 17053.87 (CCH CALIFORNIA TAX REPORTS, ¶16-956).

Comparable Federal: None.

California Form: FTB 3592 (College Access Tax Credit).

For taxable years beginning on or after January 1, 2014, and before January 1, 2018, a credit is allowed for cash contributions made to the College Access Tax Credit Fund. Taxpayers claiming the credit must first obtain a certification from the California Educational Facilities Authority (CEFA). The CEFA must certify the contribution amount eligible for the credit within 45 days following receipt of the contribution, allocate and certify tax credits, and provide the Franchise Tax Board with a copy of each credit certificate issued. (Sec. 17053.86, Rev. & Tax. Code; Sec. 17053.87, Rev. & Tax. Code)

• *Credit amount*

The credit allowed is equal to the following:

— for taxable years beginning during 2014, 60% of the amount contributed by the taxpayer, as allocated and certified by the CEFA;

— for taxable years beginning during 2015, 55% of the amount contributed by the taxpayer, as allocated and certified by the CEFA; and

— for taxable years beginning during 2016 and 2017, 50% of the amount contributed by the taxpayer, as allocated and certified by the CEFA.

The maximum aggregate amount of credits that may be allocated and certified in any calendar year is $500 million, plus for taxable years beginning before 2017 any previously unallocated and uncertified credit amounts.

• *Planning considerations*

The issues discussed below may affect taxpayers claiming the college access credit.

Credit limitations.—No deductions will be allowed for amounts taken into account in calculating the credit.

Carryforward provisions.—Unused credits may be carried over for up to six taxable years.

¶157 New Employment Credit (Post-2013 Tax Years)

Law: Sec. 17053.73 (CCH CALIFORNIA TAX REPORTS, ¶ 16-875b).

Comparable Federal: None.

California Form: FTB 3554 (New Employment Credit).

Beginning with the 2014 tax year, a nonrefundable credit is available to qualified employers that hire qualified full-time employees to work in a designated geographic area (DGA) provided the taxpayer pays qualified wages and satisfies other procedural requirements. (Sec. 17053.73, Rev. & Tax. Code)

The credit replaces the former new jobs credit that was in effect prior to the 2014 taxable year.

Practitioner Comment: Comparison to Enterprise Zone Credit

Among other restrictions and requirements, the new hiring tax credit is only available to employers that create a net increase in jobs statewide, which was not required under the EZ hiring credit. Also taxpayers that terminate a qualified employee within 36 months of hire may be subject to recapture provisions. Moreover, this new hiring credit is not available to some businesses, such as retailers, food service, and temporary employment agencies. Interestingly, the legislation states that the credit is not available to taxpayers "primarily engaged in" providing food services. Yet, taxpayers that simply "provide" temporary help services and retail trade services are similarly barred from the credit. It is unclear why the modifier "primarily" was omitted for temporary help services and retail trade services and whether this omission carries any significance or was an unintentional oversight.

Chris Whitney, Contributing Editor

• *Definitions*

Designated geographic areas.—Eligible DGAs are comprised of designated census tracts and economic development areas. A "designated census tract" is a census tract determined by the Department of Finance to be in the top 25% of California census tracts in terms of civilian unemployment and poverty rates. For purposes of this credit, "economic development areas" are all prior enterprise zones (in existence on 12/31/2011) and LAMBRAs (in existence on 7/11/2013), except in census tracts within those zones with low unemployment and low poverty levels. (Sec. 17053.73(b)(7) and (8), Rev. & Tax. Code)

Comment: Mapping Tool Available

A mapping tool is available on the Franchise Tax Board's (FTB) website to assist taxpayers in identifying the DGAs. The tool allows employers to search specific addresses to see if a location is contained in a DGA.

Qualified employee.—A "qualified employee" is an employee who meets all of the following criteria:

— Works at least 50% of the time in the designated census tract or economic development area.

— Is paid wages at least equal to 150% of the minimum wage.

— Is hired after 2013.

— Is hired by a qualified taxpayer after the census tract is designated by the Department of Finance or the economic development area is determined not to be in a designated census tract.

— Works on average at least 35 hours per week or is considered a full-time salaried employee under Labor Code § 515.

In addition, immediately prior to being hired, the employee must be one of the following:

— Unemployed for at least six months.

— A veteran who separated from service in the U.S. Armed Forces within the 12-month period prior to being hired.

— A recipient of the federal earned income tax credit in the previous tax year.

— An ex-offender previously convicted of a felony.

— A recipient of CalWORKs or general assistance.

Practice Tip: Post-graduate unemployment

Individuals who have received a baccaulaureate, post-graduate, or other professional degree must have completed their program of study at least 12 months prior to being hired in order to qualify under the "unemployed" category above.

(Sec. 17053.73(b)(10), Rev. & Tax. Code)

Qualified taxpayer.—Except for small businesses, a qualified taxpayer does not include any taxpayer involved in the following industries:

— temporary help services

— retail trade

— food services

— casinos or casino hotels

— sexually-oriented businesses

(Sec. 17053.73(b)(11), Rev. & Tax. Code)

A "small business" is a trade or business that has aggregate gross receipts (including both business and nonbusiness income), less returns and allowances reportable to California, of less than $2 million during the previous taxable year, but does not include a sexually-oriented business. (Sec. 17053.73(b)(14), Rev. & Tax. Code)

Qualified wages.—"Qualified wages" are the amount of wages paid in excess of 150% of the minimum wage up to 350% of the minimum wage, between $15 and $35 per hour for 2016. The credit may be claimed only for wages paid during the employee's first 60 months of employment. (Sec. 17053.73(b)(12), Rev. & Tax. Code)

Comment: 60-Month Period

A 60-month period does not "recommence" upon an employee's reemployment, even for seasonal employees. The credit may be claimed for qualified employees for the full 60-month period provided that the employee was hired prior to an area being "dedesignated." However, the credit may not be claimed for employees hired after the area is "dedesignated."

For qualified employees employed in a designated pilot area, qualified wages are those wages paid in excess of $10 per hour or an equivalent amount for salaried employees up to 350% of minimum wage ($35 for 2016). The Governor's Office of Business and Economic Development may designate up to a total of five pilot areas, which must be located within a designated census tract or an economic development area with average wages less than the statewide average wages. Designations last for a period of four years, but may be extended for an additional three years. Designations may not last beyond 2020. On April 24, 2014, pilot areas in Fresno, Merced, and Riverside were designated. The designations are in effect until December 31, 2017, but may be extended for an additional three years.

Practice Tip: Estates and trusts

Qualified wages for any taxable year are apportioned between the estate or trust and the beneficiaries on the basis of the trust's or estate's income allocable to each. Any beneficiary who has had wages so apportioned is treated as the employer for purposes of the credit. (Sec. 17053.73(j), Rev. & Tax. Code)

• *Credit amount*

The credit is equal to 35% of qualified wages paid for each net new qualified full-time employee hired.

Comment: Additional Comparison to Enterprise Zone Hiring Credit

The credit may be applied against all of a taxpayer's California taxable income. Unlike the enterprise zone hiring credits, the credit is not limited to the income attributable to a particular designated area. (*New Employment Credit—Frequently Asked Questions*, Franchise Tax Board (2013) (CCH California Tax Reports, ¶ 405-940))

The number of full-time employees hired is determined on the basis of the increased number of full-time employees statewide during the tax year over the base year, which is 2013 for currently existing businesses and businesses commencing in 2014. For businesses commencing after 2014, the base year is the taxable year immediately preceding the taxable year in which a qualified full-time employee was first hired by the qualified taxpayer. (Sec. 17053.73(b), Rev. & Tax. Code)

Net increase in employment.—The net increase in qualified full-time employees is determined on an annual full-time equivalent basis, determined on an hourly basis for hourly employees and a weekly basis for salaried employees. "Annual full-time equivalent" (FTE) means either of the following:

— In the case of a full-time employee paid hourly qualified wages, annual full-time equivalent means the total number of hours worked for the taxpayer by the employee (not to exceed 2,000 hours per employee) divided by 2,000.

— In the case of a salaried full-time employee, annual full-time equivalent means the total number of weeks worked for the taxpayer by the employee divided by 52.

(Sec. 17053.73(b)(10), Rev. & Tax. Code)

All employees of trades or businesses that are treated as related under IRC §§ 267, 318, or 707 are treated as employed by a single taxpayer. All employees of non-incorporated trades or businesses that are under common control are also treated as employed by a single employer. (Sec. 17053.73(d) and (h), Rev. & Tax. Code)

Employees working for a business that is acquired are not included in the "net increase." (Sec. 17053.73(c)(1), Rev. & Tax. Code)

All new hires are treated as a net-increase for taxpayers who first commence doing business in California during the taxable year. (Sec. 17053.73(d), Rev. & Tax. Code)

Comment: Relocated Businesses

Taxpayers relocating to a DGA may claim the credit for employees hired in the new location only if the taxpayer provides employees at the former location a written offer of employment in the new location with comparable compensation. This requirement does not apply to small businesses and only applies to taxpayers that have an increase in employment in a DGA and a decrease in the number of full-time employees within the last twelve months in California locations outside of DGAs. (Sec. 17053.73(a)(3), Rev. & Tax. Code)

• *Planning considerations*

Credit reservations.—Upon hiring a new employee, a taxpayer must request a tentative credit reservation from the FTB within 30 days of complying with the Employee Development Department's new hire reporting requirements on a form to be prescribed by the FTB. (Sec. 17053.73(e), Rev. & Tax. Code) The applications may only be submitted online.

Claiming the credit.—The credit may only be claimed on a timely-filed original return for qualified employees for whom the taxpayer has received a tentative credit reservation. (Sec. 17053.73(a)(4), Rev. & Tax. Code)

Annual reporting requirements.—The taxpayer must provide the FTB with an annual certification of employment with respect to each qualified full-time employee hired in a previous taxable year by the 15th day of the third month of the taxable year. The certification is submitted online through the FTB's website. (Sec. 17053.73(e)(23), Rev. & Tax. Code)

Credit carryovers.—Unused credit may be carried forward for up to five years. (Sec. 17053.73(k), Rev. & Tax. Code)

Credit recapture.—The credit is subject to recapture if the employee does not remain employed for at least three years, unless specified exceptions apply. (Sec. 17053.73(i), Rev. & Tax. Code)

Sunset.—The credit is subject to repeal on December 1, 2024, and unless extended is available only for qualified wages paid to employees hired prior to 2021. (Sec. 17053.73(n), Rev. & Tax. Code)

Public information.—The FTB must develop and post a searchable database on its website, which provides employer names, credit amounts claimed, and number of new jobs created for each taxable year. (Sec. 17053.73f(4), Rev. & Tax. Code)

¶158 Earned Income Tax Credit

Law: Sec. 17052, 19852, 19853 (CCH CALIFORNIA TAX REPORTS, ¶16-820).

Comparable Federal: Sec. 32 (CCH U.S. MASTER TAX GUIDE ¶1322).

California Form: FTB 3514 (California Earned Income Tax Credit), FTB 3596 (Paid Preparer's California Earned Income Tax Credit Checklist).

California provides a refundable earned income tax credit (EITC) to certain low-income individuals, in modified conformity with the federal EITC provisions. The California EITC will be operative only for tax years for which resources are authorized in the annual Budget Act for overseeing and auditing returns associated with the EITC. (Sec. 17052, Rev. & Tax. Code)

Differences between the California EITC and the federal EITC include the following:

— California allows the EITC only for wage income earned in California that is subject to California withholding;

— California does not allow the EITC for self-employment income;

— for California purposes, nonresident taxpayers must have earned income from working in California;

— the California income limitations differ from the federal income limitations;

— taxpayers may elect to include military combat pay in earned income for California purposes, whether or not they elect to include it for federal purposes; and

— for California purposes, the "eligible individual" and a "qualifying child" must have a principal place of abode in California.

For California purposes, both the taxpayer's adjusted gross income and earned income (for 2016) must be less than the following:

— $6,718 if there are no qualifying children;

— $10,088 if there is one qualifying child; and

— $14,162 if there are two or more qualifying children.

The California EITC begins to phase out when the taxpayer's earned income (for 2016) exceeds the following amounts:

— $3,359 if there are no qualifying children;

— $5,044 if there is one qualifying child; and

— $7,081 if there are two or more qualifying children.

Also, the taxpayer's investment income, such as interest, dividends, royalties, and capital gains, must not exceed $3,471 (for 2016) for the entire tax year.

The amount of California EITC allowed is equal to a percentage of earned income (7.65%, 34%, 40%, or 45%, depending on the number of qualifying children), subject to phaseout above the earned income levels described above, and multiplied by an annual adjustment factor (as specified in the annual Budget Act—85% for 2016). A worksheet and tax tables for determining the amount of the California EITC allowed are provided in the instructions for FTB 3514 (California Earned Income Tax Credit). For 2016, the maximum California EITC amounts allowed are as follows:

— $217 if there are no qualifying children;

— $1,452 if there is one qualifying child;

— $2,406 if there are two qualifying children; and

— $2,706 if there are three or more qualifying children.

Practice Note: Employers Required to Provide Federal EITC Information to Employees

California employers must notify employees covered by the employer's unemployment insurance that they may be eligible for the federal and California EITCs. The notice must be provided by handing the notice directly to the employee or mailing the notice to the employee's last-known address within the one week period before or after the employer provides the employee an annual wage summary. (Sec. 19852, Rev. & Tax. Code; Sec. 19853, Rev. & Tax. Code)

PERSONAL INCOME TAX

CHAPTER 2

GROSS INCOME

¶201 Gross Income—In General

Law: Secs. 17071, 17072, 17081, 17083, 17087, 17131-36, 17139.5, 17141, 17147.7, 17151, 17153.5, 17154 (CCH CALIFORNIA TAX REPORTS, ¶ 15-510, 16-060).

Comparable Federal: Secs. 61, 62, 84-86, 88, 90, 120, 125-27, 129-132, 136, 139A (CCH U.S. MASTER TAX GUIDE ¶ 700, 716, 722, 861, 863, 869, 871, 881, 883, 884, 1005).

California Forms: Sch. CA (540) (California Adjustments - Residents), Sch. CA (540NR) (California Adjustments - Nonresidents or Part-Year Residents), Sch. D (Capital Gain or Loss Adjustment), Sch. D-1 (Sales of Business Property).

California conforms, as a general rule, to most of the federal provisions concerning gross income as of the current IRC tie-in date (¶ 103).

The following paragraphs will detail the California-federal differences as to what is included in gross income for the 2016 taxable year.

"Gross income" is broadly defined to include income derived from any source whatever, except as otherwise specifically provided by statute.

Practice Pointer: BOE Audits

Taxpayers who undergo a sales and use tax audit by the State Board of Equalization (BOE) should be aware that the BOE provides the FTB with copies of sales and use tax audit reports for the audits that result in adjustments of additional gross receipts (total sales). The FTB reviews these sales and use tax reports to determine if an income tax adjustment is warranted. (*Tax News*, California Franchise Tax Board, November 2008)

The California law incorporates the federal definition of "gross income" by reference. Except as discussed in the list below, this means that the same items are included under both laws. However, even if an item is included in both California and federal gross income, the amounts to be included may differ because of prior law or other differences. The following list highlights differences in California and federal gross income that should be reported on Sch. CA (540) or Sch. CA (540NR) (other relevant forms are indicated):

— Annuities and pension and profit-sharing plans (¶ 205, ¶ 206).

— Community Energy Authority obligation income.

— Dividends and other corporate distributions (¶ 226).

— Earthquake loss mitigation incentives (¶ 256).

— Economic incentive area investment income (FTB 3805Z and FTB 3806) (¶ 240).

— Employee ridesharing arrangement participation compensation (¶ 241).

— Family leave payments (Sec. 17087, Rev. & Tax. Code).

— Health savings accounts (¶ 219, ¶ 247).

— Holocaust and Japanese internment victims compensation (¶ 248).

— Interest income (¶ 217).

¶201

— Lottery winnings from California lottery, including amounts received pursuant to an assignment, are exempt from California tax. (Sec. 8880.68, Govt. Code) Such winnings are subject to federal tax as wagering gains, except to the extent that they may be offset by wagering losses (¶307).

However, income taxes are imposed on the income that retailers realize on the sale of lottery tickets. This also includes extra cash bonuses that the Lottery Commission pays to lottery game retailers, according to percentages of lottery prizes, because they are compensation for the sale of lottery tickets (*Letter*, FTB, CCH CALIFORNIA TAX REPORTS, ¶16-305.40).

— Native Americans' income (¶254).

— Nonresidents' income (Form 540NR, Sch. CA (540NR)) (¶231).

— Patronage allocations from cooperatives (¶232).

— Prescription drug subsidies (¶252).

— Qualified stock options (¶207).

— Railroad Retirement benefits, which include pensions, ridesharing benefits, and sick pay (Sec. 17087, Rev. & Tax. Code).

— Recycling empty beverage containers payments are exempt from California tax (Sec. 17153.5, Rev. & Tax. Code).

— Rewards received from a government authorized crime hotline (¶246).

— Sales and exchanges (Sch. D, Sch. D-1, Sch. D (541)) (¶229 and ¶501 et seq.).

— Social Security benefits (Sec. 17087, Rev. & Tax. Code).

— State income tax refunds are not taxed by California (FTB Pub. 1001, Supplemental Guidelines to California Adjustments).

— Unemployment compensation (Sec. 17087, Rev. & Tax. Code).

— Water conservation rebates are treated as refunds or price adjustments rather than as income (¶244).

In addition, California law, but not federal law, provides an exclusion for in-home support services (IHSS) supplementary payments, which are equal to the IHSS sales tax, plus any Social Security and Medicare payroll withholdings that are increased due to the supplementary payment. (Sec. 17131.9, Rev. & Tax. Code) Similarly, compensation paid by California to an individual who sustained pecuniary injury as a result of an erroneous criminal conviction and incarceration is excluded for California purposes, but not federal purposes, provided the individual did not contribute to his or her arrest. (Sec. 17157, Rev. & Tax. Code)

California does not follow the special federal provisions for Domestic International Sales Corporations (DISCs), personal holding companies, foreign investment companies, foreign trusts, etc. (Sec. 17024.5(b), Rev. & Tax. Code)

In addition, California does not incorporate federal incentives available to businesses located in renewal communities, including the gross income exclusion of capital gain from the sale or exchange of a "qualified community asset" held for more than five years and acquired after 2001 and before 2010.

¶202 Definition of "Adjusted Gross Income"

Law: Sec. 17072 (CCH CALIFORNIA TAX REPORTS, ¶15-510).

Comparable Federal: Secs. 62 (CCH U.S. MASTER TAX GUIDE ¶1005, 1006).

The California definition of "adjusted gross income" incorporates the federal definition as of a fixed date (¶103). However, California does not incorporate the federal above-the line deductions for:

— qualified expenses incurred by elementary and secondary school teachers, instructors, counselors, principals, or aides; and

— attorney's fees and court costs paid by or on behalf of the taxpayer in connection with any whistleblower award paid for providing information about violations of the tax laws.

(Sec. 17072, Rev. & Tax. Code)

Practice Pointer: Treatment of Registered Domestic Partners

Registered domestic partners (RDPs) (see ¶119) must file returns jointly or separately by applying the same standards as are applied to married taxpayers under federal income tax law. (Sec. 18521, Rev. & Tax. Code) For purposes of computing their adjusted gross income (AGI) and limitations based on AGI, a RDP or former RDP should use a pro forma federal return, treating the RDP or former RDP as a spouse or former spouse and using the same filing status that was used on the state tax return for the same taxable year. Alternatively, RDPs may use the worksheets provided in FTB Pub. 737, Tax Information for Registered Domestic Partners. (Sec. 17024.5(h), Rev. & Tax. Code)

¶203 Taxable Income

Law: Secs. 17073, 17073.5 (CCH CALIFORNIA TAX REPORTS, ¶15-510, 15-535).

Comparable Federal: Sec. 63 (CCH U.S. MASTER TAX GUIDE ¶124, 126).

The federal law defining "taxable income" is incorporated in the California law by reference. With the following exceptions listed below, California law is the same as federal law as of the current IRC tie-in date (¶103):

— California allows no deduction for personal exemptions. Instead, California law allows personal exemption credits (¶113).

— California standard deduction amounts are different from the federal (¶335).

— California has not adopted the federal additional standard deductions for aged and blind individuals (¶335). However, California provides additional personal exemption credits for such taxpayers (¶113).

— California does not adopt the additional standard deductions for real property taxes, disaster losses, or motor vehicle sales taxes. (Sec. 17073, Rev. & Tax. Code; Sec. 17073.5, Rev. & Tax. Code)

Taking into account these differences, California "taxable income" may be defined briefly as adjusted gross income reduced either by the standard deduction or by itemized deductions.

Practice Note: Crowdfunding Income

In most cases, amounts raised through crowdfunding are included in taxable income unless specifically exempted by law. Income that is nontaxable may still need to be shown on the tax return, even if not taxed. Taxpayers in doubt about whether income is taxable should not guess. IRS Publication 525, Taxable and Nontaxable Income, can be consulted for more information. (*Tax News*, California Franchise Tax Board, June 2015, CCH CALIFORNIA TAX REPORTS, ¶406-360)

¶204 Alimony

Law: Sec. 17081 (CCH CALIFORNIA TAX REPORTS, ¶15-610).

Comparable Federal: Sec. 71 (CCH U.S. MASTER TAX GUIDE ¶771).

California Form: Sch. CA (540) (California Adjustments - Residents).

California law is generally the same as federal law as of the current IRC tie-in date (¶103), except with respect to alimony received by a nonresident alien. Generally, alimony and separate maintenance payments received pursuant to a divorce, dissolution, or legal separation are taxable to the spouse who receives the payments. Any amount received for support of minor children is not taxable. (Sec. 17081, Rev. & Tax. Code)

Alimony paid by a California resident to a nonresident is not taxable to the recipient (¶323). Alimony paid either by a nonresident or by a part-year resident during a period of nonresidence is deductible on a prorated basis (¶323, ¶337).

Practice Tip: Alimony Received or Paid by Registered Domestic Partners (RDPs)

If a court orders termination of a registered domestic partnership and a California Family Law Court awards spousal support that satisfies the requirements under tax law for alimony, the payments are taxable to the payee and deductible by the payor for California purposes. However, federal treatment of these payments is uncertain. An RDP receiving alimony not included in federal income should include that amount on line 11, column C, of his or her California RDP Adjustments Worksheet. An RDP paying alimony not included in the RDP's adjustments to income for federal purposes should enter that amount on line 31, column C, of his or her California RDP Adjustments Worksheet, as a positive amount. (FTB Pub. 737, Tax Information for Registered Domestic Partners)

In *Appeal of Karapetian* (2004) (CCH CALIFORNIA TAX REPORTS, ¶ 15-610.45), the State Board of Equalization (BOE) followed the IRS's ruling in *Baxter v. Commissioner*, T.C. Memo 1999-190, and held that payment of mortgage interest by a former husband to his ex-wife pursuant to a marital settlement agreement was taxable alimony because the marital settlement agreement provided that the obligation of the former husband to make mortgage payments on the taxpayer's home would cease upon her death. Because the payments were taxable alimony, the ex-wife was not entitled to deduct those payments as qualified residence interest. The payments were deductible only by the former husband.

In *Appeal of Sara J. Palevsky* (1979) (CCH CALIFORNIA TAX REPORTS, ¶ 15-610.205), the BOE held that certain payments received under a property settlement agreement were fully taxable, despite the fact that the payor spouse had agreed to claim an income tax deduction for only two-thirds of the payments.

¶205 Annuities

Law: Secs. 17024.5, 17081, 17085, 17087, 17131 (CCH CALIFORNIA TAX REPORTS, ¶ 15-800, 16-345).

Comparable Federal: Secs. 72, 122 (CCH U.S. MASTER TAX GUIDE ¶ 817—845, 891).

California law is substantially the same as federal law as of California's current federal conformity date (see ¶ 103). (Sec. 17081, Rev. & Tax. Code; Sec. 17085, Rev. & Tax. Code) However, California does not incorporate the federal provision governing the basis application rules for amounts contributed to an annuity as part of the compensation for services performed by a nonresident alien. (Sec. 17024.5(b), Rev. & Tax. Code)

Nor does California allow the federal exclusion from taxable distributions from annuity and life insurance contracts the cost of a qualified long-term care insurance coverage rider that is charged against the cash or cash surrender value of the contract. The amendments are effective for federal purposes for contracts issued after 1996, but only with respect to tax years beginning after 2009. (Sec. 17085(e), Rev. & Tax. Code)

California and federal law provide, in general, that amounts paid under an annuity contract must be included in gross income. However, amounts representing a return of capital may be excluded. The excludable portion is determined by dividing the cost of the annuity by the expected return and multiplying the result by the annuity payment received. Detailed rules are provided for various special situations.

See ¶215 for a discussion of the rules applicable when an annuity is transferred for consideration. A discussion of the penalty on premature distributions is at ¶206.

• *Self-employed retirement plans, IRAs*

For discussion of treatment of annuities or other payments received under a self-employed retirement plan or an individual retirement account, see ¶206.

• *Annuities received under Railroad Retirement Act*

Annuity or pension payments received under the federal Railroad Retirement Act are exempt from California tax. (Sec. 17087, Rev. & Tax. Code)

• *Inherited annuity*

See ¶405 for discussion of the *Kelsey* case, where annuity income earned by a decedent outside California was taxed to a survivor under the rules for income from annuities, although the income was classified as "income in respect of a decedent" and could not have been taxed to the decedent if he had become a California resident.

• *Annuities held by non-natural persons*

Annuities held by partnerships, trusts, and other non-natural persons are not entitled to the same preferential treatment as are annuities held by individuals. Instead, tax is imposed on the excess of

— the sum of the net surrender value of the contract at the end of the tax year plus any amounts distributed under the contract to date, over

— the investment in the contract (the aggregate amount of premiums paid under the contract minus policyholder dividends or the aggregate amounts received under the contract that have not been included in income).

This special rule applies for both California and federal purposes with respect to amounts invested in annuity contracts after February 28, 1986. (Sec. 17081, Rev. & Tax. Code; Sec. 17085, Rev. & Tax. Code)

¶206 Income from Pension and Profit-Sharing Plans

Law: Secs. 17085, 17501, 17501.5, 17501.7, 17504, 17506, 17507, 17508.2, 17551, 17952.5, 23712 (CCH CALIFORNIA TAX REPORTS, ¶16-685, 15-800, 16-345, 16-545).

Comparable Federal: Secs. 72, 401, 402-03, 408-20, 457, 530 (CCH U.S. MASTER TAX GUIDE ¶817 et seq., 898, 2153 et seq.).

California Forms: Sch. G-1 (Tax on Lump-Sum Distributions), FTB 3805P (Additional Taxes on Qualified Plans (Including IRAs) and Other Tax-Favored Accounts).

The general plan of taxing income from pension and profit-sharing plans is the same under California law and federal law as amended to date. California incorporates federal law relating to pension, profit-sharing, stock bonus plans, etc., unless otherwise provided, without regard to taxable year to the same extent as applicable for federal purposes. (Sec. 17501, Rev. & Tax. Code)

CCH Comment: Registered Domestic Partnerships

Although registered domestic partners (RDPs) or former RDPs are generally required to be treated as married taxpayers or former spouses under California income and franchise tax laws, an RDP will not be treated as a spouse if such treatment would result in disqualification of a federally qualified deferred compensation plan or disqualification of tax-favored accounts, such as individual retirement accounts, Archer medical savings accounts, qualified tuition programs, or Coverdell education savings accounts. (Sec. 17021.7, Rev. & Tax. Code)

An RDP may have an adjustment to income if the RDP has a California-only basis in an IRA, which is recoverable from an IRA distribution. For example, an RDP may have a California-only basis in an IRA if the RDP's partner is covered by an employer-provided retirement plan and, based on the RDPs' combined adjusted gross income, the available deduction for an IRA contribution is reduced for California income tax purposes. The amount disallowed for the IRA contribution would create a California-only basis in the IRA. RDPs must keep track of their California-only basis in order to recover it tax-free from IRA distributions reported in future years. (FTB Pub. 737, Tax Information for Registered Domestic Partners)

CCH Caution Note: Potential Future Differences

California limits the maximum amount of elective deferrals that may be excluded from gross income under IRC Sec. 402(g), as in effect on January 1, 2010. The basis in any plan, account, or annuity must be increased for California income tax purposes to reflect the amount of elective deferrals not excluded. Any income not excludable as a result of California's limitation will be includible in the gross income of the individual for whose benefit the plan or account was established in the year the income is distributed. Similar limits apply to deferred compensation under IRC Sec. 457, relating to deferred compensation salary reduction plans for state, municipal, and tax-exempt organization employees.

Generally, with the exception of qualified charitable distributions from IRAs made in 2006 through 2009, both California and federal laws tax benefits received under qualified pension or profit-sharing plans to the employee only when actually distributed to the employee. Such distributions are usually taxed as though they were an annuity, under the rules set forth in ¶205, the consideration for which is the amount (if any) contributed by the employee under the plan. Certain nonforfeitable rights to receive annuities are taxed in the year in which the employer pays for the annuity contract. Certain lump-sum distributions are subject to special treatment, as explained below. See also ¶330.

Qualified retirement income received by a former California resident is not taxable by California. (Sec. 17952.5, Rev. & Tax. Code) See ¶405 for a more detailed discussion.

• *Special rules for some organizations*

Special rules are provided for the taxation of employee annuities where the employer is a tax-exempt charitable-type organization or school, where the plan is not subject to the rules discussed above. Such annuities are only partially taxable, under a formula providing for an "exclusion allowance." The California rules are the same as the federal rules. (Sec. 17551, Rev. & Tax. Code)

• *Nonqualified plans*

Both California and federal laws provide special rules for taxing the beneficiary of a *nonqualified* employee pension or profit-sharing plan or annuity, in cases where the employee's rights are forfeitable at the time the employer's contribution is made. The general effect is to tax the employee in the year the employee's rights are no longer subject to a substantial risk of forfeiture. (Sec. 17501, Rev. & Tax. Code) California does not incorporate the federal provision (IRC Sec. 457A) that requires the current inclusion in income of some deferred compensation paid by foreign corporations when there is no substantial risk of forfeiture of the rights to the compensation, applicable for federal purposes to amounts deferred that are attributable to services performed after 2008. (Sec. 17551(g), Rev. & Tax. Code)

Under both California and federal law, if certain operational or design failures occur in a nonqualified deferred compensation plan, the deferred amounts, including compensation deferred under the plan in prior years and notional or actual income attributable to the deferred compensation, is included in the affected plan participants' gross income immediately unless it is still subject to a substantial risk of forfeiture. The tax on the compensation required to be included is increased by interest on the portion of the compensation that was deferred in prior years and by an amount equal to 20% (5% for California purposes beginning with the 2013 tax year) of the compensation required to be included. (Sec. 17508.2, Rev. & Tax. Code) The interest is the amount of interest at the underpayment rate plus one percentage point on the underpayments that would have occurred had the deferred compensation been includible in gross income for the tax year in which it was deferred or, if later, the first tax year in which it was not subject to a substantial risk of forfeiture.

Practice Tip: Noncompliance With IRC Sec. 409A Requirements

The FTB is following Internal Revenue Service (IRS) Notice 2007-100, which allows taxpayers to correct certain unintentional operational failures of nonqualified deferred compensation plans in order to comply with IRC Sec. 409A. Unlike the IRS requirement that taxpayers submit attachments to their federal income tax returns stating that they are relying upon Notice 2007-100 with respect to a correction of a failure to comply with Sec. 409A, the FTB only requires taxpayers to retain the statements instead of submitting them with their California tax returns. (*Announcement*, California Franchise Tax Board, April 18, 2008)

• *Lump-sum distributions*

If an employee's benefits are paid in one taxable year of the employee because of death or termination of employment, the taxable amount is subject to special treatment as a "lump-sum distribution." The taxable amount is the total distribution less (1) employee contributions and (2) any unrealized appreciation on employer securities included in the distribution. (Sec. 17501, Rev. & Tax. Code)

Both California and federal law have eliminated capital gain treatment for lump-sum distributions made after 1986 that are at least partially attributable to pre-1974 participation in a qualified pension plan. However, a taxpayer who reached age 50 before 1986 may elect to apply an exception that allows capital gain treatment.

• *Self-employed plans*

For purposes of both federal law and California law, the rules for self-employed plans are generally the same as for employee plans, as set forth above. However, there will be differences in the *amounts* taxable in California and federal returns because of differences in the deductibility of contributions in prior years. As explained at ¶ 330, for pre-1987 tax years, California allowed smaller deductions than federal. Also, the interest element in the redemption of certain federal retirement bonds issued before 1984 was recoverable tax-free for California purposes. (Sec. 17085, Rev. & Tax. Code; Sec. 17507, Rev. & Tax. Code)

The difference between allowable California and federal contributions is recoverable free of California tax. See below for summary of amounts recoverable tax-free.

As to the *timing* of the tax-free recovery, where distributions are received over a period of years, it has been the Franchise Tax Board's (FTB) policy to treat the amounts involved as part of the "investment in the contract" that is recoverable tax-free under the annuity rules.

For a discussion of the taxability of distributions from self-employed plans when the taxpayer's status changed from resident to nonresident, or vice-versa, see ¶ 405.

• *Individual retirement accounts*

The California treatment of distributions from IRAs is the same as the federal, except that California permits tax-free recovery of the following:

— Contributions that were not allowed as California deductions (see ¶ 330).

— Interest earned in 1975 or 1976 on a 1975 contribution, as explained below.

(Sec. 17507, Rev. & Tax. Code)

Practice Note: Distributions from IRAs to Health Savings Accounts

Although California generally conforms to federal deferred compensation provisions as amended to date, because California does not recognize health savings accounts (HSAs) (see ¶ 247) it does not conform to an amendment made to IRC Sec. 408 that authorizes a one-time tax-free distribution from an IRA to an HSA, effective for tax years beginning after 2006. Consequently, a California taxpayer who makes such a distribution is required to include the distribution in his or her gross income and the distribution is subject to California's penalty on premature withdrawals.

As to the *timing* of the tax-free recovery of amounts contributed prior to 1987 or after 2006, the amount of contributions not allowed as California deductions is considered to be the cost basis of the IRA account and no income is reportable for California purposes until the basis is recovered. Each year, the amount reportable federally is reduced for California purposes by California basis until such basis is recovered.

As for the recovery of post-1986 contributions, or at the election of the taxpayer, contributions made after July 1, 1986, the federal annuity rule is adopted in California and the portion of each distribution recognized federally is recognized for California purposes. Under this rule, the amount invested is recovered ratably, depending on the period of expected return. (Sec. 17501, Rev. & Tax. Code)

Tax-free basis of IRA account of taxpayers who have changed residency: A nonresident is treated as though he or she were a resident for all items of deferred income, including IRAs. (Sec. 17041(i)(3), Rev. & Tax. Code) Thus, only contributions not allowed as a deduction for California purposes are used to determine the tax-free basis of the IRA.

Practice Pointer: Canadian Registered Retirement Savings Plan

The Franchise Tax Board has taken the position that a Canadian Registered Retirement Savings Plan (RRSP) will be treated as a savings account rather than a functional equivalent to an IRA for California personal income tax purposes. This is contrary to federal treatment. Consequently, unlike under federal law, California taxpayers may not elect to defer taxation on RRSP earnings until a taxpayer begins receiving distributions, and must add such earnings to their taxable income. After taxpayers pay tax on these earnings, the earnings will also be treated as a capital investment in the RRSP. When taxpayers receive distributions from their RRSP, the amount consisting of the contributions and the previously taxed earnings is treated as a nontaxable return of capital. Under federal law, such earnings will be subject to tax when distributed. Consequently, taxpayers may subtract these distributions from federal adjusted gross income in the year of distribution. (*Tax News*, California Franchise Tax Board, May/June 2003)

• *1975 contribution to IRA*

For California tax purposes, any 1975 contribution to an IRA is treated, in effect, as a separate grantor trust. Any interest earned on a 1975 contribution in 1975 or 1976 was subject to California tax as earned, and of course will not be subject to California tax when it is distributed at a later time. However, as a result of 1977 legislation, any income earned after 1976 on a 1975 contribution is not taxable until it is distributed. So far as contributions to the account for years subsequent to 1975 are concerned, the account automatically qualifies under California law even though it was established before the California law providing for IRAs was enacted. (Sec. 17507, Rev. & Tax. Code)

• *Roth IRAs*

As explained in further detail at ¶330, both California and federal law recognize a "Roth IRA." For both California and federal purposes, earnings from a Roth IRA are tax-free and qualified distributions are not included in gross income or subject to a penalty on early withdrawals. (Sec. 17501, Rev. & Tax. Code)

Caution: Allowable Roth IRA Contribution for RDPs

For California income tax purposes, if RDPs contribute to a Roth IRA, the RDPs must review the income phase-out limitations. The allowable Roth IRA contribution may be reduced based on the RDPs' combined federal modified AGI. For example, if RDP One made a contribution to his Roth IRA of $5,000 in 2014 and his federal modified AGI is $90,000, and RDP Two made a contribution to his Roth IRA of $5,000 in 2014 and his federal modified AGI is $105,000, the RDPs' combined federal AGI exceeds the $191,000 income limitation for an allowable Roth IRA contribution for 2014. Thus, for California purposes, the Roth IRA contributions of both RDPs are treated as excess contributions. However, California does not impose the 6% excise tax that is imposed under federal law on excess contributions to Roth IRAs. If either RDP later receives a qualified distribution from his Roth IRA, the qualified distribution is tax-free and is not includible in their California taxable income. This tax-free treatment applies even if the qualified distribution includes earnings attributable to a previous excess contribution for California purposes. (FTB Pub. 737, Tax Information for Registered Domestic Partners)

• *Coverdell Education Savings Accounts*

As explained in further detail at ¶330, under both California law and federal law, taxpayers with modified adjusted gross income below certain levels may contribute up to $2,000 per child per year to a Coverdell Education Savings Account (previously known as an "Education IRA"). Earnings on contributions will be distributed tax-free provided that they are used to pay the child's post-secondary education expenses and/or elementary or secondary education expenses. (Sec. 23712, Rev. & Tax. Code)

Additional tax on amounts not used for education: An additional tax of 2.5% (10% for federal purposes) is imposed on amounts distributed and not used for qualified higher education expenses. (Sec. 23712, Rev. & Tax. Code) The additional penalty does not apply to the following distributions:

— made to a beneficiary's estate after the beneficiary's death;

— attributable to the beneficiary's being disabled;

— used for the beneficiary's attendance at a U.S. Armed Forces related academy;

— made on account of a scholarship received by the account holder to the extent that the amount of the distribution does not exceed the amount of the scholarship; or

— that constitute the return of excess contributions and earnings therein (although earnings are includable in income).

• *Income attributable to nondeductible contributions to traditional IRAs*

As explained at ¶330, California law provides that any income attributable to the nondeductible portion of contributions to traditional IRAs is not taxable to the beneficiary until the income is distributed.

• *Simplified employee pension (SEP) plans*

As explained at ¶330, California law conforms generally to federal law permitting employer contributions to an employee's individual retirement plan through a "simplified employee pension" (SEP) plan. The employer's contributions to the employee's SEP-IRA are excluded from the employee's gross income. The employee's contributions to the SEP-IRA are separate and apart from the employer's contributions and may be deducted from the employee's gross income in the same manner, and to the same extent, as any IRA contribution (¶330). SEP distributions are subject to tax on the basis of the same rules that apply to distributions from an IRA (see above). (Sec. 17201, Rev. & Tax. Code; Sec. 17501, Rev. & Tax. Code)

• *Savings incentive match plans for employees (SIMPLE plans)*

Certain small employers may establish SIMPLE plans structured as IRAs or as qualified cash or deferred arrangements. Employees are not taxed on account assets until distributions are made, and employers generally may deduct contributions to such plans. SIMPLE plans are not subject to nondiscrimination rules or some of the other complex requirements applicable to qualified plans. (Sec. 17501, Rev. & Tax. Code)

¶206

- *Summary of amounts recoverable free of California tax*

SELF-EMPLOYED PLANS

1963-1970: All 1963-1970 contributions recoverable tax-free (no California deduction).

1971-1973: No 1971-1973 contributions recoverable tax-free (California deduction same as federal).

1974-1986: Excess of 1974-1986 federal deduction over California deduction recoverable tax-free.

1987 and subsequent years: No contributions recoverable tax-free (California deduction same as federal).

All years: Interest element in redemption of "retirement bonds" issued before 1984 recoverable tax-free.

DEDUCTIBLE INDIVIDUAL RETIREMENT ACCOUNTS

1975: All 1975 contributions recoverable tax-free (no California deduction).

1975 and 1976: Income from 1975 contributions recoverable tax-free (income was taxed currently).

1976-1981: No 1976-1981 contributions recoverable tax-free (California deduction same as federal).

1982-1986: Excess of 1982-1986 federal deduction over California deduction recoverable tax-free.

1987 and subsequent years: No contributions recoverable tax-free (California deduction same as federal).

2007-2009: Increased contributions made by individuals who participated in a bankrupt employer's 401(k) plan or for active participants in an employer-sponsored retirement plan or whose spouse was an active participant in an employer-sponsored plan. (California did not conform to increased deduction)

All years: Interest element in redemption of "retirement bonds" issued before 1984 recoverable tax-free.

ROTH INDIVIDUAL RETIREMENT ACCOUNTS

1998 and subsequent years: All contributions and earnings recoverable tax free (contributions taxed currently).

SIMPLIFIED EMPLOYEE PENSION PLANS

1979-1986: Excess of 1979-1986 federal deduction over California deduction recoverable tax-free.

1987 and subsequent years: No contributions recoverable tax-free (California deduction same as federal).

NOTE: This summary assumes that the taxpayer was a California resident during the contribution year, as well as during the year of distribution. In case there has been a change of residence, see ¶ 405.

- *Government and nonprofit pension plans*

California incorporates federal law, generally as amended to date, governing plans maintained for governmental employees; see ¶ 330. (Sec. 17551, Rev. & Tax. Code)

- *Premature distributions*

Both California and federal laws impose a penalty tax on premature distributions (before age 59^1/$_2$) from self-employed plans, annuity plans, IRAs, and "modified endowment contracts," to the extent the distribution is includible in income. The California penalty is 2.5% of the distribution, while the federal penalty is generally 10% of the distribution. The penalty is inapplicable to premature distributions from IRAs if the distributions are used to pay the following:

— medical expenses in excess of 7.5% of a taxpayer's adjusted gross income;

— health insurance premiums if a taxpayer is unemployed and either received 12 consecutive weeks of unemployment compensation or, if self-employed, would have received such benefits but for the fact that he or she was self-employed;

— qualified first-time home buyer expenses; or

— qualified higher education expenses. (Sec. 17085(c)(1), Rev. & Tax. Code)

CCH Practice Pointer: Withdrawals Made by Active Duty Reservists and Emergency Service Personnel

California incorporates federal provisions that waive the early withdrawal penalty for certain

— distributions to qualified public safety employees who separate from service after age 50, and

— withdrawals by qualified members of the National Guard or the Reserve who are called to active duty.

Practice Note: Early Distribution to Pay Qualified Expenses of RDPs

Because federal law does not recognize RDPs, a taxpayer may take an early distribution from an IRA or other tax-favored account to pay certain expenses, such as qualified higher education expenses, of an RDP or an RDP's child and may incur premature distribution penalties with respect to that distribution for federal income tax purposes, but not for California income tax purposes. However, for both federal and California tax purposes, the RDP would need to include in taxable income the early distribution from the IRA, unless the RDP has a basis in the IRA that may be recovered tax-free. (FTB Pub. 737, Tax Information for Registered Domestic Partners)

Also, the penalty does not apply to distributions from a qualified retirement plan or IRA if the distribution is made on account of an FTB notice to withhold from the plan or IRA (an IRS levy on the plan or IRA for federal purposes).

CCH Practice Pointer: Requirement to File FTB 3805P

A taxpayer that is liable for the penalty tax on premature distributions is required to file form FTB 3805P whether or not he or she meets the threshold individual income tax filing requirements. The return filing deadline is the same for filing the individual income tax return (¶ 108).

• *Transfer of excess pension assets to retiree health accounts*

California incorporates federal law permitting employers, under strictly limited conditions, to transfer excess pension assets to retiree health accounts without disqualifying either the pension or health plan, and without including the transferred assets in gross income. (Sec. 17501, Rev. & Tax. Code)

Generally, only one such transfer may be made in any tax year.

• *Excess contributions, accumulations, or distributions*

California does not have taxes similar to those imposed under IRC Sec. 4973 (tax on excess contributions to individual retirement arrangements) or IRC Sec. 4974 (tax on excess accumulation in qualified retirement plans).

• *Rollovers*

Both California and federal laws permit tax-free "rollovers" from one tax-qualified retirement plan to another, under certain conditions.

• *Cross references*

See ¶ 205 regarding taxability of payments received under the Railroad Retirement Act. See ¶ 330 for deductions available for retirement plan contributions. See ¶ 405 regarding taxability of distributions from self-employed plans after change of residence.

¶207 Employee Stock Options and Purchase Plans

Law: Secs. 17081, 17501, 17502 (CCH CALIFORNIA TAX REPORTS, ¶ 15-800, 16-345).

Comparable Federal: Secs. 83, 421-24 (CCH U.S. MASTER TAX GUIDE ¶ 1928, 1929).

Except as noted below, California law is substantially the same as federal law as of the current IRC tie-in date (see ¶ 103). (Sec. 17081, Rev. & Tax. Code; Sec. 17501, Rev. & Tax. Code) For a discussion of the issues arising when a taxpayer changes residency, see ¶ 405.

• *California qualified stock options*

The favorable tax treatment afforded by federal law to incentive and employee stock options applies for California purposes to California qualified stock options. Accordingly, a taxpayer who exercises a qualifying stock option may postpone paying tax until disposing of the option or the underlying stock. (Sec. 17502, Rev. & Tax. Code)

A "California qualified stock option" is a stock option

— designated by the corporation issuing the stock option as a California qualified stock option at the time the option is granted,

— issued by a corporation to its employees after 1996 and before 2002, and

— exercised by a taxpayer either while employed by the issuing corporation or within three months after leaving the employ of the issuing corporation.

A taxpayer who becomes permanently and totally disabled may exercise the option within one year of leaving the employ of the issuing corporation.

The favorable tax treatment of California qualified stock options is available only to a taxpayer whose earned income from the corporation granting the option does not exceed $40,000 for the taxable year in which the option is exercised, and only to the extent that the number of shares transferable by the taxpayer's exercise of qualified options does not exceed a total of 1,000 shares and those shares have a combined fair market value of less than $100,000 (determined at the time the options are granted). (FTB Pub. 1001, *Supplemental Guidelines to California Adjustments*)

¶208 Services of Child

Law: Sec. 17081 (CCH CALIFORNIA TAX REPORTS, ¶ 15-515).

Comparable Federal: Secs. 73, 6201 (CCH U.S. MASTER TAX GUIDE ¶ 114).

California law is the same as federal law.

Income from services of a child is includible in the gross income of the child, and not in the income of the parent. All expenditures, by parent or child, attributable to such income are treated as paid or incurred by the child. (Sec. 17081, Rev. & Tax. Code)

Under certain circumstances, an assessment on the child's income is treated as an assessment against the parent as well as the child.

¶209 Prizes and Awards

Law: Sec. 17081 (CCH CALIFORNIA TAX REPORTS, ¶ 15-780).

Comparable Federal: Sec. 74 (CCH U.S. MASTER TAX GUIDE ¶ 785).

California law is the same as federal law as of California's current federal conformity date (¶103). (Sec. 17081, Rev. & Tax. Code)

Prizes and awards are specifically designated as being includible in taxable income, with two exceptions. The exceptions relate to

— the value of certain employee achievement awards, and

— amounts received in recognition of achievement of charitable, scientific, artistic, etc., nature.

To be eligible for the charitable award exemption the recipient must be selected without any action on his or her part and must not be required to render substantial future services. Also, the award must be transferred by the payor to a charity designated by the recipient. The federal law is incorporated in California by reference.

Because of California's federal conformity date (¶103), California has not conformed to an amendment made by the United States Appreciation for Olympians and Paralympians Act of 2016 (P.L. 114-239) that allows prize money awarded to a U.S. athlete by the U.S. Olympic Committee (USOC), as well as the value of any medal awarded in the Olympic Games or the Paralympic Games, to be excluded from the athlete's gross income, provided the athlete's adjusted gross income for the taxable year does not exceed $1 million ($500,000 for a married individual filing separately). The provision is effective for federal purposes for prizes and awards received after December 31, 2015.

See ¶201 for the tax treatment applied to lottery winnings.

¶210 Dealers in Tax-Exempt Securities

Law: Sec. 17081 (CCH CALIFORNIA TAX REPORTS, ¶16-075).

Comparable Federal: Sec. 75 (CCH U.S. MASTER TAX GUIDE ¶1970).

California follows the federal rules. (Sec. 17081, Rev. & Tax. Code)

Dealers in tax-free municipal bonds may be required to make an adjustment to gross income with respect to such securities sold during the year. The cost, or other basis, of certain municipal bonds sold by a dealer must be reduced by an amount equivalent to the amortization of bond premiums that would otherwise be allowable as a deduction if the interest on the bonds were fully taxable.

Exceptions are provided for certain cases where the bonds are sold within 30 days after acquisition, or where the bonds mature, or are callable, more than five years after acquisition. Special rules are provided where dealers use different inventory methods.

The federal law is incorporated in California's by reference. However, in view of the fact that certain municipal bond interest is taxable for California but not federal purposes, and interest on U.S. bonds is taxable for federal but not California purposes, there will be cases where the rules apply under one law but not under the other.

¶211 Commodity Credit Loans

Law: Sec. 17081 (CCH CALIFORNIA TAX REPORTS, ¶15-515).

Comparable Federal: Sec. 77 (CCH U.S. MASTER TAX GUIDE ¶769).

California follows the federal law. (Sec. 17081, Rev. & Tax. Code)

The taxpayer may elect to treat as income amounts received as loans from the Commodity Credit Corporation.

¶212 Employees' Group Term Life Insurance

Law: Secs. 17020.12, 17081 (CCH CALIFORNIA TAX REPORTS, ¶15-515).

Comparable Federal: Secs. 79, 7701(a)(20) (CCH U.S. MASTER TAX GUIDE ¶721).

California follows the federal law. (Sec. 17081, Rev. & Tax. Code)

An employee must include in income an amount equivalent to his or her employer's cost of group term life insurance to the extent the cost exceeds (1) the cost of $50,000 of coverage plus (2) any contribution by the employee to purchase the insurance. Exceptions are provided where the employer, or a charitable organization, is the beneficiary. An exemption is also provided for insurance under a qualified pension or profit-sharing plan (¶206).

The federal law is incorporated in California's by reference, including federal rules concerning the determination of cost under a discriminatory plan.

¶213 Certain Death Benefits

Law: Secs. 17131, 17132.5 (CCH CALIFORNIA TAX REPORTS, ¶15-655, 16-036).

Comparable Federal: Sec. 101 (CCH U.S. MASTER TAX GUIDE ¶803, 813).

California generally incorporates federal law as of California's current federal conformity date (¶103). (Sec. 17131, Rev. & Tax. Code)

See ¶225 for the tax treatment of military death benefits and the income tax exemption for terrorist victims.

• *Life insurance*

In general, life insurance proceeds are nontaxable except for the interest element. (However, see ¶215 for an exception to the general rule.) The interest received is fully taxable if proceeds are held by an insurer under an agreement to pay interest. The interest element is also taxable if the proceeds are paid in installments that include an interest element. California law is the same as federal law.

Although California incorporates the federal limit on the exclusion for employers holding a life insurance policy as a beneficiary that covers the life of an employee (IRC Sec. 101(a) and (j)), different effective dates apply. Under both California and federal law, the employer's exclusion is limited to an amount equal to the amount paid for the policy as premiums or other payments unless the employer satisfies several requirements, including notice and consent requirements. The limitation is applicable generally for federal purposes to life insurance contracts issued after August 17, 2006, but only applies for California purposes to contracts issued after January 1, 2010, with some limited exceptions. Consequently, to the extent the exclusion is limited for federal income tax purposes but not California purposes for contracts issued prior to 2010, taxpayers may subtract the difference between the full amount of the benefits paid, less certain interest, and the amount of the federal exclusion. (Sec. 17131(d), Rev. & Tax. Code)

• *Survivors of state employees, etc.*

Both California and federal law exclude from gross income certain survivor benefits paid as an annuity to the spouse, former spouse, or child of a public safety officer killed in the line of duty. (Sec. 17131, Rev. & Tax. Code) However, California does not allow the federal exclusion of survivor annuities paid on the death of a public safety officer killed in the line of duty with respect to individuals who died prior to 1997. (Sec. 17132.5, Rev. & Tax. Code)

¶214 Life Insurance—Other Than Death Benefits

Law: Secs. 17081, 17085 (CCH CALIFORNIA TAX REPORTS, ¶15-800).

Comparable Federal: Sec. 72 (CCH U.S. MASTER TAX GUIDE ¶817 et seq.).

California law conforms to the federal provisions as of California's current federal conformity date (see ¶103), regarding the taxability of amounts received on life insurance contracts other than death benefits, interest, or annuities. (Sec. 17081, Rev. & Tax. Code)

Under these provisions, the proceeds from life insurance or endowment contracts are includible in income subject to an exclusion factor determined by reference to the investment in, and expected return from, such contracts. Lump-sum proceeds will not be deemed to be constructively received if an insured elects within 60 days after maturity of a policy to take the proceeds as an annuity rather than a lump sum.

California also incorporates the federal penalty on premature distributions from "modified endowment contracts," but substitutes a different penalty rate (¶ 206). (Sec. 17085, Rev. & Tax. Code)

¶215 Life Insurance or Annuity Transferred for Consideration

> *Law:* Secs. 17081, 17131 (CCH California Tax Reports, ¶ 15-655, 15-800).
>
> *Comparable Federal:* Secs. 72(g), 101(a), 101(g) (CCH U.S. Master Tax Guide ¶ 807).

California follows federal law. (Sec. 17081, Rev. & Tax. Code)

Where the recipient of the proceeds has acquired a life insurance contract for a valuable consideration, the general rule is that the proceeds are exempt only to the extent of the consideration given and the premiums subsequently paid. An exception to the general rule exempts life insurance proceeds from taxation in cases where the transferee is the insured, a partner of the insured, or a corporation in which the insured is an officer or shareholder. Also exempt are transfers where basis for the contract is determined by reference to basis in the hands of the transferor.

As to annuities transferred for a valuable consideration, the general rule is that the cost of the annuity (determined for purposes of computing the tax-free recovery of cost) is computed by reference to the actual value of the consideration paid on transfer, plus premiums and other sums subsequently paid. An exception is provided for certain tax-free exchanges.

• *Accelerated death benefits*

California conforms to federal law allowing an exclusion from gross income when accelerated death benefits are received under a life insurance contract on the life of a terminally or chronically ill individual or when amounts are received from the sale or assignment to a viatical settlement provider of any portion of the death benefits under a life insurance contract on the life of a terminally or chronically ill individual. In the case of a chronically ill individual

— the exclusion applies only if amounts are received under a rider or other provision of a contract that is treated as a qualified long-term care insurance contract, and

— the excludable amount is capped at a specified amount.

(Sec. 17131, Rev. & Tax. Code)

¶216 Gifts, Inheritances, Tips, etc.

> *Law:* Sec. 17131 (CCH California Tax Reports, ¶ 15-715).
>
> *Comparable Federal:* Sec. 102 (CCH U.S. Master Tax Guide ¶ 847).

California law incorporates the federal law by reference. The value of property received as a gift, bequest, devise, or inheritance is nontaxable but the income from such property is taxable. (Sec. 17131, Rev. & Tax. Code)

Tips received by a waiter are taxable income and are not exempt as gifts. See *Hugo Rihn v. Franchise Tax Board* (1955) (CCH California Tax Reports, ¶ 15-715.55), decided by the California Court of Appeal.

The State Board of Equalization (BOE) held in *Appeal of Ida A. Rogers* (1956) (CCH California Tax Reports, ¶ 15-715.47) that voluntary payments by a corporation to the widow of one of its employees constituted gifts and were not taxable income. A similar result was reached by the BOE in *Appeal of Irma Livingston* (1956) (CCH California Tax Reports, ¶ 15-715.47), as to voluntary payments to surviving children of a deceased employee.

¶217 Tax-Free Interest

Law: Secs. 17088, 17133, 17143, 17145 (CCH California Tax Reports, ¶¶15-185, 15-720, 16-075, 16-280).

Comparable Federal: Secs. 103, 141-50, 852, 1286 (CCH U.S. Master Tax Guide ¶729, 731, 1952, 2307).

California Forms: Form 540 (California Resident Income Tax Return), Sch. CA (540) (California Adjustments - Residents).

California's treatment of interest on certain governmental obligations differs from federal rules, as explained below.

See ¶305 for treatment of interest expense related to tax-free interest.

• *Interest exempt*

Interest on the following obligations is exempt from California tax:

(1) Bonds and other obligations of the United States, U.S. territories, and Puerto Rico. (31 U.S.C. 3124) (Interest on Philippine Islands obligations issued on or after March 24, 1934, is not exempt. Interest on District of Columbia obligations issued after December 24, 1973, is not exempt.)

(2) Bonds (not including other obligations) of the State of California or of political subdivisions thereof, issued after November 4, 1902.

(Sec. 17143, Rev. & Tax. Code) Interest from Build America Bonds is also exempt.

Practitioner Comment: Taxation of Out-of-State Obligations

It should be noted that the constitutionality of taxing out-of-state municipal bond interest under provisions similar to those described above under California law was called into question in Kentucky. On January 6, 2006, the Kentucky Court of Appeals in *Davis v. Department of Revenue*, No. 2004-CA-001940-MR, held that these provisions were facially discriminatory in favor of in-state bonds in violation of the Commerce Clause. On August 17, 2006, the Kentucky Supreme Court denied the Kentucky Department of Revenue's motion for discretionary review. On May 21, 2007, the U.S. Supreme Court granted certiorari and on May 19, 2008, upheld the state's preferential tax treatment of interest from in-state bonds, seemingly laying to rest any speculation as to whether taxpayers in other states, including California, might be entitled to refunds on interest from out of state municipal bonds.

Chris Micheli, Esq., Carpenter, Snodgrass & Associates, Sacramento, CA

If there is a separation of the ownership between the tax-exempt bond and the right to receive interest, the payments or accruals on the stripped bond and stripped coupon are treated in the manner provided under the federal law, which requires allocation of basis to prevent artificial losses.

The exemption set forth in (1), above, does not extend to interest received on refunds of U.S. taxes. This point is not covered in the regulations or any published ruling, but it has been the Franchise Tax Board's (FTB) administrative policy to deny the exemption. The Attorney General has ruled (NS 4570, 10-28-42) that interest on postal savings accounts is taxable. Interest on bonds of other States is not exempt.

See ¶513 for the treatment of gain or loss from the sale of such bonds.

Interest on Housing Authority bonds (issued by housing projects created under the Housing Authorities Law) is exempt if the bonds are issued by a project located in California, but is taxable if the bonds are issued by a project located outside the state. Such interest would presumably be exempt from federal tax.

• *California-federal differences*

The above exemptions are quite different from those under federal law, which exempt interest on obligations of *any* state or political subdivision thereof and which extend only limited exemptions to certain U.S. obligations.

Interest on "arbitrage bonds" or private activity bonds issued by state or local governments is subject to federal tax. California has not adopted these provisions so the interest on any such bonds issued in California would be exempt from California tax. (The federal rule would have no effect on California tax so far as interest on bonds of other states is concerned, because California already taxes interest on such bonds.) (Sec. 17143, Rev. & Tax. Code)

• *Status of federal agency obligations*

Whether interest from federal agency obligations is taxable for California purposes is generally governed by federal law.

Practice Note: Taxable Bonds

The following are not considered U.S. obligations for California purposes and, therefore, interest earned on these obligations is subject to tax: Federal National Mortgage Association (Fannie Maes); Government National Mortgage Association (Ginnie Maes); and Federal Loan Home Mortgage Corporation (Freddie Macs) (FTB Pub. 1001, Supplemental Guidelines to California Adjustments).

The FTB has indicated that interest on the following obligations is not subject to tax: Student Loan Marketing Association (SLMA), Federal Home Loan banks, the Resolution Funding Corporation, the Production Credit Association, Federal Farm Credit banks, and the Commodity Credit Corporation. Interest from CATS (Certificates of Accrual on Treasury Securities) and TIGRS (Treasury Investment Growth Receipts) is also exempt because those obligations have been found to be government securities under federal law.

• *Interest on notes*

In *Appeal of M.G. and Faye W. Odenheimer* (1964) (CCH CALIFORNIA TAX REPORTS, ¶ 202-481), the State Board of Equalization held that interest on a promissory note of a California municipality, issued for purchase of land to be used as a parking lot, qualified for exemption from the California personal income tax.

• *Mutual funds*

California generally adopts the federal treatment of regulated investment companies (RICs) and their shareholders. Sec. 17088, Rev. & Tax. Code However, California has its own rules governing exempt-interest dividends and does not adopt the federal treatment of undistributed capital gains. (Sec. 17145, Rev. & Tax. Code)

As to the pass-through of tax-exempt income, California provides that the flow-through treatment is allowed if, as of the close of each quarter, at least 50% of the value of a RIC's total assets consists of obligations that, when held by individuals, pay interest that is exempt from taxation by California. State and federal tax-exempt obligations may be combined for purposes of meeting the 50% test. (Sec. 17145, Rev. & Tax. Code)

Also, California conforms to a federal provision that limits the amount of a distribution allowable as an exempt-interest dividend. With respect to the company's taxable year, if the aggregate amount of dividends reported by the company as exempt-interest dividends is greater than the excess of

— the amount of interest it received on obligations, the interest on which, if held by an individual, would be exempt from California taxation, over

— the amounts that, if the RIC were treated as an individual, would be disallowed as deductions for expenses related to exempt income under California or federal law,

the portion of the reported exempt-interest dividend amount that will be allowed as an exempt-interest dividend is the excess of the reported exempt-interest dividend amount over the portion of the excess reported amount that bears the same ratio to the excess reported amount as the reported exempt-interest dividend amount bears to the aggregate reported amount. A special allocation rule applies to non-calendar year RICs with excess reported amounts.

It should be noted that the flow-through treatment applies to interest from federal obligations that would be exempt if held directly by an individual. Therefore, interest received from certain agency bonds (*e.g.*, GNMA, FNMA, etc.) is not exempt interest from federal obligations.

Amounts designated as "exempt-interest dividends" are treated by recipients as nontaxable income.

See ¶206 regarding exemption of interest element upon redemption of individual retirement bonds.

¶218 Compensation for Injury or Sickness

Law: Secs. 17131, 17132.7, Rev. & Tax. Code (CCH CALIFORNIA TAX REPORTS, ¶15-640, 15-650, 16-235).

Comparable Federal: Sec. 104 (CCH U.S. MASTER TAX GUIDE ¶851, 852).

California adopts by reference the federal law as of the current IRC tie-in date (¶103). (Sec. 17131, Rev. & Tax. Code)

Amounts received as accident or health insurance benefits, damages, workers compensation, etc., on account of personal injuries or sickness, are tax-exempt. Payments made to individuals under Sec. 103(c)(10) of the Ricky Ray Hemophilia Relief Act of 1998 are treated as tax-exempt damages. (Sec. 17132.7, Rev. & Tax. Code)

The exemption does not apply to amounts received as reimbursement for medical expenses that were allowed as deductions in prior years. Nor does it apply to

— punitive damages, whether or not related to a claim for damages from personal injury or sickness, or

— damages for emotional distress, except to the extent of any amounts received for medical care attributable to the emotional distress or attributable to a physical injury or sickness.

Consequently, the State Board of Equalization has disallowed the deduction for sex discrimination settlement proceeds (*Evenson* (2001) (CCH CALIFORNIA TAX REPORTS, ¶15-650.551)) and damages received from an age discrimination suit (*Allison* (2001) (CCH CALIFORNIA TAX REPORTS, ¶15-650.25)).

Also, this exemption generally does not cover employer contributions to accident and health plans for *employees*; see ¶219 for discussion of special rules covering such plans. These rules are the same as the federal rules. However, the amount includible in income on account of reimbursed medical expenses may be different because of a difference in the extent to which the expenses were deductible in an earlier year.

¶219 Amounts Received Under Accident and Health Plans

Law: Secs. 17021.7, 17087, 17131, 17131.4, 17141, 17141.3 (CCH CALIFORNIA TAX REPORTS, ¶15-165, 15-705, 16-100, 16-345).

Comparable Federal: Secs. 105-06, 7702B (CCH U.S. MASTER TAX GUIDE ¶853—859).

California generally conforms to federal law as of California's current federal conformity date. (Sec. 17131, Rev. & Tax. Code) However, California does not incorporate the federal provision requiring that sick pay benefits received under the Railroad Unemployment Insurance Act be included in gross income. (Sec. 17087(c), Rev. & Tax. Code) Nor does California incorporate the exclusion for employer contributions to health savings accounts. (Sec. 17131.4, Rev. & Tax. Code)

Practice Pointer: California Excludes Reimbursements Related to Older Children

California follows the federal exclusion from gross income for reimbursements made under an employer-provided accident or health insurance plan for medical care expenses associated with any child of the employee who is under age 27 at the end of the tax year. Consequently, for both California and federal purposes, a child no longer has to be considered a dependent of the taxpayer to qualify for the exclusion. For a child that is age 26 or less at the end of the tax year, the exclusion applies even if the child provides more than one-half of his or her own support, earns more income than the exemption amount, or does not live with the taxpayer, or any other restriction prevents the employee from claiming a dependency exemption for the child under either qualifying child or qualifying relative rules. (Sec. 17131, Rev. & Tax. Code)

Certain amounts paid under an employer-financed accident or health plan to reimburse an employee for expenses incurred by the employee for medical care of the employee or the employee's spouse or dependents are excludible from gross income, unless received in reimbursement for medical expenses previously deducted. These rules also cover payments made for loss of use of a member or function of the body, or for disfigurement. Such plans are subject to detailed rules designed to prevent discrimination. (Sec. 17131, Rev. & Tax. Code)

Employer-provided coverage under an accident or health plan (including amounts contributed to an employee's medical savings account) are also excluded from an employee's gross income. However, employer-provided coverage for long-term care service provided through a flexible spending or similar arrangement must be included in an employee's gross income.

In *Appeal of Frank A. Aiello* (1987) (CCH CALIFORNIA TAX REPORTS, ¶ 15-705.40), lump-sum payments made by a former employer to "buy out" its obligations to provide retired employees with group health benefits was taxable income and not an excludable health benefit.

• *Registered domestic partners and same-sex married couples*

California, but not federal law, treats a registered domestic partner as a spouse for purposes of determining the amounts received under accident and health plans that may be excluded. (Sec. 17021.7, Rev. & Tax. Code) Both California and federal law require same-sex couples to file joint returns, see ¶ 119 for details.

For the 2013—2018 tax years, California law also excludes employer-provided reimbursements paid to compensate an employee for additional federal income taxes that are incurred by the employee on employer-provided health-care benefits because the employee's same-sex spouse or domestic partner is not (or was not prior to the recognition of same-sex marriages) considered the employee's spouse for federal income tax purposes. The exclusion also applies to any amount of the health-care compensation paid to an employee that represents the "grossed-up" amount that an employer includes to offset additional federal income taxes incurred on such compensation. Although current federal law allows same-sex married couples to exclude such reimbursements on their federal return, this does not apply to registered domestic partners. (Sec. 17141.3, Rev. & Tax. Code)

¶220 Rental Value of Parsonages

Law: Sec. 19827.5, Govt. Code; Secs. 17131, 17131.6, Rev. & Tax. Code (CCH CALIFORNIA TAX REPORTS, ¶ 15-155).

Comparable Federal: Sec. 107 (CCH U.S. MASTER TAX GUIDE ¶ 875).

California Forms: Sch. CA (540) (California Adjustments - Residents).

The California exemption for the rental value of a minister's dwelling is the same as under the federal law as of California's current federal conformity date (¶ 103). (Sec. 17131, Rev. & Tax. Code) However, unlike federal law, California law does not limit the exclusion to the fair market rental value of the home, including furnishings and appurtenances, plus the cost of utilities. (Sec. 17131.6, Rev. & Tax. Code)

CCH Caution: Establishment Clause Challenge Filed

Taxpayers should note that California's provision is currently being challenged in the courts as an unconstitutional violation of the Establishment Clause in *Freedom From Religion, Inc. v. Geithner*, U.S. District Court, Eastern District of California, May 21, 2010 (CCH CALIFORNIA TAX REPORTS, ¶ 405-191)

In addition, California allows state-employed members of the clergy to allocate up to 50% of their gross salary to either the rental value of a home furnished to him or her or to the rental allowance paid to him or her to rent a home. (Sec. 19827.5, Govt. Code) The taxpayer may claim a subtraction if, as a result of this provision, the federal exclusion is less than the California exclusion. If the federal exclusion is greater than the California exclusion, the taxpayer is required to make an addition adjustment.

In *Appeal of Nickolas Kurtaneck* (1987) (CCH CALIFORNIA TAX REPORTS, ¶ 15-155.25), the State Board of Equalization (BOE) reviewed applicable federal regulations and rulings and denied the housing exclusion to an ordained minister who taught biblical studies at an independent, nonaffiliated university. The BOE held that the institution was not operated as an integral agency of a church.

¶221 Discharge of Indebtedness

Law: Secs. 17131, 17132.11, 17134, 17144, 17144.5 (CCH CALIFORNIA TAX REPORTS, ¶ 15-680).

Comparable Federal: Secs. 108, 382 (CCH U.S. MASTER TAX GUIDE ¶ 791, 885).

California Forms: Form 540 (California Resident Income Tax Return), Sch. CA (540) (California Adjustments - Residents).

California generally incorporates federal law as of the current IRC tie-in date (see ¶ 103), which provides that, if a debt of a taxpayer is canceled or forgiven, the taxpayer must include the canceled amount in gross income. Exceptions to the general conformity rule are provided in bankruptcy situations, where the debtor/taxpayer is insolvent, or where the canceled debt is qualified real property business indebtedness or qualified farm indebtedness. (Sec. 17131, Rev. & Tax. Code)

Under the discharge of indebtedness rules, the income-tax consequences of debt discharge may be deferred—but not permanently avoided—by reducing tax "attributes" such as capital losses or capital loss carryovers and the basis of depreciable property. Certain debt reductions are treated as purchase-price adjustments.

CCH Practice Tip: COD Compliance Issues

Taxpayers should make sure that the 1099-Cs and 1099-As are reflecting the proper amount of income. The FTB has found that more than 50% of the taxpayers reporting cancellation of debt (COD) income had received inaccurate information from their lenders on the 1099-Cs. Taxpayers claiming a COD income exclusion must attach federal Form 982, Reduction of Tax Attributes Due to Discharge of Indebtedness, to their California return rather than reporting the income/exclusion on other statements within the return. Similarly, Form 982 must be attached by taxpayers claiming insolvency. Those who claim insolvency must also reduce tax attributes as required by IRC §§ 108 and 1017 due to the potential impact of basis in remaining real property holdings. Finally, taxpayers must report COD income, gain, or loss from foreclosed property on the return and include a copy of their federal return, including Form 982 and Section 1082 Basis Adjustment, with their original California tax return. (*FTB Tax News*, October 2011, CCH CALIFORNIA TAX REPORTS, ¶ 405-517)

• *Discharge of qualified principal residence indebtedness*

Although California previously partially conformed to the federal exclusion for mortgage debt forgiveness, California currently does not conform to the federal exclusion (which is in effect through 2016). (Sec. 17144.5, Rev. & Tax. Code)

CCH Practice Tip: Short Sales

In a letter issued on September 19, 2013, the IRS had stated that under California Code of Civil Procedure § 580e, a taxpayer would not have COD income arising from a short sale of specified property. However, upon further examination, the IRS has determined that its initial interpretation was overly broad and has now based its reasoning on a different section of the California Code for its analysis than that relied upon in its previous letter. The IRS has now taken the position that pursuant to California Code of Civil Procedure § 580b(a)(3) a purchase money loan between a lender and a mortgagor is from its inception a nonrecourse loan and, thus, a short sale involving such a loan does not result in COD income. Under § 580b(a)(3) a purchase money loan is a loan that is used to pay part or all of the purchase price of an owner-occupied dwelling for not more than four families and that is secured by that property. (*Letter*, Internal Revenue Service, April 29, 2014, CCH CALIFORNIA TAX REPORTS, ¶ 406-147)

• *Cancellation of student loans*

California incorporates federal law allowing an exclusion from gross income for income from the discharge of qualified student loans. (Sec. 17131, Rev. & Tax. Code) In addition, California allows an exclusion from gross income for any student loan amount repaid by the U.S. Secretary of Education or canceled pursuant to the federal income-based repayment program (20 U.S.C. Section 1098e). (Sec. 17132.11, Rev. & Tax. Code)

The discharge of a loan made pursuant to the California State University's Forgivable Loan Program is also excludable from California gross income if the discharge is made in connection with the recipient's performance of services for the California State University. (Sec. 17134, Rev. & Tax. Code)

Furthermore, for discharges of student loans occurring from 2015 to 2019, an additional gross income exclusion is available if the taxpayer:

— is granted a discharge of his or her student loan pursuant to the agreement between ECMC Group, Inc., Zenith Education Group, and the Consumer Financial Protection Bureau concerning the purchase of certain assets of Corinthian Colleges, Inc., dated February 2, 2015;

— is granted a discharge of his or her student loan pursuant to Paragraph 23 of the William D. Ford Federal Direct Loan Program Borrower's Rights and Responsibilities Statement because (1) the individual could not complete a program of study because the school closed, or (2) the individual successfully asserts that the school did something wrong or failed to do something that it should have done; or

— attended a Corinthian Colleges, Inc., school on or before May 1, 2015, is granted a discharge of any student loan made in connection with attending that school, and that discharge is not excludable from gross income as a result of the reasons listed above.

(Sec. 17144.7, Rev. & Tax. Code)

Finally, an exclusion is allowed for the discharge of a student obligation note or other debt evidencing a loan to any individual for the purpose of attending a for-profit higher education company or for the purpose of consolidating or refinancing a loan used to attend a for-profit higher education company, which is either a guaranteed student loan, an educational loan, or a loan eligible for consolidation or refinancing under Part B of Title IV of the Higher Education Act of 1965 (20 U.S.C. Sec. 1071 et seq.). This exclusion also applies to discharges occurring from 2015 to 2019. (Sec. 17144.7, Rev. & Tax. Code)

• *Reacquisition of business debt instruments*

California does not incorporate IRC Sec. 108(i), which allowed taxpayers to elect to defer the recognition of cancellation of debt income (CODI) in connection with the reacquisition of business debt instruments after December 31, 2008, and before January 1, 2011, for a period of five taxable years for CODI generated in 2009, or four taxable years for CODI generated in 2010. (Sec. 17144(f), Rev. & Tax. Code) For federal tax purposes, at the end of the deferral period (taxable years beginning on or after January 1, 2014, and before January 1, 2019), the income is reported ratably over a five-tax-year period. If for California purposes the CODI was included in income during previous tax years and for federal purposes the CODI is recognized in the current year, the CODI may be subtracted in the current year. (*Instructions, Sch. CA (540), California Adjustments—Residents*)

• *California-federal differences*

Although, as stated above, federal law concerning discharge of indebtedness income has generally been incorporated by California, federal and California results may be quite different because of federal credit carryovers that do not apply to California. For example, federal law requiring the reduction of tax attributes refers to foreign tax credit carryovers, which are not applicable for California tax purposes.

In addition, for purposes of both the reduction of tax attributes and the exclusion of income from the discharge of qualified farm indebtedness, California's treatment of other credit carryovers is slightly modified. Under federal law, a taxpayer who does not elect to reduce the basis of depreciable assets or inventory realty by the amount of a discharged obligation must instead reduce certain listed tax attributes, including general business credit carryover reductions of $33^1/_3$¢ for each dollar excluded. California modifies this provision to (1) refer instead to carryovers of credits allowed under California law and (2) require reduction of only 11.1¢ for each dollar excluded. For both federal and California purposes, a taxpayer may elect to apply the amount discharged to reduce the basis of his or her depreciable property in lieu of applying the excluded amount against tax attributes. (Sec. 17144, Rev. & Tax. Code)

Under both California and federal law, income from the discharge of certain farm indebtedness may be excluded even if the farmer is not insolvent or bankrupt, but the amount that may be excluded is limited to the sum of (1) the aggregate adjusted bases of the taxpayer's trade, business, and income-producing property in the year following the discharge year and (2) the taxpayer's "adjusted" tax attributes. For federal purposes, the taxpayer adjusts the general business credit carryover attribute by tripling it. For California purposes, the taxpayer multiplies the credit carryover figure by nine rather than by three. (Sec. 17144(d), Rev. & Tax. Code)

¶222 Lessee Improvements

Law: Sec. 17131 (CCH CALIFORNIA TAX REPORTS, ¶15-740).

Comparable Federal: Sec. 109 (CCH U.S. MASTER TAX GUIDE ¶764).

An exemption is granted to lessors on income derived upon termination of a lease in the form of improvements made by a lessee. The federal law is incorporated into California's by reference. (Sec. 17131, Rev. & Tax. Code)

¶223 Lessee Construction Allowances

Law: Sec. 17131 (CCH CALIFORNIA TAX REPORTS, ¶15-740).

Comparable Federal: Sec. 110 (CCH U.S. MASTER TAX GUIDE ¶764).

Under both California and federal law, certain tenants may exclude from gross income construction allowances received from lessors and used for additions or improvements to retail space. The exclusion applies only with respect to nonresidential real property that is (1) held under a lease of 15 years or less and (2) used in the tenant's retail trade or business. (Sec. 17131, Rev. & Tax. Code)

¶224 Recoveries of Bad Debts, Prior Taxes, etc.

Law: Secs. 17131, 17142 (CCH CALIFORNIA TAX REPORTS, ¶ 15-810, 16-120, 16-327).

Comparable Federal: Sec. 111 (CCH U.S. MASTER TAX GUIDE ¶ 799).

The federal law is incorporated in California's by reference. (Sec. 17131, Rev. & Tax. Code)

Amounts may be excluded from gross income to the extent they represent recovery of prior-year deductions that did not reduce income tax. The portion of the federal provision dealing with credit and credit carryovers is modified to refer to California credits. (Sec. 17142, Rev. & Tax. Code) Detailed rules are provided.

• *California-federal difference*

The California rule is the same as the federal rule, but the effect of the rule may be different under the two laws because the deduction in the earlier year of the item recovered may have resulted in a tax benefit under one law but not under the other. This could result from a difference in treatment of the item in question in the year of deductibility, or it could be the result of differences in taxable income having no relation to the item in question.

• *Cases decided by State Board of Equalization*

In *Appeal of Boeddeker* (2001) (CCH CALIFORNIA TAX REPORTS, ¶ 15-810.35), the BOE held that taxpayers could exclude from their gross income an amount equal to one-half of the accrued but unpaid interest that they had previously deducted upon the restructuring of a mortgage that resulted in the cancellation of all accrued but unpaid interest and the reduction of principal. Because the taxpayers received a tax benefit, in the form of net operating loss carryovers, for only one-half of the canceled interest that was allocated to them, only that portion of the canceled interest was includible in their gross income for the year. The remaining one-half of the canceled interest was a recovery exclusion, which was nontaxable.

In *Appeal of Percival M. and Katharine Scales* (1963) (CCH CALIFORNIA TAX REPORTS, ¶ 15-810.40), the BOE held that taxes and carrying charges on real property deducted in one period, without a corresponding reduction in tax liability, could not be excluded from income when recovered in a subsequent year upon sale of the property. The BOE said the "tax benefit" rule was not intended to have such broad application. To the same effect, see *Appeal of H.V. Management Corporation* (1981) (CCH CALIFORNIA TAX Reports ¶ 10-910.50), a case that involved gain on sale of a partnership interest. Also to the same effect, see *Appeal of Argo Petroleum Corporation* (1982) (CCH CALIFORNIA TAX REPORTS, ¶ 10-910.50), which involved sale of an oil and gas lease.

¶225 Military and Terrorist Victims' Compensation

Law: Secs. 17131, 17132.4, 17140.5, 17142.5, 17731 (CCH CALIFORNIA TAX REPORTS, ¶ 15-175).

Comparable Federal: Secs. 112, 122, 134, 692 (CCH U.S. MASTER TAX GUIDE ¶ 895, 896, 2533).

Except as discussed below, the California exemptions for military pay are the same as the federal as of the current IRC tie-in date (¶ 103). This applies also to forgiveness of taxes of service members who die as a result of serving in a "combat zone" or "qualified hazardous duty area" (as defined in ¶ 109).

The following military compensation is exempt from California tax:

— educational benefits received under federal or state law;

— compensation, including reenlistment bonuses, earned by enlisted personnel and warrant officers for active service in a "combat zone" or "qualified hazardous duty area" or while hospitalized as a result of such service; and

— military compensation of a person not domiciled or taxable in California, but attributable to a resident spouse because of community property laws. Members serving on active duty and domiciled in community property states

(Arizona, Idaho, Louisiana, Nevada, New Mexico, Texas, Washington, Wisconsin, or Puerto Rico) with California resident spouses may subtract half of their military pay from federal AGI.

(Sec. 17131, Rev. & Tax. Code; Sec. 17140.5, Rev. & Tax. Code)

For commissioned officers, other than commissioned warrant officers, the monthly tax exclusion is capped at the highest enlisted pay, plus any hostile or imminent danger pay received.

Expenses attributable to service pay that is exempt from tax are not deductible (¶336).

• *Victims of terroristic or military actions; astronauts*

Taxpayers who died as a result of injuries or wounds from a terroristic or military action directed against the United States or one of its allies incurred while the individual was a U.S. military or civilian employee are exempt from tax during the taxable year of the taxpayer's death and in any prior taxable year beginning with the last taxable year ending before the taxable year in which the wounds or injury were incurred. Federal law, but not California law, provides a $10,000 minimum tax relief benefit. (Sec. 17731(b), Rev. & Tax. Code)

California law, but not federal law, excludes the entire amount of a $10,000 death benefit paid by the state of California to the surviving spouse of, or a beneficiary designated by, any member of the California National Guard, State Military Reserve, or Naval Militia, who dies or is killed in the performance of duty. (Sec. 17132.4, Rev. & Tax. Code)

• *Effect of residence status on taxability*

Under the federal Servicemembers Civil Relief Act, a nonresident serviceperson may not be taxed by California on service pay received for services in California, even though he or she may be stationed in the state during the entire year, and despite the fact that such income would be considered taxable to a nonresident under the regular rules. (Sec. 17140.5, Rev. & Tax. Code) However, all other income of a nonresident serviceperson from California sources is subject to California tax. Under FTB Legal Ruling No. 300 (CCH CALIFORNIA TAX REPORTS, ¶202-877), a person who enters military service from California will be treated as a nonresident when he or she leaves the state under permanent military orders to serve at another post of duty (¶105).

California law conforms to the federal Servicemembers Civil Relief Act (SCRA) (P.L. 108-189). Among the provisions of this legislation are the following:

— The military compensation of a servicemember not domiciled in California may not be used to increase the tax liability imposed on other income earned by that servicemember or that servicemember's spouse.

— The running of the statute of limitations is suspended for the period of a servicemember's military service.

— The interest rate is limited to a maximum of 6% per year on any underpayment incurred before the servicemember enters military service.

— A servicemember not domiciled in California does not become a resident by reason of being present in the state solely in compliance with military orders.

— Military compensation of a servicemember not domiciled in California is not income for services performed or from sources within the state.

— Native American servicemembers whose legal residence or domicile is a federal Indian reservation are treated as living on the federal Indian reservation and the compensation for military service is deemed to be income derived wholly from federal Indian reservation sources.

(Sec. 17140.5, Rev. & Tax. Code)

Prior to California's conformity with the SCRA, although a nonresident's military pay was excluded from gross income subject to California personal income tax,

California included a nonresident's military pay in the computation used to determine the tax rate applied to California-source income subject to California personal income tax; see ¶116 for more details (*Brownell* (2001) (CCH California Tax Reports, ¶403-171)).

¶226 Dividends and Other Corporate Distributions

Law: Secs. 17024.5(b), 17088, 17321, 17322 (CCH California Tax Reports, ¶15-645).

Comparable Federal: Secs. 301-46, 851-60, 951-52, 995 (CCH U.S. Master Tax Guide ¶733 et seq., 2301 et seq., 2465, 2468).

California Forms: Sch. CA (540) (California Adjustments - Residents), Sch. CA (540NR) (California Adjustments - Nonresidents or Part-Year Residents).

Although California and federal law regarding dividends and other corporate distributions are generally the same as of the current IRC tie-in date (see ¶103), California has not completely conformed to current federal law. (Sec. 17321, Rev. & Tax. Code) In addition, prior differences in California and federal law may still affect the cost basis of property. Both current California-federal differences and prior-year differences are discussed below.

The principal provisions of the federal law to which California conforms may be summarized very briefly as follows:

— Any distribution out of earnings and profits of the current year or out of earnings and profits accumulated after February 28, 1913, is a "dividend" (IRC Sec. 316).

— Certain liquidating distributions are treated as payments in exchange for stock (IRC Sec. 302-03).

— A redemption of stock that is "essentially equivalent to the distribution of a taxable dividend" is to be treated as such. This may apply to acquisition of a corporation's stock by an affiliated corporation (IRC Sec. 304). Detailed rules are provided for some situations. Certain types of redemptions are not to be treated as taxable dividends. These include "disproportionate distributions," termination of a shareholder's interest, and redemption of stock to pay death taxes.

— Certain stock dividends may be nontaxable (IRC Sec. 305).

— Detailed rules are provided for the computation of "earnings and profits" so that a determination can be made regarding the taxability of a corporate distribution in the hands of shareholders (IRC Sec. 312).

• *Distributions from mutual funds*

California generally adopts the federal tax treatment of regulated investment companies (RICs) and their shareholders (IRC Sec. 852). (Sec. 17088, Rev. & Tax. Code) with certain modifications. See ¶217 for a discussion of the pass-through of RIC income that is exempt from California personal income tax.

• *Constructive dividends*

Following federal cases involving the same issue, the State Board of Equalization held in *Appeal of Howard N. and Thelma Gilmore* (1961) (CCH California Tax Reports, ¶201-861) that unsupported travel and entertainment expenses disallowed to a closely-held corporation were taxable as constructive dividends to the individual shareholders. Later cases have been decided to the same effect.

• *Current California-federal differences*

Current differences between California and federal law are summarized briefly as follows:

— Federal law provides for "consent dividends" (applicable to "personal holding companies," etc.). There is no comparable California provision.

— Federal limitations periods for waivers of stock attribution are modified for California purposes. (Sec. 17132, Rev. & Tax. Code)

— California has not adopted a special federal rule governing generation-skipping transfers. (Sec. 17024.5(b), Rev. & Tax. Code)

— The federal provision relating to distributions by foreign corporations, foreign investment companies, and foreign personal holding companies is not applicable for California purposes. (Sec. 17024.5(b), Rev. & Tax. Code)

— Under both California and federal law, a corporate distribution may be a nontaxable return of capital if there are no "earnings and profits" out of which the distribution is made. However, the amount of "earnings and profits" of a corporation may be different for California tax purposes than it is for federal tax purposes. Such a difference may result in a particular distribution being nontaxable under one law but a taxable dividend under the other.

— California does not incorporate the special federal provisions for Domestic International Sales Corporations (DISC). Accordingly, a DISC is taxed under California law in the same manner as other corporations, and the special federal treatment of its dividends has no effect for California tax purposes. (Sec. 17024.5(b), Rev. & Tax. Code)

— California, unlike federal law, does not apply a lower tax rate to qualified dividend distributions.

• *Prior-year differences*

In addition to the differences listed above, there were prior-year differences that may continue to affect computations of basis. These prior-year differences concern the following:

— federal rules for distributions by World War I "personal service corporations";

— rules for corporate liquidations in 1954, 1955, and 1956;

— special California provisions for 1935 or 1936 distributions by a "personal holding company";

— effective dates (all before 1972) of provisions regarding redemption of stock through an affiliate, and "collapsible corporations";

— various amendments in 1954 and 1955, regarding distribution of stock dividends and rights, etc.;

— various amendments, in 1981 and before, relating to special rules for redemption of stock to pay death taxes;

— 1958 federal amendments to special rules for 12-month liquidations;

— 1964-1978 difference in rules for "sidewise attribution" in stock ownership rules;

— 1954-1961 difference in special rules regarding distributions of property with a government-secured loan; and

— 1969-1971 differences in rules for taxation of stock dividends.

¶227 Scholarship and Fellowship Grants

Law: Secs. 17131 (CCH CALIFORNIA TAX REPORTS, ¶ 15-685).

Comparable Federal: Sec. 117 (CCH U.S. MASTER TAX GUIDE ¶ 879).

California conforms to federal law as of California's current federal conformity date (see ¶ 103). (Sec. 17131, Rev. & Tax. Code)

Certain scholarship and fellowship grants and tuition grants are excluded from taxable income, as long as the grant or scholarship does not represent compensation for services performed as a condition of the grant. In the case of graduate teaching or research assistants of exempt educational institutions, the amount of *any* tuition reduction for education at the employing institution may be excluded.

¶227

¶228 Meals and Lodging Furnished by Employer

Law: Sec. 17131 (CCH CALIFORNIA TAX REPORTS, ¶15-705).

Comparable Federal: Sec. 119 (CCH U.S. MASTER TAX GUIDE ¶873).

California conforms to the federal law as of the current tie-in date (see ¶103). (Sec. 17131, Rev. & Tax. Code)

The value of meals and lodging furnished by an employer for the convenience of the employer is excluded from gross income, provided (1) the meals are furnished on the business premises of the employer and (2) the employee is required to accept the lodging on the employer's premises as a condition of employment.

Under both California and federal law, all meals furnished to employees on the employer's premises are treated as furnished for the convenience of the employer as long as more than 50% of the employees to whom such meals are provided are furnished the meals for the convenience of the employer.

¶229 Gain on Sale or Exchange of Personal Residence

Law: Secs. 17131, 17152 (CCH CALIFORNIA TAX REPORTS, ¶15-710, 16-070, 16-270).

Comparable Federal: Sec. 121 (CCH U.S. MASTER TAX GUIDE ¶1705).

Both California and federal law allow an individual taxpayer to exclude from his or her gross income up to $250,000 ($500,000 for married taxpayers or registered domestic partners (RDPs) filing jointly) of gain realized on the sale or exchange of his or her residence if the taxpayer owned and occupied the residence as a principal residence for an aggregate period of at least two of the five years prior to the sale or exchange. Under both California and federal law, if a taxpayer does not meet the two-year ownership and use requirement due to a change in place of employment, health, or unforeseen circumstances, the exclusion may be prorated. (Sec. 17131, Rev. & Tax. Code)

Practice Pointer: Registered Domestic Partners

A registered domestic partner (see ¶119) who was subject to the $250,000 limit discussed above on his or her federal return, would be able to claim up to $500,000 if the registered domestic partner and his or her partner file a married, filing joint California personal income tax return.

With the exception of RDPs, the exclusion amount is based on federal filing status, and not on California filing status. The exclusion applies only to one sale or exchange every two years. The California rules are generally the same as the federal rules, except that under California law, but not federal, a portion of the two-year ownership and use requirement is waived for individuals who served in the Peace Corps (the period waived is the length of the time of service, up to a maximum of 18 months). (Sec. 17152, Rev. & Tax. Code) In addition, the $500,000 exclusion limit applies to RDPs under California, but not federal law. (Sec. 17021.7, Rev. & Tax. Code)

However, under both California and federal law, uniformed or foreign service personnel called to active duty away from home may elect to suspend the five-year test period for a period of up to five years. A federal election, or lack thereof, is binding for California purposes. (Sec. 17152(e), Rev. & Tax. Code)

California does not incorporate a federal provision that extends eligibility for the exclusion to estates, heirs, and qualified revocable trusts. (Sec. 17152(f), Rev. & Tax. Code)

See ¶503 concerning a provision that allows nonrecognition of gain in situations involving involuntary conversion.

¶230 Employees of Foreign Country

Law: Sec. 17146 (CCH CALIFORNIA TAX REPORTS, ¶15-700).

Comparable Federal: Sec. 893.

Exemption is granted for compensation for services of an employee of a foreign country, provided certain conditions are met. California law incorporates the federal law by reference. (Sec. 17146, Rev. & Tax. Code)

¶231 Gross Income of Nonresidents

Law: Secs. 17041, 17951-17955; Regs. 17951-4, 17951-6 (CCH CALIFORNIA TAX REPORTS, ¶15-105, 15-115, 15-120, 15-515, 16-505, 16-510, 16-515, 16-520, 16-525, 16-530, 16-540, 16-545, 16-550, 16-555, 16-560, 16-565, 16-570).

Comparable Federal: Secs. 861-65, 911-12, 931-33 (CCH U.S. MASTER TAX GUIDE ¶2402 et seq., 2429, 2440, 2463).

California Forms: Form 540NR (California Nonresident or Part-Year Resident Income Tax Return), Sch. CA (540NR) (California Adjustments - Nonresidents or Part-Year Residents), Sch. R (Apportionment and Allocation of Income).

For purposes of determining a nonresident's taxable income (¶116) gross income of nonresidents includes only gross income from sources within California. (Sec. 17951, Rev. & Tax. Code)

A nonresident member of a partnership or similar organization must include his or her distributive share of income from California sources. A nonresident beneficiary of an estate or trust must include distributable income of the estate or trust from California sources. (Sec. 17953, Rev. & Tax. Code)

Nonresidents are taxed as though they were residents but with the tax computed on the basis of a prorated taxable income formula. (Sec. 17041, Rev. & Tax. Code) See ¶116 for details. FTB Pub. 1100, Taxation of Nonresidents and Individuals Who Change Residency, provides extensive discussion and examples of the attribution rules for income from various sources.

A part-year resident is taxed on income regardless of source during the period of California residence and on income from California sources during the period of nonresidency. (Sec. 17041, Rev. & Tax. Code)

• *Pension income*

A former California resident's qualified retirement income received after leaving California is not subject to California income tax, even if accrued while the nonresident resided in California. The current exclusion from gross income encompasses income or distributions received from most tax-exempt trusts, simplified employee pensions, annuity plans and contracts, individual retirement plans, government plans, and deferred compensation plans of state and local governments and tax-exempt organizations, and it also encompasses specified distributions from nonqualified plans. (Sec. 17952.5, Rev. & Tax. Code)

Practice Pointer: Nonresident Partners

P.L. 109-264 (H.R. 4019), Laws 2006, amended 4 U.S.C. Sec. 114 to provide that the prohibition against taxing former resident's pension income applies to the retirement income of a nonresident retired partner, as well as a nonresident retired employee, and that the application of a predetermined formula cap or a cost-of-living adjustment in a nonqualified deferred compensation plan does not make the retirement income of such nonresidents subject to state taxation.

• *Income from tangible property*

Any income from ownership, control, management, sale or transfer of real or tangible personal property in California is income from California sources. (Reg. 17951-3, 18 CCR) In *Appeal of L.N. Hagood* (1960) (CCH CALIFORNIA TAX REPORTS,

¶16-550.77), the State Board of Equalization (BOE) held that since U.S. oil and gas leases of lands in California are real property, the income arising out of the granting of purchase options relative thereto is taxable income from California sources to a nonresident.

• *Income from intangible property*

In general, income of nonresidents from intangible property has its source at the state of residence of the owner and is therefore not taxable by California (but see next paragraph). Alimony income is considered to be derived from an intangible asset and is not taxable to a nonresident. (Sec. 17952, Rev. & Tax. Code)

Income from intangible personal property, including gain on its sale or exchange, is attributable to California if the property has a business situs in the state. Such property is deemed to have a business situs in the state if it is employed as capital in California or its use and value become an asset of a business, trade, or profession in the state. Even if the property does not have a business situs in California, if a nonresident deals in the property in California with sufficient regularity as to constitute doing business in the state, the income from such activity is taxable in California. (Sec. 17952, Rev. & Tax. Code)

The source of gains and losses from the sale or other disposition of intangible personal property is determined at the time of the sale or disposition of that property. Consequently, gain from an installment sale of intangible property made by a California resident taxpayer continues to be sourced to California even if the taxpayer subsequently becomes a nonresident. In addition, a California nonresident who sells intangible personal property that had a business situs in California at the time of the sale would be taxed by California on gain as it is recognized upon receipt of future installment payments. (Regulation 17952, 18 CCR)

In *Appeal of Robert M. and Ann T. Bass et al.* (1989) (CCH CALIFORNIA TAX REPORTS, ¶16-565.672), the BOE held that a nonresident's distributive share of income from a limited partnership that was headquartered in California and that was engaged in the acquisition, holding, monitoring, and disposition of stocks and other securities was not subject to California income tax, because the limited partnership was not doing business in California.

Income from qualifying investment securities is not taxable by California if an individual's only contact with the state with respect to the securities is through a broker, dealer, or investment adviser located in California. Special rules apply in the case of income from qualifying investment securities distributed to a nonresident by an investment partnership, a qualifying estate or trust, or a regulated investment company. Income from qualifying investment securities is taxable by California if

— the income is from investment activity that is interrelated with a California trade or business in which the nonresident owns an interest and the primary activities of the trade or business are separate and distinct from the acts of acquiring, managing, or disposing of qualified investment securities and

— the income is from qualifying investment securities that are acquired with the working capital of a California trade or business in which the nonresident owns an interest. (Sec. 17955, Rev. & Tax. Code)

Practice Pointer: Derivatives Treated as Qualified Investment Securities

Although derivatives are not specifically mentioned in the statutory provisions, the FTB determined that the statutory definition of qualified investment securities appears to encompass such securities, as it includes "stock and bond index securities and futures contracts, and other similar financial securities and futures contracts on those securities." (*Information Letter 2010-4*, California Franchise Tax Board, August 17, 2010, CCH CALIFORNIA TAX REPORTS, ¶405-237) A similar conclusion was reached by the FTB Chief Counsel concerning commodity-linked derivatives. (*Chief Counsel Legal Ruling 2010-01*, California Franchise Tax Board, March 25, 2010, CCH CALIFORNIA TAX REPORTS, ¶405-221)

- *Payment for contract termination*

In *Appeal of Edward and Carol McAneeley* (1980) (CCH CALIFORNIA TAX REPORTS, ¶16-570.411), the taxpayer, a professional hockey player, was a Canadian resident employed by a California team. He received a $17,500 payment for termination of his California contract. The BOE held that the termination payment was not taxable by California, because the payment was for the sale of an intangible property right that had its situs in Canada.

- *Income from business*

Income of a business, trade, or profession carried on within the state is taxable. If such income is derived from both within and without the state, and if the part conducted outside the state is distinct and separate, only the gross income from the California operations need be reported. However, gross income from the entire business must be reported if there is any business relationship between the parts within and without the state (flow of goods, etc.) so that the net income from sources outside the state cannot be accurately determined. In such cases, a portion of the net income is attributed to California, ordinarily—but not always—by use of the apportionment formula described at ¶1305. (Reg. 17951-4, 18 CCR; Reg. 25128.5(c), 18 CCR)

Practice Pointer: Use of Single Sales Factor by Partnership

Beginning with the 2013 taxable year, an apportioning trade or business, regardless of the form of ownership (e.g., sole proprietorship, partnership, limited liability company, or corporation), that carries on business within and without California is required to apportion business income using the single sales factor. The same would be true for a partner's distributive share. Whether the trade or business is the partnership's business (if not unitary with the trade or business of its partner), or the partnership interest when combined with the partner's trade or business (if the partnership's activities are unitary with the activities of its partner, notwithstanding ownership requirements), the business income of the trade or business must be apportioned using the single sales factor under the provisions of Rev. & Tax. Code § 25128.7 unless the trade or business meets one of the specified exceptions. (Reg. 25128.5(c), 18 CCR; *FTB Tax News* (April 2013) CCH CALIFORNIA TAX REPORTS, ¶405-867)

The source of net income of a nonresident sole proprietor, partner, S corporation shareholder, or limited liability company (LLC) member from a business, trade, or profession that is not business income must be determined in accordance with the sourcing rules discussed in Rev. & Tax. Code Secs. 17951 through 17956 and the regulations thereunder, and not by reference to the nonbusiness allocation rules of the Uniform Division of Income for Tax Purposes Act (UDITPA). The business activity of a partnership, LLC, or S corporation will not ordinarily be considered part of a unitary business with another business activity unless the partner, member, or shareholder owns, directly or indirectly, a 20% or more capital or profits interest in a partnership, LLC, or S corporation. In addition, the FTB has discretion to treat business activities as part of a unitary business if it determines such combination is appropriate after conducting a comparable uncontrolled price examination. (Reg. 17951-4, 18 CCR)

Taxpayers complete Sch. R for purposes of determining the amount of business income apportionable to California. See Chapter 13 for discussion of methods of apportionment, what constitutes business income subject to apportionment, etc. Regulation 17951-4 provides detailed explanations concerning sourcing of income for unitary multistate sole proprietorships, partnerships, S corporations, and LLCs and clarifies how to determine the 20% threshold discussed above. Special rules apply to professional corporations.

Practice Pointer: Market-Based Sourcing Rules Apply

Nonresident taxpayers with an apportioning trade or business that in the past may have had little or no income that was sourced to California may find that they now have more California-sourced income. This is especially true if the taxpayer's business income is derived from the sale of intangibles or services. For post-2012 taxable years, all apportioning trades or businesses must assign sales of other than tangible personal property under the new market-based rules. Receipts from services must be sourced to the location where the customer receives the benefit of the service, and receipts from intangibles must be assigned to California to the extent that the property was used in California. Detailed rules are discussed at ¶ 1309. (*FTB Tax News* (2013), CCH CALIFORNIA TAX REPORTS, ¶ 405-969)

In *Appeal of Chester A. and Mary E. Johnson* (1981) (CCH CALIFORNIA TAX REPORTS, ¶ 16-515.30), the taxpayers were Australian residents whose pet-food business operated in both California and Iowa. The taxpayers computed their income attributable to California by using a federal formula provided by Internal Revenue Code Section 911. The BOE upheld the Franchise Tax Board (FTB) in requiring the use of the three-factor formula required under prior law.

• *Compensation for services*

Compensation (including stock options) for personal services performed in California is considered attributable to California. (Reg. 17951-5, 18 CCR) This includes fees of nonresidents for professional services. However, California may not tax the income received from the following individuals to the extent prohibited under federal law (Amtrak Reauthorization and Improvement Act of 1990 (P.L. 101-322)):

— a nonresident who performs regularly-assigned duties while engaged as a pilot, master, officer, or crewman on a vessel operating on the navigable waters of more than one state;

— a nonresident employee of an airline, if 50% or less of the pay received by the employee is earned in California;

— a nonresident employee of a railroad, if the employee performs services in two or more states;

— a nonresident employee of an interstate motor carrier, if the employee performs services in two or more states; and

— a nonresident member of the U.S. Armed Forces who is stationed in California.

In addition, when a nonresident receives pension income that is based on services rendered in California, the income is not taxable by California (¶ 405).

Practice Pointer: Income From Restricted Stock Unit Plan

The FTB has issued a ruling on the proper method of determining the portion of California source income received by a taxpayer from a restricted stock unit (RSU) plan. The ruling specifically addresses the sourcing of income under the following scenarios: (1) the taxpayer lived in California on the date of grant of the RSUs, but became a nonresident of California prior to the vesting date; and (2) the taxpayer was a nonresident of California on the date of grant of the RSUs, but performed services for the employer in California prior to the vesting date. When restricted stock is granted, the taxpayer must recognize compensation for the performance of personal services only when the restricted stock is vested. When a taxpayer performs services in California during the period from the date of the grant of the restricted stock to the date of the vesting of the restricted stock and during this period becomes a nonresident, the taxpayer must use a reasonable apportionment method to determine the portion of California source income received. According to the FTB, the most reasonable apportionment method appears to be to multiply the compensation received by a ratio of California working days from the grant date to the vest date over the total working days anywhere during the same period. (*Chief Counsel Ruling 2014-01*, California Franchise Tax Board, May 13, 2014, CCH CALIFORNIA TAX REPORTS, ¶ 406-245)

The FTB's Legal Division has responded to an inquiry regarding the sourcing of income earned by a mixed martial arts fighter for a fight in California that would be televised to pay-per-view subscribers in 40 states. The FTB has said that if the athlete is in the business or profession of boxing, the compensation that is paid based on pay-per-view revenues would be apportioned to California based on the number of subscribers located in California in comparison to total subscribers. (*E-Mail*, California Franchise Tax Board, May 1, 2014, CCH CALIFORNIA TAX REPORTS, ¶ 406-133)

In *Appeal of Hearst* (2002) (CCH CALIFORNIA TAX REPORTS, ¶ 16-570.416), athletes' signing bonuses constituted compensation for services subject to apportionment under the duty days apportionment formula, and not true signing bonuses allocable 100% to their state of residence. Because the language of the signing bonus riders obligated the players to repay a proportionate share of the bonuses for any period of time in which they refused to practice or play, the bonuses represented compensation for services, and not mere consideration for signing the contracts.

In *Wilson et al. v. Franchise Tax Board* (1993) (CCH CALIFORNIA TAX REPORTS, ¶ 16-570.415), a nonresident professional football player's income was properly apportioned to California on the basis of the ratio of the athlete's duty days spent in California to the athlete's total duty days. "Duty days" included all days from the beginning of the official preseason training through the last game, including post-season games, in which the team competed during the taxable year.

In *Paul L. and Joanne W. Newman v. Franchise Tax Board* (1989) (CCH CALIFORNIA TAX REPORTS, ¶ 16-570.222), a nonresident actor's income from a motion picture was properly apportioned according to a formula that divided his working days in California by his total working days on the picture, with "working days" including all the days on which, by contract, he was exclusively committed to his employer and on call at the employer's discretion, and not merely those days on which he actually performed.

In *Appeal of Joseph Barry Carroll* (1987) (CCH CALIFORNIA TAX REPORTS, ¶ 16-570.414), compensation paid to a nonresident professional basketball player employed by the Golden State Warriors was apportioned to California on the basis of a "working day" or "duty day" formula that included days spent in training camp, practice sessions, and team travel. The taxpayer argued that he was paid for games only, and not practice or travel days, but produced no evidence to that effect. Accordingly, the BOE computed his California-source income on the basis of the ratio of training camp, practice, travel, and game days spent in California to total training camp, practice, travel, and game days.

In *Appeal of Edwin O. and Wanda L. Stevens* (1986) (CCH CALIFORNIA TAX REPORTS, ¶ 16-570.38), the BOE held that benefits, sick leave, and vacation pay earned while working and residing in California are California-source income and taxable in the state, even though the right to such benefits accrued during employment and residence in another state.

In *Appeal of Karl Bernhardt* (1984) (CCH CALIFORNIA TAX REPORTS, ¶ 400-983), the taxpayer was a member of the Canadian Armed Forces who worked temporarily for Sperry Univac in California as a part of his service training. His salary was paid into a Canadian bank in Canadian funds. The BOE held that the salary was subject to California tax.

In *Appeal of George and Sheila Foster* (1984) (CCH CALIFORNIA TAX REPORTS, ¶ 16-570.413), the taxpayer was an Ohio resident, where he played professional baseball for Cincinnati. He contended that $400,000 of his $985,000 salary for 1979 represented a "signing bonus" for signing a renegotiated contract, and that the "bonus" was not subject to apportionment by California according to the usual "working-days" formula. The BOE held that the $400,000 was a "playing bonus," subject to apportionment, and was not a "signing bonus" attributable to the state of residence.

In *Appeal of Dennis F. and Nancy Partee* (1976) (CCH CALIFORNIA TAX REPORTS, ¶ 16-570.41), the taxpayer was a nonresident professional football player with the San

Diego Chargers. Here also, the BOE upheld the FTB's determination of the portion of the taxpayer's total salary allocable to California on the basis of the number of "working days" spent in the State. The taxpayer argued for use of the "games-played" formula used in other sports—see the *Krake* case, discussed below.

In *Appeals of Philip and Diane Krake, et al.* (1976) (CCH CALIFORNIA TAX REPORTS, ¶ 16-570.412), the twelve taxpayers were nonresident members of the Los Angeles Kings professional hockey team. The BOE upheld the FTB's application of the "games-played" formula to total salaries, to determine the portion allocable to California. The taxpayers argued that a portion of their salary should be allocated to off-season activities before applying the "games-played" formula. However, the BOE agreed with the FTB's contention that the "games-played" method, as applied to regular season games, is a practical and reasonable method that produces approximately the same result as the "working-days" method for baseball, basketball, and hockey players.

• *Airline personnel*

Wages of nonresident flight personnel are not taxable by California unless 50% of the employee's schedule flight time is in California. If the 50% threshold is met, then wages are apportioned on the ratio of the time spent in California to total scheduled flight time. (FTB Pub. 1031, Guidelines for Determining Residence Status)

• *Burden of proof*

Appeal of Robert L. Webber (1976) (CCH CALIFORNIA TAX REPORTS, ¶ 16-570.223), involved an actor who was a New York resident. Part of his earnings for his personal services came from a wholly-owned corporation. The question at issue was the amount of his income for services performed in California. The BOE held that the taxpayer had submitted sufficient evidence to shift the burden of proof to the FTB, concluding that the latter had not borne that burden and holding in favor of the taxpayer. For another case involving similar issues, see *Appeal of Janice Rule* (1976) (CCH CALIFORNIA TAX REPORTS, ¶ 16-570.22). See also *Appeal of Oscar D. and Agatha E. Seltzer* (1980) (CCH CALIFORNIA TAX REPORTS, ¶ 16-570.332); in this case a corporate executive who was an Oregon resident was subjected to California tax on one-third of his income, because he did not overcome the presumption of correctness of the FTB's determination.

• *Royalty income*

In Legal Ruling No. 345 (1970) (CCH CALIFORNIA TAX REPORTS, ¶ 16-570.49), it was held that royalty income received by an author on the sale of books is compensation for personal services and is taxable at the place the services are performed. Where a nonresident author's writing was done in California, his royalties received from a New York publisher were subject to California tax.

• *Covenant not to compete*

Under Reg. 17951-6, 18 CCR, income from a covenant not to compete executed in connection with the sale of a business conducted entirely within California or within and without California is California-source income to the extent the income is assigned to California. Income is assigned to locations within the area covered by the covenant not to compete according to a formula that consists of the average of the property, payroll, and sales factors of the business that was sold, weighted in accordance with the apportionment formula as in effect for the tax year of sale (currently single-sales factor).

In general, UDITPA and the applicable statutes and regulations apply, except that for purposes of computing the numerator and the denominator of the sales factor, all sales of tangible personal property are assigned to the state of the purchaser where the property is delivered or shipped, and the statutory throwback provisions do not apply. In addition, the FTB may use apportionment factors for another year or years or employ another method of assigning income if this formula does not accurately reflect the nature of the prohibited activities expressed or reasonably implied from the covenant not to compete, or if they do not accurately represent the location of the recent business activities of the business that was sold, such that there is a gross distortion of income assigned within the covered area.

CCH Comment: Covenant Not Sourced To California

Despite the FTB's regulations and policies, taxpayers should determine whether the covenant not to compete has any true value in California. A California court of appeal reversed the FTB's taxation of a nonresident's covenant not to compete, finding that California's taxation of the covenant violated the U.S. Commerce Clause because none of the payments received on the covenant arose from California activities or from capital located in or associated with California. The record demonstrated that the covenant had no value in California. The business that was sold had 100% of the California market and any potential competitor would have to invest a substantial amount of capital. (*Milhous v. FTB* (2005) (CCH CALIFORNIA TAX REPORTS, ¶ 403-843))

In *Appeal of Stephen D. Bragg* (2003) (CCH CALIFORNIA TAX REPORTS, ¶ 16-525.454), the BOE held that the FTB properly apportioned a taxpayer's income from a covenant-not-to-compete using the three-factor apportionment formula used by the business that made the payments to the taxpayer.

• *Change of residence status*

See ¶ 405 regarding determination of income subject to California tax when status changes from resident to nonresident or vice versa.

• *California-federal differences*

Although the federal law includes some rules comparable to the California law, the differences are so numerous that no attempt is made here to describe them. Any such comparison would be applicable only to nonresident aliens, because U.S. citizens and resident aliens are taxable for federal purposes on all their income from whatever source, with certain specific exemptions. California law has nothing comparable to the special federal provisions for earned income and deductions of Americans living and working abroad.

¶232 Patronage Allocations from Cooperatives

Law: Sec. 17086 (CCH CALIFORNIA TAX REPORTS, ¶ 15-170).

Comparable Federal: Secs. 1381-83, 1385 (CCH U.S. MASTER TAX GUIDE ¶ 698).

California Form: Sch. CA (540) (California Adjustments - Residents).

With the exception of its treatment of agricultural cooperative patronage dividends, California's treatment of patronage allocations from cooperatives is the same as federal law. (Sec. 17086, Rev. & Tax. Code)

California provides optional methods of taxing non-cash patronage allocations from farmers' cooperatives and mutual associations. An election must be made to include such allocations in income either in the year the dollar amount of allocations is made known, or in the year the allocation is redeemed or realized. For a detailed discussion of the rules for such elections, see *Appeal of J.H. Johnson and Sons, Inc.* (1979) (CCH CALIFORNIA TAX REPORTS, ¶ 15-170.25).

Generally, the federal rules require that allocations be included in income in the year they are received. The federal rules provide that cooperatives will not be allowed a deduction for patronage dividends and per-unit retain certificates unless the patrons include such amounts in taxable income, whether they are actually received or merely allocated.

¶233 S Corporation Shareholders

> *Law:* Secs. 17087.5, 17951, 18006, 18535, 23800-10 (CCH California Tax Reports, ¶ 15-185, 16-565).
>
> *Comparable Federal:* Secs. 1361-79 (CCH U.S. Master Tax Guide ¶ 309 et seq.).

The California taxation of shareholders of federal S corporations that have elected S corporation status for California purposes is the same as federal law as of the current IRC tie-in date (¶ 103). (Sec. 17087.5, Rev. & Tax. Code) (See ¶ 806 for a discussion of S corporations generally). Essentially, S corporation shareholders are treated in the same manner as that of partners in partnerships. (*Valentino et al. v. Franchise Tax Board* (2001), CCH California Tax Reports, ¶ 15-185.72)

Under long-standing federal law, as adopted by California, the shareholders of qualified S corporations report the current corporate income as though they had earned it individually, thus avoiding a tax at the corporate level for federal purposes and most of the corporate tax for California purposes (California imposes a reduced corporate tax rate on S corporation income prior to its pass-through to shareholders) (¶ 806). Shareholders are entitled to a credit for their pro rata share of taxes paid to another state by the S corporation on income also taxed by California (¶ 128, ¶ 129).

CCH Comment: Reporting of Withholding Amounts on Schedule K-1

An S corporation must report withholding payments made from the S corporation that are allocated to all shareholders based on their stock ownership, as well as payments withheld-at-the-source on nonresident shareholders. The total withholding amount must be reported on each shareholder's Schedule K-1 (100S), line 14, and the S corporation must provide each shareholder with a completed Form 592-B, Nonresident Withholding Tax Statement. Shareholders must attach Form 592-B to the front of their California tax returns to claim the withheld amounts. (Instructions, Schedule K-1 (100S), Shareholder's Share of Income, Deductions, Credits, etc.; Instructions, Form 592-B, Nonresident Withholding Tax Statement)

In *Appeal of Merwyn P. Merrick, Sr. and Margaret F. Merrick* (1975) (CCH California Tax Reports, ¶ 15-185.51), the stockholders of a "tax-option" (S) corporation received distributions representing the proceeds of sale of the corporation's plant. The BOE held that the distributions were taxable as ordinary dividends.

See discussion at ¶ 718 of the *Winkenbach* case, involving the application of the doctrine of "equitable recoupment" where income was erroneously taxed to a corporation and later taxed to the individual stockholders.

CCH Comment: Basis Adjustments Related to Items From Closed Tax Years

The FTB has issued a technical advice memorandum (TAM) that addresses how a shareholder's basis in an S corporation is calculated when some years are closed by the statute of limitations. The TAM concludes that in situations when an S corporation has both items of income and deduction for the closed years and the shareholder failed to report these items on the shareholder's personal income tax return for the closed years, the shareholder's basis is not increased for items of income, but basis is decreased for items of deduction, but not below zero. Because the shareholder has not reported the items of loss or deduction, the shareholder may carry over any items of loss or deduction in excess of basis to future years. In instances when an S corporation has both items of income and deduction for the closed years and the shareholder reports all of these items on the shareholder's personal income tax return, basis is increased for items of income and basis is decreased for items of loss and deduction, but not below zero. Because the shareholder has reported and received the benefit of claiming these items of loss or deduction, the shareholder may not carry over any items of loss or deduction in excess of basis to future years.

The FTB has also taken the position that IRC Sec. 1016, the duty of consistency and/or the tax benefit rule, does not require a shareholder that reported items of loss and deduction in excess of the shareholder's basis in a closed year to increase the shareholder's income in an open year by the amount of the erroneous items of income and loss reported. In addition, a worthless loss deduction claimed in an open tax year generated from income items in an open tax year is not a double deduction, even if a shareholder reported losses in excess of basis in a closed year. The worthless loss deduction is not a double deduction with respect to the previous loss deductions. The basis that permits the taxpayer to take a deduction was generated from the income items in the open year. It is not attributable to any basis that was previously used. (*Technical Advice Memorandum 2003-305*, FTB, June 4, 2005, CCH California Tax Reports, ¶404-567)

• *Nonresident shareholders*

Nonresident shareholders are taxed on the portion of their distributive shares of an S corporation's income or loss, as modified for California purposes, that is derived from sources within the state. (Sec. 17951, Rev. & Tax. Code)

S corporations are required to withhold tax at a rate of 7% on distributions of California source income paid to their nonresident shareholders if the annual distributions to a shareholder are at least $1,500. (Sec. 18662, Rev. & Tax. Code; FTB Pub. 1017, Resident and Nonresident Withholding Guidelines) These shareholders typically must file California Form 540NR, California Nonresident or Part-Year Resident Income Tax Return, to report such income and pay any additional tax due or claim a refund. However, these shareholders may request a waiver of the withholding requirement using Form 588, Nonresident Withholding Waiver Request, or may elect to file a group nonresident return, which is discussed in detail at ¶619. (*Tax News*, California Franchise Tax Board, December 2006) See ¶714 for details.

CCH Practice Tip: Nonresident Group Returns

Nonresident shareholders should carefully weigh whether it makes sense to file a Form 540NR (California Nonresident Income Tax Return) or elect to file a group return. The group return is much less cumbersome. However, because taxpayers are precluded from claiming the personal exemption credit and a net operating loss on the group return and are also limited to claiming only those credits generated by the S corporation, the tax is often higher on the group return than if the nonresident completes an individual Form 540NR.

• *Part-year resident shareholders*

A part-year resident shareholder's distributive share of S corporation income is taxed based on the shareholder's period of residency and nonresidency during the S corporation's taxable year. The allocation of income between the period of residency and the period of nonresidency must be made in a manner that reflects the actual date of realization. In the absence of information that reflects the actual date of realization, the S corporation income for the corporation's taxable year must be allocated on a proportional basis between the two periods, using a daily pro rata method. (FTB Pub. 1100, Taxation of Nonresidents and Individuals Who Change Residency, CCH California Tax Reports, ¶403-885)

Practitioner Comment: Sourcing of Pass-Through Income

In Legal Ruling 2003-1, CCH California Tax Reports, ¶403-434, the FTB explains the computation of California income for owners of pass-through entities that change residency status during the year. Ch. 920 (A.B. 1115), Laws 2001, requires owners of pass-through entities to treat the items of income, deduction, and credit earned by such entities as if the items were earned by the owners at the same time and in the same manner as earned by the pass-through entity.

As noted in the ruling, the computation method is a significant shift from the method used in pre-2002 taxable years, which employed an accrual concept of accounting and looked to the individual's residency status on the last day of the pass-through entity's tax year. Under the prior method, if an individual moved out of California before the pass-through entity's year-end, the nonresident individual would only be taxed on his or her distributive share of pass-through entity income derived from California sources.

Taxpayers should keep in mind that the change to the sourcing of pass-through entity income described in the FTB's ruling is by no means clear in the provisions of A.B. 1115, so we may well see some taxpayers challenge the position outlined in the ruling.

Chris Whitney, Contributing Editor

¶234 Merchant Marine Act Exemptions

Law: Sec. 17088.3 (CCH CALIFORNIA TAX REPORTS, ¶192-869).

Comparable Federal: Sec. 7518.

California Form: Sch. CA (540) (California Adjustments - Residents).

Under Sec. 607 of the federal Merchant Marine Act, commercial fishermen and carriers can deposit part of their income in a special reserve fund to acquire or construct vessels, and can reduce their federal taxable income accordingly. Federal law, as adopted by California, provides detailed rules for treatment of deposits, withdrawals from the fund, etc. (Sec. 17088.3, Rev. & Tax. Code)

¶235 Cost-of-Living and Peace Corps Allowances

Law: None (CCH CALIFORNIA TAX REPORTS, ¶16-060).

Comparable Federal: Sec. 912.

California Form: Sch. CA (540) (California Adjustments - Residents).

California has no provisions comparable to a federal law specifically excluding from income certain cost-of-living allowances of civilian officers and employees of the U.S. Government residing outside the U.S., and certain allowances of Peace Corps volunteers. In *Appeal of Sammie W. and Harriet C. Gillentine* (1975) (CCH CALIFORNIA TAX REPORTS, ¶16-060.20), the taxpayer (presumably a California resident) received a cost-of-living allowance as a U.S. Government employee stationed in Hawaii. The State Board of Equalization held that the allowance was subject to California income tax.

¶236 Relocation Payments

Law: Sec. 7269, Government Code (CCH CALIFORNIA TAX REPORTS, ¶16-332).

Comparable Federal: Public Law 91-646.

Both California and federal laws provide that a person who is displaced from real property by a public entity may receive tax-exempt governmental assistance in the form of relocation payments.

California law also allows taxpayers to exclude from gross income tenant relocation assistance payments if such payments are required by state law or local ordinance. (Sec. 7269, Govt. Code)

¶237 Income from Original Issue Discount

Law: Secs. 17024.5, 17224, 18151, 18178 (CCH CALIFORNIA TAX REPORTS, ¶15-720, 16-075, 16-280).

Comparable Federal: Secs. 163(e), 1271-88, 6706 (CCH U.S. MASTER TAX GUIDE ¶1859 et seq., 1952 et seq.).

California Forms: Sch. CA (540) (California Adjustments - Residents), Sch. CA (540NR) (California Adjustments - Residents or Part-Year Residents).

The reporting of income from original issue discount by the holder of debt instruments is the same under California law as federal as of the current IRC tie-in date (¶103).

"Original issue discount" is the excess of the stated redemption price of a debt instrument at maturity over its issue price.

Although California generally conforms to the federal interest deduction allowed under IRC Sec. 163, an addition adjustment may be required by issuers of original issue discount (OID) for debt instruments issued in 1985 and 1986. Unlike federal law, an issuer is required to deduct the amount of OID attributable to the instrument each year. However, different rules applied in California for debt instruments issued in 1985 or 1986 and California law requires that any differences between state and federal law concerning the OID for these instruments be taken into account in the year that the debt instrument matures, is sold, exchanged, or otherwise disposed of. (Sec. 17224, Rev. & Tax. Code) Consequently, issuers of the debt instruments must make an addition adjustment to the extent that the amount eligible for deduction for California personal income tax purposes exceeds the amount reported on the federal return. A subtraction is allowed if the federal deduction exceeds the California deduction.

California conforms to the federal law used to determine how much original issue discount a purchaser of tax-exempt stripped bonds or coupons must attribute to those bonds or coupons. California also conforms to the federal provision that splits the yield on certain high-yield OID obligations into a deductible interest element and a nondeductible element representing return on equity. (Sec. 18151, Rev. & Tax. Code; Sec. 18178, Rev. & Tax. Code)

The Franchise Tax Board has taken the position that OID on "stripped" U.S. Treasury obligations is interest on U.S. obligations and is exempt from California taxation. Such obligations include securities such as TIGRs and CATs, which are issued by investment firms (¶217).

¶238 Expense Reimbursements

Law: Secs. 17081, 17131 (CCH CALIFORNIA TAX REPORTS, ¶15-515, 15-760).

Comparable Federal: Secs. 82, 123, 132 (CCH U.S. MASTER TAX GUIDE ¶877, 1076).

Specific rules are provided for certain types of expense reimbursement. California law incorporates federal law by reference as of the current IRC tie-in date (see ¶103). (Sec. 17081, Rev. & Tax. Code; Sec. 17131, Rev. & Tax. Code)

• *Moving expenses*

California adopts federal law allowing a taxpayer to exclude from gross income as a qualified fringe benefit any amount received by the taxpayer from an employer for moving expenses that would have been deductible by the taxpayer if they had not been reimbursed. (Sec. 17081, Rev. & Tax. Code)

The source of reimbursed moving expenses is the state to which the taxpayer moves, regardless of the taxpayer's place of residence when the reimbursement is made. (FTB Pub. 1031, Guidelines for Determining Residency Status)

Moving expense deductions are discussed at ¶328.

• *Loss on sale of home*

Generally, reimbursement for a loss on sale of a personal residence would be includible in income because the loss would be a personal one and nondeductible. However, where the loss is incurred in another state in connection with a move to California, the taxpayer might take the position that the reimbursement is compensation for services outside California during the period before he or she became a California resident and therefore is not taxable in California (¶405). On the other hand, the Franchise Tax Board (FTB) has taken the position that such a reimbursement is, in effect, a bonus for future services in California and is taxable.

CCH Practice Tip: Reimbursement of Loss May Be Excludable

Under the FTB's reasoning, it would appear that reimbursement for a loss on the sale of a personal residence in connection with a move from California to another state would not be includible in California income.

Appeal of William H. Harmount and Estate of Dorothy E. Harmount (1977) (CCH CALIFORNIA TAX REPORTS, ¶205-777) involved a taxpayer who moved in 1970 from Illinois to California. As an inducement to accept employment in California, the new employer reimbursed the taxpayer for certain expenses, including $5,031 for expenses in connection with the sale of an Illinois home. The State Board of Equalization held that the reimbursement represented compensation for services to be performed in California, subject to California tax. To the same effect, see *Appeal of Peter M. and Anita B. Berk* (1984) (CCH CALIFORNIA TAX REPORTS, ¶ 15-535.33). See also the *Frame* case, discussed at ¶ 405, holding in effect that the source of the reimbursement income is irrelevant if the income "accrues" after the taxpayer becomes a California resident.

- *Living expenses*

Reimbursement from an insurance company for excess living expenses paid as a result of destruction (or threatened destruction) of the taxpayer's home by fire or other casualty is excluded from gross income under both California (Sec. 17081, Rev. & Tax. Code) and federal law (IRC Sec. 123).

¶239 Community Income

Law: Sec. 771, Family Code (CCH CALIFORNIA TAX REPORTS, ¶ 15-125).

Comparable Federal: Secs. 66, 879 (CCH U.S. MASTER TAX GUIDE ¶ 710).

In general, in the absence of an agreement to the contrary, earnings of spouses and registered domestic partners (RDPs) who are domiciled in California and are not permanently separated are community property. On separate returns, any community income or deductions must be split equally between the spouses or RDPs. The credit for a dependent supported by community funds may be taken by either spouse or RDP.

Caution Note: Registered Domestic Partners

California's community property tax laws also apply to registered domestic partners (RDPs) (see ¶ 119). Consequently, RDPs who file separate income tax returns must each report one-half of the combined income earned by both RDPs, as spouses do, rather than their respective individual incomes for the taxable year. (Uncodified Sec. 1, Ch. 802 (S.B. 1827), Laws 2006)

FTB Pub. 1031 (Guidelines for Determining Residency Status) provides a useful chart that demonstrates how income should be reported if a spouses or RDPs are residents of different states and how to treat their respective incomes, depending on whether the state of residency is a community property or separate property state.

Where the spouses or RDPs are separated with no intention of resuming the marital relationship, the earnings of each spouse or RDP during the period of separation are his or her separate property. This is the effect of a provision of the Family Code. (Sec. 771, Fam. Code)

Both California and federal law provide relief for the "innocent spouse" in certain community-property situations and empower the Internal Revenue Service/ Franchise Tax Board to treat community income as separate under certain conditions (¶ 107).

Where one spouse is a nonresident alien, community property laws are inapplicable to some extent for federal income tax purposes; California has not conformed to this federal treatment.

Several decisions of the State Board of Equalization (BOE) have held a California-resident wife taxable on one-half of her nonresident husband's earnings, on the ground that the husband was domiciled in California and his earnings were therefore community property. See *Appeal of Annette Bailey* (1976) (CCH CALIFORNIA TAX REPORTS, ¶ 15-125.252), where the husband was a resident of Canada and *Appeal of Nancy B. Meadows* (1980) (CCH CALIFORNIA TAX REPORTS, ¶ 15-252.259), where the husband was a resident of Alabama.

Also, see *Appeal of George F. and Magdalena Herrman* (1962) (CCH CALIFORNIA TAX REPORTS, ¶ 15-125.25), where the husband was a resident and domiciliary of the State of Washington: the BOE held the wife taxable on one-half of the husband's income because she was entitled to it under Washington law. To the same effect, see *Appeal of Roy L. and Patricia A. Misskelley* (1984) (CCH CALIFORNIA TAX REPORTS, ¶ 15-125.255); in this case the husband was a resident and domiciliary of Nevada.

In *Appeal of Richard and Eva Taylor* (1989) (CCH CALIFORNIA TAX REPORTS, ¶ 15-125.257), a wife was liable for tax on her community share of her husband's foreign earnings, and he was liable for tax on his community share of her California earnings because even though the husband established and maintained foreign residence, both spouses remained California domiciliaries.

¶240 Income from Investments in Depressed Areas

Law: Sec. 17235 (CCH CALIFORNIA TAX REPORTS, ¶ 16-280).

Comparable Federal: None.

California Forms: FTB 3805Z (Enterprise Zone Deduction and Credit Summary).

California allows a deduction for net interest received prior to January 1, 2014, from loans made to a trade or business located in an enterprise zone (¶ 104). It does not apply to anyone who has an ownership interest in the debtor. The deduction is repealed beginning with the 2014 taxable year. (Sec. 17235, Rev. & Tax. Code)

According to the Instructions to the FTB 3805Z, Enterprise Zone Deduction and Credit Summary, the deduction may only be claimed for payments received on or before the zone's expiration date.

The deduction for interest received from loans made to an enterprise zone business is reported on FTB 3805Z.

¶241 Ridesharing and Employee Commuter Deductions

Law: Secs. 17090, 17149 (CCH CALIFORNIA TAX REPORTS, ¶ 15-705, 16-065, 16-265).

Comparable Federal: Sec. 132 (CCH U.S. MASTER TAX GUIDE ¶ 863).

California Forms: Sch. CA (540) (California Adjustments - Residents), Sch. CA (540NR) (California Adjustments - Nonresidents or Part-Year Residents).

Compensation or the fair market value of nonwage benefits furnished by an employer to an employee for participation in any employer-sponsored ridesharing program in California is excluded from the employee's California gross income. This includes compensation or benefits received for the following items:

— commuting in a vanpool, subscription taxipool, carpool, buspool, private commuter bus, or ferry;

— transit passes for use by employees or their dependents, other than transit passes for use by dependents who are elementary or secondary school students;

— free or subsidized parking for employees who participate in ridesharing arrangements;

— bicycling to or from work;

— travel to or from a telecommuting facility; or

— use of any other alternative transportation method that reduces the use of a motor vehicle by a single occupant for travel to or from that individual's place of employment.

(Sec. 17149, Rev. & Tax. Code)

Unlike the California gross income exclusion for ridesharing and employee commuter deductions, including the value of parking provided to ridesharing participants, the federal exclusion is subject to a cap.

Cash allowances received by an employee pursuant to a parking cash-out program (¶ 343), unless used for ridesharing purposes, must be included in the employee's gross income. (Sec. 17090, Rev. & Tax. Code)

¶242 Employee Educational Assistance Plans

Law: Sec. 17151 (CCH CALIFORNIA TAX REPORTS, ¶15-685).

Comparable Federal: Sec. 127 (CCH U.S. MASTER TAX GUIDE ¶871).

California law is substantially the same as federal law concerning the exclusion of up to $5,250 of employer-provided educational assistance benefits from an employee's gross income. (Sec. 17151, Rev. & Tax. Code)

¶243 Payments for Conservation and Environmental Protection

Law: Secs. 17131, 17135.5 (CCH CALIFORNIA TAX REPORTS, ¶15-690, 16-260).

Comparable Federal: Sec. 126 (CCH U.S. MASTER TAX GUIDE ¶881).

California incorporates the federal exclusion for cost-sharing payments received under certain conservation and environmental protection programs. (Sec. 17131, Rev. & Tax. Code)

• *Payments received by forest landowners*

In addition, California provides a specific exclusion from gross income for cost-share payments received by forest landowners from the Department of Forestry and Fire Protection pursuant to the California Forest Improvement Act of 1978 or from the United States Department of Agriculture, Forest Service, under the Forest Stewardship Program and the Stewardship Incentives Program, pursuant to the federal Cooperative Forestry Assistance Act. The amount of any excluded payment must not be considered for a determination of the basis of property acquired or improved or in computation of any deduction to which the taxpayer may otherwise be entitled. (Sec. 17135.5, Rev. & Tax. Code)

¶244 Water Conservation Rebates and Vouchers

Law: Secs. 17138, 17138.2 (CCH CALIFORNIA TAX REPORTS, ¶16-260).

Comparable Federal: None.

California Forms: Sch. CA (540) (California Adjustments - Residents), Sch. CA (540NR) (California Adjustments - Nonresidents or Part-Year Residents).

California law treats certain water conservation rebates and vouchers received by taxpayers from local water or energy agencies or suppliers as excludable refunds or price adjustments rather than as taxable income for personal income tax purposes. To qualify, a rebate/voucher must be for the taxpayer's expenses in purchasing or installing

— water conservation water closets or urinals that meet specified performance standards and use no more than (1) 1.6 gallons per flush in the case of a water closet or (2) 1 gallon per flush in the case of a urinal;

— a water and energy efficient clothes washer; and/or

— a plumbing device necessary to use recycled water for toilet and urinal flushing in structures if required by a state or local agency.

(Sec. 17138, Rev. & Tax. Code)

For taxable years beginning after 2013 and before 2019, California also excludes from gross income any amount received as a rebate, voucher, or other financial incentive issued by a local water agency or supplier for participation in a turf removal water conservation program. (Sec. 17138.2, Rev. & Tax. Code)

¶245 Energy Conservation Subsidies and Federal Energy Grants

Law: Secs. 17131, 17131.3, 17138.1, Rev. & Tax. Code; Secs. 25433.5 and 25434.5, Public Resources Code (CCH CALIFORNIA TAX REPORTS, ¶ 15-690, 16-260, 112-001).

Comparable Federal: Sec. 136 (CCH U.S. MASTER TAX GUIDE ¶ 884).

California incorporates the federal gross income exclusion for subsidies received from a public utility for the purchase or installation of an energy conservation measure designed to reduce the consumption of electricity or natural gas or to improve the management of energy demand with respect to a dwelling unit. (Sec. 17131, Rev. & Tax. Code)

In addition, like federal law, California excludes from gross income and alternative minimum taxable income federal energy grants provided in lieu of federal energy credits. However, the basis of the property purchased with the grant is reduced by 50% of the amount of the grant. (Sec. 17131.3, Rev. & Tax. Code)

Energy-efficient home improvement grants awarded by the State Energy Resources Conservation and Development Commission to an individual with a gross annual income equal to or less than 200% of the federal poverty level are excluded from the individual's gross income (Sec. 25433.5, Pub. Res. Code).

California specifically excludes from gross income any amount received as a rebate, voucher, or other financial incentive issued by the California Energy Commission, the California Public Utilities Commission, or a local public utility for the purchase or installation of the following:

— thermal energy systems

— solar energy systems

— wind energy systems that produce electricity, and

— fuel cell generating systems that produce electricity.

(Sec. 17138.1, Rev. & Tax. Code)

¶246 Crime Hotline Rewards

Law: Sec. 17147.7 (CCH CALIFORNIA TAX REPORTS, ¶ 16-325).

Comparable Federal: None.

California Forms: Sch. CA (540) (California Adjustments - Residents), Sch. CA (540NR) (California Adjustments - Nonresidents or Part-Year Residents).

Rewards received from a crime hotline are excludable from gross income if the hotline is established by a government agency or a California nonprofit charitable organization and is authorized by a government entity. Employees of a government agency or nonprofit charitable organization that contributes reward funds to the crime hotline are ineligible to claim this exclusion. (Sec. 17147.7, Rev. & Tax. Code)

¶247 Medical and Health Savings Accounts

Law: Secs. 17131.4, 17131.5, 17201, 17215, 17215.1 (CCH CALIFORNIA TAX REPORTS, ¶ 15-755, 16-100).

Comparable Federal: Secs. 138, 220, 223 (CCH U.S. MASTER TAX GUIDE ¶ 860).

California Form: FTB 3805P (Additional Taxes on Qualified Plans (Including IRAs) and Other Tax-Favored Accounts).

Except as noted below, California incorporates federal law concerning medical savings accounts (MSAs), but does not follow the federal treatment of health savings accounts (HSAs).

• *Medical savings accounts*

With the exception of the amount of penalties imposed on unauthorized withdrawals, California law is the same as federal law as of the current IRC tie-in date (¶ 103). Employer's contributions to an Archer MSA and any interest or dividends earned on an Archer MSA are excluded from a taxpayer's gross income. (Sec. 17201, Rev. & Tax. Code)

Withdrawals made from an Archer MSA are also exempt if used to pay unreimbursed qualified medical expenses of the taxpayer, spouse, and dependents (which are essentially the same as those expenses that qualify for an itemized deduction). Distributions from an Archer MSA for nonmedical purposes are treated as taxable income and are subject to a 10% penalty for California purposes (increased to 12.5% for disbursements made during taxable years beginning on or after January 1, 2016), unless the distribution is made after the taxpayer reaches age 65, becomes disabled, or dies. (Sec. 17215, Rev. & Tax. Code) For federal purposes, the penalty is 20%. The penalty is reported for California purposes on FTB 3805P.

CCH Comment: Registered Domestic Partners

Although registered domestic partners (RDPs) or former RDPs are required to be treated as married taxpayers or former spouses under California income and franchise tax laws, an RDP will not be treated as a spouse if such treatment would result in disqualification of an Archer medical savings account. (Sec. 17021.7, Rev. & Tax. Code)

• *Medicare Plus Choice MSAs/Medicare Advantage MSAs*

Under both California and federal law, certain seniors are permitted to establish Medicare Plus Choice MSAs (renamed the Medicare Advantage MSA under federal law). (Sec. 17201, Rev. & Tax. Code) The tax treatment of Medicare Plus Choice MSAs is similar to that of regular MSAs, with the following exceptions:

— tax-free distributions from the Medicare Plus Choice MSA may be used only for the qualified medical expenses of the account holder;

— the Secretary of Health and Human Services, rather than the account holder's employer, makes tax-free contributions to the Medicare Plus Choice MSA; and

— a Medicare Plus Choice MSA may only be used in conjunction with a high deductible Medicare Plus Choice MSA health plan (MSA health plan).

• *Health savings accounts*

California does not incorporate the federal gross income exclusion of employer contributions to HSAs. (Sec. 17131.4, Rev. & Tax. Code; Sec. 17131.5, Rev. & Tax. Code) Nor does California incorporate the federal deduction for taxpayer contributions to an HSA (see ¶326).

Planning Note: Employer Contributions Excluded From W-2 Wages

Because employers are required to exclude HSA contributions made to eligible employees from their W-2 wages, employers must reflect California and federal wage differences on their employees' Form W-2s.

Interest and dividends earned on HSAs are also subject to California personal income tax. Because such amounts are excluded from federal adjusted gross income, an addition adjustment is required for the excluded interest and dividends.

Finally, amounts rolled over from a medical savings account into an HSA are excluded from federal income tax, but subject to California personal income tax. (Sec. 17215.1, Rev. & Tax. Code) The amount withdrawn from the MSA is subject to California's penalty on nonqualified withdrawals (discussed above).

Practice Note: Treatment of Nonqualified Distributions

Nonqualified distributions from HSAs are subject to federal tax. However, because contributions to and earnings on HSAs are subject to California personal income tax, such distributions are not subject to California personal income taxation. The adjustment is made on Sch. CA (540), line 21f, column B. (Instructions, Sch. CA (540), California Adjustments—Residents)

¶248 Holocaust, Internment, and Genocide Victim Compensation

Law: Secs. 17131.1, 17131.2, 17155, 17155.5, 17156.5 (CCH CALIFORNIA TAX REPORTS, ¶ 16-335).

Comparable Federal: United States-Federal Republic of Germany Income Tax Convention; Sec. 803 of the Economic Growth and Tax Relief Reconciliation Act of 2001 (P.L. 107-16) (CCH U.S. MASTER TAX GUIDE ¶ 802).

California Form: Sch. CA (540) (California Adjustments - Residents).

California law mirrors federal law (Sec. 803, P.L. 107-16) that excludes from gross income Holocaust restitution payments and related interest received by an eligible individual or the individual's heirs or estate. In addition, California provides exclusions for Canadian government reparation payments paid to persons of Japanese ancestry and to Armenian genocide settlement payments. (Sec. 17131.1, Rev. & Tax. Code)

• *Holocaust restitution payments*

For purposes of the exclusion for Holocaust restitution payments, an eligible individual is a person who was persecuted by Nazi Germany, any other Axis regime, or any other Nazi-controlled or Nazi- allied country on the basis of the person's race, religion, physical or mental disability, or sexual orientation. An excludable restitution payment is a payment or distribution to an individual or the individual's heirs or estate that is one of the following:

(1) payable by reason of the individual's status as an eligible individual;

(2) the direct or indirect return of, or compensation or reparation for, assets stolen or hidden from or otherwise lost to the individual before, during, or immediately after World War II by reason of the individual's status as an eligible individual; or

(3) interest payable as part of any payment or distribution described in (1) or (2), above.

Excludable interest is interest earned from

— escrow accounts or settlement funds established pursuant to the settlement of *In re Holocaust Victim Assets Litigation*, U.S. District Court, Eastern District of New York, C.A. No. 96-4849, August 12, 1998;

— certain funds to benefit individuals or their heirs that are created by the International Commission on Holocaust Insurance Claims; or

— similar funds subject to the administration of the U.S. courts that are created to provide excludable restitution payments to eligible individuals or their heirs or estates.

For purposes of the exclusion, the basis of any property received by an eligible individual or the individual's heirs or estate as part of an excludable restitution payment is the fair market value of the property at the time of receipt. (Sec. 17131.1, Rev. & Tax. Code)

Under California's Holocaust Victim Compensation Relief Act, as under federal law, payments or property received as compensation pursuant to the German Act Regulating Unresolved Property Claims are also excludable from an individual's gross income. The basis of any property received pursuant to the German Act is the fair market value of the property at the time of receipt by the individual. (Sec. 17155, Rev. & Tax. Code)

In addition, California law allows Holocaust victims, or their heirs or beneficiaries, to exclude from gross income settlements received for claims against any entity or individual for any recovered asset. For purposes of the expanded exclusion, "Holocaust victim" means any person who was persecuted by Nazi Germany or any Axis regime during any period from 1933 to 1945. "Recovered asset" means any asset of any kind, including any bank deposits, insurance proceeds, or artwork owned by a Holocaust victim during any period from 1920 to 1945, inclusive, and any interest earned on the asset, that was withheld from that victim or the victim's heirs or beneficiaries from and after 1945 and that was not recovered, returned, or otherwise compensated to the victim or his or her heirs or beneficiaries until after 1994. Humanitarian reparation payments made to persons required to perform slave or forced labor during World War II are excluded for California, but not federal, income tax purposes. (Sec. 17155.5, Rev. & Tax. Code)

• *Japanese internment reparation payments*

California law, but not federal law, also excludes from gross income reparation payments made by the Canadian government for the purpose of redressing the injustice done to persons of Japanese ancestry who were interned in Canada during World War II. (Sec. 17156.5, Rev. & Tax. Code)

• *Armenian genocide settlement payments*

Settlement payments and related interest received by eligible individuals (or by the heirs or estates of eligible individuals) who were persecuted on the basis of race or religion during the Armenian genocide (1915—1923) are excludable from gross income for California personal income tax purposes. (Sec. 17131.2, Rev. & Tax. Code)

¶249 Adoption Assistance Programs

Law: Sec. 17131 (CCH California Tax Reports, ¶15-605).

Comparable Federal: Sec. 137 (CCH U.S. Master Tax Guide ¶1306).

Under both California and federal law, an employee may exclude from his or her gross income amounts paid or expenses incurred for the employee's qualified adoption expenses as part of an employer's written, nondiscriminatory, adoption assistance program.

¶250 Qualified Tuition Programs

Law: Secs. 17140, 17140.3, 19304 (CCH California Tax Reports, ¶15-685).

Comparable Federal: Secs. 529, 530 (CCH U.S. Master Tax Guide ¶697).

California Form: FTB 3805P (Additional Taxes on Qualified Plans (Including IRAs) and Other Tax-Favored Accounts).

California incorporates IRC Sec. 529, as of California's current IRC conformity date (see ¶103), concerning qualified tuition programs, which excludes from the gross income of a beneficiary of, or contributor to, a qualified tuition program, qualified distributions or earnings under such program. To qualify for the exclusion, distributions must be used to pay for a beneficiary's qualified higher education expenses. However, amounts distributed to a contributor (*e.g.,* refunds to a parent or other relative) will be included in the contributor's gross income to the extent that such amounts exceed the contributions made by that person. (Sec. 17140.3, Rev. & Tax. Code)

Distributions are also not taxable under the annuity rules if they are transferred within 60 days to another qualified tuition program for the benefit of the designated beneficiary (limited to once in a 12-month period) or to the credit of another beneficiary under a qualified tuition program who is a family member of the designated beneficiary. Also, a change in beneficiary will not be treated as a distribution if the new beneficiary is a member of the previously designated beneficiary's family.

Practice Note: EGTRRA Amendments Made Permanent

The Pension Protection Act of 2006 (PPA) (P.L. 109-280) made permanent the amendments enacted by the Economic Growth and Tax Relief and Reconciliation Act (EGTRRA) (P.L. 107-16) that affect qualified tuition programs. (Uncodified Sec. 1304 of the PPA) These amendments were originally scheduled to expire at the end of 2010.

California incorporates the EGTRRA's sunset date provision "in the same manner and to the same taxable years as it applies for federal income tax purposes." (Sec. 17024.5(a)(2)(B), Rev. & Tax. Code) As the PPA made the sunset provision inapplicable to the EGTRRA amendments that impacted qualified tuition programs, it appears as though California would similarly disregard the sunset provision and make these amendments permanent for California income tax purposes as well.

Distributions not used for qualified education expenses are subject to a 2.5% penalty (10% for federal purposes). (Sec. 17140.3, Rev. & Tax. Code) The penalty is reported on FTB 3805P.

California law contains a provision specifically addressing California's qualified state tuition program, the "Golden State Scholarshare Trust," which generally mirrors the treatment of contributions to, and distributions from, a qualified tuition program. (Sec. 17140, Rev. & Tax. Code)

Practice Note: Direct Deposit of Portion of Refund

The FTB is required to revise the personal income tax return form instructions to include information about the ability of a taxpayer to directly deposit a portion of a refund of any overpayment of taxes into the Golden State Scholarshare College Savings Trust. (Sec. 19304, Rev. & Tax. Code)

Practice Pointer: Contributors May Remove Funds from Account

If the beneficiary of a Scholarshare account does not ever attend a qualified educational institution, or if there are still funds in the account after the beneficiary graduates from a qualified educational institution, the funds can be transferred to a Scholarshare account for the benefit of another family member. Alternatively, the contributor to the account may cancel the account and take back the available funds, but must pay taxes on any earnings, as well as a penalty.

¶251 Disaster Relief Payments

Law: Secs. 17131, 17131.10 (CCH CALIFORNIA TAX REPORTS, ¶ 15-675).

Comparable Federal: Secs. 139, 139A (CCH U.S. MASTER TAX GUIDE ¶ 897).

California Form: Sch. CA (540) (California Adjustments - Residents).

California conforms to federal law, which excludes from gross income qualified disaster relief payments received as a result of terroristic or military actions against the United States or one of its allies, federally-declared disasters, common carrier accidents, other events determined by the Secretary of the Internal Revenue Service to be of a catastrophic nature, or disasters determined to warrant federal, state, or local government assistance. Under federal law, as incorporated by California, these payments are excludable only to the extent the payment is not otherwise compensated for by insurance or otherwise. (Sec. 17131, Rev. & Tax. Code)

For purposes of the disaster relief payment exclusion, California treats the natural gas transmission line explosion and fire that occurred in San Bruno, California, on September 9, 2010, as a federally declared disaster even though the explosion and fire were never declared an official federal disaster. (Sec. 17131.10, Rev. & Tax. Code)

¶252 Prescription Drug Subsidies and Indian Tribe-Provided Health Care Benefits

Law: Secs. 17131, 17139.6 (CCH CALIFORNIA TAX REPORTS, ¶ 16-100).

Comparable Federal: Secs. 139A, 139D (CCH U.S. MASTER TAX GUIDE ¶ 859, 896B, 896C).

An addition adjustment is required for the federal government subsidies provided to employers to compensate them for costs incurred in a qualified retiree prescription drug plan that are excluded from the employer's federal taxable income under IRC Sec. 139A. (Sec. 17139.6, Rev. & Tax. Code)

California has incorporated the federal exclusion of qualified health care benefits provided to a member of an Indian tribe, the member's spouse, or the member's dependents under IRC Sec. 139D. Consequently, no addition adjustment is required. (Sec. 17131, Rev. & Tax. Code)

¶253 Dependent Care Assistance

Law: Secs. 17021.7, 17131 (CCH CALIFORNIA TAX REPORTS, ¶15-660).

Comparable Federal: Sec. 129 (CCH U.S. MASTER TAX GUIDE ¶869).

California generally incorporates federal law concerning dependent care assistance programs. Consequently, taxpayers who claim the exclusion of payments of up to $5,000 ($2,500 in the case of a married person filing separately) to an employee for dependent care assistance, when made under an employer's written nondiscriminatory plan, on the federal return are not required to make an adjustment on their California return. However, adjustments may be required by registered domestic partners (RDPs) who claim the deduction on their federal return. (Sec. 17021.7, Rev. & Tax. Code)

For RDPs filing a joint return, an addition adjustment must be made on the California return if the RDPs' combined exclusion exceeded $5,000 on their federal returns. Similarly, an RDP filing separately must make an addition adjustment on his or her California return if he or she excluded more than $2,500 of dependent care assistance benefits on his or her federal return. (FTB Pub. 737, Tax Information for Registered Domestic Partnerships)

¶254 Income Received by Native Americans

Law: (CCH CALIFORNIA TAX REPORTS, ¶15-180).

California Form: FTB 3504 (Enrolled Tribal Member Certification).

Income received by Native Americans from Indian country sources is exempt from personal income taxation. To be exempt, the taxpayer must be a member of a federally recognized tribe and must live in Indian country. In addition, the income earned must be from the same Indian country source where the taxpayer resides and is a tribal member. Wages earned on an Indian reservation may be subtracted on Schedule CA (540 or 540NR), line 7, column B. Other sources of income should be subtracted on Line 21(f).

Practice Tip: Reservation-Source Income Paid by Non-Tribal Employers Exempt From Tax

The Franchise Tax Board (FTB) has announced a reversal in its position concerning the exemption of income earned by a tribal member while residing on his or her tribal lands and paid by a non-tribal payer. Previously, the FTB had taken the position that the exemption applied only if the income earned was paid by a tribal payer. In April 2013, the FTB announced that taxpayers who had previously reported tribal-source income as taxable income may file a claim for refund or credit if the claim is filed within four years from the return's original due date or four years from the date the return is timely filed (including the automatic extension period), or if payment was made within one year of the date the refund claim was filed. (*Reservation Source Income—Not Subject to Taxation,* (2013), CCH CALIFORNIA TAX REPORTS, ¶405-874)

An amended return, with the notation "Reservation Source Income" marked in red at the top, should be mailed to:

Reservation Source Income Claim for Refund 347 MS F381,

Franchise Tax Board,

PO Box 1779

Rancho Cordova CA 95741-1779

Returns sent by private carrier or deliver service should be sent to

Franchise Tax Board

Reservation Source Income Claim for Refund 347 MS F381

Sacramento CA 94267-0001

A listing of federally recognized California Indian tribes is available by searching for "federally recognized" on the National Conference of State Legislatures Web site at http://www.ncsl.org. In a non-citable letter decision, the California State Board of Equalization abstained from determining whether land that was not within a specified allotment given to a tribe, but was within the exterior boundaries of the Indian reservation, constituted Indian country. (*Appeal of Miguel-Ruiz* (2009), CCH CALIFORNIA TAX REPORTS, ¶404-941)

If a P.O. Box is used as a Native American's mailing address, his or her physical residence address must be included in the blank line on Line 21(f). (*FTB Pub. 1001, Supplemental Guidelines to California Adjustments*, CCH CALIFORNIA TAX REPORTS, ¶404-588; *FTB Pub. 674, Frequently Asked Questions About the Income Taxation of Native American Indians*, revised April 2010, CCH CALIFORNIA TAX REPORTS, ¶405-371)

Planning Note: Proof of Indian Reservation Residency

Taxpayers claiming an exemption based on residency on an Indian reservation need to gather and retain documentation to support their residency claim. A statement from the Indian tribe council stating that an individual has a home on the reservation is not sufficient. Records such as homeowner's or renter's insurance policies, motor vehicle licenses, automobile insurance policies, utility bills etc, showing an Indian reservation address should be maintained. Declarations from an individual's parents, friends, or relatives verifying the individual's Indian reservation residency may also be used to support an individual's Indian reservation residency claim. (*FTB Pub. 674, Frequently Asked Questions About the Income Taxation of Native American Indians*, revised April 2010, CCH CALIFORNIA TAX REPORTS, ¶405-371)

The FTB is reviewing its standards and procedures for purposes of determining whether a Native American is residing on a reservation and is in the process of revising Pub. 674. The FTB has held a tribal leaders consultation session and is continuing to work with tribal leaders to elicit input on how to determine whether a tribal member is "living on" or "living off" his or her own tribe's reservation for purposes of California personal income tax. In its initial discussion paper, the FTB proposes to adopt a "closest connections test," as set forth in *Appeal of Bragg*, 2003-SBE-002 (May 28, 2003), to make this determination.

- *Military income*

Military income is exempt if received by an Indian tribe member who is living outside Indian country as a result of military orders. (*FTB Pub. 674, Frequently Asked Questions About the Income Taxation of Native American Indians*, revised April 2010, CCH CALIFORNIA TAX REPORTS, ¶405-371)

- *Welfare benefits*

Under federal law, payments made to or on behalf of individuals under governmental programs are included within the broad definition of gross income under IRC Sec. 61 unless an exclusion applies. However, the IRS has consistently concluded that certain payments made to or on behalf of individuals by governmental units under governmentally provided social benefit programs for the promotion of the general welfare are not included in a recipient's gross income. This is known as the "general welfare exclusion." IRS Revenue Procedure 2014-35 provides detailed information for when certain tribal government benefits may be excluded from income under the general welfare exception. Since California conforms to IRC Sec. 61 under Sec. 17071, Rev. & Tax. Code, the FTB will follow Revenue Procedure 2014-35 in applying the general welfare exception for purposes of tribal government programs to tribal members. (*Tax News*, California Franchise Tax Board, March 2015, CCH CALIFORNIA TAX REPORTS, ¶406-310)

• *Tribal casino operation distributions*

Although federal law taxes income from tribal casino operations (per capita distributions) regardless of where the tribal member resides, California does not tax per capita distributions received by tribal members who live in Indian country affiliated with their tribe that are sourced from the same Indian country where they are members. A California court of appeal has held that California may impose its personal income tax on a per capita gaming distribution made by a Native American tribe to a tribal member that resided on another tribe's reservation. (*Mike v. FTB* (2010), CCH CALIFORNIA TAX REPORTS, ¶405-129). Distributions that are exempt under California law may be subtracted from federal income by entering the amount on Sch. CA (540 or 540NR), line 21f, column B. (*FTB Pub. 674, Frequently Asked Questions About the Income Taxation of Native American Indians*, revised April 2010, CCH CALIFORNIA TAX REPORTS, ¶405-371) See ¶714 for information regarding withholding on per capita distributions.

Practice Tip: Impact of Incarceration on Residency Determination

In a nonprecedential decision, the California State Board of Equalization (BOE) held that per capita distributions received by a Native American while he was incarcerated were subject to tax because the taxpayer was not a resident of the tribal reservation at the time the distributions were received. The BOE rejected the taxpayer's contention that he was still a resident because his incarceration amounted to an involuntary absence from the reservation. (*Appeal of Andrade* (2008), CCH CALIFORNIA TAX REPORTS, ¶404-636)

• *Return filing requirements*

Native Americans with income only from the Indian country in which they reside are not required to file a California income tax return. However, if California taxes are withheld, a California resident income tax return must be filed to receive a refund of the amounts withheld. (*FTB Pub. 674, Frequently Asked Questions About the Income Taxation of Native American Indians*, revised April 2010, CCH CALIFORNIA TAX REPORTS, ¶405-371)

¶255 ABLE Accounts

Law: Sec. 17140.4 (CCH CALIFORNIA TAX REPORTS, ¶15-673).

Comparable Federal: Sec. 529A (CCH U.S. MASTER TAX GUIDE ¶870).

California Form: FTB 3805P (Additional Taxes on Qualified Plans (Including IRAs) and Other Tax-Favored Accounts).

California generally incorporates federal law concerning Achieve a Better Living Experience (ABLE) programs, under which states are authorized to establish tax-favored savings accounts that may accept contributions and make distributions to pay for the expenses of certain individuals who are blind or disabled. Consequently, distributions from an ABLE account are not includible in the recipient's gross income unless they exceed the amount of "qualified disability expenses" incurred during the tax year. If the distribution is in excess of qualified disability expenses, the amount includible in gross income is the excess amount reduced by an amount in the same ratio as the expenses bear to the distributions. An additional 2.5% tax is required for ABLE distributions that are includible in gross income (10% for federal income tax purposes), unless the distribution is made after the death of the designated beneficiary. (Sec. 17140.4, Rev. & Tax. Code)

"Qualified disability expenses" include any expense related to the eligible individual's blindness or disability that is expended for the benefit of an eligible individual who is the designated beneficiary of an ABLE account in a qualified ABLE program. These include expenses for education, housing, transportation, employment training and support, assistive technology and personal support services, health, prevention and wellness, financial management and administrative services, legal fees, oversight and monitoring, and funeral and burial expenses. (Sec. 17140.4, Rev. & Tax. Code)

¶256 Earthquake Loss Mitigation Incentives

Law: Sec. 17138.3 (CCH CALIFORNIA TAX REPORTS, ¶16-255).

Comparable Federal: None.

California gross income does not include an amount received as a loan forgiveness, grant, credit, rebate, voucher, or other financial incentive issued by the California Residential Mitigation Program or the California Earthquake Authority to assist a residential property owner or occupant with expenses paid, or obligations incurred, for earthquake loss mitigation. "Earthquake loss mitigation" means an activity that reduces seismic risks to a residential structure or its contents, or both. For purposes of structural seismic risk mitigation, a residential structure is either (1) a structure described in Section 10087(a) of the Insurance Code; or (2) a residential building of not fewer than two, but not more than 10, dwelling units. (Sec. 17138.3, Rev. & Tax. Code)

PERSONAL INCOME TAX

CHAPTER 3

DEDUCTIONS

¶300 Deductions—Generally

Law: Sec. 17201 (CCH CALIFORNIA TAX REPORTS, ¶ 15-510).

Comparable Federal: Secs. 161-222, 261-280H (CCH U.S. MASTER TAX GUIDE ¶ 901 et seq., 1001 et seq., 1101 et seq., 1201 et seq.).

California Forms: Sch. CA (540) (California Adjustments - Residents), Sch. CA (540NR) (California Adjustments - Nonresidents or Part-Year Residents), FTB 3526 (Investment Interest Expense Deduction), FTB 3805V (Net Operating Loss (NOL) Computation and NOL and Disaster Loss Limitations - Individuals, Estates, and Trusts), FTB 3885A (Depreciation and Amortization Adjustments), FTB 3885F (Depreciation and Amortization), FTB 3885L (Depreciation and Amortization), FTB 3885P (Depreciation and Amortization).

In general, California conforms to federal law as of the current IRC tie-in date (¶ 103) regarding deductions that may be taken to reduce taxable income, but there are some differences that are discussed in the following paragraphs. (Sec. 17201, Rev. & Tax. Code) As under federal law, some deductions may be used to reduce gross income and others may be used to reduce adjusted gross income. Any differences between the amounts of the California deductions and the federal deductions must be reported on Sch. CA (540) or Sch. CA (540NR) (¶ 30, ¶ 31).

Practice Note: Registered Domestic Partners

California law, unlike federal law, treats registered domestic partners (RDPs) (see ¶ 119) as married taxpayers for California income tax purposes, unless specified exceptions apply.

In addition, some deductions may be limited because they arise from passive activities (¶ 340).

¶301 Trade or Business Expenses

Law: Secs. 17021.7, 17201, 17201.5, 17203, 17257, 17257.4, 17269, 17270, 17273, 17278 (CCH CALIFORNIA TAX REPORTS, ¶ 15-165, 15-805, 16-150).

Comparable Federal: Secs. 162, 179C, 179E, 190, 280A (CCH U.S. MASTER TAX GUIDE ¶ 901 et seq., 961 et seq., 1287).

California Forms: Sch. CA (540) (California Adjustments - Residents), Sch. CA (540NR) (California Adjustments - Nonresidents or Part-Year Residents).

All ordinary and necessary expenses of a trade or business are deductible. The California law is the same as the federal law as of the current IRC tie-in date (see ¶ 803) (Sec. 17201, Rev. & Tax. Code) except as follows:

— California prohibits deduction of certain types of expenses (illegal activities, etc.), as explained at ¶ 336.

— California has not adopted special federal rules for travel expenses of state legislators. (Sec. 17270(a), Rev. & Tax. Code)

— Where a federal tax credit is allowed for wages to provide new jobs, the wages are disallowed as a federal deduction; however, such wages are still allowed as a California deduction. (However, wages subject to the various hiring credits available to employers operating in economic incentive areas, described at ¶ 104, are not allowed as a California deduction.)

— California denies a business expense deduction for expenditures made at, or payments made to, a club that engages in discriminatory practices as explained at ¶ 336. (Sec. 17269, Rev. & Tax. Code)

— California, but not federal, law treats a taxpayer's registered domestic partner as the taxpayer's spouse for purposes of determining the amount that may be deducted for self-employed individual health insurance and amounts paid or incurred by the taxpayer as to certain group health plans under IRC Sec. 162(n). (Sec. 17021.7, Rev. & Tax. Code) Also, see ¶ 119 for a discussion of California's tax treatment of same-sex married couples.

— California law, unlike federal law, does not allow a current expense deduction for qualified film and television production costs (¶ 310). (Sec. 17201.5, Rev. & Tax. Code)

— California has not adopted federal provisions that allow taxpayers to currently expense 50% of the cost of qualified refinery property, effective for properties placed in service after August 8, 2005, and 50% of the advanced mine safety equipment expenses purchased after December 20, 2006, and placed in service prior to 2017. (Sec. 17257, Rev. & Tax. Code; Sec. 17257.4, Rev. & Tax. Code)

- *"Ordinary" and "necessary" expenses*

It should not be assumed that an item of expense that is allowed under federal law will always be allowed by California, because the interpretations of different taxing authorities concerning what are "ordinary" and "necessary" business expenses are not always uniform. Also, expenses that would normally be deductible under federal law are not allowed by California when they are attributable to income that is not taxed by California (¶ 336).

- *Principal place of business*

For purposes of claiming a home office expense deduction, a taxpayer's home office qualifies as a "principal place of business" if the following conditions are satisfied:

— the office is used by the taxpayer to conduct business-related administrative or management activities;

— there is no other fixed business location where such activities take place; and

— the office is used by the taxpayer exclusively on a regular basis as a place of business.

Also, if the taxpayer is an employee, the taxpayer's use of the home office must be for the convenience of the taxpayer's employer.

Practice Pointer: Commuting from Home Office Deduction

Although the expenses of commuting from an individual's residence to a local place of business are generally classified as nondeductible commuting expenses, such expenses may be deductible as ordinary and necessary business expenses if the individual uses his or her home as a principal place of business. For example, an anesthesiologist whose residence is her principal place of business may be able to deduct the expenses of traveling between her home and the hospitals at which she performs her primary duties.

• *Self-employed health insurance costs*

For both California and federal purposes, self-employed taxpayers are allowed to deduct 100% of the amounts they have paid for medical insurance for themselves and their families, not to exceed the taxpayer's earned income from the taxpayer's trade or business. (Sec. 17201, Rev. & Tax. Code) California law provides that amounts used as "earned income" for purposes of computing a taxpayer's federal deduction (rather than the earned income computed using California amounts) must be used for purposes of computing the taxpayer's state deduction. (Sec. 17203, Rev. & Tax. Code) In addition, California law, but not federal law, treats a taxpayer's registered domestic partner as the taxpayer's spouse for purposes of determining the amount that may be deducted. (Sec. 17021.7, Rev. & Tax. Code)

This deduction may be taken even if the taxpayer does not itemize deductions.

• *Automobile expenses*

The Internal Revenue Service has followed a policy of allowing fixed per diem allowances and automobile mileage rates in lieu of itemized details for certain deductible expenses. For transportation expenses paid or incurred, the rate is 54¢ per mile for 2016. California adopts this rate as well for California income tax purposes.

California also conforms to federal law allowing a U.S. Postal Service rural mail carrier to deduct the amount of qualified reimbursements received for expenses incurred for the use of the mail carrier's vehicle for the collection and delivering of mail on the carrier's route.

• *Physicians' deduction for interindemnity payments*

California conforms to federal law allowing physicians to deduct certain inter-indemnity payments made to provide protection from malpractice liability. (Sec. 17278, Rev. & Tax. Code)

• *Architectural adaptations to accommodate the handicapped*

Both California and federal law allow a deduction of certain expenditures for the removal of architectural and transportation barriers to the handicapped and the elderly. California and federal law allowing a credit for disabled access expenditures is discussed at ¶140. Amounts for which a credit is claimed may not be deducted.

• *Repair regulations*

California follows the federal "repair regulations," which provide rules for distinguishing capital expenditures from deductible supply, repair, and maintenance costs. (*FTB Tax News* (March 2015) (CCH CALIFORNIA TAX REPORTS, ¶406-310))

¶302 Meals, Entertainment, and Travel Expenses

Law: Sec. 17201 (CCH CALIFORNIA TAX REPORTS, ¶15-805).

Comparable Federal: Secs. 162, 170, 274 (CCH U.S. MASTER TAX GUIDE ¶910 et seq.).

California law is generally the same as federal law as of the current IRC tie-in date (see ¶103). (Sec. 17201, Rev. & Tax. Code)

• *Meal and beverage expenses*

With certain exceptions, taxpayers may deduct only 50% of business-related meal and beverage expenses, including the cost of meals incurred during business travel away from home. The 50% limit is also applicable to unreimbursed expenses incurred by employees on behalf of their employer (¶329). (Sec. 17201, Rev. & Tax. Code)

Also, the deduction is generally not allowed unless taxpayers establish that (1) the meal and beverage expenses were directly related to the active conduct of their trade or business; or (2) in the case of expenses directly preceding or directly following a bona fide business discussion, that the expenses were associated with the active conduct of their trade or business.

¶302

An exception is provided allowing deductions by taxpayers for the cost of their own meals while away on business. Food and beverage expenses deemed lavish or extravagant under the circumstances are not deductible.

The deductible percentage of meals provided to employees subject to Department of Transportation hours-of-service rules is 80%. In addition, meals provided at an eating facility for employees are fully deductible by the employer, instead of possibly being subject to the 50% limitation. For this purpose, the employee is treated as having paid an amount for the meal equal to the direct operating costs of the facility that are attributable to the meal.

• *Entertainment expenses*

Under both California and federal law, business expense deductions are not allowed with respect to an activity generally considered to be entertainment, amusement, or recreation, unless (1) the taxpayer establishes that the item was directly related or associated with the active conduct of the taxpayer's trade or business, or (2) the facility (e.g., an airplane) for which the deduction is claimed is used in connection with such activity. However, such expenses are deductible if the expenses are reported by the taxpayer as compensation and wages to the employee or if the recipient is not an employee (e.g., nonemployee director) as compensation for services rendered or as a prize or award. (Sec. 17201, Rev. & Tax. Code)

Taxpayers may deduct only 50% of the cost of business entertainment expenses. They must establish that (1) the expenses were directly related to the active conduct of their trade or business; or (2) in the case of entertainment expenses directly preceding or directly following a bona fide business discussion, that the expenses were associated with the active conduct of their trade or business.

Generally, taxpayers may not deduct more than 50% of the face value of entertainment tickets. However, the full amount paid for tickets to sporting events may be deducted if (1) the event benefits a charity; (2) the proceeds go to the charity; and (3) the event uses volunteers to perform substantially all the event's work.

Both California and federal law prohibit deductions for club dues paid or incurred for membership in any business, pleasure, social, athletic, luncheon, sporting, airline, or hotel club.

• *Travel expenses*

Taxpayers may not deduct the cost of travel that in itself constitutes a form of education. For example, a language teacher may not deduct the cost of visiting a foreign country merely for the purpose of maintaining familiarity with the country's language and culture. (Sec. 17201, Rev. & Tax. Code)

In addition, a taxpayer's employment away from home for more than one year will be treated as indefinite, rather than temporary; thus, no deduction for travel expenses will be allowed in connection with such employment. However, both California and federal law allow a deduction to federal employees traveling on temporary duty status in connection with the investigation or prosecution of a federal crime, even if they are away from home for more than one year.

Charitable travel expenses may be deducted only if there is no significant element of personal pleasure, recreation, or vacation in such travel.

Also, taxpayers may not deduct the expenses of attending a convention, seminar, or similar meeting in connection with their investment activities. The convention, meeting, or seminar must relate to the taxpayer's trade or business and must offer significant business related activities, *e.g.*, participation in meetings, workshops, or lectures.

A deduction for travel expenses of a spouse, dependent, or any other individual accompanying a person on a business trip is disallowed unless the following conditions are satisfied:

— the accompanying individual is an employee of the person paying or reimbursing the travel expenses;

— the accompanying individual's travel is also for a bona fide business purpose; and

— the expenses would otherwise be deductible by the accompanying individual.

¶303 Itemized Deductions

Law: Secs. 17024.5, 17073, 17076, 17077, 17201, 17207, 17220 (CCH California Tax Reports, ¶15-545).

Comparable Federal: Secs. 63, 67, 68, 163, 164, 165 (CCH U.S. Master Tax Guide ¶1011 et seq., 1021 et seq., 1047, 1141).

California Forms: Sch. CA (540) (California Adjustments - Residents), Sch. CA (540NR) (California Adjustments - Nonresidents or Part-Year Residents).

Individuals may take the standard deduction or itemize deductions for California purposes, whether or not they itemize federally. (Sec. 17073(c), Rev. & Tax. Code) However, married/registered domestic partner taxpayers who file separate returns must either both itemize or both take the standard deduction for California purposes. (Instructions, Form 540, California Resident Income Tax Return) California has conformed to most of the federal itemized deduction provisions. (Sec. 17201, Rev. & Tax. Code; Sec. 17024.5(b)(12) and (i), Rev. & Tax. Code)

Following are the major differences between California and federal itemized deductions:

— state, local, and foreign income taxes, state disability insurance tax (SDI), and qualified sales and use taxes may be deducted for federal but not California purposes (¶306);

— the contribution carryover from pre-1987 tax years could differ;

— there may be a California-only carryover from a disaster loss (¶307);

— miscellaneous itemized deductions for expenses related to producing income taxed under federal law, but not California law, are not deductible for California purposes, and vice versa (¶336);

— the deduction for interest on certain home mortgages may differ (¶305);

— deductions including an element of gain or loss may differ because of differences in California and federal bases (¶542); and

— itemized deductions for high-income taxpayers must be reduced by 6% of adjusted gross income for California purposes instead of the federal 3% reduction (see below).

Practice Note: Registered Domestic Partners

California law, unlike federal law, treats registered domestic partners (RDPs) and former RDPs (see ¶119) as married taxpayers or former spouses for California income tax purposes, unless specified exceptions apply.

• *2% floor on miscellaneous itemized deductions*

Certain unreimbursed employee expenses, expenses of producing income, and other qualifying expenses are deducted as miscellaneous itemized deductions federally and for California purposes. For both California and federal purposes, most miscellaneous itemized deductions are subject to a 2% floor. Only the portion of the total amount of such deductions in excess of 2% of the taxpayer's federal adjusted gross income is deductible. (Sec. 17076, Rev. & Tax. Code; Sec. 17201, Rev. & Tax. Code)

Following are the most common expenses subject to the 2% floor:

— professional society dues;

— employment-related educational expenses;

— office-in-the-home expenses;

— expenses of looking for a new job;

— professional books, magazines, journals and periodicals;

— work clothes and uniforms;

— union dues and fees;

— certain unreimbursed employee business expenses;

— safe deposit box rental;

— tax counsel and assistance;

— cost of work-related small tools and supplies;

— investment counsel fees;

— fees paid to an IRA custodian; and

— certain expenses of a partnership, grantor trust, or S corporation that are incurred for the production of income.

Following are the most common expenses *not* subject to the 2% floor:

— certain adjustments when a taxpayer restores amounts held under a claim of right;

— amortizable bond premium;

— gambling losses to the extent of gambling winnings;

— deductions allowable in connection with personal property used in a short sale;

— impairment-related work expenses of a handicapped individual that are for deductible attendant care services at the individual's place of work, and other expenses in connection with the place of work that are necessary for the individual to be able to work;

— mutual fund shareholder expenses;

— nonbusiness casualty losses; and

— interest on public utility-financed loans to purchase energy-efficient equipment.

• *Overall limitation for high-income taxpayers*

California generally conforms to federal law concerning limitations on the amount of itemized deductions claimed by high-income taxpayers. (Sec. 17077, Rev. & Tax. Code) The itemized deductions of taxpayers in high-income brackets must be reduced by the lesser of (1) 6% (3% under federal law) of the excess of adjusted gross income over the threshold amount; or (2) 80% of the amount of the itemized deductions otherwise allowable for the tax year.

For 2016, the California threshold amounts are:

— $182,459 for a single taxpayer or a married/RDP taxpayer filing a separate return;

— $273,692 for a head of household; and

— $364,923 for a surviving spouse or a married/RDP taxpayer filing a joint return.

¶303

The California threshold amounts are adjusted annually for inflation.

For both California and federal purposes, the limitation does not apply to deductions for medical expenses, casualty and theft losses, wagering losses, or investment interest expenses.

¶304 Expenses for Production of Income

Law: Sec. 17201 (CCH CALIFORNIA TAX REPORTS, ¶15-730).

Comparable Federal: Sec. 212 (CCH U.S. MASTER TAX GUIDE ¶1085).

California Forms: Sch. CA (540) (California Adjustments - Residents), Sch. CA (540NR) (California Adjustments - Nonresidents or Part-Year Residents).

California law is generally the same as federal law. (Sec. 17201, Rev. & Tax. Code) Taxpayers may deduct all ordinary and necessary expenses incurred as follows:

— for the production or collection of income;

— for the management, conservation, or maintenance of property held for the production of income; or

— in connection with the determination, collection, or refund of any tax.

Practice Pointer: Application of 2% Floor

Deductions for the expenses of producing income are generally subject to the 2% floor on miscellaneous itemized deductions. However, expenses attributable to property held for the production of rents or royalties are subtracted from gross income to arrive at adjusted gross income (*i.e.*, as above-the-line deductions) and, thus, their deduction is not subject to the 2% floor.

For California purposes, deductible expenses must relate to income that is taxable by California; see ¶336. Moreover, it should be noted that, although federal and California law are formally the same, different taxing authorities may take different views concerning whether an item of expense is "ordinary" and "necessary." In practice, therefore, deductions allowed under one law may not always be allowed under the other.

Practice Pointer: Credit Card Fees

California conforms to the recent IRS conclusion that a deduction may be claimed for credit card fees paid in connection with the payment of federal income taxes. Consequently, taxpayers that claim these credit card fees on their federal return and report their itemized deductions for California purposes do not need to make an adjustment on Schedule CA. The recent IRS conclusion also applies to credit card fees paid in connection with the payment of state income taxes. (*Tax News*, California Franchise Tax Board, February 26, 2010)

In *Appeal of Glenn M. and Phylis R. Pfau* (1972) (CCH CALIFORNIA TAX REPORTS, ¶15-730.30), the taxpayers claimed a deduction for campaign expenses in an election for municipal court judge. The State Board of Equalization (BOE) denied the deduction, following a former California regulation and federal cases decided under the comparable federal statute.

In *Appeal of Bernard B. and Dorothy Howard* (1961) (CCH CALIFORNIA TAX REPORTS, ¶15-730.53), the BOE held that legal and accounting fees incurred while the taxpayer was a resident of California, but applicable to a federal tax controversy involving years prior to the establishment of California residence, were not deductible under the third item above. The BOE based its decision on the fact that such expenses were connected with income not taxable in California; therefore, they were nondeductible under the rule denying deductions for expenses applicable to tax-exempt income (¶336).

¶305 Interest

Law: Secs. 17072, 17201, 17204, 17208.1, 17224, 17225, 17230, 17280 (CCH CALIFORNIA TAX REPORTS, ¶15-720, 16-050, 16-075, 16-260, 16-280).

Comparable Federal: Secs. 163, 221, 264, 265(a)(2), 265(a)(6) (CCH U.S. MASTER TAX GUIDE ¶909, 937 et seq., 970, 1043 et seq., 1082, 1094).

California Forms: FTB 3526 (Investment Interest Expense Deduction), Sch. CA (540) (California Adjustments - Residents), Sch. CA (540NR) (California Adjustments - Non-residents or Part-Year Residents).

California conforms to federal law as of the current IRC tie-in date (¶103) concerning the deductibility of interest expenses, except as discussed below.

• *Tax-exempt interest*

Interest expense incurred to purchase or carry tax-exempt obligations is not deductible under either California or federal law (¶217). The same rule applies to shareholders of mutual funds holding such obligations and distributing tax-exempt interest on them (¶217). However, the amount of nondeductible interest may differ due to differences between California and federal law regarding tax-exempt obligations.

• *Personal interest*

No deduction for personal interest is available.

Qualified residence interest is not subject to the same treatment as personal interest (see below).

• *Investment interest*

A deduction is allowed for investment interest up to the amount of net investment income. (IRC Sec. 163; Sec. 17201, Rev. & Tax. Code) The deduction is calculated on FTB 3526, Investment Interest Expense Deduction. Net capital gain from the disposition of investment property is generally excluded from investment income. However, taxpayers may elect to include as much of their net capital gain investment income as they choose in calculating the investment interest limitation for federal purposes if they also reduce the amount of net capital gain eligible for the special federal capital gain tax. Taxpayers are allowed to make a similar election for California purposes; however, as discussed at ¶523, California treats capital gains as ordinary income.

Any amount not allowed as a deduction for any taxable year because of this limitation may be carried over and treated as deductible investment interest in the succeeding taxable year.

The limitation on itemized deductions for high-income taxpayers does not apply to investment interest expenses (¶303).

• *Mortgage interest*

A deduction is allowed for a limited amount of interest paid or accrued on (1) debts incurred to acquire a principal or second residence and (2) home equity debts. The aggregate amount of acquisition indebtedness must not exceed $1 million, and the aggregate amount of home equity indebtedness must not exceed $100,000. Interest attributable to debt over such limits is nondeductible personal interest. See ¶221 for a discussion of the exclusion available for the discharge of qualified residence indebtedness.

California law provides that payments made to the California Housing Finance Agency by first-time home buyers under a "buy-down mortgage plan" are considered payments of interest for purposes of the interest deduction. Such payments are made under Section 52514 of the Health and Safety Code, to reimburse the agency for its cost of subsidizing the borrower's interest cost. (Sec. 17230, Rev. & Tax. Code) Although there is no comparable provision in the federal law, it might be argued that the payments are made in lieu of interest and therefore should be treated as interest for federal as well as California purposes.

California does not incorporate federal law that treats qualified premiums paid for mortgage insurance in 2007 through 2016 as deductible interest. Taxpayers that claim this interest expense deduction on their federal returns must make an adjustment on their California personal income tax return. (Sec. 17225, Rev. & Tax. Code)

• *Energy-efficient equipment loan interest*

Taxpayers may claim a deduction for the amount of interest paid or incurred by a taxpayer on a public utility-financed loan or indebtedness obtained to acquire any energy-efficient product or equipment for installation in a qualified residence located in California. Examples of qualifying equipment include heating, ventilation, air-conditioning, lighting, solar, advanced metering of energy usage, windows, insulation, zone heating products, and weatherization systems. Like the home mortgage interest deduction, this deduction is not subject to the 2% floor on miscellaneous itemized deductions. (Sec. 17208.1, Rev. & Tax. Code)

• *Interest on company-owned life insurance*

An employer is generally precluded from claiming a deduction for interest paid or incurred on money borrowed to fund an insurance policy or an endowment or annuity contract covering the life of *any* individual for whom the taxpayer has an insurable interest. However, an employer may still deduct interest paid or incurred to purchase life insurance policies, annuities, and endowment contracts for a limited number of officers and 20% owners if (1) the aggregate amount of debt with respect to the policies and contracts does not exceed $50,000 per key person and (2) the interest rate does not exceed a specified amount. (Sec. 17201, Rev. & Tax. Code) See ¶301 for limitations on the deductibility of premiums on company-owned life insurance.

• *Student loan interest*

Under both California and federal law, an above-the-line deduction is allowed for interest due and paid on qualified education loans up to a maximum of $2,500. The deduction is subject to gradual phase-outs for individuals with modified adjusted gross income (AGI) of $50,000 or more ($100,000 for joint filers), with complete phase-outs for individuals with modified AGI of $65,000 or more ($130,000 for joint filers). (Sec. 17204, Rev. & Tax. Code)

For purposes of this deduction, modified AGI includes income from social security benefits as well as amounts contributed to an individual retirement account.

• *Miscellaneous interest*

See ¶327 regarding deductibility of interest by tenant-stockholders of cooperative housing corporations. See ¶414 for special rules regarding imputed interest on certain installment contracts. See ¶416 regarding capitalization of interest during the construction period of real property.

¶306 Taxes

Law: Secs. 17201, 17220, 17222, 17240 (CCH California Tax Reports, ¶15-820, 16-120, 16-145).

Comparable Federal: Secs. 164, 275 (CCH U.S. Master Tax Guide ¶920 et seq., 1021 et seq.).

California Forms: Form 540 (California Resident Income Tax Return), Sch. CA (540) (California Adjustments - Residents), Sch. CA (540NR) (California Adjustments - Non-residents or Part-Year Residents).

California law incorporates federal law as of the current IRC tie-in date (see ¶ 103), except that California specifically prohibits the deduction of "state, local, and foreign income, war profits, and excess profits taxes," and California does not allow the deduction of state or local sales and use taxes or the California SDI tax (see below). (Sec. 17024.5(b)(7), Rev. & Tax. Code; Sec. 17220, Rev. & Tax. Code; Sec. 17222, Rev. & Tax. Code) California also prohibits the deduction for personal income tax purposes of any tax imposed under the bank and corporation tax law. However, some such taxes may be used as the basis for claiming credits (¶¶ 125—131).

Under both California and federal law, the following taxes may be deducted

— state, local, and foreign real property taxes;

— state and local personal property taxes; and

— other state, local, and foreign taxes relating to a trade or business, or to property held for production of income (except income taxes—see below).

California also specifically conforms to the federal provision that denies deductions for the annual fee imposed by Section 9008 of the Patient Protection and Affordable Care Act on branded prescription manufacturers and importers. (Sec. 17240, Rev. & Tax. Code)

CCH Comment: Real Estate Tax Deduction

Real estate tax is an allowable itemized deduction for both federal and state income tax. In 2011 and 2012 the FTB had taken the position that special assessments included in the property tax bill, such as for Mello-Roos or for various services provided to specific properties, are generally not deductible. California differs from most other states in that many California property tax bills include large special assessments that are not allowable as deductions. However, the Internal Revenue Service (IRS) has issued an information notice concerning the deductibility of various real property taxes under IRC § 164, which is incorporated by California, that appears to contradict recent positions taken by the FTB as to which real property taxes may be deducted on the California personal income tax return.

The IRS states that in contrast to the federal provision governing the personal property tax deduction, there is no statutory or regulatory requirement that real property taxes be imposed on an ad valorem basis in order to be deductible. According to the IRS, assessments on real property owners, based other than on the assessed value of the property, may be deductible if they are levied for the general public welfare by a proper taxing authority at a like rate on owners of all properties in the taxing authority's jurisdiction, and if the assessments are not for local benefits (unless for maintenance or interest charges). (*IRS Information Notice 2012-0018*, CCH CALIFORNIA TAX REPORTS, ¶ 405-619)

The FTB had previously indicated that they were going to require taxpayers to provide information concerning what type of real property taxes and special assessments were paid on their real property, but has since taken the position that they will await the IRS's revised form instructions and publications prior to requiring such information.

• *Taxes based on gross receipts*

A tax on gross receipts may be deductible under the third item above, if it can avoid classification as an income tax, because it presumably is incurred "for the production or collection of income."

In *Scott Beamer v. Franchise Tax Board* (1977) (CCH CALIFORNIA TAX REPORTS, ¶ 205-694), the California Supreme Court held that the Texas "occupation tax" on oil and gas production is not "on or according to or measured by income or profits" and therefore is deductible.

• *State and foreign taxes*

Numerous rulings and decisions over the years have held specific foreign taxes nondeductible under the income-tax prohibition. Following is a partial listing, in alphabetical order by state or country:

ALASKA—gross production tax on oil royalties— *Appeal of Jesson* (1957) (CCH CALIFORNIA TAX REPORTS, ¶ 16-145.254).

ARGENTINA—tax withheld on royalties—*Appeal of Don Baxter, Inc.* (1964) (CCH CALIFORNIA TAX REPORTS, ¶ 10-561.203).

AUSTRALIA—tax withheld on dividends—*Appeal of Siff* (1975) (CCH CALIFORNIA TAX REPORTS, ¶ 16-145.352).

BRAZIL—same as Argentina, above.

CANADA—tax withheld on dividends, interest, and trust distributions—*Appeal of Bochner* (1974) (CCH CALIFORNIA TAX REPORTS, ¶ 16-145.35), *Appeal of Siff* (1975) (CCH CALIFORNIA TAX REPORTS, ¶ 16-145.352).

HAWAII—gross income tax—*Robinson et al. v. Franchise Tax Board* (1981) (CCH CALIFORNIA TAX REPORTS, ¶ 16-145.253).

ITALY—same as Argentina, above.

JAPAN—tax withheld on royalties and dividends— *Appeal of Everett* (1973) (CCH CALIFORNIA TAX REPORTS, ¶ 16-145.60), *Appeal of Siff* (1975) (CCH CALIFORNIA TAX REPORTS, ¶ 16-145.352).

MEXICO—tax withheld on royalties, dividends, and interest— *Appeal of Don Baxter, Inc.* (1964) (CCH CALIFORNIA TAX REPORTS, ¶ 10-561.203), *Appeal of Mabee* (1966) (CCH CALIFORNIA TAX REPORTS, ¶ 16-145.353), *Appeal of Blankenbeckler* (1969) (CCH CALIFORNIA TAX REPORTS, ¶ 16-145.354).

NETHERLANDS—tax withheld on dividends—*Appeal of Siff* (1975) (CCH CALIFORNIA TAX REPORTS, ¶ 16-145.352).

PHILIPPINES—same as Argentina, above.

SOUTH AFRICA—tax withheld on dividends—*Appeal of Haubiel* (1973) (CCH CALIFORNIA TAX REPORTS, ¶ 16-145.351), *Appeal of Siff* (1975) (CCH CALIFORNIA TAX REPORTS, ¶ 16-145.352).

UNITED KINGDOM—tax withheld on dividends—*Appeal of Siff* (1975) (CCH CALIFORNIA TAX REPORTS, ¶ 16-145.352).

Practitioner Comment: FTB Withdraws Guidance Regarding Whether Certain States' Taxes Qualify as Income-Based Taxes

See ¶ 131 for information on the continuing uncertainty regarding the treatment of certain taxes as income taxes or non-income taxes for California tax purposes.

See ¶ 1006 for similar rulings under the corporate income tax law. Because the personal income tax and corporate income tax provisions governing the deduction for taxes are similar, rulings under the corporate income tax law may likely be applied under the personal income tax law.

• *SDI tax*

California does not allow a deduction for the employees' tax under the unemployment insurance law (commonly referred to as SDI). (Sec. 17222, Rev. & Tax. Code) A 1977 Tax Court decision *(Trujillo)* allowed a federal deduction for the SDI tax on the ground that it is, in effect, a state income tax; however, as explained above, California denies any deduction for income taxes. See *Appeal of Arnold E. and Mildred H. Galef* (1979) (CCH CALIFORNIA TAX REPORTS, ¶ 16-125.70).

¶306

However, California does allow a credit for excess SDI if two or more of the taxpayer's employers withheld more than the maximum amount for the year (¶132).

● *Minimum tax and LLC fees*

The minimum tax imposed on limited partnerships, limited liability partnerships, and limited liability companies (¶116) is not deductible at either the entity or the partnership/shareholder level (Instructions to Form 565). However, at the time this book went to press, the LLC fee may still be deducted (see ¶625).

● *Vehicle license fees*

California motor vehicle license fees listed on vehicle registration billing notices from the Department of Motor Vehicles are deductible as personal property taxes. Other fees listed on the billing notice, such as registration fees, weight fees, county or district fees, special plate fees, and owner responsibility fees are not deductible.

● *Postponed property taxes*

Where payment of property taxes is postponed, as explained at ¶1705, the taxes are treated as if paid for income tax purposes and are deductible in the taxable year when the required certificate is submitted to the tax assessor.

● *Cross-references*

See ¶327 regarding deductibility of taxes by tenant-stockholders of cooperative housing corporations. See ¶416 regarding capitalization of taxes during the construction period of real property.

¶307 Losses

Law: Secs. 17201, 17207-07.14 (CCH CALIFORNIA TAX REPORTS, ¶15-745, 16-300).

Comparable Federal: Secs. 165, 470, 1242-44 (CCH U.S. MASTER TAX GUIDE ¶1101 et seq., 1124 et seq., 2395).

California Forms: FTB Pub. 1034 and 1034A series (California Disaster Relief Tax Provisions), FTB 3805V (Net Operating Loss (NOL) Computation and NOL and Disaster Loss Limitations - Individuals, Estates, and Trusts).

California incorporates federal law as of the current IRC tie-in date (¶103) with the modifications noted below. (Sec. 17201, Rev. & Tax. Code) Under both California and federal laws, an ordinary loss deduction is allowed for a loss that is not compensated for by insurance or otherwise. As to individual taxpayers, losses are limited to the following:

— those incurred in a trade or business;

— those incurred in a transaction entered into for profit; or

— those arising from casualty or theft, to the extent the total of such losses, after excluding the first $100 of each loss, exceeds 10% of federal adjusted gross income. Casualty, theft, and wagering losses are not subject to the limitations on high income taxpayers explained at ¶303.

Casualty losses are measured, generally, by the loss in value of the property; but are limited by the amount of the cost or other basis of the property. (See *Appeal of Dominic and Mary Barbaria* (1981) (CCH CALIFORNIA TAX REPORTS, ¶15-745.241), where a deduction was denied because the property lost had been fully depreciated.)

Federal law disallows income tax deductions for certain losses if the losses may be claimed as federal estate-tax deductions. Although California law generally provides that references to federal estate tax should be ignored, the Franchise Tax Board has announced that estate administration expenses can be deducted for California income tax purposes or California estate "pickup" tax purposes, but not both. (*Tax News*, FTB, May 1988)

• *Theft losses*

Theft losses are deductible only in the year of discovery, unlike other losses, which are deductible in the year sustained. (Sec. 17201, Rev. & Tax. Code)

CCH Tip: Ponzi Losses

Internal Revenue Service Revenue Ruling 2009-9 and Revenue Procedure 2009-20, concerning the income tax treatment of losses from Ponzi-type investment schemes, both apply for California purposes to the extent federal law and California law are the same. Taxpayers using the federal safe harbor can choose to treat Ponzi-type losses as theft losses for California purposes. Taxpayers not using the safe harbor for California purposes may file a claim for refund for prior years, assuming the statute of limitations is open. The FTB will hold these taxpayers' amended returns as protective claims for refund until the law related to the treatment of Ponzi schemes is clarified. Taxpayers should write "Protective Claim - Ponzi scheme" in red at the top of the first page of their amended return and should also include the statement, "This is a claim for refund for (taxpayer's name) - Ponzi Scheme & (name of investment or promoter)" in a statement attached to the amended return or in the Explanation of Changes part of the amended return. (*Tax News*, California Franchise Tax Board, July 2009)

• *Disaster losses*

California generally conforms to IRC Sec. 165(i), which allows taxpayers to claim a deduction for losses occurring in certain disaster areas. For the 2014 to 2023 taxable years, the California deduction is available for any loss sustained as a result of a disaster occurring in any city, county, or city and county in the state that is proclaimed by the Governor to be in a state of emergency. The deduction can be claimed for the taxable year in which the disaster occurred or for the immediately preceding taxable year. (Sec. 17207.14, Rev. & Tax. Code) An appraisal for the purpose of obtaining a loan of federal funds or a loan guarantee from the federal government as a result of a presidentially declared disaster may be used to establish the amount of any disaster loss to the extent provided in federal regulations or other guidance. (Sec. 17207.4, Rev. & Tax. Code)

In 2016, the Governor declared a state of emergency for the following disasters:

— Wildfires in Lake, San Bernardino, San Luis Obispo counties in August 2016;

— Wildfires in Los Angeles and Monterey counties in July 2016; and

— Wildfires in Kern County in June 2016.

In addition, California law allows excess losses due to the following causes, including related casualties, to be carried forward for up to 15 years if they were sustained in federally declared disaster areas or in California counties or cities proclaimed to be in a state of disaster by the Governor:

— San Simeon earthquake or aftershocks in Santa Barbara and San Luis Obispo counties in December 2003;

— Fires and related floods, mudflows, and debris flows in Los Angeles, Riverside, San Bernardino, San Diego, and Ventura counties in October and November 2003;

— Levee break in San Joaquin County in June 2004;

— Wildfires in Shasta County, commencing August 11, 2004;

— Rainstorms, related flooding, and slides in Kern, Los Angeles, Orange, Riverside, San Bernardino, San Diego, Santa Barbara, and Ventura counties in December 2004 through March 2005, or June 2005;

— Rainstorms, related flooding, and landslides, and any other related casualties that occurred in Alameda, Alpine, Amador, Butte, Calaveras, Colusa,

Contra Costa, Del Norte, El Dorado, Fresno, Humboldt, Kings, Lake, Lassen, Madera, Marin, Mariposa, Mendocino, Merced, Monterey, Napa, Nevada, Placer, Plumas, Sacramento, San Joaquin, San Luis Obispo, San Mateo, Santa Cruz, Shasta, Sierra, Siskiyou, Solano, Sonoma, Stanislaus, Sutter, Trinity, Tulare, Tuolumne, Yolo, and Yuba counties in December 2005, and January, March, and April 2006;

— Wildfires in San Bernardino County in July 2006;

— Wildfires in Riverside and Ventura counties that occurred during the 2006 calendar year;

— Freeze in El Dorado, Fresno, Imperial, Kern, Kings, Madera, Merced, Monterey, Riverside, San Bernardino, San Diego, San Luis Obispo, Santa Barbara, Santa Clara, Stanislaus, Tulare, Venture, and Yuba counties that occurred in January 2007;

— Wildfires in El Dorado County that occurred in June 2007;

— Zaca Fire in Santa Barbara and Ventura counties that occurred during the 2007 calendar year;

— Wildfires during the 2007 calendar year in Inyo, Los Angeles, Orange, Riverside, San Bernardino, San Diego, Santa Barbara, and Ventura counties;

— Strong winds in October 2007 in Riverside County;

— Wildfires during May or June of 2008 in Butte, Kern, Mariposa, Mendocino, Monterey, Plumas, Santa Clara, Santa Cruz, Shasta, and Trinity counties;

— Wildfires in July 2008 in Santa Barbara County;

— Rainstorms, floods, landslides, or accumulation of debris during July 2008 in Inyo County;

— Wildfires that started during May 2008 in Humboldt County;

— Wildfires in Santa Barbara County that started in November 2008;

— Wildfires in Los Angeles and Ventura counties in October and November 2008;

— Wildfires in Orange, Riverside, and San Bernardino counties in November 2008;

— Wildfires in Santa Barbara County in May 2009;

— Earthquake in Humboldt County in January 2010;

— Wildfires in Placer, Los Angeles, and Monterey counties in August 2009;

— Winter storms in Calaveras, Imperial, Los Angeles, Orange, Riverside, San Bernardino, San Francisco, and Siskiyou counties in January and February 2010;

— Earthquake in Imperial County in April 2010;

— Wildfires in Kern County in July 2010;

— Fire and explosion in San Mateo County in September 2010; and

— Tsunami in Mendocino County in March 2011.

"Excess disaster loss" means a disaster loss that exceeds the taxpayer's adjusted taxable income for the taxable year in which the loss is first claimed (*i.e.*, the taxable year in which the disaster occurred or the immediately preceding taxable year). (Sec. 17207, Rev. & Tax. Code; Sec. 17207.2, Rev. & Tax. Code; Sec. 17207.3, Rev. & Tax. Code; Sec. 17207.6, Rev. & Tax. Code; Sec. 17207.7, Rev. & Tax. Code; Sec. 17207.8, Rev. & Tax. Code)

¶307

For disasters that occurred in the 2004 through 2011 taxable years, taxpayers are allowed to carryover 100% of the excess loss. For disaster losses incurred in the 2000 through 2003 taxable years, taxpayers can deduct any excess loss that remains after the initial five-year carryover period for up to 10 more years at the following percentage rates:

— 55% for disasters incurred in the 2000 and 2001 taxable years; and

— 60% for disasters incurred in the 2002 and 2003 taxable years.

(*FTB Pub. 1034, Disaster Loss: How to Claim a State Tax Deduction*, revised 2-2016, CCH CALIFORNIA TAX REPORTS, ¶ 406-590)

For the 2016 disasters listed above and the following disasters that were presidentially declared with no subsequent California legislation, excess disaster losses can be carried forward for up to 20 years:

— Rainstorms in Inyo, Kern, and Los Angeles counties in October 2015;

— Wildfires in Amador, Calaveras, Lake, and Napa counties in September 2015;

— Rainstorms in Imperial, Kern, Los Angeles, Riverside, San Bernardino, and San Diego counties in July 2015;

— Wildfires in Lake and Trinity counties in July 2015;

— Wildfires in Butte, El Dorado, Humboldt, Lake, Madera, Napa, Nevada, Sacramento, San Bernardino, San Diego, Shasta, Solano, Tulare, Tuolumne, and Yolo counties in June 2015;

— Oil spill in Santa Barbara County in May 2015;

— Rainstorms in Humboldt, Mendocino, and Siskiyou counties in February 2015;

— Wildfires in Mono County in February 2015;

— Winter storms in Alameda, Contra Costa, Del Norte, Humboldt, Lake, Los Angeles, Marin, Mendocino, Monterey, Orange, San Francisco, San Mateo, Santa Clara, Shasta, Sonoma, Tehama, Ventura, and Yolo counties in November 2014;

— Wildfires in El Dorado and Siskiyou counties in September 2014;

— Earthquake in Napa, Solano, and Sonoma counties in August and September 2014;

— Wildfires in Siskiyou County in August 2014;

— Wildfires in Amador, Butte, El Dorado, Humboldt, Lassen, Madera, Mariposa, Mendocino, Modoc, Shasta, and Siskiyou counties in July 2014;

— Wildfires in San Diego County in May 2014; and

— Rainstorms in Los Angeles County in February 2014; and

— Rim fires in Tuolumne, Mariposa, and San Francisco counties in August and October 2013.

(*FTB Pub. 1034, Disaster Loss: How to Claim a State Tax Deduction*, revised 2-2016, CCH CALIFORNIA TAX REPORTS, ¶ 406-590)

CCH Tip: Interplay with Net Operating Loss (NOL) Deduction

Any law, other than Sec. 17276.20, Rev. & Tax. Code, that suspends, defers, reduces, or otherwise diminishes an NOL deduction (discussed at ¶ 309) does not apply for the 2014 to 2023 taxable years to an NOL attributable to a loss sustained as a result of any disaster occurring in any city, county, or city and county in this state that is proclaimed by the Governor to be in a state of emergency. (Sec. 17207.14(c), Rev. & Tax. Code) If a taxpayer has both disaster loss carryovers and NOL carryovers, they must be used in the order that the taxpayer incurred them. There is no requirement to deduct NOL carryovers before disaster loss carryovers. (*FTB Pub. 1034, Disaster Loss: How to Claim a State Tax Deduction*, revised 2-2016, CCH CALIFORNIA TAX REPORTS, ¶ 406-590)

• *Wagering losses*

Wagering losses are deductible only to the extent of wagering gains. However, see ¶ 336 regarding disallowance of deductions for expenses of illegal activities or California lottery losses. (Sec. 17201, Rev. & Tax. Code)

• *Worthless securities*

Losses from worthless securities that are capital assets are considered losses from the sale or exchange of the securities on the last day of the taxable year in which the securities become worthless. As under federal law, such losses are therefore subject to the limitations on deduction of capital losses. (Sec. 17201, Rev. & Tax. Code)

In *Appeal of Everett R. and Cleo F. Shaw* (1961) (CCH CALIFORNIA TAX REPORTS, ¶ 15-745.952), the State Board of Equalization held that a worthless stock loss was not deductible in the year claimed, where the company that issued the stock later expressed an intent to continue operations with a possibility of future earnings.

• *Losses on "small business corporation" stock*

Under both California and federal law losses of up to $50,000 ($100,000 on joint returns) on stock of small business investment companies created under the Small Business Investment Company Act of 1958 are deductible from ordinary income. (Sec. 17201, Rev. & Tax. Code) In addition, any loss treated as ordinary loss under this provision must also be treated as attributable to a trade or business of the taxpayer for purposes of applying the net operating loss deduction provisions (discussed at ¶ 309). Current treatment of gains on small business corporation stock is discussed at ¶ 525.

• *Tax-exempt lease losses*

California generally follows federal law (IRC Sec. 470), which applies loss deferral rules in the case of property leased to tax-exempt entities. (Sec. 17551, Rev. & Tax. Code)

• *Violation of public policy*

A loss deduction may be disallowed on the ground that the loss is the result of actions that are violative of public policy. See *Appeal of Anthony H. Eredia* (1981) (CCH CALIFORNIA TAX REPORTS, ¶ 15-745.7858), involving a loss of money advanced to a narcotics dealer.

• *Cross references*

See ¶ 535 for treatment of losses on redemption of U.S. Savings Bonds. See ¶ 338 for discussion of special rules regarding farm and hobby losses. See ¶ 339 for "at risk" limitations on deductible losses. See ¶ 340 for a discussion of passive losses.

See ¶ 523 regarding losses on "capital assets." See ¶ 527 regarding disallowance of loss on "wash sales."

¶308 Bad Debts

Law: Sec. 17201 (CCH CALIFORNIA TAX REPORTS, ¶ 15-617).

Comparable Federal: Secs. 166, 271 (CCH U.S. MASTER TAX GUIDE ¶ 1145 et seq., 1166).

California law is the same as federal law. "Nonbusiness" bad debts are treated as short-term capital losses (one year or less). (Sec. 17201, Rev. & Tax. Code)

In *Hameetman v. California Franchise Tax Board*, (2006) CCH CALIFORNIA TAX REPORTS, ¶ 404-117, a California court of appeal ruled that an individual limited partner of a property management partnership could not claim a bad debt deduction based on a defaulted loan that the individual had made in the name of the partnership, because the business of the partnership could not be imputed to the partner.

¶309 Net Operating Loss Deduction

Law: Secs. 17041, 17276-76.22 (CCH CALIFORNIA TAX REPORTS, ¶ 15-765, 16-105, 16-310).

Comparable Federal: Sec. 172 (CCH U.S. MASTER TAX GUIDE ¶ 1173 et seq.).

California Forms: FTB 3805D (Net Operating Loss (NOL) Computation and Limitation - Pierce's Disease), FTB 3805V (Net Operating Loss (NOL) Computation and NOL and Disaster Loss Limitations - Individuals, Estates, and Trusts), FTB 3805Z (Enterprise Zone Deduction and Credit Summary), FTB 3806 (Los Angeles Revitalization Zone Deduction and Credit Summary), FTB 3807 (Local Agency Military Base Recovery Area Deduction and Credit Summary), FTB 3809 (Targeted Tax Area Deduction and Credit Summary).

California generally conforms to the federal net operating loss (NOL) deduction for losses incurred in taxable years beginning after 1984, with the exception of the following:

— for tax years beginning in 2008—2011, California did not allow NOL deductions other than for qualified small businesses (see discussion below); however, the NOL carryover period for which a deduction was not allowed as a result of the suspending provisions during those years is extended by one year for losses incurred during the 2010 tax year, two years for losses incurred during the 2009 tax year, three years for losses incurred during the 2008 tax year, and four years for NOLs incurred prior to 2008 (Sec. 17276.21, Rev. & Tax. Code, *FTB Legal Ruling 2011-04*, CCH CALIFORNIA TAX REPORTS, ¶ 405-514);

— prior to the 2013 taxable year, California did not allow an NOL carryback to prior years, including the extended NOL carryback deduction allowed federally for losses incurred during the 2001 and 2002 tax years, or the extended federal NOL carryback deductions for specified NOLs in 2008 and 2009. Furthermore, California limits the NOL carryback for 2013 to 50% of the NOL and for 2014 to 75% of the NOL (Sec. 17276(c), Rev. & Tax. Code; Sec. 17276.22, Rev. & Tax. Code);

— although California adopts the federal 20-year carryover period beginning with the 2008 taxable year, previously the carryover period was limited to 10 years (five years for losses incurred prior to the 2000 taxable year) (Sec. 17276, Rev. & Tax. Code);

— for NOLs incurred prior to 2004, except for NOLs sustained during the 2002 and 2003 taxable years, California law generally allows a specified percentage of the loss to be carried forward for up to 10 years (five years for losses incurred prior to the 2000 taxable year) rather than the federal 100% carryover for up to 20 years (15 years for NOLs incurred in tax years beginning before August 6, 1997) (Sec. 17276(b), Rev. & Tax. Code);

— for tax years beginning in 2002 and 2003, California did not allow NOL deductions; however, California extends the carryover period (1) by one additional year for an NOL sustained in a tax year beginning in 2002 and (2) by two additional years for an NOL sustained in a tax year beginning before 2002 (Sec. 17276.3, Rev. & Tax. Code);

— special rules apply to NOLs incurred by bankrupt taxpayers and prior to the 2014 tax year to qualified enterprise zone and local agency military base recovery area businesses, and former targeted tax area and Los Angeles Revitalization Zone businesses (see below); and

— an NOL sustained by a nonresident or part-year resident is limited to the sum of (1) the portion of the NOL attributable to the part of the year in which the taxpayer is a resident, plus (2) the portion of the NOL that, during the portion of the year when the taxpayer is not a resident, is attributable to California-source income and deductions (Sec. 17041(i), Rev. & Tax. Code).

Practice Pointer: Small Business Exemption From 2008—2011 NOL Suspension

Qualified small businesses were exempt from the 2008—2011 NOL suspension and could continue to claim NOL deductions in these tax years. Different qualifying thresholds applied, depending on when the NOL was incurred or the carryover was claimed. For the 2008 or 2009 tax years, an NOL deduction or carryover could be claimed by taxpayers with less than $500,000 of net business income, whereas for the 2010 and 2011 suspension period, only taxpayers with modified adjusted gross income (MAGI) of less than $300,000 for the taxable year could claim the NOL deduction. (Sec. 17276.21(d), Rev. & Tax. Code)

For purposes of the NOL suspension exemption, "MAGI" meant adjusted gross income claimed on the taxpayer's return, determined without regard to the NOL deduction. Registered domestic partners and same sex married couples were required to compute their federal AGI as though they had completed a joint federal return. "Business income" meant:

— Income from a trade or business, whether conducted by the taxpayer or by a pass-through entity owned directly or indirectly by the taxpayer.

— Income from rental activity.

— Income attributable to a farming business.

(Sec. 17276.21(d), Rev. & Tax. Code)

Net business income is reflected, respectively, on California Schedule CA(540), line 12 and line 18, as adjusted by Column B (subtractions) and Column C (additions), and federal Schedule E, line 26, line 32, and line 40, and federal Form 4797, line 9, using California amounts. (*E-mail*, California Franchise Tax Board, December 12, 2008)

Practice Pointer: Exemption From Suspension Clarified for S Corporations and Their Shareholders

For purposes of determining eligibility for the 2008/2009 NOL suspension exemption for S corporations and their shareholders, the $500,000 limit was applied at both the entity and shareholder levels. Consequently, the S corporation could be subject to the limitation and the shareholder might not have been, and vice versa. The NOL suspension rules applied to the shareholder's business income regardless of the source of the income. (*E-mail*, California Franchise Tax Board, December 12, 2008) Presumably, similar treatment applies for purposes of the 2010/2011 NOL suspension.

• *Nonresidents and part-year residents*

As discussed at ¶116, a nonresident's or part-year resident's NOL carryover losses and suspended losses are includible or allowable only to the extent that the loss was derived from sources within this state. The NOL must be computed as if the nonresident/part-year resident was a full-year resident for the entire year using only California amounts. Taxpayers should consult FTB Pub. 1100, Taxation of Nonresidents and Individuals Who Change Residency, for detailed explanations and examples of how the NOL is computed for nonresidents and part-year residents.

• *Carryover percentages*

For NOLs incurred after 2003, 100% of the NOL incurred may be carried over. For NOLs incurred prior to 2004, the amount of loss that could be carried over was limited to a specified percentage. The specified percentage that could be carried over was

— 50% for losses incurred in taxable years beginning before 2000;

— 55% for losses incurred in taxable years beginning after 1999 and before 2002; and

— 60% for losses incurred in taxable years beginning after 2001 and before 2004.

• *Carryover and carryback periods*

Historically, California's NOL carryback and carryforward provisions have differed from federal law. However, the carryback and carryforward periods are the same for NOLs incurred after the 2012 tax year.

Carryforward period.—California's NOL carryover period is dependent upon the year in which the NOL is incurred as follows (except during the suspension periods noted above) (Sec. 17276(b), Rev. & Tax. Code):

- 20 years for NOLs incurred after 2007

- 10 years for NOLs incurred after 1999 and prior to 2008

- 5 years for NOLs incurred prior to 2000

Practice Pointer: Interplay Between the Suspension and Carryover Provisions

The interplay between California's NOL suspension provisions, NOL limitations, and carryover/carrybacks is extremely complex. As outlined above, although California law allows an extended carryover period for NOLs that could not be claimed as a result of the suspension, the extended carryover periods do not apply to NOLs that could not be claimed because there was insufficient income to offset the NOL. Consequently, when determining whether NOLs incurred in multiple tax years may be carried over or carried back, taxpayers must claim the earliest-incurred NOL. If there is insufficient income to offset an NOL during a suspension year, the extended NOL carryover provisions will not apply because the NOL deduction was not disallowed as a result of the suspension provisions. The FTB has issued Legal Ruling 2011-04 to explain these complex rules and illustrates how they are applied. (*FTB Legal Division Guidance 2011-10-01*, CCH CALIFORNIA TAX REPORTS, ¶ 405-521)

Carryback period.—Beginning with the 2013 taxable year, a two-year carryback is being phased-in. A taxpayer may carryback a 50% NOL for NOLs incurred in 2013, 75% NOL for NOLs incurred in 2014, and 100% NOL for NOLs incurred thereafter. (Sec. 17276.05, Rev. & Tax. Code; Sec. 17276(c), Rev. & Tax. Code; Sec. 17276.22, Rev. & Tax. Code).

NOL carrybacks are not allowed for California purposes prior to the 2013 taxable year, whereas on a federal return taxpayers could carry back general NOLs for two years (five years for qualified disaster losses or NOLs incurred during the 2001, 2002, 2008, and 2009 tax years or for electrical transmission equipment for NOLs generated in tax years ending in 2003, 2004, and 2005).

A taxpayer entitled to an NOL carryback period may elect to waive the carryback period. By making the election, the taxpayer is electing to carry an NOL forward only instead of first carrying it back to the previous two years. The election is made by checking the box in Part I under Section C - Election to Waive Carryback, of form FTB 3805V, and attaching form FTB 3805V to the taxpayer's tax return. If a taxpayer will claim the NOL as a carryback in any of the previous two years, the taxpayer should first file the applicable 2013 return and attach Form 3805V, and after that file the amended return(s) for 2011 and/or 2012 without attaching Form 3805V to the amended return(s).

> ### Practice Pointer: Suspension Period Inapplicable.
>
> An NOL incurred in 2013, may be carried back and claimed on an amended return for the 2011 tax year, even though NOLs were suspended during the 2011 tax year. (*FTB Legal Ruling 2011-04*, CCH CALIFORNIA TAX REPORTS, ¶ 405-514)

- *Carryover for new and small businesses*

Prior to the enactment of the current 20-year carryover of 100% of NOLs, California law allowed an "enhanced" deduction of NOLs incurred by new and small businesses, that allowed them to carryover 100% of the NOLs incurred for a longer carryover period than was available to other businesses. However, because NOLs attributable to post-2003 taxable years may be fully carried over without any limitations on the carryover amount and California conforms for post-2007 taxable years to the full 20-year federal NOL carryover period, the "new business" and "eligible small business" provisions are currently irrelevant. (*FTB Legal Division Guidance 2011-10-01*, CCH CALIFORNIA TAX REPORTS, ¶ 405-521)

- *Carryover for enterprise zone, LARZ, LAMBRA, and targeted tax area businesses*

Enterprise zones and local agency military base recovery areas (LAMBRAs) are economically deprived regions in which the state and local governments provide an array of tax and other incentives for taxpayers prior to the 2014 taxable year. The targeted tax area provided similar benefits prior to the expiration of its designation at the end of 2012 (¶ 104). The Los Angeles Revitalization Zone (LARZ) was also designated as an area in which businesses could receive a variety of tax incentives, including an NOL deduction. Because the LARZ designation was repealed December 1, 1998, qualified taxpayers may claim only NOL carryovers for LARZ losses sustained prior to the 1998 taxable year. However, a taxpayer could receive a LARZ NOL in 1998 as a pass-through NOL from a 1997 fiscal-year partnership, S corporation, or limited liability company. (Sec. 17276, Rev. & Tax. Code; Sec. 17276.1, Rev. & Tax. Code; Sec. 17276.2, Rev. & Tax. Code; Sec. 17276.4, Rev. & Tax. Code; Sec. 17276.6, Rev. & Tax. Code)

> ### Practice Pointer: Fiscal Year Taxpayers Operating in EZs and LAMBRAs
>
> All EZs and LAMBRAs are repealed on January 1, 2014. The EZ or LAMBRA NOL is allowed for losses attributable to the taxpayer's business activities within the EZ and LAMBRA through December 31, 2013, without regard to the ending date of the taxpayer's taxable year. For a taxpayer with a taxable year on a fiscal year basis, this loss is calculated by computing the EZ or LAMBRA NOL as if the EZ or LAMBRA had remained in existence the entire year, then this full year loss is pro-rated by the number of days the taxpayer operated in an EZ for the taxable year over the total number of days in the taxable year. (*Repeal of Geographically Targeted Economic Development Area Tax Incentives*, FTB, CCH CALIFORNIA TAX REPORTS, ¶ 405-974)

The NOL deduction available to taxpayers in these designated areas is the same as California's regular NOL deduction except that 100% of the NOLs incurred by businesses operating in these regions incurred prior to the repeal or expiration date of the zone or area may be carried forward for 15 years following the year of the loss. Taxpayers that also conduct business outside of the designated zone or area must apportion loss to the area by multiplying the business's total loss by a two-factor apportionment formula, comprised of the property and payroll factors.

NOLS incurred in 2013 must first be carried back two years (with the carryover amount not exceeding 50% of the NOL incurred in 2013) before being carried forward, unless the taxpayer elects to waive the carryback period. An election to waive the carryback period may be made by checking the appropriate box on Form

3805Z, Part V. If a taxpayer will claim the NOL as a carryback in any of the previous two years, the taxpayer should first file the applicable 2013 return and attach Form 3805Z, and after that file the amended return(s) for 2011 and/or 2012 without attaching Form 3805Z to the amended return(s).

Because the loss attributable to the area may be claimed only against income attributable to the area, further calculations are also required. The amount of business income is first determined using the standard apportionment formula described in ¶1305—1309. For purposes of determining the amount of business income attributable to the zone or area, however, the sales factor is eliminated from the standard apportionment formula and the income used in the apportionment formula is limited to California-based income rather than worldwide income.

In order to claim the special NOL, a taxpayer must make an irrevocable election designating whether the loss is being claimed for a business located in an enterprise zone, LARZ, LAMBRA, or targeted tax area and attach a copy of the election form to a timely tax return. An enterprise zone, LARZ, LAMBRA, or targeted tax area NOL may be used only to offset income from the zone, area, or former zone for which the NOL is claimed. In addition, if a taxpayer elects to claim an enterprise zone, LARZ, LAMBRA, or targeted tax area NOL, no other type of NOL may be carried over. A worksheet is provided in the FTB 3805Z, FTB 3806, FTB 3807, and FTB 3809 booklets to assist taxpayers in determining the most advantageous NOL.

Forms.—The NOL deduction for enterprise zone businesses is claimed on FTB 3805Z. LARZ businesses claim the NOL carryover deduction on FTB 3806 and the LAMBRA NOL is claimed on FTB 3807. The NOL deduction for targeted tax area businesses is claimed on FTB 3809. The LAMBRA NOL is subject to recapture if the taxpayer does not satisfy the net increase in jobs requirement discussed at ¶104.

• *Carryover for farming businesses impacted by Pierce's disease*

For taxable years beginning after 2000 and before 2003, a person or business that conducted a farming business that was confirmed by the California Department of Food and Agriculture as being directly impacted by Pierce's disease and its vectors could carry forward the entire amount of an NOL to the nine tax years following the tax year of loss. An NOL carryover was allowed only with respect to the taxpayer's farming business income attributable to the area affected by Pierce's disease and its vectors. A loss was apportioned to the area affected by Pierce's disease and its vectors by multiplying the total loss from the farming business by a fraction, the numerator of which was the property factor plus the payroll factor and the denominator of which was two. (Sec. 17276.1, Rev. & Tax. Code; Sec. 17276.7, Rev. & Tax. Code)

A Pierce's disease NOL was claimed on FTB 3805D.

• *Effect of certain deductions and exclusions on computation of NOL*

California generally follows federal law under which certain deductions and exclusions may not be taken into account in computing an NOL deduction. However, California modifies federal law to disallow the California gross income exclusion provided to personal income taxpayers for gain on the sale of certain small business stock (¶525).

¶310 Depreciation and Amortization

Law: Secs. 17201, 17201.5, 17250, 17250.5, 17279.6 (CCH CALIFORNIA TAX REPORTS, ¶15-670, 16-040, 16-245).

Comparable Federal: Secs. 167-68, 181, 197, 198, 198A, 280F (CCH U.S. MASTER TAX GUIDE ¶903, 977D, 1201, 1203, 1206, 1211 et seq., 1216 et seq., 1234, 1236 et seq., 1288).

California Forms: FTB 3885A (540) (Depreciation and Amortization Adjustments), FTB 3885F (541) (Depreciation and Amortization), FTB 3885L (568) (Depreciation and Amortization), FTB 3885P (565) (Depreciation and Amortization), Sch. CA (540) (California Adjustments - Residents), Sch. CA (540NR) (California Adjustments -Nonresidents or Part-Year Residents), Sch. D (California Capital Gain or Loss Adjustment).

With the exception of bonus depreciation and other provisions discussed below, California has adopted federal depreciation provisions (the modified accelerated cost recovery system, or MACRS) for personal income tax purposes as of a specified tie-in date (¶103). (Sec. 17201, Rev. & Tax. Code) However, California's asset expense deduction under IRC Sec. 179 may differ depending on the year the property is purchased (¶311).

Assets placed in service before 1987 continue to be depreciated under pre-1987 California rules (see the discussion of assets placed in service before 1987, below). Property placed in service in 1987 in a taxable year which began in 1986 is depreciated under pre-1987 California law, unless the taxpayer elects to have the post-1986 law apply.

California also does not incorporate federal renewal community incentives that allow a taxpayer who receives a revitalization allocation from a state agency to elect for qualified buildings placed in service prior to 2009 either to:

— deduct one-half of any qualified revitalization expenditures chargeable to capital account with respect to any qualified revitalization building in the tax year that the building is placed in service or

— amortize all such expenditures ratably over 120 months beginning in the month that the building is placed in service.

The following summary of MACRS applies to federal and California post-1986 asset acquisitions:

The 1986 Tax Reform Act (TRA) modified the Accelerated Cost Recovery System (ACRS) for property placed in service after 1986, except for property covered by transitional rules. Four classes of property were added:

— 7-year property;

— 20-year property;

— residential rental property (generally, 27.5 years); and

— nonresidential real property (31.5 years).

The Revenue Reconciliation Act of 1993 extended for federal purposes the recovery period for nonresidential real property acquired after May 12, 1993, to 39 years. California conforms to the 39-year recovery period for nonresidential real property, but only for property placed in service after 1996 in taxable years beginning after 1996.

The 3-year, 5-year, and 10-year classes were also revised by the TRA, and more accelerated depreciation was provided within these classes. Property within the 15-year and 20-year classes is depreciated under the TRA modifications by methods that maximize the depreciation deduction. However, commercial real estate and residential rental property are depreciated over longer periods than under pre-TRA provisions.

• *Bonus depreciation*

California does not incorporate the IRC § 168(k) bonus depreciation deduction, that allows taxpayers to claim a 30%, 50%, or 100% first-year bonus depreciation deduction, depending on when the property was purchased (see ¶312). (Sec. 17250(a)(4), Rev. & Tax. Code)

In addition, unlike federal law, California does not allow a 50% depreciation deduction for the first year that qualified disaster assistance property is placed in service. (Sec. 17250(a)(10), Rev. & Tax. Code)

• *Property on Native American reservations*

Federal law, but not California law, allows special recovery periods that permit faster write-offs for qualified Indian reservation property that is placed in service after 1993 and before 2017. (Sec. 17250(a)(3), Rev. & Tax. Code)

• *Disaster costs*

Under federal law, but not California law, taxpayers could elect to currently expense qualified disaster expenses after 2007 for disasters occurring before 2010, rather than capitalizing them. (Sec. 17279.6, Rev. & Tax. Code) To the extent such amounts were deducted from federal taxable income, and were not eligible for deduction under other California personal income tax provisions, taxpayers were required to add such amounts to federal taxable income. Amounts that were added back are eligible for increased depreciation deductions in subsequent tax years.

An addition adjustment is made on Sch. CA (540). Amounts expensed on the federal return must be treated as capitalized costs for California personal income tax purposes; therefore, a depreciation adjustment must also be made thereafter (see ¶310).

• *Qualified leasehold, restaurant, and retail improvement property*

California does not incorporate federal law that classifies "qualified leasehold improvement property," "qualified restaurant property," and "qualified retail improvement property" as 15-year MACRS property with a 15-year recovery period using the straight-line method unless the MACRS alternative depreciation system (ADS) is elected or otherwise applies. (Sec. 17250(a)(5), (6), and (7), Rev. & Tax. Code) Consequently, such property must be depreciated using the standard MACRS recovery periods for California personal income tax purposes.

• *Farm machinery and equipment*

Unlike federal law, California law does not provide a shortened recovery period for farm machinery or equipment, the original use of which begins with the taxpayer in 2009, and that is placed in service by the taxpayer in a farming business in 2009. (Sec. 17250(a)(12), Rev. & Tax. Code) Presumably, the recovery period applicable for California income tax purposes would remain 10 years for such property, rather than the 5-year period allowed under federal law.

• *Second generation biofuel and reuse and recycling property*

California does not incorporate the 50% first-year depreciation deduction for second generation biofuel property or for certain reuse and recycling property that is available under federal law. (Sec. 17250(a)(8) and (9), Rev. & Tax. Code) Consequently, California's depreciation deduction may be greater than that claimed on the federal return.

• *Electric transmission property, and natural gas lines*

Because of California's federal conformity date history, California did not incorporate until the 2010 tax year federal provisions that provide the following recovery periods under IRC Sec. 168:

— for certain electric transmission property, 15 years;

— for new natural gas gathering lines, seven years; and

— for new natural gas distribution lines, 15 years.

• *Motorsports entertainment complexes*

California incorporated the federal shortened 7-year recovery period for motorsports entertainment complexes beginning with the 2005 tax year and applicable to property placed in service prior to 2008. Federal law allows the shortened recovery period for property placed in service after October 22, 2004, and before 2017. (Sec. 17250(a)(11), Rev. & Tax. Code)

¶310

• *Depreciation methods according to class (IRC Sec. 168)*

Under the federal MACRS method as incorporated by California (Sec. 17201, Rev. & Tax. Code), there are six classes of recovery property: 3-year, 5-year, 7-year, 10-year, 15-year, and 20-year. Prescribed depreciation methods are assigned to each class, as follows:

— for 3-year, 5-year, 7-year, and 10-year classes, depreciation is by the 200% declining-balance method, switching to straight line when the latter yields a larger deduction;

— for 15-year and 20-year property, depreciation is by the 150% declining-balance method, switching to straight line when the latter yields a larger deduction; and

— for residential rental property and nonresidential real property, straight-line depreciation is to be used.

Taxpayers may make an irrevocable election to depreciate personal property using the straight-line ACRS method over the regular recovery period. Taxpayers may also make an irrevocable election to depreciate property qualified for the 200% declining-balance method under the 150% declining-balance method. If the latter election is made, depreciation may be computed over the longer class lives prescribed by the alternative depreciation system of IRC Sec. 168(g) or over *the regular tax recovery period*, applicable to property placed in service after 1998.

The above elections apply to all property in the same class that is placed in service during the same tax year. The election is to be made on the taxpayer's return for the year in which the property is placed in service.

Depreciation methods and useful lives of trade or business property must be acceptable to California. If an unacceptable method was used before the move into California, taxpayers must use the straight-line method to compute the basis in the property. (FTB Pub. 1001, Supplemental Guidelines to California Adjustments)

Nor does California incorporate federal provisions that provide a 10-year recovery period for qualified smart electric meters and smart grid systems placed in service after October 3, 2008. Consequently, such property must continue to be depreciated using the 20-year recovery period for California personal income tax purposes.

• *Alternative depreciation system (IRC Sec. 168)*

An alternative system is provided for property used predominantly outside the United States, tax-exempt use property, tax-exempt bond-financed property, and certain other property. In addition, the alternative method must be used for computing the portion of the depreciation allowance treated as a tax preference item for purposes of the alternative minimum tax. The allowable depreciation deductions for luxury cars and listed property used 50% or less in business are also determined under the alternative system.

Under this alternative depreciation system, the cost of property is recovered over the property's Asset Depreciation Range (ADR) midpoint life by the straight-line method. In computing the depreciation preference for alternative minimum tax purposes, recovery of the cost of personal property is calculated by the 150% declining-balance method.

An irrevocable election may be made to use the alternative depreciation system for all property in any class.

• *Disease-infested vineyards*

The depreciation period under MACRS for any grapevine replaced in a California vineyard is reduced from the 10-year period normally allowed for fruit-bearing vines to a five-year period if the vine is replaced (1) in a taxable year beginning after 1991 as a direct result of phylloxera infestation or (2) in a taxable year beginning after 1996 as a direct result of Pierce's Disease infestation. If an election is made to use the alternative depreciation method (discussed above), such grapevines will have a 10-year class life rather than the 20-year class life normally specified for such vines. (Sec. 17250, Rev. & Tax. Code)

• *Luxury autos (IRC Sec. 280F)*

There are limits on the allowable recovery deduction for passenger automobiles in a given tax year. For automobiles first placed in service during 2016, the federal and California limits are as follows: $3,160 for the first recovery year; $5,100 for the second year; $3,050 for the third year; and $1,875 for each succeeding tax year in the recovery period. The limits for trucks and vans, including sport utility vehicles (SUVs) and minivans that are built on a truck chassis, first placed in service during 2016, are $3,560, $5,700, $3,350, and $2,075, respectively.

Practice Pointer: Limits Apply to All Auto Depreciation

The limits on depreciation deductions for passenger automobiles used in a trade or business apply to all types of depreciation deductions for automobiles, including IRC Sec. 179 asset expense deductions.

Under both California and federal law, the amount of the deduction that may be claimed for electric passenger vehicles built by an original equipment manufacturer is tripled and the cost of an installed device that equips a nonclean-burning fuel vehicle to be propelled by clean-burning fuel is exempt from the deduction limitations. The higher depreciation limits for clean-fuel vehicles may be claimed for years following the regular depreciation period, as well as during the regular depreciation period.

• *Listed property (IRC Sec. 280F)*

Special depreciation rules apply to property that is classified as "listed property" that is not used more than 50% of the time for business purposes. The depreciation of such property must be determined using the alternative depreciation method discussed above. If the percentage of business use was originally more than 50% and drops below that percentage in a subsequent tax year, the excess depreciation deduction claimed in the years that it was predominantly used in a trade or business must be recaptured.

"Listed property" includes the following:

— a passenger automobile,

— other property used as transportation,

— property that is generally used for purposes of entertainment, recreation, or amusement,

— computers or peripheral equipment (except those used exclusively at regular business establishments), and

— for California purposes prior to the 2015 tax year and for federal purposes prior to the 2010 tax year, cellular telephones and other similar telecommunications equipment.

- *Effective date differences*

Because of California's federal conformity date history, California did not incorporate the following federal provisions until the 2010 tax year:

— the 75% deduction of qualified capital costs paid or incurred during the tax year for the purpose of complying with the Highway Diesel Fuel Sulfur Control Requirements of the EPA, which is available to a small business refinery, effective for federal purposes for expenses incurred after 2002 in tax years ending after 2002;

— the five-year amortization period for expenses paid or incurred in creating or acquiring a musical composition or a copyright to a musical composition, effective for property placed in service in tax years beginning after December 31, 2005 and before 2011, for federal purposes; and

— the shortened recovery period (from seven to three years) for young racehorses placed in service after 2008 and before 2014. Also, California has not conformed to the federal extension of the three-year recovery period for racehorses placed in service through 2016.

Consequently, adjustments will be required for such property placed in service prior to the 2010 tax year.

Assets Placed in Service Before 1987

The California rules for depreciation of assets placed in service before 1987 are the same as the federal rules in effect before the 1981 introduction of ACRS, except for the California prohibition against use of the "ADR" ranges. However, there are differences in the special rules for depreciation (or amortization) for certain classes of property, as explained below. Also, there have been many differences in prior years that may still have an effect on current depreciation; because of this possible effect, the prior-year differences are explained in some detail.

The basic rules for depreciation in the federal law (IRC Sec. 167) were incorporated in the California law by reference. However, California did not adopt the federal ACRS provisions (IRC Sec. 168) that apply to assets placed in service after 1980 and before 1987.

The federal law was amended in 1984, 1985, and 1986 to provide special rules for ACRS depreciation of luxury automobiles and of property not used principally in business. The California law applicable to pre-1987 assets was amended in 1985 to conform in principle to the pre-1986 federal rules; however, the California rules are based on the depreciation allowances under the ADR system, discussed below, rather than on the ACRS system.

- *California depreciation rules for pre-1987 assets*

In general, California depreciation methods and rates for pre-1987 assets are the same as the federal methods and rates applicable to assets placed in service during the years 1971 to 1980, inclusive. California has not conformed for pre-1987 assets to the mandatory federal Accelerated Cost Recovery System (ACRS) that was adopted in 1981 for tangible assets placed in service after 1980, except for certain residential property as explained at ¶318. The federal ACRS allows generally a much faster write-off of tangible depreciable property; however, the pre-1981 rules still apply to current federal depreciation on assets acquired before 1981, and also to depreciation on assets that are not covered by ACRS.

- *Depreciation based on useful life*

Under the California rules for pre-1987 assets, property must be depreciated over its estimated useful life (economic life as well as physical life). The taxpayer could determine the useful life by any means that produced a reasonable result, or could elect to use the useful life that is specified under the Federal Class Life Asset

Depreciation Range System (known as ADR). The ADR system was in effect for federal purposes during the years 1971 to 1980, and is still applicable to assets acquired during that period and to assets not covered by ACRS. California adopted the ADR system in 1976, for assets placed in service after 1970, and it is still in effect for assets placed in service before 1987, although California uses only the standard ADR rates and does not permit use of the "ranges" of 20% above or below the standard rate.

• Useful life under ADR system

Under the ADR system, the useful life for each class of property is specified in Federal Revenue Procedure 83-35, which superseded Revenue Procedure 77-10. The classes of assets and their prescribed useful life (called the "Asset Guideline Period") are listed in previous editions of the *Guidebook*.

There are no ADR classes for buildings, except for farm buildings. A taxpayer that elected ADR could determine the useful life of buildings by using the old federal guideline lives under Revenue Procedure 62-21 as in effect from 1962 to 1970, or may determine the useful life in some other way that produced a reasonable result. The old guideline lives for buildings were as follows:

Apartment buildings, hotels, theaters	40 years
Factories, garages, machine shops, office buildings, dwellings	45 years
Loft buildings, banks	50 years
Wholesale and retail business buildings, warehouses, grain elevators	60 years

A complete table with guideline lives can be found in Revenue Procedure 83-35, 1983-1 CB 745, or see pre-1988 editions of the *Guidebook To California Taxes*.

In *Appeal of Morris M. and Joyce E. Cohen* (1973) (CCH CALIFORNIA TAX REPORTS, ¶ 16-040.753), the State Board of Equalization (BOE) overruled the FTB and allowed the taxpayers to use a shorter life for 1968 depreciation than the guideline life shown in Rev. Proc. 62-21, discussed above. The taxpayers used a 25-year life for a new apartment building. The FTB used the 40-year life shown in Rev. Proc. 62-21, but offered no explanation or evidence to support the use of the longer life. The BOE stated that Rev. Proc. 62-21 was only a guide and could not be arbitrarily applied with no objective standard, and concluded that the FTB's action in the particular circumstances of this case was "arbitrary and capricious."

• California depreciation methods

In accordance with federal rules for property that is not covered by the Accelerated Cost Recovery System, California permits a variety of depreciation methods for assets placed in service before 1987 as follows:

(1) *Straight-line method:* This is the time-honored method, applicable to both tangible and intangible property (other methods, described below, apply only to tangible property). Under this method, the cost basis of the property, less salvage value, is written off ratably over the property's estimated useful life.

(2) *200% declining-balance method:* This method may be used only for new personal property with a useful life of three years or more, and for certain new residential rental property on which at least 80% of the gross rentals come from dwelling units.

(3) *Sum-of-the-years-digits method:* This method may be used wherever the 200% declining-balance method may be used.

(4) *150% declining-balance method:* This method may be applied to used personal property and to new real estate.

(5) *125% declining-balance method:* This method may be applied to used residential rental property having a remaining useful life of 20 years or more.

(6) Other "consistent methods" (*e.g.*, sinking-fund method), with limitations on the total amount deductible during the first two-thirds of the useful life.

In accordance with the federal rules for property not covered by ACRS, California ordinarily allowed only a part of a full year's depreciation in the first year, based on the portion of the year in which the property was in service. A taxpayer that elected the ADR system could also elect to use one of two first-year conventions (1) the half-year convention, or (2) the modified half-year convention. In the year property is sold the depreciation allowable may be reduced or eliminated, in cases where excessive depreciation was taken in prior years; this conforms to a 1962 federal ruling (Rev. Rul. 62-92, 1962-1 C.B. 29).

● *Salvage value*

In computing California depreciation for pre-1987 asset additions, salvage value must be taken into account in two ways. First, in all methods except declining-balance, salvage value must be deducted from the asset's cost basis in computing the annual write-off based on useful life. Second, regardless of method, no asset may be depreciated below a reasonable salvage value. However, as to depreciable personal property (except livestock) with a useful life of three years or more, the salvage value taken into account may be reduced by up to 10% of the basis of the property.

Generally, salvage value is the amount estimated to be recoverable by the taxpayer at the end of the asset's useful economic life.

● *Change of depreciation method*

California follows the federal rules for changing depreciation methods for pre-1987 asset additions, as set forth in Revenue Ruling 74-11. Application for permission to change should be made within the same time as the application to the Internal Revenue Service, and a copy of the federal form should be submitted to the FTB. California follows the federal rules in permitting changes from certain accelerated methods to the straight-line method without consent.

● *Prior-year differences*

There have been many differences over the years between California and federal rules for depreciation. Since these differences may still affect current depreciation computations or the adjusted basis of property, they are summarized briefly in the following comments.

Any such formula is subject to FTB approval. It appears, however, that use of such a formula would not be practicable where federal depreciation is determined under ACRS.

Prior to the introduction of the ADR system in 1971, the federal rules provided guidelines for depreciation rates, published in 1962 in Revenue Procedure 62-21. Assets placed in service after 1970 and before 1987 are governed by the ADR system.

The original federal provisions for accelerated depreciation methods were enacted in 1954, but California did not conform until 1959. During the period 1954-1958 the FTB maintained the position that in failing to adopt conforming legislation in those years the California legislature had issued a mandate that the accelerated depreciation methods were not allowable for California purposes. The FTB was sustained in this position by the BOE in *Appeal of Garrett Freightlines, Inc.* (CCH CALIFORNIA TAX REPORTS, ¶ 200-754) in 1957, and in *Appeal of William S. and Camilla A. Andrews* (CCH CALIFORNIA TAX REPORTS, ¶ 201-442) in 1959. Where this situation created a difference between California and federal depreciation in the years 1954-1958, the FTB permitted taxpayers to eliminate this difference over a period of years on a somewhat arbitrary basis, in order to avoid the necessity of continuing detailed separate computations of depreciation for California tax purposes.

Use of the 200% declining-balance and sum-of-the-years-digits methods was suspended under federal law for the period October 10, 1966, to March 9, 1967. California did not follow this federal suspension.

The California law was amended in 1977 to conform to a 1976 federal amendment permitting a change from accelerated methods to the straight-line method on real estate. The California amendment permitted the change in the first taxable year ending after 1976; the federal amendment applied to the first year ending after 1975. (The corporation tax law was not amended in 1977 to conform to this personal income tax amendment.)

Special Depreciation and Amortization Rules

• *Motion picture films, books, copyrights, etc.*

Special rules have been applied over the years to the depreciation or amortization of production costs of motion picture films. The major film studios maintaining their own distribution systems amortize such costs over estimated useful lives as have been established by their own experience, or by industry averages.

Independent producers, on the other hand, are permitted to use an estimated receipts method to develop a formula for cost amortization. This formula uses estimated total receipts as the denominator and periodic receipts as the numerator in arriving at the proportion of production cost to be amortized in each period. The use of this formula by independent producers was upheld by the BOE in *Appeal of Filmcraft Trading Corporation* (1957) (CCH CALIFORNIA TAX REPORTS, ¶10-905.551). The rule was further clarified in *Appeal of King Bros. Productions, Inc.* (1961) (CCH CALIFORNIA TAX REPORTS, ¶10-905.551). Similar treatment is accorded production costs of television films. The federal rules are substantially the same.

Taxpayers may elect to compute depreciation using the income forecast method for property such as film, video tape, sound recordings, copyrights, books, patents, and other property of a similar character approved by federal regulation. If such an election is made, the depreciation claimed must take into account the amount of income expected to be earned in connection with the property before the close of the 10th tax year following the tax year that the property was placed in service, which means that 11 tax years are taken into account.

Depreciation is determined using the income forecast method by multiplying the property's cost (less estimated salvage value) by a fraction, the numerator of which is the income generated by the property during the year and the denominator of which is the total estimated income to be derived from the property during its useful life. The income forecast method may not be used to compute depreciation for intangible property amortizable under IRC Sec. 197 or for consumer durables subject to rent-to-own contracts.

Although California conforms to federal law concerning the income forecast method, unlike federal law, California law does not prohibit taking distribution costs into account for purposes of determining the depreciation deduction using the income forecast method. (Sec. 17250.5(a)(3), Rev. & Tax. Code) Nor does California incorporate the federal provision providing special rules for depreciating participations and residuals, allowing taxpayers to currently deduct participations and residuals rather than depreciate them using the income forecast method. (Sec. 17250.5(a)(4), Rev. & Tax. Code)

As a result of California's federal conformity date history (¶103), California does not incorporate until the 2010 tax year federal amendments that allow amortization of expenses paid or incurred in creating or acquiring a musical composition or a copyright to a musical composition over five-years, effective for property placed in service in tax years beginning after 2005 and before 2011.

In addition, California does not conform to federal law that allows film productions to expense the first $15 million ($20 million in specified low-income or distressed communities) of "qualified" film or television production expenses rather than depreciate or amortize such costs. (Sec. 17201.5, Rev. & Tax. Code) The federal election is applicable to qualified film and television productions commencing after October 22, 2004, and before 2015. Consequently, taxpayers that claim the deduction on their federal return, must make an addition adjustment on their California return, but will also be able to increase the depreciation deduction claimed for any depreciable property for which the federal current expense deduction was claimed.

- *Geological and geophysical expenditures*

   California does not follow the federal provision that allows the amortization of geological and geophysical expenditures over a two-year period (seven years for major integrated oil companies). (Sec. 17250.5(b), Rev. & Tax. Code)

- *"Safe harbor" transactions*

   The federal Economic Recovery Act of 1981 permits the transfer of depreciation benefits and investment tax credits between taxpayers under certain conditions. This is accomplished by so-called "safe harbor" rules that treat as a lease what would otherwise be treated as a sale. Because California has not conformed to these federal provisions, California follows prior federal rulings and may treat as a sale a transaction that is treated as a lease under the federal rules. See Legal Ruling 419 (1981) (CCH CALIFORNIA TAX REPORTS, ¶ 206-665) for discussion of the effect of this difference on the taxpayers involved.

¶311 Asset Expense Election (IRC "Sec. 179" Election) and Other Current Expense Deductions

> **Law:** Secs. 17201, 17255, 17257, 17257.2, 17257.4 (CCH CALIFORNIA TAX REPORTS, ¶ 16-040).
>
> *Comparable Federal:* Secs. 179, 1400N (CCH U.S. MASTER TAX GUIDE ¶ 1208).
>
> *California Forms:* FTB 3885A (Depreciation and Amortization Adjustments), Sch. D (California Capital Gain or Loss Adjustment).

Although California has adopted the federal asset expense election for assets placed in service after 1986, California does not incorporate federal provisions that make the following changes:

— increased the maximum federal deduction amount for property placed in service during taxable years after 2002 (see below for specific amounts allowed in specific years) and allow enhanced deductions for property purchased by qualified disaster victims or for qualified disaster property;

— increased the phase-out amount to $400,000 (adjusted for inflation) for property placed in service after 2002 and before 2007; $500,000 for property placed in service in 2007; $800,000 for property placed in service in 2008 or 2009; or $2 million for property placed in service after 2009 (adjusted annually for inflation beginning with the 2016 tax year); and

— allow the deduction to be claimed for off-the-shelf computer software purchased, qualified real property (i.e., qualified leasehold improvement property, qualified restaurant property, and qualified retail improvement property), or for air conditioning and heating units after 2015.

(Sec. 17201, Rev. & Tax. Code; Sec. 17255, Rev. & Tax. Code)

California's maximum current expense deduction is $25,000 for property placed in service after 2002, as opposed to the federal maximums listed below. Currently, there are no California and federal differences on maximum deduction limits for sports utility vehicles. Federal provisions limit the asset expense deduction to $25,000 for SUVs with loaded weights between 6,000 and 14,000 pounds, applicable to vehicles placed in service after October 22, 2004. SUVs placed in service after 2002 and before October 23, 2004, qualified for the higher deduction on a taxpayer's federal, but not California, return. California also does not adopt the increased expense deduction available for federal purposes for qualified property used in a renewal community.

The following chart lists the maximum deductions for both California and federal purposes for post-1992 tax years:

MAXIMUM CURRENT EXPENSE DEDUCTION

Property placed in service in:	California Law	Federal Law
2016	$25,000	$500,000
2015	$25,000	$500,000
2014	$25,000	$500,000
2013	$25,000	$500,000
2012	$25,000	$500,000
2011	$25,000	$500,000
2010	$25,000	$500,000
2008-2009	$25,000	$250,000
2007	$25,000	$125,000
2006	$25,000	$108,000
2005	$25,000	$105,000
2004	$25,000	$102,000
2003	25,000	100,000
2001-2002	24,000	24,000
2000	20,000	20,000
1999	19,000	19,000
1998	16,000	18,500
1997	13,000	18,000
After 1992 and before 1997	10,000	17,500

Because depreciable basis must be reduced by any IRC Sec. 179 deduction, the depreciable basis of property may differ for federal and state purposes.

For California purposes, the deduction is reduced, but not below zero, by the excess of the total investment in qualified property over $200,000 in the tax year. (Sec. 17255(b), Rev. & Tax. Code) For federal purposes, the $200,000 limit is increased to $400,000 for federal purposes for property placed in service after 2002 and before 2007 ($410,000 for the 2004 tax year, $420,000 for the 2005 tax year, and $430,000 for the 2006 tax year, as indexed for inflation); $500,000 for property placed in service during 2007; $800,000 for property placed in service during 2008 or 2009; and $2 million for property placed in service after 2009 (adjusted annually for inflation beginning with the 2016 tax year).

The excess of the deduction over otherwise allowable depreciation is recaptured if the property ceases to be used predominately in the trade or business before the end of its recovery period. The deduction cannot exceed the taxable income derived from the trade or business during the tax year.

In addition, California does not incorporate the federal provision that allows taxpayers to make, revoke, or modify an IRC Sec. 179 election without IRS permission on an amended return. (Sec. 17255(e), Rev. & Tax. Code) Presumably, a taxpayer would be required to obtain the California Franchise Tax Board's permission to make, revoke, or amend an election on the California return.

• *Married and registered domestic partner taxpayers*

Married and registered domestic partner (RDP) taxpayers who file a joint return are to be treated as one taxpayer for purposes of the dollar limitations. For married taxpayers filing separate returns, unless otherwise elected, 50% of the cost of the qualifying property that is to be expensed is allocated to each spouse. RDPs may be required to make adjustments on their California return, see ¶119.

• *Other current expense deductions*

California does not incorporate other federal provisions that allow taxpayers to currently deduct expenses associated with:

— certain refineries under IRC Sec. 179C (Sec. 17257, Rev. & Tax. Code);

— energy efficient commercial buildings under IRC Sec. 179B (Sec. 17257.2, Rev. & Tax. Code); and

— advanced mine safety equipment under IRC Sec. 179E (Sec. 17257.4, Rev. & Tax. Code).

¶312 Additional First-Year Depreciation

Law: Sec. 17250 (CCH CALIFORNIA TAX REPORTS, ¶ 16-040).

Comparable Federal: Sec. 168(k) (CCH U.S. MASTER TAX GUIDE ¶ 1237).

California Forms: FTB 3885A (Depreciation and Amortization Adjustments), Sch. D (California Capital Gain or Loss Adjustment).

California does not incorporate federal law allowing an additional 30%, 50%, or 100% first-year bonus depreciation deduction for qualified property acquired and placed in service during 2008—2019 (through 2020 in the case of property with a long production period and certain noncommercial aircraft). (Sec. 17250(a)(4), Rev. & Tax. Code) Consequently, any bonus depreciation deduction claimed on the federal return must be added back to federal adjusted gross income, and the basis of property for which the federal bonus deduction was claimed will be different under California law.

¶313 Amortization of Cost of Acquiring a Lease

Law: Sec. 17201 (CCH CALIFORNIA TAX REPORTS, ¶ 15-615).

Comparable Federal: Sec. 178 (CCH U.S. MASTER TAX GUIDE ¶ 1234).

California law incorporates the federal law by reference.

For purposes of amortizing the cost of acquiring a lease, the term of the lease includes all renewal options (and any other period for which the parties to the lease reasonably expect the lease to be renewed) if less than 75% of such cost is attributable to the unexpired term of the lease on the date of its acquisition. In determining the unexpired term of the lease, the taxpayer may not take into consideration any period for which the lease may subsequently be renewed, extended, or continued pursuant to an option exercisable by the lessee. (Sec. 17201, Rev. & Tax. Code)

¶314 Amortization of Pollution Control Facilities

Law: Sec. 17250 (CCH CALIFORNIA TAX REPORTS, ¶ 15-615, 16-015).

Comparable Federal: Sec. 169 (CCH U.S. MASTER TAX GUIDE ¶ 1287).

California Form: FTB 3580 (Application to Amortize Certified Pollution Control Facility).

California incorporates federal law allowing an accelerated (60-month) write-off of pollution control facilities, with the following modifications (Sec. 17250, Rev. & Tax. Code):

— the California deduction is available only for facilities located in California; and

— the "state certifying authority" in cases involving air pollution is the State Air Resources Board and in cases involving water pollution is the State Water Resources Control Board.

Also, California did not conform to federal amendments that expanded the amortization deduction for atmospheric pollution control facilities until the 2010 tax year. The amendments allow the amortization deduction to be claimed for qualified air pollution control facilities placed in service after April 11, 2005, even if not used in connection with a plant that was in operation before January 1, 1976. However, the amortization period applicable to taxpayers eligible under the expanded criteria is extended from 60 months to 84 months. To the extent taxpayers only qualified for the amortization deduction on their pre-2010 federal tax return under the expanded eligibility criteria, the taxpayers were required to make an addition adjustment on their pre-2010 tax year California tax return and are required to make corresponding adjustments in subsequent tax years.

FTB 3580 may be used to file an election with the Franchise Tax Board for an accelerated write-off.

¶315 Amortization of Reforestation Expenditures

Law: Secs. 17201, 17278.5 (CCH CALIFORNIA TAX REPORTS, ¶ 15-690, 16-055).

Comparable Federal: Sec. 194 (CCH U.S. MASTER TAX GUIDE ¶ 1287).

California Form: FTB 3885A (Depreciation and Amortization Adjustments).

California law is the same as federal as of the current IRC tie-in date (see ¶ 103), except that California limits the deduction to expenses associated with qualified timber located in California. (Sec. 17201, Rev. & Tax. Code; Sec. 17278.5, Rev. & Tax. Code) Under both California and federal law taxpayers may currently deduct up to $10,000 ($5,000 for married taxpayers or registered domestic partners filing separately) in qualified reforestation expenses and to amortize any remaining costs over a period of 84 months.

¶316 Accelerated Write-Offs for Economic Incentive Areas

Law: Secs. 17266, 17267.2, 17267.6, 17268, 18036 (CCH CALIFORNIA TAX REPORTS, ¶ 16-040).

Comparable Federal: None.

California Forms: FTB 3805Z (Enterprise Zone Deduction and Credit Summary), FTB 3807 (Local Agency Military Base Recovery Area Deduction and Credit Summary), FTB 3809 (Targeted Tax Area Deduction and Credit Summary), Sch. D (California Capital Gain or Loss Adjustment).

Under the tax incentive programs enacted by California and in effect prior to 2014, explained at ¶ 104, accelerated write-offs are allowed for certain property as explained below.

• *Property used in enterprise zones, LAMBRAs, and the targeted tax area*

Prior to the 2014 tax year, taxpayers could expense 40% of the cost of IRC Sec. 1245 property that was purchased for use exclusively in a business conducted in an enterprise zone, or a local agency military base recovery area (LAMBRA). The deduction was required to be claimed in the year the property was placed into service. (Sec. 17267.2, Rev. & Tax. Code; Sec. 17268, Rev. & Tax. Code) A similar deduction was available to businesses located in a targeted tax area (TTA) prior to the TTAs designation expiration on January 1, 2013. A business expense deduction could not be generated in a TTA after 2012, however a deduction claimed prior to 2013 could still be subject to recapture. (Sec. 17267.6, Rev. & Tax. Code)

The cost that may be taken into account is limited to $100,000 for the taxable year that an area is designated as a qualifying zone or LAMBRA, $100,000 for the first taxable year thereafter, $75,000 for the second and third taxable years after the year of designation, and $50,000 for each taxable year after that. For businesses located in an enterprise zone expansion area, the amount of the deduction was determined using the original zone's designation date.

CCH Practice Tip: Property Must Be Placed In Service

To qualify for the accelerated write-off, the property had to be placed in service within the zone or area prior to the expiration of the zone's or area's designation.

Taxpayers that elected the accelerated write-off for property located in economic incentive areas could not claim the IRC Sec. 179 asset expense election described at ¶311 on their California returns for the same property. The election is not available to estates or trusts or for property acquired from certain related persons.

The expense deduction is recaptured if the property ceases to be used in the zone or area at any time before the close of the second taxable year after the property was placed in service. The deduction claimed by LAMBRA businesses may also be recaptured if the taxpayer does not satisfy the net increase in jobs requirement (¶104).

A taxpayer's basis in the property must be adjusted to reflect the expense deduction. Conversely, if the deduction is subject to recapture, the depreciable basis of the property may be increased by the amount recaptured. (Reg. 17267.1, 18 CCR)

The enterprise zone deduction is claimed on FTB 3805Z, the LAMBRA deduction is claimed on FTB 3807, and the targeted tax area deduction was claimed on FTB 3809; see ¶104. The deduction must be claimed on the original return and may not be claimed on an amended return.

¶317 Domestic Production Activities Deduction

Law: Sec. 17201.6 (CCH CALIFORNIA TAX REPORTS, ¶16-085).

Comparable Federal: Sec. 199 (CCH U.S. MASTER TAX GUIDE ¶245).

California Forms: Sch. CA (540) (California Adjustments - Residents), Sch. CA (540NR) (California Adjustments - Nonresidents or Part-Year Residents).

California does not incorporate the federal deduction of income from qualified domestic production activities. (Sec. 17201.6, Rev. & Tax. Code) Consequently, any deduction claimed on the federal return must be added back for California personal income tax purposes.

¶318 Refiners' Sulfur Rules Compliance Costs

Law: Secs. 17201.4, 17255.5 (CCH CALIFORNIA TAX REPORTS, ¶16-055, 16-220).

Comparable Federal: Sec. 179B.

California Forms: Sch. CA (540) (California Adjustments - Residents), Sch. CA (540NR) (California Adjustments - Nonresidents or Part-Year Residents).

California does not incorporate the federal deduction available for capital costs incurred in complying with Environmental Protection Agency (EPA) sulfur regulations. (Sec. 17201.4, Rev. & Tax. Code). However, prior to the 2009 tax year California did allow small business refiners to elect to deduct up to 75% of qualified capital costs paid or incurred during the taxable year to bring California facilities into compliance with EPA or California Air Resources Board regulations. The California deduction was applicable to qualified capital costs paid or incurred by the taxpayer during any taxable year that included the period beginning after 2003 and ending on May 31, 2007. California's deduction was similar to the deduction allowed under federal law (IRC Sec. 179B), but differed from federal law concerning its definition of "small refiners" and "qualified capital costs." (Former Sec. 17255.5, Rev. & Tax. Code)

Taxpayers that claimed the deduction were required to reduce the basis of the property by the amount of the deduction claimed. In addition, if the property was of a character that would be subject to depreciation, the amount of the deduction claimed had to be treated as an allowance for depreciation for purposes of IRC Sec. 1245, relating to the gain from dispositions of depreciable property, and related California provisions. (Sec. 17255.5, Rev. & Tax. Code)

California provides a credit for the qualified capital costs paid or incurred by a qualified small refiner at a California facility used to produce ultra-low sulfur diesel fuel (see ¶151).

¶319   Depletion and Natural Resources

Law: Secs. 17681, 17681.3, 17681.6 (CCH CALIFORNIA TAX REPORTS, ¶ 15-665, 16-037).

Comparable Federal: Secs. 611-14, 636, 638 (CCH U.S. MASTER TAX GUIDE ¶ 1289, 1291).

With the exception of the federal extension of the exemption for owners of marginal oil and gas wells, California law is the same as federal as of the current IRC tie-in date (see ¶ 103) for tax years beginning after 1992. (Sec. 17681, Rev. & Tax. Code)

• *Percentage depletion*

Both California and federal law allow percentage depletion on specified types of depletable assets. This allowance is computed as a percentage of gross income from the property, with a limitation based on 50% of the taxable income from the property before the depletion allowance (100% in the case of oil and gas properties). However, California does not incorporate the federal suspension of the 100% taxable income limit on percentage depletion deductions for oil and gas production from marginal properties. (Sec. 17681.6, Rev. & Tax. Code) The suspension applies for federal purposes for the 2009—2011 tax years and for tax years beginning after 1997 and before 2008.

California also does not incorporate the IRC Sec. 613A(d)(4) increase in the barrel limitation from 50,000 to 75,000 for purposes of small refiners qualifying as independent producers eligible to use the percentage depletion method. (Sec. 17681.3, Rev. & Tax. Code) Therefore, small refiners that produce more than 50,000 barrels may have to make an addition adjustment on their California return.

• *Oil and gas wells and geothermal deposits*

California fully conforms to the federal law on percentage depletion for oil and gas wells and geothermal deposits. Under the incorporated federal law, the following depletion rates apply:

     — 22% for domestic regulated natural gas and natural gas sold under a fixed contract;

     — 10% for qualified natural gas from geopressurized brine;

     — 15% for domestic crude oil and natural gas from wells of certain independent producers and royalty owners, limited to 65% of the taxpayer's taxable income before the depletion allowance; and

     — 15% for geothermal deposits located in the United States.

For taxable years beginning before 1993, instead of conforming to federal law, California provided a 22% depletion rate for oil, gas, and geothermal wells, up to a maximum of 50% of the taxpayer's taxable income from the property before the depletion allowance. California also imposed a limit on depletion, applicable when the accumulated depletion allowed or allowable exceeded the taxpayer's adjusted interest in the property.

• *Depletable assets other than oil, gas, and geothermal*

California also adopts federal percentage depletion provisions for depletable assets other than oil, gas, and geothermal deposits. (17681, Rev. & Tax. Code)

In pre-1987 tax years California law provided its own depletion percentages. See the 1986 and prior editions of this *Guidebook*.

• *Continental shelf areas*

California law conforms to IRC Sec. 638, concerning continental shelf areas. Therefore, natural resources include those located in seabeds and the subsoil of submarine areas adjacent to the territorial waters of the United States over which the

United States has exclusive rights, in accordance with international law, in regard to the exploration and exploitation of natural resources. (Sec. 17681, Rev. & Tax. Code)

¶320 Development and Exploration Expenses of Mines, etc.

Law: Secs. 17260, 17681 (CCH California Tax Reports, ¶15-665).

Comparable Federal: Secs. 193, 263(c), 616-17 (CCH U.S. Master Tax Guide ¶987 et seq.).

Development and exploration expenditures in connection with a mine or other mineral deposit (other than an oil, gas, or geothermal wells) may be deducted currently or may be deferred (as to development expenses only), at the taxpayer's election, subject to the following general rules:

— Exploration expenses are those paid or incurred prior to the development period. Deductions for such expenses are subject to "recapture" when the mine reaches the productive stage.

— Development expenses are those paid or incurred after the existence of ores or minerals in commercially marketable quantities has been established. There is no dollar limitation on such deductions.

— Alternatively, development expenses may be capitalized and amortized on a ratable basis over a ten-year period depending on the units of ores or minerals produced and sold. However, the election to capitalize and amortize applies only to the excess of development expenditures paid or incurred during the taxable year over the net receipts during the year from the sale of ores or minerals produced. California has adopted federal rules for post-1986 expenditures.

Both California and federal laws permit the taxpayer to elect to expense intangible drilling and development costs of oil, gas, and geothermal wells. (Sec. 17681, Rev. & Tax. Code)

Unlike federal law, California law does not allow taxpayers to currently deduct expenditures for tertiary injectants. Such expenditures must be depreciated for California personal income tax purposes. (Sec. 17260, Rev. & Tax. Code)

¶321 Contributions

Law: Secs. 17201, 17275.5 (CCH California Tax Reports, ¶15-625, 16-220).

Comparable Federal: Secs. 170, 501(k) (CCH U.S. Master Tax Guide ¶1058 et seq.).

California Forms: Sch. CA (540) (California Adjustments - Residents), Sch. CA (540NR) (California Adjustments - Nonresidents or Part-Year Residents).

The current California contribution deduction is generally the same as the federal deduction as of the current IRC tie-in date (¶103), with the exception of the excise tax on premiums concerning split dollar insurance arrangements (see below). (Sec. 17201, Rev. & Tax. Code) In addition, subtraction adjustments may also be required as a result of California's nonconformity with the federal provisions limiting deductions for contributions to donor advised funds and disallowing the deduction for contributions of certain interests in buildings located in registered historic districts unless the requisite filing fee is paid. (Sec. 17275.5(d) and (e), Rev. & Tax. Code)

As a result of California's current IRC tie-in date, California does not conform to the increase in the amount of the charitable deduction to 50% (100% for farmers and ranchers) of a taxpayer's contribution base that may be taken for contributions of qualified conservation real property. Consequently, conservation contributions of capital gain real property are subject to the same limitations and carryover rules as other charitable contributions of capital gain property. Also, because of the IRC tie-in date, California does not conform to the federal law providing special treatment for certain agricultural research organizations for contributions made on or after December 18, 2015. California also does not conform to federal provisions that allow enhanced charitable contributions for wholesome food inventories. (Sec. 17275.2, Rev. & Tax. Code)

• *Carryovers*

California follows federal law, which allows a five-year carryover of contributions that exceed the percentage limit and specifies how the carryover is to be absorbed in succeeding tax years. (Sec. 17201, Rev. & Tax. Code)

• *Automobile expense*

California conforms to federal law allowing taxpayers to claim a fixed automobile mileage rate (14¢ per mile for 2016) for use of an automobile in activities for the benefit of an organization that qualifies for deductible contributions. (Sec. 17201, Rev. & Tax. Code)

Practice Note: Purchase of Special Interest License Plate Qualifies for Charitable Deduction

The portion of the fee paid by a purchaser of a California Arts Council license plate that exceeds the amount normally paid for a license plate and that is paid to support the Art Council's programs for children and communities qualifies for a personal income tax charitable deduction. (*FTB Information Letter 2009-02*, CCH CALIFORNIA TAX REPORTS, ¶ 405-025)

• *Split dollar insurance arrangements*

California incorporates federal law that generally denies a charitable deduction for a transfer of money to a charitable organization if, in connection with the transfer (1) the charitable organization directly or indirectly pays a premium on a life insurance, annuity, or endowment contract, and (2) the transferor, any member of the transferor's family, or any other person (other than a charity) chosen by the transferor is a direct or indirect beneficiary under the contract. However, a federal provision requiring payment of an excise tax equal to the amount of nondeductible premiums does not apply for California purposes. (Sec. 17275.5, Rev. & Tax. Code)

• *Substantiation*

California conforms to federal provisions as of the current IRC tie-in date (see ¶ 103) that allow a deduction for charitable contributions only if the contributions are verified under regulations prescribed by the Secretary of the Treasury (the Franchise Tax Board for California purposes). (Sec. 17201, Rev. & Tax. Code)

All cash contributions, regardless of amount, require either a bank statement, receipt from the charity, or a payroll deduction record. For cash donations of $250 or more, a written acknowledgment from the charitable organization is also required. Noncash contributions require additional documentation that varies depending on the value of the donation as follows:

— *Less than $250:* Receipt from charity with name, date, and donation description.

— *Greater than $250 but less than $500:* Contemporaneous written acknowledgment from charity.

— *Greater than $500 but less than $5,000:* Written acknowledgment plus file IRS Form 8283, Noncash Charitable Contributions.

— *Greater than $5,000 (not including stock, art, and autos):* Qualified appraisal and IRS Form 8283.

Substantiation requirements for stock, art, and autos are outlined in IRS Publication 526, Charitable Contributions. Taxpayers who donate clothing and household items and receive only a receipt from the charity with a date should keep detailed descriptions of items donated as well as the condition of the items in order to substantiate the value of the donation. Taxpayers may want to take pictures of the items so they will be able to prove "good used condition or better" if need be during an audit. (*FTB Tax News* (March 2012) (CCH California Tax Reports, ¶405-595))

In *Appeal of James N. Harger* (2003) (CCH California Tax Reports, ¶15-625.704) the California State Board of Equalization upheld the FTB's disallowance of a charitable contribution deduction for a residential structure because the taxpayer failed to prove that he actually delivered the structure to the charity. The charity's acknowledgment of its receipt of the structure, by itself, was insufficient evidence of actual delivery because the charity was providing bogus appraisals to other donors of structures that were to be demolished rather than donated to the charity. In addition, the taxpayer's contention that he observed the disassembling of the residence in preparation for its removal and reassembly elsewhere was too self-serving to be credible.

¶322 Designated Contributions

Law: Secs. 18705—18900.26 (CCH California Tax Reports, ¶89-224).

Comparable Federal: None.

California Form: Form 540 (California Resident Income Tax Return).

California permits taxpayers to make certain contributions by designating the desired amounts (full dollar amounts) on their returns as additions to their tax liability. Thus, the designated amounts increase the balance payable on the return or reduce the refund, if any. The contributions, funds, and accounts listed on the 2016 returns are as follows:

— Rare and Endangered Species Preservation Program.
— Alzheimer's Disease and Related Disorders Fund.
— California Breast Cancer Research Fund.
— California Firefighters' Memorial Fund.
— Emergency Food for Families Fund.
— California Peace Officer Memorial Foundation Fund.
— California Sea Otter Fund.
— California Cancer Research Fund.
— Child Victims of Human Trafficking Fund.
— School Supplies for Homeless Children Fund.
— State Parks Protection Fund/Parks Pass Purchase.
— Protect Our Coast and Oceans Fund.
— Keep Arts in Schools Fund.
— State Children's Trust Fund for the Prevention of Child Abuse.
— Prevention of Animal Homelessness and Cruelty Fund.
— Revive the Salton Sea Fund.
— California Domestic Violence Victims Fund.
— Special Olympics Fund.
— Type 1 Diabetes Research Fund.

In addition, a taxpayer who is 65 years of age or older and who is entitled to claim an additional personal exemption credit may designate an amount not to exceed the amount of the credit as a contribution to the California Seniors Special Fund. The amount of the contribution need not be reduced to reflect any income-based reduction in the amount of the credit.

All the above designated contributions are permitted as charitable contributions (¶321).

¶323 Alimony

Law: Secs. 17201, 17302 (CCH CALIFORNIA TAX REPORTS, ¶ 15-610, 16-012).

Comparable Federal: Sec. 215 (CCH U.S. MASTER TAX GUIDE ¶ 771).

California Forms: Sch. CA (540) (California Adjustments - Residents), Sch. CA (540NR) (California Adjustments - Nonresidents or Part-Year Residents).

Alimony payments includible in income of the spouse who receives the payments (¶ 204) are deductible in computing adjusted gross income of the California resident spouse who makes the payments. (IRC Sec. 215; Sec. 17201, Rev. & Tax. Code) Taxable alimony payments include payments made to a third party, including cash payments to a third party to provide a residence for a former spouse (*i.e.*, rent, mortgage, utilities, etc.), medical cost payments, or other such expenses incurred by the recipient.

The following types of payments are not considered alimony:

— property settlement payments, even if required by the divorce decree or other written instrument or agreement;

— retirement benefits that the other spouse is entitled to receive;

— voluntary payments made before they are required by a divorce decree or agreement; and

— child support payments.

(*Alimony—Frequently Asked Questions*, California Franchise Tax Board, February 14, 2008, CCH CALIFORNIA TAX REPORTS, ¶ 404-562)

Nonresidents and part-year residents are allowed a deduction for alimony paid in the same ratio that California adjusted gross income for the entire year (computed without regard to the alimony deduction) bears to total adjusted gross income (computed without regard to the alimony deduction). (Sec. 17302, Rev. & Tax. Code)

Questions frequently arise concerning the relationship of alimony with child support payments and family support payments. Payments designated as child support are not deductible. The Franchise Tax Board has taken the position that if the payor is required to pay both alimony and child support, but pays less than the total amount required, the payments are applied first to child support and any remaining amount is considered alimony.

Payments designated as family support in a divorce decree or separation instrument are considered alimony, unless the decree or instrument designates a portion of the payments as child support. (*Alimony—Frequently Asked Questions*, California Franchise Tax Board, February 14, 2008, CCH CALIFORNIA TAX REPORTS, ¶ 404-562)

Practice Tip: Alimony Received or Paid by Registered Domestic Partners (RDPs)

If a court orders termination of a registered domestic partnership and a California Family Law Court awards spousal support that satisfies the requirements under tax law for alimony, the payments are taxable to the payee and deductible by the payor for California purposes. However, federal treatment of these payments is uncertain. An RDP receiving alimony not included in federal income should include that amount on line 11, column C, of his or her California RDP Adjustments Worksheet. An RDP paying alimony not included in the RDP's adjustments to income for federal purposes should enter that amount on line 31, column C, of his or her California RDP Adjustments Worksheet, as a positive amount. (FTB Pub. 737, Tax Information for Registered Domestic Partners)

A California-federal difference could arise in a case in which a California court holds a foreign divorce invalid. For federal tax purposes, the deductibility of alimony paid under a state divorce decree is not affected by another state's declaration that the divorce is invalid. The rule is designed to avoid the uncertainty that could arise from conflicting state determinations regarding the validity of divorces.

• *Attorney fees*

Only those attorney fees attributable to alimony payments may be deducted. Those associated with a property settlement are subject to tax. Taxpayers should be careful as to how stipulation agreements are worded to ensure the proper allocation of deductions. (*Appeal of Zornes* (2009) CCH CALIFORNIA TAX REPORTS, ¶405-072)

• *Paid to nonresident*

Alimony paid by a California resident is deductible even if paid to a former spouse who is not a California resident, although the former spouse is not taxable on the income. This has been the policy of the Franchise Tax Board for many years, following two 1951 decisions of the California Court of Appeal. These cases are *Ada Davis Francis, Executrix v. McColgan* (CCH CALIFORNIA TAX REPORTS, ¶15-610.65) and *M.B. Silberberg, Executor v. Franchise Tax Board* (CCH CALIFORNIA TAX REPORTS, ¶15-610.65).

• *Mortgage payments*

In *Appeal of Karapetian* (2004) (CCH CALIFORNIA TAX REPORTS, ¶15-610.45), the State Board of Equalization followed the IRS's ruling in *Baxter v. Commissioner*, T.C. Memo 1999-190, and held that mortgage payments made by a former husband on behalf of his ex-wife pursuant to a marital settlement agreement was taxable alimony because the marital settlement agreement provided that the obligation of her former husband to make mortgage payments on the taxpayer's home would cease upon her death. Because the payments were taxable alimony, the ex-wife was not entitled to deduct those payments as qualified residence interest. The payments were deductible only by the former husband.

¶324 Amortization of Bond Premium

Law: Secs. 17201 (CCH CALIFORNIA TAX REPORTS, ¶15-615).

Comparable Federal: Sec. 171 (CCH U.S. MASTER TAX GUIDE ¶1967).

California Forms: FTB 3885A (Depreciation and Amortization Adjustments).

Deduction is allowed at the taxpayer's election for amortization of premium on bonds the income of which is taxable under California law. California law incorporates the federal law by reference. (Sec. 17201, Rev. & Tax. Code) However, the amortization may apply to different bonds because of the differences in taxability of government bond interest. This means that amortization may be deductible on a given bond on the California return and not on the federal, or vice versa. Both federal and California law treat amortizable bond premium deductions as interest.

As to nontaxable bonds, no deduction is allowed but amortization of premium must nevertheless be taken into account in computing the adjusted basis of the bond at time of sale or other disposition. This adjustment may be different for California purposes than for federal because the particular bond involved may be taxable for California purposes but not federal, or vice versa.

In some computations of adjusted basis involving amortization of premium on bonds, the result will be different for California purposes than for federal. This is because California did not conform to certain amendments to federal law affecting the computation of amortization until subsequent years, so that the computations of amortization may be different even though the two laws are now the same.

Amortization is not allowed on any portion of bond premium attributable to conversion features of the bond.

Special rules are provided for dealers in tax-exempt securities. See ¶210.

¶325 Medical Expenses

Law: Secs. 17021.7, 17201, 17241 (CCH CALIFORNIA TAX REPORTS, ¶15-165, 15-755).

Comparable Federal: Sec. 213 (CCH U.S. MASTER TAX GUIDE ¶1015 et seq.).

California Forms: Sch. CA (540) (California Adjustments - Residents), Sch. CA (540NR) (California Adjustments - Nonresidents or Part-Year Residents).

With the exception of the treatment of registered domestic partners, California law is the same as federal with respect to the deductibility of medical expenses, including the disallowance of a medical expense deduction for unnecessary cosmetic surgery. (Sec. 17201, Rev. & Tax. Code) California, but not federal law, treats a taxpayer's registered domestic partner as the taxpayer's spouse for purposes of determining the amount that may be deducted. (Sec. 17021.7, Rev. & Tax. Code)

A deduction is permitted for medical and dental expenses, not compensated for by insurance or otherwise, to the extent that such expenses paid for medical and dental care of the taxpayer, a spouse, and dependents exceed a certain percentage of adjusted gross income. The applicable percentage is 7.5% of federal adjusted gross income for California purposes and for taxpayers age 65 or older for 2013, 2014, 2015, and 2016 for federal purposes, and 10% for all other taxpayers for federal purposes. (Sec. 17241, Rev. & Tax. Code). The definition of "dependent" is the same as for purposes of the exemption credit for dependents (¶115), and is determined without reference to the gross income of the dependent.

The definition of "medical care" includes amounts paid for qualified long-term care services and eligible long-term care premiums paid under qualified long-term care insurance contracts. For the 2016 taxable year, "eligible long-term care premiums" must not exceed the following amounts:

— $390 for persons attaining age 40 or less by the close of the taxable year;

— $730 for persons attaining an age over 40 but not over 50 by the close of the taxable year;

— $1,460 for persons attaining an age over 50 but not over 60 by the close of the taxable year;

— $3,900 for persons attaining an age over 60 but not over 70 by the close of the taxable year; and

— $4,870 for persons attaining an age over 70 by the close of the taxable year.

The limitation on itemized deductions for high-income taxpayers does not apply to medical expenses (¶303).

¶326 Medical and Health Savings Accounts

Law: Secs. 17201, 17215, 17215.4 (CCH CALIFORNIA TAX REPORTS, ¶15-755, 16-100).

Comparable Federal: Secs. 138, 220, 223 (CCH U.S. MASTER TAX GUIDE ¶860, 1286).

Although California incorporates federal law concerning medical savings accounts (MSAs), California does not recognize the federal treatment of health savings accounts (HSAs).

- *Medical savings accounts*

California law is the same as federal law concerning MSAs as of the current IRC tie-in date (¶103), with the exception of the penalty amount imposed on withdrawals from an MSA that are used for nonqualified expenses and the imposition by California of penalties on rollovers from MSAs to health savings accounts (see ¶247 for a discussion of the penalty). (Sec. 17201, Rev. & Tax. Code; Sec. 17215, Rev. & Tax. Code)

CCH Comment: Registered Domestic Partners

Although RDPs or former RDPs are generally required to be treated as married taxpayers or former spouses under California income tax laws, an RDP will not be treated as a spouse if such treatment would result in disqualification of an Archer medical savings account. (Sec. 17021.7, Rev. & Tax. Code) See ¶119 for a discussion of adjustments required to be made RDPs and the California tax treatment of same-sex married couples.

Taxpayers that claim a federal deduction for contributions to an Archer MSA or MedicarePlus Choice MSA may claim the same deduction on their California return. The deduction is not subject to the 7.5% floor for itemized medical expense deductions (discussed at ¶325). Under both California and federal law, a contribution made after the end of the taxable year is considered to have been made on the last day of the year, provided that the contribution is on account of such taxable year and is made no later than the due date of the return.

- *Health savings accounts*

Unlike federal law, California does not recognize HSAs. Consequently, an individual's contributions to HSAs that were deducted on the federal tax return, must be added back for California personal income tax purposes. (Sec. 17215.4, Rev. & Tax. Code) Other addition requirements are required as a result of California's nonconformity with federal exclusions of employer contributions to HSAs and interest and dividends earned on HSAs (see ¶247).

¶327 Tenant Expenses—Cooperative Apartment and Housing Corporations

Law: Sec. 17201 (CCH CALIFORNIA TAX REPORTS, ¶15-515).

Comparable Federal: Sec. 216 (CCH U.S. MASTER TAX GUIDE ¶1040).

California law is the same as federal as of the current IRC tie-in date (¶103).

Deductions are allowed to tenant-stockholders in cooperative apartment and housing corporations for amounts representing taxes and interest paid to such corporations. (Sec. 17201, Rev. & Tax. Code)

¶328 Moving Expenses

Law: Secs. 17072, 17076 (CCH CALIFORNIA TAX REPORTS, ¶15-760).

Comparable Federal: Sec. 217 (CCH U.S. MASTER TAX GUIDE ¶1073 et seq.).

California adopts federal provisions that allow an above-the-line deduction for moving expenses incurred in connection with the commencement of work at a new principal place of work. (Sec. 17072, Rev. & Tax. Code; Sec. 17076, Rev. & Tax. Code)

The treatment of an employer's moving expense reimbursements for purposes of calculating an employee's gross income is discussed at ¶238.

¶329 Employee Business Expenses

Law: Secs. 17072, 17076, 17201 (CCH CALIFORNIA TAX REPORTS, ¶15-685, 15-805).

Comparable Federal: Secs. 62(a), 67, 68, 162, 274 (CCH U.S. MASTER TAX GUIDE ¶910 et seq., 941, 1011).

California and federal unreimbursed employee business expenses are considered miscellaneous itemized deductions rather than adjustments to gross income. As explained at ¶303, only the total amount of miscellaneous itemized deductions in excess of 2% of the taxpayer's federal adjusted gross income is deductible. (Sec. 17072, Rev. & Tax. Code; Sec. 17076, Rev. & Tax. Code; Sec. 17201, Rev. & Tax. Code)

California also incorporates the 50% limit on deductions for business meals and entertainment expenses (¶302). The 50% limit is computed before the 2% floor is applied. A deduction is allowed even if reimbursement comes from a third party rather than from the employer. Reimbursed employee business expenses that are included in the taxpayer's gross income are deducted from gross income.

¶330 Payments to Pension or Profit-Sharing Plans and Education Savings Accounts

Law: Secs. 17201, 17203, 17501, 17504-09, 17551, 17563.5, 23712 (CCH CALIFORNIA TAX REPORTS, ¶15-800, 16-135).

Comparable Federal: Secs. 194A, 219, 402, 404-420, 430-436, 457, 530 (CCH U.S. MASTER TAX GUIDE ¶2147 et seq.).

California Forms: Form 5498-ESA (Coverdell ESA Contribution Information), Form 1099-Q (Payments from Qualified Education Programs).

California generally conforms to the federal rules for deduction of contributions to retirement plans by employers, employees, and the self-employed. Unlike California's incorporation of most IRC provisions, which are tied to a specified federal conformity date (¶103), the incorporated federal provisions concerning retirement benefits and deferred compensation plans (IRC Sec. 401—IRC Sec. 420), minimum funding standards and benefit limitations (IRC Sec. 430—IRC Sec. 436), and governmental deferred compensation plans (IRC Sec. 457) are incorporated into California law without regard to the taxable year, to the same extent as applicable for federal purposes. However, the maximum amount of elective deferrals that may be excluded from gross income under IRC Sec. 402(g) and the maximum amount of deferred compensation that may be excluded under IRC Sec. 457, as applicable for state purposes, is capped at the amount established under federal law as in effect on January 1, 2010. (Sec. 17501, Rev. & Tax. Code)

Although California incorporates Part I and Part III of Subchapter D of Chapter 1 of Subtitle A of the Internal Revenue Code (IRC Sec. 401 through IRC Sec. 420 and IRC Sec. 430 through IRC Sec. 436), California does not automatically incorporate federal amendments made to Part II of Subchapter D of Chapter 1 of Subtitle A of the Internal Revenue Code. Consequently, the federal provisions governing certain stock options (IRC Sec. 421—IRC Sec. 424) are incorporated by California, but only as of California's current federal conformity date (¶103).

CCH Comment: Registered Domestic Partners

Although registered domestic partners (RDPs) or former RDPs are generally required to be treated as married taxpayers or former spouses under California income tax laws, an RDP will not be treated as a spouse if such treatment would result in disqualification of a federally qualified deferred compensation plan or disqualification of tax-favored accounts, such as individual retirement accounts, Archer medical savings accounts, qualified tuition programs, or Coverdell education savings accounts. (Sec. 17021.7, Rev. & Tax. Code) See ¶119 for a discussion of adjustments required to be made RDPs.

Beginning with the 1987 taxable year, California law has followed federal law fairly closely. For taxable years beginning before 1987, California law provided important differences, as explained below.

Under both California and federal law, a contribution made after the end of the taxable year is considered to have been made on the last day of the year, provided the contribution is on account of such taxable year and is made no later than the due date of the return. Except for IRAs, the due date for this purpose includes any extensions.

• *Payments by employers*

Detailed rules are provided for deduction of employers' payments made under an employees' trust or annuity plan or other arrangement for deferring compensation. The California rules are the same as the federal, except for the differences explained below.

California has not conformed to federal provisions that impose special excise taxes on insufficient distributions, inadequate funding, prohibited transactions, etc. However, California does impose a penalty tax on premature distributions (before age $59^1/_2$) from self-employed plans and individual retirement accounts although at a lower rate than under federal law (¶206).

See below regarding employer contributions to self-employed retirement plans and to individual retirement accounts.

To the extent the California and federal laws are comparable, it is the stated policy of the FTB to follow all federal rules and regulations. Where the federal rules require advance approval of a plan, California will accept the federal approval and it is not necessary to file a separate application with the state.

• *Self-employed retirement plans (Keoghs)*

Both California and federal laws allow deductions for contributions to self-employed retirement plans, commonly known as "H.R. 10" or "Keogh" plans. California incorporates federal law concerning limits on deductible contributions to Keogh plans. California law requires that amounts used as "earned income" for purposes of computing a taxpayer's federal deduction (rather than the earned income computed using California amounts) must be used for purposes of computing the corresponding state deduction.

For pre-1987 tax years, California had allowed a deduction of 10% of earned income for contributions to these plans, with a maximum of $2,500 and no minimum. The federal law had allowed a deduction with varying limits that have been higher than California's since 1974.

• *Individual retirement accounts—Current law*

Both California and federal laws allow deductions for contributions to individual retirement accounts or for the purchase of individual retirement annuities or bonds. These arrangements are commonly known as "IRAs." The California IRA deduction in taxable years beginning after 1986 is generally the same as the federal.

Caution: IRA Deductions for RDPs

For California income tax purposes, if one or both RDPs are covered by an employer-provided retirement plan, then the California deduction for an IRA contribution may be limited. For example, assume RDP One made an IRA contribution of $5,000 in 2014, his federal modified AGI is $80,000, and he is not covered by an employer-sponsored retirement plan. On his separate federal return, RDP One deducted his entire IRA contribution. RDP Two is covered by an employer-sponsored retirement plan, did not make an IRA contribution in 2014, and his federal AGI is $150,000. The RDPs' combined modified federal AGI exceeds the $191,000 limitation (for 2014), so they cannot deduct an IRA contribution for California purposes. When they recalculate their federal modified AGI for California purposes, as if they were married, they must make a $5,000 adjustment. (FTB Pub. 737, Tax Information for Registered Domestic Partners)

Practice Pointer: Catch-Up Contributions and Certain Limitations

Because of California's federal conformity date history (see ¶103), California did not incorporate amendments made to IRC Sec. 219(b) that allowed qualifying individuals who participated in a bankrupt employer's 401(k) plan to make additional IRA contributions of up to $3,000 for 2007 through 2009. Nor did California incorporate until the 2010 tax year the indexing for inflation of the income limits for:

> — deductible contributions to a traditional IRA for active participants in an employer-sponsored retirement plan or whose spouse is an active participant in an employer-sponsored plan; and

> — Roth IRA contributions.

Federal law allows the indexing of these limits beginning in 2007.

In addition, beginning with the 2010 tax year, California follows the federal provisions that include differential wages in compensation for purposes of determining the annual limitations on contributions to traditional IRAs and Roth IRAs, which are effective for federal purposes beginning with the 2009 taxable year. A differential wage payment is any payment made by an employer to an employee for any period during which the employee is performing qualified military service to compensate the employee for the difference between the employee's military pay and the amount the employee would have received as wages from the employer.

Consequently, taxpayers who were able to make additional IRA contributions on their federal return as a result of these amendments, or who qualified to make contributions on their federal return as a result of the increased income limits, were required to make adjustments on their pre-2010 California personal income tax returns. Also, the amount of a distribution that is subject to California taxation may differ from the amount that is subject to federal taxation because the basis in the IRA may differ for federal and California income tax purposes.

"Roth IRAs": California law is the same as federal law in its treatment of Roth IRAs.

Practice Pointer: Roth IRA Conversions

California automatically conforms to the federal rule that defers income recognition of 2010 Roth IRA conversions to 2011 and 2012. Consequently, unless the taxpayer affirmatively elected to include the income in 2010, any amount otherwise required to be included in gross income for the 2010 taxable year was not included in that taxable year but was instead included in gross income in equal amounts for the 2011 and 2012 taxable years. California automatically recognized the federal election. However, if a taxpayer elected out of the deferral for federal purposes, California allowed a separate election to not opt out of the deferral for California purposes and vice versa. Taxpayers that changed residency after a Roth conversion must include a portion of the IRA distribution in their California taxable income. The FTB will apply the same rules to such distributions as were outlined in *Legal Ruling 98-3, Taxation of IRA Distributions Rolled Over to a Roth IRA Followed by a Change of Residence Status,* in regards to the tax treatment of taxpayers who converted a traditional IRA to a Roth IRA in 1998 and then changed their residence status during the four-year period. (*FTB Tax News,* December 2010)

Deemed IRAs: Under both California and federal laws, if a qualified plan allows employees to make voluntary employee contributions to a separate account or annuity established under the plan and, under the terms of the plan, the account or annuity meets the requirements for a traditional IRA or a Roth IRA, the account or annuity will be deemed an individual retirement plan and not a qualified plan.

¶330

• *Individual retirement accounts—Pre-1987 law*

Because of important differences in pre-1987 California and federal deductible contribution limits, there could be a difference in the California and federal taxable amounts of IRA distributions (¶ 206).

• *Simplified employee pension (SEP) plans*

Under both California and federal law, an employer may provide for a simplified employee pension (SEP) plan for his or her employees. California's treatment of SEP plans is the same as the federal treatment.

• *Savings Incentive Match Plans for Employees (SIMPLE Plans)*

Both California and federal law authorize Savings Incentive Match Plans for Employees (SIMPLE plans). California's treatment of SIMPLE plans is the same as the federal treatment.

"*SIMPLE IRAs*": Contributions to a SIMPLE IRA are limited to employee elective contributions and required employer matching contributions. Employees may make elective contributions up to the amounts discussed above, even though the maximum amount that may be contributed to a traditional IRA is lower (see traditional IRA discussion above). Employers may adopt a SIMPLE IRA for noncollectively bargained employees, even if the employer also maintains a qualified plan for collectively bargained employees.

• *Contributions to union pension plans*

California conforms to the federal rules regarding deductibility of members' contributions to union pension plans. This means, generally, that the contributions are not deductible, because the employee ordinarily has a vested interest or the right to a return of his or her contributions. See *Appeal of Allen B. Crane* (1978) (CCH CALIFORNIA TAX REPORTS, ¶ 15-805.96) and *Appeal of Allan I. and Ivy L. Berr* (1980) (CCH CALIFORNIA TAX REPORTS, ¶ 15-805.961) (5% of the contributions in question was allowed as a deduction, because that portion was forfeitable upon termination of union membership).

• *Coverdell Education Savings Accounts (formerly known as education IRAs)*

Under both California law and federal law joint filers with modified adjusted gross income below $190,000 ($95,000 for single filers) may contribute up to $2,000 per child per year to a Coverdell education savings account. Earnings on contributions will be excluded from gross income and distributed tax-free provided that they are used to pay the child's post-secondary education expenses or a child's elementary or secondary education expenses. A federal election, or lack thereof, to waive the application of the exclusion is binding for California purposes. (Sec. 23712, Rev. & Tax. Code)

The $2,000 annual contribution is phased out for joint filers with modified adjusted gross income of $190,000 to $220,000, and for single filers with modified adjusted gross income of $95,000 to $110,000. The $2,000 maximum annual contribution is reduced by an amount that bears the same ratio to $2,000 as the excess of the contributor's modified adjusted gross income for the tax year over $190,000, or $95,000, bears to $30,000 for joint filers or $15,000 for single filers.

Under both California and federal law an individual may contribute a military death gratuity or payment under the Servicemembers' Group Life Insurance (SGLI) program to a Coverdell education savings account (Coverdell ESA), notwithstanding the $2,000 annual contribution limit and the income phase-out of the limit that would otherwise apply. (Sec. 23712(f), Rev. & Tax. Code)

Taxpayers may make deductible contributions for the tax year up until the time for filing the return (without extensions).

Form 5498-ESA, Coverdell ESA Contribution Information, is used to report Coverdell education savings account contributions. Distributions are reported on Form 1099-Q, Payments from Qualified Education Programs.

CCH Practice Tip: Transfer of Coverdell Education Savings Account Balances

Before a beneficiary reaches age 30, the balance of a Coverdell education savings account may be transferred or rolled over to another Coverdell education savings account for a member of the former beneficiary's family in order to further defer or possibly avoid payment of tax on the earnings in the account.

¶331 Research and Experimental Expenditures

Law: Sec. 17201 (CCH CALIFORNIA TAX REPORTS, ¶15-795).

Comparable Federal: Secs. 59(e), 174 (CCH U.S. MASTER TAX GUIDE ¶979).

Research and experimental expenditures may be deducted currently, or may be amortized over a 60-month period at the election of the taxpayer. For both California and federal purposes, the option to deduct or amortize research and experimental expenditures applies only to expenditures that are "reasonable under the circumstances." (Sec. 17201, Rev. & Tax. Code)

Both California law and federal law allow a credit for certain increases in research expenditures (¶148).

¶332 Trademark or Trade Name Expenditures

Law: Sec. 18151 (CCH CALIFORNIA TAX REPORTS, ¶15-615, 15-620).

Comparable Federal: Former Sec. 167(e), Sec. 1253 (CCH U.S. MASTER TAX GUIDE ¶1775).

California incorporates special federal rules governing the deductibility of payments made in connection with the transfer of a trademark, trade name, or franchise. Such amounts, when paid or incurred in the conduct of a trade or business during the taxable year, are currently deductible if they satisfy the following conditions:

— they are contingent on the productivity, use, or disposition of the trademark, trade name, or franchise;

— they are paid as part of a series of amounts payable at least annually throughout the term of the transfer agreement; and

— the payments are substantially equal in amount or are to be paid pursuant to a fixed formula. (Sec. 18151, Rev. & Tax. Code)

Transfer payments that do not meet the above requirements are generally subject to amortization over a 15-year period for post-August 10, 1993, transfers (¶310).

¶333 Goodwill and Other Intangibles

Law: Sec. 17279 (CCH CALIFORNIA TAX REPORTS, ¶15-615).

Comparable Federal: Sec. 197 (CCH U.S. MASTER TAX GUIDE ¶1288).

California incorporates IRC Sec. 197 as of the current IRC tie-in date (see ¶103), which provides for the amortization, over a 15-year period, of goodwill and certain other intangibles used in a trade or business or for the production of income. (Sec. 17279, Rev. & Tax. Code)

The following intangibles are subject to amortization unless specifically excluded by federal law:

— goodwill, going concern value, and covenants not to compete entered into in connection with the acquisition of a trade or business;

— workforce in place;

— information base;

— know-how;

— any customer-based intangible;

— any supplier-based intangible;

— any license, permit, or other right granted by a governmental unit or agency; and

— any franchise, trademark, or trade name.

¶334 Start-Up Expenditures

Law: Sec. 17201 (CCH CALIFORNIA TAX REPORTS, ¶ 15-805, 16-150).

Comparable Federal: Sec. 195 (CCH U.S. MASTER TAX GUIDE ¶ 904).

California law incorporates the federal law as the current IRC tie-in date (¶ 103). (Sec. 17201, Rev. & Tax. Code)

Under both California and federal law, taxpayers may

— currently deduct up to $5,000 in start-up expenditures (reduced by the amount by which the expenditures exceed $50,000) in the year the trade or business begins; and

— amortize any remainder over a period of 15 years.

¶335 Standard Deduction

Law: Sec. 17073.5 (CCH CALIFORNIA TAX REPORTS, ¶ 15-540).

Comparable Federal: Sec. 63 (CCH U.S. MASTER TAX GUIDE ¶ 126).

California Forms: Form 540 (California Resident Income Tax Return), Form 540 2EZ (California Resident Income Tax Return).

California conforms to federal law allowing taxpayers to elect a standard deduction in lieu of itemizing deductions, with the exception of the amount of the deduction. (Sec. 17073.5, Rev. & Tax. Code)

For 2016, the California standard deduction for a head of household, surviving spouse, or a married couple or registered domestic partnership filing a joint return is $8,258. For others, the deduction is $4,129.

Both federal and California law limit the standard deduction of a person who is claimed as a dependent. For 2016, the deduction is limited to the greater of (1) $1,050, or (2) the earned income of the dependent plus $350.

CCH Example: Deduction for Employed Dependent

Matthew, age 16, has $100 of interest income from a savings account and $2,000 of earned income from a summer job in 2016. Assuming Matthew is eligible to be claimed as a dependent on his parents' tax return, his standard deduction for 2016 is $2,350: the greater of (1) $1,050, or (2) the $2,000 of earned income plus $350.

Both federal and California law provide for inflation adjustments to the standard deduction.

As under federal law, the following taxpayers may not take the standard deduction:

— a married individual filing separately when the other spouse itemizes (the same applies to registered domestic partners for California purposes only);

— an individual making a short-period return because of a change in the annual accounting period; or

— an estate, trust, common trust fund, or partnership.

Federal law also denies the standard deduction to nonresident aliens, but California does not.

¶336 Items Not Deductible

Law: Secs. 17201, 17228, 17269, 17270, 17274-75, 17280-82, 17286, 17299.8-9.9, Rev. & Tax. Code; Sec. 11135, Govt. Code (CCH CALIFORNIA TAX REPORTS, ¶15-735, 15-775, 16-110, 16-150, 16-290, 16-315).

Comparable Federal: Secs. 162, 183, 261-68, 273, 274, 276, 280A, 280B, 280C, 280E, 280G (CCH U.S. MASTER TAX GUIDE ¶903, 907, 909, 910, 961, 963, 965, 966, 969, 999, 1044, 1195, 1214, 1286, 1330, 1343, 1527).

California Forms: Sch. CA (540) (California Adjustments - Residents), Sch. CA (540NR) (California Adjustments - Nonresidents or Part-Year Residents).

Federal law making certain items expressly nondeductible is incorporated in California's law by reference as of the current IRC tie-in date (¶103). (Sec. 17201, Rev. & Tax. Code)

In addition, there are several specific differences between California law and federal law that are explained below.

• *California-federal differences*

California provides for the following categories of nondeductible items not provided under federal law:

— expenses of certain illegal activities in addition to those specified federally, or of other activities that directly tend to promote or are otherwise related to such activities (Sec. 17282, Rev. & Tax. Code);

— certain expenses attributable to substandard housing, as explained below;

— abandonment fees on open-space easements and timberland tax-recoupment fees, as explained below;

— in connection with the denial of deductions for illegal bribes, etc., California provides for disallowance of certain payments that would be unlawful under U.S. laws (Sec. 17286, Rev. & Tax. Code);

— remuneration for personal services that is not reported in required statements to employees (¶715) or in required information returns (¶713) may be disallowed at the discretion of the Franchise Tax Board;

— interest, taxes, depreciation, and amortization are denied to property owners who fail to file proper information returns, as explained at ¶713;

— business expense deductions for expenditures made at, or payments made to, a club that engages in discriminatory practices on the basis of sex, race, color, religion, ancestry, national origin, ethnic group identification, age, mental disability, physical disability, medical condition, genetic information, marital status, or sexual orientation (Sec. 17269, Rev. & Tax. Code; Sec. 11135, Govt. Code); and

— for taxable years beginning on or after January 1, 2014, league-imposed fines or penalties paid or incurred by an owner of all or part of a professional sports franchise (Sec. 17228, Rev. & Tax. Code).

Federal law that generally prohibits a current deduction for capital expenditures (IRC Sec. 263(a)) does not apply to expenditures for which a deduction is allowed under California law for enterprise zone property.

Also, although California conforms to federal law generally disallowing a deduction for a loss on the sale or exchange of property to certain related parties, because of California's federal conformity date (see ¶103), California has not conformed to a federal provision preventing the transfer of loss from tax indifferent parties. The federal provision applies to sales and other dispositions of property acquired after December 31, 2015.

Practice Tip: Repair Regulations

California follows the federal "repair regulations," which provide rules for distinguishing capital expenditures from deductible supply, repair, and maintenance costs. (*FTB Tax News* (March 2015) (CCH CALIFORNIA TAX REPORTS, ¶406-310))

• *Illegal activities*

In addition to incorporating federal law disallowing deductions for illegal drug trafficking expenditures, California prohibits taxpayers from claiming deductions for any income received directly derived from any act or omission of criminal profiteering activity (as defined in Calif. Penal Code § 186.2 or as defined in Chapter 6 (commencing with Section 11350) of Division 10 of the Health and Safety Code, or Article 5 (commencing with Section 750) of Chapter 1 of Part 2 of Division 1 of the Insurance Code), which includes, but is not limited to illegal activities associated with lotteries, gaming, horseracing, prostitution, pornography, burglary, larceny, embezzlement, drug trafficking, and insurance fraud. (Sec. 17282, Rev. & Tax. Code) (Sec. 17282, Rev. & Tax. Code).

The deduction may only be disallowed if the taxpayer is found guilty of the specified illegal activities in a criminal proceeding before a California state court or any proceeding in which the state, county, city and county, city, or other political subdivision was a party. California taxpayers deriving income from the specified illegal activities are taxed on gross income without allowance of any business deductions, including cost of goods sold. (Sec. 17282, Rev. & Tax. Code)

CCH Practice Tip: Cost of Goods Sold

Unlike IRC Sec. 280E, which still allows taxpayers involved in illegal drug trafficking to claim a deduction for cost of goods sold, the California provision prohibits taxpayers involved in the specified illegal activities from excluding the cost of goods sold. For example, an owner of a medical marijuana dispensary would be prohibited form claiming business expense deductions under IRC Sec. 280E, as followed by California for personal income tax purposes, but would be able to take an adjustment for cost of goods sold, unless the taxpayer was found guilty of the specified illegal activities by a California superior court or other California criminal proceeding.

The law specifically provides that wagering losses may be deducted as an offset to wagering gains, but it has been held that this does not apply to bookmakers. See *Appeal of M.R. and J.V. Van Cleave* (1955) (CCH CALIFORNIA TAX REPORTS, ¶200-346), decided by the State Board of Equalization (BOE), and *Herman E. Hetzel v. Franchise Tax Board* (1958) (CCH CALIFORNIA TAX REPORTS, ¶16-150.36), decided by the California District Court of Appeal. These cases disallowed deductions claimed by bookmakers for wagering losses and taxed them on their entire gross winnings. The BOE reached a similar result in cases regarding payouts to pinball machine winners—see *Appeals of C.B. Hall, Sr., et al.* (CCH CALIFORNIA TAX REPORTS, ¶16-150.41) and *Appeal of Arnerich et al.* (CCH CALIFORNIA TAX REPORTS, ¶16-150.53).

• *Substandard rental housing*

California denies deductions for interest, taxes, depreciation, or amortization attributable to substandard rental housing. This applies to both occupied and unoccupied housing that violates laws or codes relating to health, safety, or building, where (1) the property is not renovated within six months after notice of violation is given or (2) good faith compliance efforts have not been commenced. It also applies to employee housing that has not been brought into compliance with the conditions stated in a written notice of violation issued under the Employee Housing Act within 30 days of the date of such notice or the date prescribed in the notice. (Sec. 17274, Rev. & Tax. Code)

Exceptions to the disallowance of deductions are provided for cases where the substandard condition results from a natural disaster or from a change in standards (unless there is danger to occupants), or where failure to renovate is due to unavailability of credit.

This deduction prohibition was applied to deny deductions for interest, taxes, and depreciation in *Appeal of Robert J. and Vera Cort* (1980) (CCH CALIFORNIA TAX REPORTS, ¶ 16-150.73). Other cases have held to the same effect. In *Appeal of Bryan H. Hillstrom* (1983) (CCH CALIFORNIA Tax Reports, ¶ 15-974.36), deductions were disallowed even though the notice of violation had been issued to a prior owner and the current owner was not aware of the notice or the substandard condition.

• *Fees under environmental laws*

California denies deductions for abandonment fees paid to terminate an open-space easement, and also for tax recoupment fees imposed by the Government Code under the program for timberland preserves (see also ¶ 559). (Sec. 17275, Rev. & Tax. Code)

• *Expenses for which credits are allowable*

California incorporates the portions of IRC Sec. 280C that (1) disallow a deduction for that portion of qualified research expenses or basic research expenses that is equal to the amount of the credit allowed for such expenses (¶ 148), and (2) disallow a deduction or credit for that portion of the qualified clinical testing expenses otherwise available as a deduction that is equal to the amount of the clinical testing tax credit allowable under IRC Sec. 28.

California does not incorporate the rest of IRC Sec. 280C, which disallows a deduction for that portion of expenses for which other federal credits, including the federal employment credit, are allowed. Because California law makes federal provisions relating to federal credits inapplicable (Sec. 17024.5(b), Rev. & Tax. Code), unless specifically incorporated, federal provisions that disallow deductions for expenses for which federal credits were claimed are inapplicable. Consequently, California taxpayers may subtract these amounts from federal AGI in computing California taxable income.

• *Other nondeductible items*

Differences between federal and California rules as to what is tax-exempt income may also result in differences in expenses that are nondeductible. For example, California exempts certain interest income, whereas federal does not. Expenses attributable to such income that would be deductible for federal tax purposes would not be deductible for California purposes. Also, California does not permit deduction of expenses attributable to income that was not taxed by California.

CCH Example: Nondeductible Lottery Expenses

California lottery losses may not be deducted from lottery winnings for California purposes, because the expenses are attributable to the production of income not taxed by California.

See the following paragraphs for other possible federal or California nondeductible items:

¶ 305 Interest.

¶ 338 Farm and hobby losses.

¶ 339 "At risk" limitations.

¶ 416 Construction-period interest and taxes.

¶ 532 Gain or loss on options.

¶337 Deductions of Nonresidents

Law: Secs. 17041, 17301-10 (CCH CALIFORNIA TAX REPORTS, ¶ 15-105).

Comparable Federal: None.

California Form: Sch. CA (540NR) (California Adjustments - Nonresidents or Part-Year Residents).

As explained at ¶ 116, the tax on nonresidents and part-year residents is determined on the basis of the taxable income of a nonresident or part-year resident. In computing either California adjusted gross income or a nonresident's or part-year resident's taxable income for this purpose, only deductions that are attributable to California are allowable. (Sec. 17041(i), Rev. & Tax. Code)

Nonresidents and part-year residents may prorate their itemized deductions, including, deductions for alimony paid, or the standard deduction by the ratio that California adjusted gross income bears to total adjusted gross income. (Sec. 17301, Rev. & Tax. Code)

A net operating loss carryover (¶ 309) is deductible for California purposes even if the loss was sustained while the taxpayer was not a state resident, as long as the loss was attributable to California sources. (Sec. 17041(i)(2), Rev. & Tax. Code)

In computing the tax that would be payable if the taxpayer were a full-year resident, the usual rules for itemizing deductions are applicable; that is, deductions should normally be itemized if they amount to more than the standard deduction (¶ 335).

¶338 Farm and Hobby Losses

Law: Sec. 17201 (CCH CALIFORNIA TAX REPORTS, ¶ 15-745).

Comparable Federal: Sec. 183 (CCH U.S. MASTER TAX GUIDE ¶ 1195).

California conforms to federal law (¶ 103).

California and federal law provide special rules to restrict the tax benefit of farm and hobby losses. These rules disallow loss deductions under certain conditions and "recapture" prior deductions when property is sold. (IRC Sec. 183; Sec. 17201, Rev. & Tax. Code)

¶339 "At Risk" Limitations

Law: Sec. 17551 (CCH CALIFORNIA TAX REPORTS, ¶ 15-745).

Comparable Federal: Sec. 465 (CCH U.S. MASTER TAX GUIDE ¶ 2045).

California law is the same as federal as of the current IRC tie-in date (¶ 103). (Sec. 17551, Rev. & Tax. Code)

Detailed rules are provided to limit the deduction of certain losses to the amount of the taxpayer's economic risk. These provisions, which were designed to restrict the use of various types of tax shelters, apply to any activity engaged in as a trade or business or for the production of income. The federal law is incorporated in California's by reference.

In *Haggard and Williams* (1994) (CCH CALIFORNIA TAX REPORTS, ¶402-752) the State Board of Equalization held that losses arising from a taxpayer's investment in a tax shelter that involved the purchase and leaseback of computer equipment were not deductible, because the taxpayer was protected against loss by the provisions of his purchase agreement. Although business losses generated by the leasing of depreciable property may be deducted to the extent that a taxpayer is "at risk," a taxpayer is not considered "at risk" with respect to amounts protected against loss through nonrecourse financing, guarantees, stop loss agreements, or similar arrangements.

¶340 Passive Activity Losses and Credits

Law: Secs. 17551, 17561 (CCH CALIFORNIA TAX REPORTS, ¶15-745, 16-095).

Comparable Federal: Sec. 469 (CCH U.S. MASTER TAX GUIDE ¶2053 et seq.).

California Forms: Sch. CA (540) (California Adjustments - Residents), Sch. CA (540NR) (California Adjustments - Nonresidents or Part-Year Residents), FTB 3801 (Passive Activity Loss Limitations), FTB 3801-CR (Passive Activity Credit Limitations).

California incorporates, with the changes noted below, the federal law as of the current IRC tie-in date (¶103) that generally prohibits the use of passive losses to reduce nonpassive income. (Sec. 17551, Rev. & Tax. Code)

California makes the following three modifications to the federal rule as incorporated:

(1) under IRC Sec. 469(d)(2), certain federal passive income credits may be carried over to later tax years if they exceed the tax attributable to the passive activity; for California purposes, credits that may be carried over are the credits for research expenses and low-income housing and the former credits for targeted jobs and orphan drug research;

(2) for purposes of California's low-income housing credit, California substitutes a $75,000 limitation in place of the federal $25,000 limitation on use of passive activity losses or credits against nonpassive rental income; and

(3) unlike federal law, California law has not eased application of the passive activity loss rules to rental real estate losses suffered by certain taxpayers who materially participate in a real property trade or business. For California purposes, all rental activities are passive activities, regardless of the level of participation. (Sec. 17561, Rev. & Tax. Code)

• *Computation*

All California taxpayers who engage in passive activities must segregate California adjustments that relate to passive activities from California adjustments that relate to nonpassive activities. On FTB 3801, taxpayers must make adjustments to items of federal adjusted gross income that relate to passive activities and as to which California and federal law differ (*e.g.,* depreciation).

On FTB 3801, the taxpayer first adjusts passive activity losses to reflect any California/federal differences (as in depreciation) and then subjects the modified figure to the passive activity loss limitation rules. The resultant figure, which is the California passive activity loss, is transferred to the form or schedule normally used to report the California adjustment amount. The adjustment is computed and then entered on the appropriate line of Schedule CA (540) or Schedule CA (540NR).

If there is no California schedule or form to compute the passive activity loss adjustment (*e.g.,* for rental real estate losses), the adjustment is computed on a special worksheet on FTB 3801 and then transferred directly to the corresponding line in either the subtraction or addition section of Schedule CA (540) or Schedule CA (540NR). To compute passive activity loss adjustment amounts for Schedule CA (540) or Schedule CA (540NR), the taxpayer should use total adjusted gross income amounts and should not start with federal income amounts.

Taxpayers should consult FTB Pub. 1100, Taxation of Nonresidents and Individuals Who Change Residency, for detailed explanations and examples of how the passive activity loss limitations impact nonresidents and part-year residents.

Unallowed (*i.e.*, excess) passive activity losses and credits may be carried forward and subtracted from passive activity income in succeeding tax years.

Practice Tip: Dispositions

Unallowed passive activity credits, unlike passive activity losses, are not allowable when a taxpayer disposes of his or her interest in an activity in a taxable transaction. However, a taxpayer may elect to increase the basis (by the amount of the original basis reduction) to the extent that the credit has not been used. (Instructions to FTB 3801-CR).

¶341 Expenses of Soil Conservation, etc.

Law: Sec. 17201 (CCH CALIFORNIA TAX REPORTS, ¶ 15-170).

Comparable Federal: Secs. 175, 180 (CCH U.S. MASTER TAX GUIDE ¶ 982, 985).

California law concerning the expensing of soil and water conservation expenses is the same as federal as of the current federal conformity date (see ¶ 103). (Sec. 17201, Rev. & Tax. Code)

• *Soil and water conservation*

Farmers may deduct expenditures for soil and water conservation and the prevention of erosion on farmland.

• *Expenditures for fertilizer, etc.*

Farmers are permitted to elect to deduct expenditures for fertilizer and other materials designed to improve farm land, where the costs would otherwise be chargeable to capital account.

¶342 Circulation Expenditures of Periodicals

Law: Sec. 17201 (CCH CALIFORNIA TAX REPORTS, ¶ 15-515).

Comparable Federal: Sec. 173 (CCH U.S. MASTER TAX GUIDE ¶ 971).

Expenditures to "establish, maintain, or increase" the circulation of a periodical are deductible. This provision permits deduction of costs of increasing circulation, which would otherwise have to be capitalized, with elective three-year amortization of such expenditures. California law incorporates the federal law by reference. (Sec. 17201, Rev. & Tax. Code)

¶343 Employee Parking Cash-Out Programs

Law: Sec. 17202 (CCH CALIFORNIA TAX REPORTS, ¶ 16-365).

Comparable Federal: Sec. 162 (CCH U.S. MASTER TAX GUIDE ¶ 863).

California law allows employers a business expense deduction for expenses incurred in connection with an employee parking cash-out program. Under such a program, an employer provides a cash allowance to an employee in an amount equal to the parking subsidy that the employer would otherwise pay to provide the employee with a parking space. (Sec. 17202, Rev. & Tax. Code)

¶344 Tuition and Related Expenses

Law: Sec. 17204.7 (CCH CALIFORNIA TAX REPORTS, ¶ 16-050).

Comparable Federal: Sec. 222 (CCH U.S. MASTER TAX GUIDE ¶ 1082).

California Forms: Sch. CA (540) (California Adjustments - Residents), Sch. CA (540NR) (California Adjustments - Nonresidents or Part-Year Residents).

Unlike federal law, California does not allow an above-the-line deduction for qualified tuition and related expenses incurred by individual taxpayers. (Sec. 17204.7, Rev. & Tax. Code) Federal law allows such a deduction for tax years beginning after 2001 and before 2017. Taxpayers who claim the deduction on their federal return are required to make an addition adjustment on Sch. CA (540).

¶345 Energy Efficient Commercial Property Costs

Law: Sec. 17257.2. (CCH CALIFORNIA TAX REPORTS, ¶ 16-055).

Comparable Federal: Sec. 179D (CCH U.S. MASTER TAX GUIDE ¶ 977D).

California Forms: FTB 3885A (540) (Depreciation and Amortization Adjustments), FTB 3885F (541) (Depreciation and Amortization), FTB 3885L (568) (Depreciation and Amortization), FTB 3885P (565) (Depreciation and Amortization), Sch. CA (540) (California Adjustments - Residents), Sch. CA (540NR) (California Adjustments -Nonresidents or Part-Year Residents), Sch. D (California Capital Gain or Loss Adjustment).

California does not incorporate the federal deduction available for a portion of the costs of installing energy-efficient systems in commercial buildings (Code Sec. 179D), which is available for qualified commercial property placed in service after 2005 but before 2017. (Sec. 17257.2, Rev. & Tax. Code)

Taxpayers that claim the federal deduction for such costs must add these amounts to federal adjusted gross income (AGI) when computing their California taxable income. The expenses added back to federal AGI may then be depreciated on the California personal income tax return.

¶346 Expensing of Environmental Remediation Costs

Law: Sec. 17279.4. (CCH CALIFORNIA TAX REPORTS, ¶ 16-055).

Comparable Federal: Sec. 198 (CCH U.S. MASTER TAX GUIDE ¶ 977D).

California Forms: FTB 3885A (540) (Depreciation and Amortization Adjustments), FTB 3885F (541) (Depreciation and Amortization), FTB 3885L (568) (Depreciation and Amortization), FTB 3885P (565) (Depreciation and Amortization), Sch. CA (540) (California Adjustments - Residents), Sch. CA (540NR) (California Adjustments - Nonresidents or Part-Year Residents), Sch. D (California Capital Gain or Loss Adjustment).

Under federal law applicable to pre-2012 expenditures, but not California law, taxpayers may elect to currently deduct costs paid or incurred in connection with the abatement or control of hazardous substances at a qualified contaminated site. California allowed the deduction prior to 2004. (Sec. 17279.4, Rev. & Tax. Code)

Absent federal legislation, an addition adjustment is made on Sch. CA (540) for pre-2012 expenditures only. Amounts expensed on the federal return must be treated as capitalized costs for California personal income tax purposes; therefore, a depreciation adjustment must also be made (see ¶ 310).

The federal deduction may only be claimed for expenditures incurred prior to 2012. Once the federal deduction expires, no addition adjustment is required. However, depreciation adjustments may still be required for post-2011 taxable years.

PERSONAL INCOME TAX

CHAPTER 4
ACCOUNTING METHODS AND BASES, INVENTORIES

¶ 400 Accounting Periods and Methods—In General

Law: Secs. 17551-70 (CCH CALIFORNIA TAX REPORTS, ¶ 15-455—15-480, 16-070, 89-102).

Comparable Federal: Secs. 441-83 (CCH U.S. MASTER TAX GUIDE ¶ 1501, 1515).

California generally incorporates federal law governing accounting periods and methods of accounting as of the current tie-in date (¶ 103). (Sec. 17551, Rev. & Tax. Code) However IRC Sec. 457, relating to deferred compensation plans of state and local governments and tax-exempt organizations, is incorporated by California as amended to date (see ¶ 206 for details). California's requirements in connection with annualized short-period returns are somewhat different (¶ 403). In addition, California has a special rule with no federal counterpart authorizing the Franchise Tax Board to allocate income between separately filing spouses (¶ 412) and California does not incorporate IRC Sec. 457A, which requires that any compensation that is deferred under a nonqualified deferred compensation plan of a nonqualified entity be included in gross income when there is no substantial risk of forfeiture of the rights to the compensation. (Sec. 17551(g), Rev. & Tax. Code)

CCH Comment: Doctrine of Election

Legislation enacted in 2012 clarified that the doctrine of election applies to any election affecting the computation of California franchise or income tax, meaning that the election must be made on an original timely filed return for the taxable period for which the election is to apply, and once made is binding. This provision is declarative of existing law, so its effective date is retroactive. (Sec. 4, Ch. 37 (S.B. 1015), Laws 2012) However, under Proposition 26 (2010), a two-thirds vote is required in both houses of the California Legislature to pass legislation resulting in "any taxpayer paying a higher tax." Since the 2012 legislation did not pass with the required super-majority, it might be challenged in the courts.

• *Taxable year of inclusion*

California incorporates federal law providing that income must be included in the year of receipt unless properly accounted for in another period under an acceptable method of accounting. Amounts accrued only by reason of the death of an accrual-basis taxpayer are not included for the taxable period of the taxpayer's death.

California does not incorporate federal law allowing taxpayers to elect to recognize qualified gain from a qualifying electric transmission transaction over an eight-year period applicable to pre-2017 transactions. (Sec. 17551(f), Rev. & Tax. Code) Consequently, taxpayers must recognize the entire gain for California purposes in the year of the transaction. Presumably, this difference is reflected on Sch. D (540 or 540NR).

Production flexibility contracts: California law mirrors Sec. 2012 of the Tax and Trade Relief Extension Act of 1998, which allows farmers to include in their taxable income production flexibility contract payments made under the Federal Agriculture Improvement and Reform Act of 1996 (P.L. 104-127) in the taxable year of actual receipt, even though the contract grants the farmer the option to receive payments earlier. (Sec. 17552.3, Rev. & Tax. Code)

• *Taxable year of deduction*

California incorporates federal law as of California's current federal conformity date (see ¶103) to provide that deductions must be taken in conformance with the method of accounting employed by the taxpayer. (Sec. 17551, Rev. & Tax. Code) However, California does not incorporate a federal provision that limits the amount of net Schedule F losses from farming activities that may be claimed by taxpayers, other than C corporations, who receive Commodity Credit Corporation loans or certain other farm subsidies. (Sec. 17560.5, Rev. & Tax. Code) Consequently, taxpayers whose losses were limited on their federal returns as a result of this provision will be able to claim a greater loss on their California returns.

¶401 Accounting Periods

Law: Secs. 17551, 17565 (CCH CALIFORNIA TAX REPORTS, ¶ 15-455, 89-102).

Comparable Federal: Secs. 441, 444, 645 (CCH U.S. MASTER TAX GUIDE ¶ 1501 et seq.).

California incorporates federal law as of a specified tie-in date (¶103). (Sec. 17551, Rev. & Tax. Code) The taxpayer's tax year must be the same as federal unless a different period is initiated or approved by the Franchise Tax Board. (Sec. 17565, Rev. & Tax. Code)

The taxpayer may report on a calendar year or fiscal year basis, in accordance with the taxpayer's books. If no books are kept, the taxpayer must report on the calendar year basis. A 52-53 week year may be used under certain circumstances; special rules are provided for determining the effective date of law changes in such cases.

If a fiscal year is to be established by a new taxpayer, the year must be adopted on or before the time prescribed by law (not including extensions) for filing the return for that year.

In *Appeal of P.A. Reyff* (1958) (CCH CALIFORNIA TAX REPORTS, ¶ 15-455.25), the State Board of Equalization held that the taxpayer was required to report on a calendar year basis for the particular year in question because he kept no books, even though returns were filed and accepted in later years on a fiscal year basis. The later years were not in question.

¶402 Change of Accounting Period

Law: Secs. 17551, 17556 (CCH CALIFORNIA TAX REPORTS, ¶ 15-455).

Comparable Federal: Sec. 442 (CCH U.S. MASTER TAX GUIDE ¶ 1513).

California law is essentially the same as federal law, including the provisions on accounting-period changes by partnerships, S corporations, trusts, and personal service corporations (and the effects of the taxable income of partners, S corporation shareholders, etc.).

Federal law regarding changes of accounting period is incorporated in California law by reference. (Sec. 17551, Rev. & Tax. Code)

Generally, a change of accounting period requires the approval of the taxing authorities. However, an estate may change its annual accounting period one time without the approval of the FTB. (Sec. 17556, Rev. & Tax. Code) Application for change should be filed by the 15th day of the second month following the close of the short period. Under the conformity rules, an application for federal purposes is considered an application for California purposes also, and federal approval will apply for California purposes as long as the following conditions are met:

— California has conformed to the underlying law that is being applied;

— the FTB has authority for granting the request; and

— the FTB has not announced that it will decline to follow the federal procedure being relied upon.

However, federal forms must be submitted to the Franchise Tax Board, as prescribed, if the taxpayer cannot rely on a federally approved change request, desires a change different from the federal change, or desires a change for state tax purposes only (FTB Notice 2000-8 (2000) (CCH CALIFORNIA TAX REPORTS, ¶ 15-455.321)).

Federal Form 3115, Application for Change in Accounting Method, or federal Form 1128, Application to Adopt, Change, or Retain a Tax Year, must be submitted to the FTB by the due date specified in California law or, if none is specified, by the due date for a federal change request if a federal change request has been submitted to the IRS for that change. Other than specified identifying information, the federal forms must be completed using appropriate California tax information and not federal tax information, taking into account differences in federal and California law (e.g., different depreciation methods).

A cover letter must be attached to the front of federal Form 3115 or Form 1128, clearly indicating that a "Change in Accounting Period" or a "Change in Accounting Method" is being requested. The application and the accompanying cover letter should be sent to:

Franchise Tax Board

Change in Accounting Periods and Methods, Coordinator

P.O. Box 1998

Sacramento, CA 95812

The FTB will acknowledge receipt of the request within 30 days and will issue a response in writing once the request has been reviewed. (FTB Notice 2000-8 (2000) (CCH CALIFORNIA TAX REPORTS, ¶ 15-455.321))

Practice Tip: Repair Regulations

California follows the federal "repair regulations," which provide rules for distinguishing capital expenditures from deductible supply, repair, and maintenance costs. However, one issue that may arise with regard to the repair regulations is that there may be a difference between the federal and California depreciable basis, useful life, or method of depreciation. According to the FTB, to the extent that California follows the federal provision for which a federal approval for a change in accounting method was granted, the federal approval will still apply for California purposes, even though the resulting federal numbers may be different than the California numbers. In cases where there is a federal/California difference, taxpayers should attach to their California tax return both a copy of the federal Form 3115 and a *pro forma* Form 3115 with the numbers adjusted for California. In addition, California follows IRS Revenue Procedure 2015-20, which allows qualifying small businesses to apply certain repair regulations on a prospective basis without the need to file Form 3115. (*FTB Tax News* (March 2015) (CCH CALIFORNIA TAX REPORTS, ¶ 406-310))

See ¶ 616 for a discussion of the taxable year of a partnership.

¶403 Return for Short Period—Annualization of Income

Law: Secs. 17551, 17552 (CCH CALIFORNIA TAX REPORTS, ¶ 15-455, 89-102).

Comparable Federal: Sec. 443 (CCH U.S. MASTER TAX GUIDE ¶ 1505).

California law is the same as federal law with minor exceptions noted below. (Sec. 17551, Rev. & Tax. Code)

California law, unlike federal law, requires a short-period return when a taxpayer's year is terminated by the Franchise Tax Board because of a jeopardy assessment. (Sec. 17552, Rev. & Tax. Code)

California requires a proportional reduction in the amount allowed for exemption credits when a short-period return is filed. Federal law requires a similar reduction for exemption deductions.

¶404 Optional Method for Short-Period Returns

Law: Sec. 17551 (CCH CALIFORNIA TAX REPORTS, ¶ 15-455, 89-102).

Comparable Federal: Sec. 443 (CCH U.S. MASTER TAX GUIDE ¶ 1515).

California law is the same as federal law (¶ 103). (Sec. 17551, Rev. & Tax. Code)

¶405 Change of Status, Resident or Nonresident

Law: Sec. 17041(b) and (i) (CCH CALIFORNIA TAX REPORTS, ¶ 16-510, 16-535, 16-545, 16-550, 16-555, 16-560, 16-570).

Comparable Federal: None.

For California personal income tax purposes, the term "taxable income of a nonresident or part-year resident" includes the following:

— for any part of the taxable year during which the taxpayer was a resident of this state, all items of gross income and all deductions, regardless of source; and

— for any part of the taxable year during which the taxpayer was not a resident of this state, gross income and deductions derived from sources within this state.

(Sec. 17041(i)(1), Rev. & Tax. Code)

Practice Pointer: Attribution and Accrual Rules

Taxpayers should consult FTB Pub. 1100, Taxation of Nonresidents and Individuals Who Change Residency, for the FTB's interpretation of the attribution and accrual rules. The publication provides numerous examples to illustrate how the current attribution and accrual rules apply.

For pre-2002 taxable years, if the status of the taxpayer changed from resident to nonresident, or vice versa, the determination of whether or not income was subject to California tax was made on the accrual basis, even though the taxpayer reported on the cash basis of accounting. The period in which the income was actually to be reported, however, was determined under the regular rules relating to the taxpayer's method of accounting. The purpose of the pre-2002 rules, as interpreted by the State Board of Equalization (BOE) in the cases discussed below, was to treat cash-basis taxpayers the same as accrual-basis taxpayers when a change of residency occurred.

Practitioner Comment: Sourcing of Pass-Through Income

See ¶233 for discussion of an FTB ruling on the sourcing of income for owners of pass-through entities that change residency status during the year.

• *Installment sales*

The FTB has taken the position that installment proceeds received by a California resident from the sale of property located outside California are taxable by California. Conversely, installment proceeds received by a former California resident from the sale of property located outside California are not taxable by California (FTB Pub. 1100, Taxation of Nonresidents and Individuals Who Change Residency, revised 11-2007, CCH CALIFORNIA TAX REPORTS, ¶404-599).

• *Individual retirement accounts, employer-sponsored retirement plans, and compensation*

Taxpayers who move into California do not receive a stepped-up basis for annual contributions and earnings on individual retirement accounts (IRAs) for contributions made when they are nonresidents. Because part-year residents are treated as residents for all prior years for all items of deferred income, which includes IRAs, taxpayers are allowed a basis for contributions actually made, even if they would not have been allowed under California law before they became California residents.

Compensation received by a California resident is taxable by California, even if it accrued prior to becoming a resident. However, taxpayers may be eligible to claim a credit for taxes paid to the other state (FTB Pub. 1100, Taxation of Nonresidents and Individuals Who Change Residency).

• *Stock options*

Nonstatutory stock options.—California taxes the wage income received by a nonresident taxpayer from nonstatutory stock options on a source basis, whether the taxpayer was always a nonresident or was formerly a California resident. On the other hand, if a taxpayer is granted nonstatutory stock options while a nonresident and later exercises the options while a California resident, the resulting compensation is taxable by California because the wage income is recognized while the taxpayer is a California resident. The taxable wage income is the difference between the fair market value of the stock on the exercise date and the option price. (FTB Pub. 1004, Stock Option Guidelines; FTB Pub. 1100, Taxation of Nonresidents and Individuals Who Change Residency)

Example: Nonresident: On February 1, 2007, while a California resident, the taxpayer was granted nonstatutory stock options. The taxpayer performed all of his services in California from February 1, 2007, to May 1, 2012, the date he left the company and permanently moved to Texas. On June 1, 2012, he exercised his nonstatutory stock options. The income resulting from the exercise of his nonstatutory stock options is taxable by California because the income is compensation for services having a source in California, the state where he performed all of his services.

¶405

Example: *Move-in to California:* On March 1, 2007, while a Nevada resident, the taxpayer was granted nonstatutory stock options. On April 1, 2012, the taxpayer retired and permanently moved to California. On May 1, 2012, the taxpayer exercised her options. The compensation resulting from the exercise of her nonstatutory stock options is taxable by California because she was a California resident when the income was recognized.

Statutory stock options.—California taxes the capital gain income received by a former nonresident from the sale of stock in a qualifying disposition of statutory stock options because the stock is sold while the taxpayer is a resident. (FTB Pub. 1004, Stock Option Guidelines; FTB Pub. 1100, Taxation of Nonresidents and Individuals Who Change Residency)

Example: *Move-in to California:* On February 1, 2003, while a Texas resident, the taxpayer was granted incentive stock options. On February 1, 2011, the taxpayer exercised his options. On December 1, 2011, the taxpayer permanently moved to California, and on March 1, 2012, the taxpayer sold his stock for a gain. The resulting capital gain is taxable by California because the taxpayer was a California resident when he sold the stock.

In the reverse situation, if statutory stock options are granted to a taxpayer while he or she works in California, but are exercised and sold in a qualifying disposition after the taxpayer moves out of California, the capital gain on the sale of the stock would not be taxed by California. (Question 14, California Society of CPAs 2001 Liaison Meeting with FTB, November 14, 2001; FTB Pub. 1004, Stock Option Guidelines)

• *Rules for application of accrual provision (prior law)*

The purpose and application of this former provision are discussed in some detail in *Appeal of Virgil M. and Jeanne P. Money* (1983) (CCH CALIFORNIA TAX REPORTS, ¶ 16-545.255). The opinion reasons that the purpose was merely to prevent differing treatment of cash- and accrual-basis taxpayers, and concluded that the provision was applicable only if;

— California's sole basis for taxation was the taxpayer's residency; and

— taxation would differ depending on whether the taxpayer used the accrual or cash method of accounting.

Applying these criteria to a situation where a California taxpayer received a military pension that started when he was a nonresident, the BOE held that the second condition was not satisfied and, therefore, the pension was taxable by California.

In the *Money* opinion, the BOE stated specifically that it had reversed its earlier reasoning regarding the intent of the law. Cases decided before 1983 should be reconsidered in the light of the rationale of the *Money* case. Some such older cases have been cited in the discussion below, because the conclusions reached in the cited cases would presumably be the same under the *Money* rationale.

• *Distributions from qualified plans for deferred compensation*

In *Appeal of Frank W. and Harriet S. Walters* (1984) (CCH CALIFORNIA TAX REPORTS, ¶ 16-545.256), the BOE applied the rationale of the *Money* case, discussed above, to distributions from a qualified deferred-compensation plan. The taxpayer earned future benefits in Missouri, and moved to California after his retirement. The BOE held that his benefit payments were taxable by California, since there is no distinction between cash- and accrual-basis taxpayers in the treatment of distributions from qualified plans. Also, to the same effect, see *Appeal of Edward A. and Leonora F. Kodyra* (1985) (CCH CALIFORNIA TAX REPORTS, ¶ 16-545.253); in this case, the pension of a retired New York policeman was taxed by California even though it was exempt from state and local taxation under New York law. Similarly, in *Daks v. Franchise Tax Board* (1999) (CCH CALIFORNIA TAX REPORTS, ¶ 16-545.258) a California court of appeal held that pension benefits earned by a taxpayer as a participant in his employer's noncontributory, qualified, defined-benefit pension plan while the taxpayer was a resident of New York were taxable in California because the benefits were received by the taxpayer while he was a resident of California.

The BOE has also cited and followed the *Money* decision in a case involving a lump-sum distribution from a qualified plan. In *Appeal of Lawrence T. and Galadriel Blakeslee* (1983) (CCH CALIFORNIA TAX REPORTS, ¶ 400-716), the taxpayer became entitled to a lump-sum distribution in 1976, before moving to California from Florida; however, she did not receive the distribution until 1978, after she became a California resident. The BOE held that the distribution was taxable by California, on the ground that California makes no distinction between cash- and accrual-basis taxpayers in the treatment of lump-sum distributions; this principle was affirmed in *Appeal of Ralph G. and Martha E. McQuoid* (1989) (CCH CALIFORNIA TAX REPORTS, ¶ 16-545.257).

Similar reasoning was applied by a California court of appeal in *Paine v. Franchise Tax Board* (2004) (CCH CALIFORNIA TAX REPORTS, ¶ 16-545.2591), in determining that deferred compensation payments from a partnership that were received by taxpayers residing in California were subject to California personal income tax even though the payments began before the taxpayers became California residents. The court ruled that the second prong of the *Money* test was not met, because the partnership elected to use a cash method of accounting and the taxpayers were bound by that election. Consequently, the taxpayers were required to recognize the income they received after they became California residents.

It should be observed that California taxation of pensions earned elsewhere does not depend on the rationale of the *Money* case. Many earlier cases held that such pensions were taxable to California residents because the right to receive the pensions was contingent upon the taxpayer's survival and therefore the income had not "accrued" when the change of residence occurred.

Under current law, all income from qualified plans for deferred compensation are taxable by California if received by a California resident, even if the compensation "accrued" prior to the taxpayer's California residency.

• *Sale of out-of-state real estate*

In the *Appeal of Estate of Albert Kahn, Deceased, and Lillian Kahn* (1986) (CCH CALIFORNIA TAX REPORTS, ¶ 401-307), the taxpayers, having established residence in California on May 21, 1976, were not allowed to deduct rental expenses on out-of-state real estate even though the expenses were paid at the escrow for the sale of the property and even though the gain from the sale was taxable. Although binding agreements of sale had been executed prior to the establishment of California residency, escrow closed afterwards, and the gain was realized during the period of residency. The BOE applied the rationale of the *Money* case and held that the rental expenses were accrued prior to the establishment of California residency.

• *Distributions from self-employed (Keogh) or IRA plans*

Retirement income attributable to services performed outside California but received after the taxpayer becomes a resident is taxable in its entirety by California. California does not impose tax on retirement income, including income from a self-employed (Keogh) plan or an individual retirement account (IRA), received by a nonresident. (FTB Pub. 1005, Pension and Annuity Guidelines; FTB Pub. 1100, Taxation of Nonresidents and Individuals Who Change Residency)

See ¶ 206 for a discussion of (1) a possible recoverable tax-free California basis of a self-employed plan resulting from pre-1987 differences between California and federal law on deductibility of contributions to such a plan and (2) how to calculate the California basis of an IRA of a California resident that made nondeductible contributions to an IRA while a nonresident.

• *Income from annuities*

In *Appeal of Preston T. and Virginia R. Kelsey* (1976) (CCH CALIFORNIA TAX REPORTS, ¶ 16-435.41), the taxpayer was the current beneficiary of her deceased father's retirement annuity. The annuity had been earned entirely in Pennsylvania. The BOE held that the taxpayer, as a California resident, was fully taxable under the rules for income from annuities, even though the payments were properly classifiable as "income in respect of a decedent" (¶ 413).

• *Liquidation of corporation*

The case of *Sweetland et al.* (1961) (CCH CALIFORNIA TAX REPORTS, ¶ 16-550.92), involved a large gain realized by a shareholder upon liquidation of a corporation. The taxpayer contended that his gain was not taxable because it was the result of appreciation in value prior to the time he became a resident (and also prior to the time the California income tax law was enacted in 1935). A California court of appeal held that the entire gain was taxable in the year of liquidation, because there was no realization of income until that year. Other cases have held to the same effect.

• *Installment sales (prior law)*

In cases decided before the *Money* decision, discussed above, the BOE held that installments received by nonresidents on a sale made when they were California residents were subject to California tax. See *Appeal of Sherwood R. and Marion S. Gordon* (1983) (CCH CALIFORNIA TAX REPORTS, ¶ 16-550.47). Presumably these cases are not affected by the *Money* decision, since the income is from a California source and is therefore taxed regardless of residence. As to installments received by a California resident on an out-of-state sale made before becoming a California resident, the installments are not subject to California tax because the right to receive the income accrued during nonresidency. Any interest from installment sales is taxable while the taxpayer is a resident.

• *Disputed or contingent income*

In *Appeal of David D. and Linda D. Cornman* (1984) (CCH CALIFORNIA TAX REPORTS, ¶ 16-825.252), the taxpayer earned income in Alaska during the years 1974-1977 when he was a resident of that state. The amount of the income was subject to litigation, which was settled in 1979 after he had become a California resident. The BOE held that the income was subject to California tax.

In *Appeal of Louis E. and Echite M. Dana* (1979) (CCH CALIFORNIA TAX REPORTS, ¶ 16-570.28), the taxpayer received income after he became a California resident, under a contingent-fee contract executed with other attorneys when he was a Michigan resident. The BOE held that the income was taxable by California, because uncertainty regarding the amount to be received prevented its accrual before the change of residence.

The issue of "disputed" or "contingent" income is moot under current law if the income is received while the taxpayer is a current resident, as all income received by a California resident is subject to tax.

• *Expense reimbursement*

In *Appeal of James H. and Heloise A. Frame* (1979) (CCH CALIFORNIA TAX REPORTS, ¶ 16-535.331), the taxpayer received approximately $50,000 from IBM as reimbursement for expenses of moving to California. The right to receive the reimbursement was clearly established before the taxpayer became a California resident; however, the BOE held that the reimbursement (partly offset by about $11,000 of deductions allowed) was taxable by California, because uncertainty as to the amount prevented accrual before the change of residence. See ¶238 for further discussion of treatment of reimbursed expenses when a taxpayer moves to or from California.

The issue of "disputed" or "contingent" income is moot under current law if the income is received while the taxpayer is a current resident, as all income received by a California resident is subject to tax.

¶406 Tax Rate Change During Taxable Year

Law: Sec. 17034 (CCH CALIFORNIA TAX REPORTS, ¶191-645).

Comparable Federal: Sec. 15 (CCH U.S. MASTER TAX GUIDE ¶2561).

California law differs from federal in situations involving rate changes during the taxable year.

The general California rule is that, unless an amending act specifies otherwise, changes affecting the imposition or computation of taxes (including rates), credits, penalties, and additions to tax are applicable to taxable years beginning on or after January 1 of the year in which the amending act takes effect. All other tax-related provisions are applied beginning on the date the act takes effect. (Sec. 17034, Rev. & Tax. Code)

¶407 Accounting Methods—General

Law: Secs. 17201, 17207, 17551, 17564 (CCH CALIFORNIA TAX REPORTS, ¶15-460, 15-465, 15-470, 15-745).

Comparable Federal: Secs. 165, 263A, 446-48, 451, 455-56, 458, 460, 461, 464, 467-68B, 481 (CCH U.S. MASTER TAX GUIDE ¶1515 et seq.).

California Form: FTB 3834 (Interest Computation Under the Look-Back Method for Completed Long-Term Contracts).

With minor exceptions, California law is the same as federal law as of the current IRC tie-in date (¶103). (Sec. 17551, Rev. & Tax. Code; Sec. 17564, Rev. & Tax. Code)

• *Automatic consent procedure for accounting method change*

California does not follow federal law that provides for an automatic consent procedure for a change in accounting method for purposes of claiming the full deduction for any previously unclaimed depreciation or amortization allowed—see IRS Rev. Proc. 96-31; FTB Notice 96-3 (CCH CALIFORNIA TAX REPORTS, ¶402-880).

• *Timing of excess disaster-loss deductions*

Both California law and federal law allow taxpayers to elect to deduct in the prior year certain excess casualty losses sustained after the end of the year in a disaster area, as determined by the President. (Sec. 17201, Rev. & Tax. Code; Sec. 17207, Rev. & Tax. Code) California law provides similar treatment for specified categories of excess losses sustained in a disaster area declared by the Governor. Under California law, losses from specified disasters may also be carried forward to subsequent years from the year claimed. For a discussion of disaster losses, see ¶307.

• *Special rules for accounting methods*

See ¶310 for special rules regarding production costs of films, books, etc. See ¶416 for special rules regarding construction-period interest and taxes. See ¶620 for special rules regarding partnership accounting.

¶408 Election to Accrue Income on Noninterest-Bearing Obligations Issued at Discount

Law: Secs. 17551, 17553 (CCH CALIFORNIA TAX REPORTS, ¶ 15-465).

Comparable Federal: Sec. 454.

California law is the same as federal as of the current IRC tie-in date (¶ 103). (Sec. 17551, Rev. & Tax. Code)

A cash-basis taxpayer may elect to accrue the increment in value of noninterest-bearing bonds issued at a discount and redeemable for fixed amounts increasing at stated intervals. The election is binding for subsequent years. On certain short-term obligations issued at a discount, the discount is not considered to accrue until the obligation is disposed of.

Federal law includes a special rule for income from U.S. Savings Bonds. Because interest from such bonds is exempt from California tax (¶217), this rule is not applicable to California. (Sec. 17553, Rev. & Tax. Code)

See also ¶ 237, regarding special rules for discount bonds.

¶409 Inventories

Law: Secs. 17201, 17551, 17570 (CCH CALIFORNIA TAX REPORTS, ¶ 15-475).

Comparable Federal: Secs. 263A, 471, 475 (CCH U.S. MASTER TAX GUIDE ¶ 1553 et seq.).

California law is the same as federal law as of the current IRC tie-in date (¶ 103). (Sec. 17551, Rev. & Tax. Code)

Inventories are required where the production, purchase, or sale of merchandise is an income-producing factor. Valuation must conform to the best practice in the industry and must clearly reflect income. California follows federal regulations that provide detailed rules for inventory valuation.

• *Mark-to-market accounting*

California incorporates federal law requiring securities dealers to use the mark-to-market method of accounting in identifying and valuing inventory. (Sec. 17551, Rev. & Tax. Code; Sec. 17570, Rev. & Tax. Code)

¶410 Inventories—Last-In, First-Out Method

Law: Sec. 17551 (CCH CALIFORNIA TAX REPORTS, ¶ 15-475).

Comparable Federal: Secs. 472-74 (CCH U.S. MASTER TAX GUIDE ¶ 1564, 1565).

A taxpayer may elect to use the last-in, first-out (LIFO) method of inventory valuation. California law is the same as federal law (¶ 103), including the limitation on the election of the simplified dollar-value LIFO method for small businesses. (Sec. 17551, Rev. & Tax. Code)

See ¶ 806 for special rules concerning the LIFO method of reporting for S corporations.

¶411 Installment Sales

Law: Secs. 17551, 17560 (CCH CALIFORNIA TAX REPORTS, ¶ 15-460).

Comparable Federal: Secs. 453, 453A, 453B (CCH U.S. MASTER TAX GUIDE ¶ 1801 et seq.).

California Form: FTB 3805E (Installment Sale Income).

California law is the same as federal as of the current IRC tie-in date (¶ 103). (Sec. 17551, Rev. & Tax. Code) However, income reported federally on the installment basis may differ from that reported for California purposes because of federal/California differences in basis of property sold and differences in installment reporting rules applicable to the year of sale.

Practitioner Comment: Significant Uncertainty Regarding Contingent Consideration

California adopts IRC Sec. 453A, which imposes an interest charge on tax which is deferred under the installment sale rules. Although expressly called for by the statute, regulations have not been issued to date that explain how these provisions should apply where contingent consideration is concerned. Possibilities would include a "wait and see" approach that retroactively assesses interest based upon the amount ultimately collected and a "fair market value" approach that bases the interest charge upon the fair market value of the contingent note.

In one non-citable letter decision the State Board of Equalization (BOE) held that the interest charge should be based upon the fair market value of the note at the end of each year despite the fact that no amount was ultimately collected. See *Appeal of Kingston Technology Corporation, et al.*, Nos. 286420, 286421 and 288052, August 17, 2006 (hereinafter "Kingston I"). The BOE similarly held that fair market value should be used in its letter decision in the *Appeal of Rawlings*, No. 343163, June 1, 2007, but subsequently granted a petition for rehearing in the *Kingston II*. On February 28, 2008, the BOE issued a letter decision in *Kingston I* concluding in that case that the taxpayer's use of the wait and see method was appropriate. Given that the BOE has upheld the use of the fair market value method in *Rawlings* and, on rehearing, has upheld the use of the wait and see method in *Kingston I*, until a published decision or regulations are issued, significant uncertainty will persist in this area.

It should be noted that the BOE issued a letter decision on December 14, 2010 in an appeal involving a second Franchise Tax Board (FTB) assessment issued to Kingston Technology Corporation and its shareholders relating to the same transaction but involving the application of IRC Sec. 453B upon the cancellation of the contingent installment note in 1999. See *Appeal of Kingston Technology Corporation* (2010), CCH California Tax Reports, ¶ 405-397 (hereinafter "Kingston II"). IRC Sec 453B requires gain recognition upon the sale, transfer or other disposition of installment sale obligations, generally in an amount equal to the difference between the fair market value of the obligation and its basis. In *Kingston II*, the BOE upheld a reduced assessment based upon an updated fair market value analysis using data at the time of the note's cancellation in 1999. The BOE's use of a reduced fair market value in *Kingston II* for purposes of IRC 453B stands in contrast with its use of the wait and see approach on rehearing in *Kingston I* in which the BOE held that no IRC 453A interest was due since no amount was ultimately received on the contingent note.

[CCH Note: The BOE once again upheld the use of the fair market value method in two additional non-citable letter decision in *Appeal of Blanks et al.*, (2009), CCH CALIFORNIA TAX REPORTS, ¶ 404-940 and *Appeal of Canter* (2009), CCH CALIFORNIA TAX REPORTS, ¶ 20090522046.]

Chris Whitney, Contributing Editor

Income from casual sales of real or personal property other than inventory is reported on FTB 3805E if payments are received in a year after the year of sale.

• *Law applicable when installments received*

The taxation of installment sales is governed by the law in effect at the time each installment is received. To this effect, see *William S. Andrews et al. v. Franchise Tax Board* (1969) (CCH CALIFORNIA TAX REPORTS, ¶ 15-460.24), involving the percent of gain to be taken into account after the law was changed in 1959. See also *Appeal of Herbert J. and Sheila Frankel* (1978) (CCH CALIFORNIA TAX REPORTS, ¶ 15-620.52), holding that the percent of gain to be taken into account on a 1974 installment was governed by the law as amended in 1972, although the installment sale was made in 1970.

• *Change of residence*

See ¶ 405 for discussion of treatment of installments received after an interstate move, where an installment sale was made before the change of residence.

¶412 Allocation of Income and Deductions—Related Organizations, etc.

Law: Secs. 17201, 17287, 17555 (CCH CALIFORNIA TAX REPORTS, ¶ 15-315, 15-480).

Comparable Federal: Secs. 269A-69B, 482 (CCH U.S. MASTER TAX GUIDE ¶ 1573, 1575).

California law, otherwise the same as federal law, contains a unique marital provision that applies when spouses file separate returns. This provision empowers the Franchise Tax Board to make any adjustments necessary to reflect the proper income of the spouses. (Sec. 17555, Rev. & Tax. Code) Presumably, this would apply to registered domestic partners as well (see ¶ 119).

Under both federal and California law, the tax authorities are given broad powers to allocate income or deductions among related organizations, trades, or businesses where necessary to prevent evasion of taxes or to clearly reflect income. (Sec. 17551, Rev. & Tax. Code) Specific authority is given for treatment of personal service corporations formed, or availed of, to avoid or evade income tax.

¶413 Income and Deductions in Respect of Decedents

Law: Secs. 17024.5, 17731 (CCH CALIFORNIA TAX REPORTS, ¶ 15-160).

Comparable Federal: Sec. 691 (CCH U.S. MASTER TAX GUIDE ¶ 182 et seq.).

Income and deductions of a decedent, not reportable during his or her life, are includible in the return of the decedent's estate or heir when received or paid. (Sec. 17731, Rev. & Tax. Code)

Despite the inclusion of federal law in California law by reference (¶103), California does not allow a deduction for federal death tax attributable to the income reported. Any provision relating to federal estate tax is ignored for California purposes. Also, no deduction is allowed for the California estate tax allowed as a credit against the federal tax. (Sec. 17024.5, Rev. & Tax. Code)

In *Appeal of Estate of Marilyn Monroe, Deceased* (1975) (CCH CALIFORNIA TAX REPORTS, ¶16-825.45), the estate received substantial income under contracts providing for payment of a percentage of the earnings of certain films in which the actress Marilyn Monroe had appeared. She was not a California resident when she died. The State Board of Equalization held that to the extent the films were made in California, the income was from a California source and was taxable by California as "income in respect of a decedent."

See ¶405 for discussion of the *Kelsey* case, where annuity income earned by a decedent outside California was classified as "income in respect of a decedent" but was taxed to a survivor under the rules for income from annuities.

¶414 Imputed Interest—Loans with Below-Market Interest

Law: Secs. 17024.5, 17551, 18180 (CCH CALIFORNIA TAX REPORTS, ¶ 15-465).

Comparable Federal: Secs. 483, 7872 (CCH U.S. MASTER TAX GUIDE ¶ 795, 1868, 1872).

California law generally is the same as federal law as of California's current federal conformity date (see ¶103). (Sec. 17551, Rev. & Tax. Code) California generally incorporates IRC Sec. 7872, which concerns taxation of "foregone interest" on loans with below-market interest rates. However, unlike federal law, California law did not relax the requirements of exemption from the below-market interest loan rules for loans to continuing care facilities for a five-year period. (Sec. 18180, Rev. & Tax. Code)

When property is sold on a deferred payment basis and no provision is made for interest, or an unreasonably low rate of interest is provided, a portion of the deferred payments is treated as interest to the buyer and to the seller.

¶415 Claim of Right—Effect of Repayment

Law: Secs. 17049, 17076 (CCH CALIFORNIA TAX REPORTS, ¶ 15-635).

Comparable Federal: Sec. 1341 (CCH U.S. MASTER TAX GUIDE ¶ 1543).

California allows a claim of right adjustment similar to the adjustment allowed under federal law. Under the claim of right provision, if an individual includes an item of income in his or her gross income for a preceding taxable year(s), and a deduction in excess of $3,000 is allowable for the taxable year based on the repayment of the item by the individual during the taxable year, then the tax imposed on the individual for the taxable year will be the lesser of:

(1) the tax for the taxable year computed without regard to the deduction; or

(2) an amount equal to the tax for the taxable year computed without that deduction, minus the decrease in tax for the prior taxable year(s) that would result solely from the exclusion of the item or portion thereof from the gross income required to be shown on the individual's California return for the preceding taxable year(s).

If the decrease in tax for the preceding taxable year(s) exceeds the tax imposed for the taxable year, computed without the deduction, the excess will be considered a payment of tax on the last day prescribed for the payment of tax for the taxable year, and will be refunded or credited in the same manner as if it were an overpayment for the taxable year. (Sec. 17049, Rev. & Tax. Code)

The above provisions do not apply to any deduction allowable with respect to an item that was included in gross income by reason of the sale or other disposition of stock in trade of the taxpayer, or other property of a kind that would properly have been included in the inventory of the taxpayer if on hand at the close of the prior taxable year, or property held by the taxpayer primarily for sale to customers in the ordinary course of his or her trade or business. (Sec. 17049, Rev. & Tax. Code)

Detailed rules apply if the exclusion of the item for prior taxable years would have resulted in a net operating loss or a capital loss. (Sec. 17049, Rev. & Tax. Code)

Amounts restored under a claim of right are exempt from the 2% floor for miscellaneous itemized deductions; see ¶ 303. Deductions of $3,000 or less are subject to the 2% adjusted gross income floor for miscellaneous itemized deductions. An individual eligible to claim the adjustment who included the income in prior taxable years when he or she was a nonresident may make the claim of right adjustment only for income that was attributable to California during the preceding years.

See the Instructions to Schedule CA(540), line 41 for details.

¶416 Construction-Period Interest and Taxes

Law: Sec. 17201 (CCH CALIFORNIA TAX REPORTS, ¶ 15-775).

Comparable Federal: Former Sec. 189, Sec. 263A (CCH U.S. MASTER TAX GUIDE ¶ 1029).

California conforms to federal rules requiring capitalization under the uniform capitalization rules of interest and taxes incurred during the construction period of real property. (Sec. 17201, Rev. & Tax. Code)

PERSONAL INCOME TAX

CHAPTER 5

SALES AND EXCHANGES, GAIN OR LOSS, BASIS

¶501 Gain or Loss—General Rule

Law: Secs. 18031, 18042 (CCH California Tax Reports, ¶15-710).

Comparable Federal: Secs. 1001, 1042 (CCH U.S. Master Tax Guide ¶1601, 1733, 2394).

California Forms: Sch. D (Capital Gain or Loss Adjustment), Sch. D-1 (Sales of Business Property).

Gain or loss on disposition of property is the difference between the adjusted basis and the amount realized. The entire gain or loss is recognized except where specifically exempted or deferred. Exceptions to the general rule are discussed in subsequent paragraphs. (Sec. 18031, Rev. & Tax. Code; Sec. 18042, Rev. & Tax. Code)

Although California law is generally the same as federal law, the *effect* may be different because (1) of a difference in the basis of the property and (2) California law, unlike federal law, does not apply a lower tax rate to capital gains.

¶502 Transfers Between Spouses/Registered Domestic Partners

Law: Secs. 17021.7, 18031 (CCH California Tax Reports, ¶15-710).

Comparable Federal: Sec. 1041 (CCH U.S. Master Tax Guide ¶1693).

California law is the same as federal law with respect to the treatment of transfers between spouses. (Sec. 18031, Rev. & Tax. Code) No gain or loss is recognized on a transfer of property from an individual to, or in trust for the benefit of (1) a spouse or (2) a former spouse if the transfer is incident to a divorce. However, gain is recognized with respect to the transfer of property in trust to the extent that the liabilities assumed, plus the amount of any liabilities to which the property is subject, exceeds the total of the adjusted basis of the property transferred.

However, while California law extends this treatment to transfers of property to registered domestic partners (RDPs) and former RDPs, federal law does not, see ¶119. (Sec. 17021.7, Rev. & Tax. Code) Consequently, a subtraction adjustment may be made by RDPs who are required to recognize such gain on their federal income tax returns. (FTB Pub. 737, Tax Information for Registered Domestic Partners).

¶503 Involuntary Conversion

Law: Secs. 18031, 18037, 18154 (CCH CALIFORNIA TAX REPORTS, ¶15-710, 16-070).

Comparable Federal: Sec. 1033 (CCH U.S. MASTER TAX GUIDE ¶1713 et seq.).

California Forms: Sch. D (Capital Gain or Loss Adjustment), Sch. D-1 (Sales of Business Property).

California law is generally the same as federal as of the current IRC tie-in date (¶103). (Sec. 18031, Rev. & Tax. Code)

Loss (but not gain) is recognized on involuntary conversion of property due to destruction, theft, condemnation, etc. Gain is recognized, however, to the extent (1) the proceeds are not used to acquire other property similar or related in service or use or (2) the taxpayer purchases the replacement property or stock from related persons. However, a taxpayer, other than a C corporation or a partnership with majority corporate partners, may defer gain recognition if the aggregate of the amount of gain realized on the property is $100,000 or less.

The taxpayer may elect not to recognize gain even though the proceeds of the involuntary conversion are not expended *directly* on the replacement property. In this case the replacement property must be purchased within a limited period of time as specified in the law. A longer period may be allowed upon application by the taxpayer. Replacement property may consist of stock in a corporation owning qualified replacement property, provided control of the corporation is acquired. "Control" for this purpose is defined as 80% of the voting stock, plus 80% of all other classes of stock outstanding.

Special rules limit the amount of gain a taxpayer must recognize on the receipt of insurance proceeds for the taxpayer's principal residence (including a rented residence) or its contents that are involuntarily converted as a result of a federally-declared disaster. In addition, if business or investment property is compulsorily or involuntarily converted as the result of a federally-declared disaster, *any* tangible property of a type held for productive use in a trade or business will be treated for nonrecognition purposes as "similar or related in service or use" to the converted property.

CCH Example: Disaster-Related Involuntary Conversion

Paul's coffee cart was destroyed as a result of a federally-declared disaster. Before the disaster, Paul sold coffee, juices, and pastries from the cart outside a local hospital. Within two months of the cart's destruction, Paul received related insurance proceeds and immediately used all of the proceeds to purchase a computer for use in the word processing business he runs from his home. The computer will be treated as similar or related in use to the coffee cart, and Paul may elect not to recognize gain with respect to the involuntarily converted cart.

¶504 Sale of Residence

Law: Sec. 18031 (CCH CALIFORNIA TAX REPORTS, ¶15-710).

Comparable Federal: Sec. 121 (CCH U.S. MASTER TAX GUIDE ¶1705).

California law is generally the same as federal law as of the current IRC tie-in date (¶103). (Sec. 18031, Rev. & Tax. Code) See ¶229 for details.

Gain from the sale or exchange of the taxpayer's own residence is taxable as a capital gain because the residence is a "capital asset" (¶524). Loss from such a sale or exchange is not deductible, either as a capital loss or as an ordinary loss (¶307).

Taxpayers who sell or exchange property that they owned and occupied as a principal residence for at least two of the five years preceding the sale or exchange can elect up to a $250,000 ($500,000 for joint filers) exclusion from gross income of gain realized on the sale or exchange. Gain that is allocable to periods of nonoccupancy is not excluded. However, as discussed at ¶ 229, certain exceptions apply to the two-year and five-year use and test periods and California treats registered domestic partners as spouses, whereas federal law does not.

¶505 Gain from Sale of Assisted Housing

Law: Sec. 18041.5 (CCH CALIFORNIA TAX REPORTS, ¶ 16-270).

Comparable Federal: Former Sec. 1039.

No gain is recognized on the sale of an assisted housing development to a tenant association, organization, agency, or individual that obligates itself and its successors to make the development affordable to low-income families for (1) 30 years from the date of sale or (2) for the remaining term of existing federal government assistance, whichever is longer. The proceeds from the sale must be reinvested in residential real property, other than a personal residence, within two years of the sale. An "assisted housing development" is a multifamily rental housing development that receives federal government assistance. (Sec. 18041.5, Rev. & Tax. Code)

¶506 Liquidation Under S.E.C. Order

Law: Sec. 18031 (CCH CALIFORNIA TAX REPORTS, ¶ 15-710).

Comparable Federal: Former Sec. 1081 (CCH U.S. MASTER TAX GUIDE ¶ 2247).

California law is the same as federal law as of the current IRC conformity date (¶ 103). (Sec. 18031, Rev. & Tax. Code)

¶507 Exchange of Property for Like Property

Law: Secs. 18031, 18032 (CCH CALIFORNIA TAX REPORTS, ¶ 15-710).

Comparable Federal: Sec. 1031 (CCH U.S. MASTER TAX GUIDE ¶ 1721 et seq.).

California law is generally the same as federal law as of the current IRC tie-in date (¶ 103). (Sec. 18031, Rev. & Tax. Code)

Generally, no gain or loss is recognized if property held for productive use or investment is exchanged for property of a like kind. However, under both federal and state law, an exchange of foreign real property for real property located within the United States may not qualify as a like-kind exchange. This disqualification from nonrecognition of gain extends to exchanges of *personal property* predominantly used outside the United States for personal property predominantly used in the United States.

CCH Practice Tip: Replacement Period

Under federal law, followed by California, the replacement property must be purchased within the earlier of 180 days from the transfer of the relinquished property or the due date (determined with regard to extensions) of the taxpayer's federal tax return. California follows the federal treatment, regardless of whether or not an extended California return was filed. Therefore, the federal extended due date should be used in determining whether the property is qualifies for like-kind treatment. (*FTB Tax News* (2012), CCH CALIFORNIA TAX REPORTS, ¶ 405-721)

Caution: Like-Kind Exchange of Tenancy-In-Common Interest

The Franchise Tax Board has identified a trend that is resulting in many audit adjustments, with respect to like-kind exchanges of tenancy-in-common (TIC) interests. A TIC interest is considered like-kind property for purposes of the like-kind exchange provisions. A partnership interest, however, is not treated as such.

The FTB has identified a number of cases in which the property interest exchanged is more closely aligned with a partnership interest than a TIC. If a property interest is found, in substance, to be a partnership interest, then the property is not considered like-kind property, and deferring gain is not allowed. The FTB will continue to consider IRS Rev. Proc. 2002-22 (relating to rental real property), on which taxpayers are relying to support their position that they hold a TIC interest and are entitled to defer gain, but will continue to make determinations based on existing law and the facts and circumstances of each case. (*Tax News*, California Franchise Tax Board, November 2007, CCH CALIFORNIA TAX REPORTS, ¶ 404-487)

California law, unlike federal law, does not extend like-kind exchange treatment to an exchange of certain mutual ditch, reservoir, or irrigation company stock completed after May 22, 2008. (Sec. 18031.5, Rev. & Tax. Code) However, under California law, mutual water companies that were formed before September 26, 1977, are allowed to transfer assets to community services districts tax-free. (*FTB's Summary of 2008 Federal Legislative Changes*)

• *Exchanges by nonresidents*

The Franchise Tax Board has taken the position that a nonresident's gain or loss from the exchange of real or tangible property located within California for real or tangible property located outside California is sourced to California. California also taxes the gain realized on the sale of California property in a non-deferred transaction, even if the sale is of property that was exchanged for out-of-state property while the taxpayer was a nonresident. However, the taxpayer is eligible for a credit for taxes paid to the other state on any gain that was deferred from the original transaction (FTB Pub. 1100, Taxation of Nonresidents and Individuals Who Change Residency, revised 11-2007, CCH CALIFORNIA TAX REPORTS, ¶ 404-599).

Applicable to exchanges of property that occur in taxable years beginning after 2013, taxpayers that defer any gain or loss on their California tax return pursuant to an IRC § 1031 like-kind exchange must file an information return with the FTB if the transaction involves California property that is exchanged for like-kind property located outside California. The return must be filed for the taxable year of the exchange and for each subsequent taxable year in which the gain or loss from that exchange has not been recognized. Taxpayers that fail to file the required information return and fail to file a tax return reporting the deferred gain or loss may be subject to the same penalties, interest, and assessments that may be proposed for failure to file a return. The FTB is authorized to make an estimate of the net income from the exchange using any available information, including the amount of deferred gain or loss reported in the year of the exchange. (Sec. 18032, Rev. & Tax. Code)

The reporting requirement applies to all individuals, estates, trusts, and all business entities regardless of their state of residency or commercial domicile. The seller/exchanger is required to file Form FTB 3840, California Like-Kind Exchanges, even if the seller/exchanger is not required to file any other California franchise, income, or information return. For those with a California franchise and/or income tax return filing requirement, the Form FTB 3840 should be attached to the tax return. For those sellers/exchangers who do not have a California return filing requirement, the Form FTB 3840 must be mailed to the FTB by the return due date as if the taxpayer had a California filing requirement. (*FTB Tax News*, October 2014 (CCH CALIFORNIA TAX REPORTS, ¶ 406-241))

Practitioner Comment: California Reporting Requirement for IRC §1031 Like-Kind Exchanges of California Property for Out-of-State Property Raises Constitutional and Reporting Concerns

A.B. 92, the legislation that enacted the IRC § 1031 information return reporting requirement, may be subject to a constitutional challenge because it appears to unduly impose an additional burden on out-of-state exchanges as compared to in-state exchanges. In particular, the law creates the burden of annual reporting on businesses that follow federal and state laws allowing legitimate deferral of gains and imposes consequences on nonfilers (i.e., those who do not file either a personal or corporate California return) that fail to report the exchanges. However, A.B. 92 appears to provide no consequences to California filers that fail to comply with the disclosure requirement.

There are also the practical considerations. For example, the mechanics of the provision are unclear as applied to pass through entities where the owners can change over time. Query whether if a gain is triggered, the incidence of tax would fall on the owners at the time of the original exchange or the current pass through entity owners. Furthermore, from a policy perspective the reporting requirement appears to be unnecessary for multistate business taxpayers filing in California since the ultimate sale of the out of state business property acquired in such an exchange would be reportable on the return in any event and would typically generate apportionable business income.

On February 3, 2016, the Franchise Tax Board (FTB) held an Interested Parties Meeting to discuss modifications to California like-kind exchange regulations, 18 California Code of Regs. Secs. 17951-7 and 25137(e). The regulation project is focusing on how to treat gains and losses disclosed under the reporting requirements of A.B. 92 after the ultimate sale of the property. Additionally, the FTB discussed the ambiguities of whether to use current year or historical apportionment percentages when corporations apportion gain from the ultimate sale of like-kind exchanged property.

Chris Whitney, Contributing Editor

CCH Practice Tip: Common Audit Issues

One of the FTB's top audit issues continues to be like-kind exchanges, also known as 1031 exchanges. The FTB has identified the following most common audit issues:

— sourcing of gains to California upon disposition of replacement property received in a California deferred exchange even if the replacement property was not located in California;

— taxpayer receives other property (boot) in the exchange but does not report the boot on its return;

— taxpayers do not meet identification or other technical requirements of IRC § 1031;

— relinquished and/or replacement property are not held for investment or for productive use in a trade or business (i.e., property is used for personal purposes or is held primarily for sale); and

— the taxpayer who transfers relinquished property is a different taxpayer than the party who acquires replacement property.

The FTB continues to review certain "drop and swap" or "swap and drop" transactions. Where the form does not support the economic realities or substance of the transaction, the FTB will recharacterize the taxpayer's transaction as appropriate.

The FTB also notes that the Board of Equalization recently upheld its recharacterization of transactions involving 1031 exchanges in the following appeals:

— *Appeal of Aries*, No. 464475 (swap and drop);

— *Appeal of Marcil*, No. 458832 (different taxpayer acquired replacement property, rehearing granted); and

— *Appeal of Brief*, Appeal No. 5308782 (deemed contribution to a partnership).

(*FTB Tax News* (January 2012), CCH CALIFORNIA TAX REPORTS, ¶ 405-551)

¶508 Exchange of Insurance Policies

Law: Secs. 18031, 18037.5 (CCH CALIFORNIA TAX REPORTS, ¶15-710).

Comparable Federal: Sec. 1035 (CCH U.S. MASTER TAX GUIDE ¶1724).

California law is generally the same as federal law as of California's current federal conformity date (¶103).

No gain or loss is recognized on (1) the exchange of a life insurance contract for another life insurance contract or (2) certain exchanges involving endowment or annuity contracts. (Sec. 18031, Rev. & Tax. Code) However, California law, unlike federal law, does not apply the tax-free exchange treatment of certain insurance and annuity contracts to exchanges involving long-term care insurance contracts. (Sec. 18037.5, Rev. & Tax. Code)

¶509 Exchange of Stock for Stock

Law: Sec. 18031 (CCH CALIFORNIA TAX REPORTS, ¶15-710).

Comparable Federal: Sec. 1036 (CCH U.S. MASTER TAX GUIDE ¶1728).

California law is the same as federal law (¶103). (Sec. 18031, Rev. & Tax. Code)

No gain or loss is recognized on an exchange of a corporation's (1) common stock for common stock of the same corporation or (2) preferred stock for other shares of its preferred stock.

¶510 Exchange of Certain U.S. Obligations

Law: Sec. 18031 (CCH CALIFORNIA TAX REPORTS, ¶15-710).

Comparable Federal: Sec. 1037 (CCH U.S. MASTER TAX GUIDE ¶1726, 1925).

California law is the same as federal law (¶103). (Sec. 18031, Rev. & Tax. Code)

Certain designated U.S. obligations (bonds issued under chapter 31, title 31, of the United States Code) may be exchanged tax-free for other obligations issued under the same chapter.

¶511 Reacquisition of Property After Installment Sale

Law: Sec. 18031 (CCH CALIFORNIA TAX REPORTS, ¶15-710).

Comparable Federal: Sec. 1038 (CCH U.S. MASTER TAX GUIDE ¶1841, 1843).

California law is the same as federal law (¶103). (Sec. 18031, Rev. & Tax. Code)

Certain limitations are imposed on a seller's recognized gain or loss upon repossession of certain *real* property if the property had previously been sold on the installment method.

¶512 Sale or Exchange of Property for Stock

Law: Sec. 17321 (CCH CALIFORNIA TAX REPORTS, ¶15-710).

Comparable Federal: Sec. 351 (CCH U.S. MASTER TAX GUIDE ¶203, 1731, 2205, 2233, 2257).

California law is the same as federal law as of the current IRC tie-in date (¶103). Generally, no gain or loss is recognized on a transfer of property to a corporation in exchange for its stock or securities, when the transferrers are in control after the exchange. (Sec. 17321, Rev. & Tax. Code)

¶513 Sale or Exchange of Tax-Exempt Bonds

Law: Sec. 17133.5 (CCH CALIFORNIA TAX REPORTS, ¶15-710).

Comparable Federal: None.

The gain or loss from the sale or transfer of bonds yielding tax-exempt interest is not exempt. Federal law is the same regarding state and municipal obligations. (Sec. 17133.5, Rev. & Tax. Code)

¶514 Sale of Stock to ESOPs or Cooperatives

Law: Sec. 18042 (CCH CALIFORNIA TAX REPORTS, ¶ 15-170, 16-070).

Comparable Federal: Sec. 1042 (CCH U.S. MASTER TAX GUIDE ¶ 1733, 2109).

California generally conforms to federal law allowing taxpayers to sell qualified securities to an employee stock ownership plan (ESOP) or worker-owned cooperative and to replace such securities with other securities without recognition of the gain. However, California does not incorporate the federal provision that allows a taxpayer to defer the recognition of gain from the sale of stock of a qualified agricultural refiner or processor to an eligible farm cooperative. (Sec. 18042, Rev. & Tax. Code)

¶515 Sale of Small Business Stock

Law: Secs. 18038.4, 18038.5, 18152.5, 18153 (CCH CALIFORNIA TAX REPORTS, ¶ 15-710, 16-070).

Comparable Federal: Sec. 1045 (CCH U.S. MASTER TAX GUIDE ¶ 2397).

Legislation enacted in 2013 (Ch. 546 (A.B. 1412)), retroactively reinstated a modified version of California's qualified small business stock (QSBS) gain deferral provision for 2008—2012 tax years. (Sec. 18038.5, Rev. & Tax. Code; Sec. 18152.5, Rev. & Tax. Code) California's original QSBS gain deferral provision, which was based on the QSBS exclusion eligibility provision, was struck down in *Cutler v. Franchise Tax Board* (2012) 146 Cal.Rptr.3d 244, 208 Cal.App.4th (CCH CALIFORNIA TAX REPORTS, ¶ 405-704), as an unconstitutional violation of the dormant Commerce Clause because it was only available to taxpayers that invested in corporations that had a significant presence in California. In response to the court's decision in *Cutler*, which did not address the remedy issue, the Franchise Tax Board (FTB) issued *FTB Notice 2012-03* (CCH CALIFORNIA TAX REPORTS, ¶ 405-750), which retroactively denied the deferral and exclusion provisions for all taxpayers for all open tax years.

California law generally mirrors federal law allowing a taxpayer, other than a C corporation, to elect to roll over capital gain from a sale of qualified small business stock held for more than six months, provided that the gain from the sale was used to purchase other qualified small business stock within 60 days from the date of the original sale. The election must generally be made on an original return filed on or before the due date (including extensions) for filing the income tax return for the taxable year in which the qualified small business stock is sold. (Sec. 18038.4, Rev. & Tax. Code; Sec. 18038.5, Rev. & Tax. Code) However, prior to being struck down as unconstitutional in *Cutler*, California law, unlike federal law, also required that:

— at least 80% of the corporation's payroll measured by total dollar value, had to be attributable to employment located within California and

— at least 80% (by value) of the assets of the corporation used by the corporation had to be in the active conduct of one or more qualified trades or businesses in California. (Sec. 18152.5(c)(2)(A), Rev. & Tax. Code)

The modified provisions enacted in 2013 by A.B. 1412, and effective retroactively to the 2008—2012 tax years, eliminated the previous requirement that 80% percent of business activity occur in California during the holding period. However, the QSBS must still meet the 80% California payroll requirement at the time of the stock's acquisition to claim the gain exclusion or deferral, but the 80% California-employment level need no longer be maintained for all periods for which the exclusion is claimed.

CCH Practice Tip: Procedures to claim 2008—2012 deferral

The FTB has released procedures for taxpayers to follow as a result of the retroactive reinstatement of the QSBS gain deferral for tax years 2008 to 2012. The procedures to follow are dependent upon whether the taxpayer has filed a return as yet and/or whether the FTB has contacted the taxpayer concerning the QSBS gains.

Taxpayers who have not filed their 2012 tax return: Eligible taxpayers may claim the QSBS gain deferral on Form 540, Schedule D. Taxpayers should report the entire amount of gain from the sale of QSBS on Form 540, Schedule D. Immediately underneath that line taxpayers should write "QSBS deferral" and report the exclusion or deferral amount as a negative number (loss).

Taxpayers who filed their 2008—2012 tax returns and were contacted by the FTB regarding their QSBS election: Taxpayers will be notified by the FTB of the following:

— The FTB is withdrawing pending notices of proposed assessments based on the *Cutler* decision or FTB Notice 2012-3.

— Closing letters will be sent to taxpayers who signed a limited QSBS waiver for 2008.

— Unpaid tax, interest, or penalty assessed as a result of the *Cutler* decision/ FTB Notice 2012-3 will be abated.

The FTB will automatically issue refunds for payments received related to the *Cutler* decision/FTB Notice 2012-3. Taxpayers are not required to file refund requests or take any further action. However, if a taxpayer has not heard from the FTB concerning this issue by November 30, 2013, the taxpayer should contact the FTB at (916) 845-3030.

Taxpayers who filed their 2008—2012 tax returns but did not claim the QSBS election: As noted above, amendments made by A.B. 1412 eliminate the previous requirement that 80% of business activity occur in California during the holding period. However, the QSBS must still meet the 80% California payroll requirement at the time of acquisition to claim the gain deferral. Refund claims must also be filed within the statute of limitations period. Generally, the statute of limitations is four years from the date the return was filed (if filed within the extension period), or one year from the date of the overpayment, whichever is later. However, taxpayers are given until June 30, 2014, to file a QSBS claim for refund for tax year 2008.

Amended returns should state in red "QSBS CLAIM FOR REFUND" at the top of the return, include the computed refund amount, and be mailed to the following address:

Cutler Claim for Refund 347 MS F381

Franchise Tax Board

C/O FTB Notice 2012-03

P.O. Box 1779

Rancho Cordova, CA 95741-1779

Refund claims sent by courier service delivery or private courier mail should be addressed to the following:

Franchise Tax Board

Sacramento, CA 95827

(*Qualified Small Business Stock Update*, California Franchise Tax Board (2013) (CCH CALIFORNIA TAX REPORTS, ¶ 405-973))

CCH Comment: Interest/penalty waivers

No penalties or interest will accrue with respect to any addition to tax that may result from the A.B. 1412 amendments described above or, if the provisions discussed above are struck down by an appellate court, to any addition to tax to the extent that the increase is attributable to the implementation of the appellate court's decision invalidating the provisions as amended, coupled with the implementation of the decision of the appellate court's decision in *Cutler*. (Sec. 18153, Rev. & Tax. Code)

Practitioner Comment: California Court of Appeal Deems Qualified Small Business Stock Statute Unconstitutional

On August 28, 2012, the California Court of Appeal concluded in *Cutler v. FTB*, 146 Cal.Rptr.3d 244, 208 Cal.App.4th 1247 (2012), CCH CALIFORNIA TAX REPORTS, ¶ 405-704, that Cal. Rev. & Tax. Code § 18038.5, which allows for the deferral of capital gains on the sale of "qualified small business stock", is unconstitutional. The California provision generally mirrors the federal provision, except that in California "qualified small business stock" is limited to stock issued by corporations that used 80% of their assets in the conduct of business in California and that maintained 80% of their payrolls in California. *Cutler* held that because the statute affords taxpayers a deferral for income received from the sale of stock in corporations maintaining assets and payroll in California, while no deferral is afforded for income from the sale of stock in corporations that maintain assets and payroll elsewhere, the deferral provision discriminates on its face and is unconstitutional. However, the Court of Appeal remanded the case back to the trial court to fashion a remedy.

The issue in *Cutler* is similar to that presented in *Farmer Bros.* and *Abbott*. In *Farmer Bros.* the courts concluded that the California dividends received deduction (DRD) at Cal Rev. & Tax Code § 24402 was discriminatory on its face because it favored dividend-paying corporations doing business in and paying taxes to California over dividend-paying corporations that did not do business in or pay taxes to California. *Abbott* determined that the appropriate remedy was to invalidate the entire provision (i.e., deny the DRD to all taxpayers), not reform the portion deemed unconstitutional by making the DRD available to all taxpayers.

Moreover, while in *Cutler* the court only addressed the deferral provision in Cal. Rev. & Tax. Code § 18038.5, it would appear that the same rational would apply to the exclusion provision under Cal. Rev. & Tax. Code § 18152.5. The exclusion provision limits the benefit to stock in California companies similar to the deferral provision that the court found was unconstitutional.

The FTB issued Notice 2012-03 on December 21, 2012, in response to the *Cutler* decision. It announced that all taxpayers would be denied the QSBS exclusion/deferral for 2008 and later. In effect, the FTB took the position that the provision should be struck in its entirety instead of reforming it to allow deferral for all "qualified small business stock," regardless of the location of the corporation's assets and payroll. The FTB began sending Notices of Proposed Assessment (NPAs) to taxpayers who claimed a small business stock benefit on their 2008 returns in April 2013.

On October 4, 2013, California Governor Jerry Brown signed A.B. 1412, which removes the active in-state requirements, thus applying the QSBS exclusion deferral investments in:

> — in-state businesses that remain predominantly in-state; and

> — in-state businesses that may have expanded to include out-of-state business operations.

Because the legislation applies retroactively, the FTB announced on October 7, 2013, that it will withdraw the NPAs it had previously issued.

California taxpayers should consider filing refund claims for gains realized in prior years that may have otherwise qualified for gain exclusion/deferral but for the in-state business requirement. Because the statute of limitations in California is generally four years, the 2008 tax year would typically close in 2013. The legislation, however, provides a special statute of limitations that permits taxpayers to file refund claims for the 2008 tax year until June 30, 2014. The FTB posted FAQs on its website that provide guidance to taxpayers seeking refunds under these provisions (see discussion above).

Interestingly, A.B. 1412 still requires that the QSBS must meet the 80% California payroll requirement at the time of acquisition to claim the 50% gain exclusion or deferral in order to file an amended return (claim for refund) if the statute of limitations is open. Although the statute no longer has the California assets test and only applies the 80% California payroll test at the time of stock acquisition (versus during the entire holding period as previously required), it is questionable whether A.B. 1412 would withstand constitutional scrutiny. Indeed, it appears that the Legislature anticipates litigation on this issue since the bill expressly states that to the extent any provision in the statute is deemed invalid, that invalidity applies to the entire statute, except the provision that prohibits imposing penalties and interest against taxpayers that properly claimed QSBS exclusion/deferral under the statute deemed unconstitutional in *Cutler*.

Chris Whitney, Contributing Editor

CCH Comment: Replacement Stock Purchases by Partnerships

For purposes of the requirement to acquire replacement stock, a taxpayer could use a partnership other than the one selling the qualified small business stock to acquire the replacement stock, and an individual could use a partnership to acquire replacement stock on his or her behalf. This FTB position was based on final federal Reg. 1.1045-1. (*Tax News*, California Franchise Tax Board, October 2007, CCH California Tax Reports, ¶404-468)

Reporting requirements.—To qualify as a small business, corporations must file a completed Form FTB 3565, Small Business Stock Questionnaire, with the FTB, and mail copies to each of its shareholders. A corporation's failure to complete and file a Form FTB 3565 will not disqualify stockholders from claiming the exclusion. However, the stockholders must prove that the stock satisfies the statutory definition of "small business stock". (*FTB Notice 96-2*, Franchise Tax Board, May 6, 1996, CCH California Tax Reports, ¶402-840)

¶516 Exchange in Connection with Reorganization

Law: Sec. 17321 (CCH California Tax Reports, ¶15-710).

Comparable Federal: Secs. 354, 368 (CCH U.S. Master Tax Guide ¶2205).

California law is the same as federal law as of the current IRC tie-in date (¶103). (Sec. 17321, Rev. & Tax. Code)

No gain or loss is recognized if stock or securities in a corporation that is a party to a reorganization are exchanged solely for other stock or securities in the corporation or for stock or securities in another corporation that is a party to the reorganization (a "B" type reorganization). "Reorganization" and other terms are specifically defined.

¶517 "Spin-Off" Reorganization

Law: Sec. 17321 (CCH California Tax Reports, ¶15-710).

Comparable Federal: Sec. 355 (CCH U.S. Master Tax Guide ¶2201).

California law is the same as federal law as of the current IRC tie-in date (¶103). (Sec. 17321, Rev. & Tax. Code) However, because of its IRC conformity date, California has not adopted federal amendments enacted by the federal Protecting Americans from Tax Hikes (PATH) Act of 2015 and effective generally for distributions on or after December 7, 2015, providing that IRC Sec. 355 will not apply to any distribution if either the distributing corporation or the controlled corporation is a real estate investment trust (REIT).

No gain is recognized in a "spin-off" type of reorganization, provided certain tests of the business purpose of the transaction are met. This type of reorganization involves the transfer of part of a corporation's assets to a new corporation and the distribution of the new corporation's stock to the shareholders of the old corporation. Both corporations must be engaged in the active conduct of a trade or business that has been operating for at least five years, and it must be shown that the transaction was not used principally as a "device for the distribution of earnings and profits."

Practitioner Comment: California-Federal Differences

California's lagging conformity to the Internal Revenue Code (IRC) could result in certain transactions that qualified as tax-free spin-offs for federal income tax purposes being treated as taxable dividends for California tax purposes. Prior to the 2010 tax year, California had conformed to the IRC as of January 1, 2005. However, on May 17, 2006, IRC Sec. 355(b)(3) was enacted in order to simplify the active trade or business test by treating all members of both the distributing and the controlling entity(ies)'s affiliated group as one corporation. Because this enactment was subsequent to the January 1, 2005 conformity date in effect prior to the 2010 tax year, certain spin-off transactions that were nontaxable for federal purposes could be taxable for California income tax purposes.

The Franchise Tax Board (FTB) in Chief Counsel Ruling 2007-3, July 17, 2007, CCH CALIFORNIA TAX REPORTS, ¶404-447, acknowledged that a taxpayer could restructure in order to meet the active trade or business requirements. Further, although such was intended to avoid adverse California tax consequences, the FTB indicated that it would not regard the restructuring as a non-economic substance transaction or "NEST" otherwise subject to potential penalties under RTC Section 19774.

It should be noted that S.B. 401, enacted April 10, 2010, updated the IRC conformity date to January 1, 2009, effective for tax years beginning on or after January 1, 2010. As a result, beginning in 2010 California conformed to the changes made to IRC Section 355 in 2006. It should be noted, however, that the passage of Proposition 26 on November 2, 2010, has raised some questions concerning the continuing validity of S.B. 401 for the reasons discussed below.

Specifically, Proposition 26 amended Section 3 of Article XIII of the California Constitution to require a 2/3 super-majority vote for legislation that results in any taxpayer paying higher taxes in California and expanded the definition of taxes to include fees. Although S.B. 401 was scored as a "revenue neutral" bill, it may increase taxes for taxpayers in certain circumstances and it did not garner a 2/3 super-majority vote. Proposition 26 by its own terms is applicable to legislation enacted after January 1, 2010 and provides that affected legislation which was not properly enacted after such date but prior to the effective date of the proposition (November 3, 2010) will become void 12 months after such effective date (i.e., November 3, 2011) if not reenacted with a 2/3 super-majority vote prior to that date. Since S.B. 401 was not reenacted with a super-majority vote prior to November 3, 2011, the continuing validity of S.B. 401 beginning on such date has been called into question, leaving taxpayers uncertain as to which IRC reference date (i.e., January 1, 2005 or January 1, 2009) currently applies.

The FTB has issued Legal Guidance 2011-01-01 indicating that it will continue to apply the January 1, 2009, conformity date per S.B. 401 until such time as a California Court of Appeal holds that S.B. 401 has been rendered void. Note that the California Legislature attempted to bolster the validity of S.B. 401 in A.B. 154 by stating "it is the intent of the Legislature to confirm the validity and ongoing effect of Senate Bill No. 401 of the 2009-10 Regular Session." It is unclear whether this language in A.B. 154 is sufficient to remedy any potential issues with S.B. 401.

Note that with the passage of A.B. 154 (which passed with a 2/3 super-majority vote) the Legislature updated California's IRC conformity date to January 1, 2015, effective for tax years beginning on or after January 1, 2015. As a result, while some uncertainty remains as to the validity of spins pursuant to IRC Sec. 355 occurring between January 1, 2009, and January 1, 2015, A.B. 154 updates California to conform to federal treatment for those spins occurring after January 1, 2015.

Chris Whitney, Contributing Editor

¶518 Exchanges Not Solely in Kind

Law: Sec. 17321 (CCH CALIFORNIA TAX REPORTS, ¶15-710).

Comparable Federal: Sec. 356 (CCH U.S. MASTER TAX GUIDE ¶2237).

California law is the same as federal law as of the current IRC tie-in date (¶103). (Sec. 17321, Rev. & Tax. Code)

Where exchanges would be exempt except for the fact that money or other property ("boot") is received, gain is recognized up to the amount of money or other property, but no loss may be recognized. Where a distribution has the effect of a taxable dividend, it is subject to tax up to the amount of gain recognized on the transaction.

¶519 Exchanges Involving Foreign Corporations

Law: Sec. 17321 (CCH CALIFORNIA TAX REPORTS, ¶16-079).

Comparable Federal: Sec. 367 (CCH U.S. MASTER TAX GUIDE ¶2267).

California law is the same as federal law as of the current IRC tie-in date (¶103). (Sec. 17321, Rev. & Tax. Code)

Certain exchanges involving foreign corporations lose their exempt status unless property is transferred to the foreign corporation for use in its active conduct of a trade or business.

¶520 Transfers of Property to Foreign Trusts and Estates

Law: Sec. 17760 (CCH CALIFORNIA TAX REPORTS, ¶16-398a).

Comparable Federal: Sec. 684.

California does not incorporate federal law, which provides special gain recognition rules for certain transfers to foreign trusts and estates. (Sec. 17760, Rev. & Tax. Code)

¶521 Foreign Currency Transactions

Law: Sec. 17078 (CCH CALIFORNIA TAX REPORTS, ¶15-700, 16-520).

Comparable Federal: Sec. 988 (CCH U.S. MASTER TAX GUIDE ¶2498).

California law is the same as federal law (¶103), except that the federal provision relating to the source of income or loss does not apply for California purposes. Gains and losses resulting from foreign currency transactions are characterized as ordinary income and classified as interest income or expense. (Sec. 17078, Rev. & Tax. Code)

¶522 Liquidation of Corporation

Law: Secs. 17024.5, 17321 (CCH CALIFORNIA TAX REPORTS, ¶15-645).

Comparable Federal: Secs. 331-46 (CCH U.S. MASTER TAX GUIDE ¶2253 et seq.).

California law is the same as federal law as of the current IRC tie-in date (¶103), except for provisions relating to domestic international sales corporations (DISCs) that are not recognized by California. (Sec. 17024.5(b), Rev. & Tax. Code; Sec. 17321, Rev. & Tax. Code)

Gain or loss to a stockholder upon liquidation of a corporation is ordinarily a capital gain or loss because it results from the exchange of stock for assets distributed in liquidation (see also ¶226).

• *Relief for minority shareholders*

Relief is provided for minority shareholders in corporate liquidations if the liquidation is tax-free to a parent corporation owning 80% or more of the stock. Accordingly, minority shareholders are protected from the double impact of corporate tax on the sale of appreciated property and a personal income tax on the distribution from the corporate liquidation (see also ¶1216).

¶523 Capital Gains and Losses—General Rules

> *Law:* Secs. 18151, 18152.5, 18155, 18155.6, 18171, 18178, 18181 (CCH CALIFORNIA TAX REPORTS, ¶15-620).
>
> *Comparable Federal:* Secs. 1201-57, 1260 (CCH U.S. MASTER TAX GUIDE ¶1735 et seq.).
>
> *California Form:* Sch. D (Capital Gain or Loss Adjustment).

California law is the same as federal law as of the current IRC tie-in date (¶103), with the exceptions of the tax rate applied to capital gains and other differences discussed below. (Sec. 18151, Rev. & Tax. Code)

Because California treats capital gains as ordinary income, the amount of California tax is not dependent on the holding period, and the distinction between long-term and short-term capital gains has less significance for California purposes. Because lower capital gains rates apply for federal purposes for long-term capital gains (gain from sales or exchanges of property held for more than 12 months) the concept of long-term capital gains and holding periods still plays a significant role for federal taxation purposes.

Certain gains and losses are classified as "capital" gains and losses and are subject to special rules. Generally, capital losses are subject to restrictions, as explained at ¶525, ¶526. Ordinarily, a gain or loss constitutes a "capital" gain or loss only if

— the asset disposed of is a "capital asset" (¶524) or a noncapital asset that, under a special rule, is treated as a "capital asset" (¶537),

— the gain or loss results from a *sale or exchange*, including a sale or exchange of specified securities futures contracts, or from something that, under a special rule, is treated as a sale or exchange (¶529, ¶540), and

— the gain or loss is attributable to the cancellation, lapse, expiration, or other termination of a right or obligation (other than a securities futures contract) with respect to a capital asset or an IRC Section 1256 contract that is a capital asset in the hands of the taxpayer.

The last item does not apply to the retirement of a debt instrument.

• *Special rules*

Worthlessness of securities is arbitrarily treated as a sale or exchange (¶307). A nonbusiness bad debt is treated as a capital loss (¶308). Losses from the destruction or theft of property may also be treated as a sale or exchange under some circumstances (¶537). Gain or loss on liquidation of a corporation is ordinarily capital gain or loss (¶522). Losses on wash sales are not allowable (¶527), and limits are placed on the losses attributable to straddles (¶532).

Losses resulting from abandonment are not subject to capital loss limitations, because they do not result from sale or exchange.

The general rules for capital gains and losses discussed above are provided under federal law incorporated by California. However, there are a number of differences between California and federal law in the numerous special rules. The differences are discussed in later paragraphs. See also ¶226 for special federal capital-gain treatment of dividends from mutual funds.

Taxpayers are allowed to report capital gain distributions from mutual funds on Form 540 2EZ. (Instructions, Form 540 2EZ)

• *Federal-California differences*

—California does not incorporate a federal provision that allows an exclusion for gain from the sale of certain small business stock, but adopted a substantially similar provision for pre-2013 tax years that was limited to a 50% exclusion (¶525). (Sec. 18152, Rev. & Tax. Code; Sec. 18152.5, Rev. & Tax. Code)

—California does not permit capital loss carrybacks (¶526). (Sec. 18155, Rev. & Tax. Code)

—California renders inoperative for specified periods certain federal rules relating to recapture of excess depreciation (¶539). (Sec. 18171, Rev. & Tax. Code)

—As noted above, California does not adopt the special federal tax rates imposed on long-term capital gains.

—California does not incorporate the federal provisions providing special treatment for certain passive foreign investment companies. (Sec. 18181, Rev. & Tax. Code)

—California does not incorporate federal incentives available to businesses located in renewal communities, including the gross income exclusion of capital gain from the sale or exchange of a "qualified community asset" held for more than five years and acquired after 2001 and before 2010.

—California references to specific subsections of IRC Sec. 1223 are different than the federal internal references beginning with the 2010 tax year. (Sec. 18155.6, Rev. & Tax. Code)

¶524 Definition of "Capital Assets"

Law: Sec. 18151 (CCH California Tax Reports, ¶15-620).

Comparable Federal: Sec. 1221 (CCH U.S. Master Tax Guide ¶1741).

California law is the same as federal law as of the current IRC tie-in date (¶103).

Under both California and federal law, the term "capital assets" includes all property *except:*

— inventoriable assets;

— property held for sale in the ordinary course of business;

— depreciable business property;

— real property used in business;

— certain copyrights, books, artistic works, etc. (however, see discussion below);

— accounts or notes receivable acquired in the ordinary course of business through sales or services;

— certain government publications;

— most commodities derivative financial instruments held by a commodities derivative dealer;

— hedging transactions; and

— supplies of a type regularly consumed in the ordinary course of business. (Sec. 18151, Rev. & Tax. Code)

See ¶537—¶540 for items that, although they are not actually capital assets, are treated under some circumstances as though they were.

¶525 Capital Gains and Losses—Amount Taken into Account

Law: Secs. 18038.5, 18151, 18151.5 18152, 18152.5, 18153 (CCH CALIFORNIA TAX REPORTS, ¶ 15-620).

Comparable Federal: Secs. 1202, 1222, 1260 (CCH U.S. MASTER TAX GUIDE ¶ 1740, 1742, 1777).

Both California and federal law measure the amount of capital gains in the same manner, except as noted below. (Sec. 18151, Rev. & Tax. Code)

• *Small business stock*

For pre-2013 tax years, California generally followed federal law allowing 50% of the gain from the sale or exchange of qualified small business stock (QSBS) held for more than five years to be excluded from gross income under certain conditions, provided the issuing corporation met specified active business requirements within California. (Sec. 18152, Rev. & Tax. Code; Sec. 18152.5, Rev. & Tax. Code) However, California did not follow federal amendments that increased the exclusion from 50% to 75% for stock acquired after February 17, 2009, and to 100% for stock acquired after September 27, 2010, and before January 1, 2014, if it is held for more than five years. See ¶ 515 for a discussion of the rollover of gain allowed for sales of certain small business stock.

Legislation enacted in 2013 (Ch. 546 (A.B. 1412)), retroactively reinstated a modified version of California's QSBS gain exclusion provisions for the 2008—2012 tax years. (Sec. 18038.5, Rev. & Tax. Code; Sec. 18152.5, Rev. & Tax. Code) California's original QSBS gain deferral provision, which was based on the QSBS exclusion eligibility provision, was struck down in *Cutler v. Franchise Tax Board* (2012) 146 Cal.Rptr.3d 244, 208 Cal.App.4th 1247, (CCH CALIFORNIA TAX REPORTS, ¶ 405-704) as an unconstitutional violation of the dormant Commerce Clause because it was only available to taxpayers that invested in corporations that had a significant presence in California. In response to the court's decision in *Cutler*, which did not address the remedy issue, the Franchise Tax Board (FTB) issued *FTB Notice 2012-03* (CCH CALIFORNIA TAX REPORTS, ¶ 405-750), which retroactively denied both the deferral and exclusion provisions for all taxpayers for all open tax years.

California's QSBS provisions were generally identical to the federal provisions. However, unlike federal law, to qualify for the California exclusion in effect prior to the *Cutler* decision, California also required that:

— at least 80% of the corporation's payroll measured by total dollar value, had to be attributable to employment located within California and

— at least 80% (by value) of the assets of the corporation used by the corporation had to be in the active conduct of one or more qualified trades or businesses in California. (Sec. 18152.5(c)(2)(A), Rev. & Tax. Code)

The modified provisions enacted by A.B. 1412 in 2013, and effective retroactively to the 2008—2012 tax years, eliminated the previous requirement that 80% percent of business activity occur in California during the holding period. However, the QSBS must still meet the 80% California payroll requirement at the time of the stock's acquisition to claim the gain exclusion, but the 80% California-employment level need no longer be maintained for all periods for which the exclusion is claimed. The reinstatement of the 50% gain exclusion applies to sales, including installment sales, occurring in each taxable year beginning after 2007 and before 2013, and to installment payments received in taxable years beginning after 2007, for sales of QSBS made in taxable years beginning before 2013.

CCH Practice Tip: Procedures to claim 2008—2012 deferral/exclusion

The FTB has released procedures for taxpayers to follow as a result of the retroactive reinstatement of the QSBS 50% gain exclusion for tax years 2008 to 2012. The procedures to follow are dependent upon whether the taxpayer has filed a return as yet and/or whether the FTB has contacted the taxpayer concerning the QSBS gains.

Taxpayers who have not filed their 2012 tax return: Eligible taxpayers may claim the QSBS gain exclusion on Form 540, Schedule D. Taxpayers should report the entire amount of gain from the sale of QSBS on Form 540, Schedule D. Immediately underneath that line taxpayers should write "QSBS exclusion" and report the exclusion amount as a negative number (loss). Taxpayers should also report 50% of the QSBS exclusion amount on Form 540 Schedule P (Line 10), as an alternative minimum tax (AMT) preference item.

Taxpayers who filed their 2008—2012 tax returns and were contacted by the FTB regarding their QSBS election: Taxpayers will be notified by the FTB of the following:

— The FTB is withdrawing pending notices of proposed assessments based on the *Cutler* decision or FTB Notice 2012-3

— Closing letters will be sent to taxpayers who signed a limited QSBS waiver for 2008.

— Unpaid tax, interest, or penalty assessed as a result of the *Cutler* decision/FTB Notice 2012-3 will be abated

The FTB will automatically issue refunds for payments received related to the *Cutler* decision/FTB Notice 2012-3. Taxpayers are not required to file refund requests or take any further action. However, if a taxpayer does not hear from the FTB concerning this issue by November 30, 2013, the taxpayer should contact the FTB at (916) 845-3030.

Taxpayers who filed their 2008—2012 tax returns but did not claim the QSBS election: As noted above, amendments made by A.B. 1412 eliminate the previous requirement that 80% of business activity occur in California during the holding period. However, the QSBS must still meet the 80% California payroll requirement at the time of acquisition to claim the gain exclusion. Refund claims must also be filed within the statute of limitations period. Generally, the statute of limitations is four years from the date the return was filed (if filed within the extension period), or one year from the date of the overpayment, whichever is later. However, taxpayers are given until June 30, 2014, to file a QSBS claim for refund for tax year 2008.

Amended returns should state in red "QSBS CLAIM FOR REFUND" at the top of the return, include the computed refund amount, and be mailed to the following address:

Cutler Claim for Refund 347 MS F381

Franchise Tax Board

C/O FTB Notice 2012-03

P.O. Box 1779

Rancho Cordova, CA 95741-1779

Refund claims sent by courtier service delivery or private courier mail should be addressed to the following:

Franchise Tax Board

Sacramento, CA 95827

(*Qualified Small Business Stock Update*, California Franchise Tax Board (2013) (CCH CALIFORNIA TAX REPORTS, ¶ 405-973))

CCH Comment: Interest/penalty waivers

No penalties or interest will accrue with respect to any addition to tax that may result from the A.B. 1412 amendments described above or, if the provisions discussed above are struck down by an appellate court, to any addition to tax to the extent that the increase is attributable to the implementation of the appellate court's decision invalidating the provisions as amended, coupled with the implementation of the decision of the appellate court's decision in Cutler. (Sec. 18153, Rev. & Tax. Code)

Practitioner Comment: California Court of Appeal Deems Qualified Small Business Stock Statute Unconstitutional

On August 28, 2012, the California Court of Appeal concluded in *Cutler v. FTB*, 146 Cal.Rptr.3d 244, 208 Cal.App.4th 1247 (2012), CCH CALIFORNIA TAX REPORTS, ¶ 405-704, that Cal. Rev. & Tax. Code § 18038.5, which allows for the deferral of capital gains on the sale of "qualified small business stock", is unconstitutional. The California provision generally mirrors the federal provision, except that in California "qualified small business stock" is limited to stock issued by corporations that used 80% of their assets in the conduct of business in California and that maintained 80% of their payrolls in California. *Cutler* held that because the statute affords taxpayers a deferral for income received from the sale of stock in corporations maintaining assets and payroll in California, while no deferral is afforded for income from the sale of stock in corporations that maintain assets and payroll elsewhere, the deferral provision discriminates on its face and is unconstitutional. However, the Court of Appeal remanded the case back to the trial court to fashion a remedy.

The issue in *Cutler* is similar to that presented in *Farmer Bros.* and *Abbott*. In *Farmer Bros.* the courts concluded that the California dividends received deduction (DRD) at Cal Rev. & Tax Code § 24402 was discriminatory on its face because it favored dividend-paying corporations doing business in and paying taxes to California over dividend-paying corporations that did not do business in or pay taxes to California. *Abbott* determined that the appropriate remedy was to invalidate the entire provision (i.e., deny the DRD to all taxpayers), not reform the portion deemed unconstitutional by making the DRD available to all taxpayers. It remains to be seen whether the *Cutler* court will follow the *Abbott* court and strike the entire deferral provision, or reform it to allow deferral for all "qualified small business stock," regardless of the location of the corporation's assets and payroll.

Moreover, while in *Cutler* the court only addressed the deferral provision in Cal. Rev. & Tax. Code § 18038.5, it would appear that the same rational would apply to the exclusion provision under Cal. Rev. & Tax. Code § 18152.5. The exclusion provision limits the benefit to stock in California companies similar to the deferral provision that the § court found was unconstitutional.

The FTB issued Notice 2012-03 on December 21, 2012, in response to the *Cutler* decision. It announced that all taxpayers would be denied the QSBS exclusion/deferral for 2008 and later. In effect, the FTB took the position that the provision should be struck in its entirety instead of reforming it to allow deferral for all "qualified small business stock," regardless of the location of the corporation's assets and payroll. The FTB began sending Notices of Proposed Assessment (NPAs) to taxpayers who claimed a small business stock benefit on their 2008 returns in April 2013.

On October 4, 2013, California Governor Jerry Brown signed A.B. 1412, which removes the active in-state requirements, thus applying the QSBS exclusion deferral investments in:

— in-state businesses that remain predominantly in-state; and

— in-state businesses that may have expanded to include out-of-state business operations.

Because the legislation applies retroactively, the FTB announced on October 7, 2013, that it will withdraw the NPAs it had previously issued.

California taxpayers should consider filing refund claims for gains realized in prior years that may have otherwise qualified for gain exclusion/deferral but for the in-state business requirement. Because the statute of limitations in California is generally four years, the 2008 tax year would typically close in 2013. The legislation, however, provides a special statute of limitations that permits taxpayers to file refund claims for the 2008 tax year until June 30, 2014. The FTB posted FAQs on its website that provide guidance to taxpayers seeking refunds under these provisions (see discussion above).

Chris Whitney, Contributing Editor

In a nonprecedential letter decision, the California State Board of Equalization held in *Appeal of Anderson* (2006) (CCH CALIFORNIA TAX REPORTS, ¶ 15-620.83) that family limited partnerships (FLPs) were ineligible to exclude gain from the sale of qualified small business stock sold by the FLPs. Because the small business stock was acquired at original issue by the founding partners and not by the partnerships, the stock did not constitute qualified small business stock for purposes of the exclusion.

Amounts excluded from gross income are treated as a tax preference item in a computation of the alternative minimum tax (¶ 117).

• *Gain or loss from sale or exchange of Fannie Mae or Freddie Mac preferred stock*

California does not incorporate the federal provision that provides ordinary gain or loss treatment to the sale or exchange of Fannie Mae or Freddie Mac preferred stock by certain financial institutions. (Sec. 18151.5, Rev. & Tax. Code) Consequently, a transaction in Fannie Mae or Freddie Mac preferred stock receives treatment as capital gain or loss for California tax purposes and would be subject to the capital loss limitation rules. Consequently, addition and subsequent subtraction modifications may be required.

¶ 526 Deductible Capital Losses—Carryovers, Carrybacks

Law: Secs. 18151, 18155 (CCH CALIFORNIA TAX REPORTS, ¶ 15-620).

Comparable Federal: Secs. 1211-12 (CCH U.S. MASTER TAX GUIDE ¶ 1752, 1754).

California Form: Sch. D (Capital Gain or Loss Adjustment).

Capital losses are deductible in full both federally and for California purposes against capital gain. In addition, up to $3,000 ($1,500 for married or registered domestic partner (see ¶ 119) taxpayers filing separately) of any excess of capital loss over capital gain is also deductible against ordinary income. (Sec. 18151, Rev. & Tax. Code)

Practice Pointer: Registered Domestic Partners

RDPs who claimed capital losses on their federal returns may need to recompute the amount that may be claimed on their California personal income tax returns to stay within the limits specified above (see ¶ 119).

• *Current treatment of carryovers*

Any unused net capital loss may be carried forward, indefinitely, to offset capital gains in subsequent years and may be deducted from ordinary income up to the limitation discussed above. The California rule is the same as the federal rule. (Sec. 18151, Rev. & Tax. Code)

• *No carrybacks*

California law does not permit capital loss carrybacks by individuals under any circumstances. (Sec. 18155, Rev. & Tax. Code) Federal law, on the other hand, allows individuals to claim capital loss carrybacks with respect to capital losses from "marked to market" contracts (regulated futures contracts, foreign currency contracts, nonequity options, and dealer equity options).

¶ 527 Loss from Wash Sales

Law: Sec. 18031 (CCH CALIFORNIA TAX REPORTS, ¶ 15-620).

Comparable Federal: Sec. 1091 (CCH U.S. MASTER TAX GUIDE ¶ 1935, 1939).

California law is the same as federal law as of the current IRC tie-in date (¶ 103). (Sec. 18031, Rev. & Tax. Code) Losses on disposition of stock or securities are disallowed where substantially identical property is acquired within 30 days before or after the sale. The wash sale rules apply to a contract or option to acquire or sell stock or securities solely by reason of the fact that the option or contract is, or could be, settled in cash or property other than the stock or securities.

Rules similar to the rules disallowing losses on such wash sales also apply to certain short sales of stock or securities. Any loss realized on the closing of a short sale of stock or securities, including securities futures contracts to sell, is disallowed if within a period beginning 30 days before the date of closing and ending 30 days after that date (1) substantially identical stock or securities were sold, or (2) another short sale of substantially identical stock or securities was entered into.

¶528 Holding Period—Special Rules

Law: Secs. 18151, 18155.5 (CCH California Tax Reports, ¶ 15-620).

Comparable Federal: Sec. 1223 (CCH U.S. Master Tax Guide ¶ 1777, 1941).

California law as to the character of gain or loss as long or short term is the same as federal law as of the current tie-in date (¶ 103). (Sec. 18151, Rev. & Tax. Code; Sec. 18155.5, Rev. & Tax. Code)

Special rules are provided for determining the holding period in situations where (1) property was received in a tax-free exchange, and (2) stock was acquired through exercise of rights. Where property is acquired from a decedent and sold within one year after his or her death, the property is considered to have been held for more than one year.

Under both California and federal law, the holding period for the surviving spouse's share of community property dates from the date of original acquisition.

¶529 Gain or Loss on Short Sales

Law: Sec. 18151 (CCH California Tax Reports, ¶ 15-620).

Comparable Federal: Sec. 1233 (CCH U.S. Master Tax Guide ¶ 1944).

California law as to the character of gain or loss as capital or ordinary or long-term or short-term is the same as federal law as of the current IRC tie-in date (¶ 103). (Sec. 18151, Rev. & Tax. Code)

Gains or losses on short sales are treated as capital gains or losses to the extent the property used to close the short sale is a "capital asset." The law regarding short sales includes many special rules for determining holding period, etc., intended to close certain "loopholes" that permitted tax avoidance through conversion of short-term gains into long-term gains.

¶530 Sale or Exchange of Patents

Law: Sec. 18151 (CCH California Tax Reports, ¶ 15-620).

Comparable Federal: Secs. 1235, 1249 (CCH U.S. Master Tax Guide ¶ 1741, 1767, 2489).

California law as to the character of gain or loss as (1) capital or ordinary and (2) long-term or short-term is generally the same as federal law as of the current IRC tie-in date (¶ 103). (Sec. 18151, Rev. & Tax. Code)

Capital gain treatment is accorded investors and certain others on gain from the sale or exchange of patent rights, or interests therein. This treatment pertains even though the transaction has certain characteristics of a license rather than a sale. The provision does not apply to transfers between certain family members, controlled corporations, etc. California law incorporates the federal law by reference, except for the federal provision that denies capital gains treatment on transactions with controlled foreign corporations.

¶531 Transfers of Trademarks, Trade Names, and Franchises

Law: Sec. 18151 (CCH CALIFORNIA TAX REPORTS, ¶15-620).

Comparable Federal: Sec. 1253 (CCH U.S. MASTER TAX GUIDE ¶1774, 1775).

California law as to the character of gain or loss as (1) capital or ordinary and (2) long-term or short-term is the same as federal law as of the current IRC tie-in date (¶103). (Sec. 18151, Rev. & Tax. Code)

Detailed rules govern the transfer of a franchise, trademark, or trade name. Generally, the transaction is denied capital gain treatment if the transferor retains any significant power, right, or continuing interest.

¶532 Gain or Loss on Options

Law: Sec. 18151 (CCH CALIFORNIA TAX REPORTS, ¶15-620).

Comparable Federal: Secs. 1092, 1234, 1256 (CCH U.S. MASTER TAX GUIDE ¶1919, 1926, 1948).

California law as to the character of gain or loss as capital or ordinary or long-term or short-term is the same as federal law as of the current IRC tie-in date (¶103). (Sec. 18151, Rev. & Tax. Code)

Gain or loss attributable to the sale or exchange of (or loss arising from failure to exercise) a privilege or option to buy or sell property may or may not be a capital gain or loss. The character of the gain or loss depends on the character of the optioned property in the hands of the taxpayer.

The law provides special rules designed to prevent tax avoidance by means of option transactions, including the use of straddle options. Certain futures contracts must be marked to market under these rules and 40% of the gain or loss is treated as short-term while 60% is treated as long-term. The special marked-to-market rules do not apply to hedging transactions.

California incorporates IRC Sec. 1092, as of California's current federal conformity date (¶103), which provides rules relating to the recognition of gain or loss on transactions involving straddles. (Sec. 18031, Rev. & Tax. Code) However, California did not incorporate until the 2010 tax year federal amendments that modified the basis adjustment provisions of the straddle rules, effective for federal purposes after October 21, 2004, and the straddle identification rules, effective for federal purposes for straddles acquired after December 29, 2007.

¶533 Dealers in Securities

Law: Sec. 18151 (CCH CALIFORNIA TAX REPORTS, ¶15-620).

Comparable Federal: Sec. 1236 (CCH U.S. MASTER TAX GUIDE ¶1760).

California law as to the character of gain or loss as capital or ordinary or long-term or short-term is the same as federal law as of the current IRC tie-in date (¶103). (Sec. 18151, Rev. & Tax. Code) For a discussion of the accounting methods applicable to security dealers, see ¶409.

Securities dealers are subject to special rules designed to prevent switching of securities in and out of the capital asset category for the purpose of realizing capital gains and ordinary losses.

¶534 Appreciated Financial Positions

Law: Sec. 18151 (CCH CALIFORNIA TAX REPORTS, ¶15-620).

Comparable Federal: Sec. 1259 (CCH U.S. MASTER TAX GUIDE ¶1944).

California incorporates federal law as of the current IRC tie-in date (see ¶103), which treats specified hedging transactions as constructive sales that require the immediate recognition of gain (but not loss). The provision generally applies to "short sales against the box," futures or forward contracts, notional principal contracts, and to any other transactions as prescribed by regulations. (Sec. 18151, Rev. & Tax. Code)

¶535 Retirement of Bonds, etc.

Law: Secs. 17024.5, 18151 (CCH California Tax Reports, ¶15-620).

Comparable Federal: Secs. 1271-74 (CCH U.S. Master Tax Guide ¶1952, 1954, 2431).

California law as to the character of gain or loss as capital or ordinary or long-term or short-term is the same as federal law as of the current IRC tie-in date (¶103). (Sec. 18151, Rev. & Tax. Code)

Amounts received upon retirement of bonds, etc., are ordinarily treated as amounts received in exchange therefore. The purpose of this provision is to permit such transactions to qualify for capital gain treatment. However, capital gain treatment does not apply to any obligation issued before July 2, 1982, if the issuer was neither a corporation nor a governmental unit or political subdivision.

¶536 Real Estate Subdivided for Sale

Law: Sec. 18151 (CCH California Tax Reports, ¶15-620).

Comparable Federal: Sec. 1237 (CCH U.S. Master Tax Guide ¶1762).

California law as to the character of gain or loss as capital or ordinary or long-term or short-term is the same as federal law as of the current IRC tie-in date (¶103). (Sec. 18151, Rev. & Tax. Code)

In general, profits from land subdivision activities will be treated as ordinary income. However, at least a part of the gain may be treated as long-term capital gain if the taxpayer can comply fully with certain very restrictive conditions in the law. Detailed rules are provided, including a requirement that the property be held at least five years, a prohibition against substantial improvements to the property, etc.

¶537 Sales of Property Used in Business, etc.

Law: Sec. 18151 (CCH California Tax Reports, ¶15-620).

Comparable Federal: Secs. 1231, 1239 (CCH U.S. Master Tax Guide ¶1747 et seq.).

California Forms: Sch. D (Capital Gain or Loss Adjustment), Sch. D-1 (Sales of Business Property).

California law as to the character of gain or loss as capital or ordinary or long-term or short-term is the same as federal law as of the current IRC tie-in date (¶103). (Sec. 18151, Rev. & Tax. Code)

Capital gain treatment applies to the disposition of certain property that would not otherwise qualify for such treatment because the property is not a "capital asset" or because it is not sold or exchanged. In applying the rule, the following three classes of transactions are lumped together:

— sales or exchanges of "property used in the trade or business";

— involuntary conversions (including losses upon destruction, theft, or condemnation) of business property; and

— involuntary conversions of capital assets held for more than one year.

If, during the taxable year, the gains on all three classes of transactions exceed the losses (using 100% of each gain or loss regardless of holding period), all transactions are treated as sales or exchanges of capital assets. This means that all of the gains or losses involved are treated as capital gains or losses, applying the rules discussed in ¶525 in determining the amount to be taken into account in computing taxable income. If the total gains do not exceed the total losses, all gains and losses are treated as "ordinary" gains and losses. Thus, involuntary conversions of *capital assets* resulting in a loss would give rise to a fully-deductible "ordinary" loss if there were no offsetting gains.

Nonresidents net only California source IRC Sec. 1231 gains and losses for purposes of computing California taxable income (FTB Pub. 1100, Taxation of Nonresidents and Individuals Who Change Residency, revised November 2007, CCH CALIFORNIA TAX REPORTS, ¶ 404-599).

- *"Property used in trade or business"*

Federal law is incorporated in California law by reference.

For this purpose "property used in the trade or business" includes:

— depreciable and real property used in a trade or business, held for more than one year;

— cattle and horses held for draft, breeding, dairy, or sporting purposes, provided they are held for two years or longer, and other livestock held for such purposes provided they are held for one year or longer;

— unharvested crops sold with land used in a trade or business and held for more than one year; and

— timber, coal, and iron ore, under certain circumstances (¶ 540).

However, depreciable and real property used in a business is *not* "property used in the trade or business" for capital gain treatment purposes if it is any of the following:

— inventoriable property;

— property held primarily for sale in the ordinary course of business;

— copyrights, etc., of the type included in the fifth item listed in ¶ 524; and

— certain government publications.

- *Transactions between related taxpayers*

Capital gain treatment is denied on the sale or exchange, directly or indirectly, of depreciable property between spouses and, for California purposes only, between registered domestic partners (see ¶ 119). This rule applies also to transactions between:

— an individual and a corporation that is 50% or more owned by such individual,

— an executor and beneficiary of an estate, except in the case of a sale or exchange in satisfaction of a pecuniary bequest, and

— certain related individuals.

¶538 Sale of Stock of Foreign Investment Companies, etc.

Law: Sec. 17024.5 (CCH CALIFORNIA TAX REPORTS, ¶ 15-515, 15-620).

Comparable Federal: Sec. 1248 (CCH U.S. MASTER TAX GUIDE ¶ 2487, 2488).

California has not adopted federal provisions that treat as ordinary income, rather than capital gain, the gain arising out of the sale or exchange of certain stock investments in foreign investment companies and other foreign corporations. (Sec. 17024.5, Rev. & Tax. Code)

¶539 Recapture of Excess Depreciation, etc.

Law: Secs. 18151, 18165, 18171, 18171.5 (CCH CALIFORNIA TAX REPORTS, ¶15-620).

Comparable Federal: Secs. 1239, 1245, 1250-55 (CCH U.S. MASTER TAX GUIDE ¶1744, 1779).

California law as to the character of gain or loss as capital or ordinary or long-term or short-term is the same as federal law as of the current IRC tie-in date (¶103). (Sec. 18151, Rev. & Tax. Code)

The law contains several "recapture" provisions intended to prevent possible abuse of the capital gain benefits permitted on the sale of various kinds of business property as explained at ¶537. The recapture provisions treat as ordinary income a portion of the gain realized upon disposition of certain property that has been subject to depreciation deductions. The amount "recaptured" depends on (1) the type of property, (2) the method of depreciation used, and (3) the period during which depreciation has been deducted. The types of property subject to this treatment are prescribed in IRC Secs. 1245 and 1250, which are incorporated into California law by reference.

California provides for the following differences from the federal rules:

— federal provisions regarding the disposal of certain multiple IRC Sec. 197 assets (intangibles) did not apply to California for pre-2010 dispositions (Sec. 18165(b), Rev. & Tax. Code);

— special federal rules for Subchapter S corporations do not apply to California for pre-1987 tax years;

— federal provisions for recapture on pollution control facilities do not apply to California;

— federal provisions for recapture of pre-1983 amortization of trademarks do not apply to California;

— California provides for some exceptions to the federal rules for certain low-income housing (for pre-1987 tax years) and historic structures;

— California substitutes different dates for various dates in the federal law, as follows:

— December 31, 1970, for July 24, 1969, and December 31, 1969,

— January 1, 1971, for January 1, 1970,

— December 31, 1976, for December 31, 1975, and

— January 1, 1977, for January 1, 1976; and

— the federal provision treating certain deductions as deductions allowable for amortization is modified for California purposes to also apply to enterprise zone, former Los Angeles Revitalization Zone, local agency military base recovery area, and former targeted tax area asset expense allowance deductions (discussed at ¶316). (Sec. 18165, Rev. & Tax. Code; Sec. 18171, Rev. & Tax. Code; Sec. 18171.5, Rev. & Tax. Code)

Even where the applicable California and federal recapture provisions are the same, the amount of recapture may of course be different because of differences in amounts deducted in prior years.

¶540 Gain or Loss in the Case of Timber, Coal, or Domestic Iron Ore

Law: Sec. 17681 (CCH CALIFORNIA TAX REPORTS, ¶15-620, 15-665).

Comparable Federal: Sec. 631 (CCH U.S. MASTER TAX GUIDE ¶1772).

California law as to the character of gain or loss as capital or ordinary or long-term or short-term is the same as federal law as of the current IRC tie-in date (¶103).

Special rules allow a taxpayer to elect to apply capital gain treatment to the cutting of timber held for more than one year or the disposal of coal or domestic iron ore held for more than one year. This is accomplished by including gains or losses from such cutting or disposal in the class of transactions designated the first item in the first list in ¶537, above. (Sec. 17681, Rev. & Tax. Code)

¶541 Cancellation of Lease or Distributor's Agreement

Law: Sec. 18151 (CCH CALIFORNIA TAX REPORTS, ¶15-650).

Comparable Federal: Sec. 1241 (CCH U.S. MASTER TAX GUIDE ¶1751).

California law as to the character of gain or loss as capital or ordinary or long-term or short-term is the same as federal law as of the current IRC tie-in date (¶103). (Sec. 18151, Rev. & Tax. Code)

The law provides for capital gain treatment on (1) amounts received by a lessee for the cancellation of a lease and (2) amounts received by a distributor for cancellation of a distributor's agreement, provided the distributor has a substantial capital investment in the distributorship.

¶542 Basis, General Rule

Law: Sec. 18031 (CCH CALIFORNIA TAX REPORTS, ¶15-710).

Comparable Federal: Secs. 1012, 1059A (CCH U.S. MASTER TAX GUIDE ¶1701).

Except where otherwise provided, the "basis" of property is its cost. California law is the same as federal law as of the current IRC tie-in date (¶103). (Sec. 18031, Rev. & Tax. Code)

Prior to 1961 for California purposes (and prior to 1954 for federal), certain real property taxes paid by the buyer were not deductible and were required to be capitalized. Any such taxes are includible in the basis of the property.

¶543 Basis, Inventoriable Property

Law: Sec. 18031 (CCH CALIFORNIA TAX REPORTS, ¶15-710).

Comparable Federal: Sec. 1013 (CCH U.S. MASTER TAX GUIDE ¶1601).

The basis of inventoriable property is the last inventory value thereof. California law incorporates the federal law by reference as of the current IRC tie-in date (¶103). (Sec. 18031, Rev. & Tax. Code)

¶544 Basis of Property Acquired by Gift

Law: Secs. 17081, 18031 (CCH CALIFORNIA TAX REPORTS, ¶15-710).

Comparable Federal: Secs. 84, 1015 (CCH U.S. MASTER TAX GUIDE ¶1630).

California law is the same as federal law as of the current IRC tie-in date (¶103). (Sec. 17081, Rev. & Tax. Code; Sec. 18031, Rev. & Tax. Code)

The basis of property acquired by gift after 1920 is generally determined by reference to the donor's basis, except that for the purpose of determining loss, the basis is limited to the fair market value at the date the gift was made. The basis of property acquired by gift before 1921 is the fair market value at the date the gift was made.

• *Adjustment for gift tax*

The basis may be increased by federal gift tax paid, but there is a limitation on this adjustment. For gifts before 1977, the gift tax adjustment is limited to the excess of fair market value over the donor's adjusted basis. For gifts after 1976, the adjustment is limited to an amount proportionate to the appreciation in value over the donor's adjusted basis. (Sec. 18031, Rev. & Tax. Code)

Prior to 1985, the California limitation on gifts after 1976 was the same as for earlier gifts.

• *Transfers between spouses*

The federal law was amended in 1984 to provide a special rule for transfers between spouses. Such transfers are treated as gifts, with carryover of basis to the transferee and with no limit on the transferee's basis for determining loss. California conformed in 1985. (Sec. 18031, Rev. & Tax. Code) Presumably, California law, but not federal law, extends this treatment to transfers between registered domestic partners (see ¶119).

• *Procedure where facts unknown*

Where the necessary facts for determination of basis are unknown to the donee, the Franchise Tax Board (FTB) is required to obtain the facts. If the FTB can not obtain sufficient facts to make the determination, the basis is the fair market value, as determined by the FTB, as of the date the property was acquired by the donor. (Sec. 18031, Rev. & Tax. Code)

The provision for FTB determination of basis of gift property was applied in *Appeal of Victor and Evelyn Santino* (1975) (CCH CALIFORNIA TAX REPORTS, ¶15-710.281). The State Board of Equalization upheld the FTB's finding, based on 1926 records and market values.

¶545 Basis of Property Acquired by Transfer in Trust

Law: Sec. 18031 (CCH CALIFORNIA TAX REPORTS, ¶15-710).

Comparable Federal: Sec. 1015 (CCH U.S. MASTER TAX GUIDE ¶1630, 1678).

California law is the same as federal law as of the current IRC tie-in date (¶103). (Sec. 18031, Rev. & Tax. Code)

The basis of property acquired by a transfer in trust (other than by gift, bequest or devise) after 1920 is the grantor's basis adjusted for gain or loss recognized to the grantor on the transfer. For such transfers before 1921, the basis is the fair market value at the date of the transfer.

The federal law was amended in 1984 to provide special basis rules for inter-spousal transfers in trust, and California conformed in 1985 (¶544).

¶546 Basis of Property Transmitted at Death

Law: Secs. 18031, 18035.6, 18036.6 (CCH CALIFORNIA TAX REPORTS, ¶15-710).

Comparable Federal: Secs. 1014, 1022 (CCH U.S. MASTER TAX GUIDE ¶1633).

Federal law regarding basis of property transmitted at death is incorporated by California by reference as of the current IRC tie-in date (¶103). (Sec. 18031, Rev. & Tax. Code) However, the California law provides for important differences from the federal rules as explained below.

— Ordinarily, the basis of property acquired by bequest, devise, or inheritance (or deemed to be so acquired) is the fair market value at date of death.

— If federal estate tax is calculated on the basis of the value of the property at the "optional" valuation date (six months after death), that value becomes the basis. California conformed to the federal law in 1985.

— If family farms or businesses are valued for federal estate tax purposes at less than fair market value, the reduced valuation becomes the basis. California conformed to the federal law in 1985.

— Federal (but not California) law contains special rules for the basis of stock in certain foreign personal holding companies and Domestic International Sales Corporations (DISCs). The federal rule concerning foreign personal holding companies is repealed, effective for tax years of foreign corporations beginning after 2004 and for tax years of U.S. shareholders with or within which such tax years of foreign corporations end.

— If death occurred between January 1, 1977, and November 6, 1978, and a carryover basis was elected, the basis is the carryover basis.

— If appreciated property is received by a decedent as a gift within one year before death and the same property reverts to the donor (or spouse), a carryover basis applies.

— The basis of individual retirement accounts and retirement bonds is zero. However, as to the portion attributable to contributions that were not deductible for state purposes, the California basis would be fair market value.

— Special rules are provided for community property, quasi-community property, and joint tenancy property. The California and federal rules are different, as explained below.

— California does not incorporate the federal repeal of the "stepped-up" basis rule and adoption of a modified carryover basis rule with respect to decedents dying after 2009. (Sec. 18035.6, Rev. & Tax. Code; Sec. 18036.6, Rev. & Tax. Code)

• *Community property*

Each spouse has a one-half interest in California community property. With the exception of cases in which a carryover basis was elected (as discussed above), the California basis of the *decedent spouse's* one-half interest in the hands of the surviving spouse (or other party) is fair market value at date of death. See ¶119 for a discussion of community property rules concerning registered domestic partners.

• *"Quasi-community" property*

In determining the basis of property acquired from a decedent, quasi-community property is treated as community property.

"Quasi-community" property generally refers to property that was acquired while the taxpayer was domiciled outside of California and that would have been community property had the taxpayer been domiciled in California.

• *Interest of surviving spouse*

The basis of the *surviving spouse's* one-half interest varies according to date of death and other circumstances. Under federal law, for deaths occurring after 1947, the basis of a surviving spouse's one-half interest is fair market value. California basis is also fair market value for deaths occurring after 1986. Prior to 1987, the California basis of the surviving spouse's one-half interest was valued at cost.

• *Joint tenancy property*

The basis of joint tenancy property transmitted at death is not covered by the general rule stated at the beginning of ¶546, because such property is not received by "bequest, devise or inheritance." However, federal law provides that, in the case of decedents whose deaths occurred after 1953, such property is considered to have been acquired from the decedent as to the portion of the property that is includible in the estate for federal death-tax purposes. As to that portion, the basis is fair market value, under the rule stated at the beginning of ¶546. As to the survivor's interest, the basis is cost. This federal provision was incorporated in California law by reference so that the California basis is now the same as the federal.

Prior-Year Basis Rules

The many changes in the inheritance tax and income tax laws over the years are reflected in the following summary of the California rules for determining the basis of California community property in the hands of the survivor, covering both the decedent's and the surviving spouse's interests in the property:

(1) **if death occurred prior to April 9, 1953:** basis of decedent's one-half interest is fair market value at date of death and basis of surviving spouse's one-half interest is cost;

(2) **if death occurred after April 8, 1953, and before September 15, 1961:**

(a) if wife was survivor, basis of entire property is fair market value;

(b) if husband was survivor and all of wife's one-half interest went to others, basis of entire property is fair market value; and

(c) if husband was survivor and he received any part of wife's one-half interest, basis of decedent wife's one-half interest is fair market value and basis of surviving husband's one-half interest is cost;

(3) **if death occurred after September 14, 1961, and before January 1, 1987:**

(a) if decedent's entire interest went to others than the surviving spouse (prior to June 8, 1982), basis of entire property is fair market value; and

(b) if any part of decedent's interest went to surviving spouse, basis of decedent's one-half interest is fair market value and basis of surviving spouse's one-half interest is cost (excepted from this rule is the period from January 1, 1981, to June 8, 1982; see below).

(4) **if death occurred after December 31, 1986:** basis of entire property is fair market value—the same as the federal basis.

• *Death 1965-1975—Conversion of separate property*

There is a special rule for community property that was converted from separate property, applicable when death occurred between September 17, 1965, and December 31, 1975. In this case, the basis of the entire property is fair market value. Under the present law, there is no special treatment of such converted property.

• *Decisions of courts and State Board of Equalization*

In *Howard Mel v. Franchise Tax Board* (1981) (CCH CALIFORNIA TAX REPORTS, ¶ 15-710.256), involving four companion cases, the bulk of the deceased husband's one-half interest in community property was left in trust upon his death in 1967, with a lifetime beneficial interest to the surviving wife. The wife claimed a stepped-up basis for her one-half interest when she sold certain items of the community property. A California Court of Appeal applied rule 3(b), above, to deny a stepped-up basis on the items in question. For a later case, citing and following the *Mel* case, see *Appeal of Georgianna Brewer* (1983) (CCH CALIFORNIA TAX REPORTS, ¶ 15-710.257).

In *The Bank of California, N.A., et al. v. Franchise Tax Board* (1978) (CCH CALIFORNIA TAX REPORTS, ¶ 15-710.255), the deceased husband's one-half interest in a substantial estate of community property was left to a testamentary trust. The trust provided for payments of $1,000 per month to the surviving wife for her lifetime. The surviving wife claimed a stepped-up basis for her one-half interest in certain items of the community property. The Franchise Tax Board (FTB) applied rule 3(b), above, and denied the stepped-up basis. However, a California Superior Court overruled the FTB and allowed the stepped-up basis, concluding that it was the legislative intent to conform the California law to the federal. However, see discussion above of the *Howard Mel* case, in which the Court of Appeal overruled the trial court and reached the opposite conclusion.

In *Appeals of Estate of William S. Hatch et al.* (1976) (CCH CALIFORNIA TAX REPORTS, ¶ 15-710.30), community property (a citrus grove) was in escrow when the husband died, under an almost-completed contract of sale. The State Board of Equalization (SBE) held, following federal precedents, that decedent's one-half of the property constituted a right to receive "income in respect of a decedent" and that neither one-half of the property was entitled to a stepped-up California basis.

In *Appeal of Estate of Philip Rosenberg, Deceased* (1975) (CCH CALIFORNIA TAX REPORTS, ¶ 15-710.253), the question was whether the surviving wife was entitled to a stepped-up California basis on her one-half interest in community property. The husband died in 1966, leaving the community property in trust for the surviving wife and children. The situation fell squarely within item (3)(b) of the discussion above. The SBE's opinion deplored the fact that the California result was different from the federal, but upheld the FTB in limiting the survivor's basis to her cost and denying a step-up to the value at date of death. See also *Appeal of Louis (L.M.) Halper Marital Trust* (1977) (CCH CALIFORNIA TAX REPORTS, ¶ 15-710.254), to the same effect.

• *Non-California community property*

The basis provisions of the income tax law apply to property held "under the community property laws of any state, territory or possession of the United States or any foreign country." However, the basis of non-California community property may be different from the basis of California community property as discussed above, because of differing treatment under the inheritance tax law. See the following discussion of quasi-community property.

• *"Quasi-community" property (prior law)*

"Quasi-community" property is property acquired outside California that would have been California community property if the spouse acquiring the property had been domiciled in California at the time of acquisition. Under the California inheritance tax law from 1957 to 1980, one-half of such property was includible in the estate.

• *Joint tenancy property*

Prior to 1985 California law provided a rule that was similar in principle to the federal rule, but California permitted a stepped-up basis only on the portion of the property that was subject to California inheritance tax. Since the California inheritance tax was repealed on June 8, 1982, in case of death after that date and subsequent disposition of the property before 1985, it appears that the basis of the entire property would be cost.

• *Death between January 1981 and June 1982*

Under the California inheritance tax law in effect from January 1, 1981, to June 8, 1982, property transferred to the spouse of the decedent was exempt from the tax. Thus, none of such property has a basis of fair market value, and the basis of the entire property in the hands of the surviving spouse is cost.

• *Surviving joint tenant other than spouse*

When death occurred during the period January 1, 1955, to June 8, 1982, and the surviving joint tenant is other than the spouse, the basis of the decedent's interest is fair market value. However, when death occurred prior to 1955, the basis of the entire property is cost; this applies also when the surviving joint tenant was the spouse.

• *Decedent spouse's interest—Death before 1981*

When the surviving joint tenant is the spouse and death occurred prior to 1981, the basis of the decedent's interest is usually fair market value. This applies back to 1955 in cases in which the property was originally separate property of the spouses; the decedent's interest is determined by contribution to the original cost. It applies back to September 15, 1961, in cases where the property was originally "quasi-community" property (as defined in the gift tax law); the decedent is deemed to have had a one-half interest. It applies back to 1976 in cases where the property was originally California community property; the decedent's interest was one-half of the total property. When death occurred prior to 1976 and the property was originally California community property, the basis of the decedent's interest is usually cost; however, there are some exceptions, and it is suggested that the FTB be consulted in case of any question.

• *Decision of BOE*

Appeal of William F. and Dorothy M. Johnson (1976) (CCH CALIFORNIA TAX REPORTS, ¶ 15-710.331) involved the basis to the survivor of joint tenancy property that had its source in community property, where death occurred in 1967. The BOE held that the basis was original cost, applying the rule set forth above.

• *California-federal differences*

The federal basis of joint tenancy property in the hands of the survivor may be different from the California basis because of differences in the death tax treatment and differences between the two laws in prior years. Where death occurred prior to 1954, the federal basis of the entire property is cost. Where death occurred after 1953, the federal basis is fair market value for the portion includible in the estate (unless a carryover basis applied under prior law) and cost for the remainder of the property. Note that the decedent's interest is always "includible in the estate" for federal estate tax purposes, even though the property may be completely relieved of tax by the marital deduction. In the case of joint tenancy property of husband and wife, where death occurs after 1981, the decedent's interest is deemed to be one-half of the property regardless of which spouse furnished the consideration.

¶547 Basis of Property Acquired in Tax-Free Exchange

Law: Sec. 17321 (CCH CALIFORNIA TAX REPORTS, ¶ 15-710).

Comparable Federal: Sec. 358 (CCH U.S. MASTER TAX GUIDE ¶ 2201, 2205).

California law is the same as federal law as of the current IRC tie-in date (¶ 103).

The basis of property acquired after February 28, 1913, in a tax-free exchange is the same as that of the property exchanged, with adjustment for "boot" received, for any amount treated as a dividend in the exchange, and for any gain or loss recognized upon the exchange. (Sec. 17321, Rev. & Tax. Code)

¶548 Basis of Property Acquired in Corporate Liquidation

Law: Sec. 17321 (CCH CALIFORNIA TAX REPORTS, ¶ 15-645, 15-710).

Comparable Federal: Sec. 334 (CCH U.S. MASTER TAX GUIDE ¶ 2261).

California law is the same as federal law as of the current IRC tie-in date (¶ 103). (Sec. 17321, Rev. & Tax. Code)

Generally, the basis of property received by an individual stockholder in a corporate liquidation is the fair market value of the property at the date of liquidation.

¶549 Basis of Stock After "Spin-Off" Reorganization

Law: Sec. 17321 (CCH CALIFORNIA TAX REPORTS, ¶ 15-710).

Comparable Federal: Sec. 358 (CCH U.S. MASTER TAX GUIDE ¶ 2201, 2205).

California law is the same as federal law as of the current IRC tie-in date (¶ 103). (Sec. 17321, Rev. & Tax. Code)

When stock of a new corporation is distributed to stockholders of another corporation in a "spin-off" type reorganization (¶ 517), the adjusted basis of the old stock is allocated between the old and new stocks.

¶550 Basis of Property Acquired upon Involuntary Conversion

Law: Secs. 18031 (CCH CALIFORNIA TAX REPORTS, ¶ 15-710).

Comparable Federal: Sec. 1033 (CCH U.S. MASTER TAX GUIDE ¶ 1713, 1715).

California law is the same as federal law as of the current IRC tie-in date (¶ 103). (Sec. 18031, Rev. & Tax. Code)

The basis of property acquired as a result of involuntary conversion (¶ 503) is the same as that of the property converted, with adjustment for any part of the proceeds not reinvested as required by the law and for any gain or loss recognized upon the conversion.

¶551 Basis of FNMA Stock

Law: Sec. 18031 (CCH CALIFORNIA TAX REPORTS, ¶ 15-710).

Comparable Federal: Sec. 1054.

Basis is reduced for the excess of cost over fair market value (deductible as a business expense) of Federal National Mortgage Association (FNMA) stock issued to an initial holder. California law incorporates the federal law by reference as of the current IRC tie-in date (¶ 103). (Sec. 18031, Rev. & Tax. Code)

¶552 Redeemable Ground Rents

Law: Sec. 18031 (CCH CALIFORNIA TAX REPORTS, ¶ 15-710).

Comparable Federal: Sec. 1055 (CCH U.S. MASTER TAX GUIDE ¶ 1611).

Redeemable ground rents are treated as being the equivalent of a mortgage. California law incorporates the federal law by reference as of the current IRC tie-in date (¶ 103). (Sec. 18031, Rev. & Tax. Code)

¶553 Basis of Securities Acquired in Wash Sale

Law: Sec. 18031 (CCH CALIFORNIA TAX REPORTS, ¶ 15-710).

Comparable Federal: Sec. 1091 (CCH U.S. MASTER TAX GUIDE ¶ 1939).

The basis of stock or securities acquired in a "wash sale" is the same as that of the securities sold, increased, or decreased, as the case may be, by the difference between the cost of the new securities and the selling price of the securities that were subject to the "wash sale" rules. California law incorporates the federal law by reference as of the current IRC tie-in date (¶ 103). (Sec. 18031, Rev. & Tax. Code)

¶554 Basis Prescribed by Personal Income Tax Law of 1954

Law: Sec. 18039 (CCH CALIFORNIA TAX REPORTS, ¶ 15-710).

Comparable Federal: Sec. 1052.

The basis of property acquired after February 28, 1913, in certain transactions covered by the California Personal Income Tax Law of 1954, is as prescribed in that Law. (Sec. 18039, Rev. & Tax. Code)

The federal law contains a somewhat comparable provision that refers to federal Revenue Acts of 1932 and 1934. Prior to 1983 California law contained a conforming provision.

¶555 Basis of Partnership Property

Law: Sec. 17851 (CCH CALIFORNIA TAX REPORTS, ¶ 15-185).

Comparable Federal: Secs. 701-61 (CCH U.S. MASTER TAX GUIDE ¶ 443, 459, 467).

California law is the same as federal law as of the current IRC tie-in date (¶ 103). (Sec. 17851, Rev. & Tax. Code)

Except as noted above, the basis of property transferred to a partnership is the transferor's basis, adjusted for any gain or loss recognized upon the transfer.

• *Property distributions to a partner*

The rules for determining basis of property distributed by a partnership to a partner may be summarized very briefly as follows:

— generally, the basis of property in the hands of the partner-distributee is the same as the basis in the hands of the partnership;

— the basis of property distributed in liquidation of a partner's interest is the properly allocable part of the basis of the partner's partnership interest;

— special rules to prevent tax avoidance are provided for the treatment of inventories, "unrealized receivables," and depreciable property subject to "depreciation recapture" provisions that are distributed to a partner (there are minor federal-California differences in these rules, as explained at ¶618);

— under some conditions, the partnership may adjust the basis of its assets remaining after the distribution to reflect the step-up or step-down of basis in the transfer from the partnership to the partner; and

— the partnership may elect to adjust the basis of partnership assets to reflect the purchase price paid by a new partner for his or her interest; under some conditions the same type of adjustment may be made by a partner who receives a distribution of partnership property within two years after acquiring an interest.

¶556 Basis of Property Acquired Before March 1, 1913

Law: Sec. 18031 (CCH CALIFORNIA TAX REPORTS, ¶15-710).

Comparable Federal: Sec. 1053.

For property acquired before March 1, 1913, when the fair market value at March 1, 1913, was greater than the adjusted basis otherwise determined as of that date, the basis for determining gain is such fair market value. Federal law is incorporated in California law by reference as of the current IRC tie-in date (¶103). (Sec. 18031, Rev. & Tax. Code)

¶557 Basis of Property Acquired Pursuant to S.E.C. Order

Law: Sec. 18031 (CCH CALIFORNIA TAX REPORTS, ¶15-710).

Comparable Federal: Sec. 1082.

The basis of securities received in certain liquidations under order of the federal Securities and Exchange Commission is the same as that of the securities exchanged. Federal law is incorporated in California law by reference as of the current IRC tie-in date (¶103). (Sec. 18031, Rev. & Tax. Code)

¶558 Basis of Rights to Acquire Stock

Law: Sec. 17321 (CCH CALIFORNIA TAX REPORTS, ¶15-645).

Comparable Federal: Sec. 307 (CCH U.S. MASTER TAX GUIDE ¶1907).

California law is the same as federal law as of the current IRC tie-in date (¶103). (Sec. 17321, Rev. & Tax. Code)

If the fair market value of stock rights is less than 15% of the value of the stock on which the rights are issued, the basis of the rights is zero unless the taxpayer elects to allocate to the rights a portion of the basis of the stock.

As to the following rights, the basis of the stock is allocated between the stock and the rights according to their respective values at the time the rights are issued:

— all rights acquired in a taxable year beginning before 1937, *except* as to certain rights acquired before 1935 (see below); and

— nontaxable rights acquired in a taxable year beginning after December 31, 1936, where the value of the rights is more than 15% or the taxpayer elects to allocate as explained above.

If a stock right was acquired prior to 1935 and it constituted income under the Sixteenth Amendment to the Federal Constitution, the basis of the right is its fair market value when acquired.

If stock rights were acquired and sold in a taxable year beginning after 1934 and prior to 1941 and the entire proceeds were reported as income, the basis of the stock is determined without any allocation to the rights.

California law incorporates the federal law by reference. California has conformed closely to the federal law for many years, although there have been minor differences in the effective dates of prior-year amendments.

¶559 Adjusted Basis

Law: Secs. 17024.5, 18031, 18036 (CCH CALIFORNIA TAX REPORTS, ¶15-710, 16-020).

Comparable Federal: Secs. 1011, 1016-21 (CCH U.S. MASTER TAX GUIDE ¶1604, 1701).

Although California generally incorporates federal law (IRC Sec. 1016) as of California's current federal conformity date (¶103), concerning adjustments to basis, many of the federal adjustments are inapplicable for California purposes because California does not incorporate the federal credits or deductions that require the basis adjustments. In addition, when applying the incorporated provisions of IRC Sec. 1016(a) to make California basis adjustments, any references in IRC Sec. 1016 to other IRC provisions must be treated as including California modifications to those other IRC provisions. (Sec. 17024.5(i), Rev. & Tax. Code)

The following federal basis adjustments, although contained in federal law, are inapplicable under California law (Sec. 18036, Rev. & Tax. Code):

— adjustments for amounts related to a shareholder's stock in a controlled foreign corporation (Sec. 17024.5(b)(9), Rev. & Tax. Code);

— adjustments for certain federal investment tax credits (Sec. 17024.5(b)(10), Rev. & Tax. Code); and

— adjustments to the basis of a U.S. taxpayer's stock in a foreign personal holding company to reflect certain undistributed income of the company (Sec. 17024.5(b)(4), Rev. & Tax. Code).

The following basis adjustments required under federal law are examples of provisions technically incorporated by California but that have no practical effect because California does not incorporate the underlying credit or deduction. Thus, for California personal income tax purposes, no adjustments are required for the following:

— adjustments for amounts specified in a shareholder's consent made under IRC Sec. 28 of the 1939 Internal Revenue Code;

— adjustment for amortization under IRC Sec. 811(b) of premium and accrual of discount on bonds and notes held by a life insurance company;

— adjustment for certain carryover basis property acquired from a decedent under IRC Sec. 1023;

— adjustments to the basis of stock required by IRC Sec. 1059, concerning a basis reduction for extraordinary dividends;

— adjustment for adoption costs for which a taxpayer has claimed a federal credit under IRC Sec. 23;

— adjustment with respect to property the acquisition of which resulted in the nonrecognition of gain on the rollover of empowerment zone investments under IRC Sec. 1397B;

— adjustment required with respect to property for which a federal employer-provided child care credit was claimed under IRC Sec. 45F, although California requires a similar basis adjustment for taxpayers who claimed the former California employer's credit for child care programs (¶134); and

— adjustment required under IRC Sec. 1016(d) for certain automobiles for which a taxpayer is required to pay the federal "gas guzzler tax".

Adjustments must also be made for certain deducted enterprise zone, former Los Angeles Revitalization Zone (LARZ), and local agency military base recovery area (LAMBRA) business expenses. No comparable basis adjustments are required under federal law.

Finally, in addition to the adjustments required under IRC Sec. 1016, proper adjustments must be made for the following:

— upon the sale of depreciable property for amounts for which the federal bonus deprecation deduction or increased federal IRC Sec. 179 asset expense election was claimed;

— for amounts that were formerly allowed as deductions as deferred expenses under former Sec. 17689, Rev. & Tax. Code (b) or Sec. 17689.5, Rev. & Tax. Code, relating to certain exploration expenditures, and that resulted in a reduction of the taxpayer's California personal income taxes; and

— for certain deducted enterprise zone, former LARZ, and LAMBRA business expenses (¶316). No comparable basis adjustments are required under federal law. (Sec. 18036, Rev. & Tax. Code)

See ¶221 regarding basis adjustment upon discharge of indebtedness. See ¶561 regarding basis adjustment for lessee improvements.

¶560 Substituted Basis

Law: Sec. 18031 (CCH CALIFORNIA TAX REPORTS, ¶15-710).

Comparable Federal: Sec. 1016 (CCH U.S. MASTER TAX GUIDE ¶1607).

"Substituted basis" is defined as the basis determined (1) by reference to the basis in the hands of a transferor or (2) by reference to other property held at any time by the taxpayer. California law incorporates federal law by reference as of the current IRC tie-in date (¶103). (Sec. 18031, Rev. & Tax. Code)

¶561 Lessor's Basis for Lessee's Improvements

Law: Sec. 18031 (CCH CALIFORNIA TAX REPORTS, ¶15-710).

Comparable Federal: Sec. 1019 (CCH U.S. MASTER TAX GUIDE ¶1601).

Where the value of improvements by a lessee is excluded from income (¶222), there is no effect on the basis of the property to the lessor. Where the value of such improvements was included in the lessor's income, in a taxable year beginning before 1943, the basis of the lessor's property is adjusted accordingly. California law incorporates federal law by reference as of the current IRC tie-in date (¶103). (Sec. 18031, Rev. & Tax. Code)

¶562 Basis for Depreciation and Depletion

Law: Secs. 17201, 17681 (CCH CALIFORNIA TAX REPORTS, ¶15-665).

Comparable Federal: Secs. 167, 612-13 (CCH U.S. MASTER TAX GUIDE ¶1203, 1289).

The basis for depreciation and for cost depletion is the adjusted basis for purposes of determining gain upon sale of the property, except that certain deferred development and exploration expenses includible in basis are disregarded for this purpose (¶320). California law incorporates federal law by reference as of the current IRC tie-in date (¶103). (Sec. 17201, Rev. & Tax. Code; Sec. 17681, Rev. & Tax. Code)

CCH Practice Tip: Basis of Out-of-State Property

California follows the same federal basis rules, regardless of whether the depreciation occurred outside of California. Thus, the gain from the sale of out-of-state property for which prior depreciation deductions were claimed on a federal return is the same for California purposes even though the taxpayers never claimed the depreciation deduction on a California return. (*Appeal of Varma* (2011), CCH CALIFORNIA TAX REPORTS, ¶405-455)

For rules regarding percentage depletion, see ¶319.

¶563 Allocation of Transferred Business Assets

Law: Sec. 18031 (CCH CALIFORNIA TAX REPORTS, ¶15-710).

Comparable Federal: Sec. 1060 (CCH U.S. MASTER TAX GUIDE ¶1620).

California has adopted the federal residual method for allocating purchases of assets that constitute a trade or business (¶103). Generally, under the residual method, the purchase price is allocated first to the assets to the extent of their fair market value, and then, if there is any excess, to goodwill and going concern value. However, if a transferor and a transferee agree in writing as to the allocation of consideration for transferred business assets, their agreement will generally be binding for tax purposes. (Sec. 18031, Rev. & Tax. Code)

PERSONAL INCOME TAX

CHAPTER 6

ESTATES AND TRUSTS, PASS-THROUGH ENTITIES

¶601 Application of Tax to Estates and Trusts

Law: Secs. 17041, 17731, 17731.5, 17734.6, 18505, 18635.5, 19136 (CCH California Tax Reports, ¶15-210, 15-215, 15-225, 15-270, 89-104).

Comparable Federal: Secs. 641, 643, 644, 646, 665, 6034A, 6048 (CCH U.S. Master Tax Guide ¶518, 520 et seq.).

California Forms: Forms 541 (California Fiduciary Income Tax Return), 541-A (Trust Accumulation of Charitable Amounts), 541-B (Charitable Remainder and Pooled Income Trusts), 541-ES (Estimated Tax for Fiduciaries), 541-QFT (California Income Tax Return for Qualified Funeral Trusts), 541-T (California Allocation of Estimated Tax Payments to Beneficiaries).

The personal income tax law applies to the income of estates and to property held in trust, whether the income is accumulated or distributed. The federal law is incorporated by California as of the current IRC tie-in date (¶103). (Sec. 17731, Rev. & Tax. Code) However, California does not incorporate the federal provision that allows an electing Alaska Native Settlement Trust to elect to pay tax on its income at the lowest tax rate applicable to individuals and allows beneficiaries to exclude from their gross income amounts contributed to the electing trust. (Sec. 17734.6, Rev. & Tax. Code)

The tax rates for estates and trusts are the same as for resident individuals, including the mental health services tax. (Sec. 17041(e), Rev. & Tax. Code) The highest individual tax rate is applied to an electing small business trust's income (¶116). (Sec. 17731.5, Rev. & Tax. Code) The alternative minimum tax, discussed at ¶117, applies to estates and trusts as well.

• *Estimated tax*

Generally, trusts and estates make estimated tax payments in the same manner as individuals (¶111). However, under both California and federal law, this general rule is inapplicable to the following:

       — private foundations;

       — charitable trusts that are taxed on unrelated business income;

       — any estate in the first two tax years following the decedent's death; or

       — any trust in the first two tax years following the grantor's death if (1) the trust receives the residual of a probate estate under the grantor's will or, (2) the grantor died without a will and the trust is primarily responsible for the estate's taxes, debts, and administrative expenses.

(Sec. 19136, Rev. & Tax. Code)

Under both California and federal law, a trust or, for its final year, a decedent's estate, may elect to have any part of its estimated tax payments treated as made by a beneficiary or beneficiaries. For California purposes, the election is made on Form 541-T, which must be filed by the 65th day after the close of the estate's or trust's taxable year.

• *Consistency rule*

Under both California and federal law, beneficiaries of an estate or trust are required to (1) file their returns in a manner consistent with that reported on the trust's or estate's return or (2) file a notice of inconsistent treatment with the Franchise Tax Board (FTB) (the Secretary for federal purposes) that identifies the inconsistent items. (Sec. 18635.5, Rev. & Tax. Code) If a beneficiary fails to comply with these requirements, any adjustment necessary in order to make the treatment of the items consistent will be treated as a mathematical or clerical error subject to summary assessment procedures. A negligence penalty will also be imposed if the noncompliance was the result of the beneficiary's negligence (¶712).

• *Returns*

Form 541 is used to report the tax information of estates and trusts unless otherwise indicated.

Fiduciaries who file Form 541, California Fiduciary Income Tax Return, may e-file their returns beginning January 2, 2014. Fiduciaries are not included in the individual e-file mandate discussed at ¶108 at this time. (*FTB Tax News* (2013), CCH CALIFORNIA TAX REPORTS, ¶405-969)

• *Notice of administration*

A personal representative of an estate or an estate attorney must provide notice of administration of an estate subject to California probate law to the FTB within 90 days after the estate's personal representative has been issued letters in probate. (Sec. 9202, Probate Code).

¶602 Effect of Residence upon Taxability

    Law: Secs. 17742-45 (CCH CALIFORNIA TAX REPORTS, ¶15-205).

    Comparable Federal: None.

In the case of an estate, the following rules apply:

       — if the decedent was a resident of California at the time of his or her death, all of the estate's net income is taxable, regardless of source;

— if the decedent was a nonresident, only income of the estate from California sources is taxable, unless income is distributed to California beneficiaries; if income is not distributed, it does not matter that either the fiduciary or beneficiary, or both, are California residents ("income in respect of a decedent" may be from a California source and therefore taxable, even though the decedent was a nonresident, where the income arose from personal services in California, see ¶413); and

— any income distributed to a beneficiary who is a California resident is taxable to the beneficiary, regardless of the source of the income.

(Sec. 17742, Rev. & Tax. Code)

See ¶605 for taxation of nonresident and part-year resident beneficiaries.

In the case of a trust, taxability depends on the residence of the fiduciaries and noncontingent beneficiaries (contingent beneficiaries are not relevant). All of the income is taxable, regardless of source, if either the fiduciary (or all fiduciaries, if more than one) or the beneficiary (or all beneficiaries, if more than one) is a California resident. (Sec. 17742, Rev. & Tax. Code) This applies only to any net income that is taxable to the trust, as distinguished from the beneficiaries. It does not apply to distributed (or distributable) income that is taxable to the beneficiaries; see ¶605 for treatment of such income.

Practitioner Comment: Passive Fiduciaries and Contingent Beneficiaries

The California State Board of Equalization (BOE) held in an unpublished decision on October 2, 2007 in the *Appeals of Yolanda King Family Trust and Mary L. Tunney Jr. Trust*, CCH CALIFORNIA TAX REPORTS, ¶404-483, that a trust with trustees as well as income beneficiaries who were California residents was nonetheless not subject to tax in California. The BOE agreed that the trustees had delegated all of their authority to an out-of-state bank and should not be considered. Further, the BOE agreed that income beneficiaries of a discretionary trust were contingent beneficiaries which were excluded from consideration under the statute.

Chris Whitney, Contributing Editor

See also *Appeal of The First National Bank of Chicago, Trustee* (1960) (CCH CALIFORNIA TAX REPORTS, ¶15-205.201), decided by the State Board of Equalization, in which a nonresident trustee was held taxable on the undistributed income of a trust only because its beneficiaries were California residents. In *Robert P. McCulloch v. Franchise Tax Board* (1964) (CCH CALIFORNIA TAX REPORTS, ¶15-235.341), the California Supreme Court held that the tax on income accumulated by a nonresident trust could be collected from a resident trustee-beneficiary in the year of distribution to him.

The residence of a corporate fiduciary is determined by reference to the place where the corporation transacts the major portion of its administration of the trust. (Sec. 17742, Rev. & Tax. Code)

If the taxability of the trust depends on the residence of the fiduciary and there are two or more fiduciaries, not all of whom are residents of California, the taxable income from sources outside California is apportioned to California according to the number of California fiduciaries in relation to the total number of fiduciaries. (Sec. 17743, Rev. & Tax. Code) For example, suppose a trust has two fiduciaries, only one of whom is a California resident, and has net income of $10,000 from property located in New York. One-half of the income of the trust, or $5,000, is taxable for California income tax purposes. This rule has no application to income derived from sources within California (¶231); such income is fully taxable in California regardless of the residence of the fiduciary, beneficiary, or settlor.

If the taxability of the trust depends on the residence of the beneficiary and there are two or more beneficiaries, not all of whom are California residents, the taxable income from sources outside California is apportioned to California to the extent the income will eventually be distributed to beneficiaries who are California residents. (Sec. 17744, Rev. & Tax. Code) To illustrate, suppose A, a resident, and B, a nonresident, are equal beneficiaries of the income of a trust established by a nonresident settlor and having a nonresident fiduciary. Its income of $10,000 is all derived from property located in New York State. All of the income is accumulated in the trust. One-half of the income, or $5,000, is taxable for California income tax purposes. As in the rule discussed in the preceding paragraph, this rule has no application to income derived from California sources.

Where there are multiple fiduciaries and also multiple beneficiaries, some of whom are California residents and some nonresidents, the practice of the Franchise Tax Board has been to apply the above rules consecutively; that is first to the fiduciaries and then to the beneficiaries, or vice versa. For example, suppose there are two fiduciaries, one of whom is a California resident, and two (equal) beneficiaries, one of whom is a California resident. One-half of the income taxable to the trust would be considered attributable to California because of the resident fiduciary. Of the remaining one-half, 50% would then be considered as California income because of the resident beneficiary, the result being that 75% of the total income is attributed to California. This practice is explained in some detail in Legal Ruling No. 238 (1959) (CCH CALIFORNIA TAX REPORTS, ¶ 15-205).

Where a nonresident trust has a resident trustee who is also a beneficiary, taxability of the trust's income has been held to be determined only by reference to the resident's status as a trustee. See *Robert P. McCulloch v. Franchise Tax Board*, cited above.

Qualified settlement funds

A fiduciary must file a Form 541 on behalf of a qualified settlement fund (including designated settlement funds) as defined under IRC Sec. 468B, if (1) the court or government agency administering the fund is located in California or (2) the fund receives or expects to receive income from California sources.

¶603 Income of Estate from Community Property

Law: Reg. 17742, 18 CCR (CCH CALIFORNIA TAX REPORTS, ¶ 15-215).

Comparable Federal: None.

Franchise Tax Board Reg. 17742, 18 CCR provides that the estate of a deceased spouse is taxable on the income from that part of his or her one-half of the community property that is subject to administration. Income received by the estate, but derived from the surviving spouse's share of the community property, is taxable to the surviving spouse.

Under the California Probate Code, the decedent's share of community property may pass to the surviving spouse without administration. In this case, the entire income is taxable to the surviving spouse. (Secs. 13500 et. seq., Prob. Code)

¶604 Taxable Income of Estate or Trust

Law: Secs. 17076, 17731, 17731.5, 17735-36, 17750, 17751, 18038 (CCH CALIFORNIA TAX REPORTS, ¶ 15-215).

Comparable Federal: Secs. 67, 641-45, 651, 661, 1040 (CCH U.S. MASTER TAX GUIDE ¶ 520 et seq., 528 et seq., 537 et seq.).

The taxable income of an estate or trust is computed the same as for individuals, as explained in Chapters 2—5 of this *Guidebook,* inclusive, with the following exceptions:

(1) unlimited deduction is allowed for income paid or set aside by an estate or complex trust under the terms of the will or trust instrument for certain charitable-type purposes (see discussion below);

(2) deduction is allowed for income required to be distributed currently to beneficiaries, the deduction not to exceed the "distributable net income"; and

(3) deduction is allowed to certain types of trusts ("complex" trusts—see ¶605) for other amounts properly paid or credited or required to be distributed.

The federal law is incorporated in California's by reference as of the current IRC tie-in date (¶103). (Sec. 17731, Rev. & Tax. Code) However, California does not incorporate a federal provision that limits the amount of gain that is taxable to an estate or trust that transfers appreciated farm property or closely held business real estate that has been valued for estate tax purposes under the "special-use" valuation method of IRC Sec. 2032A to a "qualified heir." (Sec. 18038, Rev. & Tax. Code)

In the case of an estate, prior to the 2014 tax year, California allows no deduction under items (2) and (3), above, for distributions that are taxable to a nonresident beneficiary if the fiduciary fails to obtain a tax-clearance certificate as explained at ¶613. (Sec. 17735, Rev. & Tax. Code) The tax clearance certificate requirement is repealed beginning with the 2014 tax year.

• *Expenses of administration*

Expenses of administration of an estate are ordinarily deductible. However, estate administration expenses can be deducted for California income tax purposes or California estate "pickup" tax purposes, but not both (*Tax News*, FTB, May 1988, CCH CALIFORNIA TAX REPORTS, ¶15-215.751). Note that California's "pick-up" tax is no longer in effect, see ¶1601.

• *Unlimited deduction*

The deduction described in (1), above, is subject to some restrictions. (Sec. 17736, Rev. & Tax. Code) Generally, the unlimited deduction is reduced or denied where the trust has "unrelated business income" or where it engages in certain "prohibited transactions." The deduction is allowed only for income actually paid out and not for income set aside by a trust. A trust claiming the unlimited deduction presumably would be classified as a charitable trust and treated as a corporation for California tax purposes, as explained at ¶606.

For both federal and California tax purposes, the above deductions are not miscellaneous itemized deductions subject to the 2% floor (¶303). (Sec. 17076, Rev. & Tax. Code)

• *Electing small business trusts*

The portion of a small business trust that consists of stock in one or more S corporations is treated as a separate trust for purposes of computing the income tax attributable to the S corporation stock held by the trust and is taxed at the highest rate applicable to individuals. (Sec. 17731.5, Rev. & Tax. Code) Special rules also apply to the income attributable to the S corporation stock, treatment of capital losses, deductions, exemptions, and credits.

• *Treatment of revocable trust as part of estate*

A qualified revocable trust may make an irrevocable election to be treated for income tax purposes as part of a decedent's estate, provided the election is made jointly by the trustee of the revocable trust and the executor of the decedent's estate by the due date for filing the estate's income tax return for its first tax year. (Sec. 17731, Rev. & Tax. Code) A federal election, or lack thereof, is binding for California purposes. (Sec. 17751, Rev. & Tax. Code)

¶604

¶605 Income Taxable to Beneficiaries

Law: Secs. 17731, 17734, 17745, 17779, 18631 (CCH CALIFORNIA TAX REPORTS, ¶ 15-235, 89-104).

Comparable Federal: Secs. 642, 652, 662-68 (CCH U.S. MASTER TAX GUIDE ¶ 554 et seq., 567).

California Form: FTB 5870A (Tax on Accumulation Distribution of Trusts).

Federal law pertaining to income taxable to beneficiaries is incorporated in California law by reference as of the current IRC tie-in date (¶ 103). (Sec. 17731, Rev. & Tax. Code) However, California provides special rules to cover various residence situations, as explained below.

Amounts deductible under (2) and (3) of ¶ 604 are includible in the income of the beneficiaries.

Income retains the same character (capital gain, exempt income, etc.) in the hands of the beneficiary that it had in the hands of the estate or trust. In other words, the estate or trust is treated as merely a "conduit" for income that is taxable to the beneficiaries. Depreciation is apportioned between the trust or estate and the beneficiaries according to the terms of the trust instrument or on the basis of the income allocable to each.

• *Notice to estate or trust beneficiaries*

The fiduciary of an estate or trust must furnish each beneficiary (or nominee) (1) who receives a distribution from an estate or trust or (2) to whom any taxable item is allocated, a statement (in accordance with IRC Sec. 6034A) containing information necessary for the beneficiary to file his or her California income tax return. (Sec. 18631, Rev. & Tax. Code)

• *Nonresident and part-year resident beneficiaries*

Nonresident beneficiaries are taxed on their distributive shares of estate or trust income only to the extent the income and deductions are derived from sources within California. (Sec. 17734, Rev. & Tax. Code) Thus, four beneficiaries who were residents of Sweden were required to pay California income tax on distributions from their brother's estate because the distributions were from the sale of real estate located in California (*Appeals of Folke Jernberg et al.* (1986), CCH CALIFORNIA TAX REPORTS, ¶ 15-205.302); the accumulated income from these holdings was also taxable.

A part-year resident beneficiary's distributive share of certain trust income is taxed based on the beneficiary's period of residency and nonresidency during the trust's taxable year (¶ 605). The allocation of income between the period of residency and the period of nonresidency must be made in a manner that reflects the actual date of realization. In the absence of information that reflects the actual date of realization, the annual amount of trust income must be allocated on a proportional basis between the two periods, using a daily pro rata method (FTB Pub. 1100, Taxation of Nonresidents and Individuals Who Change Residency, revised 11-2007, CCH CALIFORNIA TAX REPORTS, ¶ 404-599).

• *Miscellaneous provisions*

In *Estate of Dehgani-Fard* (2006) (CCH CALIFORNIA TAX REPORTS, ¶ 404-038), a California court of appeal ruled that a state university that was among several beneficiaries of a decedent's estate was not liable for any portion of the California personal income tax attributable to the after-discovered assets of the estate, where the income tax on those assets was paid before the income was distributed, and the estate, on its tax returns, had already claimed and received a partial tax exemption based on the university's status as a tax-exempt organization.

In *Appeal of Proctor P. and Martha M. Jones* (1983) (CCH CALIFORNIA TAX REPORTS, ¶ 15-235.342), the taxpayer, a California resident, was one of several beneficiaries of an out-of-state trust. The State Board of Equalization held that tax-exempt California municipal bond income of the trust was properly allocated exclusively to the taxpayer.

Where accumulated income is distributed by a nonresident trust to a resident beneficiary, the distribution is fully taxable to the beneficiary in the year of distribution if it has not previously been taxed in California. If the beneficiary was not a resident during the period of accumulation, the income may or may not be taxable in the year of distribution (¶ 405). However, credit will be allowed for taxes paid to other states (¶ 130). California law also provides the following:

(1) where taxes have not been paid on the income of a trust because a resident beneficiary's interest was merely contingent, and not vested, the income is taxable to the resident beneficiary when distributed, or distributable, to the beneficiary;

(2) even though the trust instrument provides that income accumulations are to be added to corpus, the income is nevertheless taxable as distributed, or distributable, to a resident beneficiary, if the trust failed to pay the tax when due, or no tax was paid by the trust because the interest of the resident beneficiary was merely contingent during the period of accumulation;

(3) the tax attributable to the inclusion of trust distributions in income by a resident beneficiary under (1), above, is the total amount of tax that would have been paid by the beneficiary if he or she had included a ratable amount in his or her income for the shorter of the following two periods: (a) the year of distribution and the five preceding years, or (b) the period that the trust acquired or accumulated the income (the "throwback" rules discussed below do not apply in this situation); and

(4) where a resident beneficiary leaves California within 12 months prior to the date of distribution of accumulated income and returns within 12 months after the receipt of such distribution, the beneficiary is presumed to be a resident throughout the entire intervening period of distribution.

(Sec. 17745, Rev. & Tax. Code)

In *Robert P. McCulloch v. Franchise Tax Board* (1964) (CCH CALIFORNIA TAX REPORTS, ¶ 15-235.341), the California Supreme Court held that where income was accumulated by a nonresident trust, and the tax on that income was not paid over to the state when due, it was properly includible in the resident beneficiary's income when distributed in a later year in proportion to the amount that should have been taxed to the trust in prior years.

The law divides trusts into two classes. The first type—commonly known as the "simple" trust—is one that is required to distribute all of its income currently. All other trusts and decedents' estates are included in the other category, commonly called "complex" trusts. Separate rules are provided for the determination of the amount taxable to beneficiaries of "simple" and of "complex" trusts. (Sec. 17731, Rev. & Tax. Code)

Relief is provided to beneficiaries in some cases in the year of termination of an estate or trust. If the deductions of the estate or trust exceed the gross income for the last year, the excess deductions may be carried over and allowed to the beneficiaries. The same procedure applies to unused capital loss carryovers.

If the taxable year of the beneficiary is different from that of the estate or trust, the amount of distributable income that the beneficiary reports is based upon the income of the estate or trust for the taxable year of the estate or trust that ends within the beneficiary's taxable year.

¶606 Charitable Trusts

Law: Secs. 17009, 17731, 17755, 18635 (CCH CALIFORNIA TAX REPORTS, ¶15-215, 15-235, 89-104).

Comparable Federal: Secs. 501(c)(3), 642(c), 664, 681, 4940-48, 6034 (CCH U.S. MASTER TAX GUIDE ¶590 et seq.).

Under California law, a charitable trust is treated as a corporation. (Sec. 17009, Rev. & Tax. Code) (This is accomplished by including trusts operated for charitable purposes within the definition of "corporation.") This means that a charitable trust should apply for tax exemption under Section 23701d of the corporation tax law and should comply with the reporting requirements discussed at ¶811. (Sec. 18635, Rev. & Tax. Code)

The special federal treatment of "charitable remainder annuity trusts" and "charitable remainder unitrusts" is incorporated in California law by reference. (Sec. 17731, Rev. & Tax. Code) However, for taxable years beginning after 2013, if a charitable remainder annuity trust or charitable remainder unitrust has unrelated business taxable income, instead of the excise tax imposed under federal law, a tax will be imposed on unrelated business taxable income for California purposes at the graduated personal income tax rates set forth in Sec. 17651, Rev. & Tax. Code (see ¶116). For taxable years beginning before 2014, California did not conform to the federal law subjecting charitable remainder annuity trusts and charitable remainder unitrusts with unrelated business taxable income to an excise tax; instead, for California purposes, charitable remainder trusts with unrelated business taxable income previously lost their tax exempt-status. (Sec. 17755, Rev. & Tax. Code)

Although California has conformed in principle to federal law by creating a special category of organizations classified as "private foundations," California has not adopted many of the complicated federal provisions relating to such organizations. California does not impose a tax on the investment income of "private foundations," nor does California impose any of the excise taxes (on self-dealing, income-accumulation, prohibited investments, lobbying, termination, etc.) that are included in the federal law. The California provisions regarding "private foundations" are almost all in the corporation tax law (¶811).

Both California and federal laws require specified trusts, including "private foundations," to include certain provisions in their governing instruments in order to maintain their tax-exempt status, unless a state statute accomplishes the same result. The California Civil Code provides that the required provisions are deemed to be included automatically in the governing instruments of all trusts to which the requirement applies, and further provides that any provisions of trust instruments that are inconsistent or contrary are of no effect.

¶607 Employees' Trusts

Law: Secs. 17501, 17504, 17510, 17631-40, 18506, 19518 (CCH CALIFORNIA TAX REPORTS, ¶15-800).

Comparable Federal: Secs. 401-7, 501-14, 4971-75, 6047, 7701 (CCH U.S. MASTER TAX GUIDE ¶2101 et seq.).

California law is generally the same as federal law. (Sec. 17501, Rev. & Tax. Code)

A trust forming part of an employees' stock bonus, pension, or profit-sharing plan is exempt from taxation provided it meets certain requirements as summarized very briefly as follows:

— contributions must be made for the exclusive benefit of employees or their beneficiaries and it must be impossible for any part of the corpus or income to be diverted to any other purpose; and

— the plan must benefit the employees generally, under certain specific rules, and must not discriminate in favor of officers, shareholders, supervisory employees, etc.

The employee benefits under an exempt plan are taxed to the employee only when actually distributed to the employee (see ¶206).

California rules for employees' trusts (including self-employed plans and individual retirement accounts) conform generally to federal rules. See ¶206 and ¶330 for a detailed discussion.

An exempt employees' trust need not file a California return unless it changes its character, purpose, or method of operation, or unless it has unrelated business income. (Sec. 18506, Rev. & Tax. Code) However, both California and federal laws require trustees and insurers to file information returns regarding payments made under self-employed retirement plans. (Sec. 19518, Rev. & Tax. Code) Also, as to individual retirement accounts, California requires trustees and others to file copies of federal reports with the Franchise Tax Board.

¶608 Trusts Taxable to Grantor

Law: Secs. 17731, 17760.5 (CCH California Tax Reports, ¶15-215).

Comparable Federal: Secs. 671-79, 685 (CCH U.S. Master Tax Guide ¶571 et seq.).

California law is the same as federal law as of the current IRC tie-in date (¶103). (Sec. 17731, Rev. & Tax. Code)

Where the grantor retains an interest, as specifically defined in the Code sections cited above, in either corpus or income, the income is taxable to the grantor and not to the trust or the beneficiaries. However, under both California and federal law, qualified pre-need funeral trusts may not be treated as grantor trusts. (Sec. 17760.5, Rev. & Tax. Code) Consequently, the tax on the annual earnings of a funeral trust is payable by the trustee, if a trustee elects this special tax treatment. A federal election to receive such treatment for a qualified pre-need funeral trust is binding for California purposes and a separate California election is not allowed.

Where income of a trust may be used to satisfy the grantor's legal obligation to support a beneficiary, the income is taxed to the grantor to the extent—and only to the extent—that the income is so used.

In *Appeal of Blake and Alice Hale* (1960) (CCH California Tax Reports, ¶15-215.907), the State Board of Equalization held that income from a voluntary trust was taxable to the grantor when the trust instrument did not specifically provide that the trust was irrevocable, and partial or total revocations were contemplated in certain provisions.

Where the grantor in a trust of the type under discussion is not a California resident, he or she is taxed on the income of the trust only to the extent it is derived from sources within California.

There are special federal rules for taxing the income of foreign trusts to their U.S. grantors, under certain conditions. In addition, the U.S. beneficiary of a foreign trust may be treated as the grantor of the trust in certain cases in which the grantor trust rules would otherwise be frustrated.

Fiduciaries of certain grantor trusts are not required to file a return for the trust; the income, deductions, and credits of the trust are reported on the grantor's return.

¶609 Real Estate Investment Trusts

Law: Sec. 17088 (CCH CALIFORNIA TAX REPORTS, ¶10-360).

Comparable Federal: Secs. 856-60 (CCH U.S. MASTER TAX GUIDE ¶2326 et seq.).

California generally adopts by reference the federal provisions as of the current IRC tie-in date (¶103); see ¶805 for additional information. (Sec. 17088, Rev. & Tax. Code) California law, unlike federal law, does not apply a lower tax rate to qualified dividend distributions made by a real estate investment trust (REIT).

A REIT is ordinarily treated as a business trust subject to the corporation income tax, as explained at ¶805. The corporation tax law allows such organizations a deduction for income distributed, as explained at ¶1021.

¶610 Financial Asset Securitization Investment Trusts

Law: Sec. 17088 (CCH CALIFORNIA TAX REPORTS, ¶10-370).

Comparable Federal: Former Secs. 860H—860L (CCH U.S. MASTER TAX GUIDE ¶2369).

California incorporates federal provisions concerning financial asset securitization investment trusts (FASITs) as of the current IRC tie-in date (¶103). (Sec. 17088, Rev. & Tax. Code) The FASIT provisions are repealed under both California and federal law, generally effective January 1, 2005. However, the repeal does not apply to any FASIT in existence on October 22, 2004, to the extent that regular interests issued by the FASIT before such date continue to remain outstanding in accordance with the original terms of issuance.

A FASIT is a pass-through entity that may be used to securitize debt obligations such as credit card receivables, home equity loans, and auto loans. Securities issued by a FASIT are treated as debt for federal income tax purposes, regardless of whether instruments with similar terms issued by an entity other than a FASIT would be characterized as equity ownership interests. Consequently, a FASIT may be used to avoid imposition of a corporate level tax on investors' income and to ensure that interest paid to investors will be deductible by the loan pool's sponsor.

¶611 Alimony Trusts

Law: Secs. 17731, 17737 (CCH CALIFORNIA TAX REPORTS, ¶15-215).

Comparable Federal: Sec. 682 (CCH U.S. MASTER TAX GUIDE ¶775).

Income of "alimony trusts" is taxable to the beneficiary and is not taxable to the trustor. (Sec. 17731, Rev. & Tax. Code) This rule does not apply to any part of such income that is payable for the support of minor children. (Sec. 17737, Rev. & Tax. Code)

California law incorporates federal law by reference as of the current IRC tie-in date (¶103).

¶612 Lien for Tax on Trust Income

Law: Secs. 19221, 19223-24 (CCH CALIFORNIA TAX REPORTS, ¶89-172).

Comparable Federal: Sec. 6321.

California law provides that under certain conditions the amount of taxes imposed upon the grantor of a trust on the trust income (¶608) constitutes a lien on the trust property. (Sec. 19221, Rev. & Tax. Code) Although federal law contains certain provisions for liens for unpaid taxes, it contains no rule similar to this one.

¶613 Liability of Fiduciary

Law: Secs. 19071-74, 19512-17 (CCH CALIFORNIA TAX REPORTS, ¶89-166).

Comparable Federal: Secs. 6501, 6901, 6903, 6905 (CCH U.S. MASTER TAX GUIDE ¶512).

California Forms: Form 541 (California Fiduciary Income Tax Return), FTB 3571 (Request for Estate Income Tax Certificate).

California law is the same as federal law as of the current IRC tie-in date (¶103).

The fiduciary is personally liable for the taxes on an estate or trust under certain conditions. (Sec. 19073, Rev. & Tax. Code; Sec. 19074, Rev. & Tax. Code) Federal law provides for discharge of an executor's liability under certain circumstances. There is no comparable California provision.

Prior to January 1, 2014, if the asset value of an estate exceeded $1 million and assets valued at more than $250,000 were distributable to one or more nonresident beneficiaries, the fiduciary of an estate was required to file with his or her final accounting a certificate from the Franchise Tax Board (FTB) to the effect that all California income taxes had been paid or otherwise provided for. (Former Sec. 19513, Rev. & Tax. Code; Reg. 19513, 18 CCR) Issuance of the certificate did not relieve the estate of any taxes due or that might become due from the decedent or the estate, nor did it relieve the fiduciary from personal liability for taxes or expenses. (Former Sec. 19515, Rev. & Tax. Code; Sec. 19516, Rev. & Tax. Code)

A fiduciary (or other person liable for the tax) of an estate or trust may by written request filed with the FTB shorten the period of limitations on assessment, etc., to 18 months. (Sec. 19517, Rev. & Tax. Code) The comparable federal provision is limited to the fiduciary of an estate.

A fiduciary should give the FTB notice in writing of the assumption of the duties, rights, etc., attaching to the fiduciary capacity. A fiduciary who wishes to be relieved of fiduciary responsibilities must give the FTB a written termination notice, accompanied by evidence of such termination. (Sec. 19512, Rev. & Tax. Code) The California rule is the same as the federal rule.

In *Appeals of Dunham et al.* (1963) (CCH CALIFORNIA TAX REPORTS, ¶ 89-166.40), the State Board of Equalization (BOE) held that the co-executors of an estate remained liable for additional California income tax imposed on the estate after they had been discharged from their duties by a superior court. The BOE held that failure to notify the FTB of discharge by a superior court left them responsible, in their representative capacities, for the additional tax.

¶614 Common Trust Funds

Law: Secs. 17671, 17677 (CCH CALIFORNIA TAX REPORTS, ¶ 15-515).

Comparable Federal: Sec. 584 (CCH U.S. MASTER TAX GUIDE ¶ 595).

California law is the same as federal law as of the current IRC tie-in date (¶ 103). (Sec. 17671, Rev. & Tax. Code)

Special rules are provided for common trust funds maintained by banks or trust companies. The general plan is to treat such funds as reporting entities, only the individual shares of income being taxed to the participants, as is the manner for partnerships.

¶615 Real Estate Mortgage Investment Conduits

Law: Secs. 17088, 24874 (CCH CALIFORNIA TAX REPORTS, ¶ 10-365).

Comparable Federal: Secs. 860A—860G (CCH U.S. MASTER TAX GUIDE ¶ 2343 et seq.).

California law is the same as federal law as of the current IRC tie-in date (¶ 103). (Sec. 17088, Rev. & Tax. Code), except that California does not impose an excise tax on prohibited transactions, but subjects real estate mortgage investment conduits (REMICs) to a minimum tax. (Sec. 24874, Rev. & Tax. Code)

Trusts or partnerships that meet specified requirements may elect to be treated as a REMIC. A REMIC, which is a fixed pool of mortgages with multiple classes of interests held by investors, is not taxed on its income, but its income is taxable to the holders of its interests.

¶616 Partnerships—Method of Taxing

> *Law:* Secs. 17008, 17008.5, 17551, 17851, 17935, 17941, 17948, 23081, 23097, 24637 (CCH CALIFORNIA TAX REPORTS, ¶10-220, 15-455, 15-185).
>
> *Comparable Federal:* Secs. 444, 701-61, 7701, 7704 (CCH U.S. MASTER TAX GUIDE ¶403, 404, 416).
>
> *California Form:* Form 565 (Partnership Return of Income).

California law is the same as federal law as of the current IRC tie-in date (¶103) (Sec. 17851, Rev. & Tax. Code), except for a minimum tax imposed by California on limited partnerships, limited liability partnerships (LLPs), and limited liability companies (LLCs) treated as partnerships (¶116) that are organized or registered in California or doing business in California. See ¶804 for a discussion of "doing business."

The minimum tax must be paid for each taxable year until a certificate of cancellation is filed with the office of the Secretary of State (SOS). (Sec. 17935, Rev. & Tax. Code; Sec. 17941, Rev. & Tax. Code; Sec. 17948, Rev. & Tax. Code) Ceasing operations, filing a "final return", and filing a certificate of dissolution with the Secretary of State's Office, without filing a certificate of cancellation with the Secretary of State's office, was insufficient to relieve a limited partnership from liability for the minimum tax. (Uncitable decision, *Third Pine Associates, L.P. and 1319 Promenade, L.P.* (2006), CCH CALIFORNIA TAX REPORTS, ¶89-210.544) See ¶623 for further details.

Partnerships are not taxable as such but are treated as reporting entities only, the distributive shares of the partners being reported and taxed in their individual returns. (Sec. 17851, Rev. & Tax. Code) "Partnership" may include a syndicate, group, pool, joint venture, or other unincorporated organization. (Sec. 17008, Rev. & Tax. Code)

California adopts the federal provision that treats publicly traded partnerships as corporations unless (1) 90% or more of their gross income consists of qualifying passive income or (2) they are grandfathered publicly traded partnerships exempt from corporate treatment. (Sec. 17008.5, Rev. & Tax. Code) However, a grandfathered publicly traded partnership that elects to continue its partnership status is subject to a California tax equal to 1% of its California-source gross income attributable to the active conduct of any trade or business (a 3.5% tax on gross income attributable to the active conduct of any trade or business for federal purposes).

For a detailed discussion of limited liability partnerships, see ¶623. For a discussion of limited liability companies classified as partnerships, see ¶625.

• *Taxable year*

Generally, a partnership must use the same taxable year as the taxable year of a majority of its partners (usually a calendar year). However, certain partnerships may elect to change to a taxable year with a three-month deferral period. (Sec. 17551, Rev. & Tax. Code) Federal law requires an entity making the election federally to make certain "required payments" to the IRS in exchange for deferral of the tax. California does not adopt the "required payments" requirement.

Partnership information is reported on Form 565 unless otherwise indicated.

¶617 Transactions Between Partner and Partnership

> *Law:* Sec. 17851 (CCH CALIFORNIA TAX REPORTS, ¶16-417, 16-428).
>
> *Comparable Federal:* Secs. 704, 707, 721-24, 731-36 (CCH U.S. MASTER TAX GUIDE ¶421, 425, 428, 432, 435, 443, 453 et seq.).

California law generally is the same as federal law as of the current IRC tie-in date (¶103). (Sec. 17851, Rev. & Tax. Code)

In keeping with the theory that a partnership is not a separate taxable entity, it has been the general rule that no gain or loss is recognized when property is transferred from a partner to a partnership or *vice versa*. Special rules applicable to specific situations have, to some extent, eroded that general rule, however. Distributions of money and distributions in liquidation of a partner's interest are subject to special rules under which gain or loss is sometimes recognized. Also, recognition treatment is accorded to distributions of appreciated property contributed by a partner when the property is distributed within seven years of its contribution. See ¶555 for rules regarding basis of property contributed to or distributed by a partnership.

California incorporates federal law that dramatically limits the ability of partners and partnerships to shift or duplicate losses by (1) placing restrictions on certain partnership allocations traceable to built-in loss property and (2) limiting elections not to make partnership basis adjustments under IRC Secs. 743 and 734 in "substantial" loss situations.

When a partner engages in a transaction with the partnership in a non-partner capacity, the partner is generally treated as an outsider. This provision does not apply, however, in the case of losses on such transactions where the partner holds more than a 50% interest in the partnership. Also, capital gain treatment is denied on certain sales or exchanges where a partner holds more than a 50% interest in a partnership or where the same group owns more than a 50% interest in two partnerships.

¶618 Transfer of Partnership Interest

Law: Secs. 17024.5, 17851, 17855-57 (CCH CALIFORNIA TAX REPORTS, ¶15-190).

Comparable Federal: Secs. 736, 737, 741-55 (CCH U.S. MASTER TAX GUIDE ¶438, 440, 454).

The sale of a partnership interest is generally considered to be the sale of a capital asset, with exceptions for cases where there are "unrealized receivables" or appreciated inventory.

The federal law is incorporated in California law by reference as of the current IRC tie-in date (¶103). (Sec. 17851, Rev. & Tax. Code) However, there are some specified California differences, as explained below.

The law provides special rules for treatment of "unrealized receivables" and appreciated inventory in the sale or liquidation of a partnership interest. The purpose is to prevent tax avoidance by converting profit on such items from ordinary income to capital gain. The federal definition of "unrealized receivables" includes the following items that are not included in the California definition:

— stock in a Domestic International Sales Corporation (DISC);

— stock in certain foreign corporations; and

— certain oil, gas, and geothermal property.

(Sec. 17024.5(b)(2) and (5), Rev. & Tax. Code; Sec. 17855, Rev. & Tax. Code)

Under both California and federal law, if the partner receiving property in liquidation does not have enough available basis to cover the full amount of the partnership's basis in unrealized receivables and inventory, the shortfall in available basis must be accounted for. The difference between the partnership's basis in the unrealized receivables and inventory and the partner's substituted basis available for allocation is treated as a basis "decrease." The decrease is allocated first to properties with unrealized depreciation. Any remaining decrease is allocated to the properties in proportion to their respective adjusted bases.

For an example of ordinary-income treatment of "unrealized receivables" upon sale of a partnership interest, see *Appeal of Gerald H. and Dorothy A. Bense* (1979) (CCH CALIFORNIA TAX REPORTS, ¶ 15-190.57).

CCH Caution Note: Variant of Son-of-Boss Transaction Treated as Sham Transaction

In a rarely-issued formal opinion, the California State Board of Equalization (BOE) upheld a personal income tax assessment and accuracy-related penalty imposed as a result of unreported gain that a taxpayer attempted to shield through a series of sham transactions. The transactions were a variant of the "Son of Boss" transactions, in which the taxpayer claimed significant losses stemming from a series of complicated transactions involving several partnerships, a short-sale of securities, and losses from the sale of other assets. All of these transactions were undertaken to offset the taxpayer's personal income tax liabilities stemming from a multimillion dollar gain received from a real estate foreclosure. Although the BOE did not affirm the FTB's reasoning that the obligation to return borrowed securities in a short-sale transaction was a liability for purposes of IRC Sec. 752, the BOE upheld the assessment and penalty on the basis that the whole transaction was a sham transaction from which the taxpayer could not receive any tax benefit. (*Appeal of Alyn* (2009) CCH CALIFORNIA TAX REPORTS, ¶ 404-949)

¶619 Nonresident and Part-Year Resident Partners

Law: Secs. 17951, 18535 (CCH CALIFORNIA TAX REPORTS, ¶ 16-565, 89-102).

Comparable Federal: None.

California Forms: Form 540NR (California Nonresident or Part-Year Resident Income Tax Return), Sch. CA (540NR) (California Adjustments - Nonresidents or Part-Year Residents), FTB 3864 (Group Nonresident Return Election).

Nonresident partners

Nonresident partners are taxable on the portion of their distributive share of partnership income that is derived from sources within California. Such partners are taxable on any such income and may deduct their share of any loss attributable to California sources. (Sec. 17951, Rev. & Tax. Code) See ¶231 for a discussion of taxable income of nonresidents and ¶129 for a credit nonresident partners may take on taxes paid other states on income also taxed by California. Withholding requirements for distributions to nonresident partners is discussed at ¶714.

A nonresident partner in an investment partnership is not subject to California taxation on income from qualifying investment securities. However California tax applies to income from an investment activity that is interrelated with a California trade or business in which the nonresident owns an interest and the primary activities of the trade or business are separate and distinct from the acts of acquiring, managing, or disposing of qualified investment securities. Likewise, income from qualifying investment securities that are acquired with the working capital of a California trade or business in which the nonresident owns an interest is taxable by California. (Sec. 17955, Rev. & Tax. Code)

Group returns

An election to file a group nonresident personal income tax return (Form 540NR, California Nonresident or Part-Year Resident Personal Income Tax Return) is available to nonresident partners of California partnerships or partnerships having California source income (this provision also applies to nonresident shareholders of S corporations and nonresident members of a limited liability company; see ¶233 and ¶625, respectively). The election may be made on behalf of a single nonresident partner. (Sec. 18535, Rev. & Tax. Code)

An irrevocable election must be made by the partnership each year. Election to file a group return relieves a nonresident partner of the responsibility of filing individually. A nonresident may only participate in the group return if he or she is an individual, was a nonresident for the full year, and has no income from any other California source (other than another business entity that files a nonresident group return on behalf of the individual). Individuals with taxable income in excess of $1 million who are subject to the mental health services tax (see ¶116) may be included in a group return. (Sec. 18535, Rev. & Tax. Code)

A calendar year should be used for the group nonresident return, even if the partnership has a fiscal year end. Any estimated tax payments should also be made on a calendar year basis. A Schedule 1067B should be used to authorize the FTB to move estimated tax payments from the group to an individual's account, or from an individual's account to the group. It will take the FTB six to eight weeks to move the estimated tax payments and make them available to be claimed on the group nonresident return. (FTB Pub. 1067, Guidelines for Filing a Group Form 540NR)

The tax rate applicable to each partner's distributive share will be the highest marginal rate, including, when applicable, the additional 1% mental health services tax applied to individuals with taxable income in excess of $1 million. Only distributive deductions, those necessary to determine each partner's distributive share, are permitted (an exception is made for deferred-compensation deductions attributable to the partner's earned income from the partnership, provided this is the only earned income the partner has). Credits are restricted to those directly attributable to the partnership (*e.g.*, as net income taxes paid to other states by the partnership) and do not include credits to which the nonresident may be otherwise entitled as an individual.

Planning Note: Pros and Cons of Group Returns

On a group nonresident return, only the California source pass-through income or director's compensation is reported. The upside to the group return is that worldwide income does not need to be reported individually. However, the income reported on the group nonresident return is taxed at the highest marginal rate, currently at 12.3%. (*FTB Tax News* (April 2013), CCH CALIFORNIA TAX REPORTS, ¶405-867)

Once the group nonresident return is filed, the return cannot be amended to either include or exclude a nonresident member. Similarly, if a nonresident member is included in the group nonresident return, the member may not subsequently file an individual nonresident return.

For more information concerning nonresident group returns, see FTB Pub. 1067, Guidelines for Filing a Group Form 540NR.

The Franchise Tax Board may adjust the income of an electing nonresident taxpayer included in a group return to properly reflect income. (Sec. 18535, Rev. & Tax. Code)

Part-year resident partners

A part-year resident partner's distributive share of partnership income is taxed based on the partner's period of residency and nonresidency during the partnership's taxable year (¶605). The allocation of income between the period of residency and the period of nonresidency must be made in a manner that reflects the actual date of realization. In the absence of information that reflects the actual date of realization, the annual amount of partnership income must be allocated on a proportional basis between the two periods, using a daily pro rata method (FTB Pub. 1100, Taxation of Nonresidents and Individuals Who Change Residency, revised May 2013, CCH CALIFORNIA TAX REPORTS, ¶405-932).

¶620 Computation of Partnership Income

Law: Secs. 17201, 17851-54, 17858 (CCH CALIFORNIA TAX REPORTS, ¶10-220, 15-805).

Comparable Federal: Secs. 195, 702, 703, 709 (CCH U.S. MASTER TAX GUIDE ¶417, 419, 427).

California law is substantially the same as federal law as of the current IRC tie-in date (¶103), except that California deductions are not allowed to the partnership for state income taxes. (Sec. 17851, Rev. & Tax. Code; Sec. 17853, Rev. & Tax. Code) In addition, California does not incorporate federal law providing special treatment for small partnerships.

Under both California and federal law, the taxable income of a partnership is computed in the same way as that of an individual, except that no deduction is allowed for charitable contributions or for personal items such as medical expenses. The individual partners are permitted to pick up their shares of the partnership contributions in their individual returns. Capital gains and losses of the partnership are segregated from other income so that the individual partners' shares may be picked up and combined with other capital gains and losses on their individual returns.

Guaranteed payments to partners for salary and interest are treated as though paid to an outsider, and are reported by the partners as separate items. For purposes of computing a nonresident's taxable income (¶116), guaranteed payments received by a nonresident are included in gross income from California sources in the same manner as if those payments were a distributive share of that partnership. (Sec. 17854, Rev. & Tax. Code)

A partner's share of a partnership loss may be deducted only to the extent of the adjusted basis of the partner's interest in the partnership at the end of the partnership year. However, such losses may be deducted in a subsequent year when the partner has sufficient basis to offset the loss.

Generally, elections affecting the computation of partnership income, such as depreciation, must be made on the partnership return; thus, the amount of depreciation is not recalculated by individual partners. (Sec. 17858, Rev. & Tax. Code) However, certain elections are made by each partner separately.

See ¶1304 and ¶1305 regarding computation of California partnership income where a partnership is engaged in a unitary business with a corporate partner.

Special rules are provided for determining income of partnerships and partners, as part of the effort to restrict the use of various forms of tax shelters. These provisions include "at risk" limitations on losses (¶339), restrictions on the ability of partners and partnerships to shift or duplicate losses (¶617), limitations on deduction of syndication and organization expenses, specific rules for apportionment of income among partners, restrictions on deductions by farming syndicates, and use of the accrual method of accounting by certain farming partnerships.

Under both California and federal law (IRC Sec. 195) partnerships may currently deduct up to $5,000 of their organizational expenditures, reduced by the amount by which such expenditures exceed $50,000, for the tax year in which the partnership begins business. The remainder of any organizational expenses can be deducted ratably over the 180-month period beginning with the month in which the partnership begins business. (Sec. 17201, Rev. & Tax. Code)

¶621 Taxable Year in Which Income of Partner Includible

Law: Sec. 17851 (CCH CALIFORNIA TAX REPORTS, ¶15-190).

Comparable Federal: Secs. 706, 708 (CCH U.S. MASTER TAX GUIDE ¶404, 416).

California law is the same as federal law (¶103). (Sec. 17851, Rev. & Tax. Code)

A partner must report a distributive share of the partnership income for the taxable year (or years) of the partnership ending within or with the partner's taxable year. A partnership is limited in its choice of a taxable year (¶616). In order to adopt a taxable year other than that of its principal partners, the partnership must establish a business purpose. (Sec. 17851, Rev. & Tax. Code)

¶622 Partnership Returns

Law: Secs. 18409, 18633, 19172 (CCH CALIFORNIA TAX REPORTS, ¶89-102, 89-206).

Comparable Federal: Secs. 6011(e), 6031, 6698 (CCH U.S. MASTER TAX GUIDE ¶404 et seq.).

California Form: Form 565 (Partnership Return of Income).

Partnership returns are made on Form 565 and for taxable years beginning on or after January 1, 2016, must be filed by the 15th day of the third month after the close of the partnership's taxable year. For taxable years beginning before January 1, 2016, the return due date was the 15th day of the fourth month after the close of the partnership's taxable year. Automatic extensions of up to six months are available (¶108). (Sec. 18633, Rev. & Tax. Code) Partnership returns may be filed electronically.

CCH Tip: Schedule EO, Pass-Through Entity Ownership

Schedule EO, Pass-Through Entity Ownership, is used to report pass-through entity ownership interests in entities that file federal Form 1065 or that are disregarded. This schedule is completed by partnerships and LLCs taxable as partnerships that hold partial ownership interest in other partnerships, LLCs taxable as partnerships, and/or own disregarded entities, including Single Member Limited Liability Companies (SMLLC) that are disregarded. Taxpayers must identify by name, Secretary of State number, and Federal Employee Identification Number all partnerships (including LLCs taxable as partnerships), in which the taxpayer holds a partial interest and for disregarded entities in which the taxpayer has full ownership. In addition, the taxpayer must indicate which entities received California source income, and must provide the profit and loss sharing percentages used to compute the amount of income received by the owner. S corporations do not complete this schedule nor are partnerships or LLCs required to report S corporation pass-through income. (Schedule EO Instructions)

Returns must be filed by all partnerships (including real estate mortgage investment conduits treated as partnerships) having income from sources in California or engaging in a trade or business within California. Regardless of where the trade or business of the partnership is located, a partnership is considered to be doing business in California if any of its partners (general or limited) or other agents is conducting business in California on behalf of the partnership.

CCH Tip: Required signature

Form 565 is not considered a valid return unless it is signed by a general partner.

Pertinent information from the return must be furnished to each partner and to each person who holds a partnership interest as a nominee for another person. The provision is the same as federal law. California also conforms to the federal reporting requirements of a partnership that has one or more exempt partners subject to the unrelated business tax. (Sec. 18633, Rev. & Tax. Code) However, California does not conform to the federal requirement that all partnerships having more than 100 partners file returns on magnetic media. (Sec. 18409, Rev. & Tax. Code)

California law imposes a special penalty, in addition to other penalties discussed at ¶712, for failure to file a timely and proper partnership return. The penalty is $18 per month per partner, for a maximum of 12 months ($10 per month for a maximum of 5 months for returns filed prior to 2011). (Sec. 19172, Rev. & Tax. Code) This conforms generally to a federal penalty that is imposed at the rate of $50 per month per partner. However, the federal exception to the imposition of penalties for certain small partnerships does not apply for California purposes.

A partnership carrying on no business in California and having no income from sources in California is not required to file a partnership return, even if the partnership consists of one or more California residents. However, if any partner is a California resident, a return must be filed if there is an election required to be made by the partnership, and the partners wish to obtain different California treatment with respect to the election than that chosen for federal purposes (e.g., installment method, exclusion from partnership provisions, etc.).

Even if there are no partnership elections to be made and a return is not filed, a resident partner of a nonresident partnership may be required to submit information to determine whether or not there is any liability for California tax on partnership income; this may include information regarding the apportionment factors discussed in Chapter 13, as well as a copy of federal Form 1065.

Limited partnerships and limited liability partnerships that have a certificate on file or are registered with the Secretary of State must file a return even if they are not doing business in California. However, if the limited partnership has no income from California sources and is not carrying on any business in California, its reporting requirements may be reduced.

For information concerning a partnership's obligation to withhold on payments and distributions to nonresident partners, see ¶714.

¶623 Limited Liability Partnerships

Law: Sec. 12189, Government Code; Secs. 16101, 16951, 16953, 16956, 16959, Corporation Code; Secs. 17948—17948.2, Revenue and Taxation Code (CCH CALIFORNIA TAX REPORTS, ¶10-225).

Comparable Federal: None.

California Form: Form 565 (Partnership Return of Income).

The formation of registered limited liability partnerships (LLPs) and the registration of foreign LLPs by legal, accounting, and architectural firms is authorized in California. (Sec. 16951, Corp. Code) A qualifying partnership, other than a limited partnership, may register as an LLP if all of the firm's partners are licensed, registered, or authorized to practice any of the following, either in California or in another jurisdiction:

— public accountancy;

— law;

— until January 1, 2019, architecture; or

— until January 1, 2016, engineering or land surveying.

(Sec. 16101, Corp. Code)

A partnership that is related to an LLP and provides services related or complementary to the professional services provided by the LLP or provides services to the LLP may also register as an LLP. A partnership is considered related to an LLP if it meets one of the following requirements:

— at least a majority of the partners in one partnership are also partners in the other partnership;

— at least a majority in interest in each partnership hold interest or are members in another entity and each renders services pursuant to an agreement with that other entity; or

— one partnership controls, is controlled by, or is under common control with the other partnership. (Sec. 16101, Corp. Code)

• *LLPs subject to minimum tax*

An LLP must pay an annual nondeductible minimum tax if the LLP is doing business in California or has had its certificate of registration issued by the Secretary of State and has had a taxable year of more than 15 days. (Sec. 17948, Rev. & Tax. Code; Sec. 17948.2, Rev. & Tax. Code) An LLP must continue to pay the tax until one of the following requirements are satisfied:

— the LLP files a notice of cessation with the California Secretary of State,

— a foreign LLP withdraws its registration, or

— the registered LLP or foreign LLP dissolves and is finally wound up.

See ¶ 816 for the minimum tax rate.

In addition, a registered LLP is relieved of liability for the minimum tax if it

— files a timely final annual tax return for a taxable year with the Franchise Tax Board (FTB),

— does not do business in California after the end of the taxable year for which the final annual tax return was filed, and

— files a notice of cessation or similar document with the Secretary of State's Office before the end of the 12-month period beginning with the date the final annual tax return was filed.

(Sec. 17948.3, Rev. & Tax. Code)

• *Registration requirements*

To register as an LLP or foreign LLP, a partnership must file a registration statement with the Secretary of State and pay a fee of $70. A foreign LLP that transacts intrastate business in California without registration is subject to a penalty of $20 per day, up to a maximum of $10,000. In addition, as part of the registration requirement, all LLPs are required to provide specified amounts of security against any claims that might arise against the LLP. (Sec. 12189, Gov't. Code; Sec. 16953, Corp. Code; Sec. 16956, Corp. Code; Sec. 16959, Corp. Code)

¶624 Electing Large Partnerships

Law: Sec. 17865 (CCH California Tax Reports, ¶ 10-230).

Comparable Federal: Secs. 771-777 (CCH U.S. Master Tax Guide ¶ 482 et seq.).

California does not incorporate the federal provisions that authorize electing large partnerships, which may use simplified reporting systems and significantly reduce the number of items that must be separately reported to their partners. (Sec. 17865, Rev. & Tax. Code) Consequently, such electing large partnerships are required to file California's partnership returns and comply with other California partnership reporting responsibilities (see ¶ 622).

An "electing large partnership" is any nonservice partnership that elects to apply certain simplified reporting provisions, provided that the number of qualifying partners in the partnership was at least 100 during the preceding tax year. An electing large partnership combines most items of partnership income, deduction, credit, and loss at the partnership level and passes through net amounts to the partners. Netting of capital gains and losses occurs at the partnership level, and passive activity items are separated from capital gains stemming from partnership portfolio income. Special rules apply to partnerships engaging in oil and gas activities.

¶625 Limited Liability Companies

Law: Sec. 17060, Corporations Code; Secs. 17087.6, 17941-46, 18535, 18633.5, 18662, 18666, 19172, 19394, 23038 (CCH CALIFORNIA TAX REPORTS, ¶ 10-240, 89-102, 89-206).

Comparable Federal: Reg. 301.7701-2 (CCH U.S. MASTER TAX GUIDE ¶ 402A, 402B).

California Forms: Form 568 (Limited Liability Company Return of Income), FTB 3522 (Limited Liability Company Tax Voucher), FTB 3832 (Limited Liability Company Non-resident Members' Consent), Sch. K-1 (568) (Member's Share of Income, Deductions, Credits, etc.).

California authorizes the formation of limited liability companies (LLCs), whether or not for profit, and also allows foreign LLCs to qualify to do business in California. California conforms to federal "check-the-box" rules, and an LLC will be classified for California tax purposes according to the classification the LLC elects for federal purposes. (Sec. 23038, Rev. & Tax. Code)

However, an entity that is a previously existing foreign single member LLC that was classified as a corporation under pre-1997 California law but became a disregarded entity for federal purposes for post-1996 taxable years may continue to be classified differently for California and federal tax purposes. Such an entity may make an irrevocable election to be disregarded for California tax purposes as well, unless specified exceptions apply. The election is made on FTB 3574, Special Election for Business Trusts and Certain Foreign Single Member LLCs. (Reg. 23038, 18 CCR; Instructions, FTB 3574, Special Election for Business Trusts and Certain Foreign Single Member LLCs)

CCH Caution: LLCs Classified as Corporations

The taxes and fees discussed below apply to LLCs classified as partnerships or that are disregarded and taxed as a sole proprietorship for California tax purposes. LLCs classified as corporations remain subject to the same tax return and tax payment requirements as any other corporation.

California authorizes the formation of single member LLCs and allows a member of an LLC to have alter ego liability for the LLC's debts or other liabilities.

Each series in a Delaware Series LLC is considered a separate LLC and must file its own return and pay its own separate LLC fee and tax. (FTB Pub. 3556, Limited Liability Company Filing Information, July 2008, CCH CALIFORNIA TAX REPORTS, ¶ 404-737)

• *Minimum tax*

An LLC that is classified as a partnership or that is disregarded and treated as a sole proprietorship for California tax purposes must pay an annual minimum tax of $800 if the LLC (1) is doing business in California or (2) has had its articles of organization accepted or a certificate of registration issued by the Secretary of State. The LLC is not liable for the tax if it did no business in California during the taxable year and the taxable year was 15 days or less.

CCH Caution: "Doing Business" Threshold Quite Low

In a nonprecedential decision, the State Board of Equalization (BOE) has ruled that the activities undertaken by a foreign LLC's California-resident managers on behalf of the LLC constituted "doing business" and therefore subjected the LLC to the minimum tax even though the LLC, which was formed to acquire and manage real estate, was not registered in California, its primary asset was real estate located in Montana, and the day-to-day management of the real estate was performed by a Montana real estate management company. The property purchasing negotiations conducted by the California-resident members were sufficient for purposes of satisfying the "doing business" threshold requirements, as was a loan transaction between the LLC and one of its members. The BOE held that it is not where property is located that is most germane to determining whether the LLC was conducting business in California, but where the activity of the business that owns that property occurred. (*Appeal of Mockingbird Partners, LLC* (2006), CCH CALIFORNIA TAX REPORTS, ¶ 404-012)

A similar ruling was reached in another nonprecedential BOE decision concerning a Nevada LLC whose sole member was a California resident. The BOE found that the activities undertaken by the member constituted doing business in California because there was no evidence produced to demonstrate that he left California to conduct LLC business. (*International Health Institute, LLC* (2006) CCH CALIFORNIA TAX REPORTS, ¶ 10-240.221)

However, the FTB's Taxpayers' Rights Advocate has stated that the FTB will not consider a single-member out-of-state LLC whose sole property is an out-of-state vacation home to be doing business in California if the only use of the residence is personal use by the owner of the LLC and the sole expenses and activities are those associated with mere ownership of the property, such as paying taxes. (*Tax News*, California Franchise Tax Board, May 2010, CCH CALIFORNIA TAX REPORTS, ¶ 405-181)

A tiered entity is considered doing business in California if it is a nonregistered foreign LLC that is a member of an LLC doing business in California or it is a general partner in a limited partnership that is doing business in California. Beginning with the 2011 taxable year, LLCs that are limited partners in a limited partnership may be considered to be doing business in California, see ¶ 804. (FTB Pub. 3556, Limited Liability Company Filing Information (2011), CCH CALIFORNIA TAX REPORTS, ¶ 405-528)

An LLC is relieved of liability for the minimum tax if it

— files a timely final annual tax return for a taxable year with the Franchise Tax Board (FTB),

— does not do business in California after the end of the taxable year for which the final annual tax return was filed, and

— files a certificate of dissolution (LLC-3) or certificate of cancellation (Form LLC-4/7) with the Secretary of State's Office before the end of the 12-month period beginning with the date the final annual tax return was filed.

(Sec. 17947, Rev. & Tax. Code)

Also, a domestic LLC that has not conducted any business in California and that files a short-form certificate of cancellation (Form LLC-4/8) with the Secretary of State's Office within 12 months from the date that the articles of organization were filed is exempt from the minimum tax, provided that the following criteria are satisfied:

— the LLC has no debts or liabilities, other than tax liabilities;

— the known assets of the LLC have been distributed to the entitled persons;

— the LLC has filed or will file a final tax return with the FTB;

— the dissolution of the LLC is authorized by a majority of the members or managers, or the person or majority of persons who signed the articles of organization; and

— all payments the LLC has received for interests from investors have been returned to the investors.

¶625

However, the LLC will not be entitled to a refund of any taxes or fees already paid. (Sec. 17941, Rev. & Tax. Code) (Instructions, Form 568, Limited Liability Company Return of Income) See ¶816 for the minimum tax rate.

CCH Caution: Exemption From Minimum Tax Available to Certain LLCs Owned by Military Personnel on Deployment

An LLC that is a small business with total income from all sources derived from, or attributable to, the state of $250,000 or less that is solely owned by a deployed member of the U.S. Armed Forces is not subject to the annual LLC tax for any taxable year that the owner is deployed and the LLC operates at a loss or ceases operation. The exemption is available for the 2010—2017 tax years. (Sec. 17941(f), Rev. & Tax. Code)

In situations where the entity is winding up its business operations, the entity may be considered to have ceased operations for tax purposes if it:

— is not engaged in any active business operations beyond the close of its taxable year;

— files final tax returns with the IRS and the FTB and delivers a certificate of dissolution or a certificate of cancellation to the California Secretary of State within 12 months of the filing date of the final return;

— has zero gross income and zero gross expenses for the taxable year;

— discontinues all business operations during the taxable year, but during the following year must defend itself in a lawsuit in state or federal court;

— discontinues all business operations during the taxable year, but resumes operations during the following taxable year, provided that it (1) ceases operations contemporaneously with the deployment; (2) ceases operations for at least one month during the taxable year; (3) does not resume operations during the taxable year; and (4) ceases operations for at least three months, even if this period extends into the following taxable year.

(*FTB Legal Ruling 2011-03*, CCH California Tax Reports, ¶405-438)

The tax is due by the 15th day of the fourth month after the beginning of the taxable year. (The taxable year of an LLC that was not previously in existence begins when the LLC is organized, registered, or begins doing business in California.) If the 15th day of the fourth month of the taxable year has passed before an existing foreign LLC commences business in California or registers with the Secretary of State, the tax should be paid immediately after commencing business in California or registering with the Secretary of State. The LLC is liable for the tax until it files a certificate of dissolution or cancellation of registration or of articles of organization with the California Secretary of State.

CCH Example: When to Pay the Annual LLC Tax

DDLLC, a newly formed calendar-year taxpayer, organizes as an LLC in Delaware on June 1. DDLLC registers with the California Secretary of State on August 12, and begins doing business in California on August 13. Because DDLLC's initial tax year began on June 1, it must pay an annual LLC tax by September 15 (the 15th day of the fourth month of its short-period taxable year). Thereafter, its annual LLC tax is due on April 15 of each year.

The minimum tax is submitted with FTB 3522, LLC Tax Voucher and should not be submitted along with the Form 568. (Instructions, Form 568, Limited Liability Company Return of Income)

¶625

• *Fee*

Additionally, other than exempt title-holding companies, every LLC classified as a partnership or treated as a sole proprietorship and subject to the minimum tax must pay an annual fee. The fees are permanently set as follows (Sec. 17942, Rev. & Tax. Code):

— $900 if the total income of the LLC from all sources derived from or attributable to California for the taxable year is at least $250,000 but less than $500,000;

— $2,500 if the LLC's total income derived from or attributable to California is at least $500,000 but less than $1 million;

— $6,000 if the LLC's total income derived from or attributable to California is at least $1 million but less than $5 million; and

— $11,790 if the total income derived from or attributable to California is $5 million or more.

For purposes of these provisions, California-source income is determined using the rules for assigning sales under California's apportionment provisions, other than those provisions that exclude receipts from the sales factor. (Sec. 17942, Rev. & Tax. Code)

CCH Tip: Deductibility of Fee

The LLC fee is generally considered an ordinary and necessary expense paid or incurred in carrying on the LLC's trade or business and is deductible on the LLC's Form 568 as an "other deduction." (*FTB Tax News*, August 2011, CCH CALIFORNIA TAX REPORTS, ¶405-488)

Excluded from total income derived from or attributable to California are allocations or attributions of income, gain, or distributions to one LLC in its capacity as a member of, or holder of an economic interest in, another LLC if the allocations or attributions are directly or indirectly attributable to income that is included in determining the annual fee payable by the other LLC. A regulation clarifies that even if the LLC that makes the distribution does not actually pay the LLC fee because it did not have enough total California-source income to be liable for the fee, the distribution would be excluded because the LLC making the distribution was still subject to the LLC fee. If, however, multiple LLCs are formed primarily to reduce the annual fees payable by members of a group of commonly controlled LLCs, the FTB may determine that the total income of a commonly controlled LLC is the aggregate total income of *all* the commonly controlled group members. (Sec. 17942, Rev. & Tax. Code; Reg. 17942, 18 C.C. R)

CCH Tip: Calculation of Fee

In a situation involving a California LLC with two or more members that is classified as a partnership for tax purposes and that holds real property for sale to customers in the ordinary course of its trade or business, if the LLC sells the property that was held for sale to customers in the ordinary course of its trade or business, the adjusted basis in the property will be added back to the LLC's gross income for purposes of calculating the LLC fee. On the other hand, if the LLC sells real property that was held for investment purposes, the adjusted basis in the property will not be added back to the LLC's gross income for purposes of calculating the LLC fee. (*Legal Ruling 2016-01*, July 14, 2016, CCH CALIFORNIA TAX REPORTS, ¶406-528)

CCH Tip: Simplified Calculation of Fee

A regulation allows an LLC with a sales factor numerator in excess of $5 million to simply use its sales factor numerator, without adjustment, as a proxy for "total income from all sources derived from or attributable to this state" for purposes of calculating the LLC fee without having to look at each item of income individually, because the LLC will already exceed the threshold for imposition of the maximum LLC fee. An LLC with a sales factor numerator of less than $5 million may use the sales factor numerator amount as the starting point for the calculation of its fee, but then must: (1) assign all items of total income from all sources that were previously assigned as nonbusiness income for apportionment purposes; (2) assign all items of total income from all sources that were excluded from the sales factor numerator; and (3) remove all items of total income that were derived from or attributable to other LLCs that were subject to the LLC fee. (Reg. 17942, 18 C.C. R)

Prior to the 2007 taxable year, the fee was based on an LLC's worldwide income rather than on the LLC's California-source income.

CCH Comment: Constitutionality of Former LLC Fee Scheme

A California court of appeal has ruled that California's pre-2007 taxable year LLC fee scheme as applied to an out-of-state LLC that had registered as an LLC with the California Secretary of State's office but that had no income from activities in California amounted to an unfairly apportioned tax in violation of the U.S. Constitution's Commerce and Due Process Clauses. The court ordered a refund of all LLC fees paid by the out-of-state LLC, plus interest and penalties and the FTB did not appeal the portion of the ruling declaring the tax unconstitutional as applied to the taxpayer. (*Northwest Energetic Services, LLC v. California Franchise Tax Board*, (2008) 159 Cal.App. 4th 841, CCH CALIFORNIA TAX REPORTS, ¶404-550) Another California court of appeal also found that the LLC fee was an unconstitutional unapportioned tax, but held that in the case of a taxpayer with income from both inside and outside California, the proper remedy to be applied to the unapportioned tax was to refund the difference between the amount of the fee paid by the taxpayer and the amount of the fee that would have been required had the fee been fairly apportioned. (*Ventas Finance I, LLC v. California Franchise Tax Board*, (2008) 165 Cal.App.4th 1207, petition for review denied, California Supreme Court, No. S166870, November 13, 2008, CCH CALIFORNIA TAX REPORTS, ¶404-709, petition for certiori denied, U.S. Supreme Court, Dkt. 08-1022, April 6, 2009). Two other cases that challenge the constitutionality of the LLC fee as applied to an LLC that conducted all of its activities in California have been filed (*Bakersfield Mall, LLC v. Franchise Tax Board*, San Francisco Superior Court, No. CGC-07-462728 and *CA-Centersie II, LLC v. Franchise Tax Board*, Fresno Superior Court, No. 10CECG00434). These cases have been consolidated as *FTB LLC Tax Refund Cases Judicial Council Coordination Proceeding No. 4742* and proceedings are being held to determine whether these actions may proceed as a class action.

The FTB has outlined the procedures that taxpayers with no income from activities in California should follow to have their refunds processed in light of the California Court of Appeal's final decision in *Northwest Energetic Services*, see *FTB Notice 2008-2*, April 14, 2008, CCH CALIFORNIA TAX REPORTS, ¶404-656. *FTB Notice 2009-04*, May 22, 2009, CCH CALIFORNIA TAX REPORTS, ¶404-916, outlines the refund procedures to be followed by LLCs with income attributable to sources both inside and outside California. LLCs with income attributable solely to California should follow the protective claim procedures outlined by the FTB on its Web site.

Legislation enacted in 2007 (Ch. 381 (A.B. 198), Laws 2007), revised the basis of the fee from one based on the LLC's total income to the LLC's total income apportionable to California, but only on a prospective basis. The Legislature stated its intent that no inference be drawn in connection with the legislative amendments for any taxable year beginning before 2007. However, for refund actions filed after October 10, 2007, or for refund actions filed prior to such date that are not final as of October 10, 2007, if the LLC fee as imposed prior to the 2007 taxable year is finally adjudged to be discriminatory or unfairly apportioned under California or federal law, the fee of any disfavored taxpayer that files a timely claim for refund asserting discrimination or unfair apportionment will be recomputed, but only to the extent necessary to remedy the discrimination or unfair apportionment. Such refunds will be limited to the amount by which the fee paid, plus any interest assessed, exceeds the amount of the fee that would have been assessed if the fee had been determined pursuant to the new provisions. (Sec. 19394, Rev. & Tax. Code)

Estimated fee payment: LLCs are required to make an estimated LLC fee payment equal to 100% of the taxpayer's liability for the current year by the 15th day of the sixth month of the current taxable year. (Sec. 17942(d), Rev. & Tax. Code) A 10% underpayment penalty will be imposed if the estimated fee paid by the LLC is less than the amount of the fee actually due and payable with the LLC's return. However, no penalty will be imposed if the estimated fee equals or exceeds the amount of the fee paid by the LLC in the preceding taxable year.

CCH Caution: Differences From Corporate Estimated Tax Exceptions

Unlike the corporation estimated tax prior tax year exception, there is no requirement that the prior tax year be a full 12 months and no penalty will be imposed for the LLC's first year filing in California. However, the LLC estimated fee penalty may not be waived for reasonable cause. (*Tax News*, California Franchise Tax Board, May 31, 2010, CCH CALIFORNIA TAX REPORTS, ¶405-193)

• *Returns*

LLCs classified as partnerships: An LLC classified as a partnership must file a return (Form 568) by the 15th day of the third month after the close of its taxable year. For taxable years beginning before January 1, 2016, the return due date was the 15th day of the fourth month after the close of its taxable year. (Sec. 18633.5, Rev. & Tax. Code) LLC returns may be filed electronically. The LLC must attach to the return a Schedule K-1 (568) for each member containing the member's name, address, and taxpayer identification number and the amount of the member's distributive share of the LLC's income, deductions, credits, etc. Also, when the LLC files its return, it must do one of the following:

— attach the agreement of each nonresident member to file a return, make timely tax payments, and be subject to personal jurisdiction in this state for purposes of the collection of income taxes (FTB 3832) (see ¶619 for details), or

— pay tax on behalf of each nonconsenting nonresident member, computed by multiplying the member's distributive share of income by the highest marginal tax rate in effect.

CCH Tip: Schedule EO, Pass-Through Entity Ownership

Schedule EO, Pass-Through Entity Ownership, is used to report pass-through entity ownership interests in entities that file federal Form 1065 or that are disregarded. This schedule is completed by partnerships and LLCs taxable as partnerships that hold partial ownership interest in other partnerships, LLCs taxable as partnerships, and/or own disregarded entities, including single member limited liability companies (SMLLC) that are disregarded. Taxpayers must identify by name, Secretary of State file number, and Federal Employee Identification Number all partnerships (including LLCs taxable as partnerships) in which the taxpayer holds a partial interest and all disregarded entities in which the taxpayer has full ownership. In addition, the taxpayer must indicate which entities received California source income, and must provide the profit and loss sharing percentages used to compute the amount of income received by the owner. S corporations do not complete this schedule, nor are partnerships or LLCs required to report S corporation pass-through income. (Instructions, Schedule EO, Pass-Through Entity Ownership)

The return must be verified by a written declaration that it is made under the penalties of perjury, and it must be signed by one of the LLC members or managers. A copy of each member's Schedule K-1 (568) must be provided to that member. Unrelated business taxable income of an LLC must be separately stated to the members.

Penalties are authorized for the failure to file an LLC return or provide LLC information as required by the FTB. (Sec. 19172, Rev. & Tax. Code) Penalties are discussed in detail at ¶712.

CCH Tip: Use Proper Form to Avoid Penalties

Many LLCs classified as partnerships, especially foreign LLCs, mistakenly file a Form 565, Partnership Return, rather than a Form 568, LLC Return. According to the FTB, when such LLCs file a Form 565, the FTB processes the return as a partnership and creates a new account and applies any payments made to that new account number. Because a Form 568 isn't filed, the FTB also issues a delinquent notice and assess penalties for not filing. In some instances, though the incorrect tax return was filed, the correct LLC Tax Voucher (Form 3522) was submitted with the payment. The payment is then applied to the LLC account, but the return is on the new account number.

LLCs may file a Form 565 if they meet the requirements for *Finanz* status (see *Appeal of Amman & Schmid Finanz AG, et-al* (1986) CCH CALIFORNIA TAX REPORTS, ¶402-852). Generally, only foreign LLCs that are limited partners of partnerships doing business in the state qualify. Additionally, post-2010 changes to the definition of "doing business" in Rev. & Tax. Code §23101 (see ¶804) may result in entities previously eligible for *Finanz* treatment being disqualified. (*FTB Tax News*, March 2011, CCH CALIFORNIA TAX REPORTS, ¶405-386)

LLCs treated as sole proprietorships: An owner of an LLC that is disregarded and treated as a sole proprietorship is required to file a California return if the LLC is doing business in California, is organized in California, or is registered with the Secretary of State. The return must contain information necessary to verify the tax liability for the minimum tax and LLC fees and must be filed by the 15th day of the fourth month after the close of the owner's taxable year. If the owner fails to comply with the reporting and payment requirements, the LLC will be liable for California tax at an amount equal to the highest marginal tax rate and will be subject to penalties and interest for failure to timely pay the amount due.

LLCs with nonresident members: An LLC with nonresident members must file FTB 3832, Limited Liability Company Nonresident Members' Consent, along with Form 568, when one of its members is a nonresident of California. Form FTB 3832 must be filed for the first taxable period for which the LLC became subject to tax with nonresident members and for any taxable year in which the LLC had a nonresident member not previously listed on form FTB 3832 (Instructions, Form FTB 3832, Limited Liability Company Nonresident Members' Consent). The LLC is required to pay the tax on the member's distributive share of income at that member's highest marginal tax rate if the member fails to sign FTB 3832.

Nonregistered foreign LLCs: Nonregistered foreign LLCs that are not doing business in, but that are deriving income from California or that are filing to report an election on behalf of a California resident, should file Form 565, Partnership Return of Income. Nonregistered foreign LLCs that are members of an LLC doing business in California or general partners in a limited partnership doing business in California are considered doing business in California and are required to file a Form 568, Limited Liability Company Return of Income. (Instructions, Form 568 Booklet, Limited Liability Return of Income)

CCH Comment: LLC Suspension/Forfeiture Program

The FTB will suspend/forfeit the rights, powers, and privileges of LLCs for nonpayment of taxes, penalties, or interest, and/or failure to file a return. The FTB will send notification to all entities at their last known addresses, 60 days before imposing the suspension/forfeiture. Nonregistered LLCs acting and filing in California will be subject to contract voidability. The reasons for contract voidability are the same as for suspension/forfeiture: failure to file a return, and/or failure to pay taxes, penalties, or interest. (*FTB Tax News* (October 2008), CCH CALIFORNIA TAX REPORTS, ¶404-769)

¶625

• *Withholding*

An LLC may be subject to three different withholding requirements. An LLC is required to withhold on amounts paid to nonresident domestic members, but only if the income paid to the nonresident exceeds $1,500 during the calendar year or the LLC is directed to withhold by the FTB. (Sec. 18662, Rev. & Tax. Code; Reg. 18662-2, 18 CCR) The tax is equal to 7% of the amount actually distributed to the member. (Sec. 18662, Rev. & Tax. Code; Reg. 18662-3, 18 CCR)

Different rules apply to the withholding required for LLCs treated as partnerships for amounts paid to nonresident foreign members. These amounts are subject to withholding at the highest personal income tax rate and are applied to the nonresident's distributive share of income. (Sec. 18666, Rev. & Tax. Code)

Finally, if the LLC fails to file an nonresident member agreement to file a California return, the LLC must pay withholding on behalf of the nonresident member in an amount equal to the highest marginal tax rate in effect multiplied by the member's distributive share of LLC income, and reduced by any withholding amounts previously paid under either of the withholding requirements discussed above. (Sec. 18633.5, Rev. & Tax. Code). This is referred to as the nonconsenting nonresident's (NCNR) withholding tax. Because the NCNR tax is imposed at the same rate and on the same tax base as the foreign nonresident withholding tax, an LLC is not required to pay any additional NCNR withholding tax for nonresident foreign members for whom an agreement to file and pay tax was not filed.

However, an LLC must pay additional NCNR withholding tax on behalf of nonresident domestic members for whom an agreement was not filed. The withholding applies to those domestic nonresident members that do not satisfy the $1,500 threshold requirement of the domestic member withholding tax and also applies to the difference between the highest tax rate (up to 12.3% for individuals and up to 8.84% for corporations) and the 7% tax rate imposed under Sec. 18662. Additional amounts may also be due as a result of the different tax bases. The domestic nonresident member withholding tax is imposed on the amount actually distributed to members, while the NCNR withholding tax is imposed on the nonresident's distributive share of income allocable to California.

> **Example:** *Computing the NCNR withholding tax.* A nonresident domestic member had a $1,000 distributive share of income allocable to California, and only $900 was actually distributed. Under the domestic nonresident withholding requirements, the LLC is required to pay the $63 in withholding tax ($900 x 7%). If the LLC does not timely file the agreement, then the LLC is responsible for paying an additional NCNR member's tax of $30.00. This is equal to the difference between $93.00 (the tax due by multiplying 9.3% x $1,000) and the $63 previously paid.

For more detailed information concerning an LLC's withholding at source requirements and procedures, see ¶714.

• *Returns of LLC members*

Persons with membership or economic interests in an LLC are required to include in their California taxable income their share of the LLC's California-source income in the same manner as partners must include their distributive share of partnership income in their taxable income (¶619, ¶620). (Sec. 17087.6, Rev. & Tax. Code) As with nonresident partners of a partnership, nonresident members of an LLC may elect to file a group income tax return in lieu of filing individual returns (¶619). (Sec. 18535, Rev. & Tax. Code) The filing of FTB 3832, Limited Liability Company Nonresident Members' Consent, does not relieve the nonresident member from filing a California tax return.

Planning Note: Pros and Cons of Group Returns

On a group nonresident return, only the California source pass-through income or director's compensation is reported. The upside to the group return is that worldwide income does not need to be reported individually. However, the income reported on the group nonresident return is taxed at the highest marginal rate, currently at 12.3%. (FTB Tax News (April 2013) CCH CALIFORNIA TAX REPORTS, ¶ 405-867)

Planning Note: Inconsistent Items

Generally, members must report tax items shown on their Sch. K-1s and any attached schedules, the same way the LLC treated the items on its tax return. If the treatment on a member's return is inconsistent with the LLC treatment, or the LLC did not file a return, the member is required to attach a statement explaining the difference or to note that an LLC return has not been filed. Failure to attach this statement may result in the imposition of an accuracy-related penalty (see ¶712). (Instructions, Schedule K-1 (568), Members' Share of Income, Deductions, Credits, etc.)

• *Report to Secretary of State*

LLCs are required to file with the Secretary of State a biennial report showing names of managers or members and other information. The first report must be filed within 90 days of filing original articles of organization. Thereafter, reports are due biennially by the date indicated by the Secretary of State on the form mailed to the LLC. LLCs may file a brief statement in lieu of the biennial report in cases where no changes have occurred during the filing period. (Sec. 17060, Corp. Code)

PERSONAL INCOME TAX

CHAPTER 7
ADMINISTRATION, DEFICIENCIES, REFUNDS

¶701 Administration of Tax—General

Law: Secs. 5054, 22250–22255, Bus. & Prof. Code; Sec. 13943.1, Govt. Code; Secs. 18624-25, 19167, 19501-11, 19525, 19717, 21001-26, Rev. & Tax. Code (CCH CALIFORNIA TAX REPORTS, ¶34-601, 89-054—89-060, 89-064, 89-068, 89-222, 89-226).

Comparable Federal: Secs. 6060, 6107, 6109, 6694-96, 7421, 7430, 7811 (CCH U.S. MASTER TAX GUIDE ¶2517, 2518, 2719, 2796, 2707).

California income tax law is administered by the Franchise Tax Board (FTB), composed of the State Controller, the Director of the Department of Finance, and the Chairman of the State Board of Equalization. The chief administrative officer is the Executive Officer of the FTB. The FTB has broad powers to prescribe necessary rules and regulations, etc.

Practice Tip: Taxpayer Information Available on FTB's Web Site

The *My FTB Account* service available on the FTB's Web site enables taxpayers and practitioners to view the following information for a particular taxpayer:

— a taxpayer's last 25 estimated tax payments, estimate transfers, and extension payments made as a prepayment of the taxes owed;

— up to 60 recent payments made by a taxpayer and applied to a balance due and the total current balance due;

— a summary of up to 10 tax years with a balance and the total amount due;

— a summary of each tax year with a balance due;

— a maximum of four years of California wage and withholding information;

— up to three years of FTB-issued 1099-G and 1099-INT information; and

— a subscription to the FTB's estimated tax payment e-mail reminder service.

Additionally taxpayers may make a payment through WebPay or by credit card online. To access the information currently available, enter "myftb account" in the search bar of the FTB's Web site at http://www.ftb.ca.gov.

If an audit of a return is concluded with no change, the FTB will notify the taxpayer to that effect; this procedure is similar to the federal one. For the procedure in case of underpayment or overpayment, see subsequent paragraphs in this chapter.

The FTB and the Internal Revenue Service have exchanged tax-related data for many years. When an audit is conducted by either the FTB or the IRS, the results are reported to the other entity. See ¶106 regarding required California reporting of federal changes by taxpayers.

Practitioner Comment: U.S. Supreme Court Limits Nevada Supreme Court Judgment Against FTB

On April 19, 2016, the U.S. Supreme Court ruled in *Franchise Tax Board v. Gilbert Hyatt*, 576 U.S. __ (2016), that the full faith and credit clause does not require a state to substitute for its own statute the statute of another state, if doing so would violate the state's public policy, so long as it does not embody a policy of discrimination against the other state. Additionally, due to the Court's 4-4 split on the issue, it upheld the ability of private citizens to sue states in the courts of their sister states.

The genesis of the case began in 1991, when the taxpayer, Gilbert Hyatt (then a resident of California), allegedly relinquished his California residency to become a resident of Nevada (a state with no personal income tax). Hyatt asserts he became a Nevada resident in October of 1991, shortly before receiving substantial licensing fees from a patent he owned. The FTB, however, claims Hyatt remained a California resident until April of 1992 and issued notices of proposed assessments for 1991 and 1992.

Hyatt sued the FTB in Nevada state court alleging claims of negligence, intentional infliction of emotional distress, fraud, invasion of privacy, abuse of process, and breach of a confidential relationship, based in part on allegations that FTB auditors went through Hyatt's mail and garbage, and made anti-Semitic remarks in reference to him. In 2003, the case went before the U.S. Supreme Court, which held that Nevada was not required to provide the FTB with full immunity from suit as required by the applicable California statute, but rather Nevada was correct in providing only partial immunity from negligence claims consistent with Nevada law. *Franchise Tax Bd. Of Cal. v. Hyatt*, 538 U.S. 488 (2003). As a result, Hyatt's suit against the FTB for intentional torts was allowed to continue, and eventually a Nevada jury awarded Hyatt damages for emotional distress, invasion of privacy, fraud and punitive damages. See *Franchise Tax Bd. Of Cal. V. Hyatt*, 335 P.3d 125, 134 (2014). The Nevada Supreme Court remanded the claim for emotional distress, and reduced the damages for fraud; however, the court refused to apply the statutory cap of $50,000 per claim on damages that would have applied to Nevada agencies. Id. at 130.

On March 23, 2015, the FTB petitioned the U.S. Supreme Court to review the Nevada Supreme Court's decision, and on June 30, 2015, the Court granted certiorari as to whether: 1) Nevada may refuse to extend to sister states hauled into Nevada courts the same immunities Nevada enjoys in those courts, and 2) whether *Nevada v. Hall*, 440 U.S.

410 (1979), which permits a sovereign state to be hauled into the courts of another state without consent, should be overruled.

In its April 19, 2016, opinion, the U.S. Supreme Court held that the full faith and credit clause does not require a state to substitute for its own statute the statute of another state, if doing so would violate the state's public policy. However, the state's decision not to apply those laws must not embody a policy of discrimination against the other state. In explaining its refusal to apply Nevada's statutory cap of $50,000 for damages, the Nevada Supreme Court stated that California's system failed to provide adequate recourse to Nevada's citizens. The U.S. Supreme Court wrote that absent sufficient policy considerations to justify a special rule, Nevada's disregard for its own ordinary legal principles reflects a policy of hostility to the public acts of its sister state. As a result, the California Franchise Tax Board will receive protection under Nevada's $50,000 damage cap, as if the California FTB were a Nevada state agency.

On the issue of overruling *Nevada v. Hall*, the U.S. Supreme Court was split 4 - 4. Although Justice Scalia was present during oral arguments, he passed away before the court issued its final decision. Stephen Vladeck, a law professor at American University, suggests that if Justice Scalia had been part of the Court's opinion, the FTB may have succeeded in overruling *Nevada v. Hall*. However, being equally divided on the jurisdiction issue, the Court effectively upheld *Hall*. As a result, private citizens retain the ability to sue states in the courts of their sister states.

The fight between Hyatt and the FTB over residency status began over 20 years ago and the U.S. Supreme Court's decision does not end it. What remains includes a retrial on Hyatt's emotional distress damage claim, a residency determination before the California State Board of Equalization, and an additional dispute ongoing at the 9th Circuit Court of Appeals concerning Hyatt's suit for violation of Equal Protection and Due Process because of excessive delays. (*Hyatt v. Chiang*, No. 14-849, 2015 WL 545993 (E.D. Cal. Feb. 10, 2015), appeal docketed, No. 15-15296 (9th Cir. Feb. 19, 2015)). It appears that the Hyatt saga is likely to continue for some time.

Chris Whitney, Contributing Editor

• *Tax-return preparers*

Tax preparers must do the following:

— maintain a $5,000 bond for each individual preparing tax returns for another person;

— provide in writing to each customer the tax preparer's name, address, telephone number, and evidence of compliance with the bonding requirements before rendering tax return preparation services; and

— meet stringent educational requirements.

(Sec. 22250, Bus. & Prof. Code; Sec. 22252, Bus. & Prof. Code; Sec. 22255, Bus. & Prof. Code)

Conversely, tax preparers are prohibited from doing the following:

— making deposits instead of complying with the bonding requirements;

— making false, fraudulent, or misleading statements;

— having taxpayers sign documents containing blank spaces to be filled in after they have been signed;

— failing to sign taxpayers' returns;

— failing to maintain copies of returns prepared for customers; and

— failing to return taxpayers' records upon request.

(Sec. 22253, Bus. & Prof. Code)

Currently licensed public accountants, active members of the State Bar of California, employees of certain trust companies, financial institutions regulated by the state or federal government, and enrolled agents who practice before the IRS are exempt from these compliance provisions. (Sec. 22258, Bus. & Prof. Code)

Practice Tip: Signature Requirements

California tax returns, including corporation franchise and income, personal income, and sales and use tax returns, that are prepared by an employee of a tax preparer who is exempt from the California Tax Education Council (CTEC) registration requirements must be signed by a California certified public accountant, attorney, enrolled agent, or a tax preparer who is registered with the CTEC. However, this requirement does not apply to employees who are themselves exempt from the CTEC registration requirements, who are registered with the CTEC, or who are employees of a trust company or financial institution, at least with respect to the returns prepared within the scope of their employment. Tax return preparation includes inputting of tax data into a computer (Sec. 22258, Bus. & Prof. Code).

Tax preparers must be at least age 18. (Sec. 22250, Bus. & Prof. Code)

An individual or firm holding a valid and current license, certificate, or permit to practice public accountancy from another state may prepare tax returns for natural persons who are California residents or estate tax returns for the estates of natural persons who were clients at the time of death without obtaining a California permit to practice public accountancy or a practice privilege so long as the individual or firm does not physically enter California to practice public accountancy, does not solicit California clients, and does not assert or imply that the individual or firm is licensed or registered to practice public accountancy in California. (Sec. 5054, Bus. & Prof. Code)

Both federal and California laws also provide for the regulation of "income tax preparers." California law conforms to federal requirements for furnishing copies of returns to taxpayers, retaining certain records, and providing identification numbers (social security numbers or IRS-approved alternatives) of preparers on returns and refund claims. (Sec. 18624, Rev. & Tax. Code; Sec. 186245, Rev. & Tax. Code)

California Tax Education Council.—The California Tax Education Council (CTEC) is the governing body charged with issuing tax preparer registrations, reviewing application, taking disciplinary actions, and establishing and charging various fees in association therewith. (Sec. 22251.2, Bus. & Prof. Code) Registrations must be renewed annually. (Sec. 22251.3, Bus. & Prof. Code)

Violations.—The FTB is required to notify the CTEC when it identifies an individual who has violated specific provisions regulating tax preparers. The CTEC is required to notify the Attorney General, a district attorney, or a city attorney of the violation, and the person so notified may do any of the following:

— cite individuals preparing tax returns in violation of provisions governing tax preparers;

— levy a fine on such individuals not to exceed $5,000 per violation; and

— issue a cease and desist order effective until the tax preparer is in compliance with the registration requirement. (Sec. 22253.2, Bus. & Prof. Code)

In addition, the FTB is authorized to impose a penalty of up to $5,000 ($2,500 for first-time offenders) against a tax preparer that fails, without reasonable cause, to register with the CTEC. The penalty must be waived if proof of registration is provided to the FTB within 90 days from the date notice of the penalty is mailed to the tax preparer. The penalty will not be imposed unless there is an appropriation in the FTB's budget to implement the penalty or the CTEC agrees to finance the program. (Sec. 19167, Rev. & Tax. Code)

Other penalties are discussed at ¶712.

¶701

Confidentiality.—A tax preparer is prohibited, except in specified circumstances, from disclosing confidential information concerning a client or a prospective client without obtaining the client's written consent. However, tax preparers are allowed to make the following disclosures:

— in compliance with a subpoena or a summons enforceable by an order of court;

— regarding a client or prospective client to the extent the tax preparer reasonably believes it is necessary to maintain or defend himself or herself in a legal proceeding initiated by the client or prospective client;

— in response to an official inquiry from a federal or state government regulatory agency;

— to another tax preparer in connection with a proposed sale or merger of the tax preparer's professional practice;

— to another tax preparer to the extent necessary for purposes of professional consultation;

— to organizations that provide professional standards review and ethics or quality control peer review; and

— when specifically required by law.

(Sec. 22252.1, Bus. & Prof. Code)

• *Third-party designees*

Taxpayers may authorize a third party designee directly on their personal income tax returns by entering the designee's name and telephone number in the space provided below the taxpayer's signature. Designees may discuss information with the FTB needed to process the taxpayers' current year tax return; inquire about the status of a taxpayer's refunds or payments; respond to FTB notices about math errors, offsets, and return preparation; and also request copies of notices for the authorized tax year. However, designees may not discuss any other tax year with the FTB, receive any refund checks, make binding agreements on behalf of the taxpayer, or otherwise represent the taxpayer before the FTB.

A third-party designation authorization automatically ends no later than the due date (without regard to extensions) for filing the next year's return. Authorization may be revoked prior to that date by contacting the FTB at (800) 852-5711 or writing to: FTB, P.O. Box 942840 Sacramento, CA 94240-0040. (*Announcement*, California Franchise Tax Board, December 2, 2008)

• *Issuance of rulings by FTB*

See ¶ 703 for a discussion.

• *FTB audit and procedure manuals*

The FTB has issued several audit and procedure manuals for the guidance of its staff. These manuals may be purchased from the Technical Analysis Section of the FTB; prices will be quoted upon request. The manuals are also available on-line at http://www.ftb.ca.gov/aboutFTB/manuals/index.shtml.

Effective January 1, 2014, California launched a pilot program that established the Revenue Recovery and Collaborative Enforcement Team, comprised of participants from the State Board of Equalization (BOE), Franchise Tax Board (FTB), Employment Development Department (EDD), and Department of Justice (DOJ) to collaborate, share data, and criminally prosecute those who evade state sales and use, excise, corporate and personal income, and employment taxes. (Sec. 15910, Govt. Code, et seq.)

¶701

• *Recovery of litigation costs*

California law follows federal provisions that permit a taxpayer to recover litigation costs in a civil income tax proceeding if the taxpayer has exhausted all available administrative remedies, including the filing of an appeal before the State Board of Equalization, and the State is unable to establish that its position in the proceeding was substantially justified. (Sec. 21021, Rev. & Tax. Code)

Practitioner Comment: Taxpayer is Reimbursed Litigation Costs by California

On August 15, 2005, the California Court of Appeal, Fourth Appellate District, ruled in an uncitable decision that taxpayers were entitled to recover attorney fees incurred in litigation contesting the California FTB's denial of their California personal income tax refund claim. According to the Court, the FTB's position in the litigation was not substantially justified, so reimbursement of the taxpayers' attorney fees incurred during the trial, as well as the fees associated with filing the initial refund claim, participating in settlement negotiations, and opposing the FTB's motion for summary judgment was appropriate. The Court also ruled, however, that the lower court acted within its discretion in denying reimbursement for (1) attorney fees incurred in filing an unsuccessful cross-motion for summary judgment and (2) amounts billed the attorneys for outside paralegal services. (*Milhous v. Franchise Tax Board*, California Court of Appeal, Fourth Appellate District, No. D044362, August 15, 2005, CCH CALIFORNIA TAX REPORTS, ¶403-845)

The holding in *Milhous* makes it clear that while the FTB's position does not have to be a winning one, it does have to be justified. The Court stated, "...there is no basis upon which the FTB could attribute the lump sum payment the Milhouses received (at the close of the sale and before the buyers had control of the business) to capital in this state . . . .there was a good deal which undermined the FTB's position that income from the covenant was attributable to activities in this state. In particular, we note the quantum of evidence in the record which demonstrated that the covenant had no value in California because as a practical matter it was not possible to compete here."

Taxpayers should keep in mind that even if they prevail against the FTB, they still must exhaust all administrative remedies and they bear the burden of proving the FTB's position is not "substantially justified."

Attorney fees were also awarded to taxpayers in *American General Realty Investment Corp. v. Franchise Tax Board*, San Francisco Sup. Court, No. CGC-03-425690, April 28, 2005, CCH CALIFORNIA TAX REPORTS, ¶403-794, and *Fujitsu IT Holdings, Inc. v. Franchise Tax Board*, 120 Cal.App.4th 459, 15 Cal.Rptr.3d 473 (2004), CCH CALIFORNIA TAX REPORTS, ¶403-655.

Chris Whitney, Contributing Editor

Practitioner Comment: California Judge Awards Costs to Comcast in Tax Dispute with FTB

On February 9, 2015, a California state trial court judge ruled in favor of Comcast finding that it was the "prevailing party" under Code of Civil Procedure Sec. 1032. As the "prevailing party," Comcast was entitled to recover litigation costs. Sec. 1032 defines "prevailing party" to include the party with a "net monetary recovery."

Prior to litigation, Comcast paid the FTB approximately $28 million as required by Article XIII, Section 32 of the California Constitution to litigate the matter in court. Although the FTB largely prevailed at trial and retained $25 million, the judge ruled in favor of Comcast on the issue of whether it was unitary with QVC. Prevailing on this issue resulted in a $3 million refund to Comcast and therefore entitled Comcast to litigation costs. The judge rejected the FTB's position that Comcast did not receive a net monetary recovery because, after trial, the FTB retained much more of the tax paid than refunded as a result of the litigation. The judge also rejected the FTB's argument that it was the prevailing party because the $25 million it obtained at audit was money recovered for purposes of Sec. 1032's "net monetary recovery" requirement. The FTB asserted that a taxpayer in a refund action would only be successful if it received a refund of more than 50% of what was paid to the FTB prior to litigation. The judge rejected the FTB's interpretation of Sec. 1032 because it would treat tax refund actions differently than other civil litigation where courts have concluded prevailing party status in actions where a plaintiff was less than completely successful but still had a net monetary recovery. Further, the court noted that the FTB did not in essence "gain any money" because the money Comcast paid prior to litigation was required to be paid under the state constitution and the FTB was not required to take an action to obtain the funds.

Chris Whitney, Contributing Editor

• *Taxpayers' bill of rights*

The legislature provides for the safeguarding of taxpayer privacy and property rights during the tax collection process. See ¶702 for a discussion.

• *Enforcement program*

Additional information returns, including returns of tax-shelter promoters, are required as explained at ¶713 and ¶727. The FTB is empowered to employ private in-state as well as out-of-state collection agencies and add their compensation to the amount of tax due. The FTB may establish a reward program for information leading to the collection of underreported taxes.

• *Discharge of tax debts*

The FTB is authorized to discharge and extinguish the following liabilities for unpaid taxes, fees, or other uncollectible amounts due the state:

— a liability of less than $500;

— a liability of a person who has been deceased for more than four years for whom there is no active probate;

— a liability of a person with a permanent financial hardship; or

— a liability that has been unpaid for more than 30 years.

(Sec. 13943.1, Govt. Code)

¶702 Taxpayers' Bill of Rights

Law: Secs. 19225, 21001-28 (CCH California Tax Reports, ¶89-222).

Comparable Federal: Sec. 7811 (CCH U.S. Master Tax Guide ¶2755, 2707, 2708).

Taxpayers dealing with the Franchise Tax Board (FTB) are given a wide range of protections under the "Katz-Harris Taxpayers' Bill of Rights". (Sec. 21001, Rev. & Tax. Code) The provisions contained in the "Bill of Rights" are applicable to both the personal income and corporation franchise and income taxes. Similar "bills of rights" apply to unemployment insurance tax matters involving the Employment Development Department (¶715) and property and sales and use tax matters involving the State Board of Equalization (BOE) (¶1510, ¶1709).

• *Hearing and appeal procedures*

Protest hearings before the FTB's audit or legal staff must be held at times and places that are reasonable and convenient to the taxpayer. Prior to the hearing, the taxpayer must be informed of the right to have a designated agent present. Hearings may be recorded only with prior notice to the taxpayer, who is entitled to receive a copy of any such recording. (Sec. 21001, Rev. & Tax. Code) Protest hearings are discussed further at ¶704.

Taxpayers who appeal to the BOE and who are successful may be awarded reimbursement for reasonable fees and expenses related to the appeal that were incurred after the date of the notice of proposed deficiency assessment. The decision to make such an award is discretionary with the BOE, which must determine, in ruling on a reimbursement claim filed with the BOE, whether action taken by the FTB's staff was unreasonable, and in particular, whether the FTB has established that its position in the appeal was substantially justified. Fees may be awarded in excess of the fees paid or incurred if the fees paid or incurred are less than reasonable fees. (Sec. 21013, Rev. & Tax. Code) See ¶701 for more details.

For appeals to the BOE from an action of the FTB on a deficiency assessment protest or refund claim, the burden of proving the correctness of certain items of income reported by third parties on information returns filed with the FTB also shifts to the FTB if the taxpayer asserts a reasonable dispute with respect to the reported amounts and fully cooperates with the FTB. The items of income to which the shift applies are the same as under federal law. (Sec. 21024, Rev. & Tax. Code)

Appeals to the BOE are discussed further at ¶705 and ¶717.

• *Tax levy protections*

The FTB must send a notice of levy to a taxpayer at least 30 days prior to issuing a levy for unpaid tax. Also, if the FTB holds the collection of unpaid tax in abeyance for more than six months, the FTB is generally required to mail the taxpayer an additional notice prior to issuing a levy. A taxpayer may, within the 30-day period, request an independent administrative review and if a review is requested the levy action will be suspended until 15 days after there is a final determination in the review. (Sec. 21015.5, Rev. & Tax. Code)

Except in the case of property seized as a result of a jeopardy assessment, a previously issued tax levy must be released in the following situations:

— the expense of selling the property levied upon would exceed the taxpayer's liability;

— the proceeds of the sale would not result in a reasonable reduction of the taxpayer's debt;

— a determination is made by the Taxpayer Rights Advocate that the levy threatens the health or welfare of the taxpayer or the taxpayer's family;

— the levy was not issued in accordance with administrative procedures;

— the taxpayer has entered into an installment payment agreement with the FTB to satisfy the tax liability for which the levy was made, and nothing in the agreement or any other agreement allows for the levy;

— the release of the levy will facilitate the collection of the tax liability or will be in the best interest of the taxpayer and the State; or

— the FTB otherwise deems the release of the levy appropriate.

(Sec. 21016, Rev. & Tax. Code)

Certain household and other goods are exempted from levy under California's Code of Civil Procedure. The taxpayer must be notified in writing of these exemptions prior to the sale of any seized property. (Sec. 21017, Rev. & Tax. Code)

The FTB must release a levy on salary or wages as soon as practicable upon agreement with the taxpayer that the tax is not collectible. However, this requirement does not apply to any levy issued with respect to a debt that has been discharged because the tax debtor and/or the tax debtor's assets cannot be located, unless the debt is satisfied. (Sec. 21016, Rev. & Tax. Code)

• *Civil actions against the FTB; litigation costs*

Taxpayers aggrieved by the reckless disregard of the FTB's published procedures on the part of an officer or employee of the FTB may bring a superior court action against the state for actual damages. In determining damages, the court must take

¶702

into consideration any contributing negligence on the taxpayer's part. A taxpayer who prevails in such an action is entitled to reasonable litigation costs, but there is a penalty of up to $10,000 for filing frivolous claims. (Sec. 21021, Rev. & Tax. Code)

Taxpayers may also file a civil action against the State for direct economic damages and costs totaling up to $50,000 if an officer or employee of the FTB intentionally entices an attorney, certified public accountant, or tax preparer representing the taxpayer into disclosing taxpayer information in exchange for a compromise or settlement of the representative's tax liability. However, the action is not allowed if the information was conveyed by the taxpayer to the representative for the purpose of perpetuating a fraud or crime. The action must be brought within two years after the date the activities creating the liability were discoverable by the exercise of reasonable care. (Sec. 21022, Rev. & Tax. Code)

• *Reimbursement of third-party charges and fees*

A taxpayer may be reimbursed for third-party charges and fees assessed against a person as a result of an erroneous levy, erroneous processing action, or erroneous collection action by the FTB. The charges and fees that may be reimbursed are limited to the usual and customary charges and fees imposed by a business entity in the ordinary course of business. (Sec. 21018, Rev. & Tax. Code)

• *Reliance on FTB written opinions; taxpayers' remedies*

See ¶703 for a complete discussion.

• *Tax liens*

Practice Tip: Lien Threshold

Beginning in July 2013, the FTB increased the general guideline amount at which a new income tax lien will be filed from $1,000 to $2,000. The $2,000 amount is a guideline only, and the FTB reserves the right to file a lien for a balance less than this amount based on individual facts and circumstances. (*FTB Tax News* (July 2013) CCH CALIFORNIA TAX REPORTS, ¶405-903)

A taxpayer is entitled to preliminary notice of the proposed filing or recording of a tax lien, mailed at least 30 days beforehand, and an opportunity in the interim to demonstrate by substantial evidence that the lien would be in error. Also, at least five business days after the date the notice of lien is filed the FTB must notify taxpayers in writing of the filing or recording of a notice of state tax lien and the taxpayer's right to an independent administrative review. A taxpayer must request a review during the 15-day period beginning on the day after the five-day period described above. (Sec. 21019, Rev. & Tax. Code)

The FTB must mail a release to the taxpayer and the lien recorder within seven working days if it finds that its action was in error. The FTB may also release a lien if it determines that the release will facilitate the collection of tax or will be in the best interest of the taxpayer and the State.

Practice Tip: Relief Available to Taxpayers Facing Financial Hardships

The FTB can assist taxpayers facing financial hardships by establishing payment plans, granting relief from state tax liens, or delaying some collection actions. The FTB can generally grant relief from state tax liens within two weeks for financially distressed homeowners trying to sell or refinance their homes. The FTB may be able to remove its tax lien to assist a homeowner to complete a home sale when a home sells for less than the loan balance. The tax lien remains in effect on any other property the taxpayer currently holds or later acquires. The FTB can also help individuals who are refinancing or modifying an existing home loan by allowing the new or modified loan to have priority over the tax lien. (*Press Release*, California Franchise Tax Board, January 23, 2009)

• *Unassociated payments*

If the FTB receives a payment from a taxpayer that the FTB cannot associate with the taxpayer's account, the FTB must make reasonable efforts to notify the taxpayer of this situation within 60 days after receipt of the payment. (Sec. 21025, Rev. & Tax. Code)

• *Annual notice of tax delinquencies*

The FTB must mail an annual notice to each taxpayer who has a delinquent tax account, indicating the amount of the delinquency as of the date of the notice, unless a previously mailed notice has been returned to the FTB as undeliverable or the account has been discharged from accountability. (Sec. 21026, Rev. & Tax. Code)

• *Client/tax practitioner communications*

California conforms to federal law extending the lawyer-client privilege to communications between clients and federally authorized tax practitioners with respect to non-criminal tax matters before the FTB, the BOE, or the Employment Development Department. The privilege does not apply to written communications concerning the promotion of the direct or indirect participation in any abusive tax shelters. (Sec. 21028, Rev. & Tax. Code)

• *Other provisions*

The Taxpayers' Bill of Rights also obligates the FTB to undertake extensive taxpayer education and information programs; report annually to the legislature concerning areas of noncompliance with the tax laws; develop simplified written statements of taxpayer rights and FTB procedures; develop and implement an employee and officer evaluation program; and draw up plans to reduce the time required to resolve amended return claims for refunds, protests, and appeals. (Sec. 21001, Rev. & Tax. Code) The FTB is authorized to settle certain civil tax disputes (¶722) and the Taxpayers' Rights Advocate is authorized to abate penalties, interest, fees, and additions to tax under specified circumstances (¶712). FTB officers and employees are prohibited from authorizing, requiring, or conducting an investigation or surveillance of taxpayers for reasons unrelated to tax administration. (Sec. 21014, Rev. & Tax. Code)

¶703 Reliance on FTB's Advice

Law: Sec. 21012 (CCH CALIFORNIA TAX REPORTS, ¶89-222, 89-226).

Comparable Federal: Sec. 6404(f) (CCH U.S. MASTER TAX GUIDE ¶2813, 2838).

Under the "Taxpayers' Bill of Rights" (¶702), taxpayers may be relieved from penalties, interest, and even tax liability itself in certain cases in which there was detrimental reliance on written advice from the Franchise Tax Board (FTB). (Sec. 21012, Rev. & Tax. Code)

• *Taxpayer's reliance on FTB rulings*

The following concerns the waiver of tax, penalties, and interest in situations in which the taxpayer relied on the FTB's own written advice (*FTB Notice No. 2009-8*, CCH CALIFORNIA TAX REPORTS, ¶404-992). A taxpayer may not rely on a Chief Counsel Ruling issued to another taxpayer.

—*Waiver of tax:* If a taxpayer's failure to timely file or pay is due to reasonable reliance on a Chief Counsel Ruling or an Opinion Letter, the taxpayer may be relieved—under the proper conditions (see below)—of having to pay *the tax itself*, as well as any interest, penalty, or addition to the tax.

—*Waiver of penalties, interest, and additions to tax only:* If the taxpayer relies on FTB correspondence other than Chief Counsel Rulings or Opinion Letters, such as standard computer-generated letters issued in response to frequently asked questions, the taxpayer may be relieved—under the proper conditions (see below)—of having to pay any interest, penalty, or addition to the tax. The taxpayer will not be relieved of having to pay the tax itself.

—*Conditions for waiver:* All of the following conditions must be met for the taxpayer to receive a waiver:

— the taxpayer must have made a written request that the FTB indicate whether a particular activity or transaction is taxable and must have described in the request all of the facts and circumstances involved;

— the FTB must have responded in writing, stating whether the activity was taxable or the conditions under which it would be taxable;

— the taxpayer must have failed to remit tax in reliance on the FTB's advice;

— the FTB's ruling must not have been revoked before the taxpayer relied on it; and

— there must have been no change in applicable state or federal law or in the facts or circumstances of the taxpayer's case.

• *How to make a proper advance ruling request*

A written request for an advance ruling must contain the taxpayer's name, identifying number, a statement of all facts relating to the transaction, entity, plan, or arrangement from which the tax question arises, and true or certified copies of all contracts, deeds, agreements, instruments, or other documents. In addition, the request must disclose if the same question arose in a prior year's return, an ongoing audit, protest, or appeal, or litigation involving the taxpayer. If the requestor is a professional preparer or paid representative acting on behalf of the taxpayer, the requestor must provide (1) his or her legal analysis, including legal authority and his or her conclusion, (2) a draft of the requested ruling, and (3) a draft redacted version of such ruling for release to the public. (*FTB Notice No. 2009-8*, CCH CALIFORNIA TAX REPORTS, ¶404-992)

Practice Tip: How a Taxpayer May Seek Relief

If the FTB acts in a way that appears inconsistent with its written advice to the taxpayer, the taxpayer may seek relief following one of two courses. If the advice was not issued by the FTB's legal division, the taxpayer must file FTB 3910 (Request for Waiver of Tax, Penalty or Interest). If the advice was issued by the FTB's Chief Counsel or another member of the FTB's legal division, the taxpayer must mail a written request for relief to the Chief Counsel, enclosing the following:

— a copy of the original written request for an opinion and the FTB's written response,

— documentation of the adverse action subsequently taken by the FTB, and

— a sworn statement that describes the activity or transaction in which the taxpayer engaged and that states that the failure to remit tax was due to reliance on the FTB's opinion. The request for relief must be made separately from any protest or appeal filed by the taxpayer.

(*FTB Notice No. 2009-9*, CCH CALIFORNIA TAX REPORTS, ¶404-993) Also, see ¶712 for a discussion of the Taxpayers' Rights Advocate's authority to abate penalties, interest, and additions to tax under specified circumstances.

• *Oral advice*

The FTB may also respond to individual queries with nonbinding oral advice, which is purely advisory. A taxpayer who relies on such advice is not entitled to the relief provisions of the Taxpayers' Bill of Rights (*FTB Notice No. 2009-8*, CCH CALIFORNIA TAX REPORTS, ¶404-992).

• *Effect of federal regulations and procedures*

The FTB will generally follow federal regulations, procedures, and rulings in situations in which the California provisions substantially conform to those of federal law. However, federal rulings and procedures are not binding on the FTB if the FTB has publicly indicated in writing that the federal ruling or procedure will not be followed (FTB Notice No. 89-277, *supra*).

¶704 Deficiencies—Procedure, Protests

Law: Secs. 18416, 19031-36, 19041-44, 19050-51, 19133 (CCH CALIFORNIA TAX REPORTS, ¶ 89-164, 89-228, 89-238, 89-240).

Comparable Federal: Secs. 6103, 6201, 6211-13 (CCH U.S. MASTER TAX GUIDE ¶ 2711—2713).

If the Franchise Tax Board (FTB) determines after examining an original or amended return or related electronically stored return that additional tax is payable, it may proceed in any one of the following ways:

— if the additional tax is due to a mathematical error, the FTB sends the taxpayer a notice and requests payment of the tax; the taxpayer has no right of protest or appeal in such cases (Sec. 19051, Rev. & Tax. Code);

— if the FTB is of the opinion that collection of the deficiency will be jeopardized by delay, it may make a jeopardy assessment (¶707);

— if the taxpayer fails to make a required return after notice and demand by the FTB, the FTB may estimate the income and levy the tax from any available information; in such cases the tax is immediately due and payable, without administrative remedies prior to payment, and a special penalty of 25% of the tax is added (¶712); and

— in other cases the FTB will mail to the taxpayer a notice of proposed deficiency assessment (sometimes referred to as an NPA), which must include an explanation of the adjustments made, a computation of the deficiency, and the date determined by the FTB as the last day on which the taxpayer may file a written protest.

(Sec. 19033, Rev. & Tax. Code)

These procedures may also be followed if the return or data is unavailable and the taxpayer fails to provide the return within 30 days (60 days if good cause exists) of a request by the FTB.

Comment: Notice Procedures

The FTB must mail notices to the taxpayer's last known address, which is defined as the address that appears on the taxpayer's last return filed with the FTB, unless the taxpayer has provided to the FTB clear and concise written or electronic notification of a different address, or the FTB has an address it has reason to believe is the most current address for the taxpayer. (Sec. 18416, Rev. & Tax. Code) In addition, all notices concerning proposed and final deficiencies must include a U.S. postal service postmark. (Sec. 19033, Rev. & Tax. Code, Sec. 19049, Rev. & Tax. Code)

In *Appeal of Holland* (2004) (CCH CALIFORNIA TAX REPORTS, ¶ 89-164.451), a case in which a taxpayer failed to report federal changes made to a tax return filed more than 10 years earlier, the State Board of Equalization (BOE) held that the FTB's estimate of the taxpayer's income that was based on the use of an income figure in the median amount of taxable income corresponding to a zero tax liability was arbitrary and unreasonable given that the federal returns for the corresponding year showed the taxpayer's taxable income to be less than the FTB's estimate by more than $300,000. Because the FTB had access to the federal returns and to electronically stored data concerning the taxpayer's income for the taxable year at issue, the BOE refused to uphold the FTB's estimated income figure.

Similarly, in *Appeal of Degnan* (2009) (CCH CALIFORNIA TAX REPORTS, ¶405-117), the BOE modified the FTB's proposed assessment that was based on the FTB's finding that 100% of the previously unreported partnership/trust income of taxpayers who were either nonresidents or part-year residents for the tax year in question was California source income. According to the BOE, the FTB's assessment had no reasonable and rational basis and was arbitrary. The federal determination upon which the California assessment was based did not address whether any portion of the unreported federal taxable income was from California sources, and the FTB provided no explanation as to why it classified all of the income shown in the federal determination as California source income. Although a presumption exists that the FTB's reconstruction was correct, the absence of adequate tax records did not give the FTB "carte blanche for imposing Draconian absolutes."

In *Appeal of Melvin D. Collamore* (1972) (CCH CALIFORNIA TAX REPORTS, ¶16-825.89), involving the personal income tax, and in *Appeal of Kung Wo Company, Inc.* (1953) (CCH CALIFORNIA TAX REPORTS, ¶89-144.70), involving the franchise tax, the BOE held that the FTB can properly make two deficiency assessments against a taxpayer for the same taxable year.

• *Carryover adjustments*

The FTB may serve a taxpayer with notice of a proposed carryover adjustment in regards to any amount of credit, loss, deduction, or any other item shown on a return, including an amended return reporting federal adjustments, if the FTB determines that the amount disclosed by the taxpayer is greater than that disclosed by the FTB's own examination. The proposed adjustment becomes final 30 days after its determination, unless either the FTB or the taxpayer files a petition for rehearing within that 30-day period. Once final, the FTB's carryover adjustment is binding and conclusive except in certain circumstances. A taxpayer's failure to comply with a final carryover adjustment in subsequent tax years is treated as a mathematical error, precluding a taxpayer from subsequent appeals. (Sec. 19043.5, Rev. & Tax. Code)

• *Protest*

A taxpayer who does not agree with the notice of proposed deficiency assessment may file a protest. The protest must be filed within 60 days from the mailing date of the notice of proposed assessment. Other than extensions available for military personnel serving in combat zones (¶109) and disaster victims (Sec. 18572, Rev. & Tax. Code), there is no provision for extension of time for filing a protest. Any protest filed by the last day for filing the protest, as specified by the FTB in a notice of proposed deficiency assessment, will be treated as timely filed. (Sec. 19041, Rev. & Tax. Code)

CCH Comment: Faxing of Protest

Taxpayers may send a protest of a notice of proposed assessment by faxing the protest to (916) 364-2754. (*Tax News*, California Franchise Tax Board, February 26, 2010)

The FTB has established internal procedures pursuant to which it will attempt to process all docketed protests within a two-year period. Protests will be categorized as 12-month, 18-month, or 24-month protests depending upon whether the protest involves an issue for which the FTB already has an established litigating position, the number and complexity of the legal issues involved, and how much factual development is required. (*FTB Notice 2006-6*, California Franchise Tax Board, October 27, 2006, CCH CALIFORNIA TAX REPORTS, ¶404-078)

• *Oral hearing*

A request for an oral hearing must be made in the protest. Unless otherwise specified in the request, the hearing usually will be arranged at the branch office of the FTB nearest to the taxpayer's address. A taxpayer who wishes to be represented by others at the hearing should so state in the written protest; arrangements will be made accordingly. The oral hearings are informal. (Sec. 19044, Rev. & Tax. Code)

• *Power of attorney*

No power of attorney is required as evidence of the authority of the taxpayer's representative to discuss the case, provided the taxpayer has indicated, in the protest or otherwise, a desire to be so represented. However, a representative may not take any definite action on the taxpayer's behalf without a power of attorney definitely authorizing the representative to act. The FTB provides FTB 3520 for this purpose. There is no requirement that representatives be admitted to practice or have particular qualifications to be eligible to represent taxpayers.

Joint filers must complete and submit a separate FTB Form 3520 for each spouse/registered domestic partner. Taxpayers may authorize their representatives to represent them for all matters regardless of income or tax year. This authority automatically expires four years from the date the power of attorney is signed or when a new one is filed.

¶705 Deficiencies—Appeal to State Board of Equalization

Law: Secs. 19045-48 (CCH California Tax Reports, ¶89-234).

Comparable Federal: Secs. 6211-15 (CCH U.S. Master Tax Guide ¶2711).

Upon receiving notice of action by the Franchise Tax Board (FTB) on the taxpayer's protest, the taxpayer may appeal to the State Board of Equalization (BOE). The appeal must be filed by the appeal filing date specified in the FTB's notice (within 30 days of the date of the FTB's notice). The FTB's action becomes final at the expiration of the 30-day period if no appeal is filed. (Sec. 19045, Rev. & Tax. Code)

Two copies of the appeal and two copies of any supporting documents must be sent to the BOE in Sacramento, which will send a copy of each document to the FTB. (Sec. 19046, Rev. & Tax. Code)

• *Requirements for appeal*

BOE Regulation 5420 covering hearing procedures before the BOE provides that the appeal must be in writing, should state the fact that an appeal is being made, and should include the following information:

— name of appellant (or appellants);

— the social security number or taxpayer identification number of each appellant;

— the address and telephone number of each appellant and each appellant's authorized representative;

— amounts (including tax, penalties, fees, and interest) and years involved;

— copy of the FTB notice from which the appeal is made;

— statement of facts;

— points and authorities in support of the taxpayer's position;

— statement of portion of tax the taxpayer concedes is owing; and

— signature of appellant (or appellants) or authorized representative.

The appeal may be supplemented at a later date, provided the original appeal is filed timely. If additional data is requested by the BOE and it is not provided by the taxpayer within the time requested (including reasonable extensions of time granted by the BOE), the appeal may be dismissed. Upon receipt of an appeal, the BOE gives the FTB an opportunity to file an answer, and gives the taxpayer an opportunity to file a reply if desired.

• *Hearing on appeal*

The BOE will set a time and place for hearing on the appeal and will so notify the taxpayer or the taxpayer's representatives. Hearings are more formal than the oral hearings before the FTB, sworn testimony being taken and other formalities observed. Taxpayers' representatives are not required to be admitted to practice before the BOE.

After the hearing, the BOE notifies the taxpayer and the FTB of its determination. (Sec. 19047, Rev. & Tax. Code) Either the taxpayer or the FTB may file a petition for rehearing within 30 days of the time of the determination. If such petition is not filed, the determination becomes final at the expiration of the 30-day period. If a petition is filed, the determination becomes final 30 days after the BOE issues its opinion on the petition. (Sec. 19048, Rev. & Tax. Code)

The BOE has published a booklet entitled "Appeals Procedures" and will supply a copy upon request.

Practitioner Comment: Legislation Requires BOE to "Publish" Its Decisions

Effective January 1, 2013, Cal. Rev. & Tax. Code § 40 requires the BOE to publish on its website a written formal opinion, a written memorandum opinion, or a written summary decision for each decision in which the amount in controversy is at least five hundred thousand dollars ($500,000). The decision must be published within 120 days of the date upon which the board rendered its decision. Each opinion is required to include the following:

— Findings of fact

— The legal issue or issues presented

— Applicable law

— Analysis

— Disposition

— Names of adopting board members

Concurring and dissenting opinions are permitted and are required to be published as well. Formal and memorandum opinions are precedential unless the opinion has been depublished, overruled, or superseded. Summary decisions may not be cited as precedent. Consent calendar actions, which are cases where the taxpayer waives its right to an oral hearing, are not required to be published.

The BOE staff's legislative bill analysis states that the impetus for the legislation is to help restore the BOE's twin goals of transparency and sound governance. However, the California Department of Finance has refused to approve the BOE's budget change proposal ("BCP") to request additional funds to implement the legislative mandate. The BOE is grappling with how to fulfill its obligations under Cal. Rev. & Tax. Code § 40 within its available budget.

Note that CCR § 5552(d) defines "amount in controversy" as "the total amount of taxes, fees, penalties, interest and or/other charges directly contested by the parties to an appeal as of the date the Board's vote to decide that appeal becomes final."

Chris Whitney, Contributing Editor

At the time this book went to press, the BOE was working on defining "the amount of controversy."

• *Suit to establish residence*

See ¶ 105 for a description of a special procedure whereby a person who is alleged to be a California resident can file a suit to determine the issue of residency without first paying the tax. Otherwise, there is no provision in California law for filing suit until after the tax is paid. See ¶720 regarding suits for refund.

¶706 Final Assessment of Deficiency

Law: Secs. 19042, 19049 (CCH California Tax Reports, ¶89-228).

Comparable Federal: Secs. 6213, 6402 (CCH U.S. Master Tax Guide ¶2711).

A deficiency assessment becomes final, in the absence of protest, at the expiration of the 60-day period allowed for protest after mailing of the notice of proposed deficiency. (Sec. 19042, Rev. & Tax. Code) If a protest is filed, the assessment becomes final at a later date as explained above in ¶704, ¶705. When the assessment becomes final, the Franchise Tax Board mails to the taxpayer a notice and demand for payment of the tax and interest. Except as noted below, the amount is due and payable within 15 days of the date of the notice and demand. (Sec. 19049, Rev. & Tax. Code)

The IRS may offset past-due, legally enforceable state income tax debts that have been reduced to judgment against any federal tax refunds due to the same taxpayer.

¶707 Jeopardy Assessments

Law: Secs. 19081-86, 19093 (CCH California Tax Reports, ¶89-168, 89-178).

Comparable Federal: Secs. 6851, 6861 (CCH U.S. Master Tax Guide ¶2713).

If the Franchise Tax Board (FTB) finds that the collection of a tax or deficiency for any year will be jeopardized by delay, it may make an immediate assessment. (Sec. 19081, Rev. & Tax. Code) As to the current period, it may declare the taxable period immediately terminated. (Sec. 19082, Rev. & Tax. Code) Any such assessment is immediately due and payable, but the taxpayer may stay collection by filing within 30 days a bond in the amount of the tax and accrued interest, or other security in such amount as the FTB may require. (Sec. 19083, Rev. & Tax. Code) Any jeopardy assessment is also a deficiency assessment, if such an assessment has not already been issued for that tax year and amount. (Sec. 19081, Rev. & Tax. Code)

No jeopardy assessment may be made and no levy may be issued less than 30 days after notice and demand is mailed for payment or for a return and payment, unless the Chief Counsel of the FTB or the Chief Counsel's delegate personally approves, in writing, the assessment or levy. (Sec. 19084, Rev. & Tax. Code)

The taxpayer may file a petition for reassessment within 30 days after the FTB furnishes the taxpayer with a written statement of the information upon which it relied in issuing the notice and demand. If the taxpayer so requests, an oral hearing will be granted, and under certain conditions the taxpayer may appeal to the State Board of Equalization (BOE). If no petition for reassessment is filed, the assessment becomes final at the end of the 30-day period. (Sec. 19084, Rev. & Tax. Code)

The taxpayer or the FTB may file a civil action within 60 days in superior court to appeal the decision of the BOE. If no civil action is commenced, the BOE's determination is final.

In *Pierre Roland Dupuy* (1975) (CCH California Tax Reports, ¶89-236.26), the taxpayer sought an injunction against seizure and sale of his property under a jeopardy assessment. The matter reached the California Supreme Court, which discussed the constitutional questions involved and concluded that an injunction may be issued in some circumstances in the interests of "due process."

¶708 Bankruptcy and Receiverships

Law: Secs. 19088-91, Reg. 19089 (CCH California Tax Reports, ¶89-170).

Comparable Federal: Secs. 6871-73 (CCH U.S. Master Tax Guide ¶2750).

California law is generally the same as federal law.

Special provisions apply to taxpayers in bankruptcy or receivership. In such cases the tax may be assessed immediately. The running of the statute of limitations is suspended under certain circumstances. Claims for tax are adjudicated by the court before which the bankruptcy or receivership procedure is pending, despite any appeal which may be pending before the State Board of Equalization. (Sec. 19088 et seq., Rev. & Tax. Code)

Anyone who is appointed trustee, receiver, assignee, or other fiduciary in a receivership or bankruptcy situation is required to give the Franchise Tax Board (FTB) notice of the appointment. Notice procedures are discussed at length in Reg. 19089. Failure to give timely notice may suspend the running of the period of limitations on assessments. (Sec. 19089, Rev. & Tax. Code) The notices of qualification should be sent by fax to (916) 845-9799 or by mail to:

Bankruptcy Section Manager MS A340

Franchise Tax Board

PO Box 2952

Sacramento, CA 95812-2952

(*FTB Notice 2013-02*, CCH CALIFORNIA TAX REPORTS, ¶405-864)

CCH Comment: Discharge in Bankruptcy

A bankruptcy court may enjoin the FTB from collecting prepetition nonpriority personal income taxes discharged in a bankruptcy proceeding in which the FTB declined to participate (*Goldberg v. Elliott*, U.S. Ct. of Appeals, 9th Cir., No. 00-15128, July 16, 2001, CCH CALIFORNIA TAX REPORTS, ¶89-170.27). However, a U.S. District Court overturned a bankruptcy court's discharge of delinquent taxes when the FTB failed to participate in a bankruptcy proceeding as a result of the FTB's reliance on the taxpayer's statement in the bankruptcy notice that the delinquent taxes at issue were less than one-third of the amount actually due and shown on the taxpayer's tax returns filed after the bankruptcy claims bar date for government entities had expired. (*Franchise Tax Board v. Joye*, United States District Court for the Northern District of California, No. C 06-2145 SC, March 23, 2007, CCH CALIFORNIA TAX REPORTS, ¶404-248) Similarly, a court of appeal upheld a lower court's decision to not discharge the pre-petition taxes assessed by the FTB finding that the taxpayer failed to provide adequate notice when the taxpayer listed an incorrect Social Security number on the notice provided to the FTB, even though the notice contained the taxpayer's correct name and address. (*Ellett v. Stanislaus*, 506 F.3d 774 (9th Cir. 2007), CCH CALIFORNIA TAX REPORTS, ¶404-485)

In addition, the Ninth Circuit has held that the FTB could not file a post-petition claim for outstanding personal income taxes for a tax year that concluded prior to the taxpayers' filing their bankruptcy petition, but for which the return filing and payment due date fell after the filing of the petition, because the outstanding taxes for that tax year had been discharged in the bankruptcy proceeding. (*Joye v. Franchise Tax Board*, U.S. Court of Appeals for the Ninth Circuit, No. 07-15676, August 21, 2009, CCH CALIFORNIA TAX REPORTS, ¶404-968)

CCH Comment: FTB May Pursue Collections During Ch. 13 Bankruptcy Proceedings

The Ninth Circuit Court of Appeal has held that the FTB was not precluded from collecting an outstanding tax liability during the taxpayer's earlier Chapter 13 bankruptcy proceedings. The bankruptcy automatic stay provisions applied only to collection actions against the property of the bankruptcy estate. As the bankruptcy estate's property revested in the taxpayer once the bankruptcy court confirmed the taxpayer's Chapter 13 plan, the taxpayer's property no longer was vested with the bankruptcy estate and the FTB could have pursued its collection activities during the gap period between the date the tax debt became due and the date of the taxpayer's second bankruptcy filing. In so holding, the court found that the taxpayer's debt was discharged in a subsequent Chapter 7 bankruptcy proceeding as the debt arose prior to the three-year look-back period and the FTB was not precluded from collecting the debt during the taxpayer's earlier Chapter 13 bankruptcy proceedings. (*In Re Jones* (2011), CCH California Tax Reports, ¶ 405-471)

¶709 Transferee Liability

Law: Secs. 18669, 19006, 19071-74 (CCH California Tax Reports, ¶ 89-166).

Comparable Federal: Secs. 6013, 6901-4 (CCH U.S. Master Tax Guide ¶ 2745).

The law contains provisions permitting assessment and collection of tax from persons secondarily liable. The period of limitations is extended for assessments against transferees and fiduciaries. (Sec. 19071, Rev. & Tax. Code; Sec. 19072, Rev. & Tax. Code) California law is the same as federal law.

Both California and federal laws provide for suspension of the running of the period of limitations against the transferee while the taxpayer is exercising an administrative remedy. (Sec. 19073, Rev. & Tax. Code)

California law also provides that the spouse who controls the disposition of, as well as the spouse who is taxable on, community income is liable for the tax on such income. (Sec. 19006, Rev. & Tax. Code) There is no comparable federal provision.

In *Appeal of Robert D. Burch* (1968) (CCH California Tax Reports, ¶ 89-234.25), the Franchise Tax Board held a husband liable for an additional assessment against his former wife, because the husband controlled the disposition of the community income involved, but contended that the husband was not entitled to appeal the wife's assessment. The State Board of Equalization permitted the appeal.

• *Withholding*

A successor to a business that is sold, transferred, or dissolved must withhold in trust a part of the purchase price or set aside money to cover the taxes required to be withheld. The successor's liability is limited to the fair market value of the assets acquired. The successor (including heirs, distributees, or other persons acquiring assets of the business) may request that the FTB issue a statement showing the amount of tax due from the employer, and if no certificate is issued within 60 days, the successor is relieved of any tax liability. If a statement is issued showing that taxes are due, the successor must pay the amount within 30 days of the date the statement is delivered or on the day the business or assets are acquired, whichever is later. If no statement is requested, the taxes must be paid by the successor on the day the business or assets are acquired. Failure to pay the taxes within the prescribed time period results in a 10% penalty. The successor is personally liable for the amount due. A statement to the successor from the FTB that no taxes are due or failure of the FTB to issue a statement releases only the successor from further liability, and not the original payer. The business entity (payer) remains liable for the amount due, less any amounts collected from any successor(s). (Sec. 18669, Rev. & Tax. Code)

¶710 Statute of Limitations on Assessments

Law: Secs. 17024.5, 18529, 18572, 18622, 19057-67, 19087, 19255, 19371, 19444, 19755, 24672 (CCH California Tax Reports, ¶ 89-144).

Comparable Federal: Secs. 1311-14, 6501-4, 7508A (CCH U.S. Master Tax Guide ¶ 2537, 2712, 2726 et seq.).

The California statute of limitations on assessments applies to the date for mailing a notice of proposed deficiency assessment, whereas the federal law applies to the date of the actual assessment of tax. The California rules governing time limits on assessment are summarized below. (The statute of limitations on tax *collection* is discussed below under "Statute of limitations on collections.")

(a) **General rule**—Taxes may be assessed up to four years after the return required to be filed by the taxpayer is filed. A return filed before the "last day prescribed by law for filing," determined without regard to any extension of time for filing, is deemed to have been filed on such last day. The federal limitation period is three years, with the same rule about returns filed before the regular due date. (Sec. 19057, Rev. & Tax. Code; Sec. 19066, Rev. & Tax. Code)

(b) **Waivers**—The taxpayer may agree to an extension of the limitation period. The Franchise Tax Board (FTB) must notify a taxpayer of his or her right to (1) refuse to extend the statute of limitations for assessments or (2) limit the extension to a particular period of time. This is the same as the federal rule. The California law has an additional provision that *automatically* extends the limitation period whenever the taxpayer has signed a waiver extending the statute of limitations for federal purposes. The automatic extension runs to six months after the expiration date of the federal waiver. (Sec. 19065, Rev. & Tax. Code; Sec. 19067, Rev. & Tax. Code)

(c) **Omission of over 25% of income**—Where a taxpayer's return omits gross income in excess of 25% of the gross income stated in the return, the limitation date is six years after the return was filed. This provision is comparable to the federal rule. (Sec. 19058, Rev. & Tax. Code; Sec. 19066, Rev. & Tax. Code) It should be noted that the six-year limitations period does not apply if the return contains sufficient information so that the FTB can tell the nature and amount of the income that is not included on the return. (*Tax News*, California Franchise Tax Board, May 31, 2010, CCH CALIFORNIA TAX REPORTS, ¶405-193)

(d) **False or no return**—Where no return or a false or fraudulent return was filed, there is no period of limitation on assessment or collection of tax. The California rule is the same as the federal one. (Sec. 19057, Rev. & Tax. Code)

(e) **Failure to report changes or amendment of federal returns**—Where the taxpayer fails to report any change of income or deductions made by federal authorities or fails to file an amended California return when required (¶106), a notice of proposed deficiency may be mailed at any time after the change or amended return is reported to or filed with the federal government. This rule applies only to the effect of the adjustments made by the federal authorities, or to the items changed in an amended federal return. (Sec. 19060, Rev. & Tax. Code) The California Supreme Court has ruled that this extended limitation period is an exception to the general four-year limitation period discussed in (a) above. (*Ordlock v. Franchise Tax Board* (2006) (CCH CALIFORNIA TAX REPORTS, ¶404-022))

(f) **Amended return filed or federal change reported**—When the taxpayer does file an amended return or otherwise reports a federal change within the required time (¶106), the limitation date for deficiencies "resulting from such adjustments" is two years after the filing of the amended return or report, or the date provided in (a) or (c), above, whichever is later. If an amended return is filed or a federal change is reported by the taxpayer after the prescribed time for doing so has expired, the limitation period for deficiencies is four years from the date the amended return or report is filed. The two-year limitation period applies to notifications made by the IRS, as well as by the taxpayer, within six months of the final federal determination or filing of an amended federal return. (Sec. 18622, Rev. & Tax. Code; Sec. 19059, Rev. & Tax. Code; Sec. 19060, Rev. & Tax. Code)

(g) **Change from separate to joint returns**—Where taxpayers elect to change from separate to joint returns (¶107), the otherwise applicable limitation period includes one additional year after the date of filing on the new basis. (Sec. 18529, Rev. & Tax. Code)

(h) **Involuntary conversion**—If the taxpayer elects not to recognize gain on involuntary conversion where replacement property is purchased (¶503), the limitation period is extended to four years from the date the FTB receives notice from the taxpayer regarding the replacement, etc. The federal period is three years. (Sec. 17024.5(g), Rev. & Tax. Code)

(i) **"Federally registered partnerships"**— The limitation date for assessments against partners is extended under certain conditions. (Sec. 19063, Rev. & Tax. Code)

(j) **Installment sales between related parties**—The limitation period may be extended under certain circumstances. (Sec. 24672, Rev. & Tax. Code)

(k) **Additional tax liability shown within 60 days of limitation date for assessment**—Where, within the 60-day period ending on the limitation date for assessment, the FTB receives from the taxpayer a signed document, other than an amended return or report required to be filed due to a federal change or correction (¶106), showing that the taxpayer owes an additional amount of tax for the taxable year, the period for assessment of that additional amount is extended to 60 days after the document is received by the FTB. (Sec. 19057(c), Rev. & Tax. Code)

(l) **Subpoenaed person's intervention**—The statute of limitations for assessment is suspended in certain cases involving actions by taxpayers to quash subpoenas to other persons. This conforms to federal law. (Sec. 19064, Rev. & Tax. Code)

(m) **Abusive tax shelters**—The statute of limitations for issuing proposed deficiency assessments related to abusive tax avoidance transactions is generally 12 years after the return is filed, applicable to notices issued on or after August 1, 2011, for taxable years that are not closed by the statute of limitations as of that date (previously, eight years after the return was filed). (Sec. 19755, Rev. & Tax. Code)

CCH Comment: Imposition of Penalties

In a nonprecedential decision, the California State Board of Equalization ruled in *Expert Dealer Services, LLC* (2006) (CCH CALIFORNIA TAX REPORTS, ¶89-206.352) that the four-year statute of limitations period applies only to the assessment of tax deficiencies and not to the imposition of penalties or interest.

• *Special rules*

In the case of members of the Armed Forces, disaster victims, and certain other taxpayers who are outside the United States for a period of time, the statute of limitations is automatically extended under certain conditions. Collection actions may also be suspended for National Guard members and army reservists called into service (¶109, ¶110).

The limitation period for an estate or trust may be shortened to 18 months (¶613).

CCH Comment: LLC Fees

There is no statute of limitations for assessing an LLC fee because the fee is not a tax. (*Tax News*, California Franchise Tax Board, August 30, 2010, CCH CALIFORNIA TAX REPORTS, ¶405-239)

The running of the period of limitations is suspended for any period during which the FTB is precluded from action by bankruptcy laws and for 30 days thereafter; the California rule is the same as the federal one. (Sec. 19089, Rev. & Tax.

Code) Also, the running of the period of limitations may be suspended where a fiduciary fails to give timely notice of his or her appointment (¶708).

California law contains nothing similar to IRC Secs. 1311-14, which mitigate the effect of the statute of limitations in certain situations where an inconsistent position is maintained.

• *Statute of limitations on collections*

California's statute of limitations on court actions to collect tax deficiencies, penalties, and interest is ten years. The period runs from the time the taxpayer's liability for tax, penalties, or interest is first determined, but does not apply in situations in which a tax lien is properly in force. (Sec. 19371, Rev. & Tax. Code)

A 20-year statute of limitations applies to collections of unpaid income tax liabilities, including penalties and interest. The limitations period runs from (1) the date of the latest tax liability for a taxable year or (2) the date any other liability that is not associated with a taxable year becomes due and payable. The 20-year period is extended for any period during which the FTB pursues a civil action or files a probate claim and does not expire until that liability, probate claim, or judgment against the taxpayer is satisfied or becomes unenforceable. (Sec. 19255, Rev. & Tax. Code)

• *Decisions of State Board of Equalization*

Appeal of Orville H. and Jeanne K. Haag (1977) (CCH CALIFORNIA TAX REPORTS, ¶89-144.354) involved the application of rule (c) above. The taxpayers failed to report $67,257 of dividends received from an S corporation. The omitted income exceeded 25% of the gross income on the return. However, the reconciliation in the return between federal and state income showed that S corporation income was reported on the federal but not on the state return. The State Board of Equalization (BOE) held that the reconciling item was sufficient to put the FTB on notice as to the possibility of additional California income; it followed that the statute of limitations was not extended and the proposed assessment was not timely.

In *Appeal of Phillip Yordan* (1958) (CCH CALIFORNIA TAX REPORTS, ¶89-144.403), the BOE applied rule (e) above in a situation where the taxpayer did report the federal adjustments but did not do so within the specified time limit. Similarly, see *Appeal of the Pullman Company* (1972) (CCH CALIFORNIA TAX REPORTS, ¶89-144.408), involving the comparable provision of the corporation tax law. In the *Pullman* case, state assessments for the years 1938 through 1943 were not made until 1957, based on a Tax Court settlement that became final in 1955. See also *Appeal of Vinemore Company, etc.* (1972) (CCH CALIFORNIA TAX REPORTS, ¶11-361.15), holding that notice of a Federal Revenue Agent's Report did not constitute the required notice where the final determination was made later in a Tax Court proceeding.

¶711 Interest on Deficiencies

> *Law:* Secs. 17140.5, 19101-20, 19521, 19738, 19777-78 (CCH CALIFORNIA TAX REPORTS, ¶89-192, 89-204, 89-210).

> *Comparable Federal:* Secs. 6404, 6601, 6621, 6622, 6631 (CCH U.S. MASTER TAX GUIDE ¶2838 et seq.).

> *California Form:* FTB 3701 (Request for Abatement of Interest).

Interest is charged upon deficiencies or other delinquent payments of tax (see ¶110 for interest charged during extension periods). Interest is compounded daily. (Sec. 19521, Rev. & Tax. Code) As to certain individuals, the running of interest may be suspended for a period because of their absence from the United States (¶109).

California imposes interest on tax underpayments at the federal underpayment rate. However, while the federal rate changes on a quarterly basis, the California rate is adjusted semiannually. In addition, California does not follow the federal provision that eliminates the imposition of interest on overlapping periods of tax overpayments and underpayments.

Interest rates are as follows:

January 1, 2013—December 31, 2013	3%
January 1, 2014—December 31, 2014	3%
January 1, 2015—December 31, 2015	3%
January 1, 2016—December 31, 2016	3%
January 1, 2017—June 30, 2017	4%

• *Interest is mandatory*

The imposition of interest is not a penalty, but is considered to be compensation for the taxpayer's use of money. The assessment of interest is mandatory, regardless of the reason for the late payment of tax. See *Appeal of Robert M. and Mildred Scott* (1981) (CCH California Tax Reports, ¶89-202.37), and other cases involving this point. However, as noted below, under some circumstances interest may be waived.

• *Special rules for related taxpayers or items*

In certain cases involving related taxpayers or related items where overpayments are offset against deficiencies, no interest is charged on the portion of the deficiency extinguished by the credit for overpayment for the period subsequent to the date the overpayment was made. This rule applies in the following situations:

(1) where a deficiency owed by one spouse is offset by an overpayment by the other spouse for the same year; presumably this rule would apply to registered domestic partners (RDPs) as well (see ¶119) (Sec. 19107, Rev. & Tax. Code);

(2) where a deficiency owed by a taxpayer for any year is offset by an overpayment by the same taxpayer for any other year (Sec. 19108, Rev. & Tax. Code); and

(3) in the cases of estates, trusts, parents and children (including in-laws), spouses, or RDPs, where the correction of an error results in a deficiency for one taxpayer and an overpayment for a related taxpayer (Sec. 19110, Rev. & Tax. Code).

There are no comparable federal provisions with respect to the first and third items. The second item is somewhat similar to a federal provision whereby interest is not imposed on deficiencies satisfied by overpayment credits under certain conditions.

In *Appeal of John L. Todd* (1952) (CCH California Tax Reports, ¶89-202.53), the State Board of Equalization (BOE) considered the effect of this rule in a case where the tax was paid in installments. The case involved a deficiency against the husband and an overpayment of exactly the same amount by the wife. The BOE held that there was no overpayment by the wife until she paid her last installment, so interest was properly chargeable on the husband's deficiency from the due date of the return to the date of the last installment.

• *Military personnel*

The maximum rate of interest on any underpayment incurred by a service member, or the service member and the service member's spouse jointly, before the service member enters military service may not exceed 6% per year during the period of military service. (Sec. 17140.5, Rev. & Tax. Code)

• *Potentially abusive tax shelters*

For interest penalties related to abusive tax shelters see ¶727.

¶1711

• *Rules for imposition of interest*

The law contains detailed rules regarding interest on deficiencies. Principal provisions of these rules are as follows:

— interest is assessed, collected, and paid in the same manner as the tax (Sec. 19101, Rev. & Tax. Code);

— interest is assessed on tax deficiencies from the due date of the tax without regard for any extension of time that may have been granted and without regard to any notice of jeopardy assessment issued prior to the last date prescribed for the payment of such deficiency (Sec. 19101, Rev. & Tax. Code);

— interest is normally assessed on a penalty from the date of notice and demand for payment if the penalty is not paid within 15 days from notice and demand for payment; however, as to certain penalties, interest is imposed from the due date of the return (Sec. 19101, Rev. & Tax. Code);

— if an amount is paid within 15 days following notice and demand for payment, no interest will be charged for the period after the date of the notice and demand (Sec. 19101, Rev. & Tax. Code);

— if tax is satisfied by an overpayment credit, interest is not imposed on such tax for any period during which interest was allowable on the overpayment (Sec. 19113, Rev. & Tax. Code);

— interest may be assessed and collected any time during the period within which the related tax may be collected (Sec. 19114, Rev. & Tax. Code); and

— no interest may be imposed for the period between 45 days after the date of final audit review and the date a notice of proposed assessment is sent to the taxpayer (Sec. 19105, Rev. & Tax. Code).

Practice Note: Interest Computation Adjustments

The FTB has announced that a limited number of individuals or business entities meeting specific criteria might be subject to interest computation adjustments as a result of the rulings in *May Department Stores v. United States* (IRS Rev. Rul. 99-40) and Corporate Interest Netting (IRS Rev. Proc. 94-60). Regarding *May Department Stores* interest calculations, the review is centered on individuals or business entities that (1) filed an amended return for additional tax or received a deficiency assessment after the original return was filed for the same tax year; (2) on the original return, elected an overpayment transfer to the subsequent year's estimated tax; and (3) in the subsequent year, had a required first quarter estimated payment that was less than the requested overpayment transfer amount. Regarding corporate interest netting adjustments, the review is centered on corporations with a previous refund or payment transfer and a subsequent deficiency or amended return for additional tax with interest for the same tax year. The FTB will be issuing refunds/credits and sending letters of explanation to impacted taxpayers. (*Tax News*, California Franchise Tax Board, October 2015, CCH CALIFORNIA TAX REPORTS, ¶ 406-422)

• *Suspension of interest*

The Franchise Tax Board (FTB) must suspend the imposition of interest if an individual files a timely return and the FTB fails to issue a notice specifically stating the taxpayer's liability and the basis for such liability within 36 months following the later of the original due date of the return, the date on which a timely return is filed, or the date when documents showing the taxpayer owes additional tax are filed. The suspension period commences on the date after the 36-month period expires until 15 days after the FTB sends the required notice. The suspension does not apply to the following:

— penalties for failure to file or failure to pay,

— penalties, additions to tax, or additional amounts involving fraud,

— penalties, additions to tax, or additional amounts shown on the return,

— criminal penalties,

— penalties, additions to tax, or additional amounts related to any gross misstatement,

— penalties, additions to tax, or additional amounts related to reportable transactions for which specified requirements are not met and listed transactions, or

— taxpayers with taxable income greater than $200,000 that have been contacted by the FTB regarding the use of a potentially abusive tax shelter.

(Sec. 19116, Rev. & Tax. Code)

Federal law is similar.

Special rules apply when a taxpayer is required to report a federal change or correction to the state. In that case, the FTB has either one or two years from the date the taxpayer or the IRS reports the federal change or correction to issue a notice before interest is suspended, depending on whether the change or correction is reported within six months or more than six months after the final federal determination.

CCH Example: Suspension of Interest

Ken received an automatic extension of time to file his 2011 California personal income tax return and timely filed on September 1, 2012. Ken inadvertently failed to include $1,000 of interest income on the return. The FTB sent Ken the required notice on June 1, 2016, and Ken paid the tax deficiency on July 15, 2016. Ken owes interest on the tax deficiency from April 15, 2012 (the original due date of the return), through September 1, 2015 (the last day of the 36-month period). Interest is suspended from September 2, 2015, through June 15, 2016. Interest runs again from June 16, 2016 (the 15th day after notice was provided), until July 15, 2016 (the date of payment of the tax deficiency).

• *Notice of interest charges*

Each notice that states an amount of interest required to be paid must include the code section under which the interest is imposed and a description of how the interest is computed. Upon request of the taxpayer, the FTB must also provide a computation of the interest. (Sec. 19117, Rev. & Tax. Code)

• *Waiver and abatement of interest*

Interest may be waived for any period for which the FTB determines that the taxpayer cannot pay because of extreme financial hardship caused by catastrophic circumstance. (Sec. 19112, Rev. & Tax. Code) In addition, the FTB is authorized to abate the assessment of interest whenever the following occurs:

— the interest on a deficiency is attributable at least in part to an unreasonable error or delay of an FTB officer or employee, or

— the interest on a delay in payment is the result of dilatory conduct on the part of an FTB officer or employee performing a ministerial or managerial act in an official capacity, or

— a deficiency is based on a final federal determination of tax for the same period that interest was abated on the related federal deficiency amount, provided that the error or delay to which the deficiency is attributable occurred on or before the issuance of the final federal determination.

(Sec. 19104, Rev. & Tax. Code)

In *Appeal of Hall* (2012) (CCH CALIFORNIA TAX REPORTS, ¶89-210.2140), a non-precedential decision, the State Board of Equalization (BOE) ordered that interest be abated on the portion of a deficiency assessment that arose as a result of the FTB erroneously applying the taxpayers' payment of an assessment for the 2006 tax year to their 2008 tax year tax liability and then erroneously refunding the 2006 tax payment as a 2008 overpayment. The BOE found that an employee made an unreasonable error in applying the taxpayers' payment to the wrong tax year. The taxpayers' check was included with their protest letter and amended 2006 return, and the check's memo line indicated it was associated with the 2006 amended return. The BOE found that the check was a "record" that was temporarily lost through its erroneous application to another tax year during the processing of the taxpayers' case for 2006 and that the taxpayers played no significant part in the FTB's error.

Conversely, in *Appeal of Medeiros* (2004) (CCH CALIFORNIA TAX REPORTS, ¶89-210.32), the BOE determined that the FTB's failure to change a taxpayer's "last-known address" of record after the taxpayer sent an attachment to his return indicating that his address had changed was not an unreasonable error given the volume of returns received by the FTB. Consequently, the BOE therefore refused to abate the interest imposed on a deficiency even though the notice of proposed assessment was sent to the wrong address. Under the law in effect at the time, the taxpayer's last-known address was the address shown on the taxpayer's most recently filed return, unless the FTB is given clear and concise notice of a different address. Under the BOE's ruling, an attachment to a return indicating a change of address did not satisfy the "clear and concise notice of a different address" requirement. However, the BOE did abate the interest imposed for the period after the FTB's "request for a tax return" was returned by the post office as undeliverable, because the FTB was then put on notice that the address they had for the taxpayer was not valid and the FTB had the correct address in its records.

A request for such an abatement may be made by submitting FTB 3701 to the FTB. A taxpayer may appeal an interest abatement denial to the BOE. The appeal must be filed within 30 days in the case of unpaid interest or within 90 days in the case of any paid interest. A taxpayer may treat the FTB's failure to make a determination within six months as a denial. A request for abatement may accompany a written protest or appeal of the underlying deficiency. If a deficiency is final, the interest accruing prior to the deficiency becoming final may not be abated. The FTB may also waive interest in certain cases in which the taxpayer has relied on the FTB's written advice (¶703).

In addition, both California and federal law require the abatement of interest imposed against any taxpayer located in a federally-declared disaster area for any period that the FTB (IRS for federal purposes) (1) extended the taxpayer's period for filing an income tax return and paying income tax with respect to such return and (2) waived any corresponding penalties. California differs from the federal law by (1) extending relief to taxpayers in Governor-declared disaster areas and (2) requiring taxpayers seeking relief to have incurred a loss, in addition to being located in a disaster area. The FTB may also abate interest in situations in which the interest accrued as the result of the FTB's delay in mailing a notice or other correspondence as a result of a presidentially or gubernatorially declared disaster, even if the taxpayer was not directly impacted by the disaster. (Sec. 19109, Rev. & Tax. Code)

Finally, see ¶712 for a discussion of the FTB's Taxpayers' Rights Advocate's authority to abate the imposition of interest under specified circumstances.

Practitioner Comment: FTB's Errors and Delays May Justify Abatement

The State Board of Equalization held in a published decision in the *Appeal of Alan and Rita Shugart* (2005) CCH CALIFORNIA TAX REPORTS, ¶403-816, on July 1, 2005, that the cumulative effect of multiple documented errors and delays on the part of the FTB during the audit and protest process justified an abatement of interest. Although legislation requiring the FTB to suspend the imposition of interest on individual taxpayers if the FTB fails to issue a notice of proposed assessment within 18 months of the tax return being filed may mitigate the need for taxpayers to seek to have some or all of their interest abated, in circumstances when this suspension of interest does not apply, taxpayers who experience delays that they believe are unreasonable at audit or protest should maintain careful records documenting the causes of the delays and consider filing a request for interest abatement.

Chris Whitney, Contributing Editor

• *Interest on erroneous overpayment to taxpayer*

Interest may be assessed and collected if the FTB makes an erroneous overpayment to a taxpayer. Interest accrues from the date the refund is erroneously paid but will be abated for the period from the date the refund is made until 30 days after the FTB makes a demand for repayment if payment is made within the 30-day period. (Sec. 19104, Rev. & Tax. Code; Sec. 19411, Rev. & Tax. Code)

¶712 Penalties

Law: Secs. 17299.8, 17299.9, 18633.5, 19011, 19116, 19131-36.3, 19141, 19164, -67, 19169, 19170, 19172-79, 19181-87, 19444, 19701-01.5, 19705-06, 19708-09, 19711-15, 19720-21, 19730-38, 19772-74, 19777.5 (CCH California Tax Reports, ¶89-192, 89-206—89-210).

Comparable Federal: Secs. 6111-12, 6404, 6651-53, 6657-58, 6662, 6663, 6671-6674, 6682, 6693-95, 6698, 6700-06, 6707, 6721-24, 7201-07, 7408 (CCH U.S. Master Tax Guide Chapter 28).

California Forms: FTB 2300 PIT (Amnesty Application - Individuals).

[NOTE: See ¶703 for a discussion of relief provisions under the Taxpayers' Bill of Rights.]

California imposes a variety of civil and criminal penalties for failure to comply with the personal income tax law. Some of these penalties may be waived for reasonable cause.

Practice Note: New Reasonable Cause Abatement Form

The FTB has created a new form for personal income taxpayers to use to request penalty abatement due to reasonable cause: FTB 2917, Reasonable Cause – Individual and Fiduciary Claim for Refund. The new form allows the FTB to scan and associate forms with taxpayers, properly route requests to the proper workbasket and agent, easily identify claims for refund, and reduce unnecessary correspondence. The FTB recommends that taxpayers use the new form, but it will also continue to accept and process handwritten reasonable cause abatement letter requests. Taxpayers may consult FTB 1024, Franchise Tax Board Penalty Reference Chart, for a list of penalties eligible for abatement due to reasonable cause. (*Public Service Bulletin 14-26*, California Franchise Tax Board, September 4, 2014)

Penalties related to abusive tax shelters are discussed at ¶727. Other personal income tax penalties are provided as follows. The FTB also provides a penalty reference chart (FTB 1024), which lists the penalty codes numerically by Rev. & Tax. Code Sections and the comparable IRC sections.

• *Civil penalties*

Failure to file/timely file penalties

— failure to file return without reasonable cause—5% per month, up to 25%; for individuals, after 60 days, at least the lesser of $135 or 100% of tax; if fraudulent, 15% per month, up to a 75% maximum (Sec. 19131, Rev. & Tax. Code)

— failure to timely file a return concerning medical savings accounts, qualified tuition programs, or education savings accounts—$50 per failure (Sec. 19184, Rev. & Tax. Code)

— failure to file partnership return—$18 multiplied by the number of partners for each month that the failure continues, up to a maximum of 12 months (Sec. 19172, Rev. & Tax. Code)

Practice Note: Partnership Late Filing Penalty Misapplied to Certain SMLLCs

The FTB discovered that a partnership late filing penalty was misapplied to certain single member limited liability companies (SMLLCs) treated as disregarded entities for tax purposes. The FTB indicated that it would correct accounts and issue refunds/ credits (with interest) or cancel the unpaid penalty for tax years and/or payments within the statute of limitations for refunds as of June 26, 2013 (the date the FTB discovered the misapplication of the penalty). The FTB also determined that a late filing penalty payment made by an SMLLC outside the statute of limitations may be treated as an "over collection," meaning that the FTB can repay SMLLC late filing penalty payments that would otherwise be nonrefundable due to the statute of limitations. Because an "over collection" is not considered a payment towards tax, it is not eligible to receive interest. Beginning in May 2014 and through the subsequent 12 months, affected SMLLCs that had this penalty "over collected" and that are in good standing will receive a letter from the FTB indicating their eligibility for repayment without interest, with a check to follow. (*Single Member LLC (SMLLC) Penalty FAQs*, California Franchise Tax Board, February 4, 2014; *Tax News*, California Franchise Tax Board, April 2014, CCH CALIFORNIA TAX REPORTS, ¶ 406-092)

Failure to pay penalties

— failure to timely pay amount of tax when due or within 15 days of notice and demand without reasonable cause—5% of unpaid amount plus 0.5% per month of remaining tax, up to 25% of unpaid amount (Sec. 19132, Rev. & Tax. Code)

— failure of LLC to pay the income tax liability of a nonresident member when required to do so—5% of unpaid amount plus 0.5% per month of remaining tax, up to 25% of unpaid amount (Sec. 19132, Rev. & Tax. Code)

Practitioner Comment: U.S. Supreme Court Declines to Address Whether Penalty for Failing to Pay Tax Is a "Tax" Barred from Federal Court Jurisdiction Under Tax Injunction Act

On June 10, 2016, a California taxpayer, Roger Huang, filed a petition asking the U.S. Supreme Court to resolve a circuit conflict on whether the Tax Injunction Act ("TIA") bars cases challenging a state tax penalty from being filed in federal court. The petition stated, "The Second, Sixth, Seventh, and Tenth Circuits correctly hold that a tax penalty is a penalty, not a tax, so that a suit challenging the penalty but not the tax is not barred by the [TIA]". Conversely," the Fifth and Ninth Circuits incorrectly hold that a tax penalty is a tax, not a penalty." On October 11, 2016, the U.S. Supreme Court denied Huang's petition for certiorari, leaving the circuit split in place.

The circuit decision in *Huang* as well as the decisions of the Fifth and Ninth circuit courts appear in contrast to the California Third District Court of Appeals' decision in *California Taxpayers' Association v. FTB* (190 Cal. App. 4th 1139), decided in 2010. In that case, the court concluded that the recently enacted large corporate understatement penalty (LCUP) was in fact a "penalty" and not a "tax," and therefore did not require a two-thirds majority vote pursuant to California Constitution Article 13A, Section 3 (Proposition 13). Of course, a full analysis of the issue requires consideration of the nature of the tax or penalty and the specific statutory language.

The distinction between a "tax" and a "penalty" has ramifications beyond the TIA and Proposition 13. In 2010, Californians passed Proposition 26, which requires that any new legislation that increases the tax for any single taxpayer (regardless of whether the overall change is revenue neutral or not), must be passed by a two-thirds majority vote. Proposition 26 does specifically exempt some penalties from this requirement; however, the absence of a specific reference to all penalties may even further complicate the discussion.

Chris Whitney, Contributing Editor

Notice and demand penalties

— failure to furnish requested information or to file return on notice and demand by the FTB without reasonable cause—25% of deficiency or of tax amount for which information was requested (Sec. 19133, Rev. & Tax. Code)

Underpayment/understatement penalties

— estimated tax underpayment penalties (see ¶111)

— negligence, substantial underpayment, etc. without reasonable cause—20% of underpayment attributable to violation; 40% for gross valuation misstatements (see ¶727 for provisions relating to underpayments resulting from abusive tax shelters) [Note: Federal amendments that lowered the threshold for imposing the substantial and valuation misstatement penalties apply to returns filed after 2010 (after August 17, 2006, for federal purposes)] (Sec. 19164, Rev. & Tax. Code)

— fraud—75% of underpayment attributable to fraud (Sec. 19164, Rev. & Tax. Code)

— aiding or abetting understatement of tax liability—$1,000 (Sec. 19178, Rev. & Tax. Code)

— substantial and gross valuation misstatements attributable to incorrect appraisals—the lesser of (1) the greater of $1,000 or 10% of the tax underpayment amount attributable to the misstatement or (2) 125% of the gross income received by the appraiser for preparing the appraisal (Sec. 19185, Rev. & Tax. Code)

E-filing/payment penalties

— failure to remit payment by electronic funds transfer when required without reasonable cause—10% of amount paid (Sec. 19011, Rev. & Tax. Code)

Failure to report penalties

— failure to report personal services remuneration—disallowance of deduction; unreported amount multiplied by the highest personal income tax rate (Sec. 17299.8, Rev. & Tax. Code; Sec. 19175, Rev. & Tax. Code)

— failure to report real estate transaction—disallowance of related deductions (Sec. 17299.8, Rev. & Tax. Code)

— failure to make small business stock report without reasonable cause—$50 per report; $100 if failure due to negligence or intentional disregard (Sec. 19133.5, Rev. & Tax. Code)

— failure to file information return or furnish payee statement—up to $100 per violation, not to exceed $1.5 million per year; the greater of $250 or 5% or 10% of the items to be reported, depending on the return involved, if intentional disregard of requirements (Sec. 19183, Rev. & Tax. Code)

— failure to provide written explanation—$10 per failure up to $5,000 (Sec. 19183, Rev. & Tax. Code)

— failure to file information report regarding individual retirement account (IRA) or annuity—$50 per failure (Sec. 19184, Rev. & Tax. Code)

— failure to meet original issue discount reporting requirements—1% of aggregate issue price, up to $50,000 per issue (Sec. 19181, Rev. & Tax. Code)

— failure to file statement of information for limited liability company—$250 (Sec. 19141, Rev. & Tax. Code)

Miscellaneous penalties

— dishonored check or electronic funds transfer—the lesser of $25 or amount of check; 2% of amount of check if check is for $1,250 or more (Sec. 19134, Rev. & Tax. Code)

— making false statements in connection with withholding—$500 (Sec. 19176, Rev. & Tax. Code)

— frivolous return—$500; $5,000 if frivolous tax submission (Sec. 19179, Rev. & Tax. Code)

— overstatement of nondeductible IRA contributions without reasonable cause—$100 per overstatement (Sec. 19184, Rev. & Tax. Code)

— instituting frivolous protest or refund proceedings—$5,000 maximum (Sec. 19174, Rev. & Tax. Code)

— fraudulent identification of exempt use property—$10,000 (Sec. 19186, Rev. & Tax. Code)

Tax preparer penalties

— understatement by return preparer—$250 per return; $1,000 if noncompliance with reportable transaction requirements, listed transaction, or gross misstatement; $5,000 if willful or reckless (Sec. 19166, Rev. & Tax. Code)

— failure of tax preparer to give taxpayer copy of return, furnish identifying number, or retain copy or list—$50 for each failure up to $25,000 per return period (Sec. 19167, Rev. & Tax. Code)

— negotiation or endorsement of client's refund check by tax preparer—$250 per check plus criminal penalty (misdemeanor) of up to $1,000 and/or up to 1 year in jail, and costs of prosecution (Sec. 19172, Rev. & Tax. Code)

— failure to file mandatory electronic return, except when failure is due to reasonable cause, which may include a taxpayer-client electing not to e-file (see ¶ 108)—$50 per non-electronic return (Sec. 19170, Rev. & Tax. Code)

— failure of tax preparer to register with California Tax Education Council—$5,000 ($2,500 for first offense) (Sec. 19167, Rev. & Tax. Code)

— failure of tax preparer to exercise due diligence in determining eligibility for earned income credit—$500 per failure (Sec. 19167, Rev. & Tax. Code)

Practitioner Comment: 2010 Legislation Lowers Preparer Penalty Standard in California

California's basic conformity to the federal preparer penalty standards set forth in IRC Sec. 6694 is contained in RTC Sec. 19164. Prior to amendment in 2010, California's adoption of IRC Sec. 6694 was based upon IRC Sec. 6694 as it existed at January 1, 2005, but was modified such that preparers faced a "more likely than not" standard to avoid penalty imposition relating to assessments based upon undisclosed tax positions, as opposed to the "realistic possibility of being sustained on its merits" standard found in the IRC at the time. IRC Sec. 6694 was subsequently modified to raise the federal standard to "substantial authority" (greater than 40% chance of being sustained).

In contrast, California law is in substantial conformity to the federal accuracy related penalty imposed upon taxpayers contained in IRC Sec. 6662, which generally provides an exception to penalty imposition for undisclosed tax positions which are based upon substantial authority, a standard lower than the "more likely than not" standard. The different standards had the potential to create conflicting interests between taxpayers and their tax preparers as to when tax positions should or should not be disclosed.

As part of S.B. 401, enacted April 10, 2010, and which updated the IRC conformity date to January 1, 2009, effective for tax years beginning on or after January 1, 2010,

California now conforms to the federal substantial authority standard for purposes of the tax preparer penalty in most cases, as a result of which taxpayers and tax preparers have essentially the same standard for purposes of the accuracy related and preparer penalties. It should be noted that higher standards continue to apply for certain tax positions, such as listed transactions, etc.

Note that with the passage of A.B. 154, the Legislature updated California's IRC conformity date to January 1, 2015, effective for tax years beginning on or after January 1, 2015, but for only those IRC sections specifically noted, which did not include IRC Sec. 6694. A.B. 154 only references IRC Sec. 6694(a)(1) in the context of permitting the Franchise Tax Board to prescribe a list of positions for which it believes there is not substantial authority or there is no reasonable belief that the tax treatment is more likely than not the proper tax treatment. As a result, A.B. 154 does not alleviate the uncertainty from S.B. 401 related to California's date of conformity to IRC Sec. 6694 with regard to the preparer standard.

Chris Whitney, Contributing Editor

The failure to file and failure to timely pay penalties may be imposed simultaneously but may not exceed 25% combined.

The FTB is authorized by law to waive or not impose the penalty for failure to comply with EFT requirements under certain conditions. In Legal Ruling 96-4 (CCH CALIFORNIA TAX REPORTS, ¶89-206.64), the FTB provides examples of situations in which it will or will not use this authority.

The penalty for instituting frivolous protest or refund proceedings, imposed under Rev. & Tax. Code Sec. 19714 (formerly, Sec. 19414), conforms to IRC Sec. 6673. In *Appeals of Fred R. Dauberger et al.* (1982) (CCH CALIFORNIA TAX REPORTS, ¶89-164.506), the State Board of Equalization (BOE) commented on the flood of California "tax protester" cases and used the following language: "We take this opportunity to advise all individuals who proceed with frivolous cases that serious consideration will be given to the imposition of damages under Section 19414." (This case involved a consolidation of appeals for 32 different taxpayers.) In numerous later decisions involving similar facts, the BOE has imposed the penalty.

CCH Comment: Zero Returns

The State Board of Equalization has taken the position that returns that do not contain sufficient data from which the FTB can compute and assess the tax liability of a particular taxpayer or that do not demonstrate an honest and genuine endeavor to satisfy the requirements of California's tax law (including "zero returns") are not valid returns and may subject filers of such returns to late filing penalties or penalties for failure to file upon notice and demand (*Appeal of Lavonne A. Hodgson* (2002) (CCH CALIFORNIA TAX REPORTS, ¶89-206.6094, 89-206.7596)).

• *Criminal penalties*

The following criminal penalties are authorized under the Revenue and Taxation Code:

— failure to file return or to furnish information repeatedly over a period of 2 years or more or filing false or fraudulent return or information, resulting in an underpayment of at least $15,000; aiding or abetting tax evasion; willfully failing to pay tax or estimated Tax—$5,000 maximum plus criminal penalty (misdemeanor) of up to $5,000 and/or up to 1 year in jail, and costs of prosecution (Sec. 19701, Rev. & Tax. Code)

— obtaining, endorsing, or negotiating a tax refund generated by the filing of a return knowing the recipient is not entitled to the refund—$5,000 maximum plus criminal penalty (misdemeanor) of up to $10,000 and/or up to 1 year in jail, and costs of investigation and prosecution; $10,000 maximum if done willfully and with intent to defraud plus criminal penalty (misdemeanor/felony) of up to $50,000 and/or up to 1 year in jail or up to 3 years in prison, and costs of investigation and prosecution (Sec. 19720, Rev. & Tax. Code; Sec. 19721, Rev. & Tax. Code)

— forging spouse's signature—misdemeanor; up to $5,000 and/or up to 1 year in jail (Sec. 19701.5, Rev. & Tax. Code)

— willfully making or signing a return or document containing a declaration made under penalty of perjury that the maker or signer does not believe to be materially true or correct—felony; up to $50,000 and/or up to 3 years in prison, and costs of investigation and prosecution (Sec. 19705, Rev. & Tax. Code)

— willfully aiding preparation or presentation of a false return or document—felony; up to $50,000 and/or up to 3 years in prison, and costs of investigation and prosecution (Sec. 19705, Rev. & Tax. Code)

— falsely executing or signing a bond, permit, entry, or required document—felony; up to $50,000 and/or up to 3 years in prison, and costs of investigation and prosecution (Sec. 19705, Rev. & Tax. Code)

— removing, depositing, or concealing taxable goods to evade tax—felony; up to $50,000 and/or up to 3 years in prison, and costs of investigation and prosecution (Sec. 19705, Rev. & Tax. Code)

— concealing property or destroying or falsifying records in regard to a tax settlement, closing agreement, compromise, or offer in compromise—felony; up to $50,000 and/or up to 3 years in prison, and costs of investigation and prosecution (Sec. 19705, Rev. & Tax. Code)

— willfully failing to file return or supply information with intent to defraud—misdemeanor/felony; up to $20,000, and/or up to 1 year in jail or 3 years in prison, and costs of investigation and prosecution (Sec. 19705, Rev. & Tax. Code)

— willfully making, signing, or verifying false return or statement with intent to evade tax——misdemeanor/felony; up to $20,000 and/or up to 1 year in jail or 3 years in prison (Sec. 19706, Rev. & Tax. Code)

— failure to collect and pay withholding—felony; up to $2,000 and/or up to 3 years in prison (Sec. 19708, Rev. & Tax. Code)

— failure to withhold or pay over nonresident withholding—misdemeanor; up to $1,000 and/or up to 1 year in jail, and costs of prosecution (Sec. 19709, Rev. & Tax. Code)

— filing false information with employer—misdemeanor; $1,000 and/or up to 1 year in jail (Sec. 19711, Rev. & Tax. Code)

— failure to set up withholding account—misdemeanor; up to $5,000 and/or up to 1 year in jail (Sec. 19713, Rev. & Tax. Code)

— willful failure of check cashing business to file information return (see ¶713)—felony; up to $25,000 ($100,000 for a corporation), and or up to 1 year in prison in a county jail or a state prison, plus costs of prosecution (Sec. 18631.7, Rev. & Tax. Code)

• *Effect of automatic extension of time*

Under the automatic-extension procedure (¶108), reasonable cause is assumed and a late-payment penalty will not be imposed if at least 90% of the tax is paid by the regular due date and the balance is paid (with the return) by the extended due date. This conforms to federal practice. (Sec. 19132, Rev. & Tax. Code)

¶712

- *Procedures for imposing penalties*

Each notice that imposes a penalty must include the name of the penalty, the code section under which it is imposed, and a description of the computation of the penalty. Upon request of the taxpayer, the FTB must also provide a computation of the penalty imposed. (Sec. 19187, Rev. & Tax. Code)

Further, penalties may not generally be imposed unless the initial determination of the imposition of the penalty receives written approval by an authorized FTB supervisor. However, supervisory approval is not required for any penalty (1) for failure to file or failure to pay, (2) calculated through automated means, or (3) resulting from a federal change or correction required to be reported to the state.

- *Taxpayers' Rights Advocate abatement of penalties and interest*

The FTB's Taxpayers' Rights Advocate may abate any penalties, fees, additions to tax, or interest assessed against a taxpayer if (1) relief is not otherwise available, (2) the error or delay was not attributable to the taxpayer, and (3) the advocate determines that the penalties, fees, additions to tax, or interest have been assessed as a result of any of the following:

— the FTB's erroneous action or erroneous inaction in processing the taxpayer's documents or payments;

— the FTB's unreasonable delay; or

— erroneous written advice that does not otherwise qualify for relief by the Chief Counsel.

Effective January 1, 2016, such relief may be granted only in consultation with the Chief Counsel. The determination regarding whether to grant relief is not subject to administrative or judicial review.

The relief must be submitted to the FTB's executive officer for concurrence if the total reduction in the amounts owed exceeds $500. The total relief granted pursuant to this authority must not exceed $7,500 (increased to $10,000 beginning January 1, 2016, and adjusted for inflation in years thereafter). Refunds resulting from the advocate's granting of relief may only be granted if a written request for relief was filed with the advocate's office within the statute of limitations period for filing a refund claim. (Sec. 21004, Rev. & Tax. Code)

- *Review of noneconomic substance penalties*

The FTB has established a process to determine whether the noneconomic substance penalty (NEST) under Sec. 19774, Rev. & Tax. Code should be reduced or withdrawn. To dispute a NEST penalty, taxpayers should file a protest of the penalty within the required 60-day period and also file a Form FTB 626, Request for Chief Counsel To Relieve Penalties. The Chief Counsel will issue a nonappealable determination on the request for penalty relief. Taxpayers may also contest the penalty after paying the full amount and filing a claim for refund with the FTB, and may appeal to the BOE or file an action in court after the refund claim is denied or deemed denied. (*Tax News*, California Franchise Tax Board, September 2008, CCH CALIFORNIA TAX REPORTS, ¶ 404-742)

- *Suspension of penalties*

If an individual files a timely return and the FTB fails to issue a notice specifically stating the taxpayer's liability and the basis for such liability within 36 months following the later of the original due date of the return or the date on which a timely return is filed, the FTB must generally suspend the imposition of civil penalties, additions to tax, or additional amounts during the period beginning from the date after the 36 month-period expires until 15 days after the FTB sends the required notice. The suspension does not apply to any of the following:

— penalty for failure to file or failure to pay;

— penalty, addition to tax, or additional amount involving fraud;

— penalty, addition to tax, or additional amount shown on the return;

— criminal penalties;

— penalty, addition to tax, or additional amounts related to any gross misstatement;

— penalty, addition to tax, or additional amounts related to reportable transactions for which specified requirements are not met and listed transactions; or

— applicable to notices provided, or amended returns filed, on or after January 1, 2012, interest, penalty, addition to tax, or additional amount relating to any abusive tax avoidance transaction (see ¶727).

(Sec. 19116, Rev. & Tax. Code)

Federal law is similar.

• *Relief for innocent spouse*

Under both California and federal law, in cases involving joint returns an innocent spouse may be relieved from penalties in certain cases of wrongdoing or in divorce settlement decrees. See ¶107 for details.

• *Misdemeanor prosecutions*

The FTB may not pursue misdemeanor prosecution of any person for failing to file a return or furnish required information, aiding another person to evade tax, filing a false or fraudulent return or statement, or supplying false or fraudulent information unless the violations occur over a period of two or more years and result in an estimated delinquent tax liability of $15,000 or more. Also, the FTB may not pursue misdemeanor prosecution of any person for failure to pay any tax, including any estimated tax, if the person is mentally incompetent or suffers from dementia, Alzheimer's disease, or a similar condition. (Sec. 19701, Rev. & Tax. Code)

• *Bankruptcy proceedings*

Both California and federal laws provide for relief from penalties in cases where failure to pay is due to rules applicable in bankruptcy proceedings. (Sec. 19161, Rev. & Tax. Code)

• *Collection and filing enforcement fees*

A collection cost recovery fee will be imposed on any taxpayer who fails to timely pay any amount of tax, penalty, addition to tax, interest, or other liability if the FTB has mailed a notice advising the taxpayer that continued failure to pay that amount may result in a collection action, including the imposition of a collection cost recovery fee. A filing enforcement cost recovery fee will be imposed on any taxpayer who fails to file a required tax return within 25 days after formal legal demand is mailed to the taxpayer by the FTB. The fees for the state's 2016—2017 fiscal year are $266 and $81, respectively. Collection and filing enforcement fees are subject to annual adjustment to reflect actual costs. (Sec. 19254, Rev. & Tax. Code)

• *Decisions of State Board of Equalization*

In *Appeal of Auto Theft R.F. Systems, LLC* (2011) (CCH CALIFORNIA TAX REPORTS, ¶405-452), a summary decision not to be cited as precedent, the BOE held that the taxpayer was not entitled to a refund of late payment penalties paid on a deficiency associated with a "risky" tax position. The taxpayer underpaid its LLC fee because it based its position on its liability on the theory of a commonly controlled LLC. However the taxpayer's CPA at the time warned the taxpayer that such a position was "aggressive" and advised the taxpayer to consult an LLC attorney before computing its liability on the basis of such a theory. However, the taxpayer failed to demonstrate that it had actually contacted an attorney, and there was no evidence that the CPA had followed through on the advice of FTB staff to submit a letter to the FTB explaining the taxpayer's position in order to receive a ruling.

In *Appeal of Freshman* (2006) (CCH CALIFORNIA TAX REPORTS, ¶ 89-210.243), a summary decision not to be cited as precedent, the BOE abated a penalty imposed for late filing of a California personal income tax return. The BOE determined that the taxpayers' reliance on their previous accountant's advice that they did not have a California personal income tax return filing requirement constituted reasonable cause. The taxpayers immediately filed a California nonresident return when they discovered that they were required to file a return and had an established history of timely filing their federal and resident state tax returns.

In *Appeal of Tuason* (2005) (CCH CALIFORNIA TAX REPORTS, ¶ 89-210.275), a summary decision not to be cited as precedent, the BOE abated a penalty imposed for late payment of California personal income tax by the same percentage that the Internal Revenue Service abated the taxpayer's federal late payment penalty, even though the taxpayer did not provide sufficient evidence to support her claim of reasonable cause and the IRS work papers did not specify that the penalty was abated for reasonable cause.

In several cases the BOE has upheld the presumptive correctness of the FTB's imposition of penalties. For example, in *Appeal of Harold G. Jindrich* (1977) (CCH CALIFORNIA TAX REPORTS, ¶ 89-224.7494), the taxpayer failed to file a return and did not respond to the FTB's notice and demand for a return. The BOE upheld the imposition of two 25% penalties, under items (4) and (6) above, on the income as computed by the FTB.

In *Appeal of Terry L. Lash* (1986) (CCH CALIFORNIA TAX REPORTS, ¶ 89-206.36), the taxpayer failed to prove to the BOE that the failure to respond to notice and demand to file was due to a reasonable cause and not willful neglect. The taxpayer also failed to prove that not filing a timely return in the subsequent year was due to a reasonable cause. Reasonable cause was tested in both years by the standards of a normally intelligent and prudent businessperson.

In *Appeal of Philip C. and Anne Berolzheimer* (1986) (CCH CALIFORNIA TAX REPORTS, ¶ 89-206.901), the BOE held that an underpayment penalty was properly assessed. A New York law firm, acting as the taxpayers' agent, had filed a timely request for an extension of time for filing the taxpayers' 1981 California income tax return. Due to a programming error in the agent's computer tax software program, the capital gains for the year were incorrectly computed, resulting in an underpayment of the amount required to be paid with the extension request. The FTB assessed an underpayment penalty.

In holding that the underpayment was due to willful neglect and not reasonable cause, the BOE found inapplicable the U.S. Supreme Court rule that it is reasonable for a taxpayer to rely on the advice of an accountant or attorney on a matter of tax law. The underpayment was not due to a mistake of law; it was due to a simple mistake in computation of tax due. It is not "reasonable cause" so as to overcome a presumption of "willful neglect" to rely on an accountant or attorney for a simple computational problem as distinguished from a matter of law.

In *Appeal of Greg L. Dexter* (1986) (CCH CALIFORNIA TAX REPORTS, ¶ 89-206.82), the BOE held that a return with the verification above the signature altered was not filed and signed under penalty of perjury and was an invalid return. Since the taxpayer had not filed a valid return, penalties for negligence and failure to respond were upheld and calculated on the entire tax liability.

¶712

Failure to receive a tax form does not constitute reasonable cause for failure to file—see *Appeal of Thomas P.E. and Barbara Rothchild* (1973) (CCH CALIFORNIA TAX REPORTS, ¶ 89-206.566).

In *Appeal of Frank E. and Lilia Z. Hublou* (1977) (CCH CALIFORNIA TAX REPORTS, ¶ 89-206.85), the taxpayers failed to respond to a notice and demand for a return. The return, as filed later, showed a tax liability of $213 which was more than offset by a $419 credit for tax withheld from salary, resulting in a refund. The BOE upheld the FTB in imposing a 25% penalty on the $213 tax liability, under item (6) above. To the same effect, see *Appeal of Sal J. Cardinalli* (1981) (CCH CALIFORNIA TAX REPORTS, ¶ 89-206.60), involving penalties imposed under items (6) and (10) above. In *Appeal of Irma E. Bazan* (1982) (CCH CALIFORNIA TAX REPORTS, ¶ 89-206.605), the BOE's opinion points out that the penalty described in item (6), above, is properly measured by the FTB's estimate of the tax liability rather than the actual tax as later determined.

In *Appeal of Estate of Marilyn Monroe, Deceased* (1975) (CCH CALIFORNIA TAX REPORTS, ¶ 89-206.80), the estate contended that there was reasonable cause for failure to file California returns, because of uncertainties as to whether the estate was subject to tax and the fact that the executor believed in good faith that no tax was due. The BOE upheld imposition of penalties ($12,810) for failure to file, commenting that "mere uninformed and unsupported belief, no matter how sincere . . . is insufficient to constitute reasonable cause . . . ."

In *Appeal of Horace H. and Mildred E. Hubbard* (1961) (CCH CALIFORNIA TAX REPORTS, ¶ 89-206.6092), the BOE upheld the penalty for failure to file, where the taxpayers had repeatedly ignored the demand of the FTB for a return based on a federal audit report.

In *Appeals of Leonard S. and Frances M. Gordon* (1960) (CCH CALIFORNIA TAX REPORTS, ¶ 89-206.6795), the BOE held that taxpayers, having previously been found guilty of filing fraudulent federal income tax returns, were also subject to the California fraud penalty provisions. (But see the *Brown* case, cited at ¶ 106, to the opposite effect.)

In *Appeal of Thomas* (1955) (CCH CALIFORNIA TAX REPORTS, ¶ 89-206.80), the BOE held that a new resident of California was subject to a delinquency penalty for failure to file a return for his first year in the state. The taxpayer's income was from salary earned in California; the BOE held that he could reasonably have been expected to make inquiry regarding possible liability for California tax. However, in *Appeal of Estate of Anna Armstrong* (1964) (CCH CALIFORNIA TAX REPORTS, ¶ 89-206.907), the BOE held that the taxpayer's failure to file a timely return was due to reasonable cause when she relied on the advice of competent professional tax advisors.

Both California and federal laws provide special provisions for injunctive relief to prevent taxpayers from engaging in certain conduct (abusive tax shelters, etc.) subject to penalty.

• *Tax Amnesty*

The enhanced interest penalties do not apply to taxpayers that have entered into an installment agreement with respect to amounts payable under the agreement. (Sec. 19738, Rev. & Tax. Code)

The FTB has stated that although a taxpayer cannot file a formal protest of a post-amnesty penalty before payment, and there are no formal prepayment protest rights, the FTB will administratively review and correct a post-amnesty penalty before payment if the taxpayer believes that the penalty was computed incorrectly. (*Tax News*, California Franchise Tax Board, June 2006)

A taxpayer may not file a claim for refund or credit for any amounts paid in connection with the enhanced interest penalty unless the penalty was improperly computed by the FTB. (Sec. 19777.5(e), Rev. & Tax. Code)

¶713 Information at Source

Law: Secs. 18631-32, 18639-61, 19175, 19182 (CCH CALIFORNIA TAX REPORTS, ¶ 89-104).

Comparable Federal: Secs. 6039, 6039D, 6041-50R, 6052-53, 6111 (CCH U.S. MASTER TAX GUIDE ¶ 628, 797, 871, 2004, 2565, 2607).

Under California law, the Franchise Tax Board (FTB) *may* require individuals, partnerships, corporations, or other organizations engaged in trade or business in California, making payments in the course of such trade or business, to make information returns and to furnish copies to recipients of the payments. The following are some of the payments that are covered. See Sec. 18631, Rev. & Tax. Code for a complete listing.

— *as to payees whose last known address is in California:*

— payments of any fixed or determinable income (*i.e.,* group term life insurance, gambling winnings, medical payments, remuneration for personal services, but excludes compensation subject to withholding as explained at ¶715) amounting to $600 or more;

— "service-recipients" required to make a return under IRC Sec. 6041A must also make a return to California;

— payments of dividends if the payor was required to file an information return (1099) under federal law;

— payments of interest if the payor was required to file an information return (1099) under federal law;

— specified payments of interest and exempt-interest dividends aggregating $10 or more if the interest is from other states' bonds exempt from federal income tax but taxable by California (see discussion below);

— group life insurance benefits provided to employees, to the extent the cost of such benefits exceeds the cost of $50,000 of coverage plus the amount contributed by the employee;

— corporate liquidating distributions amounting to $600 or more to any stockholder;

— patronage dividends of cooperatives amounting to $100 or more; and

— original issue discount paid on a publicly offered debt instrument; and

— *as to payees who are not residents of California;*

— payments of compensation for services rendered in California; and

— payments of rents or royalties on property located in California.

See ¶716 for reporting requirements for dispositions of real property.

• *Reporting not required*

The following payments need not be reported, regardless of amount:

— payments to a corporation, other than payments for attorneys' fees;

— partnership, estate, or trust distributions shown on their returns;

— rent payments to a real estate agent having a place of business in California;

—, payments to a nonresident that are reported by the withholding agent on Forms 592 and 592-B (¶714);

— payments of income exempt from California income tax;

— payments by those not engaged in a trade or business;

— payments for merchandise, etc.;

— certain payments to employees of interstate carriers;

— certain payments by bankers acting as collection agents.

(Reg. 18631--18681(b), 18 CCR)

• *Information on cash received in trade or business*

The FTB *must* require a copy of the federal information return relating to cash received in a trade or business (Form 8300) if a federal information return was required under IRC Sec. 6050I. Under federal law, any person required to be named in the return must be furnished with written notice of the name and address of the person required to file the Form 8300 and the amount of cash required to be specified on Form 8300 as received from the person named. California has not adopted this requirement. (Sec. 18631(c)(10), Rev. & Tax. Code)

• *Information on tax-exempt interest and dividends*

Brokerages and mutual fund companies are required to report to the FTB payments of interest and exempt-interest dividends aggregating $10 or more in any calendar year to any person if the interest and dividends are from other states' bonds that are exempt from federal income taxation but taxable by California. (Sec. 18631(c)(8), Rev. & Tax. Code)

• *Procedure for reporting*

Payments are reported on federal Form 1099. Except as noted below, 1099-B returns must be filed on magnetic tape; other information reports may be made on magnetic tape if the volume exceeds specified limits, conforming to the federal procedure. Reports are for the calendar year and are due generally on February 28th of the following year (March 31 if filed using the Internet). Extension of time for filing may be obtained by written request to the FTB. Copies of individual forms should be furnished to recipients by January 31. (FTB Pub. 4227, Information Returns (Forms 1098, 1099, 5498, W-2G))

Practice Note: Relationship to Federal Filing

Taxpayers that file paper information returns such as Form 1099s with the IRS are not required to file the returns with the FTB as the IRS will forward the information to the FTB. Similarly, if a taxpayer e-files these returns through the IRS Combined Federal/ State Filing Program, the returns need only be filed once. Generally, electronic returns may be filed by March 31; however, the IRS has not extended the deadline for filing Form 5498 electronically. If different figures are required to be reported for state and federal purposes, taxpayers must file separate returns with the IRS and the FTB. Although the FTB encourages taxpayers to file these returns electronically, a taxpayer is not required to e-file such returns unless the taxpayer files 250 or more returns. (*Tax News*, California Franchise Tax Board, February 26, 2010. CCH CALIFORNIA TAX REPORTS, ¶ 405-127)

• *Nontaxable distributions*

In the case of corporate distributions believed to be nontaxable, complete information should be supplied to the FTB not later than February 1, for the preceding year. The FTB will then advise the distributing corporation regarding the taxability of the distribution.

• *Stock options*

Corporations transferring stock under certain stock options are required to furnish statements (by January 31 of the following year) to the individuals involved. California incorporates the federal requirement. (Sec. 18631(c)(2), Rev. & Tax. Code)

• *Tips*

The California recordkeeping and reporting requirements for tips are generally the same as the federal regulations. However, under federal law, certain food or beverage establishments employing ten or more workers on a typical business day in the preceding year are required to file annual information returns for the purpose of increasing taxpayer compliance in reporting income from tips. California has no comparable requirement. (Reg. 4350-1)

• *Tax-shelter promoters*

Tax shelter promoters are subject to stringent reporting requirements; see ¶727 for details.

• *Property owners*

Owners and transferors of real property or a mobile home assessed by a California assessor, except for property covered by a homeowner's exemption (¶1704), may be required to file returns requested and prescribed by the FTB. The returns include the owner's social security number or other identification number prescribed by the FTB, identification of the property interest, and other information the FTB may request. Owners who fail to file within 60 days of the due date or who file a misleading return will be denied deductions for interest, taxes, depreciation, or amortization paid or incurred with respect to the property. (Sec. 18642, Rev. & Tax. Code)

• *Check cashing businesses*

Any check cashing business that cashes checks other than one-party checks, payroll checks, or government checks totaling more than $10,000 in one transaction or in two or more transactions for the same person within the calendar year must file an information return with the FTB no later than 90 days after the end of the calendar year. (Sec. 18631.7, Rev. & Tax. Code)

• *Penalties*

As stated at ¶712, severe civil and criminal penalties may be imposed for various offenses, including failure to comply with the requirements for information returns. Also, as stated at ¶336, certain deductions may be disallowed in cases where required information returns are not filed.

The failure to file information returns on remuneration for personal services is also penalized under the Unemployment Insurance Code. If the failure to file is punishable under the Revenue and Taxation Code as well as the Unemployment Insurance Code, only the latter penalty will be applied. (Sec. 19175, Rev. & Tax. Code)

¶714 Withholding of Tax at Source—General

Law: Secs. 18536, 18662, 18664, 18665, 18666, 18668-77, 19002 (CCH CALIFORNIA TAX REPORTS, ¶16-605, 16-635, 16-640, 16-650, 16-655, 89-056, 89-176).

Comparable Federal: Secs. 1445, 1446, 3406 (CCH U.S. MASTER TAX GUIDE ¶2329, 2492, 2645).

California Forms: Forms 587 (Nonresident Withholding Allocation Worksheet), 588 (Nonresident Withholding Waiver Request), Form 589 (Nonresident Reduced Withholding Request), 590 (Withholding Exemption Certificate), 590-P (Nonresident Withholding Exemption Certificate for Previously Reported Income), 592 (Resident and Nonresident Withholding Statement), 592-A (Payment Voucher for Foreign Partner or Member Withholding), 592-B (Resident and Nonresident Withholding Tax Statement), 592-F (Foreign Partner or Member Annual Return), 592-V (Payment Voucher for Resident and Nonresident Withholding), 594 (Notice to Withhold Tax at Source), 595 (Entertainment Withholding Reduction), 1023S (Resident and Nonresident Withholding Electronic Submission Requirements).

Below is a discussion of the withholding requirements for payments to residents, nonresidents, and foreign partners.

CCH Comment: Withholding Agents

Anyone can be a withholding agent. The requirement to withhold is not limited to business entities. Any individual or business entity who makes payments that fit the requirements below is considered a withholding agent. (*FTB Tax News* (2012), CCH CALIFORNIA TAX REPORTS, ¶405-721)

• *Back-up withholding*

California requires payors to withhold 7% from specified reportable payments. California's provision is similar to the federal backup withholding provisions under IRC Sec. 3406. However, California's requirements apply to rents, prizes and winnings, compensation for services, including bonuses, and other fixed or determinable annual or periodic gains, profits, and income, but do not apply to payments of interest and dividends or any release of loan funds made by a financial institution in the normal course of business. (Sec. 18664, Rev. & Tax. Code)

Generally, with the exceptions noted above, back-up withholding is required if a payer issues a payment of more than $600 to a payee that is subject to federal backup withholding, and the payee is a California resident or is a nonresident of California and the payment is sourced to California.

Back-up withholding is required when a payee submits an IRS Form W-9 that: does not provide a taxpayer identification number (TIN); provides an invalid TIN; or fails to certify exemption from backup withholding. There is no waiver available for back-up withholding, but back-up withholding does not apply to real estate withholding and government entities, tax-exempt organizations, and other payers listed on IRS Form W-9 as exempt from back-up withholding.

A payer who back-up withholds in error or back-up withholds too much may refund the incorrect amount withheld if payment has not yet been sent to the FTB. The refund must be made prior to the end of the calendar year. If the payer has already sent the incorrect amount to the FTB, then the payer may adjust subsequent remittances of withholding. (*Tax News*, California Franchise Tax Board, October 1, 2009)

• *Nonresidents*

As to nonresidents, withholding is generally required on payments of compensation for personal services performed in California (including payments to independent contractors), rents, patent royalties, prizes, etc., provided the income is attributable to California (see ¶231 for discussion of income from sources within the state). In addition, the Franchise Tax Board (FTB) requires withholding on payments of pass-through entity income to domestic nonresident owners. (Sec. 18662, Rev. & Tax. Code; Reg. 18662-2, 18 CCR) FTB Pub. 1017, *Resident and Nonresident Withholding Guidelines*, also specifies that withholding must be made on payments from the following sources:

— payments made to nonresident entertainers for services rendered in California, including, but not limited to, guaranteed payments, overages, royalties, and residual payments;

— payments received for a covenant not to compete in California;

— payments releasing a contractual obligation to perform services in California;

— income from options received for performing personal services in California;

— bonuses paid for services performed in California; and

— distributions of California source taxable income.

However, under Reg. 18662-2, 18 CCR, withholding is not required unless the income payments to a payee by the same payor exceed $1,500 during the calendar year or the payor is directed to withhold by the FTB.

Nonresidents include nonresident individuals, nonresident estates and trusts, and corporations and pass-through entities that do not have a permanent place of business in California and are not registered with the California Secretary of State's Office (SOS). A corporate payee that is not qualified through the SOS and does not have a permanent place of business in this state, but is included in the combined report of a corporation that does have a permanent place of business in California, is also subject to nonresident withholding. However, the corporation may request a waiver from the FTB by submitting Form 588, Nonresident Withholding Waiver Request. (FTB Pub. 1017, *Resident and Nonresident Withholding Guidelines*)

The tax to be withheld for nonresident individuals and business entities is generally computed at the rate of 7% of gross income. (Reg. 18662-3, 18 CCR) However, in cases such as those involving entertainers where deductible expenses are likely to be large, the FTB may upon application (through the payor's submission of a Form 588, Nonresident Withholding Waiver Request) waive the withholding requirements in whole or in part. According to the Instructions to Form 588, reasons for a waiver request include the following:

— the vendor/payee has California state tax returns on file for the two most recent taxable years in which the vendor/payee has a filing requirement, and the vendor/payee is considered current on any outstanding tax obligations with the FTB;

— the vendor/payee is making timely estimated tax payments for the current taxable year, and the vendor/payee is considered current on any outstanding tax obligations with the FTB;

— the vendor/payee, S corporation shareholder, partner, or member is a corporation not qualified to do business and does not have a permanent place of business in California but is filing a tax return based on a combined report with a corporation that does have a permanent place of business in California; or

— the vendor/payee, shareholder, partner, or member is a newly admitted S corporation shareholder, partner, or LLC member.

If none of the above reasons apply, a taxpayer may still submit a request but must attach a specific reason and a calculation of the reduced rate. Waivers may not be granted for withholding on foreign partners. Different procedures apply to waivers for withholding on sales of California real estate.

CCH Practice Pointer: Partnership Distributions Representing a Return of Capital

Waiver requests are not required if a partnership's distribution represents a return of capital. However, the partnership will be subject to penalties for failure to withhold if, upon audit, the FTB determines that the distribution represented taxable income. (FTB Pub. 1017, Resident and Nonresident Withholding Guidelines)

Waivers are effective for a maximum of two years from the date the waiver is granted.

Domestic nonresidents use Form 589, Nonresident Request for Reduced Withholding, to request a reduction in the standard 7% withholding amount that is applicable to California source payments to nonresidents. The payee must complete Form 589 before receiving payment for services and must

— complete the form based on expenses, costs, or other special circumstances that would justify a reduced withholding amount;

— calculate the proposed reduced withholding amount as 7% of the net California source payment, which is the gross payment minus expenses or costs identified on the form; and

— certify under penalty of perjury that the expenses and resulting reduced withholding calculations are true and correct.

After the FTB analyzes Form 589, it will issue a letter to the payee and the withholding agent notifying them of its determination and the amount to be withheld. The FTB has indicated that receiving Form 589 at least 10 business days before the withholding agent pays the nonresident payee will help it meet requests as quickly as possible. (*FTB Tax News* (November 2007), CCH CALIFORNIA TAX REPORTS, ¶404-487)

Waivers or reduced rates.—The FTB applies Federal Treasury Reg. 1.1446-6 procedures, which allow foreign partners to request reduced or no withholding of California tax on effectively connected taxable income from California sources allocable to a foreign partner. A foreign partner may request reduced withholding annually before the first installment period using FTB Form 589, Nonresident Reduced Withholding Request. A completed and signed IRS Form 8804-C, Certificate of Partner-Level Items to Reduce Section 1446 Withholding, must be submitted with FTB Form 589. The FTB has provided a chart summarizing how to request and report foreign partner reduced withholding. The foreign partner claims credit for the withholding by attaching a copy of FTB Form 592-B when filing a California tax return. (*Tax News*, California Franchise Tax Board, June 2011, CCH CALIFORNIA TAX REPORTS, ¶405-440)

Practice Note: Treatment of Withholding on Payments to Pass-Through Entities

As a general rule, withholding on payments to pass-through entities must be passed through and credited against the pass-through entity owners' tax liabilities in proportion to their ownership interests. However, pass-through entities may claim the withholding against any entity level tax or fees that may be owing prior to passing through the withholding credit to its owners. The entity level taxes include the annual tax imposed on partnerships, limited liability companies, and S corporations; the LLC fees; and the 1.5% tax imposed against S corporations. (FTB Pub. 1017, *Resident and Nonresident Withholding Guidelines*)

S corporations may not claim a refund of California income tax withholding at source in excess of their tax liability. Any remaining withholding at source credit in excess of their tax liability must be allocated to their shareholders using Form 592, Quarterly Resident and Nonresident Withholding Statement. (*FTB Public Service Bulletin 10-09, New Withhold at Source Rule for 2009 Form 100S* (2010), CCH CALIFORNIA TAX REPORTS, ¶405-150)

Certain nonresident individual owners of S corporations, partnerships, or LLCs may elect to file a group nonresident return using Long Form 540NR, California Nonresident or Part-Year Resident Income Tax Return, in which case the business entity would file a group nonresident return for its qualified nonresident pass-through entity owners. In order for withholding to be credited to a nonresident group return, the proper Form 592 showing the allocation of these withholding credits needs to be filed. If Form 592 is not filed, withholding may not be properly credited to the group nonresident return. If the withholding credit was not allocated to the nonresident group return, Schedule 1067A, Nonresident Group Return Schedule, must be used to allow the FTB to move withholding credits to the group. It will take the FTB six to eight weeks to move the withholding credits and make them available to be claimed on the group return. (*FTB Tax News*, August 2012, CCH CALIFORNIA TAX REPORTS, ¶405-697)

• *Foreign partners*

California incorporates the federal provision (IRC Sec. 1446) that requires the withholding of tax on all amounts paid by U.S. partnerships to foreign partners that

¶1714

are connected to the partnership's U.S. activities. (Sec. 18666, Rev. & Tax. Code) Also, the FTB applies Federal Treasury Regulation 1.1446-6 procedures to reduce or eliminate withholding of California tax on effectively connected taxable income from California sources allocable to a foreign partner or member. (Instructions, Form 588, Nonresident Withholding Waiver Request) However, the California tax is withheld at the maximum applicable California rate, rather than at the rate specified in the federal provision, and California's withholding is limited to California-source amounts. The $1,500 minimum filing threshold is not applicable to the withholding for foreign partners.

• *Teachers' Replacement Benefit Program payments*

Annual benefits payable under the Teachers' Replacement Benefits Program are subject to withholding of California personal income and employment taxes. The disbursements under this program represent amounts in excess of federal limitations on annual benefits applicable to a government plan (Sec. 24260, Education Code).

• *Per capita distributions made to Native American tribe members*

An alternative personal income tax withholding procedure is available for per capita income distributed by Native American tribes to their resident tribal members. Tribes may send the withheld amounts directly to the FTB using Form 592, Quarterly Resident and Nonresident Withholding Statement, in lieu of making payments to the EDD and filing form DE-6 with the Employment Development Department. The Form 592 includes a Schedule of Payees section to identify the payment recipients and the income and withholding amounts. The tribe will also need to provide a Form 592-B, Resident and Nonresident Withholding Tax Statement, to the tribal member. The member should include the Form 592-B with his or her personal income tax return for purposes of claiming his or her withholding credit. (*Tax News*, California Franchise Tax Board, May 4, 2009)

• *Procedures and returns*

A payor who receives a Nonresident Withholding Allocation Worksheet (Form 587) from the payee may rely on that certification to determine if withholding is required provided the form is accepted in good faith. A payor is relieved of the obligation to withhold if he or she obtains a Withholding Exemption Certificate (Form 590) or Nonresident Withholding Exemption Certificate for Previously Reported Income of Partners and Members (Form 590-P). (Reg. 18662-7, 18 CCR) Foreign (non-U.S.) partners or members may not file a Form 590-P as there is no exemption from withholding available to a foreign partner or member. (Instructions to Form 590-P) Penalties (fine, or imprisonment, or both) are provided for violation of withholding requirements.

Compliance Tip: Incomplete Exemption Certificates Invalid; Substitutes Allowed

If the withholding agent receives an incomplete certificate, the withholding agent is required to withhold tax on payments made to the payee until a valid certificate is received. In lieu of a completed certificate on the preprinted form, the withholding agent may accept as a substitute certificate a letter from the payee explaining why the payee is not subject to withholding. The letter must contain all the information required on the certificate in similar language, including the under penalty of perjury statement and the payee's taxpayer identification number. The withholding agent must retain a copy of the certificate or substitute for at least five years after the last payment to which the certificate applies, and provide it upon request to the FTB. (Instructions for Form 590, Withholding Exemption Certificate)

Tax withheld on California source payments is remitted to the FTB on a quarterly basis (similar to estimated tax payments, see ¶111) using Form 592, Resident and

Nonresident Withholding Statement. Form 592 includes a schedule of payees section that requires the withholding agent to identify the payment recipients, the income, and the withholding amounts. Withholding agents are not required to submit Form 592-B, Resident and Nonresident Withholding Tax Statement, to the FTB for each payee, but must still provide each payee with a paper Form 592-B to show the total amount withheld for the year.

Partnerships and LLCs withholding on foreign partners or members must file Form 592-A *Payment Voucher for Foreign Partner or Member Withholding*, along with their withholding. Form 592-A is filed on the 15th day of the fourth, sixth, ninth, and twelfth months of the partnership's or LLCs taxable year. At the close of the taxable year, the partnership or LLC must complete Form 592-F, Foreign Partner or Member Annual Return, to report the total withholding for the year and allocate the income or gain and related withholding to the foreign partners or members. When filing Form 592-F, the withholding agent is not required to submit Form 592-B to the FTB for each partner or member. However, withholding agents must provide the partners or members with paper Forms 592-B.

For realty dispositions, Form 593, Real Estate Remittance Statement, is used to report and transmit the amount withheld, see ¶716.

Practice Tip: Voluntary Disclosure Program

A Withholding Voluntary Compliance Program (WVCP) is available that allows eligible withholding agents to remit past-due, nonwage personal income tax and real estate withholding for the previous two calendar years, including interest, in exchange for having specified withholding tax liabilities and penalties waived. See ¶725 for details.

Practice Tip: SWIFT Filings

Withholding agents must use the FTB's Secure Web Internet Filing Transfer (SWIFT) process to submit the withholding data electronically. Publication 923, SWIFT Guide for Resident, Nonresident, and Real Estate Withholding, contains technical information for preparing withholding forms for submission through SWIFT. Additional information is available on the FTB's Web site at http://ftb.ca.gov/individuals/wsc/electronic_filing.shtml#New_Features. Questions or comments can be sent via e-mail to WSCS.SWIFT@ftb.ca.gov. (*Announcement*, California Franchise Tax Board, September 17, 2010)

• *Interest on late remittances*

The interest on deficiencies (¶709) applies to delayed remittances of amounts withheld from fixed or determinable gains, profits, and income and from remittances of partnership income to foreign partners. (Sec. 18668, Rev. & Tax. Code)

• *Delinquent taxes*

In addition to withholding from payments of income to nonresidents, the FTB may require withholding of delinquent taxes due from both resident and nonresident taxpayers. The FTB may, by notice and demand, require such withholding and payment to the FTB by anyone, including state agencies, who is in possession or control of credits or property belonging to a delinquent taxpayer or belonging to a person who has failed to withhold as required under the law. (Sec. 18670, Rev. & Tax. Code)

In *Greene v. Franchise Tax Board* (1972) (CCH CALIFORNIA TAX REPORTS, ¶89-176.60) the California Court of Appeal upheld the FTB's use of the withholding procedure to collect delinquent tax of $72. In *Franchise Tax Board v. Construction Laborers Vacation Trust for Southern California* (1983) (CCH CALIFORNIA TAX REPORTS, ¶89-176.602), the issue was whether the FTB was precluded by federal law (ERISA) from requiring a union vacation trust fund to withhold for unpaid personal income tax owed by union members. The U.S. Supreme Court held that federal courts did not have jurisdiction in the matter, and referred the case back to California Superior Court. In *Franchise Tax Board of California v. United States Postal Service* (1984) (CCH CALIFORNIA TAX REPORTS, ¶ 89-176.80), the U.S. Supreme Court held that the Postal Service could be required to withhold delinquent California tax from its employees.

An employer is liable for unremitted amounts, plus interest, if the FTB determines that an employer withheld earnings pursuant to an earnings withholding order for taxes but failed to remit the withheld earnings to the FTB, and the employer also fails to remit the withheld earnings following notice from the FTB. A deficiency assessment may be issued for such amount within seven years from the date that the amount, in the aggregate, was first withheld. When the assessment against the employer becomes final, the taxpayer's account may be credited for that amount. Collection action against the taxpayer is stayed until the earlier of the time the credit is applied or the assessment against the employer is withdrawn or revised and the taxpayer is notified thereof. (Sec. 18673, Rev. & Tax. Code)

• *Date tax deemed paid*

For the purpose of filing claims for refund, any tax withheld under the California withholding provisions is deemed to have been paid on the due date (without regard to extensions of time) of the return for the taxable year with respect to which the withheld tax is allowed as a credit. (Sec. 19002, Rev. & Tax. Code) Under the proposed regulations, special rules would apply to end-of-the year payments and distributions. (Proposed Reg. 19002, 18 CCR)

¶715 Withholding on Wages

Law: Secs. 18408, 18551, 18662-66, 19002, 19009, 19852, 19853; Secs. 1088, 1112.1, 1151-1153, 1233—1236, 1870-1875, 13004, 13009, 13020, 13021, 13028, 13059, Unemployment Insurance Code (CCH CALIFORNIA TAX REPORTS, ¶ 16-610, 16-615, 16-620, 16-630, 16-645, 16-660, 89-102, 89-106, 89-186, 89-210).

Comparable Federal: Secs. 31, 3401-05, 3501-05, 6051, 6053 (CCH U.S. MASTER TAX GUIDE ¶ 2601 et seq.).

California Forms: DE-4 (Employee's Withholding Allowance Certificate), W-2 (Wage and Tax Statement), DE-9 (Quarterly Contribution Return and Report of Wages), DE-0C (Quarterly Contribution Return and Report of Wages (Continuation)), Form 592-V (Payment Voucher for Resident and Nonresident Withholding), FTB 3525 (Substitute for W-2, Wage and Tax Statement, or Form 1099-R, Distributions from Pensions, Annuities, Retirement or Profit-Sharing Plans, IRAs, Insurance Contracts, Etc.).

The California wage withholding system conforms closely to the federal system. For this reason, the following discussion will deal principally with the differences between the California and federal rules.

• *California-federal differences*

Employers are required to withhold on all "wages," as defined below, of California residents and on "wages" of nonresidents for services performed in California. (Sec. 13020, Unempl. Ins. Code) As in the federal rules, "wages" includes all remuneration for services of an employee, with specified exceptions for agricultural labor, domestic service, and other categories. Wages includes compensation that is deductible under IRC Sec. 162 that is paid to a member of a limited liability company filing a federal corporate income tax return. Following are differences between the California and federal rules in what is subject to withholding:

> — California excludes wages paid to members of a crew on a vessel engaged in foreign, coastwise, intercoastal, interstate, or noncontiguous trade; federal law has no such exclusion;

— federal law excludes compensation paid under certain bond purchase plans; California has no such exclusion;

— federal law excludes certain foreign service; California has no such exclusion; however, such compensation would be excluded under California law if the employee is not a California "resident," as defined at ¶105;

— California specifies that whether an individual provides equipment shall be ignored in determining whether the individual is an "employee" (Sec. 13004, Unempl. Ins. Code); and

— federal law considers certain payments of gambling winnings as wages, whereas California withholding law does not. (Sec. 13009, Unempl. Ins. Code) However, California does require withholding from prizes and winnings. (Reg. 18662-2, 18 CCR)

The California rules for withholding on pensions, annuities, sick pay, supplemental unemployment benefits, and other deferred income conform generally to the federal rules.

• *Employee vs. independent contractor*

In *Hunt Building Corp. v. Michael S. Bernick* (2000) (CCH CALIFORNIA TAX REPORTS, ¶16-615.80), a California court of appeal held that a general contractor was subject to California personal income tax withholding and unemployment compensation fund and disability insurance contribution requirements as if it were the employer of its unlicensed subcontractors' employees. State law defined the unlicensed subcontractors and their employees as employees of the general contractor, rather than independent contractors, because their services required the general contractor to obtain a state contractor license. Although the construction work performed by the unlicensed subcontractors' employees was performed for the U.S. government on federal lands, federal law provided no relief from the state requirements, because federal law deferred to state law defining employer/employee relationships.

• *Withholding methods*

California provides two methods for computing the amount of tax to be withheld, as follows:

Method A—WAGE BRACKET TABLE METHOD (similar to federal "wage bracket" method); and

Method B—EXACT CALCULATION METHOD (similar to the federal "percentage" method).

California permits use of other methods in special situations, upon application. Federal rules also permit alternative methods.

With respect to supplemental wages (bonuses, overtime, commissions, sales awards, back pay including retroactive wage increases, reimbursement of nondeductible moving expenses, and stock options), an employer may either

— add supplemental wages to regular wages and compute withholding on the whole amount or

— apply a flat percentage rate to the supplemental wages alone, without allowance for exemptions or credits.

California's supplemental withholding rate is 6.6%. The withholding rate on stock options and bonus payments that constitute wages is 10.23%. (Sec. 13043, Unempl. Ins. Code; Sec. 18663, Rev. & Tax. Code)

¶715

Practice Pointer: Withholding Rate Increased

The payroll withholding rate was increased in the wage withholding tables by 10%, effective for wages paid after October 31, 2009. (Sec. 18663(a)(2), Rev. & Tax. Code) The increased withholding rate is voluntary and taxpayers may adjust the amount withheld to counteract the increase.

• *Instruction booklet*

Detailed instructions for determining the amount to be withheld, with tables and formulas, are included in a booklet entitled "Employer's Tax Guide for the Withholding, Payment, and Reporting of California Income Tax." This booklet can be obtained from offices of the FTB or the EDD or on the EDD's Web site at: http://www.edd.ca.gov/Payroll_Taxes/Rates_and_Withholding.htm.

• *Employee forms*

California provides a form (Form DE-4) for the employee's exemption certificate to determine the number of California withholding exemptions. The employee has the option of using California Form DE-4. Otherwise, the employee must use federal Form W-4 to determine the number of California exemptions. The employee is considered married if the employer cannot determine the employee's marital status from either Form DE-4 or W-4.

California conforms fully to the federal rules for exemption certificates. Thus, any certificate that complies with the federal rules is accepted also for California purposes. The requirements for complete exemption, based on absence of federal income tax liability, are the same for California as for federal; that is, a certificate that eliminates federal withholding also eliminates California withholding. An employer who makes the required special report to the Internal Revenue Service where a large number of exemptions is claimed need not make a report to the state. The FTB may require employers to submit copies of withholding exemption certificates. The law sets forth procedures to be followed if the FTB determines that the withholding exemption certificate is invalid. (Sec. 13040, Unempl. Ins. Code; Sec. 13041, Unempl. Ins. Code; Sec. 18667, Rev. & Tax. Code; Reg. 4340-1, 22 CCR)

• *Filing of returns*

Withheld tax must be reported and paid monthly or quarterly, depending on the amounts involved, as explained below.

Statements must be furnished to employees, using federal Form W-2, by January 31 and upon termination. The Form W-2 must show the amount of disability insurance contributions (SDI) withheld. (Sec. 13050, Unempl. Ins. Code)

Practice Note: Earned Income Tax Credit Information Must Be Provided to Employees

California employers must notify employees covered by the employer's unemployment insurance that they may be eligible for the federal and California earned income tax credits (EITCs). The EITC notice must be provided by handing the notice directly to the employee or mailing the notice to the employee's last-known address within the one week period before or after the employer provides the employee an annual wage summary. Sec. 19852, Rev. & Tax. Code, Sec. 19853, Rev. & Tax. Code.

Generally, a report of wages (Form DE-9 and Form DE-9C) must be submitted each calendar quarter showing the total tax withheld for each employee and the amounts withheld from pensions, annuities, and other deferred compensation. (Sec. 13021, Unempl. Ins. Code; Sec. 13050, Unempl. Ins. Code)

¶715

The due date of a withholding return, report, or statement may be extended if an employer's failure to timely file or pay tax is attributable to a state of emergency declared by the Governor. (Sec. 13059, Rev. & Tax. Code)

Electronic filing.—Effective January 1, 2017, all employers with 10 or more employees must file their report of contributions, quarterly return, and report of wages electronically. Effective January 1, 2018, the requirement is extended to all employers to file the report of contributions, quarterly return, and report of wages electronically. However, an employer may request a waiver from the electronic filing requirements. The Employment Development Department may grant a waiver if the employer establishes to the satisfaction of the director that there is a lack of automation, a severe economic hardship, a current exemption from filing electronically for federal purposes, or other good cause. An approved waiver will be valid for one year or longer, at the discretion of the director. (Sec. 1088, Unempl. Ins. Code) Beginning January 1, 2019, an employer that is required to file a quarterly return electronically and without good cause fails to file electronically will be subject to a penalty of $50, in addition to any other penalties that may apply. (Sec. 1112.1, Unempl. Ins. Code)

• *Payment of tax*

An employer who is required to remit withheld federal income taxes pursuant to IRC Sec. 6302 and who has accumulated withheld state income taxes in the amount of $500 or more must remit the withheld state income taxes within the same number of business days specified for withheld federal income taxes. The $500 threshold amount is adjusted annually for inflation. For 2016, the threshold amount is $500. An employer who is required to withhold tax, but who is not required to remit payment in accordance with IRC Sec. 6302, must remit the amount withheld during each month of each calendar quarter by the 15th day of the subsequent month if the amount withheld for any month, or cumulatively for two or more months within the quarter, is $350 or more. (Sec. 13021, Unempl. Ins. Code)

Prior to January 1, 2017, any employer whose cumulative average payment during any deposit period is $20,000 or more must remit the withheld state income taxes by way of electronic funds transfer within the same number of business days specified in IRC Sec. 6302, for withheld federal income taxes. Effective January 1, 2017, all employers subject to the electronic filing requirements of Sec. 1088, Unemp. Ins. Code, must remit the total amount of income tax withheld by electronic funds transfer. The electronic funds transfer requirement may be waived if the average withholding payment exceeding the threshold amount is not representative of the taxpayer's actual tax liability and was the result of an unprecedented occurrence.

Employers not required to pay by electronic means may elect to do so with the approval of the EDD. Payment by electronic means will generally be deemed complete on the date the transfer is initiated.

Any income tax withheld that is not covered by any of the above requirements must be remitted to the state by the last day of the month following the end of the quarter. Any amounts withheld for employees' disability-insurance contributions (¶1808) are due and payable at the same time as the payments for income-tax withholding, regardless of the amounts involved.

Employers who are subject to certain requirements for accelerated payment of withheld federal taxes are required to remit withheld California taxes on the same time schedule.

The law provides detailed rules for collection of tax, liabilities and obligations of employers and employees, penalties, etc. An employer or withholding agent is liable for personal income tax required to be deducted and withheld or, withheld and not timely remitted. The employer or withholding agent is generally liable whether or not the tax was collected and withheld. (Sec. 13070, Unempl. Ins. Code; Sec. 18668, Rev. & Tax. Code; Reg. 4370-1, 22 CCR) If the tax for which an employer is liable is paid or if the employee reports the wages to the FTB, the employer is relieved of liability for the tax itself but not for penalties or additions to the tax arising out of the failure to withhold. (Sec. 13071, Unempl. Ins. Code)

Upon sale of a business, the purchaser may be liable for unsatisfied obligations of the seller. (Sec. 18669, Rev. & Tax. Code) EDD Reg. 4320-1, 22 CCR, specifies procedures to be followed when employers are required to withhold other-state taxes from wages paid to California residents. In these cases, where the other state's withholding requirement is greater than the California amount, no California withholding is required.

Withholding is required on judgments for lost past and future wages. Adopting the prevailing federal view, the California Court of Appeal, Second District, held in *Cifuentes v. Costco Wholesale Corporation* (2015) (CCH CALIFORNIA TAX REPORTS, ¶16-615.851) that an employer was required to withhold federal and California personal income and payroll taxes from a judgment to a former employee for "lost past wages" (back pay) and "lost future wages" (front pay).

• *Compromise of withholding tax liability*

The EDD is authorized to accept partial payment in satisfaction of final, nondisputed withholding tax liabilities of certain employers if the amount offered in compromise is more than could reasonably be collected through involuntary means during the four-year period beginning on the date the offer is made. (Sec. 1870 et seq., Unempl. Ins. Code)

Practice Pointer: Making an Offer in Compromise

Form DE 999CA, Multi-Agency Form for Offer in Compromise, may be used by individuals to make an offer in compromise for personal income, sales and use, and other taxes owed to the FTB, BOE, and EDD. Corporations, partnerships, and limited liability companies should continue to use Form FTB 4905BE, Offer in Compromise for Business Entities, for FTB offers, and Form BOE-490-C, Offer In Compromise Application For Corporations, Limited Liability Companies, Partnerships, Trusts, and Unidentified Business Organizations, for BOE offers. (*News Release*, California Tax Service Center, August 23, 2006)

• *Penalties*

As stated at ¶712, severe civil and criminal penalties are imposed on employers, employees, and others for various offenses. Also, as stated at ¶322, deductions for remuneration for personal services may be disallowed for failure to report the payments in required statements to employees or to independent contractors.

• *Settlement authority*

The Director of the EDD may approve the settlement of any civil tax dispute involving a reduction of tax of $7,500 or less on his or her own authority. However, the proposed settlement must be submitted to an administrative law judge for approval if any of the following circumstances apply:

— an appeal has been filed with the Unemployment Insurance Appeals Board;

— the appeal has been assigned to an administrative law judge; and

— a notice of hearing has been issued.

(Sec. 1236, Unempl. Ins. Code)

¶715

Proposed settlements of $5,000 or more must be reviewed by the Attorney General prior to final approval, and settlements involving amounts over $7,500 must also be approved by the Unemployment Insurance Appeals Board.

• *Waiver for reliance on written advice*

The EDD is authorized to waive tax assessments, interest, additions to tax, or penalties imposed as a result of a taxpayer's failure to make a timely return or payment if the taxpayer's failure was due to the taxpayer's reasonable reliance on the written advice of a ruling by the Director or the Director's designee. If the taxpayer's action was due to reasonable reliance on written advice other than a ruling by the director or director's designee, the EDD is authorized to waive interest, additions to tax, or penalties. All of the following conditions must be met before the EDD may provide relief:

— the taxpayer must request advice regarding the tax consequences of a particular activity or transaction and the activity or transaction must be fully described;

— the EDD must issue a written ruling or opinion;

— the taxpayer must have reasonably relied on that advice; and

— the tax consequences expressed in the EDD's advice must not have been changed by a later issued opinion, statutory or case law, federal interpretation, or material facts or circumstances relating to the taxpayer.

(Sec. 111, Unempl. Ins. Code)

No relief will be provided if the taxpayer's request for written advice contained a misrepresentation or omission of a material fact.

Nonprofit organizations and governmental agencies are specifically excluded from the relief provisions discussed above. Relief from the assessment of unemployment insurance taxes is conditioned upon approval from the U.S. Secretary of Labor; however, relief from any corresponding interest and penalties may still be provided.

¶716 Withholding on Dispositions of California Realty

Law: Secs. 18662, 18668 (CCH CALIFORNIA TAX REPORTS, ¶16-625, 89-102, 89-206).

Comparable Federal: Sec. 1445 (CCH U.S. MASTER TAX GUIDE ¶2442).

California Forms: Forms 593 (Real Estate Withholding Tax Statement), 593-C (Real Estate Withholding Certificate), 593-I (Real Estate Withholding Installment Sale Acknowledgement), 593-E (Real Estate Withholding - Computation of Estimated Gain or Loss), 593-V (Payment Voucher for Real Estate Withholding Electronic Submission), FTB Pub. 1016 (Real Estate Withholding Guidelines).

Applicable to dispositions of real property interests by resident individuals, nonresident individuals, corporations with no permanent place of business in California, and out-of-state partnerships, transferees (including intermediaries or accommodators in a deferred exchange) are required to withhold an amount equal to $3\frac{1}{3}\%$ of the sales price of the California real property conveyed.

Alternatively, transferors may to elect to withhold at the corporation franchise tax rate (currently, 8.84%), bank and financial corporation tax rate (currently, 10.84%), or highest personal income tax rate of 12.3%, as applicable, multiplied by the reportable gain on the sale rather than at the current withholding rate of 31/3% on the sales price of California real property conveyed. For this purpose, the highest personal income tax rate is determined without regard to the additional 1% surtax (*a.k.a.* the mental health services tax) on income in excess of $1 million.

The alternative withholding rate for S corporations is 13.8% of the gain (the current S corporation tax rate of 1.5% plus the highest personal income tax rate of 12.3%). For S corporations that are financial corporations, the alternative withholding rate is 15.8%. (Sec. 18662, Rev. & Tax. Code)

However, no withholding is required if any of the following circumstances apply:

— the sales price of the California real property conveyed is $100,000 or less;

— written notification of the withholding requirements was not provided by a real estate escrow person (this exception does not apply to an intermediary or an accommodator in a deferred exchange);

— the transferee acquires the property at a sale pursuant to a power of sale under a mortgage or deed of trust, at a sale pursuant to a decree of foreclosure, or by a deed in lieu of foreclosure;

— the transferor is a bank acting as a trustee other than a trustee of a deed of trust;

— the property being conveyed is (1) the principal residence of the transferor or decedent, or (2) the last use of the property being conveyed was use by the transferor as the transferor's principal residence, even if the transferor does not satisfy the two out of the last five years requirement or other special circumstances;

— the property was the subject of an IRC Sec. 1033 compulsory or involuntary conversion and the transferor intends to acquire property similar or related in service or use so as to be eligible for nonrecognition of gain;

— the transaction will result in either a net loss or a net gain not required to be recognized for California income or franchise tax purposes;

— the property being conveyed is exchanged, or will be exchanged, for IRC Sec. 1031 like-kind property, but only to the extent of the amount of the gain not required to be recognized for California purposes under IRC Sec. 1031;

— the transferor is a California partnership (including an LLC treated as a partnership); or

— the transferor is a corporation with a permanent place of business in California.

(Sec. 18662, Rev. & Tax. Code)

Practice Tip: Transfers by Trusts

Whether withholding is required on transfers of property by trusts is dependent upon the type of trust and whether certain exemptions apply. The FTB has prepared a flow chart that illustrates how the rules are applied.

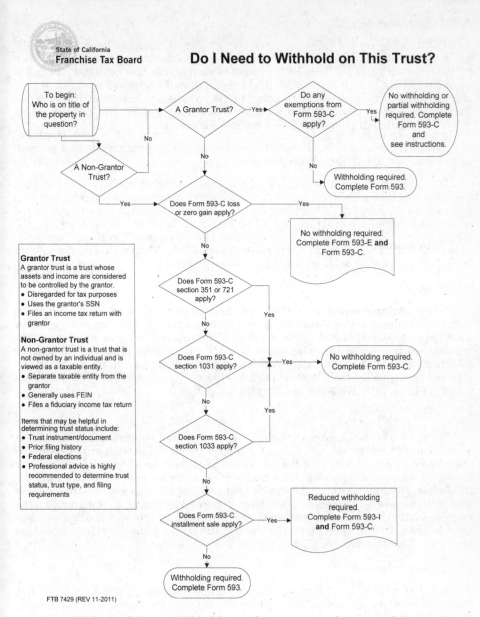

State of California
Franchise Tax Board

Do I Need to Withhold on This Trust?

To begin:
Who is on title of the property in question?

A Grantor Trust? — Yes →

Do any exemptions from Form 593-C apply? — Yes →

No withholding or partial withholding required. Complete Form 593-C and see instructions.

No ↓

No ↓

A Non-Grantor Trust?

No ↓

Withholding required. Complete Form 593.

— Yes →

Does Form 593-C loss or zero gain apply? — Yes →

No withholding required. Complete Form 593-E **and** Form 593-C.

No ↓

Grantor Trust
A grantor trust is a trust whose assets and income are considered to be controlled by the grantor.
• Disregarded for tax purposes
• Uses the grantor's SSN
• Files an income tax return with grantor

Does Form 593-C section 351 or 721 apply?

No ↓

Yes →

Non-Grantor Trust
A non-grantor trust is a trust that is not owned by an individual and is viewed as a taxable entity.
• Separate taxable entity from the grantor
• Generally uses FEIN
• Files a fiduciary income tax return

Does Form 593-C section 1031 apply? — Yes →

No withholding required. Complete Form 593-C.

No ↓

Items that may be helpful in determining trust status include:
• Trust instrument/document
• Prior filing history
• Federal elections
• Professional advice is highly recommended to determine trust status, trust type, and filing requirements

Yes →

Does Form 593-C section 1033 apply?

No ↓

Does Form 593-C installment sale apply? — Yes →

Reduced withholding required. Complete Form 593-I **and** Form 593-C.

No ↓

Withholding required. Complete Form 593.

FTB 7429 (REV 11-2011)

Form 593-E, Real Estate Withholding—Computation of Estimated Gain or Loss, must be used by those claiming an exemption due to a loss or zero gain or electing the optional gain on sale withholding. Sellers should retain this form for five years.

Form 593-C, Real Estate Withholding Exemption Certificate, must be used by individual and non-individual sellers to certify that they meet one of the withholding requirement exceptions above. Withholding agents should retain a copy of this form for five years.

Tax-exempt entities, insurance companies, IRAs, qualified pension plans, charitable remainder trusts, and profit sharing plans are also exempt from the withholding requirements. (FTB Pub. 1016, Real Estate Withholding Guidelines)

¶716

• *Installment sales*

Withholding on the full sales price on installment sales can be deferred if the buyer agrees to withhold $3^1/3$% (or the installment withholding percentage specified by the seller on Form 593-I) on the principal of each installment payment. The buyer must complete and sign Form 593-I, Real Estate Withholding Installment Sale Agreement. This form must be sent with a copy of the promissory note, the withholding on the first installment payment, and the seller's certified Form 593. (Instructions, Form 593-I, Real Estate Withholding Installment Sale Agreement)

The buyer must withhold on each installment sale payment made to a nonresident seller. (Sec. 18662, Rev. & Tax. Code)

If a seller elects not to report the sale on the installment method (IRC § 453[d]), the seller must file a California tax return and report the entire sale on Schedule D-1, Sale of Business Property. After filing the tax return and reporting the entire gain, the seller must submit a written request to the Franchise Tax Board (FTB) to release the buyer from withholding on the installment sale payments. Once the request is received, the FTB will issue an approval or denial within 30 days. (Instructions, Form 593-I, Real Estate Withholding Installment Sale Agreement)

• *Multiple sellers*

When multiple sellers in a California real property hold interest or interests within the same escrow, withholding is required by each seller unless the seller qualifies for an exemption. A sale of multiple California real property interests within the same escrow constitutes one transaction for withholding purposes. Each seller uses Form FTB 593-C, Real Estate Withholding Exemption Certificate, to determine whether they qualify for a full or partial withholding exemption. (*FTB Tax News* (March 2015), CCH CALIFORNIA TAX REPORTS, ¶ 406-310)

• *Penalties*

Those who fail, without reasonable cause, to withhold required tax in connection with a realty disposition or to timely submit such tax are subject to a penalty equal to the greater of $500 or 10% of the amount that should have been withheld. Any transferor who knowingly executes a false certificate for the purpose of avoiding the withholding requirements is liable for twice this amount. A real estate escrow person who fails to give a transferee (other than a transferee that is an intermediary or accommodator in a deferred exchange) written notice of this withholding requirement is liable for the same penalty if the tax due on the transaction is not paid on time. (Sec. 18668, Rev. & Tax. Code)

• *Procedures and returns*

A payor who in good faith receives a Withholding Exemption Certificate and Waiver Request for Real Estate Sales (Form 590-W) from the payee, is relieved of the obligation to withhold.

For realty dispositions, Form 593, Real Estate Withholding Tax Statement, must be used to report and transmit the amount withheld. For information regarding electronic filing, see FTB Pub. 923, Secure Web Internet File Transfer (SWIFT) Guide for Nonresident and Real Estate Withholding. Funds withheld on individual transactions by real estate escrow persons may, at the option of the real estate escrow person, be remitted by the 20th day of the month following the month in which the transaction occurred, or may be remitted on a monthly basis in combination with other transactions closed during that month. (Sec. 18662, Rev. & Tax. Code)

See ¶ 714 for a discussion of returns required to be filed.

¶716

Practice Tip: Withholding Credits

To claim a real estate withholding credit, a taxpayer should report the sale or transfer on an appropriate tax return, enter the withholding amount from Form 593 on the line designated for real estate withholding on the tax return, and attach a copy of Form 593 to the lower front of the tax return, Side 1. If the real estate sale or transfer is reported on an original return but the taxpayer fails to claim the withholding credit on that return, the FTB requests that the taxpayer file an amended return to properly report the credit and to preserve the taxpayer's administrative appeal rights. The FTB's system will not generate a Return Information Notice (RIN) when real estate withholding is not reported because the current system is not able to associate unclaimed withholding with tax returns during processing. The FTB is working to improve its system and practices and expects to have the ability to notify taxpayers of unclaimed withholding credits beginning at the end of 2013 or in early 2014. (*FTB Tax News* (November 2012), CCH CALIFORNIA TAX REPORTS, ¶ 405-732)

¶717 Overpayments and Refunds—Procedure

Law: Secs. 19301-19302, 19307, 19321-19323 (CCH CALIFORNIA TAX REPORTS, ¶ 89-224).

Comparable Federal: Secs. 6401-02 (CCH U.S. MASTER TAX GUIDE ¶ 2759 et seq.).

California Form: Form 540X (Amended Individual Income Tax Return).

Claims for refund must be in writing, signed by the taxpayer or the taxpayer's representative, and must state the specific grounds upon which they are based. They should ordinarily be filed on Form 540X, Amended Individual Income Tax Return. Claims should be filed with the Franchise Tax Board (FTB) at Sacramento, California. (Sec. 19322, Rev. & Tax. Code)

Practitioner Comment: Tax Authorities May be Equitably Estopped From Asserting a Claim is Invalid Where the Taxpayer Had Reasonably Relied on Instructions From Such Tax Authority

In *D.R. Systems, Inc. v. Cal. State Bd. of Equalization*, Cal Ct.App., Dkt. No. D060856 (March 7, 2013) (unpublished), a California court of appeal held that a taxpayer's evidence of communications with a State Board of Equalization (BOE) agent presented triable issues of material fact regarding the application of equitable estoppel. D.R. Systems, Inc. asserted that it filed a valid sales tax refund claim with the BOE because it wrote a letter stating that it was owed a "large credit balance" as instructed by a BOE agent.

In order to state a valid claim for refund of sales and use tax, Rev. & Tax. Code § 6904(a) [Rev. & Tax. Code § 19322 is the analogous income and franchise tax code section] requires that the claim must be in writing and state the specific grounds upon which it is founded. The BOE argued that the taxpayer's letter was not a valid refund claim because it did not specify grounds for a refund and that, consequently, the taxpayer had not exhausted its administrative remedies before filing suit.

Notwithstanding that the court agreed that the taxpayer's communications did not constitute a valid refund claim under the statute, the court determined that estoppel may be appropriate in "a situation where the claim is that a government agent has negligently or intentionally caused a claimant to fail to comply with a procedural precondition, and the failure to invoke estoppel would cause an injustice to the claimant." In order to prevail at trial on its estoppel argument, the taxpayer must show that it was reasonable to rely on the BOE agent's instruction, which requires additional factual development.

Although an unpublished decision, to the extent that a taxpayer submits its claim in reliance on the instructions of a revenue agent, *D.R. Systems* potentially lowers the standard required to file a valid claim as stated in Rev. & Tax. Code § § 6904(a) and 19322, and analyzed in *Newman v. Franchise Tax Bd.*, 208 Cal.App.3d 972 (1989) and *J.H. McKnight Ranch, Inc. v. Franchise Tax Bd.*, 110 Cal.App.4th 978 (2003).

Chris Whitney, Contributing Editor

Claims for refund made on behalf of a class of taxpayers must be both authorized in writing and signed by each taxpayer.

Upon examination of a refund claim, the FTB must notify the taxpayer of its action on the claim and state its reasons for disallowing any refund claim. It is the FTB's practice to grant the taxpayer an informal hearing, if desired, before the claim is acted upon or within 90 days after the mailing of a notice of disallowance. The law provides that the FTB may reconsider a disallowed claim at any time within the period allowed for filing a suit for refund (¶720). (Sec. 19324, Rev. & Tax. Code)

A return filed within the statutory period for filing refund claims, showing a credit of more than $1 for estimated tax paid in excess of the tax due, is treated as a claim for refund. At the taxpayer's election, such overpayment may be either refunded or applied on the following year's estimated tax. (Sec. 19307, Rev. & Tax. Code)

Legal Ruling No. 386 (1975) (CCH California Tax Reports, ¶89-224.75) discusses the question of what constitutes a valid refund claim. The ruling states that it is not necessary to use a particular form, provided the necessary information is provided. A federal revenue agent's report, filed by the taxpayer or a representative and accompanied by a refund request, will constitute a claim if sufficient explanation is provided in the report or otherwise.

Under some circumstances the FTB may initiate a refund action in the absence of a proper claim. See *Newman v. Franchise Tax Board* (1989) (CCH California Tax Reports, ¶89-224.753); in this case, the California Court of Appeal held that a statement entitled "protest" qualified as a sufficient claim for refund because it put the FTB on notice that a right was being asserted with respect to an overpayment of tax.

A California court of appeal held that payment of interest was not a prerequisite to seeking judicial review. (*Chen et al. v. Franchise Tax Board*, CCH California Tax Reports, ¶89-224.67)

In case of a joint return, an overpayment may be credited against taxes due from both taxpayers and any balance is refunded to both taxpayers. In *Appeal of Elam* (1997) (CCH California Tax Reports, ¶89-224.61), the State Board of Equalization ordered the FTB to refund to a divorced taxpayer her portion of an overpayment from a prior year's tax return filed jointly with her ex-husband, even though the FTB had erroneously refunded the entire overpayment to the ex-husband.

Practice Tip: Misdirected Direct Deposits

The FTB receives over 60,000 misdirected direct deposit refunds (DDR) each year. Tax preparers are asked to check with their clients to see if their banking information has changed during the year and to verify the banking information on the return before submitting the return for processing. A client that has not received the DDR should wait at least 25 working days from the authorized date of the refund (seven days for e-file returns and eight weeks for paper-filed returns) before calling the FTB. Taxpayers will need to fax the FTB a bank statement showing that the deposit was not made to their account and will be sent a FTB 3851, Taxpayer Affidavit of Misdirected Refund Deposit, to complete and return to the FTB. In addition, the taxpayer must notify the taxpayer's bank or financial institution in writing of the error and file a police report. Copies of the letter and the report must be attached to FTB 3851. After the FTB receives the FTB 3851 from the taxpayer, the FTB will contact the bank or financial institution where the misdirected refund was deposited to request information on the account holder who received the misdirected refund. Although the information is required to be sent within seven days, it frequently takes longer. Once the FTB receives the information from the bank or financial institution, a paper check refund will be issued to the correct taxpayer. (*Tax News*, California Franchise Tax Board, April 2, 2012, CCH California Tax Reports, ¶405-618)

¶717

¶718 Refund Claims—Appeal to State Board of Equalization

Law: Secs. 19324-35, 19343, Rev. & Tax. Code (CCH CALIFORNIA TAX REPORTS, ¶ 89-234).

Comparable Federal: Secs. 6401-02.

A taxpayer may appeal the Franchise Tax Board's (FTB) disallowance of a refund claim. The appeal must be made to the State Board of Equalization (BOE) within 90 days from the date of mailing of the notice of disallowance. (Sec. 19324, Rev. & Tax. Code; Sec. 19343, Rev. & Tax. Code) A taxpayer may consider a claim disallowed and file an appeal with the BOE if the FTB fails to take action on a claim for six months (120 days in certain bankruptcy situations) after the claim is filed. (Sec. 19348, Rev. & Tax. Code)

Procedure on an appeal to the BOE on a refund claim is the same as on a proposed deficiency, as outlined in ¶705, above. Some proceedings that start out as deficiency appeals are converted into refund appeals because the taxpayer pays the tax while the proceeding is pending. In such cases the proceeding is considered after payment of the tax as an appeal from the denial of a claim for refund.

See ¶720 regarding suits for refund.

¶719 Statute of Limitations on Refund Claims

Law: Secs. 18572, 19041.5, 19052, 19066, 19306-16, 19322.1 (CCH CALIFORNIA TAX REPORTS, ¶ 89-224).

Comparable Federal: Secs. 1311-14, 6511, 6603, 7508A (CCH U.S. MASTER TAX GUIDE ¶ 2763).

The period of limitation for filing refund claims is outlined below.

(a) **General rule**—Generally, a refund claim must be made by the later of (1) four years after the last day prescribed for filing the return (determined without regard to any extension of time for filing), (2) one year from the date of overpayment, or (3) four years from the date the return was filed, if filed by the prescribed date for filing the return (including extensions). This may be compared with the federal rule of the earlier of three years from the date the return was filed or two years from the date the tax was paid. If a return is filed before the actual due date, it is treated as filed on the due date. (Sec. 19306, Rev. & Tax. Code)

A deposit in the nature of a cash bond made by a taxpayer to stop the running of interest after the Franchise Tax Board (FTB) has mailed a notice of proposed deficiency assessment is not a payment of tax for purposes of determining the limitations period for filing a refund claim or converting an administrative refund claim into a judicial refund action, unless the taxpayer provides a written statement to the FTB specifying that the deposit is a payment of tax or the deposit is actually used to pay a final tax liability. (Sec. 19041.5, Rev. & Tax. Code) The FTB will generally follow federal interpretations and procedures relating to tax deposits. (*FTB Notice 2005-6* (CCH CALIFORNIA TAX REPORTS, ¶ 403-924))

An "informal" refund claim may be made, which allows a taxpayer to file a refund claim without full payment of the assessed or asserted tax. An informal refund claim is deemed filed only for purposes of tolling the four-year statute of limitations. For all other purposes, the claim is deemed filed on the date the tax is paid in full. An "informal" refund claim is deemed perfected for purposes of commencing the formal administrative claims procedure (including the deemed six month denial) when all outstanding tax, penalties, and interest are paid. The informal claim procedure does not apply to deficiency amounts that are not finalized. (FTB Notice 2003-5 (2003) (CCH CALIFORNIA TAX REPORTS, ¶ 89-224.451))

CCH Comment: Refund of Voluntary Payment

California does not follow the federal law that requires the IRS to refund voluntary payments made after the statute of limitations has lapsed. Under California law, the FTB is required to refund payments made after the limitations period has lapsed only if there was an actual overpayment. If a taxpayer fails to establish that the amounts self-assessed on the taxpayer's return for the tax years at issue were incorrect, the FTB is not required to refund the amounts paid that were associated with the amounts reflected on the taxpayer's returns. (*Appeal of Auto Theft R..F. Systems, LLC* (2011), CCH CALIFORNIA TAX REPORTS, ¶ 405-452)

CCH Comment: Withholding Agents

The one-year and four-year statute of limitations periods under Rev. & Tax. Code Sec. 19306 apply to withholding agents. Therefore, they limit the period in which the FTB may allow a refund or credit to a withholding agent of the failure to withhold liability. The four-year limitations period starts to run from the due date of the original information return filed on FTB Form 592 or FTB Form 593. If no information return is filed, the statute of limitations period for a withholding agent claiming a refund or credit of the failure to withhold liability begins to run on the due date of the original information return that was required to be filed with respect to that withholding amount. (*Technical Advice Memorandum 2016-02*, California Franchise Tax Board, February 24, 2016, CCH CALIFORNIA TAX REPORTS, ¶ 406-487)

(b) **Waivers**—Where a waiver has been executed, *either* for California tax purposes or for federal tax purposes, extending the running of the statute of limitations on deficiency assessments, the limitation date for refunds is the same as that for mailing notices of proposed additional assessments. This is different from the federal rule, which extends the limitation period for refunds six months beyond the period for deficiency assessments. It should be noted, however, that where the California refund limitation date is based on a federal waiver, the date is six months after the expiration of the period for *federal* deficiency assessments, and not six months after the date for additional *California* assessments. (Sec. 19308, Rev. & Tax. Code; Sec. 19065, Rev. & Tax. Code)

The limitation date for a California refund claim, if based upon a federal waiver, may be the same as that for a federal claim.

(c) **Special seven-year rule**—Where the claim is based on (1) a bad debt loss, (2) a worthless security loss, or (3) erroneous inclusion of certain recoveries of no-tax-benefit deductions, the limitation period is extended to seven years from the last day prescribed for filing the return. As to bad debt and worthless security losses, this is the same as the federal. As to erroneous inclusion of certain recoveries, there is no comparable federal rule. (Sec. 19312, Rev. & Tax. Code)

(d) **Changes or corrections to federal returns**—When a change or correction to the taxpayer's federal return is made or allowed by federal authorities, as explained at ¶ 106, the limitation period is extended to a date two years after the notice or amended return is filed with the FTB, if such date is later than that set forth in (a) or (b), above, or the extended date established by reason of financial disability as described below. (Sec. 19311, Rev. & Tax. Code) In a nonprecedential summary decision, the BOE applied this extended statute of limitations provision to allow a taxpayer to claim a refund of late filing penalties within two years from the date on which the IRS had abated the corresponding federal late payment penalties, even though the general four-year limitations period had lapsed. The BOE held that because the federal abatement changed the amount of the taxpayer's federal tax liability, the taxpayer had two years from the federal determination to file a state refund claim. (*Appeal of Mart* (2006) CCH CALIFORNIA TAX REPORTS, ¶ 89-224.7482)

CCH Comment: Limitations on Refund Claims Based on Federal Adjustment

The claim for refund is limited to overpayments resulting from the federal adjustment and must be based on a federal adjustment to an original or amended federal return that affects the tax shown on a previously filed original or amended California return. The federal adjustment may result in a claim for refund for a tax year different from the tax year in which the federal adjustment occurred. This commonly occurs where there is a federal carryforward or carryback that is not applicable under California law or where there is a California-only credit or credit carryforward in the year of the federal adjustment. (*Tax News*, California Franchise Tax Board, August 2010, CCH CALIFORNIA TAX REPORTS, ¶ 405-223)

(e) **Refunds related to taxes paid to another state**—Taxpayers may file claims for refund or credit for taxes paid to other states within one year from the date the tax is paid to the other state even if the standard statute of limitations period has lapsed. (Sec. 19311.5, Rev. & Tax. Code)

CCH Comment: Shareholder's Limitation Period to File Refund Claim Not Extended

A refund claim filed by an S corporation shareholder that was based on amendments made on the S corporation's return was denied as untimely because the refund claim was filed after the limitations period had lapsed. The taxpayer claimed that the S corporation's original return on which the shareholder based his original personal income tax return was grossly inaccurate and that it was not until the S corporation filed an amended return five years later that he became aware that he was eligible to claim a research and development credit passed through from the S corporation. However, while there are numerous statutory exceptions from the statute of limitations period that allow the FTB to impose deficiency assessments after the four-year limitations period has lapsed, these exceptions do not toll the statute of limitations period for claiming a refund of overpaid tax. (*Appeal of Tinker* (2009), CCH CALIFORNIA TAX REPORTS, ¶ 405-084)

• *Taxpayers outside United States; disaster victims*

In the case of members of the armed forces and certain other taxpayers who are outside the United States for a period of time, the statute of limitations is automatically extended under certain conditions (¶ 109). See ¶ 110 for a discussion of extensions available to victims of disasters or terroristic or militaristic actions. (Sec. 18570, Rev. & Tax. Code; Sec. 18571, Rev. & Tax. Code)

• *Financially disabled persons*

California follows federal law by suspending the statute of limitations periods discussed above for personal income tax refund claims when an individual is financially disabled, as established under the procedures and requirements specified by the FTB. (Sec. 19316, Rev. & Tax. Code)

An individual is "financially disabled" if that individual is unable to manage his or her financial affairs by reason of a medically determinable physical or mental impairment that is either deemed to be a terminal impairment or is expected to last for a continuous period of not less than 12 months. Receipt of social security disability benefits does not in and of itself establish that a taxpayer is unable to manage his or her financial affairs. (*Appeal of Meek* (2006) CCH CALIFORNIA TAX REPORTS, ¶ 89-224.395) A suspension is not available if the individual's spouse or any other person is legally authorized to act on that individual's behalf in financial matters. However, it should be noted that California follows the federal interpretation that suspends the limitations period for refunds for purposes of a financially disabled spouse's one-half community property interest in any overpayment on the couple's tax account. (*Appeal of Sim*, (2009) CCH CALIFORNIA TAX REPORTS, ¶ 405-062)

• *Offset of refund against deficiency*

A refund that is barred under the above rules may be allowed as an offset against a deficiency, where the refund and deficiency both result from the transfer of income or deductions from one year to another. Such offset is also allowed where the refund is for the same year as the deficiency and is due to a related taxpayer. The offset must be made within seven years from the due date of the return on which the refund (overpayment) is determined. (Sec. 19314, Rev. & Tax. Code)

In *Appeal of Paritem and Janie Poonian* (1971) (CCH CALIFORNIA TAX REPORTS, ¶ 89-102.554), the State Board of Equalization (BOE) applied the seven-year limitation strictly to deny an offset (an offset had been allowed earlier in settling the federal tax liability, presumably because the federal limitation period had not yet run).

In *Appeal of Earl and Marion Matthiessen* (1985) (CCH CALIFORNIA TAX REPORTS, ¶ 89-224.7491), the taxpayers claimed a barred refund as an offset to a deficiency for a later year. A refund claim had been filed within the seven-year period, but the offset was not claimed until after the deficiency had been paid. The BOE denied the claim.

In *Appeal of Wilfred and Gertrude Winkenbach et al.* (1975) (CCH CALIFORNIA TAX REPORTS, ¶ 89-102.5592), individuals were taxed on income that had been taxed to a corporation in an outlawed year. The situation did not permit an offset of the barred refund due the corporation against the individuals' deficiency, under the rules discussed above, because the corporation and the individuals were not "related" taxpayers as specifically defined in the law. However, the BOE allowed the offset under the doctrine of "equitable recoupment."

• *Credit refunds*

Adjustments to refundable credits are treated as mathematical errors by the FTB, and a taxpayer may claim a refund of such adjusted amounts within the time limits specified above.

• *Effect of federal litigation*

In *Appeal of Valley Home Furniture* (1972) (CCH CALIFORNIA TAX REPORTS, ¶ 89-224.741), the taxpayer's refund claim was based on the allowable deduction of certain salaries paid to an officer-stockholder. The Tax Court had allowed the deduction for federal tax purposes, and the officer-stockholder had paid both federal and California income tax on the salaries. Nevertheless, the refund was denied because the claim was not filed within the required period of one year after the date of overpayment. The BOE commented that the taxpayer "could easily have filed protective claims for refund pending the outcome of the federal litigation."

• *No California relief provision*

California law contains nothing similar to IRC Secs. 1311-14, which mitigate the effect of the statute of limitations in certain situations where an inconsistent position is maintained. In *Appeal of Skaggs Pay Less Drug Stores* (1959) (CCH CALIFORNIA TAX REPORTS, ¶ 89-144.501), the taxpayer attempted to obtain a refund for an outlawed year to conform with a federal adjustment made under IRC Sec. 1311; the BOE held that no refund could be made.

¶720 Suits for Refund

Law: Secs. 19041.5, 19381-92 (CCH CALIFORNIA TAX REPORTS, ¶ 89-236).

Comparable Federal: Secs. 6532, 6603, 7421-22 (CCH U.S. MASTER TAX GUIDE ¶ 2790).

Generally, suits for refund may be instituted only after the taxpayer has filed a claim for refund, and they must be based on the grounds set forth in the claim. (Sec. 19382, Rev. & Tax. Code) However, if the FTB is on notice and aware of an issue, a taxpayer will not be precluded from pursing judicial relief for failure to specifically state the issue on the claim for refund (*J.H. McKnight Ranch, Inc. v. Franchise Tax Board* (2003) CCH CALIFORNIA TAX REPORTS, ¶89-236.303). Time limits for bringing suit are the later of the following:

— four years from the due date of the return;

— one year from the date the tax was paid;

— 90 days after notice of action by the Franchise Tax Board (FTB) on a claim for refund; or

— 90 days after notice of action by the State Board of Equalization (BOE) on an appeal from the action of the FTB on a refund claim.

(Sec. 19384, Rev. & Tax. Code)

A deposit in the nature of a cash bond made by a taxpayer to stop the running of interest after the FTB has mailed a notice of proposed deficiency assessment is not a payment of tax for purposes of the limitations period for converting an administrative refund claim into a judicial refund action or filing a suit for refund, unless the taxpayer provides a written statement to the FTB specifying that the deposit is a payment of tax or the deposit is actually used to pay a final tax liability. (Sec. 19041.5, Rev. & Tax. Code). The FTB will generally follow federal interpretations and procedures relating to tax deposits. (*FTB Notice 2005-6* (CCH CALIFORNIA TAX REPORTS, ¶403-924))

Practice Pointer: Procedural Issues Addressed

Exhaustion of administrative remedies.—Although a taxpayer is not required to pursue an administrative appeal before the BOE prior to bringing a judicial action challenging a refund denial or deemed denial, a taxpayer is precluded from recovering any litigation costs, including attorney fees, incurred in pursuing a judicial action unless the taxpayer has exhausted administrative remedies, including filing an administrative appeal with the BOE. (*Information Letter 2007-2*, California Franchise Tax Board, August 23, 2007, CCH CALIFORNIA TAX REPORTS, ¶404-448)

Payment of proposed assessments.—In *City National Corp. v. Franchise Tax Board*, an appellate court held that payment of proposed assessments of California corporation franchise and income taxes was not a prerequisite for filing a suit for refund of taxes involving the same tax years because the proposed assessments had not yet become final. The California Supreme Court denied a petition for review of the case. (*City National Corp. v. Franchise Tax Board* (2007), CCH CALIFORNIA TAX REPORTS, ¶404-200; pet. for review denied, Cal SCt, No. S150563, April 11, 2007)

Tax deposit forms.—Forms 3576-3579, Tax Deposit Voucher, should be used to designate a remittance as a tax deposit for a specific tax year. Form 3581, Tax Deposit Refund or Transfer Request, should be used to request a tax deposit refund, designate the application of a tax deposit to a different tax year, or apply a tax deposit to convert an administrative protest or appeal to an administrative refund action.

If the tax deposit amount is not enough to pay the final deficiency amount, including penalties, fees, and interest, the claim will become an informal claim, and the taxpayer will receive a bill for the remaining amount due. The FTB cannot act on a claim until it is perfected by full payment. The same procedures apply when a taxpayer has appealed the denial of a protested proposed assessment to the BOE and wishes to convert the deficiency appeal to an appeal from the denial of a refund claim. The "deemed denial" period does not start to run until the claim is perfected by full payment. (*Tax News*, California Franchise Tax Board, September 2006; FTB 3581, Tax Deposit Refund and Transfer Request)

A taxpayer may consider a claim disallowed and bring a suit for refund if the FTB fails to take action on a refund claim within six months (120 days in certain bankruptcy situations) after the claim is filed. (Sec. 19385, Rev. & Tax. Code)

Under the California procedure, the taxpayer may appeal to the BOE and, following an adverse decision, may then appeal to the courts by filing suit for refund. The FTB has no right to appeal an adverse decision of the BOE.

Caution Note: Scope of Liability Issues

The FTB is not limited to the issues raised by a taxpayer in a suit to refund, but may raise any and all liability issues in order to defeat the refund claim (*Marken v. Franchise Tax Board* (2002) (CCH CALIFORNIA TAX REPORTS, ¶89-224.79)).

See ¶105 for the special procedure whereby a person who is alleged to be a California resident can file a suit to determine the issue without first paying the tax.

The California rules regarding suits for refund are different from the federal in several respects. Due to the technical nature and limited applicability of these provisions, no attempt is made here to explain the differences.

CCH Note: Right to Jury Trial

The California Supreme Court has ruled that a taxpayer does not have a right to a jury trial in a refund action to collect personal income taxes. (*Franchise Tax Board v. The Superior Court of the City and County of San Francisco* (2011) (CCH CALIFORNIA TAX REPORTS, ¶405-441))

¶721 Disclosure of Information

Law: Secs. 6835, 6850, 19195, 19266, 19291, 19377.5, 19504.5, 19528, 19530, 19542.3, 19544-65, Revenue and Taxation Code; Sec. 17530.5, Business and Professions Code (CCH CALIFORNIA TAX REPORTS, ¶89-134, 89-222).

Comparable Federal: Secs. 6103-10, 7213-16 (CCH U.S. MASTER TAX GUIDE ¶2892).

Under the California Business and Professions Code, it is a misdemeanor for anyone to disclose any information obtained in the business of preparing federal or state income tax returns or in assisting taxpayers to prepare their returns, unless the disclosure is

— authorized by written consent of the taxpayer,

— authorized by law,

— necessary to the preparation of the return, or

— pursuant to court order.

(Sec. 17530.5, Bus. & Prof. Code)

California and federal laws provide for reciprocal exchange of information in administration of tax laws. The Franchise Tax Board (FTB) and the Internal Revenue Service have a continuing program of informing each other of findings resulting from their examinations of tax returns. To avoid duplication of effort, the two agencies may agree that a particular taxpayer's return will be examined by one or the other. Any improper disclosure or use of such information is a misdemeanor. (Sec. 19551, Rev. & Tax. Code)

State law also authorizes reciprocal exchange programs between the FTB and California cities, counties, or a city and county that assesses a city business tax or that require a city business license. (Sec. 19551, Rev. & Tax. Code—Sec. 19551.5, Rev. & Tax. Code)

A state licensing board must provide the FTB, upon request, with a licensee's individual taxpayer identification number (ITIN), in addition to the other license information required to be provided to the FTB. (Sec. 19528, Rev. & Tax. Code)

Also, upon request from the State Department of Public Health, the FTB may provide information verifying the adjusted gross income, tax-exempt interest, tax-exempt Social Security benefits, and foreign earned income of an applicant for, or recipient of, human immunodeficiency virus treatment services from the state. (Sec. 19548.2, Rev. & Tax. Code)

CCH Comment: Reciprocal Collection Agreements

The California State Board of Equalization (BOE) and the FTB are also authorized to enter into agreements to collect any delinquent tax debt due to the IRS or any other state imposing an income tax, a tax measured by income, sales and use tax, or a similar tax, provided that the IRS and the other states agree to collect delinquent tax debts due to the BOE and the FTB. Under any such agreement, the California Controller would offset any delinquent tax debt due to that other state from a person or entity against any refund to that person or entity under the California sales and use tax law, personal income tax law, or corporation tax law. (Sec. 6835, Rev. & Tax. Code, Sec. 6850, Rev. & Tax. Code, Sec. 19291, Rev. & Tax. Code, Sec. 19377.5, Rev. & Tax. Code)

Practitioner Comment: FTB Announces Reciprocal Agreement With New York to Exchange Refund Offsets

In a public service bulletin dated October 14, 2013, the Franchise Tax Board (FTB) informed their staff that beginning October 29, 2013, the FTB will exchange refund offsets with New York State. This means that any California refund due to an individual can be directed to New York for a New York personal income tax debt of that individual, and vice versa. The authority for this reciprocity comes from the Delinquent Taxpayer Accountability Act, dated October 4, 2011, which added Rev. & Tax. Code § 19377.5.

The reciprocal agreement is a pilot project and currently limited only to monies available on individual amounts. However, given that the FTB stated "[t]hese agreements enhance our ability to collect from taxpayers who reside out of state," if this agreement is successful, the FTB may seek to expand the agreement to other business entities (e.g., corporations, partnerships, LLCs, S Corps) as well as with other jurisdictions.

Chris Whitney, Contributing Editor

The California Revenue and Taxation Code provides rules and procedures regarding personal and confidential information in the files of state agencies; these rules are designed to insure privacy of such information. (Sec. 19545, Rev. & Tax. Code) The FTB is required to redact the first five digits of a Social Security number on personal income and corporation franchise and income tax lien abstracts and any other public records created by the FTB that are disclosable under the Public Records Act. (Sec. 15705, Govt. Code)

CCH Comment: Privacy in the Electronic Age

California law requires that all businesses use safeguards to ensure the security of Californians' personal information and to contractually require third parties to do the same. (Sec. 1798.81.5, Civil Code) Businesses are also prohibited from requiring a customer to transmit unencrypted Social Security numbers over a nonsecure connection. (Sec. 1798.85, Civil Code)

CCH Comment: Public Disclosure of Tax Delinquencies

The FTB is authorized to make available as a matter of public record an annual list of the 500 largest uncontested tax delinquencies in excess of $100,000 under the Personal Income Tax Law and the Corporation Tax Law. Before making a delinquency a matter of public record, however, the FTB must provide written notice to the person or persons liable by certified mail and provide an opportunity for the taxpayer to comply. (Sec. 19195, Rev. & Tax. Code)

Generally, a state licensing agency that issues professional or occupational licenses (including drivers licenses), certificates, registrations, or permits must suspend, revoke, and refuse to issue a license if the licensee's name is included on the delinquency lists. (Sec. 494.5, Bus. & Prof. Code) In addition, state agencies generally are prohibited from entering into any contract for the acquisition of goods or services with a contractor whose name appears on either of the lists. (Sec. 10295.4, Pub. Cont. Code)

Special safeguards are provided to prevent improper disclosure by the FTB of trade secrets or other confidential information with respect to any software that comes into the FTB's possession or control in connection with a tax return examination. (Sec. 19504.5, Rev. & Tax. Code) Computer software source code and executable code are considered return information for disclosure purposes. Any person who willfully makes known to another person any computer software source code or executable code obtained in connection with a tax return examination may be punished by a fine or imprisonment or both. (Sec. 19542.3, Rev. & Tax. Code)

•*Financial institutions record matching (FIRM) system*

The FTB is mandated to establish a financial institutions record match (FIRM) system with specified financial institutions doing business in California for purposes of improving collections from taxpayers with outstanding California income tax liabilities or other debts that the FTB is required to collect, as well as outstanding tax liabilities owed to the Employment Development Department and the State Board of Equalization. Under the FIRM system, financial institutions must provide the FTB quarterly reports including the account holder's name, record address, and other addresses, Social Security number or other taxpayer identification number, and other identifying information for each delinquent tax debtor, as identified by the FTB. Financial institutions that fail to comply, without reasonable cause, are subject to a penalty equal to $50 for each record not provided, up to a total of $100,000 annually. Financial institutions may be reimbursed for specified program implementation costs. (Sec. 19266, Rev. & Tax. Code; Sec. 19560.5, Rev. & Tax. Code)

¶722 Interest on Overpayments

Law: Secs. 19325, 19340-51, 19363 (CCH California Tax Reports, ¶89-204).

Comparable Federal: Sec. 6611 (CCH U.S. Master Tax Guide ¶2765).

Interest is paid upon overpayments of tax. The interest rate is the same as the rate for deficiencies, as explained at ¶711. (Sec. 19340, Rev. & Tax. Code) The law contains specific rules regarding the period for which interest will be paid, depending on whether the tax is refunded or allowed as a credit.

With the exception discussed below, no interest will be allowed if refund or credit is made within 45 days of the date of filing a return, or within 45 days after the due date (without regard to extensions of time). In case of a late return, no interest will be allowed for any day before the date of filing. (Sec. 19341, Rev. & Tax. Code)

The law contains a provision to prevent payment of interest on overpayments that are made deliberately for the purpose of obtaining interest. (Sec. 19349, Rev. & Tax. Code) In any case where the Franchise Tax Board disallows interest on a refund, the taxpayer may appeal to the State Board of Equalization (BOE) and may bring suit if the action of the BOE is not favorable. (Sec. 19343, Rev. & Tax. Code) Detailed rules are provided for such appeals. There are no comparable federal provisions.

Where a refund is made under the special seven-year limitation period for claims based on bad debt and worthless security losses, the amount of interest paid is limited.

¶723 Closing Agreements

Law: Secs. 19441, 19442 (CCH CALIFORNIA TAX REPORTS, ¶89-186).

Comparable Federal: Sec. 7121 (CCH U.S. MASTER TAX GUIDE ¶2721).

The Franchise Tax Board (FTB) and a taxpayer may enter into a "closing agreement" with respect to the tax for any taxable period. Such an agreement is binding and may not be reopened except upon a showing of fraud, etc. The California provision is substantially the same as the federal. (Sec. 19441, Rev. & Tax. Code)

In addition, the Executive Officer and the Chief Counsel of the FTB may approve the settlement of all tax liabilities for a specified year involving a reduction of tax of $7,500 (adjusted annually for inflation) or less without the Attorney General's review or the FTB's approval. (Sec. 19442, Rev. & Tax. Code) For reduction of tax settlements in excess of the annually adjusted amount, the Executive Officer and the Chief Counsel are required to submit the proposed settlements to the Attorney General for review prior to presenting their recommendations to the FTB. However, an assessment or refund may still be issued as a result of a federal tax change.

FTB Notice No. 2007-02, CCH CALIFORNIA TAX REPORTS, ¶404-303, addresses the procedures for initiating and processing a request for a settlement agreement. Taxpayers seeking to initiate the settlement of a civil tax dispute should write to:

Patrick J. Bittner
Director, Settlement Bureau, Mail Stop A270
Franchise Tax Board
P.O. Box 3070
Rancho Cordova, CA 95741-3070
Telephone (916) 845-5624
FAX (916) 845-4747
Message Line (916) 845-5034

Written requests should include the following:

— the taxpayer's name and current address;

— if the taxpayer is represented by another, the representative's name, current address, fax, and telephone number, and a copy of the representative's power of attorney, unless a valid form is already on file with the FTB;

— the taxpayer's Social Security number or taxpayer identification number;

— the taxable year(s) involved;

— the tax amount(s) involved;

— the present status of the dispute (*i.e.,* protest, appeal, or claim for refund);

— a good faith settlement offer, including the factual and legal grounds in support of the offer;

— identification and discussion of all issues in contention, including legal and factual grounds for positions taken by the taxpayer; and

— a listing of all notice(s) of proposed assessment (NPA) and claim(s) for refund for the taxable year(s) involved that are not part of the settlement request, including the present status of each NPA(s) and claim(s) for refund and the amount(s) involved.

Practice Tip: Acceptance by Settlement Bureau

A request for settlement will likely be accepted by the FTB's Settlement Bureau for review if the FTB determines that there is a bona fide factual or legal dispute. However, if the FTB determines that there is a negligible litigation risk to the FTB's position in the case or that the facts have not been sufficiently developed to allow proper settlement consideration, the case will be not be accepted into the settlement program. Such a decision is completely discretionary with the FTB. (*FTB Notice No. 2007-02*, CCH CALIFORNIA TAX REPORTS, ¶ 404-303)

The FTB attempts to reach tentative settlement agreements within nine months of the case being accepted into the program.

If the FTB neither approves nor disapproves a recommendation for settlement within 45 days after receiving the recommendation, the recommendation is deemed approved. Disapproval requires a majority vote of the FTB, and a disapproved settlement may be resubmitted to the FTB. All settlements are final and nonappealable, except upon a showing of fraud or material misrepresentation.

CCH Comment: Evidence of Settlement Negotiations Inadmissible

Evidence of a settlement offer made during settlement negotiations between a taxpayer and the FTB is inadmissible in any subsequent adjudicative proceeding or civil action, including any appeal to the BOE. In addition, no evidence of any conduct or statements related to the settlement negotiations is admissible to prove liability for any tax, penalty, fee, or interest, except to the extent provided for in Sec. 1152 of the Evidence Code. (Sec. 19442, Rev. & Tax. Code)

In *Appeal of Wesley G. Pope* (1958) (CCH CALIFORNIA TAX REPORTS, ¶ 89-186.20), the State Board of Equalization held that a check marked "payment in full" does not follow the statutory requirements of a closing agreement. Hence, the FTB was justified in making subsequent assessments after the receipt of such a payment.

¶724 Compromise of Tax Liability

Law: Sec. 19443 (CCH CALIFORNIA TAX REPORTS, ¶ 89-186).

Federal: Sec. 7122 (CCH U.S. MASTER TAX GUIDE ¶ 2723).

The executive officer and chief counsel of the Franchise Tax Board (FTB), or their delegates, jointly, may administratively compromise any final tax liability in which the reduction of tax is $7,500 or less. The FTB, itself, upon recommendation by its executive officer and chief counsel, jointly, may compromise a final tax liability in which the reduction of tax is in excess of $7,500 but less than $10,000. (Sec. 19443, Rev. & Tax. Code)

For an amount to be administratively compromised, the taxpayer must establish the following:

— the amount offered in payment is the most that can be expected to be paid or collected from the taxpayer's present assets or income, and

— the taxpayer has no reasonable prospects of acquiring increased income or assets that would enable the taxpayer to satisfy a greater amount of the liability than that offered.

In addition, the FTB must determine that the acceptance of the offer in compromise is in the best interest of the state.

Practice Pointer: Best Offer

The FTB requires taxpayers to prove that the amount offered is the most the FTB could expect to receive based on their present assets and income. In addition, the FTB determines whether taxpayers have reasonable prospects of acquiring additional income or assets that would allow them to satisfy a greater amount of the liability than the offered amount within a reasonable period. Depending on other factors, five years is usually considered a reasonable period. (*Tax News*, California Franchise Tax Board, August 2010, CCH CALIFORNIA TAX REPORTS, ¶ 405-223)

In the case of joint and several liability, the acceptance of an offer in compromise from one spouse does not relieve the other spouse from paying the liability. However, the amount of the liability must be reduced by the amount of the accepted offer.

Also, it is of course possible under California procedures, as under federal, to negotiate a "compromise" of doubtful items of income, expense, etc., in dealing with representatives of the FTB upon examination of returns or during appeal proceedings or to make a settlement of a suit after litigation has begun.

See ¶ 715 for a discussion of compromises of withholding tax liabilities.

Practice Pointer: Making an Offer of Compromise

Form DE 999CA, Multi-Agency Form for Offer in Compromise, may be used to make an offer in compromise by individuals for personal income, sales and use, and other taxes owed to the FTB, BOE, and EDD. Corporations, partnerships, and limited liability companies should continue to use Form FTB 4905BE, Offer in Compromise by Business Entities, for FTB offers, and Form BOE-490-C, Offer In Compromise Application For Corporations, Limited Liability Companies, Partnerships, Trusts, and Unidentified Business Organizations, for BOE offers. (*News Release*, California Tax Service Center, August 23, 2006)

¶725 Voluntary Disclosure Agreements and Filing Compliance Agreements

Laws: Secs. 19191-94 (CCH CALIFORNIA TAX REPORTS, ¶ 89-186, 89-210).

Comparable Federal: None.

California Form: FTB 4925 (Application for Voluntary Disclosure), FTB 4827, *Withholding Voluntary Compliance Program Application.*

Two programs are available to encourage taxpayers to comply with California's reporting and registration requirements. The voluntary disclosure program is a statutory program that has very specific requirements and applies to a limited class of eligible applicants. In contrast, the filing compliance program is a Franchise Tax Board (FTB) initiated program based on the FTB's authority to abate penalties for reasonable cause under various statutory provisions. Unlike a voluntary disclosure agreement, a filing compliance agreement is not limited to a specific look-back period.

• *Voluntary disclosure program*

The FTB is authorized to enter into voluntary disclosure agreements with the following:

— qualified business entities that in good faith have previously failed to comply with California's registration and reporting requirements;

— qualified S corporation shareholders who in good faith have failed to comply with California's registration, reporting, and payment requirements;

— qualified trusts and qualified beneficiaries of those trusts; and

— limited liability companies (LLCs) and their qualified members.

(Sec. 19191 et. seq., Rev. & Tax. Code)

Under the terms established in a voluntary disclosure agreement, the FTB may waive penalties for noncompliance with specified reporting and payment requirements for the six taxable years immediately preceding the FTB's signing of the agreement. For taxable years ending more than six years prior to the agreement, the business's income taxes, additions to tax, fees, or penalties may also be waived. However, the FTB may not waive penalties for any of the six years immediately preceding the signing of the agreement in which an S corporation shareholder or LLC member was a California resident required to file a California tax return. In addition, for purposes of qualified shareholders and LLC members, the FTB's waiver authority is limited to penalties or additions to tax attributable to the shareholder's California source income from the S corporation or the LLC member's California source income from the LLC.

A "qualifying business entity" includes any out-of-state bank or non-exempt corporation (including any predecessors to the business entity) that voluntarily comes forward prior to any contact from the FTB and that has never filed a California income tax return or been the subject of an FTB inquiry regarding income tax liability.

A "qualified shareholder" is a nonresident shareholder of an S corporation that has applied for a voluntary disclosure agreement and disclosed all material facts pertaining to the shareholder's liability. A "qualified member" is an individual, corporation, or LLC that is a nonresident individual on the signing date of the voluntary disclosure agreement or a corporation not qualified or registered with the California Secretary of State's office. The LLC of which the individual or entity is a member must have applied for a voluntary disclosure agreement under which all material facts pertinent to the member's liability would be disclosed.

To participate in a voluntary disclosure agreement, an LLC must agree to pay all LLC fees, in addition to any tax, interest, and penalties not waived by the FTB for each of the six taxable years ending immediately preceding the signing date of the written agreement. In addition, LLCs and other entities that participate in the voluntary disclosure program are liable for the minimum tax for their first year of business in California.

A "qualified trust" is a trust that has never been administered in California and that has had no resident beneficiaries in California for six taxable years ending immediately preceding the signing date of the voluntary disclosure agreement, other than a beneficiary whose interest in the trust is contingent. A "contingent beneficiary" is a beneficiary that has not received any distribution from a qualified trust at any time during the six taxable years ending immediately preceding the signing date of the voluntary disclosure agreement. A "qualified beneficiary" is an individual who is a beneficiary of a qualified trust and is a nonresident on the signing date of the voluntary disclosure agreement and for each of the preceding six taxable years.

• *Withholding voluntary compliance program*

The FTB has a withholding voluntary compliance program (WVCP) that allows eligible withholding agents to remit past-due, nonwage and real estate withholding for the previous two calendar years, including interest, in exchange for having specified withholding tax liabilities and penalties waived. The limited amnesty program is available to both business and individual withholding agents who have a requirement to withhold resident, nonresident, and real-estate withholding and have not previously withheld.

Withholding agents who participate in the program are eligible for the following benefits:

— Waiver of information return penalties for the two-year look-back period.

— Elimination of withholding audits prior to the two-year look-back period.

— Limitation of the tax withholding liability to the look-back period, plus interest.

Withholding agents are ineligible to participate in the program if they:

— Participated in the 2008 nonresident withholding incentive program.

— Have been audited by the FTB for nonwage withholding.

— Have had a withholding liability or information return penalty for nonwage withholding assessed against them by the FTB.

Eligible agents should submit a completed FTB 482, Withholding Voluntary Compliance Program Application, along with an estimate of the amount of withholding for each calendar year covered, and pay the required withholding amount, plus interest. (*FTB Tax NewsFlash—Withholding Voluntary Compliance Initiative* (2013), CCH CALIFORNIA TAX REPORTS, ¶ 405-906)

• *Filing compliance program*

Taxpayers with corporation franchise and income tax and personal income tax liabilities that are ineligible for the voluntary disclosure program (VDP) discussed above but that can show reasonable cause for their failure to file may obtain relief from specified penalties by entering into a filing compliance agreement (FCA) with the FTB.

Taxpayers eligible to enter into an FCA are those taxpayers in the class of taxpayers described in the authorizing statute for the VDP discussed above, but who failed to satisfy an eligibility requirement. In addition, partnerships, limited partnerships, and limited liability partnerships and the nonresident partners of those partnerships are also eligible. A shareholder of an S corporation, a beneficiary, a member of an LLC, or a partner, who is a nonresident, may apply for agreement if the entity also files an FCA request.

The primary differences between an FCA and the VDP are the following:

— a taxpayer may enter into an FCA even if the taxpayer was first contacted by the FTB, whereas a taxpayer may not enter into the VDP if the taxpayer was contacted by the FTB prior to applying for the program. However, a taxpayer is ineligible to participate in an FCA if the FTB sent a notice requesting a tax return;

— relief from penalties and additions to tax is limited to a six year look-back period under the VDP, whereas there is no specified look-back period under the FCA program; and

— the underpayment of estimated tax penalty may be waived under the VDP, but not under the FCA program.

A taxpayer interested in participating in an FCA should send a completed FTB 5841, Request for Filing Compliance Agreement to: Attn: Larry Womac, State of California, Complex Filing Enforcement Unit, Franchise Tax Board, P.O. Box 1779, Rancho Cordova, California 95741-1779.

Taxpayers allowed to enter into an FCA must submit the required tax returns and payment by the date specified in the agreement. Full payment is usually due within 30 days from the date of the agreement, unless the taxpayer enters into an installment payment agreement.

The FCA will be voided if at any time the information supplied by the taxpayer is subsequently determined by the FTB to be inaccurate or false.

¶726 Recovery of Erroneous Refunds

Law: Secs. 19054, 19368, 19411-13 (CCH CALIFORNIA TAX REPORTS, ¶ 89-190).

Comparable Federal: Secs. 6532, 6602, 7405 (CCH U.S. MASTER TAX GUIDE ¶ 2738).

The Franchise Tax Board may recover erroneous refunds, with interest, subject to certain conditions. The California law is generally similar to the federal law. (Sec. 19368, Rev. & Tax. Code)

In *Appeal of Albert A. Ellis, Jr.* (1972) (CCH CALIFORNIA TAX REPORTS, ¶ 89-202.671), the State Board of Equalization (BOE) allowed interest on recovery of an erroneous refund, although the tax assessment in question was not a "deficiency" under the law then in effect. In *Appeal of Bruce H. and Norah E. Planck* (1977) (CCH CALIFORNIA TAX REPORTS, ¶ 89-190.301), the BOE held that assessment of an erroneous refund was a "deficiency" and that interest was properly imposed under the rules for interest on deficiencies (¶ 711).

¶727 Abusive Tax Shelters

Law: Secs. 18407, 18628, 18648, 19164, 19164.5, 19173, 19174, 19177, 19179, 19182, 19751-54, 19761-64, 19772, 19774, 19777, 19778 (CCH CALIFORNIA TAX REPORTS, ¶ 89-102, 89-186, 89-206, 89-210).

Comparable Federal: Secs. 6011, 6111, 6112 (CCH U.S. MASTER TAX GUIDE ¶ 2001 et seq.).

California conforms to the federal rules as of the current California federal conformity date (¶ 103) that govern reporting of abusive tax shelters with the following modifications that:

— expand the definition of a "reportable transaction" to include any transaction of a type that either the IRS or the Franchise Tax Board (FTB) determines as having a potential for tax avoidance or evasion (either federal or state tax), including deductions, basis, credits, entity classification, dividend elimination, or omission of income; and

— expand the definition of a reportable "listed transaction" to include a transaction that is the same as, or substantially similar to, a transaction specifically identified by the IRS or the FTB as a federal or state tax avoidance transaction, including deductions, basis, credits, entity classification, dividend elimination, or omission of income.

(Sec. 18628, Rev. & Tax. Code)

An "abusive tax avoidance transaction" is:

— a California tax shelter;

— a reportable transaction that is not adequately disclosed;

— a listed transaction;

— a gross misstatement, which includes both the omission of income equal to more than 25% of the gross income reported on a return and the substantial undervaluation of property as described in IRC § 6662(e) and (h)(2); or

— a transaction subject to the noneconomic substance transaction (NEST) penalty.

(Sec. 19777(b), Rev. & Tax. Code; *FTB Tax News*, October 2011, CCH CALIFORNIA TAX REPORTS, ¶ 405-517)

The FTB is required to identify and publish "listed transactions" through the use of FTB notices, other published positions, and the FTB Web site.

CCH Tip: Reportable Transaction Rules for Enterprise Zone Credits

Transactions involving a refundable or contingent fee relating to an enterprise zone hiring credit (EZ hiring credit) against personal income tax or corporation franchise and income tax are exempt the from contractual protection reportable transaction disclosure and reporting rules. Consequently, taxpayers are not required to disclose to the FTB such transactions and material advisors are not required to report such transactions or maintain lists of such advisees, unless the transactions fall under one of the other reportable transactions categories required to be disclosed under Treasury Regulation § 1.6011-4(b). The exemption applies to all transactions in which the refundable or contingent fee relates to the EZ hiring credit, regardless of when the transaction was entered into, that otherwise would have been required to be disclosed by the taxpayer or reported by the material advisor after 2008. (*FTB Notice 2009-2*, CCH CALIFORNIA TAX REPORTS, ¶ 404-879)

Generally, taxpayers that are involved in a reportable transaction and/or a listed transaction must attach a copy of the federal Form 8666 to their original or amended California return. A copy must also be sent to the FTB's Abusive Tax Shelter Unit (ATSU), at ATSU 398 MS: F385, Franchise Tax Board, P.O. Box 1673, Sacramento, California, 95812-9900, the first time a reportable transaction is disclosed on the taxpayer's return. (FTB Notice 2007-3, CCH CALIFORNIA TAX REPORTS, ¶ 404-326; Chapter 656 (SB 614/AB 1601) - General Information: Registration & Reporting Requirements—Reportable Transaction Disclosure Requirements, California Franchise Tax Board, July 19, 2006, CCH CALIFORNIA TAX REPORTS, ¶ 404-333)

Practitioner Comment: Reportable Transaction Clarification

The FTB has clarified that it will follow Internal Revenue Service Notice 2006-6 and no longer require the reporting of transactions with substantial book-tax differences to the extent captured on Federal Schedule M-3 unless the transaction is described in one of the other categories of reportable transactions. For transactions with a California-only substantial book-tax difference, reporting on Schedule M-1 is sufficient disclosure.

Chris Whitney, Contributing Editor

Practitioner Comment: California "Listed Transactions"

Cal. Rev. & Tax. Code Sec. 8407(a)(4) states that a "listed transaction" includes any transaction that is the same as, or substantially similar to, a transaction specifically identified by the Secretary of the Treasury under IRC § 6011 for federal income tax purposes or a transaction identified by the Franchise Tax Board (FTB). Currently, there are four California specific listed transactions identified by the FTB. Two listed transactions were identified in the FTB's initial guidance following comprehensive California tax legislation enacted in 2003. In *Chief Counsel Announcement 2003-1*, dated December 31, 2003, the FTB includes as "listed transactions" certain real estate investment trust (REIT) and regulated investment company (RIC) transactions. With respect to the former transactions, the FTB specifically identified as a listed transaction any "transactions involving [REITs] where the REIT takes a deduction for a consent dividend." The guidance notes that California does not conform to the federal consent dividend regime under IRC § 565. As noted in the guidance, in applying the federal REIT provisions under California law, the REIT is not entitled to deduct consent dividends and the REIT is subject to California tax for amounts treated as consent dividends under federal tax law. Accordingly, the deduction for dividends paid may differ for federal and California purposes.

It is important to note that the FTB's decision to include REIT consent dividends as a listed transaction is not limited to so-called "captive" REITs. In some cases, publicly held REITs deduct consent dividends for valid business reasons. Under the FTB's guidance, these REITs may have listed transactions under California's tax shelter provisions.

The FTB identified the third listed transaction on January 6, 2011, in *Notice 2011-01*, where it identifies as a listed transaction the use by corporate taxpayers of one or more partnerships to inflate the denominator of the sales factor, thereby reducing the amount of business income apportioned to California.

In this regard it should be noted that California Code of Regs § 25137-1(f)(3)(A)(i) provides that sales made by a taxpayer to a unitary partnership are eliminated from the sales factor to the extent of the taxpayer's interest in the partnership while (A)(ii) provides that sales by a unitary partnership to a taxpayer are eliminated in an amount not to exceed the taxpayer's interest in all partnership sales. In addition, (f)(3)(B) of this regulation explicitly states that sales made to nonpartners are to be included in the sales factor denominator in an amount "equal to such taxpayer's interest in the partnership." These regulatory provisions suggest that sales between a corporation and a partnership in which the corporation is not a partner should not be eliminated, even when such corporation is included in a combined report with one or more corporations that are partners in such partnership.

Lastly, on August 4, 2011, the FTB withdrew Notice 2011-03 and issued Notice 2011-04, which identifies as a listed transaction capital contributions "without any outlay of cash or property" to increase the basis in subsidiary stock made by corporate taxpayers in contemplation of a sale of a subsidiary. The transactions described in Notice 2011-04 are, in the FTB's view, designed for the purpose of exploiting and abusing California's nonconformity to a substantial portion of the IRC § 1502 federal consolidated return regulations. Specifically, California has no provisions similar to the investment adjustments required for federal purposes under Treasury Reg. § 1.1502-32. The FTB intends to attack such transactions using substance over form, sham transaction, and the step transaction doctrine when such transactions fail to reflect an economic change of position of a parent company with respect to its investment in subsidiary stock. Note that pursuant to Reg § 25106.5-1(f)(1)(B)(2), a DISA can be reduced or eliminated through subsequent capital contributions. While there is not direct guidance stating that reducing or curing a DISA with subsequent capital contributions prior to a triggering event is substantially similar to the listed transaction in Notice 2011-04, it is unlikely to be the case since the DISA regulation specifically permits curing or reducing a DISA in this manner.

It should be noted that several taxpayers have argued that California's lack of conformity to the federal adjustment provisions results in double taxation of a unitary subsidiary's earnings. The State Board of Equalization and California Court of Appeal, however, have both nonetheless held that there was no basis in California statutes or regulations to support making Treasury Reg § 1.1502-32 investment adjustments to subsidiary stock basis. See Appeal of Rapid-American, State Board of Equalization, 97-SBE-019 (1997) and Jim Beam Brands v. Franchise Tax Board, 133 Cal. App. 4th 514 (2005).

Tax practitioners should keep in mind what the FTB may consider as substantially similar when advising clients on strategies that are similar to these recently listed transactions, as California listed transactions are subject to disclosure and reporting requirements and penalties under the state's noneconomic substance transaction (NEST) provisions.

Chris Whitney, Contributing Editor

Practitioner Comment: FTB "Reaches Out" to Taxpayers with California and Federal Listed Transaction

California corporate franchise and individual income taxpayers that participated to any degree in a potentially abusive tax shelter, including a federal or California listed transaction, and that did not participate in the California Voluntary Compliance Initiative may receive a notice of intent to audit from the FTB. The notice offers two options for an expedient resolution: (1) admit to the use of a potentially abusive tax shelter, file an amended return, and pay the additional tax, interest and applicable penalties; or (2) choose to be audited subject to all applicable penalties. Under the first alternative, the 100% interest-based penalty will be waived, but all other tax shelter penalties will apply.

The FTB, using information obtained from promoter filings submitted during the California Voluntary Compliance Initiative Program and from the IRS, has identified individual and corporate taxpayers that may have been involved in potentially abusive tax shelters. Based on that information, the FTB sends notices of intent to conduct an examination to select taxpayers. The notices describe the transaction at issue and request extensive information with respect to the transaction, including the business purpose for the transaction; any offering prospectus or other literature that describes the transaction, and the related fees paid to participate or structure the transaction; the federal and state tax treatment of the transaction; and other supporting information. Of note, the notices caution taxpayers to retain all relevant documentation, both physical and electronic.

Chris Whitney, Contributing Editor

Bogus optional basis transactions.—The FTB is closely scrutinizing the use of bogus optional basis (BOB) transactions, in which a partnership uses an IRC §754 election to inappropriately increase the basis of its property. In some cases, the basis of assets is increased before their disposition. In other cases, taxpayers are using the additional basis to claim increased depreciation or amortization deductions. Depending upon the facts and circumstances, a BOB transaction may be disregarded or be recast to properly reflect California income, or the basis step-up might be disallowed. (*Tax News*, California Franchise Tax Board, September 2007, CCH CALIFORNIA TAX REPORTS, ¶404-446)

• *Information returns*

Information returns.—California incorporates, with modifications, federal law (IRC Sec. 6111) requiring specified material advisors to file information returns disclosing reportable transactions. Material advisors are required to send a duplicate of federal Form 8918, Material Advisor Disclosure Statement, or the same information required to be provided on the federal reportable transactions return for California reportable transactions to the Franchise Tax Board (FTB) by the last day of the month that follows the end of the calendar quarter in which the advisor became a material advisor with respect to a reportable transaction or in which the circumstances necessitating an amended disclosure statement occur. Additional information may be required if specified in an FTB Notice. (Sec. 18628, Rev. & Tax. Code)

For transactions entered into after September 1, 2003, and before August 3, 2007, if a transaction becomes listed after the filing of the taxpayer's return reflecting the taxpayer's participation in the listed transaction, the taxpayer is required to file the Form 8886 with the next filed California return after the transaction is listed, regardless of the year in which the taxpayer participated in the transaction. For transactions entered into after August 2, 2007, the taxpayer must file Form 8886 with the FTB within 90 calendar days of the date listing the transaction in the FTB Notice. Failure to file the required Form 8886 or filing an incomplete form may result in the assessment of a penalty for failure to include information on reportable transactions. California listed transactions entered into prior to September 2, 2003, are not required to be disclosed unless the transaction falls under one of the other categories of reportable transactions defined under Treasury Reg. 1.6011-4(b). (*Tax News Flash*, California Franchise Tax Board, February 3, 2011)

Comment: FTB Reporting Requirements

Taxpayers are required to attach IRS Form 8886 to the back of their California return. If this is the first time the reportable transaction is disclosed on the return, a copy of the federal form must also be sent to the FTB at:
Tax Shelter Filing, ATSU 398 MS F385
Franchise Tax Board
P.O. Box 1673
Sacramento, CA 95812-9900

Alternatively, the Form may be sent by private carrier services to Tax Shelter Filing, Franchise Tax Board, Sacramento, CA 95827

Material advisors are subject to the California reporting requirements if they are:

— organized in California;

— doing business in California;

— deriving income from California sources; or

— providing any material aid, assistance, or advice with respect to organizing, managing, promoting, selling, implementing, insuring, or carrying out any reportable transaction with respect to a taxpayer that is organized in California, does business in California, or derives income from California sources.

In addition, material advisors are required to file returns with the FTB for any transactions that become listed transactions at any time for federal income tax purposes or for any transactions that are identified by the FTB as listed transactions for California corporation franchise or income tax purposes. The returns must be filed within 60 days after (1) entering into the transaction, or (2) the transactions become a listed transaction.

More than one advisor.—If more than one material advisor is required to file a form for the same transaction, the material advisors may designate by agreement a single material advisor to file the required form. The designation agreement should be attached to the form filed with the FTB. The designation of one material advisor to file does not relieve the other material advisors from the obligation to file if the designated material advisor fails to file. (*FTB Notice 2005-7* (2005), CCH CALIFORNIA TAX REPORTS, ¶ 403-941)

Filing of request for letter ruling.—If a material advisor sends the FTB a copy of a request for a letter ruling filed with the IRS on or before the date the information return is due with respect to a particular transaction, the FTB will suspend the due date for disclosing that transaction until 60 days from the date of the IRS ruling that the transaction is a reportable transaction or, if the request is withdrawn, 60 days from the date of the request to withdraw. (*FTB Notice 2005-7* (2005), CCH CALIFORNIA TAX REPORTS, ¶ 403-941)

List of advisees.—California also conforms to federal law, requiring material advisors of reportable transactions to keep lists of advisees. The lists must be maintained for California purposes in the form and manner prescribed by the FTB. The lists must be provided to the FTB by the later of 60 days after entering into the transactions, or 60 days after the transaction becomes a listed transaction. (Sec. 18648, Rev. & Tax. Code)

CCH Tip: If It Looks Like a Tax Shelter . . .

According to the Franchise Tax Board if a taxpayer can answer "yes" to any of the following questions, he or she is likely involved in an abusive tax scheme:

—Is the tax loss, deduction, or credit a significant amount and used to offset income from unrelated transactions?

—Is the taxpayer's economic and out-of-pocket loss minimal compared to the tax benefits realized from the transaction?

—Does the transaction lack a business purpose other than the reduction of income taxes?

—Does the transaction lack a reasonable possibility of making a profit?

—Are multiple entities involved to unnecessarily complicate the transaction?

—Does the tax position ignore the true intent of relevant statutes and regulations?

—Does the transaction produce a tax result that is too good to be true?

Common schemes involve:

—*basis shifting*, in which foreign corporations and instruments are utilized to artificially increase and shift the basis of stock held by a foreign shareholder who is not subject to U.S. taxation to stock owned by U.S. shareholders. The taxpayers ultimately sell their stock and report an inflated loss despite incurring no or minimal economic loss.

—*inflated basis,* in which transactions that are characterized as contingent are utilized to inflate an owner's basis in a pass-through entity investment. Taxpayers contribute cash or securities to a pass-through entity and obtain a basis in the entity equal to the value of the cash or cost of the securities contributed. Simultaneously, taxpayers contribute an alleged liability, obligation, or deferred income item to the entity, which should reduce the taxpayers' basis in the entity for the amount of that liability or deferral. But taxpayers involved in such transactions do not reduce their basis in the pass-through entity, claiming that the liability or income item is contingent or deferred for tax purposes. In this manner, taxpayers create an artificially inflated basis for the pass-through entity interest that is then used to deduct ordinary losses or to compute a large loss on liquidating distributions received from the entity. The most common variations of this type of scheme include the contribution of short sale proceeds and liabilities to a partnership, or the contribution of debt instruments that include contingencies or premiums that taxpayers ignore for purposes of computing basis.

—*commercial domicile,* in which taxpayers are told that they can avoid California income taxes if they incorporate in states such as Delaware or Nevada that do not impose an income tax. Although there are many variations of this scheme, the most conspicuous version has, in the past, involved a business incorporating in Nevada, electing S corporation status for federal purposes, but electing C corporation status for California purposes. Individual business owners contribute a highly appreciated intangible asset, such as stock, to the Nevada corporation tax-free. The corporation then sells the asset, recognizing a gain, and claims that the source of the gain from the intangible asset is Nevada, because the commercial domicile of the corporation is Nevada and the corporation is not doing business in California. The individual business owners ultimately receive the proceeds from the stock sale through shareholder loans or via dividends once the shareholders change their state of residence.

(*Tax News,* California Franchise Tax Board, September 2003)

- *Tax professionals*

Tax professionals are subject to special registration and "list of investors" requirements if they are engaged in any of the following activities:

— participation in the organization of a potentially abusive tax shelter;

— advising a potentially abusive tax shelter;

— providing an opinion on a potentially abusive tax shelter;

— promoting a potentially abusive tax shelter;

— selling a potentially abusive tax shelter; or

— managing a potentially abusive tax shelter.

(*Information Release, E-mail,* California Franchise Tax Board, February 10, 2004)

- *Reporting procedures*

Reporting procedures.—Taxpayers submitting information required by California statutory provisions regarding tax shelter registration must provide the applicable California business entity number. The California business entity number of the key corporation must likewise be provided if a business entity is a corporation included in a group return for a combined reporting group (*FTB Notice 2004-1,* California Franchise Tax Board, Legal Department, January 30, 2004).

Practice Tip: Reporting Electronically

Taxpayers can file IRS Form 8886, Reportable Transaction Disclosure, with the California e-file return. E-filers must also file a separate IRS Form 8886 for the first time the reportable transaction is disclosed. The copy should show exactly the same information, word for word, provided with the electronically filed return. Mail a duplicate copy of IRS Form 8886 to the attention of "Tax Shelter Filing" at the Franchise Tax Board, P.O. Box 1673, Sacramento, CA 95812-1673.

Inquiries relating to abusive tax shelters may be e-mailed to the FTB at TaxShelter@ftb.ca.gov.

• *Penalties*

The following penalties relate to abusive tax shelters:

(1) failure to maintain list of advisees—$10,000 for each day of failure if not provided within 20 days of request (Sec. 19173, Rev. & Tax. Code);

(2) material advisor's failure to maintain list—an additional penalty equal to the greater of (1) $100,000 or (2) 50% of advisor's gross income from activity (Sec. 19173, Rev. & Tax. Code);

(3) failure to maintain records to substantiate tax shelter promoter return—$1,000 multiplied by number of investors (Sec. 19174, Rev. & Tax. Code);

(4) promoting abusive tax shelter—$1,000 or 100% of gross income derived or to be derived from violation, whichever is less; except 50% of gross income derived or to be derived from violation if a person makes or causes another to make a statement that the person knows or has reason to know is false or fraudulent as to a material matter (Sec. 19177, Rev. & Tax. Code);

(5) failing to furnish information concerning a reportable transaction—$50,000 (Sec. 19182, Rev. & Tax. Code);

(6) failure to furnish information concerning listed transaction—the greater of (1) $200,000 or (2) 50% (100% if intentional) of gross income derived with respect to transaction (Sec. 19182, Rev. & Tax. Code);

(7) failure by taxpayer with taxable income greater than $200,000 to include reportable or listed transaction information with return—maximum $15,000 per failure ($5,000 in the case of a natural person) for reportable transaction; maximum $30,000 per failure ($15,000 in the case of a natural person) if listed transaction; minimum $2,500 penalty ($1,250 in the case of a natural person) (Sec. 19772, Rev. & Tax. Code);

(8) accuracy-related penalty on reportable transaction understatements (¶727)—20% of understatement; 30% if undisclosed on return (Sec. 19164.5, Rev. & Tax. Code);

(9) deficiency and contacted by FTB concerning an abusive tax avoidance transaction (ABAT)—100% of interest payable for period beginning on the last day of payment (without extensions) until date notice or proposed assessment mailed; 50% of interest attributable to ABAT if amended return filed after being contacted by the FTB but before notice of proposed assessment is issued (Sec. 19777, Rev. & Tax. Code); and

(10) noneconomic substance transaction (NEST) penalty—40% of the understatement; 20% for underpayments to which the facts were disclosed in the return (Sec. 19774, Rev. & Tax. Code). A transaction that the IRS examines and determines lacks economic substance is subject to California's NEST and accuracy-related penalties.

The tax shelter penalties under (1) and (2), above, may be assessed within eight years from the date of the failure. (Sec. 19173, Rev. & Tax. Code)

• *Penalty waivers and abatements*

No penalty will be imposed for failure to comply with providing information concerning reportable transactions required by the FTB if it was not identified in a FTB notice issued prior to the date the transaction or shelter was entered into. (Sec. 19182(c), Rev. & Tax. Code)

The Chief Counsel of the FTB may rescind all or any portion of the accuracy-related reportable transaction penalty or any penalty imposed for failure to maintain a list of advisees or to provide information concerning reportable transactions, or the penalty applicable to taxpayers with taxable income greater than $200,000 that fail to include reportable transactions information with their return if all of the following apply:

— the violation is with respect to a reportable transaction other than a listed transaction;

— the person on whom the penalty is imposed has a history of complying with the requirements of the California franchise or income tax laws;

— the violation is due to an unintentional mistake of fact;

— imposing the penalty would be against equity and good conscience; and

— rescinding the penalty would promote compliance with the requirements of the California franchise or income tax laws and effective tax administration.

(Sec 19164.5(d), Rev. & Tax. Code; Sec. 19173, Rev. & Tax. Code; Sec. 19182(d), Rev. & Tax. Code; Sec. 19772, Rev. & Tax. Code)

Also, the Chief Counsel may rescind all or any portion of any penalty imposed for filing a frivolous return if both of the following apply:

— imposing the penalty would be against equity and good conscience; and

— rescinding the penalty would promote compliance with the requirements of the California franchise or income tax laws and effective tax administration.

(Sec. 19179, Rev. & Tax. Code)

If the notice of proposed assessment of additional tax has been sent with respect to a noneconomic substance transaction understatement, only the Chief Counsel may compromise the penalty or any portion thereof. (Sec. 19774, Rev. & Tax. Code)

The FTB Chief Counsel may rescind the penalties associated with non-listed activities in (1) and (2) and for the omissions listed in (7), above, if the taxpayer has a history of compliance and can demonstrate that the failure/omission was the result of an unintentional mistake of fact.

• *Interest penalties*

A penalty equal to 100% of the accrued interest on the underpayment is assessed against taxpayers contacted by the FTB regarding the use of a potentially abusive tax shelter. The penalty accrues from the due date of the return, without regard to extensions, and ends on the date that the notice of assessment is mailed. (Sec. 19777, Rev. & Tax. Code)

Interest at a rate equal to 150% of the interest rate above applies to understatements of tax related to the use of a reportable transaction by taxpayers who have not previously been contacted by the IRS or FTB regarding their investment in a potentially abusive tax shelter. (Sec. 19778, Rev. & Tax. Code)

• *Voluntary Compliance Initiative Two*

Practitioner Comment: Taxpayers Who Have Been "Contacted" Regarding An ATAT

S.B. 86, Laws 2011, created a second Voluntary Compliance Initiative or "VCI 2" that ended on October 31, 2011. Among other things, the VCI 2 legislation adopted a uniform definition of an "Abusive Tax Avoidance Transaction" or "ATAT." Prior to the legislation, taxpayers who had been contacted regarding reportable, listed, or certain other transactions could avoid the 100% interest penalty imposed by CRTC Section 19777 by filing an amended return to report the transaction prior to the issuance of the notice of proposed assessment ("NPA"). Under the VCI 2 legislation, taxpayers who file amended returns after such contact remain subject to a 50% interest penalty under this statute. It is our understanding that the FTB regards the mass mailings it issued regarding the VCI 2 initiative as constituting "contact" for this purpose. Finally, it should also be noted that the legislation increases the statute of limitations for assessment for ATATs from 8 to 12 years.

Chris Whitney, Contributing Editor

Practice Tip: Appeal Rights Waived

An election to participate in the VCI Two results in the abandonment of any rights to file an appeal or a claim for refund with respect to those transactions. (S.B. 86, Final Bill Analysis, California Franchise Tax Board, March 24, 2011)

PART IV

TAXES ON CORPORATE INCOME

FEDERAL-CALIFORNIA CROSS-REFERENCE TABLE AND INDEX

Showing Sections of California Bank and Corporation Tax Law (Revenue and Taxation Code) Comparable to Sections of Federal Law (1986 Internal Revenue Code)

Federal	California	Subject	Paragraph
IRC Sec. 11	Secs. 23151, 23501	Tax imposed	¶805, ¶816
IRC Sec. 15	Secs. 23058, 24251	Tax rate changes during year	¶1105
IRC Sec. 30	. . . .	Low emission motor vehicle credit	. . . .
IRC Sec. 38	. . . .	General business credit	. . . .
IRC Sec. 39	. . . .	Unused credits	. . . .
IRC Sec. 40		Alcohol fuel credit	. . . .
IRC Sec. 41	Sec. 23609	Qualified research credit	¶818
IRC Sec. 42	Secs. 23610.4-10.5	Low-income housing credit	¶818
IRC Sec. 43	Sec. 23604	Enhanced oil recovery credit	¶818
IRC Sec. 44	Sec. 23642	Disabled access credit	¶818
IRC Sec. 45(a)	Sec. 23684	Renewable resources credit	¶818
IRC Sec. 45C	. . . .	Clinical testing credit	¶818
IRC Sec. 45D	. . . .	New markets tax credit	. . . .
IRC Sec. 45E		Credit for small employer pension plan startup costs	
IRC Sec. 45F	Sec. 23617	Employer-provided child care credit	¶134
IRC Sec. 45G		Railroad track maintenance credit	
IRC Sec. 45H	Sec. 23662	Low sulfur diesel fuel production credit	¶818
IRC Sec. 45I	. . . .	Marginal well production credit	
IRC Secs. 46-50	. . . .	Investment in depreciable property	¶818
IRC Secs. 51, 52	Sec. 23621	Work opportunity credit	. . . .
IRC Sec. 53	Sec. 23453	Minimum tax credit	¶817, ¶818
IRC Secs. 55-59	Secs. 23400, 23455-59	Alternative minimum tax	¶817, ¶1011
IRC Sec. 59A	. . . .	Environmental tax	
IRC Sec. 61	Secs. 24271, 24314, 24308, 24315, 24323	Gross income	¶901
IRC Sec. 63	Sec. 24341	Taxable income defined	¶815
IRC Sec. 64	Sec. 23049.1	Ordinary income defined	. . . .
IRC Sec. 65	Sec. 23049.2	Ordinary loss defined	. . . .
IRC Sec. 72	Secs. 24272.2, 24302	Annuities	¶903, ¶904
IRC Sec. 75	. . . .	Dealers in tax-exempt securities	. . . .
IRC Sec. 77	Sec. 24273	Community credit loans	¶912
IRC Sec. 78	. . . .	Dividends from foreign corporations	¶909
IRC Sec. 80	. . . .	Restoration of value of certain securities	. . . .
IRC Sec. 83	Sec. 24379	Transfer of property in exchange for services	¶1001, ¶1017
IRC Sec. 84	. . . .	Property transferred to political organizations	¶901
IRC Sec. 87		Alcohol and biodiesel fuel credits	¶901
IRC Sec. 88	Sec. 24275	Nuclear plant expenses	¶901
IRC Sec. 90	Sec. 24276	Illegal federal irrigation subsidies	. . . .
IRC Sec. 101	Secs. 24301, 24302, 24305	Life insurance proceeds	¶902, ¶904
IRC Sec. 102	. . . .	Gifts and inheritances	. . . .
IRC Sec. 103	Secs. 24272, 24301	Interest on government bonds	¶910
IRC Sec. 108	Secs. 24301, 24307	Income from discharge of indebtedness	¶908
IRC Sec. 109	Secs. 24301, 24309	Improvements by lessee	¶905
IRC Sec. 110	Sec. 24309.5	Lessee construction allowances	¶906
IRC Sec. 111	Secs. 24301, 24310	Recovery of bad debts and prior taxes	¶907

Federal	California	Subject	Paragraph
IRC Sec. 114	. . . .	Extraterritorial income	¶ 825, ¶ 901
IRC Sec. 118	Secs. 24324, 24325	Contributions to capital of corporation	¶ 913
IRC Sec. 126	Secs. 24301, 24308.5	Cost-sharing payments	¶ 923
IRC Sec. 136	Secs. 24301, 24308.1, 24326	Energy conservation subsidies	¶ 922
IRC Sec. 139	Sec. 24329	Disaster relief payments	¶ 927
IRC Sec. 139A	. . . .	Prescription drug subsidies	¶ 901, ¶ 926
IRC Secs. 141-50	Sec. 24272	Private activity bonds	¶ 910
IRC Sec. 161	Secs. 24415, 24436.5, 24441, 24447, 24448	Allowance of deductions	. . . .
IRC Sec. 162	Secs. 24343, 24343.2, 24343.5, 24343.7	Deductions for business expense	¶ 1001, ¶ 1023
IRC Sec. 163	Secs. 24344, 24344.5, 24344.7	Interest expense deduction	¶ 1004, ¶ 1312
IRC Sec. 164	Secs. 24345, 24346	Deduction for taxes	¶ 1006
IRC Sec. 165	Secs. 24347-47.14	Losses-deductions	¶ 1007, ¶ 1010
IRC Sec. 166	Sec. 24347	Deduction for bad debts	¶ 1009
IRC Sec. 167	Secs. 24349-5.4, 24368.1	Depreciation	¶ 1011, ¶ 1250
IRC Sec. 168	Secs. 24349, 24355.4, 24355.5	Accelerated cost recovery system	¶ 1011
IRC Sec. 169	Sec. 24372.3	Amortization of pollution control facilities	¶ 1011
IRC Sec. 170	Secs. 24357-59.1	Charitable contributions	¶ 1014, ¶ 1312
IRC Sec. 171	Secs. 24360-63.5	Amortizable bond premium	¶ 1015
IRC Sec. 172	Secs. 24416-16.22, 25110	Net operating loss deduction	¶ 1024
IRC Sec. 173	Sec. 24364	Circulation expenditures	¶ 1003
IRC Sec. 174	Sec. 24365	Research expenditures	¶ 1011
IRC Sec. 175	Sec. 24369	Soil and water conservation expenditures	¶ 1002
IRC Sec. 176	. . . .	Social security payments for employees of foreign subsidiaries	. . . .
IRC Sec. 178	Sec. 24373	Depreciation or amortization of lessee improvements	¶ 1011
IRC Sec. 179	Secs. 24356, 24356.8	Asset expense election	¶ 1011
IRC Sec. 179B	Sec. 24356.4	Refiners' sulfur rules compliance costs	¶ 1026
IRC Sec. 179C	. . . .	Expensing of qualified refinery property	¶ 1001
IRC Sec. 179D	. . . .	Expensing of energy efficient commercial building costs	¶ 1027
IRC Sec. 180	Sec. 24377	Farm fertilizer expenses	¶ 1002
IRC Sec. 181	. . . .	Qualified film and television productions	¶ 1011
IRC Sec. 183	. . . .	Hobby losses	. . . .
IRC Sec. 186	Secs. 24675, 24677, 24678	Recovery of antitrust damages	¶ 1106
IRC Sec. 190	Sec. 24383	Architectural adaptations for the handicapped	¶ 1001
IRC Sec. 192	. . . .	Contributions to black lung benefit trust	¶ 1014
IRC Sec. 193	. . . .	Tertiary injectants	¶ 1013
IRC Sec. 194	Sec. 24372.5	Amortization of reforestation expenses	¶ 1011
IRC Sec. 194A	. . . .	Contributions to employer liability trusts	¶ 1016
IRC Sec. 195	Sec. 24414	Start-up expenses	¶ 1018
IRC Sec. 196	Sec. 23051.5	Unused investment credits	. . . .
IRC Sec. 197	Sec. 24355.5	Amortization of goodwill	¶ 1011
IRC Sec. 198	. . . .	Environmental remediation costs	¶ 1011
IRC Sec. 198A	. . . .	Qualified disaster expenses	. . . .
IRC Sec. 199	. . . .	Domestic production deduction	¶ 925
IRC Sec. 216	Sec. 24382	Foreclosure of cooperative housing corporation stock	¶ 1022
IRC Sec. 220	Sec. 24343.3	Archer MSAs	. . . .
IRC Sec. 241	Sec. 24401	Special deductions	. . . .
IRC Secs. 243-247	Secs. 24401, 24402, 24410, 24411	Dividends received by corporations	¶ 909, ¶ 1020
IRC Sec. 248	Secs. 24407-09	Organizational expenditures	¶ 1011
IRC Sec. 249	Sec. 24439	Deductions of bond premium on repurchase	¶ 1004, ¶ 1223
IRC Sec. 261	Sec. 24421	Disallowance of deductions	¶ 1023
IRC Sec. 263	Secs. 24422-23	Capital expenditures	¶ 1013, ¶ 1023
IRC Sec. 263A	Sec. 24422.3	Inventory capitalization—inclusion	¶ 1106, ¶ 1107
IRC Sec. 264	Sec. 24424	Payments on life insurance contracts	¶ 1004, ¶ 1023
IRC Sec. 265	Sec. 24425	Deductions allocable to tax-exempt income	¶ 1004, ¶ 1023
IRC Sec. 266	Sec. 24426	Taxes and carrying charges	¶ 1023

Federal	California	Subject	Paragraph
IRC Sec. 267	Sec. 24427	Transactions between related individuals	¶1023
IRC Sec. 268	. . . .	Sale of land with unharvested crop	¶1023
IRC Sec. 269	Sec. 24431	Acquisitions made to avoid tax	¶1110
IRC Sec. 269A	. . . .	Personal service corporations formed to evade taxes	¶1110
IRC Sec. 269B	. . . .	Stapled interests	¶1110
IRC Sec. 271	Sec. 24434	Debts owed by political parties	¶1009, ¶1023
IRC Sec. 272	. . . .	Disposal of coal or iron ore	. . . .
IRC Sec. 274	Sec. 24443	Disallowance of entertainment and gift expenses	¶1001, ¶1023
IRC Sec. 275	Secs. 24345, 24345.5	Certain taxes	¶1006
IRC Sec. 276	Sec. 24429	Indirect contributions to political parties	¶1023
IRC Sec. 277	Sec. 24437	Deduction limitation for social clubs	¶1023
IRC Sec. 279	Sec. 24438	Interest deduction on corporate acquisition indebtedness	¶1004
IRC Sec. 280B	Sec. 24442	Demolition of historic structures	¶1023
IRC Sec. 280C	Sec. 24440	Expenses for which credit allowed	¶818, ¶1023
IRC Sec. 280E	Secs. 24436.1	Illegal sale of drugs	¶1023
IRC Sec. 280F	Sec. 24349.1	Depreciation-luxury cars	¶1011
IRC Sec. 280G	Sec. 24349.2	Golden parachutes	¶1023
IRC Sec. 280H	Sec. 24442.5	Amounts paid to employee owners	. . . .
IRC Sec. 291	Sec. 24449	Preference items	¶817
IRC Secs. 301-385	Secs. 24451-81	Corporate distributions and adjustments	¶Various
IRC Secs. 401-424	Secs. 23701p, 24601-12, 24685.5	Deferred compensation	¶909, ¶1016, ¶1017
IRC Sec. 430-436	. . . .	Minimum funding for single-employer and multi-employer plans	¶909, ¶1016
IRC Sec. 441	Secs. 24631, 24632, 24633.5	Accounting periods	¶1101
IRC Sec. 442	Sec. 24633	Change in accounting period	¶1102
IRC Sec. 443	Secs. 23113, 24634-36	Short-period returns	¶1103
IRC Sec. 444	Sec. 24637	Election to keep same tax year—S Corporations	¶806, ¶1104
IRC Sec. 446	Sec. 24651	Accounting methods	¶1106
IRC Sec. 447	Secs. 24652-52.5	Accounting for farm corporations	¶1106
IRC Sec. 448	Sec. 24654	Cash method of accounting restricted	¶1106
IRC Sec. 451	Secs. 24661, 24661.5, 24661.6	Taxable year of inclusion	¶1106
IRC Sec. 453	Secs. 24667, 24668.1	Installment method	¶1109
IRC Sec. 453A	Sec. 24667	Installment method	¶1109
IRC Sec. 453B	Sec. 24667	Installment method	¶1109
IRC Sec. 454	Sec. 24674	Obligation issued at discount	¶1111
IRC Sec. 455	Sec. 24676	Prepaid subscription income	¶1106
IRC Sec. 456	. . . .	Prepaid dues income	¶1106
IRC Sec. 457	. . . .	Deferred compensation plans-state governments	. . . .
IRC Sec. 457A	. . . .	Nonqualified deferred compensation from certain tax indifferent parties	¶1100
IRC Sec. 458	Sec. 24676.5	Returned magazines, paperbacks, records	¶1106
IRC Sec. 460	Secs. 24673, 24673.2	Long-term contracts	¶1106
IRC Sec. 461	Sec. 24681	Taxable year of deduction	¶1004, ¶1106
IRC Sec. 464	Sec. 24682	Farming expenses	¶1106
IRC Sec. 465	Sec. 24691	Deductions limited to amount at risk	¶1023, ¶1025
IRC Sec. 467	Sec. 24688	Deferred rental payments	¶1106
IRC Sec. 468	Sec. 24689	Waste disposal costs	¶1106
IRC Sec. 468A	Sec. 24690	Nuclear decommissioning funds	. . . .
IRC Sec. 468B	Sec. 24693	Designated settlement funds	¶807, ¶1106
IRC Sec. 469	Sec. 24692	Passive losses and credits	¶1005, ¶1106
IRC Sec. 470	Sec. 24694	Tax-exempt use losses	¶1007
IRC Sec. 471	Sec. 24701	Inventories-general rule	¶1107
IRC Sec. 472	Sec. 24701	Inventories-LIFO	¶1108
IRC Sec. 473	. . . .	Liquidation of LIFO inventories	¶1108
IRC Sec. 474	Sec. 24708	Simplified dollar value LIFO	¶1108
IRC Sec. 475	Sec. 24710	Mark to market accounting	¶1107
IRC Sec. 481	Sec. 24721	Adjustments required by changes in method	¶1106

Federal	California	Subject	Paragraph
IRC Sec. 482	Sec. 24725	Allocation of income among taxpayers	¶1106, ¶1110
IRC Sec. 483	Sec. 24726	Imputed interest	¶1106, ¶1112
IRC Sec. 501	Secs. 23701-01y, 23703.5, 23704, 23704.4, 23704.5, 23706	Exempt organizations and trusts	¶808, ¶809
IRC Sec. 502	Sec. 23702	Feeder organizations	¶809
IRC Sec. 503	Secs. 23736-36.4	Requirements for exemption	¶809
IRC Sec. 504	Sec. 23704.6	Status after disqualification for lobbying	¶808
IRC Sec. 505	Sec. 23705	Special rules—VEBAs, etc.	¶808
IRC Sec. 507	Sec. 23707	Private foundation status terminated	¶808
IRC Sec. 508	Sec. 23708	Presumption that organization is private foundation	¶808
IRC Sec. 509	Sec. 23709	"Private foundation" defined	¶808
IRC Sec. 511	Sec. 23731	Unrelated business income	¶809
IRC Sec. 512	Sec. 23732	Unrelated business taxable income	¶809
IRC Sec. 513	Secs. 23710, 23734	Unrelated trade or business	¶809
IRC Sec. 514	Sec. 23735	Unrelated debt-financed income	¶809
IRC Sec. 515	. . . .	Taxes, possessions, and foreign countries	¶809
IRC Sec. 521	. . . .	Farmers' cooperatives-exemption	¶1021
IRC Sec. 526	. . . .	Shipowners' protection associations	. . . .
IRC Sec. 527	Sec. 23701r	Political organizations	¶808
IRC Sec. 528	Sec. 23701t	Homeowners' associations	¶808, ¶915
IRC Sec. 529	Secs. 18645, 23711, 23711.5, 24306	Qualified state tuition program	¶808, ¶924
IRC Sec. 529A	Sec. 23711.4	ABLE accounts	¶255
IRC Sec. 530	Sec. 23712	Education IRAS	¶250, ¶330
IRC Secs. 531-37	. . . .	Corporations improperly accumulating surplus	. . . .
IRC Secs. 541-47	Sec. 23051.5	Personal holding companies	. . . .
IRC Secs. 561-65	Sec. 24402	Deduction for dividends paid	. . . .
IRC Sec. 581	Sec. 23039	Definition of bank	
IRC Sec. 582	Sec. 24347	Bad debts, losses, and gains	¶1009
IRC Sec. 585	Sec. 24348	Deduction for bad debts—banks and S and L's	¶1009
IRC Sec. 591	Secs. 24370, 24403	Deduction for dividends paid on deposits	¶1021
IRC Sec. 593	Sec. 24348	Deduction for bad debts—federal mutual savings banks	¶1009
IRC Sec. 594	. . . .	Mutual savings banks conducting life insurance business	. . . .
IRC Sec. 597	Sec. 24322	FSLIC financial assistance	¶913
IRC Secs. 611-12	Sec. 24831	Natural resources	¶1012, ¶1250
IRC Sec. 613	Sec. 24831	Percentage depletion	¶1012, ¶1250
IRC Sec. 613A	Secs. 24831, 24831.3, 24831.6	Oil and gas wells	¶1012
IRC Sec. 614	Sec. 24831	"Property" defined	¶1012
IRC Sec. 616	Sec. 24831	Mine development expenditures	¶1012, ¶1013
IRC Sec. 617	Sec. 24831	Mine exploration expenditures	¶1012, ¶1013
IRC Sec. 631	Sec. 24831	Timber, coal, iron ore	¶1012
IRC Sec. 636	Sec. 24831	Mineral production payments	¶1012
IRC Sec. 638	Sec. 24831	Continental shelf areas	¶1012
IRC Secs. 641-92	Sec. 24271	Estates, trusts, and beneficiaries	. . . .
IRC Secs. 701-777	Secs. 23081, 23083, 23091-99.5, 24271	Partnerships	¶616, ¶1246
IRC Secs. 801-848	. . . .	Insurance companies	. . . .
IRC Secs. 851-855	Secs. 24870, 24872	Regulated investment companies	¶805, ¶1021
IRC Secs. 856-860	Secs. 24870-72.7	Real estate investment trusts	¶805, ¶1021
IRC Secs. 860A-860G	Secs. 24870, 24873, 24874	Real estate mortgage investment conduits	¶805
IRC Secs. 860H-860L	Secs. 24870, 24875	Financial asset securitization trusts	¶805
IRC Secs. 861-865	Sec. 25110	Income from sources within or without U.S.	¶825, ¶1309
IRC Secs. 871-879	. . . .	Foreign government investment income	. . . .
IRC Secs. 881-882	Sec. 24321	Income of foreign corporations	. . . .
IRC Sec. 883	Sec. 24320	Operation of foreign aircraft or ships	¶916

Federal	California	Subject	Paragraph
IRC Secs. 884-891	. . . .	Foreign corporations and nonresident aliens	. . . .
IRC Sec. 892	Sec. 24327	Income of foreign governments and of international organizations	. . . .
IRC Secs. 901-907	. . . .	Foreign tax credit	. . . .
IRC Sec. 908	. . . .	Reduction of credit for international boycott participation	. . . .
IRC Secs. 931-937	. . . .	U.S. possessions	
IRC Secs. 951-964	Sec. 25110	Controlled foreign corporations	¶825, ¶909
IRC Sec. 965		Temporary dividends received deduction	¶1309
IRC Secs. 970-971	. . . .	Export trade corporations	. . . .
IRC Secs. 985-989	Sec. 24905	Foreign currency transactions	¶1204
IRC Sec. 988	Secs. 24905, 24905.5	Hedging transactions	¶1204, ¶1222
IRC Secs. 991-996	Sec. 23051.5	DISC corporations	¶909
IRC Sec. 1001	Secs. 24901, 24902, 24955	Determination of gain or loss	¶1201
IRC Sec. 1011	Secs. 24911, 24964	Adjusted basis	¶1247
IRC Sec. 1012	Sec. 24912	Basis of property—cost	¶1226
IRC Sec. 1013	Sec. 24913	Basis of property in inventory	¶1227
IRC Sec. 1014	. . . .	Basis of property acquired from decedent	¶1230
IRC Sec. 1015	Secs. 24914, 24915	Basis of property acquired by gift or transfer in trust	¶1228, ¶1229
IRC Sec. 1016	Secs. 24916, 24916.2, 24917	Adjustments to basis	¶1247 -48
IRC Sec. 1017	Sec. 24918	Discharge of indebtedness	¶1247, ¶1251
IRC Sec. 1019	Sec. 24919	Improvements to property by lessee	¶1247, ¶1249
IRC Sec. 1021	. . . .	Sale of annuities	¶1247
IRC Sec. 1031	Secs. 24941, 24941.5	Exchange of property held for productive use	¶1206
IRC Sec. 1032	Secs. 19061, 24942	Exchange of stock for property	¶1224
IRC Sec. 1033	Secs. 19061, 24941-49.5	Involuntary conversions	¶1202, ¶1235
IRC Sec. 1035	Sec. 24950	Exchanges of insurance policies	¶1207
IRC Sec. 1036	Sec. 24951	Exchange of stock	¶1208
IRC Sec. 1037	. . . .	Exchanges of U.S. obligations	¶1209
IRC Sec. 1038	Sec. 24952	Reacquisitions of real property	¶1210
IRC Sec. 1042	Secs. 24954-54.1	Securities sales to ESOPs	¶1213
IRC Sec. 1044	Sec. 24956	Rollover of publicly traded securities	¶1222
IRC Sec. 1051	Sec. 24961	Basis of property acquired from affiliated corporation	¶1237
IRC Sec. 1052	Sec. 24962	Basis provisions from prior codes	¶1238
IRC Sec. 1053	Sec. 24963	Basis of property acquired before March 1, 1913	¶1238
IRC Sec. 1054	Sec. 24965	Basis of stock issued by FNMA	¶1240
IRC Sec. 1055	. . . .	Redeemable ground rents	¶1241
IRC Sec. 1057	. . . .	Transfers of property to foreign trust	. . . .
IRC Sec. 1059	Sec. 24966	Basis after extraordinary dividend	¶1226
IRC Sec. 1059A	Sec. 24966.1	Basis of property imported from related persons	¶1226, ¶1227
IRC Sec. 1060	Sec. 24966.2	Allocation of asset acquisitions	¶1226, ¶1252
IRC Sec. 1091	Sec. 24998	Wash sales of stock or securities	¶1008, ¶1236
IRC Sec. 1092	Sec. 24998	Straddles	¶1225
IRC Secs. 1201-60	Secs. 23051.5, 24990, 24990.4-90.8	Capital gains and losses	¶1011, ¶1201, ¶1217, ¶1222
IRC Secs. 1271-74A	Sec. 24990	Debt instruments	¶911, ¶1223
IRC Sec. 1275	Secs. 24990, 24991	Definitions and special rules relating to debt instruments	¶910, ¶911
IRC Secs. 1276-78	Sec. 24990	Market discount on bonds	¶911, ¶1222
IRC Secs. 1281-83	Secs. 24990, 24991	Discount on short term obligations as income	¶1222
IRC Secs. 1286-88	Sec. 24990	Miscellaneous provisions	¶1222
IRC Secs. 1291-98	Secs. 24990, 24995	Passive foreign investment companies	¶1222
IRC Secs. 1311-14	. . . .	Mitigation of effect of limitations	¶1409
IRC Sec. 1341	. . . .	Repayment of income received under claim of right	¶1106
IRC Sec. 1351	. . . .	Recovery of foreign expropriation losses	. . . .
IRC Secs. 1361-79	Secs. 23800-11, 23813	"Subchapter S" corporations	¶806
IRC Sec. 1381	Secs. 24404-06	Cooperatives	¶1021
IRC Sec. 1382	Secs. 24404-06	Taxable income of cooperatives	¶1021
IRC Sec. 1383	Secs. 24404-06.5	Nonqualified notices of allocation redeemed by cooperative	¶1021

Federal	California	Subject	Paragraph
IRC Sec. 1385	Sec. 24273.5	Amounts includible in patron's gross income	¶914
IRC Sec. 1388	Sec. 24406.6	Net earnings of cooperatives	¶1021
IRC Sec. 1441	. . . .	Withholding on nonresident aliens	¶1413
IRC Sec. 1445	. . . .	Withholding on U.S. real estate sales	¶1413
IRC Sec. 1501	Secs. 23362, 23364a	Consolidated return of affiliated group	¶812
IRC Sec. 1502	Secs. 23363, 25106.5	Regulations	¶812
IRC Sec. 1503	Sec. 23364	Computation and payment of tax	¶812
IRC Sec. 1504	Sec. 23361	"Affiliated group" defined	¶812
IRC Sec. 4911	Sec. 23740	Excess expenditures to influence legislation	¶1023
IRC Secs. 4940-48	. . . .	Taxes on private foundations	¶808
IRC Secs. 4971-75	. . . .	Tax on failure to meet pension funding requirements	¶1016
IRC Sec. 6011	Sec. 18407	Tax shelter reporting requirements	¶1424
IRC Sec. 6012	Various	Returns required	¶810, ¶811
IRC Sec. 6031	Secs. 18535, 18633-33.5	Return of partnership income	. . . .
IRC Sec. 6033	Sec. 23772	Annual returns by exempt organizations	¶811
IRC Sec. 6037	Sec. 18601	S corporation returns	¶806
IRC Sec. 6038	Sec. 19141.2	Information returns on foreign corporations	¶1413, ¶1414
IRC Sec. 6038A	Sec. 19141.5	Report of 25% foreign-owned corporations	¶1414
IRC Sec. 6038B	Sec. 19141.5	Report on transfers to foreign persons	¶1414
IRC Sec. 6038C	Sec. 19141.5	Report of foreign corporation doing U.S. business	¶1414
IRC Sec. 6038D	Sec. 19141.5	Information with respect to foreign financial assets	¶1414
IRC Sec. 6039	Sec. 18631	Information returns for foreign interests	¶1412
IRC Sec. 6039I	Sec. 18631	Information returns for employer-owned life insurance contracts	¶1412
IRC Sec. 6039J	Sec. 18631	Information returns for commodity credit corporation transactions	¶1412
IRC Sec. 6041	Secs. 18631, 25111	Information at source	¶1412
IRC Sec. 6041A	Sec. 18631	Reporting certain payments	¶1412
IRC Sec. 6042	Sec. 18639	Returns for corporate earnings and profits	¶1412
IRC Sec. 6043	. . . .	Returns for dividends on liquidation	. . . .
IRC Sec. 6044	Sec. 18640	Returns for cooperatives	. . . .
IRC Sec. 6045	Secs. 18631, 18642	Returns for brokers	¶1412
IRC Sec. 6049	Sec. 18630	Returns for payment of interest	¶1412
IRC Sec. 6050A	Sec. 18644	Returns for fishing boat operators	¶1412
IRC Sec. 6050I-50W	Sec. 18631	Information returns	¶1411, ¶1412
IRC Sec. 6062	. . . .	Signing of corporation returns	. . . .
IRC Sec. 6065	Secs. 18606, 18621	Verification of return	¶810
IRC Sec. 6072	Sec. 18566	Time for filing returns	¶810
IRC Sec. 6081	Secs. 18567, 18604	Extension of time for filing return	¶810
IRC Sec. 6091	Sec. 18621	Place for filing returns or other documents	. . . .
IRC Sec. 6102	Sec. 18623	Fractional dollar calculations	¶810
IRC Secs. 6103-04	Secs. 19543-49, 19551-55, 19562, 19565, 21023	Confidentiality of returns	. . . .
IRC Sec. 6107	Sec. 18625	Duties of tax prepares	¶1401
IRC Sec. 6109	Sec. 18624	Identifying numbers required on documents	¶1401
IRC Sec. 6111	Sec. 18628	Reportable transactions	¶1424
IRC Sec. 6112	Sec. 18648	Listed transactions	¶1424
IRC Sec. 6115	Sec. 18648.5	Disclosure related to quid pro quo information	¶1014
IRC Sec. 6151	Secs. 19001, 19004-06	Payment of tax	¶814
IRC Sec. 6155	. . . .	Payment on notice and demand	¶1405
IRC Secs. 6161-64	Sec. 19131.5	Extensions of time for payment	¶814
IRC Sec. 6201	Sec. 21024	Burden of proof	¶1402
IRC Sec. 6211	. . . .	"Deficiency" defined	¶1403, ¶1404
IRC Sec. 6212	Secs. 19031-36, 19049, 19050	Notice of deficiency	¶1403, ¶1404
IRC Sec. 6213	Secs. 19041-48, 19332-34, 19051	Deficiencies—petition to tax court	¶1403, ¶1404, ¶1405

Federal	California	Subject	Paragraph
IRC Sec. 6225	Sec. 19063	SOL for partnership items	¶1409
IRC Sec. 6325	Sec. 19226	Release of liens	. . . .
IRC Sec. 6331	Secs. 19231, 19236, 19262, 21019	Levy to collect tax	. . . .
IRC Sec. 6335	Sec. 19262	Sale of seized property	. . . .
IRC Sec. 6338	Sec. 19263	Certificate of sale	. . . .
IRC Sec. 6342	Sec. 19263	Disposition of proceeds of levy or sale	. . . .
IRC Secs. 6401-08	Secs. 19104, 19107, 19116, 19349, 19354, 19362-63, 19431, 21012	Abatements, credits, and refunds	¶1410, ¶1415, ¶1416
IRC Sec. 6425	. . . .	Adjustment of overpayment of estimated income tax	¶813
IRC Secs. 6501, 6503(i)	Secs. 19057-58, 19065-67, 19087, 19371	Limitations on assessments	¶1403, ¶1409
IRC Sec. 6511	Secs. 19306, 19308-14	Time limitation on filing claim for credit or refund	¶1417
IRC Sec. 6532	Sec. 19384	Limitation periods on suits	¶1418, ¶1423
IRC Sec. 6601	Secs. 19101, 19104, 19108, 19112-14	Interest on tax due	¶814, ¶1410
IRC Sec. 6602	Sec. 19411	Interest on erroneous refund	¶1423
IRC Sec. 6611	Secs. 19340, 19341, 19349, 19351	Interest on overpayments	¶813, ¶1419
IRC Sec. 6621	Sec. 19521	Determination of rate of interest	¶1410
IRC Sec. 6651	Secs. 19131-32.5	Failure to file return or pay tax	¶1411
IRC Sec. 6652	Secs. 19133.5, 23772	Failure to file return	¶811, ¶1411
IRC Sec. 6653	. . . .	Failure to pay stamp tax	¶1411
IRC Sec. 6655	Secs. 19004, 19010, 19023-27, 19142-51	Estimated tax	¶813
IRC Sec. 6657	Sec. 19134	Bad checks	¶1411
IRC Sec. 6658	Sec. 19161	Timely payments during pending bankruptcy	¶1411
IRC Sec. 6662	Secs. 19164, 19772-74	Accuracy-related penalty	¶1411
IRC Sec. 6663	Secs. 19164, 19772-74	Fraud penalty	¶1411
IRC Sec. 6664	Sec. 19164	Definitions and special rules	¶1411
IRC Sec. 6665	Sec. 19164	Applicable rules	¶1411
IRC Sec. 6673	Sec. 19714	Penalty for delay	¶1411
IRC Sec. 6693	Sec. 19184	Failure to file return	¶1411
IRC Sec. 6694	Sec. 19166	Understatement by preparer	¶1411
IRC Secs. 6695-96	Secs. 19167, 19168, 19185, 19712	Tax preparer penalties	¶1411
IRC Sec. 6700	Sec. 19177	Penalty for promoting abusive tax shelters	¶1424
IRC Sec. 6701	Sec. 19178	Penalty for aiding understatement of tax liability	¶1411
IRC Sec. 6702	Sec. 19179	Penalty for frivolous tax returns	¶1411
IRC Sec. 6703	Sec. 19180	Rules for penalties	¶1411
IRC Sec. 6706	Sec. 19181	Original issue discount reporting	¶911, ¶1411
IRC Secs. 6707-08	Secs. 19173, 19182, 19772, 19774	Abusive shelter penalties	¶1424
IRC Sec. 6714	Sec. 19182.5	Penalty for failure to disclose quid pro quo information	. . . .
IRC Sec. 6720B	Sec. 19186	Penalty for fraudulent identification of exempt-use property	¶1411
IRC Secs. 6721-24	Sec. 19183	Penalty for nonfiling	¶1411
IRC Sec. 6751	Sec. 19187	Procedures for penalties	¶1411
IRC Sec. 6861	Secs. 19081, 19086, 19092	Jeopardy assessments	¶1406
IRC Sec. 6863	Sec. 19083	Jeopardy assessments stay of collection	¶1406
IRC Sec. 6867	Sec. 19093	Presumption for large amount of cash not identified	. . . .
IRC Sec. 6871	Secs. 19088, 19090	Receivership—immediate assessment	¶1407
IRC Sec. 6872	Sec. 19089	Suspension of period on assessment	¶1407
IRC Sec. 6873	Sec. 19091	Unpaid claims	¶1407
IRC Secs. 6901-04	Secs. 19071-74	Liability of transferees and fiduciaries	¶1408
IRC Sec. 7121	Sec. 19441	Closing agreements	¶1420
IRC Sec. 7122	Sec. 19441	Compromise of tax liability	¶1421
IRC Sec. 7201	. . . .	Attempt to evade or defeat tax	. . . .
IRC Sec. 7202	Secs. 19708, 19709	Wilful failure to collect or pay over tax	¶1411
IRC Sec. 7203	Sec. 19706	Wilful failure to file return	¶1411
IRC Sec. 7206	Secs. 19701, 19705	Fraud and false statements	¶1411

Federal	California	Subject	Paragraph
IRC Sec. 7207	. . . .	Fraudulent returns, statements, or other documents	. . . .
IRC Sec. 7213	Secs. 19542, 19542.3, 19552	Unauthorized disclosure of information	. . . .
IRC Sec. 7405	Sec. 19411	Recovery of erroneous refunds	¶1423
IRC Sec. 7421	Secs. 19081, 19381	Prohibition of suits to restrain assessment	¶1419
IRC Sec. 7422	Secs. 19382, 19383, 19387	Actions for refunds	¶1419
IRC Sec. 7428	. . . .	Exempt status declaratory judgments	¶808
IRC Sec. 7430	Secs. 19717, 21013	Recovery of litigation costs	¶1401
IRC Sec. 7502	Sec. 21027	Mailing/delivery of returns	¶1402
IRC Sec. 7508A	Sec. 18572	Disaster relief extensions	¶810, ¶814, ¶1409, ¶1417
IRC Sec. 7518	Sec. 24272.5	Capital construction funds for vessels	¶917
IRC Sec. 7524	Sec. 21026	Annual notice of delinquency	¶1402
IRC Sec. 7602	Secs. 19504, 19504.7	Examination of books and witnesses	¶1403
IRC Sec. 7609	Sec. 19064	Third-party summonses	¶1403, ¶1409
IRC Sec. 7612	Sec. 19504.5	Software trade secrets	¶1401
IRC Sec. 7701	Secs. 23031-38, 23041-51	Definitions	¶805, ¶1106
IRC Secs. 7702, 7702A	Sec. 23045	Modified endowment contracts	. . . .
IRC Sec. 7704	Sec. 23038.5	Publicly traded partnerships	¶804, ¶805
IRC Sec. 7806	Secs. 23030, 23051.5, 23060	Construction of title	. . . .
IRC Sec. 7811	Secs. 21001-27	Taxpayers' bill of rights	¶1401, ¶1402
IRC Sec. 7872	Sec. 24993	Imputed interest	¶1112

CALIFORNIA-FEDERAL CROSS-REFERENCE TABLE AND INDEX

Showing Sections of Federal Law (1986 Internal Revenue Code) Comparable to Sections of California Bank and Corporation Tax Law (Revenue and Taxation Code)

California	Federal	Subject	Paragraph
Secs. 18401-03	. . . .	General application of administrative provisions	. . . .
Sec. 18405	. . . .	Relief upon noncompliance with new provisions	. . . .
Sec. 18405.1	. . . .	Perfection of water's-edge election	¶1311
Sec. 18407	IRC Sec. 6011	Tax shelter reporting	¶1424
Sec. 18408	IRC Sec. 6011	Computerized returns	. . . .
Sec. 18410	. . . .	Federal holidays	¶810
Secs. 18412-17	IRC Sec. 7807	Continuity of provisions with prior law	. . . .
Secs. 18416	. . . .	Last known address	. . . .
Secs. 18416.5	. . . .	Electronic communications	. . . .
Sec. 18510	. . . .	Use tax reporting	¶814
Sec. 18536	. . . .	Group returns for nonresident corporate directors	¶714
Sec. 18572	IRC Sec. 7508A	Disaster relief extensions	¶810, ¶814, ¶1409, ¶1417
Sec. 18601	IRC Secs. 6012(a), 6037, 6072	Annual income or franchise tax return	¶810
Sec. 18602	. . . .	Paying wrong tax	¶810
Sec. 18604	IRC Sec. 6081	Extension of time for filing return	¶810
Sec. 18606	IRC Sec. 6012(b)	Returns by receivers, trustees, or assignees	¶810
Sec. 18621	IRC Secs. 6065, 6091	Verification of return	¶810
Sec. 18621.5	. . . .	Electronic filing verification	¶810
Sec. 18621.10	. . . .	Electronic filing mandate	¶810
Sec. 18622	. . . .	Change in federal income tax return	¶810
Sec. 18623	IRC Sec. 6102	Fractional dollar calculations	¶810
Sec. 18624	IRC Sec. 6109	Identifying numbers	¶1401
Sec. 18625	IRC Sec. 6107	Copy to taxpayer	¶1401
Sec. 18628	IRC Sec. 6111	Reportable transaction reporting requirements	¶1424
Sec. 18631	IRC Secs. 6034, 6034A, 6039, 6039C, 6039I, 6039J, 6041, 6041A, 6042, 6045, 6049, 6050H-W, 6052	Information return filing requirements	¶1412
Sec. 18631.7	. . . .	Check cashing business information return	¶1411, ¶1412
Sec. 18633.5	IRC Sec. 6031	Limited liability companies	¶805
Sec. 18639	IRC Secs. 6041-43, 6049	Returns for interest, dividends, collections	¶1412
Sec. 18640	IRC Sec. 6044	Returns by cooperatives	¶1412
Sec. 18642	IRC Sec. 6045	Information returns of property owners	¶1412
Sec. 18644	IRC Sec. 6050A	Fishing boat operators— reporting requirements	¶1412
Sec. 18648	IRC Sec. 6112	Listed transactions	¶1412
Sec. 18648.5	IRC Sec. 6115	Disclosure related to quid pro quo information	¶1014
Sec. 18649	IRC Sec. 1275	Information furnished to FTB	¶1412
Sec. 18661	IRC Sec. 3402	Recipient of income	¶1413
Sec. 18662	IRC Secs. 1445, 3402	Withholding of corporate tax	¶716, ¶1413
Sec. 18665	. . . .	Change in withholding due to legislative enactments	¶1413
Sec. 18667	IRC Sec. 3402	Withholding exemption certificates	¶1413
Sec. 18668	IRC Sec. 3403	Withholding penalties	¶1413
Sec. 18669	. . . .	Sale, transfer, or disposition of business	¶1413
Sec. 18670	. . . .	Notice to withhold	¶1413
Sec. 18670.5	. . . .	Electronic notice to withhold	. . . .
Sec. 18671	. . . .	Withholding—state agencies	¶1413
Sec. 18672	. . . .	Liability for failure to withhold	¶1413
Sec. 18674	. . . .	Requirements for withholding agent	¶1413

California	Federal	Subject	Paragraph
Sec. 18675	IRC Sec. 6414	Taxpayer remedies when order to withhold	¶1413
Sec. 18676	. . . .	Notice to withhold to state agencies	¶1413
Sec. 18677	IRC Sec. 3505	Lender, surety, or other person liable	¶1413
Sec. 19001	IRC Sec. 6151	Payment of tax	¶814
Sec. 19002	IRC Sec. 6513	Credit for amount withheld	¶810
Sec. 19004	IRC Sec. 6151	Early tax payment	¶814
Sec. 19005	IRC Sec. 6151	Tax payable to FTB	¶814
Sec. 19007	IRC Sec. 6315	Payments of estimated taxes	¶813
Sec. 19009	IRC Sec. 7512	Failure to pay collected taxes	¶1413
Sec. 19010	IRC Sec. 6655	Assessing delinquent estimated taxes	¶813
Sec. 19011	IRC Sec. 6302	Electronic funds transfer	¶814
Sec. 19021	. . . .	Bank and financial corporation tax	¶813, ¶814
Sec. 19023	IRC Sec. 6655(g)	"Estimated tax" defined	¶813
Sec. 19025	IRC Sec. 6655(c), (d)	Installment payments of tax	¶813
Sec. 19026	IRC Sec. 6655	Revised estimate of taxes	¶813
Sec. 19027	IRC Sec. 6655	Short-year estimated tax payments	¶813
Sec. 19031	IRC Sec. 6212	Deficiency assessments—FTB authority	¶1403
Sec. 19032	IRC Sec. 6212	FTB authorized to examine return	¶1403
Sec. 19033	IRC Sec. 6212	Notice of additional assessment	¶1403
Sec. 19034	IRC Sec. 6212	Contents of notice	¶1403
Sec. 19036	IRC Sec. 6212	Interest, penalties, additions to tax as deficiency assessments	¶1403
Sec. 19041	IRC Sec. 6213	Filing protest	¶1403
Sec. 19041.5	. . . .	Treatment of deposits	¶1417, ¶1418
Sec. 19042	IRC Sec. 6213	60-day protest period	¶1403, ¶1405
Sec. 19043	IRC Sec. 6211	Deficiency defined	¶1403
Sec. 19043.5	. . . .	Carryover adjustments	¶1403
Sec. 19044	IRC Sec. 6213	Protest hearing	¶1403
Sec. 19045	. . . .	Finality of action upon protest	¶1403
Sec. 19046	IRC Sec. 6213	Appeal to SBE	¶1403, ¶1404
Sec. 19047	IRC Sec. 6213	Determination of appeal	¶1403, ¶1404
Sec. 19048	IRC Sec. 6213	Finality of determination	¶1403, ¶1404
Sec. 19049	IRC Sec. 6212	Notice and demand	¶1403, ¶1405
Sec. 19050	IRC Sec. 6212	Certificate of mailing	¶1403
Sec. 19051	IRC Sec. 6213	Mathematical error	¶1403
Sec. 19054	IRC Sec. 6201	Overstatement of credit	¶1403
Sec. 19057	IRC Sec. 6501	Limitation on assessment	¶1403, ¶1409
Sec. 19058	IRC Sec. 6501(e)	Limitation period extended	¶1403, ¶1409
Sec. 19059	. . . .	Assessment of deficiencies on amended returns	¶1409
Sec. 19060	. . . .	Failure to file amended return	¶1409
Sec. 19061	IRC Secs. 1032, 1033(a)(2)(A)-(a)(2)(D)	Deficiency after involuntary conversion	¶1409
Sec. 19063	IRC Secs. 6501(a), 6225	Items of federally registered partnership	¶1409
Sec. 19064	IRC Sec. 7609	Motion to quash subpoena	¶1403, ¶1409
Sec. 19065	IRC Sec. 6501(c)	Federal extension for assessing deficiencies	¶1403, ¶1409
Sec. 19066	IRC Sec. 6501(b)	Time return deemed filed	¶1403, ¶1409
Sec. 19066.5	IRC Sec. 6501(c)	Suspension of SOL	¶1409
Sec. 19067	IRC Sec. 6501(c)	Extension by agreement	¶1403, ¶1409
Sec. 19071	IRC Sec. 6901	Collection from other than taxpayer	¶1408
Sec. 19072	IRC Sec. 6901	Collection from person secondarily liable	¶1408
Sec. 19073	IRC Sec. 6901	Assessment and collection from transferees and fiduciaries	¶1408
Sec. 19074	IRC Sec. 6901	Limitations period for assessment of transferee or fiduciary	¶1408
Sec. 19081	IRC Secs. 6851, 6861	Jeopardy assessments	¶1406
Sec. 19082	IRC Sec. 6862	Jeopardy assessments	¶1406
Sec. 19083	IRC Sec. 6863	Jeopardy assessments—stay of collection	¶1406
Sec. 19084	IRC Sec. 6863	Jeopardy assessments	¶1406
Sec. 19085	IRC Sec. 6863	Jeopardy assessments	¶1406
Sec. 19086	IRC Sec. 6861	Evidence of jeopardy	¶1406
Sec. 19087	IRC Sec. 6501(c)	Estimated assessments	¶1403
Sec. 19088	IRC Sec. 6871	Receivership—immediate assessment	¶1407

California	Federal	Subject	Paragraph
Sec. 19089	IRC Secs. 6036, 6872	Notice by receiver to FTB	¶1407
Sec. 19090	IRC Sec. 6871	Adjudication in receivership proceeding	¶1407
Sec. 19091	IRC Sec. 6873	Unpaid claims	¶1407
Sec. 19092	IRC Sec. 6861	Regulations	. . . .
Sec. 19101	IRC Sec. 6601(a)	Interest on tax due	¶1410
Sec. 19104	IRC Sec. 6404	Interest on deficiency	¶1410
Sec. 19108	IRC Sec. 6601	Overpayment applied to another year's deficiency	¶1410
Sec. 19109	. . . .	Abatement of interest	¶1410
Sec. 19113	IRC Sec. 6601(f)	Satisfaction by credit	¶1410
Sec. 19114	IRC Sec. 6601(g)	Collection and assessment of interest	¶1410
Sec. 19120	. . . .	Interest on erroneous refunds	¶1410
Sec. 19131	IRC Sec. 6651	Penalty for failure to file return	¶1411
Sec. 19131.5	IRC Sec. 6164	Extensions for corporations expecting carrybacks	¶814
Sec. 19132	IRC Sec. 6651	Penalty for underpayment of tax	¶1411
Sec. 19133	. . . .	Penalty for failure to furnish information	¶1411
Sec. 19134	IRC Sec. 6657	Bad checks	¶1411
Sec. 19135	. . . .	Penalty—unqualified and doing business	¶1411
Sec. 19136.8	. . . .	Waiver of estimated tax underpayment penalty	¶813
Sec. 19138	. . . .	Large corporate underpayment penalty	¶1411
Sec. 19141	. . . .	Failure to file annual statement	¶1411
Sec. 19141.2	IRC Sec. 6038	Information returns on foreign corporations	¶1414
Sec. 19141.5	IRC Secs. 6038A-38D	Information returns on foreign-owned and foreign corporations, transfers to foreign persons	¶1411, ¶1414
Sec. 19141.6	. . . .	Penalty for failure to keep water's-edge records	¶1411
Sec. 19142	IRC Sec. 6655(a)	Underpayment of estimated tax	¶813
Sec. 19144	IRC Sec. 6655(b)	Amount of underpayment	¶813
Sec. 19145	IRC Sec. 6655(e)	Period of underpayment	¶813
Sec. 19147	IRC Sec. 6655(d)	Exceptions to underpayment	¶813
Sec. 19148	IRC Sec. 6655	Underpayment of estimated tax	¶813
Sec. 19149	IRC Sec. 6655	Calculation of addition to tax	¶813
Sec. 19150	IRC Sec. 6655	Underpayment for income years of less than 12 months	¶813
Sec. 19151	IRC Sec. 6655	Underpayment not applicable to exempt corporation until certificate revoked	¶813
Sec. 19161	IRC Sec. 6658	Timely payments during pending bankruptcy	¶813, ¶1411
Sec. 19164	IRC Secs. 6662-65	Accuracy- and fraud-related penalties, special rules	¶1411, ¶1424
Sec. 19164.5	IRC Secs. 6662A	Reportable transaction accuracy-related penalty	¶1424
Sec. 19166	IRC Sec. 6694	Penalty—preparer understatement	¶1411
Sec. 19167	IRC Sec. 6695(a), (c), (d)	Penalty—tax preparers	¶1411
Sec. 19168	IRC Sec. 6696	Penalty—tax preparers	¶1411
Sec. 19169	IRC Sec. 6695(f)	Penalty—negotiating client's refund check	¶1411
Sec. 19171	. . . .	Penalty—electronic filing	¶1411
Sec. 19172-72.5	. . . .	Penalty—late filing of S corporation and partnership return penalties	¶1411
Sec. 19173	IRC Sec. 6708	Penalty—tax shelters	¶1411
Sec. 19174	IRC Sec. 6700	Penalty—tax shelters	¶1411
Sec. 19176	IRC Sec. 6682	Penalty—withholding	¶1411
Sec. 19177	IRC Sec. 6700	Penalty—abusive tax shelters	¶1411
Sec. 19178	IRC Sec. 6701	Penalty—aiding and abetting	¶1411
Sec. 19179	IRC Sec. 6702	Penalty—frivolous return	¶1411
Sec. 19180	IRC Sec. 6703	Rules for penalties	¶1411
Sec. 19181	IRC Sec. 6706	Penalty for failure to report original issue discount	¶1411
Sec. 19182	IRC Sec. 6707	Penalty for tax shelter providers	¶1411
Sec. 19182.5	IRC Sec. 6714	Penalty for failure to disclose quid pro quo information	. . . .
Sec. 19183	IRC Secs. 6721-24	Penalty for failure to file information return	¶1411

California	Federal	Subject	Paragraph
Sec. 19184	IRC Sec. 6693	Penalty for failure to properly report IRA	¶1411
Sec. 19186	IRC Sec. 6720B	Penalty for fraudulent identification of exempt use property	¶1411
Sec. 19187	IRC Sec. 6751	Procedures for penalties	¶1411
Secs. 19191-94	. . .	Voluntary disclosure agreements	¶1423
Secs. 19195	. . .	Public disclosure of large delinquent taxpayers	¶721
Sec. 19201	. . .	Request for judgment	. . .
Sec. 19202	. . .	Judgment for taxes	. . .
Sec. 19221	IRC Sec. 6321	Perfected tax lien	. . .
Sec. 19222	IRC Sec. 6311	Lien for dishonored checks	. . .
Sec. 19225	. . .	Administrative review	¶1402
Sec. 19226	IRC Sec. 6325	Release of third-party liens	. . .
Sec. 19231	IRC Sec. 6331	Warrant for collection of tax	. . .
Sec. 19232	. . .	Warrant as writ of execution	. . .
Sec. 19233	. . .	Fees for warrant	. . .
Sec. 19234	. . .	Fees as obligation of taxpayer	. . .
Sec. 19235	. . .	Costs associated with sale of property	. . .
Sec. 19236	IRC Sec. 6331	Seizure of property	. . .
Sec. 19251	. . .	Remedies cumulative	. . .
Sec. 19252	. . .	FTB as representative	. . .
Sec. 19253	. . .	Priority of tax lien	. . .
Sec. 19253.5	. . .	Tax practitioner disbarment; suspension	. . .
Sec. 19254	. . .	Collection and filing enforcement fees	¶1411
Sec. 19255	IRC Sec. 6502	Limitations period for collections	¶1409
Sec. 19256	IRC Sec. 7504	Fractional dollar amounts	. . .
Sec. 19262	IRC Secs. 6331, 6335	Seizure and sale of personal property	¶1411
Sec. 19263	IRC Secs. 6338, 6342	Bill of sale; disposition of excess	. . .
Sec. 19264	. . .	Earnings withholding tax orders	. . .
Sec. 19266	. . .	Financial institutions record matching (FIRM) system	¶721
Sec. 19291	. . .	Reciprocal collection agreements with IRS/other states	¶721
Sec. 19301	IRC Sec. 6402(a)	Overpayment—credit or refund	¶1415
Sec. 19302	. . .	Credit and refund approval	¶1417
Sec. 19306	IRC Sec. 6511(a)	Time limitation on filing claim for credit or refund	¶1417
Sec. 19307	. . .	Return as claim for refund	¶1415, ¶1417
Sec. 19308	IRC Sec. 6511(c)	Effect of assessment extension	¶1415, ¶1417
Sec. 19309	IRC Sec. 6511(c)	Claims file before assessment extension	¶1415, ¶1417
Sec. 19311	IRC Sec. 6511	Time limit following federal adjusted return	¶1415, ¶1417
Sec. 19312	IRC Sec. 6511(d)	Time limit where bad debts or worthless securities	¶1415, ¶1417
Sec. 19313	IRC Sec. 6511(g)	Federally registered partnerships	¶1415, ¶1417
Sec. 19314	. . .	Overpayment allowed as offset	¶1415, ¶1417
Sec. 19321	. . .	Refund claim where final action	¶1415
Sec. 19322	. . .	Claim for refund—grounds	¶1415
Sec. 19322.1	. . .	Informal refund claim	¶1417
Sec. 19323	. . .	Notice of disallowance	¶1415
Sec. 19324	. . .	Finality of action upon claim	¶1415
Sec. 19325	. . .	Disallowance of interest on claims resulting from change in federal law	¶1419
Sec. 19331	. . .	Presumption of disallowance	¶1415
Sec. 19332	IRC Sec. 6213	Mailing of appeals	¶1415, ¶1416
Sec. 19333	IRC Sec. 6213	SBE's determination	¶1415, ¶1416
Sec. 19334	IRC Sec. 6213	Petition for rehearing	¶1415, ¶1416
Sec. 19335	. . .	Appeal as claim for refund	¶1415
Sec. 19340	IRC Sec. 6611(b)	Interest on overpayments	¶1419
Sec. 19341	IRC Sec. 6611(e)	Time period for payment without interest	¶1419
Sec. 19342	. . .	Notice of disallowance	¶1419
Sec. 19343	. . .	Finality of notice	¶1419
Sec. 19344	. . .	Appeal to SBE	¶1419
Sec. 19345	. . .	Determination of appeal	¶1419
Sec. 19346	. . .	Finality of determination	¶1419
Sec. 19347	. . .	Suit to recover interest	¶1419

California	Federal	Subject	Paragraph
Sec. 19348	. . . .	Failure of FTB to give notice	¶1419
Sec. 19349	IRC Secs. 6401, 6611	Payments not entitled to refunds	¶1419
Sec. 19350	. . . .	No interest on portion of barred claim	¶1419
Sec. 19351	IRC Sec. 6611(b)	Determining limitation period for interest	¶1419
Sec. 19355	. . . .	Refunding excess	. . . .
Sec. 19361	IRC Sec. 6414	Employer's overpayment	. . . .
Sec. 19362	IRC Sec. 6402	Credits against estimated tax	. . . .
Sec. 19363	IRC Sec. 6402	Interest on overpayments of estimated tax	¶813, ¶1419
Sec. 19364	. . . .	Overpayments of tax	¶813
Sec. 19365	. . . .	S corporation transfer of estimated tax	¶806
Sec. 19368	. . . . , . .	erroneous refunds	¶1423
Sec. 19371	IRC Sec. 6502	Writ of attachment	. . . .
Sec. 19372	. . . .	Suit for tax	. . . .
Sec. 19373	. . . .	Prosecution of suit	. . . .
Sec. 19374	. . . .	Evidence of tax due	. . . .
Sec. 19375	. . . .	Bringing of action	. . . .
Sec. 19376	. . . .	Collection of tax	¶1401
Secs. 19377, 19377.5	IRC Sec. 6301	Agreements with collection agencies/other taxing agencies	. . . .
Sec. 19378	IRC Sec. 6301	Collection and transfer of funds	. . . .
Sec. 19381	IRC Sec. 7421	Injunction to prevent assessment prohibited	¶1418
Sec. 19382	IRC Sec. 7422	Action to recover void tax	¶1418
Sec. 19383	IRC Sec. 7422	Credit of overpayment	¶1418
Sec. 19384	IRC Sec. 6532	Time limitation on action	¶1418
Sec. 19385	IRC Sec. 6532	FTB's failure to mail notice	¶1418
Sec. 19387	IRC Sec. 7422	Service upon FTB	¶1418
Sec. 19388	IRC Sec. 6532	Place of action	¶1418
Sec. 19389	IRC Sec. 6532	Defense of action	¶1418
Sec. 19390	. . . .	Bar of action	¶1418
Sec. 19391	IRC Sec. 6612	Interest on judgment rendered for overpayment	¶1418
Sec. 19392	. . . .	Judgment against FTB	¶1418
Sec. 19393	. . . .	Recomputation of discriminatory bank tax	. . . .
Sec. 19411	IRC Secs. 6602, 7405	Action to recover refund erroneously made	¶1423
Sec. 19412	. . . .	Location of trial	¶1423
Sec. 19413	. . . .	Prosecution of action	¶1423
Sec. 19431	IRC Sec. 6404	Cancellation of illegal levy	. . . .
Sec. 19432	. . . .	Cancellation of tax for inactive corporations	. . . .
Sec. 19441	IRC Secs. 7121-23	Closing agreements	¶1420
Sec. 19442	. . . .	Settlement of tax disputes	¶1411, ¶1420
Sec. 19443	. . . .	Offers in compromise	¶1421
Sec. 19501	IRC Sec. 7621(a)	FTB's powers	¶1401
Sec. 19502	IRC Sec. 7621(b)	FTB—establishment of districts	¶1401
Sec. 19503	IRC Sec. 7805	FTB—rules and regulations	¶1401
Sec. 19504	IRC Sec. 7602	FTB—audits	¶1401
Sec. 19504.5	IRC Sec. 7612	Software trade secrets	¶1401
Sec. 19504.7	IRC Sec. 7602	Notice of contact of third parties	¶1401
Sec. 19521	IRC Secs. 6621, 6622	Determination of rate of interest	¶1410
Sec. 19525	IRC Sec. 7623	Reward program	¶1401
Sec. 19530	. . . .	Preservation of returns	¶1401
Sec. 19531	. . . .	Fees for publications	. . . .
Secs. 19532-33	. . . .	Priority for application of collected amounts	. . . .
Secs. 19542-42.3	IRC Secs. 6103, 7213	Unauthorized disclosure by FTB	. . . .
Sec. 19543	IRC Sec. 6103(b)	Nondisclosure of extraneous matters	. . . .
Sec. 19544	IRC Sec. 6103(b)	Nondisclosure of audit methods	. . . .
Sec. 19545	IRC Sec. 6103(h)	Disclosure in tax administration proceedings	. . . .
Secs. 19546-46.5	IRC Sec. 6103(f)	Disclosure to legislative committee	. . . .
Sec. 19547	IRC Sec. 6103(h)	Matters represented by Attorney General	. . . .
Sec. 19548.5	. . . .	Disclosure to state health organizations	. . . .
Sec. 19549	IRC Sec. 6103(b)	Definitions	. . . .
Sec. 19551	IRC Sec. 6103(d)	Disclosure to proper authorities	. . . .
Sec. 19551.1-51.5	. . . .	Disclosure to city officials	. . . .

California	Federal	Subject	Paragraph
Sec. 19552	IRC Sec. 7213	Unauthorized disclosure	. . . .
Sec. 19559	. . . .	Disclosure of tourist industry information	. . . .
Sec. 19562	IRC Sec. 6103	Charge for reasonable cost	. . . .
Sec. 19563	IRC Sec. 6108	Publication of statistics	. . . .
Sec. 19565	IRC Sec. 6104	Inspection of exempt organizations' applications	. . . .
Sec. 19570	. . . .	Use of Information Practices Act	
Sec. 19571-72	. . . .	Disclosure to/from state licensing agencies	. . . .
Sec. 19590-92	. . . .	Tax service fees	
Sec. 19701	IRC Sec. 7206	Failure to file—aiding and abetting	¶1411
Sec. 19703	. . . .	Evidence of failure to file	¶1411
Sec. 19704	. . . .	Time limit on prosecution	¶1411
Sec. 19705	IRC Sec. 7206	False statements and fraud	¶1411
Sec. 19706	IRC Sec. 7203	Wilful failure to file return	¶1411
Sec. 19707	. . . .	Venue	. . . .
Sec. 19708	IRC Sec. 7202	Failure to collect or pay over tax	¶1411
Sec. 19709	IRC Sec. 7202	Failure to withhold tax as misdemeanor	¶1411
Sec. 19710	. . . .	Writ of mandate	¶1411
Sec. 19712	IRC Sec. 6695	Endorsing client's refund check as misdemeanor	¶1411
Sec. 19713	IRC Sec. 7215	Failure to collect and pay withholding tax	¶1411
Sec. 19714	IRC Sec. 6673	Delay tactics	¶1411
Sec. 19715	IRC Sec. 7408	Penalties—injunctive relief	¶1411
Sec. 19717	IRC Sec. 7430	Recovery of litigation costs	¶1401
Sec. 19719	. . . .	Penalty for doing business after suspension	¶1412
Secs. 19720-21	. . . .	Fraudulently obtaining refunds	¶1412
Secs. 19730-38	. . . .	Amnesty	¶1411
Secs. 19751-54	. . . .	Abusive tax shelter voluntary compliance initiative	¶1424
Sec. 19755	. . . .	Abusive tax shelter limitations period	¶1409
Secs. 19761-73	. . . .	Voluntary Compliance Initiative Two	¶1424
Sec. 19772	Sec. 6707A	Omission of reportable transaction penalty	¶1424
Secs. 19774	. . . .	Nondisclosure of reportable transactions	¶1424
Sec. 19777	. . . .	Interest-based penalty—abusive tax shelter deficiency	¶1424
Sec. 19777.5	. . . .	Amnesty-enhanced interest penalty	¶1410, ¶1411
Sec. 19778	. . . .	Interest—reportable transaction understatement	¶1410
Secs. 21001-28	IRC Secs. 6103(e)(8), 6201(d)(4), 6323, 6331, 6404(f), 7430, 7433, 7435, 7502, 7521, 7524, 7811	Taxpayers' bill of rights	¶810, ¶1401, ¶1402, ¶1411, ¶1414
Sec. 23002	IRC Sec. 7851	Application of Bank and Corporation Law	. . . .
Sec. 23004	IRC Sec. 7805	Regulation authorization	. . . .
Sec. 23030	IRC Sec. 7806	Definitions	. . . .
Secs. 23031-35	IRC Secs. 7701(a)(10), (11), (24), (25), 7704	Definitions	. . . .
Sec. 23036	IRC Sec. 26	"Tax" defined	¶817, ¶818
Sec. 23036.1	. . . .	Natural heritage preservation credit	¶817, ¶818
Sec. 23036.2	. . . .	2008-2009 credit limitations	¶818
Sec. 23037	IRC Sec. 7701(a)(14)	"Taxpayer" defined	
Sec. 23038	IRC Sec. 7701(a)(3)	"Corporation" defined	¶804, ¶805
Sec. 23038.5	IRC Sec. 7704	Publicly-traded partnerships	¶804, ¶805
Sec. 23039	IRC Sec. 581	"Bank" defined	
Sec. 23040	. . . .	"Income from sources within State" defined	¶805, ¶909
Sec. 23040.1	. . . .	Income from qualifying investment securities	¶909
Sec. 23041	IRC Sec. 7701(a)(23)	"Taxable year" defined	. . . .
Sec. 23042	. . . .	"Income year" defined	. . . .
Sec. 23043.5	IRC Sec. 7701(g)	"Fair market value—Property subject to nonrecourse debt	. . . .
Sec. 23044	. . . .	"International banking facility" defined	. . . .

California	Federal	Subject	Paragraph
Sec. 23045	IRC Secs. 7702, 7702A-B	Modified endowment contracts	. . . .
Sec. 23045.1	IRC Sec. 7701(a)(42)	"Substituted basis" defined	¶1106
Sec. 23045.2	IRC Sec. 7701(a)(43)	"Transferred basis" defined	¶1106
Sec. 23045.3	IRC Sec. 7701(a)(44)	"Exchanged basis" defined	¶1106
Sec. 23045.4	IRC Sec. 7701(a)(45)	"Nonrecognition transaction" defined	¶1106
Sec. 23045.5	IRC Sec. 7701(a)(19)	"Domestic building & loan association" defined	. . . .
Sec. 23045.6	IRC Sec. 7701(a)(20)	Employee defined	. . . .
Sec. 23046	IRC Sec. 7701(a)(46)	Collective bargaining agreements	. . . .
Sec. 23046.5	IRC Sec. 7701(n)	Convention or association of churches	¶808
Sec. 23047	IRC Sec. 7701(e)	Lease vs. service contracts	. . . .
Sec. 23048	IRC Sec. 7701(i)	"Taxable mortgage pools" defined	. . . .
Sec. 23049	IRC Sec. 7701(h)	Motor vehicle operating leases	¶1011
Sec. 23049.1	IRC Sec. 64	"Ordinary income" defined	. . . .
Sec. 23049.2	IRC Sec. 65	"Ordinary loss" defined	. . . .
Sec. 23050		Specific definitions	. . . .
Sec. 23051	IRC Sec. 7701(a)(29)	Definition of BCTL of 1954	. . . .
Sec. 23051.5	Various	References to federal law	¶Various
Sec. 23051.7	. . . .	Effect of amendments	¶802, ¶818
Secs. 23052-57	IRC Secs. 7807, 7852	Applications and effects	. . . .
Sec. 23058	IRC Sec. 15	Tax rate changes during year	¶1105
Sec. 23101	. . . .	"Doing business" defined	¶804
Sec. 23101	. . . .	"Doing business" defined	¶804
Sec. 23101.5	. . . .	Activities not constituting doing business	¶804
Sec. 23102	. . . .	Status of holding companies	¶804
Sec. 23104	. . . .	Convention and trade show activities	¶804
Sec. 23113	IRC Sec. 443	Short year returns	. . . .
Sec. 23114	. . . .	Tax attaches irrespective of short period	¶816
Sec. 23151	IRC Sec. 11	Franchise and corporation income tax rate	¶816
Sec. 23151.1	. . . .	Rate of tax of commencing or ceasing corporations	¶819, ¶820
Sec. 23151.2	. . . .	Franchise tax when corporation dissolves or withdraws	¶821
Sec. 23153	. . . .	Minimum franchise tax	¶816
Sec. 23154	. . . .	Tax imposed in lieu of other taxes	¶816
Sec. 23155	. . . .	Credit for erroneous taxes	. . . .
Sec. 23181	. . . .	Imposition of tax on banks	¶816, ¶819, ¶820
Sec. 23182	. . . .	In lieu of other taxes	¶816
Sec. 23183	. . . .	Annual tax on financial corporation	¶816, ¶819, ¶820
Sec. 23183.1	. . . .	Financial corporations— determination of tax	¶816 -20
Sec. 23183.2	. . . .	Tax when financial corporation dissolves or withdraws	¶821
Sec. 23186	. . . .	Rate of tax on banks	¶816, ¶1411
Sec. 23187	. . . .	Tax receipts	¶816
Sec. 23188	. . . .	Erroneous assessment	¶816
Sec. 23201	. . . .	Determination of credit in year of dissolution	¶821
Sec. 23202	. . . .	Transferees in reorganization	¶821
Sec. 23203	. . . .	Submission of evidence for credit	¶821
Sec. 23204	. . . .	Statute of limitations	¶821
Sec. 23221	. . . .	Minimum tax prepayment	¶819
Sec. 23222	. . . .	Prepayment basis for first and subsequent years	¶819
Sec. 23222a	. . . .	Computation in case of short periods	¶819
Sec. 23223	. . . .	Commencing business in year other than incorporation or qualification	¶819
Sec. 23224	. . . .	Computation basis upon change from corporation income to franchise tax	¶819
Sec. 23224.5	. . . .	Doing business after 12/31/71	¶819
Sec. 23225	. . . .	Due date for payment in excess of minimum	¶819
Sec. 23226	. . . .	FTB may apportion income	¶819

California	Federal	Subject	Paragraph
Sec. 23251	IRC Sec. 368	"Reorganization" and "control" defined	¶822
Sec. 23253	IRC Sec. 381	Reorganization—procedure taxable to transferee	¶822
Sec. 23281	. . . .	Resuming business after voluntary discontinuance	¶821
Sec. 23282	. . . .	Computation after suspension or forfeiture	¶821
Sec. 23301	. . . .	Suspension of corporate powers for nonpayment	¶824
Sec. 23301.5	. . . .	Suspension for failure to file	¶824
Sec. 23301.6	. . . .	Application of suspension on foreign corporation	¶824
Sec. 23302	. . . .	Transmittal of names by FTB to Secretary of State	¶824
Sec. 23303	. . . .	Doing business while suspended—taxability	¶824
Sec. 23304.1	. . . .	Contracts made during suspension	¶824
Sec. 23304.5	. . . .	Court order rescission of contract	¶824
Sec. 23305	. . . .	Application for certificate of revivor	¶824
Sec. 23305a	. . . .	Endorsement of corporation's name by Secretary of State	¶824
Sec. 23305b	. . . .	Revival without tax payment	¶824
Sec. 23305c	. . . .	Revival sent to Secretary of State	¶824
Sec. 23305d	. . . .	FTB's certificate as evidence of suspension	¶824
Sec. 23305e	. . . .	Letters of good standing	¶824
Sec. 23305.1	. . . .	Relief from contract voidability	¶824
Sec. 23305.2	. . . .	Revival with bond or other security	¶824
Sec. 23305.5	. . . .	Suspension of LLC corporate powers	¶824
Sec. 23331	. . . .	Effective date of dissolution or withdrawal	¶821
Sec. 23332	. . . .	Corporations dissolving or withdrawing before 1/1/73	¶820, ¶821
Sec. 23332.5	. . . .	Tax on financial corporations	¶821
Sec. 23333	. . . .	Maximum tax on withdrawal or dissolution	¶821
Sec. 23334	. . . .	Issuance of tax clearance certificate by FTB	¶821
Sec. 23335	. . . .	Request of tax clearance certificate	¶821
Sec. 23361	IRC Sec. 1504	"Affiliated group" defined	¶812
Sec. 23362	IRC Sec. 1501	Consolidated return of affiliated group	¶812
Sec. 23363	IRC Sec. 1502	FTB's regulations	¶812
Sec. 23364	IRC Sec. 1503	Parent and each subsidiary severally liable	¶812
Sec. 23364a	IRC Sec. 1501	Computation of tax	¶812
Secs. 23400, 23453-59	IRC Secs. 55-59	Alternative minimum tax	¶817
Sec. 23453	IRC Sec. 53	Minimum tax credit	¶817, ¶818
Sec. 23455.5	. . . .	AMT exclusion for small corporations inapplicable	¶817
Sec. 23456	IRC Sec. 56	AMT adjustments	¶817
Sec. 23456.5	IRC Sec. 56(g)	Extraterritorial AMT adjustments	¶817
Sec. 23457	IRC Sec. 57	Tax preference items	¶817
Sec. 23459	IRC Sec. 59	AMT special rules	¶817
Sec. 23501	IRC Sec. 11(b)	Rate of tax	¶805, ¶816
Sec. 23503	. . . .	Franchise tax offset	¶805, ¶817
Sec. 23504	. . . .	Change to corporation income tax liability	¶820
Sec. 23561	. . . .	Tax payment before termination	¶821
Sec. 23601.5	. . . .	Energy conservation credit	¶818
Sec. 23604	IRC Sec. 43	Enhanced oil recovery credit	¶818
Sec. 23608	. . . .	Credit for transportation of donated agricultural products	¶818
Sec. 23608.2	. . . .	Farmworker Housing credit	¶818
Sec. 23608.3	. . . .	Credit for farmworker housing development loans	¶818
Sec. 23609	IRC Sec. 41	Reseach expense credit	¶818
Sec. 23610	. . . .	Rice straw credit	¶818
Secs. 23610.4-10.5	IRC Sec. 42	Credit for low-income housing	¶818
Sec. 23612.2	. . . .	Sales tax credit	¶818

California	Federal	Subject	Paragraph
Secs. 23621	IRC Secs. 51-52	Jobs tax credit	¶818
Sec. 23622.7	. . . .	Enterprise zone wage credit	¶818
Sec. 23622.8	. . . .	Manufacturing enhancement area wage credit	¶818
Sec. 23624	. . . .	Prison inmate labor credit	¶818
Sec. 23626	. . . .	Post-2013 new jobs credit	¶818
Sec. 23630	. . . .	Natural heritage preservation credit	¶818
Sec. 23633	. . . .	Targeted tax area's qualified property sales and use tax credit	¶818
Sec. 23634	. . . .	Targeted tax area's employer's wages credit	¶818
Sec. 23636	. . . .	Advanced strategic aircraft program credit	¶818
Sec. 23642	IRC Sec. 44	Disabled access credit	¶818
Sec. 23645	. . . .	Sales tax credit	¶818
Sec. 23646	. . . .	Employers' wage payment credit	¶818
Sec. 23649	. . . .	Manufacturing and research property credit	¶818
Sec. 23657	. . . .	Community development investment credit	¶818
Secs. 23662	IRC Sec. 45H	Low-sulfur diesel fuel production credit	¶818
Secs. 23663	. . . .	Assignment of credits to unitary group members	¶1310
Sec. 23685	. . . .	Motion picture production credit	¶818
Secs. 23686, 23687	. . . .	College access tax credit	¶818
Secs. 23688, 23688.5	. . . .	Agricultural products donation credit	¶818
Sec. 23689	. . . .	California competes credit	¶818
Sec. 23695	. . . .	New motion picture production credit	¶818
Sec. 23701	IRC Sec. 501(a), (b)	Exemption for employee trusts	¶808
Sec. 23701a	IRC Sec. 501(c)(5)	Labor, agricultural, horticultural organizations	¶808
Sec. 23701b	IRC Sec. 501(c)(8)	Fraternal orders	¶808
Sec. 23701c	IRC Sec. 501(c)(13)	Cemetery companies	¶808
Sec. 23701d	IRC Sec. 501(c)(3), (j)	Religious, charitable, educational organizations	¶808
Sec. 23701e	IRC Sec. 501(c)(6)	Business leagues, chambers of commerce	¶808
Sec. 23701f	IRC Sec. 501(c)(4)	Civic leagues or organizations	¶808
Sec. 23701g	IRC Sec. 501(c)(7)	Nonprofit recreational clubs	¶808
Sec. 23701h	IRC Sec. 501(c)(2)	Companies holding title for exempt organizations	¶808
Sec. 23701i	IRC Sec. 501(c)(9)	Employees' beneficiary associations	¶808
Sec. 23701j	IRC Sec. 501(c)(11)	Teachers' retirement associations	¶808
Sec. 23701k	IRC Sec. 501(d)	Religious organizations	¶808
Sec. 23701l	IRC Sec. 501(c)(10)	Domestic fraternal societies	¶808
Sec. 23701n	IRC Sec. 501(c)(17)	Supplemental unemployment compensation plan	¶808
Sec. 23701p	IRC Sec. 401	Self-employed individual retirement plans	¶808, ¶1016
Sec. 23701r	IRC Secs. 527, 6012(a)(6)	Political organizations	¶808
Sec. 23701s	IRC Sec. 501(c)(18)	Employee funded pension trust—pre-6/25/59	¶808
Sec. 23701t	IRC Secs. 528, 6012(a)(7)	Homeowners' associations	¶808, ¶915
Sec. 23701u	. . . .	Nonprofit public benefit corporations	¶808
Sec. 23701v	IRC Sec. 501(c)	Mobile home owners	. . . .
Sec. 23701w	IRC Sec. 501(c)(19)	Veterans organizations	. . . .
Sec. 23701x	IRC Sec. 501(c)(25)	Title holding companies	¶808
Sec. 23701y	IRC Sec. 501(c)(14)	Credit unions	¶808
Sec. 23701z	IRC Sec. 501(n)	Nonprofit insurance risk pools	¶808
Sec. 23702	IRC Sec. 502	Feeder organizations	¶808, ¶809
Sec. 23703	. . . .	Failure to file with attorney general	¶808, ¶811
Sec. 23703.5	IRC Sec. 501(p)	Terrorist organizations	¶808
Sec. 23704.3	IRC Sec. 501(o)	Participation in provider-sponsored organization	¶808
Sec. 23704.4	IRC Sec. 501(e)	Child care organizations	¶808
Sec. 23704.5	IRC Sec. 501(h)	Expenditures to influence legislation	¶808
Sec. 23704.6	IRC Sec. 504	Status after disqualification for lobbying	¶808
Sec. 23705	IRC Sec. 505	Nondiscrimination requirement	¶808

California	Federal	Subject	Paragraph
Sec. 23706	IRC Sec. 501(c)(1)	Exemptions for state instrumentalities	. . . .
Sec. 23707	IRC Sec. 507	Private foundation status terminated	¶808
Sec. 23708	IRC Sec. 508	Presumption that organization is private foundation	¶808
Sec. 23709	IRC Sec. 509	"Private foundation" defined	¶808
Sec. 23710	IRC Sec. 513	Bingo games	¶808
Sec. 23711	IRC Sec. 529	Qualified state tuition program	¶808, ¶924
Sec. 23711.4	IRC Sec. 529A	ABLE accounts	¶255
Sec. 23711.5	. . . .	Golden State Scholarshare Trust	¶808, ¶924
Sec. 23712	IRC Sec. 530	Coverdell Education Savings Accounts	. . . .
Sec. 23731	IRC Secs. 501(b), 511	Unrelated business income	¶805, ¶809
Sec. 23732	IRC Sec. 512	Unrelated business income	¶809
Sec. 23734	IRC Sec. 513	"Unrelated trade or business" defined	¶809
Sec. 23735	IRC Sec. 514	Unrelated debt-financed income	¶809
Sec. 23736	IRC Sec. 503(a)	Prohibited transactions	¶809
Sec. 23736.1	IRC Sec. 503(b)	"Prohibited transactions" defined	¶809
Sec. 23736.2	IRC Sec. 503(a)(1)	Denial of exemption to organizations engaged in prohibited transactions	¶809
Sec. 23736.3	IRC Sec. 503(a)(2)	Taxable years affected	¶809
Sec. 23736.4	IRC Sec. 503(c)	Future status of organizations denied exemption	¶809
Sec. 23737	. . . .	Grounds for denial of exemption	¶809
Sec. 23740	IRC Sec. 4911	Excess expenditures to influence legislation	¶808
Sec. 23741	. . . .	Churches receiving rental income from other churches	¶809
Sec. 23771	IRC Sec. 6012	Returns required	¶809, ¶811
Sec. 23772	IRC Secs. 6033, 6072(e)	Annual returns by exempt organizations	¶811
Sec. 23774	. . . .	Annual return of exempt corporation	¶811
Sec. 23775	. . . .	Exempt corporation's failure to file return	¶811
Sec. 23776	. . . .	Reinstatement of exempt corporation	¶811
Sec. 23777	. . . .	Revocation of exemption	¶811
Sec. 23778	. . . .	Reestablishing exemption	¶811
Sec. 23800	IRC Secs. 1361-79	S corp determination	¶806
Sec. 23800.5	IRC Sec. 1361	Application	. . . .
Sec. 23801	IRC Sec. 1362	Election	¶806, ¶1310
Sec. 23802	IRC Sec. 1363	Tax rate	¶806, ¶816
Sec. 23802.5	IRC Sec. 1366	Determination of shareholders tax liability	. . . .
Sec. 23803	IRC Sec. 1361	Credit carryover	¶806
Sec. 23804	IRC Sec. 1367	Cross references	¶806
Sec. 23806	IRC Sec. 1371	IRC Sec. 338 election	¶806
Sec. 23807	IRC Sec. 1372	Partnership references	¶806
Sec. 23808	IRC Secs. 1373, 1379	Nonconformity to Federal	¶806
Sec. 23809	IRC Sec. 1374	Substituted California tax rate	¶806
Sec. 23811	IRC Sec. 1375	Tax on passive income	¶806
Sec. 23813	IRC Sec. 1377	Determinations	¶816
Sec. 24251	IRC Sec. 15	Tax rate changes during year	¶1105
Sec. 24271	IRC Secs. 61, 641-92, 701-77	Gross income	¶901
Sec. 24272	IRC Secs. 103, 141-50	Interest on government bonds	¶910
Sec. 24272.2	IRC Sec. 72	Annuities	¶904
Sec. 24272.5	IRC Sec. 7518	Capital construction funds for vessels	¶917
Sec. 24273	IRC Sec. 77	Commodity credit loans	¶912
Sec. 24273.5	IRC Sec. 1385	Noncash patronage allocations from farmers' cooperatives	¶914
Sec. 24275	IRC Sec. 88	Nuclear decommissioning costs	¶901
Sec. 24276	IRC Sec. 90	Illegal federal irrigation subsidies	. . . .
Sec. 24301	IRC Secs. 101-36	Exclusions from gross income	. . . .
Sec. 24303	Sec. 1603 of the American Recovery and Reinvestment Tax Act of 2009	Renewable energy grant exclusion	¶922, ¶904
Sec. 24305	IRC Sec. 101(f)	Life insurance proceeds	¶902
Sec. 24306	IRC Sec. 529	Qualified state tuition program	¶924
Sec. 24307	IRC Sec. 108	Income from discharge of indebtedness	¶908
Sec. 24308	IRC Sec. 61	Forest Service payments	¶901

California	Federal	Subject	Paragraph
Sec. 24308.1	IRC Sec. 136	Energy conservation subsidy exclusion	¶922
Sec. 24308.2	. . . .	Turf removal water conservation program incentive exclusion	¶921
Sec. 24308.5	IRC Sec. 126	Cost-share payments received by forest landowners	¶923
Sec. 24308.7	. . . .	Earthquake loss mitigation incentives	¶928
Sec. 24309	IRC Sec. 109	Improvements by lessee	¶905
Sec. 24309.5	IRC Sec. 110	Qualified lessee construction allowances	¶906
Sec. 24310	IRC Sec. 111	Recovery of bad debts and prior taxes	¶907
Sec. 24314	IRC Sec. 61	Gain or loss from exempt bond	¶1212
Sec. 24315	IRC Sec. 61	Recycling income	¶919
Sec. 24320	IRC Sec. 883	Operation of foreign aircraft or ships	¶916
Sec. 24321	IRC Secs. 881-82	Local governmental units prohibited	¶916
Sec. 24322	IRC Secs. 118, 597	Contributions to capital	¶913
Sec. 24323	IRC Sec. 61	Rebates for water-conservation devices	¶921
Sec. 24324	IRC Sec. 118	Exclusion of utilities	. . . .
Sec. 24325	IRC Sec. 118	Contributions to capital	¶913
Sec. 24326	IRC Sec. 136	Energy conservation subsidies	¶922
Sec. 24327	IRC Sec. 892	Foreign government investment income	. . . .
Sec. 24329	IRC Sec. 139	Disaster relief payment exclusions	¶927
Sec. 24330	. . .	Qualified health care service plan income exclusion	¶929
Sec. 24341	IRC Sec. 63	"Net income" defined	¶815
Sec. 24343	IRC Sec. 162	Deductions for business expenses	¶1001
Sec. 24343.2	IRC Sec. 162	Expenses incurred at discriminatory clubs	. . . .
Sec. 24343.3	IRC Sec. 220	Medical savings account deduction	. . . .
Sec. 24343.5	IRC Sec. 162	Subsidization of employees' ridesharing	¶1019
Sec. 24343.7	IRC Sec. 162	Deductions for business expenses	¶1001, ¶1023
Sec. 24343.8	. . . .	Professional sports league-imposed fines or penalties	¶1023
Sec. 24344	IRC Sec. 163	Interest expense deduction	¶1004, ¶1311, ¶1312
Sec. 24344.5	IRC Sec. 163	Deduction for discount bonds	¶911, ¶1004
Sec. 24344.7	IRC Sec. 163	Limitation on interest expense deduction	¶1004
Secs. 24345, 24345.5	IRC Secs. 164, 275	Deduction for taxes	¶1006
Sec. 24346	IRC Sec. 164	Apportionment of taxes on real property	¶1006
Sec. 24347	IRC Secs. 165, 166, 582	Losses—deductions	¶1007, ¶1009, ¶1010
Secs. 24347.4-47.14	IRC Sec. 165	Disaster losses	¶1007
Sec. 24348	IRC Secs. 166, 585, 593	Deduction for bad debts	¶1009
Sec. 24349	IRC Secs. 167(a), 168	Depreciation	¶1011
Sec. 24349.1	IRC Sec. 280F	Depreciation-luxury cars	¶1011
Sec. 24349.2	IRC Sec. 280G	Golden parachute payments	¶1023
Sec. 24350	. . . .	Limitations on use of methods and rates	¶1011
Sec. 24351	. . . .	Agreement as to useful life—depreciation	¶1011
Sec. 24352	. . . .	Depreciation—change in method	¶1011
Sec. 24352.5	. . . .	Depreciation—salvage method	¶1011
Sec. 24353	IRC Sec. 167(c)	Basis for depreciation	¶1011, ¶1250
Sec. 24354	IRC Sec. 167(d)	Life tenants and beneficiaries	¶1011
Sec. 24354.1	. . . .	Rules for Sec. 18212 property	¶1011
Sec. 24355	IRC Sec. 167(f)	Intangibles ineligible for amortization	¶1011
Sec. 24355.4	IRC Sec. 168	Depreciation of rent-to-own property	¶1011
Sec. 24355.5	IRC Sec. 168(i)(16)	Useful life of Alaska natural gas pipeline	¶1011
Sec. 24355.5	IRC Sec. 197	Amortization of goodwill	¶1011
Sec. 24356	IRC Sec. 179	Bonus depreciation	¶1011
Sec. 24356.4	IRC Sec. 179B	Sulfur regulation compliance costs	¶1026

California	Federal	Subject	Paragraph
Sec. 24356.6	. . . .	Election to expense 40% of cost in targeted tax property	. . . .
Sec. 24356.7	. . . .	Accelerated write-off for enterprise zone property	¶1011
Sec. 24356.8	IRC Sec. 179	Accelerated write-off	¶1011
Sec. 24357	IRC Sec. 170(a), (f)(8), (9), (j)	Charitable contributions	¶1014, ¶1312
Sec. 24357.1	IRC Sec. 170(e)	Contributions of ordinary income and capital gain property	¶1014
Sec. 24357.2	IRC Sec. 170(f)(3)	Partial interest in property	¶1014
Sec. 24357.3	IRC Sec. 170(f)(4)	Valuation of remainder interest in real property	¶1014
Sec. 24357.4	IRC Sec. 170(f)(5)	Reduction for certain interest	¶1014
Sec. 24357.5	IRC Sec. 170(f)(1)	Disallowance of deduction	¶1014
Sec. 24357.6	IRC Sec. 170(f)(6)	Out-of-pocket expenditures	¶1014
Sec. 24357.7	IRC Sec. 170(h)	Qualified conservation expenditures	¶1014
Sec. 24357.8	IRC Sec. 170(e)	Scientific property used for research—deduction	¶1014
Sec. 24357.9	IRC Sec. 170	Contribution of computer technology to schools	¶1014
Sec. 24357.10	IRC Sec. 170(l)	Contributions in connection with athletic events	¶1014
Sec. 24357.11	IRC Sec. 170	Contributions in connection with Haiti earthquake relief efforts	¶1014
Sec. 24358	IRC Sec. 170(b)	Limitations on corporate contributions	¶1014
Sec. 24359	IRC Sec. 170(c)	Charitable contribution defined	¶1014
Sec. 24359.1	IRC Sec. 170(e)	Credit or deduction for scientific equipment donated	¶1014
Sec. 24360	IRC Sec. 171(a)	Amortizable bond premium	¶1015
Sec. 24361	IRC Sec. 171(b)	Determination of bond premium	¶1015
Sec. 24362	IRC Sec. 171(c)	Election as to taxable bonds	¶1015
Sec. 24363	IRC Sec. 171(d)	Bond defined	¶1015
Sec. 24363.5	IRC Sec. 171(e)	Offset to interest payments	¶1015
Sec. 24364	IRC Sec. 173	Circulation expenditures	¶1003
Sec. 24365	IRC Sec. 174	Research expenditures	¶1011
Sec. 24368.1	IRC Sec. 167(e)	Trademark expenditures	¶1011
Sec. 24369	IRC Sec. 175	Soil and water conservation expenditures	¶1002
Sec. 24369.4	IRC Sec. 198	Environmental remediation expenses	¶1011
Sec. 24370	IRC Sec. 591	Deductions for dividends paid on deposits	¶1021
Sec. 24372.3	IRC Sec. 169	Amortization of pollution control facilities	¶1011
Sec. 24372.5	IRC Sec. 194	Amortization of reforestation expenses	¶1011
Sec. 24373	IRC Sec. 178	Depreciation or amortization of lessee improvements	¶1011
Sec. 24377	IRC Sec. 180	Farm fertilizer expenses	¶1002
Sec. 24379	IRC Sec. 83	Transfer of property for services	¶1017
Sec. 24382	IRC Sec. 216	Foreclosure of cooperative housing corporation stock	¶1022
Sec. 24383	IRC Sec. 190	Architectural adaptations for the handicapped	¶1001
Sec. 24384.5	IRC Sec. 163	Interest received-depressed areas	¶918
Sec. 24401	IRC Sec. 241	Special deductions	. . . .
Sec. 24402	IRC Secs. 243-47, 561-565	Dividends received by corporations taxed by California	¶909, ¶1020
Sec. 24403	IRC Sec. 591	Deductions for credits to withdrawable shares	¶1021
Sec. 24404	IRC Secs. 1381-83	Agricultural cooperatives	¶1021
Sec. 24405	IRC Secs. 1381-83	Other cooperatives	¶1021
Sec. 24406	IRC Secs. 1381-83	Cooperative corporations	¶1021
Sec. 24406.5	IRC Sec. 1381	Gas producers' cooperatives	¶1021
Sec. 24406.6	IRC Sec. 1388	Net earnings of cooperatives	¶1021
Sec. 24407	IRC Sec. 248(a)	Organizational expenditures	¶1011
Sec. 24408	IRC Sec. 248(b)	"Organizational expenditures" defined	¶1011
Sec. 24409	IRC Sec. 248(c)	Organizational expenditures—period of election	¶1011
Sec. 24410	IRC Secs. 243-47	Dividends from subsidiary insurance company	¶909, ¶1020
Sec. 24411	IRC Secs. 243-47	Unitary business water's edge election	¶812, ¶1311
Sec. 24414	IRC Sec. 195	Start-up expenses	¶1018
Sec. 24415	IRC Sec. 161	Interindemnity payments	¶1001

California	Federal	Subject	Paragraph
Secs. 24416-16.22	IRC Secs. 172	Net operating loss carryovers	¶806, ¶1024
Sec. 24421	IRC Sec. 261	Disallowance of deductions	¶1011, ¶1023
Sec. 24422	IRC Secs. 263, 263A	Capital expenditures	¶1011, ¶1023, ¶1107
Sec. 24422.3	IRC Sec. 263A	Capitalization of inventory-related expense	¶1023, ¶1107
Sec. 24423	IRC Sec. 263	Drilling and development costs—oil and gas	¶1013, ¶1023
Sec. 24424	IRC Sec. 264	Payments on life insurance contracts	¶1004, ¶1023
Sec. 24425	IRC Sec. 265	Deductions allocable to tax-exempt income	¶1023
Sec. 24426	IRC Sec. 266	Taxes and carrying charges	¶1023
Sec. 24427	IRC Sec. 267	Transaction between related individuals	¶1023
Sec. 24429	IRC Sec. 276	Indirect contributions to political parties	. . . .
Sec. 24431	IRC Sec. 269	Acquisitions made to avoid tax	¶1110
Sec. 24434	IRC Sec. 271	Debts owed by political parties	¶1009
Sec. 24436.1	IRC Sec. 280E	Illegal activities	¶1023
Sec. 24436.5	IRC Sec. 161	Deductions on substandard housing	¶1023
Sec. 24437	IRC Sec. 277	Deduction limitation for social clubs	¶1023
Sec. 24438	IRC Sec. 279	Interest deduction on corporate acquisition indebtedness	¶1004
Sec. 24439	IRC Sec. 249	Deductions of bond premium on repurchase	¶1004, ¶1223
Sec. 24440	IRC Sec. 280C(b), (c)	Federal credits	¶818, ¶1021
Sec. 24441	IRC Sec. 161	Abandonment or tax recoupment fees	¶1023
Sec. 24442	IRC Sec. 280B	Demolition of historic structures	¶1023
Sec. 24442.5	IRC Sec. 280H	Limitation on amounts paid to employee-owners	¶1023
Sec. 24443	IRC Sec. 274	Disallowance of entertainment expenses	¶1001, ¶1023
Secs. 24447-48	IRC Sec. 161	Expenses disallowed	¶1023, ¶1024
Sec. 24449	IRC Sec. 291	Preference items	¶817
Sec. 24451	IRC Secs. 301-85	Corporate distributions and adjustments	Various
Sec. 24452	IRC Sec. 301	Special rule for distributions received by 20% shareholder	¶909
Sec. 24453	IRC Sec. 302	Termination of interest	¶909
Sec. 24454	IRC Sec. 304	Special rule in case of foreign acquiring corporation	¶909
Sec. 24456	IRC Sec. 306	Source of gain—IRC Sec. 306(f) inapplicable	¶909
Sec. 24458	. . . .	Treatment of banks" built-in losses	¶822
Sec. 24459	IRC Sec. 382(n)	Special rule for certain ownership changes	¶822
Sec. 24461	IRC Sec. 337	Effective dates of 1986 TRA changes as to liquidations	¶1221
Sec. 24462	IRC Sec. 355	Corporate reorganizations and spin-offs	¶1215
Sec. 24465	. . . .	Gain on transfers to insurance companies	¶1211, ¶1214, ¶1216, ¶1218
Sec. 24471	IRC Sec. 381	Items of distributor or transferor corporation	¶909, ¶1221
Sec. 24472	IRC Sec. 382	Discharge of indebtedness	¶908
Sec. 24473	. . . .	Mutual water company reorganization	. . . .
Sec. 24481	IRC Sec. 383	Special limits on certain excess credits, etc.	¶909, ¶1221
Secs. 24601-12	IRC Secs. 401-24	Deferred compensation	¶909, ¶1001, ¶1016, ¶1017
Sec. 24631	IRC Sec. 441	Accounting periods	¶1101
Sec. 24632	IRC Sec. 441	Income year	¶1101, ¶1102
Sec. 24633	IRC Sec. 442	Change in accounting period	¶1102
Sec. 24633.5	IRC Sec. 441	Change of accounting period	¶806, ¶1102
Sec. 24634	IRC Sec. 443	Short-period returns	¶1103
Sec. 24636	IRC Sec. 443	Computation of tax in short period return	¶1106
Sec. 24637	IRC Sec. 444	Election to Keep Same Tax Year—S Corporations	¶806, ¶1104
Sec. 24651	IRC Sec. 446	Accounting methods	¶1106
Sec. 24652	IRC Sec. 447	Accounting for farm corporations	¶1106

California	Federal	Subject	Paragraph
Sec. 24654	IRC Sec. 448	Cash method of accounting restricted	¶1106
Sec. 24661	IRC Sec. 451	Taxable year of inclusion	¶1106
Sec. 24661.3	. . . .	Production flexibility contracts	¶1106
Sec. 24667	IRC Secs. 453, 453A, 453B	Installment method	¶1109
Sec. 24668.1	IRC Sec. 453	Installment method—property condemnations	¶1109
Sec. 24672	. . . .	Installment income on cessation of business	¶1109
Sec. 24673	IRC Sec. 460	Percentage of completion accounting	¶806, ¶1106
Sec. 24673.2	IRC Sec. 460	Long term contracts	¶1106
Sec. 24674	IRC Sec. 454	Obligations issued at discount	¶1111
Sec. 24675	IRC Sec. 186	Patent infringement damages	¶1106
Sec. 24676	IRC Sec. 455	Prepaid subscription income	¶1106
Sec. 24676.5	IRC Sec. 458	Returned magazines, paperbacks, records	¶1106
Sec. 24677	IRC Sec. 186	Breach of contract award	¶1106
Sec. 24678	IRC Sec. 186	Damages received under Clayton Act	¶1106
Sec. 24679	. . . .	Fractional part of month	¶1106
Sec. 24681	IRC Sec. 461	Taxable year of deduction	¶1006, ¶1106
Sec. 24682	IRC Sec. 464	Farming expenses	¶1106
Sec. 24685	. . . .	Accrual of vacation pay	¶1106
Sec. 24685.5	IRC Sec. 404	Accrued vacation and sick pay	¶1016
Sec. 24688	IRC Sec. 467	Deferred rental payments	¶1106
Sec. 24689	IRC Sec. 468	Waste disposal costs	¶1106
Sec. 24690	IRC Sec. 468A	Nuclear decommissioning funds	¶1106
Sec. 24691	IRC Sec. 465	At risk	¶1023, ¶1025
Sec. 24692	IRC Sec. 469	Passive activity losses	¶1005, ¶1106
Sec. 24693	IRC Sec. 468B	Designated settlement funds	¶807
Sec. 24701	IRC Secs. 471, 472	Inventories—general rule	¶1107, ¶1108
Sec. 24708	IRC Sec. 474	Simplified dollar value LIFO	¶1108
Sec. 24710	IRC Sec. 475	Mark-to-market accounting	¶1107, ¶1222
Sec. 24721	IRC Sec. 481	Adjustments required by changes in method	¶1106
Sec. 24725	IRC Sec. 482	Allocation of income among taxpayers	¶1106, ¶1110
Sec. 24726	IRC Sec. 483	Interest on deferred payments	¶1106, ¶1112
Sec. 24831	IRC Secs. 611-38	Natural resources	¶1012, ¶1013, ¶1250
Secs. 24831.3, 24831.6	IRC Secs. 613A	Percentage depletion for marginal properties	¶1012
Secs. 24870-75	IRC Secs. 851-60L	RICs, REITs, REMICs, and FASITs	¶805, ¶1021
Sec. 24900	. . . .	Deemed dividends for overcapitalized insurance companies	¶909
Sec. 24901	IRC Sec. 1001	Determination of gain or loss	¶1201
Sec. 24902	IRC Sec. 1001	Recognition of gain or loss	¶1201
Sec. 24905	IRC Sec. 988	Foreign currency transactions	¶1204
Sec. 24905.5	IRC Sec. 988	Hedging transactions	. . . .
Sec. 24911	IRC Sec. 1011	Adjusted basis	¶1247
Sec. 24912	IRC Sec. 1012	Basis of property—cost	¶1226
Sec. 24913	IRC Sec. 1013	Basis of property in inventory	¶1227
Sec. 24914	IRC Sec. 1015	Basis of property acquired by gift or transfer in trust	¶1228, ¶1229
Sec. 24915	IRC Sec. 1015	Adjustment for gift taxes paid	¶1228
Sec. 24916	IRC Sec. 1016	Adjustments to basis	¶1247
Sec. 24916.2	IRC Sec. 1016	Abandonment fees, open-space easement	¶1247
Sec. 24917	IRC Sec. 1016	Substituted basis	¶1248
Sec. 24918	IRC Sec. 1017	Discharge of indebtedness	¶1251
Sec. 24919	IRC Sec. 1019	Improvements to property by lessee	¶1249
Sec2. 24941, 24941.5	IRC Sec. 1031	Exchange of property held for productive use	¶1206
Sec. 24942	IRC Sec. 1032	Exchange of stock for property	¶1224
Sec. 24943	IRC Sec. 1033(a)	Involuntary conversions	¶1202
Sec. 24944	IRC Sec. 1033(a)(2), (A), (B)	Conversion into money or unrelated property	¶1202
Sec. 24945	IRC Sec. 1033(a)(2)(C)	Time for assessment of deficiency attributable to gain	¶1202
Sec. 24946	IRC Sec. 1033(a)(2)(D)	Time for assessment of other deficiencies	¶1202
Sec. 24947	IRC Sec. 1033(b)	Basis of property	¶1235
Sec. 24948	IRC Sec. 1033(c)	Property sold pursuant to reclamation laws	¶1202

California	Federal	Subject	Paragraph
Sec. 24949	IRC Sec. 1033(d)	Diseased livestock	¶1202
Sec. 24949.1	IRC Sec. 1033(e)	Livestock sold on account of drought	¶1202
Sec. 24949.2	IRC Sec. 1033(g)	Condemnation of real property held for productive use	¶1202
Sec. 24949.3	IRC Sec. 1033(f)	Environmental contamination— replacement of livestock	¶1202
Sec. 24949.5	IRC Sec. 1033(h)	Applicability of federal involuntary conversion rules	¶1202
Sec. 24950	IRC Sec. 1035	Exchanges of insurance policies	¶1207
Sec. 24951	IRC Sec. 1036	Exchange of stock	¶1208
Sec. 24952	IRC Sec. 1038	Reacquisitions of real property	¶1210
Sec. 24953	IRC Sec. 1031	Like-kind exchange reporting requirement	¶1206
Sec. 24954	IRC Sec. 1042	Deferral of gain on roll-over sales of stock to ESOP	¶1213
Sec. 24954.1	IRC Sec. 1042(g)	Sales to agricultural refiners and cooperatives	¶1213
Sec. 24955	IRC Sec. 1001	Rollover sales of low-income housing	¶1203
Sec. 24956	IRC Sec. 1044	Rollover of publicly traded securities gain	¶1222
Sec. 24961	IRC Sec. 1051	Basis of property acquired from affiliated corporation	¶1237
Sec. 24962	IRC Sec. 1052	Basis provisions from prior codes	¶1238
Sec. 24963	IRC Sec. 1053	Basis of property acquired before March 1, 1913	¶1238
Sec. 24964	IRC Sec. 1011	Property received from controlled corporation	¶1243
Sec. 24965	IRC Sec. 1054	Basis of stock issued by FNMA	¶1240
Sec. 24966	IRC Sec. 1059	Basis after extraordinary dividend	¶1226
Sec. 24966.1	IRC Sec. 1059A	Basis of property imported from related persons	¶1226, ¶1227
Sec. 24966.2	IRC Sec. 1060	Allocation of transferred business assets	¶1226, ¶1252
Secs. 24990, 24990.2, 24990.5, 24990.8	IRC Secs. 1201-97	No capital gains or losses	¶1011, ¶1222, ¶1223
Sec. 24990.6	IRC Sec. 1245	Character of gain or loss	. . . .
Sec. 24990.7	IRC Sec. 1248	Gain on sales in foreign corporations	¶1217
Sec. 24991	IRC Sec. 1275	Definition of tax-exempt obligation	¶910, ¶911
Sec. 24993	IRC Sec. 7872	Imputed interest	¶911, ¶1112
Sec. 24995	IRC Secs. 1291-98	Passive foreign investment companies	¶1222
Sec. 24998	IRC Secs. 1091, 1092	Wash sales of stock or securities	¶1008, ¶1225, ¶1236
Sec. 25101	. . . .	Apportionment	¶823, ¶1302, ¶1313
Sec. 25101.3	. . . .	Property factor—aircraft	¶1307
Sec. 25101.15	. . . .	In-state income of two or more taxpayers	¶1310
Sec. 25102	. . . .	Combined return of controlled taxpayers	¶1110, ¶1310
Sec. 25103	. . . .	Corporate transactions to evade tax	¶1110
Sec. 25104	. . . .	Consolidated report	¶1310
Sec. 25105	. . . .	Determination of control	¶1310
Sec. 25106	. . . .	Income from intercompany dividend distribution	¶909
Sec. 25106.5	IRC Sec. 1502	Affiliated corporations— Combined reporting	¶812, ¶1310
Sec. 25107	. . . .	Apportionment of income of international banking facility	¶1307, ¶1308, ¶1309
Sec. 25108	IRC Sec. 172	Net operating loss	¶1024
Secs. 25110-16	. . . .	Unitary business water's-edge election	¶1024, ¶1311
Sec. 25120	. . . .	Definitions	¶1302
Sec. 25121	. . . .	Allocation and apportionment of income	¶1302
Sec. 25122	. . . .	Taxability in another state	¶1302
Sec. 25123	. . . .	Nonbusiness income	¶1303
Sec. 25124	. . . .	Rents and royalties from real and tangible personal property	¶1303

California	Federal	Subject	Paragraph
Sec. 25125	. . . .	Capital gains and losses from sales of real and personal property	¶ 1303
Sec. 25126	. . . .	Allocation of interest and dividends	¶ 1303
Sec. 25127	. . . .	Allocation of patent and copyright royalties	¶ 1303
Sec. 25128	. . . .	Apportionment formula	¶ 1304, ¶ 1305
Sec. 25128.5	. . . .	Optional single sales factor apportionment formula	¶ 1305
Sec. 25128.7	. . . .	Mandatory single sales factor apportionment formula	¶ 1305
Sec. 25129	. . . .	Property factor	¶ 1307
Sec. 25130	. . . .	Property valuation	¶ 1307
Sec. 25131	. . . .	Average value of property	¶ 1307
Sec. 25132	. . . .	Payroll factor	¶ 1308
Sec. 25133	. . . .	Allocation of compensation	¶ 1308
Sec. 25134	. . . .	Sales factor	¶ 1309
Sec. 25135	. . . .	Sales of tangible personal property	¶ 1309
Sec. 25136	. . . .	Sales other than sales of tangible personal property	¶ 1309
Sec. 25136.1	. . . .	Special sourcing rules for qualified cable companies	¶ 1309
Sec. 25137	. . . .	Adjustment of formula	¶ 1304, ¶ 1305, ¶ 1306
Sec. 25138	. . . .	Purpose of act	. . . .
Sec. 25139	. . . .	Title	. . . .
Sec. 25140	. . . .	Intercompany dividends	. . . .
Sec. 25141	. . . .	Professional sports	¶ 1306

TAXES ON CORPORATE INCOME

CHAPTER 8
IMPOSITION OF TAX, RATES, EXEMPTIONS, RETURNS

¶ 801 Overview of Corporation Franchise and Income Taxes

The franchise tax was first imposed in 1929; the corporation income tax in 1937. The law is known as the Corporation Tax Law, and constitutes Part 11 of Division 2 of the Revenue and Taxation Code. Administrative provisions affecting both corporate and personal income taxpayers are in Part 10.2 of Division 2 of the Revenue and Taxation Code.

The Law is administered by the Franchise Tax Board, composed of the State Controller, the Director of the Department of Finance, and the Chair of the State Board of Equalization.

The franchise tax is imposed for the privilege of exercising the corporate franchise in California. It is imposed upon corporations organized in California and upon out-of-state ("foreign") corporations that are doing business in the state.

Special rules are provided for beginning corporations, dissolving corporations, and corporations involved in a reorganization (¶ 819—¶ 822). Banks and financial corporations are taxed at a higher rate than other corporations, and in turn are relieved of certain other taxes as explained at ¶ 816.

The corporation income tax is imposed upon net income, at the basic rate of the franchise tax (¶ 816). It is intended to be complementary to the franchise tax, to apply to corporations that derive income from California sources but that are not subject to the franchise tax. Because the franchise tax applies in the great majority of cases (¶ 804), the income tax is applicable only to a relatively small number of corporations (¶ 805).

The franchise and income tax rate applied to general C corporations is 8.84%. (Sec. 23151(e), Rev. & Tax. Code) For banks and financial corporations, the tax rate is 10.84%. (Sec. 23186, Rev. & Tax. Code) S corporations are taxed at a reduced rate of 1.5% (3.5% for S corporations that are financial corporations). (Sec. 23802, Rev. & Tax. Code) For a discussion of the minimum tax, see ¶ 816.

The computation of income for both the franchise tax and the income tax generally follows the pattern of the federal income tax, and interpretations of the federal law by the Treasury Department and the courts are usually followed in the administration of comparable provisions of the California law. However, there are many differences between the federal and California laws. See ¶ 803 for an explanation of the federal conformity program established in 1983. There is also one important difference between the two California laws, as explained at ¶ 910interest on obligations of the United States is not taxable for income tax purposes although it is included in the measure of the tax for franchise tax purposes.

Some corporations are exempt from both franchise and income taxes. These include insurance underwriting companies (subject to special taxes—see ¶ 1902), several categories of nonprofit organizations, and others, as explained at ¶ 808.

¶802 Scope of Chapter

This chapter discusses the two taxes imposed on, or measured by, corporate income: (1) the bank and corporation franchise tax; and (2) the corporation income tax. It covers the question of who is subject and who is exempt, requirements for filing returns and payment of tax, the base upon which the taxes are imposed, the rates of tax and credits against tax, and the extent to which the taxes apply in certain special situations.

¶803 Federal Conformity Program

> *Law:* Sec. 23051.5 (CCH CALIFORNIA TAX REPORTS, ¶ 10-510, 10-515).
>
> *Comparable Federal:* None.

The federal conformity program adopted in 1983 for the personal income tax, as explained at ¶ 103, has not been applied as thoroughly to corporation taxes. However, in a number of areas—including gross income, deductions, and accounting periods and methods—California corporation franchise and income tax law consists largely of incorporated federal provisions.

Comment: Incorporation of Federal Exclusions and Deductions

California's corporation tax law is structured differently than California's personal income tax law as it relates to items of income, exclusions, and deductions. Under California's personal income tax law, Revenue and Taxation Code Sections 17081, 17131, and 17201 incorporate entire subchapters of the IRC that govern the treatment of items of gross income, exclusions, and deductions. The California Revenue and Taxation Code sections that follow these specific provisions then modify or specifically decouple from the IRC provisions within those subchapters. Thus, Sec. 17201 specifically incorporates the part of the IRC that contains all of the provisions governing deductions for individual and corporate taxpayers, including the IRC Sec. 199 deduction for domestic production activities income. However, because California personal income tax law contains another provision, Rev. & Tax. Code Sec. 17201.6, that specifically decouples from the IRC Sec. 199 deduction, California does not allow a deduction for domestic production activities income for personal income tax purposes, and an addition adjustment is required.

In contrast, the corporation tax law governing items of gross income and net income, does not have general provisions analogous to Rev. & Tax. Code Secs. 17081, 17131, and 17201 in the personal income tax law. Consequently, unless the corporate income tax law specifically incorporates a federal provision governing items of income, exclusions, or deductions, California does not incorporate the federal law. Using the example above, because there is no specific corporation tax law provision either directly incorporating IRC Sec. 199, nor mirroring its provisions, California does not follow federal law concerning the deduction for domestic production activities income and taxpayers that use the federal reconciliation method of computing their California tax liability will be required to make an addition adjustment on the corporation tax return.

As under the personal income tax law, with the exception of provisions dealing with retirement and deferred compensation plans, water's-edge elections, and certain S corporation and real estate investment trust (REIT) provisions, which conform to the IRC as amended to date (¶806, ¶1311), references to the Internal Revenue Code (and to uncodified federal laws that relate to Internal Revenue Code provisions) are updated periodically through conforming legislation. Such references in the California law are now updated to January 1, 2015 (previously to January 1, 2009). (Sec. 23051.5, Rev. & Tax. Code) Consequently, California has not conformed to amendments made by the following federal laws:

— Slain Officer Family Support Act of 2015 (P.L. 114-7);

— Medicare Access and CHIP Reauthorization Act of 2015 (P.L. 114-10);

— Don't Tax Our Fallen Public Safety Heroes Act (P.L. 114-14);

— Highway and Transportation Funding Act of 2015 (P.L. 114-21);

— Defending Public Safety Employees' Retirement Act (P.L. 114-26);

— Trade Preferences Extension Act of 2015 (P.L. 114-27);

— Surface Transportation and Veterans Health Care Choice Improvement Act of 2015 (P.L. 114-41); and

— Protecting Americans From Tax Hikes Act of 2015 (P.L. 114-113).

Practitioner Comment: California Updates IRC Conformity Reference Date

See the Practitioner Comment at ¶103 for additional insight regarding California's IRC conformity date change.

Planning Note: EGTRRA Sunset Provision Incorporated

California incorporates the federal provision of the Economic Growth and Tax Relief and Reconciliation Act of 2001 (P.L. 107-134) that provides that all provisions of, and amendments made by, the 2001 Act will not apply to taxable, plan, or limitation years beginning after 2010. However, to the extent that any of these provisions are extended or the sunset date repealed, California will incorporate the extension, whether the extension is temporary or permanent (Sec. 23051.5(a)(2), Rev. & Tax. Code) The sunset dates for all of these federal provisions were extended an additional two years by the federal Jobs Creation Act of 2010 and eliminated by the Taxpayer Relief Act of 2012, thus making the EGTRRA provisions permanent.

California adopts both temporary and final federal regulations to the extent that the federal regulations do not conflict with California law or California regulations.

• *Federal elections*

A proper election, application, or consent filed in accordance with the Internal Revenue Code is effective for California purposes, unless otherwise specified. To obtain different California treatment than federal treatment, a California taxpayer must file a separate election, application, or consent with the Franchise Tax Board. (Sec. 23151(e), Rev. & Tax. Code)

Federal income tax elections, or lack thereof, made before becoming a California taxpayer are binding for California corporation franchise and income tax purposes, unless a separate election is specifically authorized by a California law or regulation.

• *Taxable income computation methods*

California gives corporations the option of choosing how to compute their net income. Under the federal reconciliation method, the starting point for computing California corporation franchise or income tax is the federal taxable income from federal Form 1120 or Form 1120A, the corporation's federal tax return, before claiming the net operating loss and special deductions. (Instructions, Form 100, California Corporation Franchise or Income Tax Return) The federal amount, after required California additions and subtractions, constitutes the corporation's net income subject to California taxation. (Sec. 24341, Rev. & Tax. Code) The necessary additions and subtractions are discussed in the following chapters.

In lieu of the federal reconciliation method, corporations that are not required to file a federal return or that maintain separate records for state purposes may compute their net income using the California computation method on California Form 100, Schedule F, Computation of Net Income. Generally, if ordinary income is computed under California law, no state adjustments are necessary. (Instructions, Form 100, California Corporation Franchise or Income Tax Return)

Corporations using the California computation method to compute net income must transfer the amount from Schedule F, line 30, to Form 100, Side 1, line 1. Corporations should complete Form 100, Side 1, line 2 through line 17, only if applicable. (Instructions, Form 100, California Corporation Franchise or Income Tax Return)

¶804 Corporations Subject to Franchise Tax

Law: Sec. 191, Corporations Code; Secs. 23038, 23038.5, 23101-04, 23151, Rev. & Tax. Code (CCH CALIFORNIA TAX REPORTS, ¶ 10-075, 10-210, 10-235, 10-240).

Comparable Federal: Sec. 7704 (CCH U.S. MASTER TAX GUIDE ¶ 403).

California Form: Form 100 (California Corporation Franchise or Income Tax Return).

Every corporation doing business in California is subject to the franchise tax, unless specifically exempted as set forth in ¶ 808. (Sec. 23151, Rev. & Tax. Code) A corporation incorporated in California or qualified to do business in California, but not actually doing business in the state, and not expressly exempt, is subject only to the minimum franchise tax (¶ 816). However, if such a corporation has income from California sources, it is subject to the income tax, as explained at ¶ 805. If there is income from both within and without the state, a portion of the total is assigned to California as explained in Chapter 13.

For purposes of the franchise tax, a corporation includes associations (including nonprofit associations that perform services, borrow money, or own property), other than banking associations, and Massachusetts or business trusts. (Sec. 23038, Rev. & Tax. Code)

• *What is "doing business"*

Beginning with the 2011 tax year, the law defines "doing business" as "actively engaging in any transaction for the purpose of financial or pecuniary gain or profit," or meeting one of the bright-line, factor-based thresholds discussed below. Prior to the 2011 tax year, there were no factor-based thresholds.

Practice Tip: Two Tests Are Independent

An out-of-state taxpayer that has less than the threshold amounts of property, payroll, and sales in California may still be considered doing business in this state if the taxpayer actively engages in any transaction for the purpose of financial or pecuniary gain or profit in California. For example, an out-of-state partnership whose only connection with California is its employees who work out of their homes in California selling and providing warranty work to California customers will still be considered to be doing business in California even if the property, payroll, and sales in California fall below the threshold amounts. The partnership would be considered doing business in California through its employees because those employees are "actively engaging" in transactions for profit on behalf of the partnership. (*FTB's General Information on New Rules for Doing Business in California*, CCH CALIFORNIA TAX REPORTS, ¶ 405-387)

Taxpayers who are unsure of whether they are "doing business" under the "actively engaging in any transaction for the purpose of financial or pecuniary gain or profit" test can petition the Franchise Tax Board for a determination through a chief counsel ruling (FTB Notice 2011-06, CCH CALIFORNIA TAX REPORTS, ¶ 405-518). According to FTB legal counsel, it can take up to four months to issue a ruling.

A taxpayer is considered to be doing business in California during a taxable year if it satisfies one of the following:

— the taxpayer is organized or commercially domiciled in California;

— the taxpayer's California sales, including sales by an agent or independent contractor, exceed the lesser of $547,711 for 2016 ($536,446 for 2015; $529,562 for 2014; $518,162 for 2013; $509,500 for 2012; $500,000 for 2011) or 25% percent of the taxpayer's total sales;

— the taxpayer's California real property and tangible personal property exceed the lesser of $54,771 for 2016 ($53,644 for 2015; $52,956 for 2014; $51,816 for 2013; $50,950 for 2012; $50,000 for 2011) or 25% of the taxpayer's total real property and tangible personal property; or

— the amount paid in California by the taxpayer for compensation exceeds the lesser of $54,771 for 2016 ($53,644 for 2015; $52,956 for 2014;$51,816 for 2013; $50,950 for 2012; $50,000 for 2011) or 25% of the total compensation paid by the taxpayer.

The figures above are adjusted annually for inflation. In addition, the sales, property, and payroll of the taxpayer include the taxpayer's pro rata or distributive share of partnerships or S corporations. (Sec. 23101, Rev. & Tax. Code)

These thresholds apply to out-of-state corporations and pass-through entities (partnerships, S corporations, limited liability companies (LLCs) treated as partnerships) and their partners/shareholders/members that have property, payroll or sales in California. (*FTB's General Information on New Rules for Doing Business in California*, CCH CALIFORNIA TAX REPORTS, ¶ 405-387)

Practice Note: Determining Sales for Purposes of Factor-Based Thresholds

The Franchise Tax Board's Chief Counsel has ruled that a taxpayer was required to aggregate the proceeds from sales of tangible personal property (TPP) with royalties received to determine whether it met California's economic nexus standard for doing business in the state. The gross amounts realized from both sales of TPP and royalties received (sales of other than TPP) were "gross receipts" for purposes of the doing business determination. (*Chief Counsel Ruling 2016-03*, July 5, 2016, CCH CALIFORNIA TAX REPORTS, ¶ 406-541).

Practitioner Comment: LLC Corporate Members Not "Doing Business" in California if the LLC's Sole California Activity Consists of Registering to Do Business or Being Organized In the State

In *Legal Ruling 2014-01*, July 22, 2014, CCH CALIFORNIA TAX REPORTS, ¶ 406-180, the FTB concluded that LLC corporate members are not "doing business" in the state when the LLC's only California activity consists of registering to do business or being organized in the state. As a result, corporate members of these LLCs are not subject to the requirement to file a tax return based on "doing business" in California and are not subject to the state's franchise tax regime. The ruling also reiterated that it is still the FTB's position that corporate members are doing business in California if the LLC is commercially domiciled or otherwise doing business in the state. Note, however, in *Swart* (see practitioner comment), the California trial court held that simply having a 0.2% ownership interest in an LLC was not sufficient to create nexus for the owner. The FTB has appealed the trial court decision.

Chris Whitney, Contributing Editor

Practitioner Comment: Nexus and California Disregarded Entities

Under *FTB Legal Ruling 2011-01*, California activities performed by a disregarded entity are treated as activities of its owner, and cause the disregarded entity's owner to have nexus and be subject to the California franchise tax. Disregarded entities include Qualified Subchapter S Subsidiaries ("QSubs") and Single Member Limited Liability Companies ("SMLLCs").

It should be noted that the nexus and apportionment implications of membership in disregarded LLCs was litigated in California. Specifically, in *Bunzl Distribution v. Franchise Tax Board*, San Francisco Superior Court, Case No. GC10506344, the taxpayer was challenging whether the FTB properly imposed California tax on an out of state SMLLC owner that had not given its consent to California tax jurisdiction under Cal. Rev. & Tax. Code § 18633.5. Cal Rev. & Tax. Code § 18633.5 provides that in the absence of such consent, the LLC is to pay tax on behalf of non-consenting members based upon their share of the LLC's income. The FTB in *Bunzl* asserted, among other things, that these provisions do not preclude California from imposing tax directly upon the out-of-state SMLLC member by attributing the LLC's income and apportionment factors to such member. The Superior Court found in favor of the FTB on a summary judgment motion concluding that the withholding of consent to California jurisdiction by a non-resident member of a SMLLC on an information return per Cal. Rev. & Tax. Code § 18633.5 does not obviate the requirement to pay California franchise tax based on the LLC's apportionment factors pursuant to the Uniform Division of Income for Tax Purposes Act. Bunzl appealed the superior court's ruling, which is currently in the briefing stage in the First Appellate District. Note, while *Bunzl* continues to be appealed, the California trial court in *Swart* (see practitioner comment), held that simply having a 0.2% ownership interest in an LLC was not sufficient to create nexus for the owner. The FTB has appealed the trial court decision.

Chris Whitney, Contributing Editor

Practitioner Comment: An LLC Ownership Interest May not Necessarily Constitute "Doing Business" in California

In *Swart Enterprises, Inc. v. California Franchise Tax Board*, Superior Court of California, Fresno County, No, 13CECG02171 (11/14/14), a California trial court held that a corporate member of an LLC was not doing business in California based solely on its 0.2% interest in the LLC and therefore not subject to the minimum California corporate franchise tax. The LLC was a manager-managed LLC where only the manager had authority to manage and control the LLC's business. The taxpayer was not the LLC's manager and had no connection to California aside from its LLC interest.

The FTB argued that an LLC electing to be taxed as a partnership is essentially electing to treat all of its members as general partners, which is the same position the FTB has long asserted informally and eventually memorialized in its July 2014 *Legal Ruling 2014-01*. Essentially, the FTB has sought to limit the holding in *Amman & Schmid* to limited partners in limited partnerships. There, the BOE held that an out-of-state corporation whose only tie to California was as a limited partner in limited partnerships was not doing business in the state and therefore not subject to the minimum California corporate franchise tax.

Swart rejected the FTB's narrow interpretation of *Amman & Schmid*, explaining that there was "no legal authority" for its interpretation. The court in *Swart* held that the doing business exception is dependent on a member's lack of right to manage or control the decision making process of the entity. Since Swart did not have such control, the court held that the taxpayer could not be deemed to be doing business in the state simply as a result of its 0.2% membership interest in an LLC doing business in California.

The FTB appealed the trial court's decision and the case is now before the Fifth District Court of Appeal. Although *Swart* is not binding on the FTB or citable by taxpayers, it is noteworthy that a court rejected the line of reasoning the FTB asserted and formalized in *Legal Ruling 2014-01*.

Chris Whitney, Contributing Editor

Certain corporations, the activities of which are limited to the receipt and disbursement of dividends and interest on securities, are not to be considered as doing business. (Sec. 23101, Rev. & Tax. Code) Additionally, a corporation is not "doing business" in California for franchise tax purposes if the following apply:

— it is not incorporated under the laws of California;

— its sole activity in California is engaging in convention and trade show activities for seven or fewer calendar days during the taxable year; and

— it derives no more than $10,000 of gross income reportable to California from convention and trade show activities during the taxable year.

(Sec. 23104, Rev. & Tax. Code)

Below are decisions made and positions taken under the pre-2011 tax year definition of "doing business."

Practitioner Comment: In-State Presence of a Telecommuting Employee Creates Substantial Nexus

In the *Matter of Warwick McKinley, Inc.* (2012) (CCH California Tax Reports, ¶10-075.853), the BOE ruled in a summary decision that may not be cited as precedent that an out-of-state company had substantial nexus with California where it had an authorized California-based representative. Warwick McKinley, Inc. ("Warwick"), a Massachusetts-based taxpayer, provided marketing and recruiting consulting services to clients in the environmental, engineering/construction, and green technology sectors. Warwick did not maintain an office in California nor have clients in the state. However, Warwick did have an employee that relocated to California. The employee later became an independent contractor and worked from her home in Venice, California.

The FTB asserted that it became aware the taxpayer was doing business in California when it received information from the California Employment Development Department (EDD) that the taxpayer paid payroll taxes to this state because one of its employees was working in California. As a result, the FTB assessed the taxpayer with unpaid corporate franchise taxes as well as various penalties. Warwick protested, arguing that the presence of a single employee was not sufficient to create substantial nexus and that it was protected under Public Law 86-272. The company also protested the fact that the FTB's assessment, which was based on the average income of a business in Warwick's industry, attributed all of the taxpayer's income to California.

The BOE ruled that the presence of the in-state employee was sufficient to create substantial nexus. By operating through its employee in California, the taxpayer was afforded substantial and enduring benefits and protections of the state that enabled it to generate business for its recruiting services. The BOE concluded that Warwick's regular and systematic physical presence in California established substantial nexus for corporate franchise tax purposes. In addition, Public Law 86-272 did not apply to Warwick because it was in the business of providing services, not selling tangible personal property.

Turning to Warwick's other arguments, the BOE noted that Warwick had repeatedly failed to respond to the FTB's requests for documentation. As such, there was no evidence that the FTB's proposed assessment did not reflect Warwick's business activities in California.

Chris Whitney, Contributing Editor

Practitioner Comment: Corporations With No In-State Physical presence Have Nexus Based on Agency Relationship With Affiliate

On May 28, 2015, a California court of appeal issued *Harley-Davidson, Inc. v. Franchise Tax Board*, 237 Cal.App.4th 193 (2015), finding that two corporations with no California physical presence had substantial nexus with California due to the activities of an in-state affiliate. The corporations at issue were established as bankruptcy remote special purpose entities (SPEs) and were engaged in securing loans for their parent and affiliated corporations that did business in California. The court concluded that an in-state affiliate had an agency relationship with the SPEs and consequently the SPEs had sufficient nexus to satisfy both the Due Process and Commerce Clauses.

There existed an agency relationship between the affiliate and the SPEs because (1) the SPEs were specifically formed so that the affiliate could obtain a more favorable pricing for securitization investors, (2) the SPEs did not have any employees of their own and acted entirely through the affiliate's employees, (3) the affiliate controlled selection of the pools of loans to securitize, administered the sale of the SPEs' securities to underwriters, and indemnified the underwriters, (4) the affiliate undertook collection activities on the SPEs' loans, and (5) an employee of the affiliate visited an auction house in California on 17 days total to assist in the auction process—a process designed to ensure the value of the collateral securing the loans held by the SPEs.

The court of appeal found Due Process nexus because, inter alia, the SPEs' agent targeted California by attending 17 auctions there to assist in maintaining the value of the motorcycles that secured the loans held by the SPEs. Regarding Commerce Clause nexus, Harley-Davidson cited *Tyler Pipe Industries v. Dept. of Revenue*, 483 U.S. 232, 250 (1987), for the proposition that "third parties may give rise to nexus for [an] out-of-state company if... their activities were 'significantly associated with the taxpayer's ability to establish and maintain a market in th[e]state.'" Harley–Davidson interpreted this to require that the third-party's conduct must be sales-related, and argued that since the SPEs' market for the sale of securities are underwriters, not California consumers which is whom the affiliate's in-state activities targeted, the SPEs did not have California nexus. The court, however, rejected this argument, stating that "the third-party's in-state conduct need not be sales-related; it need only be 'an integral and crucial aspect of the business.'" (citing *Illinois Commercial Men's Assn. v. State Bd. Of Equalization*, 34 Cal.3d 839 (1983)).

Chris Whitney, Contributing Editor

In *Appeal of Amman & Schmid Finance AG et al.* (1996) (CCH CALIFORNIA TAX REPORTS, ¶ 10-210.262), foreign corporations with interests in limited partnerships were not subject to the California franchise tax, because the corporations' only contact with the state was the receipt of distributive shares of the limited partnerships' California source income. Accordingly, they did not meet the active participation requirement for "doing business" in the state.

The FTB has taken the position that an out-of-state limited partner in a limited partnership is not subject to the California minimum tax simply because it holds an interest in a limited partnership that is doing business in California. The FTB's position, in effect, extends the holding in *Amman & Schmid Finance AG et al.* to all limited partners, including corporate and limited partnership limited partners. In addition, the FTB has indicated that it will apply this holding to an LLC to the extent that the LLC is a limited partner in a limited partnership (*Tax News*, FTB, January 1997).

FTB Reg. 23101, 18 CCR, provides, generally, that a foreign corporation that has stocks of goods in California and that makes deliveries in California pursuant to orders taken by employees in California is doing business in the state and is subject to the franchise tax. On the other hand, Regulation 23101 provides that a foreign corporation engaged wholly in interstate commerce is not subject to the franchise tax. (Note that these rules apply to the *franchise* tax. For the application of the corporation *income* tax, see ¶805).

In *Appeal of Hugo Neu-Proler International Sales Corporation* (1982) (CCH CALIFOR-NIA TAX REPORTS, ¶400-444), the taxpayer was a Domestic International Sales Corporation (DISC) subject to special treatment under federal income tax law. The corporation had no employees or physical assets in California. The BOE held that the corporation was doing business in California and subject to the franchise tax, because "the exercise of appellant's corporate powers and privileges was essential to the performance of the various transactions it entered into" in California.

In *Appeal of Putnam Fund Distributors Inc., et al.* (1977) (CCH CALIFORNIA TAX REPORTS, ¶11-520.8291), the BOE held that a Massachusetts corporation engaged in promoting California sales of mutual fund shares by brokers was doing business and was subject to the franchise tax. The BOE approved the imposition of 25% failure-to-file penalties (¶1411) for a period of 10 years.

In *Appeal of Kimberly-Clark Corp.* (1962) (CCH CALIFORNIA TAX REPORTS, ¶10-210.239), the BOE held that a foreign corporation qualified to do business in California was subject to the franchise tax even though it did not maintain a stock of goods within the state. It conducted extensive activities and had substantial stocks of samples, displays, and sales promotion materials in the state.

A corporation may be "doing business" even though it is in the process of liquidation. The BOE held to this effect in the case of *Appeal of Sugar Creek Pine Co.* (1955) (CCH CALIFORNIA TAX REPORTS, ¶10-210.51). The corporation's activities involved principally perfecting title to properties that it had previously contracted to sell.

In *Appeal of American President Lines, Ltd.* (1961) (CCH CALIFORNIA TAX REPORTS, ¶10-075.56), the BOE held that a corporation that is principally engaged in interstate and foreign commerce is nevertheless subject to the *franchise* tax on the basis of its entire income attributable to sources within the state when it engages in some *intrastate* business in California.

• *Foreign lending institutions*

The Corporations Code specifies the activities in which a foreign lending institution may engage in California without being deemed to be "doing business" in the state. The permissible activities include purchasing or making loans, making appraisals, enforcement of loans, etc., provided the activities are carried on within the limitations set forth in the law. (Sec. 191, Corp. Code)

• *Exemption for limited activities*

The law authorizes the FTB to determine that a corporation is not subject to franchise or income tax if its only activities in California are within specified limits. A corporation may petition the FTB for such a determination. The limited activities are the following:

¶804

— purchasing of personal property or services in California for its own or its affiliate's use outside the state if (1) the corporation has no more than 100 employees in California whose duties are limited to specified activities, or (2) the corporation has no more than 200 employees in California whose duties are limited, as specified, and the items purchased are used for the construction or modification of a physical plant or facility located outside the state; however, the combined number of employees in this state for purposes of both (1) and (2) may not exceed 200; and/or

— presence of employees in California solely for the purpose of attending school.

(Sec. 23101.5, Rev. & Tax. Code)

• *Certain organizations treated as corporations*

The tax law includes "professional corporations" within the definition of "corporation" for franchise tax purposes. Charitable trusts are also treated as "corporations" (¶606). (Sec. 23038, Rev. & Tax. Code)

Under both federal and California law, publicly traded partnerships are treated as "corporations" for income tax purposes unless 90% or more of their gross income consists of qualifying passive activities or they are grandfathered publicly traded partnerships exempt from corporate treatment. However, a grandfathered publicly traded partnership that elects to continue its partnership status is subject to a California tax equal to 1% of its California-source gross income attributable to the active conduct of any trade or business (a 3.5% tax on gross income attributable to the active conduct of any trade or business for federal purposes). The tax is due from the partnership at the time the partnership return is filed (see ¶622). Otherwise, the tax is paid, collected, and refunded in the same manner as corporate franchise and income taxes. (Sec. 23038.5, Rev. & Tax. Code)

Limited liability companies classified as corporations are discussed at ¶805.

¶805 Corporations Subject to Income Tax

Law: Secs. 18633.5, 23038, 23038.5, 23501, 23503, 23731, 24870-75 (CCH California Tax Reports, ¶10-015, 10-075, 10-210, 10-235, 10-240, 10-245, 10-355, 10-360, 10-365, 10-370).

Comparable Federal: Secs. 851-860G, 7701, 7704, Former Secs. 860H-860L (CCH U.S. Master Tax Guide ¶403, 2301—2323, 2326—2340, 2343—2367, 2369).

California Form: Form 100 (California Corporation Franchise or Income Tax Return).

Generally, the corporation income tax applies to those corporations (including associations, Massachusetts or business trusts, and real estate investment trusts) that derive income from sources within California but are not subject to the franchise tax. If there is income from both within and without the state, a portion of the total is assigned to California as explained in Chapter 13. (Sec. 23501, Rev. & Tax. Code)

• *Application of income tax*

The most common application of the income tax is to foreign corporations that engage in some business activity in California but that are not "doing business" in the state so as to subject them to the franchise tax. One example is a corporation that maintains a stock of goods in California from which deliveries are made to fill orders taken by independent dealers or brokers. Another example might be a corporation that has employees operating in California but has no stock of goods or other property in the state; however, the state's right to tax in such a situation may be limited under the federal legislation discussed below. Where a corporation maintains only a stock of samples in California, having no other property or agents or other activity in the state, it has generally been considered not subject to tax in California.

The income tax, rather than the franchise tax, is imposed on the unrelated business income of an exempt organization. (Sec. 23731, Rev. & Tax. Code)

• *Limited activities—Application of P.L. 86-272*

The scope of the California income tax is limited by federal legislation enacted in 1959. This legislation was intended to overcome the effect of two decisions of the U.S. Supreme Court earlier in 1959: *Northwestern States Portland Cement Co. v. Minnesota* and *Williams v. Stockham Valves and Fittings, Inc.,* 358 U.S. 450, 79 S.Ct. 357. These cases ruled that individual states had broad powers to levy taxes on the income of foreign state corporations even though the business conducted within the state was exclusively in interstate commerce. The federal law (P.L. 86-272) prohibits a state from imposing a tax on income derived from interstate commerce, provided:

> — the activities within the state are limited to the solicitation of orders for sales of tangible personal property by employees or other representatives;

> — orders are sent outside the state for approval; and

> — orders are filled from stocks of goods maintained outside the state.

The prohibition against tax applies also to a corporation that sells through a sales office maintained within the state by independent contractors whose activities consist solely of making sales or soliciting orders.

Practice Tip: P.L. 86-272 Inapplicable to Minimum Tax

Although P.L. 86-272 exempts qualified taxpayers engaged in the selling of tangible personal property from paying the franchise or income tax if their only connection to the state is solicitation of sales, P.L. 86-272 does not provide immunity from the minimum tax because the minimum tax is not based upon net income. Consequently, for post-2010 tax years a taxpayer whose only connection with California is selling tangible personal property to California customers over the Internet must file a return and pay the minimum tax if its sales exceed the minimum threshold of $500,000 (adjusted for inflation) or 25% of its total sales.

Similarly, if a taxpayer's only connections to California are sales of services and intangibles to California customers, which services are performed outside of the state, the taxpayer is still subject to the minimum tax if the sales exceed the threshold levels. This is because the market-based approach for sourcing sales must be used for purposes of determining whether a taxpayer is doing business in California. Thus, the taxpayer would be liable for the minimum tax even though it has no California-source income. (*FTB's General Information on New Rules for Doing Business in California,* CCH CALIFORNIA TAX REPORTS, ¶ 405-387)

A taxpayer in this situation should file the appropriate form (California Form 100, 568, or 565) if it is doing business within California, and pay the applicable tax and fee. Partnerships, LLCs, and S corporations are also required to fill out a California Schedule K-1 for each partner/members/shareholder. For purposes of reporting the information from Column (e) of the California Schedule K-1, the entity must complete Schedule R, to determine the entity's income from California sources. If the activities of the business entity are protected under P.L. 86-272, taxpayers should provide that information on Schedule R. It is best to attach a statement explaining why the apportioning percentage and the business income are zero. (*FTB Tax News* (April 2013), CCH CALIFORNIA TAX REPORTS, ¶ 405-867)

In a nonprecedential summary decision, the State Board of Equalization (BOE) held that P.L. 86-272 did not provide protection from the establishment of taxable nexus where the solicitation of advertising sales involved sales of a service and not sales of tangible personal property. (*Personal Selling Power, Inc.* (2009), CCH CALIFORNIA TAX REPORTS, ¶ 404-881)

The Franchise Tax Board (FTB) has issued a guide to its interpretation of P.L. 86-272 (FTB 1050, Application and Interpretation of Public Law 86-272). The guide discusses various types of activity that will, or will not, cause a business to lose its state-tax immunity. Activities that will subject a corporation to California taxation include property repairs, credit investigations, and collection of delinquent accounts. Certain activities that are incidental to the solicitation of sales will not cause a business to lose its state-tax immunity. However, if at any time during the taxable year, a company conducts activities that are not protected, all sales in this state or income earned by the company attributed to this state during any part of the taxable year are subject to California taxation.

The guide also discusses various other problems, including use of display rooms, use of independent contractors, maintaining facilities in the state, and application of the throwback rule. It states that the protection of P.L. 86-272 does not apply to California or foreign-nation corporations or to California residents or domiciliaries. The guide can be found at the FTB's Web site at the following address: http://www.ftb.ca.gov/forms/misc/1050.pdf.

In *The Reader's Digest Assoc., Inc. v. Franchise Tax Board*, 94 Cal. App.4th 1240 (2001) (CCH CALIFORNIA TAX REPORTS, ¶ 10-210.26), the court ruled that an out-of-state corporation was doing business in California and subject to tax in the state as a result of activities provided by an in-state affiliate because the in-state affiliate was not an independent contractor to the out-of-state corporation. The court's conclusion that a subsidiary cannot be an independent contractor when the parent has a right to exercise control over the subsidiary is one approach that states may take in challenging a taxpayer's claim of P.L. 86-272 protection.

In Legal Ruling No. 372 (1974) (CCH CALIFORNIA TAX REPORTS, ¶ 16-851.20), the FTB held that the protection of P.L. 86-272 does not extend to salesmen soliciting orders in California; such salesmen are subject to withholding of California income tax.

As explained at ¶ 804, the FTB may determine that a corporation is subject to neither franchise nor income tax if its only activities in California are within specified limits.

Appeal of Riblet Tramway Co. (1967) (CCH CALIFORNIA TAX REPORTS, ¶ 10-075.97) involved a Washington state manufacturer of ski lift facilities that were installed in California by others. The company usually inspected the facilities after they were installed. The State Board of Equalization (BOE) held that this inspection activity went beyond "solicitation" and subjected the company to California tax.

Similarly, in *Brown Group Retail, Inc. v. Franchise Tax Board* (1996) (CCH CALIFORNIA TAX REPORTS, ¶ 10-075.216), an out-of-state shoe manufacturer and distributor that had no facilities or property in the state was not immune from California franchise tax under P.L. 86-272, because services performed by the taxpayer's employees went beyond the mere solicitation of orders. Although the taxpayer made no direct sales in the state, the presence in California of two of the taxpayer's employees who assisted current and potential customers with financial analysis, lease and loan negotiations, site selection, store design, marketing, etc., established a sufficient nexus with the state to subject the taxpayer to California's franchise tax.

• *Cases decided favorably to taxpayer*

In *Appeal of John H. Grace Co.* (1980) (CCH CALIFORNIA TAX REPORTS, ¶ 10-075.51), the taxpayer was an Illinois corporation that leased railroad cars to industrial companies. The cars sometimes passed into or through California in interstate commerce, and the taxpayer paid the private car tax (¶ 1905) on the average number of cars per day in California. The BOE held that the corporation was not subject to California income tax, because it had no "activities" within the state and the railroad cars were not under its control when they were in the state.

¶805

In *Appeal of E.F. Timme & Son, Inc.* (1969) (CCH CALIFORNIA TAX REPORTS, ¶ 10-075.98), the FTB contended that P.L. 86-272 was not applicable because the taxpayer did not own the goods it was selling in California. The BOE overruled the FTB and held that the taxpayer was exempt from California tax.

• *Cases unfavorable to taxpayer*

In *Harley-Davidson, Inc. v. FTB* (2015) (CCH CALIFORNIA TAX REPORTS, ¶ 10-075.13) the appellate court held that Harley-Davidson's two special purpose entity subsidiaries (SPEs) had sufficient nexus with California for corporation franchise and income tax purposes to overcome Due Process and Commerce Clause limitations on taxing foreign entities. Even though the SPEs were separate entities with no direct presence or business activity in California, various other subsidiaries were found to be agents for the SPEs. Further, the SPEs' agents had participated in 17 auctions in California during the years at issue. The California Supreme Court has denied review.

In *William Wrigley, Jr., Co. v. Wisconsin Department of Revenue* (1992) (CCH CALIFORNIA TAX REPORTS, ¶ 10-075), the U.S. Supreme Court held that an Illinois-based corporation that had sales representatives in Wisconsin to store goods, replace goods, and restock retailers' display racks was not immune from Wisconsin franchise taxes under P.L. 86-272, because those activities went beyond mere "solicitation."

In *Appeal of Aqua Aerobic Systems, Inc.* (1985) (CCH CALIFORNIA TAX REPORTS, ¶ 10-075.93), the BOE held that an Illinois manufacturer's warranty repairs exceeded "solicitation" and went beyond the protection of P.L. 86-272.

In *Appeal of Ramfjeld and Co., Inc.* (1981) (CCH CALIFORNIA TAX REPORTS, ¶ 10-075.67), the taxpayer warehoused in California canned fish that it sold to U.S. military installations in California and Asia. The taxpayer was a New York corporation, with no office or employees in California. The BOE held that the corporation was subject to California income tax.

In *Appeal of CITC Industries, Inc.* (1979) (CCH CALIFORNIA TAX REPORTS, ¶ 10-075.94), the taxpayer was the U.S. sales representative for a Japanese manufacturer and maintained a sales office in California. The BOE held that the taxpayer's activities went beyond the protection of P.L. 86-272. See also *Appeal of Schmid Brothers, Inc.* (1980) (CCH CALIFORNIA TAX REPORTS, ¶ 10-075.991), to the same effect.

In *Appeal of Kelsey-Hayes Company* (1978) (CCH CALIFORNIA TAX REPORTS, ¶ 11-525.59), the taxpayer corporation had an active California division that admittedly subjected the corporation to the franchise tax. The corporation also had limited activity in California in an entirely unrelated business. The BOE held that P.L. 86-272 was not applicable and the limited activity could be taxed on a unitary basis with related out-of-state operations, because P.L. 86-272 must be applied to the totality of the corporation's California activities.

In *Appeal of Knoll Pharmaceutical Company, Inc.* (1977) (CCH CALIFORNIA TAX REPORTS, ¶ 10-075.32), an out-of-state manufacturer had employees soliciting sales in California. The sales were approved and filled by a California consignee from a stock of goods maintained in the state. The BOE held that the corporation's activities went beyond the protection of P.L. 86-272. See also *Consolidated Accessories Corp. v. Franchise Tax Board* (1984) (CCH CALIFORNIA TAX REPORTS, ¶ 10-075.22), to the same effect.

In *Appeal of Nardis of Dallas, Inc.* (1975) (CCH CALIFORNIA TAX REPORTS, ¶ 10-075.99), an out-of-state corporation sold clothing through a California showroom. The BOE held that the corporation was not protected from California tax under P.L. 86-272, because the California salesman was an employee—not an independent contractor—and the showroom was maintained by the company, even though it was leased in the salesman's name.

In *Appeal of Snap-On Tools Corporation* (1958) (CCH CALIFORNIA TAX REPORTS, ¶ 10-075.34), the BOE held that where an out-of-state corporation operated in California solely through independently owned distributorships, it was not doing business in the state so as to be subject to the franchise tax. However, because the corporation maintained consigned stocks of goods in California from which withdrawals were made by the independent distributors, it was held subject to the income tax.

• *Noncorporate organizations subject to tax*

California adopts IRC Sec. 7704 as of the current IRC tie-in date (see ¶803), under which publicly traded partnerships are taxed as corporations, unless 90% or more of their gross income is qualifying passive income or they are grandfathered publicly traded partnerships exempt from corporate treatment. However, a grandfathered publicly traded partnership that elects to continue its partnership status is subject to a California tax equal to 1% of its California-source gross income attributable to the active conduct of any trade or business (a 3.5% tax on gross income attributable to the active conduct of any trade or business for federal purposes). The tax is due from the partnership at the time the partnership return is filed (see ¶622). Otherwise, the tax is paid, collected, and refunded in the same manner as corporate franchise and income taxes. (Sec. 23038.5, Rev. & Tax. Code)

The income tax applies to certain other organizations that may be said generally to have the characteristics of a corporation. It applies to certain associations, to Massachusetts or business trusts, and to some non-publicly traded limited partnerships. FTB Reg. 23038 (a), 18 CCR, and Reg. 23038 (b), 18 CCR, contain detailed rules in this regard.

Note that a business trust that was classified as a corporation for California corporation franchise tax purposes but was classified as a partnership for federal purposes prior to January 1, 1997, may make an irrevocable election to be classified as a partnership for California tax purposes as well, unless specified exceptions apply. The election is made on FTB 3574, Special Election for Business Trusts and Certain Foreign Single Member LLCs. (Reg. 23038, 18 CCR; Instructions, FTB 3574, Special Election for Business Trusts and Certain Foreign Single Member LLCs)

• *Regulated investment companies*

California adopts federal provisions dealing with regulated investment companies (RICs) (commonly known as "mutual funds") (¶803), with exceptions that (1) allow RICs to deduct exempt interest dividends distributed to shareholders to the extent that the interest was included in gross income and (2) modify the provisions concerning the computation of investment company taxable income taxable to RIC shareholders. (Sec. 24870, Rev. & Tax. Code; Sec. 24871, Rev. & Tax. Code)

At the federal level, the deduction for exempt interest dividends is denied because interest from state and local bonds is excluded from federal gross income; however, because such interest is included in gross income for California purposes (¶910), California permits the deduction. California taxes a RIC the same as a taxable C corporation, except that its California "net income" is the same as its federal "investment company taxable income" with specified modifications.

For purposes of calculating a RIC's investment company taxable income, California incorporates federal law except that

(1) California, unlike federal law, does not exclude a RIC's net capital gain from its taxable income;

(2) California denies the California net operating loss (NOL) deduction rather than the federal NOL deduction;

(3) California disallows the former California dividends received deduction for corporations taxed by California rather than the federal dividends received deduction;

(4) California denies the deductions for (a) an intercompany dividend received from corporations that are members of the unitary group, (b) patronage refunds from certain cooperative corporations, and (c) dividends received from insurance companies;

(5) California, unlike federal law, includes a deduction for capital gain and exempt interest dividends for purposes of computing the deduction for dividends paid;

(6) federal law, but not California, allows taxpayers to pass on the foreign tax credit to its shareholders;

(7) federal law, but not California, provides for reduced rates for qualified dividend income distributed to investors by RICs; and

(8) California imposes a lower tax rate in instances in which a RIC fails the "asset test." The California tax is equal to $12,500 tax or the product of California's highest corporate tax rate applied against the net income generated during the period of asset test failure by the assets that caused the RIC to fail the asset test, rather than the $50,000 tax or application of the highest federal corporate tax rate in instances in which the non de minimis savings provisions apply.

(Sec. 24871, Rev. & Tax. Code)

• *Real estate investment trusts*

An organization that qualifies as a "real estate investment trust" (REIT) for federal income tax purposes is treated as a business trust subject to the corporation income tax. California generally follows federal law as of the current IRC tie-in date (¶803), except that a REIT's California "net income" is the same as its federal "real estate investment company taxable income" with specified modifications. (Sec. 24870, Rev. & Tax. Code; Sec. 24872, Rev. & Tax. Code, through Sec. 24872.7, Rev. & Tax. Code)

Federal law, but not California law, provides for reduced rates for qualified dividend income distributed to investors by REITs. In addition, unlike federal law, California law does not impose tax on income from foreclosure property or prohibited transactions. Nor does California impose a tax in the case of a failure to meet certain requirements. (Sec. 24872, Rev. & Tax. Code)

Also, due to California's IRC conformity date (¶803), California has not conformed to the federal repeal of the preferential dividend rule for publicly offered REITs, which applies to distributions in taxable years beginning after December 31, 2014, or federal amendments to the computation of earnings and profits of a REIT, which apply to taxable years beginning after December 31, 2015.

Practice Tip: Minimum Tax

REITs are subject to the minimum tax (see ¶816), but a qualified real estate investment trust subsidiary (QREITS) is not, according to informal guidance issued by the Franchise Tax Board. A QREITS and its parent real estate investment trust (REIT) are treated as a single tax entity for California tax purposes. In addition, because the QREITS is disregarded as a separate entity for California income tax purposes, its activities are the activities of its parent REIT for purposes of Rev. & Tax. Code § 23101 (doing business). Thus, a QREITS's parent REIT is subject to the minimum franchise tax, but the QREITS itself is not subject to the tax. (*FTB Legal Division Guidance 2011-06-02*, CCH California Tax Reports, ¶ 405-448)

A federal election, or lack thereof, to qualify as a REIT is binding for California corporation franchise and income tax purposes. The same applies to a federal election to treat certain REIT property as foreclosure property. (Sec. 24872.4, Rev. & Tax. Code; Sec. 24872.6, Rev. & Tax. Code) Although California law technically only adopts federal amendments adopted prior to California's IRC conformity date, because

California recognizes any federal REIT election or termination thereof, California effectively conforms to all amendments to the federal REIT provisions impacting eligibility, elections, and terminations, even those enacted after California's latest conformity date.

The FTB has identified transactions that involve REIT consent dividends as a "listed transaction"; see ¶727 for details.

• *Real estate mortgage investment conduits*

California follows federal law as of the current IRC tie-in date (¶803), exempting from income or franchise taxation corporations that qualify as "real estate mortgage investment conduits" (REMICs). The income of such an entity is taxable to the holders of its interests. There are two separate interests in a REMIC, with each taxed under a different set of complex rules. California does not incorporate the federal provision that imposes a 100% tax on the net income from prohibited transactions. A REMIC is subject to the minimum tax, but not to the franchise tax, and a REMIC's income is taxable to the holders of its interests (¶804). (Sec. 24870, Rev. & Tax. Code; Sec. 24873, Rev. & Tax. Code; Sec. 24874, Rev. & Tax. Code)

• *Financial asset securitization investment trusts*

California incorporates the former federal provisions concerning financial asset securitization investment trusts (FASITs) as of the current IRC tie-in date (¶803), with modifications. California also incorporates the federal repeal of the FASIT provisions, effective January 1, 2005, including the exceptions to the federal repeal that are applicable to FASITs in existence on October 22, 2004, to the extent that regular interests issued by the FASIT before October 22, 2004, continue to remain outstanding in accordance with the original terms of issuance. (Sec. 24870, Rev. & Tax. Code; Sec. 24875, Rev. & Tax. Code)

• *Limited liability companies*

A limited liability company (LLC) that is classified as a corporation for California tax purposes is subject to the same tax return and tax payment requirements as any other corporation. LLCs that are classified as partnerships or that are disregarded and treated as sole proprietorships are discussed at ¶625.

Note that an entity that was a previously existing foreign single member LLC that was classified as a corporation under California law but elected to be treated as a disregarded entity for federal purposes for pre-1997 taxable years may continue to be classified differently for California and federal tax purposes. However, such an entity, may make an irrevocable election to be disregarded for California tax purposes as well, unless specified exceptions apply. The election is made on FTB 3574, Special Election for Business Trusts and Certain Foreign Single Member LLCs. (Reg. 23038, 18 CCR; Instructions, FTB 3574, Special Election for Business Trusts and Certain Foreign Single Member LLCs) (Sec. 18633.5(h), Rev. & Tax. Code; Sec. 23038, Rev. & Tax. Code)

• *Credit for franchise tax*

A corporation subject to the income tax is allowed a credit for any franchise tax imposed for the same period. (Sec. 23503, Rev. & Tax. Code)

¶806 S Corporations

Law: Secs. 18535, 19365, 23153, 23800-13, 24416, 24633.5, 24637 (CCH CALIFORNIA TAX REPORTS, ¶10-215).

Comparable Federal: Secs. 1361-79 (CCH U.S. MASTER TAX GUIDE ¶301—349).

California Form: Form 100S (California S Corporation Franchise or Income Tax Return).

California conforms to federal S corporation provisions as of the current IRC tie-in date (see ¶803), with substantial modifications. (Sec. 23800, Rev. & Tax. Code)

Caution Note: Conformity Issues

Although California only technically incorporates federal law as of California's current conformity date (see ¶803), because S corporations that have a valid S corporation election for federal purposes are treated as S corporations for California corporation franchise and income tax purposes (Sec. 23801(a), Rev. & Tax. Code), California essentially incorporates the IRC provisions governing S corporation qualifications, elections, and terminations (IRC Sec. 1361 and IRC Sec. 1362) as currently amended.

However, California's conformity to federal provisions recognizing S corporations as pass-through entities is partial in that:

— California imposes both a 1.5% tax and the minimum tax at the corporate level, and

— California imposes a minimum tax on qualified subchapter S subsidiaries. (Sec. 23802, Rev. & Tax. Code; Sec. 23153, Rev. & Tax. Code)

Practice Tip: S Corporations with Total Assets of $10 Million or More

For taxable years beginning on or after January 1, 2014, the Internal Revenue Service allows S corporations with total assets of at least $10 million but less than $50 million on the last day of the year to complete Schedule M-1 (Form 1120S) in place of Schedule M-3 (Form 1120S) Parts II and III. However, Schedule M-3 (Form 1120S), Part I, is required for these corporations. For California purposes, the S corporation must complete the California Schedule M-1 and do one of the following: (1) attach a copy of the federal Schedule M-3 (Form 1120S) and related attachments or (2) attach a complete copy of the federal return. The FTB will accept a Schedule M-3 (Form 1120S) in a spreadsheet format if it is more convenient. (Instructions, Form 100S, S Corporation Franchise or Income Tax Return)

• *Character of pass-through entity*

Under federal law, S corporations enjoy the tax advantages of partnerships while at the same time benefiting from the corporate characteristic of limited liability. Tax is not paid by the corporation, as such. Generally, items of income, loss, and credits are passed through to shareholders on a pro-rata basis. California has adopted a hybrid version of the S corporation in which both a reduced corporate tax is paid at the corporate level and income and tax attributes are passed through to shareholders. (Sec. 23800, et. seq., Rev. & Tax. Code)

• *Nonresident shareholders*

S corporations are required to remit California income tax withholding on behalf of their nonresident shareholders (see ¶714).

S corporations are allowed to file group (composite) returns and to make composite tax payments on behalf of electing nonresident shareholders. A single 100% nonresident S corporation may also file a group return, see ¶619 for details. (Sec. 18535, Rev. & Tax. Code)

• *S corporation's taxable year*

California incorporates IRC Sec. 444, under which S corporations may elect a fiscal year that is the same as the corporation used in its last tax year. (Sec. 24637, Rev. & Tax. Code) See ¶1104.

• *Reduced tax at corporate level*

S corporations that are not financial corporations compute the corporate franchise or income tax on Form 100S, but pay this tax at the rate of 1.5% instead of the normal corporate tax rate discussed at ¶816. For purposes of the 1.5% tax, S corporations compute depreciation and amortization deductions using MACRS (see ¶310). (Sec. 23802, Rev. & Tax. Code)

In *Handlery Hotels, Inc.* (1995) (CCH CALIFORNIA TAX REPORTS, ¶10-215.217), a California court of appeal held that a corporation that made a valid election to be treated as an S corporation was not entitled to apply the lower S corporation franchise tax rate until the first income year following the corporation's valid election.

As under federal law, S corporations are not subject to the alternative minimum tax (¶817). However, they are subject to the minimum tax (¶816). (Sec. 23153, Rev. & Tax. Code)

• *Financial S corporation*

The tax rate for S corporations that are also financial corporations is 3.5%. (Sec. 23802, Rev. & Tax. Code)

• *Qualified subchapter S subsidiaries*

Under both California and federal law an S corporation may own a qualified subchapter S subsidiary (QSub). However, under California (but not federal) law, a QSub is subject to the California corporate minimum tax if it is incorporated in California, qualified to transact business in California, or doing business in California. In addition, the activities of a QSub are imputed to the S corporation for purposes of determining whether the S corporation is "doing business" in California. An S corporation's federal election to treat a corporation as a QSub is binding for California purposes and no separate election is allowed. (Sec. 23800.5, Rev. & Tax. Code)

In a nonprecedential decision, the BOE ruled that an S corporation was liable for $1,600 in minimum tax imposed on its two QSubs for the two days of the S corporation's taxable year remaining when it acquired the QSubs, even though each of the QSubs had already paid an $800 minimum franchise tax or QSub tax for their short taxable year ending the day before they were acquired by the S corporation. The BOE ruled that the QSubs became new entities, with a new taxable year, when they were acquired by the S corporation, and the taxes in question were payable per entity, per taxable year. (*Appeal of The Greystone Group, Inc.* (2006) (CCH CALIFORNIA TAX REPORTS, ¶10-380.451))

• *Separate tax on excess net passive investment income*

A separate tax is imposed on excess net passive investment income from California sources, using the full tax rate that applies to general corporations, but only when the taxpayer has excess net passive income for federal purposes. This tax is not reduced by any tax credits; however, the amount of the income subject to this tax is deductible from net income for purposes of computing the 1.5% tax. (Sec. 23811, Rev. & Tax. Code)

• *NOL deductions*

An S corporation is allowed to deduct a net operating loss (NOL) incurred during a year in which it is treated as an S corporation. An S corporation may pass the full amount of such loss through to its shareholders in the year the loss is incurred. If a shareholder is unable to use the full amount of the loss in the year it is incurred, the shareholder may carry over or carry back the NOL deduction as allowed for C corporations (see ¶1024). (Sec. 23802(d), Rev. & Tax. Code)

S corporations may also qualify for the 100% NOL carryover deduction available to (1) taxpayers engaged in the conduct of qualified businesses in enterprise zones, the former Los Angeles Revitalization Zone, local agency military base recovery areas, and the former targeted tax area; and (2) "new" and "small" businesses (¶1024).

¶806

According to the Instructions to FTB 3805Q, an S corporation that converted from a C corporation may apply an NOL carryover from a period in which it was a C corporation only against the tax on built-in gains and not against the standard 1.5% tax imposed on S corporations. If an S corporation converts to a C corporation, any NOLs incurred by the S corporation are lost.

• *Combined reporting of members of a unitary business*

A corporation that elects to be treated as an S corporation is, by virtue of its election, required to be excluded from a combined report of the unitary group. However, the law contains enforcement provisions to help the FTB prevent tax avoidance or evasion (¶1110). (Sec. 23801, Rev. & Tax. Code)

• *Separate tax on built-in capital gains*

A "built-in gains" tax is imposed on gains from sales of assets, as determined under IRC Sec. 1374. The tax applies only to gains from California source income. The tax is not reduced by any credits, even credits carried over from years prior to an S corporation election. The full corporate tax rate (¶816) is applied to this income. (Sec. 23809, Rev. & Tax. Code)

For corporations required to convert to S corporations for California tax purposes as a result of their federal S corporation election (see the discussion under "S corporation election, termination of status" below), the effective date of the S corporation election for purposes of determining the California tax on built-in gains is the same as the federal S corporation election date.

Because of California's current IRC conformity date (see ¶803), California does not follow the federal amendment made to IRC Sec. 1374 by the American Recovery and Reinvestment Tax Act of 2009, the Small Business Jobs Act, or the American Taxpayer Relief Act of 2012 (ATRA), which, for the 2009 and 2010 tax year, eliminates the built-in gains tax on an S corporation's net unrecognized built-in gain if the seventh tax year in the corporation's 10-year recognition period preceded its 2009 or 2010 tax year. The 2010 Jobs Act and ATRA shortened the recovery-period to five years for post-2010 tax years. California still follows the 10-year recognition period.

• *Credits available to S corporations*

Corporate credits may be claimed against the 1.5% (or 3.5% for financial S corporations) tax, with no pass-through to shareholders. The credits are reduced to one-third of their total value because the tax rate is much lower than the regular corporate tax rate discussed at ¶816. Unused portions of the credit, but not the two-thirds that is denied, may be carried forward. Credit carryovers from years prior to making an S election are also subject to the one-third limitation, but not in subsequent years. Shareholders, however, are able to take the full amount of credits to which they may be entitled as individual taxpayers. (Sec. 23803, Rev. & Tax. Code)

Planning Tip: Pass-Through of Credits

Credits available only against the corporation franchise and income tax may be applied only against the 1.5% S corporation tax and may not be passed through to shareholders. The credit must be reduced by two-thirds and the one-third may be applied against the S corporation tax and/or carried over. If a credit may be claimed only against the personal income tax, the full amount of the credit may be passed through to the shareholders and none of it may be applied against the S corporation's 1.5% tax. If the credit may be claimed against both the corporation franchise and personal income taxes, the S corporation may use one-third of the credit to offset the S corporation tax or it may be carried over, if allowed. The remaining two-thirds must be disregarded and may not be carried over. The full amount of the credit, as calculated under the Personal Income Tax Law, may also be passed through to the shareholders. (Form 100S Booklet, S Corporation Tax Booklet)

For California purposes, credits and credit carryovers may not reduce the minimum franchise tax, built-in gains tax, excess net passive income tax, credit recaptures, the increase in tax imposed for the deferral of installment sale income, or an installment of last-in first-out (LIFO) recapture tax.

S corporations may claim withholding at source credits on their returns only to the extent of their tax liability. Any remaining withholding at source credit in excess of the tax liability must be allocated to shareholders using Form 592, Quarterly Resident and Nonresident Withholding Statement. S corporations may no longer claim refunds on Form 100S of any withholding at the source in excess of their tax liability. (*Public Service Bulletin 10-09* (2010) (CCH CALIFORNIA TAX REPORTS, ¶ 405-150))

• *Passive activity losses and at-risk rules*

The federal limitations on losses and credits from passive activities (IRC Sec. 469) and the at-risk rules (IRC Sec. 465) are applied in the same manner as if the corporation were an individual (see ¶ 339 and ¶ 340). For this purpose, "adjusted gross income" of the S corporation is its "net income," as modified for California purposes, but without any charitable contributions deduction. However, the material participation rules apply as if the S corporation was a closely held corporation. (Sec. 23802, Rev. & Tax. Code)

See the discussion under "Qualified subchapter S subsidiaries," above, for special provisions concerning the disposition of S corporation stock by a QSub for purposes of applying the passive activity loss and at-risk limitations.

Practitioner Comment: California Conforms to Federal LIFO Recapture Income for Estimated Payments

California conforms to federal law by excluding a last-in, first-out (LIFO) recapture amount from estimated tax payments in any taxable year that an annual installment of LIFO recapture is due. For federal tax purposes, a corporation that uses the LIFO method of accounting for its inventory for the taxable year before its election to become an S corporation takes effect must include the LIFO recapture amount in its taxable income and report and pay tax on the recaptured income in four equal annual installments. However, the recapture amount is not included in the amount of federal quarterly estimated tax payments that are made during the years in which an installment payment is due.

Chris Whitney, Contributing Editor

• *S corporation election; termination of status*

A corporation that has in effect a valid federal S corporation election is treated as an S corporation for California tax purposes and no separate election is allowed. (Sec. 23801, Rev. & Tax. Code)

The federal election date is deemed to be the California S corporation election date for corporations that elect to be S corporations after 2001. The federal election applies for purposes of determining shareholders' California income tax liability, even if the corporation is not qualified to do business in California or is not incorporated in California. A termination of a federal S corporation election that is not an inadvertent termination simultaneously terminates the corporation's S corporation status for California tax purposes.

The Secretary for federal purposes (Franchise Tax Board (FTB) for California purposes) has the authority to validate invalid elections that have resulted from the following:

— an entity's inadvertent failure to qualify as a small business corporation;

— failure to obtain required shareholder consents; or

— late filing of an election with reasonable cause.

A corporation may also perfect an S corporation election for California purposes in instances when the corporation merely failed to timely file a federal S corporation election. The corporation and its shareholders must have filed with the IRS for relief and received notification from the IRS of the acceptance of an untimely filed S corporation election.

Planning Tip: Consider Timing of Elections

Taxpayers considering making an S corporation election may want to consider the timing of making the election. If they make an S corporation election mid-year, they will have to file two short-year returns and pay for two entities. (*Tax News*, California Franchise Tax Board, February 2010)

Under both federal and California law, once a valid election for S corporation treatment has been filed, S corporation status continues for as long as the corporation remains in existence, unless the election is terminated. Termination of a federal election occurs when an S corporation:

(1) ceases to qualify as a small business corporation;

(2) has passive investment income that amounts to more than 25% of its gross receipts for each of three consecutive tax years, and has accumulated earnings and profits at the end of each of those years; or

(3) deliberately revokes its S corporation election by filing a revocation statement to which the majority of the shareholders consent.

The termination under (2), above, is not recognized in California unless the election is terminated for federal income tax purposes. Dividends received by an S corporation from a C corporation subsidiary are not treated as passive investment income to the extent such dividends are attributable to the earnings and profits of the C corporation derived from the active conduct of a trade or business.

If an S corporation terminates its election, it is ineligible to make another S corporation election for five years.

• *Other differences from federal treatment*

The federal provisions dealing with coordination with the investment credit recapture are inapplicable as are the provisions dealing with foreign (non-U.S.) income. (Sec. 23051.5, Rev. & Tax. Code) A C corporation resulting from an S corporation termination must annualize its taxable income for the short taxable year under both California and federal law. However, taxpayers must annualize their income on a monthly basis for California corporation franchise and income tax purposes and on a daily basis for federal income tax purposes. (Sec. 23801(f), Rev. & Tax. Code)

• *Taxation of shareholders*

Taxation of shareholders is discussed at ¶233.

¶807 Designated Settlement Funds

Law: Sec. 24693 (CCH CALIFORNIA TAX REPORTS, ¶10-520).

Comparable Federal: Sec. 468B (CCH U.S. MASTER TAX GUIDE ¶1539).

California follows IRC Sec. 468B as of California's current federal conformity date (¶803), relating to the taxation of designated settlement funds, except that the tax imposed is at the regular California income tax rate, see ¶ 816. The tax is in lieu of any other income tax. (Sec. 24693, Rev. & Tax. Code)

¶808 Exempt Corporations

Law: Secs. 23046.5, 23701-11.5, 23740, 23741 (CCH California Tax Reports, ¶ 10-245, 10-250, 10-525).

Comparable Federal: Secs. 501, 504-05, 507-09, 527-29, 4940-48, 7428 (CCH U.S. Master Tax Guide ¶ 601—698).

California Form: FTB 3500 (Exemption Application), FTB 3500A (Submission of Exemption Request).

The following organizations are exempt from both corporation franchise and income taxes:

(1) labor, agricultural, or horticultural organizations, with some exceptions (see comment below) (Sec. 23704, Rev. & Tax. Code);

(2) fraternal organizations providing insurance benefits to their members or devoting earnings exclusively to certain charitable-type and fraternal purposes (Sec. 23701b, Rev. & Tax. Code);

(3) nonprofit cemetery or crematory companies (Sec. 23701c, Rev. & Tax. Code);

(4) nonprofit religious, charitable, scientific, literary, or educational organizations (including certain cooperative hospital service organizations and certain amateur athletic associations) (Sec. 23701d, Rev. & Tax. Code);

(5) nonprofit business leagues, chambers of commerce, etc. (Sec. 23701f, Rev. & Tax. Code);

(6) nonprofit civic leagues, etc. (Sec. 23701u, Rev. & Tax. Code);

(7) nonprofit social and recreational clubs (Sec. 23701g, Rev. & Tax. Code);

(8) nonprofit title holding corporations (Sec. 23701h, Rev. & Tax. Code);

(9) voluntary employees' beneficiary associations (Sec. 23704, Rev. & Tax. Code);

(10) teachers' retirement associations (Sec. 23701j, Rev. & Tax. Code);

(11) certain religious or apostolic organizations, provided the income is reported by the individual members (Sec. 23701k, Rev. & Tax. Code), including the expanded definition of convention or association of churches (Sec. 23046.5, Rev. & Tax. Code);

(12) certain employee-funded pension plans created before June 25, 1959 (Sec. 23701s, Rev. & Tax. Code);

(13) organizations providing child care to the general public (Sec. 23704.4, Rev. & Tax. Code);

(14) insurance underwriting companies (this is a constitutional exemption; see discussion below. Insurance companies are subject to special taxes—see ¶ 1902);

(15) nonprofit corporations engaged in port and terminal protection and development (Sec. 10703, Corp. Code);

(16) trusts that provide for the payment of supplemental unemployment compensation benefits (Sec. 23701n, Rev. & Tax. Code);

(17) trusts or plans that meet the requirements of the federal Self-Employed Individual Tax Retirement law, if not otherwise exempt as an employees' trust (Sec. 23701p, Rev. & Tax. Code);

(18) political organizations (see discussion below) (Sec. 23701r, Rev. & Tax. Code);

(19) homeowners' associations (¶915) (Sec. 23701t, Rev. & Tax. Code);

(20) tenant organizations established to purchase mobile home parks for conversion into condominiums, stock cooperatives, or other resident ownership interests (Sec. 23701v, Rev. & Tax. Code);

(21) veterans' organizations (Sec. 23701w, Rev. & Tax. Code);

(22) nonprofit public benefit organizations (Sec. 23701u, Rev. & Tax. Code);

(23) nonprofit insurance risk pools (Sec. 23701z, Rev. & Tax. Code);

(24) qualified tuition programs (Sec. 23711, Rev. & Tax. Code); and

(25) state-chartered and federally chartered credit unions (Sec. 23701y, Rev. & Tax. Code).

California incorporates the tightened federal eligibility requirements for credit counseling organizations to qualify as exempt social welfare organizations or charitable or educational organizations, but modifies the federal provision to substitute internal cross references. (Sec. 23703.7, Rev. & Tax. Code)

• *California-federal comparisons*

The California exemptions are largely the same as the federal exemptions as of the current IRC tie-in date (¶803), although there are several differences.

The following exemptions are the same as the federal:

Item above	California law	Federal law
(1)	23701a	501(c)(5)
(2)	23701b, 23701 *l*	501(c)(8), (c)(10)
(3)	23701c	501(c)(13)
(4)	23701d, 23704	501(c)(3), 501(e), 501(j)
(7)	23701g	501(c)(7)
(8)	23701h, x	501(c)(2), (c)(25)
(9)	23701i	501(c)(9)
(10)	23701j	501(c)(11)
(11)	23701k	501(d)
(12)	23701s	501(c)(18)
(13)	23704.4	501(k)
(16)	23701n	501(c)(17)
(17)	23701p	401(a)
(21)	23701w	501(c)(19)
(24)	23711	529
(25)	23701y	501(c)(14)

Item (1) above (Sec. 23701a) is substantially the same as IRC Sec. 501(c)(5). The California exemption for agricultural cooperatives applies only if the organization is determined by the Internal Revenue Service to be exempt (see also ¶1021).

Item (5) above (Sec. 23701e) is the same as IRC Sec. 501(c)(6) except that the federal provision includes professional football leagues and California does not.

Item (6) above (Sec. 23701f) is the same as IRC Sec. 501(c)(4) except that the California law requires that the organization's assets be irrevocably dedicated to exempt purposes.

Item (12) above (Sec. 23701s) is the same as IRC Sec. 501(c)(18) except that California does not impose a tax on excess contributions to employee-funded pension plans.

Item (23) above (Sec. 23701z) applies to any organization established pursuant to the Nonprofit Corporation Law by three or more corporations to pool self-insurance claims or losses of those corporations. Federal law provides a similar exemption to "qualified charitable risk pools" organized under state law.

Item (25) above (Sec. 23701y) applies to California state-chartered credit unions only. Federally-chartered unions are exempt from California taxation by operation of the Federal Credit Union Act.

The federal law contains a number of exemptions not included in the California law. On the other hand, there are no specific exemptions in the federal law comparable to California items (14), (15), (20), and (22), above.

The Franchise Tax Board publishes a monthly-updated list, on its Web site, of all organizations exempt from California corporation franchise and income taxes. The list can be viewed by going to the FTB's website at http://ftb.ca.gov and searching for the term "exempt organizations."

• *Political organizations*

The California exemption for political organizations—item (18) above—with minor exceptions, is the same as the federal exemption. However, the California definition of "political organization" is slightly different from the federal. Also, California has not conformed to federal provisions that tax a nonpolitical organization on certain amounts when such organization engages in political activity. (Sec. 23701r, Rev. & Tax. Code)

An unincorporated political organization is automatically exempt, and is not required to file the usual application for exemption. Likewise, an *incorporated* political organization is not required to file the usual application for exemption. As explained at ¶811, an exempt political organization is required to file an income tax return if it has taxable income in excess of $100.

• *Insurance companies*

The gross premiums tax imposed on insurance companies is "in lieu" of all other state and local taxes and licenses, including the franchise tax (see ¶1902).

• *Title holding companies*

Federally exempt title holding companies that are limited liability companies classified as a partnership or as a disregarded entity are exempt from income taxes, including the fees imposed on LLCs under the personal income tax law (¶625). (Sec. 23701x, Rev. & Tax. Code)

• *Dedication of assets required*

Under California law, a charitable organization is not eligible for exemption under item (4) above unless its assets are irrevocably dedicated to exempt purposes. The California law (Sec. 23701d, Rev. & Tax. Code) provides specific rules for determining whether the assets are so dedicated, and requires a provision to that effect in the articles of organization. Federal law does not include this requirement; however, the governing instrument of a charitable organization must include specific provisions regarding distribution of income, prohibited acts, etc.

• *Use of accumulated income defeated exemption*

The State Board of Equalization (BOE) held in *Appeal of Boys Incorporated of America* (1960) (CCH CALIFORNIA TAX REPORTS, ¶10-245.92) that the organization was not operated exclusively for exempt purposes, where it was shown that accumulated income had been used to liquidate indebtedness rather than for its avowed charitable purposes.

• *Application for exemption*

Charitable trusts are treated as corporations for California corporation income and franchise tax purposes (see also ¶606).

IRC Sec. 501(c)(3) organizations, and effective January 1, 2014, IRC Sec. 501(c)(4), (5), (6), and (7) organizations that are granted tax-exempt status under federal law may submit FTB 3500A, Submission of Exemption Request, along with a copy of their IRS issued tax-exempt status notice to the FTB to establish their California tax-exempt status. The effective date of an organization's California tax-exempt status will be no later than the effective date of that organization's federal tax-exempt status. (Sec. 23701(d), Rev. & Tax. Code)

These IRC provisions apply to the following types of organizations:

— 501(c)(3): Charitable organizations.

— 501(c)(4): Civic leagues, social welfare organizations (including certain war veterans' organizations), or local employee associations.

— 501(c)(5): Labor, agricultural, or horticultural associations.

— 501(c)(6): Business leagues, chambers of commerce, etc.

— 501(c)(7): Social clubs.

An organization that incorporated prior to receiving its federal exempt status and that wants to receive state-exempt status retroactively in order to avoid the imposition of the minimum franchise or annual tax should file FTB 3500, Exemption Application, and not Form FTB 3500A, to request exemption retroactive to its date of incorporation.

Receipt of a federal group exemption letter issued and substantiation that the organization is included in the federal group exemption letter as a subordinate organization will qualify the group and all its affiliates for acknowledgment from the FTB that the organization is exempt from California corporation franchise and income taxes, other than the tax on unrelated business income. The effective date of an organization's exemption from state income tax will be no later than the effective date of the organization's recognition of exemption from federal income tax as an IRC Sec. 501(c)(3) organizaiton, or effective January 1, 2014, an IRC Sec. 501(c)(4), (5), (6), or (7) organization or its status as a subordinate organization under a federal group exemption letter, as applicable.

Organizations that are not issued a 501(c)(3), (4), (5), (6), or (7) federal tax-exempt status notice must file an application (FTB 3500) with the FTB, along with a $25 filing fee. This does not apply to insurance underwriting companies, which are exempt under the state constitution. Neither does it apply to political organizations except that an *incorporated* political organization must either pay the minimum tax (¶816) or obtain a certificate of exemption. (Sec. 23701d, Rev. & Tax. Code)

IRC Sec. 501(c)(3), (4), (5), (6), or (7) organizations must still fulfill California's exemption law requirements to receive the FTB's affirmation of federal tax exemption. This includes California's filing requirements for FTB Form 199, California Exempt Organization Annual Information Return; FTB Form 109, California Exempt Organization Business Income Tax Return; or FTB Form 100, Corporation Tax Return. Furthermore, an inactive organization is not entitled to exemption. Organizations seeking to obtain and retain California exempt status must meet requirements that they are organized and operating for nonprofit purposes within the provisions of their exempt code section. (Sec. 23701d, Rev. & Tax. Code) (*FTB Notice 2008-3, May 30, 2008*, CCH CALIFORNIA TAX REPORTS, ¶404-679; *Tax News*, FTB, December 2007, CCH CALIFORNIA TAX REPORTS, ¶404-503)

Planning Note: Effect of Federal Exemption/Suspension/Revocation

The FTB may still refuse to grant an exemption or may revoke an organization's exempt status if the organization is not organized or operated in accordance with state or federal law, including being listed with the Secretary of State's Office or the FTB as being suspended or forfeited. Taxpayers are required to notify the FTB of any federal tax-exempt status suspension or revocation. Upon receipt of such notice, the FTB may suspend or revoke the organization's state tax-exempt status.

Expedited Services

For a fee of $40, the FTB will expedite an application for exempt status. Qualified entities requesting tax exempt status must submit Form FTB 3500 (Exemption Application), along with all necessary documentation, to the Sacramento or Los Angeles FTB district office. (Reg. 19591, 18 CCR; *FTB Notice 2004-09*, California Franchise Tax Board, December 17, 2004, CCH CALIFORNIA TAX REPORTS, ¶ 403-722)

Certain organizations are required by federal law to give notice that they are applying for tax-exempt status. In these cases, the organizations are required to file a copy of the federal notice with the FTB.

California law provides that an exempt organization shall not be disqualified on the basis that it conducts bingo games authorized by law, provided the proceeds are used exclusively for charitable purposes. (Sec. 23710, Rev. & Tax. Code) Federal law provides for exemption of income from bingo games under certain conditions (¶ 809).

• *Retroactivity of exemption*

The FTB may grant exempt status retroactively to years that the organization can prove it satisfied the exemption requirements. (Sec. 23701, Rev. & Tax. Code) All applications for refunds must be timely filed (¶ 1417).

• *Private foundations*

Although California has conformed in principle to federal law by creating a special category of charitable organizations classified as "private foundations," California has not adopted many of the complicated federal provisions relating to such organizations. Also, whereas federal law imposes a tax on the investment income of such organizations and a series of excise taxes on self-dealing, income-accumulation, prohibited investments, lobbying, termination, etc., California imposes no special taxes on "private foundations" as such. (Sec. 23707, Rev. & Tax. Code)

Corporations classified as "private foundations" are required to include certain provisions in their governing instruments in order to maintain their tax-exempt status, unless a state statute accomplishes the same result. The California Corporations Code imposes the restrictions of federal law on every corporation that is deemed to be a "private foundation" under federal law. The law further provides that any provisions of a corporation's governing instruments that are inconsistent or contrary are of no effect.

Organizations exempt under Sec. 23701d of the law (item (4), above) may lose their exemption by engaging in certain "prohibited transactions" or by accumulating income under certain conditions.

In *Appeal of Vinemore Company, etc.* (1972) (CCH CALIFORNIA TAX REPORTS, ¶ 10-245.40), the BOE revoked a hospital corporation's charitable exemption retroactively six years after the exemption was granted; the FTB had not been informed earlier of the corporation's improper activities.

• *Permissible lobbying activities*

Both California and federal laws provide for permissible levels of lobbying activities that a tax-exempt organization, which elects to apply these provisions, can engage in without losing its exempt status. (Sec. 23704.5, Rev. & Tax. Code) However, California has not conformed to the federal provisions imposing a 25% tax on "excess expenditures." (Sec. 23740, Rev. & Tax. Code; Sec. 23741, Rev. & Tax. Code)

¶808

• *No California provision for court review*

The federal law provides for court review of Internal Revenue Service rulings regarding tax-exempt status under certain conditions; there is nothing comparable in the California law.

¶809 Taxation of Business Income of Exempt Corporations

Law: Secs. 23702, 23731-37, 23741, 23771 (CCH CALIFORNIA TAX REPORTS, ¶10-245).

Comparable Federal: Secs. 501-03, 511-15 (CCH U.S. MASTER TAX GUIDE ¶655— 685).

California law concerning the taxation of unrelated business income of exempt organizations is substantially the same as federal law as of the current IRC tie-in date (¶803), except that certain rentals received by one exempt church from another are exempt from California tax. Unrelated business income is subject to California income tax, rather than franchise tax. (Sec. 23731 et seq., Rev. & Tax. Code)

A U.S. circuit court of appeals has held that the California statute that imposed tax on the unrelated business taxable income (UBTI) of otherwise tax-exempt trusts was not preempted by the federal Employee Retirement Income Security Act of 1974 (ERISA). (*Hattem v. Schwarzenegger* (2006) (CCH CALIFORNIA TAX REPORTS, ¶15-215.91))

California adopts by reference federal law for treatment of "unrelated debt-financed income" as of the current IRC tie-in date (¶803). Under the rule, tax-exempt organizations in partnership with taxable entities treat income from debt-financed real property as unrelated business taxable income if partnership allocations are neither (1) qualified allocations nor (2) permissible disproportionate allocations. The purpose of the federal rule is to prevent the allocation of tax losses to the taxable partner.

Income from bingo games conducted by exempt organizations is exempt from California tax (Sec. 23710, Rev. & Tax. Code); however, income from games of chance is subject to the federal tax on unrelated business income.

• *Return required for business income*

Organizations otherwise exempt that are subject to tax on unrelated business income are required to file returns reporting their income from taxable activities and to pay tax on such income, under the rules applicable to organizations that are not exempt (¶811).

¶810 Returns—Time and Place for Filing

Law: Secs. 1502, 1502.1, 2117, 2117.1, Corporations Code; Secs. 18410, 18510, 18572, 18601-23, 21027, Rev. & Tax. Code (CCH CALIFORNIA TAX REPORTS, ¶3-015, 3-020, 89-102—89-112).

Comparable Federal: Secs. 6065, 6072, 6081, 6102, 7508A (CCH U.S. MASTER TAX GUIDE ¶211, 2460, 2505, 2537, 2557).

California Forms: Form 100 (California Corporation Franchise or Income Tax Return), Form 100S (California S Corporation Franchise or Income Tax Return), Form 100X (Amended Corporation Franchise or Income Tax Return), FTB 3539 (Payment for Automatic Extension for Corps and Exempt Organizations), FTB 3586 (Payment Voucher for Corporation E-filed Returns), FTB 8453-C (California e-file Return Authorization for Corporations), FTB 8633 (California Application to Participate in the e-file Program).

For taxable years beginning on or after January 1, 2016, C corporations subject to tax are required to file an annual income or franchise tax return by the 15th day of the fourth month after the close of the taxable year. For taxable years beginning prior to January 1, 2016, the C corporation return due date was the 15th day of the third month after the close of the taxable year. This is the same as the federal due date. The filing date for S corporations is the 15th day of the third month after the close of the taxable year. The filing date for farmers' cooperative associations is the 15th day of the ninth month after the close of the taxable year. (Sec. 18601, Rev. & Tax. Code)

CCH Comment: Federal Holidays

Any federal legal holiday recognized by the Internal Revenue Service under IRC §7503 will automatically be considered a legal holiday for California corporation franchise and income tax purposes. (Sec. 18410, Rev. & Tax. Code)

Practitioner Comment: California Conforms to Federal Due Dates for Partnership and C Corporation Returns

On September 14, 2016, Governor Jerry Brown signed A.B. 1775, which conforms California to federal tax due dates for partnerships and corporations. For years beginning on or after January 1, 2016, partnerships, S Corporations, and LLCs treated as partnerships will have a due date of the 15th day of the third month following the end of their taxable year, which is a month earlier for partnerships and LLCs. C Corporations and LLCs treated as corporations will have a due date of the 15th day of the fourth month following the end of their taxable year.

The Franchise Tax Board may grant a filing extension of no more than seven months for taxpayers subject to the Corporation Tax Law, and no more than six months for entities subject to the Personal Income Tax Law. The Franchise Tax Board indicated in FTB Notice 2016-04 that for tax years beginning on or after January 1, 2016, it will allow pass-through extensions for calendar-year taxpayers of no later than September 15 (previously October 15) and corporate or corporate equivalent extensions for calendar-year taxpayers of no later than October 15 (also previously October 15).

Taxpayers should be wary that the due date changes would also apply to short period returns for years beginning on or after January 1, 2016. As such, the importance of these changes could have effect before the calendar year filing season.

Chris Whitney, Contributing Editor

Information returns are discussed at ¶1412. See ¶811 for a discussion of exempt organization returns. Group returns that may be filed by corporations on behalf of their nonresident directors are discussed at ¶714.

• *Short-period returns*

A California short-period return is due the same day as the federal short-period return, which is the 15th day of the third calendar month following the close of the short period. If a federal short-period return is not required, the California short-period return is due within two months and 15 days after the close of the short period. (Sec. 18601, Rev. & Tax. Code)

• *Qualified use taxes*

Corporations not required to hold a seller's permit or to register with the California State Board of Equalization may self-report their qualified use tax liabilities on their timely filed original corporation franchise or income tax returns. Persons electing to report such taxes are required to report and remit the tax on a franchise or income tax return that corresponds to the taxable year in which the use tax liability was incurred. Payments made on a franchise or income tax return of a taxpayer that reports use tax on the return must be applied first to satisfy the use tax liability, with any excess amount then being applied to the outstanding taxes, penalties, and interest owed to the FTB. (Sec. 6452.1, Rev. & Tax. Code; Sec. 18510, Rev. & Tax. Code) See ¶1511 for details concerning the payment of use taxes.

• *Extensions of time*

An automatic six-month extension will be granted for filing C corporation franchise or income tax returns (unless the corporation is suspended on the original

¶810

due date for the return), if the return is filed by the 15th day of the 10th month following the close of the taxable year (October 15 for calendar-year taxpayers). The extended due date for S corporations is the 15th day of the 9th month following the close of the taxable year (September 15 for calendar year taxpayers). The extended due date for farmers' cooperative associations is the 15th day of the 15th month following the close of the taxable year (March 15 of the year following close of taxable year for calendar year taxpayers). The extended due date for exempt organizations filing a Form 199 or Form 109 is the 15th day of the 11th month following the close of the taxable year (November 15 for calendar-year taxpayers). Employees' trusts and IRAs filing Form 109 must file by the 15th day of the 10th month following the close of the trusts' taxable year (October 15 for calendar-year taxpayers). (Sec. 18604, Rev. & Tax. Code; *FTB Notice 2016-04*, CCH CALIFORNIA TAX REPORTS, ¶406-588; FTB 3539, Payment for Automatic Extension for Corps and Exempt Organizations)

An extension of time for filing does not extend the time for paying the underlying tax. Interest and late payment penalties will still accrue from the date the original return was due.

Tax payments must be accompanied by FTB 3539 (Payment for Automatic Extension for Corps and Exempt Orgs). A single FTB 3539 may be filed for all affiliated corporations filing a combined report (¶1313). Corporations required to pay their tax liability by electronic funds transfer (EFT) (¶814) must remit all payments by EFT to avoid penalties and, thus, do not submit FTB 3539.

California incorporates federal law that extends filing deadlines for victims of Presidentially-declared disasters or terroristic or militaristic actions for a period of up to one year and also allows the one-year extension for victims of gubernatorially-declared disasters. (Sec. 18572, Rev. & Tax. Code)

The deadlines that may be postponed are the same as those that may be postponed by reason of a taxpayer's service in a combat zone (¶109).

• *Interest on late payments*

Interest is charged from the regular due date of the return to the date of payment, if the amount paid by the regular due date of the return (without regard to extensions) is less than the tax payable with the return. However, interest is abated for late payments made by corporations located in disaster areas (¶711). Interest is charged on late payments, at the rate charged on deficiencies as explained at ¶1410. See ¶1411 regarding the penalty for failure to pay by the regular due date, in cases where an extension is granted for filing.

• *Filing by mail*

Returns and requests for extension of time filed by mail are deemed to be filed on the date they are placed in the U.S. mail, provided they are properly addressed and the postage is prepaid. When the due date falls on a Saturday, Sunday, or other legal holiday, returns may be filed on the following business day. The date of the postmark is ordinarily deemed to be the date of mailing. Although it may be possible to prove that the return was actually mailed on an earlier date, it is obviously desirable to mail early enough to be sure the postmark is timely. (Note that a postage meter date is not a "postmark.") If private delivery services are used, items should be sent in time to be *received* by the deadline. (Sec. 11003, Govt. Code)

Returns should be mailed to the FTB in Sacramento, or filed with any area or district office. The Sacramento mailing address is shown in the return instructions.

• *Filing using electronic technology*

Certain business entity returns that are prepared using tax preparation software must be filed using electronic technology in a form and manner prescribed by the FTB, unless a waiver is granted. The requirement applies to original or amended franchise and income tax returns required to be filed by corporations, S corporations, partnerships, limited liability companies, and exempt organizations, other than returns for unrelated business taxable income. (Sec. 18621.10, Rev. & Tax. Code) For taxable years beginning on or after January 1, 2017, a penalty may be imposed for failure to comply with the e-filing requirement (see ¶1411).

Practitioner Comment: California Business Entity E-file Requirement

During the FTB's meeting in December 2013, board members voted to approve a legislative proposal regarding e-filing requirements of business returns. On September 19, 2014, this proposed legislation, (A.B. 2754), was signed into law (Cal. Rev. & Tax. Code § 18621.10). As a result, effective January 1, 2015, for taxable years beginning on or after January 1, 2014, any business (corporation, limited liability company, partnership, and certain exempt organizations) that prepares an original or amended tax return using tax preparation software, is required to electronically (e-file) its return with the FTB.

Cal. Rev. & Tax. Code § 18621.10 is effective January 1, 2015, and businesses that fail to comply will be subject to a penalty if the failure to e-file is due to willful neglect and not reasonable cause. The penalty for the initial e-file failure is $100 and $500 for each subsequent failure, and is applied at the entity level. The penalty will take effect starting January 1, 2017.

A waiver may be obtained due to, but not limited to, the following reasons: 1) technology constraints, 2) undue financial burden, and 3) other circumstances that constitute reasonable cause and not willful neglect. The waiver must be requested annually and may be submitted online through the FTB's website. For combined reporting filers, only one waiver is required for the parent and all taxpayer members of the group. The waiver request may be made at any time before return filing.

Chris Whitney, Contributing Editor

California conforms to federal income tax provisions allowing electronic postmarks as proof of the date electronically filed returns are deemed filed.

• *Alternative signatures*

Unlike the IRS, the FTB does not offer an electronic signature option for its business e-file program. The business taxpayer, electronic return originator, and paid preparer must sign the California e-file Return Authorization Form (FTB 8453-C, FTB 8453-P, FTB 8453-LLC, or FTB 8453-EO) prior to the transmission of the e-file return. This form may be retained by the preparer or business taxpayer or be scanned and included as an attachment to the business e-file return, but should not be mailed to the FTB. (*Frequently Asked Questions*, FTB, http://www.ftb.ca.gov/professionals/busefile/profaq.shtml#9)

• *Form for return*

Form 100 is used to file a California corporation franchise or income tax return. Schedules on the California return provide for adjustments and other information needed for state purposes. Corporations may substitute federal schedules for California schedules as long as they attach all supporting federal schedules and reconcile any differences between federal and California figures.

Corporations with total assets of at least $10 million but less than $50 million as of the last day of the taxable year must complete the California Schedule M-1 and must attach either: (1) a copy of the federal Schedule M-3 (Form 1120/1120-F) and related attachments; (2) a complete copy of the federal return; or (3) the federal Schedule M-3 (Form 1120/1120-F) in a spreadsheet format. Corporations using the federal reconciliation method must transfer the amount from line 28 of Form 1120 to line 1, side 1, of Form 100, and attach the federal return and all pertinent schedules, or copy the information from page 1 of Form 1120 onto Schedule F and transfer the amount from line 30, Schedule F, to line 1, side 1, of Form 100. (Instructions, Form 100, Corporation Franchise or Income Tax Return)

S corporations file Form 100S.

CCH Comment: Attaching Letters To Forms Inadvisable

The FTB advises tax practitioners against attaching letters to their clients' corporation franchise and income tax returns, stating that in most cases tax practitioners will get faster results by calling the FTB's Tax Practitioner Hotline at (916) 845-7057 to ask specific questions regarding their clients' tax returns or other issues requiring timely action. The Tax Practitioner Hotline is open from 8 a.m. to 5 p.m., Monday through Friday. Questions may also be sent by fax to (916) 845-6377, 24 hours a day, seven days a week. Often letters attached to returns are not answered until they have traveled through the FTB's entire return processing system and are ultimately rerouted to the FTB's Taxpayer Service Center for a reply, which may take many weeks. Also, letters are sometimes inadvertently filed without a reply. (*Tax News*, California Franchise Tax Board, July/August 2005)

- *Whole dollar reporting*

The California law conforms to federal law with respect to whole dollar reporting (sometimes referred to as "cents-less" reporting). Under these rules, if any amount required to be shown on a return, statement, or other document is other than a whole dollar, the fractional part of a dollar may be rounded to the nearest dollar; that is, amounts under 50¢ are dropped and amounts from 50¢ to 99¢ increased to the next dollar. (Sec. 18623, Rev. & Tax. Code)

- *Reporting federal changes*

A taxpayer filing an amended federal return is required to file an amended California return within six months if the change increases the amount of California tax due. Corporate taxpayers are required to report changes or corrections to any item required to be reported on a federal tax return within six months of the federal determination of the change or correction, regardless of whether the change or correction increases the amount of tax due. The "date of the final federal determination" is defined as the date that each adjustment or resolution resulting from an IRS examination is assessed pursuant to IRC Sec. 6203. (Sec. 18622, Rev. & Tax. Code)

The taxpayer is required to concede the accuracy of the federal determination or state where the determination is erroneous. Failure to comply with these requirements may result in extending the running of the statute of limitations on deficiency assessments (¶1409). In *LSI Logic Corp. and Subsidiaries* (2009), CCH CALIFORNIA TAX REPORTS, ¶404-846, the State Board of Equalization held that the taxpayers failed to timely report federal changes, because the date of the final federal determination was the date that the adjusted liability of the taxpayers was recorded on the taxpayers' federal business master file, not the date of execution of the closing agreement.

- *Exempt organizations*

If an exempt-organization return (¶811) is filed in good faith and the organization is later held to be taxable, the return filed is deemed a valid taxable return for the organization. Receivers, trustees in bankruptcy, or assignees operating the property or business of a corporation are required to file returns.

- *Report to Secretary of State*

Sections 1502 and 2117 of the Corporations Code require domestic and foreign corporations to file with the Secretary of State an annual report showing names of officers and directors and other information. The first report must be filed within 90 days of incorporation. Thereafter, reports are due annually by the date indicated by the Secretary of the State on the form mailed to the corporation. The tax law provides for assessment by the FTB of a penalty for failure to file this report (¶1411). Corporations may file a brief statement in lieu of the biennial report in cases where no changes have occurred during the filing period.

In addition to the annual report, publicly traded corporations and foreign corporations must annually file a sworn statement on a form provided by the Secretary of State that contains certain information, including the following:

— the name of the independent auditor that prepared the most recent report on the corporation's annual financial statements as well as the name of the independent auditor employed by the corporation on the date of the statement if different from the auditor that prepared the report;

— a description of any other services performed for the corporation during its two most recent fiscal years and the period between the end of its most recent fiscal year and the date of the statement by the independent auditor, its parent corporation, or a subsidiary or corporate affiliate of the independent auditor or its parent corporation;

— the compensation for the corporation's most recent fiscal year that is paid to each member of the board of directors and paid to each of the five most highly compensated executive officers who are not members of the board as well as the chief executive officer's compensation if not already included. Compensation that must be reported includes any shares issued, options for shares granted, and similar equity-based compensation;

— a description of any loan, including the loan amount and terms, made to any corporate board member during the corporation's two most recent fiscal years.

— a statement indicating whether an order for relief has been entered in a bankruptcy case with respect to the corporation, its executive officers, or corporate board members during the previous 10 years;

— a statement indicating whether any board members or corporate executive officer was convicted of fraud during the previous 10 years unless the conviction was overturned or expunged; and

— a description of any material pending legal proceedings, other than ordinary routine litigation incidental to the business, to which the corporation or any of its subsidiaries is a party or of which any of their property is the subject, as specified by Item 103 of Regulation S-K of the Securities Exchange Commission (Section 229.103 of Title 12 of the Code of Federal Regulations). Also, a description of any material legal proceeding during which the corporation was found legally liable by entry of a final judgment or final order that was not overturned on appeal during the previous five years must be provided.

(Sec. 1502, Corp. Code; Sec. 1502.1, Corp. Code; Sec. 2117, Corp. Code; Sec. 2117.1, Corp. Code)

The statement is due within 150 days after the end of the corporation's fiscal year and will be open for public inspection.

• *Effect of failure to file or pay*

A corporation that fails to file a return or to make required payments may have its corporate rights suspended (¶824).

• *Filing date for DISCs*

California has nothing comparable to the special federal provisions for Domestic International Sales Corporations (DISCs). (Sec. 23051.5, Rev. & Tax. Code) Accordingly, the special federal filing date for such corporations has no application to California returns. See *Appeal of Cerwin Vega International* (1978) (CCH CALIFORNIA Tax

Reports ¶ 89-202.40), in which penalties were imposed on a DISC for underpayment of estimated tax and late payment of tax.

¶811 Returns of Exempt Organizations

Law: Secs. 23703, 23771-78 (CCH CALIFORNIA TAX REPORTS, ¶ 10-245).

Comparable Federal: Secs. 6012(a), 6033, 6652 (CCH U.S. MASTER TAX GUIDE ¶ 537, 625, 2145).

California Forms: Form 109 (California Exempt Organization Business Income Tax Return), Form 199 (California Exempt Organization Annual Information Return), FTB 3539 (Payment for Automatic Extension for Corporations and Exempt Organizations).

Exempt organizations (including charitable trusts) are required to file annual information returns (Form 199). (Sec. 23771, Rev. & Tax. Code) The Form 199 may be filed electronically.

• *Exceptions to filing requirement*

The filing of information returns is not required for the following organizations and activities:

— churches;

— religious orders; and

— exempt organizations, except private foundations, with gross receipts of $50,000 or less.

(Sec. 23772, Rev. & Tax. Code)

According to the Instructions to Form 199, a three-year average is used to compute the $50,000 threshold discussed in the third item above. New organizations must file Form 199 if their gross receipts are $75,000 or less for their first year of existence or if their average gross receipts are $60,000 or less for their first two years of existence.

Some other organizations are excepted under discretionary authority of the Franchise Tax Board (FTB).

A religious organization that refuses to file because of religious convictions may be permitted to submit a notarized statement instead. (Sec. 23774, Rev. & Tax. Code)

Organizations exempt from the information return filing requirements as a result of the $50,000 threshold requirement, or who have been excused from the annual return filing requirements by the FTB, must file an annual informational notice, FTB Form 199N, California e-Postcard by the 15th day of the fifth month after the close of the organization's tax year. The Form 199N provides identifying information for the organization, such as the organization's legal name, mailing and Internet Web site addresses, name and address of a principal officer, and evidence of the continuing basis for the organization's exemption. These organizations are also required to alert the FTB upon the termination of their existence.

Failure to provide the required annual statement for three consecutive years will result in the organization's exempt status being revoked. Once revoked, the organization must reapply for reinstatement, regardless of whether the organization was originally required to make an application for tax-exempt status. However, the FTB may at its discretion retroactively reinstate the exemption upon a showing of reasonable cause. Income received between the revocation date and renewed exemption date may be taxable. (Sec. 23772, Rev. & Tax. Code; *FTB Technical Advice Memorandum 2011-4*, CCH CALIFORNIA TAX REPORTS, ¶ 405-447)

CCH Comment: Substantiation Requirements

If an organization does not have financial records to support its claim that it did not exceed the $50,000 threshold, the FTB may accept a signed statement of a duly elected officer or board member attesting to the fact that the entity did not have gross receipts normally exceeding $50,000 for certain years. The FTB has the authority to exercise judgment to determine what supporting documentation is sufficient. (FTB *Technical Advice Memorandum 2011-4*, CCH CALIFORNIA TAX REPORTS, ¶405-447)

• *Requirements for returns*

Although the California requirements for information returns are generally similar to the federal requirements, there are some differences and the FTB should be consulted in case of any question.

Each controlling organization required to file an exempt organization information return must include on its information return a listing of a variety of transactions between the controlling organization and its controlled entities. (Sec. 23772(b)(12), Rev. & Tax. Code)

• *Private foundations*

California private foundations file Form 199 as do other exempt organizations. Instead of completing certain parts of the form, a private foundation may submit a completed copy of the current Form RRF-1, Registration/Renewal Fee Report (including federal Form 990) or a completed copy of federal Form 990-PF with appropriate schedules.

• *Filing with Registrar of Charitable Trusts*

In addition to the information return requirements discussed above, a charitable corporation, association, or a trustee holding property for charitable purposes is required to register with the Registrar of Charitable Trusts, in the office of the Attorney General in Sacramento, and to file an annual report (RRF-1) with the Registry. (Some types of organizations, including churches, schools, and hospitals, are specifically exempted from this requirement.) An organization that fails to file a required registration or annual report with the Registry on or before the due date (four months and 15 days after the close of the organization's calendar or fiscal year) or extended due date may be subject to assessment of the minimum tax and loss of its tax exemption for the period of noncompliance.

Once the Attorney General notifies the FTB that a corporation is out of compliance with the registration and reporting requirements, the FTB mails a notice to the corporation indicating that the corporation has 120 days to get back into compliance, otherwise the FTB will revoke the corporation's tax-exempt status. (Sec. 23703, Rev. & Tax. Code) The organization's tax exemption or corporate status may be revoked for failure to pay the minimum tax assessed within one year after the close of the organization's accounting period. (Sec. 23775, Rev. & Tax. Code)

Charities with gross receipts or total assets of $25,000 or more must also file a copy of IRS Form 990, 990-EZ, or 990-PF and attachments with the Registry of Charitable Trusts (Instructions to Form RRF-1).

• *Filing fees*

The information returns discussed above (Form 199), with limited exceptions, must be accompanied by a $10 fee if filed on time (including extensions), or by a $25 fee if filed later. (Sec. 23772, Rev. Tax. Code)

• *Time for filing/penalties*

The due date for information returns and statements, including statements from Coverdell education savings accounts, is the 15th day of the fifth month (fourth month for Coverdell education savings accounts) following the end of the organization's taxable year. Employees' trusts and IRAs must file by the 15th day of the fourth month following the close of the taxable year. (Sec. 23771, Rev. & Tax. Code; FTB 3539, Payment for Automatic Extension for Corps and Exempt Organizations) An exempt organization that fails to timely file an information return without reasonable cause is subject to a penalty for late filing, at the rate of $5 per month, with a maximum of $40. Also, a special penalty of $5 per month, with a $25 maximum, may be imposed where a private foundation fails to respond to a demand for filing. (Sec. 23772, Rev. & Tax. Code)

• *Organizations penalized for failure to file*

In *Appeal of Young Women's Christian Association of Santa Monica* (1971) (CCH CALIFORNIA TAX REPORTS, ¶ 10-245.75), the BOE upheld the imposition under prior law of the $100 minimum tax, plus interest, for failure to file annual information returns, despite the fact that the Internal Revenue Service did not require federal information returns for the years involved. The organization did not come within the exception for filing of returns by charitable organizations, because it did not establish compliance with the exception's requirement that the organization be "primarily supported by contributions of the general public."

• *Effect of failure to file or pay*

An exempt organization that fails to file required reports or to pay any tax due within 12 months from the close of its taxable year may have its corporate rights suspended or forfeited. Provision is made for relief from such suspension under certain conditions. Further, the FTB may revoke the organization's exemption if it fails to file any corporation franchise or income tax return or pay any tax due. (Sec. 23775 et. seq., Rev. & Tax. Code)

• *Extensions of time*

Exempt organizations will be granted an automatic six-month "paperless" extension. The extended due date is the 15th day of the eleventh month following the close of the taxable year (fiscal year filers) or November 15 (calendar year filers). For employees' trusts and IRAs, the extended due date is the 15th day of the tenth month following the close of the taxable year (fiscal year filers) or October 15 (calendar year filers). An extension of time for filing does not extend the time for paying tax. Tax payments must be accompanied by FTB 3539 (Payment for Automatic Extension for Corps and Exempt Orgs). (Reg. 25402, 18 CCR; *FTB Notice 2016-04*, CCH CALIFORNIA TAX REPORTS, ¶ 406-588; FTB 3539, Payment for Automatic Extension for Corps and Exempt Organizations)

• *Organizations with nonexempt income*

Exempt political organizations are not required to file the annual information returns or statements discussed above. (Sec. 23701r, Rev. & Tax. Code) However, such organizations that have more than $100 of income from sources other than contributions, dues, and political fund-raising ("exempt function income") should file a corporation income tax return. (See ¶ 808 for discussion of exemption for political organizations.)

Exempt homeowners' associations that have more than $100 of income from sources other than membership dues, fees, and assessments should file a corporation income tax return (¶ 915). (Sec. 23701t, Rev. & Tax. Code)

An exempt organization, other than a political organization, a homeowner's association, or an organization controlled by the state carrying out a state function, must file an exempt organization business income tax return (Form 109) in addition to its annual information return (Form 199) if it has gross income of $1,000 or more from an unrelated trade or business. The electronic funds transfer requirements discussed at ¶814 also apply to nonprofit corporations with nonexempt income.

• *Filing with Secretary of State*

Sections 6210 and 8210 of the California Nonprofit Corporation Law require nonprofit corporations to file with the Secretary of State an annual report showing names of officers and other information. The tax law provides for assessment by the FTB of a penalty for failure to file this report (¶1411).

¶812 Consolidated Returns

Law: Sec. 23361-64a (CCH CALIFORNIA TAX REPORTS, ¶89-102).

Comparable Federal: Sec. 1501-4 (CCH U.S. MASTER TAX GUIDE ¶295).

The law contains provision for filing of consolidated franchise tax returns by certain groups of railroad corporations, where the degree of affiliation through a common parent corporation is 80% or more. Unlike federal law, California law contains no general provisions allowing affiliated groups of corporations other than railroads the privilege of making consolidated returns. However, the Franchise Tax Board may require any affiliated corporations to file a consolidated return to prevent tax evasion or to clearly reflect income earned by the corporations from business in this state (¶1110). (Sec. 23361 et seq., Rev. & Tax. Code)

Although California permits only railroad corporations to file *consolidated returns*, California does permit or require *combined reports* by corporations owned or controlled by the same interests, under some conditions. See ¶1310 for further discussion of combined reporting.

Because California does not incorporate IRC Sec. 1504, which defines affiliated groups, California does not adopt amendments to IRC Sec. 1504, that allowed corporations to offset their income with net operating losses incurred by an Alaska Native Corporation. (*The Pillsbury Co. v. Franchise Tax Board* (2004) (CCH CALIFORNIA TAX REPORTS, ¶10-515.61))

¶813 Estimated Tax

Law: Secs. 19010, 19021-27, 19136.8, 19142-61, 19363-64, 26081.5 (CCH CALIFORNIA TAX REPORTS, ¶89-104, 89-206, 89-210).

Comparable Federal: Secs. 6611, 6655 (CCH U.S. MASTER TAX GUIDE ¶225 et seq., 2765, 2890).

California Forms: Form 100-ES (Corporation Estimated Tax), FTB 5806 (Underpayment of Estimated Tax by Corporations).

All corporations and exempt organizations subject to franchise or income tax, other than REMICs, are required to pay estimated tax during the taxable year. The estimated tax of a corporation subject to the franchise tax cannot be less than the minimum tax (¶816). (Sec. 19025, Rev. & Tax. Code) Instructions to FTB 5806 state that a newly formed or qualified corporation is required to make estimated tax payments based on its estimated tax liability after credits for its first taxable year. To avoid a penalty, the taxpayer should use its annualized current year income.

If an S corporation has a qualified subchapter S subsidiary (QSub) (discussed at ¶806), the S corporation's estimated tax payments must not be less than the S corporation's minimum tax plus the subsidiary's minimum tax. (Reg. 25562, 18 CCR) California law does not require corporations to file declarations, but they must file their estimated tax with payment vouchers (Form 100-ES). Banks and financial corporations should compute their estimated tax at the special rate for such taxpayers explained at ¶816. California has not adopted the federal provision that waives the underpayment penalty if the tax shown on the return is less than $500.

See ¶814 for a discussion of taxpayers required to submit estimated tax payments through electronic funds transfer. Such corporations do not submit a Form 100-ES.

• *Computation of estimated tax payments*

Practice Note: "Tax" Defined

For purposes of the estimated tax requirements, "tax" includes the alternative minimum tax, taxes from Schedule D, excess net passive income tax, and the minimum franchise tax. (Instructions, FTB 5806, Underpayment of Estimated Tax by Corporations).

If the estimated tax is not over the minimum tax, the entire amount is payable on the 15th day of the fourth month of the corporation's taxable year. For S corporations, this includes the minimum tax for a QSub incorporated in California, qualified to do business in California, or doing business in California. If the QSub is acquired after the due date for the first installment, the minimum tax for the QSub is due with the next required installment. (Sec. 19025, Rev. & Tax. Code) (Instructions, Form 100-ES, Corporation Estimated Tax)

Estimated tax over the minimum tax is payable in installments on the 15th day of the fourth, sixth, ninth, and 12th months of the taxable year, respectively. The amount of the installment payments is equal to 30% of the estimated amount due for the first installment, 40% for the second installment, 0% for the third installment, and 30% for the fourth installment. The first installment generally may not be less than the minimum tax, unless the taxpayer is a newly formed or qualified corporation, has been granted an exemption by the Franchise Tax Board, or is subject to income tax only (rather than franchise tax) under California law.

If the requirements for making payments of estimated tax are first met after the first day of the fourth month, the payments are spread over the appropriate remaining quarters, depending on the quarter in which the requirements are first met, as in the case of the federal tax.

Corporations not required to make an estimated tax payment for the first quarter must make estimated tax payments of 60%, 0, and 40% for the second, third, and fourth quarter installments, respectively. Corporations not required to make an estimated tax payment for the first and second quarter must make estimated tax payments of 70% and 30%, for third, and fourth quarter installments, respectively. (*Tax News*, California Franchise Tax Board, May 31, 2010)

• *Penalty for underpayment*

A penalty, in the form of an addition to the tax, is imposed when there has been an underpayment of estimated tax. (Sec. 19142, Rev. & Tax. Code) The additional tax is computed as a percentage of the amount of the underpayment, for the period of underpayment. (Sec. 19144, Rev. & Tax. Code)

The penalty rate is the same as the interest rate on deficiencies and refunds, which is established semiannually (see ¶711 for rates). However, the penalty rate is not compounded.

An underpayment is defined as the excess of the amount that would be required to be paid on each installment of estimated tax if the estimated tax were equal to 100% of the tax shown on the return, over the amount actually paid on or before the due date of each installment. The tax shown on an amended return filed after the original due date, including extensions, or the tax as finally determined, is not to be used in computing underpayment penalties. If the tax due is the minimum tax and the corporation is not a "large corporation" (see discussion below), then the addition to the tax because of underpayment of any installment is calculated on the amount of the minimum tax. (Sec. 19144, Rev. & Tax. Code; Sec. 19147, Rev. & Tax. Code)

The period of underpayment runs from the due date of each installment to the normal due date of the return, or to the date on which the underpayment was paid, if payment was made prior to the due date of the return. (Sec. 19145, Rev. & Tax. Code)

• *Exceptions to underpayment penalty*

No penalty may be imposed for underpayment of estimated tax to the extent the underpayment was created or increased as the direct result of the following:

— an erroneous levy, erroneous processing action, or erroneous collection action by the FTB (Sec. 19136.7, Rev. & Tax. Code); or

— legislation chaptered and operative for the taxable year of the underpayment. (Sec. 19142(b), Rev. & Tax. Code).

CCH Comment: *Federal Legislation*

The relief discussed above does not apply to federal law changes that may create an underpayment of state tax, because federal law is enacted without being chaptered. (Bill Analysis, Ch. 242 (S.B. 14), Laws 2005, Senate Floor, August 23, 2005)

CCH Comment: *No Excuses*

Except as noted above, the estimated tax underpayment penalty is mandatory and will be imposed unless one of the six exceptions below applies. There is no good cause or lack of willful neglect exception. (Sec. 19147, Rev. & Tax. Code; Sec. 19148, Rev. & Tax. Code)

California shields a corporation from penalty if the following conditions are satisfied:

— total payments equal or exceed the tax shown on the prior year's return, prorated to each installment (this exception has limited application to "large corporations");

— the installment meets the required percentage of the tax due, computed by placing the taxpayer's net income (or alternative minimum taxable income, if applicable) on an annualized basis as outlined by statute;

— the required percentage of the tax for the taxable year was paid by withholding;

— the required percentage of the net income for the taxable year consisted of items subject to withholding and the amount of the first installment was at least equal to the minimum tax.

(Sec. 19147, Rev. & Tax. Code)

Practitioner Comment: *Upon Challenge—Exception to Annualized Income Exception*

In a non-citable summary decision, the State Board of Equalization abated a corporation's penalty for underpayment of estimated tax for the first and fourth quarters, when it met the "annualized income" exception. The corporation was still liable for the penalty in the second and third quarters. Under Cal. Rev. & Tax. Code Sec. 19147, taxpayers claiming the "annualized income" exception must meet the applicable percentages in all four quarters. Accordingly, where the FTB imposes a material estimated tax penalty, taxpayers may want to consider an appeal if the annualized income exception is met in one or more of the quarters. (*Howard Hughes Medical Institute*, California State Board of Equalization, No. 246269, August 24, 2004, CCH CALIFORNIA TAX REPORTS, ¶ 89-206.33)

Chris Whitney, Contributing Editor

• *Reporting of underpayment*

Where the figures on the return indicate that there has been an underpayment of estimated tax, FTB 5806 should be attached to show the computation of penalty or to explain why no penalty is due. (Federal forms should not be used with California returns.)

To request a waiver of underpayment penalties created or increased by a provision of law chaptered and operative for the taxable year of the underpayment, taxpayers should:

— use FTB 5806 to compute the full underpayment penalty that would normally be due;

— write "Waiver" across the top of FTB 5806;

— attach an explanation to FTB 5806 giving the specific law change that caused the underpayment and showing the computation and the amount of penalty to be waived; and

— attach FTB 5806 to the face of the return.

A second form FTB 5806, clearly marked "Second form FTB 5806" may be used to show the computation of any penalty not related to a change in the law. (Instructions, FTB 5806, Underpayment of Estimated Tax by Corporations)

• *Penalty strictly applied*

In *Appeal of Bechtel Incorporated* (1978) (CCH CALIFORNIA TAX REPORTS, ¶ 89-210.301), the taxpayer made estimated-tax payments in irregular amounts, totaling $495,000, against an ultimate liability of $1,059,849. The taxpayer claimed relief from penalty on the ground that the total payments exceeded the tax of $459,795 shown on its return for the preceding year. The State Board of Equalization (BOE) held that an underpayment penalty of $13,547 was properly imposed on the first two installments, because they did not meet the specific requirements for avoidance of penalty based on the preceding year's tax.

In *Appeal of Decoa, Inc.* (1976) (CCH CALIFORNIA TAX REPORTS, ¶ 89-210.302), the taxpayer was a Florida corporation that began doing business in California in 1973. The corporation failed to pay estimated tax for its 1973 income year. The BOE held that the underpayment penalty was mandatory and could not be excused because of "extenuating circumstances." Relief was not available under the rules based on the preceding year's return, because such a return had not been filed and was not required to be filed. See also *Appeal of International Business Machines Corporation* (1979) (CCH CALIFORNIA TAX REPORTS, ¶ 89-210.303) and *J.F. Shea Co., Inc.* (1979) (CCH CALIFORNIA TAX REPORTS, ¶ 89-210.302); in the latter case an underpayment of $1,100 resulted in a penalty of $8,500.

In *Appeal of Uniroyal, Inc.* (1975) (CCH CALIFORNIA TAX REPORTS, ¶ 89-206.58), the taxpayer could have avoided an underpayment penalty by timely payment of estimated tax of $100 (based on preceding year's tax, before the minimum was increased to $200). However, because the corporation was unable to prove it had filed or paid estimated tax, the penalty was based on the actual tax of $77,895, in accordance with the definition of "underpayment" set forth above. See also *Appeal of Lumbermans Mortgage Company* (1976) (CCH CALIFORNIA TAX REPORTS, ¶ 89-210.302), to the same effect.

• *Refund/credit of overpayment*

Where payments of estimated tax are made and the total amount of tax due on the completed return is subsequently determined to be less than the estimated tax payments, the balance will be refunded or will be credited against other taxes. An overpayment from a prior year return will be credited as of the first estimated installment due date or the date of payment, whichever is later. No interest is payable on overpayments for the period prior to the due date of the return. Further, no interest will be payable if the refund or credit is made within 90 days after the due date or 90 days after the return is filed, whichever is later. See also ¶1419.

If any overpayment of tax is claimed as a credit against estimated tax for the succeeding taxable year, that amount shall be considered as payment of the tax for the succeeding taxable year (whether or not claimed as a credit in the return of estimated tax for the succeeding taxable year), and no claim for credit or refund of that overpayment will be allowed for the taxable year in which the overpayment occurred. (Sec. 19002(e), Rev. & Tax. Code)

• *Combined reports*

In the case of corporations entitled or required to file a combined report, a combined payment of estimated taxes may be made for the group by the parent or other designated "key" corporation, under the procedure described at ¶1313. Alternatively, each member may make its own payments and have its payments applied against the ultimate tax liability of the combined group. (FTB Pub. 1061, Guidelines for Corporations Filing a Combined Report)

• *DISCs required to file*

California has nothing comparable to the special federal provisions for Domestic International Sales Corporations (DISCs). (Sec. 23051.5, Rev. & Tax. Code) Accordingly, such corporations are subject to the regular California rules for payment of estimated tax. See *Appeal of Cerwin-Vega International* (1978) (CCH CALIFORNIA TAX REPORTS, ¶89-206.481), in which penalties were imposed on a DISC for underpayment of estimated tax and late payment of tax.

¶814 Payment of Tax

Law: Secs. 18572, 18604, 19001, 19004, 19005, 19008, 19011, 19021, 19131.5; Reg. 19591, 18 CCR (CCH CALIFORNIA TAX REPORTS, ¶89-108).

Comparable Federal: Secs. 6151, 6161, 6601, 7508A (CCH U.S. MASTER TAX GUIDE ¶215, 2529, 2537).

California Form: FTB 3593 (Extension of Time for Payment of Taxes by a Corporation Expecting a Net Operating Loss Carryback).

Unless a taxpayer enters into an installment agreement (see below), taxpayers, including banks and financial corporations, must pay, on or before the due date of the return, the entire balance of tax due after applying the advance payments made under the estimated tax procedure outlined at ¶813. (Sec. 19001, Rev. & Tax. Code) Payment in the form of a check must be payable in U.S. funds. (Sec. 19005, Rev. & Tax. Code) To expedite processing, it is suggested that payments for balance due and for estimated payments should not be combined in one check. The corporation number should be shown on each check.

• *Extension of time*

An extension of time for filing the return does not extend the time for payment of the tax (¶810). (Sec. 18604, Rev. & Tax. Code) However, various filing and payment deadlines may be extended for victims of federally or gubernatorially-declared disasters or terroristic or militaristic actions for a period of up to one year.

The deadlines that may be postponed are the same as those that may be postponed by reason of a taxpayer's service in a combat zone (¶109). (Sec. 18572, Rev. & Tax. Code)

In addition, California generally conforms to the federal provision (IRC §6164) that allows a corporation expecting a net operating loss (NOL) carryback to extend the time for payment of taxes for the immediately preceding taxable year. IRC §6164(d)(2), relating to the period of extension if an application for tentative carryback adjustment is filed, is inapplicable for California purposes. (Sec. 19131.5, Rev. & Tax. Code) Form FTB 3593 is used to obtain the extension. The payment of tax that can be postponed cannot exceed the expected overpayment from the carryback of the NOL. Only payments of tax that are required to be paid after the filing of form FTB 3593 are eligible for extension. If all the required payments have been paid or were required to have been paid, FTB 3593 should not be filed. For corporations that file a combined report, the parent or key corporation should file a FTB 3593 to obtain the extension for the members in the combined reporting group. FTB 3593 should be filed after the start of the taxable year of the expected NOL but before the tax for the preceding taxable year is required to be paid. In general, the extension for paying the tax expires at the end of the month in which the return for the taxable year of the expected NOL is required to be filed (including extensions). The FTB can terminate the extension if it believes that any part of the form contains erroneous or unreasonable information. The FTB can also terminate the extension if it believes it may not be able to collect the tax. (Instructions, FTB 3593, Extension of Time for Payment of Taxes by a Corporation Expecting a Net Operating Loss Carryback)

• *Payment by mail*

Under Sec. 11002, Govt. Code, a payment is deemed to be made on the date it is mailed, provided the envelope is properly addressed and the postage is prepaid. The federal rule is similar.

•*Payment by credit card*

Corporations, partnerships, and limited liability companies may use Discover, MasterCard, Visa, or American Express credit cards to make their estimated tax payments, extension payments, or payments of amounts due on their current year or prior year tax returns.

• *Payment by electronic funds transfer*

The Franchise Tax Board (FTB) must allow payments to be made by electronic funds transfer (EFT). Such payments will generally be deemed complete on the date the transfer is initiated. A taxpayer whose estimated tax liability exceeds $20,000 or more with respect to any installment, or whose total tax liability exceeds $80,000 in any taxable year must remit payment by such electronic means. (Sec. 19011, Rev. & Tax. Code)

Once a taxpayer is required to make payments by EFT, all subsequent payments must be made by EFT regardless of the taxable year to which the payments apply. However, a taxpayer may elect to discontinue making payments in this manner if the threshold amounts set forth above were not met for the preceding taxable year.

A taxpayer required to remit estimated tax payments electronically may satisfy the requirement by means of an international funds transfer.

A penalty of 10% is imposed if mandated payments are made by other means, unless it is shown that failure to use EFT was for reasonable cause.

• *Web Pay*

Businesses can make the following types of payments online via Web Pay:
— corporate estimated taxes;
— limited liability company taxes and fees;

— current year and amended tax return balances;

— extension payments;

— amounts owed for prior years;

— notices of proposed assessment payments; and

— tax deposit payments for pending audits.

• *Installment agreement*

The FTB may enter into an agreement with a taxpayer that allows the taxpayer to pay the full or partial amount of outstanding corporation franchise or income taxes, interest, and penalties due in installments if the FTB determines that the taxpayer's situation is one of financial hardship. (Sec. 19008, Rev. & Tax. Code)

Comment: Business Entity Applications

Business entities inside the U.S. may request an installment payment arrangement for the payment of unpaid California corporation franchise or income taxes by calling the FTB at 1-888-635-0494. Corporations outside the U.S. should call (916) 845-7033, LLCs outside the U.S. should call (916) 845-7166, and partnerships outside the U.S. should call (916) 845-7165. The fee for business entities to enter into an installment payment plan is $50. (Reg. 19591, 18 CCR)

¶815 Tax Base

Law: Sec. 24341 (CCH California Tax Reports, ¶10-505).

Comparable Federal: Sec. 63 (CCH U.S. Master Tax Guide ¶126).

The California franchise tax and income tax are imposed generally upon net income. "Net income" is defined as the gross income less the deductions allowed. (Sec. 24341, Rev. & Tax. Code) For a discussion of "gross income," see Chapter 9; for "deductions," see Chapter 10.

For taxpayers using the federal reconciliation method (¶803), a corporation begins its net income computation with its federal taxable income, modifies it to account for differences between California and federal law, and, if the corporation also does business in other states, allocates and apportions the modified amount to determine the portion taxable by California.

¶816 Tax Rates

Law: Secs. 17942, 23114, 23151-54, 23181-88, 23501, 23802, 24330 (CCH California Tax Reports, ¶10-215, 10-340, 10-380).

Comparable Federal: None.

The rate of franchise tax and income tax on corporations other than banks and financial corporations or S corporations is 8.84%. (Sec. 23151, Rev. & Tax. Code; Sec. 23501, Rev. & Tax. Code)

• *S corporation rate*

California subjects all S corporations, other than financial corporations, to franchise and income tax at a special 1.5% rate. Financial corporations that are S corporations are taxed at a higher rate of 3.5%. (Sec. 23802, Rev. & Tax. Code)

• *Bank and financial corporation rate*

Financial institutions pay a higher rate, commonly called the "bank rate," designed to equalize the tax burden between financial institutions and other taxpayers. The bank rate is simply equal to the franchise tax rate on nonfinancial corporations plus 2%. Currently, the rate is 10.84%. (Sec. 23802, Rev. & Tax. Code; Sec. 23186, Rev. & Tax. Code)

The reason for the special bank rate is that banks and financial corporations are not subject to personal property taxes and license fees. The additional tax imposed by the bank rate is in lieu of the personal property taxes and license fees that are paid by nonfinancial corporations.

• *Constitutionality of bank rate upheld*

In *Security-First National Bank of Los Angeles, et al. v. Franchise Tax Board* (1961) (CCH CALIFORNIA TAX REPORTS, ¶ 10–105.30), the California Supreme Court upheld the constitutional right of the state to tax banks at the special bank rate. The court held that, because the purpose of the special rate is to equalize tax burdens within the state, it is within the power of the legislature to authorize such taxing procedure and the tax is constitutional.

• *Minimum tax*

The amount of the minimum tax is $800, with some exceptions. The minimum tax is $25 for (1) corporations engaged in gold mining that have been inactive since 1950, and (2) corporations engaged in quicksilver mining that have been inactive since 1971 or have been inactive for a period of 24 consecutive months. In addition, credit unions and nonprofit cooperative associations that are certified by their local board of supervisors are exempt from any minimum tax. However, a credit union must prepay a tax of $25 when it incorporates under the laws of California or when it qualifies to transact business in California. (Sec. 23153, Rev. & Tax. Code)

The minimum tax should not be confused with the alternative minimum tax (¶ 817).

Corporations that incorporate or qualify to do business in California are not subject to the minimum franchise tax for the corporations' first taxable year. (Sec. 23153, Rev. & Tax. Code) This exemption does not apply to limited partnerships, LLCs, limited liability partnerships, regulated investment companies, real estate investment trusts, real estate mortgage investment conduits, financial asset securitization investment trusts, and qualified Subchapter S subsidiaries.

Practice Tip: Nonqualified Corporations Ineligible for Exemption

An out-of-state corporation doing business in California that fails to register with the California Secretary of State is ineligible for the exemption from the minimum tax. However, the nonqualified corporation may still be able to receive first year relief if it subsequently qualifies with the Secretary of State's Office and files a claim for refund within the statute of limitations. (*FTB Tax News*, August 2011, CCH CALIFORNIA TAX REPORTS, ¶ 405-488)

For the 2010 through 2017 tax years, a corporation that is a small business (total income from all sources derived from, or attributable to, the state of $250,000 or less) and that is solely owned by a deployed member of the U.S. Armed Forces will not be subject to the minimum tax for any taxable year that the owner is deployed and the LLC operates at a loss or ceases operation. (Sec. 23153, Rev. & Tax. Code)

Also, a qualified health care service plan that is subject to the managed care organization provider tax (see ¶ 1902) and that has no income other than qualified health care service plan income that is excluded from gross income for California corporation franchise and income tax purposes (see ¶ 929) will be exempt from the $800 minimum franchise tax. (Sec. 24330, Rev. & Tax. Code)

A domestic bank or corporation that files a certificate of dissolution with the Secretary of State and does no business thereafter is not subject to minimum tax for taxable years beginning on or after the date of the filing. (Sec. 23153, Rev. & Tax. Code)

Practitioner Comment: California Clarifies the Minimum Tax Requirement for Certain Entities

The California Franchise Tax Board (FTB) issued Chief Counsel Rulings 2016-01 and 2016-02, stating that a regulated investment company ("RIC") that is organized as a Massachusetts business trust ("MBT") or a Delaware business trust ("DBT") does not qualify as a corporation under Chapter 2 of the California Revenue and Taxation Code and therefore is not liable for the annual minimum franchise tax.

It should be noted that an RIC that is not organized as an MBT or a DBT would generally be subject to both the minimum tax requirement of the corporate franchise tax under Chapter 2 and also the income tax under Chapter 3 of the Revenue and Taxation Code. As a practical matter, RICs are provided a dividends paid deduction for all distributed income and, as such, generally will not incur an income tax liability to the extent the income is not retained in the RIC. Even without an income tax liability, the RICs organized as entities other than these specific business trusts will be subject to the corporate franchise minimum tax.

Further, LLCs registered or doing business in California are subject to the minimum tax, even when disregarded for tax purposes and owned by tax exempt entities. In Chief Counsel Rulings 2015-02 and 2016-04, the California FTB reiterated that the filing and minimum tax requirement for a single-member LLC that is disregarded for income/franchise tax purposes but is doing business in the state will not be removed simply because its single member is a tax-exempt organization.

Chris Whitney, Contributing Editor

A corporation is also not subject to the minimum tax if it did no business in the state during the taxable year and its taxable year was 15 days or less. (Sec. 23114, Rev. & Tax. Code)

Practice Tip: 15-Day Rule

The 15-day rule does not normally apply to entities involved in a conversion, because they are usually continuously doing business during the both periods involved, so both the converting entity and the converted entity will each have a filing requirement. (*FTB Tax News*, November 2012, CCH California Tax Reports, ¶405-732)

In addition, a domestic limited liability company (LLC) that has not conducted any business in California and that has obtained a certificate of cancellation within 12 months from the date that the articles of organization were filed is exempt from the minimum tax. However, the LLC will not be entitled to a refund of any taxes or fees already paid. (Sec. 17941, Rev. & Tax. Code)

Liability for the tax commences with the earlier of the date of incorporation, qualification, or commencing to do business within California, until the effective date of dissolution or withdrawal, or, if later, the date the corporation ceases to do business within California. (Sec. 23153, Rev. & Tax. Code) Once articles of incorporation are filed with the California Secretary of State, a corporation is subject to the franchise tax unless it is specifically exempt—see *Appeal of Mammouth Academy* (1973) (CCH California Tax Reports, ¶10-210.27).

See also *Appeal of Mission Valley East* (1974) (CCH California Tax Reports, ¶10-380.47). In this case the Secretary of State permitted the filing of articles of incorporation, but there was a conflict of corporate name and the corporation was not permitted to pursue its business activity. The State Board of Equalization (BOE) held that the corporation was nevertheless subject to the franchise tax. If the foreign corporation is qualified in the state, it is required to pay the minimum franchise tax even though it does not engage in business in the state; see *Appeal of Tip Top Delights, Inc.* (1970) (CCH California Tax Reports, ¶10-380.261).

¶816

Final year.—A corporation is not required to pay the minimum tax if it does the following:

— files a timely final franchise tax return for a taxable year with the FTB;

— does not do business in this state after the end of the taxable year for which the final franchise tax return was filed; and

— files a certificate of dissolution or surrender with the Secretary of State's Office before the end of the 12-month period beginning with the date the final franchise tax return was filed. (Sec. 23332, Rev. & Tax. Code)

Taxpayers do not need to provide a tax clearance certificate from the FTB prior to obtaining a certificate of dissolution or surrender.

Practitioner Comment: Timely Filing of Certificates of Dissolution for Inactive Entities Can Save Minimum Tax

A limited partnership was found to be liable for the $800 minimum partnership tax for years after it had transferred all of its assets to a limited liability company and ceased operations because the limited partnership failed to file a cancellation certificate, the California State Board of Equalization (BOE) ruled. Under Cal. Rev. & Tax. Code Sec. 17935, every limited partnership that has filed a certificate of limited partnership with the state must pay the annual tax until a certificate of cancellation is filed. As it was undisputed that the limited partnership failed to file a cancellation certificate, the BOE held that the minimum partnership tax was due, notwithstanding the fact that the transferee LLC filed and paid tax as an LLC for the same years [Uncitable Summary Decision, *Appeal of Cinema Plaza Partners, LP.*, Cal. State Bd. of Equal., No. 207907, November 18, 2003 (CCH CALIFORNIA TAX REPORTS, ¶ 10-225.30)].

Similarly, a corporation was liable for the minimum tax for the year in which it surrendered its operations to another corporation because a certificate of dissolution was not timely filed with the Secretary of State. Despite the fact that the corporation had filed a "final" tax return and had clearly surrendered its business operations, state law provides that a corporation remains subject to the minimum tax until it files a certificate of dissolution with the Secretary of State. In the instant case, the certificate was not filed until more than two years after the "final" return was filed (*Red Bud Industries*, Cal. State Bd. of Equal., No. 224004, March 23, 2004 (CCH CALIFORNIA TAX REPORTS, ¶ 10-215.35)).

Chris Whitney, Contributing Editor

• *What is a "financial corporation"*

Reg. 23183, 18 CCR, defines a "financial corporation" as one that deals predominantly in money or moneyed capital in substantial competition with the business of national banks. The definition explicitly excludes corporations that are principally engaged in the business of leasing tangible personal property. A corporation deals "predominantly" in money or moneyed capital if over 50% of its gross income is attributable to such dealings. However, a corporation's status does not change as a result of an occasional year in which its gross income from money dealings goes over or under the 50% level.

A corporation's classification as a financial (or nonfinancial) corporation changes only if there is a shift in the predominant character of its gross income for two consecutive years and the average of its gross income in the current and two immediately preceding years satisfies (or fails) the predominance test. Substantial amounts of gross income arising from incidental or occasional asset sales (such as the sale of a headquarters building) are excluded for these purposes.

In Legal Ruling 94-2 (CCH CALIFORNIA TAX REPORTS, ¶ 10-340.98), the FTB stated its position that corporations whose principal business activity is the finance leasing of tangible personal property are properly classified as financial corporations because such corporations predominantly deal in money or moneyed capital in substantial competition with the business of national banks. A "finance lease" is a lease that is of the type permitted to be made by national banks and is the economic equivalent of an extension of credit.

In Chief Counsel Ruling 2007-1 (CCH California Tax Reports, ¶ 404-330), the FTB stated that income from nonfinancial activities did not equate to "financial income" for purposes of satisfying the 50% gross income threshold. At issue was whether interest income and gains on sales from intangibles generated from a nonfinancial activity could be considered financial income if it was of the same character as income earned from a bank. However, the FTB concluded that the gross measurement test focuses on the activity that generated the income, not the character of the income generated.

Financial classification may result when only a portion of a corporation's income is derived from financial activities, but the financial corporation rate will nevertheless apply to its entire taxable income.

• *Decisions of courts and State Board of Equalization*

For a discussion of the principal factors that have been considered by the courts and the State Board of Equalization (BOE) in determining financial-corporation status, see *Appeals of Delta Investment Co., Inc. and Delta Investment Research Corporation* (1978) (CCH California Tax Reports, ¶ 10-340.82). In that case the taxpayers were held to be taxable as financial corporations, although their loans were made primarily to affiliated corporations and they contended that their financial activities did not constitute the major aspect of their operations.

In *Appeal of Cascade Acceptance Corp.* (2009) (CCH California Tax Reports, ¶ 10-340.72), the taxpayer made loans mainly to high risk customers who were unable to acquire traditional financing. The taxpayer's loans were typically short-term in nature, and had a higher than average rate of interest. The BOE found that even though the taxpayer's business and the business of national banks were not exactly the same, competition could exist between those businesses, and therefore the taxpayer was subject to tax at the financial corporation rate.

In *Appeal of Southern Securities Corporation* (1977) (CCH California Tax Reports, ¶ 10-340.81), the taxpayer was engaged in several activities, including use of surplus funds for real estate loans. The BOE held that the taxpayer was taxable as a "financial corporation."

In *Appeal of Cal-West Business Services, Inc.* (1970) (CCH California Tax Reports, ¶ 10-340.84), the BOE held that a corporation that purchased small retail customers' accounts and performed credit, billing, and bookkeeping services on the purchased accounts was taxable as a financial corporation. The BOE found that the taxpayer was in "substantial competition" with national banks in its locality, although testimony showed that the banks generally would not be interested in purchasing the same accounts. See also *Appeal of Atlas Acceptance Corporation* (1981) (CCH California Tax Reports, ¶ 10-340.97), to the same effect; this case involved the purchase and the collection of health spa membership contracts.

In *Appeal of the Diners' Club, Inc.* (1967) (CCH California Tax Reports, ¶ 10-340.91), the BOE held that a credit card company was taxable as a financial corporation because the corporate business was to deal in money and was in substantial competition with national banks.

In *Appeal of Stockholders Liquidating Corp.* (1963) (CCH California Tax Reports, ¶ 10-340.90), the BOE held that a mortgage loan correspondent, servicing mortgages it placed with an insurance company, was taxable as a financial corporation. It was determined that the taxpayer dealt in money and competed with national banks. To the same effect, see *Marble Mortgage Co. v. Franchise Tax Board* (1966) (CCH California Tax Reports, ¶ 10-340.79), decided by the California District Court of Appeal.

¶816

In *Appeal of Humphreys Finance Co., Inc.* (1960) (CCH CALIFORNIA TAX REPORTS, ¶10-340.692), the BOE held that a corporation engaged solely in the purchase of conditional sales contracts arising out of the sale of personal property by a corporation affiliated with it through common control was properly classified as a financial corporation. It was determined that the taxpayer met the two tests for classification as a financial corporation: (1) it dealt primarily in money, as distinguished from other commodities; and (2) it was in substantial competition with national banks.

In *Appeal of Motion Picture Financial Corporation* (1958) (CCH CALIFORNIA TAX REPORTS, ¶10-340.94), the BOE held that a corporation organized to finance motion pictures was a "financial corporation," even though it made loans which a national bank would not make and such loans were made only to a controlling shareholder.

¶817 Alternative Minimum Tax

Law: Secs. 23036, 23036.1, 23400, 23453, 23455, 23455.5, 23456, 23456.5, 23457, 23459, 24449 (CCH CALIFORNIA TAX REPORTS, ¶10-385).

Comparable Federal: Secs. 53, 55-59, 291 (CCH U.S. MASTER TAX GUIDE ¶1370, 1401—1480).

California Form: Sch. P (100) (Alternative Minimum Tax and Credit Limitations—Corporations).

California imposes an alternative minimum tax (AMT) on corporations, other than S corporations, in substantial conformity to the federal AMT. (Sec. 23400, Rev. & Tax. Code)

The California AMT is calculated in the same manner as the federal AMT, except California requires modifications to the federal adjustments made in computing alternative minimum taxable income (AMTI) and items of tax preference. For California purposes, "regular tax," used in the calculation of the AMT, means either the California corporation franchise tax, the California corporate income tax, or the California tax on unrelated business income of an exempt organization or trust, before application of any credits. (Sec. 23455, Rev. & Tax. Code)

California does not conform to the federal law providing an AMT exemption for small corporations. (Sec. 23455.5, Rev. & Tax. Code)

The tentative minimum tax, used for the calculation of the California AMT, is equal to 6.65% (the federal rate is 20%) of the amount by which AMTI for the taxable year exceeds the exemption amount.

In computing AMTI California makes the following modifications:

— for purposes of the alternative tax net operating loss deduction, California does not incorporate the federal increase in the limits placed on the alternative tax net operating loss deduction for NOLs generated or claimed in 2001 or 2002 and does not incorporate the increased AMTI NOL deduction for federally declared disaster areas. Additionally, federal references to December 31, 1986, and January 1, 1987, are modified to refer to December 31, 1987, and January 1, 1988, respectively;

— adjustments for mining exploration/development costs are applicable only to years beginning after 1987 (after 1986 for federal purposes);

— the adjustment available for pollution control facilities may be made for California purposes only if the facility is located in California and certified by the State Air Resources Board or the State Water Resources Control Board; and

— California (but not federal) law requires that if a corporation elected to depreciate a grapevine that was replanted in a vineyard as a result of phylloxera or Pierce's Disease infestation over 5 years instead of 20 years for regular tax purposes (¶1011), it must depreciate the grapevine over 10 years for AMT purposes. (Sec. 23456, Rev. & Tax. Code)

California adopts the federal adjustments on the basis of adjusted current earnings, as specified in IRC Sec. 56(g), with the following modifications:

— although California adopts federal provisions enacted under the Revenue Reconciliation Act of 1993 that eliminate the depreciation adjustment to adjusted current earnings for corporate property placed in service after December 31, 1993, the adjustment is applicable for California purposes in taxable years beginning after 1997;

— depreciation allowed on non-ACRS property placed in service after 1980 and before 1987 is the amount that would have been allowable had the taxpayer depreciated the property under the straight-line method for each year of the useful life for which the property had been held; depreciation allowed on non-MACRS property placed in service after 1986 and before 1990 is the amount determined under the Alternate Depreciation System of IRC Sec. 168(g);

— California does not follow IRC Sec. 56(g)(4)(C)(ii), (iii), and (iv) relating to the federal dividend deduction;

— California follows IRC Sec. 56(g)(4)(D)(ii) in disallowing the current deduction of circulation expenditures and the amortization of organizational expenditures; however, such deduction or amortization could be different under federal and California law, and an appropriate modification must be made to reflect the difference;

— corporations subject to the income tax and, therefore, not subject to the minimum franchise tax, limit the interest income included in adjusted current earnings to the amount included for purposes of the regular tax;

— the interest expense deducted in determining adjusted current earnings is the same as the interest deduction for purposes of the regular California tax; a modification must be made to reflect any differences between the California and federal interest deductions in computing the regular taxes;

— California law requires corporations whose income is subject to allocation and apportionment to calculate their adjustments based on adjusted current earnings by allocating and apportioning adjusted current earnings in the same manner as net income is allocated and apportioned for purposes of the regular tax;

— Although California technically conforms to the provisions of IRC Sec. 56(g)(4)(C) that allow deductions for purposes of computing adjusted current earnings for amounts deductible under IRC Sec. 199 (domestic production deduction) and under IRC Sec. 965 (temporary special dividends received deduction allowed to U.S. shareholders from controlled foreign corporations), because California does not allow any IRC Sec. 199 or IRC Sec. 965 deductions generally, there is no IRC Sec. 199 or IRC Sec. 965 deduction allowed for purposes of determining California adjusted current earnings. In addition, although California technically conforms to the provisions of IRC Sec. 56(g)(4)(B)(i) that allow an exclusion for purposes of computing adjusted current earnings for amounts excludable under IRC Sec. 139A for subsidies allowed for prescription drugs provided under a qualified retiree prescription drug plan and under IRC Sec. 1357 for income subject to the federal tonnage tax, because California does not allow any IRC Sec. 139A or IRC Sec. 1357 exclusions generally, there is no IRC Sec. 139A or IRC Sec. 1357 exclusion allowed for purposes of determining California adjusted current earnings.

(Sec. 23456, Rev. & Tax. Code)

California modifies federal items of tax preference as follows:

— federal treatment of tax-exempt interest as a tax preference item is inapplicable; and

— the excess of depreciation taken on IRC Sec. 1250 property (real property) placed in service before 1987 over the amount allowable under the straight-line method is an item of tax preference. (Sec. 23457, Rev. & Tax. Code)

The AMT applies to commencing and dissolving corporations that are subject to special rules as discussed at ¶ 819 and ¶ 820.

● *Exemption amount*

For both federal and California purposes, the first $40,000 of alternative minimum taxable income is exempt from the AMT. However, the exemption amount is reduced (but not below zero) by an amount equal to 25% of the amount by which the taxpayer's alternative minimum taxable income exceeds $150,000. (Sec. 23400, Rev. & Tax. Code)

● *Ten-year writeoff of certain tax preferences*

For both federal and California purposes, certain enumerated expenditures that would otherwise constitute tax preferences may be deducted ratably over an extended period instead of being deducted in the taxable year of the expenditure. The expenditures covered include:

— circulation expenses—three year period;

— research expenses—10 year period; and

— intangible drilling costs—five year period.

(Sec. 24365, Rev. & Tax. Code; Sec. 24423, Rev. & Tax. Code; Sec. 24364, Rev. & Tax. Code)

● *Credits against AMT*

Under federal law as incorporated by California, the AMT is equal to the excess, if any, of the tentative minimum tax over the regular tax for the taxable year. If the regular tax exceeds the tentative minimum tax so that the AMT does not apply, the taxpayer may not then apply tax credits to reduce the regular tax below the tentative minimum tax. For California purposes, an exception is made so that certain credits may reduce the regular tax below the tentative minimum tax, after the allowance of the minimum tax credit. (Sec. 23453, Rev. & Tax. Code)

The following credits discussed at ¶ 818, may reduce the regular tax below the tentative minimum tax:

— solar energy, commercial solar energy, or commercial solar electric system (carryovers);

— research and development expenditures;

— clinical testing expenses (carryovers);

— low-income housing;

— sales and use tax paid or incurred in connection with the purchase of qualified property used in an enterprise zone, former targeted tax area, local agency military base recovery area (LAMBRA), or former Los Angeles Revitalization Zone (LARZ);

— qualified hiring within an enterprise zone, former targeted tax area, LAMBRA, or former LARZ;

— former manufacturing investment credit;

— natural heritage preservation credit;

— original motion picture production credit;

— California Competes credit;

— college access tax credit; and

¶817

— new motion picture production credit (for taxable years beginning on or after January 1, 2016).

(Sec. 23036(d)(1), Rev. & Tax. Code; Sec. 23036.1, Rev. & Tax. Code)

Practitioner Comment: FTB Notice Creates Significant Uncertainty Regarding Which Credits Can Reduce the Alternative Minimum Tax

Unlike under federal law, the California AMT is determined separately before the application of credits as the excess of Tentative Minimum Tax (TMT) over regular tax. In contrast to federal law, California credits can not reduce the AMT in California. However, because the California AMT is in addition to the regular tax, most credits can still be used to reduce regular tax below the TMT.

For example, assume a corporation has TMT of $120 and regular tax of $100, before credits, and a $50 research credit. The corporation's tax liability (ignoring the $800 minimum tax) would be $70, consisting of $20 of AMT ($120 TMT – $100 regular tax before credits) and $50 of regular tax ($100 regular tax before credits – $50 research credit).

A published State Board of Equalization (BOE) decision has called the above approach into question. On November 17, 2010, the BOE held in the *Appeal of NASSCO* that enterprise zone credits could be used to reduce the AMT because the AMT was included in the statutory definition of the tax that could be offset by credits. The BOE subsequently denied the FTB's petition for rehearing.

The FTB issued *Notice 2011-02* to provide guidance regarding the application of *NASSCO* and purportedly limited its application to corporate taxpayers liable for AMT. The Notice also states that *NASSCO* applies only to EZ and MIC credits, and does not permit a corporate taxpayer to apply any of the other credits listed in Cal. Rev. & Tax. Code § 23036(d)(1) (e.g., research and experimental (R&E) credit) to offset the AMT. In addition, the Notice requires taxpayers to demonstrate the credits were not "allowed or allowable" against corporate AMT in prior years. To the extent the credits were "allowable" in prior years, taxpayers are not permitted to claim them in later taxable years.

The FTB's attempts to limit *NASSCO* to only EZ and MIC credits, and distinguish R&E credits seem questionable and appear ripe for future litigation. Therefore, notwithstanding the FTB's position in *Notice 2011-02*, taxpayers should consider filing refund claims to claim the R&E credit against AMT to protect against potential "allowed or allowable" issues in the event a subsequent court or BOE decision applies NASSCO to R&E credits.

Chris Whitney, Contributing Editor

Caution Note: Application of NASSCO Decision

An FTB notice explains that the decision in *Appeal of NASSCO, Inc.*, discussed immediately above, applies only to corporate taxpayers claiming the MIC and EZ credits against the AMT in post-2003 tax years. Corporate taxpayers that are or were liable for AMT in any taxable year after 2003, which had or have valid EZ or MIC credits, may need to revise their tax credit carryover amounts and/or file claims for refund with the FTB, provided the claims are not barred by the statute of limitations. If the claim is not barred, the taxpayer must demonstrate that the credits were not allowed or allowable against corporate AMT in a taxable year prior to the taxable year for which the claim for refund is made. Similarly, if the taxpayer is recomputing the amount of the credit carryover from prior tax years, the taxpayer must demonstrate that the credit could not be applied previously. If a corporate taxpayer was entitled to apply those same credits in a prior taxable year, the corporate taxpayer is not entitled to claim them in the later taxable year as those credits were "allowable" in such earlier year. The same rules apply to credits that are being assigned to another member of the taxpayer's unitary group. (*FTB Notice 2011-02*, CCH CALIFORNIA TAX REPORTS, ¶ 405-390)

• *Credit for prior year minimum tax*

California incorporates the federal credit provisions applicable to taxpayers who have incurred California AMT in prior years but not in the current tax year. (Sec. 23455, Rev. & Tax. Code) See ¶818 for a discussion.

• *Short taxable year*

The AMT for a short taxable year is computed on an annual basis, in the same manner as under federal law. (Sec. 24636, Rev. & Tax. Code)

¶818 Credits Against Tax

Law: Secs. 23036, 23051.7, 23453, 23601.5, 23604, 23608-25, 23630, 23633, 23634, 23636, 23642-46, 23649, 23657, 23684, 23685, 23686, 23687, 23688, 23688.5, 23695; former Secs. 23601, 23601.3, 23601.4, 23603, 23605, 23606, 23606.1, 23607, 23608, 23612.5, 23623, 23662, 23666, 23803, 24440; 18 CCR Regs. 23636-0—23636-9, 23637-0—23637-11 (CCH CALIFORNIA TAX REPORTS, ¶12-001—12-150).

Comparable Federal: Secs. 38, 41, 42, 45(a), 45C, 48, 53, 280C (CCH U.S. MASTER TAX GUIDE ¶1323, 1326, 1330, 1334, 1339, 1343, 1344, 1353).

California Forms: FTB 3507 (Prison Inmate Labor Credit), FTB 3503 (Natural Heritage Preservation Credit), FTB 3508 (Solar or Wind Energy System Credit), FTB 3511 (Environmental Tax Credit), FTB 3521 (Low Income Housing Credit), FTB 3523 (Research Credit), FTB 3534 (Joint Strike Fighter Credits), FTB Form 3527 (New Jobs Credit), FTB 3531 (California Competes Tax Credit), FTB 3540 (Credit Carryover Summary), FTB 3541 (California Motion Picture and Television Production Credit), FTB 3551 (Sale of Credit Attributable to an Independent Film), FTB 3546 (Enhanced Oil Recovery Credit), FTB 3547 (Donated Agricultural Products Transportation Credit), FTB 3548 (Disabled Access Credit for Eligible Small Businesses), FTB 3592 (College Access Tax Credit), FTB 3802 (Corporate Passive Activity Loss and Credit Limitations), FTB 3805Z (Enterprise Zone Deduction and Credit Summary), FTB 3807 (Local Agency Military Base Recovery Area Deduction and Credit Summary), FTB 3808 (Manufacturing Enhancement Area Credit Summary), FTB 3809 (Targeted Tax Area Deduction and Credit Summary), FTB 3811 (Donated Fresh Fruits or Vegetables Credit), Sch. C (100S) (S Corporation Tax Credits).

• *Tax credits—In general*

As in the personal income tax law (¶126), the corporation tax law provides rules for the order in which various tax credits are to be applied. The law provides that credits shall be allowed against "tax" (defined as the franchise or income tax, the tax on unrelated business taxable income, and the tax on S corporations).

The priority for claiming credits is as follows:

(1) credits, except the credits in categories 4 and 5, below, with no carryover or refundable provisions;

(2) credits with carryovers that are not refundable, except for those that are allowed to reduce "net tax" below the tentative minimum tax (see ¶117);

(3) credits with both carryover and refundable provisions;

(4) the minimum tax credit;

(5) credits that are allowed to reduce "net tax" below the tentative minimum tax (see ¶117);

(6) credits for taxes withheld.

(Sec. 23036, Rev. & Tax. Code)

As discussed at ¶817, only certain specified credits may reduce a taxpayer's regular tax below the tentative minimum tax.

Also, some credits may be limited because they arise from passive activities. The taxpayer must file FTB 3802 (Corporate Passive Activity Loss and Credit Limitations) if the taxpayer claims any of the following credits from passive activities: the orphan drug research credit carryover; the low-income housing credit; or the research and development credit.

Practitioner Comment: Do Certain States' Taxes Qualify as Income-Based Taxes?

See ¶131 for information on the continuing uncertainty regarding the treatment of certain taxes as income taxes or non-income taxes for California tax purposes.

• *S corporations*

An S corporation is limited to one-third of the amount of any credit against corporation franchise (income) tax, see ¶806. (Sec. 23036, Rev. & Tax. Code)

• *Pass-through entities*

Credits that become inoperative that are passed through (in the first tax year after they become inoperative) to a taxpayer who is a partner or shareholder of an eligible pass-through entity may be claimed in the year of the pass-through. An eligible pass-through entity is any partnership or S corporation that files a fiscal year return and is entitled to a credit in the last year that the credit is operative. (Sec. 23036, Rev. & Tax. Code)

Practitioner Comment: Credits Generated By Disregarded Entities are Subject to Special Limitations

Cal. Rev. & Tax. Code Secs. 17039(i) and 23036(i) provide special limitations with respect to the utilization of credits generated by disregarded entities (DREs), such as single member limited liability companies (LLCs) that have not elected to be taxed as corporations for federal income tax purposes. The amount of such credits and credit carryovers that may be applied to their owner's tax liability is limited to the excess of the taxpayer's tax determined by including the DRE's income over the amount of regular tax determined by excluding the income of such DRE. It is not clear how this limitation is to be computed for an apportioning taxpayer. The FTB has issued FAQs on its website indicating that if a credit generated by a DRE is assigned under the credit assignment provisions enacted in 2008, the FTB will treat the assignee as continuing to be subject to the DRE credit limitations.

Chris Whitney, Contributing Editor

Caution Note: Temporary Limitation on Credit Amounts Lifted

The amount of credits and credit carryovers that could be claimed by taxpayers on a corporation franchise and income tax return were limited to 50% of a taxpayer's tax during the 2008 and 2009 tax years. Thereafter, the credits may be claimed in full. Any unused credit may be carried over and the carryover period is extended by the number of taxable years the credit, or any portion thereof, was not allowed as a result of the 50% limitation. A taxpayer with net business income of less than $500,000 for the taxable year was exempt from the 50% limitation. (Sec. 23036.2, Rev. & Tax. Code)

• *Unitary groups*

For a discussion of the treatment of credits claimed by unitary group members, see ¶1310.

• *Research and development credit*

California provides a credit for research and development expenditures that is generally the same as that provided by federal law (Sec. 41), with the following exceptions:

¶818

—The applicable California percentage is 15% of the excess of qualified expenses over a specified percentage of the taxpayer's average annual gross receipts for the four preceding taxable years (the "base amount") and 24% of basic (university) research payments (the federal percentage is 20% of the excess of qualified expenses over a base amount and 20% of basic research payments).

—California substitutes 1.49%, 1.98%, and 2.48% for the former federal alternative incremental credit (AIC) method percentages of 3%, 4%, and 5%, respectively, effective generally for tax years ending after 2006. California does not adopt the federal repeal of the AIC, applicable to taxable years beginning after 2008.

—California does not incorporate the use of a third method, the alternative simplified credit, generally effective for federal purposes in tax years ending after 2006.

—Research must be conducted in California (federal law requires that it be conducted within the United States, Puerto Rico, or other U.S. possessions).

—The California credit may be carried over (the federal credit is part of the general business credit subject to the limitations imposed by Sec. 38).

—The California credit for basic research payments includes payments for applied research. Also, for California purposes only, the credit is extended to payments that are made by taxpayers engaged in specified biopharmaceutical or biotechnology activities for university hospitals and special cancer research facilities.

—For purposes of determining the base amount under California law, only the gross receipts from the sale of property that is held primarily for sale to customers in the ordinary course of the taxpayer's trade or business and delivered or shipped to a purchaser within California, regardless of F.O.B. point or other conditions of sale, may be taken into account.

—California law, unlike federal law, prohibits a taxpayer from claiming the credit for expenses paid or incurred for property for which a sales and use tax exemption for teleproduction or other postproduction services may be claimed.

—California has not adopted federal provisions that (1) allow a taxpayer to claim 20% of amounts paid or incurred by the taxpayer during the tax year to an energy research consortium and (2) repeal the limitation on contract research expenses paid to eligible small businesses, universities, and federal laboratories for qualified energy research.

(Sec. 23609, Rev. & Tax. Code)

Practice Tip: Maintain Records to Support Validity of Carryforwards

The Franchise Tax Board (FTB) may examine and disallow a corporation's carryforwards of research and development credit generated in closed tax year to the extent the carryforwards affect open tax years. The lack of authority to "determine" a tax for a tax year not in issue can be distinguished from the authority to "compute" a tax for a tax year not in issue when the computation is necessary to determine the correct tax liability for a tax year at issue. Thus, corporations should maintain records supporting the validity of their credit carryforwards until the credit carryforwards are exhausted. (*Appeal of Eclipse Solutions, Inc.* (2009) (CCH CALIFORNIA TAX REPORTS, ¶12-065.30))

Practitioner Comment: California Gross Receipts and Substantiation Requirements

The California FTB issued Legal Division Guidance 2012-03-01 (superseding Legal Division Guidance 2011-06-01, which was subsequently withdrawn by 2011-07-01) indicating that California law modifies the I.R.C. §41(c)(6) definition of "gross receipts" to include only California sales of property held primarily for sale to customers in the regular course of business that has been delivered or shipped to purchasers located within California. The guidance also explains that a taxpayer with California qualified research expenses and no California gross receipts may still claim the regular incremental research and development credit. In this circumstance, the California credit would generally be equal to 7.5% of the qualified research expenses for the credit year (15% of qualified research expenses in excess of the "minimum base amount" of 50% of qualified research expenses), or the reduced credit under I.R.C. §280(c)(3). If a taxpayer has no gross receipts in the base period (i.e., 1984-1988), the "start-up" provisions in I.R.C. §41(c)(3)(B) apply.

The guidance also indicates that taxpayers with gross receipts that can not substantiate their base amount or fixed base percentage calculations for any reason are not entitled to the credit for lack of substantiation. This conclusion seems unreasonable, particularly given the challenges taxpayers face in gathering documentation from the 1984 - 1988 base period as well as the fact that for many California taxpayers the fixed base percentage has no impact on the amount of California credit to begin with. Because the maximum fixed base percentage is 15% and is applied to California, not total gross receipts, in many cases the minimum base amount of 50% of qualified research expenses applies in practice in California. To deny a taxpayer a research credit because it cannot substantiate a fixed base percentage that mathematically has no impact on the credit calculation seems unreasonable.

Chris Whitney, Contributing Editor

Practitioner Comment: BOE Holds That Project Accounting Is Not Required For R&D Credit

Significant controversy at both the federal and state level has surrounded the sufficiency of taxpayer documentation needed to substantiate research and experimentation credits ("research credits") claimed under IRC §41 and California Rev. & Tax. Code §23609, respectively. In *The Appeal of Pacific Southwest Container, Inc.*, et al., California State Board of Equalization, (March 25, 2011), in sustaining 100% of the taxpayers, credit, the BOE rejected the idea that project accounting was required to support the credit, finding that the taxpayer's cost center based records along with related employee time surveys was sufficient to support the credit. It should be noted that certain federal courts have also recognized the use of reasonable estimates under the "Cohan rule" as providing support for research credits. The "Cohan rule" stands for the proposition that when it is apparent that some business expense, deduction or credit should be allowed, but available records are inadequate to accurately determine the amount, a reasonable estimate may be used based upon the best available evidence. See *Cohan v. Commissioner* (2nd Cir. 1930) 39 F.2d 540.

Chris Whitney, Contributing Editor

California has adopted the portion of IRC Sec. 280C that bars taxpayers from taking a business deduction for that portion of the research expenditures that is equal to the amount of the allowable credit (¶1023). (Sec. 24440, Rev. & Tax. Code)

Combined groups.—For taxpayers filing on a combined group basis, all members of the combined group must use the same method. To compute either the regular research credit or the AIC, all members of a controlled group are treated as a single taxpayer. The credit amount is then divided and proportionately allocated to each member of the controlled group. (*Tax News*, California Franchise Tax Board, September 2006)

Practitioner Comment: Treatment of R&D Credit Allocation

On August 17, 2006, the California Supreme Court in *General Motors Corp. v. Franchise Tax Board*, 39 Cal. 4th 773 (2006), (CCH CALIFORNIA TAX REPORTS, ¶404-044) held that only the taxpayer that incurred the research and development expenses may use the research and development credit so generated. In so holding, the Court's decision was consistent with an earlier State Board of Equalization decision (*Appeal of Guy F. Atkinson Company*,

No. 96R-0051, March 19, 1997, CCH CALIFORNIA TAX REPORTS, ¶403-307) as well as the unpublished Court of Appeal decision, *Guy F. Atkinson Company v. Franchise Tax Board*, (No. A985075). [CCH Note: Legislation enacted in 2008 allows combined group members to assign credits to other group members, see ¶1310 for details]

Chris Whitney, Contributing Editor

- *Credit for prior year minimum tax*

California allows a credit in the form of a carryover to corporate taxpayers who have incurred California alternative minimum tax in prior years but not in the current tax year. (Sec. 23453, Rev. & Tax. Code)

The credit is computed in the same manner as the federal credit with the substitution of certain California figures in place of the federal. The credit is taken against the "regular tax" but may not reduce liability to less than the "tentative minimum tax." Both the federal and California credits are based on the amount of alternative minimum tax paid on "deferral preferences" (items that defer tax liability) as distinct from "exclusion items" (items that permanently reduce tax liability).

- *Low-income housing credit*

Corporations may qualify for a low-income housing credit, based upon federal law (IRC Sec. 42). The credit is the same as under personal income tax law and is discussed at ¶138. (Sec. 23610.5, Rev. & Tax. Code)

A corporation that is entitled to the low-income housing credit may elect to assign any portion of the credit to one or more affiliated banks or corporations for each taxable year in which the credit is allowed.

- *Prison inmate job tax credit*

Employers may claim a credit equal to 10% of the wages paid to each prison inmate hired under a program established by the Director of Corrections. This credit is identical to the one provided under the personal income tax law (¶154). (Sec. 23624, Rev. & Tax. Code)

- *New employment credit*

Beginning with the 2014 taxable year, the former jobs credit is repealed and replaced with a nonrefundable credit equal to 35% of qualified wages paid for each net new qualified full-time employee hired to work in a designated geographic area. See ¶157. (Sec. 23626, Rev. & Tax. Code)

- *Tax-incentive credit—Sales tax equivalent*

The corporation tax law allows a tax credit for the amount of sales or use tax paid on the pre-2014 purchase of "qualified property" by businesses located in an enterprise zone or local agency military base recovery area (LAMBRA), or the pre-2013 purchase of qualified property by businesses located in a targeted tax area. The conditions for allowance of the credit are the same as those for the personal income tax credit, as explained at ¶144, except that the corporate credit applies to purchases up to a value of $20 million. (Sec. 23612.2, Rev. & Tax. Code; Sec. 23633, Rev. & Tax. Code; Sec. 23645, Rev. & Tax. Code)

Practitioner Comment: Overview of Enterprise Zone Credit Repeal

With A.B. 93 and S.B. 90, signed into law on July 11, 2013, the California legislature phases out California's Enterprise Zone ("EZ") Credit Program and replaces it with a new, temporary regime that went into effect on January 1, 2014, and sunsets December 31, 2020. The new program consists of a hiring tax credit (¶158), a partial sales and use tax manufacturing exemption (¶1509), and an incentive fund (¶134) (the latter two features are discussed in separate Practitioner's Comments).

The new regime creates a credit for hiring qualified full-time employees in (i) designated census tracts with high unemployment and poverty rates, (ii) certain former Enterprise Zones, or (iii) local agency military base recovery areas ("LAMBRAs"). This hiring credit can offset California personal and corporate income taxes from January 1, 2014 until December 31, 2020. The EZ reform also eliminates the retroactive vouchering process. Previously employers were permitted to voucher qualified employees and claim the EZ credit in tax years after hiring to the extent the income tax statute of limitations period was still open. Under the new regime, taxpayers must request a tentative credit reservation ("TCR") from the FTB within 50 days of the hire date, claim the credit on the original tax return, and provide certification to the FTB annually that the qualified employee remains employed.

Subsequent legislation, A.B. 106, extended the time frame to voucher employees hired before December 31, 2013, to January 1, 2015. The bill also allayed concerns raised by the announcement of certain zone coordinators that they would discontinue vouchering prior to 2014.

Among other restrictions and requirements, the new hiring tax credit is only available to employers that create a net increase in jobs state-wide, which was not required under the EZ hiring credit. Also, taxpayers that terminate a qualified employee within 36 months of hire may be subject to certain recapture provisions. Moreover, this new hiring credit is not available to some businesses, such as retailers, food service and temporary employment agencies. Interestingly, the legislation states that the credit is not available to taxpayers "primarily engaged in" providing food services. Yet, taxpayers that simply "provide" temporary help services and retail trade services are similarly barred from the credit. It is unclear why the modifier "primarily" was omitted for temporary help and retail trade services and whether this omission carries any significance or was an unintentional oversight.

Additionally, A.B. 93 cuts the previously unlimited EZ credit carry-forward period for credits earned prior to January 1, 2014 to 10 years. A.B. 106 clarified that the 10 year carry-forward period commences January 1, 2014, and not from the date the credit was originally generated.

Chris Whitney, Contributing Editor

• *Tax-incentive credit—Employers' hiring credit*

Employers may claim a credit for a portion of "qualified wages" paid to certain disadvantaged individuals who are hired to work in an enterprise zone or LAMBRA prior to 2014 or in a targeted tax area, or a manufacturing enhancement area prior to 2013. The conditions for allowance of the credit are the same as those for the personal income tax, as explained at ¶145 and ¶147 through ¶149, respectively. (Sec. 23622.7, Rev. & Tax. Code; Sec. 23646, Rev. & Tax. Code; Sec. 23634, Rev. & Tax. Code; Sec. 23622.8, Rev. & Tax. Code)

Practitioner Comment: Enterprise Zone Credit Repeal May be Challenged on Constitutional Grounds

See ¶145 for information on the potential challenges that might be made to the constitutionality of the legislation repealing the enterprise zone credit.

Practitioner Comment: Assignment of Enterprise Zone Credits May Render Credits Unusable in Some Cases According to FTB

Enterprise zone (EZ) credits are available for qualified wages as well as sales and use taxes paid in connection with acquiring manufacturing, computer and certain telecommunications equipment for use in a designated EZ. The EZ credits that may be utilized in any given year are limited to the tax liability attributed to the EZ based upon the ratio of property and payroll located within the EZ as compared to California property and payroll. FTB Form 3805Z requires that a separate form, including zone credit limitation, be submitted for each EZ in which credits are claimed.

Under FAQs on its website, the FTB has indicated that the EZ credit limitations discussed above will continue to apply to credits assigned to other unitary group members under Rev. & Tax. Code § 23663. Specifically the FTB has indicated in its FAQs that the assignee in such situations is limited based upon its own activity (or lack thereof) within the specific EZ, not the assignor's activity. As a result, taxpayers that assign EZ credits to unitary members that do not conduct activity within the same EZ in which the credits were originally generated may be unable to utilize the assigned credits.

Chris Whitney, Contributing Editor

- *Disabled access expenditures credit*

California allows eligible small businesses a credit for 50% of up to $250 of the disabled access expenditures paid or incurred by those businesses to comply with the federal Americans with Disabilities Act. The conditions for allowance of the credit are the same as those for the personal income tax, as explained at ¶140. (Sec. 23642, Rev. & Tax. Code)

- *Enhanced oil recovery credit*

California allows certain independent oil producers an enhanced oil recovery credit equal to $1/3$ of the federal credit allowed under IRC Sec. 43 as of the current IRC tie-in date (see ¶803), provided the costs for which the credit is claimed are attributable to projects located within California. The conditions for the allowance of the credit are the same as those for the personal income tax, as explained at ¶153. (Sec. 23604, Rev. & Tax. Code)

- *Agricultural products donation credits*

California allows a credit against net tax for 50% of the costs paid or incurred in connection with the transportation of agricultural products donated to nonprofit charitable organizations. A credit is also available to farmers who donate fresh fruit and/or vegetables to California food banks. The conditions for the allowance of the credits are the same as those for the personal income tax, as explained at ¶141. (Sec. 23608, Rev. & Tax. Code, Sec. 23688, Rev. & Tax. Code; Sec. 23688.5, Rev. & Tax. Code)

- *Community development investment credit*

For taxable years beginning before 2017, California allows a credit in an amount equal to 20% of each qualified investment made into a community development financial institution. The conditions for the allowance of the credit are the same as those for the personal income tax, as explained at ¶156. (Sec. 23657, Rev. & Tax. Code)

- *Natural heritage preservation credit*

A taxpayer may claim a credit equal to 55% of the fair market value of qualified real property donated before July 1, 2020, for conservation to the California Resources Agency (CRA), a local government, or a nonprofit land and water conservation organization designated by the CRA or local government to accept donations. The corporation franchise and income tax credit is identical to the personal income tax credit discussed at ¶143. (Sec. 23630, Rev. & Tax. Code)

- *Ultra-low sulfur diesel fuel production credit*

A credit is available for ultra low-sulfur diesel fuel produced by a qualified small refiner at a California facility, effective for taxable years beginning before 2018. The corporation franchise and income tax credit is identical to the personal income tax credit discussed at ¶151. (Sec. 23662, Rev. & Tax. Code)

¶818

- *Film and television production credit*

A motion picture production credit is available against personal income tax, corporation franchise and income taxes, or state sales and use taxes. The credit is equal to 20% (25% if the qualified motion picture is a television series that relocated to California or an independent film) of the qualified expenditures attributable to the production of a qualified motion picture in California. The credit is claimed for all qualified expenditures incurred in all taxable years for the qualified motion picture, but may be claimed only in the taxable year that the California Film Commission issues a credit certificate. See ¶ 137. (Sec. 23685, Rev. & Tax. Code) Also, for taxable years beginning on or after January 1, 2016, a new credit is available for motion picture production expenditures paid or incurred, which is provided in addition to the previously existing (original) motion picture production credit. However, the new credit will not be allowed for any expenditures for which the original credit has been claimed. See ¶ 137a. (Sec. 23695, Rev. & Tax. Code)

- *California competes credit*

A California competes credit against personal income and corporation franchise and income taxes is available for the 2014 through 2024 taxable years to taxpayers that apply to the Governor's Office of Business and Economic Development (GO-Biz). The credit will be awarded on a competitive basis based on specified criteria. See ¶ 134. (Sec. 23689, Rev. & Tax. Code)

- *College access credit*

For taxable years beginning on or after January 1, 2014, and before January 1, 2018, a credit is allowed for cash contributions made to the College Access Tax Credit Fund. The corporation franchise and income tax credit is identical to the personal income tax credit discussed at ¶ 156. (Sec. 23686, Rev. & Tax. Code)

- *New advanced strategic aircraft program employment credit*

For taxable years beginning on or after January 1, 2016, and before January 1, 2031, qualified taxpayers who manufacture property for a new advanced strategic aircraft for the U.S. Air Force are allowed a nonrefundable credit for qualified wages paid to qualified full-time employees. A "qualified taxpayer" is either a prime contractor awarded a prime contract or a major first-tier subcontractor awarded a subcontract to manufacture property for ultimate use in or as a component of a new advanced strategic aircraft for the U.S. Air Force. The credit is allowed in an amount equal to 17.5% of the qualified wages paid or incurred during the taxable year to qualified full-time employees, subject to the limitations discussed below. The total aggregate amount of the credit that may be allowed to all qualified taxpayers is set at $25 million annually for the first five years, $28 million annually for the next five years, and $31 million annually for the final five years (for a 15-year total of $420 million). Also, the aggregate number of total annual full-time equivalents of all qualified taxpayers with respect to which a credit amount may be allowed for a calendar year must not exceed 1,100. (Sec. 23636, Rev. & Tax. Code)

The credit will not be allowed unless it was reflected within the bid upon which the prime contract or subcontract to manufacture property is based by reducing the amount of the bid by a good faith estimate of the amount of the credit allowable. The FTB will allocate the credit on a first-come, first-served basis, determined by the date the taxpayer's timely filed original tax return is received. If the returns of two or more qualified taxpayers are received on the same day and the amount of credit remaining to be allocated is insufficient to be allocated fully to each, the credit remaining will be allocated to those taxpayers on a pro-rata basis.

If a taxpayer is allowed this credit for qualified wages, no other credit will be allowed with respect to those wages. Unused credit may be carried over to reduce tax in the following year and the seven succeeding years, if necessary, until the credit is exhausted.

Practitioner Comment: Aerospace Income Tax Credit and Temporary Changes to the Capital Investment Incentive Program are Aimed to Benefit Certain Taxpayers and Industries

Governor Jerry Brown signed A.B. 2389 on July 10, 2014. The legislation creates the aerospace income tax credit ("ATC") and temporarily expands the capital investment incentive program ("CIIP"). The legislation is aimed at creating and retaining aerospace industry jobs in California by providing up to $420 million in tax credits over 15 years. This program will be administered by the Governor's Office of Business and Economic Development (GO-Biz).

The ATC is an income tax credit available to "qualified taxpayers" for taxable years beginning on or after January 1, 2016, and before January 1, 2031. The credit is equal to 17.5% of qualified wages paid to qualified full-time employees during the taxable year. "Qualified taxpayer" includes any taxpayer that is a major first-tier subcontractor awarded a subcontract to manufacture property for ultimate use in or as a component of a new advanced strategic aircraft for the U.S. Air Force. A "major first-tier subcontractor" is a subcontractor that was awarded a subcontract in an amount of at least 35 percent of the amount of the initial prime contract awarded for the manufacturing of a new advanced strategic aircraft for the U.S. Air Force.

The changes to the CIIP are temporarily effective between July 10, 2014, and June 30, 2015. The changes consist of a temporary increase in the amount of property tax incentives available under the CIIP, and a temporary limitation of the definition of "qualifying manufacturing facility" to those operated by taxpayers with North American Industry Classification System (NAICS) codes 3364 (Aerospace Product and Parts Manufacturing) and 3359 (Other Electrical Equipment and Component Manufacturing) (see ¶1711).

The Bill Analysis indicates that the ATC is intended to help the Lockheed Martin Aerospace Company while the changes to the CIIP were intended to benefit Tesla Motors, which was searching for a location for its so-called "Battery Gigafactory" at the time the bill was passed. Tesla subsequently selected a site in Nevada for this factory.

It is well publicized that other states have been pursuing California-based companies with lucrative incentives such as the significant package Nevada offered Tesla Motors to locate its battery factory in its state. California historically did not have an incentives program until the California Competes Credit, which is administered by GO-Biz and effective beginning fiscal year 2014-2015. However, the California Competes Credit, which permits only a six-year carryforward and is not refundable, is not as attractive as incentives available in other states.

A.B. 2389 may suggest Governor Brown and the Legislature are willing to work collaboratively with companies to develop competitive incentives packages outside the scope of the California Competes Credit. Since the Democrats currently control both the governor's office and the Legislature, they have an increased ability to offer incentive packages via legislative action.

Chris Whitney, Contributing Editor

• *Carryover credits*

Expired credits for which carryovers may be claimed (and the years for which the credits were available) include the following:

— solar pump credit (1981—1983);

— solar energy credit (1985—1988);

— energy conservation credit (1981—1986);

— ridesharing credits (1981—1986 and 1989—1995);

— credit for donation of computer or scientific equipment (1983—1986);

— credit for donation of computer software (1986—1987);

— commercial solar energy credit (1987—1988);

— orphan drug research credit (1987—1992);

— commercial solar electric system credit (1990—1993);

— recycling equipment credit (1989—1995);

— low-emission vehicles credit (1991—1995);

— salmon and steelhead trout habitat credit (1995—1999);

— rice straw credit (1997—2007);

— farmworker housing credits (1997—2008);

— employer childcare program credit (1994—2011);

— employer childcare contribution credit (1994—2011);

— targeted tax area sales and use tax credit (1998—2012);

— local agency military base recovery area credit (1996—2013); and

— new jobs credit (2009—2013).

All of the above credit carryovers may be claimed on FTB 3540, except for the LARZ hiring and sales and use tax credits, targeted tax area sales and use tax credit, and LAMBRA sales and use tax credit. See prior editions of the *Guidebook* for details about these credits.

¶819 Franchise Tax on Commencing Corporations

Law: Secs. 23151.1, 23153, 23181, 23183, 23221-26 (CCH California Tax Reports, ¶10-210, 10-240, 10-340, 10-380).

Comparable Federal: None.

New corporations are exempt from the minimum franchise tax for their first taxable year. However, a credit union that incorporates in or qualifies to transact intrastate business in California must prepay a tax equal to $25. (Sec. 23153, Rev. & Tax. Code)

However, a corporation is still liable for the regular tax for it's first taxable year. The tax is computed according to or measured by its net income for the taxable year. (Sec. 23151.1(c)(2), Rev. & Tax. Code)

Franchise Tax Board Reg. 23222, 18 CCR, provides that where a commencing corporation is in existence or is qualified in California for no more than one-half month prior to the end of its accounting period, such period may be disregarded provided the corporation was not doing business in and received no income from sources within the state during the period. The corporation is not required to file a return or pay a tax for such a period, but may be required to file affidavits to establish its right to come under this special rule. This rule does not apply to limited partnerships, which are subject to a minimum franchise tax (¶616).

CCH Example: Corporation Not Required to File or Pay

ABC Corporation files its articles of incorporation with the Secretary of State on December 17, and elects to file on a calendar year basis. However, ABC does no business in California and receives no income from California sources for the period from December 17 through December 31. In this case, no return would be required and no tax would be due for the period from December 17 through December 31. However, if ABC had filed its articles on December 10th, it would be required to file a return, even if it remained inactive and received no income during the period from December 10 through December 31.

• *Cross references*

Special rules apply when a reorganization is involved (¶822).

¶820 Franchise Tax on Corporations Discontinuing Business

Law: Secs. 23151.1, 23181, 23183, 23332, 23504; Reg. 23334, 18 CCR (CCH CALIFORNIA TAX REPORTS, ¶10-210, 10-340).

Comparable Federal: None.

The tax for a corporation's taxable year of cessation is imposed on the corporation's net income for the taxable year, which may not be less than the minimum tax discussed at ¶816. (Sec. 23151.1, Rev. & Tax. Code)

A corporation that commenced to do business before 1972 may be allowed a credit, in the year of dissolution or withdrawal, for tax paid during its commencing period (¶821).

A corporation that discontinues business but does not dissolve or withdraw until a later year is subject to the minimum franchise tax until it dissolves or withdraws. See ¶821.

¶821 Franchise Tax upon Dissolution or Withdrawal

Law: Secs. 23151.2, 23201-04, 23223, 23281-82, 23331-35, 23561 (CCH CALIFORNIA TAX REPORTS, ¶10-210, 10-340).

Comparable Federal: None.

California Form: FTB 3555A (Request for Tax Clearance Certificate—Exempt Organizations).

The franchise tax for the year of dissolution or withdrawal is based on the income of the year of discontinuing business, unless that income was previously taxed. (Sec. 23151.2, Rev. & Tax. Code) In the usual situation where dissolution or withdrawal occurs in the same year as discontinuance of business, there is of course no additional tax beyond that described at ¶820. In any event, the minimum tax is applicable unless certain conditions are satisfied (see below). Credit may be allowable for tax paid during the corporation's commencing years, as explained below.

• *Effective date of dissolution*

The effective date of dissolution is the date on which a "Certificate of Winding Up," if necessary, and the "Certificate of Dissolution," or certified copy of a court order of dissolution, is filed with the Secretary of State. The effective date of withdrawal is the date on which a certificate of withdrawal is filed with the Secretary of State. (Sec. 23331, Rev. & Tax. Code) See *Appeal of Mount Shasta Milling Company* (1960) (CCH CALIFORNIA TAX REPORTS, ¶10-210.452); also, *Appeal of Air Market Travel Corporation* (1978) (CCH CALIFORNIA TAX REPORTS, ¶10-210.452).

The California Attorney General has taken the position that the California Secretary of State is not required to accept for filing a certificate of voluntary dissolution of a nonprofit corporation that contains facsimile signatures rather than original signatures of the directors (*Opinion No. 02-514*, Office of the California Attorney General, September 5, 2002 (CCH CALIFORNIA TAX REPORTS, ¶10-210.454)).

In *Appeal of Rogers* (1950) (CCH CALIFORNIA TAX REPORTS, ¶10-210.56), the State Board of Equalization (BOE) considered the question of the date on which a certificate of dissolution was "filed" for purposes of the rule described above. In that case the corporation offered a proper and adequate certificate to the Secretary of State on October 14, 1948, but the Secretary returned the certificate to the corporation for more information. The certificate was sent back to the Secretary, with the information requested, and was accepted for filing on November 1, 1948. The BOE held that the certificate was "filed" on October 14, the date it was first offered to the Secretary of State.

- *Shareholders' assumption of liability*

In *Appeal of B.&C. Motors, Inc.* (1962) (CCH CALIFORNIA TAX REPORTS, ¶ 10-210.455), the BOE held that an assumption of liability executed by shareholders of a dissolving corporation imposes an obligation on the shareholders for all franchise taxes of the corporation, even though (1) the taxes apply to a period prior to the time the shareholders acquired their stock, and (2) the tax liability was not disclosed until after the assumption was executed.

- *Special rules*

When a corporation is suspended in one year and is not revived in the same year, but is revived in a later year, its tax for the year of revivor is computed as though it were a new corporation (¶ 819). (Sec. 23282, Rev. & Tax. Code)

- *Credit for prepaid tax*

A corporation that commenced to do business before 1972 is allowed a credit in the year of dissolution or withdrawal for tax paid during the commencing period. The credit allowed is the excess of the tax paid over the minimum tax, for the first taxable year that constituted a full 12 months of doing business. The reason for this is that under the old commencing-corporation rules tax was paid twice on some income of the commencing years; this doubling up usually applied to the income of the first full year of doing business. (The doubling up was justified by the fact that under the old rules there was no tax on income of the corporation's final year.) (Sec. 23223, Rev. & Tax. Code)

The law provides that the credit is allowable only upon submission by the taxpayer of evidence establishing the amount paid. If the taxpayer does not have a copy of the tax return or other competent evidence that shows the commencing-corporation tax it paid, the FTB will—upon request, and for a fee—supply the necessary information from its files if available.

Corporations that first became subject to the franchise tax before 1933 may encounter special problems in determining the credit; these issues are discussed in Legal Ruling No. 382 (1975) (CCH CALIFORNIA TAX REPORTS, ¶ 205-238).

The credit may be allowed to a transferee corporation for tax paid by a transferor, where there is a "reorganization" as explained at ¶ 822. In this case the credit is not allowed to the transferor.

¶822 Franchise Tax on Reorganized Corporations

Law: Secs. 23251-53, 24458, 24459.

Comparable Federal: Secs. 338, 368, 381(b), 382 (CCH U.S. MASTER TAX GUIDE ¶ 2209, 2277).

In cases involving certain types of reorganizations, the transferor and transferee corporations are treated in effect as one continuing corporation for franchise tax purposes. For this purpose the term "reorganization" is defined in IRC Sec. 368. (Sec. 23251 et. seq., Rev. & Tax. Code)

Practice Note: Apportionment of IRC Sec. 338 deemed asset sales

The Franchise Tax Board's *Legal Ruling 2006-03*, May 6, 2006, CCH CALIFORNIA TAX REPORTS, ¶ 10-540.21, and *Chief Counsel Ruling 2008-2*, September 15, 2008, CCH CALIFORNIA TAX REPORTS, ¶ 404-925 provide information regarding how to apportion the gains resulting from an IRC Sec. 338(h)(1) or IRC Sec. 338(g) election to treat the sale or purchase of stock as a sale or purchase of assets for California corporation franchise and income tax purposes.

• *Procedure after reorganization*

In the case of a reorganization, IRC Sec. 381(b) shall apply in determining the close of the taxable year. This federal law provides that the taxable year of the transferor shall end on the date of the transfer.

IRC Sec. 382(n), which provides an exception from the loss limitation rules following corporate mergers and acquisitions for certain ownership changes, does not apply for California purposes. (Sec. 24459, Rev. & Tax. Code)

• *Effect of insurance-company exemption*

In *First American Title Insurance and Trust Company v. Franchise Tax Board* (1971) (CCH CALIFORNIA TAX REPORTS, ¶ 10-540.803), the transferee corporation took over four subsidiary corporations that were in the escrow business. The transaction was a "reorganization" as described in this paragraph. The transferee was exempt from franchise tax (¶ 808), except for its trust business. The court of appeal overruled the Franchise Tax Board and held that the transferee was not required to include the transferors' income for the preceding year in the measure of its tax, because the income came within the protection of the transferee's insurance-company exemption.

• *Transferee's credit for transferor's tax*

Under the system for taxing the income of a corporation's final year, as explained at ¶ 820 and ¶ 821, a transferee corporation may be allowed credit for tax paid by a transferor. Where there has been a "reorganization," as defined above, the transferee is allowed credit for tax that was paid by the transferor during the commencing period of the transferor. The credit is allowed in a later year when the transferee dissolves or withdraws, under the rules outlined at ¶ 821—it is not allowed in the year of the reorganization. This conforms to the idea of treating transferor and transferee as though they were one continuing corporation for franchise tax purposes. Thus, when the transferee corporation dissolves or withdraws, it gets the benefit of a credit for the transferor's commencing-corporation tax as well as for its own.

• *Treatment of losses*

Internal Revenue Service (IRS) Notice 2008-83, 2008-42 I.R.B. 905, issued on October 20, 2008, relating to the treatment of deductions under Internal Revenue Code Sec. 382(h) following an ownership change, is inapplicable for California corporation franchise and income tax purposes with respect to any ownership change occurring at any time. (Sec. 24458, Rev. & Tax. Code) Federal Notice 2008-83 exempted banks from the IRC Sec. 382 limitations on loss carryovers in change-of-ownership circumstances. The American Recovery and Reinvestment Act of 2009 repealed IRS Notice 2008-83 for federal purposes, but repealed it prospectively only.

California also has not incorporated amendments made to IRC Sec. 382 that provide an exception to the rule that limits the offset of taxable income post-change tax years by pre-change net operating losses, certain built-in gains, and deductions for a loss corporation that experiences an ownership change as a result of specified restructuring plans required by the Treasury Department.

¶823 Tax on Corporations Having Income from Within and Without the State

Law: Secs. 25101, 25120-40 (CCH CALIFORNIA TAX REPORTS, ¶ 10-800, 11-510 et seq.).

Comparable Federal: None.

Corporations having income from both within and without the state are taxed only on the income attributable to California. See Chapter 13 for full discussion of this subject. (Sec. 25101, Rev. & Tax. Code)

Because income from sources outside the state is not subject to California tax, it is presumed that no income will be subject to tax by California and also by another state. Accordingly, California does not allow credit against the California tax for taxes paid to other states or countries. This is contrary to the treatment in the California personal income tax (¶127—131), and is also unlike the federal treatment of domestic corporations that have income from foreign sources.

¶824 Suspension and Revivor of Corporate Powers

Law: Secs. 23301-23305.5 (CCH CALIFORNIA TAX REPORTS, ¶10-210).

Comparable Federal: None.

California Forms: FTB 3557BC (Application for Certificate of Revivor), FTB 3557LLC (Application for Certificate of Revivor).

Except for the purpose of amending the articles of incorporation to change the corporate name or filing an application for exempt status, all of the powers, rights, and privileges of a corporation or limited liability company (LLC) may be suspended (or, in the case of a foreign corporation or LLC, forfeited) for failure to file a return or for nonpayment of taxes, penalties, or interest. Generally, these nonpayment provisions come into play if payment is not made within the following time limitations: (1) tax shown on return, by close of year following taxable year and (2) tax payable upon notice and demand, by close of 11th month after due date. (Sec. 23301, Rev. & Tax. Code; Sec. 23301.5, Rev. & Tax. Code) Also, contracts made by a suspended or forfeited taxpayer may be voided. (Sec. 23304.1, Rev. & Tax. Code)

Comment: *Treatment of Foreign Nonqualified LLCs*

By including foreign nonqualified LLCs within the definition of a "taxpayer" for purposes of the suspension and revivor provisions, foreign nonqualified LLCs are made subject to the same provisions relating to contract voidability that apply to all other LLCs and corporations. A foreign nonqualified LLC without an FTB-assigned account number that fails to file a required tax return will be subject to contract voidability during the period beginning on the later of January 1, 2014, or the first day of the taxable year for which the taxpayer has failed to file a return, and ending when the LLC qualifies with the Secretary of State or obtains an FTB account number. A foreign nonqualified LLC with an FTB-assigned account number that fails to file a tax return or fails to pay delinquent taxes, penalties, fees, or interest within 60 days of the FTB's mailing a written demand therefor will be subject to contract voidability during the period beginning with the end of the 60-day demand period and ending on the earlier of the date relief from contract voidability is granted or the date the LLC qualifies with the Secretary of State. (Sec. 23304.1, Rev. & Tax. Code; Sec. 23305.5, Rev. & Tax. Code)

A corporation or LLC desiring to be relieved of the suspension described above may apply to the Franchise Tax Board (FTB) for a certificate of revivor. The application must be accompanied by payment of all delinquent amounts, unless the FTB determines that prospects for collection will be improved by not imposing this requirement. (Sec. 23305, Rev. & Tax. Code; Sec. 23305b, Rev. & Tax. Code)

Practice Note: *Revivor Without Full Payment*

If collection of the full amount due cannot be secured because of the suspension, FTB collection staff has the discretion to consider reviving the entity to good standing without full payment to allow the entity to receive funds or other assets used to pay any amounts due in full. A specific future source or method of collection must be identified and secured, and the entity must provide any requested documentation to support the decision to revive the entity. Under this procedure, an entity may be revived without full payment; however, all missing returns must be filed. If there is a financial hardship, an installment agreement may be approved. (*FTB Tax News*, November 2012, CCH CALIFORNIA TAX REPORTS, ¶ 405-732)

Practitioner Comment: Expedited Requests for Corporate Revivor

The fee for submitting expedited service requests for corporation revivor requests is $56 and must be paid in guaranteed funds such as cashier's checks, certified checks, money orders, or cash. Personal checks will not be accepted. Expedited corporation revivor requests are made by submitting the necessary returns, paperwork, and payments at one of the FTB district offices that accept walk through applications, including the Los Angeles, Oakland, Sacramento, San Diego, San Francisco, or Santa Ana district offices. (Reg. 19591, 18 CCR; *FTB Notice 2004-09* (2004) (CCH CALIFORNIA TAX REPORTS, ¶ 403-722))

Chris Whitney, Contributing Editor

Corporations or LLCs may also be relieved of the contract voidability and penalty provisions imposed for failure to comply with reporting and payment requirements by entering into a voluntary disclosure agreement with the FTB (¶ 1422).

The FTB is authorized to provide entity status letters verifying the status of a corporation or LLC with the FTB and may charge a fee for the reasonable costs of responding to requests for such letters. (Sec. 23305e, Rev. & Tax. Code)

The law provides that even though a corporation may be suspended, it remains taxable on any income received during the period of suspension. (Sec. 23303, Rev. & Tax. Code)

In *Appeal of Lomita Plaza, Inc.* (1961) (CCH CALIFORNIA TAX REPORTS, ¶ 10-210.854), the State Board of Equalization (BOE) held that a corporation could not file a valid appeal against a proposed assessment of franchise tax at a time when the corporation was under suspension, even though the corporation was kept in existence for the sole purpose of defending against the proposed assessment and was subsequently revived. Similarly, in *Appeal of RJ Standard Corp.* (2004) (CCH CALIFORNIA TAX REPORTS, ¶ 10-210.55), the BOE held that a formerly suspended corporation could not pursue a refund claim that was filed during the period of its suspension after the corporation was revived. The statute of limitations had lapsed during the suspension period and the limitations period was not "tolled" during such period.

The California Supreme Court has upheld the BOE's reasoning in *Appeal of RJ Standard Corp.* as applies to instances when the statute of limitations has lapsed. However, it has held that a corporation that filed notices of appeal while its corporate powers were suspended for nonpayment of its corporation franchise taxes could proceed with the appeals after those powers were revived, even if the revival occurred after the time to appeal had expired. (*Bourhis v. Lord,* (2013), CCH CALIFORNIA TAX REPORTS, ¶ 10-210.859)

A California court of appeal has held that an assignee was not precluded from pursuing a court action to enforce an agreement against a third party even though the assignor's corporate powers were suspended subsequent to the assignment. The rights of an assignor are measured at the time of the assignment, and the rights of the assignee are independent of, and unaffected by, the incapacity of its assignor subsequent to the assignment (*Fidelity Express Network, Inc. v. Mobile Information Systems, Inc.* (2004) (CCH CALIFORNIA TAX REPORTS, ¶ 89-206.946)).

Reference should be made to the law or regulations for detailed rules relating to this subject and the effect on the voidability of a contract of a corporation or LLC during suspension.

¶824

¶825 Interest-Charge DISCs

Law: Sec. 23051.5(b) (CCH CALIFORNIA TAX REPORTS, ¶ 10-515).

Comparable Federal: Sec. 114 (CCH U.S. MASTER TAX GUIDE ¶ 2471).

California law specifically disallows any application of the IRC provisions on DISCs (Domestic International Sales Corporations). (Sec. 23051.5(b), Rev. & Tax. Code) For California purposes, DISCs, including interest-charge DISCS (IC-DISCs), are treated in the same manner as other corporations.

The FTB has issued *Legal Ruling 15-02* (2015) (CCH CALIFORNIA TAX REPORTS, ¶ 10-255.83), clarifying treatment of transactions between an IC-DISC and its owner(s) for California corporation franchise and income tax and personal income tax purposes. IC-DISCs are not applicable for California purposes; however, in many instances, corporations that are designated as IC DISCs for federal tax purposes, and their owner(s), have a return-filing obligation with California.

Practitioner Comment: FTB Issues Guidance on the Treatment of Transactions Between IC DISCs and Their Owners

The Franchise Tax Board ("FTB") issued *Legal Ruling 2015-02* to clarify the proper California tax treatment of transactions between corporations designated as Interest Charged Domestic International Sales Corporations (IC DISCs) for federal tax purposes, and their owners. IC DISCs are a federally-created tax savings mechanism aimed at spurring the export of U.S. goods. IC DISCs are not directly subject to federal tax. Instead, the owners of IC DISCs are subject to tax on deemed or actual dividends received from the IC DISC. Given the lower income tax rate applicable to dividends available to individuals for federal income tax purposes, IC DISCs are typically owned by either pass-through entities or individuals, as opposed to C corporations.

Pursuant to Cal. Rev. & Tax. Code § 23051.5(b)(1), the IC DISC provisions are not adopted under California law and IC DISCs are treated as C corporations. The purpose of the ruling is to provide overall guidance to taxpayers who own interests in IC DISCs given the intricacies of these provisions, including the above -mentioned dividend income inclusion.

As explained in the ruling, an IC DISC can be structured in two ways. Under a buy/sell DISC structure, the taxation of profits on export sales up to $10 million which are attributed to the IC DISC through a series of accounting entries is deferred, with an interest charge on the deferred amount. Profits on export sales above this figure are deemed distributed to the owner as a dividend. Alternatively, an IC DISC can be structured as a commission DISC with the owner paying a commission to the IC DISC which is ultimately taxed to the owner as a dividend.

The ruling focuses on both situations with five examples, concluding that because the IC DISC is essentially a shell entity which lacks economic substance, all transactions with the IC DISC will be re-attributed back to the pass-through entity or owner under Cal. Rev. & Tax. Code § 25102, which gives the FTB the authority to "distribute, apportion, or allocate gross income or deductions" between persons (e.g., individuals or entities) "if it determines that such consolidation, distribution, apportionment, or allocation is necessary in order to reflect the proper income of such persons."

As noted in the ruling, IC DISCs which are commonly controlled along with other C corporations would generally file a combined report, within which the transactions between the corporations would be offset or eliminated and without effect. This is not the case with pass-through entities (e.g., partnerships, LLCs taxed as partnerships, and S corporations) which are generally not combinable with C corporations. In this regard, the ruling appears to be at odds with the FTB Multistate Audit Technique Manual ("MATM"). Although MATM sections 5220 and 7550 expressly state that DISCs are "treated the same as any other corporation," the ruling treats the transactions pass-through entities have with a DISC differently than its transactions with other corporations.

Chris Whitney, Contributing Editor

TAXES ON CORPORATE INCOME

CHAPTER 9
GROSS INCOME

¶901 Gross Income—In General

Law: Sec. 3294.5, Civ. Code; Secs. 24271, 24275, Rev. & Tax. Code (CCH CALIFORNIA TAX REPORTS, ¶10-505, 10-515).

Comparable Federal: Secs. 61, 87, 114, 139A, 199 (CCH U.S. MASTER TAX GUIDE ¶71, 2471).

California Form: Form 100 (California Corporation Franchise or Income Tax Return).

"Gross income" is generally the same as under federal law as of the current IRC tie-in date (see ¶103), except that California law specifically includes all interest on federal, state, and municipal bonds for franchise tax purposes (¶910). (Sec. 24271, Rev. & Tax. Code) However, it may not be assumed from this that the items to be included are always the same under federal and California laws. For one thing, the exclusions are different in several respects, as set forth in succeeding paragraphs. It is also possible for the law to be interpreted differently for California purposes than for federal. Any case involving a specific item of income should be checked against the exclusions listed in this chapter and, if there appears to be any question as to its status, should be checked further against the regulations or a more detailed reference work.

Gross income is reported on Form 100, unless otherwise indicated.

Practice Pointer: BOE Audits

Taxpayers who undergo a sales and use tax audit by the State Board of Equalization (BOE) should be aware that the BOE provides the FTB with copies of sales and use tax audit reports for the audits that result in adjustments of additional gross receipts (total sales). The FTB reviews these sales and use tax reports to determine if an income tax adjustment is warranted. (*Tax News*, California Franchise Tax Board, November 2008)

¶902 Life Insurance—Death Benefits

Law: Sec. 24305 (CCH CALIFORNIA TAX REPORTS, ¶10-515).

Comparable Federal: Sec. 101 (CCH U.S. MASTER TAX GUIDE ¶803).

Although California law mirrors federal law (IRC Sec. 101) concerning the exclusion from gross income of life insurance benefits paid upon the death of an insured, other than certain interest, differences may arise as regards the treatment of benefits from a life insurance policy held by an employer. Although California incorporates IRC Sec. 101(j), which limits the exclusion for employers holding a life insurance policy as a beneficiary that covers the life of an employee, different effective dates apply. California incorporates the limits applicable generally to life insurance contracts issued after January 1, 2010, whereas the limits generally apply for federal purposes to life insurance contracts issued after August 17, 2006. (Sec. 24305, Rev. & Tax. Code)

¶903 Life Insurance—Other Than Death Benefits

Law: Sec. 24302 (CCH CALIFORNIA TAX REPORTS, ¶10-708, 10-906).

Comparable Federal: Sec. 72 (CCH U.S. MASTER TAX GUIDE ¶817 et seq.).

California Form: Form 100 (California Corporation Franchise or Income Tax Return).

Amounts received, other than death benefits, on life insurance, endowment, or annuity contracts are nontaxable until the amount received exceeds the aggregate premiums or other consideration paid. This is different from federal law. See also ¶214. (Sec. 24302, Rev. & Tax. Code)

¶904 Life Insurance, Endowment, or Annuity Contract Transferred for Consideration—Other Than Death Benefits

Law: Secs. 24272.2, 24302 (CCH CALIFORNIA TAX REPORTS, 10-708, 10-906).

Comparable Federal: Secs. 72, 101 (CCH U.S. MASTER TAX GUIDE ¶803, 817 et seq.).

California law is substantially the same as federal law.

Generally, when amounts are received other than by reason of the death of the insured under a life insurance, endowment, or annuity contract that has been acquired for valuable consideration, they are includible in income to the extent that they exceed the consideration paid, plus any subsequent premiums. When the cost basis of such contracts carries over from the transferor to the transferee, or when the transferee is a corporation in which the insured is an officer or shareholder, the basis carried over, plus subsequent premiums, may be recovered tax-free. However, annuities held by corporations and other nonnatural persons are not entitled to the same preferential treatment as annuities held by individuals. Instead, a corporate annuity holder is taxed on the excess of:

— the sum of the net surrender value of the contract at the end of the tax year plus any amounts distributed under the contract to date; over

— the investment in the contract (the aggregate amount of premiums paid under the contract minus policyholder dividends or the aggregate amounts received under the contract that have not been included in income).

(Sec. 24272.2, Rev. & Tax. Code)

¶905 Lessee Improvements

Law: Sec. 24309 (CCH CALIFORNIA TAX REPORTS, ¶ 10-515).

Comparable Federal: Sec. 109 (CCH U.S. MASTER TAX GUIDE ¶ 764).

Same as personal income tax (¶ 222).

¶906 Lessee Construction Allowances

Law: Sec. 24309.5 (CCH CALIFORNIA TAX REPORTS, ¶ 10-515).

Comparable Federal: Sec. 110 (CCH U.S. MASTER TAX GUIDE ¶ 764).

Same as personal income tax (¶ 223).

¶907 Recoveries of Bad Debts, Prior Taxes, etc.

Law: Sec. 24310 (CCH CALIFORNIA TAX REPORTS, ¶ 10-703, 10-911).

Comparable Federal: Sec. 111 (CCH U.S. MASTER TAX GUIDE ¶ 799).

California Form: Form 100 (California Corporation Franchise or Income Tax Return).

Same as personal income tax (¶ 224).

¶908 Discharge of Indebtedness

Law: Secs. 24307, 24472 (CCH CALIFORNIA TAX REPORTS, ¶ 10-701).

Comparable Federal: Sec. 108 (CCH U.S. MASTER TAX GUIDE ¶ 791).

Same as personal income tax (¶ 221).

Practitioner Comment: California Tax Attribute Reduction Due to Cancellation-of-Debt Income Should Be Applied According to Post-Apportioned Income

The California Franchise Tax Board ("FTB") issued Technical Advice Memorandum (TAM) 2015-02, dated December 22, 2015, CCH CALIFORNIA TAX REPORTS, ¶ 406-457, which addressed the reduction of certain tax attributes in instances when cancellation-of debt income ("CODI") is excluded from gross income for California purposes. The TAM specifies that the post-apportioned, rather than the pre-apportioned, excluded CODI should be used to reduce the tax attributes.

IRC Sec. 61(a)(12) provides the general rules that gross income includes CODI. An exemption exists under IRC Sec. 108(a)(1), incorporated by reference into Rev. & Tax. Code Sec. 24307(a). Under IRC Sec. 108(a)(1), CODI is not included in gross income if the debt is discharged due to bankruptcy or to the extent of the taxpayer's insolvency. If CODI is excluded pursuant to this exception, IRC Sec. 108(b)(1) requires that certain tax attributes, such as net operating loss (NOL) carryover, certain tax credits, capital loss carryover, and basis in property, be reduced to the extent CODI is excluded from gross income.

The TAM was issued to address whether multistate taxpayers excluding CODI from gross income should reduce tax attributes by pre-apportioned or post-apportioned CODI. The TAM clarifies that post-apportioned excluded CODI should be used to reduce tax attributes when applying IRC Sec. 108.

The implications of the TAM are very significant for multistate taxpayers. State application of attribute reduction on a pre-apportionment basis could result in a far greater reduction of state attributes in the aggregate. Assume a taxpayer with $4 million of CODI and $10 million of federal NOL carryforward. The taxpayer operates in 10 states with a 10% apportionment factor in each state and, accordingly, has a $1 million NOL carryover in each state. For federal purposes, the $10 million NOL would be reduced by $4 million to $6 million. For state purposes, on a pre-apportioned basis, the $4 million reduction per state would disallow each $1 million state NOL carryforward, effectively disallowing $10 million of aggregate state carryovers. A post-apportioned approach, as per the TAM, would allow each state to apportion the $4 million CODI at 10%, reducing the attributes by $400,000 per state, and allowing $6 million in state NOLs in the 10 states in aggregate.

Chris Whitney, Contributing Editor

¶909 Dividends and Other Corporate Distributions

Law: Secs. 23040, 23040.1, 24402, 24410, 24451-481, 24601, 24611, 24900, 25106 (CCH CALIFORNIA TAX REPORTS, ¶ 10-540, 10-630, 10-810, 11-515, 11-520, 11-540, 11-550).

Comparable Federal: Secs. 78, 243-47, 301-46, 404, 951-52 (CCH U.S. MASTER TAX GUIDE ¶ 237, 733 et seq., 742 et seq., 2101, 2465).

California Forms: Form 100 (California Corporation Franchise or Income Tax Return), Sch. H (100) (Dividend Income Deduction).

Except for the provisions discussed below regarding deduction of dividends where the income has been subjected to tax in the hands of the payor, the corporation tax provisions regarding dividends and other corporate distributions are generally the same as in the personal income tax law as outlined at ¶ 226. As under the personal income tax law, federal law governing corporate distributions is generally incorporated by reference for corporate tax purposes. (Sec. 24451 et seq., Rev. & Tax. Code)

• *Use of appreciated property to redeem stock*

California incorporates the federal provision (IRC Sec. 311) under which, with some exceptions, a corporation is taxed on the appreciation of value of property used to redeem its own stock. (Sec. 24451, Rev. & Tax. Code)

• *Distributions in kind*

When property is distributed in kind, it is valued in the hands of the recipient at its fair market value. California incorporates the federal rule in this area with minor modifications.

• *IRC Sec. 78 gross-up of dividends*

The California Corporation Tax Law has no provision comparable to IRC Sec. 78, which requires a domestic corporation that elects the foreign tax credit for a proportionate part of foreign taxes paid by a foreign corporation from which the domestic corporation has received dividends to include in gross income not only the actual dividends received from such foreign corporation, but also the foreign taxes it is deemed to have paid. Consequently, California corporations may deduct from gross income the amount of their IRC Sec. 78 gross-up of dividends (*Letter to CCH*, FTB, March 25, 1987, CCH CALIFORNIA TAX REPORTS, ¶ 401-491).

• *Deduction for dividends received*

California's dividends received deduction was struck down as unconstitutional in *Farmer Brothers Co. v. Franchise Tax Board* (2003) (CCH CALIFORNIA TAX REPORTS, ¶ 403-464). A California court of appeal found Rev. & Tax. Code Sec. 24402, which tied the California general corporation dividends received deduction to the payor's level of California in-state activity, created an unconstitutional burden on interstate commerce and was, therefore, invalid. The ruling adopts in large part the court's reasoning in *Ceridian Corp. v. Franchise Tax Board* (2000) (CCH CALIFORNIA TAX REPORTS,

¶909

¶403-121), which held that former Rev. & Tax. Code Sec. 24410, which limited the deduction for dividends received from an insurance company based on the insurer's level of California business activity, was discriminatory on its face in violation of the Commerce Clause. The California Supreme Court denied the California Franchise Tax Board's (FTB) petition for review, and the U.S. Supreme Court denied the FTB's petition for certiorari.

Practitioner Comment: California Court of Appeals finds California's Dividends Received Deduction Statute to be Unconstitutional

The California Court of Appeals ruling in *Farmer Brothers Co. v. Franchise Tax Board* (2003) (CCH CALIFORNIA TAX REPORTS, ¶403-464) is a mixed decision for California corporate taxpayers that earned dividend income in open tax years. The decision struck down as unconstitutional the California dividend received deduction (Rev. & Tax. Code Section 24402) that tied the deduction to the payor's level of activity in the state. The ruling obligates the FTB to apply the provisions of the Due Process Clause and provide "meaningful backward-looking relief" to rectify an unconstitutional deprivation.

The FTB has announced that it will allow a dividend received deduction to all qualified corporate taxpayers for tax years ending before December 1, 1999, but will disallow the deduction for all later tax years.

For dividends deducted under Cal. Rev. & Tax. Code § 24402 (e.g., dividends received in years ending before December 1, 1999), taxpayers will need to carefully consider the implications of the expense disallowance rules of Cal. Rev. & Tax. Code § 24425 (discussed at ¶1023). While it has been the FTB's policy to disallow deductions prorated to deductible dividends under a fungibility of money concept, it should be noted that the California Court of Appeal rejected this approach in *Apple Computer v. Franchise Tax Board*, Cal.App.4th 1, September 12, 2011. In *Apple*, the court found that the taxpayer had met its burden of demonstrating that the dominant purpose for which the underlying funds had been borrowed was for domestic as opposed to foreign investment. In this regard, the *Apple* decision stands for the proposition that direct evidence of the purpose and actual use of borrowed funds can be used to overcome the pro rata approach that would otherwise apply in the absence of such specific evidence. Note that the California Supreme Court denied Apple's petition for review relating to the dividend ordering issue.

Several taxpayers have objected to the FTB's Farmer Brothers policy of disallowing a DRD for tax years ending on or after December 1, 1999, in effect arguing that the unconstitutional portions of the statute can be severed with the rest of the statute continuing to provide a DRD based solely upon stock ownership in the dividend paying corporation.

On July 21, 2009, the California Court of Appeal issued a published opinion on rehearing in *Abbott Laboratories v. FTB* (2009) (CCH CALIFORNIA TAX REPORTS, ¶404-938) upholding the Superior Court's earlier decision that the taxpayer was not entitled to a DRD under Cal. Rev. & Tax. Code § 24402 for dividends received in 1999 and 2000 from a 50% owned out-of-state corporation. Abbott filed a petition for review with the California Supreme Court on August 26, 2009, which was subsequently denied on October 28, 2009. On July 15, 2010, the California Court of Appeal issued a published opinion in *River Garden Retirement Home v. FTB* (CCH CALIFORNIA TAX REPORTS, ¶405-214), similarly rejecting a DRD under § 24402 for dividends received in 1999 and 2000. River Garden's petition for review with the California Supreme Court was denied, thereby making the Court of Appeal decision final.

Chris Whitney, Contributing Editor

FTB's internal policy outlined.—In an internal memorandum sent to the FTB's audit staff, the FTB outlined its policies for dealing with returns in which a dividends received deduction was claimed under Sec. 24402 since it was declared unconstitutional in *Farmer Bros.* (*Memorandum*, California Franchise Tax Board, Multistate Audit Program Bureau, May 17, 2004, CCH CALIFORNIA TAX REPORTS, ¶403-646).

• *Intercompany dividends*

Intercompany dividends between members of a controlled group filing a combined report are excluded from income, to the extent such dividends are paid out of unitary income. (Sec. 25106, Rev. & Tax. Code) Dividends received from noncontrolled affiliated corporations may be treated as "business" income, apportionable within and without the state as described in Chapter 13 (¶ 1302).

Practice Pointer: Dividends Paid Up the Corporate Chain

The FTB Chief Counsel has taken the position that distributions paid up the corporate chain from lower tier subsidiaries to the ultimate parent of a unitary group each constituted dividends, creating unitary income to the respective payees within the meaning of Rev. & Tax. Code Sec. 25106, so that the third in the series of three distributions qualified for the intercompany dividend elimination from income. Furthermore, the Chief Counsel clarified that for purposes of the dividend elimination provision, California follows an earnings and profits ordering rule for dividend payments similar to the federal rules, whereby dividends are deemed paid out of current earnings and profits first and then layered back on a last-in, first-out basis. (*Chief Counsel Ruling 2007-4*, California Franchise Tax Board, January 3, 2008, CCH California Tax Reports, ¶ 404-710; *Chief Counsel Ruling 2007-5*, California Franchise Tax Board, February 22, 2008, CCH California Tax Reports, ¶ 404-927)

Dividend elimination is available whether or not the members of the group are California taxpayers. Dividends paid by a group member may be eliminated even if no group members were subject to California taxation at the time the income was earned as long as the income would have been included in a California combined report had any of the group members been subject to California taxation at the time that the income was earned. (Sec. 25106, Rev. & Tax. Code)

The law provides that intercompany dividends may also be eliminated if paid from the unitary group's income to a newly formed corporation if the recipient corporation was part of the unitary group from the time it was formed until the time the dividends were received. (Sec. 25106, Rev. & Tax. Code)

Tax evasion.—The FTB may deny the elimination of intercompany dividends available to members of a unitary combined reporting group if the FTB determines that the transaction is entered into or structured with a principal purpose of evading California corporation franchise or income taxes. (Sec. 25106, Rev. & Tax. Code)

• *Dividends from insurance subsidiary*

A deduction is allowed for a portion of the qualified dividends received by a corporation or by members of the corporation's commonly controlled group (if any) from an insurance company subsidiary, regardless of whether the insurance company is engaged in business in California, if at the time of each dividend payment, at least 80% of each class of stock of the insurer was owned by the corporation receiving the dividend. The deduction is equal to 85% of the qualified dividends received. (Sec. 24410, Rev. & Tax. Code)

Disincentives to overcapitalization of insurance company subsidiaries.—Dividends qualifying for the deduction must be reduced on the basis of an overcapitalization percentage. The overcapitalization percentage is calculated by dividing the five-year average of net written premiums for all insurance companies in the insurance company's commonly controlled group by the five-year average of total income for all insurance companies in the insurance company's commonly controlled group. The dividends qualifying for the deduction will not be reduced if the overcapitalization percentage is 70% or greater. If the overcapitalization percentage is greater than 10% and less than 70%, the dividends qualifying for the deduction will be ratably reduced for each percentage point by which the overcapitalization percentage falls below 70%.

¶909

The dividends qualifying for the reduction will be reduced to zero if the overcapitalization percentage is 10% or less. (Sec. 24410, Rev. & Tax. Code)

Special rules for dividends from self-insurance companies.—Special rules apply to dividends received from an insurance company that insures risks of a member of its commonly controlled group. Premiums received or accrued from another member of the insurance company's commonly controlled group will not be included in the overcapitalization ratio calculation. Furthermore, dividends attributable to premiums received or accrued by the insurance company from a member of the insurance company's commonly controlled group will not qualify for the dividends received deduction. (Sec. 24410, Rev. & Tax. Code)

Legislative intent.—The provisions of Sec. 24410 set forth above are intended to provide equitable tax treatment for insurance company dividends in light of the California court of appeal's decision in *Ceridian Corp. v. Franchise Tax Board*, 85 Cal.App.4th 875 (2000) (see below). The legislature has declared that the tax treatment of insurance company dividends under Section 24410 is unrelated to and distinguishable from the tax treatment of general corporation dividends under Section 24402 and from the application of Section 24425 to deductions allocable to those dividends, and that no inference should be drawn with respect to Section 24402 (see above) or the application of Section 24425 (see ¶1023) from the changes with respect to Section 24410. (Uncodified Sec. 6, Ch. 868 (A.B. 263), Laws 2004)

Prior law.—Rev. & Tax. Code Sec. 24410 previously allowed only California-domiciled corporations a deduction for dividends received from a California subsidiary insurance company that was subject to the gross premiums tax. A California appellate court determined that the deduction allowed to California-domiciled corporations for dividends received by a California subsidiary insurance company was unconstitutional because it facially discriminated against interstate commerce without compelling justification, in violation of the Commerce Clause of the U.S. Constitution. According to the court, the statute unconstitutionally favored domestic corporations over foreign competitors by disallowing deductions based on property owned and people employed outside California by a dividend-declaring insurer (*Ceridian Corp. v. Franchise Tax Board*, (2000) CCH CALIFORNIA TAX REPORTS, ¶403-121; *aff'g* SuperCt, No. 983377, May 7, 1998, CCH CALIFORNIA TAX REPORTS, ¶402-996).

Deemed dividends.—The FTB may include a deemed dividend from an insurance company subsidiary in the gross income of the parent corporation (or a member of the corporation's combined reporting group), if all insurance companies in the commonly controlled group have a capitalization percentage not exceeding 15% and the earnings and profits of the insurance company subsidiary have been accumulated to avoid income taxes of any state. The deemed dividend equals the corporation's pro rata share (or the combined reporting group member's pro rata share) of the insurance companies' earnings and profits for the taxable year. However, the amount of the deemed dividend is limited to a particular insurance company's net income attributable to investment income less that insurance company's net written premiums received for the year. The amount included is treated as a dividend received from an insurance company during the taxable year, which may be deductible under Sec. 24410, above. (Sec. 24900, Rev. & Tax. Code)

• *Expenses attributable to dividend income*

The FTB has taken the position in some cases that general and administrative expenses attributable to dividend income are not deductible. This is on the ground that expenses attributable to tax-exempt income are nondeductible. (Sec. 24425, Rev. & Tax. Code) See ¶1021 and ¶1023.

• *Dividends paid to employee stock ownership plan*

California conforms to federal law (IRC Sec. 404(k)) allowing a deduction for specified dividends paid on stock held by an employee stock ownership plan. The deduction is unavailable to S corporations under both California and federal law. (Sec. 24601, Rev. & Tax. Code)

• *Income from qualifying investment securities*

A corporation's distributive share of interest, dividends, and gains from qualifying investment securities that are sold or exchanged by an investment partnership in which the corporation is a partner is not income derived from sources within California and thus is not subject to the corporation income tax, provided that the following conditions are satisfied:

(1) the income is the corporation's only income derived from sources within California;

(2) the corporation does not participate in the management of the investment partnership's investment activities; and

(3) the corporation is not engaged in a unitary business with another corporation or partnership that does not meet the requirements of (1) and (2), above.

In response to a taxpayer's inquiry, the FTB's chief counsel has ruled that the taxpayer's proposed investments in commodity-linked derivative securities are qualified investment securities. (*Chief Counsel Ruling 2010-01* (2010), CCH CALIFORNIA TAX REPORTS, ¶405-221)

Income, gain, or loss from stocks or securities received by an alien corporation is also exempt if the corporation's sole activity in California involves trading stocks or securities for its own account. The exemption does not apply to an alien corporation that has income attributable to California sources or that is engaged in a unitary business with another corporation that has California source income other than the income, gain, or loss from stocks or securities described above. Dealers in stocks and securities are also ineligible to claim this exemption. (Sec. 23040.1, Rev. & Tax. Code)

• *Special rules for liquidations*

See ¶1220 for special rules regarding certain corporate liquidations.

¶910 Interest on Government Bonds

Law: Sec. 24272 (CCH CALIFORNIA TAX REPORTS, ¶10-610).

Comparable Federal: Secs. 103, 141-150 (CCH U.S. MASTER TAX GUIDE ¶729 et seq.).

California Form: Form 100 (California Corporation Franchise or Income Tax Return).

Although federal law generally prohibits states from taxing obligations issued by the U.S. government, this prohibition does not apply to the imposition of a nondiscriminatory corporate franchise tax. Accordingly, corporations that are subject to the California franchise tax must include in gross income all interest received from federal obligations. Interest income from state, municipal, or other bonds must also be included in gross income for franchise tax purposes. (Sec. 24272, Rev. & Tax. Code)

However, because the California corporate income tax is subject to the federal prohibition described above, corporations subject to the corporate income tax may exclude U.S. bond interest from gross income. Income from bonds issued by the state of California or by a local government within the state are similarly exempt from the corporate income tax.

The exemption of U.S. obligations does not extend to interest received on refunds of federal taxes (¶217). See ¶1212 for the treatment of gain or loss on the sale of government bonds.

Under federal law, interest on the obligations of a state or its political subdivisions and on obligations issued by the federal government are generally exempt from state tax.

¶911 Income from Bond Discount, etc.

Law: Secs. 23051.5, 24344.5, 24991-93 (CCH CALIFORNIA TAX REPORTS, ¶ 10-640, 10-815).

Comparable Federal: Secs. 1271-88, 6706 (CCH U.S. MASTER TAX GUIDE ¶ 1952 et seq.).

California Forms: Form 100 (California Corporation Franchise or Income Tax Return), Sch. D (100) (California Capital Gains and Losses), Sch. D-1 (Sales of Business Property).

Same as personal income tax (¶ 237).

¶912 Commodity Credit Loans

Law: Sec. 24273 (CCH CALIFORNIA TAX REPORTS, ¶ 10-515).

Comparable Federal: Sec. 77 (CCH U.S. MASTER TAX GUIDE ¶ 769).

As under federal law, a taxpayer may elect for California purposes to treat as income amounts received as loans from the Commodity Credit Corporation. (Sec. 24273, Rev. & Tax. Code)

¶913 Contributions to Capital of a Corporation

Law: Secs. 24322, 24325 (CCH CALIFORNIA TAX REPORTS, ¶ 10-340, 10-515).

Comparable Federal: Sec. 118.

California incorporates federal law that excludes a contribution to capital from a corporate taxpayer's income. (Sec. 24325, Rev. & Tax. Code)

Where property is contributed to capital by someone other than a shareholder, the corporation is required to reduce the basis of property by the amount of the contribution (¶ 1234).

¶914 Patronage Allocations from Cooperatives

Law: Sec. 24273.5 (CCH CALIFORNIA TAX REPORTS, ¶ 10-250).

Comparable Federal: Sec. 1385 (CCH U.S. MASTER TAX GUIDE ¶ 698).

Same as personal income tax (¶ 232).

¶915 Condominiums and Co-ops

Law: Sec. 23701t (CCH CALIFORNIA TAX REPORTS, ¶ 10-245, 89-102).

Comparable Federal: Sec. 528 (CCH U.S. MASTER TAX GUIDE ¶ 699).

California Form: Form 100 (California Corporation Franchise or Income Tax Return).

Nonprofit homeowners' associations, such as condominium management associations and timeshare associations, are usually tax-exempt. However, any income from sources other than membership dues, fees, and assessments ("exempt-function income") is taxable if it exceeds $100 a year. Associations that have such taxable income should file a corporation income tax return, in addition to the usual information return or statement as explained at ¶ 811. The California law conforms generally, but not completely, to the federal law. (Sec. 23701t, Rev. & Tax. Code)

As one of the conditions required for exemption, California requires that any "exempt-function income" not expended for association purposes during the taxable year be "transferred to and held in trust" for proper use in the association's operations. There is nothing comparable in the federal law.

¶916 Income from Foreign Aircraft or Ships

Law: Secs. 24320-21 (CCH CALIFORNIA TAX REPORTS, ¶ 10-704, 10-913).

Comparable Federal: Sec. 883 (CCH U.S. MASTER TAX GUIDE ¶ 2455).

California Form: Form 100 (California Corporation Franchise or Income Tax Return).

Income from the operation of foreign aircraft or ships is exempt under certain conditions. The aircraft or ships must be registered or documented in a foreign country, and the income of the corporation must be exempt from national income taxes under a reciprocal agreement between the United States and the foreign country. The federal law contains a similar exemption. (Sec. 24320, Rev. & Tax. Code; Sec. 24321, Rev. & Tax. Code)

In *Appeals of Learner Co. et al.* (1980) (CCH CALIFORNIA TAX REPORTS, ¶ 11-520.43), the State Board of Equalization held that this exemption did not apply where the ship involved was documented in Liberia, because there was no reciprocal agreement between the United States and Liberia.

¶917 Merchant Marine Act Exemption

Law: Sec. 24272.5 (CCH CALIFORNIA TAX REPORTS, ¶ 10-515).

Comparable Federal: Sec. 7518.

California conforms to federal law. U.S. citizens that own or lease qualified vessels may establish tax-deferred reserve funds, called capital construction funds, under Section 607 of the Merchant Marine Act of 1936, for the replacement or addition of vessels. Generally, amounts deposited into a capital construction fund are deductible from taxable income, and earnings from the investment of amounts held in the fund are not taken into account.

Withdrawals made for the acquisition, construction, or repair of a qualified vessel are "qualified withdrawals" and do not generate income. Nonqualified withdrawals generate income and are taxed in the year they are made. (Sec. 24272.5, Rev. & Tax. Code)

¶918 Income from Investments in Depressed Areas

Law: Sec. 24384.5 (CCH CALIFORNIA TAX REPORTS, ¶ 10-845).

Comparable Federal: None.

California Form: Form 100 (California Corporation Franchise or Income Tax Return).

The corporation tax law allows a deduction for net interest received or accrued prior to January 1, 2014, from loans made to a trade or business located in an enterprise zone (¶ 104). It does not apply to any taxpayer that has an ownership interest in the debtor. (Sec. 24384.5, Rev. & Tax. Code)

Qualified loans made to nonprofit organizations qualify for the enterprise zone net interest deduction if the debtor meets all the other required qualifications. (*Tax News*, FTB, July 2009, CCH CALIFORNIA TAX REPORTS, ¶ 404-930)

¶919 Income from Recycled Beverage Containers

Law: Sec. 24315 (CCH CALIFORNIA TAX REPORTS, ¶ 10-860).

Comparable Federal: None.

California Form: Form 100 (California Corporation Franchise or Income Tax Return).

Same as personal income tax (¶ 201).

¶920 Relocation Payments

Law: Sec. 7269, Government Code (CCH CALIFORNIA TAX REPORTS, ¶ 10-912).

Comparable Federal: Public Law 91-646 (CCH U.S. MASTER TAX GUIDE ¶ 702).

California Form: Form 100 (California Corporation Franchise or Income Tax Return).

Same as personal income tax (¶ 236).

¶921 Incentives for Water Conservation

Law: Secs. 24308.2, 24323 (CCH CALIFORNIA TAX REPORTS, ¶ 10-860).

Comparable Federal: None.

California Form: Form 100 (California Corporation Franchise or Income Tax Return).

Under California law, but not federal law, certain water conservation rebates received by taxpayers from local water agencies or suppliers for the purchase or installation of specified water closets are treated as excludable refunds or price adjustments rather than as taxable income. (Sec. 24323, Rev. & Tax. Code)

Also, for taxable years beginning on or after January 1, 2014, and before January 1, 2019, certain financial incentives received for participation in a turf removal water conservation program are excluded from gross income, as explained at ¶ 244. (Sec. 24308.2, Rev. & Tax. Code)

¶922 Energy Conservation Subsidies and Federal Energy Grants

Law: Secs. 24303, 24308.1, 24326 (CCH CALIFORNIA TAX REPORTS, ¶ 10-515, 10-860).

Comparable Federal: Sec. 136 (CCH U.S. MASTER TAX GUIDE ¶ 884).

California Form: Form 100 (California Corporation Franchise or Income Tax Return).

Same as personal income tax (¶ 245).

¶923 Cost-Share Payments Received by Forest Landowners

Law: Sec. 24308.5 (CCH CALIFORNIA TAX REPORTS, ¶ 10-860).

Comparable Federal: Sec. 126 (CCH U.S. MASTER TAX GUIDE ¶ 881).

California Form: Form 100 (California Corporation Franchise or Income Tax Return).

California provides an exclusion from gross income for cost-share payments received by forest landowners from the Department of Forestry and Fire Protection pursuant to the California Forest Improvement Act of 1978 or from the U.S. Department of Agriculture, Forest Service, under the Forest Stewardship Program and the Stewardship Incentives Program, pursuant to the federal Cooperative Forestry Assistance Act. The amount of any excluded payment must not be considered when determining the basis of property acquired or improved or when computing any deduction to which the taxpayer may otherwise be entitled. (Sec. 24308.5, Rev. & Tax. Code)

¶924 Earnings on Qualified Tuition Programs

Law: Secs. 23711, 23711.5, 24306 (CCH CALIFORNIA TAX REPORTS, ¶ 10-245, 10-515).

Comparable Federal: Sec. 529 (CCH U.S. MASTER TAX GUIDE ¶ 697).

California incorporates federal law excluding from a contributor's gross income any earnings under a qualified tuition program. Distributions to a corporation as a result of a refund or credit on the qualified tuition program or savings account is includible in the corporation's gross income to the extent the distribution exceeds the amounts actually contributed. See ¶ 250 for more details. (Sec. 23711, Rev. & Tax. Code)

California has established a qualified state tuition program entitled the Golden State Scholarshare Trust.

¶925 Foreign Source Income

Law: None (CCH CALIFORNIA TAX REPORTS, ¶ 10-707).

Comparable Federal: Secs. 114, 199 (CCH U.S. MASTER TAX GUIDE ¶ 245, 2471).

Unlike federal law, California does not provide any special treatment for foreign source income. Foreign source income is treated as ordinary income for California corporation franchise and income tax purposes. In addition, California does not incorporate the federal domestic production activities deduction (IRC Sec. 199).

Taxpayers that use the federal reconciliation method (¶ 803) must make an adjustment on their California corporation franchise or income tax return, adding back any amounts excluded.

¶926 Federal Prescription Drug Subsidies

Law: None (CCH CALIFORNIA TAX REPORTS, ¶ 10-709).

Comparable Federal: Sec. 139A.

California does not incorporate and does not have any provision similar to IRC Sec. 139A, which allows taxpayers to exclude special federal subsidies for prescription drug plans received under Sec. 1860D-22 of the Social Security Act. Taxpayers that use the federal reconciliation method (¶ 803) must make an addition adjustment to the extent such amounts are excluded from federal taxable income.

¶927 Federal Disaster Relief Payments

Law: Sec. 24329 (CCH CALIFORNIA TAX REPORTS, ¶ 10-515).

Comparable Federal: Sec. 139 (CCH U.S. MASTER TAX GUIDE ¶ 897).

Same as personal income tax (¶ 251).

¶928 Earthquake Loss Mitigation Incentives

Law: Sec. 24308.7 (CCH CALIFORNIA TAX REPORTS, ¶ 10-919).

Comparable Federal: None.

Same as personal income tax (¶ 256).

¶929 Qualified Health Care Service Plan Income

Law: Sec. 24330 (CCH CALIFORNIA TAX REPORTS, ¶ 10-920).

Comparable Federal: None.

California provides an exclusion from gross income for qualified health care service plan income accrued by a health care service plan that is subject to the managed care organization provider tax with respect to enrollment or services that occur on or after July 1, 2016, and on or before June 30, 2019 (see ¶ 1902). Also, a qualified health care service plan with no income for a taxable year other than qualified health care service plan income that is excluded from gross income pursuant to this provision will be exempt from the minimum franchise tax (see ¶ 816) for that year. (Sec. 24330 Rev. & Tax. Code)

"Qualified health care service plan income" means any of the following revenue that is associated with the operation of a qualified health care service plan and that is required to be reported to the Department of Managed Health Care:

— premiums (commercial);

— copayments, COB, subrogation;

— Title XIX Medicaid;

— point-of-service premiums;

— risk pool revenue;

— capitation payments;

— Title XVIII Medicare;

— fee-for-service;

— interest; and

— aggregate write-ins for other revenues, including capital gains and other investment income. (Sec. 24330 Rev. & Tax. Code)

TAXES ON CORPORATE INCOME

CHAPTER 10
DEDUCTIONS

¶1001 Trade or Business Expenses

Law: Secs. 24343, 24343.7, 24383, 24415, 24443, 24602 (CCH CALIFORNIA TAX REPORTS, ¶10-515, 10-595, 10-645, 10-830, 10-880).

Comparable Federal: Secs. 83, 162, 190, 274 (CCH U.S. MASTER TAX GUIDE ¶713, 901—999, 1287).

California Form: Form 100 (California Corporation Franchise or Income Tax Return).

Same as personal income tax, as explained at ¶301 and ¶302, except for provisions that, by their terms, do not apply to corporations. (Sec. 24343, Rev. & Tax. Code; Sec. 24343.7, Rev. & Tax. Code; Sec. 24383, Rev. & Tax. Code; Sec. 24415, Rev. & Tax. Code; Sec. 24443, Rev. & Tax. Code; Sec. 24602, Rev. & Tax. Code)

Corporations are specifically precluded by California law from claiming business expense deductions for granting California qualified stock options (see ¶207 for a discussion of the favorable tax treatment afforded to California qualified stock options).

¶1002 Expenses of Soil Conservation, etc.

> *Law:* Secs. 24369, 24377 (CCH CALIFORNIA TAX REPORTS, ¶ 10-515).
>
> *Comparable Federal:* Secs. 175, 180 (CCH U.S. MASTER TAX GUIDE ¶ 982, 985).

Same as personal income tax (¶ 341).

¶1003 Circulation Expenditures of Periodicals

> *Law:* Sec. 24364 (CCH CALIFORNIA TAX REPORTS, ¶ 10-515).
>
> *Comparable Federal:* Sec. 173 (CCH U.S. MASTER TAX GUIDE ¶ 971).

Same as personal income tax (¶ 342).

¶1004 Interest

> *Law:* Secs. 24344, 24344.5, 24344.7, 24424, 24438-39, 24451 (CCH CALIFORNIA TAX REPORTS, ¶ 10-210, 10-515, 10-540, 10-815, 11-515).
>
> *Comparable Federal:* Secs. 163, 249, 264, 265, 279, 385, 461(g) (CCH U.S. MASTER TAX GUIDE ¶ 341, 533, 909, 940, 970, 1044, 1055, 1056).
>
> *California Form:* Form 100 (California Corporation Franchise or Income Tax Return).

California incorporates by reference as of the current IRC tie-in date (¶ 803) the federal rule generally providing a deduction for all interest paid or accrued on business debts. (Sec. 24344, Rev. & Tax. Code) In *Hunt-Wesson, Inc. v. Franchise Tax Board* (2000), (CCH CALIFORNIA TAX REPORTS, ¶ 403-071), the U.S. Supreme Court held that a California interest offset provision that reduced a non-California corporation's interest expense deduction by the amount of the corporation's nonbusiness income not allocable to California was unconstitutional because it imposed tax on income outside California's jurisdictional reach. According to the Court, the state's attribution of all taxpayer borrowing first to nonunitary investment, even if none of the funds borrowed were actually invested in the nonunitary business, was not a reasonable allocation of taxpayer expense deductions to the income that the expense generated.

• *FTB clarification of post-**Hunt-Wesson** interest expense deductions*

The California Franchise Tax Board has issued *FTB Notice 2000-9* (CCH CALIFORNIA TAX REPORTS, ¶ 403-120) to explain the limitations on the deductibility of interest expense in light of the U.S. Supreme Court decision in *Hunt-Wesson.* The FTB policy is that the interest-offset provision invalidated in *Hunt-Wesson* will not be applied to nondomiciliary corporations, but that all other provisions in the interest-offset rules will continue to be applied.

FTB Notice 2000-9 explains the treatment of interest expense deductions and the interest offset in the aftermath of *Hunt-Wesson.* Based on the notice, domestic and foreign corporations must compute their allowable interest expense deduction differently. Foreign (*i.e.,* non-California) corporations allocate their interest expense between apportionable and nonapportionable income as follows:

(1) A deduction for interest expense equal to business interest income may be claimed in computing income subject to apportionment.

(2) A deduction for interest expense in excess of business interest income may be claimed in computing income subject to apportionment in an amount equal to the amount of nonbusiness interest and dividend income.

(3) Any interest expense in excess of interest income and nonbusiness dividend income may be assigned to other types of nonbusiness income, such as rents and royalties, under authority of Reg. 25120 (d), 18 CCR. Interest expense assigned to such nonbusiness income items would not be deductible in determining apportionable income. Note, however, that the FTB will not apply Reg. 25120 (d), 18 CCR to

assign interest expense to assets that have the potential to generate interest and dividend income. In other words, the FTB will not use the regulation to assign interest expense to capital gains or losses from sales or other exchanges of stocks, bonds and similar instruments.

(4) Any remaining interest expense (after applying steps 1 through 3) is deductible against apportionable income.

For domestic (*i.e.*, California) corporations, interest expense is allocated in the same manner, except that step 2 is modified to provide that interest expense in excess of business interest income may reduce nonbusiness interest and dividend income allocable to California in an amount equal to the amount of nonbusiness interest and dividend income. In other words, California corporations continue to enjoy a full offset of interest expense against nonbusiness interest and dividend income.

Practitioner Comment: Interest Offset Provisions Continue to Benefit In-State Companies

As noted above, FTB policy after *Hunt-Wesson* is to require the dollar-for-dollar offset of interest expense against nonbusiness interest and dividend income only with respect to such nonbusiness income items that are allocable to California. This approach can provide a substantial benefit for taxpayers domiciled in California. A.B. 1618, which passed the legislature in 2007, would have repealed the interest offset provisions of Cal. Rev. & Tax. Code Sec. 24344(b). The Governor vetoed this legislation on October 11, 2007. As a result, for the time being these provisions will continue to benefit California domiciled businesses.

Chris Whitney, Contributing Editor

• Pre-**Hunt-Wesson** *decisions*

In *Appeal of F.W. Woolworth Co. et al.* (1998) (CCH CALIFORNIA TAX REPORTS, ¶ 10-815.33), a California court of appeal held that the interest expense deducted by a parent corporation and its wholly owned subsidiary was properly reduced by the amount of its nonunitary dividend income. However, the U.S. Supreme Court has remanded this case in light of the *Hunt-Wesson, Inc.* case (discussed above).

The exclusion of dividends deductible under former Sec. 24402 applied to foreign domiciliary corporations as well as to California corporations—see Legal Ruling No. 379 (1975) (CCH CALIFORNIA TAX REPORTS, ¶ 11-520.55).

Application of the rule limiting deductibility of interest expense was discussed in *Appeal of Kroehler Mfg. Co.* (1964) (CCH CALIFORNIA TAX REPORTS, ¶ 11-520.53). The rule (as it stood prior to the 1967 amendment relating to intercompany dividends) was also discussed at length in the 1972 decision of the California Supreme Court, in *The Pacific Telephone and Telegraph Company v. Franchise Tax Board* (1972) (CCH CALIFORNIA TAX REPORTS, ¶ 11-515.352).

In *Appeal of Sears, Roebuck and Co., et al.* (1970) (CCH CALIFORNIA TAX REPORTS, ¶ 11-520.532), the State Board of Equalization (BOE) held that carrying charges on installment sales may not be treated as interest income in applying the rules set forth above. The BOE held that the special provisions permitting the buyer to treat a portion of carrying charges as interest (¶ 305) had no application to the seller.

The Franchise Tax Board ruled in Legal Ruling No. 59 (1958) (CCH CALIFORNIA TAX REPORTS, ¶ 10-815.92) that interest on federal tax deficiencies was subject to the foregoing limitations.

• *Prepaid interest*

Both California and federal law require cash-basis taxpayers to deduct prepaid interest over the period to which it applies. (Sec. 24681, Rev. & Tax. Code)

¶1004

• *Interest on company-owned life insurance*

California incorporates federal law, disallowing a deduction by an employer for interest expenses paid or accrued that are associated with debt incurred by the employer to purchase life insurance policies or endowment or annuity contracts for *any* individual for whom the employer has an insurable interest. However, an employer may still deduct interest paid or incurred on debt to purchase life insurance policies, annuities, and endowment contracts for a limited number of officers and 20% owners if (1) the aggregate amount of debt with respect to the policies and contracts does not exceed $50,000 per person, and (2) the interest rate does not exceed a specified amount. (Sec. 24424, Rev. & Tax. Code)

• *California-federal differences*

California and federal rules regarding deduction of interest differ in that:

— Federal law has nothing comparable to the special California rules for multistate corporations, discussed above.

— Federal law disallows interest on indebtedness incurred or continued to carry tax-exempt obligations. California has no comparable provision regarding interest, although the same result presumably would be achieved under the California provision disallowing expenses allocable to tax-exempt income (¶1023). Such interest is deductible generally by financial institutions as a business expense. However, federal deductions for such interest are reduced as a result of a provision reducing the benefits of certain tax preferences. For private activity bonds and certain other obligations not meeting federal qualifications issued after August 7, 1986, interest indebtedness expense is not deductible under federal law.

— California has not conformed to special federal rules regarding bond registration requirements.

California conforms to the federal law regarding computation of deductions for original issue discount (OID) as of the current IRC tie-in date (see ¶803).

¶1005　Passive Activity Losses and Credits

Law: Sec. 24692 (CCH CALIFORNIA TAX REPORTS, ¶10-635).

Comparable Federal: Sec. 469 (CCH U.S. MASTER TAX GUIDE ¶2053 et seq.).

California Form: FTB 3802 (Corporate Passive Activity Loss and Credit Limitations).

Same as personal income tax (¶340).

¶1006　Taxes

Law: Secs. 24345-46 (CCH CALIFORNIA TAX REPORTS, ¶10-515, 10-615, 10-840, 11-515).

Comparable Federal: Secs. 164, 275 (CCH U.S. MASTER TAX GUIDE ¶532, 1025).

California Form: Form 100 (California Corporation Franchise or Income Tax Return).

The California deduction for taxes is the same as the federal deduction as of the current IRC tie-in date (¶803), except for the following differences:

— unlike federal law, California does not permit deduction of the California franchise or income tax, or of any other tax based on income or profits and levied by any foreign country or by any state, territory, or taxing subdivision thereof; neither are such taxes allowed as a credit against the California tax (¶823);

— California law permits deduction of water or irrigation district general assessments levied on all lands within the district; there is nothing comparable under federal law; and

— California does not permit an increase in basis for sales tax for which a credit is claimed by enterprise zone, former Los Angeles Revitalization Zone, local agency military base recovery area, and former targeted tax area taxpayers, as explained at ¶818.

(Sec. 24345, Rev. & Tax. Code; Sec. 24345.5, Rev. & Tax. Code; Sec. 24346, Rev. & Tax. Code)

The prohibition against deduction of income taxes is the same as under the personal income tax law. See the discussion at ¶306, including cases holding that the prohibition does not apply to some taxes based on *gross receipts*. However, the prohibition does apply to taxes based on *gross income*. See *MCA, Inc. v. Franchise Tax Board* (1981) (CCH CALIFORNIA TAX REPORTS, ¶10-561.202), in which the Court of Appeal disallowed deductions for foreign taxes paid on film rentals and record royalties. The Court's opinion makes a careful distinction between "gross receipts" and "gross income."

• *Treatment of various taxes*

The following outlines the treatment of various state, federal, and foreign taxes. Addition adjustments are only necessary for those taxes that are nondeductible under California law.

Canadian mining taxes.—Nondeductible (*Alloys, Inc.* (1984) CCH CALIFORNIA TAX REPORTS, ¶400-493)

Federal minimum tax.—Nondeductible (*Coachella Valley Savings and Loan Assn.* (1987) CCH CALIFORNIA TAX REPORTS, ¶401-499)

Federal social security taxes paid by employers.—Deductible (Reg. 24345-5, 18 CCR)

Foreign income taxes.—Nondeductible (*California Response to CCH Multistate Corporate Income Tax Survey*, California Franchise Tax Board, July 21, 2003, CCH CALIFORNIA TAX REPORTS, ¶403-506)

Kentucky license tax.—Deductible (*California Response to CCH Multistate Corporate Income Tax Survey*, California Franchise Tax Board, July 21, 2003, CCH CALIFORNIA TAX REPORTS, ¶403-506)

Libyan petroleum tax surcharge.—Deductible (*Occidental Petroleum Corp.* (1983) CCH CALIFORNIA TAX REPORTS, ¶403-394)

Michigan single business tax (MSBT).—Deductible (*Kelly Service, Inc.* (1997) CCH CALIFORNIA TAX REPORTS, ¶402-935; *Dayton Hudson Corp.* (1994) CCH CALIFORNIA TAX REPORTS, ¶402-678)

New Hampshire business profits tax.—Nondeductible (*California Response to CCH Multistate Corporate Income Tax Survey*, California Franchise Tax Board, July 21, 2003, CCH CALIFORNIA TAX REPORTS, ¶403-506)

New York franchise taxes.—Nondeductible (*Coro, Inc.* (1955), CCH CALIFORNIA TAX REPORTS, ¶200-306)

Ohio franchise tax-net worth portion.—Deductible (*California Response to CCH Multistate Corporate Income Tax Survey*, California Franchise Tax Board, July 21, 2003, CCH CALIFORNIA TAX REPORTS, ¶403-506)

Texas franchise tax-net worth portion.—Deductible (*California Response to CCH Multistate Corporate Income Tax Survey*, California Franchise Tax Board, July 21, 2003, CCH CALIFORNIA TAX REPORTS, ¶403-506)

Unemployment insurance tax contributions paid by employers.—Deductible (Reg. 24345-5, 18 CCR)

Washington business and occupation tax.—Deductible (*California Response to CCH Multistate Corporate Income Tax Survey*, California Franchise Tax Board, July 21, 2003, CCH CALIFORNIA TAX REPORTS, ¶ 403-506)

West Virginia business and occupation tax.—Deductible (*California Response to CCH Multistate Corporate Income Tax Survey*, California Franchise Tax Board, July 21, 2003, CCH CALIFORNIA TAX REPORTS, ¶ 403-506)

Practitioner Comment: FTB Withdraws Guidance Regarding Whether Certain States' Taxes Qualify as Income-Based Taxes

See ¶ 131 for information on the continuing uncertainty regarding the treatment of certain taxes as income taxes or non-income taxes for California tax purposes.

¶1007 Losses

Law: Secs. 24347-47.13, 24694 (CCH CALIFORNIA TAX REPORTS, ¶ 10-515, 10-685, 10-820, 10-875).

Comparable Federal: Secs. 165, 198A, 470, 582 (CCH U.S. MASTER TAX GUIDE ¶ 1101—1195).

California Form: Form 100 (California Corporation Franchise or Income Tax Return).

California incorporates federal law as of the current IRC tie-in date (¶ 803), which allows a deduction for losses sustained and not compensated for by insurance or otherwise. (Sec. 24347, Rev. & Tax. Code)

California also incorporates federal law disallowing deductions for losses associated with tax-exempt use property to the extent the losses exceed the income from the leases of the property. Amounts disallowed as tax-exempt use losses are carried over to the next year and are treated as a federal deduction with respect to the property, again limited to the income received from the property leases. (Sec. 24694, Rev. & Tax. Code)

The corporate provisions regarding the deduction and carryover of disaster losses are the same as the provisions for personal income (¶ 307). (Sec. 24347.4, Rev. & Tax. Code; Sec. 24347.5, Rev. & Tax. Code)

See Chapter 12 of this *Guidebook* for a discussion of capital losses.

See ¶ 1223 for treatment of losses on redemption of U.S. Savings Bonds. See ¶ 1023 regarding disallowance of certain losses.

¶1008 Wash Sales

Law: Sec. 24998 (CCH CALIFORNIA TAX REPORTS, ¶ 10-640).

Comparable Federal: Sec. 1091 (CCH U.S. MASTER TAX GUIDE ¶ 2361).

Same as personal income tax (¶ 527).

¶1009 Bad Debts

Law: Secs. 24347, 24348, 24434 (CCH CALIFORNIA TAX REPORTS, ¶ 10-340, 10-515, 10-685, 10-875).

Comparable Federal: Secs. 166, 271, 582, 593, 595 (CCH U.S. MASTER TAX GUIDE ¶ 1128, 1157—1163).

California law governing the deduction of bad debts is the same as federal law as of the current IRC tie-in date (see ¶ 803) with the following modifications:

— with respect to partially worthless debts, if a portion of a debt is deducted in any year, no deduction is allowable in a subsequent year for any portion of the debt that was charged off in a prior year, whether claimed as a deduction in the prior year or not; and

— California incorporates federal law relating to bad debts with respect to securities held by financial institutions, but modifies a federal limitation on foreign corporations so that the limitation applies only to foreign corporations that have a water's-edge election in effect for the taxable year.

(Sec. 24347, Rev. & Tax. Code; Sec. 24348, Rev. & Tax. Code; Sec. 24434, Rev. & Tax. Code)

California allows banks, at the discretion of the FTB, to claim a deduction for bad debt reserves in conformance with federal law. (Sec. 24348, Rev. & Tax. Code)

• *Bad debt vs. capital contribution*

For a loan to qualify as a bad debt deduction, the taxpayer must have a reasonable expectation of repayment and a debtor-creditor relationship must exist. If a purported advance of funds is essentially a capital investment placed at the risk of the business, it does not qualify as a loan for a bad debt deduction.

• *Decisions of State Board of Equalization*

In *Appeal of Southwestern Development Company* (1985) (CCH California Tax Reports, ¶ 10-875.24), the State Board of Equalization (BOE) upheld the FTB's position that items deducted by the taxpayer as bad debts were actually capital contributions and, hence, not deductible. Funds placed at the risk of the business with no reasonable expectation of repayment were capital contributions. Advances made during the formation period of a business and later funds to protect the initial investment were also capital contributions. The BOE also held that losses from a business could not be claimed as totally worthless in a year when the business continued in operation beyond that particular year.

In *Appeal of San Fernando Valley Savings and Loan Association* (1975) (CCH California Tax Reports, ¶ 10-340.23), the taxpayer made inadequate additions to its bad-debt reserve in 1968 and 1969, resulting in a debit balance in the reserve. Adequate additions would have resulted in net operating losses for those years. In 1970 the taxpayer claimed a deduction for an addition to the reserve to reduce the debit balance built up in 1968 and 1969. The BOE upheld the FTB's disallowance of the 1970 deduction, pointing out that the taxpayer's accounting had the effect of a net operating loss carryover, which was not allowed under California law in effect at that time.

In *Appeal of Culver Federal Savings and Loan Association* (1966) (CCH California Tax Reports, ¶ 10-340.57), the BOE held that a reserve for bad debts entered on its books by the taxpayer and deducted for federal income tax purposes, but not for California, could nevertheless be claimed later to obtain a refund of California tax. The FTB applied the rationale of this case in Legal Ruling No. 417 (1981) (CCH California Tax Reports, ¶ 10-340.261), which provides that a savings and loan association may retroactively increase its bad debt deduction up to the amount of the year's addition to the reserve as shown on the association's books, but not beyond that amount.

¶1010 Worthless Securities

Law: Sec. 24347 (CCH California Tax Reports, ¶ 10-340, 10-515, 10-685, 10-820).

Comparable Federal: Sec. 165 (CCH U.S. Master Tax Guide ¶ 1764).

Same as personal income tax (¶ 307).

¶1011 Depreciation and Amortization

Law: Secs. 24349-56.8, 24365, 24368.1, 24369.4, 24372.3-73, 24407-09, 24421-22, 24990 (CCH California Tax Reports, ¶ 10-385, 10-515, 10-640, 10-670, 10-680, 10-690, 10-800, 10-845, 10-900, 10-915).

Comparable Federal: Secs. 59, 167-69, 174, 178, 179, 181, 194, 197, 198, 248, 280F (CCH U.S. MASTER TAX GUIDE Chapter 12).

California Forms: FTB 3580 (Application to Amortize Certified Pollution Control Facility), FTB 3805Z (Enterprise Zone Deduction and Credit Summary), FTB 3807 (Local Agency Military Base Recovery Area Deduction and Credit Summary), FTB 3809 (Targeted Tax Area Deduction and Credit Summary), FTB 3885 (Corporation Depreciation and Amortization), Sch. B (100S) (S Corporation Depreciation and Amortization).

A corporate taxpayer is permitted a deduction for depreciation of real or personal property used in a trade or business or held for the production of income. (Sec. 24349, Rev. & Tax. Code) The California depreciation provisions are generally the same as those contained in the pre-1987 personal income tax law (see "Assets Placed in Service Before 1987" at ¶310). However, beginning with the 2005 taxable year, the useful life of motor sports entertainment complexes and Alaska natural gas pipelines is seven years. (Sec. 24355.3, Rev. & Tax. Code; Sec. 24355.5, Rev. & Tax. Code) This is the same as under federal law, except that the seven-year useful life does not apply to motor sports entertainment complexes after 2009 for California purposes.

Except as discussed below, the federal accelerated cost recovery system (ACRS) depreciation method for assets placed in service after 1980 and the federal modified accelerated cost recovery system (MACRS) depreciation method for assets placed in service after 1986 have not been adopted into the California corporation tax law.

Practitioner Comment: Corporate Partners Need Not Recompute Their Distributive Share of Income for Depreciation Items

While California does not conform to IRC Sec. 168 (so called "MACRS" depreciation) under the Bank and Corporate Tax Law, it does so in the Personal Income Tax Law. The Franchise Tax Board's longstanding view has been that corporate partners need not recompute their share of partnership income, even though such may have been based on federal depreciation methods not adopted under the Bank and Corporate Tax Law. See *FTB Notice 89-129* (CCH CALIFORNIA TAX REPORTS, ¶401-175).

Chris Whitney, Contributing Editor

Written agreements may be made between the taxpayer and the Franchise Tax Board (FTB) as to the useful life and depreciation rate of a particular property. (Sec. 24351, Rev. & Tax. Code; Sec. 24352, Rev. & Tax. Code)

• *ACRS depreciation allowed for S corporations*

An S corporation's deduction for depreciation and amortization is computed under the personal income tax law (¶310, ¶311). (Sec. 17201, Rev. & Tax. Code)

• *IRC Sec. 179 asset expense election*

Taxpayers may elect to claim an IRC Sec. 179 asset expense election for corporation income and franchise tax purposes in lieu of the first-year additional bonus depreciation deduction discussed below. California's asset expense election is limited to $25,000 per taxable year, while the federal limit is $500,000 for tax years after 2009 (adjusted annually for inflation beginning with the 2016 tax year); $250,000 during the 2008 and 2009 tax years; $125,000 during the 2007 tax year; and $100,000 (subject to adjustments for inflation) for the 2003 through 2006 tax years. (Sec. 24356(b), Rev. & Tax. Code)

Other differences between California and federal law are as follows:

— the phase-out threshold for the cost of the qualified property is $200,000 for California purposes in contrast to the federal phase-out threshold of $2 million for tax years after 2009 (adjusted annually for inflation beginning with the 2016 tax year); $800,000 during the 2008 and 2009 tax years; $500,000 during the 2007 tax year; and $400,000 (subject to adjustments for inflation) during the 2003 through 2006 tax years;

— federal law, unlike California law, allows the election to be made for purchases of off-the-shelf computer property, qualified real property (i.e., qualified leasehold improvement property, qualified restaurant property, and qualified retail improvement property), and air conditioning and heating units;

— California does not allow taxpayers to make, modify, or revoke the election without the consent of the FTB, whereas taxpayers may unilaterally make, modify, or revoke the election for federal purposes; and

— California law, unlike federal law, does not raise the deduction amount for disaster-related purchases.

If a taxpayer elects this deduction, the depreciable basis of the subject property must be reduced by the IRC Sec. 179 expense. (Instructions, FTB 3885F, Corporation Depreciation and Amortization) Because the maximum California deduction has differed from the maximum federal deduction, the depreciable basis of property will differ for federal and state purposes.

• *Residential rental property*

Although California does not incorporate MACRS or ACRS, California allows the use of these federal depreciation methods to determine a reasonable depreciation allowance for California purposes. Accordingly, under federal law as incorporated by California, corporate taxpayers are permitted to treat residential rental property on which construction began after 1986, and before July 1, 1988, as either 18-year real property, 27.5-year residential rental property, or asset depreciation range property. (*Letter*, FTB, September 13, 1988, CCH CALIFORNIA TAX REPORTS, ¶ 401-662)

• *Phylloxera infested vineyards*

The useful life for any grapevine replaced in a California vineyard is five-years if the grapevine was replaced as a direct result of (1) phylloxera infestation, or (2) Pierce's Disease infestation. However, a taxpayer may elect to use the federal alternative depreciation system (¶ 310). If the taxpayer chooses to use this method and if the taxpayer elected not to capitalize the costs of replacing the infested vines, the replacement vines will have a class life of 10 years rather than the 20-year class life normally specified under federal law for fruit-bearing vines. (Sec. 24349(c), Rev. & Tax. Code)

• *Luxury automobiles and listed property*

For corporate income tax purposes, California adopts a modified version of IRC Sec. 280F, which imposes a limitation on depreciation deductions for luxury automobiles and other listed property, including computers and peripheral equipment. The limitation is similar to that imposed under the personal income tax law (¶ 310), except that for corporate purposes, the terms "deduction" or "recovery deduction" relating to ACRS mean amounts allowable as a deduction under the bank and corporation tax law. (Sec. 24349.1, Rev. & Tax. Code)

• *Property leased to tax-exempt entities*

California has adopted the IRC 168(h) limitation on deductions for property leased to tax-exempt entities for taxable years after 1986. For taxable years beginning after 1990, the amount of such deductions is limited to the amount determined under IRC Sec. 168(g), concerning the alternative depreciation system. (Sec. 24349(d), Rev. & Tax. Code)

• *Salvage reduction*

The amount of salvage value to be taken into consideration in computing the amount subject to depreciation may be reduced by up to 10% of the depreciable basis of the property, except with respect to property for which California allows the use of the current federal depreciation methods. (Sec. 24352.5, Rev. & Tax. Code)

- *Additional first-year depreciation*

Planning Note: Additional First-Year Bonus Depreciation Not Allowed

California does not incorporate the IRC Sec. 168(k) 50% bonus depreciation deduction for property purchased in 2008 through 2010, the 100% bonus depreciation applicable to property acquired after September 8, 2010, and before January 1, 2020 (before January 1, 2021 in the case of property with a long production period and certain noncommercial aircraft) and subject to possible extension if federal "extenders" legislation is enacted, nor the IRC Sec. 168(k) additional 30% or 50% bonus depreciation deduction for property purchased after September 10, 2001, and before 2005. California also does not incorporate the additional 30% first-year bonus depreciation deduction allowed for qualified New York Liberty Zone property. However, California does allow a limited 20% first-year bonus depreciation deduction as discussed below.

California does allow a corporate taxpayer to take an additional 20% first-year (bonus) depreciation deduction on personal property having a useful life of six years or more. It is limited to 20% of the cost of such property, and may be claimed only with respect to $10,000 of property additions each year and is taken in lieu of the IRC Sec. 179 deduction discussed above. (Sec. 24356, Rev. & Tax. Code; Reg. 24356-1, 18 CCR; Reg. 24356(d), 18 CCR)

The limitation is applied to each taxpayer, and not to each taxpayer's trade or business. In determining the allowable first-year depreciation bonus, all members of an affiliated corporation are treated as one taxpayer. The basis of the property used for regular depreciation purposes must be reduced by the amount of bonus depreciation claimed.

- *Safe-harbor leases*

California recognizes safe harbor leases under former IRC Sec. 168(f). (*California Response to CCH Multistate Corporate Income Tax Survey*, California Franchise Tax Board, July 21, 2003, CCH CALIFORNIA TAX REPORTS, ¶ 403-506).

- *Pollution control facilities*

Same as personal income tax (¶ 314). (Sec. 24372.3, Rev. & Tax. Code)

CCH Practice Tip: Preference Item Reduction

Because California incorporates the IRC Sec. 291 tax preference item treatment for C corporations and for elections made during the first three taxable years following a C corporation conversion to an S corporation, only 80% of the facility's adjusted basis may be amortized over 60 months. Accordingly, for corporations, the amortizable basis for such facilities for which a rapid amortization election is made must be reduced by 20%. (Instructions, FTB 3580, Application to Amortize Certified Pollution Control Facility)

- *Trademark, trade name, and franchise transfer payments*

Same as personal income tax (¶ 332). (Sec. 24368.1, Rev. & Tax. Code)

- *Films, video tapes, sound recordings, and similar property*

Same as personal income tax (¶ 310). (Sec. 24349(f), Rev. & Tax. Code; Sec. 24355.4, Rev. & Tax. Code)

- *Indian reservation property*

Same as personal income tax (¶ 310).

¶1011

- *Environmental remediation expenses*

    Same as personal income tax (¶346).

- *Reforestation expenses*

    A corporate taxpayer may elect to currently deduct up to $10,000 of qualified reforestation expenses in the year paid and to capitalize and amortize any remaining amount over a seven-year period. This applies to direct costs of forestation or reforestation, including seeds, labor, equipment, etc. The amortization period begins on the first day of the second half of the taxable year of the expenditures. The deduction is taken from adjusted gross income and is limited to $10,000 per taxable year. (Sec. 24372.5, Rev. & Tax. Code)

- *Research and experimental expenditures*

    Same as personal income tax (¶331). (Sec. 24365, Rev. & Tax. Code; Reg. 24365-24368(a) —Reg. 24365-24368(d), 18 CCR)

- *Amortization of cost of acquiring a lease*

    Same as personal income tax (¶313). (Sec. 24373, Rev. & Tax. Code)

- *Organizational expenditures*

    As under federal law, taxpayers may currently deduct up to $5,000 (temporarily increased to $10,000 for the 2010 tax year only) in start-up expenses and amortize any remainder over a 15-year period. (Sec. 24407, Rev. & Tax. Code)

- *Term property interests*

    California adopts federal law, under which no depreciation or amortization deduction is allowed for any term property interest (such as a life interest, an interest for a term of years, or an income interest in a trust) for any period during which the remainder interest is held, directly or indirectly, by a related person. The basis of such property for which a depreciation or amortization deduction has been allowed must be reduced by the amount of the disallowed deduction, and the basis of the remainder interest in such property must be increased by the same amount. (Sec. 24368.1, Rev. & Tax. Code)

- *Accelerated write-offs for depressed areas*

    Same as personal income (¶316), except that in addition to disallowing the IRC Sec. 179 asset expense election if the write-offs are claimed by enterprise zone, local agency military base recovery area, former targeted tax area, or former Los Angeles Revitalization Zone businesses, the additional first-year depreciation is disallowed. (Sec. 24356.7, Rev. & Tax. Code; Sec. 24356.8, Rev. & Tax. Code; Former Sec. 24356.4, Rev. & Tax. Code)

- *Goodwill and other intangibles*

    Same as personal income tax (¶333). (Sec. 24355.5, Rev. & Tax. Code)

¶1012 Depletion

Law: Secs. 24831, 24831.3, 24831.6 (CCH CALIFORNIA TAX REPORTS, ¶10-515, 10-850).

Comparable Federal: Secs. 611-38 (CCH U.S. MASTER TAX GUIDE ¶1289 et seq.).

California Form: Form 100 (California Corporation Franchise or Income Tax Return).

Same as personal income tax (¶319, ¶540).

¶1013 Development and Exploration Expenses of Mines, etc.

Law: Secs. 24423, 24831 (CCH CALIFORNIA TAX REPORTS, ¶10-515, 10-850).

Comparable Federal: Secs. 193, 263(c), 263(i), 616-17 (CCH U.S. MASTER TAX GUIDE ¶987—990, 1779).

California Form: Form 100 (California Corporation Franchise or Income Tax Return).

Except for minor technical differences, the corporation tax law is the same as the personal income tax law, as explained at ¶320. The corporation tax law also specifically provides for deduction of intangible drilling and development costs of oil and gas wells. (Sec. 24423, Rev. & Tax. Code; Sec. 24831, Rev. & Tax. Code)

California has no provision comparable to the federal provision that provides a deduction for expenses incurred for tertiary injectants.

¶1014 Contributions

Law: Secs. 18648.5, 24357-59.1 (CCH CALIFORNIA TAX REPORTS, ¶10-650, 10-705, 10-880, 10-900).

Comparable Federal: Secs. 170, 6115 (CCH U.S. MASTER TAX GUIDE ¶1058—1071).

California Form: Form 100 (California Corporation Franchise or Income Tax Return).

Corporations are allowed a California deduction for contributions paid to certain organizations, up to a limit of 10% of net income computed without the benefit of this deduction or certain other special deductions (dividends received, building and loan dividends paid, certain deductions of cooperatives, etc.). Contributions in excess of the 10% limit may be carried over to the next five succeeding taxable years. (Sec. 24357, Rev. & Tax. Code; Sec. 24358, Rev. & Tax. Code)

• *California-federal differences*

—There are differences in the adjustments to income for purposes of computing the limitation. For federal purposes, income is adjusted for net operating loss carryovers and other special deductions not applicable to California. For California purposes, income is adjusted, as shown above, for special deductions not applicable to the federal computation. (Sec. 24357, Rev. & Tax. Code)

—There are slight differences in the rules for contributions of appreciated property. California ordinarily reduces the contribution by the amount of the untaxed gain; in effect, the deduction is limited to the cost basis of the property. The federal law similarly limits the deduction to the donor's basis in the property. However, federal law retains an exception for donations of appreciated stock to certain private foundations. (Sec. 24357.1, Rev. & Tax. Code)

—Federal law, unlike California law, allows a deduction for certain contributions of research property to a California college or university, the amount being the basis of the property plus one-half of the appreciation, limited to twice the basis.

—California allows a deduction for charitable contributions only if the contributions are verified under regulations prescribed by the Franchise Tax Board. For federal purposes, charitable contributions may be deducted only if the contributions are verified under regulations prescribed by the Secretary of the Treasury. (Sec. 24357, Rev. & Tax. Code)

—California has no provision similar to the federal provision disallowing the deduction for transfers made in split-dollar insurance arrangements.

—California does not adopt federal provisions that limit the charitable contributions deduction for patents and most other intellectual property donated to a charitable organization to the lesser of the donor's basis in the property or its fair market value, but allow limited additional deductions for such contributions if the donee has income attributable to the donation during the 12 years after the property is donated. Nor has California conformed to the limits placed on the amount of deductions that may be claimed for vehicles, boats, and aircraft and the increased substantiation requirements for such property (see ¶321 for details).

—California has not adopted federal provisions that allow an enhanced deduction for donations of food from the taxpayer's inventory.

—California does not follow the federal provision that with certain exceptions, makes qualified contributions to donor advised funds fully deductible.

Because the contribution deduction is limited to the adjusted basis of the assets being contributed and the income from which the contributions are deducted, taxpayers must add back the federal contributions deduction and recalculate the amount that may be deducted for California corporation franchise and income tax purposes. The computation is completed on a separate worksheet, using the Form 100, California Corporation Franchise or Income Tax Return, as a format and adding in any federal contribution deduction on Line 8, Form 100. An additional worksheet is also provided in the Form 100, Instructions to Line 14, to complete the computation. (Instructions, Form 100, California Corporation Franchise or Income Tax Return)

The California limitation may also be affected by the apportionment of income within and without the state (¶1312).

¶1015 Amortization of Bond Premium

Law: Secs. 24360-63.5 (CCH CALIFORNIA TAX REPORTS, ¶10-610).

Comparable Federal: Sec. 171 (CCH U.S. MASTER TAX GUIDE ¶1967).

California Form: Form 100 (California Corporation Franchise or Income Tax Return).

Deduction is allowed, at the taxpayer's election, for amortization of premium on bonds owned. (Sec. 24360, Rev. & Tax. Code through 24363.5, Rev. & Tax. Code) The general rule is the same as the federal rule, but there may be a difference in its application because of differences in taxability of government bond interest or because the taxpayer may elect to amortize for California purposes and not for federal, or vice versa. This may result in a difference in the adjusted cost basis, and consequently a difference in gain or loss, when bonds are sold. For California purposes, the premium of a taxable bond is allocated to the interest from the bond. In lieu of being deducted, the premium is applied against (and reduces) interest income from the bond.

No amortization is allowable on any portion of bond premium attributable to conversion features of the bond.

The federal law provides that the amortization period is to be determined with reference to the maturity date of the bonds, except that if use of an earlier call date results in a smaller amortization deduction, then the call date is to be used.

The California law contains nothing comparable to the federal provision that requires securities dealers to amortize premium paid on certain short-term municipal bonds. Because of the difference in treatment of interest on municipal bonds for franchise tax purposes, there would be no point in having such a provision in the California law.

¶1016 Payments to Pension or Profit-Sharing Plans

Law: Secs. 24601-12, 24685.5 (CCH CALIFORNIA TAX REPORTS, ¶10-515, 10-520, 10-595).

Comparable Federal: Secs. 194A, 401-20, 4971-75 (CCH U.S. MASTER TAX GUIDE Chapter 21).

Same as personal income tax, except that the corporation tax law incorporates by reference only those federal provisions that deal with employer deductions (¶330, ¶607). (Sec. 24601 et. seq., Rev. & Tax. Code; Sec. 24685.5, Rev. & Tax. Code)

¶1017 Employee Stock Options

Law: Secs. 24379, 24601-12 (CCH California Tax Reports, ¶10-515, 10-520, 10-595, 10-645).

Comparable Federal: Secs. 83, 421-24 (CCH U.S. Master Tax Guide ¶1919— 1934A).

Except with respect to California qualified stock options, the California rules regarding an employer's treatment of employee stock options and other transfers of property for services are the same as federal. (Sec. 24379, Rev. & Tax. Code; Sec. 24601 et. seq., Rev. & Tax. Code)

An employer corporation is precluded by California law from claiming a business expense deduction for granting a California qualified stock option (see ¶207 for a discussion of the favorable tax treatment afforded California qualified stock options). (Sec. 24602, Rev. & Tax. Code)

¶1018 Start-Up Expenditures

Law: Sec. 24414 (CCH California Tax Reports, ¶10-210, 10-515).

Comparable Federal: Sec. 195 (CCH U.S. Master Tax Guide ¶481, 984).

Same as personal income tax (¶334).

¶1019 Subsidization of Employees' Ridesharing and Parking

Law: Sec. 24343.5 (CCH California Tax Reports, ¶10-830).

Comparable Federal: None.

California Form: Form 100 (California Corporation Franchise or Income Tax Return).

The corporation tax law permits employers to claim a business expense deduction for specific benefits paid or incurred relating to employee ridesharing and parking. These benefits are the following:

— subsidizing employees commuting in buspools, private commute buses, carpools, and subscription taxipools;

— subsidizing monthly transit passes to employees and their dependents;

— compensating employees who do not require free parking;

— providing free or preferential parking to carpools, vanpools, and any other vehicle used in a ridesharing arrangement;

— making facility improvements to encourage employees to participate in ridesharing arrangements, to use bicycles, or to walk (corporations are allowed a 36-month depreciation deduction for these improvements);

— providing company commuter van or bus service to employees for commuting to and from their homes; improvements (capital costs) to the vehicle are not allowed as a business expense deduction;

— providing employee transportation services that are required as part of the employer's business activities, if the employee is not reimbursed and there is no available ridesharing incentive program; and

— providing cash allowances to employees in amounts equal to the parking subsidies that the employer would otherwise pay to secure parking spaces for those employees.

(Sec. 24343.5, Rev. & Tax. Code)

¶1020 Deduction for Dividends Received

Law: Secs. 24402, 24410 (CCH California Tax Reports, ¶10-810).

Comparable Federal: Secs. 243-47 (CCH U.S. Master Tax Guide ¶237 et seq.).

California law provided a deduction for dividends received when the income distributed had been subjected to tax in the hands of the paying corporation. However, as discussed at ¶909, this deduction was held unconstitutional as applied to non-California corporations. (Sec. 24402, Rev. & Tax. Code) California does allow a deduction for dividends paid from insurance company subsidiaries (¶909). California also allows an intercompany dividend elimination for members of a combined unitary group (¶909).

¶1021 Deductions Allowed to Special Classes of Organizations

Law: Secs. 24370, 24403-06.6, 24870-74 (CCH CALIFORNIA TAX REPORTS, ¶10-250, 10-340, 10-355, 10-360, 10-365, 10-370, 10-701).

Comparable Federal: Secs. 521, 591, 851-60, 1381-83 (CCH U.S. MASTER TAX GUIDE ¶698, 2301, 2317, 2320, 2323, 2326, 2329, 2337, 2339, 2383).

California Form: Form 100 (California Corporation Franchise or Income Tax Return).

The California law allows special deductions to certain classes of organizations, as follows:

— building and loan associations: dividends on shares allowed as a deduction (Sec. 24403, Rev. & Tax. Code);

— agricultural cooperative associations: income from nonprofit activities allowed as a deduction (Sec. 24404, Rev. & Tax. Code);

— other cooperative associations: income from certain nonprofit activities allowed as a deduction (see below) (Sec. 24405, Rev. & Tax. Code);

— retail cooperatives: certain allocated patronage refunds allowed as a deduction (see below) (Sec. 24406, Rev. & Tax. Code);

— mutual savings banks: certain interest on deposits allowed as a deduction for franchise tax purposes (Sec. 24370, Rev. & Tax. Code);

— real estate investment trusts (REITs): income distributed during the year, or within a certain period after the year, is allowed as a deduction (see also ¶805);

— regulated investment companies (RICs): exempt interest dividends distributed to shareholders allowed as a deduction (see also ¶805) (Sec. 24870 et. seq., Rev. & Tax. Code);

— gas producers' cooperatives: patronage refunds paid to patrons allowed as a deduction (Sec. 24406, Rev. & Tax. Code); and

— credit unions: income arising from business with credit union members and income from investments of surplus member savings capital (see *Christian Community Credit Union* (2003) (CCH CALIFORNIA TAX REPORTS, ¶10-250.24) for the formula established by the BOE for computing this deduction) and income resulting from reciprocal transactions with member credit unions are allowed as a deduction.

Income allocations to members of agricultural cooperatives may be made within 8 1/2 months after the close of the taxable year and still be considered as having been made on the last day of the taxable year, provided the members are advised of the dollar amount of such allocations.

Income earned by credit unions from third-party investments are not exempt from tax as income from business done for credit union members, and share dividends paid by the credit unions to their members are not deductible as patronage dividends, interest, or ordinary and necessary business expenses. (*Educational Employees Credit Union v. Franchise Tax Board* (2006) CCH CALIFORNIA TAX REPORTS, ¶10-250.4191)

Agricultural cooperatives are permitted to deduct all income, regardless of source, that is properly allocated to members. See Legal Ruling No. 389 (1975) (CCH CALIFORNIA TAX REPORTS, ¶ 10-250.25) and Legal Ruling No. 418 (1981) (CCH CALIFORNIA TAX REPORTS, ¶ 10-250.34).

Retail cooperatives are permitted to deduct patronage refunds allocated to their patrons, provided the refunds are made and allocated within specific restrictions set forth in the law. (Sec. 24406, Rev. & Tax. Code)

In *Appeal of Certified Grocers of California, Ltd.* (1962) (CCH CALIFORNIA TAX REPORTS, ¶ 10-250.35), the State Board of Equalization (BOE) held that a wholesale grocery cooperative could deduct patronage dividends and interest on members' accounts, following long-standing federal practice, irrespective of the fact that the California law did not provide specifically to this effect in the year involved.

California law, like federal law, allows a cooperative to pay a dividend on capital stock or other proprietary capital interest of the organization without reducing net earnings, to the extent that the organizational documents provide that the dividend is in addition to amounts otherwise payable to patrons. (Sec. 24406.6, Rev. & Tax. Code)

• *Some expenses not deductible*

In *Security-First National Bank v. Franchise Tax Board* (1961) (CCH CALIFORNIA TAX REPORTS, ¶ 10-210.361), it was held that a cooperative association could not deduct expenses allocable to income for which special deductions discussed above were allowable. To the same effect, see *Anaheim Union Water Company v. Franchise Tax Board* (1972) (CCH CALIFORNIA TAX REPORTS, ¶ 10-250.393), involving the deductibility of operating losses of a nonprofit mutual water company against income from certain profit-making activities. The Court of Appeal held that the losses in question were nondeductible because they were allocable to exempt income. Also, to the same effect, see *Appeal of Los Angeles Area Dodge Dealers Association* (1978) (CCH CALIFORNIA TAX REPORTS, ¶ 10-250.55), involving interest on short-term certificates of deposit. See also ¶ 1023.

In *Appeal of San Antonio Water Company* (1970) (CCH CALIFORNIA TAX REPORTS, ¶ 10-250.39), the BOE held that gain on sale of land to a member of a cooperative was not deductible under the third item above.

For a good discussion of the accounting rules applicable to organizations covered by the other cooperative associations, above, see *Appeal of Redwood Mutual Water Company* (1980) (CCH CALIFORNIA TAX REPORTS, ¶ 10-250.391).

In *Appeal of Imperial Hay Growers' Association* (1970) (CCH CALIFORNIA TAX REPORTS, ¶ 10-250.27), the BOE held that a loss on plant abandonment was outside the scope of the special provisions described above and was deductible against income derived from nonmembers.

The federal law allows some special deductions somewhat comparable, in a general way, to the California deductions described above. In view of the many differences, no attempt is made here to compare the two laws.

¶1022 Tenant Expenses—Cooperative Apartment and Housing Corporations

Law: Sec. 24382 (CCH CALIFORNIA TAX REPORTS, ¶ 10-515).

Comparable Federal: Sec. 216 (CCH U.S. MASTER TAX GUIDE ¶ 1028, 1040).

California law is generally the same as federal law in allowing certain expenses of tenant-stockholders to be deducted. (Sec. 24382, Rev. & Tax. Code)

¶1023 Items Not Deductible

Law: Secs. 24343.2, 24343.7, 24343.8, 24349.2, 24421-29, 24436.1-37, 24441-48, 24691 (CCH CALIFORNIA TAX REPORTS, ¶10-250, 10-515, 10-520, 10-525, 10-595, 10-645, 10-665, 10-800, 10-810, 10-830).

Comparable Federal: Secs. 162, 261-68, 271, 274, 276-77, 280B, 280C, 280E, 280G (CCH U.S. MASTER TAX GUIDE ¶293, 673, 901, 903, 907, 909, 910 et seq., 969, 970, 972, 990 et seq., 1029, 1122, 1166, 1330, 1343, 1551, 1553, 1717, 1747, 2028, 2257).

California Form: Form 100 (California Corporation Franchise or Income Tax Return).

Certain items are made expressly nondeductible, the principal items being:

(a) capital expenditures, certain life insurance premiums, interest on indebtedness incurred in connection with certain life insurance and annuity contracts, expenses allocable to tax-exempt income, carrying charges that the taxpayer elects to capitalize, etc. (Sec. 24422, et seq., Rev. & Tax. Code);

(b) losses, expenses, and interest with respect to certain transactions between related taxpayers (Sec. 24427, Rev. & Tax. Code);

(c) expenses of certain illegal activities or of other activities that tend to promote or are otherwise related to such illegal activities, as explained at ¶336;

(d) criminal profiteering expenses, including those associated with drug trafficking and insurance fraud, as explained at ¶336;

(e) certain expenses attributable to substandard housing, as explained at ¶336;

(f) abandonment fees on open-space easements and timberland tax-recoupment fees, as explained at ¶336;

(g) certain expenses in connection with entertainment activities, business gifts, and foreign conventions, as explained at ¶302;

(h) deductions for remuneration of personal services that are not reported in required statements to employees (¶715) or in required information returns (¶713) may be disallowed at the discretion of the Franchise Tax Board (FTB);

(i) deductions for interest, taxes, depreciation, and amortization are denied to property owners who fail to file proper information returns as explained at ¶713;

(j) business expenses incurred at a discriminatory club, as explained at ¶336;

(k) expenses of advertising in political programs or for admission to political fundraising functions and similar events (Sec. 24429, Rev. & Tax. Code);

(l) deductions for golden parachute payments (although California does not adopt the federal excise tax) (Sec. 24349.2, Rev. & Tax. Code); and

(m) certain league-imposed fines paid or incurred by professional sports franchise owners, as explained at ¶336 (for taxable years beginning on or after January 1, 2014).

Practice Tip: Repair Regulations

California follows the federal "repair regulations," which provide rules for distinguishing capital expenditures from deductible supply, repair, and maintenance costs. (*FTB Tax News* (March 2015) (CCH CALIFORNIA TAX REPORTS, ¶406-310))

• *California-federal differences*

(a) Federal law contains a special provision disallowing expenses attributable to the production of an unharvested crop in certain cases when the land is sold after having been used in a trade or business. There is no necessity for a comparable California rule, because California has no special alternative method of computing the tax on capital gains.

(b) Federal law that generally prohibits a current deduction for capital expenditures does not apply for California purposes to expenditures for which a deduction is allowed under California law for enterprise zone, local agency military base recovery area, or former targeted tax area property.

(c) Because of California's federal conformity date (see ¶803), California has not conformed to a federal provision preventing the transfer of loss from tax indifferent parties. The federal provision applies to sales and other dispositions of property acquired after December 31, 2015.

(d) There are no federal provisions comparable to items (d), (f), (g), and (k), above, except for a federal provision that prohibits deductions and credits for illegal drug trafficking. Otherwise, the California rules are generally similar to the federal rules, as they relate to corporations.

CCH Practice Tip: Illegal Drug Activities

California's Corporation Franchise and Income Tax Law does not incorporate IRC § 280E, which prohibits taxpayers from claiming deductions or credits for amounts paid or incurred in the trade or business of illegal trafficking of drugs listed in the Controlled Substances Act (such as marijuana, cocaine, heroin, LSD, opium, amphetamines, etc.). However, as discussed at ¶336, California does prohibit taxpayers from claiming deductions for any income received that is directly derived from any act or omission of criminal profiteering activity if the taxpayer is found guilty of the specified illegal activities in a criminal proceeding before a California state court or any proceeding in which the state, county, city and county, city, or other political subdivision was a party. This distinction could be important for businesses such as medical marijuana dispensaries. It would appear that dispensaries subject to the corporation franchise and income tax would be allowed to deduct their trade and business expenses for California purposes as long as they are not found guilty of criminal profiteering. This treatment is different than that under the personal income tax law.

• *Entertainment and gifts*

California law is the same as federal law. (Sec. 24443, Rev. & Tax. Code)

• *Shipping company and oil/gas drilling rig employee's meal expenses*

Both California and federal law allow a 100% deduction (rather than 50%) of meals to employees on offshore oil or gas rigs and to employees who are crew members of certain commercial vessels (¶302).

• *Expenses allocable to exempt income*

Like federal law (IRC Sec. 265(a)), a California deduction of expenses allocable to tax-exempt income is not allowed. (Sec. 24425, Rev. & Tax. Code) Under the allocation and apportionment provisions (see ¶1301 *et seq.*), if some income is not included within a corporation's measure of tax, any deductions in connection with the production of such income may not be deducted from income attributable to such sources. (Reg. 25120, 18 CCR)

Also, under California law, no deduction is allowed for specified interest and other expenses paid or incurred to an insurer, if the insurer is a member of the taxpayer's commonly controlled group and the amount paid or incurred would constitute income to the insurer if the insurer were subject to California corporation franchise or income tax (see Sec. 24425(b) for details).

There may be a difference between federal and California treatment of expenses allocable to tax-exempt income, as referred to in item (a), above, in that certain items may be excludable or deductible from income for California purposes, but not for federal. Examples include interest earned by certain cooperative associations, income from bonds exempt under California law, but not federal law, etc. See ¶1021 for cases involving credit unions and cooperative associations, and ¶1004 regarding unallowable interest on indebtedness incurred to acquire property from which the income is allocable to sources outside California. Also see ¶909 for a discussion of this in relation to the dividends received deduction.

In *Appeal of Mission Equities Corporation* (1975) (CCH CALIFORNIA TAX REPORTS, ¶10-800.402), the State Board of Equalization (BOE) followed the *Great Western Financial* case, below, in disallowing expenses allocable to dividends received from California subsidiaries. The BOE approved the FTB's allocation of indirect expenses between taxable and nontaxable income in proportion to the amount of each, the same formula having been approved by the Supreme Court in the *Great Western Financial* case.

In *Great Western Financial Corporation v. Franchise Tax Board* (1971) (CCH CALIFORNIA TAX REPORTS, ¶204-497), the FTB disallowed deductions for interest and for general and administrative expenses of a parent corporation, on the ground that the deductions were allocable to income from dividends received from subsidiary California corporations and that such dividends were "exempt" income because they were deducted as explained in ¶909. The California Supreme Court held for the FTB, and concluded that "expenses incurred by a taxpayer in producing or receiving dividend income are properly deductible only when that taxpayer's dividend income is taxable."

Practitioner Comment: Deemed Intention

In *American General Realty Investment Corp., Inc. v. Franchise Tax Board*, California Superior Court for the City and County of San Francisco, No. CGC-03-425690, April 28, 2005, CCH CALIFORNIA TAX REPORTS, ¶403-794, the Court held that the California Franchise Tax Board (FTB) erred in disallowing a portion of a taxpayer's interest expense deduction, because all of the interest expense was directly traceable to the active conduct of the taxpayer's consumer finance and real estate businesses, both of which generated taxable income.

Notably, in this decision the Court found that, under the rules of statutory construction, Section 24344(b) is applied before 24425. In other words, if there is no excess of business interest expense over business interest income, there is simply nothing to disallow. Before *Ceridian* the FTB's administrative position was that Section 24344(b) applies first, as outlined in FTB Legal Ruling 374, FTB Legal Ruling 424, and FTB Notice 2000-9. After the *Ceridian* decision, the FTB argued the opposite—that Section 24425 applies first.

The FTB alternately argued that IRC Sec. 265(a)(2) and Rev. Proc. 72-18 would apply to disallow the interest expense as well. The Court rejected both positions. With respect to Rev. Proc. 72-18, the Court firmly rejected the FTB's assertions and held that the taxpayer had met its burden of proving that no debt was incurred for the purposes of receiving exempt income.

American General Realty Investment Corp. is not binding precedent. However, in a letter decision the BOE has ruled that the FTB improperly disallowed a portion of the interest expense deductions claimed by a taxpayer's unitary group. The BOE ruled for the taxpayer and allowed the full deduction. The BOE did not give an explanation of its decision. However, the result in the letter decision is consistent with *American General Realty Investment Corp.* (Appeal of Beneficial California, Inc. (2005) CCH CALIFORNIA TAX REPORTS, ¶403-851)

It is not clear at this point whether the FTB will follow the decision. In any event, the case does not resolve the issue of how to apply Section 24425 to other expenses that the FTB may attempt to allocate to insurance company dividend income, as Section 24344(b) only applies to interest.

It is possible that the FTB may attempt to disallow an amount of interest expense that actually exceeds the dividend deduction, or to disallow interest expense in years when no dividend income was received.

As to the disallowance of expenses other than interest expenses, the Superior Court on July 1, 2008, rejected the FTB's attempt to disallow certain overhead expenses which were charged by a corporate parent to its insurance company subsidiaries under the theory that "but for" such expenses the insurance companies would have been unable to conduct business and hence pay dividends to their parent. Instead, the court agreed that the expenses were directly traceable to the management fees received the subsidiaries and should be allowed. See *Mercury General Corporation v. Franchise Tax Board*, Superior Court, San Francisco Case No. CGC-07-462688. It should be noted that Superior Court decisions are not citable and cannot be relied on as precedent.

Chris Whitney, Contributing Editor

In *Appeal of Zenith National Insurance Corporation* (1998) (CCH CALIFORNIA TAX REPORTS, ¶ 10-800.40), the FTB determined that the income from the taxpayer's sale of debentures and purchase of preferred stock contributed to both the taxpayer's taxable and nontaxable activities and, therefore, utilized a general formula to allocate the interest expense in accordance with the ratio of the taxpayer's tax-exempt income to the taxpayer's gross income. However, the BOE found that the taxpayer incurred the expense for the purpose of producing taxable income for three of the four income years at issue and, thus, could claim the full deduction for those three years.

• *Expenses for which credits are allowable*

California incorporates, as of the current IRC tie-in date (see ¶ 803), the portion of IRC Sec. 280C that disallows a deduction for (1) qualified clinical testing expenses that were otherwise available, to the extent that such expenses were claimed for the federal clinical testing tax credit, and (2) that portion of qualified research expenses or basic research expenses that equals the credit amount allowed for such expenses under IRC Sec. 41 (¶ 818).

California does not incorporate the rest of IRC Sec. 280C, which disallows a deduction for expenses for which other federal credits are claimed, such as the federal work opportunity credit and the low sulfur diesel fuel production credit. Because federal provisions dealing with federal credits are inapplicable under California law (Sec. 23051.5(b), Rev. & Tax. Code), these provisions are inapplicable and taxpayers utilizing the federal reconciliation method (¶ 803) would be allowed to subtract such expenses on their federal return.

See ¶ 1004 regarding deduction of prepaid interest. See ¶ 1106 regarding certain deductions of farming corporations.

¶ 1024 Net Operating Loss Carryover and Carryback

Law: Secs. 24416-16.22, 24451, 24458, 24459, 24471, 25108, 25110 (CCH CALIFORNIA TAX REPORTS, ¶ 10-385, 10-805, 11-550).

Comparable Federal: Secs. 172, 269, 381, 382, 384 (CCH U.S. MASTER TAX GUIDE ¶ 1173—1188).

California Forms: FTB 3805Q (Net Operating Loss (NOL) Computation and Disaster Loss Limitations - Corporations), FTB 3805Z (Enterprise Zone Deduction and Credit Summary), FTB 3806 (Los Angeles Revitalization Zone Deduction and Credit Summary), FTB 3807 (Local Agency Military Base Recovery Area Deduction and Credit Summary), FTB 3809 (Targeted Tax Area Deduction and Credit Summary).

Same as personal income tax (¶ 309), except as discussed below. (Sec. 24416 et. seq., Rev. & Tax. Code)

CCH Practice Tip: Small Business Exemption from NOL Suspension

While businesses with less than $500,000 of taxable income were exempt from the 2008 and 2009 NOL suspension, only businesses with preapportioned income of less than $300,000 for the taxable year were exempt from the 2010 and 2011 NOL suspension. "Preapportioned income" means net income, including business and nonbusiness income, after state adjustments and before the application of California's apportionment and allocation provisions. It should be noted that for taxpayers included or includable in a combined report, preapportioned income is determined at the aggregate level for all members included in a combined report, and not at the individual group member level. Thus, a parent company with $250,000 of preapportioned income could not claim an NOL deduction in 2010 if the preapportioned income of the parent company's unitary group exceeded $300,000. This aggregation provision did not apply to the exemption for the 2008 and 2009 taxable years. (Sec. 24416.21(d) and (e), Rev. & Tax. Code)

Practitioner Comment: Carryover Period for NOLs May Not Always Be Extended as a Result of the 2008-2009 and 2010-2011 NOL Suspensions

California has suspended NOL utilization for tax years beginning in 1991 and 1992, 2002 and 2003, 2008 and 2009, and with the enactment of S.B. 858 on October 8, 2010, for 2010 and 2011. Each of the NOL suspension provisions indicates that carryover periods are to be extended for the tax years for which the NOL suspension applied. For example, if a taxpayer had an NOL carryforward from 2001, the carryover period would be increased by the two years for which NOLs were suspended in 2002 and 2003.

Unlike prior NOL suspensions, the 2008-2009 and 2010-2011 suspensions do not apply to taxpayers with less than $500,000 and $300,000 of net business income, respectively (the latter threshold is determined on a pre-apportionment basis). Since these NOL suspension periods do not apply to taxpayers with income below these thresholds (and presumably those with losses as well), it is not clear whether the NOL carryover period would be extended in such cases.

On September 23, 2011, the FTB issued Legal Ruling 2011-04 in which it concludes that the carryover period extension applies only to the extent that the NOL carryover could otherwise have been used if the suspension had not been enacted. Three examples are provided in the ruling. In the first, the taxpayer has NOLs from both 2006 and 2007 and has sufficient income to be subject to the suspension in 2008 and 2009, but we are told to assume has no income or loss in 2010 and 2011. The NOLs from 2006 and 2007 each exceed 2008 and 2009 apportioned income.

In the first example, the FTB concludes that four years would be added to the carryover period of the 2006 NOL, but none would be added to the carryover period of the 2007 NOL. In reaching this conclusion, FTB reasons that absent the NOL suspension provisions, the 2007 NOLs would not have been utilized since the 2006 NOL would have completely offset the 2008 and 2009 apportioned income. This conclusion seems at odds with the statutory language that states that the NOL suspension provisions, and the extended carryover periods, simply apply where income exceeds the specified thresholds. This language suggests that additional years should be added to the carryover period of both the 2006 and 2007 NOLs.

In the second example, the FTB similarly concludes that an extra two years would only be added to a pre-2002 NOL carryover to the extent the NOL could have otherwise been used during the suspension period. It is interesting to note that the statute governing the 2002-2003 NOL suspension did not contain language limiting its application to taxpayers with income above certain thresholds and that FTB's instructions to Form 3805Q say only that additional years should be added to the carryover period of NOLs generated prior to the final year of the suspension period.

The third and final example illustrates the application of the NOL carryback provisions and the impact of such on the carryover of 2012 and 2013 NOLs.

Taxpayers should analyze the impact of the FTB's legal ruling on their ability to utilize their California NOLs. It would also seem that the FTB's conclusions may be susceptible to legal challenge particularly for the reasons that are suggested above.

Moreover, note that the suspension legislation contains a trap for the unwary. A NOL, or portion thereof depending on the year generated, from a taxable year beginning on or after January 1, 2013, must be carried back two years even where a NOL deduction is otherwise suspended. A taxpayer is permitted to elect to "relinquish" the entire carryback period with respect to a NOL for any taxable year. If the taxpayer elects to relinquish the carryback period, the NOL is carried forward only to the years eligible

¶1024

under the applicable carryover period. However, if a taxpayer does not make an election to relinquish the carryback, or if an attempted election is invalid, the taxpayer must carry the NOL back each year in the carryback period before carrying the NOL forward. Therefore, a taxpayer that does not elect to relinquish the carryback period and fails to carryback eligible NOLs, may subsequently lose those NOLs. Specifically, when the statute of limitations for the carryback years closes, the FTB may in an audit of a later year reduce a taxpayer's NOL carryover by the amount of NOLs that should have been carried back under the allowed versus allowable rubric.

Chris Whitney, Contributing Editor

• *Water's-edge corporations*

A multinational corporation that has made a water's-edge election for the current taxable year may not fully deduct a net operating loss (NOL) carryover from a prior taxable year in which it had no water's-edge election in effect. Rather, the deduction is denied to the extent that the NOL carryover reflects income and apportionment factors of affiliated entities that would not have been taken into account had a water's-edge election been in effect for the year of the loss. (Sec. 24416(c), Rev. & Tax. Code)

In Legal Ruling 99-2 (1999) (CCH CALIFORNIA TAX REPORTS, ¶ 10-805), the Franchise Tax Board clarified that, despite a prior legal ruling stating the contrary, in determining whether a water's-edge taxpayer is an "eligible small business" or a "new business" for NOL purposes, the procedures for computing business assets and gross receipts do not deviate from the procedures used for other taxpayers.

• *Corporations subject to allocation and apportionment*

California modifies federal law by providing that for multistate corporations subject to allocation and apportionment and corporations electing intrastate combined reporting, an NOL may be deducted from the sum of the net income or loss of a corporation apportionable or allocable to California. The effect of this modification is to limit the deduction to the amount specifically allocable to the company that generated the loss. (Sec. 25108, Rev. & Tax. Code)

• *Combined reporting*

Corporations that are members of a unitary group filing a single return must use intrastate apportionment, separately computing the loss carryover for each corporation in the group using its individual apportionment factors and completing a separate FTB 3805Q for each taxpayer included in the combined report. Unlike the loss treatment for a federal consolidated return, a California loss carryover for one member in a combined report may not be applied to the income of another member included in the combined report. (Instructions, Form 3805Q, Net Operating Loss (NOL) Computation and NOL and Disaster Loss Limitations—Corporations)

• *Mergers and acquisitions*

California generally follows, as of California's current IRC conformity date, IRC § 269 anti-abuse rules, IRC § 381 carryover rules, and IRC § 382 and § 384 loss limitation rules that govern the use of NOLs following corporate mergers and acquisitions. (Sec. 24451, Rev. & Tax. Code) However, California does not follow Internal Revenue Service Notice 2008-83, 2008-42 I.R.B. 905, issued on October 20, 2008, relating to the treatment of deductions under IRC § 382(h) following an ownership change, with respect to any ownership change occurring at any time. (Sec. 24458, Rev. & Tax. Code) Also, IRC § 382(n), which provides an exception from the application of the IRC § 382 limitations for certain ownership changes, does not apply for California purposes. (Sec. 24459, Rev. & Tax. Code) In addition, although California incorporates IRC Sec. 381, California law substitutes references to the federal general business credit and credit for prior year minimum tax liability that may be carried over to the acquiring corporation with references to the allowable California credits. (Sec. 24471, Rev. & Tax. Code)

¶1025 "At Risk" Limitations

Law: Sec. 24691 (CCH CALIFORNIA TAX REPORTS, ¶10-060).

Comparable Federal: Sec. 465 (CCH U.S. MASTER TAX GUIDE ¶2045).

California conforms to federal law (¶803). (Sec. 24691, Rev. & Tax. Code) A brief explanation of the federal provisions is covered at ¶339.

¶1026 Refiners' Sulfur Rules Compliance Costs

Law: Sec. 24356.4 (CCH CALIFORNIA TAX REPORTS, ¶10-860).

Comparable Federal: Sec. 179B (CCH U.S. MASTER TAX GUIDE ¶1285).

Same as personal income tax (¶318).

¶1027 Energy Efficient Commercial Building Costs

Law: None (CCH CALIFORNIA TAX REPORTS, ¶10-665).

Comparable Federal: Sec. 179D (CCH U.S. MASTER TAX GUIDE ¶977D).

Same as personal income tax (¶345).

TAXES ON CORPORATE INCOME

ACCOUNTING METHODS AND BASES, INVENTORIES

¶1100 Accounting Periods and Methods—In General

Law: Secs. 24631-726 (CCH CALIFORNIA TAX REPORTS, ¶10-520).

Comparable Federal: Secs. 441-83 (CCH U.S. MASTER TAX GUIDE Chapter 15).

California generally conforms to, and in some cases incorporates, federal law governing accounting periods, accounting methods, year of inclusion and deduction, inventories, and adjustment. Differences are noted in the following paragraphs. (Sec. 24631 et seq., Rev. & Tax. Code)

However, California does not incorporate nor have a provision similar to IRC Sec. 457A, which provides rules for compensation from nonqualified deferred compensation plans maintained by foreign corporations.

CCH Comment: Doctrine of Election

Legislation enacted in 2012 clarified that the doctrine of election applies to any election affecting the computation of California franchise or income tax, meaning that the election must be made on an original timely filed return for the taxable period for which the election is to apply, and once made is binding. This provision is declarative of existing law, so its effective date is retroactive. (Sec. 4, Ch. 37 (S.B. 1015), Laws 2012) However, under Proposition 26 (2010), a two-thirds vote is required in both houses of the California Legislature to pass legislation resulting in "any taxpayer paying a higher tax." Since the 2012 legislation did not pass with the required super-majority, it might be challenged in the courts.

¶1101 Accounting Periods

Law: Secs. 24631, 24632 (CCH CALIFORNIA TAX REPORTS, ¶10-520).

Comparable Federal: Sec. 441 (CCH U.S. MASTER TAX GUIDE ¶1501).

Same as personal income tax (¶401).

¶1102 Change of Accounting Period

Law: Secs. 24632, 24633, 24633.5 (CCH California Tax Reports, ¶ 10-520).

Comparable Federal: Sec. 442 (CCH U.S. Master Tax Guide ¶ 1513).

The taxable year of a corporation must be the same as the tax year used by the corporation for federal income tax purposes, unless a change in accounting period is initiated or approved by the Franchise Tax Board. (Sec. 24632, Rev. & Tax. Code; Sec. 24633, Rev. & Tax. Code; Sec. 24633.5, Rev. & Tax. Code)

Practice Tip: Repair Regulations

California follows the federal "repair regulations," which provide rules for distinguishing capital expenditures from deductible supply, repair, and maintenance costs. However, one issue that may arise with regard to the repair regulations is that there may be a difference between the federal and California depreciable basis, useful life, or method of depreciation. According to the FTB, to the extent that California follows the federal provision for which a federal approval for a change in accounting method was granted, the federal approval will still apply for California purposes, even though the resulting federal numbers may be different than the California numbers. In cases where there is a federal/California difference, taxpayers should attach to their California tax return both a copy of the federal Form 3115 and a *pro forma* Form 3115 with the numbers adjusted for California. In addition, California follows IRS Revenue Procedure 2015-20, which allows qualifying small businesses to apply certain repair regulations on a prospective basis without the need to file Form 3115. (*FTB Tax News* (March 2015) (CCH California Tax Reports, ¶ 406-310))

¶1103 Return for Short Period—Annualization of Income

Law: Secs. 24634-36 (CCH California Tax Reports, ¶ 10-520).

Comparable Federal: Sec. 443 (CCH U.S. Master Tax Guide ¶ 1505).

California law incorporates federal law, except that California still requires a short-period return when a taxpayer's year is terminated for jeopardy by the Franchise Tax Board. (Sec. 24634, et seq., Rev. & Tax. Code)

¶1104 Change of Taxable Year—S Corporations

Law: Sec. 24637 (CCH California Tax Reports, ¶ 10-520).

Comparable Federal: Sec. 444 (CCH U.S. Master Tax Guide ¶ 1501).

California incorporates federal law by reference (¶ 803) with one modification relating to "required payments." (Sec. 24637, Rev. & Tax. Code)

Both federal and California law allow S corporations to elect to change to a taxable year with a three-month deferral period, or its previous taxable year deferral period, whichever is shorter.

Federal law requires that such an entity making the election federally must make certain "required payments" on April 15th of each calendar year following the calendar year in which the election begins (IRC Sec. 444(c)). California does not adopt the "required payments" requirement.

¶1105 Tax Rate Change During Taxable Year

Law: Secs. 23058, 24251 (CCH California Tax Reports, ¶ 10-380).

Comparable Federal: Sec. 15 (CCH U.S. Master Tax Guide ¶ 2561).

The general rule is the same as for personal income tax (¶ 406). (Sec. 23058, Rev. & Tax. Code)

The corporation tax law also specifies that, except as otherwise provided, the tax of a fiscal year taxpayer in a year in which the law is changed equals the sum of;

    — a portion of a tax computed under the law applicable to the first calendar year, based on the portion of the fiscal year falling in the first calendar year; and

— a portion of a tax computed under the law applicable to the second calendar year, based on the portion of the fiscal year falling in the second calendar year.

(Sec. 24251, Rev. & Tax. Code)

¶1106 Accounting Methods—General

Law: Secs. 24633, 24651-54, 24661, 24661.3, 24661.6, 24673, 24673.2, 24675-79, 24681-82, 24685, 24688-90, 24692, 24693, 24701, 24721, 24725, 24726 (CCH CALIFORNIA TAX REPORTS, ¶10-520, 10-706, 10-915).

Comparable Federal: Secs. 186, 263A, 446-48, 451, 455-56, 458, 460-61, 464, 467-69, 481-83, 1341, 7701 (CCH U.S. MASTER TAX GUIDE ¶759, 1029, 1515 et seq., 1531, 1533 et seq., 1541, 1543, 1551, 1553, 1573, 1868, 2053 et seq.).

California Form: FTB 3834 (Interest Computation Under the Look-Back Method for Completed Long-Term Contracts).

With minor exceptions, California incorporates by reference federal accounting methods and definitions, including limitations on the cash method of accounting (IRC Sec. 448), as of the current IRC tie-in date (¶803). (Sec. 24651, Rev. & Tax. Code)

California does not incorporate federal law allowing a taxpayer to elect to recognize qualified gain from a qualifying electric transmission transaction over an eight-year period beginning in the tax year of the transaction. (Sec. 24661.6, Rev. & Tax. Code) The federal provision is applicable to transactions before 2017. Consequently, taxpayers must recognize the total gain in the year of the transaction for California income tax purposes.

The corporation tax rules for accounting methods generally are the same as those for personal income tax (¶407) except for those provisions which, by their nature, are applicable only to individuals. The differences between California and federal laws discussed at ¶407 are applicable to corporation tax as well as to personal income tax. Provisions applicable only to corporations are discussed below.

• *Change in accounting periods and methods*

Although California law specifies that a taxpayer must receive approval from the Franchise Tax Board (FTB) for a change in accounting periods or methods (Sec. 24633, Rev. & Tax. Code; Sec. 24651, Rev. & Tax. Code), the FTB has taken the position that it will automatically accept an IRS approved change as long as the following conditions are met:

— California has conformed to the underlying law that is being applied;

— the authority for granting the request is within the FTB's authority; and

— the FTB has not announced that it will not follow the federal procedure being relied upon.

(*FTB Notice 2000-8* (2000), CCH CALIFORNIA TAX REPORTS, ¶403-112)

If a California taxpayer (1) cannot rely on a federally approved request for permission to change an accounting period or method, (2) desires to obtain a change different from the federal change, or (3) desires a change for California tax purposes only, a federal Form 3115, Application for Change in Accounting Method, or federal Form 1128, Application to Adopt, Change, or Retain a Tax Year, must be submitted to the FTB. The application must be submitted by the due date specified in California law or, if none is specified, by the due date for a federal change request if a federal change request had been submitted to the IRS for that change. Other than specified identifying information, the federal forms must be completed using appropriate California tax information and not with federal tax information, taking into account differences in federal and California law (e.g., different depreciation methods).

A cover letter must be attached to the front of the federal Form 3115 or Form 1128, clearly indicating that a "Change in Accounting Period" or a "Change in Accounting Method" is being requested. The application and the accompanying cover letter should be sent to: Franchise Tax Board, Change in Accounting Periods and Methods, Coordinator, P.O. Box 1998, Sacramento, CA 95812. The FTB will acknowledge receipt of the request within 30 days and will issue a response in writing once the request has been reviewed. (*FTB Notice 2000-8* (2000), CCH CALIFORNIA TAX REPORTS, ¶ 403-112)

CCH Note: *Subsidiary Must Obtain Consent To Change Period*

Subsidiaries included in a consolidated return must obtain the FTB's consent for a change of accounting period for California corporation franchise or income tax purposes, even though no such consent is required under federal law. The California State Board of Equalization (BOE) has ruled that the exemption available to corporate subsidiaries from obtaining IRS consent prior to changing accounting periods for purposes of filing a consolidated return does not apply for California corporation franchise and income tax purposes. California, unlike federal law, does not permit the filing of consolidated returns; therefore, the rules governing the filing of consolidated returns are inapplicable for California income tax purposes. (*NIF Liquidating Co.* (1980) CCH CALIFORNIA TAX REPORTS, ¶ 206-429)

California does not follow IRS Rev. Proc. 96-31 allowing an automatic consent procedure for a change of accounting method involving previously unclaimed allowable depreciation or amortization (see *FTB Notice 96-3* (1996), CCH CALIFORNIA TAX REPORTS, ¶ 10-520.204).

• *"Spreadback" relief*

Special rules providing "spreadback" relief in certain cases for income attributable to several years, repealed for federal purposes in 1964 and replaced by the allowance of deductions (IRC Sec. 186), are still in effect for California purposes. These rules apply to the following:

— income from patent infringement awards (Sec. 24675, Rev. & Tax. Code);

— damages received for breach of contract, or breach of fiduciary relationship (Sec. 24677, Rev. & Tax. Code); and

— lump sum antitrust awards under the Clayton Act (Sec. 24678, Rev. & Tax. Code).

• *Prepaid subscription income*

California has a special provision that treats prepaid subscription income, not previously reported when a corporation ceases to do business, as includible in the measure of tax in the last year the corporation is subject to tax. (Sec. 24676, Rev. & Tax. Code)

• *Farm corporations*

Under California and federal law, corporations engaged in farming must use the accrual method of accounting and capitalize preproductive-period expenses. (Sec. 24652, Rev. & Tax. Code; Sec. 24652.5, Rev. & Tax. Code) However, the following are exempt from the accrual method rule:

— S corporations;

— corporations operating nurseries or sod farms or raising or harvesting trees other than fruit and nut trees;

— family farm corporations with gross receipts of $25 million or less in each taxable year; and

— all other corporations with gross receipts of $1 million or less in each taxable year.

Under both California and federal law, a corporation is required to change from the cash method to the accrual method of accounting in a year in which gross receipts exceed $1 million (or, in the case of a family farm corporation, $25 million).

• *Production flexibility contracts*

California law mirrors Sec. 2012 of the Tax and Trade Relief Extension Act of 1998, which allows farmers to include in their taxable income production flexibility contract payments made under the Federal Agriculture Improvement and Reform Act of 1996 (P.L. 104-127) in the taxable year of actual receipt, even though the contract grants the farmer the option to receive payments earlier. (Sec. 24661.3, Rev. & Tax. Code)

• *Long-term contracts*

California incorporates IRC Sec. 460, which generally requires the use of the percentage-of-completion method of accounting for long-term contracts. A look-back rule is generally applied to correct errors in estimates of contract price or costs. A taxpayer may elect not to apply the look-back rule if, for each prior contract year, the cumulative taxable income or loss under the contract, as determined using estimated contract price and costs, is within 10% of the cumulative taxable income or loss, as determined using actual contract price and costs. (Sec. 24673, Rev. & Tax. Code; Sec. 24673.2, Rev. & Tax. Code)

California has a special provision (Sec. 24673, Rev. & Tax. Code) authorizing the FTB to require that income from a contract be reported on the percentage-of-completion basis if the contract period exceeds one year, even if the corporation regularly uses the completed contract basis of accounting. The corporation may prevent such action by furnishing security guaranteeing the payment of a tax measured by the income received upon completion of the contract, *even though* the corporation is not doing business in California in the year subsequent to the year of completion. The principal purpose of this provision is to prevent avoidance of tax by foreign corporations that perform contracts in California.

• *Inventory shrinkage*

Under both California and federal law, a business may determine its year-end closing inventory by taking a reasonable deduction for shrinkage, even if a year-end inventory has not been taken to measure the actual amount of shrinkage. (Sec. 24701, Rev. & Tax. Code)

Shrinkage is generally inventory loss due to undetected theft, breakage, or bookkeeping errors. In order to claim the deduction for estimated shrinkage, a business must normally take a physical count of its inventories at each business location on a regular, consistent basis. It also must make proper adjustments to its inventories and to its estimating methods to the extent its estimates are more or less than the actual shrinkage.

• *Nuclear decommissioning reserve funds and designated settlement funds*

Although California incorporates federal law (IRC Sec. 468A and IRC Sec. 468B), concerning deductible payments to designated settlement funds and nuclear decommissioning reserve funds, respectively, California modifies the provisions to (1) substitute California's franchise tax rate rather than the highest federal tax rate; and (2) specify that the California franchise tax is in lieu of any other tax that may be imposed under either the Personal Income Tax Law or the Corporation Tax Law. (Sec. 24690, Rev. & Tax. Code; Sec. 24693, Rev. & Tax. Code)

• *Other California-federal differences*

There is no California corporation franchise or income tax statute comparable to IRC Sec. 1341, which permits adjustment of income in certain situations where income received under a "claim of right" is later refunded. However, it is clear from the case law that California does apply the claim-of-right doctrine. See *Appeal of J.H. McKnight Ranch, Inc.* (1986) (CCH CALIFORNIA TAX REPORTS, ¶ 10-520.85). See also ¶ 415.

• *Accrual basis required in final return*

In *Appeal of Williams & Glass Accountancy Corporation* (1982) (CCH CALIFORNIA TAX REPORTS, ¶ 10-520.39), a cash-basis taxpayer distributed in liquidation accounts receivable that represented earned income. The State Board of Equalization upheld the FTB in its use of the accrual method of accounting in the corporation's final return.

¶1107 Inventories

Law: Secs. 24422.3, 24701 (CCH CALIFORNIA TAX REPORTS, ¶ 10-515, 10-520).

Comparable Federal: Secs. 263A, 471, 475 (CCH U.S. MASTER TAX GUIDE ¶ 475, 1553, 1561, 1564).

Same as personal income tax (¶ 409).

¶1108 Inventories—Last-In, First-Out Method

Law: Secs. 24701, 24708 (CCH CALIFORNIA TAX REPORTS, ¶ 10-520).

Comparable Federal: Secs. 472-74 (CCH U.S. MASTER TAX GUIDE ¶ 1565, 1567).

California incorporates by reference IRC Sec. 472, authorizing the use of the last-in, first-out (LIFO) method of inventory identification, and IRC Sec. 474, permitting eligible small business to elect to use a simplified dollar-value LIFO method to account for their inventories. However, California has not incorporated IRC Sec. 473, which prescribes accounting procedures to be employed when qualified liquidations of LIFO inventories are made. (Sec. 24701, Rev. & Tax. Code; Sec. 24708, Rev. & Tax. Code)

¶1109 Installment Sales

Law: Secs. 24667-72 (CCH CALIFORNIA TAX REPORTS, ¶ 10-520).

Comparable Federal: Secs. 453, 453A, 453B, former Sec. 453C (CCH U.S. MASTER TAX GUIDE ¶ 1801 et seq.).

The same as under the personal income tax law (¶ 411). (Sec. 24667 et seq., Rev. & Tax. Code)

• *Installment obligations in liquidation of subsidiary*

Both California and federal laws provide that no gain or loss will be recognized if installment obligations are distributed in a complete liquidation of a subsidiary into its parent corporation (¶ 1216); however, there is a difference between the two laws where the parent corporation is tax-exempt under California law.

The State Board of Equalization held in *Appeal of C.M. Ranch Co.* (1976) (CCH CALIFORNIA TAX REPORTS, ¶ 10-520) that a tax-exempt corporation technically is not a "corporation" under the corporation tax law. Consequently it cannot qualify as a parent "corporation" so as to enable the distributing corporation to avoid recognition of gain or loss on distribution of installment obligations. This reasoning is not applicable under federal law, because the federal definition of "corporation" does not exclude a tax-exempt corporation.

• *Repossession of installment obligations*

See ¶ 511 regarding limitations on recognition of gain on installment sales of real property where repossession occurs in a subsequent year.

¶1110 Related Taxpayers, Acquisitions to Avoid Tax, etc.

Law: Secs. 24431, 24725, 25102-03 (CCH CALIFORNIA TAX REPORTS, ¶10-515, 10-520, 10-835, 11-550).

Comparable Federal: Secs. 269, 269A, 269B, 482 (CCH U.S. MASTER TAX GUIDE ¶273, 1573, 1575).

California law, incorporating by reference IRC Sec. 482, gives the Franchise Tax Board (FTB) broad power to distribute or allocate income or deductions among related taxpayers—if the FTB determines that it is necessary to do so in order to prevent evasion of taxes or clearly reflect income. (Sec. 24725, Rev. & Tax. Code) In addition, the FTB may require combined or consolidated reports and adjust the income or tax of related taxpayers. (Sec. 25102, Rev. & Tax. Code; Sec. 25103, Rev. & Tax. Code) See Chapter 13 for discussion of the apportionment formula as it relates to business done within and without the state.

In *Appeal of Baldwin and Howell* (1968) (CCH CALIFORNIA TAX REPORTS, ¶10-520.702), the State Board of Equalization upheld an increase made by the FTB in the income of a parent corporation that was accomplished by transferring certain income from a subsidiary to the parent and by increasing the parent's charge to the subsidiary for the services of loaned employees.

California law is the same as federal law providing for the disallowance of tax benefits upon the acquisition of the stock or property of a corporation when the principal purpose of the acquisition is to evade or avoid tax. (Sec. 24431, Rev. & Tax. Code)

California has not conformed to federal loophole-closing provisions regarding personal service corporations (IRC Sec. 269A) and "stapled interests" (IRC Sec. 269B). Nor does California conform to federal law and regulations (Treasury Regulation 1.482-1 (h)(3)(ii)) that allow taxpayers that make an election under IRC Sec. 936 to use the profit-split method to allocate income and deductions of a possessions corporation affiliate. Under the water's-edge rules, the FTB is specifically directed to use IRC Sec. 482 to make income adjustments among affiliates within and without a water's-edge combined group (FTB Legal Ruling 2003-2 (2003), CCH CALIFORNIA TAX REPORTS, ¶11-550.28).

¶1111 Election to Accrue Income on Noninterest-Bearing Obligations Issued at Discount

Law: Sec. 24674 (CCH CALIFORNIA TAX REPORTS, ¶10-520).

Comparable Federal: Sec. 454 (CCH U.S. MASTER TAX GUIDE ¶1537).

A cash-basis taxpayer may elect to accrue the increment in value of noninterest-bearing bonds issued at a discount and redeemable for fixed amounts increasing at stated intervals. The election is binding for subsequent years. This rule is the same as the federal one, except that California law does not conform to a federal provision relating to the inclusion in income of the accrued increment in value of obligations owned at the beginning of the year in which the election is made. (Sec. 24674, Rev. & Tax. Code)

See also ¶911, regarding special rules for discount bonds.

¶1112 Imputed Interest

Law: Secs. 24726, 24993 (CCH CALIFORNIA TAX REPORTS, ¶10-520, 10-640).

Comparable Federal: Secs. 483, 7872 (CCH U.S. MASTER TAX GUIDE ¶795, 1859, 1868).

California law adopts by reference (¶803) federal provisions concerning both imputed interest on certain deferred payment contracts and "foregone interest" on loans with below-market interest rates. (Sec. 24726, Rev. & Tax. Code; Sec. 24993, Rev. & Tax. Code)

TAXES ON CORPORATE INCOME

CHAPTER 12

SALES AND EXCHANGES, GAIN OR LOSS, BASIS

¶1201 Gain or Loss—General Rule

Law: Secs. 24901-02 (CCH California Tax Reports, ¶ 10-640, 10-825).

Comparable Federal: Secs. 1001, 1221-57 (CCH U.S. Master Tax Guide ¶ 1601, 1735 et seq.).

California Forms: Form 100 (California Corporation Franchise or Income Tax Return), Schedule D (100) (California Capital Gains and Losses), Sch. D-1 (Sales of Business Property).

Gain or loss on the disposition of property is the difference between the property's adjusted basis and the amount realized. In general, California has adopted federal general and special rules for determining capital gains and losses. (Sec. 24901, Rev. & Tax. Code; Sec. 24902, Rev. & Tax. Code) However, unlike federal law, California has not adopted lower capital gains tax rates.

For California corporation franchise and income tax purposes, a taxpayer's gain or loss is computed on Schedule D (100), California Capital Gains and Losses, and Schedule D-1, Sales of Business Property. The actual amount of gain recognized is transferred to Form 100, California Corporation Franchise or Income Tax Return.

¶1202 Involuntary Conversion

Law: Secs. 24943-49.5 (CCH California Tax Reports, ¶ 10-640).

Comparable Federal: Sec. 1033 (CCH U.S. Master Tax Guide ¶ 1713 et seq.).

California has its own corporate tax provisions governing computation of gain and loss on involuntary conversions and does not generally incorporate the federal law in this area for corporate tax purposes, as it does for personal income tax purposes. However, the rules are generally the same (¶ 503), including the special rules for property damaged by federally-declared disasters. (Sec. 24943 et. seq, Rev. & Tax. Code)

¶1203 Gain from Sale of Assisted Housing

Law: Sec. 24955 (CCH California Tax Reports, ¶ 10-640).

Comparable Federal: Former Sec. 1039.

Same as personal income tax (¶ 505).

¶1204 Foreign Currency Transactions

Law: Sec. 24905 (CCH California Tax Reports, ¶ 10-640).

Comparable Federal: Sec. 988 (CCH U.S. Master Tax Guide ¶ 2498).

Same as personal income tax (¶ 520).

¶1205 Liquidation Under S.E.C. Order (Prior Law)

Law: Former Sec. 24981 (CCH California Tax Reports, ¶10-640, 10-690).

Comparable Federal: Former Sec. 1081 (CCH U.S. Master Tax Guide ¶2247).

Same as personal income tax (¶506).

¶1206 Exchange of Property for Like Property

Law: Secs. 24941, 24941.5, 24953 (CCH California Tax Reports, ¶10-640).

Comparable Federal: Sec. 1031 (CCH U.S. Master Tax Guide ¶1721 et seq.).

Same as personal income tax (¶507).

¶1207 Exchange of Insurance Policies

Law: Sec. 24950 (CCH California Tax Reports, ¶10-640).

Comparable Federal: Sec. 1035 (CCH U.S. Master Tax Guide ¶1724).

Same as personal income tax (¶508).

¶1208 Exchange of Stock for Stock

Law: Sec. 24951 (CCH California Tax Reports, ¶10-640).

Comparable Federal: Sec. 1036 (CCH U.S. Master Tax Guide ¶1728).

Same as personal income tax (¶509).

¶1209 Exchange of Certain U.S. Obligations

Law: None (CCH California Tax Reports, ¶10-640).

Comparable Federal: Sec. 1037 (CCH U.S. Master Tax Guide ¶1726, 1925).

The California corporation tax law has nothing comparable to the federal provisions for the tax-free exchange of obligations of the United States issued under the Second Liberty Bond Act.

¶1210 Reacquisition of Property After Installment Sale

Law: Sec. 24952 (CCH California Tax Reports, ¶10-640).

Comparable Federal: Sec. 1038 (CCH U.S. Master Tax Guide ¶1841, 1843).

California has its own corporate tax provisions governing computation of gain and loss upon a seller's repossession of real property following an installment sale and does not incorporate the federal law in this area for corporate tax purposes, as it does for personal income tax purposes. However, the rules are generally the same (¶511). (Sec. 24952, Rev. & Tax. Code)

¶1211 Exchange of Property for Stock

Law: Secs. 24451, 24465 (CCH California Tax Reports, ¶10-210, 10-540).

Comparable Federal: Sec. 351 (CCH U.S. Master Tax Guide ¶203, 1731, 2205, 2233, 2257).

California Form: Form 3725 (Assets Transferred From Parent Corporation to Insurance Company Subsidiary)

Same as personal income tax (¶512), except as noted below. (Sec. 24451, Rev. & Tax. Code)

• *Transfers to insurance companies*

The nonrecognition rules do not apply and gain is recognized on property transferred from a corporation to an insurance company in an IRC Sec. 332 exchange, unless an exception applies. An exception does not apply if the transfer or exchange has the effect of removing the property from the corporation tax base. Deferral of gain recognition is allowed if the transferred asset is used in the active conduct of the insurer's trade or business. In order to provide the FTB with sufficient notice of the status of such transferred assets and any deferred gain, until the assets are subsequently disposed of and gain is fully recognized, an annual statement must be filed with the FTB. (Sec. 24465, Rev. & Tax. Code) A regulation provides a non-exhaustive list of data to be provided on the annual statement, prescribes when and how the annual statement is to be filed, and specifies record retention requirements. (Reg. 24465-3, 18 CCR) Form 3725, Assets Transferred From Parent Corporation to Insurance Company Subsidiary, is used to track the assets transferred from a parent corporation to an insurance company subsidiary.

Practitioner Comment: Expanded Reporting Requirements on Transfers of Appreciated Property to Insurers

Effective April 1, 2015, the FTB adopted Reg. 24465-3, 18 CCR, expanding the reporting requirements under Cal. Rev. & Tax. Code § 24465 related to transfers of appreciated property from corporations to insurance companies occurring in tax years beginning on or after January 1, 2015.

Cal. Rev. & Tax. Code § 24465, applicable to transactions and certain related contracts occurring on or after June 23, 2004, provides that when a corporation transfers appreciated property to an insurance company, the gain is deferred if the property transferred to the insurer is used in the active conduct of a trade or business of the insurer. The gain is triggered when the property is no longer owned by an insurer in the taxpayer's commonly controlled group (or a member of the taxpayer's combined reporting group), or the property is no longer used in the active conduct of the insurer's trade or business (or the trade or business of another member in the taxpayer's combined reporting group), or the holder of the property is no longer held by an insurer in the commonly controlled group of the transferor (or a member of the taxpayer's combined reporting group). The purpose of the triggering provision is to limit the ability of corporations, subject to the corporate income or franchise tax, to erode the tax base by transferring appreciated property to insurance companies that are not subject to the corporate income or franchise tax. Note that the triggering year apportionment factors are applied to apportioned deferred gain that is business income.

In order to defer gain under Cal. Rev. & Tax. Code § 24465, the taxpayer must provide the FTB with sufficient notice of the status of such transferred assets. Cal. Rev. & Tax. Code § 24465(c) provides that until the asset is subsequently disposed of and gain is fully recognized, an annual statement must be filed with the FTB. The newly adopted regulation prescribes the specific content, filing methodology, and required record retention for the annual statement (California Form 3725).

Reg. 24465-3, 18 CCR, provides that an annual statement shall include 18 specific items. Previous reporting requirements included general information about the asset transfer, deferred capital gains, asset disposition, and reported capital gains. The new requirements include information about stock ownership changes, if equity interests become worthless, and a signature from both the transferor and insurer. Transactions entered into before June 23, 2004, are not subject to these reporting requirements.

The following are new requirements:

(1) If shares of stock were transferred to an insurer, the percentage of insurer or transferred stock (measured by relative fair market value) that was subsequently transferred or disposed of.

(2) Whether an insurer or transferred entity issued additional or canceled existing shares of stock during the taxable year. If so, indicate number of shares outstanding before and after such issuance or cancellation.

(3) Whether an insurer or transferred entity issued another class of stock or type of equity interest.

(4) Whether the equity interest in the transferred entity became worthless.

(5) Signatures of transferor and insurer.

The annual statement for transfers of appreciated property to insurers is made on California Form 3725 and is attached to the transferor's tax return. If a taxpayer fails to provide California Form 3725, the FTB may require the transferor to take those gains into account in the first taxable year in which the current ownership of the property is not reported. However, the FTB will not require triggering of the deferred gain if the property is still owned by the transferee, and the failure to provide the information is due to reasonable cause and not willful neglect. (Reg. 24465-3, 18 CCR, 24465(c)) Caution should be used to ensure proper filing of the required California Form 3725 because reasonable cause can be a difficult standard to satisfy.

Chris Whitney, Contributing Editor

¶1212 Sale or Exchange of Tax-Exempt Bonds

Law: Sec. 24314 (CCH CALIFORNIA TAX REPORTS, ¶ 10-640).

Comparable Federal: None.

The gain or loss from the sale or transfer of bonds yielding tax-exempt interest is not exempt. Federal policy is the same as to state and municipal obligations. (Sec. 24314, Rev. & Tax. Code)

¶1213 Sale of Stock to ESOPs or Cooperatives

Law: Sec. 24954.1 (CCH CALIFORNIA TAX REPORTS, ¶ 10-640).

Comparable Federal: Sec. 1042 (CCH U.S. MASTER TAX GUIDE ¶ 1733, 2109).

Same as personal income tax (¶ 514).

¶1214 Exchange in Connection with Reorganization

Law: Secs. 24451, 24465 (CCH CALIFORNIA TAX REPORTS, ¶ 10-210, 10-540).

Comparable Federal: Secs. 354, 355, 357, 361, 368 (CCH U.S. MASTER TAX GUIDE ¶ 203, 1789, 2205 et seq., 2229, 2233).

California Form: Form 3725 (Assets Transferred From Parent Corporation to Insurance Company Subsidiary)

California incorporates federal law governing computation of gain and loss in connection with corporate reorganizations as of the current IRC tie-in date (¶ 803). (Sec. 24451, Rev. & Tax. Code) However, because of its IRC conformity date, California has not adopted federal amendments enacted by the federal Protecting Americans from Tax Hikes (PATH) Act of 2015 and effective generally for distributions on or after December 7, 2015, providing that IRC Sec. 355 will not apply to any distribution if either the distributing corporation or the controlled corporation is a real estate investment trust (REIT).

No gain or loss is recognized if stock or securities in a corporation that is a party to a reorganization are exchanged solely for stock or securities in such corporation, or in another corporation that is a party to the reorganization. Also, no gain or loss is recognized if a corporation exchanges property solely for stock or securities in connection with a reorganization. "Reorganization" and other terms are specifically defined.

In addition, the assumption of liabilities in connection with certain types of tax-free reorganizations is not considered to be money or property and does not prevent the exchange from being tax-free, unless the assumption of liabilities is a device to avoid tax on the exchange, or if the transfer is not made for a bona fide business purpose.

Nonqualified preferred stock received in exchange for stock other than nonqualified preferred stock is treated as "boot" rather than stock, and gain, but not loss, is recognized on such an exchange.

• *Transfers to insurance companies*

Generally, the nonrecognition rules do not apply and gain is recognized on property transferred from a corporation to an insurance company in an exchange governed by IRC Sec. 354 or 361, unless an exception applies. An exception does not apply if the transfer or exchange has the effect of removing the property from the corporation tax base. Deferral of gain recognition is allowed if the transferred asset is used in the active conduct of the insurer's trade or business. In order to provide the FTB with sufficient notice of the status of such transferred assets and any deferred gain, until the assets are subsequently disposed of and gain is fully recognized, an annual statement must be filed with the FTB. (Sec. 24465, Rev. & Tax. Code) A regulation provides a non-exhaustive list of data to be provided on the annual statement, prescribes when and how the annual statement is to be filed, and specifies record retention requirements. (Reg. 24465-3, 18 CCR) Form 3725, Assets Transferred From Parent Corporation to Insurance Company Subsidiary, is used to track the assets transferred from a parent corporation to an insurance company subsidiary.

¶1215 "Spin-Off" Reorganization

Law: Sec. 24451, 24462 (CCH CALIFORNIA TAX REPORTS, ¶ 10-210, 10-540).

Comparable Federal: Sec. 355 (CCH U.S. MASTER TAX GUIDE ¶ 2201).

California incorporates federal law under which certain distributions of the stock or securities of a corporation controlled by the distributor in connection with a "spin-off," "split-up," or "split-off" reorganization may be received by distributees without recognition of gain or loss. (Sec. 24451, Rev. & Tax. Code) However, because of its IRC conformity date, California has not adopted federal amendments enacted by the federal Protecting Americans from Tax Hikes (PATH) Act of 2015 and effective generally for distributions on or after December 7, 2015, providing that IRC Sec. 355 will not apply to any distribution if either the distributing corporation or the controlled corporation is a real estate investment trust (REIT).

California also incorporates the federal rules governing the taxability of the distributing corporations, including a provision under which distributing corporations may be required to recognize gain on certain distributions resembling outright sales of subsidiaries.

Practitioner Comment: California-Federal Differences

See ¶ 517 for a discussion of ways in which California law may differ from federal law in this area.

Compliance Note: Satisfying the Active Trade or Business Requirement of IRC Sec. 355(b)

The FTB has indicated that it will apply Internal Revenue Service Rev. Rul. 2007-42, 2007-28 I.R.B. 44, to attribute the business activities of a partnership to a corporate partner for purposes of satisfying the active trade or business requirement of IRC Sec. 355(b) for California corporation franchise tax purposes. (*Chief Counsel Ruling 2009-1* (2009) (CCH CALIFORNIA TAX REPORTS, ¶ 10-540.21))

¶1216 Complete Liquidation of Subsidiary

Law: Secs. 24451, 24465 (CCH CALIFORNIA TAX REPORTS, ¶ 10-210, 10-540).

Comparable Federal: Sec. 332 (CCH U.S. MASTER TAX GUIDE ¶ 2241, 2261).

California Form: Form 3725 (Assets Transferred From Parent Corporation to Insurance Company Subsidiary)

No gain or loss is recognized upon the receipt by a corporation of property distributed in complete liquidation of a subsidiary corporation; 80% ownership is required and other conditions must be satisfied. California incorporates the IRC provisions as of the current IRC tie-in date (¶ 803). (Sec. 24451, Rev. & Tax. Code)

Under federal law, as incorporated by California, any amount that a liquidating regulated investment company (RIC) or real estate investment trust (REIT) takes as a deduction for dividends paid with respect to an otherwise tax-free liquidating distribution must be included in the income of the corporation receiving the distribution.

In *C.M. Ranch Co.*, discussed at ¶ 1109, it was held that the California provision for tax-free liquidation does not apply where the parent corporation is tax-exempt, because such a corporation is technically not a "corporation" under the corporation tax law.

• *Transfers to insurance companies*

Generally, the nonrecognition rules do not apply and gain is recognized on property transferred from a corporation to an insurance company in an exchange governed by IRC Sec. 332, unless an exception applies. An exception does not apply if the transfer or exchange has the effect of removing the property from the corporation tax base. Deferral of gain recognition is allowed if the transferred asset is used in the active conduct of the insurer's trade or business. In order to provide the FTB with sufficient notice of the status of such transferred assets and any deferred gain, until the assets are subsequently disposed of and gain is fully recognized, an annual statement must be filed with the FTB. (Sec. 24465, Rev. & Tax. Code) A regulation provides a non-exhaustive list of data to be provided on the annual statement, prescribes when and how the annual statement is to be filed, and specifies record retention requirements. (Reg. 24465-3, 18 CCR) Form 3725, Assets Transferred From Parent Corporation to Insurance Company Subsidiary, is used to track the assets transferred from a parent corporation to an insurance company subsidiary.

¶1217 Exchanges of Stock in 10%-Owned Foreign Corporations

Law: Sec. 24990.7 (CCH CALIFORNIA TAX REPORTS, ¶ 10-640).

Comparable Federal: Sec. 1248 (CCH U.S. MASTER TAX GUIDE ¶ 2488).

California does not currently adopt the federal provision that taxes as a dividend the portion of gain on the sale or exchange of stock in a 10%-owned foreign corporation attributable to earnings and profits of the corporation accumulated in taxable years beginning after 1962, and during the period or periods the stock was owned by the taxpayer. (Sec. 24990.7, Rev. & Tax. Code)

¶1218 Exchanges Not Solely in Kind

Law: Secs. 24451, 24465 (CCH CALIFORNIA TAX REPORTS, ¶ 10-210, 10-540).

Comparable Federal: Sec. 356 (CCH U.S. MASTER TAX GUIDE ¶ 2237).

California Form: Form 3725 (Assets Transferred From Parent Corporation to Insurance Company Subsidiary)

Same as personal income tax (¶ 518). (Sec. 24451, Rev. & Tax. Code)

• *Transfers to insurance companies*

Generally, the nonrecognition rules do not apply and gain is recognized on property transferred from a corporation to an insurance company in an exchange governed by IRC Sec. 356, unless an exception applies. An exception does not apply if the transfer or exchange has the effect of removing the property from the corporation tax base. Deferral of gain recognition is allowed if the transferred asset is used in the active conduct of the insurer's trade or business. In order to provide the FTB with sufficient notice of the status of such transferred assets and any deferred gain, until the assets are subsequently disposed of and gain is fully recognized, an annual statement must be filed with the FTB. (Sec. 24465, Rev. & Tax. Code) A regulation provides a non-exhaustive list of data to be provided on the annual statement, prescribes when and how the annual statement is to be filed, and specifies record retention requirements. (Reg. 24465-3, 18 CCR) Form 3725, Assets Transferred From Parent Corporation to Insurance Company Subsidiary, is used to track the assets transferred from a parent corporation to an insurance company subsidiary.

¶1219 Exchanges Involving Foreign Corporations

Law: Sec. 24451 (CCH CALIFORNIA TAX REPORTS, ¶ 10-210, 10-540).

Comparable Federal: Sec. 367 (CCH U.S. MASTER TAX GUIDE ¶ 2267).

Same as personal income tax (¶ 519).

¶1220 Liquidation of Corporation

Law: Sec. 24451 (CCH CALIFORNIA TAX REPORTS, ¶ 10-210, 10-540).

Comparable Federal: Secs. 331, 334, 336-38 (CCH U.S. MASTER TAX GUIDE ¶ 2253, 2257, 2261, 2265).

Gain or loss is ordinarily recognized to a corporate stockholder upon liquidation of a corporation, the gain or loss being measured by the difference between the basis of the stock and the value of the property received. California incorporates the federal law (¶ 803). (Sec. 24451, Rev. & Tax. Code)

• *Liquidation of subsidiary*

See ¶ 1216 for special rules applying to the complete liquidation of a subsidiary.

• *California-federal differences*

Federal law contains special provisions for treatment of liquidating distributions by certain types of corporations, where corporate income has been taxed directly to shareholders. This applies particularly to Domestic International Sales Corporations and successor entities. Because such special corporations have no counterparts in the California law (Sec. 23051.5(b), Rev. & Tax. Code), their liquidating distributions are subject to the regular rules for California tax purposes.

¶1221 Carryovers in Corporate Acquisitions

Law: Secs. 24451, 24471, 24481 (CCH CALIFORNIA TAX REPORTS, ¶ 10-210, 10-540).

Comparable Federal: Secs. 381-84 (CCH U.S. MASTER TAX GUIDE ¶ 2277, 2281).

California incorporates federal provisions regarding carryover of certain corporate attributes in reorganizations and in liquidations of subsidiaries, with minor modifications substituting certain California credits for those enumerated in the federal law. (Sec. 24451, Rev. & Tax. Code; Sec. 24471, Rev. & Tax. Code; Sec. 24481, Rev. & Tax. Code)

¶1222 Capital Gains and Losses

Law: Former Sec. 24905.5, Secs. 24956, 24990, 24990.2, 24990.5, 24990.6, 24990.7, 24990.8, 24995 (CCH CALIFORNIA TAX REPORTS, ¶ 10-640).

Comparable Federal: Secs. 988, 1044, 1201-88 (CCH U.S. MASTER TAX GUIDE ¶ 1735 et seq., 2498).

California Form: Sch. D (Capital Gain or Loss Adjustment).

California law adopts by reference as of the current IRC tie-in date (¶803) the federal treatment of capital gains and losses except for the following differences:

— the federal alternative tax on corporations is inapplicable (Sec. 24990(a), Rev. & Tax. Code);

— California allows a five-year carryover, but no carryback, of capital losses; federal law provides for a three-year carryback in addition to a five-year carryover (Sec. 24990.5, Rev. & Tax. Code);

— the provisions dealing with the treatment of certain passive foreign investment companies do not apply for California purposes (Sec. 24995, Rev. & Tax. Code);

— provisions relating to gain from certain foreign stock sales or exchanges do not apply for California purposes (Sec. 24990.7, Rev. & Tax. Code);

— provisions that allow certain financial institutions to receive ordinary income or loss treatment, rather than capital gain or loss treatment, on the sale or exchange of preferred stock in the Federal National Mortgage Association ("Fannie Mae") or the Federal Home Loan Mortgage Corporation ("Freddie Mac") do not apply for California purposes (Sec. 24990.2, Rev. & Tax. Code); and

— internal references to various provisions governing capital assets are different for California and federal law (Sec. 24990.8, Rev. & Tax. Code).

- *"Small business" stock*

The limited exclusion for gain on the sale of small business stock that was available for personal income tax purposes prior to the 2013 tax year (¶525) is not available for corporation franchise or income tax purposes. (Sec. 24956, Rev. & Tax. Code)

¶1223 Retirement of Bonds, etc.

Law: Secs. 24439, 24990 (CCH California Tax Reports, ¶10-515, 10-640).

Comparable Federal: Secs. 249, 1271-74A (CCH U.S. Master Tax Guide ¶1952, 1954, 2431).

Except for U.S. Savings Bonds, gain on retirement of bonds is taxable income and loss is fully deductible. There is a difference between the franchise tax and the income tax in the treatment of gain or loss on redemption of savings bonds, resulting from the difference in the treatment of interest income as explained at ¶910.

Under the corporation income tax, a gain on redemption of Savings Bonds is not taxable and a loss is not deductible, as outlined at ¶535 for the personal income tax. Under the franchise tax, however, such a gain is fully taxable and such a loss is fully deductible, because interest on U.S. obligations is fully taxable for franchise tax purposes. (Sec. 24990, Rev. & Tax. Code)

Where a corporation redeems bonds that were issued at a discount after May 27, 1969, a corporate holder's California gain may be different from the federal gain, because the federal gain will reflect the fact that the federal cost basis of the bonds has been increased by the amount of discount that has been reported as income as explained at ¶911. Although current California law provides for the same addition to basis, it did not become effective for taxable years before 1987.

California law is the same as federal in restricting the amount of deduction for premium paid by a corporation on the repurchase of bonds convertible into stock. The deduction is limited to the amount of a normal call premium. (Sec. 24439, Rev. & Tax. Code)

Original issue discount on bonds is discussed at ¶911.

¶1224 Corporation Dealing in Own Stock

Law: Sec. 24942 (CCH California Tax Reports, ¶10-640).

Comparable Federal: Sec. 1032 (CCH U.S. Master Tax Guide ¶203, 1729).

Under both California and federal law, no gain or loss is recognized to a corporation on the receipt of money or other property in exchange for the corporation's stock, including treasury stock. In addition, a corporation is not required to recognize gain or loss upon any acquisition of an option, or with respect to a securities futures contract, to buy or sell its stock (including treasury stock) or when an option to buy its stock lapses. (Sec. 24942, Rev. & Tax. Code)

In *Federal Employees Distributing Company v. Franchise Tax Board* (1968) (CCH California Tax Reports, ¶10-015.20), the California District Court of Appeals held that fees collected for memberships by a nonprofit nonstock corporation were the corporation's sole source of equity capital and therefore were exempt under Sec. 24942 from franchise tax.

¶1225 Limitation of Straddle Losses

Law: Sec. 24998 (CCH California Tax Reports, ¶10-640).

Comparable Federal: Sec. 1092 (CCH U.S. Master Tax Guide ¶1948).

California law is the same as federal law as of the current IRC tie-in date (see ¶803), which prevents taxpayers from using various tax-motivated straddles (positions in a transaction that balance or offset each other) to defer income or to convert short-term capital gain into long-term capital gain. Losses from actively traded personal property are deferred to the extent that the taxpayer had gains in offsetting positions that were not closed out by year-end. Straddle rules deal with "contracts" (including securities futures contracts), "options," or "rights" involving possible price fluctuations as the result of future events and a taxpayer's attempts to reduce the risk of loss on such investments, but do not apply to hedging transactions. (Sec. 24998, Rev. & Tax. Code)

¶1226 Basis, General Rule

Law: Secs. 24912, 24966-66.2 (CCH California Tax Reports, ¶10-640).

Comparable Federal: Secs. 1012, 1059, 1059A, 1060 (CCH U.S. Master Tax Guide ¶237, 315, 1611, 1743).

Same as personal income tax (¶542). California law parallels and in some instances incorporates federal law in this area. The general rule is that the basis of an item of property is its cost. Exceptions are discussed in the following paragraphs. (Sec. 24912, Rev. & Tax. Code; Sec. 24966, Rev. & Tax. Code; Sec. 24966.1, Rev. & Tax. Code; Sec. 24966.2, Rev. & Tax. Code)

¶1227 Basis, Inventoriable Property

Law: Secs. 24913, 24966.1 (CCH California Tax Reports, ¶10-640).

Comparable Federal: Secs. 1013, 1059A (CCH U.S. Master Tax Guide ¶1553 et seq.).

Same as personal income tax (¶543).

¶1228 Basis of Property Acquired by Gift

Law: Secs. 24914-15 (CCH California Tax Reports, ¶10-640).

Comparable Federal: Sec. 1015 (CCH U.S. Master Tax Guide ¶1630, 1678).

Same as personal income tax (¶544) except that the corporation tax law does not provide for property acquired before 1921. (Sec. 24914, Rev. & Tax. Code; Sec. 24915, Rev. & Tax. Code)

¶1229   Basis of Property Acquired by Transfer in Trust

Law: Sec. 24914 (CCH CALIFORNIA TAX REPORTS, ¶10-640).

Comparable Federal: Sec. 1015 (CCH U.S. MASTER TAX GUIDE ¶1630, 1678).

Same as personal income tax (¶545) except that the corporation tax law does not provide for property acquired before 1921. (Sec. 24914, Rev. & Tax. Code)

¶1230   Basis of Property Transmitted at Death

Law: None (CCH CALIFORNIA TAX REPORTS, ¶11-869).

Comparable Federal: Sec. 1014 (CCH U.S. MASTER TAX GUIDE ¶1633 et seq.).

The California corporation tax law has no provision for basis of property transmitted at death.

¶1231   Basis of Property Acquired in Tax-Free Exchange

Law: Sec. 24451 (CCH CALIFORNIA TAX REPORTS, ¶10-210, 10-540).

Comparable Federal: Sec. 358 (CCH U.S. MASTER TAX GUIDE ¶2201, 2205).

Same as personal income tax (¶547).

¶1232   Basis of Stock After "Spin-Off" Reorganization

Law: Sec. 24451 (CCH CALIFORNIA TAX REPORTS, ¶10-210, 10-540).

Comparable Federal: Sec. 358 (CCH U.S. MASTER TAX GUIDE ¶2201, 2205).

Same as personal income tax (¶549).

¶1233   Basis of Property Acquired in Reorganization

Law: Sec. 24451 (CCH CALIFORNIA TAX REPORTS, ¶10-210, 10-540).

Comparable Federal: Sec. 362 (CCH U.S. MASTER TAX GUIDE ¶1666).

In the case of property acquired by a corporation in a "reorganization," the property takes the transferor's basis, with adjustment for gain recognized upon the transfer. California incorporates federal law as of the current IRC tie-in date (¶803). (Sec. 24451, Rev. & Tax. Code)

¶1234   Basis of Property Acquired by Issuance of Stock or Contribution to Capital

Law: Sec. 24551 (CCH CALIFORNIA TAX REPORTS, ¶10-210, 10-540).

Comparable Federal: Sec. 362 (CCH U.S. MASTER TAX GUIDE ¶1660).

In the case of property acquired by a corporation by issuance of stock in a tax-free transaction under IRC Sec. 351 (¶512), or as a contribution to capital, the basis of the property is the transferor's basis, with adjustment for gain recognized on the transfer. However, if a contribution to capital is received from other than a share-holder, the corporation is required to reduce the basis of property by the amount of the contribution.

The California law is the same as the federal law. (Sec. 24451, Rev. & Tax. Code)

¶1235 Basis of Property Acquired upon Involuntary Conversion

Law: Sec. 24947 (CCH California Tax Reports, ¶10-640).

Comparable Federal: Sec. 1033 (CCH U.S. Master Tax Guide ¶1713, 1715).

California has its own corporate tax provision regarding the basis of property acquired upon an involuntary conversion and does not generally incorporate the federal law in this area for corporate tax purposes, as it does for personal income tax purposes. However, the rules are generally the same (¶550). (Sec. 24947, Rev. & Tax. Code)

¶1236 Basis of Securities Acquired in Wash Sale

Law: Sec. 24998 (CCH California Tax Reports, ¶10-640).

Comparable Federal: Sec. 1091 (CCH U.S. Master Tax Guide ¶1939).

Same as personal income tax (¶553).

¶1237 Basis of Property Acquired During Affiliation

Law: Sec. 24961 (CCH California Tax Reports, ¶10-640).

Comparable Federal: Sec. 1051.

In the case of property acquired by a corporation from an affiliated corporation during a period of affiliation, the basis of the property is determined under special rules, the general effect of which is to disregard the transfer from the affiliate. The California provision contains several references to federal law and is generally the same as the federal provision. (Sec. 24961, Rev. & Tax. Code) There are some differences, however, and there may be important differences in the effect of the two laws because the periods of affiliation may be different under one law than under the other. Reference should be made to the law or regulations or to a more detailed reference work in case of any question involving this provision.

¶1238 Basis Prescribed by Revenue Acts of 1932 or 1934

Law: Sec. 24962 (CCH California Tax Reports, ¶10-640, 10-690).

Comparable Federal: Sec. 1052.

The basis of property acquired after February 28, 1913, in an income year beginning prior to 1937, where the basis was prescribed by the federal Revenue Acts of 1932 or 1934, is as prescribed in those Acts. The California provision parallels the federal one, except that the federal provision applies only to transfers in tax years beginning prior to 1936. (Sec. 24962, Rev. & Tax. Code)

¶1239 Basis of Property Acquired Before March 1, 1913

Law: Sec. 24963 (CCH California Tax Reports, ¶10-640, 10-690).

Comparable Federal: Sec. 1053.

Same as personal income tax (¶556).

¶1240 Basis of FNMA Stock

Law: Sec. 24965 (CCH California Tax Reports, ¶10-640).

Comparable Federal: Sec. 1054.

The basis of stock issued by the Federal National Mortgage Association to an original holder is cost, reduced by the amount of any premium paid above face value. The premium may be deducted as an ordinary business expense in the year of purchase. The California provision parallels the federal one. (Sec. 24965, Rev. & Tax. Code)

¶1241 Basis Under Redeemable Ground Rents

> *Law:* None (CCH CALIFORNIA TAX REPORTS, ¶ 10-640).
>
> *Comparable Federal:* Sec. 1055 (CCH U.S. MASTER TAX GUIDE ¶ 1611).

The California corporate tax law contains nothing comparable to a federal provision that treats redeemable ground rents as being the equivalent of a mortgage. Presumably, California would treat redeemable ground rents as regular leases.

¶1242 Basis of Property Acquired in Corporate Liquidation or Acquisition

> *Law:* Secs. 23051.5, 23806, 24451 (CCH CALIFORNIA TAX REPORTS, ¶ 10-210, 10-540).
>
> *Comparable Federal:* Secs. 334, 338 (CCH U.S. MASTER TAX GUIDE ¶ 2261, 2265).

In an ordinary corporate liquidation, the basis of property received by a corporate stockholder is the fair market value of the property at the date of liquidation. California incorporates federal law as of the current IRC tie-in date (¶ 803). (Sec. 24451, Rev. & Tax. Code)

- *Liquidation in plan to purchase assets*

Upon the complete liquidation of a subsidiary under IRC Sec. 332 (¶ 1216) the property received by the parent corporation ordinarily takes the same basis it had in the hands of the subsidiary (transferor). However, a different result occurs if the corporation elects under IRC Sec. 338 to treat its acquisition of another business through purchase of a controlling interest (80%) in stock as the purchase of the assets of the acquired corporation. In this case, the buyer receives a fair market value basis in each asset and is entitled to claim depreciation and investment tax credit on a stepped-up basis. The tax attributes of the acquired (target) corporation disappear. In turn, the target corporation is subject to recapture tax liability.

Reg. 24519, 18 CCR permits a California taxpayer to elect out of the federal election of IRC Sec. 338(g), which allows the purchasing corporation to have a stock purchase treated as an acquisition of assets.

CCH Caution Note: Impact of Federal Election Extensions

A taxpayer making a proper federal election under IRC Sec. 338, concerning qualified stock purchases, that makes the election using an automatic extension pursuant to federal Rev. Proc. 2003-33, is entitled to the election for purposes of California corporation franchise or income tax. However, a taxpayer making a separate California election may not rely on the federal revenue procedure to extend the time for filing the separate state election (*FTB Notice 2003-9* (2003), CCH CALIFORNIA TAX REPORTS, ¶ 10-540).

An IRC Sec. 338(h)(10) election is available when an affiliated group sells the stock of a subsidiary. Under this election, the acquired corporation must recognize any gain or loss on the deemed asset sale; however, the selling group does not recognize any gain or loss on the stock sale. Although California incorporates IRC Sec. 338, without modification, under California's general election provisions discussed at ¶ 803, taxpayers may make a separate election on their California return. (Sec. 23051.5(e), Rev. & Tax. Code) However, an S corporation and its shareholders are precluded from making a separate California election. (Sec. 23806, Rev. & Tax. Code) In an unpublished decision that may not be cited as precedence, a California court of appeal refused to accept a taxpayer's contention that the statute prohibiting a separate election applied only in instances in which the S corporation was acquiring a subsidiary, and not when it was the target of an acquisition. (*ELS Educational Services, Inc. v. Franchise Tax Board* (2011), CCH CALIFORNIA TAX REPORTS, ¶ 405-490)

Practitioner Comment: California Clarifies Treatment of IRC Sec. 338(h)(10) Election When Target Company Is Insurer

Chief Counsel Ruling 2016-05, CCH CALIFORNIA TAX REPORTS, ¶ 10-540.36, addresses the California tax consequences of an IRC Sec. 338(h)(10) election for sale of stock of a wholly owned insurance company. The ruling clarifies that an insurance company is a corporation for purposes of being an eligible target for purposes of an IRC Sec. 338 election.

Because an insurance company is not subject to corporate income or franchise tax, the provisions of Treasury Regulation Sec. 1.338(h)(10)-1(d)(3), are modified. These provisions generally treat a target corporation as if it sold all of its assets and recognized gain so that the seller does not recognize gain on the sale of the target corporation's stock nor on the deemed liquidation. Because the target corporation is an insurance company, California Rev. & Tax. Sec. 24465 provides that the seller must treat any related deemed distribution on the deemed liquidation as a distribution of the insurance company's earnings and profits. The dividend is then treated as a dividend eligible for a dividend received deduction under California Rev. & Tax. Code Sec. 24410 (see ¶ 909), subject to anti-stuffing and other restrictions.

Chris Whitney, Contributing Editor

See ¶ 1304 for a discussion of the apportionment rules applicable to IRC Sec. 338 deemed asset sales.

¶1243 Basis of Property Acquired upon Transfers from Controlled Corporations

Law: Sec. 24964 (CCH CALIFORNIA TAX REPORTS, ¶ 10-640).

Comparable Federal: None.

Where a corporation subject to the franchise tax received property after 1927, from a controlled corporation, and where gain or loss was realized but was not taken into account for franchise tax purposes, the property takes the transferor's basis. There is no comparable federal provision. (Sec. 24964, Rev. & Tax. Code)

¶1244 Basis of Rights to Acquire Stock

Law: Sec. 24451 (CCH CALIFORNIA TAX REPORTS, ¶ 10-210, 10-540).

Comparable Federal: Sec. 307 (CCH U.S. MASTER TAX GUIDE ¶ 1907).

Where the fair market value of stock rights is less than 15% of the value of the stock on which the rights are issued, the basis of the rights is zero unless the taxpayer elects to allocate to the rights a portion of the basis of the stock. This rule dates from 1954 in federal law and from 1955 in California law. (Sec. 24451, Rev. & Tax. Code)

• *Allocation of basis*

As to the following rights, the basis of the stock is allocated between the stock and the rights according to their respective values at the time the rights are issued:

— all rights acquired in an income year beginning before 1937, *except* as to certain rights acquired before 1928 (see below); and

— nontaxable rights acquired in an income year beginning 1936, where the value of the rights is more than 15% or the taxpayer elects to allocate as explained above.

If a stock right was acquired prior to 1928, and it constituted income under the Sixteenth Amendment to the Federal Constitution, the basis of the right is its fair market value when acquired.

¶1243

• *Pre-1943 transactions*

Where stock rights were acquired and sold in an income year beginning prior to 1943 and the entire proceeds were reported as income, the basis of the stock is determined without any allocation to the rights.

• *California-federal differences*

California law now incorporates the federal law, but, as discussed below, there have been the following differences in effective dates in prior years:

— In the first item listed above under "Allocation of basis," the federal dates are January 1, 1936, in both cases instead of January 1, 1937, and January 1, 1928. As to both dates, the federal refers to *years beginning* before January 1, 1936, instead of to the *period prior* to the date specified.

— In the second item listed above under "Allocation of basis," the federal date is December 31, 1935, instead of December 31, 1936.

— In the rule stated above regarding rights acquired prior to January 1, 1928, the federal law refers to rights acquired in a taxable year beginning prior to January 1, 1936. Also, the federal rule is different in that it applies only if the value of the rights was included in gross income in the year acquired, whereas the prior California rule applies to all cases where the acquisition of the rights constituted income under the Sixteenth Amendment.

— In the rule stated above regarding rights acquired and sold prior to 1943, the federal law refers to rights acquired in any tax year beginning prior to 1939.

¶1245 Basis of Property Acquired Pursuant to S.E.C. Order (Prior Law)

Law: Former Sec. 24988 (CCH CALIFORNIA TAX REPORTS, ¶10-640).

Comparable Federal: Former Sec. 1082.

Prior to the 2010 tax year, special rules were provided for determination of basis in cases involving an order of the Securities and Exchange Commission under the Public Utility Holding Company Act. California incorporated the former federal law in this area. (Former Sec. 24988, Rev. & Tax. Code)

¶1246 Basis of Property Acquired from Partnership

Law: None (CCH CALIFORNIA TAX REPORTS, ¶10-220).

Comparable Federal: Sec. 732 (CCH U.S. MASTER TAX GUIDE ¶456).

The corporation tax law contains no provision regarding basis of property distributed in kind by a partnership. However, California law provides that a corporation receiving *income* from an interest in a partnership is to treat that income in the same manner as under the Personal Income Tax Law. (Sec. 73, Ch. 35 (A.B. 1122) and Ch. 34 (S.B. 657), Laws 2002, CCH CALIFORNIA TAX REPORTS, ¶201-802) Also, see ¶555 for a discussion of the basis of corporate stock distributed by a partnership to a corporate partner that has control of the distributed corporation after the distribution.

¶1247 Adjusted Basis

Law: Secs. 24911, 24916, 24916.2 (CCH CALIFORNIA TAX REPORTS, ¶10-690).

Comparable Federal: Secs. 1011, 1016-21 (CCH U.S. MASTER TAX GUIDE ¶1604, 1701).

The adjusted basis for determining gain or loss on the sale of property is the basis of the property, as adjusted by specific California provisions. (Sec. 24911, Rev. & Tax. Code) The provision is the same as IRC Sec. 1011, as of the current California conformity date (¶803), except that, as discussed below, the federal basis adjustments are in some cases different from those provided by California law. Special rules apply to California's treatment of gains and losses and its general basis rules.

In computing gain or loss on the sale or exchange of assets, adjustments to basis must be made for depreciation allowed or allowable, for various deferred expenses taken as deductions, and for many other factors, which are discussed below. (Sec. 24916, Rev. & Tax. Code)

California law also requires that adjustments be made for certain deducted enterprise zone, LAMBRA, former targeted tax area, or former LARZ business expenses (¶316, ¶1011). No comparable basis adjustments are required under federal law.

Corporate taxpayers may be prohibited from making basis adjustments authorized by federal provisions that have not been adopted by California. For instance, in *Appeal of CRG Holdings, Inc.* (1997) (CCH CALIFORNIA TAX REPORTS, ¶11-875.201), a taxpayer was not allowed to adjust its basis in the stock of its subsidiaries based on a consent dividend that was properly reported on the taxpayer's federal return, because California has never adopted the federal provision authorizing consent dividends.

Similarly, in *Appeal of Rapid-American Corporation* (1997) (CCH CALIFORNIA TAX REPORTS, ¶11-875.20), a taxpayer that sold its stock in its unitary subsidiaries was prohibited from increasing the basis of stock by the amount of earning and profits held in the subsidiaries that had previously been reported to California on the taxpayer's combined unitary report and that had not been distributed as dividends prior to the sales of stock. Although the disputed adjustment was authorized under federal law, California has never recognized earnings and profits as an appropriate basis adjustment.

• *Identical federal and California treatment*

The treatment of the following basis adjustments is identical for both California and federal law:

— tax free stock distributions (Sec. 24916(c), Rev. & Tax. Code; IRC Sec. 1016(a)(4))

— property pledged to the Commodity Credit Corporation (Sec. 24916(d)(3), Rev. & Tax. Code; IRC Sec. 1016(a)(8))

— deferred mine development expense (Sec. 24916(e), Rev. & Tax. Code; IRC Sec. 1016(a)(9))

— deferred research and experimental expenses (Sec. 24916(g), Rev. & Tax. Code; IRC Sec. 1016(a)(14))

— rollover of gain into a specialized small business investment company (SSBIC) (Sec. 24916(j), Rev. & Tax. Code; IRC Sec. 1016(a)(23))

— lessee-made improvements to real property (Sec. 24919, Rev. & Tax. Code; IRC Sec. 1019)

— the former deduction for clean-fuel vehicles and certain refueling property allowed under IRC Sec. 179A (Sec. 24916(i), Rev. & Tax. Code)

[*CCH Note:* California incorporates the federal basis adjustment for clean fuel vehicles and refueling property even though California no longer incorporates the IRC Sec. 179A deduction]

Although California does not include the following adjustments in its provision requiring basis adjustments, California does incorporate the underlying federal provision that requires a taxpayer to make a basis adjustment. Thus, as under federal law, taxpayers under California law must make adjustments for the following:

¶1247

— adjustments to the basis of a shareholder's stock in an S corporation that are required by IRC Sec. 1367, to reflect the shareholder's portion of various items of income, nontaxable return-of-capital distributions by the S corporation, etc. (Sec. 23800, Rev. & Tax. Code); and

— a reduction in basis in qualified employer securities to employee stock ownership plans (ESOPs) or qualified worker-owned cooperatives purchased by the taxpayer for which nonrecognition of gain is available under IRC Sec. 1042. (Sec. 24954, Rev. & Tax. Code)

Also, although California does not directly incorporate federal provisions that require basis adjustments for capital costs currently deducted by small business refiners under IRC Sec. 179B and facilities for which a production of low sulfur diesel fuel credit was claimed under IRC Sec. 45H, California requires basis adjustments for the equivalent California deduction and credit available to small business refiners. (Sec. 23662(d), Rev. & Tax. Code; Sec. 24356.4(b), Rev. & Tax. Code)

- *Federal basis adjustments not followed under California law*

Under IRC Sec. 1016, but not under California law, basis adjustments must be made for the following items discussed below:

— disallowed deductions on the disposal of coal or domestic iron ore;

— amounts related to a shareholder's stock in a controlled foreign corporation;

— the amount of gas guzzler tax on an automobile;

— for pre-2005 tax years, certain amounts that must be included in the gross income of a United States shareholder in a foreign personal holding company;

— municipal bond premiums required to be amortized under federal law;

— property for which a federal investment tax credit is claimed;

— amounts specified in a shareholder's consent made under IRC Sec. 28 of the 1939 Internal Revenue Code;

— disallowed deductions on the sale of unharvested crops;

— amortization of premium and accrual of discount on bonds and notes held by a life insurance company;

— certain amounts deducted under IRC Sec. 59(e) that are not treated as tax preference items if so deducted;

— property for which a federal credit for qualified electric vehicles was claimed under the federal credit for qualified electric vehicles;

— facilities for which a federal employer-provided child care credit was claimed; and

— railroad track for which a federal credit was claimed under IRC Sec. 45G.

In addition, California has not incorporated federal provisions that require adjustments for expenses for which an IRC Sec. 179D energy efficient commercial buildings deduction was claimed. Other adjustments required relating to expenses for which federal credits are claimed are similarly inapplicable for California purposes. (Sec. 23051.5(b), Rev. & Tax. Code)

¶1248 Substituted Basis

Law: Sec. 24917 (CCH California Tax Reports, ¶ 10-640, 10-690).

Comparable Federal: Sec. 1016 (CCH U.S. Master Tax Guide ¶ 1607).

Same as personal income tax (¶ 560).

¶1249 Lessor's Basis for Lessee's Improvements

Law: Sec. 24919 (CCH CALIFORNIA TAX REPORTS, ¶10-690).

Comparable Federal: Sec. 1019 (CCH U.S. MASTER TAX GUIDE ¶1601).

When the value of improvements by a lessee is excluded from income (¶905) there is no effect on the basis of the property to the lessor. When the value of such improvements was included in the lessor's gross income for any taxable year beginning before 1942, the basis of the lessor's property is adjusted accordingly. The California provision is the same as the federal one except for the effective date for California income tax purposes. (Sec. 24919, Rev. & Tax. Code)

¶1250 Basis for Depreciation and Depletion

Law: Secs. 24353, 24831 (CCH CALIFORNIA TAX REPORTS, ¶10-515, 10-850, 10-900).

Comparable Federal: Secs. 167, 612-13 (CCH U.S. MASTER TAX GUIDE ¶1203, 1289).

Same as personal income tax (¶562).

For rules regarding percentage value depletion, see ¶319.

¶1251 Reduction of Basis—Income from Discharge of Indebtedness

Law: Sec. 24918 (CCH CALIFORNIA TAX REPORTS, ¶10-690).

Comparable Federal: Sec. 1017 (CCH U.S. MASTER TAX GUIDE ¶1672).

When the taxpayer has elected to exclude from gross income gain from discharge of indebtedness, the amount excluded is applied to reduce the basis of property held by the taxpayer. Federal references to affiliated groups are applied to unitary members under California law. The California rules generally are the same as the federal rules. (Sec. 24918, Rev. & Tax. Code)

California conforms to the federal requirement that the amount of income realized from the discharge of qualified real property business indebtedness that a taxpayer excludes from gross income must be applied to reduce the basis of business real property held by the taxpayer at the beginning of the taxable year following the taxable year in which the discharge occurs.

¶1252 Allocation of Transferred Business Assets

Law: Sec. 24966.2 (CCH CALIFORNIA TAX REPORTS, ¶10-640).

Comparable Federal: Sec. 1060 (CCH U.S. MASTER TAX GUIDE ¶1620).

California has adopted the federal residual method for allocating purchases of assets that constitute a trade or business (¶803). Generally, under the residual method, the purchase price is allocated first to the assets to the extent of their fair market value, and any excess is allocated to goodwill and going concern value. However, if a transferor and a transferee agree in writing concerning the allocation of consideration for transferred business assets, their agreement will generally be binding for tax purposes. (Sec. 24966.2, Rev. & Tax. Code)

TAXES ON CORPORATE INCOME

CHAPTER 13
ALLOCATION AND APPORTIONMENT

¶1301 Scope of Chapter

The California taxes on corporate income are measured by income derived from or attributable to sources within California only. This applies both to corporations organized in California and to out-of-state ("foreign") corporations.

Where income is derived from sources both within and without the state, it is necessary to determine the income attributable to sources within the state. This chapter discusses the method of making this determination and points out some of the problems encountered. It covers not only situations where the income of only one corporation is involved, but also situations involving affiliated corporations. As pointed out in ¶ 1310, apportionment of all of the income of an affiliated group may be required even where only one of the affiliated corporations is engaged in any activity in California.

• *Uniform Division of Income for Tax Purposes Act*

California adopted the Uniform Division of Income for Tax Purposes Act (commonly referred to as UDITPA), effective in 1967; the Act has also been adopted by many other states. The California law deviates slightly from the original UDITPA draft, the principal differences being that (1) California does not exclude financial corporations and public utilities from the operation of the Act; and (2) California's standard apportionment formula (¶1305) included a double-weighted sales factor formula prior to the 2013 tax year, and includes a "mandatory" single sales factor formula beginning with the 2013 tax year (optional for the 2011 and 2012 tax years), in addition to the Multistate Tax Compact's equally-weighted apportionment formula (available at least for pre-2011 tax years and possibly beyond, see below).

In *Appeal of American Telephone and Telegraph Co.* (1982) (CCH CALIFORNIA TAX REPORTS, ¶ 11-530.70), discussed at ¶1305 and ¶1307, the State Board of Equalization (BOE) stated that "UDITPA'S fundamental purpose is to assure that 100%, and no more and no less, of a multistate taxpayer's business income is taxed by the states having jurisdiction to tax it." The BOE cites decisions of courts of other states that have adopted UDITPA, and says that in each of those cases "the court sought to avoid an interpretation of UDITPA which would create a gap in the taxation of the taxpayer's income."

Franchise Tax Board Reg. 25121, 18 CCR, through Reg. 25137, 18 CCR, interpret UDITPA and provide detailed rules for application of the law. Regulation 25121 requires that the taxpayer be consistent in reporting to California and to other states to which the taxpayer reports under UDITPA; if the taxpayer is not consistent in its reporting, it must disclose in its California return the nature and extent of the inconsistency.

• *Multistate Tax Compact*

California previously adopted the Multistate Tax Compact, which was developed by the Council of State Governments to promote uniformity among the States and to avoid duplicate taxation. The Compact includes the allocation and apportionment rules of UDITPA, discussed above. The constitutionality of the Compact was upheld by the U.S. Supreme Court in *United States Steel Corp. et al. v. Multistate Tax Commission et al.* (1978) (CCH CALIFORNIA TAX REPORTS, ¶ 10–105). California withdrew from the Compact for post-2010 tax years. However, some legal experts question the validity of the repealing legislation, see ¶ 1305 for more details.

Practitioner Comment: U.S. Supreme Court Declines to Rule on California Supreme Court's Decision in Gillette

On October 11, 2016, the U.S. Supreme Court denied Gillette's petition for certiorari, which requested that the Court review the California Supreme Court's decision in *Gillette Co. v. Franchise Tax Board*.

On December 31, 2015, the California Supreme Court ("CSC") unanimously reversed the California Court of Appeal's decision in *Gillette Co. v. Franchise Tax Board* and held that California law precludes taxpayers from relying on the Multistate Tax Compact's equally-weighted three-factor apportionment election provision.

In reaching its decision, the CSC did not determine whether the Compact took precedence over state law. Instead, the CSC held that the Compact was not a binding reciprocal agreement between its members and the California Legislature was not required to permit the Compact's election provision. The CSC reasoned that the Compact did not create reciprocal obligations among the member states as it did not possess the indicia of a binding interstate compact under *Northeast Bancorp. v. Board of Governors*, 472 U.S. 159 (1985).

In *Northeast Bancorp.*, the U.S. Supreme Court outlined the indicia of a binding compact as including (1) whether its effectiveness depends on the conduct of other members, (2) whether any provision prohibits unilateral member action, and (3) whether a regulatory organization has been established. In *Gillette*, the CSC noted that there is a history of unilateral state action amending the Compact, pointing to Florida's elimination of Article III, and the Multistate Tax Commission's subsequent recognition of Florida as a member in good standing. With respect to the Commission, the CSC concluded that its powers are "are strictly limited to an advisory and informational role." Consequently, the CSC held that the Compact was not the type of binding compact contemplated under *Northeast Bancorp.*

In two other Compact election cases at the state level, the Minnesota high court ruled in favor of the state, and the Michigan high court declined to review the issue. Compact election cases are still pending before the Texas Supreme Court and the Oregon Supreme Court.

Chris Whitney, Contributing Editor

Practice Note: FTB's Intended Actions Following Denial of Review of Gillette

The FTB has issued a notice regarding its intended courses of action on cases involving the Compact election following the U.S. Supreme Court's denial of the petition for certiorari in *Gillette*. The FTB had been holding cases raising the Compact election issue pending resolution of the *Gillette* litigation. Now that the litigation has concluded, the FTB will process claims for refund based on the Compact election issue and audits involving the issue in the normal course of business. To stop the accrual of interest, taxpayers may make tax deposits or pay proposed deficiency assessments. Penalties will be imposed as appropriate on a case-by-case basis. (*FTB Notice 2016-03*, November 1, 2016, CCH CALIFORNIA TAX REPORTS, ¶ 406-586).

¶1302 Apportionment of Business Income—General

Law: Secs. 25101, 25120-22 (CCH CALIFORNIA TAX REPORTS, ¶ 10-800, 11-520, 11-540, 11-550).

Comparable Federal: None.

California Forms: Form 100 (California Corporation Franchise or Income Tax Return), Sch. R (Apportionment and Allocation of Income).

Subject to the limitations pointed out in ¶ 804 and ¶ 805, any corporation deriving income from California sources is subject to California tax. If all of the income is from California, it is all subject to tax and there is, of course, no problem of apportioning a portion of the total net income to the state. However, the corporation may have income from sources outside California if (1) it is "doing business" outside of California, (2) it has property outside the state, or (3) it carries on some other activity outside the state.

If an activity generates both income that is included in the measure of tax and excluded income, only factors related to the production of income should be utilized to apportion that income. (*FTB Legal Ruling 2006-01* (2006) CCH CALIFORNIA TAX REPORTS, ¶ 404-006)

• *When apportionment required*

Apportionment of income is required where business activities are *taxable* inside and outside California. (Sec. 25121, Rev. & Tax. Code) For this purpose, a taxpayer is deemed to be taxable outside California if one of the following two specific qualifications is met:

(1) the taxpayer is subject to a net income tax, a franchise tax measured by net income, a franchise tax for the privilege of doing business, or a corporate stock tax in another state; or

(2) another state has jurisdiction to levy a net income tax on the taxpayer, *whether or not* the other state actually subjects the taxpayer to the tax.

(Sec. 25122, Rev. & Tax. Code; Reg. 25122, 18 CCR)

The other state is deemed to have jurisdiction to levy a net income tax if it would be permitted to levy a tax under the limitations imposed by the federal law (P.L. 86-272) pertaining to corporations engaged solely in interstate commerce. See ¶ 805.

As used in these qualification tests, "another state" also means the District of Columbia, Puerto Rico, U.S. territories and possessions, and any foreign country or political subdivision. A foreign country is deemed to have jurisdiction to tax if it would be permitted to impose a tax under the limitations imposed by federal law or any state of the United States. It should be noted that because the sale is made outside of the United States, the sale is not considered to be in interstate commerce and thus the protections offered by P.L. 86-272 would not apply. (Reg. 25122, 18 CCR; *FTB Chief Counsel Ruling 2012-03*, CCH CALIFORNIA TAX REPORTS, ¶ 405-723)

Reg. 25122, 18 CCR, provides rules for determining whether a taxpayer is taxable in another state, and gives several examples. The Franchise Tax Board (FTB) may require proof that the taxpayer has filed a return and paid tax of the required type in another state.

CCH Practice Tip: Voluntary Payments

A taxpayer is not considered to be subject to tax in another state if it voluntarily files and pays one or more of the taxes listed above when not required to do so or pays a minimal fee for qualification, organization, or the privilege of doing business in that state but does not:

— actually engage in business activity in that state, or

— engage in sufficient business activity to establish taxable nexus and the minimum tax bears no relation to the taxpayer's business activity within that state.

(Reg. 25122(b)(1), 18 CCR)

• *Procedure to determine taxable income*

Where income is to be apportioned within and outside the state under the rule set forth above, the taxable income is determined by the following steps:

(1) eliminate from the total net income any "nonbusiness" income attributable to intangible assets or to other property not connected with the operation of the principal or unitary business (such items are considered allocable either wholly to California or wholly outside California, as explained in ¶1303);

(2) apportion the remaining net income, described as "business income," within and outside the state by means of a formula or otherwise, as explained in ¶1304 and ¶1305; and

(3) the income taxable is the amount of business income apportioned to California in step 2 plus the income (less the losses) determined in step 1 to be wholly attributable to California.

Reg. 25120, 18 CCR, provides that a single corporate entity may have more than one "trade or business." In this case the income of each business is separately apportioned inside and outside the state. Examples are provided to illustrate the determination of whether the taxpayer's activities constitute a single business or more than one. See ¶1304 for decisions of the State Board of Equalization (BOE) involving use of separate formulas.

• *Distinction between "business" and "nonbusiness" income*

Under Reg. 25120, 18 CCR, income is deemed to be "business" income, subject to apportionment, unless it is clearly classifiable as "nonbusiness" income. A series of examples is provided to illustrate the rules to be applied in determining whether income is "business" or "nonbusiness." In general, all income—including all of the types listed in ¶1303—is "business" income if it arises from the conduct of trade or business operations.

In *Hoechst Celanese Corp. v. Franchise Tax Board,* (2001) (CCH CALIFORNIA TAX REPORTS, ¶11-520.67), the California Supreme Court reversed a decision of the Court of Appeal and held that income attributable to a reversion of surplus pension plan assets constituted business income under the functional test because the pension plan assets were created to retain and attract new employees who materially contributed to its production of business income. The decision marked the first time that the California Supreme Court addressed the question of whether the business income definition contains a functional test as well as a transactional test.

Practitioner Comment: "Cessation of Business" Concept for Classifying Income from Sale of Subsidiary Fails to Pass Muster with Court of Appeal

In what is arguably the first California appellate court decision addressing the "cessation of business" and "partial liquidation" exception concepts, the California Court of Appeal, First Appellate District, held that the complete sale of a subsidiary corporation engaged in a unitary business with the taxpayer resulted in business income under the functional test. (*Jim Beam Brands Co. v. Franchise Tax Board* (2005) CCH CALIFORNIA TAX REPORTS, ¶403-904, pet. for review denied, Cal SCt, No. S139031, January 4, 2006) As part of its analysis, the court rejected the concept—advanced by the taxpayer and contained in court decisions of other states—that where the sale of an asset of a unitary business results in the cessation of that line of business activity, the proceeds from that sale are treated as nonbusiness income.

The court initially objected to the taxpayer's portrayal of the partial liquidation exception as an issue of first impression for the court, finding that a 1980 Court of Appeal case (*Times Mirror Co. v. Franchise Tax Board* (1980) CCH CALIFORNIA TAX REPORTS,

¶11-520.726) and prior BOE decisions had held that sales of subsidiary stock yielded business income. In addition, relying on the decision in *Hoechst Celanese*, the court stated that focusing on the disposition of the property, as opposed to the income-producing property itself, "is contrary to California decisional law, for it focuses on the nature of the transaction, rather than on the relationship between the property sold and the taxpayer's regular trade or business operations."

Chris Whitney, Contributing Editor

CCH Comment: Integration of Subsidiary

In *Appeal of Occidental Petroleum*, 83-SBE-119, the State Board of Equalization held that the classification of income from intangibles under the functional test of business income must be made on the basis of the relationships between the intangible and the taxpayer's unitary business. Sales of stock in entities that were fully integrated and functioning parts of the taxpayer's existing unitary business gave rise to apportionable income. Sales of stock in corporations that were intended to be integrated into the taxpayer's business, but at the time of the sales were not yet integrated, generated nonbusiness income. This distinction—between the intent and potential for integration, on the one hand, versus actual integration, on the other—has led to confusion as to what the result should be where the two corporations have had a preexisting business relationship beyond that involved in the mere acquisition of stock, yet the purpose for the acquisition of the stock is based on intent to integrate the target into the taxpayer's unitary business operations. If the integration does not occur, and the intent of the taxpayer is frustrated, questions have arisen as to whether a sale of the stock should properly give rise to nonbusiness income even though there are preexisting operational ties unrelated to the acquisition of the stock. The FTB has issued a legal ruling that addresses this issue and provides examples of the application of the law to various situations. According to the FTB, in making the determination of business or nonbusiness income, it is the actual operational ties and the significance of such ties that are most important. While the taxpayer's intent, along with other factors, may support a determination that an operational relationship did or did not exist, the frustration of the taxpayer's intended purpose for the acquisition of the stock is not a determining factor. (*FTB Legal Ruling 2012-01*, CCH CALIFORNIA TAX REPORTS, ¶405-703)

Practitioner Comment: FTB Guidance on the Business/Nonbusiness Characterization on Sale of Stock

FTB issued Legal Ruling 2012-01 to provide guidance with respect to the business/nonbusiness characterization of income arising from the disposition of stock in a corporation where there is a pre-existing business relationship between the entities concerned on the one hand, and a plan to integrate the operations of the two companies which is never realized on the other.

The taxpayer in all three factual scenarios provided in the legal ruling purchased and later sells a minority interest in a target corporation. In the first scenario, Corporations A and B have no prior business relationship and their operations are never integrated. When Corporation A's plan to acquire a majority interest in Corporation B is thwarted because Corporation C acquires a majority interest, Corporation A sells its stock in Corporation B. In the second scenario, Corporation D acquires an interest in Corporation E in order to gain information regarding the latter's technology, based on which Corporation D enters into an exclusive license to use such technology and after which Corporation D sells the Corporation E stock. In the third scenario, Corporations F and G have an ongoing business relationship and Corporation F becomes the predominant distributor of Corporation G's products after acquiring the minority interest. Unable to acquire a majority interest in Corporation G, Corporation F later sells the minority interest.

In its analysis, the FTB cites the California Supreme Court's decision in *Hoechst Celanese Corp. v. FTB*, (2001) 25 Cal. 4th 508, CCH CALIFORNIA TAX REPORTS, ¶403-142, which firmly established the alternative "transactional" and "functional" tests for determining whether income is apportionable business income or allocable nonbusiness income. In regard to the functional test, which focuses on the role of the underlying asset in the taxpayer's trade or business, the FTB cited several State Board of Equalization (BOE) decisions, most notably the *Appeal of Occidental Petroleum*, 83-SBE-119 (1983), CCH CALIFORNIA TAX REPORTS, ¶00567 as standing for the proposition that intentions to integrate are not sufficient to meet the functional test. Instead, actual operational integration is required.

Applying these standards to the scenarios in question, the FTB concluded that because Corporation A had no preexisting or ongoing business relationship or operational involvement with Corporation B, the gain or loss on the sale of Corporation B stock would be nonbusiness income. On the other hand, because Corporation D gained useful information regarding Corporation E's technology and had an ongoing business relationship, such effectively integrated Corporation E's stock into its unitary business thereby causing the sale of stock to produce business income. Finally, the ongoing business relationship between Corporations F and G would also support business income treatment.

The legal ruling focuses on the functional test and does not address whether the sale of stock might have been considered business income under the transactional test. In addition, although the legal ruling cites *Hoechst Celanese*, it omits reference to where the Court went on to state that "[t]he property must be so interwoven into the fabric of the taxpayer's business operations that it becomes 'indivisible' or inseparable from the taxpayer's business activities with both 'giving value' to each other," which suggests that the flow of value should be "two way." This two-way flow of value concept was one area of focus during the BOE hearing in *Appeal of Pacific Bell Telephone Company & Affiliates*, Cal. St. Bd. of Equal., Case No. 521312, heard Sept. 20, 2011 (nonprecedential decision), CCH CALIFORNIA TAX REPORTS, ¶405-572, in which the BOE held that income arising from minority stock holdings was properly characterized as nonbusiness income. It is unclear from the limited facts presented in the ruling how consideration of such a concept might have impacted the conclusions reached with respect to each of the scenarios.

Chris Whitney, Contributing Editor

Practitioner Comment: Gain on the Subsequent Sale of Stock Received in Connection with an Earlier Sale of Business Assets was Nonbusiness Income Where the Stock Received Played no Part in the Seller's Regular Trade or Business Operations

The California State Board of Equalization's (BOE's) nonprecedential summary decision in *Appeal of ConAgra Foods, Inc.*, Nos. 597512, 785058, and 799162, 06/26/2015 (CCH CALIFORNIA TAX REPORTS, ¶11-510.23), concluded that gain on the sale of publicly traded stock received in exchange for the taxpayer's chicken processing business was nonbusiness income. The BOE explained that the stock received in the earlier transaction was not an integral part of the taxpayer's regular trade or business operations at the time of the subsequent sale.

Specifically, the taxpayer sold its chicken processing business to Pilgrim's Pride in exchange for cash and publicly traded Pilgrim's Pride stock. The BOE explained that when the taxpayer acquired the Pilgrim's Pride stock, "it ended its participation in its former chicken business interest and obtained a minority interest in an independent publicly owned company." The BOE also noted that although the taxpayer's supply agreement with Pilgrim's Pride represented a continuing operational tie between the two companies, it "merely provided that [the taxpayer] would offer Pilgrim's Pride the first opportunity to provide chicken to [it] at fair market value and in volumes similar to past volumes or in such volumes as the parties might mutually agree." Most importantly, there was no evidence suggesting that the taxpayer's Pilgrim's Pride stock allowed it to exercise "continued management or control" over any assets it sold to Pilgrims' Pride. Moreover, the taxpayer sold the stock it received in the transaction as soon as permissible and it was "primarily as a result of the substantial appreciation in the price of the publicly traded stock of Pilgrim's Pride" that the taxpayer recognized substantial income. Based on these findings, the BOE held that gain on the sale of Pilgrim's Pride stock was nonbusiness income.

The SBE's holding with respect to the sale of Pilgrim's Pride stock provides an interesting contrast to the its earlier decision in *Appeal of General Dynamics Corporation*, 75-SBE-037, June 3, 1975. In *General Dynamics*, the BOE held that gain on the sale of stock it received in connection with a customer's previous bankruptcy was business income under the transactional test. Although both parties referenced *General Dynamics* in their briefs, the BOE did not address this decision in its summary decision. Perhaps the two decisions can be reconciled on the basis that the stock received by General Dynamics arose from a sale of aircraft in the course of General Dynamics' regular trade or business operations and hence met the "transactional test." In contrast, the BOE's decision in *Conagra* was based on the "functional test," which focuses on the role, or in this case, the lack thereof, that the business interest represented by the stock played in the taxpayer's trade or business.

The BOE's holding with respect to the Pilgrim's Pride stock sale may also contrast with its holding in connection with a second transaction addressed in the appeal, in which the BOE found that income from equity and debt interests from a joint venture formed in the connection with the sale of Conagra's fresh beef and pork operations was business income. In the second transaction, Conagra provided debt financing to fund the joint venture, continued to use beef and pork from its operations in its other business, and reacquired its cattle operations when sufficient funds were not produced to repay the funding provided by the taxpayer. These facts, the BOE concluded, did not result in a termination of the taxpayer's participation in fresh beef and pork operations, but rather represented a "repackaging" of the taxpayer's beef and pork operations into a joint venture that the taxpayer "continued to hold and use as an integral part of its business."

Chris Whitney, Contributing Editor

In *ComCon Production Services I, Inc. v. FTB* (2014) (CCH CALIFORNIA TAX REPORTS, ¶406-243), a California superior court ruled that a termination fee paid to one of the taxpayer's affiliates following the taxpayer's failed merger with another company was apportionable business income under both the transactional test and the functional test. The termination fee satisfied the transactional test for business income because (1) it arose from a cable company acquisition agreement, which was of the same basic nature as scores of other agreements the taxpayer regularly entered into in the course of its business; and (2) the taxpayer used the proceeds from the fee to pay down its business obligations, all of which related to the taxpayer's business as opposed to nonbusiness assets. The termination fee also satisfied the functional test for business income because the merger agreement represented intangible property rights that the taxpayer acquired, managed, and disposed of as an integral part of its regular business. Furthermore, the termination fee was a substitute for profits that the taxpayer would have earned in the regular course of its business had the merger been completed. The taxpayer has filed a notice of appeal regarding the business/nonbusiness income issue.

In *Appeal of Consolidated Freightways, Inc.* (2000) (CCH CALIFORNIA TAX REPORTS, ¶11-520.561), the BOE held that interest and dividends earned by a California-domiciled taxpayer from investments in long-term securities constituted business income under the functional test because the taxpayer had "earmarked" the funds for acquisition of a target in the same general line of business as the taxpayer.

In Legal Ruling 98-5 (1998) (CCH CALIFORNIA TAX REPORTS, ¶11-515.28), the FTB ruled that interest and dividend income generated from liquid assets in excess of current business needs and identified future business needs could not properly be characterized as business income. The fact that the excess income was available for business use did not make the income business income when neither the transactional nor functional test for business income was satisfied.

In *Appeal of Bank of Tokyo, Limited, and Union Bank* (1995) (CCH CALIFORNIA TAX REPORTS, ¶11-520.303), a California bank and a Japanese bank engaged in a unitary business were required to treat the Japanese bank's capital gains and dividends from investments in unrelated nonbanking companies as business income, even though a California bank could not have made the same type of investments, because the investment income was earned through a common practice in Japan in which banks own stock in companies to whom they lent funds.

In *Appeal of R.H. Macy & Co., Inc.* (1988) (CCH CALIFORNIA TAX REPORTS, ¶11-520.562), the BOE held that interest from short-term marketable securities bought by a New York corporation engaged in retail operations in California was business income. The securities were bought with working capital awaiting use.

In the *Appeal of Inco Express, Inc.* (1987) (CCH CALIFORNIA TAX REPORTS, ¶11-520.542), the interest earned on short-term working capital investments by a Washington-based trucking corporation was held to be business income by the BOE in the absence of a showing that the funds were earmarked for nonbusiness purposes.

In *Appeal of American Medical Buildings, Inc.* (1986) (CCH CALIFORNIA TAX REPORTS, ¶11-520.563), the short-term investment income of a unitary construction business based in Wisconsin and engaged in business in California was held to be business income by the BOE. The income was intended to help finance the corporation's construction of medical buildings and was therefore integral to the company and apportionable to California.

In *Appeal of Louisiana-Pacific Corporation* (1986) (CCH CALIFORNIA TAX REPORTS, ¶11-520.721), gain on the sale of a noncontrolling 50% stock interest in a raw materials supply affiliate was apportionable business income.

In *Appeal of Standard Oil Co. of California* (1983) (CCH CALIFORNIA TAX REPORTS, ¶11-520.372), the taxpayer received substantial dividends from noncontrolled affiliated joint venture corporations. The joint venture corporations (Aramco and CPI) were major sources of supply for the taxpayer's worldwide activities. The BOE, in a lengthy and detailed opinion, held that the dividend income was integrally related to the taxpayer's business activities and was apportionable as part of the unitary income.

In *Appeal of Occidental Petroleum Corporation* (1983) (CCH CALIFORNIA TAX REPORTS, ¶11-520.72), a California corporation contended that gains and losses on sale of stocks of five subsidiaries were business income, subject to apportionment. The BOE held that three of the subsidiaries were integrated parts of the unitary business, but that two of the subsidiaries were not; it followed that the gains on the latter two were nonbusiness income.

In *Appeal of Johns-Manville Sales Corporation* (1983) (CCH CALIFORNIA TAX REPORTS, ¶11-515.571), the taxpayer contended that a loss suffered upon disposition of its 48% interest in a Belgian corporation was a business loss subject to apportionment. The BOE held that the taxpayer had not borne the burden of proving an integral relationship between its stockholding and its unitary business.

In *Appeal of Joy World Corporation* (1982) (CCH CALIFORNIA TAX REPORTS, ¶11-520.705), the taxpayer was one of a number of subsidiaries of a Japanese corporation. The taxpayer's principal activity was the purchase of raw cotton for sale to its parent. The business of the affiliated group was admittedly unitary. The FTB included in unitary income the gain realized by the affiliated group on the sale of certain of its securities and fixed assets; the taxpayer objected to this, using as one argument the assertion that the income involved was nonbusiness income under Japanese accounting principles. The BOE upheld the FTB.

In *The Times Mirror Co. v. Franchise Tax Board* (1980) (CCH CALIFORNIA TAX REPORTS, ¶206-294), the parent corporation realized a capital gain on sale of stock of a subsidiary in 1969. The subsidiary was one of several that had been included in a combined return with the parent and had been treated for many years as parts of a unitary business for California tax purposes. The Court of Appeal held that the capital gain was "business" income, to be apportioned within and without the state along with other income of the unitary business.

Appeal of General Dynamics Corporation (1975) (CCH CALIFORNIA TAX REPORTS, ¶205-274) involved gain on the sale of certain stock in 1967. The stock had been acquired in a complicated series of transactions that arose in the course of the unitary business. The BOE held that the gain was unitary "business income" rather than "nonbusiness income" attributable to its out-of-state situs. The BOE's opinion included this significant comment: "In determining whether the income from intangibles constitutes business or nonbusiness income, the classifications normally given income, such as interest, dividends, or capital gains are of no assistance. The relevant inquiry is whether the income arises in the main course of the taxpayer's business operations." To the same effect, see *Appeal of Pacific Telephone and Telegraph Co.* (1978) (CCH CALIFORNIA TAX REPORTS, ¶11-525.80), involving business income gained on the sale of stock of an affiliated corporation that was received in a reorganization, and *Robert Half International, Inc. v. Franchise Tax Board* (1998) (CCH CALIFORNIA TAX REPORTS, ¶11-515.592), involving a nonbusiness loss incurred on the acquisition of a warrant for stock.

• *Pertinent cases under prior law*

Under pre-1967 law, there were many decisions of the BOE and the courts dealing with the question of whether certain income was "unitary" income subject to "allocation" or was nonunitary income that was attributable entirely to a particular State. The reasoning of these cases should apply, generally, under present law, to the question of whether income is "business" or "nonbusiness." (However, as pointed out in the opinion in the *Times Mirror* case, discussed above, such prior-law cases cannot be used as *precedents* under the current law; also, as pointed out in the *Standard Oil* case, the pre-1967 law regarding dividends was different from current law.)

Appeal of Capital Southwest Corporation (1973) (CCH CALIFORNIA TAX REPORTS, ¶204-818) involved a "small business investment company," with its head office outside California and a small office within the State. The BOE held that the taxpayer's income from dividends and capital gains was part of its unitary business income from long-term investments and was subject to apportionment.

In *Appeal of the Western Pacific Railroad Company* (1972) (CCH CALIFORNIA TAX REPORTS, ¶11-530.38), the BOE held in 1972 that gains and losses on sales of land were not includible in unitary income subject to apportionment. The land was sold to prospective shippers to increase rail traffic, but it was never used in the unitary operations.

In *Appeal of W.J. Voit Rubber Company* (1964) (CCH CALIFORNIA TAX REPORTS, ¶11-520.70), a California corporation sold an entire manufacturing plant located in another state. The out-of-state plant had previously been operated as part of a unitary business, and gain arising out of its sale was held to be unitary income subject to allocation within and without California. To the same effect, involving the out-of-state sale of motion pictures that had been produced in prior years in a unitary business, see *Appeal of Paramount Pictures Corp.* (1969) (CCH CALIFORNIA TAX REPORTS, ¶11-525.31).

In *Appeal of the United States Shoe Corporation* (1959) (CCH CALIFORNIA TAX REPORTS, ¶11-520.661), the BOE held that license fees received from licensees in foreign countries for technical information, services, advice, and manufacturing "know-how" were includible in unitary income, since the taxpayer's ability to furnish such advice and "know-how" arose out of its unitary business.

In *Appeal of Union Carbide & Carbon Corporation* (1957) (CCH CALIFORNIA TAX REPORTS, ¶11-520.42), the BOE held that certain government project fees were part of unitary income to be allocated by formula. These fees were received for services of a managerial and technical nature, the services having been rendered at the Oak Ridge atomic energy plant and other locations outside of California. The BOE's decision was based on the reasoning that the fees were received for the use of skills developed in the taxpayer's regular business operations.

In *Appeal of International Business Machines Corp.* (1954) (CCH CALIFORNIA TAX REPORTS, ¶11-520.661), the BOE held that royalty income of a foreign corporation was part of its unitary income and subject to allocation. In this case the corporation received large royalties for the use of its patents in foreign countries. The patents had been developed and were used in the corporation's regular business operations in this country. To the same effect, see *Appeal of National Cylinder Gas Company* (1957) (CCH CALIFORNIA TAX REPORTS, ¶11-520.66) and *Appeal of Rockwell Manufacturing Company* (1958) (CCH CALIFORNIA TAX REPORTS, ¶11-520.66).

• *Cases decided under UDITPA*

Later cases, involving the Uniform Division of Income for Tax Purposes Act that became effective in 1967, follow the pattern of the prior-law cases discussed above. In *Appeal of New York Football Giants, Inc.* (1977) (CCH CALIFORNIA TAX REPORTS, ¶11-525.512), the BOE held that compensation to an out-of-state corporation for loss of a franchise was part of unitary "business income" to be allocated by formula. In *Appeal of Borden, Inc.* (1977) (CCH CALIFORNIA TAX REPORTS, ¶11-520.701), the BOE held that losses on sale of a California plant and goodwill were "business losses" subject to formula apportionment. The BOE refused to recognize a liquidation exception to the functional test for determining whether income is business income. Similarly, see *Appeal of Imperial, Inc.* (2010) (CCH CALIFORNIA TAX REPORTS, ¶11-520.47), holding that gain from goodwill on the sale of a corporation's assets was properly classified as business income.

In *Appeal of Calavo Growers of California* (1984) (CCH CALIFORNIA TAX REPORTS, ¶11-520.703), it was held that gain on the sale of Florida citrus groves was "business income"; the groves had been acquired in an earlier year upon default of a company to which the taxpayer had made loans. In *Appeal of Triangle Publications, Inc.* (1984) (CCH CALIFORNIA TAX REPORTS, ¶11-520.702), the BOE cited and followed the *Borden* and *Calavo Growers* cases. In *Appeal of Kroehler Manufacturing Co.* (1977) (CCH CALIFORNIA TAX REPORTS, ¶11-520.721), the BOE held that rebates received upon liquidation of the pension plan of a predecessor corporation were "business income" subject to formula apportionment. In *Appeal of Thor Power Tool Company* (1980) (CCH CALIFORNIA TAX REPORTS, ¶203-306), the BOE held that gain on sale of land (former plant site) was "business income." In *Appeal of Fairchild Industries, Inc.* (1980) (CCH CALIFORNIA TAX REPORTS, ¶11-520.662) the BOE held that gain on sale of patent rights was "business income."

The cases have held that the present law provides two alternative tests for determining what is "business income": the "transactional test" and the "functional test." For a discussion of these tests, see the decision of the BOE in *Appeal of DPF, Inc.* (1980) (CCH CALIFORNIA TAX REPORTS, ¶11-520.48). In that case the BOE decided that gain on repurchase of debentures was "business income." On the other hand, in *Appeal of Beck Industries* (1982) (CCH CALIFORNIA TAX REPORTS, ¶11-520.805) the BOE applied the two tests and found that interest received on certificates of deposit was nonbusiness income; in that case the deposited funds arose from selling discontinued business interests during a bankruptcy reorganization. However, interest income from short-term investment of excess funds was held to be business income in *Appeal of A. Epstein and Sons, Inc.* (1984) (CCH CALIFORNIA TAX REPORTS, ¶11-520.837).

In two 1977 decisions involving UDITPA, the BOE held that real estate rentals were "business income" subject to formula allocation. See *Appeal of Isador Weinstein Investment Co.* (CCH CALIFORNIA TAX REPORTS, ¶11-520.692) and *Appeal of O.K. Earl Corp.* (CCH CALIFORNIA TAX REPORTS, ¶11-520.691).

¶1303 Allocation of Nonbusiness Income—General

Law: Secs. 25123-27 (CCH CALIFORNIA TAX REPORTS, ¶11-515).

Comparable Federal: None.

As explained at ¶1302, most income is deemed to be "business" income—regardless of the form or type of income involved—but some income is clearly classifiable as "nonbusiness." The law provides the following specific rules for the treatment of certain types of income, to the extent that the income constitutes "nonbusiness" income:

— Net rents and royalties from real property, and gains and losses from the sale thereof, are allocable to the state in which the property is located. (Sec. 25124, Rev. & Tax. Code)

— Net rents and royalties from tangible personal property are allocable to the state in which the property is utilized. However, if the taxpayer was not organized in, or is not taxable in, the state in which the property is utilized, such income is taxable in the state of the owner's commercial domicile. For tangible personal property utilized in more than one state, the income is allocated on the basis of the number of days of physical location within and without California during the rental or royalty period of the taxable year. If the physical location during the period is unknown or unascertainable by the taxpayer, the property is deemed utilized in the state in which the property is located at the time the payer of the rent or royalty obtained possession. (Sec. 25124, Rev. & Tax. Code)

— Gains and losses from sale of tangible personal property are allocable to the state where the property is located at the time of sale. However, if the taxpayer is not taxable in the state in which the property is located at the time of sale, the gain or loss is allocable to the state of the taxpayer's commercial domicile. (Sec. 25125, Rev. & Tax. Code)

— Interest and dividends, as well as gains and losses from sale of intangible personal property, are allocable entirely to the state of the taxpayer's commercial domicile. (Sec. 25125, Rev. & Tax. Code; Sec. 25126, Rev. & Tax. Code)

— Patent and copyright royalties are allocable to the state in which the patent or copyright is utilized by the payer of the royalties. However, if the taxpayer is not taxable in the state in which the property is utilized, the royalty income is allocable to the state of commercial domicile. Royalty income from a patent that is utilized in more than one state in production, fabrication, manufacturing, etc., or a patented product that is produced in more than one state is allocable to the states of utilization on the basis of gross royalty receipts. However, if the taxpayer fails to maintain accounting records to reflect the states of utilization, the entire amount is allocable to the state of the taxpayer's commercial domicile. A copyright is deemed to be utilized in the state in which printing or other publication originates. (Sec. 25127, Rev. & Tax. Code)

• *What is "commercial domicile"?*

The law defines "commercial domicile" as "the principal place from which the trade or business of the taxpayer is directed or managed." (Sec. 25120, Rev. & Tax. Code) This is generally similar to the pre-1967 law, so the reasoning of the 1955 decision of the California District Court of Appeal in *Pacific Western Oil Corp. v. Franchise Tax Board* (CCH CALIFORNIA TAX REPORTS, ¶ 11-515.301) presumably would be applicable under present law. In that case, the taxpayer was a Delaware corporation and received income from dividends, interest, and gains from sale of securities at its offices in New Jersey. However, it was held that the taxpayer's commercial domicile was in California and, therefore, the income from the intangibles was includible in the measure of the franchise tax. Important factors influencing the decision were:

— revenue from sales of products was greater in California than in all other states combined;

— the value of the fixed assets in California was several times greater than those located in other states;

— over 90% of the employees were performing services in California;

— the principal accounting records were kept in California;

— the income from the intangibles had not been taxed by any other state; and

— the federal income tax returns were filed in California.

In *Appeal of Vinnell Corporation* (1978) (CCH CALIFORNIA TAX REPORTS, ¶11-515.453), the taxpayer (a predecessor corporation) was a wholly-owned subsidiary of a California corporation. The taxpayer was incorporated in Panama and was engaged in the construction business entirely outside the United States. The State Board of Equalization (BOE) held that the taxpayer's commercial domicile was not in California, although there were some contacts with California. The BOE dismissed the contacts as "artificial and lacking in substance" and commented that the concept of commercial domicile that has been developed by the courts is an "intensely practical" one.

In *Appeal of Norton Simon, Inc.* (1972) (CCH CALIFORNIA TAX REPORTS, ¶11-515.45), the BOE held that the commercial domicile of a predecessor corporation (Harbor Plywood) was in California. The BOE held that "the essence of the concept of commercial domicile is that is the place where the corporate management functions, the place where real control exists ... "

In *Appeal of Bristol-Myers Company* (1972) (CCH CALIFORNIA TAX REPORTS, ¶11-515.26), a New York company suffered losses on its investment in a nonunitary subsidiary located in California. The corporation claimed deduction of the losses for franchise tax purposes, contending that it had commercial domiciles in both New York and California. The BOE held that the losses were attributable to New York, the state of the parent corporation's only domicile, and were not deductible.

Practitioner Comment: A Corporation Solely Owned by a California Resident Shareholder May Be Able to Support an Out-of-State Commercial Domicile With Adequate, Contemporaneous Documentation

In *Daniel V, Inc., v. Franchise Tax Board*, Los Angeles County Superior Court, No. BC457301, June 14, 2013, the court held that the taxpayer was commercially domiciled in Nevada, notwithstanding that its sole owner was a California resident, and awarded nearly $1.2 million in attorney fees. The litigation lasted over a decade with the taxpayer losing at the State Board of Equalization before ultimately prevailing in trial court.

During the course of the audit, the taxpayer provided contemporaneous documentation that it maintained its corporate office, a bank account, and books and records in Nevada. The taxpayer was also able to demonstrate that all of its board of directors meetings were conducted in Nevada, and that the corporation's president, who was a resident of Nevada, signed all of Daniel V's checks and handled all of its expenditures and business affairs from Nevada. The court found that the FTB did not produce sufficient direct evidence to support its assertion that Daniel V's sole owner actually managed and directed Daniel V from California. Instead, the court noted that the FTB's case was mostly circumstantial.

Therefore, the trial court agreed with the taxpayer's assertion that it was commercially domiciled in Nevada. Although the FTB filed a notice of appeal, it was dismissed.

California law provides for the award of reasonable litigation costs to a prevailing party in a civil proceeding brought by the FTB in connection with the determination of any tax, interest, or penalty if the state's position is not "substantially justified." During a June 14, 2013 hearing on the taxpayer's motion for attorney fees, the trial court judge awarded the taxpayer nearly $1.2 million in fees. The judge noted that he found "the position taken by the Franchise Tax Board in this matter was not substantially justified... the evidence was surprisingly weak in terms of a case that's gone on for... 12 years or so. And all we've got is some speculation, some supposition but evidence just wasn't there.... the conduct of the Franchise Tax Board just was not doing the right thing.... all we really had was some speculation because the corporation has their CPAs in California, that's not enough."

The *Daniel V* litigation highlights the importance of documenting tax positions, including commercial domicile, and may also be instructive in matters involving residency for personal income tax purposes and nexus positions.

Chris Whitney, Contributing Editor

¶1303

- *Share of out-of-state partnership loss*

In *Appeal of The National Dollar Stores, Ltd.* (1986) (CCH CALIFORNIA TAX REPORTS, ¶ 11-515.59), losses from an oil and gas drilling partnership in Colorado incurred by a California clothing retailer were nonbusiness income, unrelated to the retailer's unitary retail sales business. The losses were attributable to Colorado and not deductible.

In *Appeal of Custom Component Switches, Inc.* (1977) (CCH CALIFORNIA TAX REPORTS, ¶ 11-515.48), a California corporation was a manufacturer of electrical equipment and was a member of a real estate partnership. The BOE held that partnership losses attributable to out-of-state property were from sources outside California and were not deductible.

- *Intercompany dividends*

Dividends received by one member from another member of a group of affiliated corporations filing a combined California report are excluded from income, to the extent such dividends are paid out of unitary income, see ¶ 909 for details. In *Appeal of Louisiana-Pacific Corporation* (1987) (CCH CALIFORNIA TAX REPORTS, ¶ 11-515.404), the exclusion for intercompany dividends paid from unitary income did not apply to distributions made prior to the time the payor corporation became a member of the unitary business.

- *Royalty income*

In the *Appeal of Masonite Corporation* (1987) (CCH CALIFORNIA TAX REPORTS, ¶ 11-515.59), income derived from the production of oil and gas from reserves underlying taxpayer's Mississippi timberlands was nonbusiness income. The BOE held that income was unrelated to the taxpayer's unitary wood-products business because the oil production activities were, in fact, detrimental to the timberlands.

- *Allocation of gain or loss on sale of partnership interests*

An interstate or international corporation that sells a partnership interest must use an allocation formula to determine the portion of capital gain or loss realized from the sale that must be attributed to California taxable income. The allocation formula is based on the relationship that the original cost of the partnership's tangible property located in California bears to the original cost of all the partnership's tangible property. In the event that more than 50% of the partnership's assets consists of intangible property, the allocation to California income of the gain or loss realized must be determined by using the ratio of the partnership's California sales to the partnership's total sales during the first full tax period preceding the sale of the partnership interest. (Sec. 25125, Rev. & Tax. Code)

¶ 1304 Methods of Apportioning Business Income

Law: Secs. 25128, 25137 (CCH CALIFORNIA TAX REPORTS, ¶ 11-520, 11-550).

Comparable Federal: None.

The law provides detailed rules for apportionment of business income by formula. It also provides for use of separate accounting where apportionment by formula does not fairly reflect the extent of the taxpayer's business activity in the state, and permits the taxpayer to petition for use of separate accounting.

- *FTB policy on apportionment, separate accounting, and decombination*

Until the early 1990s, it was the consistent policy of the Franchise Tax Board (FTB) to find business operations unitary (and thus require apportionment or, if separate affiliates were involved, combined reporting) if sufficient, minimum unitary criteria were met. For example, operations were generally considered unitary if there was any flow of goods or benefits between the part of the business within and the part outside the state, or where one part contributed directly or indirectly to the other. Examples of such relationships would be one division purchasing materials or merchandise from another; insurance or pension plans handled jointly; advertising done on a cooperative basis; centralized purchasing, selling, engineering accounting, financing, etc.

¶ 1304

In August 1992, however, the FTB issued revised audit guidelines with respect to the unitary combination of diverse businesses (*FTB Notice No. 92-4*, CCH CALIFORNIA TAX REPORTS, ¶11-520.35). According to the revised guidelines, there is no unique test for evaluating unity in diverse business cases. Unity may be established under any of the judicially acceptable tests (the three unities, contribution or dependency, and flow of value tests) and may not be denied merely because another of those tests does not simultaneously apply, *i.e.*, the tests are not mutually exclusive. In addition, a lack of functional integration will not prevent a finding of unity. On the other hand, the fact that functionally integrated businesses may be found to be unitary does not mean that functional integration is a *requirement* for unity.

Also, presumptions of unity under Reg. 25120(b), 18 CCR, which states that the activities of a taxpayer will be considered a single business if there is evidence to indicate that the segments under consideration are integrated with, depend on, or contribute to, each other and the operations of the taxpayer as a whole, although important considerations, are not conclusive in determining unity.

Finally, the guidelines state that *Mole-Richardson, Dental Insurance Consultants,* and *Tenneco West, Inc.* (all discussed below) are controlling of the diverse business issue and that State Board of Equalization (BOE) decisions that are not in accord with these cases should not be relied upon.

If the operations of a business are "unitary" in nature, it makes no difference whether there is only one corporation or an affiliated group. Consolidation and income-apportionment of a large group of corporations may be required even where only one of the corporations is subject to California tax. See *Edison California Stores* and other cases discussed below. See also ¶1310.

The FTB has issued a legal ruling containing guidelines for determining whether the "unity of ownership" requirement for unitary treatment is satisfied (see below) (*FTB Legal Ruling No. 91-1*, CCH CALIFORNIA TAX REPORTS, ¶11-520.954).

CCH Practice Tip: Apportionment of IRC Sec. 338 Deemed Asset Sales

For information regarding how to apportion the gains resulting from an IRC Sec. 338(h)(1) or IRC Sec. 338(g) election to treat the sale or purchase of stock as a sale or purchase of assets, see the FTB's *Legal Ruling 2006-03*, May 6, 2006, CCH CALIFORNIA TAX REPORTS, ¶10-540.21, and *Chief Counsel Ruling 2008-2*, September 15, 2008, CCH CALIFORNIA TAX REPORTS, ¶404-925.

• *Leading cases*

The courts have developed the following three general tests for determining whether a business is "unitary":

— the three unities test, in the *Butler Brothers* case;

— the contribution and dependency test, in the *Edison California Stores* case; and

— the functional integration test, in the *Container* case.

The existence of a unitary business is established if any of the three tests is met.

In *Butler Brothers v. McColgan* (1942) (CCH CALIFORNIA TAX REPORTS, ¶11-520.2096), the U.S. Supreme Court upheld use of the allocation formula (equivalent to the "apportionment" formula under present law) in preference to separate accounting. In that case the taxpayer corporation operated a number of stores throughout the country, one of which was in California. The unitary nature of the business was held to have been definitely established by the presence of the following factors:

— unity of ownership;

— unity of operation as evidenced by central purchasing, advertising, accounting, and management divisions; and

— unity of use in its centralized executive force and general system of operation.

¶1304

Separate accounting showed a large loss for the California store, whereas application of the formula resulted in a substantial profit allocable to California. Nevertheless, the court upheld the use of the formula, because the taxpayer did not demonstrate convincingly that the formula produced a clearly unreasonable result and that separate accounting fairly and accurately reflected the income properly allocable to California.

In *Container Corporation of America v. Franchise Tax Board* (1983) (CCH CALIFORNIA TAX REPORTS, ¶ 11-520), the U.S. Supreme Court upheld the application of the standard three-factor apportionment formula to a domestic corporation and several foreign subsidiaries. The court held that the parent and subsidiaries were unitary because they were linked by common managerial or operational resources that produced economies of scale and transfers of value. The court stated that whether businesses are unitary is determined by whether contributions to income result from functional integration, centralization of management, and economies of scale. Other issues in *Container Corporation of America* are discussed at ¶ 1310.

In *Edison California Stores, Inc. v. McColgan* (1947) (CCH CALIFORNIA TAX REPORTS, ¶ 11-520.803), the California Supreme Court held that the allocation formula (equivalent to the "apportionment" formula under present law) was properly applicable to the combined income of a California corporation and its foreign parent corporation and other subsidiaries. The taxpayer produced evidence to show that its separate accounting for the subsidiary was reasonable and proper, but the court held that the taxpayer had not met the burden of proving that the consolidation and the allocation formula produced an unreasonable result. The court stated clearly its test of whether or not a business is unitary: "If the operation of the portion of the business done within the state is dependent upon or contributes to the operation of the business without the state, the operations are unitary . . . ."

• *Other cases holding business to be unitary*

Over the years there have been many decisions of the courts and the BOE that have followed the lead of the *Butler Brothers* and *Edison* cases and have held that businesses were unitary. The following brief summaries of these cases will provide a "feel" for the trend of the decisions.

For a later case that followed *Butler Brothers* in a somewhat similar situation, see the BOE opinion in *Appeal of Ohrbach's, Inc.* (1961) (CCH CALIFORNIA TAX REPORTS, ¶ 11-520.836). The taxpayer operated department stores in New York and California. The reasoning applied in *Edison* was applied by a California court of appeal in *Yoshinoya West, Inc. v. Franchise Tax Board* (2006) (CCH CALIFORNIA TAX REPORTS, ¶ 11-520.8396). The court ruled that a U.S. corporation that operated fast-food restaurants was unitary with its Japanese parent corporation because the U.S.-based business depended upon and contributed to the business conducted by the Japanese parent company.

In *ComCon Production Services I, Inc. v. FTB* (2014), CCH CALIFORNIA TAX REPORTS, ¶ 406-243, a California superior court ruled that a cable television company was not unitary with QVC, a company that marketed consumer products and services through a televised home shopping program broadcast. The evidence did not establish any of the hallmarks of a unitary business—centralized management, functional integration, or economies of scale. Centralized management was lacking, as the subsidiary's personnel made all meaningful business decisions without direction or shared expertise from the taxpayer. Also, the taxpayer and the subsidiary did not become functionally integrated, as they maintained separate headquarters and separate departments for the operation of their respective businesses. Due to the absence of centralized management and functional integration, there also were no economies of scale resulting from the taxpayer's ownership of the subsidiary. The FTB has filed a notice of appeal regarding the unitary business issue.

In *Appeal of PBS Building Systems, Inc., and PKH Building Systems* (1994) (CCH CALIFORNIA TAX REPORTS, ¶ 11-520.491), the BOE held that a "passive" holding company was engaged in a unitary business with its operating subsidiary for combined reporting purposes, as evidenced by a complete overlap of officers and directors and extensive intercompany financing consisting of loans, loan guarantees, debt refinancing, debt reduction, and a covenant not to compete that was purchased by the holding company for the benefit of its subsidiary. Because "passive" holding companies are fully capable of providing and receiving a flow of value to or from an operating subsidiary, the factors to consider in determining whether a holding company is unitary with its operating subsidiaries are the same factors that must be considered with respect to any other business enterprise.

In *Dental Insurance Consultants, Inc. v. State Franchise Tax Board* (1991) (CCH CALIFORNIA TAX REPORTS, ¶ 11-520.351), a court of appeal held that a dental insurance consulting corporation and its wholly owned farming subsidiary were engaged in a unitary enterprise. Although the FTB argued that the three unities test should be abandoned in favor of the functional integration test, the court determined that application of both tests was proper because they were not mutually exclusive. The court held that under both the three unities test and the functional integration test, the corporations were unitary. In addition, the court held that application of the dependency and contribution test was unnecessary because its use would result in the same conclusion yielded by the three unities test.

In *Mole-Richardson v. Franchise Tax Board* (1990) (CCH CALIFORNIA TAX REPORTS, ¶ 11-520.353), a court of appeal held that a group of commonly owned and centrally managed corporations that did business both inside and outside of California constituted a unitary business even though the business they engaged in inside California was primarily the manufacture and sale of lighting equipment and the business they engaged in outside of California was primarily ranching. The court rejected the FTB's argument that the corporations constituted two distinct business groups because they were not "functionally integrated." In doing so, the court stated that "functional integration" was not a new concept by which business enterprises must be evaluated to justify unitary treatment. Moreover, the court held that the presence of strong centralized management and economies of scale was evidence that the corporations were functionally integrated.

In *Appeal of Capital Industries—EMI, Inc.* (1989) (CCH CALIFORNIA TAX REPORTS, ¶ 11-520.8098), a California corporation that produced and sold recorded music, sheet music, and blank audio tapes was engaged in a unitary business with its British parent, which conducted similar activities on a worldwide basis. Factors considered by the BOE as supporting unity were intercompany matrix agreements, intercompany sales, transfers of key personnel, common directors, joint use of key labels, intercompany financing, mutual international promotional activities, and exercise of parental control over the distribution of the music of the parent's artists.

In *Appeal of Trails End, Inc.* (1986) (CCH CALIFORNIA TAX REPORTS, ¶ 11-520.838), the BOE denied rehearing an earlier decision that a California plastics manufacturer, a California vitamin manufacturer, and a Michigan corporation were in a unitary business relationship. The plastics manufacturer was a subsidiary of the vitamin manufacturer, which was itself a subsidiary of and engaged in a unitary business with the Michigan corporation. It is necessary in establishing unity only that the business within California is dependent upon or contributes to the business outside California, and it is the aggregate effect of one company on another that determines unity. The relationship between the plastics manufacturer and the Michigan corporation did not need to be direct to establish a unitary relationship; it was sufficient for franchise tax purposes if the unitary business relationship was indirect. Thus, because

¶1304

the plastics manufacturer was found to be engaged in a unitary business with the vitamin manufacturer, its operations could not justifiably be separated from the unitary operation of the Michigan corporation and the vitamin manufacturer.

In *Appeal of Atlas Hotels, Inc., et al.* (1985) (CCH CALIFORNIA TAX REPORTS, ¶ 11-520.8197), the taxpayer was in the hotel business and its subsidiary was in the restaurant business. The BOE found that the subsidiary became "instantly unitary" with the parent's unitary business from the date of its acquisition when there was evidence that many of the managerial and operational changes that demonstrated the subsidiary's integration with its parent not only were implemented immediately upon acquisition, but were planned or commenced well before the actual acquisition date.

In *Appeal of Allstate Enterprises, Inc., et al.* (1984) (CCH CALIFORNIA TAX REPORTS, ¶ 11-520.8197), the taxpayer and several affiliated corporations were engaged in providing vehicle financing and motor club services. Another subsidiary was engaged in the mortgage banking business, and the taxpayer contended that this corporation should not be included in the unitary group. The BOE held that the mortgage banking business was a part of a unitary operation.

In *Appeal of Lancaster Colony Corporation and August Barr, Inc.* (1984) (CCH CALIFORNIA TAX REPORTS, ¶ 11-520.82), there were seven divisions and fourteen subsidiaries engaged in a wide variety of industrial and consumer businesses. The BOE held that the operations constituted a single unitary business, based on flow of goods, supplying of administrative and technical services, interlocking officers and directors, and other indications of unity.

Appeal of Data General Corporation (1982) (CCH CALIFORNIA TAX REPORTS, ¶ 11-520.806) involved a Delaware corporation that conducted a worldwide business in computers and related products with four domestic and twelve foreign subsidiaries. The BOE held that the group met both the "unity" and "dependency" tests for a unitary operation: the BOE referred to the taxpayer's public reports as one indication of the centralization and integration of management and operations.

In *Appeal of Kikkoman International, Inc.* (1982) (CCH CALIFORNIA TAX REPORTS, ¶ 11-520.825), the taxpayer was a 70% owned California subsidiary of a prominent Japanese company. The taxpayer contended that the income attributable to California could be determined fairly only by separate accounting, because the property and payroll factors did not account for the disparity between California and Japan in property costs and wages. The BOE held that the companies were "a classic example of the type of vertically integrated enterprise to which the unitary concept has been applied" and required use of the standard apportionment formula.

See ¶ 1310 for discussion of other cases involving foreign operations, including the 1983 decision of the U.S. Supreme Court in the case of *Container Corporation of America.*

In *Appeal of Beck/Arnley Corporation of California* (1981) (CCH CALIFORNIA TAX REPORTS, ¶ 11-520.805), the taxpayer was the wholly-owned subsidiary of a New York corporation. Both corporations were engaged in the sale of automobile parts and accessories. The BOE held that the operations were unitary under either the "unity" test or the "contribution and dependency" tests.

In *Appeal of Credit Bureau Central, Inc.* (1981) (CCH CALIFORNIA TAX REPORTS, ¶ 11-520.827), a California corporation was one of 14 wholly owned subsidiaries of a Georgia corporation. All of the subsidiaries operated as collection agencies. The BOE held that the operations were unitary, based largely on centralized executive and management services.

In *Appeal of National Silver Co.* (1980) (CCH CALIFORNIA TAX REPORTS, ¶ 11-520.813), the taxpayer was engaged in the marketing of houseware products. The corporation had various relationships with two affiliated out-of-state corporations and purchased 10% of the output of one of the affiliates. The BOE held that the businesses of the three corporations were unitary.

¶1304

In *Appeal of L&B Manufacturing Co.* (1980) (CCH CALIFORNIA TAX REPORTS, ¶11-520.812), the taxpayer was a member of an affiliated group of seven corporations engaged in the restaurant and hotel furnishings business. The BOE held that the business was unitary, since the taxpayer did not carry the burden of proof to the contrary under either the "unity" or the "dependency" test.

In *Appeal of Wynn Oil Company* (1980) (CCH CALIFORNIA TAX REPORTS, ¶206-308), the taxpayer was engaged primarily in the manufacture and distribution of petrochemical products. The corporation supplied active management direction and services to a subsidiary that operated student dormitories on college campuses. The BOE held that, despite their diverse nature, the businesses of the parent and subsidiary were unitary. However, a 1990 decision of the BOE ruled that this decision has "no continuing validity as precedent" because the test following the U.S. Supreme Court decision in *Container Corporation v. FTB* requires an analysis on evidence of a functionally integrated enterprise (see *Appeal of Meadows Realty Co.* (1990), CCH CALIFORNIA TAX REPORTS, ¶12-500.90).

In *Allright Cal., Inc.* (1979) (CCH CALIFORNIA TAX REPORTS, ¶11-520.808), the taxpayer was one of 95 subsidiaries of a Texas corporation. The affiliated corporations operated a nationwide network of automobile parking lots. The BOE cited the *John Deere Plow Co.* case, discussed below (and others), and held that the operations were unitary and subject to formula apportionment. Principal unitary factors were ownership, interlocking officers and directors, centralized overhead functions, common pension plan, and parent-supplied financing and other services.

In *Appeals of Cascade Dental Laboratory, Inc., et al.* (1978) (CCH CALIFORNIA TAX REPORTS, ¶11-520.828), the taxpayers were dental-laboratory subsidiaries of a health-service company that had its headquarters in Texas. The BOE held that the business was not unitary in the first year at issue, but that the character of the operation changed to the point that the business was unitary in later years.

In *Appeal of Parador Mining Co., Inc.* (1977) (CCH CALIFORNIA TAX REPORTS, ¶11-520.8292), the taxpayer was a closely held corporation engaged in mineral exploration. Most of its business was conducted in the home of the president and chief stockholder. The BOE held that the business was unitary and that its California income must be determined by formula rather than by separate accounting.

In *Appeal of Isador Weinstein Investment Co.* (1977) (CCH CALIFORNIA TAX REPORTS, ¶11-520.692), the taxpayer's principal activity was real estate rentals. The BOE held that the operation was unitary and was subject to formula allocation. To the same effect, see *Appeal of O.K. Earl Corp.* (1977) (CCH CALIFORNIA TAX REPORTS, ¶11-520.809), involving a variety of related activities in addition to real estate rentals.

Appeal of Beecham, Inc. (1977) (CCH CALIFORNIA TAX REPORTS, ¶11-520.8293) involved a large conglomerate with an English parent company. The BOE held that the business was unitary and that the income of the entire group was subject to allocation by formula. Although the propriety of including the foreign parent and its foreign subsidiaries was not a primary issue in the case, the BOE pointed out that in earlier cases the income of foreign subsidiaries has been held to be includible in a combined report and commented: "We are unable to discern any difference when the foreign corporation is the parent rather than the subsidiary."

In *Appeal of Putnam Fund Distributors, Inc., et al.* (1977) (CCH CALIFORNIA TAX REPORTS, ¶11-520.8291), the BOE held that a Massachusetts mutual-fund-management company was engaged in a unitary operation with a 51% owned California corporation and other subsidiaries; the subsidiaries were engaged principally in sales activities.

In *Appeal of Automated Building Components, Inc.* (1976) (CCH CALIFORNIA TAX REPORTS, ¶11-520.8298), the taxpayer was a Florida corporation that had an operation

¶1304

in California and had foreign subsidiaries. The BOE held that the group was engaged in a unitary operation that required a combined report as discussed in ¶1310. The BOE's opinion discusses the general tests established in the *Butler Brothers* and *Edison California Stores* cases, and concludes that "a unitary business exists if *either* the three unities or the contribution or dependency tests are satisfied" (emphasis supplied).

In *Appeal of Grolier Society, Inc.* (1975) (CCH CALIFORNIA TAX REPORTS, ¶11-520.8299), the BOE held that five Canadian subsidiaries and four Latin American subsidiaries were engaged in a unitary business with the taxpayer, its parent, and other subsidiaries.

In *Appeal of Harbison-Walker Refractories Company* (1972) (CCH CALIFORNIA TAX REPORTS, ¶11-520.83), the BOE decided that a Pennsylvania corporation and its Canadian subsidiary were engaged in a unitary business. The corporations had common officers and directors, common purchases, intercompany purchases and sales, and an intercompany management fee.

In *Appeal of Anchor Hocking Glass Corporation* (1967) (CCH CALIFORNIA TAX REPORTS, ¶11-520.8193), the BOE held that the use of common trademarks and patents and the interchange of "know-how" were significant factors in determining the existence of a unitary business between a U.S. parent and its foreign and domestic subsidiaries.

In *Appeal of Cutter Laboratories* (1964) (CCH CALIFORNIA TAX REPORTS, ¶11-520.8194), the BOE held that a parent corporation manufacturing and selling vaccines and pharmaceuticals for both human and animal consumption was engaged in a unitary business with its wholly owned subsidiary operating in another State in the manufacture and sale of veterinary instruments and animal vaccines. The taxpayer's contention that the corporations were engaged in different types of business was rejected when the two corporations were found to be closely related through common officers and directors, interstate flow of products, and joint participation in insurance, retirement, and automobile leasing plans.

In *Appeal of Youngstown Steel Products Company of California* (1952) (CCH CALIFORNIA TAX REPORTS, ¶11-520.213), the BOE upheld the application of the allocation formula to the combined income of three corporations, only one of which operated in California, despite the fact that the California corporation operated under an "arm's-length" contractual arrangement similar to a previous arrangement with an unrelated corporation.

In *John Deere Plow Co. v. Franchise Tax Board* (1951) (CCH CALIFORNIA TAX REPORTS, ¶11-520.202), the California Supreme Court upheld the FTB in applying the allocation formula to the combined income of a parent corporation and 84 subsidiaries, only one of which was doing business in California. The taxpayer contended unsuccessfully that use of the allocation formula was unreasonable because the income of the California branch was overstated rather than understated by the use of separate accounting. The taxpayer's argument was based partly on the fact that no charge had been made to the California branch for services rendered to it by the central office of the affiliated group.

• *Unity of ownership*

The FTB has issued detailed guidelines for determining whether ownership of a group of corporations satisfies the "unity of ownership" standard (*FTB Legal Ruling No. 91-1, supra*). Generally, unity of ownership is established only when the same interests directly or indirectly own or control more than 50% of the voting stock of all members of the purported unitary group. "Indirect ownership" may include direct ownership and control of more than half the voting stock of a corporation that in turn directly owns and controls the requisite amount of voting stock in another corporation. Likewise, "indirect control" includes control exercised through ownership or control of an intermediary corporation. "Direct control" of voting stock includes ownership of the voting rights alone, pursuant to a binding and permanent legal transfer of those rights.

The requisite control may also be exercised by a group of shareholders acting in concert. In *Rain Bird Sprinkler Mfg. Corp. v. FTB* (1991) (CCH CALIFORNIA TAX REPORTS, ¶ 11-520.8092), seventeen corporations that were operated as a single business enterprise constituted a unitary business even though no *single* individual or entity held a majority interest in all of the corporations. The court held that "unity of ownership" existed because members of the same family held the majority of the voting stock in each of the corporations, and all of the stock of each corporation was subject to written stock purchase agreements prohibiting transfer to outsiders.

According to the FTB, application of the "concerted ownership or control" principle of *Rain Bird* is not limited to members of the same family. Factors to be considered in determining whether a group of shareholders exercises concerted ownership or control of several corporations include the business relationships of the corporations involved, the relationships between the shareholders, the degree of common ownership, common voting patterns, and each shareholder's relative percentage of ownership or control. A similar conclusion was reached in *Appeal of AMP, Inc.* (1996) (CCH CALIFORNIA TAX REPORTS, ¶ 11-520.95).

• *Cases holding business to be nonunitary*

In *Appeal of F.W. Woolworth Co. et al.* (1998) (CCH CALIFORNIA TAX REPORTS, ¶ 11-520.60), a California court of appeal held that a parent corporation was not engaged in a unitary business with its wholly owned subsidiary, because they were not in the same general line of business. The parent conducted a mass merchandising business in apparel and general merchandise and the subsidiary was engaged primarily in the manufacture and sale of shoes and there was not strong centralization of the management of the two corporations.

In *Appeal of Hearst Corporation* (1992) (CCH CALIFORNIA TAX REPORTS, ¶ 11-520.6091), a domestic corporation that was engaged in various business activities, including publication of newspapers, books, and magazines, was not engaged in a unitary business with its wholly owned foreign subsidiary, which published books and magazines in the United Kingdom. The taxpayer rebutted the presumption that the businesses were unitary by providing evidence that they had separate editorial, writing, and photographic staffs and that intercompany sales and use of material were extremely minimal. Additionally, the BOE found that no phase of the subsidiary's operations was actually integrated with the taxpayer's operations.

In *Tenneco West, Inc. v. Franchise Tax Board* (1991) (CCH CALIFORNIA TAX REPORTS, ¶ 11-520.352), a court of appeal held that the taxpayer, which was in the oil and gas business, and its subsidiaries, which were in the business of shipbuilding, packaging, manufacturing automotive parts, manufacturing equipment used in construction, and farming, were not unitary. The court determined that there was no strong centralized management and that the subsidiaries were engaged in diverse activities unrelated to the parent's business and thus lacked integration.

In *Appeal of Meadows Realty Company et al.* (1990) (CCH CALIFORNIA TAX REPORTS, ¶ 11-520.45), unity did not exist between a parent corporation's oil refining activities and its subsidiary's realty development activities even though the subsidiary received financial assistance and management services from the parent corporation. The BOE indicated that "functional integration" was required to establish the existence of a unitary business.

In *Appeal of Postal Press* (1987) (CCH CALIFORNIA TAX REPORTS, ¶ 11-520.609), the BOE held that a 68.3% ownership of a subsidiary's stock by a taxpayer was insufficient to prove that it was engaged in a unitary business. The taxpayer specialized in commercial printing and its subsidiary specialized in instant printing. The BOE found that, despite the stock ownership and use of similar trademarks and names, other indications of unity, such as common management and operations, were absent.

In *Appeal of Nevis Industries, Inc.,* (1985) (CCH CALIFORNIA TAX REPORTS, ¶ 11-520.952), ownership of a Nevada corporation and eight affiliated companies was shared equally (never exceeding 50%) by two brothers. The California Supreme Court

¶1304

held that the businesses were not unitary because no single entity owned more than 50% and had controlling interest in any of the involved companies. Stock owned directly or indirectly by family members is not attributed to other family members, for purposes of determining unity of ownership.

In *Appeal of Coachmen Industries of California* (1985) (CCH CALIFORNIA TAX REPORTS, ¶ 11-520.8197), the BOE found that a California company's evidence of independence from its Indiana parent was insufficient to prove it was not engaged in a unitary business. A number of factors, when taken in the aggregate, indicated that the two companies were involved in a single economic enterprise. The connections that indicated a unitary relationship included almost identical businesses, interlocking officers and directors, intercompany product flow, shared purchasing, exclusively intercompany financing, and shared group life and health insurance.

Appeal of The Grupe Company et al. (1985) (CCH CALIFORNIA TAX REPORTS, ¶ 11-520.604) was another case in which the taxpayer contended that two businesses were unitary but was overruled by the BOE. In this case, land development operations were conducted in California and an alfalfa farm was operated on leased land in Nevada.

In *Appeal of Vidal Sassoon of New York, Inc.* (1984) (CCH CALIFORNIA TAX REPORTS, ¶ 11-520.607), the taxpayer and 19 affiliated corporations operated hairdressing salons in the United States, Canada, and Europe under the common name "Sassoon." The BOE held that the operations in Europe were not unitary with those in the United States.

In *Appeals of Dynamic Speaker Corporation* and *Talone Packing Company* (1984) (CCH CALIFORNIA TAX REPORTS, ¶ 11-520.607), the parent company of the taxpayers and six subsidiaries were engaged in a variety of diverse businesses. Although there were some unitary factors, the BOE held that the operations were not unitary. To the same effect, see also *Appeal of P and M Lumber Products, Inc.* (1984) (CCH CALIFORNIA TAX REPORTS, ¶ 11-520.357) and *Appeal of Berry Enterprises, Inc.* (1986) (CCH CALIFORNIA TAX REPORTS, ¶ 11-520.952). In these cases, the taxpayers had contended that the businesses were unitary.

In *Appeals of Santa Anita Consolidated, Inc., et al.* (1984) (CCH CALIFORNIA TAX REPORTS, ¶ 11-520.6094), the taxpayer and its four subsidiaries were engaged in a variety of activities including operation of a racetrack, transportation of automobiles, real estate development, etc. Although there were some unitary factors in management and operation, the BOE held that the business did not constitute a "functionally integrated enterprise" and was not unitary.

To the same effect, see *Appeal of Bredero California, Inc., Bredero Consulting, Inc., and Best Blocks, Inc.* (1986) (CCH CALIFORNIA TAX REPORTS, ¶ 11-520.612). Also to the same effect, see *Appeals of Andreini & Company and Ash Slough Vineyards, Inc.* (1986) (CCH CALIFORNIA TAX REPORTS, ¶ 11-520.608), in which an agricultural insurance brokerage was found not to constitute a unitary business with its vineyard subsidiary.

In *Appeal of Holloway Investment Company* (1983) (CCH CALIFORNIA TAX REPORTS, ¶ 11-520.521), the taxpayer held a variety of apparently unrelated property interests in California and Illinois. Citing some of the cases discussed below and also the U.S. Supreme Court decision in *Container Corporation* (¶ 1310), the BOE held that the business was not unitary.

In *Appeal of Unitco, Inc.* (1983) (CCH CALIFORNIA TAX REPORTS, ¶ 11-520.69), the taxpayer was a closely held corporation that owned rental properties in California and three other states. The FTB contended that the operations were unitary, based largely on the similarity of activities in the four states and the personal participation of the three owner-officers in policy decisions. The BOE held that the business was not unitary, commenting that "at best, the suggested unitary connections are superficial and trivial."

In *Bay Alarm Company* (1982) (CCH CALIFORNIA TAX REPORTS, ¶11-520.601), a California corporation had a burglar alarm business in California, an investment portfolio, and a cattle ranch in New Mexico. The BOE upheld the FTB in holding that the activities did not constitute a unitary business. To the same effect, see *Appeal of Myles Circuits, Inc.* (1982) (CCH CALIFORNIA TAX REPORTS, ¶11-520.601), in which the taxpayer and its subsidiaries had a circuit breaker factory in California and a cattle ranch in Texas.

In *Appeal of Mohasco Corp.* (1982) (CCH CALIFORNIA TAX REPORTS, ¶11-520.607), the taxpayer and its Mexican subsidiaries were engaged in the manufacture and sale of carpets and related products. Although there were some intercompany relationships and transactions, the BOE found that these were insignificant in the situation as a whole and held that the operations were not unitary.

In *Appeal of Hollywood Film Enterprises, Inc.* (1982) (CCH CALIFORNIA TAX REPORTS, ¶11-520.602), the taxpayer operated wholly within California. It was a wholly owned subsidiary of a Delaware corporation with headquarters in New York and some operations in California. The two corporations were involved in diverse lines of business (although both involved motion picture films), but there were several intercompany activities of various kinds. In this case the taxpayer contended that the two businesses *should* be treated as unitary, while the FTB took the position that they should not. The BOE held that the taxpayer had not borne the required burden of proof that the businesses were unitary.

• *Use of separate accounting*

Despite the general preference for use of the allocation or apportionment formula, separate accounting may be permitted (or required) in some cases. The following are the principal situations where it may be used:

— businesses that by their nature permit accurate determination of results by separate accounting; and

— cases where a corporation is in entirely different businesses within and without the state, with no unitary factors present. (Sec. 25137, Rev. & Tax. Code)

Reg. 25137, 18 CCR provides that exceptions to the regular allocation formula will be permitted only where "unusual fact situations . . . produce incongruous results" under the regular rules. The regulation mentions specific industries that are subject to special treatment (¶1306). See ¶1307 for a more detailed explanation of deviations from the standard UDITPA formula.

• *Cases upholding use of separate accounting*

In *Appeal of The National Dollar Stores, Ltd.* (1986) (CCH CALIFORNIA TAX REPORTS, ¶11-520.607), a California clothing retail corporation was not unitary with a wholly owned subsidiary that imported and marketed Asian films. The BOE held that, though there was 100% unity of ownership, the unities of use and operation did not exist between the two. There was no evidence that either business contributed to or was dependent on the other.

In *Appeal of The Amwalt Group* (1983) (CCH CALIFORNIA TAX REPORTS, ¶11-520.6094), a closely-held California architectural firm owned 100% of a leasing subsidiary and 80% of a heavy equipment dealership. Fiscal management was centralized and there were some intercompany transactions, and the corporations filed a combined report on a unitary basis. The FTB took the position that the operations were not unitary and required separate accounting for the three corporations; the BOE agreed.

¶1304

In *Appeal of Carl M. Halvorson, Inc.* (1963) (CCH CALIFORNIA TAX REPORTS, ¶ 11-520.70), the BOE held that separate accounting more clearly reflected income attributable to California by a heavy construction contractor engaged in construction projects located within and without the State. It was further held that overhead expenses were properly allocated to such projects on the basis of direct costs incurred. However, it is the policy of the FTB to require use of the apportionment formula in the construction business "where the usual tests of unitary business are met." The FTB has issued detailed regulations for apportionment of income from long-term contracts, and also detailed rules for corporate partners in joint ventures—see below and ¶ 1306.

In *Appeal of Highland Corporation* (1959) (CCH CALIFORNIA TAX REPORTS, ¶ 11-520.358), the BOE held that a business is not unitary when the only unitary factor is centralized management. The corporation operated a lumber business in Oregon, had oil interests in New Mexico, and was in the construction business and owned rental properties in California. All activities were controlled and supervised by executives who operated out of the corporation's head office, which was in California. In this case the FTB took the position that the business was not unitary and that separate accounting should be used, and the BOE agreed. To the same effect, see *Appeal of Allied Properties, Inc.* (1964) (CCH CALIFORNIA TAX REPORTS, ¶ 11-520.357), involving a cattle ranch in Nevada and real estate investments in California.

• *Oil and gas operators*

The FTB for many years required oil and gas operators to use separate accounting in some situations, particularly where a profitable segment of an oil business was conducted in California while an extensive exploratory program was carried on in an out-of-state location of such magnitude as to produce deductions that offset or materially reduced the California income. However, the FTB was overruled by the BOE in a 1959 decision involving a situation of this type. In *Appeal of Holly Development Company* (CCH CALIFORNIA TAX REPORTS, ¶ 11-520.835), it was held that a unitary business existed where the corporation was engaged in the acquisition and development of oil properties in both California and Texas, and the evidence showed centralized management, accounting, financing, and purchasing. To the same effect, see *Superior Oil Co. v. Franchise Tax Board* (CCH CALIFORNIA TAX REPORTS, ¶ 11-520.201) and *Honolulu Oil Co. v. Franchise Tax Board* (CCH CALIFORNIA TAX REPORTS, ¶ 11-520.201), both cases decided by the California Supreme Court in 1963.

Legal Ruling No. 366 (1973) (CCH CALIFORNIA TAX REPORTS, ¶ 11-520.2091) deals with allocation questions of unitary oil operations beyond the 3-mile continental limit. The ruling states that use of the standard allocation formula is appropriate, and provides that factors relating to offshore operations should be reflected only in the denominators of the formula; thus, no income from such operations is apportioned to California. Legal Ruling No. 396 (1976) (CCH CALIFORNIA TAX REPORTS, ¶ 10-075.73) modifies the portion of Legal Ruling No. 366 pertaining to operations of drilling barges.

In the case of partnership interests in oil and gas properties that are deemed to be "tax shelters" and not part of the unitary business, income or loss has been held to be nonbusiness income allocated to the state where the oil or gas property is located. *Appeal of The National Dollar Stores, Ltd.* (1986) (CCH CALIFORNIA TAX REPORTS, ¶ 11-520.607).

• *Combination of separate accounting and formula*

Where a taxpayer has more than one trade or business as discussed at ¶ 1302, it is possible to use a combination of separate accounting and the apportionment formula. One example under prior law may be found in *Appeal of Industrial Management Corporation* (1959) (CCH CALIFORNIA TAX REPORTS, ¶ 11-520.358). In this case the corporation was engaged in the insecticide business both within and without California, and also was engaged in two businesses (sale of street improvement bonds and

¶1304

rental of real estate) solely within California. The principal office was in California. There was no unitary relationship between the insecticide business and the other two. The insecticide business showed a loss and the other two showed a profit. The BOE upheld the contention of the FTB that only the insecticide business was unitary and subject to allocation by formula; thus, the entire income of the two California businesses was taxed, with an offset for only an allocated portion of the loss on the unitary business.

In *Appeal of Hunt Foods & Industries, Inc.* (1965) (CCH CALIFORNIA TAX REPORTS, ¶11-520.8194), the FTB contended that, where the taxpayer operated a match manufacturing business and a food processing business, the income of each should be computed and allocated separately. However, the BOE held that a single allocation formula applied to the entire income of both businesses was proper, since there was common management, the products were sold in the same markets, they shared common warehouses, and other unitary factors were present.

In *Appeal of Simco, Incorporated* (1964) (CCH CALIFORNIA TAX REPORTS, ¶11-520.52), the BOE permitted a combination of separate accounting and the allocation formula. The income of fruit orchards operated entirely in California was determined by separate accounting, and the allocation formula was applied to a farming and cattle business operated in both California and Nevada. The BOE held that centralization of management and of accounting, legal, and tax services did not mean that the entire business was unitary.

In *Appeal of Halliburton Oil Well Cementing Co.* (1955) (CCH CALIFORNIA TAX REPORTS, ¶11-520.831), the taxpayer was turned down in its attempt to use a combination of separate accounting and an allocation formula. The company used separate accounting for its income from service activities and from sale of purchased goods and used a (nonstandard) formula for income from sale of its own manufactured goods. The BOE upheld the FTB in requiring the use of the standard formula for both service and merchandising activities.

In *Appeal of American Writing Paper Corporation* (1952) (CCH CALIFORNIA TAX REPORTS, ¶11-520.8392), the BOE upheld the FTB in applying the allocation formula to the entire income of a foreign corporation that sold in California the products of some—but not all—of its plants. The taxpayer was unsuccessful in its contention that the income of the plants manufacturing the product sold in California should be determined by separate accounting and the allocation formula applied only to that income instead of to the entire income from operations of all plants.

• *Use of separate formulas*

As explained at ¶1302, separate apportionment formulas may sometimes be used for different portions of a taxpayer's business. In *Appeal of Lear Siegler, Inc.* (1967) (CCH CALIFORNIA TAX REPORTS, ¶11-520.6095), a single corporation had six separate manufacturing divisions, each operating within and without California. The BOE permitted the taxpayer to apply six separate apportionment formulas to the various divisions.

In *Appeal of United Parcel Service* (1986) (CCH CALIFORNIA TAX REPORTS, ¶11-540.75), the taxpayer was a unitary business with package delivery cars that ordinarily operated within the state and tractor-trailer rigs that operated both within and without the state. The BOE, in reversing the FTB's application of separate apportionment formulas to the two classes of equipment, held that the special interim formula developed by the FTB for truckers applied to all the taxpayer's trucks whether in interstate or intrastate commerce.

• *Treatment of partnership interests*

Reg. 25137-1, 18 CCR outlines the appropriate method for apportionment and allocation of partnership income in unitary situations where a corporation has an interest in a partnership and one or both have income from sources within and without the State. The corporation is not required to own any particular percentage of the partnership for this regulation to apply. The partnership income and apportionment factors are included in determining unitary income only to the extent of the corporation's percentage of ownership interest.

In *Appeal of Powerine Oil Company* (1985) (CCH CALIFORNIA TAX REPORTS, ¶ 11-520.591), the taxpayer was engaged in oil refining and distribution and also had a 50% interest in a joint venture engaged in copper mining in California. The BOE cited the *Pittsburgh-Des Moines Steel Company* case, above, and held that the taxpayer's share of joint-venture losses could be included in determining the unitary income allocable to California.

In *Appeal of A. Epstein and Sons, Inc.* (1984) (CCH CALIFORNIA TAX REPORTS, ¶ 11-520.837), the taxpayer was a member of a group of closely-held affiliated corporations under common control of two brothers. The brothers also owned a New York partnership that had been formed (because of legal requirements) to render architectural services at cost to the corporations. The BOE held that the affiliated group of corporations was engaged in a unitary business, subject to formula allocation, but denied inclusion of the partnership in the computation. See also *The National Dollar Stores, Ltd.*, under "Oil and Gas Operators," above.

In *Appeal of Pittsburgh-Des Moines Steel Company* (1983) (CCH CALIFORNIA TAX REPORTS, ¶ 11-520.59), the taxpayer corporation was engaged in a unitary business involving various aspects of the steel business. The corporation had a 50% interest in a joint venture with a real-estate operator; the joint venture was formed to build and lease two office buildings in California. The BOE held that the corporation's share of the income and apportionment factors of the joint venture should be included in the corporation's combined report. To the same effect, see *Appeal of Willamette Industries, Inc.* (1987) (CCH CALIFORNIA TAX REPORTS, ¶ 11-520.373).

In *Appeal of Saga Corp.* (1982) (CCH CALIFORNIA TAX REPORTS, ¶ 11-520.821), the taxpayer corporation and subsidiaries supplied food service to colleges, hospitals, and other organizations throughout the United States. The corporation owned 50.51% of another corporation that developed and managed off-campus student dining and housing facilities in California and elsewhere; the subsidiary employed the taxpayer (or other subsidiaries) to provide food services in these facilities. The corporation also owned 50% of a partnership that owned and constructed a dormitory complex for which the two corporations provided management and food services. The BOE held that the subsidiary and the partnership were both parts of a unitary operation with the taxpayer, and that the partnership's income and apportionment factors should be taken into account to the extent of the taxpayer's 50% interest.

In *Appeal of Albertson's, Inc.* (1982) (CCH CALIFORNIA TAX REPORTS, ¶ 11-520.65), the taxpayer corporation operated a multistate chain of supermarkets selling principally food items. The corporation owned 50% of a partnership that operated a chain of supermarkets selling both food items and general merchandise. The corporation shared, with the other 50% owner, the overall control and direction of the partnership's management policies and also provided some financial and management assistance. The BOE held that the partnership was engaged in a unitary business with the taxpayer, and that the partnership factors should be taken into account to the extent of the taxpayer's 50% ownership interest.

In *Appeal of Pup 'n' Taco Drive Up* (1977) (CCH CALIFORNIA TAX REPORTS, ¶ 11-520.8297), the taxpayer was a California fast-food corporation with a majority interest in two out-of-state partnerships. The BOE held that the corporation and the partnerships were engaged in a unitary business and were subject to formula allocation.

¶1305 Apportionment Formula

Law: Secs. 25128, 25128.5, 25128.7, 25137 (CCH California Tax Reports, ¶11-520, 11-550).

Comparable Federal: None.

California Form: Sch. R (Apportionment and Allocation of Income).

Beginning with the 2013 tax year, a single-sales factor apportionment formula is mandatory for most taxpayers. (Sec. 25128.7, Rev. & Tax. Code) The apportionment formula is used only to compute a percentage, which is then applied to the total "business" income to determine the portion taxable in California. It should be kept in mind throughout the discussion of the formula that the items attributed to California in computing the various factors are not taxed directly, but are only used in the computation of a percentage to be applied to the net income. This point was illustrated in *Appeal of North American Aviation, Inc.* (1952) (CCH California Tax Reports, ¶11-525.27). Under the peculiar facts in that case title to certain goods sold had passed twice and technically there were two "sales." The State Board of Equalization (BOE) sustained the Franchise Tax Board (FTB) in eliminating the duplication in computing the sales factor in the allocation formula. The BOE's opinion pointed out that to include both sales would be unreasonable, in view of the purpose of the sales factor as a measure of the taxpayer's activity within and without California.

• *Single sales factor formula*

Practitioner Comment: Mandatory Single Sales Factor Effective For Tax Years Beginning on or After January 1, 2013.

In the November 2012 election, California voters approved Proposition 39, which implements a mandatory single- sales factor formula for most multistate taxpayers for tax years beginning on or after January 1, 2013. (Sec. 25128.7, Rev. & Tax. Code) While taxpayers engaged in certain industries (e.g., agricultural, financial institutions, extractive industries, and savings and loans) continue to be required to use an evenly-weighted three -factor apportionment formula, all taxpayers (other than cable companies for which special rules are provided) will be required to calculate the sales factor under California's market- based sourcing rules at Cal. Rev. & Tax. Code § 25136(b) and CCR § 25136-2, see ¶1309. As a result of Proposition 39's passage, a number of multistate companies that are based out of state are likely to see a sharp increase in their California corporate franchise tax liabilities.

Chris Whitney, Contributing Editor

For the 2011 and 2012 tax years, taxpayers, other than those taxpayers primarily engaged in an agricultural, extractive, savings and loan, or banking or financial business activity, could make an irrevocable election to apportion their business income utilizing a single sales factor apportionment formula. (Sec. 25128.5, Rev. & Tax. Code)

Making the election.—The election available during the 2011 and 2012 tax years could be made by a corporation, a partnership, or a sole proprietorship. A taxpayer engaged in more than one apportioning trade or business could make a separate election for each apportioning trade or business. (Reg. 25128.5, 18 CCR) A regulation addresses the following issues regarding the election:

— **Timeliness of the election:** The election had to be made on a timely filed (including extensions), original return for the year of the election.

— **Validity of election:** An election was valid if (1) the tax was computed in a manner consistent with the single-sales factor formula election, and (2) a written notification of election was made on Part B of schedule R-1 that was attached to the taxpayer's return.

— **Combined reporting groups:** All California taxpayer members of a combined reporting group had to make the election for the election to be valid. An election made on a group return was an election by each taxpayer member included in that group return. However, the election made on the group return had no effect if a taxpayer member of the combined reporting group filed a separate return in which no election was made, unless the business assets held by the electing group members were greater than the business assets held by the non-electing members. Special rules applied to new members and exiting members, and those who were added or deleted from the group as a result of an FTB audit.

Practitioner Comment: FTB Rejects Protective Single Sales Factor Filing

Legal Division Guidance 2012-03-02 states that a taxpayer could not file two returns for the same year, one reflecting a single sales factor (SSF) election and another filed without the election, as a way to avoid the large corporate understatement penalty (LCUP) in the event it is later determined that the taxpayer was ineligible to elect SSF. The FTB states that because the last return, or amended return, filed before the extended due date is considered the original return, the SSF election would have to be made on the last timely filed return in order to be valid. Further the LCUP would be based upon the liability reported on that last filed return.

A taxpayer that derives more than 50% of its "gross business receipts" from conducting one or more "qualified business activities" (e.g., agriculture and banking) is prohibited from making the SSF election. For some taxpayers it may be unclear as to how to classify their receipts from certain activities, creating uncertainty as to whether they are eligible to make the election. While the guidance rejects the filing of two returns as a way to mitigate this exposure, the guidance does not directly address whether a protective election of some kind could be made whereby the tax liability on a single original return is determined under the standard formula as opposed to under a SSF election, which is otherwise clearly made on the same return. Under this approach an amended return would be subsequently filed after the extended due date of the return to claim a refund pursuant to the SSF election which was made with the original return.

Note that on November 6, 2012, California voters approved Proposition 39, which now makes the single sales factor provisions mandatory for most multistate taxpayers (other than those engaged in specified industries) for tax years beginning on or after January 1, 2013.

Chris Whitney, Contributing Editor

Application to non-corporate taxpayers.—An apportioning trade or business, regardless of the form of ownership (e.g., sole proprietorship, partnership, limited liability company, or corporation), that carries on business inside and outside California is required to apportion business income using the single sales factor. The same would be true for a partner's distributive share. Whether the trade or business is the partnership's business (if not unitary with the trade or business of its partner), or the partnership interest when combined with the partner's trade or business (if the partnership's activities are unitary with the activities of its partner, notwithstanding ownership requirements), the business income of the trade or business must be apportioned using the single sales factor under the provisions of § 25128.7 unless the trade or business meets one of the specified exceptions. (*FTB Tax News* (April 2013), CCH California Tax Reports, ¶ 405-867)

• *Equally-weighted factor formula applied to specified industries*

An equally-weighted apportionment formula, comprised of property (¶ 1307), payroll (¶ 1308), and sales (¶ 1309) factors, applies in California to taxpayers that derive more than 50% of their "gross business receipts" from:

— extractive or agricultural business activity,

— savings and loan activity, or

— banking or financial business activity.

(Sec. 25128, Rev. & Tax. Code)

If the income and apportionment factors of two or more affiliated banks or corporations must be included in a combined report (¶ 1310), the above apportionment formulas apply to the combined income of those banks or corporations.

"Agricultural business activity" means soil cultivation, or any activity related to stock, dairy, poultry, fruit, fur-bearing animal, or truck farm, plantation, ranch, nursery, or range. Examples include picking, washing, inspecting, and packing activities. In addition, handling, drying, packing, grading, or storing on a farm of any agricultural or horticultural commodity in its unmanufactured state constitutes agricultural business activity, provided that the farm owner, tenant, or operator regularly produces more than one-half of the commodity so treated. However, an activity is not an agricultural business activity if a mechanical process is applied to the agricultural products to transform them into different forms for consumption, such as processing of grains into flour or the shelling of nuts. (Reg. 25128-2, 18 CCR)

Practitioner Comment: Processing Beyond Picking and Packaging is Not Qualified Agricultural Business Activity

Chief Counsel Ruling 2012-04 states that revenue from products that are the result of processing beyond picking and packaging activities do not constitute revenue from agricultural business activities under Cal. Rev. & Tax. Code § 25128(b) and (c)(1). Because the ruling is redacted, it is not clear exactly which commodities, processes, or products the taxpayer used and sold. The ruling merely states that the products at issue are "processed beyond the picking and packaging activities that are normally considered agricultural business activities;" these activities "are similar to those in Examples 1 and 3 in CCR § 25128-2(b)(3), relating to processing of grains into flour and processing of nuts by shelling;" and "[l]ike the production of flour or the shelling and processing of nuts, a mechanical process is applied to the whole ***** to transform it into a different form for consumption." Based on the foregoing, the ruling concludes that the taxpayer's activities "are not normally incident to growing and raising," and are not considered agricultural business activities subject to evenly-weighted three-factor apportionment. Furthermore, the ruling specifically states that CCR § 25128-2(c)(6)(C) is beyond its scope. CCR § 25128-2(c)(6)(C) defines agricultural business activity to include "[h]andling, drying, packing, grading, or storing on a farm [of] any agricultural or horticultural commodity in its unmanufactured state, but only if the owner, tenant, or operator of the farm regularly produces more than one-half of the commodity handled, dried, packed, graded, or stored."

The ruling confirms the diverging approaches California takes towards agricultural business activities and extractive business activities, which are both "qualified business activities" subject to evenly-weighted three-factor apportionment. The ruling generally limits agricultural business activities to harvesting and packaging commodities. Any additional processing, particularly those involving a mechanical process, that transforms the commodity into a different form for consumption is not qualified business activity. This interpretation appears congruous with the agricultural business regulation. Conversely, the plain language of the extractive business activity statute and regulations indicates processing and refining are qualified business activities.

Chris Whitney, Contributing Editor

• Standard apportionment formula

For pre-2013 tax years, the standard apportionment formula applied in California was a double-weighted sales factor formula consisting of the following factors:

    — property, both real and tangible personal property, owned or rented by the taxpayer (¶ 1307);

    — payroll, including all forms of compensation paid to employees (¶ 1308); and

    — sales, meaning all gross receipts of the taxpayer from the sale of tangible and intangible property (¶ 1309).

(Sec. 25128, Rev. & Tax. Code)

The double-weighted sales factor formula was applied by determining the ratios of the property, payroll, and two times the sales factors within California to the property, payroll, and sales factors everywhere. The sum of the ratios was divided by four and the resulting factor was applied to the total income of the taxpayer to arrive at California taxable income. The California double-weighted sales factor formula could be depicted graphically as:

Calif. Prop.	+	Calif. Payroll	+	2 × Calif. Sales				
Total Property		Total Payroll		Total Sales	/ 4	=	Calif. factor	

- *Multistate Tax Compact equally-weighted formula*

Prior to the 2011 tax year, California was a member of the Multistate Tax Compact. Under Article III of the Compact, taxpayers can elect to use either an apportionment formula enacted by the state or the Compact's equally-weighted apportionment formula. However, California enacted legislation in 1993 that, notwithstanding the Compact provision (Rev. & Tax Code § 38006), required California taxpayers to use a double-weighted sales factor apportionment formula. (Sec. 25128, Rev. & Tax. Code) Later, the state implemented a mandatory single-sales factor formula for tax years beginning after 2012. (Sec. 25128.7, Rev. & Tax. Code) In *Gillette v. FTB*, the California Supreme Court held that multistate corporate taxpayers may no longer elect to use the Compact's equally-weighted formula for California corporation franchise and income tax purposes. Instead, the court held that California taxpayers must use the apportionment formula required under California law (i.e., a double-weighted sales factor formula for tax years beginning before to 2013, or a single-sales factor formula for tax years beginning after 2012). (*Gillette v. FTB* (2015) (CCH CALIFORNIA TAX REPORTS, ¶ 406-459))

CCH Practice Note: U.S. Supreme Court Declines to Review Gillette

On October 11, 2016, the U.S. Supreme Court denied a petition to review the California Supreme Court's decision in *Gillette*. With the conclusion of litigation in the case, the FTB has issued guidance concerning post-*Gillette* refund claims, audits, interest, and penalties (see *FTB Notice 2016-03*, November 1, 2016, CCH CALIFORNIA TAX REPORTS, ¶ 406-586). See ¶ 1301 for further discussion of the *Gillette* decision.

- *Deviations from standard formula*

The Uniform Division of Income for Tax Purposes Act (UDITPA) provides for deviation from the standard formula, where necessary to fairly reflect the extent of the taxpayer's business activity in California. This may be accomplished by excluding, adding, or modifying one or more factors, or by other means, as indicated in the cases discussed below. (Some of these cases were decided under pre-1967 law, but their reasoning is applicable generally under the present law.) The FTB may require such special treatment or the taxpayer may petition for it, in which case the FTB may grant a hearing. (Sec. 25137, Rev. & Tax. Code)

Deviation is only allowed where unusual fact situations, which ordinarily will be unique and nonrecurring, produce incongruous results (Reg. 25137, 18 CCR). In *Appeal of Crisa Corp.* (2002) (CCH CALIFORNIA TAX REPORTS, ¶ 11-540.25), the BOE rejected the taxpayer's contention that Mexican hyperinflation distorted the calculation of both net income and the property factor of the apportionment formula. In ruling in favor of the FTB, the BOE focused on whether an unusual fact situation existed and rejected the use of a quantitative comparison for purposes of whether there was sufficient distortion to justify deviation from the standard UDITPA formula. Stating that there is no bright line rule that can be used, the BOE summarized the following five examples from previous cases that may justify deviation from the standard formula. Note that this guidance was issued prior to the enactment of the single sales factor apportionment formula.

— A corporation does substantial business in California, but the standard formula does not apportion any income to California. For example, the employees of a professional sports franchise render services in California while playing "away" games, but the standard formula apportions all income to the team's home state (see *Appeal of New York Football Giants; Appeal of Milwaukee Professional Sports and Services, Inc.* (1979), (CCH CALIFORNIA TAX REPORTS, ¶ 11-525.514)).

— The factors in the standard formula are mismatched to the time during which the income is generated. For example, a construction contractor reports income when long-term contracts are completed, but the standard formula requires income to be reported currently (see *Appeal of Donald M. Drake Company* (1977) (CCH CALIFORNIA TAX REPORTS, ¶ 11-540.651)).

— The standard formula creates "nowhere income" that does not fall under the taxing authority of any jurisdiction. For example, a company owns equipment, the value of which is attributed to the high seas or outer space, where it cannot be taxed by any jurisdiction (see *Appeal of American Telephone and Telegraph Company* (1982) (CCH CALIFORNIA TAX REPORTS, ¶ 11-530.70)).

— One or more of the standard factors is biased by a substantial activity that is not related to the taxpayer's main line of business. For example, the taxpayer continuously reinvests a large pool of "working capital," generating large receipts that are allocated to the site of the investment activity. However, the investments are unrelated to the services provided by the taxpayer as its primary business (see *Appeal of Pacific Telephone and Telegraph Company* (1978) (CCH CALIFORNIA TAX REPORTS, ¶ 11-535.37)).

— A particular factor does not have material representation in either the numerator or denominator, rendering that factor useless as a means of reflecting business activity. For example, because a company does not own or rent any tangible or real personal property, the numerator and denominator of the property factor are zero (see *Appeal of Oscar Enterprises, LTD* (1987) (CCH CALIFORNIA TAX REPORTS, ¶ 11-540.20)).

CCH Practice Tip: Prior Approval Required

An original return that is inconsistent with California's standard allocation and apportionment rules that is filed without having obtained prior approval from the FTB will be treated as erroneous and the FTB may impose an accuracy-related penalty, including an increased penalty for substantial understatement (see ¶ 1411). Prior approval to file an original return that is inconsistent with the standard allocation and apportionment rules will be deemed to have been provided, without having to actually obtain prior approval, only if the inconsistent treatment meets the following criteria:

—is a variation permitted in an audit manual that was operative during the taxable year or that is currently operative, and the taxpayer's facts are substantially the same as those described in the manual;

—is a variation specifically permitted in a published opinion of the California State Board of Equalization, a California court of appeal, or the California Supreme Court, and the taxpayer's facts are substantially the same as those described in the opinion;

—has been approved in writing in a prior year petition that specifically states that the variation also applies to the taxable year in question; or

—has been approved in a prior year closing agreement that by its terms also applies to the taxable year in question.

The FTB will not impose an accuracy-related penalty if the taxpayer's position is adequately disclosed, provided the taxpayer's self-assessed position is one that would have a realistic possibility of being granted by the FTB as fairly representing the extent of the taxpayer's business activity in the state. Merely entering data on California Schedule R, Apportionment and Allocation of Income, using an alternative method of allocation and apportionment will not, by itself, be considered adequate disclosure, because that cannot reasonably be expected to apprise the FTB of the nature of the potential controversy (*FTB Notice 2004-5*, (2004) (CCH CALIFORNIA TAX REPORTS, ¶ 403-663)).

In *Appeal of Evergreen Marine Corporation (Calif.), Ltd.* (1986) (CCH CALIFORNIA TAX REPORTS, ¶ 11-520.2095), the taxpayer, its parent corporation, and affiliates were engaged in various aspects of the ocean freighter business. In upholding the FTB's application of the standard formula to the unitary income of the corporate group, the BOE held that methods other than the standard formula may be used only in exceptional circumstances where UDITPA's provisions do not fairly represent the extent of the taxpayer's business activity in the state. The challenge to the formula must attack each element of the formula equation, and show that the formula as a whole unfairly apportions net income to California. Furthermore, deviations from the formula are not permitted simply because there is a better approach. If the standard formula fairly represents the extent of in-state activity it must be used.

In *American Telephone and Telegraph Co.* (1982) (CCH CALIFORNIA TAX REPORTS, ¶ 11-530.70), discussed at ¶ 1307, the FTB adjusted the California property factor by including property located in outer space and on the high seas. The BOE upheld the FTB, and expressed the belief that the law authorizes the FTB to deviate from UDITPA's standard provisions "in order to prevent some . . . business income from escaping taxation entirely."

Appeal of Universal C.I.T. Credit Corporation (1972) (CCH CALIFORNIA TAX REPORTS, ¶ 11-530.85) involved a large finance company with a Delaware parent corporation and more than fifty subsidiaries. The taxpayer agreed to the three-factor formula used in the finance company cases cited above, but contended that receivables originating in California had a business situs outside the State and therefore could not properly be attributed to California in computing the "property" factor (loans outstanding). The BOE held that the loans were a proper measure of the portion of the business emanating from California, citing as support a court decision dealing with tangible property in the property factor and expressing the belief that the same principles apply to intangible property.

In *Appeal of Public Finance Company, et al.* (1958) (CCH CALIFORNIA TAX REPORTS, ¶ 11-520.834), the corporations involved were engaged in the small loan business. The FTB used an allocation formula consisting of the factors of (1) average loans outstanding, (2) payroll, and (3) interest earned. The taxpayers contended that their income should be determined by separate accounting. The BOE held that the business was unitary and approved the formula used. See also *Appeal of Beneficial Finance Co. of Alameda and Affiliates* (1961) (CCH CALIFORNIA TAX REPORTS, ¶ 11-520.208). A similar result was reached in *Appeal of Tri-State Livestock Credit Corporation* (1960) (CCH CALIFORNIA TAX REPORTS, ¶ 11-530.464). In this case the taxpayer's only office was in California, but many loans were made outside the State. The BOE apportioned the factor of average loans outstanding entirely to California, on the theory that a loan has a business situs where it is serviced. The interest-earned factor, being somewhat comparable to the sales factor in the usual formula, was developed by assigning interest income to the places where employees solicited the loans.

• *Omission of one or more factors - pre-single-sales factor apportionment*

Where property is a negligible factor in the business, as in the case of some service corporations, the property factor might be omitted; the computation would then be made by averaging only the other two factors. The same procedure may occasionally be applied also to the wages or sales factor, in special cases where use of the factor would be meaningless or impracticable or would result in distortion. For example, in the case of a gold mining operation the sales factor might be omitted, because all gold must be sold to the U.S. Government and there is no sales activity in the usual sense.

In *Appeal of Twentieth Century-Fox Film Corporation* (1962) (CCH CALIFORNIA TAX REPORTS, ¶ 11-540.80), the BOE held that a taxpayer could not use a single factor formula (gross receipts) to determine the California portion of one segment of its income, *i.e.*, distribution of films for unrelated producers, and another formula (the usual 3-factor formula) to determine California income from distribution of its self-produced films.

In *Appeal of Farmers Underwriters Association* (1953) (CCH CALIFORNIA TAX REPORTS, ¶ 11-530.83), the taxpayer was a service corporation and contended that the property factor should be omitted from the allocation formula. The BOE sustained the FTB in requiring inclusion of the property factor, because the taxpayer used a substantial amount of property (land, buildings, furniture, office equipment, supplies, and motor vehicles) in its business. However, in *Appeal of Woodward, Baldwin & Co., Inc.* (1963) (CCH CALIFORNIA TAX REPORTS, ¶11-530.25), it was held that where a manufacturer's sales agent employed a relatively small amount of owned property in its business, the property factor should be ignored, and income allocated according to the remaining two factors of payroll and sales.

• *Cases involving professional sports*

Two 1977 decisions of the BOE involved questions of deviating from the standard formula in special situations. *Appeal of Danny Thomas Productions* (CCH CALIFORNIA TAX REPORTS, ¶11-540.55) involved production of television shows; *Appeal of New York Football Giants* (CCH CALIFORNIA TAX REPORTS, ¶11-525.512) involved a professional football team. The BOE allowed some deviations (too complicated for discussion here) and commented that the party desiring to deviate from the standard formula must bear the burden of proving that it does not produce a fair result. See also *Appeal of Milwaukee Professional Sports and Services, Inc.* (1979) (CCH CALIFORNIA TAX REPORTS, ¶11-525.514), involving a professional basketball team, and *Appeal of Boston Professional Hockey Association, Inc.* (1979) (CCH CALIFORNIA TAX REPORTS, ¶11-525.511), involving a professional hockey team. See ¶1306 for discussion of special statutory rules for professional sports teams.

¶1306 Apportionment Rules for Specialized Industries

Law: Secs. 25107, 25137, 25141; Regs. 25137-8.1, 25137-8.2 (CCH CALIFORNIA TAX REPORTS, ¶11-525, 11-530, 11-540).

Comparable Federal: None.

Over the years the Franchise Tax Board (FTB) has provided modified apportionment rules for a number of specialized industries, and for specialized types of business such as foreign operations and partnerships. Some of these rules have been issued as official regulations. In addition, Reg. 25137, 18 CCR, sets forth the circumstances under which it will permit a taxpayer to use an apportionment method other than that prescribed by law. Following is a listing of special industries and other groups (in alphabetical order) for which modified apportionment rules apply, with a brief summary for each category.

CCH Practice Tip: Impact of Mandatory Single Sales Factor Apportionment Formula

The special apportionment regulations discussed below were adopted prior to California's mandatory single sales factor apportionment formula. According to the FTB, these regulations are not moot, however, because the sales factor provisions in the special regulations still apply to the single sales factor taxpayers and all of the provisions still apply to the three-factor formula taxpayers (those primarily engaged in extractive or agricultural business activities, savings and loan activities, or banking or financial business activities). (*E-mail*, Franchise Tax Board, November 4, 2013)

• *Airlines*

The law (Sec. 25101.3, Rev. & Tax. Code) provides a special formula for the property factor, as explained at ¶1307. Reg. 25137-7, 18 CCR provides detailed rules for computation of all three of the standard factors.

• *Banks and financial corporations*

Reg. 25137-4.2, 18 CCR, provides detailed rules for computation of the property and sales factors. Loans, receivables, and other intangible assets are included in the property factor. The regulation is substantially similar to a Multistate Tax Commission model regulation, under which banks and financial corporations apportion their income using a three-factor formula consisting of equally-weighted sales, property, and payroll factors.

Reg. 25137-10, 18 CCR, details the rules regarding the computation of income of a unitary business consisting of a bank or financial corporation and a general corporation.

An international banking facility maintained by a bank within California is to be treated for purposes of the apportionment formula as though it were doing business outside the state. (Sec. 25107, Rev. & Tax. Code)

See ¶1305 for a discussion of *Appeal of Universal C.I.T. Credit Corporation* and other cases involving apportionment of income of financial corporations.

• *Commercial fishing*

Reg. 25137-5, 18 CCR, provides special rules for computation of the three standard-formula factors. Allocations are based largely on the ratio of California port days to total port days. Port days represent time spent either in port or at sea while a ship is "in operation."

• *Construction, manufacturing, and fabrication contractors*

Reg. 25137-2, 18 CCR, provides detailed rules and examples for apportioning income from long-term contracts under the completed-contract method and the percentage-of-completion method of accounting. The rule applies to long-term construction contracts and manufacturing and fabrication contracts. The three standard-formula factors are used, but special rules apply to the computation of each factor. The regulation also covers the application of the special rules for corporations that discontinue doing business in California (¶819).

Reg. 25137-1, 18 CCR, regarding partnerships (see below), provides special rules for apportionment where a corporation is a member of a construction-contractor partnership. See also *Appeal of Donald M. Drake Company* (1977) (CCH CALIFORNIA TAX REPORTS, ¶11-540.651), involving a construction contractor reporting income on the completed-contract basis. The State Board of Equalization (BOE) held that the taxpayer's share of joint ventures' property, payroll, and sales should be included in the allocation formula in the years the project is in progress rather than in the year the contract is completed.

In *Appeal of Robert E. McKee, Inc.* (1983) (CCH CALIFORNIA TAX REPORTS, ¶11-540.652), the taxpayer was engaged in numerous construction projects in California and other States. The BOE applied the methodology specified in the regulations, and cited, with approval, the *Drake* case.

• *Franchisors*

Reg. 25137-3, 18 CCR, provides rules for corporations engaged in the business of franchising. Special rules are provided for the payroll and sales factors.

The FTB's Chief Counsel's office has advised a taxpayer that receives license fees and royalties from foreign affiliates that manufacture, distribute, and/or sell products bearing the taxpayer's licensed trademarks that the taxpayer is a franchisor for purposes of the special apportionment rules. (*Chief Counsel Ruling 2010-2* (2010) (CCH CALIFORNIA TAX REPORTS, ¶405-222)).

• *Motion picture and television producers, distributors and broadcasters*

Reg. 25137-8.1 and Reg. 25137-8.2, 18 CCR, 18 CCR, provide rules for the apportionment of income of motion picture and television producers, television network broadcasters, and beginning with the 2011 tax year, distributors. Topical film properties, the cost of which is expensed for California tax purposes at the time of production, are included in the denominator of the property factor at full value for one year. Film properties, including news and sports filmed for telecast, other than films the cost of which is expensed for California tax purposes at the time of production, are included at full value for twelve years. All other film properties are included at eight times the receipts generated in an amount not to exceed the original cost of such properties.

The payroll factor is modified to specify that compensation includes payments made to talent salaries, residual and profit participation payments, and payments made by producers to other corporations for actor and director services. The sales factor is modified to specify that gross receipts include advertising revenues from films in release to theaters and television stations, networks, and telecasters, and licensing revenues from video cassettes and discs. Gross receipts are attributed to California in the ratio that the audience for such network stations (owned and affiliated) located in California or the subscribers for such telecaster location in California bears to the total audience for all such network stations (owned and affiliated) everywhere and/or the total subscribers of such telecaster everywhere. Special rules are also provided for other situations peculiar to the industry.

Practitioner Comment: Amendments to Film and TV Industry Regulation Expand Its Application to Include Advertising Revenue, News and Sports Programming, and New Technologies While Continuing to Explicitly Exclude Cable Companies

In 2012, the FTB renumbered and expanded the scope of the film and TV industry regulation. Former CCR § 25137-8 was renumbered as CCR § 25137-8.1 and effective for taxable years ending before January 1, 2011. New CCR § 25137-8.2 is effective for taxable years beginning on and after January 1, 2011. The new regulation expanded the rules to address the treatment of receipts from advertising revenue, adds news and sports filmed for telecast to the definition of films, and covers income from new technologies (e.g., video streaming and online websites) to the extent utilized by motion picture and television film producers, producers of television commercials, and television networks. The basic content of the special industry regulation, such as inclusion of film costs in the property factor or the market sourcing of the revenue based on the audience, was not altered.

Interestingly, while the definition section of the revised regulation covers new technologies (e.g., defines "advertising revenue" to include online advertising, and "producer" to include an entity that develops and creates web-based content), the sales factor rules at CCR § 25137-8.2(c)(3) do not provide direct guidance regarding the sourcing methodology for online advertising or web-based content. Furthermore, these changes conform California's treatment of advertising revenue definition of film and income from new technologies to Multistate Tax Commission Regulation IV.18(h). The regulation specifically identifies "distributors" as part of the industry covered under the regulation, but clarifies that ownership of movie theaters does not make an entity a distributor. The regulation does not contain a throwback provision unlike some of the other special industry regulations (e.g., franchisor at CCR § 25137-3(b)(2) and print media at CCR § 25137-12(c)(4)). The regulation expressly indicates that its provisions are inapplicable to "a business entity that earns receipts from the provision of cable television services.".

Chris Whitney, Contributing Editor

• *Mutual fund service providers*

Reg. 25137-14, 18 CCR requires mutual fund service providers to apportion their receipts from mutual fund services utilizing a shareholder location sales factor approach with a throwback provision using the methodology employed in *Appeal of Finnigan Corp.* (1990) (CCH CALIFORNIA TAX REPORTS, ¶ 11-525.813). Similarly, a mutual fund service provider's receipts from performing asset management services are assigned to California if the asset's beneficial owner's domicile is located in California. However, a shareholder's or beneficiary's receipts will be disregarded in computing the shareholder ratio in instances when a shareholder of record's domicile cannot reasonably be obtained.

• *Offshore drilling companies*

Legal Ruling No. 366 (1973) (CCH CALIFORNIA TAX REPORTS, ¶ 11-520.2091) deals with allocation questions of unitary oil operations beyond the 3-mile continental limit. The ruling states that use of the standard allocation formula is appropriate, and provides that factors relating to offshore operations should be reflected only in the denominators of the formula; thus, no income from such operations is apportioned to California. Legal Ruling No. 396 (1976) (CCH CALIFORNIA TAX REPORTS, ¶ 10-075.73) modifies the portion of Legal Ruling No. 366 pertaining to operations of drilling barges.

• *Partnerships*

Reg. 25137-1, 18 CCR, provides detailed rules for apportionment where a corporation is a partner. Special rules are provided for long-term contracts, intercompany transactions, etc. See also ¶ 1304.

• *Personal service companies*

See *Appeal of Farmers Underwriters Association* and *Appeal of Woodward, Baldwin & Co., Inc.*, discussed at ¶ 1305, involving questions of which factors should be used in apportioning income of service corporations.

• *Professional sports teams*

The law (Sec. 25141, Rev. & Tax. Code) provides rules for calculating the apportionment formula for all professional sports teams.

Section 25141 applies to any "professional athletic team" that:

— has at least five participating members;

— is a member of a league of at least five teams;

— has paid attendance of at least 40,000 for the year; and

— has gross income of at least $100,000 for the year.

Section 25141 provides rules for computation of each of the three standard factors in the allocation formula. The basic approach is that *all* property, payroll, and sales are to be allocated to the state or country in which the team's operations are based. The base of operations is in the state in which the team derives its territorial rights under the league's rules. Special rules are provided for cases where the team is subject to an apportioned tax in another state or country.

Entities that operate a professional sports organization are treated as corporations for purposes of the minimum franchise tax on corporations. The liability of any corporation owning a sports organization is satisfied by the minimum tax if that corporation is not otherwise doing business in the state.

See cases discussed at ¶ 1305 that involve question of deviating from the standard allocation formula by sports organizations.

• *Publishers of print media*

Reg. 25137-12, 18 CCR, provides rules for the apportionment of income of taxpayers in the business of publishing, selling, licensing, or distributing newspapers, magazines, periodicals, trade journals, or other printed material. A special circulation factor is used to determine the amount of the taxpayer's gross receipts from advertising and the sale, rental, or use of customer lists that must be included in the numerator of the sales factor.

• *Trains*

Reg. 25137-9, 18 CCR, provides special rules for computation of income from railroad operations. Generally the three standard-formula factors are used, but special rules apply to the computation of each factor.

• *Trucking companies*

Reg. 25137-11, 18 CCR, provides special rules for computation of income from trucking companies. Special rules are provided for the property and sales factor.

Practitioner Comment: Significant Uncertainty Surrounds Application of Special Apportionment Provisions to Mixed Combined Groups in Light of BOE Decision

As noted above, California has a number of regulations that set forth specialized apportionment rules for industries ranging from long term construction contractors to mutual fund service providers. Certain of these regulations provide specific rules for apportioning income of mixed combined groups which contain members in special industries. See for example CCR Section 25137-10 dealing with mixed financial and nonfinancial groups. Most of the regulations do not contain provisions regarding mixed groups, raising some uncertainty as to how the special apportionment regulations should be applied in such instances. It has generally been thought that absent a specific rule, and consistent with California's general "separate entity" approach to combined reporting group members, that the special apportionment regulations would only be applied to specific members who are engaged in special industry operations. (See CCR Section 25106.5(c)(7)(B))

Some doubt has been raised as to this view as a result of the BOE's letter decision in the *Appeal of Swift Transportation Co., Inc. and Swift Transportation Corporation* (2008), CCH CALIFORNIA TAX REPORTS, ¶ 404-616. In *Swift*, the BOE held that all members of a combined reporting group were required to use the special apportionment regulations applicable to trucking companies because that was the overall nature of Swift's unitary business even though certain members of the group did not operate as carriers of freight but instead solicited and procured customers or leased trucking equipment to the actual carrier.

Chris Whitney, Contributing Editor

¶1307 Property Factor in Apportionment Formula

Law: Secs. 25101.3, 25107, 25129-31 (CCH CALIFORNIA TAX REPORTS, ¶ 11-530, 11-540).

Comparable Federal: None.

California Form: Sch. R (Apportionment and Allocation of Income).

CCH Practice Tip: Single-Sales Factor Apportionment Formula Mandated for Post-2012 Tax Years

As discussed at ¶ 1305, taxpayers are required to utilize a single-sales factor (SSF) apportionment formula beginning with the 2013 tax year, unless the taxpayer is engaged in agricultural, extractive, or banking activities, in which case the use of an equally-weighted property/payroll/sales factor apportionment formula is required.

In computing the property factor, all real estate and tangible personal property owned or rented by the corporation and used in the business is included. (Sec. 25129, Rev. & Tax. Code) Property used to produce "nonbusiness" income is excluded from the factor, but property used to produce both "nonbusiness" and "business" income is included to the extent it is used to produce "business" income. Property owned by the corporation that is in transit between states is generally considered to be located at its destination. Reg. 25129, 18 CCR, gives examples that show what to include in the property factor in unusual situations such as a plant under construction, closing of a plant, etc., and provides specific rules for property in transit, movable property, etc.

• *Closing of plant*

In *Appeal of Ethyl Corporation* (1975) (CCH CALIFORNIA TAX REPORTS, ¶ 11-530.581), the taxpayer closed its California plant and started to sell its equipment in 1963 and contended that the property was permanently removed from the unitary business in that year. The State Board of Equalization (BOE) held that the plant was includible in the property factor until it was dismantled in 1965.

- *Property under construction*

Real property constituting "construction in progress" (CIP) of a homebuilder/ developer is excluded from the property factor because it is not regarded as property owned or rented and used in California during the taxable year. Conversely, specified items such as land that has not yet become CIP or that may be treated as CIP at some point in the future, or that is not CIP because it has been completed and is held for sale or other disposition is included in the property factor because it is treated as reserve property that is available for or capable of being used in the taxpayer's regular trade or business or property that is no longer classifiable as CIP. Such property is valued for property tax purposes by the averaging of monthly values during the taxable year if reasonably required to reflect properly the average value of the taxpayer's property, particularly in circumstances where substantial fluctuations in the values of the property exist during the taxable year or where property is acquired after the beginning of the taxable year or disposed of before the end of the taxable year.

Should the Franchise Tax Board (FTB) want to include CIP property in the property factor, the FTB would have to prove distortion and an unfair reflection of the taxpayer's business activity in California, a showing that cannot be satisfied by merely establishing that including CIP in the property factor would result in a different tax burden from one that would be imposed if the CIP is excluded from the property factor. Different rules apply in cases in which the taxpayer is a contractor using the percentage of completion method of accounting, or the completed contract method of accounting for long-term contracts. (*FTB Technical Advice Memorandum 2011-1*, CCH CALIFORNIA TAX REPORTS, ¶ 405-334)

In *Appeal of O.K. Earl Corp.* (1977) (CCH CALIFORNIA TAX REPORTS, ¶ 11-530.561), the taxpayer questioned the regulations regarding inclusion of costs of construction in progress in the property factor of construction contractors. The BOE upheld the provision that such costs are to be included only to the extent they exceed progress billings.

- *In-transit inventory*

In *Appeal of Craig Corporation* (1987) (CCH CALIFORNIA TAX REPORTS, ¶ 11-530.661), goods ceased to be "in transit" and entered the taxpayer's unitary business when received from Japan at the taxpayer's California facility for customs inspection, repackaging, and shipment to the taxpayer's regional warehouses in other states. The BOE held that within the context of a multistate unitary business it was too restrictive to interpret "destination" as the goods' ultimate storage place prior to sale. The imported goods were properly included in the California property factor numerator.

- *Property in outer space*

In *Appeal of American Telephone and Telegraph Co.* (1982) (CCH CALIFORNIA TAX REPORTS, ¶ 11-530.70), the FTB revised the California property factor by including the following property not physically located in the State: (1) the high-seas portion of certain jointly-owned California-Hawaii cables, and (2) a portion of certain leased satellite circuits in outer space. The FTB first contended that the property was "used" in California within the intent of the law, but the BOE rejected this argument. However, the BOE permitted the same result to be achieved by applying the provision of the law (discussed at ¶ 1305) that provides for deviation from the standard formula to fairly reflect the extent of California business activity. To the same effect, see the Court of Appeal decision in *Communications Satellite Corporation v. Franchise Tax Board* (1984) (CCH CALIFORNIA TAX REPORTS, ¶ 11-540.53); this case applied the same reasoning to the sales factor.

- *Property neither owned nor rented*

In *Appeal of Union Carbide Corporation* (1984) (CCH CALIFORNIA TAX REPORTS, ¶ 11-540.421), the taxpayer operated rent-free a government-owned nuclear gas-separation plant outside California. The BOE held that, under Reg. 25137 regarding deviations from the standard formula for exceptional circumstances, the property in question was properly includible in the denominator of the property factor.

• *Transportation companies*

Transportation companies present unusual problems in the property factor, and special procedures have been developed for them. The law provides a statutory formula for airlines and air taxis, based on time in California, number of arrivals and departures, etc. (Sec. 25101.3, Rev. & Tax. Code; Reg. 25137-7, 18 CCR)

Although the law does not provide specific formulas for other transportation companies, the FTB has developed a special formula for railroads and trucking companies based on "revenue miles" and a formula for sea transportation companies based on "voyage days" within and without California.

• *Use of original federal cost basis*

Property owned by the taxpayer is included in the property factor at its original cost ("basis") for *federal* income tax purposes. This means that depreciation is ignored. (Sec. 25130, Rev. & Tax. Code) However, certain adjustments are allowed, including adjustments for any subsequent capital additions or improvements, special deductions, and partial deductions because of sale, exchange, abandonment. Inventory is included in accordance with the method of valuation for *federal* income tax purposes. Reg. 25130, 18 CCR provides specific rules and examples for determining "original cost" in unusual situations such as corporate reorganizations, inherited property, etc.; in each case, the determination relates to the *federal* cost basis of the property. Leasehold improvements are included at their original cost. In the case of property acquired as a result of involuntary conversion or exchange, the original federal cost is carried over to the replacement property—see Legal Ruling No. 409 (1977) (CCH California Tax Reports, ¶ 11-530.97).

In *Appeal of Pauley Petroleum, Inc.* (1982) (CCH California Tax Reports, ¶ 11-530.591), the taxpayer had elected to expense intangible drilling and development costs for federal income tax purposes, but included them as costs in the property factor of the State apportionment formula. The BOE held that the costs could not be included in the property factor, since they were not included in the federal tax basis of the property.

• *Rental property and royalties*

Rental property is included in the property factor at eight times the net annual rental rate. (Sec. 25130, Rev. & Tax. Code) Any subrentals received—provided they constitute "nonbusiness" income—are ordinarily deducted from rentals paid to determine the net annual rate; however, Reg. 25137, 18 CCR, provides for special treatment in exceptional cases where deduction of subrentals would produce a distorted result. Reg. 25130, 18 CCR, and Reg. 25137, 18 CCR, give examples to illustrate treatment of this and other unusual situations, and also provide rules and examples for determining the "net annual rental" in cases of short-term leases, reorganizations, payments in lieu of rent, nominal rental rates, etc.

Under both Reg. 25130, 18 CCR and Reg. 25137, 18 CCR, and FTB Legal Ruling 97-2 (1997) (see CCH California Tax Reports, ¶ 11-530.44), royalty payments made by a corporation with respect to the corporation's oil and gas and/or timber rights are treated as equivalents to rental payments to the extent that the property for which the royalty payments are made is actually used.

• *Averaging for year*

The amount to be included in the property factor is the average value for the year. This is usually determined by averaging the values at the beginning and end of the year. However, the FTB may require or allow averaging by monthly values, where substantial fluctuations occur during the year or large amounts of property are acquired or disposed of during the year or where membership in the unitary group changes during the year. (Reg. 25131, 18 CCR) The FTB was sustained in this position by the BOE in *Appeal of Craig Corporation* (1987) (CCH California Tax Reports, ¶ 11-530.661).

¶1307

¶1308 Payroll Factor in Apportionment Formula

Law: Secs. 25107, 25132-33, 25137 (CCH CALIFORNIA TAX REPORTS, ¶ 11-535, 11-540).

Comparable Federal: None.

California Form: Sch. R (Apportionment and Allocation of Income).

CCH Practice Tip: Single-Sales Factor Apportionment Formula Mandated for Post-2012 Tax Years

As discussed at ¶ 1305, taxpayers are required to utilize a single-sales factor (SSF) apportionment formula beginning with the 2013 tax year, unless the taxpayer is engaged in agricultural, extractive, or banking activities, in which case the use of an equally-weighted property/payroll/sales factor apportionment formula is required.

The payroll factor includes all salaries, wages, commissions, and other compensation to employees. (Sec. 25132, Rev. & Tax. Code; Reg. 25132, 18 CCR) Officer compensation and 401(k) deferred earnings are also included in the payroll factor (California Response to CCH Multistate Corporate Income Tax Survey, California Franchise Tax Board, July 21, 2003, CCH CALIFORNIA TAX REPORTS, ¶ 403-506). The test of whether a person is an employee is the way the person is treated for payroll tax purposes; if the person is not considered to be an employee for payroll taxes the person's compensation is not included.

Compensation is attributable to California under the following scenarios:

— the employee performs services entirely within California;

— the employee performs services both within and without the state, but the services performed outside the state are merely incidental to those performed within the state;

— the employee performs some services within the state, and the base of operations is in the state, or if there is no base of operations, the place from which services are directed or controlled is in California; or

— the employee performs some services within the state and the base of operations, or the place from which services are directed or controlled, is not in any state in which some part of the services are performed, but the employee's residence is in California.

(Sec. 25133, Rev. & Tax. Code; Reg. 25133e, 18 CCR)

In *Appeal of Photo-Marker Corporation of California* (1986) (CCH CALIFORNIA TAX REPORTS, ¶ 11-535.60), wages paid principal corporate officers residing in California were includible in the California numerator because the base of operations for the officers was in California even though the corporation was headquartered in New York.

Compensation attributable to "nonbusiness" income (¶ 1303) should be excluded from the payroll factor. Capitalized payroll costs (*e.g.*, plant construction) should be included in the payroll factor, even though they also become part of the property factor.

Special rules have been developed over the years for determining the payroll factor in unusual industry situations. For example, in the case of transportation companies, payroll of traveling personnel may be apportioned according to "revenue miles" or "voyage days" as discussed in ¶ 1307.

The California payroll of an international banking facility is to be treated for purposes of the apportionment formula as payroll outside the state. (Sec. 25137, Rev. & Tax. Code)

¶1309 Sales Factor in Apportionment Formula

Law: Secs. 25107, 25134-37 (CCH California Tax Reports, ¶11-525, ¶11-540).

Comparable Federal: None.

California Form: Sch. R (Apportionment and Allocation of Income).

CCH Practice Tip: Single-Sales Factor Apportionment Formula Mandated for Post-2012 Tax Years

As discussed at ¶1305, taxpayers are required to utilize a single-sales factor (SSF) apportionment formula beginning with the 2013 tax year, unless the taxpayer is engaged in agricultural, extractive, or banking activities, in which case the use of an equally-weighted property/payroll/sales factor apportionment formula is required.

The sales factor of the apportionment formula for multistate taxpayers that derive business income from California is a fraction, the numerator of which is the total sales of the taxpayer in California during the taxable year, and the denominator of which is the total sales of the taxpayer everywhere during the taxable year. (Sec. 25134, Rev. & Tax. Code; Reg. 25134, 18 CCR)

• *Definition of sales*

"Sales" is generally defined by California income tax law as all gross receipts of the taxpayer not allocated (Sec. 25120(e), Rev. & Tax. Code), including all gross receipts derived from a taxpayer's business activities, even if the income is not from usual business sources. It does not include receipts from nonbusiness activities. (Sec. 25134, Rev. & Tax. Code; Reg. 25134, 18 CCR)

Items included.—Beginning with the 2011 taxable year, a statutory definition of "gross receipts" has been adopted for purposes of California's apportionment provisions. Under the statutory definition, "gross receipts" are the amounts realized on:

— the sale or exchange of property,

— the performance of services,

— or the use of property or capital in a transaction that produces business income, in which the income, gain, or loss is recognized (or would be recognized if the transaction were in the United States) under the Internal Revenue Code, as applicable for California corporation franchise and income tax purposes.

CCH Comment: Impact on Basis

Amounts realized on the sale or exchange of property are not reduced by the cost of goods sold or the basis of property sold. (Sec. 25120(f)(2), Rev. & Tax. Code)

The following rules apply for determining what constitutes "sales" for various taxpayers and situations:

— **Manufacturer or seller of goods or products:** "Sales" include all gross receipts from the sales of such goods or products (or other property of a kind that would properly be included in the inventory of the taxpayer if on hand at the close of the income year) held by the taxpayer primarily for sale to customers in the ordinary course of its trade or business. Gross receipts includes gross sales, less returns and allowances, and includes all interest income, service charges, carrying charges, or time-price differential charges incidental to such sales. Federal and state excise taxes (including sales taxes) are included if the taxes are passed on to the buyer or included as part of the product's selling price. (Reg. 25134(a)(1)(A), 18 CCR)

— **Cost plus fixed fee contracts:** "Sales" include the entire reimbursed cost, plus the fee. (Reg. 25134(a)(1)(B), 18 CCR)

— **Services, including research and development:** "Sales" include gross receipts from the performance of such services, including fees, commissions, and similar times. (Reg. 25134(a)(1)(C), 18 CCR)

— **Real or tangible property rentals:** "Sales" include gross receipts from the rental, lease or licensing the use of the property. (Reg. 25134(a)(1)(D), 18 CCR)

— **Intangible personal property:** "Sales" include gross receipts from the sale, assignment, or licensing of such property. (Reg. 25134(a)(1)(E), 18 CCR)

— **Sales of equipment used in trade or business:** "Sales" may include gross receipts from such transactions. For instance, a truck express company that owns and fleet of trucks and sells its trucks under a regular replacement program would include the receipts from the program in its sales factor. (Reg. 25134(a)(1)(F), 18 CCR) However, see the "occasional sale" discussion in the throwback or throwout rules discussed below.

— **Cost sharing arrangements:** Under Treasury Regulation 26 CFR § 1.482-7(b), a cost sharing arrangement (CSA) is generally defined as an arrangement under which controlled participants share the costs and risks of developing cost shared intangibles in proportion to their share of reasonably anticipated benefits. For California sales factor purposes, payments received from controlled participants pursuant to a qualified CSA for current operational research and development costs reduce expense deductions for the recipient and are not gross receipts. In contrast, payments in excess of the deductions available for the costs being reimbursed to the payee are payments in consideration for use of property or services made available to the CSA and are gross receipts for sales factor purposes. In addition, payments from controlled participants for resources or capabilities developed, maintained, or acquired externally to the CSA (whether prior to or during the course of the CSA) that are reasonably anticipated to benefit the development of cost-shared intangibles within the CSA are not reimbursements of costs under the CSA, but rather are consideration for use of the intangible property or resource and thus considered gross receipts for sales factor purposes. Furthermore, while Treasury Regulation 26 CFR § 1.482-7 allows platform contribution transaction (PCT) payments to be reduced by amounts owed to the payer, these offset amounts owed to the payee, which constitute PCT payments, are included at gross in the sales factor, subject to potential distortion analysis. (*Technical Advice Memorandum 2015-01* (CCH CALIFORNIA TAX REPORTS, ¶ 11-525.267)).

Practitioner Comment: FTB Addresses Treatment of Payments Pursuant to Cost Sharing Arrangements (CSAs) for Sales Factor Purposes

It is not uncommon for U.S.-based multinational corporations to develop intellectual property (e.g., technology, etc.) which is used by foreign affiliates in other countries. In these circumstances, foreign affiliates may enter into Cost Sharing Agreements (CSAs) under which they make Cost Sharing Transaction (CST) payments to their U.S. parent in order to share in the cost of development. In addition, such affiliates may make Platform Contribution Transaction (PCT) payments for technologies or other capabilities developed outside the CSA which benefit the development of cost shared intangibles within the CSA.

The California Franchise Tax Board (FTB) issued *Technical Advice Memorandum (TAM) 2015-01* to address the treatment of these payments for sales factor purposes, concluding that CST payments are reimbursements of costs incurred by the recipient and therefore are not gross receipts for California sales factor purposes. However, to the extent that these payments are in excess of the CSA amount being reimbursed to the taxpayer-payee, these payments are in consideration for use of property or services made available to the CSA and therefore constitute gross receipts for California sales factor purposes.

In contrast, the FTB concludes that since PCT payments are not reimbursements of costs under the CSA they constitute consideration for the use of the intangible property, services, or other resources and are thus gross receipts for California sales factor purposes under Cal. Rev. & Tax. Code §25134(a)(1)(A) or (C). The TAM also states that, "[w]hile Treasury Regulation 26 CFR § 1.482-7 allows PCT payments to be reduced by amounts owed to the payer, under authority of *General Mills v. Franchise Tax Board* (2012) 208 Cal.App.4th 1290, these offset amounts owed to the payee, which constitute PCT Payments, are included at gross in the sales factor, subject to potential distortion analysis under section 25137."

To the extent payments made are gross receipts for California sales factor purposes, they are sourced under the California statute and regulations applicable to the tax year at issue. Therefore, the cascading rules in Reg. 25136-2, 18 CCR, govern the sourcing of these receipts for years that market based sourcing applies. In the years prior to market based sourcing, these receipts should be sourced based on the location of the greater cost of performance.

It should be noted that the FTB's conclusion concerning the exclusion of CST payments at first blush seems to be at odds with the State Board of Equalization's (BOE's) decision in *In the Matter of the Appeals of Bechtel Power Corporation, et. al.,* 97-SBE-002 (3/19/1997), in which the BOE held that the taxpayer, a cost-plus contractor, should include the entire amount received, including the expense reimbursement portion of the agreement (which would be excluded under the TAM where there is a CSA), in its sales factor.

The TAM may resolve this conflict where it states that for taxable years on or after January 1, 2011, under Rev. & Tax. Code § 25120(f)(2), California's definition of "gross receipts" is tied to what is considered income, gain, or loss under the Internal Revenue Code. As noted in the TAM, for federal purposes, CSA payments are considered a contra expense item and not a receipt based on IRC § 482. The TAM also explains that although the definition of gross receipts is not tied to the Internal Revenue Code prior to 2011, "for consistency purposes California should follow federal law for earlier years as well." Interestingly, the BOE in *Bechtel* found Reg. 25134, 18 CCR, related to cost plus fixed fee contracts "most significant" and that provision is the same today as it was when *Bechtel* was decided. The FTB further concludes in the TAM, without addressing the possible conflict with *Bechtel* directly, that under a CSA no service has been provided which would justify inclusion of the CST payments in the sales factor, a fact which may distinguish CSAs from the type of contracts at issue in *Bechtel*.

Chris Whitney, Contributing Editor

Items excluded.—Specifically excluded from the statutory definition of gross receipts, even if considered business income, are the following items:

— repayment, maturity, or redemption of the principal of a loan, bond, mutual fund, certificate of deposit, or similar marketable instrument;

— the principal amount received under a repurchase agreement or other transaction properly characterized as a loan;

— proceeds from issuance of the taxpayer's own stock or from sale of treasury stock;

— damages and other amounts received as the result of litigation;

— property acquired by an agent on behalf of another;

— tax refunds and other tax benefit recoveries;

— pension reversions;

— contributions to capital (except for sales of securities by securities dealers);

— income from discharge of indebtedness;

— amounts realized from exchanges of inventory that are not recognized under the Internal Revenue Code;

— amounts received from transactions in intangible assets held in connection with a treasury function of the taxpayer's unitary business and the gross receipts and overall net gains from the maturity, redemption, sale, exchange, or other disposition of those intangible assets; and

— amounts received from hedging transactions involving intangible assets.

(Sec. 25120(f)(2), Rev. & Tax. Code)

CCH Pointer: Relationship to business/nonbusiness income classification

The exclusion of an item from the definition of gross receipts is not determinative of its character as business or nonbusiness income. (Sec. 25120(f), Rev. & Tax. Code)

CCH Comment: Effective date of gross receipts exclusions

The legislation enacting the specific list of gross receipts exclusions listed above (S.B. 15, Laws 2009, third extraordinary session) declared that although the amendments were effective beginning with the 2011 tax year, the changes made were clarifying, nonsubstantive changes. However many tax practitioners have questioned the accuracy of that statement.

Broker/dealers.—Broker-dealers may include the entire sales price from the sale of a marketable security in the sales factor, including return of capital, unless such inclusion gives rise to apportionment that unfairly represents the extent of a taxpayer's activity in California such that the Franchise Tax Board requires an alternative formula under the authority of Rev. & Tax. Code Sec. 25137. (*FTB Chief Counsel Ruling 2012-01*, CALIFORNIA TAX REPORTS, ¶ 11-525.852)

Practitioner Comment: FTB Rules that Broker-Dealers Must Include Gross Amount of Sales of Securities in Sales Factor and Distortion Based Alternative Apportionment Does Not Apply to Intrastate Apportionment

A registered broker-dealer must include the gross sales price received from the sale of securities, including the return of capital, in the sales factor as required by Cal. Rev. & Tax. Code § 25120(f)(2)(K). Additionally, California's alternative apportionment provisions at Cal. Rev. & Tax. Code § 25137 are inapplicable when determining the individual California tax liabilities of the taxpayer members of a combined reporting group.

In Chief Counsel Ruling 2012-01, a registered broker-dealer received income from buying and selling securities. Receipts from the principal trades were sourced to California and included in the broker-dealer's California sales factor numerator and denominator under Cal. Rev. & Tax. Code § 25136 because the greater cost of performance of the broker-dealer's transactions occurred in California.

Effective for tax years on or after January 1, 2011, gross receipts for California sales factor purposes includes only net gains from treasury function activities. However, under Rev. & Tax Code § 25120(f)(2)(K), a taxpayer whose primary line of business consists of trading securities must include gross receipts from sales of securities in its sales factor. As such, the FTB ruled that the taxpayer, as a registered broker-dealer, must include the gross amount from the sale, including a return of capital, in its sales factor under the standard apportionment formula.

The FTB also addressed the taxpayer's alternative apportionment inquiry. Under Rev. & Tax. Code § 25137, an alternative apportionment formula may be requested or required if the standard method does not fairly represent the extent of the taxpayer's business in the state. In this case, the issue was with respect to intrastate apportionment, which involves the assignment of California source apportioned income amongst the California taxpayer members of a unitary group. Under California law, California business income is assigned to taxable members based on the relative weight of each member's California factors. The FTB stated that § 25137 only applies where the interstate apportionment factor does not fairly reflect the activities in California. Because intrastate apportionment for combined groups does not concern interstate division of income, the FTB determined that § 25137 did not apply. It should be noted that the FTB in a footnote expressly states that issues related to distortion and alternative apportionment methodologies under § 25137 for interstate division of income is outside the scope of the Chief Counsel Ruling.

Chris Whitney, Contributing Editor

• *Sourcing rules for tax years after 2012 (after 2010 for taxpayers that elected single-sales factor apportionment formula)*

Like the Uniform Division of Income for Tax Purposes Act (UDITPA) and Multistate Tax Commission (MTC) Model Apportionment Regulations, California follows the destination test with respect to the sourcing of income from the sales of tangible personal property. Beginning with the 2013 tax year, market-based sourcing is required for all taxpayers for purposes of sourcing sales of other than tangible personal property, even taxpayers who are predominately involved with qualified business activities (e.g. agricultural, extractive, and banking) that are still required to use the equally-weighted apportionment formula. (Sec. 25136, Rev. & Tax. Code) However, a provision excludes 50% of the sales sourced to the California numerator under the market-based sourcing rules for combined reporting groups engaged in the cable network business that make a minimum investment of $250 million for the taxable year. (Sec. 25136.1, Rev. & Tax. Code) Prior to the 2013 tax year, sales of other than tangible personal property were generally sourced using the income-producing activity test. However, taxpayers using the single-sales factor apportionment formula were required to use the market-based sourcing rules to source sales of services and intangibles.

Reg. 25136-2, 18 CCR provides detailed, cascading presumptions as to the records and/or methods to use to best determine where the benefit is received or where the property is used, as outlined below. The taxpayer's books and records must be those that are kept in the taxpayer's regular course of business. A particular rule or method will be bypassed if either the information is unavailable or the taxpayer or the FTB can rebut the presumption by a preponderance of the evidence, unless a safe harbor is indicated, in which case only the taxpayer may rebut the presumption. For purposes of the market-based sourcing rules, "benefit of a service is received" means the location where the taxpayer's customer has either directly or indirectly received value from delivery of that service.

CCH Comment: Classification of Property—Threshold Issue

A threshold issue for purposes of applying these rules is to determine whether the transaction involves the sale of tangible personal property or sales of other than tangible personal property. The following our illustrative of some of the decisions in this area:

— *Sales of electricity.*—The generation and transmission of electricity sold to California customers was the sale of a service. In reaching this conclusion, the BOE found that, "for purposes of California tax law, electricity is intangible." (*Appeal of PacifiCorp.* (2002) (CCH CALIFORNIA TAX REPORTS, ¶403-326))

— *Metal fabrication.*—The fabrication of metal products constituted a service. (*Appeal of Mark IV Metal Products, Inc.*, (1982) (CCH CALIFORNIA TAX REPORTS, ¶400-268))

— *Design, manufacture, and sale of steam generating systems.*—The design, manufacture, and sale of steam generating systems constituted the sale of tangible personal property. The BOE pointed out that the property and payroll factors fairly reflected the out-of-state activity in planning, engineering, etc. (*Appeal of The Babcock and Wilcox Company* (1978) (CCH CALIFORNIA TAX REPORTS, ¶205-814))

— *Licensing of software.*—Royalties from the licensing of the right to replicate and install software constituted receipts from the licensing of an intangible personal property right and not from the sale of tangible personal property. (*Microsoft Corporation v. Franchise Tax Board* (2012) (CCH CALIFORNIA TAX REPORTS, ¶405-747))

Practitioner Comment: Off-the-Shelf Software Classified as Intangible Personal Property

In *Microsoft Corporation v. Franchise Tax Board*, Cal. Sup. Ct., San Francisco Cty., Statement of Decision, No. CGC 08-471260 (February 17, 2011), CCH CALIFORNIA TAX REPORTS, ¶405-382, the court determined that royalty income received from the license of canned software to original equipment manufacturers (OEMs) should be treated as income

¶1309

from the sale of tangible personal property ("TPP") and must be sourced based upon the location of the customer rather than based upon the cost of performance method applicable to other revenues such as revenues from services and intangibles. The court also held that Microsoft had not met its burden of demonstrating that the exclusion of intangible property from its property factor distorted the apportionment of its income to California while at the same time finding that the exclusion of Microsoft's treasury receipts from the sales factor was necessary to avoid such distortion.

Microsoft appealed the superior court's decision on the royalty sourcing issue to the California Court of Appeal. In *Microsoft Corporation v. Franchise Tax Board*, Court of Appeal, First Appellate District, No. A131964 (December 18, 2012), CCH CALIFORNIA TAX REPORTS, ¶405-747, the appellate court determined that royalties received from the license to replicate and install software during the manufacture of computers by original equipment manufacturers (OEMs) are receipts from intangible property and must be sourced based on the location of the preponderance of the costs of performance. The court relied on the plain meaning of "intangible property," California franchise and sales tax laws, and federal law to conclude that the license was intangible property for franchise tax purposes. The court concluded that because Microsoft incurred the preponderance of its costs of performance in Washington, the royalties at issue were not sourced to California for sales factor purposes.

While the court's decision may have adverse implications for California-based companies that receive license royalties, the decision has limited future applicability due to the passage of Proposition 39 in 2012, which requires taxpayers to use market based sourcing instead of cost of performance for tax years beginning on or after January 1, 2013.

Chris Whitney, Contributing Editor

Sales of tangible personal property.—Sales of tangible personal property are attributed to California if the property is delivered or shipped to a purchaser within California. Property is deemed to be delivered or shipped to a purchaser within California if the recipient is located in California, even if the property is ordered from outside the state. (Sec. 25135, Rev. & Tax. Code) The most significant exception to the California sourcing rules for sales of tangible personal property is the application of a throwback rule.

> **EXAMPLE:** *Location of purchaser.*—A taxpayer with inventory in Washington sold $100,000 of its products to a purchaser having branch stores in several states, including California. The purchase order for was placed by the purchaser's central purchasing department located in Arizona. Twenty-five thousand dollars of the purchase order was shipped directly to purchaser's branch store in California. The branch store in California is the purchaser within California with respect to $25,000 of the taxpayer's sales.

Sales of tangible personal property ultimately destined for another state but shipped to a third-party public warehouse in California for temporary storage pending shipment in the same form as received were not considered sales within California for sales factor purposes. The property was not used in California through activities such as warehousing and repackaging. Moreover, since the ultimate destination was designated at the time of the initial order and was separately billed to a division in the ultimate state of destination, the temporary storage in California was merely for purposes of further shipment elsewhere in the stream of interstate commerce. (*Chief Counsel Ruling 2013-03*, California Franchise Tax Board, September 25, 2013, CCH CALIFORNIA TAX REPORTS, ¶406-061)

Practitioner Comment: Separately Stated Shipping Charges Sourced Using Rules for TPP for Income Tax Purposes

In *Appeal of Williams-Sonoma, Inc.* Cal. St. Bd. of Equal., Case No. 519857 (June 26, 2012), CCH CALIFORNIA TAX REPORTS, ¶405-711, the BOE held in a decision that may not be cited as precedent that separately stated shipping charges associated with items purchased from catalogues, websites, and/or retail stores are considered part of the sale of the tangible personal property and therefore should be sourced consistent with the rules applicable to the sale of tangible personal property. The taxpayer argued that the shipping charges constituted a separate profit center of its business and should be considered a separate service sourced under the rules applied to sales of other than tangible personal property, which was cost of performance for the years at issue. Under cost of performance, the charges would be sourced outside of California. The BOE disagreed and held that the shipping services were incidental to the taxpayer's sales of its products and would not be performed but for the sale of the goods. As a result, the shipping charges were considered part of the sale of the tangible personal property and should be sourced accordingly.

Chris Whitney, Contributing Editor

CCH Comment: When Does Delivery Occur?

When does delivery occur?: A presumption exists that the state where the purchaser first took actual or constructive possession of goods is the state of ultimate destination. This presumption may be rebutted if the taxpayer can demonstrate that the purchaser immediately transported the property to another state. However, if goods are shipped to a physical location of a purchaser in California, or if a purchaser takes possession (or constructive possession through an agent or bailor) in California for purposes such as warehousing, repackaging, adding accessories, etc., the property is "delivered... to a purchaser within the state," and the sale is a California sale. Any subsequent transportation of the goods to another state will not affect the California assignment of the sale. (*FTB Legal Ruling 95-3* (CCH CALIFORNIA TAX REPORTS, ¶402-780)) This ruling reflects the holdings in both *McDonnell Douglas Corp. v. Franchise Tax Board*, 26 CalApp4th 808 (1994), (CCH CALIFORNIA TAX REPORTS, ¶402-701, and *Mazda Motors of America, Inc.*, (1994) (CCH CALIFORNIA TAX REPORTS, ¶402-759)).

Lease or rental of tangible personal property.—Sales from the rental, lease, or licensing of tangible personal property are in California if the property is located in California. (Sec. 25136(a)(4), Rev. & Tax. Code)

Sale, lease or rental of real property.—Sales from the sale, lease, rental, or licensing of real property are in California if the real property is located in California. (Sec. 25136(a)(3), Rev. & Tax. Code)

Sales from services to nonunitary business customers.—Sales of services to business customers, other than another combined reporting group member, are sourced to California to the extent the purchaser of the service received the benefit of the service in California as evidenced by the following:

(1) The contract between taxpayer and customer or the taxpayer's books and records;

(2) By reasonable approximation if the location cannot be determined in (1) or if presumption is overcome;

(3) The location from which the order was placed if the location cannot be determined in (1) or (2) or if the presumption is overcome; or

(4) The customer's billing address if the location cannot be determined in (1) - (3) or if the presumption is overcome.

(Reg. 25136-2(c)(2), 18 CCR) Examples are provided in (Reg. 25136-2(c)(2)(E), 18 CCR)

CCH Comment: Activities Not Treated As A Service

The term "service" does not include activities performed by a person who is not in a regular trade or business offering its services to the public, and does not include services rendered to another member of the taxpayer's combined reporting group. (Reg. 25136-2(b)(6), 18 CCR)

EXAMPLE: Reasonable approximation.—A corporation located in California provides limited bookkeeping services to clients both within and outside the state. For the past 10 years, the corporation's only records for the sales of these services have consisted of invoices with the billing address for the client. The corporation's records have been consistently maintained in this manner. If the FTB determines that the corporation cannot determine, pursuant to financial records maintained in the regular course of its business, the location where the benefit of the services it performs are received, under the rules in Reg. 25136-2, then the corporation's sales of services will be assigned to California using the billing address information maintained by the taxpayer. The corporation will not be required to alter its record keeping method for purposes of the regulation.

Sales from services to individual customer.—Sales of services to individual customers are sourced to California to the extent the customer received the benefit of the service in California as evidenced by the following cascading rules:

(1) The customer's billing addresses (safe harbor) unless the contract or the taxpayer's books or records show otherwise; or

(2) Reasonable approximation if the location cannot be determined in (1) or if the presumption is overcome.

(Reg. 25136-2(c)(1), 18 CCR)

CCH Comment: Rebutting the Safe-Harbor Presumption

To overcome the safe-harbor presumption that the benefit of the service was received at the customer's billing address, the taxpayer must prove by a preponderance of the evidence that either the contract between the taxpayer and the taxpayer's customer, or other books and records of the taxpayer kept in the normal course of business, demonstrate the extent to which the benefit of the service is received at a location other than the customer's billing address. Note that the FTB must accept the use of the customer's billing address. The reasonable approximation method may only be used if the taxpayer demonstrates that the benefit was not received at the customer's billing address and the FTB determines that the use of the contract or the taxpayer's books or records does not provide a reasonable alternative to determining where the benefit was received. Numerous examples are provided in Reg. 25136-2(c)(1)(C), 18 CCR.

Complete sale/transfer of intangible property.—The complete sale/transfer of intangible property is sourced to California to the extent the property is used in California as evidenced by the following cascading rules:

(1) As specified (a) in the contract between taxpayer and purchaser or (b) the taxpayer's books and records for the most recent 12 month taxable year prior to the time of the sale of the intangible property;

(2) By reasonable approximation if the location cannot be determined in (1) or if the presumption is overcome; or

(3) The purchaser's billing records if the location cannot be determined in (1) or (2) or if the presumption is overcome.

Special rules apply for purposes of determining the location in (1) above if the sale/transfer involves a corporate stock sale or the sale of an ownership interest in a pass-through entity, other than sales of marketable securities, or where the gross receipts from intangible property are dividends or goodwill. For business entities sold or transferred that had at least 50% of their assets consisting of real and/or tangible personal property, the sale of the stock or ownership interest will be assigned by averaging the entity's California payroll and property factors for the previous 12-month taxable year (current year's average if the sale occurs more than six months into the current taxable year). Entities with a majority of assets consisting of intangible property assign the receipts from the sale or transfer by using the entity's California sales factor for the previous 12-month taxable year (current year's average if the sale occurs more than six months into the current taxable year). (Reg. 25136-2(d)(1), 18 CCR) Examples as to how these rules are applied are provided in (Reg. 25136-2(d)(1)(D), 18 CCR)

If the gross receipts from intangible property is interest, the interest is assigned as follows:

— Interest from investments, other than certain loans from a bank or financial institution, is assigned to California if the investment is managed in the state;

— Interest from certain loans from a bank or financial institution that are secured by real property is assigned to California to the extent the real property is located in the state; and

— Interest from certain loans from a bank or financial institution that are not secured by real property is assigned to California if the borrower is located in the state.

(Reg. 25136-2(d)(1)(A)(2), 18 CCR)

Practitioner Comment: California Updates Market Sourcing Regulation for Dividends, Which May Create Practical Difficulties for Taxpayers

The California Office of Administrative Law approved the FTB's regulatory changes to its market-based sourcing regulation regarding the sourcing treatment of receipts from marketable securities, dividends, goodwill, and interest. The amendments to the regulation apply to taxable years beginning on or after January 1, 2015; however, taxpayers may elect to apply the provisions to taxable years beginning on or after January 1, 2012, if the applicable statutes of limitations remains open.

Among other changes, the amendments provide that gross receipts from the receipt of dividends and the sale of goodwill are to be sourced in the same manner as sales of corporate shares (other than sales of marketable securities) or sales of pass-through ownership interests.

According to these rules, the receipts should be sourced based on the sales factor of the distributing company (or selling company in the case of goodwill), when the company's assets are predominantly intangible, and otherwise based on the company's average property and payroll.

As a practical matter, while companies selling stock or goodwill may have access to the company's factor information, dividend payees may not. A dividend payee, particularly when the payee does not hold a controlling interest in the corporation, may encounter significant difficulty obtaining the proper sourcing information from the company.

Chris Whitney, Contributing Editor

Licensing/leasing/renting of marketing intangible property (e.g., copyright, service mark, trademark, or trade name).—The licensing/leasing/renting of marketing intangibles are sourced to California to the extent the property is used in California as evidenced by:

(1) The location of the ultimate retail customer as determined by the contract between taxpayer and licensee or the taxpayer's books and records; or

(2) Reasonable approximation if the location of the use of the intangible property is not determinable under (1) or the presumption under (1) is overcome.

A reasonable approximation of the retail customers' use of the goods, services, or other items may be based on factors such as:

— the number of licensed sites in each state;

— the volume of property manufactured, produced, or sold pursuant to the arrangement at locations in California; or

— other data that reflects the relative usage of the intangible property in California.

For purposes of the sourcing of royalties or fees from the licensing of a marketing intangible property for use in connection with sales or other transfers at wholesale rather than directly to retail customers, a reasonable approximation may be based on a percentage of the state's total population, plus the population of other countries if it is shown that the property is being used materially in other parts of the world, as compared to the total population of the geographic area in which the licensee uses the intangible to market its goods, services or other items. (Reg. 25136-2(d)(2)(A), 18 CCR)

Licensing/leasing/renting of non-marketing or manufacturing intangible property.—Revenues received from the licensing/leasing/renting of non-marketing or manufacturing intangible property, such as a patent, a copyright, or trade secret to be used in a manufacturing or other non-marketing process, are sourced to California to the extent the property is used in California as evidenced by:

(1) The contract between the taxpayer and the licensee or the taxpayer's books and records; or

(2) The licensee's billing address if the location cannot be determined in (1) or the presumption is overcome.

Special rules also apply in instances when the intangible property licensed/leased/or rented involves a mixture of marketing and non-marketing intangibles. The FTB will accept a fee statement that reasonably allocates the fees in the licensing contract if the fees are separately stated in the licensing contract. Should the FTB determine that the allocation is not reasonable, the FTB may assign the fees using a reasonable method that accurately reflects the licensing of a marketing intangible and the licensing of a non-marketing or manufacturing intangible. Where the fees to be paid in each instance are not separately stated in the contract, it will be presumed that the licensing fees are paid entirely for the license of a marketing intangible except to the extent that the taxpayer or the FTB can reasonably establish otherwise.

Special rules allow for the reasonable approximation of information under certain circumstances, such as when the necessary data of a smaller business cannot be developed from financial records maintained in the regular course of business. The rule provides details as to what information may be used to make a reasonable approximation depending upon the type of service or property involved. (Reg. 25136-2, 18 CCR)

Practitioner Comment: Receipts From Non-Marketing Services Sourced to Customer's Location, Even Though Customer's Customers Indirectly Benefited From Service

The California Franchise Tax Board (FTB) issued Chief Counsel Ruling 2015-03 (2015) (CCH CALIFORNIA TAX REPORTS, ¶406-484), to a provider of non-marketing services. The services include access to real-time news and quotes, company and portfolio analyses, and industry analysis. The FTB found that receipts from a financial information service provider's non-marketing service should be sourced based on its customer's location, despite the fact that the services also benefitted the customer's customers who were located in various states.

In the taxpayer's case, not only was there a direct benefit from the sales of the taxpayer's services, there was also an indirect benefit received by customers of the taxpayer's customer. The California statutes and regulations do not address what to do when there is both a direct and an indirect benefit from the same sale of services.

The ruling references an analogous situation, addressed in a California regulation, regarding the licensing of intangible property. Receipts from licensing marketing intangibles such as trade names and trademarks are sourced to the location of the licensee's ultimate customers. In contrast, receipts from the licenses of non-marketing intangibles (where the intangible value lies in the use in a manufacturing or non-marketing process, such as a patent) are sourced to the location where the customer uses the intangible.

The ruling applies a similar analysis regarding the sale of non-marketing services. When the value of a non-marketing service lies not in the advertising or promoting of a product, but rather in the use in the customer's business operations, then the revenues from such service should be sourced to the customer's location.

In this case, the taxpayer's web-based service of providing integrated financial information and analytical applications to its customers is not a marketing service used to sell, promote, or advertise its customer's product. Rather, the service is analogous to a non-marketing intangible that is used in its customers' business operations. Accordingly, sales receipts from the taxpayer's non-marketing services should be assigned where its customers receive the benefit of their services.

It should be noted that sourcing receipts on the basis of a customer's customer location (so called "look through") presents practical difficulties as customers are not always willing or able to conveniently provide this information to third parties such as service providers.

Chris Whitney, Contributing Editor

Marketable securities.—In the case of marketable securities, sales are in California if the customer is in the state. (Sec. 25136(a)(2), Rev. & Tax. Code)

For an individual customer, the sale is assigned to California if the customer's billing address is in the state. (Reg. 25136-2(e)(1), 18 CCR)

If the customer is a corporation or other business entity, the sale is assigned to California if the customer's commercial domicile is in the state. A customer's commercial domicile is determined from the taxpayer's books and records at the end of the taxable year. However, the customer's commercial domicile can be based on something other than the taxpayer's books and records if, based on a preponderance of the evidence, other credible documentation shows that the customer's commercial domicile is in another state. (Reg. 25136-2(e)(2), 18 CCR)

If the customer's billing address or commercial domicile cannot be determined, then the customer's location will be reasonably approximated. (Reg. 25136-2(e)(3), 18 CCR)

• *Sourcing rules for tax years before 2013*

California sourcing rules for sales of tangible personal property followed the destination test for tax years before 2013. However, prior to the 2013 tax year, sales of other than tangible personal property were attributable to California if the activity that produced the sale was performed in California, unless the taxpayer elected to use the single sales factor apportionment formula. If a single sales factor apportionment formula was elected, the taxpayer was required to use the market based sourcing rules discussed above. California generally followed the UDITPA and MTC income producing activity and cost of performance (COP) rules for sourcing of income related to sales other than sales of tangible personal property. Under the all or nothing COP rules, sales other than sales of tangible personal property were sourced to California if:

— the income-producing activity was performed entirely in California; or

— the income-producing activity was performed both inside and outside California, but a greater proportion of the income-producing activity was performed in California based on costs of performance.

(Sec. 25136, Rev. & Tax. Code; Reg. 25136, 18 CCR)

CCH Comment: Sourcing of Sales of Other Than Tangible Personal Property Under the Multistate Tax Compact

It should be noted that the Multistate Tax Compact uses the income-producing activity method for purposes of sourcing receipts from the sale of other than tangible personal property. Thus, if it is found that California's withdrawal form the Multistate Tax Compact was not valid, taxpayers that elect to use the Compact's equally-weighted apportionment formula may still be able to use the income-producing activity/cost-of-performance method to source the receipts from such sales. Taxpayers should weigh the consequences of market-based sourcing vs. cost-of-performance method when determining whether to elect the Compact's apportionment formula.

Definition of income-producing activity.—California followed the MTC apportionment regulations regarding the definition of income producing activity. The term "income producing activity" applied to each separate item of income and was defined to mean the transactions and activity directly engaged in by the person in the regular course of its trade or business for the ultimate purpose of obtaining gains or profit. Activities performed on behalf of a taxpayer by an independent contractor were treated in a similar manner as activities performed directly by a taxpayer. (Reg. 25136, 18 CCR)

Items included: "Income-producing activity" included, but was not limited to, the following:

— the rendering of personal services by employees or by an agent or independent contractor acting on behalf of the taxpayer or the utilization of tangible and intangible property by the taxpayer or by an agent or independent contractor acting on behalf of the taxpayer in performing a service.

— the sale, rental, leasing, licensing or other use of real property;

— the rental, leasing, licensing or other use of tangible personal property; and

— the sale, licensing or other use of intangible personal property.

Items excluded: The mere holding of intangible personal property was not, of itself, an income producing activity. (Reg. 25136, 18 CCR)

CCH Comment: *Treatment of Dividends*

According to the FTB, business income dividends constitute gross receipts that are generally includible in the recipient's sales factor. However, dividends are includible in the sales factor only when the holder engages in an activity that constitutes more than the mere holding of intangible property. The "mere holding" of intangible property does not constitute income producing activity. Income producing activity with respect to a dividend exists when there is participation in the management and/or the operations of the dividend payor. Moreover, the exercise of voting rights conferred by ownership of stock, the receipt and review of material normally supplied to a stockholder, and accounting for the receipt of dividend income do not constitute participation in the management and/or operations of the dividend payor. Consequently, such actions do not constitute income producing activity with respect to a dividend. (*FTB Legal Ruling 2003-3* (CCH CALIFORNIA TAX REPORTS, ¶403-576))

Definition of costs of performance.—California also followed the MTC apportionment regulations regarding the definition of costs of performance. The term "costs of performance" was defined to mean direct costs determined in a manner consistent with generally accepted accounting principles and in accordance with accepted conditions or practices in the trade or business of the person. Included in the taxpayer's costs of performance were the taxpayer's payments to an agent or independent contractor for the performance of personal services and utilization of tangible and intangible property which gave rise to the particular item of income. (Reg. 25136(c), 18 CCR)

Special rules.—Like the MTC apportionment regulations, California had special rules for determining when receipts from the performance of personal services and the rental, lease, or licensing of tangible personal property were sourced to the state.

Sale, rental, lease, or licensing of real property: Gross receipts from the sale, lease, rental or licensing of real property are in California if the real property is located in California. (Reg. 25136(d)(2)(A), 18 CCR)

Rental, lease, or licensing of tangible personal property: If the property was inside and outside California during the rental, lease or licensing period, gross receipts attributable to California were measured by the ratio of time the property was physically present or was used in California compared to the total time or use of the property everywhere during that period. (Reg. 25136(d)(2)(B), 18 CCR)

Performance of personal services: If personal services constituting a separate income producing activity were performed partly inside and partly outside California, the gross receipts from such services attributable to the state were measured by the ratio of time spent in performing the services in the state compared to the total time spent in performing the services everywhere. Time spent in performing services included the amount of time expended in the performance of a contract or other obligation giving rise to such gross receipts. Personal service not directly connected with the performance of the contract or other obligation, as for example, time expended in negotiating the contract, was excluded from the computations. (Reg. 25136(d)(2)(C), 18 CCR)

In *Chief Counsel Ruling 2012-01*, CCH CALIFORNIA TAX REPORTS, ¶ 11-525.70, the FTB advises a corporate taxpayer that specialized in matching customers with Internet publishers to have its customers' advertising published on websites that reach its customers' targeted audiences that it could treat its customers' billing addresses as the customers' commercial domicile for purposes of determining where the income-producing activity occurred. The contracts with the publishers and the customers did not contain information as to where the services were to be performed, and the taxpayer's records did not contain information as to where the customers' domicile was located. Consequently, the FTB issued a ruling authorizing the taxpayer to use its customers' billing addresses as its customers' commercial domicile for purposes of determining where the income-producing activity occurred.

Practitioner Comment: "Personal Services" Defined for Sales Factor Purposes

The FTB issued Legal Ruling 2005-1, March 21, 2005, CCH CALIFORNIA TAX REPORTS, ¶ 403-772, explaining that the term "personal services" for purposes of apportioning gross receipts, using an income-producing activity standard, includes any service performed where capital is not a material income-producing factor. Furthermore, personal services are not limited to professional services or to specialized services performed by one individual.

As the ruling explains, California regulations generally require a taxpayer to apportion receipts using a "time spread" method where the contract between a taxpayer and its customer calls for a personal service, where capital is not a material income-producing factor, and where the corporation performs the contracted-for services utilizing the labor of its employees with little or no utilization of tangible or intangible property. The time spread method requires a taxpayer to treat the time each employee, including the project manager, spends in each state as a separate income-producing activity for purposes of determining the numerator of the sales factor.

In a situation in which capital is a material income-producing factor, the special time-spread rule does not apply. Instead, the standard cost of performance rule would assign the receipts to the state with the greatest cost of performance.

Note that on November 6, 2012, California voters approved Proposition 39, which now makes the single sales factor mandatory for most multistate taxpayers (other than those engaged in specified industries) and requires market sourcing for all multistate businesses other than cable companies (for which special rules are provided) effective for years beginning on or after January 1, 2013.

Chris Whitney, Contributing Editor

Services performed on behalf of the taxpayer: An income-producing activity performed on behalf of a taxpayer by an agent or independent contractor was attributed to California if the income-producing activity was in California. The income-producing activity was in California if the taxpayer could reasonably determine at the time of filing its return that all of the income-producing activity was actually performed in California by the agent or independent contractor. For services performed on behalf of the taxpayer both inside and outside California, the following cascading rules applied for purposes of determining whether the income-producing activity was performed in California:

— The income-producing activity was assigned to California if the terms of the contract between the taxpayer and the agent/independent contractor or the taxpayer's records indicated the services were to be performed in California and the portion of the payment to the agent/independent contract associated with the performance in California could be determined under the contract.

— If the location of the income producing activity could not by determined under the rules above, the location of the income producing activity was assigned to California if the terms of the contract between the taxpayer and the taxpayer's customer or the taxpayer's records indicated that the activity was to be performed in California and the portion of the taxpayer's payment to the agent or independent contractor associated with the performance in California could be determined under the contract.

— If the location of the income producing activity could not by determined under the rules above, the location of the income producing activity was assigned to California if the taxpayer's customer's domicile/commercial domicile was in California.

— If the location of the income producing activity could not by determined under the rules above and the customer's domicile could not be determined, the income-producing activity performed on behalf of the taxpayer was disregarded in determining the taxpayer's income-producing activity.

(Reg. 25136(d)(3), 18 CCR)

Practitioner Comment: *Treatment of Combined Reporting Group Members*

In FTB *Legal Ruling 2006-02*, May 3, 2006, CCH California Tax Reports, ¶404-008, the FTB explained that the activities performed by one member of a combined reporting group "on behalf of" another member of the same combined reporting group will be considered in determining the income producing activity of the other member of the combined reporting group for sales factor purposes.

Although prior to its amendment in 2010, Reg. 25136(b), 18 CCR, always excluded from the definition of the term "income producing activity" those activities performed on behalf of a taxpayer, such as those performed by an independent contractor, the FTB takes the position that the "on behalf of" rule cannot exclude all possible actors who perform services on behalf of a taxpayer. Because a corporation is an artificial legal entity that can only act through its members, officers, or agents, someone must perform acts on its behalf.

For many years the FTB has argued that the term "taxpayer" refers to a specific legal entity, not the combined reporting group as a whole. However, in this ruling, the FTB acknowledges that the several elements of a unitary business are treated as one unit for taxation purposes. According to the FTB, it would be inconsistent to disregard the activity of one member of the combined reporting group in determining the income producing activity of another because such activities are directly proximate to the generation of the business income by the group.

However, for water's-edge elections, with respect to transactions with entities that are fully or partially excluded from the combined reporting group, the "on behalf of" rule would operate to exclude activities performed by such entities for purposes of determining where the greater costs of performance occurred.

Note that on November 6, 2012, California voters approved Proposition 39, which now makes the single sales factor mandatory for most multistate taxpayers (other than those engaged in specified industries) and requires market sourcing for multistate businesses other than cable companies (for which special rules are provided) effective for years beginning on or after January 1, 2013.

Chris Whitney, Contributing Editor

• *Throwback and throwout rules*

Sales of tangible personal property.—UDITPA and the MTC apportionment regulations provide an exception to the destination test that is referred to as the "throwback rule". California has a similar throwback rule under which sales of tangible personal property are in California if the property is shipped from an office, store, warehouse, factory or other place of storage in California and:

— the purchaser is the U.S. government; or

— the taxpayer is not taxable in the state of the purchaser.

(Sec. 25135(a), Rev. & Tax. Code)

Sales to the U.S. government include only sales for which the government makes direct payment to the seller under a contract with the seller; in other words, only prime contracts are included and subcontract sales are excluded. (Sec. 25135(b), Rev. & Tax. Code)

A taxpayer is taxable in another state if

— in that state it is subject to a net income tax, a franchise tax measured by net income, a franchise tax for the privilege of doing business, or a corporate stock tax, or

— that state has jurisdiction to subject the taxpayer to a net income tax regardless of whether, in fact, the state does or does not.

(Sec. 25122, Rev. & Tax. Code)

A taxpayer must provide proof that it is subject to one of the enumerated taxes upon the FTB's request. A taxpayer is not considered subject to one of the enumerated taxes if it voluntary files and pays one of the taxes or pays a minimal fee for qualifying to do business in that state but

— does not actually engage in business activity in that state, or

— does actually engage in some business activity, not sufficient for nexus, and the minimum tax bears no relation to the taxpayer's business activity.

(Reg. 25122(b), 18 CCR)

Jurisdiction to tax is not present if the state is prohibited from imposing the tax because of P.L. 86-272. Special rules for determining whether a taxpayer is subject to tax in another state apply to combined reporting group members, see ¶1310.

CCH Pointer: Sales to Foreign Jurisdictions

A taxpayer is subject to tax in a foreign jurisdiction if the taxpayer's activity would be sufficient to subject the taxpayer to such a tax under the constitution or statutes of the United States or a state of the United States. (Reg. 25122(c), 18 CCR; FTB Chief Counsel Ruling 2012-01 (CCH CALIFORNIA TAX REPORTS, ¶405-723))

Practitioner Comment: Interplay Between Throwback and Economic Nexus Provisions

The FTB issued Chief Counsel Ruling 2012-03 to provide guidance on the interplay between California's provisions on throwback sales and the economic nexus standard that became effective January 1, 2011. The FTB concluded that a California taxpayer is not required to throwback sales from jurisdictions in which the taxpayer meets the sales thresholds articulated in California's factor presence provision at Cal. Rev. & Tax. Code §23101. A taxpayer is deemed to be doing business in California if its sales exceed the lesser of $500,000 (as adjusted for inflation) or 25% of the taxpayer's total sales. Therefore, taxpayers that meet the factor presence standard of doing business in foreign jurisdictions are taxable for purposes of the throwback provisions. The chief counsel ruling also clarified that because California reverted back to a *Finnigan* approach, throwback is not required to the extent any member of the combined group has nexus in the destination state.

FTB also concluded in Technical Advice Memorandum (TAM) 2012-01 that for years prior to January 1, 2011, a taxpayer was not taxable for purpose of throwback where it met the sales thresholds articulated in California's factor presence provision at Cal. Rev. & Tax. Code §23101. Instead, FTB concluded that taxpayers must demonstrate physical presence in the destination jurisdiction to avoid throwback.

Under Cal. Rev. & Tax. Code §25122 and Cal. Code Reg. § 25122(c), a taxpayer is taxable in another state if it is either subject to and pays tax, or the other state is constitutionally permitted to impose tax, but does not. Regarding the latter, the TAM analyzed a few cases (e.g., *Quill Corporation v. North Dakota*, 504 U.S. 298 (1992); Appeal of Dresser Industries, Inc., 82-SBE-307, June 29, 1982, rehearing 83-SBE-118) in concluding that California historically required physical presence to establish substantial nexus (i.e., taxability) under the Commerce Clause for U.S. Constitutional standards. The TAM then explained that the amendment to Cal. Rev. & Tax. Code § 23101 fundamentally changed the taxability standard from physical presence to the factor presence standard.

The TAM may be susceptible to challenge. Assuming for the sake of argument, that California's factor presence nexus statute is constitutional to begin with, the destination jurisdiction could theoretically have imposed similar nexus standards in years prior to the effective date of California's adoption of these provisions in 2011. Because throwback does not apply when the other state is constitutionally permitted to impose tax, but does not, it is unclear why the new nexus standard would not apply for purposes of throwback in years prior to 2011.

In the *Appeal of Craigslist, Inc.*, through a decision rendered on January 15, 2016, the California Board of Equalization held that for tax years prior to the economic nexus standard in 2011, physical presence was required for a taxpayer to be taxable in a state under Cal. Rev. & Tax. Code § 25122. (*Appeal of Craigslist, Inc.*, Cal. St. Bd. of Equal. January 15, 2015). In this appeal, Craigslist had entered into a determination letter with the FTB agreeing to use an alternative apportionment methodology, and also requiring "throw-out" instead of "throw-back." The throw-out provisions would apply to sales into states where Craigslist was not taxable under "United States constitutional standards for nexus." The Taxpayer argued that because the "doing business" standard under Cal. Rev. & Tax. Code § 23101 required an economic nexus standard, it must be constitutional, and should also allow for the use of an economic nexus standard when determining whether Craigslist was taxable in other states for years prior to 2011. The Board pointed to reliance concerns and a reluctance to rule on constitutional issues when it held that physical presence was required as the constitutional standard for taxability in these years. The Board declined to address whether this decision also cast doubt on the constitutionality of Cal. Rev. & Tax. Code § 23101 and economic nexus in tax years beginning on or after January 1, 2011.

In this regard, it is worth noting that the question of whether physical presence is required in order for a state to impose an income tax on an out of state taxpayer has been litigated in many states over the years (see e.g., *Geoffrey, Inc. v. South Carolina*, 437 S.E.2d 13 (1992); *Lanco, Inc. v. Div. of Tax'n*, 908 A.2d 176 (N.J. 2006)). While most of the state courts that have addressed this issue have concluded that physical presence is not required in this context, the U.S. Supreme Court has not directly addressed this issue since the aforementioned decision in *Quill* involved use tax collection, not income tax.

Chris Whitney, Contributing Editor

Sales to U.S. government.—For sales factor purposes, California regards sales of property to the U.S. government as sales made in California if the property is shipped or delivered from California, regardless of delivery destination. (Sec. 25135(a), Rev. & Tax. Code)

Sales of tangible personal property to a contractor for use in an item for ultimate sale to the government do not qualify as sales to the U.S. government and are not necessarily included in the sales factor numerator as California sales. (Reg. 25135, 18 CCR)

The cost, as well as the fee, in a cost-plus-fee contract with the U.S. government is considered to be a sale includable in the sales factor numerator. (Reg. 25134, 18 CCR)

Occasional sales.—The occasional sale of a fixed asset or other property held or used in a taxpayer's trade or business is excluded from the sales factor. For example, the gross receipts from the sale of a factory, patent, or affiliate's stock are excluded if the receipts are "substantial." Sales of assets to the same purchaser in a single year are aggregated to determine if the combined receipts are substantial. For purposes of this rule, a sale is substantial if its exclusion results in a 5% or greater decrease in the sales factor denominator of the taxpayer or, if the taxpayer is part of a combined reporting group, a 5% or greater decrease in the sales factor denominator of the group as a whole. Also, for purposes of this rule, a sale is occasional if the transaction is outside of the taxpayer's normal course of business and occurs infrequently. (Reg. 25137(c)(1)(A), 18 CCR)

In *Appeal of Imperial, Inc.* (2010) (CCH CALIFORNIA TAX REPORTS, ¶11-525.34), the BOE ruled that the gross proceeds from goodwill on the sale of a corporation's assets were properly excluded from the sales factor because substantial amounts of the gross receipts arose from an infrequent, occasional sale of property used in the business. Furthermore, it was improper to source such gains solely to Wisconsin, where the corporation's headquarters was located, because the goodwill was inseparable from the corporation's business activities in all of the states where it had operations.

Gross receipts were excluded from the sales factor for the sale of a line of business in *FTB Chief Counsel Ruling 2015-01*(CCH CALIFORNIA TAX REPORTS, ¶11-525.401). The sale qualified as "substantial" because excluding the sale receipts from the taxpayer's sales factor denominator decreased that denominator by approximately 33%. The taxpayer sold an entire line of business in an effort to focus on its other line of business. This was apparently the only time that the taxpayer disposed of an entire line of business. Because the sale was outside the course of the taxpayer's normal business operations and it occurred infrequently, the sale was "occasional."

Practitioner Comment: Gross Receipts Excluded From the Sales Factor Under the Occasional Sale Rule Must Meet Two Subjective Criteria

The FTB in *Chief Counsel Ruling 2014-02*, June 3, 2014, CCH CALIFORNIA TAX REPORTS, ¶406-186, concluded that gross receipts from a series of eight asset sale transactions in a two-year time frame by a taxpayer while implementing a Plan of Reorganization under Chapter 11 bankruptcy were within the taxpayer's normal course of business and occurred frequently. Therefore, those receipts were not excluded from the sales factor under the occasional sale rule of CCR Sec. 25137(c)(1)(A). In order to be excluded under this provision, a sale must be both "substantial" and "occasional."

CCR Sec. 25137(c)(1)(A)(1) defines a sale as "substantial" if its exclusion results in a 5% or greater decrease in the sales factor denominator of the taxpayer or, if the taxpayer is part of a combined reporting group, a five percent or greater decrease in the sales factor denominator of the group as a whole. The determinative factor in the ruling was whether the sale was "occasional," which is an issue of facts and circumstances. The FTB explained that in order to be "occasional" under the regulation, the sale must be both (i) outside of the taxpayer's normal course of business, and (ii) occur infrequently.

The ruling explained that in order to accomplish the goal of the Plan of Reorganization, the "negotiation and implementation of asset sale transactions became part of [the][t]axpayer's normal course of business." Since the assets sales did not occur outside of the taxpayer's normal course of business, they were not "occasional sales" within the meaning of CCR Sec. 25137(c)(1)(A)(2) and therefore must be included in the taxpayer's sales factor.

According to the ruling, the determination of whether a sale is "occasional" is an issue of facts and circumstances, which means that the determination is subjective in nature. While *Chief Counsel Ruling 2014-02* concluded that the taxpayer's series of asset sale transactions became the normal course of business under the Plan of Reorganization, other taxpayers may not have a documented plan to sell assets and a record demonstrating a regular and systematic series of transactions. As a result, they may find it more difficult to satisfy the subjective criteria that a sale occurred in the ordinary course of business. There is also relevant litigation to consider. During the hearing for the *Appeal of Emmis Communications Corp.*, SBE Case No. 547964, June 11, 2013, CCH CALIFORNIA TAX REPORTS, ¶406-016, an unpublished State Board of Equalization decision, the arguments focused on the number of sales (but not purchases) that the taxpayer engaged in to determine whether the sales were a regular part of its business. In *ComCon Production Services I, Inc. v. California Franchise Tax Board*, Los Angeles Superior Ct, No. BC489779, March 6, 2014, CCH CALIFORNIA TAX REPORTS, ¶406-243, however, the court looked at both purchase and sales transactions in determining that significant acquisitive activity can become part of a taxpayer's regular trade or business for purposes of the transactional test for business income.

Chris Whitney, Contributing Editor

Incidental transactions.—Inconsequential gross receipts arising from an incidental transaction need not be included in the sales factor unless they would materially affect the amount of income apportioned to California. (Reg. 25137(c)(1)(A), 18 CCR; Reg. 25137(c)(1)(B), 18 CCR)

Income from intangibles.—If business income from intangible property cannot easily be attributed to a particular income-producing activity of the taxpayer, then the income is excluded from both the numerator and the denominator of the sales factor. For example, income produced from the mere holding of intangible personal property, such as bonds, government securities, and royalties on patents and copyrights, is excluded from both the numerator and the denominator of the sales factor. (Reg. 25137(c)(1)(C), 18 CCR) Similarly, dividends received form a taxpayers passive investment in a company are excluded from the sales factor. (*FTB Legal Ruling 2003-3* (2003), CCH CALIFORNIA TAX REPORTS, ¶403-576)

Treasury function income and receipts.—Under Reg. 25137(c)(1)(D), "treasury function" income and receipts are excluded from the sales factor. This includes interest, dividends, gross receipts and net gains, as well as receipts and gains from foreign currency hedging activity (but not hedging related to price risk of products consumed or produced by the taxpayer). A "treasury function" is defined as any pooling, managing and investing of or intangible assets for the purpose of satisfying the cash flow needs of the business. Taxpayers principally engaged in an intangible activity such as registered broker dealers and financial institutions are excluded.

Prior to California's adoption of a statutory definition of "gross receipts" and the adoption of Reg. Sec. 25137(c)(1)(D), the issue of how to treat short-term investments made by a multi-state corporation's treasury department generated a host of litigation, with taxpayers contending that all income from such investments, including return of principal, should be included in the sales factor denominator. The California Supreme Court weighed in on this issue, holding that the sales factor included all gross receipts from the sale and redemption of securities, but included only the interest income from repurchase agreements. In reaching its decisions, the Court looked to the economic reality of the transactions to determine whether the total proceeds should be included in gross receipts. In situations in which the money is received in exchange for a commodity, such as the redemption of a security, the full price was to be treated as gross receipts. (*Microsoft Corp. v. Franchise Tax Board* (2006) (CCH CALIFORNIA TAX REPORTS, ¶404-043)) In contrast, if the income was received in exchange for the use of money, such as in the case of a repurchase agreement, only the interest, not the principal, was a gross receipt. (*General Motors Corp. v. Franchise Tax Board*, (2006) (CCH CALIFORNIA TAX REPORTS, ¶404-044) A California appellate court reached a similar conclusion in *The Limited Stores, Inc. v. Franchise Tax Board* (2005) (CCH CALIFORNIA TAX REPORTS, ¶403-819)).

Although the California Supreme Court determined that total proceeds received from redemptions of securities should be included in gross receipts for sales factor purposes, the Court found that in the *Microsoft* case the FTB proved that including the receipts in the denominator was distortive. In so holding, the Court stated that "the party attempting to invoke the Revenue and Taxation Section 25137 alternative apportionment provision had the burden of proving by clear and convincing evidence that (1) the approximation provided by the standard formula is not a fair representation, and (2) its proposed alternative is reasonable." Microsoft's short-term investments produced less than 2% of the company's income, but 73% of its gross receipts. Inclusion of these receipts in the sales factor resulted in severely diminishing the impact of Microsoft's activities in those states in which the treasury department was not located and overemphasizing the impact of the business's activities in the state where its treasury department was located.

In its decision in *Microsoft Corp.*, the Court fell short of ruling that equitable apportionment would be proper in all instances involving short-term treasury investments and called on the California Legislature to address this issue, which it did in its statutory definition of gross receipts. The court noted that absent a global redefinition of gross receipts to exclude such returns, smaller distortions insufficient to trigger a reappraisal under the equitable apportionment provision could slip through the cracks, resulting in underestimation of the tax owed California. In fact, in its decision in *General Motors Corp.*, the Court remanded this issue to the appellate court to determine if there was indeed unreasonable distortion and if the FTB's approach was reasonable.

The California Supreme Court instructed two California courts of appeal to vacate their prior decisions in *Toys "R" Us, Inc. v. Franchise Tax Board* (2006) (CCH CALIFORNIA TAX REPORTS, ¶ 403-996) and *The Limited Stores, Inc. v. Franchise Tax Board* (2005) (CCH CALIFORNIA TAX REPORTS, ¶ 403-819), and to reconsider the cases in light of the decisions in *Microsoft* and *General Motors*. (*Toys "R" Us, Inc. v. Franchise Tax Board*, California Supreme Court, No. S143422, November 15, 2006; *The Limited Stores. v. Franchise Tax Board*, California Supreme Court, No. S136922, November 15, 2006) On remand, the court of appeals in the *Limited Stores, Inc.* applied reasoning similar to the California Supreme Court's reasoning in *Microsoft Corp.* to find that an alternative apportionment calculation should be applied and should only include the net income from the taxpayer's short term investments in the sales factor calculation. (*The Limited Stores, Inc. v. Franchise Tax Board* (2007) (CCH CALIFORNIA TAX REPORTS, ¶ 404-295))

In *General Mills, Inc. & Subsidiaries v. Franchise Tax Board*, (2009) CCH CALIFORNIA TAX REPORTS, ¶ 404-894, a California court of appeal ruled that commodity futures sales that were made to hedge against price fluctuations in the agricultural materials used in a cereal company's manufacturing operations should be included in the taxpayer's sales factor for purposes of apportioning the taxpayer's business income to California. Because all the sales took place outside of California, including them increased the denominator of the taxpayer's sales factor and reduced its California taxes. The court held that the full sales price of these futures contracts constituted gross receipts includable in the sales factor during the tax years at issue, but remanded the case back to the trial court to determine whether a distortion adjustment under Rev. & Tax. Code Sec. 25137 was appropriate. The California Supreme Court denied review of the case.

Practitioner Comment: General Mills Potentially Expands Application of Alternative Apportionment

In *General Mills, Inc. v. FTB*, 146 Cal.Rptr.3d 475, 208 Cal.App.4th 1290 (2012), CCH CALIFORNIA TAX REPORTS, ¶ 405-705, on appeal from the trial court's decision on remand, the California Court of Appeal held that General Mills's hedging transactions did not "fairly represent" its California business activity and therefore the FTB was permitted to apply an alternative apportionment methodology that included only net gains (as opposed to gross receipts) received from its hedging transactions. The court concluded that although the hedging transactions were integral to General Mills's main consumer foods business, the hedging transactions did not fairly represent General Mills activities in California because (1) the hedging transactions were qualitatively different from General Mills's business of selling consumer food products, and (2) inclusion of the gross receipts in General Mills's sales factor substantially distorted the percentage of its California income.

The court's decision seemed to broadly expand the circumstances where distortion may exist. *General Mills* found substantial distortion to exist where the percentage reduction in the standard apportionment figure ranged from 3.6% (TYE 1993) to 13.9% (TYE 1996), or an average of 8.2%. The court explained "[c]learly, the ultimate impact on the standard formula here is less severe than in the treasury cases. However, the case law does not indicate that this quantitative metric, or any one metric, alone is dispositive." Historically, case law generally required a higher threshold of quantitative distortion to permit alternative apportionment in circumstances where the hedging activity was related to the taxpayer's main business as compared to hedging activity not core to the taxpayer's main business. In *Hans Rees' Sons*, one of the U.S. Supreme Court's original decisions in this area, the High Court found distortion where there was approximately 250% distortion from a quantitative perspective. In *Microsoft*, the California Supreme Court concluded that an approximate 50% reduction in tax due was distortive where the treasury function was qualitatively different from the taxpayer's main business. Conversely, in *Merrill Lynch*, the BOE found that because the treasury activity was related to the taxpayer's main business, 23% to 36% quantitative distortion was not sufficient to permit alternative apportionment.

In *General Mills*, even though the underlying commodities being hedged were integral to the taxpayer's business operations, the court nevertheless found that the hedging transactions were qualitatively different from General Mills's consumer product sales because they served only a supportive function and were not intended to make a profit. The court explained that hedging transactions served a "risk management function" unrelated to the selling of products to customers. The court stated that the profit margin was a key quantitative metric. As a result, there is some question regarding the degree to which in other circumstances the analysis should focus on profit margin. For example, the decision may have implications for taxpayers with otherwise unitary operations that have widely different profit margins.

Note that effective for taxable years beginning on or after January 1, 2011, Cal. Rev. & Tax. Code §25120(f)(2)(L) has been amended to explicitly exclude amounts received from hedging transactions from the sales factor.

Chris Whitney, Contributing Editor

A U.S. bankruptcy court applied similar reasoning in upholding the FTB's use of an alternative apportionment formula to exclude from a national restaurant chain's sales factor denominator any treasury gross receipts from commercial paper investments that constituted the return-of-principal amounts to the treasury, but not that portion that constituted interest income. The FTB established that use of the standard apportionment formula would result in qualitative distortion because the taxpayer's treasury functions were qualitatively different from its principal business of operating restaurants. The standard formula would also result in quantitative distortion because the taxpayer's margin quantitative difference (53 times) and income quantitative difference (treasury activities generated 77% of gross receipts but only 5.4% of income) fit well within ranges established by recent California court decisions. For the taxable years at issue, rote application of the standard apportionment formula would treat 77% of the operator's total sales as occurring in Minnesota and over 38.5% of the income as though it were apportioned only to Minnesota solely because the operator's three-person treasury department was located there. In addition, by using the standard formula for the taxable years at issue, the income apportioned to California would be reduced on average 40% and the operator's California franchise tax liability would be reduced on average 44%. Furthermore, the alternative formula was reasonable. The operator's net receipts from its treasury activities ($15.1 million) were quite small in comparison to its non-treasury income ($233 million) and its gross receipts ($5.5 billion). (*Buffets, Inc. v. California Franchise Tax Board* (2011), CCH CALIFORNIA TAX REPORTS, ¶405-491)

In a nonprecedential corporation franchise tax letter decision, the State Board of Equalization (BOE) concluded that the FTB did not show by clear and convincing evidence that the inclusion of the gross receipts from the redemption of certain marketable securities in a taxpayer's apportionment formula sales factor resulted in distortion sufficient to invoke the alternative equitable apportionment provisions of Rev. &. Tax. Code Sec. 25137. Therefore, the BOE ordered that the action of the FTB in denying the taxpayer's claim for refund be reversed. The BOE did not state the specific basis for its decision. The hearing summary indicated that the taxpayer had calculated the gross receipts from its redemption of marketable securities as 3.3% of the total gross receipts of its unitary business, and had argued that any distortion was too insignificant to permit application of Sec. 25137. (*Appeal of Home Depot U.S.A., Inc.* (2008) CCH CALIFORNIA TAX REPORTS, ¶ 404-894, ¶ 404-820)

Outsourced investment services.—Investment services performed by unrelated third parties on behalf of a taxpayer are not considered income-producing activities of the taxpayers and, therefore, are excluded from both the sales factor numerator and denominator. (*FTB Chief Counsel Ruling 2007-2*, CCH CALIFORNIA TAX REPORTS, ¶ 404-331)

- *Effect of Public Law 86-272*

If the other state, territory, or country could tax the seller but does not actually do so, the seller is nevertheless deemed to be "taxable" there and sales shipped there from California are not attributable to California. On the other hand, when P.L. 86-272 (¶ 805) would preclude taxing of the seller by the other state, sales shipped from California are attributable ("thrown back") to California.

In Legal Ruling 99-1 (1999) (CCH CALIFORNIA TAX REPORTS, ¶ 10-105.75), the FTB ruled that a corporation's sales of tangible personal property shipped from California into Puerto Rico should be included in the corporation's sales factor for apportionment purposes because Puerto Rico had no authority to impose a tax on the corporation. The corporation was protected from Puerto Rico taxation under P.L. 86-272 because its activity there was limited to the solicitation of orders. Although a commonwealth, Puerto Rico was a destination state for purposes of P.L. 86-272.

In *McDonnell Douglas Corporation v. Franchise Tax Board* (1994) (CCH CALIFORNIA TAX REPORTS, ¶ 11-525.45), a California court of appeal held that an aircraft manufacturer was permitted to exclude from the California sales factor numerator of the apportionment formula its sales of aircraft that were destined for use outside California but that were delivered to purchasers in California.

However, in *Appeal of Mazda Motors of America, Inc.* (1994) (CCH CALIFORNIA TAX REPORTS, ¶ 11-525.451), the BOE held that an automobile importer's sales receipts for vehicles that the importer stored, assembled, serviced, repaired, and subsequently shipped to the purchaser in Texas were properly included in the numerator of the apportionment formula's sales factor for purposes of calculating the taxpayer's California taxable income. Unlike the situation in *McDonnell Douglas Corp.*, where the purchaser merely picked up the goods in this state for shipment to an out-of-state destination, the taxpayer exercised sufficient possession and control over the vehicles while they were in California to subject the goods to taxation by the state.

In *Appeal of Schwinn Sales West, Inc.* (1988) (CCH CALIFORNIA TAX REPORTS, ¶ 11-520.2099), the nonsolicitation activities in California of a regional sales manager of an Illinois bicycle manufacturer, along with the company's conducting of service schools for its California dealers, indicated that the company's activities were regular and systematic, exceeding protected solicitation.

In *Appeals of Foothill Publishing Co. and the Record Ledger, Inc.* (1986) (CCH CALIFORNIA TAX REPORTS, ¶ 11-525.818), the income derived by two California publishers for printing Nevada and Arizona publications was "thrown back" under prior law to California because under P.L. 86-272 neither Nevada nor Arizona could tax the publishers. The only business activity in those states was the solicitation of orders that were sent outside the state for approval and then delivered from California.

In *Appeal of Union Carbide Corporation* (1984) (CCH CALIFORNIA TAX REPORTS, ¶ 11-525.8192), the taxpayer's subsidiaries sold its products in various foreign countries. The taxpayer contended that it would have been taxable in those countries except for certain tax treaties; however, it did not offer any evidence that the foreign activities were extensive enough to subject it to the tax jurisdiction of the foreign countries. The BOE held that the foreign sales were properly "thrown back" to California under prior law.

In *Appeal of The Olga Company* (1984) (CCH CALIFORNIA TAX REPORTS, ¶ 11-525.8191), the taxpayer shipped its products from California to more than 30 other states. Although the taxpayer did not pay income taxes in the other states, it contended that the other states had jurisdiction to tax because of the taxpayer's extensive sales activities. The BOE held that the sales in other states should be "thrown back" to California under prior law.

In *Appeal of Dresser Industries* (1982) (CCH CALIFORNIA TAX REPORTS, ¶ 11-525.817), the taxpayer sold its products in Japan through several subsidiaries. The BOE held that these sales could not be attributed ("thrown back") to California under prior law, because the FTB did not show that Japan lacked jurisdiction to tax the parent corporation. The BOE held that the criteria of P.L. 86-272 could not be applied, because P.L. 86-272 does not apply to foreign commerce. See also the opinion on rehearing in this case.

In *Appeals of Learner Co. et al.* (1980) (CCH CALIFORNIA TAX REPORTS, ¶ 11-520.43), the taxpayer shipped scrap metal to customers in Japan. The taxpayer contended that it would have been taxable by Japan if the standards of P.L. 86-272 had been applicable there. The BOE held that the taxpayer would not have been taxable by Japan, and that the sales to Japan were properly assigned to California for purposes of the allocation formula.

In *Hoffmann-La Roche, Inc. v. Franchise Tax Board* (1980) (CCH CALIFORNIA TAX REPORTS, ¶ 11-525.57), the taxpayer questioned the constitutionality of the rule involving P.L. 86-272 discussed above. The FTB attributed to California sales that were shipped from California to certain other states, in which states the taxpayer (seller) was not taxable. A federal appellate court upheld the constitutionality of the rule.

Practitioner Comment: Total Receipts, Including Sales of Tangible Personal Property Otherwise Protected by P.L. 86-272, Considered for Purposes of Avoiding Throwback

The FTB issued Chief Counsel Ruling 2016-03 (2016) (CCH CALIFORNIA TAX REPORTS, ¶ 11-515.88), to provide guidance with respect to whether the proceeds from the sale of tangible personal property (TPP) must be aggregated with royalties received from California licensees to determine whether a taxpayer has economic nexus with the state. Additionally, the ruling addressed whether a third-party licensee's use of the taxpayer's trademarks that gives rise to royalties exceeds P.L. 86-272 protections for purposes of throwing back sales of TPP in other states.

The Chief Counsel ruled that the proceeds from the sales of TPP must be aggregated with the royalty income to determine if the taxpayer meets California's "doing business" standard under Rev. & Tax. Code Sec. 23101(b)(2). The analysis in the ruling applies to taxable years beginning on or after January 1, 2011, but does not apply to taxable years beginning prior to that date.

In addition, the Chief Counsel ruled that, where a taxpayer's aggregate sales of tangible personal property and royalties exceed California's doing business threshold, and the taxpayer's activities exceed P.L. 86-272 protection in such states, the taxpayer should not throw back to its California sales factor numerator sales of tangible property to such states. The ruling clarifies that royalties received for a third-party's use of licensed trademarks in other states is not an activity protected by P.L. 86-272 where the taxpayer purposefully avails itself of the market in that state.

The ruling suggests that a relatively small amount of unprotected licensing or service receipts coupled with otherwise P.L. 86-272-protected tangible personal property sales would constitute being "subject to tax" in the other state such that throwback would be avoided. Although not addressed in the ruling, by implication, an out of state company would appear to be subject to California tax on the same basis.

Chris Whitney, Contributing Editor

• *Installment sales*

In Legal Ruling No. 413 (1979) (CCH CALIFORNIA TAX REPORTS, ¶12-525.35), the FTB ruled that an apportioning corporation reporting a sale on the installment basis should include the total sales price in the sales factor in the year of sale, and should apportion the installment income each year according to the apportionment percentage of the year of sale.

• *Cost-plus contracts*

In *Appeal of Bechtel Power Corporation, et al.* (1997) (CCH CALIFORNIA TAX REPORTS, ¶11-525.71), the BOE ruled that in order to accurately reflect the taxpayer's economic activities in California, client-furnished materials used to fulfill a "cost-plus" contract were required to be included in the taxpayer's sales factor for apportionment purposes.

• *Special rules and decisions*

The FTB has developed special rules for the sales factor in some unusual industry situations. In the case of sea transportation companies, income from carrying cargo is attributed to California under a formula based on "voyage days" (see also ¶1307).

In *Appeal of Royal Crown Cola Co.* (1974) (CCH CALIFORNIA TAX REPORTS, ¶12-525.54), the taxpayer argued for a novel computation of the sales factor. The taxpayer contended that to avoid a distorted result, the sales of certain subsidiaries should be excluded from the sales factor and intercompany sales of the parent to the subsidiaries (normally eliminated) should be included instead. The BOE held against the taxpayer, citing several of the cases discussed above at ¶1304 and emphasizing the broad discretion vested in the FTB in apportionment matters.

• *Patent infringement awards*

In an informal decision that cannot be cited as precedent, the BOE followed the North Carolina Supreme Court's ruling in *Polaroid Corp. v. Offerman*, 349 N.C. 290 (1998), and held that the proceeds from a patent infringement lawsuit constituted unrealized lost profits that were apportionable business income rather than nonbusiness income allocable to the taxpayer's state of domicile. In so ruling, the BOE adopted the North Carolina Supreme Court's reasoning that it was irrelevant whether the income was received in the courtroom vs. the marketplace (*Appeal of Polaroid Corp.* (2003) (CCH CALIFORNIA TAX REPORTS, ¶10-075.92)). The BOE granted the appellant's petition for rehearing in this case (*Appeal of Polaroid Corp.* (2004) (CCH CALIFORNIA TAX REPORTS, ¶11-525.60)), but the appeal was dismissed and a stipulated agreement was entered on August 25, 2004.

¶1310 Affiliated Corporations—Combined Reporting

Law: Secs. 23801, 25101.15, 25101, 25102, 25104-05, 25106.5 (CCH CALIFORNIA TAX REPORTS, ¶10-640, 11-520, 11-540, 11-545, 11-550).

Comparable Federal: None.

California Forms: Form 100 (California Corporation Franchise or Income Tax Return), FTB 3544 (Election to Assign Credit Within Combined Reporting Group), FTB 3726 (Deferred Intercompany Stock Account (DISA) and Capital Gains Information).

As explained at ¶812, California law specifically provides for the filing of consolidated franchise tax returns only by certain railroad corporations. However, when a group of corporations conducts a unitary business (discussed at ¶1304), members of the group are generally required to file a combined report if the unitary activities are carried on within and without California. (Sec. 25102, Rev. & Tax. Code)

Practitioner Comment: Permitting Only Intrastate Unitary Taxpayers to Elect Separate or Combined Reporting Deemed Facially Discriminatory

The California Court of Appeal, Fourth District, in *Harley-Davidson, Inc. v. Franchise Tax Board*, 237 Cal.App.4th 193 (2015) (CCH CALIFORNIA TAX REPORTS, ¶406-342), held that a California statute which permits controlled groups of otherwise unitary companies which operate entirely within the state (i.e., intrastate unitary groups) to elect whether to file on a separate accounting or combined reporting basis was facially discriminatory since the election is not made available to unitary groups of companies operating across state lines (i.e., interstate combined groups).

The court remanded the case back to the trial court to determine whether the statute withstands strict scrutiny (i.e., whether it advances a legitimate local purpose that cannot be adequately served by reasonable nondiscriminatory alternatives).

Pursuant to Sec. 25101.15, Rev. & Tax. Code, intrastate unitary groups are permitted to elect either combined reporting or separate entity reporting. However, Sec. 25101, Rev. & Tax. Code, requires interstate unitary groups to file on a combined basis. In order to determine whether the tax scheme at issue was unconstitutionally discriminatory under the Commerce Clause, the court explained that it must determine whether:

> — the relevant aspect of California's tax scheme treats intrastate and interstate unitary businesses differently;

> — any differential treatment discriminates against interstate commerce either by benefiting intrastate businesses or burdening interstate businesses; and

> — any discriminatory differential treatment withstands strict scrutiny.

The court stated that the FTB "effectively concede[d] in its briefing that the differential-treatment prong is satisfied." For the second prong, the court discussed "[m]any federal, California, and out-of-state cases," including *Cutler v. Franchise Tax Board*, 208 Cal. App. 4th 1247 (Cal. App. Ct. 2012), *Ceridian Corp. v. Franchise Tax Board*, 85 Cal. App. 4th (Cal. App. Ct. 2000), and *Farmer Bros. Co. v. Franchise Tax Board*, 108 Cal. App. 4th 976 (Cal. App. Ct. 2003), and concluded "[a] reading of the foregoing cases leads to the unavoidable conclusion that California's statutory scheme for determining how unitary businesses compute their California tax liability discriminates on its face on the basis of an interstate element in violation of the commerce clause." (internal citations and quotation mark omitted) The court explained, "whether a unitary business computes its California tax liability using the separate accounting method or the combined reporting method is determined solely by where the unitary business engages in commerce."

Finally, since the FTB argued for the first time on appeal that the scheme withstands strict scrutiny, the court determined the record was not sufficiently developed to determine whether the FTB "identified a legitimate reason for differentiating between and discriminating against intrastate and interstate unitary businesses and, if so, whether that legitimate reason can be adequately served by reasonable nondiscriminatory alternatives." (internal citations and quotation mark omitted) As a result, the court remanded the case back to the trial court to make these determinations.

The strict scrutiny standard is a high hurdle to clear, making very real the possibility that the Court of Appeal or California Supreme Court upon review may ultimately conclude that the statute impermissibly violates the Commerce Clause and is invalid, raising the significant question as to what legal remedy might result. In prior cases where California statutes have been struck down as unconstitutional (e.g., the aforementioned *Cutler*, *Abbott Labs* and *Ceridian* decisions), the statute has been declared null and void prospectively and for all years considered open under the normal four year statute of limitations for assessment at the time the final decision was rendered. In those other cases, refunds were allowed to taxpayers who filed claims asserting nondiscriminatory application of the statute for years considered beyond the four year SOL at such time. Accordingly, multistate taxpayers should evaluate the impact of filing on a separate vs. combined basis and, if filing separately would be beneficial, consider filing refund claims on this basis.

Regarding the separate nexus issue on appeal, the court found in favor of the state and held that two corporations with no California physical presence had substantial nexus with California due to the activities of an in-state affiliate (see Practitioner Comment at ¶804). The California Supreme Court denied Harley Davidson's petition for review of the appellate court decision on the nexus issue, and did not address the lower court's separate finding that California's combined reporting scheme facially discriminates against interstate commerce, which was remanded back to the trial court to determine whether California can justify its discrimination under the strict scrutiny test.

On October 31, 2016, the San Diego Superior Court ruled on summary judgment that allowing only intrastate unitary taxpayers to make a separate or combined filing election did not violate the Commerce Clause. The court concluded that even if the election discriminated against interstate commerce, the differential treatment withstood strict scrutiny because the state has a "valid interest in preventing the manipulation and hiding of taxable income" and there was no reasonable nondiscriminatory alternative that would adequately serve the state's interest. (*Harley-Davidson, Inc. v. Franchise Tax Board*, Sup. Ct. of Cal., San Diego County, Minute Order, No. 37-2011-00100846-CU-MC-CTL, October 31, 2016, CCH CALIFORNIA TAX REPORTS, ¶406-587)

The court's conclusion that no nondiscriminatory alternative is available is suspect in light of the number of states which currently employ "separate filing" as opposed to "combined filing" and rely on arm's length pricing under IRC Sec. 482 and other means to ensure that the income and apportionment factors reported to the state are appropriate. Indeed, the FTB itself has these means at its disposal, given that California both adopts IRC Sec. 482 and the FTB is given additional authority to require combined reporting or make other adjustments among commonly controlled entities "in order to reflect the proper income of any such persons." See CRTC Sec. 25102.

Thus, the expansive nature of the FTB's arguments and the trial court's determination are at risk, particularly in light of the above nondiscriminatory alternatives already at hand, of being overturned by the California Court of Appeal, should Harley appeal.

Chris Whitney, Contributing Editor

The combined report shows the manner in which the unitary business apportions and allocates its income to California and to other states in which it does business, but should not be equated with a combined group return (discussed at ¶1313). Members of a unitary group deriving income solely from California sources may elect to file a combined return, but are not required to do so; such an election must be made annually. When computing the elements of sales, property, and payroll for a combined report, some intercompany transactions must be eliminated (see discussion below).

While Franchise Tax Board (FTB) Publication 1061, Guidelines for Corporations Filing a Combined Report, indicates that combined reporting is required whenever a unitary business conducts unitary activities both within and without the state, the applicable statutes state that combined reporting is generally required only if the corporations are members of a "commonly controlled group." A "commonly controlled group" is any of the following:

— a group of corporations connected through stock ownership (or constructive ownership) if the parent corporation owns stock possessing more than 50% of the voting power of at least one corporation and, if applicable, the parent or one or more of the other corporations own stock cumulatively representing more than 50% of the voting power of each of the corporations (other than the parent);

— any two or more corporations if stock representing more than 50% of the voting power of the corporations is owned (or constructively owned) by one person;

— any two or more corporations if more than 50% of the ownership or beneficial ownership of the stock possessing voting power in each corporation consists of stapled interests; or

— any two or more corporations if stock representing more than 50% of the voting power of the corporations is cumulatively owned (without regard to constructive ownership) by, or for the benefit of, members of the same family.

(Sec. 25105, Rev. & Tax. Code)

¶1310

A corporation eligible to be a member of more than one commonly controlled group must elect to be a member of a single group. Such membership will be terminated when stock of the corporation is sold, exchanged, or otherwise disposed of, unless the corporation meets the requirements for being a member of the same commonly controlled group within a two-year period.

A corporation that is a partner in a partnership that is part of a unitary business is not required to own more than 50% of the partnership before the partnership may be included in a combined report. Because the partnership is not a separate taxable entity, its income and apportionment factors are included only to the extent of the corporate partner's percentage of ownership interest. See cases cited at ¶1304.

Practitioner Comment: Partnership's Apportionment Factors Included in Year of Liquidation

In a nonprecedential decision, the State Board of Equalization held in the *Appeal of Eli Lilly & Co.*, (2007) (CCH CALIFORNIA TAX REPORTS, ¶404-213), that when a taxpayer liquidates its interest in a limited liability company (LLC) treated as a partnership for federal and state tax purposes, the taxpayer must include its proportionate share of the LLC's apportionment factors on its California corporate franchise tax return for the year in which the interest was liquidated.

Chris Whitney, Contributing Editor

S corporations are generally prohibited from being included in a combined report. (Sec. 23801, Rev. & Tax. Code) However, in some cases, the FTB may use combined reporting methods to clearly reflect income of an S corporation.

Under California's water's-edge law, taxpayers may elect to exclude certain foreign affiliates from a combined report. For further details, see ¶1311.

CCH Comment: Corporation Numbers Must Be Listed on Schedule R-7

Tax return preparers are reminded that when their client is the designated key corporation for a combined reporting group for California corporation franchise and income tax purposes, they should list, on Part 1 of Schedule R-7, Election to File a Unitary Taxpayers' Group Return and List of Affiliated Corporations, the California corporation numbers for the client and every member of the client's combined reporting group. In addition, when a client is a designated key corporation, tax return preparers must list, on Part 2 of Schedule R-7, any members of the client's commonly controlled group that are not listed on Part 1 of Schedule R-7 as making an election to file a single unitary group return. It is not enough to provide federal employer identification numbers. The California corporation numbers are critical because they provide the Franchise Tax Board (FTB) with the most effective and reliable way to verify information on returns, and they allow the FTB to process returns faster and more accurately. (*Tax News*, California Franchise Tax Board, May/June 2005)

On Part I, Section B, List of Taxpayers No Longer Included in the Single Group Tax Return After the Last Filing, tax return preparers must list each removed taxpayer's name, California corporation number or federal employer identification number (FEIN), and effective date of removal from the single group tax return. (Instructions, Schedule R, Apportionment and Allocation of Income)

• *Combination of general and financial corporations*

Reg. 25137-10, 18 CCR, sets forth in detail how a unitary business that consists of at least one bank or financial corporation and at least one general corporation whose predominant activity is not financial, allocates and apportions income in a combined report.

• *Insurance affiliates*

In Legal Ruling No. 385 (1975) (CCH CALIFORNIA TAX REPORTS, ¶205-232), the FTB ruled that a California corporate insurer engaged in a unitary business must be

¶1310

excluded from a combined report for apportionment of unitary income, because the state constitution exempts such organizations from franchise and income taxes.

However, in a nonprecedential decision, the BOE refused to extend this finding and held that a taxpayer's combined report was required to include its wholly owned unitary insurance subsidiary that conducted a non-insurance business within California and was not subject to California's gross premiums tax but conducted an insurance business in Texas and was classified as an insurance company under Texas law. The BOE also went on to hold that the calculation of the sales factor properly included the premiums received by the subsidiary during the course of its Texas insurance activities. (*Appeal of Electronic Data Systems Corp.* (2008) CCH CALIFORNIA TAX REPORTS, ¶ 404-727)

• *Parent company excluded*

Legal Ruling No. 410 (1979) (CCH CALIFORNIA TAX REPORTS, ¶ 206-100) involved a situation where three subsidiaries were engaged in a unitary business but their parent was not involved. The ruling concluded that the subsidiaries must be included in a combined report but the parent corporation should be excluded.

• *FTB policy*

The FTB requires combined reporting of multistate operations wherever a "unitary" business is operated within and without California. As discussed more fully at ¶ 1304, there are three judicially acceptable tests for determining whether a business is unitary. These are (1) the three unities test, (2) the contribution and dependency test, and (3) the flow of value test.

The FTB has issued audit guidelines with respect to the unitary combination of diverse businesses (*FTB Notice No. 92-4*, CCH CALIFORNIA TAX REPORTS, ¶ 402-432). According to the guidelines, there is no unique test for evaluating unity in diverse business cases. Unity may be established under any of the judicially acceptable tests and may not be denied merely because another of those tests does not simultaneously apply, *i.e.*, the tests are not mutually exclusive. In addition, a lack of functional integration will not prevent a finding of unity. On the other hand, the fact that functionally integrated businesses may be found to be unitary does not mean that functional integration is a *requirement* for unity.

Also, presumptions of unity under Reg. 25120(b), 18 CCR, which states that the activities of a taxpayer will be considered a single business if there is evidence to indicate that the segments under consideration are integrated with, depend upon, or contribute to, each other and the operations of the taxpayer as a whole, although important considerations, are not conclusive in determining unity.

Finally, the guidelines state that *Mole-Richardson, Dental Insurance Consultants,* and *Tenneco West, Inc.* (each discussed at ¶ 1304), are controlling of the diverse business issue and that State Board of Equalization (BOE) decisions that are not in accord with these cases should not be relied upon.

• *Corporations under common control*

In *Rain Bird Sprinkler Mfg. Corp. v. Franchise Tax Board* (1991) (CCH CALIFORNIA TAX REPORTS, ¶ 11-520.8092), a California court of appeal allowed seventeen corporations to file a combined report even though no single individual or entity held a majority interest in all of the corporations. The court, rejecting what it called "a host" of BOE decisions requiring ownership by a single individual or entity, held that "unity of ownership" existed because members of the same family held the majority of the voting stock in each of the corporations, and all of the stock of each corporation was subject to written stock purchase agreements prohibiting transfer to outsiders.

• *Other cases involving questions of control*

In *Appeal of Armco Steel Corp.* (1984) (CCH CALIFORNIA TAX REPORTS, ¶ 11-540.63), the taxpayer owned exactly 50% of the stock of a "captive mining corporation" that supplied iron ore to the taxpayer at cost. The captive corporation was treated as a partnership for federal tax purposes. The BOE followed the *Revere Copper and Brass* case (below) in holding that the taxpayer could not include the captive corporation's factors in its computation of unitary income, even though the factors could have been included if the captive corporation had been a partnership (see also ¶1304).

In *Appeal of Revere Copper and Brass Inc.* (1977) (CCH CALIFORNIA TAX REPORTS, ¶205-752), the taxpayer was admittedly engaged in a unitary business. The taxpayer bought a substantial portion of its raw material requirements from a subsidiary that was 50% owned by the taxpayer. The BOE held that the subsidiary was not includible in a combined return, since the taxpayer's ownership in the subsidiary was not more than 50%. To the same effect, see *Appeal of Standard Brands, Inc.* (1977) (CCH CALIFORNIA TAX REPORTS, ¶11-520.952). However, in *Appeal of Signal Oil and Gas Co.* (1970), the BOE held that a 50% owned German subsidiary of a Swiss subsidiary of a California parent should be included in the computation of unitary income, since the 50% stock ownership carried with it decisive control over the subsidiary's operations.

- *Apportionment of tax within group*

Where income of an affiliated group is combined and there are two or more corporations having activity in California, there may be a question of how the total tax on the combined income taxed by California should be divided between the corporations having income from California sources. Legal Ruling No. 234 (1959) (CCH CALIFORNIA TAX REPORTS, ¶11-520.206) prescribes the method of apportionment to be used. The apportionment is based upon the California income attributable to each member of the affiliated group, such income being assigned to each corporation on the basis of the average ratio of the California factors of each corporation to the total factors of the group. This method is illustrated in the ruling as follows:

	Corp. A	Corp. B	Corp. C	Total
Totals within and without the State:				
Property	$ 500,000	$ 64,000	$ 36,000	$ 600,000
Payroll	300,000	74,000	26,000	400,000
Sales	4,000,000	600,000	400,000	5,000,000
Totals within the State:				
Property	24,000	—0—	36,000	60,000
Payroll	14,000	—0—	26,000	40,000
Sales	150,000	450,000	400,000	1,000,000
Allocating fractions:				
Property	4.0%	—0—	6.0%	10.0%
Payroll	3.5	—0—	6.5	10.0
Sales	3.0	9.0%	8.0	20.0
Total	10.5%	9.0%	20.5%	40.0%
Average	3.5 %	3.0%	6.83 1/3%	13 1/3%

Applying the foregoing fractions to a combined business income of $1,000,000 would result in $133,333 being attributed to California sources. This amount would then be allocated to each corporation, and the tax computed at the appropriate rate, as follows:

Corp. A (3.5% of $1,000,000)	$ 35,000
Corp. B (3% of $1,000,000)	30,000
Corp. C (6.83 1/3% of $1,000,000)	68,333
Total	$133,333

- *Significance of apportionment within group*

Practitioner Comment: *Joyce vs. Finnegan* **Approach to Sourcing Receipts of Combined Reporting Group Members**

In general, sales of tangible personal property are sourced on a destination basis but are *thrown back* to the state of origin in situations where the corporation shipping the product from California lacks nexus in the destination state. The application of these rules to combined reporting groups where unitary affiliates may have nexus in the destination state has evolved over the years. For example, in 1966, the State Board of Equalization in the *Appeal of Joyce, Inc.*, 66-SBE-070 (Nov. 23, 1966), held that sales of a Florida corporation shipping product to California could not be sourced to the state because the corporation lacked nexus in California, despite the fact that its unitary affiliates had nexus in the state. However, in 1990, the State Board of Equalization in *Appeal of Finnegan Corp.*, 88-SBE-022-A (Jan. 24, 1990), held that a corporation's sales shipped from California to states where it lacked nexus could not be thrown back to California because its unitary affiliates had nexus in the destination states. In 1999, the State Board of Equalization held in *Appeal of Huffy Corp.*, 99-SBE-005 (Apr. 22, 1999) that it returned to the *Joyce* approach on a prospective basis for income years beginning on or after April 22, 1999, the date of the opinion. This prospective application was affirmed on rehearing at 99-SBE-005-A (Sep. 1, 1999).

The *Joyce* approach seems to be consistent with the separate entity approach to utilizing credits endorsed by the California Supreme Court in *General Motors*—see Practitioner Comment on "Treatment of Credits below". The FTB has made exceptions to the separate entity approach in the apportionment area. See for example the Practitioner Comment above regarding FTB Legal Ruling 2006-2. Also, as noted in ¶1306, the FTB has promulgated a regulation first effective in 2007 that provides special apportionment rules for the mutual fund service industry that use a *Finnegan* approach to sourcing mutual fund service receipts.

It should be noted that S.B.x3 15, which was enacted on February 20, 2009, essentially codifies the *Finnigan* approach for taxable years beginning after 2010, by providing that all tangible personal property sales of the combined reporting group assigned to the state are to be included in the numerator, regardless of whether the entity making the sale has nexus. It should be noted that the same legislation also codifies an economic nexus standard and market state sourcing for intangible and service receipts.

The primary effect of the *Finnigan* codification is the inclusion of the California sales of tangible personal property by out-of-state unitary affiliates that are otherwise protected from taxation by P.L. 86-272 in the sales factor numerator. On the flip side, throw back can be avoided by in-state companies shipping such product to other states where affiliates have nexus. (Sec. 25135, Rev. & Tax. Code)

Chris Whitney, Contributing Editor

In *Chief Counsel Ruling 2012-03*, CALIFORNIA TAX REPORTS, ¶405-723, the FTB notes that for purposes of determining whether the throwback rule applies, a foreign jurisdiction is treated like another state. Therefore, a taxpayer is subject to tax in a foreign jurisdiction if the taxpayer's activity would be sufficient to subject the taxpayer to such a tax under the constitution or statutes of the United States or a state of the United States, including under California's bright-line doing business test, discussed at ¶804.

• *Minimum tax applies to each corporation*

The minimum tax (discussed at ¶816) is imposed on *each* corporation in the combined group that is incorporated or qualified to do business in California, even though the combined report shows a net loss or shows taxable income that would produce a lower tax. (Instructions, Form 100, California Corporation Franchise or Income Tax Return)

• *Allocation of credits and capital gains and losses*

Practitioner Comment: Treatment of Credits

On August 17, 2006, the California Supreme Court in *General Motors Corp. v. Franchise Tax Board* (2006) (CCH CALIFORNIA TAX REPORTS, ¶404-044) held that only the taxpayer that incurred the research and development expenses may use the research and development credit so generated. In so holding, the Court's decision was consistent with an earlier State Board of Equalization decision (*Appeal of Guy F. Atkinson Company* (1997) CCH CALIFORNIA TAX REPORTS, ¶403-307) as well as the unpublished Court of Appeal decision, *Guy F. Atkinson Company v. Franchise Tax Board* (2000) (CCH CALIFORNIA TAX REPORTS, ¶403-097).

Chris Whitney, Contributing Editor

Members of a unitary group included in a combined report may assign tax credits to other eligible members of the unitary group. The members may assign any credit earned by the taxpayer in a taxable year beginning after 2007 or any credit earned in any taxable year beginning before July 1, 2008, that is eligible to be carried forward to the taxpayer's first taxable year beginning after June 30, 2008.

To be eligible to receive the credit, the assignee must have been a member of the assigning taxpayer's unitary combined group on (1) the last day of the first taxable year in which the credit was allowed to the taxpayer, and (2) the last day of the taxable year of the assigning taxpayer in which the eligible credit is assigned.

The taxpayer must make an irrevocable election on its original return for the taxable year in which the assignment is made. The election is made by completing form FTB 3544, Election to Assign Credit Within Combined Reporting Group, and attaching it to the assignor's original tax return for the taxable year the assignment is made. A separate FTB 3544 must be completed and attached for each credit being assigned. (Sec. 23663, Rev. & Tax. Code)

Any credit limitations that would apply to the assigning taxpayer in the absence of an assignment also apply to the same extent to the assignee. In addition to the requirement to separately list credits generated in different taxable years, the assignor must separately list credits that are subject to separate and distinct limitations and disclose each of those separate and distinct limitations in a statement to be attached to form FTB 3544. (Instructions, FTB 3544)

An assignee may pay consideration to the assigning taxpayer for the credit transfer. However, the assignee may not claim any deduction with respect to any amounts so paid and the assigning taxpayer may not include in its gross income any amounts received as consideration. (Sec. 23663(d), Rev. & Tax. Code)

Practitioner Comment: Assignment of Credit Provisions Can Be Used to Circumvent California's Separate Entity Application of Credits

A.B. 1452, signed into law on September 30, 2008, allows "eligible credits" to be assigned to other members of a combined reporting group for tax years beginning on or after July 1, 2008. Assignment can be made both with respect to credits generated in years beginning after that date as well as to carryovers from prior years. The assignee, however, can only use the assigned credits in a tax year beginning on or after January 1, 2010. The assignment must be made on the original return for the year of assignment. Once the election is made the credit "belongs" to the other member and cannot be reassigned nor can the election be revoked. With proper planning these provisions can be used to circumvent the separate entity limitations endorsed by the California Supreme Court's 2006 decision in *General Motors*, discussed above.

It is the FTB's position that any limitations on the assignor's use of the credit will also apply to the assignee however. For example, enterprise zone credits assigned to other members would still need to meet the enterprise zone activity limitations imposed under those provisions.

Chris Whitney, Contributing Editor

Practitioner Comment: Regulation Proposed to Clarify Treatment of Defective Credit Assignments

The Franchise Tax Board (FTB) has undertaken a regulation project regarding California Rev. and Tax. Code Sec. 23663, which permits the assignment of credits among members of the same combined reporting group. A proper election to assign credits is irrevocable and must be made with an original return on California Form 3544, Election to Assign Credit Within Combined Reporting Group.

The regulation project would attempt to address situations where, in the FTB's view, taxpayers have made "defective assignments." For example, the credits a taxpayer properly assigns may be subsequently reduced at audit, or the assignee may later be determined by FTB to have not been a member of the same combined reporting group as the assignor on the dates required under the statute. The FTB's proposed regulations would provide default allocation rules for such "defective assignments," procedures for correcting clerical errors, and the ability for taxpayers to request relief from the default rules.

The proposed default rule for a "defective assignment" where a taxpayer's available credits are less than the amount assigned to an eligible assignee(s) is to allocate to the eligible assignee(s) in order to give as full an effect to the original assignment as possible. To the extent the assignee(s) claimed the credits in a year for which the statute of limitations (SOL) is closed, the amount of credits claimed by the assignee(s) in the barred closed year are allocated to the assignee(s) for that year (essentially preserving the original assignment), and remaining credits are reallocated to the assignor. The remaining credits are then allocated to the eligible assignee(s) based first on the ratio of credits claimed and, if eligible credits remain, based on the ratio of credits assigned.

The proposed regulations also provide that, in general, if an assignment is noncompliant for any other reason (e.g., assigned to an ineligible assignee or assignor), then the assignment is treated as if it had not been made, unless a credit is claimed by an ineligible assignee in a year for which the SOL is closed. In this circumstance, the assignment is treated as if it was never made, but the amount of the assignor's credits will be reduced by the amount of credits claimed in the closed years to avoid allowing duplicate use of the same credit amount. The proposed regulations also provide guidance for the correction of defective assignments related to clerical errors, allow taxpayers to request alternative allocation of a defective assignment if certain conditions are met, and provide ordering rules in case provisions of the regulations overlap.

Based on the language and examples in the proposed regulations, there may be circumstances where an election is deemed to be defective as a result of an audit in a subsequent year that could subject a taxpayer to assessment. For example, Corporation X reported $150 of credit in 2010 and assigned $100 of such credit to corporation Y, retaining $50 of credit which it used against its tax liability in 2010. Then, under subsequent audit, the FTB reduced the amount of credit generated in 2010 from $150 to $75. Since the default rules try to give as full an effect to the original assignment as possible, X may be deemed to have assigned the entire $75 of 2010 credits to Y. As a result, X will no longer have $50 of credits to offset its 2010 liability, thereby potentially resulting in an assessment. It should be noted that while the taxpayer in this case could request relief from the default rule, in other circumstances relief may not be available. For example, the FTB may deem a prior credit assignment to have been defective based on a subsequent determination that the assignee and assignor were not unitary members of the same combined reporting group as required by statute. In this regard, it should be noted that because credit assignment must be made on a timely filed original return, taxpayers who are subsequently determined to be unitary on audit do not have an opportunity to make retroactive credit assignments to reduce assessments which may arise from such determinations.

Chris Whitney, Contributing Editor

• *Adjustments for intercompany transactions*

FTB Pub. 1061, Guidelines for Corporations Filing a Combined Report, discusses the adjustments necessary to properly reflect intercompany transactions among unitary affiliates included in the combined report. The adjustments concern inventories, intangible assets, fixed assets and capitalized items, dividends (see ¶ 909), and other factor adjustments.

Practitioner Comment: Deferral Provisions in CCR §25106.5-1 Only Apply to Intercompany Transactions Between Corporations

In Chief Counsel Ruling 2012-02 the FTB concludes that gain from the sale of a partnership interest by a member of a combined reporting group to a unitary partnership will not be deferred under CCR § 25106.5-1. CCR § 25106.5-1 contains California's rules relating to intercompany transactions between members of a combined reporting group. As stated in CCR § 25106.5-1(a)(1), gains and losses resulting from intercompany transactions between members of a combined reporting group are generally deferred. However, as set forth in CCR § 25106.5-1(b)(1)(A), by definition an intercompany transaction only occurs between *corporations* that are members of the same combined reporting group immediately after the transaction in question.

The transaction at issue in the Chief Counsel Ruling was the sale of an interest in a unitary partnership by a corporate member of a combined group to another unitary partnership, which was owned by other members of the combined group. Although the purchasing unitary partnership was entirely owned by corporate members of the group, the FTB concluded that because the unitary partnership was not a member of the group, the intercompany regulations could not be applied.

The approach taken in the Chief Counsel Ruling stands in contrast to CCR § 25137-1, which sets forth apportionment provisions dealing with partnership interests held by corporations. This regulation provides for the elimination of sales between corporate partners and unitary partnerships for sales factor purposes. In addition, it is worth noting that in FTB Notice 2011-01, the FTB indicated that a transaction by a corporation with a captive partnership that lacked economic substance should not give rise to a sale for sales factor purposes. The relevant distinction would appear to be the fact that the Chief Counsel Ruling states that the transactions in question were engaged in "for reasons other than for California franchise purposes."

Chris Whitney, Contributing Editor

Reg. 25106.5-1, 18 CCR generally conforms to Treasury Regulation Sec. 1.1502-13, concerning the treatment of intercompany transactions between seller members and buyer members of combined reporting groups. The regulation does not conform, however, to federal sourcing rules. Instead, California treats intercompany items as current apportionable business income.

Comment: Deferred Intercompany Stock Account (DISA) Disclosures

FTB 3726, Deferred Intercompany Stock Account (DISA) and Capital Gains Information, must be used to annually disclose the balance of any deferred intercompany stock account (DISA) and to report the capital gains from a DISA due to the occurrence of a triggering event. Failure to disclose the existing DISA balance for any tax year may result in the current recognition of capital gain. The corporation that must complete the form is the corporation that received the distribution. When filing a combined return, if there is more then one corporation that has a DISA, a separate form FTB 3726 must be completed for each corporation and must be attached to Form 100 or 100W. If the FTB has not contacted the corporation for an audit and the corporation needs to disclose DISA information for a prior taxable year, the corporation should file an amended return. (Instructions to FTB 3726, Deferred Intercompany Stock Account (DISA) and Capital Gains Information)

Practitioner Comment: Changes to Intercompany Transaction Regulation Allow Subsequent Capital Contributions to Reduce and Even Eliminate Deferred Intercompany Stock Accounts ("DISAs")

California adopts IRC § 301, which among other things provides that corporate distributions that exceed both the distributor's earnings and profits ("E&P") and the distributee's basis in the stock of the distributor result in gain to the distributee (see IRC § 301(c)(3)). For California purposes, IRC § 301(c)(3) gains that relate to distributions between members of the same combined reporting group are deferred. The deferred gain is maintained in a deferred intercompany stock account (DISA), which must be reported annually with the tax return on CA Form 3726. Historically, once a DISA was created it could not be reversed until triggered and recognized as income. Regulatory amendments effective April 1, 2014, allow for the reduction or even elimination of a DISA via subsequent capital contributions (the new provisions are applicable to transactions occurring on or after January 1, 2001, but a taxpayer may elect to have the changes apply prospectively starting April 1, 2014). In addition, changes would generally prevent multiple DISAs from being created by a single distribution through a chain of unitary corporations.

Chris Whitney, Contributing Editor

• *Accounting methods and periods*

Reg. 25106.5 et seq., 18 CCR, provide detailed rules concerning the accounting methods and periods to be used by a unitary group and its individual members. Under these rules, each member of a combined reporting group has its own accounting methods and elections. However, the unitary group is authorized to make an election on behalf of an individual member if that member has not otherwise made an election on a California or federal return.

The principal member's accounting period is used as a reference period for all members of the combined reporting group to aggregate and apportion combined report business income of the group. The regulations also address fiscalization issues, clarify how to incorporate/exclude a business's income that joins/leaves the unitary group mid-year, and govern the preparation of combined reports that include operations in foreign countries (see *Appeal of Crisa Corp.* (2002) (CCH CALIFORNIA TAX REPORTS, ¶ 11-540.25) for a discussion of the functional currency to be used in a combined report with unitary businesses in different countries).

¶1311 Water's-Edge Election for Multinational Unitary Businesses

Law: Secs. 18405.1, 24344, 24411, 25110-16; Reg. 25114, 18 CCR (CCH CALIFORNIA TAX REPORTS, ¶ 10-815, 11-515, 11-550).

Comparable Federal: None.

California Forms: Form 100W (California Corporation Franchise or Income Tax Return - Water's Edge Filers), Form 100-WE (Water's-Edge Election), FTB 1115 (Request for Consent for a Water's-Edge Re-Election), FTB 1117 (Request to Terminate Water's-Edge Election).

Multinational taxpayers have an option to compute their California tax base on a water's-edge basis. Taxpayers that make such an election are taxed on income from sources solely within the United States. (Sec. 25110, Rev. & Tax. Code; Reg. 25110, 18 CCR)

• *Pre-water's-edge contract intercompany sales*

The California State Board of Equalization (BOE) upheld a water's-edge group member's nonrecognition of profits realized from its sale to a third party of inventory that it had purchased from its foreign parent company the year before the water's-edge filing election, even though the unitary group's worldwide combined report for that year properly eliminated the parent seller's intercompany inventory property. Consequently, the taxpayer only had to report as income the difference between the price it had paid its parent for the inventory, including the parent's profit, and the sales price it received from the third parties rather than recognizing income equal to the difference between the parent's acquisition price and the company's sales price. Without guidance from contradictory authority, profits from selling the inventory to a third party could be excluded from the water's-edge group's combined report (*Yamaha Motor Corp., U.S.A.* (2000) (CCH CALIFORNIA TAX REPORTS, ¶ 12-650.60)).

• *IRC conformity*

Except as specifically provided in the statutory provisions governing water's-edge elections, when any of the statutory provisions governing water's-edge elections refers to a provision of the Internal Revenue Code (IRC), the reference is to the IRC, including all amendments, in effect for federal purposes for the taxable period. This overrides the general incorporation date for IRC provisions (see ¶803) so that relevant changes to federal law are applied in computing the income and deductions of a water's-edge group for California purposes. (Sec. 25116, Rev. & Tax. Code)

• *Qualifying entities*

Under the water's-edge election, California taxable income is computed based on the income and apportionment factors of only the following entities:

— any corporation (other than a bank) the average of whose U.S. property, payroll, and sales is 20% or more;

— U.S.-incorporated entities (excluding those making an election under IRC Secs. 931-936), if, generally for water's-edge elections made before January 1, 2006, more than 50% of their stock is controlled by the same interest;

— DISCs, FSCs, and Export Trade Corporations;

— a "controlled foreign corporation" (CFC) as defined in IRC Sec. 957 that, generally for water's-edge elections made before January 1, 2006, is an affiliated corporation, and has "Subpart F income" as defined in IRC Sec. 952 (the income and apportionment factors of a CFC are multiplied by a fraction representing the ratio of Subpart F income to earnings and profits. A CFC is treated as having no Subpart F income if such income is less than $1 million and represents less than 5% of the CFC's earnings and profits); and

— any entity not described above, to the extent that its income is derived from or attributable to U.S. sources.

(Sec. 25110, Rev. & Tax. Code; Reg. 25110, 18 CCR) The FTB is required to issue regulations to prevent the double taxation of income when a CFC has both U.S.-source income and Subpart F income. (Sec. 25110, Rev. & Tax. Code)

Practitioner Comment: Water's-Edge Filers Must Determine Effectively Connected Income ("ECI") Without the Benefit of U.S. Treaties

California regulations generally provide for the inclusion of foreign corporations if they have certain characteristics, including foreign corporations with U.S. source income. For federal purposes, the taxation of foreign corporations with U.S. source income turns on whether there is an applicable treaty. If there is an applicable treaty, a foreign corporation must have a permanent establishment ("PE") in the U.S. before income effectively connected with a U.S. trade or business can be taxed for federal purposes. Moreover, in order to be subject to tax under the tax treaty, the U.S. source income must be effectively connected with a PE, not just a U.S. trade or business. Conversely, if the foreign corporation is not from a treaty country, then income effectively connected with a U.S. trade or business will be taxed for federal purposes without consideration of tax treaty PE rules.

For California water's edge filers, U.S. tax treaties are not followed to the extent they limit the application of the ECI provisions. Therefore, U.S. source ECI income of foreign corporations is included in a water's-edge return and may be subject to California tax regardless of whether it is connected to a PE. The ECI merely needs to be income effectively connected with its U.S. trade or business. Non-ECI is also taxable in California to the extent the income arises from a contract or agreement a principal purpose of which was the avoidance of federal income tax or California franchise or income tax.

Chris Whitney, Contributing Editor

Practitioner Comment: CFC Dividends

In *Fujitsu IT Holdings Inc. v. Franchise Tax Bd.*, Cal.Ct.App., 120 Cal. App. 4th (2004), CCH CALIFORNIA TAX REPORTS, ¶403-655, the court held that dividends paid from one controlled foreign corporation (CFC) to its parent CFC are eliminated in determining the amount of CFC income to be included in the income of the unitary group, to the extent that the lower-tier CFC paid the dividends out of income that was included in combined income. The court also found that where the CFC receives dividends from a lower-tier subsidiary whose income and factors are fully included in the combined return of the water's-edge group, the dividends subsequently paid by the CFC are deemed first to be distributed from unitary group earnings and profits (E&P), and to that extent are completely eliminated.

The main point made by this decision is that intercompany dividends paid from a lower-tier CFC to an upper-tier CFC are not taken into account in determining the upper-tier CFC's water's-edge inclusion ratio (to the extent the dividends were paid out of combined income of the unitary group). The BOE reached a similar result in its unpublished decision in *Appeal of Baxter Healthcare Corporation* (August 1, 2002).

Another important point made by the court is that dividends paid by a partially included first-tier CFC from current E&P are treated as first coming out of the E&P eligible for elimination under Cal. Rev. & Tax. Code Sec. 25106 with any excess coming out of the E&P that was excluded from the water's-edge group (*e.g.*, E&P eligible for Cal. Rev. & Tax. Code Sec. 24411 DRD). This is significant, because of the application of the 100% dividends received deduction under Cal. Rev. & Tax. Code Sec. 25106 rather than the 75% deduction under Cal. Rev. & Tax. Code Sec. 24411. Further, dividends eligible for Cal. Rev. & Tax. Code Sec. 25106 elimination are not subject to the foreign investment interest offset rules.

Finally, the court noted that under a treaty with the United Kingdom, U.S. corporations that own 10% or more of the stock of a U.K. corporation are entitled, when the corporation pays a dividend, to a payment from the United Kingdom of half of the amount of the tax credit that an individual U.K. shareholder would receive. The court found that this U.K. "Advance Corporation Tax" (ACT) credit received with respect to dividends from its U.K. subsidiaries should be taxable as additional dividend income, either subject to elimination under Cal. Rev. & Tax. Code Sec. 25106 or a partial deduction under Sec. 24411.

Although the court clearly rejected the "pro rata" methodology in *Fujitsu*, the FTB did not accept this portion of the Court's decision until March 15, 2011, when the FTB effectively acquiesced to this portion of the decision in Technical Advice Memorandum ("TAM") 2011-02.

Some taxpayers have argued that the *Fujitsu* decision supports the position that dividends should be treated as paid from includible unitary earnings, regardless of the year in which such earnings had been earned. The FTB has strongly disagreed with this position and has maintained that the "Last In-First Out" or "LIFO" approach in its regulations is appropriate, under which dividends are deemed distributed from the most recent year's E&P first until fully exhausted.

On September 12, 2011, the California Court of Appeals in *Apple Computer v. Franchise Tax Board*, 199 Cal.App.4th 1, CCH California Tax Reports, ¶405-498, ruled in favor of the FTB vis a vis the LIFO ordering issue. On January 23, 2012, the California Supreme Court denied petition for review effectively making the Court of Appeals' decision final.

Finally, as mentioned at ¶909, the Court also addressed the question of interest expense disallowance in relation to deductible dividends. Although the Court supported the concept of direct tracing where sufficient evidence of the purpose and use of borrowed funds exists, the ongoing relevance of this portion of the court's decision is unclear given that the Cal. Rev. & Tax. Code §24411 water's-edge DRD and the related foreign investment offset provisions that apply to CFC dividends received in years ending on or after December 1, 1999 were not addressed in *Apple*.

Chris Whitney, Contributing Editor

CCH Practice Tip: U.S.-Located Income

Taxpayers that elect water's-edge treatment are only required to include income that is effectively connected with a U.S. trade or business or that is treated as effectively connected under the provisions of the Internal Revenue Code. However, because California is not a party to federal tax treaties, the immunity provisions of federal tax treaties do not apply for California purposes. Any income satisfying the definition of effectively connected income that is excluded from federal taxable income due to a tax treaty is included for California purposes. (Instructions, California 100W, California Corporation Franchise or Income Tax Return - Water's-Edge Filers).

• *Deduction of dividends*

A qualifying water's-edge group may deduct up to 75% of dividends received from a 50% owned corporation or bank if the average of the payor's U.S. property, payroll, and sales is less than 20%. The dividend deduction is computed on Schedule H of Form 100W. A special provision permits a 100% deduction of dividends from foreign construction projects whose locations are not subject to the groups' control, provided certain other water's-edge conditions are met. (Sec. 24411, Rev. & Tax. Code; Reg. 24411, 18 CCR)

To qualify for water's-edge treatment, the taxpayer must agree that dividends received by *other* unitary group members are business income if received from (1) an entity that is engaged in the same general business and that is more than 50% owned by members of the group, and (2) an entity that purchases, supplies, or sells 15% or more of either input or output from or to the unitary business. Dividends received from any other entity will be classified as business or nonbusiness income under existing provisions.

The deductible amount of qualifying foreign dividends is reduced by the amount of any interest expense incurred for purposes of foreign investment.

• *Elections and terminations*

A water's-edge election must be made on an original, timely filed return for the year of election, in the same manner as any other election. An election on an original, timely filed return will be considered valid if the tax is computed in a manner consistent with a water's-edge election and a Form 100-WE (Water's-Edge Election) is attached to the return. (Sec. 25113, Rev. & Tax. Code; Instructions Form 100W, California Corporation Franchise or Income Tax Return—Water's Edge Filers)

In lieu of establishing a water's-edge election by filing a Form 100W, California Corporation Franchise or Income Tax Return—Water's-Edge Filers, and attaching a form 100-WE, Water's-Edge Election, the FTB may consider other objective evidence of the making of a water's-edge election such as (1) a statement attached to the timely-filed, original return indicating a water's-edge election is being made or (2) the inclusion of one or more substantially completed forms associated with water's-edge combined reporting with the taxpayer's timely filed original return. Examples of such forms include FTB Form 1115, Request for Consent for a Water's-Edge Re-Election; Form 2416, Schedule of Included Controlled Foreign Corporations (CFC); or Form 2424, Water's-Edge Foreign Investment Interest Offset.

A copy of the original election should be attached to all subsequent returns filed during the election period. (Reg. 25113, 18 CCR)

CCH Practice Tip: *Perfecting an Election*

Water's-edge elections may, at the election of the FTB, be perfected during the applicable period of limitations for mailing a notice of proposed deficiency assessment or allowing a credit or refund. The statute of limitations for all taxpayers in the water's-edge group whose taxable year falls, in whole or in part, within the period of the election will remain open to receive adjustments, under claim of deficiency, consistent with the perfection of the election.

Generally, an election will be effective only if made by every member of the self-assessed combined reporting group that is subject to California corporation franchise or income tax. An election on a group return will constitute an election by each member included in the group return, unless one of the members files a separate return in which no election is made and the nonelecting member is not otherwise deemed to have elected water's-edge treatment. A group member that does not make a water's-edge election on its own return will be deemed to have made such an election if either of the following applies:

— the income and apportionment factors of the nonelecting member are included in the self-assessed combined reporting group on an electing parent corporation's original, timely filed return, including a group return; or

— the income and apportionment factors of the nonelecting member are reflected in the self-assessed combined reporting group on an electing taxpayer's original, timely filed return, and the written notification of election filed with the return is signed by an officer or other authorized agent of a parent corporation or another corporation with authority to bind the nonelecting member to an election.

For purposes of water's-edge elections, a "parent corporation" is a corporation that owns or constructively owns stock possessing more than 50% of the voting power of the taxpayer.

Members of a unitary group that are not subject to California corporation franchise or income taxation when the election is made, but subsequently become subject to the tax, are deemed to have made a water's-edge election with the other members of the combined reporting group.

A corporation engaged in more than one apportioning trade or business may make a separate election for each apportioning trade or business.

Special rules apply to taxpayers that become members of a new unitary group when at least one member has previously made a water's-edge election.

Practitioner Comment: "Deemed Elections"

If a water's-edge taxpayer becomes unitary with a non-water's-edge taxpayer, it is necessary to determine whether a water's-edge election will apply to the newly constituted unitary group. Generally, pursuant to Cal. Rev. & Tax. Code § 25113(c)(2), the filing status of the group having the largest net book value of business assets, as measured by the taxpayer members of the group, will control for determining whether the new combined filing group will be on the water's-edge or the worldwide method. It is important to note that there is not an opportunity for automatic termination of a water's-edge election following an acquisition. In order to get a result different from the "larger taxpayer prevails" result, the taxpayer will need to get FTB permission to terminate based on good cause.

Chris Whitney, Contributing Editor

Water's-edge election period: A water's-edge election on an original, timely filed return remains in effect until terminated. Except as otherwise provided, if one or more electing members becomes disaffiliated or otherwise ceases to be included in the combined reporting group, the water's-edge election will remain in effect as to both the departing members and any remaining members. (Sec. 25113, Rev. & Tax. Code)

Effect of different fiscal years: In cases involving taxpayers with different fiscal years, each member of the water's-edge group must make the election on its timely filed original return for the taxable year for which the election is being made. The election becomes effective as of the beginning of the taxable year of the last member of the water's-edge group to file its return and election. Each taxpayer in the group must compute its tax on a worldwide basis for that portion of the taxable year between the beginning of its taxable year and the date the election becomes effective, and must compute its tax on a water's-edge basis for the remaining portion of the taxable year (*FTB Notice 2004-2*, California Franchise Tax Board, May 3, 2004 (CCH CALIFORNIA TAX REPORTS, ¶ 11-550.85)).

Election termination: A water's-edge election may be terminated on an original, timely filed return without the consent of the FTB after the election has been in effect for at least 84 months. Termination is accomplished by filing a return on a worldwide basis. To be effective, the termination must be made by every member of the water's-edge group in the same manner as a water's-edge election. (Sec. 25113, Rev. & Tax. Code; Reg. 25113, 18 CCR)

An election may be terminated for good cause before the expiration of the 84-month period only with the consent of the FTB. A request to terminate for good cause must be in writing and must state how the taxpayer meets the requirements provided in Treasury Reg. Sec. 1.1502-75(c), which governs the good cause determinations for electing to discontinue filing on a consolidated basis. A taxpayer must file

FTB 1117, Request to Terminate Water's-Edge Election, with the FTB no later than 120 days prior to the due date, including extensions, of the return for which the termination would be effective. FTB 1117 must be filed separately from any other return (Reg. 25113, 18 CCR; *FTB Notice 2004-2*, California Franchise Tax Board, May 3, 2004 (CCH CALIFORNIA TAX REPORTS, ¶ 11-550.85)).

FTB 1117 outlines the conditions to which a taxpayer seeking an early termination might have to consent, unless the taxpayer can explain why the conditions are unnecessary or inapplicable:

— Dividends received during the remaining period of the election from affiliated banks or corporations not included in the water's-edge report will be considered to have been paid first out of the E&P not included in the combined report of a unitary business for purposes of computing any allowable dividend exclusion under Rev. & Tax. Code Sec. 25106. To the extent the dividends exceed such E&P, they may be subject to the exclusion.

— Gains on distribution with respect to stock that is not a dividend or from the sale or other disposition of assets received during the remaining period of the election from affiliated banks or corporations not included in the water's-edge report will not be deferred or eliminated. Losses from the sale or worthlessness of stock or from the sale or other disposition of assets of affiliated banks or corporations not included in the water's-edge report will be allowed only to the extent of dividend income or other gain recognized as a result of the change in election.

— Gains or losses on the disposition of an affiliated bank's or corporation's stock or assets that was included in a combined report prior to the election and that was excluded from the water's-edge combined report will be included in income in the first return filed after permission is granted. Losses will be included only to the extent of gain recognized as a result of the change in election.

The FTB may also terminate an election upon request by all members of a water's-edge group, if the purpose of the request is to permit the state to contract with an expatriate corporation, or its subsidiary.

Except in cases involving deemed elections, once a taxpayer terminates its water's-edge election and returns to filing on a worldwide basis, the taxpayer may not make another water's-edge election for any taxable year beginning with the 84-month period following the last day of the election period that was terminated, unless the FTB waives the application of this prohibition for good cause. FTB 1115, Request for Consent for a Water's-Edge Re-Election, must be used by the taxpayer to request a re-election for good cause. If the taxpayer's request is approved by the FTB, a taxpayer is still required to attach a Form 100-WE, Water's-Edge Election, to a timely filed Form 100W to perfect the new election. (*Instructions*, FTB 1115, Request for Consent for a Water's Edge Re-Election)

CCH Practice Tip: When Consent Not Required

The FTB's consent for a water's-edge election termination or re-election is not required if the election is being or was terminated as a result of an affiliation change as provided in Rev. & Tax. Code Sec. 25113. (Instructions, FTB 1115, Request for Consent for a Water's-Edge Re-Election; Instructions, FTB 1117, Request to Terminate Water's-Edge Election)

Factor-based "doing business" thresholds: Beginning with the 2011 tax year, California expanded the list of activities that constitute "doing business" in the state by added factor-based thresholds (see ¶ 804). Corporations that are doing business in the state are subject to the California franchise tax (i.e., they are taxpayers). Consequently, a corporation that was not a taxpayer prior to the 2011 tax year could become taxpayer after the 2011 tax year because of the expanded "doing business" standards. In addition, a taxpayer may elect to determine its income derived from or attributable to sources in California under a water's-edge election; however, the election is effective only if every member of the combined reporting group that is subject to tax makes an election.

The FTB has issued guidance covering situations where a unitary foreign affiliate of a water's-edge combined reporting group could not make an election at the time of a water's-edge election because it was not subject to tax in California, but would have been required to make an election after the "doing business" list was expanded. According to the FTB:

— If a unitary foreign affiliate has U.S. income both before and after the tax year that it becomes a taxpayer solely because of the expanded "doing business" standards, it is deemed to have made the election with the other members of the combined reporting group.

— If a unitary foreign affiliate does not have U.S. income either before or after the tax year that it becomes a taxpayer solely because of the expanded list, it would never have been includable in the water's-edge combined report despite its status as a taxpayer. However, in order to give effect to the intent of the unitary group to maintain an effective water's-edge election, the foreign affiliate is deemed to have made an election as of the tax year in which it became a taxpayer. The commencement date of the deemed water's-edge election will be the same as the commencement date of the electing taxpayers of the existing water's-edge combined reporting group. In such circumstances, the foreign affiliate may be included in the group return of the existing combined reporting group for administrative convenience.

— If a unitary foreign affiliate does not have U.S. income before the tax year that it becomes a taxpayer solely because of the expanded "doing business" standards, but has U.S. income after that point, it will be deemed to have made an election as of the tax year in which it becomes a taxpayer. The commencement date of the deemed water's-edge election will be the same as the commencement date of the electing taxpayers of the existing water's-edge combined reporting group.

If certain conditions are satisfied, the FTB will apply these treatments and not seek to terminate the water's-edge election of a water's-edge combined reporting group that is unitary with a foreign affiliate that is now a taxpayer. However, the deemed election provisions will apply only to tax years beginning within 84 months of September 9, 2016. (*FTB Notice 2016-02*, California Franchise Tax Board, September 9, 2016 (CCH CALIFORNIA TAX REPORTS, ¶406-558))

• *Recordkeeping requirements*

A taxpayer electing water's-edge treatment must retain and make available upon request by the FTB various kinds of information and documents relating to, among other things, pricing policy, methods of allocating income and expense, apportionment factors, assignment of income to the United States or to foreign jurisdictions, information filed with the IRS, and tax returns from other states. Furthermore, the taxpayer must also consent to the taking of depositions from key employees or officers of the members of the water's edge group and to the acceptance of subpoenas duces tecum requiring the reasonable production of documents.

The FTB is given broad auditing powers with respect to a water's-edge group. The FTB may apply discretion in deciding when to conduct a detailed examination of a water's-edge taxpayer's returns for noncompliance issues, including transfer pricing, based on an analysis of all factors, including the relative levels of noncompliance and materiality. (Sec. 25112, Rev. & Tax. Code; Reg. 25114, 18 CCR)

¶1312 Deductions for Interest and Contributions

Law: Secs. 24344, 24357 (CCH California Tax Reports, ¶ 10-815, 11-515).

Comparable Federal: Secs. 163, 170 (CCH U.S. Master Tax Guide ¶ 533, 1058—1071).

Adjustment of deductions for interest and contributions may be required where income is allocated within and without the State. (Sec. 24344, Rev. & Tax. Code; Sec. 24357, Rev. & Tax. Code)

The deduction for interest expense may be limited where income from interest or dividends is allocated outside California—see ¶ 1004 for details.

• *Limit on deduction for contributions*

As explained at ¶ 1014, the deduction for contributions is limited to 10% of the net income; this deduction may require adjustment in some cases where a portion of the total net income is allocated outside of California. The usual practice is to treat contributions as one of the deductions entering into the computation of the net income from unitary operations that is subject to allocation within and without the state. If this is done where the total contributions exceed 10% of total net income (and the total deduction has been limited accordingly) and where all the income and deductions relate to the unitary operations, the adjustment of the effective contributions deduction to 10% of the net income used as the measure of the tax is automatic. On the other hand, in a case where the total contributions amount to less than 10% of the net income allocated to California, there is no problem of limitation of the deduction. Under some other circumstances, however, the contributions deduction may require special treatment to limit the deduction to 10% of the net income that is used as the measure of the tax after allocation. (Sec. 24357, Rev. & Tax. Code)

¶1313 Allocation and Apportionment—Administration

Law: Secs. 25101, 25106.5; Regs. 25106.5, 25106.5-11, 18 CCR (CCH California Tax Reports, ¶ 11-520, 11-540, 11-550).

Comparable Federal: None.

California Forms: Sch. R (Apportionment and Allocation of Income).

The return form contains a separate schedule (Schedule R) for allocation of income, with instructions for its use. The schedule provides for the use of the allocation formula described above.

• *Information required from affiliated group*

Where an affiliated group of corporations is involved, the taxpayer is required by the Franchise Tax Board (FTB) to submit information regarding income and business of the group. (Sec. 25106.5, Rev. & Tax. Code: Reg. 25106.5, 18 CCR, Reg. 25106.5-11, 18 CCR) The information submitted should include, in columnar form, profit and loss statements, a combined apportionment formula disclosing for each corporation the total amount of property, payroll, and sales and the amount of California property, payroll, and sales, and schedules disclosing for each corporation:

— the various adjustments necessary to convert the combined profit and loss statement to the combined income subject to apportionment;

— any items of nonbusiness income or expense allocated to California;

— computations of the amount of the interest offset and the charitable contributions adjustment;

— the alternative minimum tax calculation;

— information required by Form 100; and

— the computation of income apportionable and allocable to California and the computation of each member's tax credits and tax liability.

The combined apportionment schedule must reflect the elimination of intercompany sales and other intercompany revenue items, intercompany rent charges, intercompany dividends, and intercompany profits in inventories, if any.

• *Corporations separate entities for some purposes*

Despite the combined reporting approach discussed above, members of the combined group are treated as separate entities for some purposes. Thus, elections to report sales on the installment basis or to use the completed-contract method of accounting should be made individually for each corporation involved. Use of accelerated depreciation methods is based upon the experience of individual group members. (Reg. 25106.5, 18 CCR)

• *Instruction booklet available*

A booklet entitled "Guidelines for Corporations Filing a Combined Report" (FTB Pub. 1061) is available from the FTB. It outlines the rules and schedule format to be followed in preparing such reports.

• *Filing of single combined return*

The FTB permits taxpayers to elect to file one combined return for all the corporations in a unitary group, in lieu of separate returns for each corporation. The parent, or other designated "key" corporation, files the return and pays the entire tax. If the parent corporation is not a California taxpayer, the key corporation should be the taxpayer with the largest value of assets in California. The election is made on Schedule R-7 (part of Sch. R). Each corporation included in the group return must satisfy the following conditions:

— be a taxpayer required to file a return in this state;

— be a member of a single unitary group for the entire taxable year; and

— have the same taxable year as the key corporation or a taxable year that is wholly included within the taxable year of the key corporation, and have the same statutory filing date as the key corporation for the taxable year.

(Reg. 25106.5, 18 CCR)

• *Separate returns for group members*

If a unitary group does not elect the combined-return procedure, a separate return must be filed for each subject corporation. Each such return should carry a notation stating that a combined report has been filed and referring to the inclusion of the necessary supporting schedules in the return of the appropriate corporation. The return of each corporation should reflect the tax on the income allocated to that corporation in the supporting schedules; or, alternatively, the minimum tax may be assessed on all returns except one, and the balance of the entire tax of the affiliated group assessed on the return of one of the group. (Reg. 25106.5, 18 CCR)

• *Reporting should be consistent*

Once a determination has been made as to whether the income should be reported on a combined basis or by separate accounting, the returns should thereafter be prepared on the agreed basis until conditions change so that the method is no longer proper. (Reg. 25106.5, 18 CCR)

TAXES ON CORPORATE INCOME

CHAPTER 14

ADMINISTRATION, DEFICIENCIES, REFUNDS

¶1401 Administration of Tax—General

Law: Sec. 10286, Public Contracts Code; Secs. 18624-25, 19376, 19501-04.7, 19525, 19530, 19717, 21001-26, Rev. & Tax. Code (CCH CALIFORNIA TAX REPORTS, ¶ 10-015, 89-054—89-060, 89-064, 89-068, 89-222).

Comparable Federal: Secs. 6107, 6109, 7430, 7811 (CCH U.S. MASTER TAX GUIDE ¶ 2517, 2707, 2796).

Same as personal income tax (¶ 701).

• *Expatriate corporations*

California state agencies are prohibited from entering into contracts with publicly held expatriate corporations, or any of their subsidiaries, if the corporations have reincorporated overseas in countries in which they have no substantial business activities to avoid paying their fair share of California corporation franchise and/or income taxes. Exceptions apply if the taxpayer was an expatriate corporation before 2004 and provides adequate shareholder protections and uses worldwide combined reporting or if the state has a compelling public interest to contract with the corporation. (Sec. 10286, Public Contracts Code)

¶1402 Taxpayers' Bill of Rights

Law: Secs. 19225, 19547.5, 21001-28 (CCH California Tax Reports, ¶ 89-222).

Comparable Federal: Sec. 7811 (CCH U.S. Master Tax Guide ¶ 2707).

Taxpayers dealing with the Franchise Tax Board (FTB) are given a wide range of protections under the "Katz-Harris Taxpayers' Bill of Rights." The provisions contained in the "Bill of Rights" govern the FTB's administration of both the personal income and corporation franchise and income taxes. (Sec. 21001 et seq., Rev. & Tax. Code)

• *Suspension of corporate powers*

The FTB may not suspend a taxpayer's corporate powers for failure to pay taxes, penalties, or interest, or for failure to file required returns or statements, without mailing the taxpayer a written notice of the suspension at least 60 days in advance. The notice must indicate the date on which the suspension will occur and the statute under which the action is being taken. (Sec. 21020, Rev. & Tax. Code)

• *Hearing and appeal procedures*

Protest hearings before the FTB's audit or legal staff must be held at times and places that are reasonable and convenient to the taxpayer. Prior to the hearing, the taxpayer must be informed of the right to have an attorney, accountant, or other agent present. Hearings may be recorded only with prior notice, and the taxpayer is entitled to receive a copy of any such recording. Further information on protest hearings is at ¶ 1403.

Taxpayers who appeal to the State Board of Equalization (BOE) and who are successful may be awarded reimbursement for reasonable fees and expenses related to the appeal that were incurred after the date of the notice of proposed deficiency assessment. The decision to make such an award is discretionary with the BOE, which must determine, in ruling upon a reimbursement claim filed with the BOE, whether action taken by the FTB's staff was unreasonable and, in particular, whether the FTB has established that its position in the appeal was substantially justified. Fees may be awarded in excess of the fees paid or incurred if the fees paid or incurred are less than reasonable fees. (Sec. 21013, Rev. & Tax. Code)

For appeals to the BOE from an action of the FTB on a deficiency assessment protest or refund claim, the burden of proving the correctness of certain items of income reported by third parties on information returns filed with the FTB also shifts to the FTB if the taxpayer asserts a reasonable dispute with respect to the reported amounts and fully cooperates with the FTB. The items of income to which the shift applies are the same as under federal law.

Further information on appeals to the BOE is at ¶ 1404 and ¶ 1416. (Sec. 21024, Rev. & Tax. Code)

• *Tax levy protections*

The FTB is generally required to send a notice of levy to a taxpayer at least 30 days prior to issuing a levy for unpaid tax. Also, if the FTB holds the collection of unpaid tax in abeyance for more than six months, the FTB must mail the taxpayer an additional notice prior to issuing a levy. If a taxpayer requests an independent administrative review within the 30-day period, the levy action will be suspended until 15 days after there is a final determination in the review. (Sec. 21015.5, Rev. & Tax. Code)

Except in the case of property seized as a result of a jeopardy assessment, a previously issued tax levy must be released whenever the following occur:

— the state's expenses in selling the property levied upon would exceed the taxpayer's liability;

— the proceeds of the sale would not result in a reasonable reduction of the taxpayer's debt;

— the levy was not issued in accordance with administrative procedures;

— the release of the levy will facilitate the collection of the tax liability or will be in the best interest of the taxpayer and the State; or

— the FTB otherwise deems the release of the levy appropriate.

(Sec. 21016, Rev. & Tax. Code)

Certain goods are exempt from levy under California's Code of Civil Procedure; the taxpayer must be notified in writing of these exemptions prior to the sale of any seized property. (Sec. 21017, Rev. & Tax. Code)

• *Civil actions against the FTB; litigation costs*

Taxpayers aggrieved by the reckless disregard of the FTB's published procedures on the part of an officer or employee of the FTB may bring a Superior Court action against the State for actual damages. In determining damages, the court must take into consideration any contributing negligence on the taxpayer's part. A taxpayer prevailing in such an action is entitled to reasonable litigation costs, but there is a penalty of up to $10,000 for filing frivolous claims. (Sec. 21021, Rev. & Tax. Code)

A taxpayer may also file a civil action against the State for direct economic damages and costs totaling up to $50,000 if an officer or employee of the FTB intentionally entices an attorney, certified public accountant, or tax preparer representing the taxpayer into disclosing taxpayer information in exchange for a compromise or settlement of the representative's tax liability. However, the action is not allowed if the information was conveyed by the taxpayer to the representative for the purpose of perpetuating a fraud or crime. The action must be brought within two years after the date the activities creating the liability were discoverable by the exercise of reasonable care. (Sec. 21022, Rev. & Tax. Code)

Practitioner Comment: *Taxpayer is Reimbursed Litigation Costs by California*

See the Practitioner Comment at ¶701 for discussion of a case in which taxpayers were entitled to recover attorney fees incurred in litigation contesting the California FTB's denial of their California tax refund claim.

A taxpayer was entitled to recover litigation costs as a "prevailing party" under Code of Civil Procedure §1032, in the California superior court decision, *ComCon Production Services I, Inc. v. FTB* (2015) (CCH CALIFORNIA TAX REPORTS, ¶89-222.256). Under §1032, a prevailing party in litigation includes the party with a "net monetary recovery." ComCon paid approximately $28 million in California taxes to the FTB prior to litigation. The litigation resulted in a refund of approximately $3 million of that amount to ComCon.

• *Reliance on FTB written opinions; taxpayers' remedies*

Under certain circumstances, taxpayers may be relieved of penalties, interest, or tax liability itself when the taxpayers relied to their detriment on written rulings from the FTB. (Sec. 21019, Rev. & Tax. Code)

The discussion at ¶703 generally applies to corporate taxpayers, with some differences regarding requests for advance rulings. The FTB will not issue advance rulings to corporate taxpayers under the following circumstances (*FTB Notice 2009-8*, CCH CALIFORNIA TAX REPORTS, ¶404-992):

— the question is of a type that the IRS has announced it will not rule on in advance (*e.g.*, hypothetical questions, alternative plans of proposed transactions, frivolous issues);

— the taxpayer's name or identifying number is omitted from the request;

— the requester is a professional preparer or taxpayer representative who has not provided the FTB with his or her own legal analysis and conclusion, a draft of the proposed ruling, and a redacted version of the proposed ruling (where required);

— the law is already clear or is the same as federal law;

— the question is primarily one of fact (*e.g.*, whether a business is unitary); or

— the issue arises in an ongoing audit, appeal, or protest involving the requesting taxpayer.

Practice Tip: Application to Exemption Rulings

These waiver provisions apply to FTB determinations of exemption from tax, but do not apply to exempt acknowledgment letters (see ¶808 for details). (*FTB Notice No. 2009-9*, CCH CALIFORNIA TAX REPORTS, ¶404-993)

Also, see ¶712 for a discussion of the Taxpayers' Rights Advocate's authority to abate penalties, interest, and additions to tax under specified circumstances.

• *Tax liens*

A taxpayer is entitled to preliminary notice of the proposed filing or recording of a tax lien, mailed at least 30 days beforehand; in the interim, the taxpayer may prevent the filing or recording by presenting substantial evidence that the lien would be in error. Also, the FTB must notify taxpayers in writing of the filing or recording of a notice of state tax lien at least five business days after the date the notice of lien is filed. The FTB must mail the taxpayer an additional notice prior to filing or recording a notice of state tax lien if the FTB has held the collection of unpaid tax in abeyance for more than six months. An independent administrative review with the FTB is available if the taxpayer makes a request within the 15-day period beginning on the day after the five-day period described above. (Sec. 21015.5, Rev. & Tax. Code; Sec. 21019, Rev. & Tax. Code)

The FTB must mail a release to the taxpayer and the lien recorder within seven working days if it finds that its action was in error. The FTB may also release a lien if it determines that the release will facilitate the collection of tax or will be in the best interest of the taxpayer and the State.

• *Reimbursement of third-party charges and fees*

A taxpayer may be reimbursed for third-party charges and fees assessed against the taxpayer as a result of an erroneous levy, erroneous processing action, or erroneous collection action by the FTB. The charges and fees that may be reimbursed are limited to the usual and customary charges and fees imposed by a business entity in the ordinary course of business. (Sec. 21018, Rev. & Tax. Code)

• *Unassociated payments*

If the FTB receives a payment from a taxpayer that the FTB cannot associate with the taxpayer's account, the FTB must make reasonable efforts to notify the taxpayer of this situation within 60 days after receipt of the payment. (Sec. 21025, Rev. & Tax. Code)

• *Annual notice of tax delinquencies*

The FTB must mail an annual notice to each taxpayer who has a delinquent tax account, indicating the amount of the delinquency as of the date of the notice, unless a previously mailed notice has been returned to the FTB as undeliverable or the account has been discharged from accountability. (Sec. 21026, Rev. & Tax. Code)

¶1402

• *Client/tax practitioner communications*

California extends the lawyer-client privilege to communications between clients and federally authorized tax practitioners with respect to non-criminal tax matters before the FTB, the BOE, or the Employment Development Department. The privilege does not apply to written communications concerning the promotion of abusive tax shelters. (Sec. 21028, Rev. & Tax. Code)

• *List of retailers, manufacturers with receipts over $100 million*

The FTB must submit to the California attorney general by November 30, 2012, and annually each November 30 thereafter, a list, based on returns filed for the previous taxable year, of retail sellers and manufacturers doing business in the state that have annual worldwide gross receipts in excess of $100 million. These retail sellers and manufacturers are required, beginning January 1, 2012, to disclose their efforts to eradicate slavery and human trafficking from their direct supply chains for tangible goods offered for sale. (Sec. 19547.5, Rev. & Tax. Code)

• *Other provisions*

The Taxpayers' Bill of Rights also requires the FTB to undertake extensive taxpayer education and information programs; report annually to the legislature concerning areas of noncompliance with the tax laws; develop simplified written statements of taxpayer rights and FTB procedures; develop and implement an employee and officer evaluation program; and draw up plans to reduce the time required to resolve amended return claims for refunds, protests, and appeals. As under the personal income tax law (¶723), the FTB is authorized to settle certain civil tax disputes. FTB officers and employees are prohibited from authorizing, requiring, or conducting the investigation or surveillance of taxpayers for reasons unrelated to tax administration.

• *Disclosure of information*

Disclosure of information is discussed at ¶721.

¶1403 Deficiencies—Procedure, Protests

Law: Secs. 19031-34, 19036-51, 19054, 19057-58, 19064-67, 19087 (CCH CALIFORNIA TAX REPORTS, ¶89-164, 89-228, 89-240).

Comparable Federal: Secs. 6211-13, 6501, 7609 (CCH U.S. MASTER TAX GUIDE ¶2709, 2711, 2726, 2778).

Same as personal income tax (¶704).

¶1404 Deficiencies—Appeal to State Board of Equalization

Law: Secs. 19045-48 (CCH CALIFORNIA TAX REPORTS, ¶89-234).

Comparable Federal: Secs. 6211-13 (CCH U.S. MASTER TAX GUIDE ¶2711, 2778, 2838).

Same as personal income tax (¶705).

The California State Board of Equalization (BOE) has taken the position that a nonqualified foreign corporation may file an appeal with the BOE to determine the corporation's California tax filing requirements and appropriate tax liability. However, the case will be dismissed if the BOE determines that the nonqualified foreign corporation transacted intrastate business in California and, therefore, should have obtained a certificate of qualification from the California Secretary of State (*Reitman Atlantic Corp.* (2001) (CCH CALIFORNIA TAX REPORTS, ¶2-020.30)). A domestic corporation that has had its corporation powers suspended is ineligible to initiate an appeal before the BOE.

Practitioner Comment: Legislation Requires BOE to "Publish" Its Decisions

See the Practitioner Comment at ¶705 for a discussion of legislation requiring the BOE to publish its decisions.

¶1405 Final Assessment of Deficiency

Law: Secs. 19042, 19049 (CCH CALIFORNIA TAX REPORTS, ¶89-228).

Comparable Federal: Secs. 6155, 6213 (CCH U.S. MASTER TAX GUIDE ¶2711, 2778).

Same as personal income tax (¶706).

¶1406 Jeopardy Assessments

Law: Secs. 19081-86 (CCH CALIFORNIA TAX REPORTS, ¶89-168).

Comparable Federal: Secs. 6861, 6863 (CCH U.S. MASTER TAX GUIDE ¶2713).

Same as personal income tax (¶707).

¶1407 Bankruptcy and Receiverships

Law: Sec. 19088 (CCH CALIFORNIA TAX REPORTS, ¶89-170).

Comparable Federal: Secs. 6871-73 (CCH U.S. MASTER TAX GUIDE ¶2736).

Same as personal income tax (¶708).

¶1408 Transferee Liability

Law: Secs. 19071-74 (CCH CALIFORNIA TAX REPORTS, ¶89-166).

Comparable Federal: Secs. 6901-04 (CCH U.S. MASTER TAX GUIDE ¶2745, 2782).

The law contains provisions permitting assessment and collection of tax from persons secondarily liable. The period of limitations is extended for assessments against transferees and fiduciaries. California law is the same as federal law. (Sec. 19071 et seq., Rev. & Tax. Code)

Both California and federal laws provide for suspension of the running of the period of limitations against the transferee while the taxpayer is exercising an administrative remedy.

¶1409 Statute of Limitations on Assessments

Law: Secs. 18572, 19057-67, 19255, 19755 (CCH CALIFORNIA TAX REPORTS, ¶89-144).

Comparable Federal: Secs. 1311-14, 6501-4, 7508A, 7609 (CCH U.S. MASTER TAX GUIDE ¶2726, 2735, 2736, 2756).

Same as personal income tax, as explained at ¶710, except that the corporation tax law extends the limitation period under certain circumstances as to transferees and fiduciaries whereas the personal income tax law does not. The running of the statute of limitations is also suspended until a taxpayer reports required information to the FTB concerning foreign corporations or transfers to foreign persons (see ¶1414 for a discussion of the reporting requirements). (Sec. 18572, Rev. & Tax. Code; Sec. 19057 et seq., Rev. & Tax. Code; Sec. 19255 Rev. & Tax. Code; Sec. 19755, Rev. & Tax. Code)

California law has no provision for a shortened period of limitations for dissolving corporations; federal law does.

¶1405

¶1410 Interest on Deficiencies

Law: Secs. 19101, 19104, 19108, 19109, 19112-14, 19120, 19521, 19777-78 (CCH CALIFORNIA TAX REPORTS, ¶ 89-192, 89-204).

Comparable Federal: Secs. 6404, 6601, 6621 (CCH U.S. MASTER TAX GUIDE ¶ 2813, 2838).

Interest is charged on deficiencies, other delinquent payments of tax, and on extensions of payment of tax and penalties. (Sec. 19101, Rev. & Tax. Code) The rules are generally the same as for the personal income tax, as outlined at ¶711. However, there is a special higher interest rate applicable to large corporate underpayments (see below).

Interest rates are as follows:

January 1, 2013—December 31, 2013	3%
January 1, 2014—December 31, 2014	3%
January 1, 2015—December 31, 2015	3%
January 1, 2016—December 31, 2016	3%
January 1, 2017—June 30, 2017	4%

The rate is determined semiannually and compounded daily, as explained at ¶711.

Both federal and California law allow the abatement of all or any portion of interest that results from errors or delays in the performance of ministerial acts by the respective taxing agencies, as explained at ¶711. (Sec. 19104, Rev. & Tax. Code) Abatement of interest is also available to victims of disasters, also discussed at ¶711. (Sec. 19109, Rev. & Tax. Code)

There is a special rule that applies to certain cases involving related items where overpayments are offset against deficiencies. In such cases, no interest is charged on the portion of the deficiency extinguished by the credit for overpayment for the period subsequent to the date the overpayment was made. (Sec. 19108, Rev. & Tax. Code)

• *Interest on large corporate underpayments*

Both California and federal law require all corporations except S corporations to pay interest on large underpayments at 2% above the regular rate. A large underpayment is one that exceeds $100,000 for any taxable period. Under federal law, the 2% interest rate increase generally applies to periods after the 30th day following the date the IRS sends either a "30-day letter" or a deficiency notice, whichever is earlier. California modifies this provision so that the increased interest rate applies to periods after the 30th day following either the date on which a proposed assessment is issued or the date when the notice and demand is sent, whichever is earlier. (Sec. 19521, Rev. & Tax. Code)

Under both California and federal law, interest does not begin to accrue until after the mailing of a letter or notice of deficiency, proposed deficiency, assessment, or proposed assessment shows an amount exceeding $100,000. FTB Notice 98-6 (1998) addresses the calculation of the additional interest imposed against unitary corporate members filing a group return (see CCH CALIFORNIA TAX REPORTS, ¶ 89-202.451).

¶1411 Penalties

Law: Secs. 18631.7, 19131-36, 19141-41.6, 19164, 19166-69, 19172.5, 19176-81, 19183, 19187, 19254, 19262, 19442, 19701-06, 19708-15, 19719-21, 19730-38, 19772-4, 19775.5, 21015, 23156, 23186 (CCH CALIFORNIA TAX REPORTS, ¶ 10-059, 89-192, 89-206—89-210).

Comparable Federal: Secs. 6038A, 6038B, 6038C, 6038D, 6050I, 6651-53, 6657-58, 6662-65, 6673, 6694, 6700-03, 6706, 6721-24, 7201-06 (CCH U.S. MASTER TAX GUIDE ¶ 510, 537, 625, 2011, 2145, 2518, 2521, 2579, 2801, 2805, 2811, 2814, 2816, 2823, 2833, 2854, 2856, 2858, 2860, 2862, 2866).

California Form: FTB 2300 BE (Franchise and Income Tax Amnesty Application - for Business Entities).

[NOTE: See ¶ 1402 for a discussion of possible relief after detrimental reliance on advice from the Franchise Tax Board (FTB).]

Same as personal income tax, including the amnesty program, as explained at ¶ 712, except as noted below.

The corporation tax law does not include provisions for the following penalties listed at ¶ 712: failure to report personal services remuneration; failure to report real estate transaction; failure to make small business stock report; and failure to file partnership return.

The corporation tax law contains provisions similar to the following penalties described at ¶ 712, but the possible fines are higher, reaching a maximum of $200,000:

— willfully making or signing a return of document containing a declaration made under penalty of perjury that the maker or signer does not believe to be materially true or correct;

— willfully aiding preparation or presentation of a false return or document;

— falsely executing or signing a bond, permit, entry, or required document;

— removing, depositing, or concealing taxable goods to evade tax; and

— concealing property or destroying or falsifying records in regard to a tax settlement, closing agreement, compromise, or offer in compromise.

¶1411

Similarly, the maximum fine for willful failure of a check cashing business to file an information return may reach $100,000 for corporate taxpayers.

For purposes of the accuracy-related penalty for substantial understatements, a substantial understatement exists for a corporation, other than an S corporation, if the amount of the understatement for the taxable year exceeds the lesser of: (1) 10% of the tax required to be shown on the return for the taxable year (or, if greater, $2,500), or (2) $5 million. For all other taxpayers, a substantial understatement exists if the amount of the understatement exceeds the greater of (1) 10% of the tax required to be shown on the return, or (2) $10,000. (Sec. 19164, Rev. & Tax. Code)

For purposes of the enhanced penalty for substantial underpayments, the "excess" is determined without regard to items to which the reportable transaction accuracy-related penalty or the noneconomic substance transaction understatement penalty is imposed. (Sec. 19164, Rev. & Tax. Code)

The corporation tax law provides the following penalties in addition to those described at ¶712:

— failing without reasonable cause to file return if a corporation or a limited liability company is doing business in the state without being qualified—$2,000 per taxable year (Sec. 19135, Rev. & Tax. Code);

— failing to file corporate organization statement—$250 ($50 for nonprofit corporation) (Sec. 19141, Rev. & Tax. Code);

— failing to furnish information concerning foreign-controlled corporation—$10,000 per year of failure (Sec. 19141.5, Rev. & Tax. Code);

— failing to furnish information concerning transfers to foreign persons— 10% of fair market value at time of exchange (Sec. 19141.5, Rev. & Tax. Code);

— failing to report transactions between foreign corporations and foreign investors—$10,000 per year of failure (Sec. 19141.5, Rev. & Tax. Code);

— failing to furnish information with respect to foreign financial assets (taxable years beginning on or after January 1, 2016)—$10,000 per year of failure (Sec. 19141.5, Rev. & Tax. Code);

— failing to keep water's edge records—$10,000 per year; if 90 days after notice by the FTB, $10,000 per 30-day period (Sec. 19141.6, Rev. & Tax. Code);

— failing to file copy of federal information return concerning large cash transactions—$50 per return, up to $100,000 maximum per year; if intentional disregard, $100 per return, or, if greater, 5% of the aggregate amount of items required to be reported (Sec. 19183, Rev. & Tax. Code);

— failing to provide information that is required to determine rate of bank and franchise tax—$5,000 and disallowance of specified deductions (Sec. 23186, Rev. & Tax. Code);

— exercising the powers of a corporation suspended for nonpayment of taxes or transacting interstate business of a forfeited foreign corporation— misdemeanor; $250 to $1,000 and/or up to one year in jail (however, the penalty does not apply to any insurer, or counsel retained by an insurer, who provides a defense for a suspended or forfeited corporation in a civil action for personal injury, property damage, or economic losses, and who prosecutes, in conjunction with that defense, any subrogation, contribution, or indemnity rights against other persons or entities in the name of the suspended or forfeited corporation) (Sec. 19179, Rev. & Tax. Code); and

— failure without reasonable cause to timely file S corporation return—$18 per month multiplied by number of shareholders, up to a 12-month maximum (Sec. 19172.5, Rev. & Tax. Code).

Practice Note: Reasonable Cause Abatement Form

The FTB has created a form for corporate taxpayers to use to request penalty abatement due to reasonable cause: FTB 2924, Reasonable Cause – Business Entity Claim for Refund. The new form allows the FTB to scan and associate forms with taxpayers, properly route requests to the proper workbasket and agent, easily identify claims for refund, and reduce unnecessary correspondence. The FTB recommends that taxpayers use the new form, but it will also continue to accept and process handwritten reasonable cause abatement letter requests. Taxpayers may consult FTB 1024, Franchise Tax Board Penalty Reference Chart, for a list of penalties eligible for abatement due to reasonable cause. (*Public Service Bulletin 14-26*, California Franchise Tax Board, September 4, 2014)

CCH Caution: Large Corporate Understatement Penalty

Business entities that understate their tax liability by more than the greater of $1 million or 20% of the tax shown on the return are subject to a 20% large corporate understatement penalty (LCUP), in addition to any other penalty that may be imposed. Taxpayers required or allowed to be included in a combined report must aggregate the group members' understatements for purposes of determining whether the $1 million threshold has been reached. An increase in tax shown on the first amended return reflecting a proper IRC §338 election (relating to certain stock purchases treated as asset line acquisitions) will be treated as an amount of tax shown on an original return for purposes of the large corporate understatement penalty. The penalty does not apply to understatements attributable to a change in law that is enacted, promulgated, issued, or becomes final after the earlier of either (1) the date the taxpayer files the return for the taxable year for which the change is operative, or (2) the extended due date for the taxpayer's return or the taxable year for which the change is operative. Nor can the penalty be imposed if the understatement resulted from the taxpayer's reliance on written advice contained in an FTB Chief Counsel Ruling. The penalty also does not apply to an understatement attributable to a change to the taxpayer's federal method of accounting, but only to the extent of understatements for taxable years where the due date of the return, without regard to any extension of time for filing the return, is before the date the Secretary of the Treasury consents to that change. Further, applicable to understatements for any taxable year for which the statute of limitations on assessments has not expired as of September 30, 2015, the penalty does not apply to an understatement attributable to the imposition of an alternative apportionment or allocation method by the FTB under the authority of Rev. and Tax. Code §25137 when the standard allocation and apportionment provisions do not fairly represent the extent of the taxpayer's business activity in the state. (Sec. 19138, Rev. & Tax. Code)

The Revenue and Taxation Code provisions governing deficiency assessment notices and hearing rights are inapplicable to the assessment and collection of this penalty. Furthermore, credits and refunds of the penalty are limited to the amount improperly calculated by the FTB. (Sec. 19138, Rev. & Tax. Code) The FTB has posted on its Web site answers to a list of frequently asked questions concerning the large corporate understatement penalty, see https://www.ftb.ca.gov/businesses/large_corporate_understatement_penalty_faqs.shtml.

A California court of appeal ruled that the large understatement penalty is a valid penalty and not an unconstitutional tax. In so holding, the court rejected a taxpayer association's claim that the governing provision was enacted for the purpose of raising revenues in order to help bridge California's large budget deficit and, therefore, was a tax that required a two-thirds vote of the Legislature in order to pass constitutional muster pursuant to Art. XIIIA, Sec. 3 (Proposition 13). The court also rejected a claim that the penalty provision violated taxpayers' procedural due process rights because it affords no pre-or post-payment review process. Although the penalty provision precludes a taxpayer from utilizing the administrative hearing venue to protest the penalty, there is nothing specifically in the statute that prohibits taxpayers from bringing a refund action in the courts, which provides a constitutionally adequate post-deprivation remedy. The California Supreme Court denied review of the decision. (*California Taxpayers' Association v. California Franchise Tax Board* (2010), CCH CALIFORNIA TAX REPORTS, ¶405-313)

Practitioner Comment: Limited Safe Harbors Exist with Respect to 20% Penalty for Large Corporate Understatements (LCUP)

As noted above, S.B. X1 28, signed into law on October 1, 2008, imposes a 20% penalty applicable to corporate franchise tax understatements in excess of $1 million for taxable years beginning on or after January 1, 2003. The penalty applies in addition to other penalties (e.g., accuracy-related, noneconomic substance transaction, underpayment penalties, etc.). There is no reasonable cause exception to the penalty, although the penalty will not be applied for tax years beginning before January 1, 2008, to the extent the tax was paid with an amended return filed on or before May 31, 2009. Otherwise, the penalty will apply unless attributable to a change in law (including regulation changes and rulings) that becomes final after the taxpayer has timely filed its return or if the taxpayer reasonably relied on a Chief Counsel Ruling. Thus, while an amnesty program was not enacted as part of the 2008 budget legislation, the 20% penalty could be avoided if taxes relating to years prior to 2008 were paid by the end of May 2009. Unlike the 2005 amnesty program, however, there was no ability to avoid the penalty by making a tax deposit. Instead the FTB indicated that an amended return disclosing the nature of the adjustments needed to be filed and the taxes paid by May 31, 2009, to avoid the penalty. Taxpayers may claim a refund after May 31, 2009, for amounts paid with those amended returns.

In addition to updating California's IRC conformity date to January 1, 2015, A.B. 154, signed into law by the governor on September 30, 2015, contains additional safe harbors to the LCUP. First, increases in tax related to a proper IRC § 338 election as reported on the first amended return are not subject to the LCUP. Furthermore, LCUPs do not apply to an understatement that is attributable to either the FTB imposing an alternative apportionment or allocation method under the authority of Cal. Rev. & Tax. Code § 25137 to prevent distortion in the allocation and apportionment of income to California, or a change to the taxpayer's federal method of accounting, but only to the extent of understatements for taxable years where the due date of the return, without regard to any extension of time for filing the return, is before the date the Secretary of the Treasury consents to that change.

Chris Whitney, Contributing Editor

Practitioner Comment: California Budget Bill Effectively Creates a De Minimis Exception to 20% Understatement Penalty

On October 8, 2010, the California Legislature enrolled S.B. 858, which had been included as part of an overall budget agreement with the Governor. The 2010-2011 Budget Bill has modified the large corporate understatement penalty to effectively include a de minimis exception. The penalty is modified for taxable years beginning on or after January 1, 2010, to apply only to understatements that exceed the greater of $1 million or 20% of the tax shown on the original return or amended return filed on or before the original or extended due date of the return. Previously, penalties applied to all understatements in excess of $1 million, including situations where the understatement only accounted for a small percentage of a large taxpayer's liability. As a result of this legislation, the penalty will apply to a fewer number of understatements.

Chris Whitney, Contributing Editor

Practitioner Comment: California's Adoption of COES Is In Addition to Existing NEST Provisions and IRS Application of Penalties Are Presumed To Be Correct for California Tax Purposes

S.B. 86, enacted March 25, 2011, amends Cal. Rev. & Tax. Code § 19774. Since 2003, § 19774 has provided for a 40% "noneconomic substance transaction penalty" ("NEST"), which is reduced to 20% if the underlying transaction is "adequately disclosed in the return." Historically, NEST penalties have been based on broad and nebulous statutory language that applies the penalties to any transaction that lacks a "valid non-tax California business purpose." S.B. 86 adds to the NEST provisions a codified presumption of correctness for any IRC § 6662A(b)(2) penalty imposed by the IRS and expands the NEST definition to include transactions described under IRC § 7701(o) (the codification of economic substance or "COES" penalties of the IRS).

Chris Whitney, Contributing Editor

See ¶ 811 for penalties imposed for late filing of returns of exempt organizations.

A penalty for the failure to file a federal information return regarding large cash transactions is imposed in accordance with federal law. (Sec. 19183, Rev. & Tax. Code)

• *Penalties imposed under Corporations Code*

The corporation tax law imposes a penalty of $250 for failure to file with the Secretary of State an annual statement required by California Corporations Code Sec. 1502 (¶ 810). The tax law also imposes a penalty of $50 for failure of a nonprofit corporation to file with the Secretary of State a statement required by Sec. 6210, Corp. Code, or Sec. 8210, Corp. Code (¶ 811). (Sec. 19141, Rev. & Tax. Code)

• *Collection and filing enforcement fees*

Collection cost recovery and filing enforcement fees similar to those discussed at ¶ 712 are imposed under the corporation tax law, but the applicable fees for the state's 2016—2017 fiscal year are $365 and $100, respectively. The fees do not apply to exempt organizations.

• *Relief from penalties*

Relief from the penalties for failure to furnish information concerning foreign controlled corporations, failure to furnish information concerning transfers to foreign persons, and failure to report transactions between foreign corporations and foreign investors may be granted, provided that the taxpayer's failure to furnish the required information neither jeopardized the best interests of the state nor resulted from the taxpayer's willful neglect or an intent not to comply. (Sec. 21015, Rev. & Tax. Code)

Also, effective January 1, 2016, the FTB must, upon written request by a qualified nonprofit corporation, abate unpaid qualified taxes, interest, and penalties, for taxable years for which the nonprofit corporation certifies, under penalty of perjury, that it was not doing business in the state. Abatement will be conditioned on the dissolution of the qualified corporation within 12 months from the date of filing the request for abatement. (Sec. 23156, Rev. & Tax. Code)

• *Cases and rulings*

Appeal of BSR USA, Ltd., and BSR North America, Ltd. (1996) (CCH CALIFORNIA TAX REPORTS, ¶ 89-206.6191) involved the imposition of the 25% penalty for failure to furnish information on notice and demand by the FTB. The corporate taxpayers failed to respond to repeated requests by the FTB for information concerning the income and apportionment factors of the taxpayers' foreign affiliates. The penalty was not subject to abatement, because the taxpayers' conduct indicated a pattern of delay and misdirection that belied their contention that the requested information was either not available or too costly to obtain.

In *Appeal of Vidal Sassoon, Inc.* (1986) (CCH CALIFORNIA TAX REPORTS, ¶ 89-206.24), the reasonable cause exception was not applicable to late extension requests and the State Board of Equalization (BOE) upheld the late-filing penalty.

In *Appeal of Krofft Entertainment, Inc.* (1984) (CCH CALIFORNIA TAX REPORTS, ¶ 89-206.74), the taxpayer claimed that its failure to file a timely franchise tax return was due to reasonable cause. The BOE upheld the imposition of a $17,436 penalty, despite the fact that the Internal Revenue Service had removed a similar federal penalty upon a finding of reasonable cause.

¶1411

In *Appeal of Avco Financial Services, Inc.* (1979) (CCH CALIFORNIA TAX REPORTS, ¶ 89-206.48), a late payment penalty was imposed in a case where 84% of the tax was paid by the regular due date. The BOE upheld the penalty, noting that the difficulty of estimating the tax on worldwide income did not constitute reasonable cause for the underpayment. To the same effect, see *Appeal of Diebold, Incorporated* (1983) (CCH CALIFORNIA TAX REPORTS, ¶ 89-206.773); in this case, the taxpayer's extensive operations required the filing of approximately 350 state and local tax returns.

¶1412 Information at Source

Law: Secs. 18631, 18639-44, 18648-49 (CCH CALIFORNIA TAX REPORTS, ¶ 89-104).

Comparable Federal: Secs. 6041, 6041A, 6042, 6050I, 6050L (CCH U.S. MASTER TAX GUIDE ¶ 2565, 2607).

Same as personal income tax (¶ 713).

¶1413 Withholding of Tax at Source

Law: Secs. 18661-62, 18665, 18667-77, 19009 (CCH CALIFORNIA TAX REPORTS, ¶ 12-705, 89-056, 89-176).

Comparable Federal: Secs. 1441, 1445 (CCH U.S. MASTER TAX GUIDE ¶ 2442, 2492).

The corporation tax law gives the Franchise Tax Board broad power to require the withholding of tax on payments to payees subject to either franchise or income tax. (Sec. 18661, Rev. & Tax. Code; Sec. 18662, Rev. & Tax. Code) Withholding of tax is required on income paid to corporations that do not have a permanent place of business in this state. A corporation has a permanent place of business in this state if it is organized under the laws of this state or if it is a foreign corporation qualified to transact business in this state.

Corporations, among others, are required to withhold tax on certain payments to nonresidents, to withhold amounts due from delinquent taxpayers, to withhold tax on dispositions of California real estate, and to withhold tax from wages (¶ 714, ¶ 715, ¶ 716).

¶1414 Reports on Foreign and Foreign-Owned Corporations, Transfers to Foreign Persons

Law: Secs. 19141.2, 19141.5, 21015 (CCH CALIFORNIA TAX REPORTS, ¶ 89-104).

Comparable Federal: Secs. 6038, 6038A, 6038B, 6038C, 6038D (CCH U.S. MASTER TAX GUIDE ¶ 2466, 2491A, 2565).

Corporations that are incorporated in California or doing business in the state and that are more than 25% foreign owned must file a copy of the information return required by IRC Sec. 6038A (federal Form 5472) with respect to transactions with related parties. Special record-keeping requirements are also imposed. Failure to comply subjects a corporation to a $10,000 penalty. (Sec. 19141.5, Rev. & Tax. Code)

In addition, California has adopted the information reporting requirements of IRC Secs. 6038B and 6038C. IRC Sec. 6038B requires the filing of information returns with respect to certain transfers of property to foreign corporations and other foreign persons and, in cases of failure to report, imposes a penalty equal to 10% of the property's fair market value, determined at the time of the exchange. IRC Sec. 6038C requires foreign corporations engaged in U.S. business to file information returns and imposes a $10,000 penalty for noncompliance. (Sec. 19141.5, Rev. & Tax. Code)

For taxable years beginning on or after January 1, 2016, California also adopts the information reporting requirements with respect to foreign financial assets as set forth in IRC Sec. 6038D. The penalty for noncompliance is $10,000 per year of failure. (Sec. 19141.5, Rev. & Tax. Code)

Relief from these penalties may be granted, provided that the taxpayer's failure to furnish the required information neither jeopardized the best interests of the state nor resulted from the taxpayer's willful neglect or an intent not to comply. (Sec. 21015, Rev. & Tax. Code)

Domestic corporations subject to California corporation franchise or income tax that own more than 50% of the combined voting power, or the value, of all classes of stock of a foreign corporation are required to file with the FTB a copy of the information return required by IRC Sec. 6038 with respect to interests in a foreign corporation (federal Form 5471). If a taxpayer fails to comply without reasonable cause and not due to willful neglect, the taxpayer is subject to a penalty equal to $1,000 for each annual accounting period in which the information is not supplied and an additional $1,000 for each 30-day period (or fraction thereof) beyond the first 90 days, up to a maximum penalty of $24,000. The penalty may be waived if (1) a copy of the information return is filed with the FTB within 90 days after notification and the taxpayer agrees to attach a copy of the information to the taxpayer's original return for subsequent taxable years, or (2) the taxpayer enters into a voluntary disclosure agreement with the FTB (¶1422). (Sec. 19141.2, Rev. & Tax. Code)

¶1415 Overpayments and Refunds—Procedure

Law: Secs. 19301-24, 19331-35 (CCH California Tax Reports, ¶89-224).

Comparable Federal: Secs. 6401-08 (CCH U.S. Master Tax Guide ¶2759 et seq.).

California Form: Form 100X (Amended Corporation Franchise or Income Tax Return).

Same as personal income tax, as explained at ¶717, except that refund claims should be filed on Form 100X (Amended Corporation Franchise or Income Tax Return).

A corporation that overpays its tax under the estimated-tax procedure may obtain a refund before the return is filed (¶813).

¶1416 Refund Claims—Appeal to State Board of Equalization

Law: Secs. 19332-34 (CCH California Tax Reports, ¶89-234).

Same as personal income tax (¶718).

¶1417 Statute of Limitations on Refund Claims

Law: Secs. 19041.5, 19306-14, 19322.1 (CCH California Tax Reports, ¶89-224).

Comparable Federal: Secs. 6511, 7508A (CCH U.S. Master Tax Guide ¶2482, 2537, 2763).

Same as personal income tax, as explained at ¶719, except that the special seven-year rule (item (c)) does not apply to worthless securities losses. (Sec. 19041.5, Rev. & Tax. Code; Sec. 19306 et seq., Rev. & Tax. Code; Sec. 19322.1, Rev. & Tax. Code)

The law permits a barred refund of one taxpayer to be offset against a deficiency of an affiliated taxpayer in cases where the tax is determined on a combined basis as discussed at ¶1310. This provision also permits a similar offset where items of income or deductions have been transferred from one year to another. However, an offset will not be allowed in either case where more than seven years have elapsed from the due date of the return on which the overpayment is determined. (Sec. 19314, Rev. & Tax. Code)

¶1418 Suits for Refund

Law: Secs. 19041.5, 19381-92 (CCH California Tax Reports, ¶89-224).

Comparable Federal: Sec. 6532 (CCH U.S. Master Tax Guide ¶2738, 2792).

Same as personal income tax (¶720).

¶1419 Interest on Overpayments

Law: Secs. 19325, 19340-51, 19363, 19521 (CCH CALIFORNIA TAX REPORTS, ¶89-204).

Comparable Federal: Sec. 6611 (CCH U.S. MASTER TAX GUIDE ¶2765).

The corporation tax rules for interest on overpayments are generally the same as for personal income tax, as explained at ¶722. The adjusted annual interest rate on overpayments of corporation franchise and income taxes is the lesser of 5% or the bond equivalent rate of a 13-week U.S. Treasury bill. (Sec. 19521, Rev. & Tax. Code)

Interest rates are as follows:

January 1, 2013—June 30, 2017 . . . . 0%

In *Appeal of MCA, Inc.* (1967) (CCH CALIFORNIA TAX REPORTS, ¶89-202.57), the State Board of Equalization allowed interest on an overpayment of franchise tax although the Franchise Tax Board had contended that such interest was not payable because the overpayment was not made "incident to a bona fide and orderly discharge of an actual liability."

¶1420 Closing Agreements

Law: Secs. 19441-42 (CCH CALIFORNIA TAX REPORTS, ¶89-186).

Comparable Federal: Sec. 7121 (CCH U.S. MASTER TAX GUIDE ¶2721).

Same as personal income tax (¶723).

¶1421 Compromise of Tax Liability

Law: Sec. 19443 (CCH CALIFORNIA TAX REPORTS, ¶89-186).

Comparable Federal: Sec. 7122 (CCH U.S. MASTER TAX GUIDE ¶2723).

Same as personal income tax (¶724).

¶1422 Voluntary Disclosure Agreements

Laws: Secs. 19191-94 (CCH CALIFORNIA TAX REPORTS, ¶89-186).

Comparable Federal: None.

California Form: FTB 4925 (Application for Voluntary Disclosure).

Same as personal income tax (¶725).

¶1423 Recovery of Erroneous Refunds

Law: Secs. 19054, 19368, 19411-13 (CCH CALIFORNIA TAX REPORTS, ¶89-190).

Comparable Federal: Secs. 6532, 6602, 7405 (CCH U.S. MASTER TAX GUIDE ¶2738).

Same as personal income tax (¶726).

¶1424 Abusive Tax Shelters

Law: Secs. 18407, 18628, 18648, 19164, 19751-54 (CCH CALIFORNIA TAX REPORTS, ¶89-102, 89-104, 89-206, 89-210).

Comparable Federal: Secs. 6011, 6111 (CCH U.S. MASTER TAX GUIDE ¶2001 et seq.).

Same as personal income tax (¶727).

Practitioner Comment: FTB Ruling Holds That Noneconomic Substance Tax Penalty Will Not Apply to Taxpayer Restructuring in Order to Meet IRC Sec. 355 Requirements

California imposes a noneconomic substance tax or "NEST" penalty on transactions lacking a "valid non-tax California business purpose." Since its enactment there has been significant uncertainty as to what constitutes a "non-tax California business purpose" and when the penalty might be applied. Taxpayers received some guidance in the case of a restructuring that was undertaken in an effort to qualify a distribution of subsidiary stock as tax free under California's adoption of IRC Sec. 355. Due to California's January 1, 2005 IRC conformity date that was in effect prior to the 2010 tax year, California was out of conformity with 2006 federal amendments made to IRC Sec. 355(b)(3) for several years, see the Practitioner Comment at ¶517. The Franchise Tax Board in Chief Counsel Ruling 2007-3, July 17, 2007, held that a taxpayer's attempts to restructure in order to satisfy California's conformity to the IRC 355 provisions prior to the 2006 amendments, although having the effect of avoiding the imposition of California corporate franchise taxes, would not be regarded as a NEST transaction to which the penalties under Rev. & Tax. Code Sec. 19774 could be applied. In reaching this conclusion, the ruling observed that the IRS has consistently held that a taxpayer can engage in a tax-free structuring for the purpose of qualifying for the active business requirement under the pre-2006 version of IRC Sec. 355. [CCH Note: Also see *Chief Counsel Ruling 2008-1*, August 11, 2008, CCH CALIFORNIA TAX REPORTS, ¶404-924.]

Chris Whitney, Contributing Editor

• *Listed transactions identified by the FTB*

The FTB has identified circular cash flow transactions as listed transactions that may subject participants to a variety of corporation franchise and income tax penalties and trigger various reporting requirements for participants and their material advisors. The transactions described by the FTB involve parent corporations that artificially increase their basis in the stock of their subsidiaries, without any outlay of cash or property, prior to the parent selling the subsidiary's stock to an unrelated third party, thereby minimizing the taxable gain from the stock sale. (*FTB Notice 2011-04*, CCH CALIFORNIA TAX REPORTS, ¶405-489)

Sales factor manipulation transactions in which apportioning corporate taxpayers use one or more partnerships to improperly inflate the denominator of their California sales factor have also been identified by the FTB as listed transactions. These manipulations reduce the amount of business income apportioned to California for franchise or income tax purposes and the FTB considers these transactions to be tax avoidance transactions and will disallow any tax benefits claimed as a result of the sales factor manipulation. (*FTB Notice 2011-01*, CCH CALIFORNIA TAX REPORTS, ¶405-331)

Practitioner Comment: California "Listed Transactions"

See the Practitioner Comment at ¶727 for further discussion of the listed transactions identified by the FTB.

PART V

SALES AND USE TAXES

CHAPTER 15
SALES AND USE TAXES

¶1501 Overview of Sales and Use Taxes

Law: Secs. 6025-31, 6051-51.5, 6201-01.5, 7200-12, 7251.1 (CCH CALIFORNIA TAX REPORTS, ¶60-010, 60-020, 60-110, 61-720).

The California sales tax was first imposed in 1933; the use tax in 1935. These taxes, which are administered by the State Board of Equalization, have become a major source of the state's revenue.

The sales tax is imposed upon retailers for the privilege of selling tangible personal property at retail. (Sec. 6051, Rev. & Tax. Code) Although the tax is not levied directly on the consumer, it is ordinarily passed on to the consumer. The use tax, enacted as a complement to the sales tax, is imposed upon the storage, use, or other consumption in California of tangible personal property purchased from a retailer without being subjected to the sales tax. (Sec. 6202, Rev. & Tax. Code)

¶1502 Imposition of Tax—Constitutional Limitations

Law: Secs. 2-4, Art. XIIIA, Cal. Constitution; Secs. 23027, 50075 et seq., Government Code; Sec. 99550, Public Utility Code (CCH CALIFORNIA TAX REPORTS, ¶61-710).

Several sections of the U.S. Constitution restrict the authority of states to levy sales and use taxes. The Commerce Clause restricts states from levying taxes that unduly burden interstate commerce. (Cl. 3, Art. I, U.S. Const.) The Due Process Clause prevents a state from taxing a business or requiring it to collect sales and use taxes, unless the business has some connection with the taxing state. (Amend. XIV, U.S. Const.) The Equal Protection Clause restricts states from creating discriminatory classifications among taxpayers. (Amend. XIV, U.S. Const.) The Import-Export Clause precludes states from enacting duties on imports or exports. (Sec. 10, Cl. 2, U.S. Const.) The Supremacy Clause restricts states from taxing the federal government or any of its agencies or instrumentalities. (Art. VI, U.S. Const.) The First Amendment limits a state's authority to impose taxes that interfere with freedom of speech or freedom of religion. (Amend. I, U.S. Const.)

Counties, cities, and special districts are prohibited from imposing "special taxes" (those levied to fund a specific governmental project or program) unless two-thirds of the local electorate approves. (Sec. 4, Art. XIIIA, Cal. Const.)

In *Richard J. Rider et al. v. County of San Diego et al.* (1991) (CCH CALIFORNIA TAX REPORTS, ¶61-710.46), the California Supreme Court invalidated a transactions and use tax imposed by the San Diego County Regional Justice Facility Financing Agency with the approval of a bare majority of the district's voters, because the agency was a "special district" and the tax it imposed was a "special tax."

The *Rider* court determined that the term "special district" includes any taxing agency created to raise funds for city or county purposes to replace revenues lost because of Proposition 13's restrictions on property taxation (see ¶1702 for a discussion of Proposition 13). Approval by a two-thirds vote was similarly required in *Howard Jarvis Taxpayers' Association et al. v. State Board of Equalization* (1993) (CCH CALIFORNIA TAX REPORTS, ¶61-710.464) for any local sales and use tax imposed by a county justice facilities financing agency in Orange, Humboldt, Los Angeles, Riverside, San Bernardino, Stanislaus, or Ventura county.

In *Hoogasian Flowers, Inc., et al. v. State Board of Equalization* (1994) (CCH CALIFORNIA TAX REPORTS, ¶61-730.39), a California court of appeal held that a local sales and use tax imposed by the San Francisco Educational Financing Authority for the general purpose of providing financial assistance to schools was invalid because it was not approved by two-thirds of the electorate voting on the measure, as required under *Rider*.

In *Santa Clara County Local Transportation Authority v. Carl Guardino et al.* (1995) (CCH CALIFORNIA TAX REPORTS, ¶61-710.465), the California Supreme Court upheld a majority vote approval requirement for "general taxes" proposed by local governments. In 1996, California voters approved a measure that specifically prohibits *all* local governments, including charter cities, from imposing, extending, or increasing any general tax after November 5, 1996, without the approval of a majority of the local electorate.

¶1503 Rate of Tax

Law: Secs. 6025-31, 6051-51.5, 6201-01.5, 7200-12, 7251.1 (CCH CALIFORNIA TAX REPORTS, ¶60-110, ¶61-735).

Effective January 1, 2017, the total statewide base sales and use tax rate is 7.25% (formerly, 7.5%). Tax rates in certain areas are higher than the total statewide base rate depending on applicable district taxes. (Secs. 6051, 6051.2, 6051.3, 6051.5, 6201, 6201.2, 6201.3, 6201.5, 7203.1, Rev. & Tax. Code; Sec. 35, Art. XIII, Cal. Const.; Sec. 36, Art. XIII, Cal. Const.)

The statewide base sales and use tax rate was increased, effective January 1, 2013, from 7.25% to 7.5%, due to the approval by California voters of Proposition 30 at the November 6, 2012, general election. Prop 30 revenues were used to support school districts, county offices of education, charter schools, and community college districts. The imposition of the additional 0.25% sales and use tax imposed pursuant to Proposition 30 is inoperative January 1, 2017. (Sec. 36(f)(1)(A), Art. XIII, Cal. Const.)

Effective January 1, 2017, the statewide base sales and use tax rate is comprised of the following components:

— a 3.6875% state (General Fund) tax. (Sec. 6051, Rev. & Tax. Code; Sec. 6201, Rev. & Tax. Code);

— a 0.25% state (General Fund) tax (Sec. 6051.3, Rev. & Tax. Code; Sec. 6201.3, Rev. & Tax. Code);

— a 0.50% state (Local Public Safety Fund) tax imposed under the California Constitution beginning January 1, 1994, to support local criminal justice activities (Sec. 35, Art. XIII, Cal. Const.);

— a 0.50% state (Local Revenue Fund) tax to support local health and social services programs (Sec. 6051.2, Rev. & Tax. Code; Sec. 6201.2, Rev. & Tax. Code);

— a 1.0625% state (Local Revenue Fund) tax (Sec. 6051.15, Rev. & Tax. Code; Sec. 6201.15, Rev. & Tax. Code); and

— a 1.25% local (county/city) tax comprised of 0.25% for county transportation funds and 0.75% for city and county operations. (Sec. 7203.1, Rev. & Tax. Code)

Effective January 1, 2017, the partial state tax exemption rate decreases by 0.25% from 5.25% to 5% for the following partial state tax exemptions:

— teleproduction or other postproduction service equipment (Reg. 1532, 18 CCR);

— farm equipment and machinery (Reg. 1533.1, 18 CCR);

— timber harvesting equipment and machinery (Reg. 1534, 18 CCR); and

— racehorse breeding stock (Reg. 1535, 18 CCR).

(Sec. 6378, Rev. & Tax. Code; Sec. 6356.5, Rev. & Tax. Code; Sec. 6357.1, Rev. & Tax. Code; Sec. 6358.5, Rev. & Tax. Code)

Effective January 1, 2017, the partial exemption provided for diesel fuel used in farming activities or food processing is decreased from 7% to 6.75%. (Sec. 6357.1, Rev. & Tax. Code; Reg. 1533.2, 18 CCR)

California cities and counties are authorized by the Bradley-Burns Uniform Local Sales and Use Tax Law to impose a total tax of 1% on the sale or use of tangible personal property. (Sec. 7202, Rev. & Tax. Code)

One of the most common local taxes other than Bradley-Burns is the transactions and use tax, a local tax imposed within the boundaries of various transit, traffic, or other districts, as allowed by state law to finance district operations. Existing law prohibits, in any county, the combined rate of all taxes imposed in accordance with the Transactions and Use Tax Law from exceeding 2%. Transactions and use tax applies in addition to the state sales and use tax. (Sec. 7251.1, Rev. & Tax. Code)

A petition for writ of mandate challenging the placement of Measure A, which would impose a 10-year 1/8 cent California local sales tax increase, on the November 2012 general election ballot by Santa Clara County was properly denied. The placement did not violate Article XIII C, Section 2, subdivision (b) of the California Constitution (Proposition 218), which requires that local tax increase measures be placed on the ballot with a regularly scheduled general election for members of the local government's governing body. (*Silicon Valley Taxpayers' Association v. Garner*, (2013) (CCH CALIFORNIA TAX REPORTS, ¶61-710.31))

Sourcing rules.—California generally sources interstate and intrastate retail sales using origin-based sourcing. (Sec. 6010.5, Rev. & Tax. Code; Sec. 6396, Rev. & Tax. Code; Sec. 7205, Rev. & Tax. Code; Sec. 7262, Rev. & Tax. Code; Sec. 7263, Rev. & Tax. Code; Reg. 1620, 18 CCR; Reg. 1802, 18 CCR) If a retailer has more than one place of business involved in a sale, the transaction is regarded as having taken place where the principal negotiations are carried on or where the order is taken. As long as title passes within the state, it is immaterial that it passes outside the taxing jurisdiction in which the retailer's business is located. (Reg. 1802, 18 CCR, Reg. 1822, 18 CCR)

The place of sale of an out-of-state retailer that does not have a permanent place of business in the state, other than a stock of tangible personal property, is the place from which delivery or shipment is made. This rule also applies if a retailer has a permanent place of business in California if the sale is negotiated out-of-state and there is no participation in the sale by the retailer's permanent place of business in this state. (Reg. 1802, 18 CCR, Reg. 1822, 18 CCR)

For transactions of $500,000 or more, if a seller is required to collect local use tax on a transaction, the seller must report the local use tax revenues derived from such transactions directly to the participating jurisdiction where the first functional use is made. Out-of-state businesses who voluntarily register with the state to collect use tax have the option of reporting such a transaction to the participating jurisdiction. (Reg. 1802, 18 CCR)

Special rules apply: (1) to determine the place of use of leased vehicles for purposes of reporting and transmitting local use tax; and (2) for sales of jet fuel. (Secs. 7205, 7205.1, Rev. & Tax. Code)

California does not currently actively participate in the Streamlined Sales Tax Project (SSTP). California will not sign onto the SSTP agreement unless the conditions outlined in Sec. 6029, Rev. & Tax. Code are satisfied. (Sec. 6025, Rev. & Tax. Code, et. seq.)

• *Local sales and use tax rates*

Local and district taxes collected within each county are reported on Form BOE-401-A2 (State, Local and District Sales and Use Tax Return) and Schedule A (Computation Schedule for District Tax).

CCH Comment: City and County Tax Rates

For current local sales and use tax rates in specific cities and counties, see http://www.boe.ca.gov/cgi-bin/rates.cgi.

¶1504 Transactions Subject to Sales Tax

Law: Secs. 6001-6294, 7284.5; Regs. 1524, 1526, 18 CCR (CCH CALIFORNIA TAX REPORTS, ¶60-230—60-770).

The sales tax applies to the gross receipts of retailers from the sale of tangible personal property, with the exceptions listed in ¶1509. (Sec. 6051, Rev. & Tax. Code) A "retail sale" is defined as a sale of tangible personal property for any purpose other than for resale in the regular course of business. (Sec. 6007, Rev. & Tax. Code) The tax applies to certain rental transactions, and to many occasional and non-recurring sales by persons who ordinarily would not be thought of as "retailers" (¶1507, ¶1510). Sales tax also applies to certain fabrication services and to certain services that are a part of the sale or lease of tangible personal property; see discussion below under "Services." (Sec. 6006, Rev. & Tax. Code)

Anyone who makes more than two retail sales within a 12-month period is a "retailer" and therefore subject to tax. (Sec. 6019, Rev. & Tax. Code) This rule has been held applicable to liquidating sales made by a federal bankruptcy trustee—see *California State Board of Equalization v. Sierra Summit, Inc.* (1989) (CCH CALIFORNIA TAX REPORTS, ¶60-020.21). Where the customer furnishes the material, the tax applies to charges for fabrication labor (but not for installation, repairs, or alterations).

• *Auctions*

The sale of tangible personal property at auction is deemed to be a taxable transaction, irrespective of the fact that the sale is made with the understanding that (1) the property will not be delivered to the successful bidder, or (2) any amount paid for the property by the successful bidder will be returned to the bidder. The tax is applied to the amount of the successful bid. (Sec. 6015, Rev. & Tax. Code; Reg. 1565, 18 CCR)

• *Assessment on fruit trees, nut trees, olive trees, and grapevines*

An annual 1% special assessment is levied on the gross sales of all deciduous pome and stone fruit trees, nut trees, olive trees, and grapevines that are produced and sold within California or produced within and shipped from California by any licensed nursery dealer. The assessment covers seeds, seedlings, rootstocks, and topstock and includes ornamental varieties of apple, apricot, crabapple, cherry, nectarine, peach, pear, and plum. (Sec. 6981, Food & Agric. Code)

The assessment is due and payable to the Secretary of the Department of Food and Agriculture by March 10 of each year. (Sec. 6981, Food & Agric. Code)

¶1504

• *Assessment on purchasers of lumber products or engineered wood products*

In addition to any other California sales and use taxes imposed by law, an assessment is imposed on a person who purchases a lumber product, as defined, or an engineered wood product, as defined, for storage, use, or other consumption in California at the rate of 1% of the sales price. The retailer is required to collect the assessment from the purchaser and remit the amounts collected pursuant to the procedures in the Fee Collection Procedures Law. A retailer is required to charge the purchaser the amount of the assessment as a charge that is separate from, and not included in, any other fee, charge, or other amount paid by the purchaser. The retailer is also required to separately state the amount of the assessment on the sales receipt given by the retailer to the person at the time of sale. (Sec. 4629.5, Pub. Res. Code)

The lumber products assessment is due and payable to the BOE quarterly on or before the last day of the month next succeeding each quarterly period. On or before the last day of the month following each quarterly period, a return for the preceding quarterly period is required to be filed with the BOE using electronic media, in the form prescribed by the BOE. (Sec. 4629.5, Pub. Res. Code)

A retailer required to collect this assessment may retain no more than $250 per location as reimbursement for startup costs associated with the collection of the assessment. This reimbursement is to be taken on the retailer's first return on which the assessment is reported, or if the amount of the collected assessment is less than the allowed reimbursement, on the retailer's next consecutive returns until the allowed reimbursement amount is retained. "Location," for these purposes, is defined as and is limited to a business location registered under the retailer's seller's permit as of January 1, 2013, where sales of products subject to the assessment are made. (Reg. 2000, 18 CCR)

A California retailer with de minimis sales of qualified lumber products and engineered wood products of less than $25,000 during the previous calendar year is not a "retailer" for purposes of the provisions regarding the assessment. An excluded retailer is required to provide a notice to a purchaser of qualified lumber products or engineered wood products regarding the purchaser's obligation to remit the assessment to the BOE. (Sec. 4629.5, Pub. Res. Code)

• *Marijuana*

On November 8, 2016, California voters approved Proposition 64, The Control, Regulate, and Tax Adult Use of Marijuana Act. As a result, effective January 1, 2018, the following taxes are imposed:

— a 15% excise tax upon retail purchasers, based on the gross receipts from the retail sale of all marijuana and marijuana products, including medical marijuana; and

— a tax on cultivators of marijuana as follows: (1) $9.25 per dry-weight ounce of marijuana flowers; and (2) $2.75 per dry-weight ounce of marijuana leaves.

(*Special Notice L-481*, California State Board of Equalization, October 2016; *Tax Guide for Medical Cannabis Businesses*, California State Board of Equalization, November 2016)

See ¶1509 for a discussion of the exemption for sales of certain medical cannabis.

• *Medi-Cal managed care plans*

Operative July 1, 2013, inoperative July 1, 2016, and repealed effective January 1, 2017, a sales tax is imposed, for the privilege of selling Medi-Cal health care services at retail, on sellers of Medi-Cal managed care plans at a rate of 3.9375% of the gross receipts of any seller from the sale of all Medi-Cal managed care plans sold at retail in California. Counties, cities, and districts are prohibited from imposing a sales or use tax on such gross receipts. A seller is required to register with the BOE and report and pay the tax to the BOE. (Sec. 6175, Rev. & Tax. Code; Sec. 6176, Rev. & Tax. Code; Sec. 6184.5, Rev. & Tax. Code)

Sellers must file returns quarterly by October 31, January 31, April 30, and July 31. Tax return forms and prepayment forms will be provided by the BOE as appropriate. If a seller's taxable gross receipts average $17,000 or more per month, two prepayments must be made within each quarter (except for the quarterly period July 1, 2013 through September 30, 2013). When a seller registers with the BOE, the BOE will notify the seller of the seller's filing basis and whether it is necessary to file prepayments. (*Special Notice L-359*, California State Board of Equalization, August 2013)

Practitioner Comment: Sales Tax on Medi-Cal Managed Care Plans Expires

S.B. 78 imposed a 3.9375 percent sales tax on the retail sale of Medi-Cal health care services in California between July 1, 2013 and June 30, 2016.

The gross receipts subject to this tax include the total amount received by a seller of Medi-Cal managed care plans in premium or capitation payments for the coverage or provision of all health care services, including, but not limited to Medi-Cal services. Excluded from the amount subject to tax are amounts received pursuant to a subcontract with a Medi-Cal managed care plan to provide health care services to Medi-Cal beneficiaries.

Importantly, any person or entity that contracts with the DHCS to provide health care services is regarded as a seller and must register with the State Board of Equalization. "Insurers," as defined in California Revenue and Taxation Code section 12003, and dental managed care plans do not fall under this sales tax program.

This sales tax on the sale of the above plan services became inoperative as of July 1, 2016. As such, California no longer imposes a sales tax on sellers of Medi-Cal managed care plans. For a discussion on the new Managed Care tax, see ¶ 1907.

Chris Whitney, Contributing Editor

• *Nonprofit organizations*

Special rules are provided for various nonprofit organizations, to the effect that under certain conditions they are not considered to be "retailers." (Sec. 6375, Rev. & Tax. Code) Special rules are provided for vending machine operators (Sec. 6359(d), Rev. & Tax. Code; Sec. 6359.2, Rev. & Tax. Code; Sec. 6359.4, Rev. & Tax. Code), flea market or swap meet operators, and special event operators (Sec. 6073, Rev. & Tax. Code). Special rules are also provided for sales of mobile homes and manufactured homes. (Sec. 6012.8, Rev. & Tax. Code; Sec. 6012.9, Rev. & Tax. Code)

• *Online travel companies (OTCs)*

In *City of Los Angeles v. Ahir* (2016), (CCH California Tax Reports, ¶ 61-710.635), a lessee and operator of a motel was liable for California local transient occupancy taxes (TOT) since he was not denied the procedural due process right to notice and opportunity to be heard at the administrative level to contest the owner's appeal hearing regarding whether he was a lessee or property manager. The operator also was not denied those rights after the appeal hearing when he was assessed with the TOT instead of the owner. The appellate court found that he had both notice of the assessment and an opportunity to be heard. The local ordinance that imposes the TOT, which is imposed on the motel operator, defines an "operator" as the person who is either the proprietor of the hotel or any other person who has the right to rent rooms within the hotel, whether in the capacity of owner, lessee, or mortgagee in possession, licensee, or any other capacity.

Although the city sent notice of the assessment to the operator at the motel and it was returned unclaimed, the city obtained information as to the operator's location in another state and served its complaint there. The operator retained counsel, appeared at trial, and presented evidence and testimony. The city put on evidence that the operator was the lessee, and pursuant to the lease and ordinance, was the motel operator. No final decision was made depriving the operator of property before he received notice and had an opportunity to be heard. Moreover, the operator was not prejudiced by the lack of notice of the owners' administrative hearing. The appellate court held that even if the operator was entitled to intervene in the audit of another taxpayer, he was not prejudiced by the failure of the city to notify him of the owners' administrative hearing. The issue of whether the operator had a tax obligation for which he was delinquent was fully adjudicated in his own trial, in which it was determined that he was a lessee, and thus, the operator obligated to pay the TOT. The operator had constitutional notice, appeared, and put on evidence and witnesses in what was effectively his own assessment hearing, and as such, he was not prejudiced.

In *Ventura Realty and Investment Company v. City of San Buenaventura* (2016), (CCH CALIFORNIA TAX REPORTS, ¶ 61-710.44), a hotel taxpayer that sought a refund of California transient occupancy taxes paid on room rates, from which it deducted portions of tax attributed to fixed charges for food and beverages, was not entitled to the declaratory relief it requested because it had failed to exhaust its administrative remedies under the local tax ordinance before filing suit. The taxpayer's nightly room rate includes a mandatory charge for food and beverages that are provided by a cafe located on the hotel premises. An audit revealed that the taxpayer was imposing the 10% tax on the entire rent, but instead of remitting the entire 10%, the taxpayer exempted the amount attributable to the nightly food and beverage charge.

The appellate court considered precedent and found that where an adequate administrative remedy is provided by statute or rule of an administrative agency, relief must first be sought from the administrative body before the courts will act. The taxpayer, however, claimed it could maintain an action for declaratory relief on the ground that the city was applying its transient occupancy tax ordinance in an unconstitutional manner, and further, that the taxpayer should be excused from the exhaustion requirement because the administrative remedies provided are ineffective and pursuing them would have been futile. The appellate court disagreed and noted that every claim asserted in the taxpayer's complaint could have been raised during the administrative review process. If the taxpayer had invoked its right to a hearing, it would have had the opportunity to appear and offer evidence that the specified tax, interest, and penalties should not be fixed, and further, it could have sought to demonstrate that at least a portion of the tax it collected on the food and beverage charges was for the payment of state sales tax and not the local transient occupancy tax. The taxpayer would have had the right to appeal any adverse decision to the city council, which would have been required to hear and consider all evidence produced by the taxpayer and other witnesses. Nothing would have restricted the city's authority to address and resolve the taxpayer's claims. As a result, the taxpayer was not entitled to the declaratory relief it sought since it did not avail itself of the opportunity to first litigate its dispute before the tax collector and city council prior to filing suit.

In *Pershadsingh v. County of Los Angeles* (2014), (CCH CALIFORNIA TAX REPORTS, ¶ 61-710.852), a taxpayer did not have standing to challenge an increase in a California local transient occupancy tax rate because he did not pay the tax. The taxpayer, who had stayed at a hotel and was billed for the tax, filed a claim in his own name and on behalf of similarly situated taxpayers for a refund and damages on the ground that the tax hike violated the voter approval requirements of Proposition 62 because the increase was passed by the Board of Supervisors and was not submitted to the electorate. However, evidence showed that the taxpayer's closely held corporation actually paid the tax. The trial court ruled that the taxpayer had no standing to challenge the tax increase and denied class certification on the ground that the taxpayer could not adequately represent the proposed class. The appellate court affirmed the decision of the trial court. The taxpayer did not have standing the challenge the tax because he did not pay it. Moreover, the taxpayer's corporation also did not have standing because it failed to file a refund claim as required by the Government Claims Act. A claim for money or damages against a government entity must comply with the act. Although the taxpayer attempted to comply by making a personal claim against the county for a refund of the tax, the evidence showed that the taxpayer did not pay the tax. Instead, the taxpayer used a debit card for an account that belonged to the corporation. The taxpayer did not suffer any injury or violation of his legally protected interests, and as such, he lacked personal standing to bring a court action for a tax refund. Since he cannot seek a tax refund, he was not an appropriate class representative since only persons who paid the disputed tax could recover their excess payments in a refund action.

In *In Re: Transient Occupancy Tax Cases*, (2014) (CCH California Tax Reports, ¶61-710.851), the California appellate court held that under the plain language of the San Francisco ordinance that imposes a California local transient occupancy tax of 6% of the rent charged by the operator on transients for the privilege of occupancy of any hotel, online travel companies (OTCs) had no tax liability. The appellate court held that the ordinance does not impose a tax on the service fees and markups charged by the OTCs. Rather, the tax is imposed on the rent charged by the hotel operator, and the tax obligations are only imposed on transients and hotel operators. The ordinance includes no provision that imposes any tax liability on any entity other than the hotel operator or the transient. The city argued that the ordinance provides that the measure of tax is the total amount shown on the guest receipt, and the guest receipt includes the OTC's markup as part of the total charged to the transient. The appellate court disagreed, however, and found that the ordinance contains language that limits the taxable rent to the amount charged for the room occupancy. Moreover, the ordinance includes a list of items included in the definition of "rent" and the list does not include OTC service fees.

Practitioner Comment: Court of Appeal Affirms Online Travel Companies are Not Responsible for Collecting Local Transient Occupancy Tax on Service Fees and Markups

Based on the plain language of San Diego's transient occupancy tax ("TOT") ordinance, the California Court of Appeal, Second District held In re Transient Occupancy Tax Cases, 225 Cal. App. 4th 56 (2d Dist. 2014) that online travel companies ("OTCs") are not responsible for collecting the City's TOT on service fees and markups charged to customers that booked rooms. The case is one of the coordinated "Transient Occupancy Tax Cases." The California Supreme Court has granted a petition for review in this case.

In its opinion, the Court of Appeal referenced its prior unpublished decisions In re Transient Occupancy Tax Cases, Nov. 1, 2012, B230457, 2012 WL 5360907 ([nonpub. opn.] (Anaheim) and In re Transient Occupancy Tax Cases (Nov. 1, 2012, B236166, 2012 WL 5360882) [nonpub. opn.](Santa Monica) where it held that the ordinances at issue did not impose a tax on the service fees charged by the OTCs. Similar to the Anaheim ordinance, San Diego's TOT ordinance specifies that the tax is imposed on the rent charged by the "hotel operator" and, as in Santa Monica, the San Diego ordinance makes it clear that the tax obligations are only imposed on "transients" and "hotel operators." The court explained that "[t] here is no provision imposing any tax liability on any entity other than the hotel operator or the transient." The court concluded that since the OTCs are not "hotel operators," their services fees and markups are not subject to the TOT. The court was also unpersuaded by San Diego's assertions that other language in its ordinance brought OTCs within its purview.

The San Diego case is just one of a number of TOT cases in California, including appeals pending involving Los Angeles and San Francisco ordinances. While the Court of Appeal's analysis in the San Diego case focused on the specific language of the city's ordinance, there are many jurisdictions with similar language in their TOTs and a California Supreme Court decision may bring some certainty to this area. However, it is not clear whether a court may reach a similar conclusion when confronted with a more broadly worded ordinance. For example, the city of Los Angeles's TOT ordinance, Article 1.7, section 21.7.2(d), defines "operators" to include "secondary operators" such as "online room resellers" and imposes the same duties and liabilities on "secondary operators" as those imposed on a "principal operator."

Chris Whitney, Contributing Editor

In *In Re: Transient Occupancy Tax Cases*, (2012) (CCH California Tax Reports, ¶ 61-710.641), an online travel service company (OTC) was not required to pay a California city's transient occupancy tax on the portion of money they kept from sums collected from transients to rent hotel rooms in the city on behalf of the transients. Under the plain language of the municipal ordinance imposing the tax, the ordinance was for revenue purposes for the financial operation of the city; the tax was limited to the amount paid to a hotel within the city; the tax specifically targeted commercial activity within the city for the purpose of raising revenue; and there was no stated or implied intention to tax amounts paid to intermediaries or travel agents.

In *City of Santa Monica v. Expedia, Inc.* (2011) (CCH California Tax Reports, ¶ 61-720.39), the court held that the Santa Monica, California transient occupancy tax is based on the room rental paid to a hotel and not on the amount paid to an online travel company by the transient. The California Superior Court reviewed the language of the local ordinance and found that the tax is calculated based on the sum paid to the hotel. Regardless of whether a transient pays a hotel directly, or a transient pays an intermediary which in turn pays room rental for the transient, the ordinance that imposes the tax provides that the tax is based on the total amount paid to the hotel for room rental, without consideration of whether the transient might have paid a different amount to an intermediary. The court found that the statute is silent with regard to whether the hotel exercises control over the price charged by a reseller or intermediary; the tax is imposed on the amount received by the hotel. As such, a charge made by a hotel to a transient within the definition of "room rental" must be interpreted to refer to charges that are paid to the hotel. The hotel does not receive the commission.

In *Priceline.com, Inc. v. City of Anaheim* (2010) (CCH California Tax Reports, ¶ 61-720.29), the court held that OTCs are not "hotel operators" under a California local transient occupancy tax ordinance, and as such, the amount collected by each OTC is not subject to tax as rent for the privilege of occupying a hotel room in the city of Anaheim. By its own terms, the Anaheim ordinance does not impose a transient occupancy tax on the retail price of hotel rooms rented by or through OTCs. The language of the ordinance provides that tax is calculated based on a percentage of the rent. Rent is calculated based on the amount charged by the hotel operator. OTCs do not run or control hotels. Although OTCs contract with hotel operators for the ability to make rooms available through reservations to consumers by use of their Web sites and market hotel rooms to consumers, those actions do not give the OTCs the right to run the business of a hotel. Moreover, OTCs are not hotel operators, hotel proprietors, or managing agents of a hotel. The city ordinance imposes tax obligations only on managing agents who have been delegated sufficient discretion to allow them to make corporate policy. The OTCs, however, have no control over the hotels' corporate pricing policies or marketing practices. The ordinance defines "rent" as the consideration charged by an operator for accommodations. Consequently, the amount charged by the OTCs is not rent. The rent for use of a hotel room is the amount charged by the hotel to the OTC for the accommodation.

In *Priceline.com, Inc. v. City of Anaheim* (2010) (CCH California Tax Reports, ¶ 61-720.71), the appellate court held that the denial of a petition for writ of mandate filed by a number of OTCs that sought to compel the city of Anaheim to litigate California local transient occupancy tax assessment proceedings without the assistance of outside counsel retained pursuant to a contingency fee agreement was proper. Case precedent does not bar contingency fee lawyers from assisting government lawyers as co-counsel in ordinary civil litigation such as the instant case. Tax assessment proceedings are civil administration actions that do not require the delicate balancing and weighing of interests and values. All that is required in the present case, according to the court, is a determination that the transient occupancy tax is due. As such, the judgment of the trial court denying the writ petition filed by the OTCs was affirmed.

• *Sale and leaseback transactions*

Sale and leaseback transactions are not subject to sales tax if (1) the tax was paid by the person selling (and leasing back) the property, and (2) the acquisition sale and leaseback is consummated within 90 days of that person's first functional use of the property. (Sec. 6010.65, Rev. & Tax. Code)

• *Services*

Because sales tax is imposed on sales of tangible personal property, service transactions are generally not subject to tax. However, the tax is specifically imposed on certain fabrication services and on incidental services performed in the sale or lease of tangible personal property. Services performed for nontaxable sales, including sales for resales, are not subject to tax. (Sec. 6006, Rev. & Tax. Code; Sec. 6011, Rev. & Tax. Code; Sec. 6012, Rev. & Tax. Code)

California taxes charges for producing, fabricating, processing, printing, or imprinting tangible personal property for consumers who themselves have furnished, either directly or indirectly, the materials used in those procedures. (Sec. 6006(b), Rev. & Tax. Code) BOE Publication 108 states that charges for fabrication are generally taxable, whether or not the consumer supplies the materials.

Practitioner Comment: Court of Appeal Finds Sales Tax Inapplicable to Non-Separately Stated Services in Mixed Transactions

The California Court of Appeal held in *Dell, Inc. vs. San Francisco Superior Court*, Cal. Ct. App. (1st District, Div. 4, No. A118657, January 31, 2008) that charges for optional customer service contracts embedded within the overall price charged for the sale of computers were exempt from sales tax. The Court distinguished bundled transactions in which goods and services are sold together yet are readily separable from "mixed transactions" such as those at issue in the case. Dell had increased the lump sum sales price of its products based upon customer-requested changes to the package configuration.

Two Dell customers brought suit alleging that Dell had improperly applied sales tax to the entire charge and Dell filed a cross complaint to allow it to recover the taxes paid in the event Dell lost the case. Dell and the BOE, while conceding that the services at issue were nontaxable, contended that taxation was justified because there was no separately stated charge for the services. The court rejected the argument of administrative convenience, noting that whether or not the charges were separately stated did not change the fact that the services were nontaxable.

This is another in a series of decisions that have eroded California's long standing policy of generally subjecting to tax the entire amount charged for "bundled transactions." The State's arguments in this case demonstrate that California will most likely continue to take an aggressive approach in such circumstances; however, taxpayers should be encouraged with the favorable treatment received in situations where the parties can demonstrate that the amount subjected to tax includes exempt components. Because bundled transactions including services appear to be 'in play' as a result of this case, we should expect to see an attempt to apply this decision to other types of bundled transactions.

Chris Whitney, Contributing Editor

CCH Comment: Purchasers of Optional Service Contracts from Dell May Be Eligible for Refund

The BOE indicates that if taxpayers purchased one or more optional service contracts covering computer hardware sold by Dell between April 8, 1999, and June 30, 2008, and paid California sales or use taxes on such service contract(s), they may be eligible to receive a refund of the taxes paid. The BOE and Dell have reached a settlement agreement in regard to litigation that involved a class of purchasers of Dell computer products and optional service contracts. California. Those eligible to receive a refund under one or both of the settlement agreements must timely file a claim or claims to receive any refund(s). Each settlement agreement has different criteria for eligibility, and taxpayers must file a claim or claims for the settlement agreement under which they are eligible. For those taxpayers who are eligible under both settlement agreements, they must file a separate claim or claims under both agreements.

Taxpayers who received a Short Form Notice And Individual Summary for the Dell Settlement or SBE Settlement are notified that Dell's records reflect that those taxpayers made one or more service contract purchases that may entitle them to compensation under the Dell or the SBE settlement agreements or both. If Dell's records reflect that a taxpayer made more than one purchase and falls into both settlement classes, those taxpayers should have received two separate notices. Taxpayers must timely file a claim to be eligible for any benefits from the settlements. (*Dell and SBE Litigation Settlement on Optional Service Contracts—Claim for Refunds*, California State Board of Equalization, January 2013; *Mohan v. Dell Inc. Class Action Settlements*, California State Board of Equalization, January 2013)

In determining whether tax applies, "producing, fabricating, and processing" include any operation resulting in, or any step in a process or series of operations resulting in, the creation or production of tangible personal property. (Reg. 1526(b), 18 CCR) For example, tax generally applies to charges for alterations to new clothing, whether or not the alterations are performed by the seller of the garment or by another person (however, special rules apply to dry cleaners). (Reg. 1524, 18 CCR) Charges for painting, polishing, and otherwise finishing tangible personal property in connection with the production of a finished product are also subject to tax, whether the article to be finished is supplied by the customer or by the finisher. Gift-wrapping services are also subject to tax.

Charges for repair or reconditioning of property to refit it for the use for which it was originally produced are exempt, if separately stated, and tax applies only to the retail value of the parts used. The labor charge for assembling an article or piece of equipment, as distinguished from its installation, is taxable. (Reg. 1546, 18 CCR)

Many services performed on customer-furnished goods are but one step in the final production of an article of personal property; as a part of the fabrication, they are subject to tax. For example, charges for firing ceramics, cutting lumber, carving and dressing meats, printing or painting textiles, or laminating or fireproofing an article of personal property are taxable. However, tax applies to the service only if it is performed for the consumer. Consequently, a service performed by a subcontractor is not a taxable fabrication service. (SUTA Series 435, Producing, fabricating, and processing property furnished by consumers—General rules.)

CCH Tip: Computer Maintenance Contracts

A California court of appeal held that optional computer service contracts sold with computers for a single lump-sum price were not subject to California sales and use taxes because the transactions were mixed transactions that involved separately identifiable transfers of goods and services. According to the court, both the computers and the contracts were distinct consumer items, each was a significant object of the transaction, and the service contracts had readily ascertainable values even without itemized invoices. In addition, there was no state statute or regulation that required service contract charges to be separately stated in order to avoid taxation. (*Dell, Inc. v. The Superior Court of the City and County of San Francisco* (2008) CCH CALIFORNIA TAX REPORTS, ¶ 60-310.55)

Sales tax applies to half of any sum charged for optional maintenance contracts sold with the sale or lease of canned software. While one-half of the transaction is deemed a sale of tangible personal property subject to sales tax, the other half of the transaction is treated as receipts from nontaxable repairs. (Reg. 1502, 18 CCR)

Reg. 1502 is amended, effective July 1, 2014, to: (1) clarify that a backup copy of a prewritten program recorded on tangible storage media may be included in a maintenance contract sold in connection with the sale or lease of the same prewritten program; (2) clarify that taxable optional maintenance contracts are still taxed the same, even if they include a backup copy of a prewritten program recorded on tangible storage

¶1504

media; and (3) maintain the bright-line rule that 50% of the lump-sum charge for an optional maintenance contract that entitles the customer to receive tangible personal property is taxable, even when such a contract is paired with a nontaxable electronic download or load-and-leave transaction. (Reg. 1502, 18 CCR)

Practitioner Comment: Sales Tax Application to Specified Optional Software Maintenance Contracts

Effective July 1, 2014, the State Board of Equalization amended California Code of Regulations (Cal. Code of Regs.) section 1502, "Computers, Programs and Data Processing." The amendment expressly clarifies that: (1) when a consumer purchases a non-custom (prewritten) computer program via an electronic download or load-and-leave transaction that does not include the transfer of tangible storage media; and (2) also purchases a separate optional maintenance contract that includes the transfer of a backup copy of the same or similar prewritten program recorded on tangible storage media, tax does not apply to the charge for the prewritten program itself. Rather the tax applies to 50% of the lump–sum charge for the optional maintenance contract. Previously, receiving a tangible backup copy could have tainted a previously exempt download or load and leave transaction.

This regulation addresses a different circumstance than the *Nortel/Lucent* litigation. Cal. Code of Regs. Section 1502 deals with purchasing the right to use prewritten computer programs (which are exempt if no tangible personal property involved) and separately purchasing an optional maintenance program. The latter is exempt if the customer never receives tangible personal property, or 50% exempt if the customer receives tangible personal property as part of the optional maintenance agreement only. *Nortel/ Lucent* deals with California's Technology Transfer Agreement (TTA) statutes. TTAs, which are exempt, relate to licensed software that is copyrighted, contains patented processes, and enables the licensee to copy the software, as well as to make and sell products (telephone calls) embodying the patents and copyrights.

Chris Whitney, Contributing Editor

• Support services

California sales tax is imposed at the rate of 6.25% on providers of support services at retail measured by the gross receipts from the sale of those services. The tax is operative provided specified federal approval requests for matching funds are granted. Sellers that are actively engaged in arranging for the retail sale of support services are required to register with the BOE, collect tax from the provider, and report and pay the tax to the BOE. Sales tax prepayments are inapplicable to sellers until no later than three months after the date that federal approval is obtained. (Sec. 6150, Rev. & Tax. Code; Sec. 6151, Rev. & Tax. Code; Sec. 6152, Rev. & Tax. Code; Sec. 6154, Rev. & Tax. Code; Sec. 6170, Rev. & Tax. Code)

"Support services," for purposes of the tax, are defined as:

— domestic services and services related to domestic services;

— heavy cleaning;

— personal care services, as defined;

— accompaniment when needed during necessary travel to health-related appointments or to alternative resource sites;

— yard hazard abatement;

— protective supervision;

— teaching and demonstration directed at reducing the need for other supportive services; and

— paramedical services that make it possible for the recipient to establish and maintain an independent living arrangement, including necessary paramedical services ordered by a licensed health care professional, as provided.

(Sec. 6150, Rev. & Tax. Code)

• *Technology transfer agreements*

Tax applies to amounts received for any tangible personal property transferred in a technology transfer agreement. However, tax does not apply to amounts received for the assignment or licensing of a patent or copyright interest as part of the agreement. The gross receipts or sales price attributable to the transfer of tangible personal property as part of the agreement is equal to the following:

— the separately stated sales price for the property, so long as this price represents a reasonable fair market value for the property;

— the separate price at which the property or similar property was previously sold, leased, or offered for sale or lease to an unrelated third party, if there is no separately stated price; or

— 200% of the combined costs of materials and labor used to produce the property, if there is no separately stated sales price and the property or similar property has not been previously sold, leased, or offered for sale or lease to an unrelated third party.

(Sec. 6011(c)(10), Rev. & Tax. Code; Sec. 6012(c)(10), Rev. & Tax. Code; Reg. 1507, 18 CCR)

A technology transfer agreement is a written agreement for the following:

— assignment or license of a copyright interest in tangible personal property for the purpose of reproducing and selling other property subject to the copyright interest (including artwork);

— assignment or license of a patent interest for the right to manufacture and sell property subject to the patent interest; or

— assignment or license of the right to use a process subject to a patent interest.

However, a technology transfer agreement is neither an agreement for the transfer of tangible personal property manufactured pursuant to a technology transfer agreement nor an agreement for the transfer of any property derived, created, manufactured, or otherwise processed by property manufactured pursuant to a transfer technology agreement. Moreover, it is not an agreement for the transfer of prewritten software.

In *Nortel Networks, Inc. v. State Board of Equalization (2011)* (CCH California Tax Reports, ¶60-310.73), the appellate court held that software licensed by a taxpayer to operate switching equipment was exempt from California sales and use tax under statutes regarding technology transfer agreements (TTA) in that the software was copyrighted, contained patented processes, and enabled the licensee to copy the software and make and sell products (telephone calls) that embodied the patents and copyright. The taxpayer, who designs, manufactures, and sells switch hardware, entered licensing agreements with a telephone company giving the company the right to use the taxpayer's software programs in the switches. The license gave the telephone company the right to produce telephonic communications without fear of infringing upon the taxpayer's patents. The appellate court noted that the TTA statutes apply when the transfer of patents and copyrights is at issue and that a licensing agreement is exempt from sales and use tax if it is a TTA. The TTA statutes cover agreements that license the right to make and sell a product or to use a process that is subject to the patent or copyright interest. The appellate court held that the licenses gave the telephone company the right to reproduce the copyrighted material on its computers. As such, the prewritten programs were nontaxable TTAs. (Reg. 1507, 18 CCR)

In *Lucent Technologies, Inc. v. State Board of Equalization of the State of California,* (2013) (CCH California Tax Reports, ¶60-310.64), software licensed by taxpayers was, as a matter of law, exempt from California sales and use tax under statutory technology transfer agreement (TTA) provisions. The taxpayers manufactured and sold switching equipment to their telephone customers that allowed the customers to provide telephone calling and other services to end customers. The switches required software, provided on storage media, in order to operate. The software was provided to the telephone customers pursuant to written agreements. The transfer involved both tangible and intangible personal property. California law provides that intangible personal property transferred with tangible personal property in any TTA is exempt from sales and use taxes provided the agreement separately states a reasonable price for the tangible personal property. A "technology transfer agreement" is statutorily defined as any agreement under which a person who holds a patent or copyright interest assigns or licenses to another person the right to make and sell a product or to use a process that is subject to the patent or copyright interest.

The BOE appealed the *Lucent* decision and the California appellate court affirmed the decision. In *Lucent Technologies, Inc. v. State Board of Equalization*, (2015) (CCH CALIFORNIA TAX REPORTS, ¶ 60-310.731), the appellate court held that the assessment of California sales tax on the intangible portions of transactions engaged in by a manufacturer who sells telecommunications equipment to telephone companies, who then use that equipment to provide telephone and Internet services to their customers, was erroneous. In those transactions, the companies paid for: (1) the equipment; (2) written instructions on how to use the equipment; (3) a copy of the computer software that makes the equipment work; and (4) the right to copy that software onto the equipment's hard drive and then use the software to operate the equipment. In *Nortel Networks Inc. v. State Board of Equalization* (2011) 191 Cal.App.4th 1259, the appellate court held that an almost identical transaction satisfied the requirements of California's technology transfer agreement statutes and, as a result, the manufacturer was liable for paying sales taxes only on the tangible portions of the transaction (the equipment and instructions), but not the intangible portions (the software and rights to copy and use it).

Despite the *Nortel* decision, the BOE assessed sales tax on the intangible portions of the transactions, the manufacturer paid the taxes, and filed an action claiming a refund. The BOE argued that the computer software was tangible personal property, but the appellate court disagreed and held that when tangible and intangible property is inextricably intertwined, the question of whether the property is subject to sales tax turns on whether the tangible property is essential or physically useful to the subsequent use of the intangible personal property. The court noted that a number of California courts have held that the transmission of software using a tape or disc in conjunction with the grant of a license to copy or use that software is not a taxable transaction because the tape or disc is merely a convenient storage medium used to transfer the copyrighted content and is not in itself essential or physically useful to the later use of the intangible personal property.

After finding that the contracts between the manufacturer and the telephone companies met the statutory definition of "technology transfer agreements," the appellate court held: (1) the manufacturer's decision to give the telephone companies copies of the software on magnetic tapes and compact discs (as opposed to over the Internet) did not convert the software itself or the rights to use it into tangible personal property subject to sales tax; (2) a technology transfer agreement, as provided, that exempts the intangible portions of a transaction involving both tangible and intangible property, can exist when the only intangible right transferred is the right to copy software onto tangible equipment; and (3) a technology transfer agreement can exist as long as the grantee of copyright or patent rights under the agreement thereafter copies or incorporates a copy of the copyrighted work into its product or uses the patented process, and any of these acts is enough to render the resulting product or process subject to the copyright or patent interest. In addition, because the BOE's opposition to the manufacturer's refund action was all but foreclosed by *Nortel* and other binding decisional and statutory law, the BOE's position was not substantially justified and the trial court did not abuse its discretion in awarding the manufacturer its reasonable litigation costs.

The California Supreme Court has declined to review the *Lucent* decision. (Petition for review denied, California Supreme Court, No. S230657, January 20, 2016)

Practitioner Comment: Under BOE's Narrow Application of the Nortel Decision Uncertainty Remains as to the Decision's Scope and the Available Refunds

In *Nortel Networks v. State Board of Equalization*, 191 Cal.App.4th 1259 (2d. Dist. 2011), petition for review denied, California Supreme Court, No. S190946, April 27, 2011, the Appellate Court held that software licensed by Nortel that was used to operate telephone switch hardware constitutes a transfer of patent and copyright interests under California's Technology Transfer Agreement (TTA) statutes and consequently is exempt from sales and use tax. The exemption applied because the licensed software is copyrighted, contains patented processes, and enables the licensee to copy the software, as well as to make and sell products (telephone calls) embodying the patents and copyrights. The court stated "the TTA statutes encompass 'any' transfer of an interest subject to a patent or copyright, which includes prewritten programs licensed by Nortel."

It should be noted that the BOE is currently limiting the exemption articulated in *Nortel* to software purchased directly from the licensor/owner of the intellectual property. For example, if Customer Y obtains pre written software from Retail Store X it is BOE's position that the X's "sale" of such software would be taxable because X does not have a patent or copyright interest in the software and the transaction does not therefore qualify as an exempt TTA.

Further, it is the BOE's view that software that is embedded and sold along with tangible property (e.g., computers and mobile devices, etc.) does not qualify as a TTA unless there is a separate agreement for the license of the software.

Finally, on audit the BOE appears to be attempting to assign an unrealistically high value to tangible personal property (e.g., diskettes) that may be provided in a transaction otherwise qualifying as a TTA and is currently discussing this issue with industry representatives who are arguing for a much lower value.

As a result of the above uncertainty, as a precautionary measure many companies are continuing to collect sales tax on software licenses. However, practitioners are advised to file protective claims for refund based on the *Nortel* decision. It should be noted that in the case of sales tax transactions the vendor must file the refund claim and in use tax transactions the party filing the claim is typically the purchaser.

In *Lucent Technologies, Inc. v. State Board of Equalization* (Court of Appeal of California, Second District, No. B257808, October 8, 2015), the appellate court affirmed the trial court's decision which followed the precedent established in *Nortel* and held that written software agreements qualified as technology transfer agreements (TTAs) exempt from sales and use tax. Note that the BOE has 30 days to appeal to the California Supreme Court. While *Lucent* essentially followed *Nortel* and therefore does not develop the case law in this area further, the decision highlights the difference in factual support the State Board of Equalization (BOE) may demand of taxpayers as compared to that required by the courts. The BOE's efforts to challenge the factual support provided by the taxpayer to satisfy the requirements necessary to qualify for a TTA evince an attempt by the BOE to shift the burden of proof back to taxpayers.

Chris Whitney, Contributing Editor

The BOE has clarified that when the holder of copyrights or patents also sells that intellectual property to another in a technology transfer agreement that includes the transfer of software, the amount charged for the copyrights or patents is excluded from the application of sales tax. According to the BOE, court decisions have confirmed that canned software is taxable and intellectual property is not subject to tax. After getting feedback from the industry, the BOE will provide further guidance on how tax applies to sales of software. (*News Release 66-11-H*, California State Board of Equalization, May 27, 2011)

CCH Tip: Mobile Telecom Sourcing Act

California adopts the provisions of the federal Mobile Telecommunications Sourcing Act. Under the Act, mobile telecommunications services are taxable in the state and locality where the customer resides or maintains its primary business address and any other state or locality is prohibited from taxing the services, regardless of where the services originate, terminate, or pass through. The Act does not apply to prepaid telephone calling services or air-ground service. (Sec. 41020, Rev. & Tax. Code)

Furthermore, the Act provides that a state or a company designated by the political subdivisions of a state may provide an electronic database identifying the proper taxing jurisdiction for each street address in that state. If the provider of mobile telecommunications services uses such a database, it will be held harmless from any tax otherwise due solely as a result of an error in the database. If no such database exists, then a provider employing an enhanced zip code and exercising due diligence in assigning a street address to a taxing jurisdiction will be held harmless for any incorrect assignment.

• True object test

The "true object" test determines whether a transaction involves a taxable sale of tangible personal property or the transfer of property incidental to the performance of a nontaxable service. If the true object sought by the purchaser is a nontaxable service, tax does not apply to the transaction, even if some property is transferred. (Reg. 1501, 18 CCR)

In *Navistar International Transportation Corp. et al. v. State Board of Equalization et al.* (1994) (CCH CALIFORNIA TAX REPORTS, ¶ 60-310.611), a library of custom computer programs produced in-house for use by a taxpayer was subject to sales tax when sold as part of the taxpayer's business because the true object of the transaction was to sell the computer programs as tangible personal property and not to provide a service. Although the service of developing or designing custom computer programs is exempt from sales tax, once the computer programs were designed for the taxpayer's in-house use, the service had been completed, and the subsequent sale involved only the transfer of tangible personal property.

In *State Board of Equalization v. Los Angeles International Airport Hotel Associates* (1996) (CCH CALIFORNIA TAX REPORTS, ¶ 60-020.25), a U.S. bankruptcy appellate court held that a hotel owner was required to pay sales tax on complimentary beverages and breakfasts provided to guests because the money paid by guests for their rooms was consideration for the hotel's duty to provide not only rooms but also beverages and breakfasts. The complimentary beverages and breakfasts had been offered to induce travelers to rent a room at the hotel. However, in *Petitions of Embassy Suites Inc., et al.* (1996) (CCH CALIFORNIA TAX REPORTS, ¶ 60-020.251), the State Board of Equalization (BOE) took the opposite position, ruling that complimentary beverages and breakfasts provided by hotels to their guests were not subject to sales tax, because the retail value of the beverages and breakfasts was *de minimis*, equaling 10% or less of the average daily rate charged for rooms. The BOE has incorporated its ruling in *Embassy Suites, Inc.* into its regulation governing taxable sales of food products. (Reg. 1603, 18 CCR)

• Virtual currencies

The California State Board of Equalization (BOE) advises that sales and use tax applies to transactions in which virtual currencies (e.g., Bitcoin, Litecoin, Dogecoin, Peercoin) are accepted by businesses and individuals as a payment method for their sales of goods and services in the same manner as transactions paid using traditional payment methods such as cash or credit card. The IRS issued a notice that explains that virtual currencies do not have legal tender status in any jurisdiction and should not be treated as United States currency or foreign currency, but instead, as property. (IRS Notice 2014-21, March 25, 2014) For the same reason, virtual currencies are not regarded as United States currency or foreign currency for purposes of the California Sales and Use Tax Law. (*Special Notice L-382*, California State Board of Equalization, June 2014)

Tax applies to sales of tangible personal property in exchange for virtual currency in the same way it does with any other sale of tangible personal property for consideration. The measure of tax is the total amount of the sale or lease, whether received in money or other consideration. Regulation 1654 provides that the measure of tax from a barter or exchange transaction includes any amount allowed by a retailer to the customer for property or services of any kind. Consequently, if a retailer enters into a contract where the consideration is virtual currency, the measure of tax from the sale of the product is the amount allowed by the retailer in exchange for the virtual currency (generally, the retailer's advertised selling price of the product). (*Special Notice L-382*, California State Board of Equalization, June 2014)

Retailers who accept virtual currencies as payment are instructed to retain documentation on the amount for which they regularly sell the same or similar property to their customers when payment is made in United States dollars (cash, check, credit or debit card). The BOE does not accept virtual currencies as a payment method for any tax or fee program. (*Special Notice L-382*, California State Board of Equalization, June 2014)

¶1505 Transactions Subject to Use Tax

Law: Secs. 6201-94, Rev. & Tax. Code, Sec. 10295.1 Public Contract Code; Reg. 1620, 18 CCR (CCH CALIFORNIA TAX REPORTS, ¶¶ 60-020, 60-025, 60-570, 60-740, 61-450).

The use tax is imposed on the storage, use, or other consumption in California of property purchased from a retailer for such storage, use, or other consumption. (Sec. 6202, Rev. & Tax. Code) It applies to certain rental transactions and to out-of-state fabrication of customer-furnished materials. Because the use tax does not apply to cases where the sale of the property is subject to the sales tax (Sec. 6401, Rev. & Tax. Code) (except when the purchase is in a district with a lower rate than the district in which the property is purchased to be used and is actually used, and in certain lease transactions—see ¶1507), the use tax generally applies to purchases made outside of California for use within the state. Although this tax is imposed upon the purchaser, any retailer engaged in business in the state is required to collect the tax and remit it to the state.

A "retailer" that has any kind of an establishment in California or representatives conducting any kind of sales activity in the state is deemed to be "engaged in business" in the state. The law applies whether the retailer is involved directly or through a subsidiary or agent. (Sec. 6005, Rev. & Tax. Code; Sec. 6015, Rev. & Tax. Code)

In *Appeal of B & D Litho, Inc.* (2001) (CCH CALIFORNIA TAX REPORTS, ¶ 61-460.90), an out-of-state corporation that held a California use tax registration certificate was required to collect California use tax on sales of property to California customers, even if it did not have nexus with the state.

• *Commerce Clause requirements*

In *National Railroad Passenger Corporation v. State Board of Equalization* (1986) (CCH CALIFORNIA TAX REPORTS, ¶ 60-450.62), the state attempted to impose a tax on railroad passenger cars that was not imposed on other passenger vehicles used by common carriers. A federal district court held that such imposition was discriminatory and, therefore, prohibited.

• *Convention or trade show participation*

An out-of-state retailer is not engaged in business in California based solely on the physical presence of the retailer or its agents at convention or trade show activities (as described in IRC Sec. 513(d)(3)(A)) for 15 or fewer days in any 12-month period that did not derive more than $100,000 of net income from those activities in

California during the prior calendar year. However, that retailer must collect use tax on any sales of tangible personal property at those activities and with respect to any such sale made pursuant to an order taken at those activities. (Sec. 6203(d), Rev. & Tax. Code; Reg. 1684(d)(3), 18 CCR)

• *Drop shipments*

Anyone who delivers tangible personal property, either to a California consumer or to a person for redelivery to a California consumer pursuant to a retail sale made to the consumer by a retailer that does not do business in California, is the retailer of the property for California sales and use tax purposes. The deliverer must include the retail selling price of the property in the gross receipts or sales price of the property. (Sec. 6007, Rev. & Tax. Code) This rule applies to out-of-state wholesalers as well as California wholesalers. (*Mason Shoe Manufacturing Co. v. California State Board of Equalization*, (2005) CCH California Tax Reports, ¶ 60-340.50)

As a general rule, a drop shipper calculates the taxable retail selling price of its drop shipments based on the selling price from the true retailer to the consumer plus a mark-up of 10%. However, if the drop shipper can show that a lower mark-up percentage accurately reflects the retail selling price charged by the true retailer, that lower percentage can be used. (Reg. 1706, 18 CCR)

• *Imports*

Use tax is not imposed on property that is purchased for use in, and actually used in, interstate or foreign commerce prior to its entry into California and that is thereafter used continuously in interstate or foreign commerce both within and without California but not exclusively in California. (Reg. 1620(b)(2), 18 CCR) In addition, the storage, use, or other consumption in California of the first $800 of tangible personal property purchased in a foreign country by an individual from a retailer and personally hand-carried into California from the foreign country within any 30-day period is exempt from use tax; the exemption does not apply to property sent or shipped to California. (Sec. 6405, Rev. & Tax. Code) The BOE and the U.S. Customs Office have an information exchange program.

• *Insurance companies*

Although insurance companies are exempt under the California Constitution from all taxes other than the gross receipts tax, the California Supreme Court ruled in *Occidental Life Insurance Company v. State Board of Equalization* (1982) (CCH California Tax Reports, ¶ 60-440.65), that retail sales of personal property to insurance companies are subject to California sales tax because the incidence of the tax is on the retailer, not the purchaser. Insurance companies are also liable for the collection of the use tax from their customers as held in *Beneficial Standard Life Insurance Company v. State Board of Equalization* (1962) (CCH California Tax Reports, ¶ 60-440.15, ¶ 60-440.25), decided by a California district court of appeal. In that case, an insurance company was required to pay use tax on purchases of automobiles and furniture from (or through) the company by its employees.

• *Interstate transactions*

In *Montgomery Ward & Co., Inc. v. State Board of Equalization* (1969) 272 CA2d 728, 78 CRptr 373, cert. den. 396 US 1040, 90 SCt 688, the state attempted to force out-of-state stores to collect use tax on over-the-counter sales in Oregon and Nevada that were billed to California residents. The Court of Appeal held that the stores could not be required to collect use tax where the goods were delivered outside the state.

In *National Geographic Society v. California State Board of Equalization* (1977) (CCH California Tax Reports, ¶ 60-020.74, 60-075.82), the U.S. Supreme Court held that the Society could be required to collect use tax on out-of-state mail order sales to California residents. The Society had two small offices in California.

¶1505

In *Matter of Hewlett Packard Co.* (2000) (CCH California Tax Reports, ¶60-450.522), the BOE ruled that donations of electronic equipment and software to out-of-state universities were not subject to use tax.

The law provides that the terms "storage" and "use" do not apply to:

— cases where property is brought into the state to be transported outside the state, or to be processed or fabricated into property which is to be transported outside the state, for use outside the state; or

— the rental of certain cargo containers for use in interstate or foreign commerce.

Consequently, such transactions are exempt from use tax.

Property purchased out of state is subject to use tax if its first functional use occurs in California. If the first functional use occurs outside California but the property is brought into California within 90 days of its purchase, the property is presumed to have been purchased for use in California. The presumption may be overcome if the property is used or stored outside the state for at least one-half of the six-month period immediately following its entry into California. Use tax is also not imposed if the property is used out of state for more than 90 days prior to its entry into the state. (Reg. 1620(b)(3), 18 CCR)

• *Irrevocable election to report use tax on income tax returns*

Taxpayers who are not required to hold a seller's permit or to be registered with the BOE may make an irrevocable election to report their qualified use tax obligations from purchases of tangible personal property on their California personal income tax, corporation franchise or income tax, partnership, limited liability company, or estate or trust tax or information returns. These provisions are inapplicable to purchases of mobile homes, vehicles, aircraft, and vessels, leases of tangible personal property, and certain purchases of cigarettes, tobacco, and tobacco products. Qualified use tax is considered timely reported and remitted if it is included with a timely filed return. The statute was enacted to make it more convenient for taxpayers to comply with their use tax obligations. "Qualified use tax" is defined as a taxpayer's actual unpaid use tax liability, as provided, to the taxpayer's purchases of tangible personal property subject to use tax. (Sec. 6452.1, Rev. & Tax. Code)

Effective January 1, 2013, and applicable to reporting periods beginning after 2011, the qualified use tax of an eligible purchaser is due and payable on or before April 15 following the close of the calendar year in which the liability for use tax was incurred. An "eligible purchaser" is one who purchases taxable tangible personal property and is either: (1) eligible to report use tax on an income tax return but does not elect to do so; or (2) is not required to file an income tax return and is not registered or required to be registered to report sales and use tax. (Sec. 6452.2, Rev. & Tax. Code)

An eligible person is authorized for one or more single non-business purchases of individual items of tangible personal property, each with a sales price of less than $1,000, to either report the estimated amount of use tax due based on the person's California adjusted gross income as reflected in the use tax table shown in the instructions of the acceptable tax return or the actual amount of use tax that was not paid to a registered retailer. (Sec. 6452.1, Rev. & Tax. Code)

• *Qualified purchasers*

A qualified purchaser is required to register with the BOE and provide the name under which the qualified purchaser transacts or intends to transact business, the location of the qualified purchaser's place or places of business, and other information as the BOE may require. Moreover, qualified purchasers are required to file a return, along with their remittance of the amount of tax due, on or before April 15. These provisions are inapplicable to the purchase of a vehicle, vessel, or aircraft, as defined. A "qualified purchaser" is defined as a person that meets all of the following conditions:

— the person is not required to hold a seller's permit;

— the person is not required to be registered, as specified;

— the person is not a holder of a use tax direct payment permit, as described;

— the person receives at least $100,000 in gross receipts from business operations per calendar year; and

— the person is not otherwise registered with the BOE to report use tax.

(Sec. 6225, Rev. & Tax. Code; Reg. 1699(j), 18 CCR)

Practitioner Comment: *Mandatory California Use Tax Registration for Non-Retail Businesses with Over $100,000 Annual Gross Receipts*

A "qualified purchaser" is required to register with the California State Board of Equalization (BOE) and report and pay use tax directly to the BOE. Qualified purchasers are non-retail businesses with at least $100,000 annual gross receipts that are not currently registered with the BOE for sales or use tax. This mandatory use tax reporting requirement applies to service businesses and pass-through entities including corporations, partnerships, limited liability companies, limited liability partnerships, and S-corporations that receive at least $100,000 in gross receipts from business operations per calendar year. This includes businesses with a location in California that provide services that are not subject to California sales tax. Failure to comply with the new law may result in a BOE audit with a look-back period of eight (8) years as well as non-filing, non-payment, and other penalty and/or interest assessments. A use tax return filing and payment is required annually by April 15.

Chris Whitney, Contributing Editor

• *Nexus*

In any sale or other taxable transaction that crosses state lines in any fashion, there has to be a determination of whether the transaction has sufficient nexus with the state to empower the state to impose its taxes. In *National Bellas Hess, Inc. v. Department of Revenue of Illinois,* 386 US 753 (1967) (CCH CALIFORNIA TAX REPORTS, ¶ 60-025), the U.S. Supreme Court held that a vendor had to have a physical presence in a state in order for that state to require the vendor to collect sales and use taxes on mail-order purchases. Physical presence within the state was required regardless of the degree to which the vendor may have availed itself of the benefits and protections of the taxing state.

Although the U.S. Supreme Court, in *Quill Corporation v. North Dakota* (1992) (CCH CALIFORNIA TAX REPORTS, ¶ 60-075.341), upheld the test of physical presence established in *National Bellas Hess, Inc.,* stating that physical presence is still required by the Commerce Clause of the U.S. Constitution to bring out-of-state retailers within the jurisdiction of a state's sales and use tax laws, such physical presence is not required to satisfy the Due Process Clause. The court held that the Due Process Clause by itself would permit a state's enforcement of its use tax against an out-of-state retailer who had an "economic presence" within the state (*i.e.,* continuous and widespread solicitation of business in the state).

A taxpayer's physical presence in a state need not be directly related to the taxed activity to establish nexus. In *National Geographic Society v. California Board of Equalization,* 430 US 551 (1977) (CCH CALIFORNIA TAX REPORTS, ¶ 60-075.82), the U.S. Supreme Court held that the presence in California of advertising sales offices owned by the society provided sufficient nexus for California to require that the society collect use tax on mail-order sales made to California residents by another division of its society. Although the activities conducted by the two advertising sales offices were unrelated to the mail-order sales, the sales offices benefited from California services and, thus, established nexus with the state. The Court applied similar reasoning in *D.H. Holmes*

Co. v. MacNamara, 486 US 24 (1988) (CCH CALIFORNIA TAX REPORTS, ¶ 60-025), in which a company with retail outlets in the state had to pay use tax on catalogs ordered from an out-of-state printer and sent by mail to the company's customers.

Furthermore, an Internet business may establish nexus as a result of activities by its "brick-and-mortar" affiliate. An out-of-state retailer of tangible personal property via the Internet was obligated to collect and remit California sales and use tax because the willingness of its authorized representative within the state to accept returned merchandise created for the retailer a substantial physical presence within the state. In *Borders Online, LLC v. State Board of Equalization* (2005) (CCH CALIFORNIA TAX REPORTS, ¶ 60-025.32), a California court of appeal held that the representative's activity on behalf of the retailer was sufficient to consider the retailer as being engaged in business in the state because such activity constituted "selling" and was an integral part of the retailer's selling efforts.

Practitioner Comment: Companies Doing Business Online

Borders Online's returns policy was posted on its Web site for less than 11 months of the 18-month audit period. However, that was sufficient for the court to find nexus for the entire audit period, noting that the question for purposes of the Commerce Clause is the "nature and extent" of the activities in the taxing state. The fact that Borders Online changed its policy did not appear to matter to the court, which found that once Borders Online entered the California market, it had nexus for the whole period. Borders Online's policy change did not "break" nexus.

Further, the court appeared to focus on the economic environment created by Borders Inc. for Borders Online, and found nexus despite an arguably slight or tenuous physical presence. In so ruling, the court extensively cited New York's highest court's decision in *Orvis Co. v. Tax Tribunal,* 86 N.Y.2d 165 (1995), and its conclusion that while physical presence is required, it need not be substantial. Rather, it must be demonstrably more than a "slightest presence," the court said, and it may be manifested by the presence in the taxing state of the vendor's property or the conduct of economic activities in the taxing state performed by the vendor's personnel or on its behalf.

Other courts have disagreed with this interpretation, but the court said that Orvis is more in keeping with the realities of 21st century marketing and technology, which, in the words of the court, "increasingly affords opportunities for out-of-state vendors to establish a strong economic presence in California by using California's 'legal-economic environment' while maintaining only a minimal or vicarious presence in the state." However, the BOE in *barnesandnoble.com* held that a retail store located in California that includes coupons for a website in its shopping bags is not sufficient to create California nexus for the online retailer.

Chris Whitney, Contributing Editor

Conversely, in *Barnesandnoble.com LLC v. State Board of Equalization* (2007) (CCH CALIFORNIA TAX REPORTS, ¶ 404-488), the San Francisco Superior Court held that the use by a brick-and-mortar company of coupons in its shopping bags that provided a discount on any one online purchase from its Internet retailer sister company did not create nexus sufficient to impose California use tax registration, collection and remittance obligations on the Internet retailer. In granting summary judgment in favor of the taxpayer, the court rejected the contention of the State Board of Equalization (BOE) that by using the shopping bags with the pre-inserted coupons issued by the taxpayer, the retail stores were acting as the taxpayer's agents or representatives. According to the court, the concept of agency requires something significantly more than the passive distribution of coupons. On May 29, 2008, the BOE approved a global settlement with Barnes & Noble.com that resolves all disputes between Barnes & Noble.com and the State of California for sales and use taxes, including pending litigation in the U.S. District Court for the Eastern District of California and the California Court of Appeal (First District). Under the settlement, two tax determinations against Barnes & Noble.com, plus all interest and penalties, were canceled by the BOE. In addition, the BOE waived all claims for sales and use taxes, interest, and penalties through November 1, 2005, the date on which Barnes & Noble.com voluntarily commenced collecting and remitting sales and use taxes to California.

Operative September 15, 2012, California imposes click-through and affiliate nexus. (Sec. 6203, Rev. & Tax. Code)

The definition of "retailer engaged in business in this state" includes any retailer who enters into an agreement under which a person in California, for a commission or other consideration, directly or indirectly refers potential purchasers of tangible personal property to the retailer, whether by an Internet-based link, a website, or otherwise, provided two conditions are met. Those conditions are: (1) that the total cumulative sales price from all of the retailer's sales within the preceding 12 months of tangible personal property to purchasers in California that are referred pursuant to such an agreement is in excess of $10,000; and (2) the retailer has total cumulative sales of tangible personal property to California purchasers in excess of $1 million within the preceding 12 months (Sec. 6203, Rev. & Tax. Code)

An "agreement," for purposes of this provision, does not include any agreement under which a retailer:

— purchases advertisements from a person in California, to be delivered on television, radio, in print, on the Internet, or by any other medium, unless the advertisement revenue paid consists of commissions or other consideration that is based upon sales of tangible personal property; or

— engages a person in California to place an advertisement on a website operated by that person, or operated by another person in the state, unless the person entering the agreement with the retailer also directly or indirectly solicits potential customers in California through the use of flyers, newsletters, telephone calls, electronic mail, blogs, micro blogs, social networking sites, or other means of direct and indirect solicitation specifically targeted at potential customers in the state.

(Sec. 6203, Rev. & Tax. Code)

In addition, the term "retailer" includes an entity affiliated with a retailer within the meaning of IRC § 1504. (Sec. 6203, Rev. & Tax. Code)

These provisions are inapplicable if the retailer can demonstrate that the person in California with whom the retailer has an agreement did not engage in referrals in the state on behalf of the retailer that would satisfy the requirements of the Commerce Clause of the U.S. Constitution. (Sec. 6203, Rev. & Tax. Code)

The term "retailer engaged in business in this state" also includes any retailer that is a member of a commonly controlled group and a combined reporting group, both as defined, that includes another member of the retailer's commonly controlled group that, pursuant to an agreement with or in cooperation with the retailer, performs services in California in connection with tangible personal property to be sold by the retailer, including but not limited to the design and development of tangible personal property sold by the retailer, or the solicitation of sales of tangible personal property on behalf of the retailer. (Sec. 6203, Rev. & Tax. Code)

In addition, the definition of a "retailer engaged in business" in California includes a retailer that has substantial nexus with California for purposes of the Commerce Clause of the U.S. Constitution and any retailer upon whom federal law permits the state to impose a use tax collection duty. (Sec. 6203, Rev. & Tax. Code)

Every retailer engaged in business in California and making sales of tangible personal property for storage, use, or other consumption in California, not otherwise exempted, must collect sales or use tax from the purchaser. "Retailer engaged in business in this state" specifically includes but is not limited to any retailer who:

— maintains, occupies, or uses, permanently or temporarily, directly or indirectly, or through a subsidiary, or agent, by whatever name called, an office, place of distribution, sales or sample room or place, warehouse or storage place, or other place of business;

— has any representative, agent, salesperson, canvasser, independent contractor, or solicitor operating in this state under the authority of the retailer or its subsidiary for the purpose of selling, delivering, installing, assembling, or the taking of orders for any tangible personal property;

— as respects a lease, derives rentals from a lease of tangible personal property situated in California;

— is a member of a commonly controlled group and a combined reporting group, as defined, that includes another member of the retailer's commonly controlled group that, pursuant to an agreement with or in cooperation with the retailer, performs services in this state in connection with tangible personal property to be sold by the retailer, including but not limited to the design and development of tangible personal property sold by the retailer, or the solicitation of sales of tangible personal property on behalf of the retailer; and

— enters into an agreement or agreements under which a person or persons in California, for a commission or other consideration, directly or indirectly refers potential purchasers of tangible personal property to the retailer, whether by an Internet-based link or an Internet website, or otherwise, provided that both of the following conditions are met: (1) the total cumulative sales price from all of the retailer's sales, within the preceding 12 months, of tangible personal property to purchasers in this state that are referred pursuant to all of those agreements with a person or persons in this state, is in excess of $10,000, and (2) the retailer, within the preceding 12 months, has total cumulative sales of tangible personal property to purchasers in this state in excess of $1 million.

(Sec. 6203, Rev. & Tax. Code; Reg. 1684(a), 18 CCR)

Affiliate nexus does not apply if a retailer can demonstrate that all of the persons with whom the retailer has agreements, as described, did not directly or indirectly solicit potential customers for the retailer in California. In addition, a retailer can demonstrate that an agreement is not an agreement subject to the affiliate nexus provision if:

— the retailer's agreement prohibits persons operating under the agreement from engaging in any solicitation activities in California that refer potential customers to the retailer including but not limited to distributing flyers, coupons, newsletters and other printed promotional materials or electronic equivalents, verbal soliciting (e.g., in-person referrals), initiating telephone calls, and sending emails;

— the person or persons operating under the agreement in California certify annually, under penalty of perjury, that they have not engaged in any prohibited solicitation activities in California at any time during the previous year; and

— the retailer accepts the certification or certifications in good faith, and the retailer does not know or have reason to know that the certification or certifications are false or fraudulent.

(Reg. 1684, 18 CCR)

A retailer can demonstrate that an agreement with an organization, such as a club or nonprofit group, is not subject to the affiliate nexus provision if, in addition to the above requirements, the agreement provides that the organization will maintain information on its website alerting its members to the prohibition against each of the solicitation activities described above, and the retailer obtains an annual certification from the organization under penalty of perjury that includes a statement certifying that its website includes information directed at its members alerting them to the prohibition against the solicitation activities described above. (Reg. 1684, 18 CCR)

A person may complete Form BOE-232, Annual Certification of No Solicitation, or any document that satisfies the regulatory requirements, to annually certify under penalty of perjury that the person has not engaged in any prohibited solicitation activities in California at any time during the previous year. An organization may complete the Additional Statement from Organization section of Form BOE-232, or any document that satisfies the regulatory requirements, to annually certify under penalty of perjury that its website includes information directed at its members alerting them to the prohibition against the solicitation activities described above. The BOE recommends taxpayers retain this form or any other document that satisfies the annual certification requirements for a minimum of eight years. (Reg. 1684, 18 CCR)

Practitioner Comment: California Imposes Click-Through and Affiliate Nexus Provisions

As noted above, existing California law requires every retailer engaged in business in California and making sales of tangible personal property for storage, use, or other consumption in this state to collect and remit sales tax from the purchaser. Effective September 15, 2012, Section 6203 of the Revenue and Taxation Code is amended to expand the definition of "retailer engaged in business in this state" to include click-through and affiliate nexus.

First, the term "retailer engaged in business in this state" now also includes any retailer that is a member of a commonly controlled group and a combined reporting group, that includes another member of the retailer's commonly controlled group that, pursuant to an agreement with or in cooperation with the retailer, performs services in California in connection with tangible personal property to be sold by the retailer, including but not limited to the design and development of tangible personal property sold by the retailer, or the solicitation of sales of tangible personal property on behalf of the retailer. This is referred to as "affiliate nexus."

Second, "retailer engaged in business in this state" is now defined to also include retailers that enter into "agreements" with an in-state person who, for a commission or other consideration, refers potential purchasers to the retailer by an Internet-based link, website or other method. In order for California to assert this "click-through" nexus, the following two conditions must be satisfied: (1) the total cumulative sales price from all of the retailer's sales within the preceding 12 months of tangible personal property to purchasers in California that are referred pursuant to such an agreement is in excess of $10,000; and (2) the retailer has total cumulative sales of tangible personal property to California purchasers in excess of $1 million within the preceding 12 months. An "agreement" for purposes of this provision excludes:

> — an agreement under which a retailer purchases advertisements from a person in California, to be delivered on television, radio, in print, on the Internet, or by any other medium, unless the advertisement revenue paid to the person in California consists of commissions or other consideration that is based upon sales of tangible personal property; and

> — an agreement under which a retailer engages a person in California to place an advertisement on an Internet Web site operated by that person, or operated by another person in California, unless the person entering the agreement with the retailer also directly or indirectly solicits potential customers in this state through use of flyers, newsletters, telephone calls, electronic mail, blogs, microblogs, social networking sites, or other means of direct or indirect solicitation specifically targeted at potential customers in this state.

"Retailer" includes an entity affiliated with a retailer within the meaning of Section 1504 of the Internal Revenue Code.

Chris Whitney, Contributing Editor

CCH Comment: State Contracts

A California department or agency may not enter into a contract for the purchase of tangible personal property from any vendor, contractor, or affiliate of a vendor or contractor unless the vendor, contractor, and all affiliates that make sales for delivery into California have a valid seller's permit or are registered with the BOE for California sales and use tax purposes. Every vendor, contractor, or affiliate of a vendor or contractor offered such a contract is required to submit a copy of its, and any affiliate's, seller's permit or certificate of registration. Exceptions are allowed if necessary to meet a compelling state interest.

• *Purchases of automobiles, boats, or airplanes*

A purchaser acquiring an automobile without the payment of sales or use tax is required to pay use tax to the Department of Motor Vehicles when applying for transfer of registration, unless the seller is a close relative (parent, grandparent, child, grandchild, spouse, registered domestic partner, or minor brother or sister) of the purchaser and is not in the automobile business. A similar rule applies to the purchase of a boat or airplane.

Vehicles entering California after being purchased outside California are deemed to have been purchased for use in California if the vehicle's first functional use is in California. (Reg. 1620, 18 CCR)

A vehicle, vessel, or aircraft bought outside of California that is brought into California within 12 months from the date of its purchase is presumptively subject to California use tax if the vehicle, vessel, or aircraft:

— was purchased by a California resident;

— is subject to California registration or property tax laws during the first 12 months of ownership; or

— is used or stored in California more than half the time during the first 12 months of ownership.

The presumption is inapplicable to any vehicle, vessel, or aircraft used in interstate or foreign commerce, and any aircraft or vessel brought into California for the purpose of repair, retrofit, or modification. Also, the presumption may be controverted by documentary evidence. (Sec. 6248, Rev. & Tax. Code)

Aircraft or vessels brought into California for the purpose of repair, retrofit, or modification are not subject to California use tax unless, during the period following the time the aircraft or vessel is brought into California and ending when the repair, retrofit, or modification of the aircraft or vessel is complete, more than 25 hours of airtime or sailing time are logged on the aircraft or vessel by the aircraft's or vessel's registered owner or by an authorized agent operating the aircraft or vessel. The return trip to a point outside California is not counted.

• *Use tax table*

The California State Board of Equalization (BOE) provides a Use Tax Lookup Table to help taxpayers pay use tax they may owe on purchases made from out-of-state online and mail order retailers. The table provides an easy way for taxpayers to determine the amount of use tax they owe even if they did not save their receipts. Taxpayers locate their adjusted gross income on the table and the table indicates the estimated use tax that is owed, which taxpayers then enter on their state income tax form. The table is included in the instructions that accompany income tax forms. For nonbusiness purchases of $1,000 or more, taxpayers may still report and pay their use tax on Forms 540, 540A, and 5402EZ. However, they must report the actual use tax due on the transactions of more than $1,000, add that amount to the lookup table estimate of their liability, and report the total on the use tax line item on the form. (Reg. 1685.5, 18 CCR)

Consumers may elect, and are not required, to use the use tax tables included in the instructions to their California Franchise Tax Board (FTB) returns to report their estimated use tax liabilities for one or more single nonbusiness purchases of individual items of tangible personal property each with a sales price of less than $1,000 on their FTB returns. However, eligible consumers may still calculate their actual use tax liabilities using the worksheets in the instructions to their FTB returns and report their actual use tax liabilities on their returns. (Reg. 1685.5, 18 CCR)

The use tax table may not be used to estimate use tax liabilities for business purchases, including purchases made by businesses required to hold a seller's permit or to register with the BOE under the Sales and Use Tax Law and report their use tax liabilities directly to the BOE. (Reg. 1685.5, 18 CCR)

The 2015 Use Tax Lookup Table is as follows:

— AGI less than $10,000 = $2 use tax liability;

— AGI of $10,000 to $19,999 = $5 use tax liability;

— AGI of $20,000 to $29,999 = $9 use tax liability;

— AGI of $30,000 to $39,999 = $12 use tax liability;

— AGI of $40,000 to $49,999 = $16 use tax liability;

— AGI of $50,000 to $59,999 = $19 use tax liability;

— AGI of $60,000 to $69,999 = $23 use tax liability;

— AGI of $70,000 to $79,999 = $26 use tax liability;

— AGI of $80,000 to $89,999 = $30 use tax liability;

— AGI of $90,000 to $99,999 = $33 use tax liability;

— AGI of $100,000 to $124,999 = $39 use tax liability;

— AGI of $125,000 to $149,999 = $48 use tax liability;

— AGI of $150,000 to $174,999 = $57 use tax liability;

— AGI of $175,000 to $199,999 = $66 use tax liability; and

— AGI more than $199,999 = multiply AGI by 0.035% (0.00035).

(Reg. 1685.5, 18 CCR; *News Release 10-16-G*, California State Board of Equalization, February 11, 2016)

This table can only be used to report use tax on the California Income Tax Return. This table may not be used to report use tax on business purchases. The table and instructions are provided in the state income tax return instructions for calendar year 2015, for forms 540 and 540 2EZ. (*News Release 10-16-G*, California State Board of Equalization, February 11, 2016)

The BOE is required to estimate, for calendar year 2013 and subsequent years, on an annual basis, the use tax due based on various U.S. Census Bureau data reported each May 1 and to make those estimates available to the FTB by July 30 of each year in the form of a use tax table for inclusion in the FTB's tax form instructions. (Reg. 1685.5, 18 CCR)

¶1506 Sales for Resale

Law: Secs. 6012, 6051, 6091-95, 6201, 6241-45 (CCH CALIFORNIA TAX REPORTS, ¶60-650).

A sale for resale is generally exempt from tax. (Sec. 6051, Rev. & Tax. Code; Sec. 6201, Rev. & Tax. Code) However, it is presumed that all gross receipts are subject to tax until the contrary is established. (Sec. 6091, Rev. & Tax. Code) To be relieved from liability, a seller must obtain a "resale certificate" from the purchaser. To be effective, the resale certificate must be taken in good faith from a person who holds a seller's permit and is engaged in the business of selling tangible personal property. (Sec. 6092, Rev. & Tax. Code) If a resale certificate is not obtained, the seller may still be able to prove by other evidence that the sale was for resale. (Reg. 1668, 18 CCR)

If tax is paid on a purchase of property that is resold prior to any use, the amount of the purchase may be deducted on the purchaser's sales tax return. (Sec. 6012(a)(1), Rev. & Tax. Code; Reg. 1701, 18 CCR)

On the other hand, a taxpayer who buys property tax-free with the intention of reselling it but uses it instead (other than for demonstration, display, etc.) must report and pay a tax on the purchase price. Even if the property is later resold, the tax on self-consumption must be paid if the property is used for anything except demonstration or display at any time before it is resold. However, if the use is limited to an accommodation loan to a customer while awaiting property purchased or leased, the tax is imposed only on the fair rental value for the duration of the loan. Also, the tax on property used for demonstration or display or for loans during repairs is measured by the rental value. (Sec. 6094(a), Rev. & Tax. Code, Reg. 1669, 18 CCR)

• *Resale certificates*

A resale certificate may be in any form, such as a note, letter, or memorandum. Although the State Board of Equalization (BOE) does not furnish resale certificates, the form approved by the BOE is reproduced in Reg. 1668. (*Publication 32, Sales to Purchasers from Mexico*, BOE)

The four border states of Arizona, California, New Mexico and Texas, together with the United Mexican States formed the Border States Caucus to develop programs to promote trade in the southwest region of the U.S. under NAFTA. Businesses buying goods for resale in these states or the northern border strip and border region of Mexico that will be transported across state and/or national borders may use the Border States Uniform Sale for Resale Certificate in lieu of a state resale certicate. The certicate must be completed by the buyer and given to the seller, who must retain the certificate. Since incomplete documents may be invalid, sellers should not accept incomplete certificates. (Border States Uniform Sale for Resale Certificate, Border States Caucus)

Licensed auto dismantlers and auto auctioneers are prohibited from accepting resale certificates from purchasers of vehicles, mobile homes, and commercial coaches, unless the purchasers are licensed dealers, dismantlers, auto repair dealers, or scrap metal processors, as specified and defined, for California sales and use tax purposes. Every qualified person making any sale of a mobilehome or commercial coach required to be registered annually under the Health and Safety Code, or of a vehicle required to be registered under the Vehicle Code or subject to identification under the Vehicle Code, or a vehicle that qualifies under the permanent trailer identification plate program pursuant to the Vehicle Code, or of any salvage certificate vehicle as defined in the Vehicle Code, as provided, is presumed to be making a sale at retail and not a sale for resale. Sales of vehicles, motorhomes, commercial coaches, and salvage vehicles by dismantlers and auctioneers are taxable unless the dismantler or auctioneer accepts a resale certificate from someone who is licensed to sell vehicles, vehicle parts, or scrap metal. (Sec. 6092.5, Rev. & Tax. Code; Reg. 1566.1, 18 CCR)

¶1507 Rental Transactions

Law: Secs. 6006-18.8, 6094.1, 6365, 6368.7, 6381, 6390, 6406, 7205.1; Reg. 1803.5, 18 CCR (CCH CALIFORNIA TAX REPORTS, ¶ 60-460, 60-570).

A lease of tangible personal property for consideration is taxable as a sale or purchase subject to certain exceptions. (Sec. 6006(g), Rev. & Tax. Code) A lease is a "continuing sale," and possession of the leased property is a "continuing purchase." (Sec. 6006.1, Rev. & Tax. Code; Sec. 6010.1, Rev. & Tax. Code) Generally, the tax applicable to leases is the use tax, which is collected by the lessor and is measured by the rental receipts; the lessor is responsible for collecting the tax and giving the lessee a receipt. The lessee remains liable for the tax until this receipt is obtained. However, the lessor has the option of paying tax upon its acquisition of the property to be leased and not collecting tax on the lease payments. (Reg. 1660(c), 18 CCR)

The tax is applicable to a lease of tangible personal property, except the following:

— motion pictures, including television, films, and tapes (except videocassettes, etc., rented for private use);

— linen supplies and similar articles by professional cleaners;

— household furnishings included in a lease of living quarters;

— mobile transportation equipment;

— tax-paid property;

— qualified manufacturing property for which a manufacturer-lessor elects to report and pay tax measured by the cost price; and

— mobile homes.

(Sec. 6006(g), Rev. & Tax. Code; Sec. 6010(e), Rev. & Tax. Code; Sec. 6365, Rev. & Tax. Code; Reg. 1660(b)(1), 18 CCR)

Special rules apply to mobile home leases. If a mobile home was originally purchased by a retailer without payment of sales or use tax and first leased before July 1, 1980, its lease is taxable unless the mobile home becomes subject to local property taxation, in which case it is exempt from sales and use tax. The lease of a *used* mobile home that was first sold new in California after July 1, 1980, is not subject to sales or use tax. The lease of a mobile home that was originally purchased by a retailer without payment of sales or use tax and first leased on or after July 1, 1980, is not subject to sales tax, but the lessor's use of the property is subject to use tax. (Reg. 1660(d)(8), 18 CCR)

"Lease" is defined to exclude the use of tangible personal property for less than one day for a charge of less than $20, where the use of the property is restricted to the business location of the seller. (Sec. 6006.3, Rev. & Tax. Code)

A contract designated as a lease is considered a sale under a security agreement rather than a lease if the lessee is bound for a fixed term and obtains title after making the required payments or has the option to purchase the property for a nominal amount. (Sec. 6006.3, Rev. & Tax. Code; Reg. 1660(a), 18 CCR)

A lease of tangible personal property is deemed to be a continuing sale by the lessor and a continuing purchase by the lessee for the entire period that the leased property is located in California. (Sec. 6006.1, Rev. & Tax. Code; Sec. 6010.1, Rev. & Tax. Code)

If a lease of tangible personal property covers property that is in substantially the same form as when it was acquired by the lessor, and the lessor has paid the sales or use tax on its acquisition, the rental receipts are not subject to tax. (Sec. 6006(g), Rev. & Tax. Code; Reg. 1660(b)(1)(E), 18 CCR) This rule does not apply to chemical toilets, and their rentals are therefore taxable. (Sec. 6010.7, Rev. & Tax. Code) As indicated above, the tax does apply where the leased property is *not* in substantially the same form as when acquired by the lessor, or where the property was acquired by the lessor in a transaction not subject to sales or use tax; *e.g.*, in an "occasional sale" transaction.

• *Local taxes*

The local use tax from long-term leases of tangible personal property is generally allocated to the lessee's residence, as that is the place where the property is used. However, the place of use for reporting and transmittal of the local use tax for leases of passenger vehicles and small pick-up trucks is:

— the lessor's place of business at which the lease is negotiated, if the lessor is a California new motor vehicle dealer or leasing company;

— the place of business of the new motor vehicle dealer or leasing company from which the vehicle is purchased, if the lessor is not a California new motor vehicle dealer or leasing company; or

— the place of the lessee's residence, if the lessor is not a California new motor vehicle dealer or leasing company and the lessor purchases either a new motor vehicle from a person other than a new motor vehicle dealer or a used motor vehicle from any source.

(Sec. 7205.1, Rev. & Tax. Code)

Generally, the place of use, once determined, is the place of use for the duration of the lease. The lessor's sale of the vehicle, assignment of the lease contract to a third party, or, in the case of the first or second places listed above, change of residence will not affect the place of use.

¶1507

¶1508 Basis of Tax

Law: Secs. 6011, 6012, 6012.3, 6055, 6203.5; Regs. 1641, 1642, 1654, 1671, 18 CCR (CCH CALIFORNIA TAX REPORTS, ¶ 61-110—61-180).

Tax is imposed upon "gross receipts" for sales tax purposes and "sales price" for use tax purposes, which are defined as the total amount for which tangible personal property is sold, leased, or rented, valued in money (whether paid in money or otherwise). Excluded from the terms "gross receipts" and "sales price" is the portion of the sales price returned to a used vehicle purchaser or the purchase price of a contract cancellation option agreement. No deduction may be claimed for the following:

— the cost of the property sold;

— the cost of materials used, labor or service costs, interest paid or charged, losses, or any other expenses; or

— the cost of transporting the property, except as otherwise provided.

(Sec. 6011, Rev. & Tax. Code; Sec. 6012, Rev. & Tax. Code)

The "total amount for which property is sold, leased, or rented" includes the following:

— any services that are a part of the sale;

— any amount for which credit is given to the purchaser by the seller; and

— in the definition of "gross receipts," all receipts, cash, credits, and property of any kind.

(Sec. 6011, Rev. & Tax. Code; Sec. 6012, Rev. & Tax. Code)

• *Bad debt deduction*

California permits a deduction for whatever portion of a tax-paid account is found to be worthless, provided that the account has been charged off for federal income tax purposes or, if the taxpayer is not required to file a federal return, the account is charged off under generally accepted accounting principles. The deduction may not include tax-exempt charges such as interest, insurance, repair, installation, or other charges, or collection expenses. (Sec. 6055, Rev. & Tax. Code; Sec. 6203.5, Rev. & Tax. Code; Reg. 1642(a), 18 CCR)

The tax must be repaid if a recovery is made on a charged-off account. In the case of a repossession, a bad debt deduction is allowed to the extent that the seller has sustained a net loss on tax-paid gross receipts. If the tax has previously been paid, the worthless accounts may be deducted from other taxable sales in the quarter in which they are determined to be worthless and charged off, or a refund may be claimed. If there is a subsequent recovery on such accounts, the amount collected must be included in the first return filed after such collection and the tax must be paid accordingly. (Sec. 6055, Rev. & Tax. Code; Sec. 6203.5, Rev. & Tax. Code; Reg. 1642(a), 18 CCR)

The original retailer, a business successor, or specified lenders are eligible to claim the deduction. If a worthless account on which a retailer previously paid tax is held by a lender, the retailer and lender may file an election with the State Board of Equalization (BOE) to designate which party is entitled to claim the deduction or a refund of the tax, but only if: (1) the contract between the retailer and lender contains an irrevocable relinquishment of all rights to the account from the retailer to the lender; and (2) the account has been found to be worthless and written off by the lender. (Sec. 6055, Rev. & Tax. Code; Sec. 6203.5, Rev. & Tax. Code; Reg. 1642(a), 18 CCR)

• *Coupons, premiums, and cash discounts*

The amount subject to tax does not include cash discounts allowed and taken on sales. The discounts are deductible only if allowed directly to the purchaser. (Sec. 6011(c)(1), Rev. & Tax. Code; Sec. 6012(c)(1), Rev. & Tax. Code; Reg. 1654(b)(2), 18 CCR)

Sellers that issue trading stamps may deduct from taxable receipts the amount that they pay to third parties that redeem the stamps (normally, trading-stamp redemption centers) for furnishing premiums to the seller's customers. The delivery of merchandise in exchange for trading stamps is a taxable retail sale, provided that the merchandise is of a kind normally subject to the sales tax. The amount subject to tax is the average amount that the "third party" (usually, a trading-stamp redemption center) charged the retailer for the stamps, *i.e.*, the per-book value of the stamps. The delivery of premium merchandise by a retailer to a customer in exchange for indicia required by the retailer constitutes a taxable retail sale of such merchandise. The applicable sales tax is measured by the retailer's cost to purchase the merchandise. (Reg. 1671, 18 CCR)

Detailed rules regarding the tax treatment of discounts, coupons, rebates and other incentives can be found in Reg. 1671.1, 18 CCR.

• *Mixed digital and tangible newspaper and periodical products*

Practitioner Comment: Board of Equalization updates regulations to address mixed digital and tangible newspaper and periodical products

The California Board of Equalization ("Board") updated Regulation 1590 referring to the treatment of newspapers and periodicals. Due the increasing number of newspaper subscriptions that include a subscription for a right to access digital content, which by itself is not subject to tax, the Board updated its rules to provide clear guidance for determining which portion of those subscriptions are taxable as sales of tangible property and which portion is considered tax free receipts from intangibles.

For sales of mixed newspaper subscriptions made on or after October 1, 2016, the regulation creates a presumption that 47% of the subscription is tangible and taxable, with the remaining 53% presumed to be the non-taxable intangible. This presumption can be overcome through proper demonstration that the non-taxable allocation is higher than 53%.

Chris Whitney, Contributing Editor

• *Trade-ins*

The value of a trade-in may not be deducted from the sales price of the property for purposes of computing the applicable sales tax. If the BOE finds that the trade-in allowance stated in the sales agreement is less than the fair market value of the property, the agreed upon allowance is presumed to be the fair market value. Although cash discounts are normally excludable from the amount subject to tax, if a transaction involves both a trade-in and a discount, the contract of sale must specify that the parties contracted for both; otherwise, the claimed discount will be treated as an overallowance on the trade-in and will not be excludable from the measure of tax. (Sec. 6011(b)(2), Rev. & Tax. Code; Sec. 6012(b)(3), Rev. & Tax. Code; Reg. 1654, 18 CCR)

• *Transportation and handling charges*

Separately stated charges for transportation from the retailer's place of business or other point from which shipment is made directly to the purchaser is excluded from the tax base, but the exclusion may not exceed a reasonable charge for transportation. However, if the transportation is provided by a third party hired by the retailer, or if the property is sold for a delivered price, this exclusion is limited to transportation that occurs after the purchase of the property is made. (Sec. 6011(c)(7), Rev. & Tax. Code; Sec. 6012(c)(7), Rev. & Tax. Code; Reg. 1628(a), 18 CCR)

• *Installation charges*

Installation charges are not subject to tax. (Sec. 6011(c)(3), Rev. & Tax. Code; Sec. 6012(c)(3), Rev. & Tax. Code; Reg. 1546(a), 18 CCR)

• *Taxes*

California excludes from the tax base specified federal excise taxes imposed on gasoline, diesel, or jet fuel. California also excludes from the amount subject to tax diesel fuel excise tax and state motor vehicle fees and taxes that are added to or measured by the vehicle's price. (Sec. 6011, Rev. & Tax. Code; Sec. 6012, Rev. & Tax. Code; Reg. 1617, 18 CCR)

Tribal taxes imposed on a stated percentage of the sales or purchase price are excluded from the California sales and use tax base, provided the tribe is in substantial compliance with California's sales and use tax laws. (Sec. 6011(c)(12), Rev. & Tax. Code; Sec. 6012(c)(12), Rev. & Tax. Code)

• *Installment, layaway, and credit sales*

Tax applies to the entire amount of an installment, lay-away (including any fees charged), or credit sale. Finance, interest, and carrying charges, however, as well as insurance charges, are excludable from the tax base, provided that the taxpayer's records segregate the charges. (Reg. 1641(a), 18 CCR)

¶1509 Exempt Transactions

Law: Secs. 6351-6423; Regs. 1521, 1618, 18 CCR (CCH CALIFORNIA TAX REPORTS, ¶ 60-360, 60-420, 60-445, 60-510, 60-590, 60-640, 61-010—61-020).

California law allows full or partial sales and use tax exemptions for a number of items, transactions, and organizations. The main sales and use tax exemption categories are the following:

— admission charges (Sec. 6006, Rev. & Tax. Code; Sec. 6016, Rev. & Tax. Code)

— advanced transportation technologies or alternative source products, components, or systems (Secs. 26003 and 26011.8, Pub. Res. Code; Reg. 10031, 4 CCR)

— aircraft gasoline and certain aircraft sales (Sec. 6357, Rev. & Tax. Code, Sec. 6366, Rev. & Tax. Code; Sec. 6366.1, Rev. & Tax. Code; Sec. 6480(b), Rev. & Tax. Code; Reg. 1593(a), 18 CCR; Reg. 1598, 18 CCR)

— animal life, feed, and medication (Sec. 6358, Rev. & Tax. Code; Sec. 6358.4, Rev. & Tax. Code; Reg. 1587, 18 CCR)

— carbon dioxide packing (Sec. 6359.8, Rev. & Tax. Code; Reg. 1630(b), 18 CCR)

— cash discounts (excluded from the measure of tax) (Sec. 6011(c)(1), Rev. & Tax. Code; Sec. 6012(c)(1), Rev. & Tax. Code; Reg. 1654(b)(2), 18 CCR)

— charitable organizations, goods made, goods donated (Sec. 6375, Rev. & Tax. Code; Reg. 1570, 18 CCR)

— common carriers, certain sales (Sec. 6357.5, Rev. & Tax. Code, Sec. 6385, Rev. & Tax. Code, Sec. 6396, Rev. & Tax. Code)

— custom computer programs (Sec. 6010.9, Rev. & Tax. Code)

— farm equipment and machinery (partial exemption) (Sec. 6356.5, Rev. & Tax. Code)

— food products and containers (however, prepared food and dietary supplements are taxable) (Sec. 6358, Rev. & Tax. Code, Sec. 6359, Rev. & Tax. Code, Sec. 6359.1, Rev. & Tax. Code, Sec. 7282.3, Rev. & Tax. Code)

— food stamp purchases (Sec. 6373, Rev. & Tax. Code)

— fuel or petroleum (Sec. 6357, Rev. & Tax. Code, Sec. 6357.5, Rev. & Tax. Code, Sec. 6358.1, Rev. & Tax. Code)

— green manufacturing exclusion (Secs. 26003, 26011.8, Pub. Res. Code; Sec. 6010.8, Rev. & Tax. Code; Reg. 10031, 4 CCR)

— ground control stations, limited (Sec. 6366, Rev. & Tax. Code)

— installation charges (excluded from the measure of tax) (Sec. 6011(c)(3), Rev. & Tax. Code; Sec. 6012(c)(3), Rev. & Tax. Code; Reg. 1546(a), 18 CCR)

— insurers, sales by (sales tax exemption only) (Sec. 12204, Rev. & Tax. Code)

— interstate and foreign commerce (Sec. 6396, Rev. & Tax. Code)

— leases, various items (¶ 1507)

— liquefied petroleum gas for agricultural or residential use (Sec. 6353, Rev. & Tax. Code)

— lodging

— lottery tickets (Sec. 8880.68, Govt. Code)

— manufacturing and research and development (R&D) equipment by biotechnology and manufacturing companies (Sec. 6377.1, Rev. & Tax. Code)

— meals delivered to homebound elderly or disabled persons (Sec. 6363.7, Rev. & Tax. Code)

— meals served by religious organizations or social clubs (Sec. 6361, Rev. & Tax. Code, Sec. 6363.5, Rev. & Tax. Code, Sec. 6374, Rev. & Tax. Code)

— meals served in health care and residential facilities or boarding houses (Sec. 6363.6, Rev. & Tax. Code, Sec. 6363.7, Rev. & Tax. Code)

— meals served to low-income elderly persons or students (Sec. 6363, Rev. & Tax. Code, Sec. 6363.7, Rev. & Tax. Code, Sec. 6374, Rev. & Tax. Code, Sec. 6376.5, Rev. & Tax. Code)

— meals and food served by nonprofit veterans' organizations for fundraising purposes (Sec. 6363.8, Rev. & Tax. Code)

— medical devices and equipment (Sec. 6018.7, Rev. & Tax. Code, Sec. 6369.1, Rev. & Tax. Code, Sec. 6369.2, Rev. & Tax. Code, Sec. 6369.5, Rev. & Tax. Code)

— military personnel (this exemption is repealed effective January 1, 2019) (Sec. 6412, Rev. & Tax. Code);

— mobile homes, used (Sec. 6379, Rev. & Tax. Code)

— motion picture production credit (also known as the "film and television credit") (Sec. 6902.5, Rev. & Tax. Code; Sec. 17053.85, Rev. & Tax. Code; Sec. 23685, Rev. & Tax. Code) and qualified motion picture production credit (Sec. 6902.5, Rev. & Tax. Code; Sec. 17053.95, Rev. & Tax. Code; Sec. 23695, Rev. & Tax. Code)

— newspapers and periodicals (see below) (Sec. 6362.7, Rev. & Tax. Code, Sec. 6362.8, Rev. & Tax. Code)

— off-reservation sales of tangible personal property to tribal governments of certain federally-recognized Native American tribes (Reg. 1616, 18 CCR)

— occasional sales (see below) (Sec. 6006.5, Rev. & Tax. Code)

— prescription medicines (Sec. 6359(c), Rev. & Tax. Code, Sec. 6369, Rev. & Tax. Code, Sec. 6369.1, Rev. & Tax. Code)

— racehorse breeding stock (partial exemption) (Sec. 6358.5, Rev. & Tax. Code; Reg. 1535, 18 CCR)

— realty (Sec. 6051, Rev. & Tax. Code)

— resales (Sec. 6092, Rev. & Tax. Code)

— returned merchandise (Reg. 1573, 18 CCR)

— "safe harbor" sale and leaseback arrangements (Sec. 6010.11, Rev. & Tax. Code, Sec. 6018.8, Rev. & Tax. Code, Sec. 6368.7, Rev. & Tax. Code)

— seeds, plants, and fertilizer (Sec. 6358, Rev. & Tax. Code)

— solar power facilities that meet certain criteria (Reg. 1533.1, 18 CCR)

— space flight property (Sec. 6380, Rev. & Tax. Code)

— stocks, bonds, and securities (Sec. 50026.5, Govt. Code)

— telegraph and telephone lines (Sec. 6016.5, Rev. & Tax. Code)

— teleproduction and postproduction property (partial exemption) (Sec. 6378, Rev. & Tax. Code)

— tangible personal property sold by a thrift store located on a military installation and operated by a designated entity that, in partnership with the U.S. Department of Defense, provides financial, educational, and other assistance to members of the U.S. Armed Forces, eligible family members, and survivors that are in need (Sec. 6363.4, Rev. & Tax. Code)

— timber harvesting equipment and machinery (partial exemption) (Sec. 6356.5, Rev. & Tax. Code)

— United States purchases, sales (Sec. 6381, Rev. & Tax. Code, Sec. 6402, Rev. & Tax. Code)

— utilities' charges (Sec. 6353, Rev. & Tax. Code)

— vehicles purchased by family members or foreigners (Sec. 6366.2, Rev. & Tax. Code)

— vessels and watercraft, limited (Sec. 6356, Rev. & Tax. Code, Sec. 6368, Rev. & Tax. Code, Sec. 6368.1, Rev. & Tax. Code)

See ¶ 1503 for a discussion of partial state tax exemption rates.

Practitioner Comment: Sales to Certain Indian Tribal Governments May be Exempt

The California State Board of Equalization released a special notice in October 2012 highlighting an amendment to California Code of Regulations section 1616, Federal Areas. This amendment allows a limited exemption from sales and use tax for off-reservation sales of tangible personal property to Indian tribal governments. To qualify for this exemption, an Indian tribe has to be officially recognized by the U.S and either does not have a reservation or does not conduct tribal business on the tribe's reservation because the reservation either lacks a building or essential utility services. The tangible personal property purchased subject to the exemption has to be for use in tribal self-governance and it has to be delivered to where the tribal government meets to conduct tribal business. Further, within the first 12 months following delivery, the property has to be used more in tribal self-governance than for any other purposes.

Under this exemption, tribal governments provide an exemption certificate attesting that the property qualifies for exemption. Retailers should request that tribal governments complete and provide the BOE-146-TSG exemption certificate with the required information that meets the sales and use tax exemption. Retailers selling to tribal governments will be relieved of any sales tax liability if they accept in good faith a valid exemption certificate from the purchaser.

Chris Whitney, Contributing Editor

• *All volunteer fire departments*

An all volunteer fire department is a consumer of, and will not be considered a retailer, for California sales and use tax purposes, of all tangible personal property sold by it, including but not limited to hot prepared food products and clothing, provided the profits are used solely and exclusively in furtherance of the department's purposes. (Sec. 6018.10, Rev. & Tax. Code)

These provisions remain in effect until January 1, 2021, and are repealed as of that date. (Sec. 6018.10, Rev. & Tax. Code)

As a result, through December 31, 2020, qualified all-volunteer fire departments are not required to report California sales tax, have a seller's permit, or file sales tax returns for the sale of tangible personal property, including clothing and hot prepared food products, when the profits are used to further the department's purposes. All-volunteer fire departments will be considered the consumer, rather than retailer, of items sold at fundraisers. As a consumer, tax applies when they make purchases of items to be sold during fundraising activities. (Sec. 6018.10, Rev. & Tax. Code; *Special Notice L-443*, California State Board of Equalization, December 2015)

To qualify for the above tax treatment, an all-volunteer fire department must:

— not pay members a regular salary, but may pay members hourly or per incident;

— have as its purpose the protection of lives, property, and environment within a designated geographical area from fire, disasters, and emergency incidents;

— be regularly organized for volunteer fire department purposes;

— qualify as a tax-exempt nonprofit organization; and

— not have gross receipts of more than $100,000 in each of the two prior calendar years.

(*Special Notice L-443*, California State Board of Equalization, December 2015)

• *Farm equipment and machinery*

California partially exempts from sales and use taxes: farm equipment and machinery, and the parts purchased for use primarily in producing and harvesting agricultural products; and timber harvesting equipment and machinery, and the parts purchased by a qualified person primarily for use in timber harvesting. (Sec. 6356.5, Rev. & Tax. Code; Reg. 1534, 18 CCR)

The partial exemption applies to all portions of the state sales and use tax rate. The partial exemption does not apply to the sales and use tax component authorized by the Bradley-Burns Uniform Local Sales and Use Tax Law or the Transaction and Use Tax Law. (Sec. 6356.5, Rev. & Tax. Code; Reg. 1534, 18 CCR; Reg. 1533.1, 18 CCR)

The BOE advises that, generally, car dealers' sales or leases of vehicles designed primarily for transportation of persons or property on a highway, including sales or leases of pickup trucks, heavy duty trucks, and tractor trucks, do not qualify for the partial sales and use tax exemption provided for farm equipment and machinery. (*Special Notice L-436*, California State Board of Equalization, January 2016)

For sales to qualified persons, a car dealer may only accept a partial exemption certificate from the purchaser and claim the partial exemption on the dealer's sales and use tax return in the limited circumstances in which the car dealer sells or leases a vehicle that meets both of the requirements to be considered "farm equipment and machinery." If the qualified person is buying the property of a kind not normally used in producing and harvesting agricultural products, such as a passenger vehicle or pickup, the car dealer should require a statement as to how the specific property purchased will be used. An exemption certificate cannot be accepted in good faith, however, in situations in which the car dealer has knowledge that the property will not be used in an exempt manner. (*Special Notice L-436*, California State Board of Equalization, January 2016)

• *Green manufacturing exclusion*

The California Alternative Energy and Advanced Transportation Financing Authority (the Authority) is authorized to approve a sales and use tax exclusion on tangible personal property used for the design, manufacture, production, or assembly of advanced transportation technologies or alternative source products, components, or systems, otherwise known as a "green manufacturing exclusion." The Authority was created to promote the development and utilization of alternative energy sources and the development and commercialization of advanced transportation technologies and is required to establish a renewable energy program to provide financial assistance, as defined, to certain entities for projects to generate new and renewable energy sources, develop clean and efficient distributed generation, and demonstrate the economic feasibility of new technologies. Specific information must be provided when applications are submitted. (Sec. 26003, Pub. Res. Code; Sec. 26011.8, Pub. Res. Code)

Effective January 1, 2013, and until January 1, 2021, this exclusion is expanded to include advanced manufacturing, as defined. "Advanced manufacturing" is defined as manufacturing processes that improve existing, or create entirely new materials, products, and processes through the use of science, engineering, or information technologies, high-precision tools and methods, a high-performance workforce, and innovative business or organizational models utilizing any of the following technology areas: micro- and nano-electronics, including semiconductors; advanced materials; integrated computational materials engineering; nanotechnology; additive manufacturing; and industrial biotechnology. (Sec. 6010.8, Rev. & Tax. Code; Sec. 26003, Pub. Res. Code)

In addition, "advanced manufacturing" includes:

— systems that result from substantive advancement, whether incremental or breakthrough, beyond the current industry standard, in the production of materials and products (such advancements include improvements in manufacturing processes and systems that are often referred to as "smart" or "intelligent" manufacturing systems that integrate computational predictability and operational efficiency); and

— sustainable manufacturing systems and manufacturing technologies that minimize the use of resources while maintaining or improving cost and performance (sustainable manufacturing systems and manufacturing technologies do not include those required to be undertaken pursuant to state or federal law or regulations, air district rules or regulations, memoranda of understanding with a governmental entity, or legally binding agreements or documents).

(Sec. 6010.8, Rev. & Tax. Code; Sec. 26003, Pub. Res. Code)

The definition of "participating party," for purposes of the exclusion, includes an entity located outside California, including an entity located overseas as a participating party eligible to apply for financial assistance in the form of the exclusion if the participating party commits to and demonstrates that the party will open a manufacturing facility in California. Moreover, the term "project" is redefined to specify that the qualifying tangible personal property must be utilized in California. (Sec. 6010.8, Rev. & Tax. Code; Sec. 26003, Pub. Res. Code)

Effective October 11, 2015, and until January 1, 2021, the types of projects that may qualify for the sales and use tax exclusion are expanded to include tangible personal property if at least 50 percent of its use is either to process recycled feedstock that is intended to be reused in the production of another product or using recycled feedstock in the production of another product or soil amendment, or tangible personal property that is used in the state for the design, manufacture, production, or assembly of advanced manufacturing, advanced transportation technologies, or alternative source products, components, or systems, as defined. "Recycled feedstock" is defined as materials that would otherwise be destined for disposal, having completed their intended end use and product lifecycle. "Project" does not include tangible personal property that processes or uses recycled feedstock in a way that would constitute disposal, as defined. (Sec. 26011.8, Pub. Res. Code)

• *Government agency transactions*

A statutory exemption applies to sales to:

— the U.S. government and its unincorporated agencies and instrumentalities;

— any incorporated agency or instrumentality of the United States that is wholly owned by the United States or by a corporation wholly owned by the United States;

— the American National Red Cross; and

— incorporated federal instrumentalities not wholly owned by the United States (unless federal law permits taxation of the instrumentality).

(Sec. 6381, Rev. & Tax. Code; Sec. 6402, Rev. & Tax. Code)

The use tax may not be imposed on the storage, use, or other consumption of property by the government unless specifically allowed under federal law. (Reg. 1614, 18 CCR) Sales to state or local governmental units are subject to the tax.

Federal contractors: Federal contractors are consumers of materials and fixtures that they furnish and install in performing their contracts. Thus, either the sales tax or the use tax applies to sales of tangible personal property—including materials, fixtures, supplies, and equipment—to contractors for use in performing their contracts with the United States for constructing improvements on or to real property or for repairing fixtures. Sales tax, but not use tax, applies when the contractor purchases property as the agent of the federal government. Federal contractors are retailers of machinery and equipment furnished in connection with construction contracts with the United States. Thus, sales of such property to federal contractors are exempt sales for resale, provided that title passes to the United States before the contractor uses the property. (Sec. 6384, Rev. & Tax. Code; Reg. 1521, 18 CCR)

There are special provisions regarding contracts with the U.S. government to furnish, or fabricate and furnish, tangible personal property when title to items purchased by the contractor for use in performing the contract passes to the United States pursuant to title provisions contained in the contract before the contractor uses the items. A federal government contractor's purchase of "direct consumable supplies" or "overhead materials" qualifies as a sale for resale to the federal government, provided that the federal government takes title pursuant to a U.S. government supply contract before the contractor uses the property for the purpose it was manufactured. Whether title to direct consumable supplies or indirect consumable supplies (i.e., overhead materials) passes to the United States under a U.S. government supply contract, and the time at which title passes, is determined according to contractual title provisions, if any exist. (Reg. 1618, 18 CCR)

See also the U.S. Supreme Court decision in *United States of America v. California State Board of Equalization* (1993) (CCH CALIFORNIA TAX REPORTS, ¶ 61-520.75).

• *Internet Tax Freedom Act*

The federal Internet Tax Freedom Act (ITFA) and its amendments (P.L. 105-277, 112 Stat. 2681, 47 U.S.C. 151 note, amended by P.L. 107-75, P.L. 108-435, P.L. 110-108) bar state and local governments from imposing multiple or discriminatory taxes on electronic commerce and taxes on Internet access for the period beginning on October 1, 1998, and ending on November 1, 2014. However, the moratorium imposed by the Act does not apply to Internet access taxes generally imposed and actually enforced prior to October 1, 1998, as long as the state has not, more than 24 months prior to the enactment of P.L. 110-108, repealed its tax on Internet access or issued a rule that it no longer applies such a tax. A second grandfather provision permitted the taxation of certain types of "telecommunications services" until June 30, 2008.

"Internet access" means a service that enables users to connect to the Internet to access content, information, or other services, including the purchase, use, or sale of telecommunications by an Internet service provider to provide the service or otherwise enable users to access content, information, or other services offered over the Internet. It also includes incidental services such as home pages, electronic mail, instant messaging, video clips, and personal electronic storage capacity, whether or not packaged with service to access the Internet. However, "Internet access" does not include voice, audio or video programming, or other products and services using Internet protocol for which there is a charge, regardless of whether the charge is bundled with charges for "Internet access."

The Second District of the California Court of Appeal held that an Internet service provider that had improperly charged its customers taxes for Internet access and who had unsuccessfully sought refunds of those taxes from the cities and counties to which the taxes had been remitted, had standing to bring an action for a tax refund. The "refund first" local ordinances are preempted by the Government Claims Act (in the California Government Code), which provides that a claim may be presented by the claimant or a person acting on his or her behalf. The act does not require that the claim be presented only by an entity that has repaid the taxes to its customers. *Sipple v. City of Hayward*, (2014) (CCH California Tax Reports, ¶ 60-445.41)

• *Interstate transactions*

California exempts sales of property to be delivered to out-of-state destinations if under the sales contract the property is required to be and is actually shipped by the seller to an out-of-state destination by means of either (1) facilities operated by the seller or (2) delivery by the seller to a carrier, customs broker, or forwarding agent, whether hired by the purchaser or not, for shipment to the out-of-state destination. (Sec. 6396, Rev. & Tax. Code) See ¶1505 for a discussion of interstate transactions exempt from use tax.

CCH Comment: Videocassettes Shipped to Foreign Airline Found Taxable

The California Court of Appeal held in an unpublished decision that videocassettes sold to an export packer for delivery to a foreign airline were not exempt from sales tax under the Import-Export clause because of the export packer's quality control and testing activities in California.

Nor did the transaction fall under the statutory exemptions discussed above because (1) there was no evidence of a contract requiring that the videocassettes be shipped to a point outside the state by specified means and (2) at the time of the sale, the export packer was contractually required to test and inspect the videocassettes prior to commencement of the export process. (*National Film Laboratories, Inc. v. California State Board of Equalization*, (2007) CCH California Tax Reports, ¶ 60-075.56)

• *Manufacturing and R&D equipment*

Operative July 1, 2014, and before July 1, 2022, a partial sales and use tax exemption is applicable to the gross receipts from the sale, storage, use, or other consumption in California of any of the following qualified tangible personal property purchased for use by:

— a qualified person to be used primarily (i.e., 50% or more of the time) in any stage of the manufacturing, processing, refining, fabricating, or recycling of tangible personal property, beginning at the point any raw materials are received by the qualified person and introduced into the process and ending at the point at which the manufacturing, processing, refining, fabricating, or recycling has altered tangible personal property to its completed form, including packaging, if required;

— a qualified person to be used primarily in R&D;

— a qualified person to be used primarily to maintain, repair, measure, or test any qualified tangible personal property described above; and

— a contractor purchasing that property for use in the performance of a construction contract for the qualified person that will use that property as an integral part of the manufacturing, processing, refining, fabricating, or recycling processes, or as a research or storage facility for use in connection with those processes.

(Sec. 6377.1, Rev. & Tax. Code)

The partial exemption from sales and use taxes is at the rate of 3.9375% from January 1, 2017 to June 30, 2022 (it is at the rate of 4.1875% from July 1, 2014 to December 31, 2016). Reg. 1525.4 provides an exemption certificate form. (Reg. 1525.4, 18 CCR)

The exemption is not allowed unless the purchaser furnishes the retailer with an exemption certificate and the retailer retains the exemption certificate in its records and furnishes it to the BOE upon request. The exemption is repealed effective January 1, 2023. (Sec. 6377.1, Rev. & Tax. Code)

"Qualified person," for purposes of the exemption, is defined as a person that is primarily engaged in those lines of business described in Codes 3111 to 3399, inclusive, 541711, or 541712 of the NAICS, 2012 edition. Examples of types of manufacturing companies represented by the applicable NAICS codes include R&D in biotechnology, physical engineering, and life sciences. (Sec. 6377.1, Rev. & Tax. Code)

The BOE advises construction contractors that they may be able to purchase and/or sell materials and fixtures at a partial sales and use tax rate (3.3125%, plus applicable district taxes) for certain jobs when contracted by qualified companies engaged in manufacturing or Research and Development (R&D). Legislation made effective July 1, 2014, allows certain companies engaged in manufacturing or R&D to make annual purchases up to $200 million of qualifying property at a reduced sales and use tax rate. The partial exemption also applies to qualifying property purchased for use in constructing or reconstructing a special purpose building. The BOE advises that the law is unusual because qualified companies can authorize the construction contractor to make purchases of materials and fixtures for the special purpose building at a reduced tax rate and pass the tax savings back to the qualified manufacturing or R&D company. (*Special Notice L-430*, California State Board of Equalization, January 2016)

The special purpose building must be used exclusively for manufacturing, processing, refining, fabricating, or recycling, or as a research or storage facility for these activities in order to qualify for the partial exemption. Buildings such as warehouses used solely to store a product after it has completed the manufacturing process are ineligible for the partial exemption. (*Special Notice L-430*, California State Board of Equalization, January 2016)

Contractors are required to get a partial exemption certificate from qualified persons. Construction contractors need to retain records that support their purchases of materials and fixtures at the reduced sales and use tax rate. There are two separate exemption certificates that construction contractors may need:

— BOE-230-M, Partial Exemption Certificate for Manufacturing, Research & Development Equipment; and

— BOE-230-MC, Construction Contracts – Partial Exemption Certificate for Manufacturing, Research & Development Equipment.

(*Special Notice L-430*, California State Board of Equalization, January 2016)

To make qualifying purchases using the partial exemption, construction contractors must first get a signed exemption certificate BOE-230-M from the manufacturing or R&D company that certifies they are a qualified person, and that the special purpose building qualifies for the partial exemption. General contractors who hire subcontractors to furnish materials, fixtures, machinery, or equipment for a qualifying job, must provide the subcontractors with a copy of the BOE-230-M partial exemption certificate received from the qualified person, and issue the subcontractor a BOE-230-MC. (*Special Notice L-430*, California State Board of Equalization, January 2016)

Once a construction contractor has obtained the BOE-230-M from the qualified person, or once a subcontractor has obtained a BOE-230-M and BOE-230-MC from the general contractor, the contractor may then issue a separate BOE-230-MC partial exemption certificate to the contractor's supplier to make qualifying purchases at the reduced sales and use tax rate. (*Special Notice L-430*, California State Board of Equalization, January 2016)

Practitioner Comment: New Partial Sales and Use Tax Exemption for Manufacturing and R&D Equipment

Effective July 1, 2014, California enacted a partial sales and use tax exemption of 4.1875% (approximately half of California's sales and use tax rate) to replace the existing EZ sales and use tax credit (which was claimed against the California corporate franchise tax) for purchases of manufacturing and research and development equipment made between July 1, 2014 and June 30, 2022 by manufacturers and certain biotechnology, physical, engineering, and life sciences companies conducting research and development. This partial sales tax exemption applies to purchases of up to $200 million in a calendar year of qualified property by a qualified person.

"Qualified person" includes persons primarily engaged (50% plus) in those lines of business described in NAICS codes 3111-3399, and is inclusive of 541711 and 541712. A qualified person may qualify as a legal entity or an establishment within a legal entity, such as a cost center. In addition, qualified property purchased by construction contractors may qualify if the property is purchased for use in the performance of a construction contract and the qualified person will use the resulting improvement to real property as an integral part of manufacturing, processing, refining, fabricating, or recycling processes or as a research or storage facility for use in connection with those processes. Certain taxpayers, including financial institutions, agricultural and extractive taxpayers, are prohibited from claiming the partial exemption.

Qualified property includes but is not limited to machinery and equipment, including component parts; equipment used to operate, control, regulate, or maintain such equipment (including computers and software); pollution control equipment; and special purpose buildings and foundations used as an integral part of the manufacturing process. The property must be used at least 50% of the time between the point when any raw materials are received and introduced into the process and ending when the process has altered the tangible personal property to its completed form. Qualified property does not include consumables with a useful life of less than one year; furniture or inventory; or property used for administration, management, or marketing.

Taxpayers should carefully track purchases made by entities in the California combined report to ensure the partial exemption is not claimed on purchases in excess of $200M. Furthermore, the partial exemption does not apply if the qualifying purchase is removed from the state or used in an unqualified manner within one year of purchase.

A.B. 93 and S.B. 90 require that property must be purchased and placed into service by December 31, 2013, to qualify for the prior EZ sales and use tax credit. This excludes property purchased prior to the deadline, but placed into service subsequent to 2013 from the credit, while at the same time such property would not have been eligible for the new sales tax exemption as it was purchased before July 1, 2014. This problem was solved by S.B. 100, which clarified that the partial exemption would be available for qualified equipment purchased before January 1, 2014 and placed into service before January 1, 2015.

Chris Whitney, Contributing Editor

● *Marijuana*

On November 8, 2016, California voters approved Proposition 64, The Control, Regulate, and Tax Adult Use of Marijuana Act. According to the BOE, effective November 9, 2016, retail sales of the following types of medical cannabis are exempt from sales and use tax:

— medical cannabis;

— medical cannabis concentrate;

— edible medical cannabis products; and

— topical cannabis (as defined in Sec. 19300.5 of the Business and Professions Code).

(*Special Notice L-481*, California State Board of Equalization, October 2016; *Tax Guide for Medical Marijuana Businesses*, California State Board of Equalization, November 2016)

To obtain the exemption, qualified patients or their primary caregiver must provide their valid Medical Marijuana Identification Card issued by the California Department of Public Health (pursuant to Sec. 11362.71 of the Health and Safety Code) and a valid government issued identification card at the time of purchase. In order to properly claim the sales and use tax exemption, a medical marijuana business should not collect sales tax reimbursement on the qualifying exempt sales of medical marijuana, and should claim a deduction on its sales and use tax return for the qualifying exempt medical marijuana sales. (*Tax Guide for Medical Marijuana Businesses*, California State Board of Equalization, November 2016)

Medical marijuana retailers can claim the exemption on their sales and use tax return. Retailers should retain supporting documentation to substantiate exempt transactions, including:

— the purchaser's nine-digit ID number and expiration date, as shown on the qualified patient's or primary caregiver's unexpired Medical Marijuana Identification Card; and

— the related sales invoice or other original record of sale.

(*Special Notice L-481*, California State Board of Equalization, October 2016; *Tax Guide for Medical Marijuana Businesses*, California State Board of Equalization, November 2016)

Retailers can verify the validity of the nine-digit ID number on the website of the California Department of Public Health at http://www.calmmp.ca.gov/MMIC_Search.aspx. (*Tax Guide for Medical Marijuana Businesses*, California State Board of Equalization, November 2016)

• *Motion picture production credits*

Motion picture production credits are discussed.

Motion picture production credit: A motion picture production credit (the credit is also referred to as the "film and television credit") is available against personal income tax, corporation franchise and income taxes, and state sales and use taxes, as specified. The credit may be claimed by qualified taxpayers for a percentage of qualified expenditures paid or incurred by the taxpayer in this state in the production of qualified motion picture. The credit is claimed for all qualified expenditures incurred in all taxable years for the qualified motion picture, but may be claimed only in the taxable year that the California Film Commission (CFC) issues a credit certificate. The California State Board of Equalization (BOE) administers the sales and use tax provisions of the credit in conjunction with the CFC and the California Franchise Tax Board (FTB). (Sec. 6902.5, Rev. & Tax. Code; Sec. 17053.85, Rev. & Tax. Code; Sec. 23685, Rev. & Tax. Code)

Qualified taxpayers, or affiliates to whom the qualified taxpayers assigned credit amounts, may either claim a refund of qualified sales and use tax paid, or a credit against qualified sales or use taxes imposed on the qualified taxpayer or affiliate that is equal to the credit amount that would otherwise be allowed under these credit provisions. "Qualified sales and use taxes" are defined as any state sales and use taxes imposed by Part 1 (commencing with Section 6001) of the Sales and Use Tax Law, but excludes taxes imposed by Section 6051.2 and 6201.2 (Local Revenue Fund), 6051.5 and 6201.5 (Fiscal Recovery Fund), Part 1.5 (Bradley-Burns Uniform Local

Sales and Use Tax Law), Part 1.6 (Transactions and Use Tax Law), or Section 35 of Article XIII of the California Constitution (Local Public Safety Fund). (Sec. 6902.5, Rev. & Tax. Code)

Taxpayers may make an irrevocable election to claim a sales and use tax credit in lieu of the personal income or corporation franchise and income tax credit. The taxpayer has the option of claiming a refundable sales and use tax credit or offsetting any excess credit against sales and use taxes due for the subsequent five reporting periods. A qualified taxpayer may make an irrevocable election to apply all or a portion of its certified credits against qualified sales and use taxes imposed on the qualified taxpayer. Irrevocable elections to apply unused certified credits against qualified sales and use taxes must be made in the form prescribed by the BOE and include a copy of the credit certificate certifying the credits being claimed. (Sec. 6902.5, Rev. & Tax. Code)

The credit is equal to 20% (25% if the qualified motion picture is a television series that relocated to California or an independent film) of the qualified expenditures attributable to the production of a qualified motion picture in California. (Sec. 6902.5, Rev. & Tax. Code; Sec. 17053.85, Rev. & Tax. Code; Sec. 23685, Rev. & Tax. Code; Reg. 5504, 10 CCR)

Qualified motion picture production credit: For taxable years beginning on or after January 1, 2016, a new California corporation franchise and income and personal income tax credit is available to qualified taxpayers for qualified motion picture production expenditures paid or incurred. The credit is provided in addition to the already existing (original) motion picture production credit (discussed above under "Motion picture production credit"). However, the new credit will not be allowed for any qualified expenditures for which the original motion picture production credit has been claimed. A qualified taxpayer may, in lieu of claiming the new credit or the original motion picture production credit, make an irrevocable election to apply the credit amount against the qualified sales and use taxes imposed on the taxpayer. (Sec. 6902.5, Rev. & Tax. Code; Sec. 17053.95, Rev. & Tax. Code; Sec. 23695, Rev. & Tax. Code)

For purposes of the new credit, a "qualified motion picture" is a motion picture that is produced for distribution to the general public, regardless of medium, that is one of the following:

— a feature with a minimum production budget of $1 million;

— a movie of the week or miniseries with a minimum production budget of $500,000;

— a new television series of episodes longer than 40 minutes each of running time, exclusive of commercials, that is produced in California, with a minimum production budget of $1 million per episode;

— an independent film;

— a television series that relocated to California; or

— a pilot for a new television series that is longer than 40 minutes of running time, exclusive of commercials, that is produced in California, with a minimum production budget of $1 million.

(Sec. 6902.5, Rev. & Tax. Code; Sec. 17053.95, Rev. & Tax. Code; Sec. 23695, Rev. & Tax. Code)

In addition, to qualify as a "qualified motion picture," all of the following conditions must be satisfied:

— at least 75% of the principal photography days must occur wholly in California or 75% of the production budget must be incurred for payment for services performed within the state and the purchase or rental of property used within the state;

¶1509

— production of the motion picture must be completed within 30 months from the date on which the taxpayer's application is approved by the California Film Commission;

— the copyright for the motion picture must be registered with the U.S. Copyright Office; and

— principal photography for the motion picture must commence after the date on which the application is approved by the commission, but not later than 180 days after the date of that approval, unless death, disability, or disfigurement of the director or a principal cast member, an act of God, terrorist activities, or government sanction has directly prevented the principal photography from commencing within the prescribed 180-day period.

(Sec. 6902.5, Rev. & Tax. Code; Sec. 17053.95, Rev. & Tax. Code; Sec. 23695, Rev. & Tax. Code)

• *Newspapers and periodicals*

An exemption applies to newspapers and periodicals issued at regular intervals that are

— distributed free of charge,

— distributed by nonprofit organizations to their members,

— published or purchased by organizations qualifying for tax-exempt status under IRC Sec. 501(c)(3), or

— sold by subscription and delivered by mail.

(Sec. 6362.7, Rev. & Tax. Code; Sec. 6362.8, Rev. & Tax. Code) In each instance, the exemption covers the sale, storage, use, or consumption of the newspaper or periodical, as well as the sale, storage, use, or consumption of tangible personal property that becomes an ingredient or component of the newspaper or periodical.

A nonprofit organization's membership publication qualifies for exemption only if it is distributed to members at least partly in return for membership fees and the costs of printing it are less than 10% of membership fees for the distribution period. An IRC Sec. 501(c)(3) organization's publication qualifies for exemption only if it either (1) accepts no commercial advertising or (2) is distributed to contributors or to members in return for payment of membership fees. (Sec. 6362.8, Rev. & Tax. Code)

All other newspapers and periodicals are subject to sales and use tax. For purposes of the tax on newspapers, a newspaper's publisher or distributor, rather than the newspaper carrier, is considered the retailer of the newspaper. Accordingly, the publisher or distributor is responsible for payment of the tax, which is measured by the price charged to the customer by the newspaper carrier. (Sec. 6015, Rev. & Tax. Code)

• *Occasional sales*

So-called occasional sales are exempt; however, this does not apply to boats or airplanes, or to automobiles required to be registered under the Motor Vehicle Code. (Sec. 6006.5, Rev. & Tax. Code) This exemption is strictly applied in practice. It may or may not apply to the sale of a going business (¶1510).

A regulation (Reg. 1595(a), 18 CCR) provides that a service enterprise's first two sales during any 12-month period of substantial amounts of tangible personal property used in the enterprise are exempt from tax as occasional sales. For subsequent sales in substantial amounts during the 12-month period, the enterprise operator is required to hold a sales and use tax permit; gross receipts from these sales are subject to tax, unless otherwise exempt.

• *Printed sales message*

An exemption exists for the gross receipts from the sale of, and the storage, use, or other consumption in California of catalogs, letters, circulars, brochures, and pamphlets that consist substantially of printed sales messages for goods and services and are printed to the special order of the purchaser and mailed or delivered by the seller, the seller's agent, or a mailing house, acting as an agent for the purchaser, through the U.S. Postal Service or by common carrier to any other person at no cost to that person who becomes the owner of such printed sales messages. (Sec. 6379.5, Rev. & Tax. Code)

Practitioner Comment: Court of Appeal Finds Sales Tax Inapplicable to Non-Separately Stated Services in Mixed Transactions

On September 4, 2009, the California Court of Appeal in *People PC, Inc. v. State Board of Equalization*, Cal. Ct. App., No. D054163 (unpublished) ruled that CDs which were mailed at no cost to prospective customers qualified for the printed sales message exemption because the purpose of the CDs was to promote the company's products and the recipients could not use the CDs to access the internet services offered without first signing up for the service. In reaching its decision, the Court explained that the printed sales message exemption is not limited to messages printed on paper.

Chris Whitney, Contributing Editor

¶1510 Sale of a Business

Law: Secs. 6006.5, 6281, 6292, 6367 (CCH California Tax Reports, ¶60-590).

California exempts an occasional or isolated sale of property that is not held or used in the course of an activity requiring a seller's permit, unless the sale is one of a series of sales sufficient in number, scope, and character to require a seller's permit. Three or more sales for substantial amounts within a period of 12 months, regardless of whether sales take place in California, requires the seller to hold a seller's permit. Likewise, a substantial number of sales in relatively small amounts requires the seller to hold a permit. (Sec. 6006.5(a), Rev. & Tax. Code; Reg. 1595, 18 CCR)

However, certain sales are not considered when determining whether the number of sales within a 12-month period:

— sales by an auctioneer on behalf of the seller;

— sales through claiming races of horses owned by the seller;

— tax exempt sales of vehicles, mobilehomes, commercial coaches, vessels, or aircraft; and

— trade-ins that are incidental to a nonselling activity.

(Reg. 1595, 18 CCR)

When a person sells a business that is required to hold a seller's permit, tax applies to the gross receipts from the retail sale of tangible personal property held or used by that business in the course of its activities requiring the holding of the seller's permit. The gross receipts subject to tax includes all consideration received by the transferor, including cash, notes, and any other property, as well as any indebtedness assumed by the transferee. (Reg. 1595, 18 CCR)

The sale of an entire business and other sales of machinery, equipment, etc., used in a business is usually subject to sales tax. The "occasional sales" exemption ordinarily does not apply to such transactions. The tax may even apply to cases where the principal activity of the business does not involve the sale of tangible personal property and where the seller does not hold a sales tax permit. (Reg. 1595, 18 CCR)

The tax would not ordinarily apply to merchandise inventory included in the sale of a business, because the inventory is sold for resale. Neither does the tax apply to any property that is attached to a building in such a way that it is classified as "real property" rather than "personal property." The tax may apply to machinery, equipment, etc., in some cases. (Reg. 1595, 18 CCR)

• *Exemption where no real change of ownership*

Tax does not apply to the sale of a business where the "real or ultimate ownership" of the business is substantially the same after the sale as it was before. Unusual problems may arise in "reorganization" transactions that are tax-free under the income tax laws. The State Board of Equalization (BOE) has ruled that statutory mergers (qualifying under IRC Sec. 368(a)(1)(A)) are not subject to sales tax, whereas the same transaction accomplished in an "assets for stock" exchange (under IRC Sec. 368(a)(1)(C)) would be taxable, at least as to those assets deemed to be "tangible personal property sold at retail."

In *Simplicity Pattern Co. v. State Board of Equalization* (1980) (CCH CALIFORNIA TAX REPORTS, ¶60-020.60, ¶60-590.33), the taxpayer sold its subsidiary's business to another company in exchange for common stock. The California Supreme Court held that the transaction was not exempt from sales tax, even though it presumably would have been exempt if cast in the form of a statutory merger.

An example where the "real or ultimate ownership" test applies to exempt the transaction from sales tax is the incorporation of an existing business by the transfer of assets from a predecessor partnership or proprietorship to the new corporation in exchange for its stock. In *Pacific Pipeline Construction Co. v. State Board of Equalization* (1958) (CCH CALIFORNIA TAX REPORTS, ¶60-590.24), the California Supreme Court held that a transfer of certain machinery and equipment in a corporate reorganization was not exempt under the "occasional sale" rule, even though the seller was not engaged in an activity normally requiring the holding of a seller's permit.

• *Other cases involving sale of business*

In *Beatrice Company v. State Board of Equalization* (1993) (CCH CALIFORNIA TAX REPORTS, ¶60-590.211), the California Supreme Court held that a parent corporation's transfer of all of the assets of one of its divisions to a commencing subsidiary corporation in exchange for stock in the subsidiary and an assumption by the subsidiary of the division's liabilities was a taxable retail sale.

In *Ontario Community Foundation, Inc. v. California State Board of Equalization* (1984) (CCH CALIFORNIA TAX REPORTS, ¶60-590.34), the California Supreme Court held that the sale of hospital equipment as part of the sale of an entire hospital was exempt as an "occasional sale," since the equipment sold had not been used in operations subject to sales tax.

In *Davis Wire Corporation v. State Board of Equalization* (1976) (CCH CALIFORNIA TAX REPORTS, ¶60-020.39, ¶60-590.28), the California Supreme Court cited the *U.S. Industries* case, among others, and held that the sale of the entire business of certain manufacturing businesses was subject to sales tax. The sellers had made no retail sales in the ordinary course of their business. The Court distinguished the *Glass-Tite* case, cited below, on the ground that in *Glass-Tite* the seller's products were component parts of a type that could not have been sold at retail, whereas in *Davis Wire* the seller's products were finished products suitable for sale at retail. To the same effect, see the decision of the District Court of Appeal in *Santa Fe Energy Co. v. The Board of Equalization of California* (1984) (CCH CALIFORNIA TAX REPORTS, ¶60-590.30).

In *Hotel Del Coronado Corporation v. State Board of Equalization* (1971) (CCH CALIFORNIA TAX REPORTS, ¶60-590.20), a California District Court of Appeal held that the sale of hotel equipment, as part of a sale of the entire property, was subject to the sales tax.

In *Glass-Tite Industries, Inc. v. State Board of Equalization* (1968) (CCH CALIFORNIA TAX REPORTS, ¶60-590.26), the seller was a manufacturer of electronic components. The District Court of Appeal held that the sale of the business was exempt from sales tax as an "occasional sale," because it was an isolated transaction and the taxpayer was not really required to have a seller's permit even though it actually had one.

¶1510

In *U.S. Industries, Inc., et al. v. State Board of Equalization* (1962) (CCH California Tax Reports, ¶ 60-590.25), a California District Court of Appeal held that the sales tax was applicable to the sale of all the tangible assets used in operating a business, in conjunction with the sale of the business. Consideration for the sale included stock and debentures, as well as cash.

• *Liability of purchaser and seller*

The purchaser of a business is personally liable for any sales or use tax liability of the seller, unless the purchaser withholds enough of the purchase price to cover the liability or obtains from the seller evidence from the BOE to the effect that any liability has been paid or that no amount is due. (Sec. 6811, Rev. & Tax. Code; Sec. 6812, Rev. & Tax. Code)

For a discussion of this provision, see *Knudsen Dairy Products Co. v. State Board of Equalization* (1970) (CCH California Tax Reports, ¶ 61-470.88), in which the provision was held applicable to the acquisition of a business in return for cancellation of indebtedness.

The seller of a business who fails to surrender a sales tax permit to the BOE upon transfer of the business is liable for any sales tax liability incurred by the purchaser if the seller has knowledge that the purchaser is using the permit. The seller's liability is generally limited to the quarter in which the business is transferred, plus the three subsequent quarters. (Sec. 6811, Rev. & Tax. Code; Sec. 6812, Rev. & Tax. Code)

¶1511 Permits, Returns, Payment, and Records

Law: Secs. 6066-74, 6451-80.23, 6591, 7053-54; Regs. 1698, 1699, 1707, 18 CCR (CCH California Tax Reports, ¶ 61-210—61-260, 61-805—61-810).

Anyone in the business of selling tangible personal property of the type subject to tax, other than certain sellers of animal feed, must obtain a sales tax permit. (Sec. 6066, Rev. & Tax. Code) Permits are also required for locations at which merchandise is stored when the retailer negotiates sales out of state but fulfills such sales from stocks of goods located within the state. (Reg. 1699, 18 CCR)

Business owners who hold a seller's permit for a permanent place of business and who also make sales at temporary locations (such as swap meets, flea markets, trade or specialty shows, fairs, festivals, and similar limited-term events) to register and hold a sub-permit for each selling location for sales and use tax purposes. Taxpayers must report the sales made at these locations when they file their sales and use tax returns. (*Special Notice L-306*, California State Board of Equalization, April 2012)

• *Alternative method of reporting use tax program*

Under the Alternative Method of Reporting Use Tax (AMRUT) program, taxpayers may report California use tax using a formula based on the percentage of their sales for which the use tax typically applies, rather than on a transaction-by-transaction basis. However, BOE approval of the type of purchase and percentage allowed is required prior to the use of the percentage formula. In addition, an Audit Sampling Plan (Form BOE-472) must be completed prior to using the percentage reporting method. To participate in this program, a taxpayer must submit a written application, have an account that is in good standing, and maintain acceptable accounting records and internal controls. (*Alternative Method of Reporting Use Tax (AMRUT) Program Guidelines*, California State Board of Equalization, November 5, 2002, ¶ 403-355)

• *Buying Companies Ineligible for Permits*

A buying company formed for the sole purpose of purchasing tangible personal property ex-tax for resale to the entity that owns or controls it, or to which it is otherwise related, in order to re-direct local sales tax from the location(s) of the vendor(s) to the location of the buying company will not be issued a seller's permit separate from the company controlling it. A company will not be treated as formed for the sole purpose of redirecting local sales tax if it adds a markup to its cost of goods sold in an amount sufficient to cover its operating and overhead expenses or issues an invoice or otherwise accounts for the transaction. However, the absence of any of these elements is not indicative of a sole purpose to redirect local sales tax. (Reg. 1699, 18 CCR)

Where a buying company is recognized as an entity separate from its relative(s), the requirements for issuing a seller's permit to that buying company are identical to those for issuing a seller's permit to any other type of entity, including the requirement that the permit be issued for a place of business where the entity engages in business as a seller of tangible personal property. A location for any business, including a buying company, is eligible for a seller's permit only if that location is a place where orders are taken, contracts are customarily negotiated, or where a stock of merchandise is stored, as specified. (*In the Matter of the Petitions for Reallocation of Local Tax Under the Uniform Local Sales and Use Tax Law of Cities of Agoura Hills*, California State Board of Equalization, November 14, 2012, ¶405-739)

• *Direct payment permits*

A qualified big business may obtain a sales tax direct payment permit that allows the business to give a seller an exemption certificate when making a purchase, thereby shifting the duty to pay sales tax from the seller to the business holding the permit. A business may obtain a sales tax direct payment permit only if it had gross receipts from sales of tangible personal property of at least $75 million and purchases of taxable tangible personal property of at least $75 million in each calendar quarter during the 12 months preceding the application. Use tax direct payment permits, which allow taxpayers to self-assess and pay state and local use tax directly to the State Board of Equalization (BOE), may be issued to (1) businesses that purchase or lease tangible personal property valuing $500,000 or more in the aggregate during the calendar year immediately preceding the application for the permit and (2) county and/or city governments and redevelopment agencies. (Sec. 7051.1, Rev. & Tax. Code; Reg. 1669.5, 18 CCR)

• *E-filing*

The BOE's online filing program allows eligible sales and use taxpayers to file returns and/or prepayments and pay amounts due over the Internet. Two payment options are available:

— ACH debit method, which allows a taxpayer to make an EFT payment when filing the return or prepayment online; or

— ACH credit method, which allows a taxpayer to file and initiate a separate payment through the taxpayer's financial institution.

(*Publication 159EFT*, California State Board of Equalization, October 2015)

• *Electronic funds transfer payment requirement*

Anyone whose estimated sales and use tax liability averages $10,000 or more per month must remit amounts due by electronic funds transfer (EFT). A business successor must continue to make payments by EFT if its predecessor was a mandatory participant. Taxpayers not required to participate in the program may, with the BOE's approval, voluntarily remit payments electronically. Taxpayers whose monthly liability falls below the $10,000 threshold must continue to make EFT payments until they receive written BOE approval to discontinue EFT payments. The EFT payment requirement is inapplicable to taxpayers who collect use taxes voluntarily. (Sec. 6479.3, Rev. & Tax. Code)

The BOE advises that as of July 1, 2016, for all taxes required to be paid by electronic fund transfer (EFT), the bank that processes EFT payments will change from Citibank to Union Bank. Taxpayers who make Automated Clearing House (ACH) debit payments through the EFT payment processor should review the BOE's new bank and payment processor http://www.boe.ca.gov/elecsrv/new_eft_pay.htm

for instructions. Taxpayer who pay by ACH credit must notify their financial institution of the new bank information to ensure the correct bank is credited. ACH credit transactions with a settlement date on or after July 1, 2016, using incorrect banking information will be returned and may be subject to penalty and interest charges. Also, any payments to Union Bank prior to July 1, 2016, will be returned and may be subject to penalty and interest charges. For taxpayers who use the BOE's online payment system to make their payments, no change is required. (*News Release 57-16-G*, California State Board of Equalization, June 30, 2016)

- *Form for return*

The sales tax return and the use tax return are combined in one form. A return showing information relating only to one tax is deemed to be a return also for the tax for which no information is shown. (*People v. Universal Film Exchanges, Inc.* 34 CalApp2d 649 (1950) (CCH CALIFORNIA TAX REPORTS, ¶ 61-520.37))

- *Installment payments*

A taxpayer may enter into a written installment payment agreement with the BOE for the payment of any taxes, penalties, and interest. The BOE may terminate the agreement if the taxpayer fails to comply with the terms of the agreement. (Sec. 6832, Rev. & Tax. Code)

- *Mobile food vendors*

The BOE provides guidance to mobile food vendors who may be unaware of their registration, reporting, and recordkeeping requirements under the state and local sales and use tax laws. "Mobile food vendors" include those who operate food trucks, stands, or carts that do not have a fixed physical location. Such vendors are required to register with the BOE, file sales and use tax returns, and maintain books and records that are adequate for sales and use tax purposes. (*Special Notices L-348 and L-348A*, California State Board of Equalization, June 2013)

Those required to hold a seller's permit must keep books and records that are necessary to accurately determine tax liability. Such books and records include sales receipts or register tapes, books of account, and bills, invoices, and other documents that support business transactions. In addition, such taxpayers should keep the schedules and working papers used to prepare tax returns. Mobile food vendors whose menu item prices include sales tax are required to post a notice for customers that states: "All prices of taxable items include sales tax." Such vendors should report sales tax at the rate in effect at the location at which the sales are made. (*Special Notices L-348 and L-348A*, California State Board of Equalization, June 2013)

Effective July 1, 2014, and applicable to sales made on and after that date, unless a separate amount for tax reimbursement is added to the price, mobile food vendors' sales of taxable items are presumed to be made on a tax included basis. However, the presumption is inapplicable when a mobile food vendor is making sales as a caterer, as defined. (Reg. 1603, 18 CCR)

- *Other provisions*

A credit against California use tax is allowed for sales or use tax paid to another state on property purchased in another state prior to its use in California. (Sec. 6901, Rev. & Tax. Code)

Where retailers collect sales and use taxes from customers in excess of amounts legally due, such excess amounts must be returned to the customers; otherwise, the excess collections become obligations due to the state and the customers may then recover such amounts directly from the state. (Sec. 6901.5, Rev. & Tax. Code; Reg. 1700, 18 CCR)

Retailers who engage in business without a permit or after a permit has been revoked are guilty of a misdemeanor. (Sec. 6071, Rev. & Tax. Code)

• *Payment by credit card*

The BOE offers several methods to pay your sales and use taxes, excise taxes, environmental fees, fuel taxes, accounts receivable and audit payments. One method is by charging sales and use tax payments using a credit card issued by American Express, Discover Network, MasterCard, or Visa. The credit card vendor will charge a convenience fee of 2.3% of the transaction amount (which is retained by the vendor and is not revenue to the BOE). The minimum fee is $1.00. (*Credit Card Payment Program For Tax & Fee Payments*, California State Board of Equalization, November 2015)

• *Penalty for failure to pay*

A penalty is imposed if prepayments are not made when required. The penalty is 6% of the prepayment if the prepayment is actually made after its due date (but no later than the due date of the quarterly return). The penalty is 6% of the amount of the actual tax liability for each month for which a prepayment should have been made if the prepayment is not made, but the quarterly return and payment are timely. The penalty is 10% if the failure to prepay is due to negligence or intentional disregard of the rules. The penalty for failure to prepay on time may be waived if a showing of reasonable cause is made. (Sec. 6477, Rev. & Tax. Code; Sec. 6479.3, Rev. & Tax. Code; Sec. 6478, Rev. & Tax. Code; Reg. 1703(c)(5), 18 CCR)

Interest is imposed on any person who is granted relief from the penalties for late prepayments. The interest rate is the same as that charged on sales and use tax deficiencies (¶1512). The BOE may relieve a person from such interest if the person's failure to make timely prepayments was due to a disaster rather than negligence or willful neglect. (Sec. 6591.5, Rev. & Tax. Code; Sec. 6592.5, Rev. & Tax. Code; Sec. 6593, Rev. & Tax. Code; Sec. 6593.5, Rev. & Tax. Code)

• *Prepayments of tax*

Generally, returns must be filed and the tax paid quarterly. However, if the BOE determines that the taxpayer's taxable transactions average $17,000 or more per month, quarterly prepayments of tax must be made. (Sec. 6471, Rev. & Tax. Code; Sec. 6472, Rev. & Tax. Code)

Alternative I prepayment schedule: In the first, third, and fourth calendar quarters, the taxpayer must prepay no less than 90% of the state and local tax liability for each of the first two months of each quarter. In the second calendar quarter, the taxpayer must make a first prepayment of 90% of the state and local tax liability for the first month of the quarter and a second prepayment of either (1) 90% of the state and local tax liability for the second month of the quarter plus 90% of the state and local tax liability for the first 15 days of the third month of the quarter, or (2) 135% of the state and local tax liability for the second month of the quarter. (Sec. 6471, Rev. & Tax. Code)

Alternative II prepayment schedule: Persons in business during the corresponding quarter of the previous year or who are successors to a business in operation during that corresponding quarter may satisfy the prepayment requirements for the first, third, and fourth quarters by paying an amount equal to one-third of the taxable receipts reported on the return filed for the previous year's corresponding quarter multiplied by the current tax rate in effect during the month for which the prepayment is made. The prepayment requirements for the second calendar quarter may be satisfied by a first prepayment equal to one-third of the taxable receipts reported and a second prepayment equal to one-half of the taxable receipts reported on the return filed for the previous year's corresponding quarter multiplied by the current tax rate. (Sec. 6472, Rev. & Tax. Code)

In the first, third, and fourth quarters, prepayments and reports are due by the 24th day following the end of the first two months of the quarter. In the second quarter, the first prepayment and report are due by the 24th day of the second month of the quarter; the second prepayment is due by the 24th day of the third month.

¶1511

• *Prepayment of tax on motor vehicle fuel*

Distributors and brokers of motor vehicle fuel, after being notified by the BOE, must collect prepayment of the retail sales tax from anyone to whom they distribute or transfer any fuel subject to the motor vehicle fuel license tax, except aviation gasoline and fuel sold to bonded distributors. (Sec. 6480.1, Rev. & Tax. Code)

Effective July 1, 2016, through June 30, 2017, the California sales tax prepayment rates (per gallon) for fuels are as follows:

— 5¢ for motor vehicle fuel (gasoline);

— 7¢ for aircraft jet fuel; and

— 17¢ for diesel fuel.

(*Sales Tax Prepayment Rates for Fuels*, California State Board of Equalization, May 2016)

The BOE is required to establish the sales tax prepayment rates on fuels by March 1 of each year. Although new prepayment rates usually take effect July 1, the price of fuels decreased significantly, resulting in prepayments that exceed the fuel retailer's sales tax liability. As a result, the BOE adjusted the prepayment rates to be effective April 1, 2015. The BOE may adjust the rates again if the price of these fuels increases or decreases. (*Special Notice L-410*, California State Board of Equalization, March 2015)

Beginning July 1, 2013, the annual adjustment of the rates is made on July 1 for the California prepaid sales taxes on motor vehicle fuel, jet aircraft fuel, and diesel fuel. Consequently, the rate of prepayment is in effect from July 1 of the year to June 30 of the following year. Prior to July 1, 2013, the annually adjusted rate for prepaid sales tax was effective April 1. For 2013, the rate of prepayment in effect on January 1 remained in effect until June 30. (Sec. 6480.1, Rev. & Tax. Code)

Returns and payments must be filed and paid on or before the 25th day of the calendar month following the prepayment. An exemption applies to motor vehicle fuel sold to qualified purchasers who resell the same fuel to the state or its instrumentalities if certain delivery and possession requirements are satisfied. (Sec. 6480.1, Rev. & Tax. Code)

The BOE is also authorized to collect retail sales tax prepayments from fuel producers, importers, and jobbers. (Sec. 6480.1, Rev. & Tax. Code)

• *Qualified itinerant vendors*

Registration and reporting requirements apply to certain United States veterans who sell goods from temporary locations. Certain itinerant veteran vendors are regarded as consumers rather than retailers of tangible personal property owned and sold by the qualified itinerant vendors, except for alcoholic beverages or items sold for more than $100. The treatment of itinerant veteran vendors as consumers has a sunset date of January 1, 2022. A "qualified itinerant vendor" is a person who:

— was a member of the armed forces of the United States who received an honorable discharge or a release from active duty under honorable conditions from service;

— is unable to obtain a livelihood by manual labor due to service-connected disability;

— is a sole proprietor with no employees for the purposes of selling tangible personal property; and

— has no permanent place of business in California.

(Sec. 6018.3, Rev. & Tax. Code)

These provisions are inapplicable to the sale of alcoholic beverages and single items sold for more than $100. Therefore, qualifying veterans continue to be regarded as retailers, rather than consumers, with respect to their sales of alcoholic beverages and single items for more than $100. Moreover, these provisions do not apply to a

¶1511

person who operates a vending machine or to a person engaged in the business of serving meals, food, or drinks to a customer at a location owned, rented, or supplied by the customer. (*Special Notice L-251*, California State Board of Equalization, March 2010)

In addition, there are differences between retailers and consumers, according to the BOE. In general, a retailer is required to hold a seller's permit and report tax based on the taxable sales of products to the retailer's customers. When certain persons are considered the consumers of tangible personal property sold by retailers, sales to those consumers are retail sales for which either the sales or use tax applies. Resale certificates may not be issued by such consumers when making purchases. Since businesses generally owe tax on sales made to consumers, a qualified itinerant vendor should expect to pay an amount as "tax" when purchasing merchandise from their suppliers. As a consumer, a qualified itinerant vendor is not required to hold a seller's permit. (*Special Notice L-251*, California State Board of Equalization, March 2010)

• *Qualified use taxes*

Taxpayers who are not required to hold a seller's permit or to be registered with the State Board of Equalization may make an irrevocable election to report their qualified use tax obligations from purchases of tangible personal property on their California personal income tax, corporation franchise or income tax, partnership, limited liability company, or estate or trust tax or information returns. These provisions are inapplicable to purchases of mobile homes, vehicles, aircraft, and vessels, leases of tangible personal property, and certain purchases of cigarettes, tobacco, and tobacco products. Qualified use tax will be considered timely reported and remitted if it is included with a timely filed return. (Sec. 6452.1, Rev. & Tax. Code)

For taxable years beginning on or after January 1, 2011, an eligible person is authorized for one or more single non-business purchases of individual items of tangible personal property, each with a sales price of less than $1,000, to either report the estimated amount of use tax due based on the person's California adjusted gross income as reflected in the use tax table shown in the instructions of the acceptable tax return or the actual amount of use tax that was not paid to a registered retailer. (Sec. 6452.1, Rev. & Tax. Code)

• *Records*

All pertinent records must be retained for at least four years (10 years in the case of taxpayers participating in the amnesty program discussed at ¶1512) unless the BOE gives written authorization for their destruction. The required records include the normal books of account together with all bills, receipts, invoices, cash register tapes, or other documents of original entry that support the entries in the books of account, as well as all schedules and working papers used in preparing tax returns. Resale and exemption certificates should also be retained to document claimed nontaxable sales. The records must be made available to the BOE or its authorized representative on request. (Sec. 7053, Rev. & Tax. Code; Reg. 1698, 18 CCR)

Practitioner Comment: *Board of Equalization updates records requirements for digital point of sale systems*

The California Board of Equalization updated Regulation 1698 regarding the retention of records to provide higher specificity when referring to electronic records. In addition to updating the language, the regulation now provides an example stating that if a taxpayer has a point of sale system that overwrites data after a period of less than four years, the taxpayer is required to transfer that information to another form of media to preserve it for the required period of time (generally four years).

Chris Whitney, Contributing Editor

• *Relief from penalties and interest*

Taxpayers can apply for relief from certain penalties and payments through the BOE's eServices system. Specifically, taxpayers can submit electronic requests for relief from penalties, interest (including penalty and interest due to a disaster), and collection cost recovery fees, as well as declarations of timely mailing and extensions of time in which to file a tax/fee return. (*News Release 104-12-H*, California State Board of Equalization, October 30, 2012)

• *Remittance of taxes by means other than EFT*

Effective January 1, 2017, and before January 1, 2022, a person issued a seller's permit for a place of business that is a "dispensary," as defined in the Medical Cannabis Regulation and Safety Act, may remit California sales and use tax amounts due for retail sales at the dispensary by a means other than electronic funds transfer (EFT). During this period, a dispensary is not subject to the general requirement to remit amounts due by EFT if its estimated tax liability averages $10,000 or more per month. (Sec. 6479.3, Rev. & Tax. Code)

• *Sales suppression devices*

Any person who purchases, installs, or uses in California any automated sales suppression device or zapper or phantom-ware with the intent to defeat or evade the determination of an amount due pursuant to the sales and use tax law and the fee collection procedures law is guilty of a misdemeanor. (Sec. 7153.6, Rev. & Tax. Code; Sec. 55363.5, Rev. & Tax. Code)

Any person who, for commercial gain, sells, purchases, installs, transfers, or possesses in California any automated sales suppression device or zapper or phantom-ware with the knowledge that the sole purpose of the device is to defeat or evade the determination of an amount due pursuant to the sales and use tax law and the fee collection procedures law is guilty of an offense punishable by a fine, as specified, by imprisonment in a county jail for not more than one year, or for 16 months, two or three years, or by both that fine and imprisonment. In addition, any person who uses an automated sales suppression device or zapper or phantom-ware will be liable for all taxes, interest, and penalties due as a result of the use of that device. (Sec. 7153.6, Rev. & Tax. Code; Sec. 55363.5, Rev. & Tax. Code)

Where a person is guilty of selling, purchasing, installing, transferring, or possessing in California, for commercial gain, such a device or zapper or phantom-ware, and the person sold, installed, transferred, or possessed three or fewer such devices, that person will be guilty of an offense punishable by a fine of not more than $5,000. Where a person is guilty of such an offense and the person sold, installed, transferred, or possessed more than three such devices or zappers or phantom-ware, that person will be guilty of an offense punishable by a fine of not more than $10,000. (Sec. 7153.6, Rev. & Tax. Code; Sec. 55363.5, Rev. & Tax. Code)

• *Time for filing returns; penalty for late filing*

Returns must be filed quarterly, on or before the last day of the month following the quarterly period. (Sec. 6451, Rev. & Tax. Code) The law authorizes the requirement of more frequent returns if deemed necessary to insure payment or facilitate collection; in practice this has resulted in monthly returns being required in some cases. (Sec. 6455, Rev. & Tax. Code)

The tax is payable in full with the return, to the extent not previously paid under the prepayment procedure. Also as discussed above, taxpayers may be eligible to report and pay qualified use taxes directly on their personal income or corporation franchise (income) tax return.

The due date for returns or payments may be extended for not more than one month, upon the filing of a request showing good cause. An extension of more than one month may be granted if the taxpayer requesting the extension is a creditor of the state who has not been paid because the Legislature failed to adopt a budget for the

State by July 1 of the tax year in question. Such an extension expires on the last day of the month following the month in which the budget is adopted or one month from the due date of the return or payment, whichever is later. (Sec. 6459, Rev. & Tax. Code; Sec. 6459.1, Rev. & Tax. Code)

A 10% penalty is imposed against taxpayers that fail to file a sales and use tax return in a timely fashion. (Sec. 6591, Rev. & Tax. Code)

For a number of taxes and fees it administers, the California State Board of Equalization may determine, under certain circumstances, that it is inequitable to compute interest on a monthly basis for late electronic payments or prepayments and instead may compute interest on a modified adjusted daily rate. Such authority was granted previously but was operative only until January 1, 2016. (Sec. 6591.6, Rev. and Tax. Code)

The daily rate can be applied only if:

— the payment or prepayment was made one business day after the date the tax or prepayment was due;

— the person was granted relief from all penalties that applied to the payment or prepayment; and

— the person filed a request for an oral hearing before the board.

(Sec. 6591.6, Rev. and Tax. Code)

¶1512 Administration, Deficiencies, and Refunds

Law: Secs. 6481-88, 6511-96, 6811-14, 6829, 6901-63, 7051-99, 7070-78 (CCH CALIFORNIA TAX REPORTS, ¶61-410, 61-420, 61-440, 61-460, 61-470, 61-520, 61-530, 61-610—61-640, 89-210).

The tax is administered by the California State Board of Equalization (BOE). The BOE maintains a staff of field auditors who examine the books of taxpayers.

• *Arbitration agreements*

In *AT&T Mobility LLC v. Concepcion* (2011) (CCH CALIFORNIA TAX REPORTS, ¶60-720.31), the U.S. Supreme Court held that in a dispute involving the collection of California sales tax on the value of phones advertised as "free," federal law preempts California case law barring the enforcement of arbitration provisions that prohibit classwide proceedings. The plaintiffs in this case were part of a putative class action in federal court alleging that AT&T had engaged in fraud and false advertising by collecting sales tax on the retail value of phones advertised as "free." AT&T asked the federal district court to enforce an arbitration provision in its cellular telephone contract with the plaintiffs. However, the district court and the U.S. Court of Appeals for the Ninth Circuit both refused to enforce the arbitration provision. The courts found the provision unconscionable under California case law because it disallowed classwide proceedings. The U.S. Supreme Court reversed in a 5-4 opinion, holding that California's prohibition on class waivers in arbitration agreements was contrary to the "liberal federal policy favoring arbitration" embodied in the Federal Arbitration Act, 9 U.S.C. §2.

• *Auditing procedures*

The BOE's auditors have commonly used a procedure known as the "test-check." For example, one or more supposedly typical periods are checked to determine the extent to which sales are improperly reported as being for resale. The percentage of error found in the test period is then assumed to run through the entire period under audit and the same percentage of error is applied to the sales of the whole period and a tax deficiency is assessed accordingly.

Another type of test-check is used where the sales appear to be too low in relation to the cost of goods sold. In such cases the auditor may test the gross profit percentage by computing the mark-up on typical items of merchandise; the percentage of mark-up computed on these items may then be applied to the total costs for the period under audit to determine the taxable sales. This procedure was approved in 1950 by the California District Court of Appeal in the case of *Maganini v. Quinn* (CCH CALIFORNIA TAX REPORTS, ¶ 61-410.21).

Auditors will frequently rely on BOE sales and use tax annotations (SUTAs) when examining a particular transaction. These annotations consist of a compilation of replies by the BOE's legal staff to questions posed by auditors and taxpayers concerning the taxability of particular transactions. In *Yamaha Corporation of America v. State Board of Equalization* (1999) (CCH CALIFORNIA TAX Reports ¶ 60-030), the California Supreme Court reversed an appellate court's decision in which the appellate court relied on an BOE annotation. The Supreme Court determined that because the annotation was merely an agency's statutory interpretation it could not be equated with an agency rule to which the courts must give judicial deference. However, on remand, and consistent with the California Supreme Court's instructions, a California court of appeal assigned "great weight" to two BOE annotations in support of its opinion because of the BOE's consistency and expertise and evidence of legislative concurrence.

Regulations prescribe the procedures for conducting sales and use tax audits. In addition to providing definitions (e.g., including "pre-audit conference," "opening conference," "status conferences," "exit conference," "information/document request," and "audit findings presentation sheet"), the regulations require BOE staff to develop an audit plan that strives for the completion of each audit within a two-year timeframe, and suggests that taxpayers submit claims for refund at the beginning of their audits. (Reg. 1698, 18 CCR; Reg. 1698.5, 18 CCR)

The regulations prescribe the location of each audit, provides procedures for taxpayers to request a change of location, and permit BOE staff to visit a taxpayer's places of business to gain a better understanding of the taxpayer's business operations even if an audit is not being conducted at the taxpayer's place of business. The regulations also explain that field audit work is conducted during normal workdays and business hours throughout the year; however, BOE staff will try to schedule field audit work so that it is performed at a time and in a manner that minimizes any adverse effects on taxpayers. (Reg. 1698, 18 CCR; Reg. 1698.5, 18 CCR)

The regulations provide that the BOE has a duty to utilize its audit resources in an efficient and effective manner and that the purpose of an audit is to efficiently determine whether the correct amount of sales and use tax has been reported. In addition, BOE staff is required to complete audits within the statutes of limitations for issuing Notices of Determination and Notices of Refund and procedures are provided for BOE staff to obtain written waivers of the statutes of limitations from taxpayers when necessary. The regulation prescribes BOE staff and taxpayer duties during the audit process, including: (1) BOE staff has a duty to apply the Sales and Use Tax Law fairly and consistently regardless of whether an audit results in a deficiency or refund of tax; (2) BOE staff has a duty to keep taxpayers informed about the status of their audits; and (3) taxpayers have a duty to maintain adequate records and make them available to BOE staff for inspection and copying upon request. (Reg. 1698, 18 CCR; Reg. 1698.5, 18 CCR)

- *Business successor liability*

The purchaser of a business on which sales and use tax is outstanding must withhold a sufficient portion of the purchase price to cover the unpaid tax until the former owner produces a receipt from the BOE showing that the tax has been paid, unless the BOE issues the purchaser a certificate stating that all liability has been paid or that no amount is due. Noncompliance with this requirement renders the purchaser personally liable for any unpaid taxes incurred by the seller or any former owner, as well as for interest and penalties. Relief from penalties otherwise due may also be available if the BOE finds that the failure to withhold resulted from reasonable cause and circumstances beyond the purchaser's control. (Sec. 6811, Rev. & Tax. Code; Sec. 6812, Rev. & Tax. Code; Sec. 6814, Rev. & Tax. Code)

• *Deficiency procedures*

The BOE must give written notice of a deficiency determination. (Sec. 6486, Rev. & Tax. Code) A petition for redetermination may be filed within 30 days of service of such notice, and an oral hearing will be granted if requested. The determination becomes final if no petition is filed by the end of the 30-day period. If a petition is filed, the BOE's order or decision on the petition becomes final 30 days after service of notice of such order or decision. (Sec. 6561, Rev. & Tax. Code; Sec. 6562, Rev. & Tax. Code) Provision is also made for jeopardy assessments when collection of the tax will be jeopardized by delay. (Sec. 6536, Rev. & Tax. Code)

The limitation period for assessing deficiencies, generally, is three years. The limitation period for taxpayers that elect to report and remit qualified use taxes on their income tax returns (¶1505) is three years (six years if qualified use taxes are underreported by 25% or more) after the last day for which an acceptable tax return is due or filed, whichever occurs later. The period is eight years when no return is filed. There is no limitation in case of fraud. The limitation period may be extended by waiver agreement and also may be extended for a redetermination of tax under certain conditions. (Sec. 6487, Rev. & Tax. Code)

The ability of the California State Board of Equalization (BOE) to collect outstanding tax and fee liabilities is enhanced in regard to taxes administered by it as follows:

— the Contractor's State License Board (CSLB) is authorized to refuse to issue, reinstate, reactivate, or renew or to suspend a contractor's license for failure to resolve any outstanding BOE-related final tax or fee liabilities provided that the CSLB's registrar has mailed a preliminary notice to the licensee at least 60 days prior to the refusal or suspension which indicates that the license will be refused or suspended by a date certain;

— the BOE is authorized to refuse to issue a seller's permit to any person who has an outstanding liability with the BOE and has not entered into an installment payment agreement, as specified; and

— the BOE is authorized to use the new employee registry information maintained by the Employment Development Department (EDD) for tax collection and enforcement purposes.

(Sec. 6070.5, Rev. & Tax. Code)

CCH Comment: Public Disclosure of Large Tax Delinquencies

The BOE is required to make available as a matter of public record a quarterly list of the 500 largest uncontested sales and use tax delinquencies in excess of $100,000. Before making a delinquency a matter of public record, however, the BOE must provide written notice to the person or persons liable by certified mail and provide an opportunity for the person(s) to comply. If the amount due is not remitted or payment arrangements are not made within 30 days after issuance of the notice, the delinquency will be included on the list. (Sec. 7063, Rev. & Tax. Code)

CCH Comment: Impact of Public Disclosure of Large Tax Delinquencies on State Licenses and Contracts

Generally, a state licensing agency that issues professional or occupational licenses, certificates, registrations, or permits must suspend, revoke, and refuse to issue a license if the licensee's name is included on the delinquency lists. Moreover, state agencies generally are prohibited from entering into any contract for the acquisition of goods or services with a contractor whose name appears on the lists. (Sec. 7057, Rev. & Tax. Code; Sec. 7057.5, Rev. & Tax. Code)

- *Deficiency procedures for out-of-state retailers and "qualifying purchasers"*

The limitation period for assessing deficiencies for "qualifying" out-of-state retailers that failed to file a return or report is three years. A "qualifying" out-of-state retailer is a retailer doing business in California that, never having previously registered with the BOE, voluntarily registers prior to being contacted by the BOE. In addition, if the BOE determines that the retailer's failure to file is due to reasonable cause, the BOE may waive any corresponding penalties. (Sec. 6487.05, Rev. & Tax. Code)

The statute of limitations is similarly reduced to three years for the collection of unreported use tax by non-California retailers for specified purchases if it was determined that the failure to report and pay the tax was due to reasonable cause. "Qualifying purchaser" means a person who voluntarily filed an individual use tax return for tangible personal property that was purchased out of state for storage, use, or other consumption in California and who never previously (1) registered with the BOE, (2) filed an individual use tax return, (3) reported an amount on his or her individual California income tax return, (4) engaged in business in California as a retailer, or (5) was contacted by the BOE regarding failure to report use tax. The reduced limitations period does not apply to purchases of vehicles, vessels, or aircraft. (Sec. 6487.06, Rev. & Tax. Code)

- *Extensions in cases of disaster*

The BOE is authorized, in the case of a disaster, to extend the time for making any report or return or paying any BOE-administered tax or fee for a period not to exceed three months. The extension may be granted at any time provided a request for relief is filed with the BOE within or before the period at issue. "Disaster" is defined as fire, flood, storm, tidal wave, earthquake, or similar public calamity, regardless of whether the disaster results from natural causes. (Sec. 6459, Rev. & Tax. Code)

- *Interest and penalties*

In connection with deficiencies, a penalty of 10% is imposed for negligence or intentional disregard of the rules, and a penalty of 25% is imposed where fraud is involved. Fraud must be established by clear and convincing evidence. (Sec. 6484, Rev. & Tax. Code; Sec. 6485, Rev. & Tax. Code) A taxpayer that is required to make payments by electronic transfer funds, who is issued a deficiency determination after failing to remit the tax in a timely fashion, will be assessed an additional 10% penalty of the amount of tax due. This penalty is exclusive of other penalties that might be imposed for delinquencies applicable to other payment methods. (Sec. 6479.4, Rev. & Tax. Code)

Any person who knowingly collects California sales tax reimbursement or use tax and who fails to timely remit those amounts to the BOE is liable for a penalty of 40% of the amount not timely remitted. However, the penalty is inapplicable to any person whose liability for unremitted tax averages $1,000 or less per month or does not exceed 5% of the total amount of tax liability for which the tax reimbursement was collected for the period in which tax was due, whichever is greater. (Sec. 6597, Rev. & Tax. Code)

CCH Comment: Daily Interest Rate

Effective January 1, 2017, the BOE may compute interest at a modified adjusted daily rate for electronic payments if, in light of all facts and circumstances, it would be inequitable to compute interest at the modified adjusted rate per month. A "modified adjusted daily rate" is equal to the modified adjusted rate per annum divided by 365. The daily rate can only be charged if:

    — the payment or prepayment was made one business day after the date the tax or prepayment was due;

    — the person was granted relief from all penalties that applied; and

    — the person files a request for an oral hearing before the BOE.

(Sec. 6591.6, Rev. & Tax. Code)

CCH Comment: Assessment of 40% Penalty

The 40% penalty will not be assessed if:

— the taxpayer failed to remit tax only once within the last three years in business;

— the unreported tax averages less than $1,000 per month;

— the unreported tax is less than 5% of the total tax liability for the reporting period;

— the taxpayer voluntarily reported or corrected errors prior to being contacted by the BOE; or

— the failure to file and pay is due to reasonable cause or circumstances beyond the taxpayer's control.

(*Special Notice L-176*, BOE, August 2007)

Interest is charged on deficiencies at a rate established semiannually. The following chart indicates the rates of interest in effect for the designated periods:

From	To	Modified Adjusted Annual Rate
January 1, 2006	June 30, 2006	9%
July 1, 2006	December 31, 2006	10%
January 1, 2007	June 30, 2007	11%
July 1, 2007	December 31, 2007	11%
January 1, 2008	June 30, 2008	11%
July 1, 2008	December 31, 2008	10%
January 1, 2009	June 30, 2009	8%
July 1, 2009	December 31, 2009	8%
January 1, 2010	June 30, 2010	7%
July 1, 2010	December 31, 2010	7%
January 1, 2011	June 30, 2011	7%
July 1, 2011	December 31, 2011	6%
January 1, 2012	June 30, 2012	7%
July 1, 2012	December 31, 2016	6%
January 1, 2017	June 30, 2017	7%

The BOE may abate all or part of the interest imposed on tax liabilities resulting from (1) an BOE employee's unreasonable error or delay or (2) the Department of Motor Vehicle's error in calculating the use tax on a vehicle or vessel. (Sec. 6594, Rev. & Tax. Code) Interest will also be abated for late payment or filing if the lateness was due to a natural disaster. (Sec. 6593, Rev. & Tax. Code) In addition, if the BOE finds that neither the person liable for payment of tax nor any person related to that person caused the erroneous refund, no interest will be imposed on the amount of the erroneous refund until 30 days after the date on which the BOE mails a notice of determination for repayment of the erroneous refund. The act of filing a claim for refund will not be considered as causing the erroneous refund. (Sec. 6964, Rev. & Tax. Code)

Criminal penalties may be imposed for a variety of reasons, including giving a resale certificate to a seller with knowledge that the property is not to be resold. (Sec. 6094.5, Rev. & Tax. Code) A penalty of 50% of the tax is imposed upon anyone who registers a vehicle, vessel, or aircraft outside California for the purpose of tax evasion. (Sec. 6485.1, Rev. & Tax. Code, Sec. 6514.1, Rev. & Tax. Code) The state is empowered to employ out-of-state collection agencies and to add their compensation to the amount of tax due. The state may establish a reward program for information leading to the collection of underreported taxes.

A $50 penalty is imposed on paid preparers of sales and use tax returns for each failure to enter their name, Social Security number, and business name and address on a return. (Sec. 6452, Rev. & Tax. Code)

• *Managed audit program*

If selected by the BOE, taxpayers may participate in a managed audit program, in which taxpayers self-audit their books and records under the BOE's guidance. (Sec. 7076, Rev. & Tax. Code) To be eligible to participate in the program, a taxpayer must meet the following criteria:

— have a business that has few or no statutory exemptions and has a small number of clearly identified tax issues;

— agree to participate; and

— have the resources to comply with BOE instructions.

Taxpayers who participate in the program are entitled to a reduced interest rate of one-half the regular rate on liabilities covered by the audit period. Participation in the managed audit program does not limit the BOE's authority to otherwise audit a taxpayer.

See ¶1511 for a discussion of the alternative method of reporting use tax program.

• *Offers in compromise*

The Executive Director and Chief Counsel of the BOE, or their delegates, may compromise a final sales and use tax liability in which the reduction in tax is $7,500 or less ($10,000 or less if the board delegates such authority). Amounts in excess of $7,500 may be compromised by the Board. (Sec. 7093.6, Rev. & Tax. Code)

Generally, offers in compromise will be considered only for liabilities generated from a business that has been discontinued or transferred, where the taxpayer making the offer no longer has a controlling interest or association with the transferred business or a controlling interest or association with a similar type of business as the transferred or discontinued business. However, through 2012, offers in compromise can be made for a "qualified final tax liability" regardless of whether the taxpayer's business has been discontinued or transferred, or whether the taxpayer has a controlling interest or association with a business similar to the discontinued or transferred business. A "qualified final tax liability" includes (along with related interest, additions to tax, penalties, and other amounts assessed), (1) assessments in which no tax, fee, or surcharges were collected, (2) business successor liabilities, and (3) consumers' use tax liabilities. Taxpayers with previous compromise agreements are ineligible.

For amounts to be compromised, the taxpayer must establish that:

— the amount offered is the most that can be expected to be paid or collected from the taxpayer's present assets or income; and

— the taxpayer does not have reasonable prospects of satisfying a greater amount of the liability within a reasonable period of time. Furthermore, the BOE must determine that acceptance of the offer is in the best interest of the state. The BOE's determination is not appealable.

When more than one taxpayer is liable for the debt, the acceptance of an offer in compromise from one liable taxpayer does not relieve the other taxpayers from paying the entire liability. However, the amount of the liability will be reduced by the amount of the accepted offer.

• *Officer/shareholder liability*

Upon termination or dissolution of a partnership, limited liability partnership, corporation, or limited liability company, certain officers, members, managers, or other persons may be held personally liable for unpaid sales and use taxes. (Sec. 6829, Rev. & Tax. Code; Reg. 1702.5, 18 CCR)

A California court of appeal held, in *State Board of Equalization v. Wirick* (2001) (CCH CALIFORNIA TAX REPORTS, ¶61-460.40), that a former officer was personally liable for a corporation's unpaid California sales tax when the corporation ceased business because he had responsibility for paying the tax when due.

Caution Note: Returns, Statute of Limitations for Determinations

The BOE has held that a responsible person must file a return in his or her own name for the Sec. 6829, Rev. & Tax. Code liability. Such return must cover the quarter during which the business was terminated. (*In the Matter of the Petition for Redetermination under the Sales and Use Tax Law of McKoon* (2007) CCH CALIFORNIA TAX REPORTS, ¶ 404-292)

The limitation period for issuing a determination under Sec. 6829 is three years from the last day of the month following the quarter in which the BOE obtains actual knowledge, through its audit or compliance activities, or by written communication by the business or its representative, of the termination, dissolution, or abandonment of the business, or eight years from the last day of the month following the quarter of termination, dissolution, or abandonment, whichever period expires later. (Sec. 6829, Rev. & Tax. Code)

• *Primary retailer's liability for tax due on concessionaire's sales*

A primary retailer is jointly and severally liable for any sales and use tax imposed or unreported during the period that a retailer operates on the primary retailer's premises as a concessionaire. The primary retailer is relieved of this liability, however, during the period that the concessionaire holds a seller's permit to operate at the primary retailer's location or if the primary retailer takes in good faith the concessionaire's written affirmation that the concessionaire holds a seller's permit for the primary retailer's location. (Reg. 1699, 18 CCR)

• *Refunds*

The limitation period for filing refund claims, generally, is three years from the due date of the return or, in the case of a deficiency or jeopardy determination or nonfiling of a return, the later of six months from the date a deficiency determination becomes final or within six months of the overpayment. However, a taxpayer has three years from the date of overpayment to file a refund claim if the overpayment was collected as a result of the BOE's collection of an outstanding tax liability through issuance of a levy, lien, or other enforcement procedure. (Sec. 6902, Rev. & Tax. Code; Sec. 6902.3, Rev. & Tax. Code; Sec. 6905, Rev. & Tax. Code)

Applicable to claims filed on or after January 1, 2017, a claim for refund involving a case in which the amount of tax, surcharge, or fee determined has not been paid in full will be deemed to be a timely filed claim for refund with all subsequent payments applied to that determination. The "amount of tax determined" means an amount of tax, interest, or penalty with respect to a single determination under the law related to the tax. Similar definitions apply for "amount of surcharge determined" and "amount of fee determined." (Sec. 6902.6, Rev. & Tax. Code)

In *Dan J. Agnew v. California State Board of Equalization* (1999) (CCH CALIFORNIA TAX REPORTS, ¶ 61-620.25), the California Supreme Court held that a taxpayer is *not* required to pay the accrued interest on a tax deficiency in addition to the tax claimed to be due and owing as a prerequisite to administrative review of a claim for refund of an alleged overpayment of sales and use tax.

The limitations period for filing a refund claim is suspended during any period that a person is unable to manage his or her financial affairs because of a physical or mental impairment that is life threatening or that is expected to last for at least 12 months. This waiver does not apply to individuals who are represented in their financial matters by their spouses or by other persons. (Sec. 6902.4, Rev. & Tax. Code)

A claimant may bring suit within 90 days after the BOE mails a notice of disallowance. (Sec. 6933, Rev. & Tax. Code) If the BOE fails to act on the claim within six months after the claim is filed, the claimant may consider the claim disallowed and proceed to bring suit. (Sec. 6934, Rev. & Tax. Code)

¶1512

Interest is payable by the State on refunds at the modified adjusted rate per month, which is the modified adjusted rate per annum divided by 12. Interest is payable on refunds from the first day of the calendar month following the month during which the overpayment was made to (1) the last day of the calendar month in which the taxpayer is notified that the claim may be filed or (2) the date the claim is approved by the BOE, whichever is earlier. Interest may be waived for a period, in cases where the taxpayer requests deferred action on a refund claim. (Sec. 6591.5, Rev. & Tax. Code)

The following chart indicates the rates of interest for the designated periods.

From	To	Applicable Period Interest Rate
January 1, 2006	June 30, 2006	3%
July 1, 2006	December 31, 2006	4%
January 1, 2007	June 30, 2007	5%
July 1, 2007	December 31, 2007	5%
January 1, 2008	June 30, 2008	5%
July 1, 2008	December 31, 2008	3%
January 1, 2009	June 30, 2009	2%
July 1, 2009	June 30, 2017	0%

• *Relief for innocent spouse/registered domestic partner*

If two spouses' or registered domestic partners' (RDPs) names appear on an application for a seller's permit and sales and use tax liability is understated by one spouse or RDP, the innocent spouse or RDP may be relieved of liability for tax, including interest, penalties, and other amounts attributable to the understatement, if the following conditions are satisfied:

— the underpayment or nonpayment is attributable to the other spouse or RDP;

— the innocent spouse or RDP can establish a lack of knowledge that was reasonable; and

— relief from liability is deemed to be equitable under the circumstances. (Sec. 6456, Rev. & Tax. Code; Reg. 1705.1, 18 CCR)

Relief is not available for either underreporting or nonpayment in any calendar quarter that is

— more than five years from the final date on an BOE determination,

— more than five years from the return due date for nonpayment on a return,

— more than one year from the first contact with the innocent spouse or RDP claiming relief, or

— closed by *res judicata*, whichever is later.

• *Relief from liability*

Relief of liability for the payment of sales and use taxes, including penalties and interest, is available when the liability resulted from the failure to make a timely return in reliance upon written advice given by the California State Board of Equalization (BOE) to a person with shared accounting and common ownership with the audited person. The amendments clarify that relief, under Sec. 6596 of the Revenue and Taxation Code, can apply to a person who the BOE would reasonably expect to rely on written advice provided by BOE staff in a prior audit of another related person because the two persons are: (1) in the same industry; (2) under common ownership; and (3) share accounting functions and accounting staff. (Reg. 1705, 18 CCR)

¶1512

Practitioner Comment: Extension of Relief from Liability for Payment of Sales and Use Taxes

Effective July 1, 2014, the State Board of Equalization amended California Code of Regulations (Cal. Code of Regs.) section 1705, "Relief of Liability." Relief from liability for the payment of sales and use taxes, including penalties and interest, is extended to a person if the liability was the result of the person relying on erroneous advice provided during the prior audit of another person. Relief is extended if the person seeking relief: (1) is engaged in the same line of business as the audited person; (2) has the same common verifiable controlling ownership of 50% or greater or a common majority shareholder with the audited person; and (3) shares accounting functions with the audited person.

Chris Whitney, Contributing Editor

Practitioner Comment: Tax Authorities May be Equitably Estopped from Asserting a Claim is Invalid Where the Taxpayer Had Reasonably Relied on Instructions from Such Tax Authority

In *D.R. Systems, Inc. v. Cal. State Bd. of Equalization*, Cal. Ct. App., Dkt. No. D060856 (March 7, 2013) (unpublished) (CCH CALIFORNIA TAX REPORTS, ¶ 61-610.42), the California Court of Appeal held that a taxpayer's evidence of communications with a State Board of Equalization (BOE) agent presented triable issues of material fact regarding the application of equitable estoppel. D.R. Systems, Inc. asserted that it filed a valid sales tax refund claim with the BOE because it wrote a letter stating that it was owed a "large credit balance" as instructed by a BOE agent.

In order to state a valid claim for refund of sales and use tax, California Revenue and Taxation Code Section 6904(a) (Revenue and Taxation Code Section 19322 is the analogous income and franchise tax code section) requires that the claim must be in writing and state the specific grounds upon which it is founded. The BOE argued that the taxpayer's letter was not a valid refund claim because it did not specify grounds for a refund and that, consequently, the taxpayer had not exhausted its administrative remedies before filing suit.

Notwithstanding that the court agreed that the taxpayer's communications did not constitute a valid refund claim under the statute, the court determined that estoppel may be appropriate in "a situation where the claim is that a government agent has negligently or intentionally caused a claimant to fail to comply with a procedural precondition, and the failure to invoke estoppel would cause an injustice to the claimant." In order to prevail at trial on its estoppel argument, the taxpayer must show that it was reasonable to rely on the BOE agent's instruction, which requires additional factual development.

Although an unpublished decision, to the extent that a taxpayer submits its claim in reliance on the instructions of a revenue agent, *D.R. Systems* potentially lowers the standard required to file a valid claim as stated in Revenue and Taxation Code Sections 6904(a) and 19322, and analyzed in *Newman v. Franchise Tax Bd.*, 208 Cal.App.3d 972 (1989) and *J.H. McKnight Ranch, Inc. v. Franchise Tax Bd.*, 110 Cal.App.4th 978 (2003).

Chris Whitney, Contributing Editor

• *Settlement of civil tax disputes*

The Executive Officer of the BOE, or his or her designee, may settle any civil tax dispute involving amounts of $5,000 or less. For civil tax disputes involving amounts in excess of $5,000, the BOE may approve the settlement recommendations made by its Executive Officer (or Chief Counsel if authorized by the Executive Officer) and reviewed by the Attorney General. (Sec. 7093.5, Rev. & Tax. Code)

• *Special refund procedure for invalid local taxes*

Retailers who reside or conduct business in a taxing district in which an invalid tax was imposed must report sales and use tax at the currently effective combined state and local rate but may claim a 0.75% credit against the total amount of taxes reported. A corresponding 0.75% reduction must be made in the amount of sales or use taxes that retailers collect from purchasers. The 0.75% credit may be claimed for taxes due on the first day of the first calendar quarter beginning at least 120 days after a final court determination that a local sales and use tax is invalid. (Sec. 7275, Rev. & Tax. Code; Sec. 7276, Rev. & Tax. Code)

A nonretailer who pays a local sales and use tax that is subsequently held invalid may file a claim for refund of the invalid tax, provided the claim states in writing the specific ground upon which it is made and is accompanied by proof of payment. However, only claims for a single purchase or aggregate purchases of $5,000 or more will be eligible for refund, and any such claim must be filed within one year of the first day of the first calendar quarter after a local sales and use tax has been held invalid. (Sec. 7277, Rev. & Tax. Code)

A California court of appeal held, in *Kuykendall v. State Board of Equalization et al.* (1994) (CCH CALIFORNIA TAX REPORTS, ¶61-610.353), that the statutory scheme of reimbursing consumers for the local sales and use tax declared unconstitutional in *Rider* (¶1502) through a sales tax rollback and through direct refunds for claims involving documented purchases of $5,000 or more did not violate constitutional guarantees of due process and equal protection.

- *Taxpayers' bill of rights*

A "bill of rights" has been enacted to protect taxpayers' privacy and property rights during the sales and use tax collection process. (Sec. 7080, Rev. & Tax. Code through Sec. 7099, Rev. & Tax. Code) It is substantially identical to the one described briefly at ¶702, relating to taxpayer rights in connection with personal income and corporate tax collections, except that the agency involved is the BOE rather than the Franchise Tax Board.

- *Voluntary use tax reporting*

The BOE provides a voluntary use tax reporting program. A deficiency determination mailed to a qualifying purchaser is limited to the three-year period beginning after the last day of the calendar month following the quarterly period for which the amount is proposed to be determined. This reduces the period of time for which the BOE may issue a determination from eight years to three years when unregistered in-state purchasers, as defined, voluntarily report to the BOE purchases subject to use tax. A "qualifying purchaser" is a person that: (1) voluntarily files an individual use tax return for tangible personal property that is purchased from a retailer outside California for storage, use, or other consumption within California; and (2) meets all of the following conditions:

> — the purchaser resides or is located within California and has not previously registered with the BOE, filed an individual use tax return with the BOE, or reported an amount on his or her individual California income tax return;

> — the purchaser is not engaged in business in California as a retailer, as defined;

> — the purchaser has not been contacted by the BOE regarding failure to report the use tax imposed as specified; and

> — the BOE has made a determination that the purchaser's failure to file an individual use tax return or to otherwise report or pay the use tax imposed, as specified, was due to reasonable cause and was not caused by reason of negligence, intentional disregard of the law, or by an intent to evade taxes.

(Sec. 6487.06, Rev. & Tax. Code)

PART VI

DEATH TAXES

CHAPTER 16
DEATH TAXES

¶ 1601	Inhertiance, Estate, and Gift Tax

¶1601 Inheritance, Estate, and Gift Tax

California's Estate Tax is covered in Revenue and Taxation Code, Division 2 Other Taxes, Part 8 Prohibition of Gift and Death Taxes. Comprehensive coverage of estate and inheritance taxes is provided in Wolters Kluwer, CCH State Inheritance Estate and Gift Tax Reporter. For more information go to CCHGroup.com or contact an account representative at 888-CCH-REPS (888-224-377).

PART VII

PROPERTY TAXES

CHAPTER 17
PROPERTY TAXES

¶1701 Scope of Chapter

California does not impose a general ad valorem tax on real and personal property. However, local governmental units throughout the state do impose such a tax. Because of the statewide character of this tax and the fact that its provisions are included in the state Revenue and Taxation Code, this chapter is included for the sake of completeness, despite the fact that the tax is not, strictly speaking, a "state tax."

The purpose of this chapter is to give a very general picture of the nature and application of the property tax and the manner of its administration. It is not intended to provide detailed coverage. It covers, generally, the questions of what property is subject to tax, the base and rate of tax, the requirements for filing returns and making payment, collections, and appeals.

¶1702 Imposition of Tax

Law: Secs. 1-4, Art. XIIIA, Sec. 1-3, Art. XIIIC, Cal. Constitution; Secs. 53720, 53739, Govt. Code.

Beginning in 1978, California voters began to assert control over the imposition of property taxation and its related processes. In a series of Propositions, the electorate approved constitutional and statutory limitations on rates and assessments, as well as on the meaning of the term "tax."

Proposition 13—1978: The impact of property taxes in California was drastically reduced by the passage of Proposition 13 adding Article XIIIA to the State Constitution. Following is a brief overview of the provisions of Article XIIIA, as enacted:

— the overall rate of property taxation is limited to 1% of "full cash value" as specifically defined for this purpose (see ¶1706 for discussion of permissible additions to the 1% limit) and also a potential adjustment for a decline in value; (Sec. 1, Art. XIII A, Cal. Const.)

— valuations of real property are frozen at the value of the property in March 1975, with an allowable adjustment of up to 2% per year for inflation. However, property is assessed at its current value when it is purchased or newly constructed or a "change of ownership" occurs, with subsequent annual adjustment (up to 2%) for inflation. Valuations of personal property are not frozen; they are determined annually as of January 1; (Sec. 2, Art. XIII A, Cal. Const.)

— no new property, sales, or transaction taxes may be imposed on real property; (Sec. 3, Art. XIII A, Cal. Const.)

— a two-thirds vote of the legislature is required for any increases in other state taxes; and (Sec. 3, Art. XIII A, Cal. Const.)

— a two-thirds vote of qualified electors is required for the imposition of special taxes by local governments. A majority vote of qualified electors is required for the imposition of any new or higher general taxes by local governments. (Sec. 4, Art. XIII A, Cal. Const.)

Practitioner Comment: California Court of Appeals Holds That a Long Term Lease Extension with Subsequent Purchase Did Not Constitute a Change in Ownership for Property Tax Reassessment Purposes.

In *Dyanlyn Two v. County of Orange*, G049269 (January 30, 2015) (Dyanlyn), an unpublished decision, the California Court of Appeal ("Appellate Court") held that here was no change in ownership for property tax purposes when a long term lease was extended past 35 years and the property subsequently was purchased by a long term lessee and a third party investor.

Under Cal. Rev. & Tax. Code Sec. 61(c), a change in ownership occurs at the time a lease with a duration of 35 years or greater is executed. Additionally, under Cal. Rev. & Tax. Code Sec. 62(g), the sale by the lessor of property subject to a long term lease does not result in a change in ownership where the remaining term on the lease is 35 years or more.

In 1977, the owners of adjacent parcels of real property entered into a 60-year ground lease with Golden Westminster Specialty Center ("Golden Westminster"). The lease contained an option for the lessee to purchase the property during either the 25th or 30th year of the ground lease. Golden Westminster subsequently built and operated a shopping center on the property. In 2006, with 31 years remaining on the original lease, the parties agreed to extend the lease term by an additional 15 years. A few weeks later, the landlord sold the property to Dyanlyn Two and two other entities as tenants-in-common (collectively, "Dyanlyn"). Two of those entities held partnership interests in Golden Westminster, while the remaining partner was a third party investor unrelated to Golden Westminster. Orange County reassessed the property value after the sale asserting that there was a change in ownership to Dyanlyn.

The trial court applied the step transaction doctrine to treat the extension of the lease and the subsequent sale of the property as one transaction taken to avoid reassessment and ruled that Orange County properly reassessed the property value. The Appellate Court reversed, holding that the sale of property at issue did not create a change in ownership. The Appellate Court concluded that the lessee's purpose in extending the lease term was to attract outside investors to help acquire the property. Because the lessee did not target any specific investor, nor did the outside investor participate in or encourage the lease extension, it could not be said that all the parties in the transactions shared the same goal "from the beginning," and thus the "end result" test for the step transaction doctrine did not apply. The "interdependence test" for the step transaction doctrine also did not apply because the lease extension had independent economic substance from the sale since the lessee desired an additional 15 years to utilize its buildings and improvements on the property, to collect rent, and improve its profit margin. The transaction served a valid purpose unrelated to the goal of acquiring the property and was not a fruitless act. Therefore, the Appellate Court held that the lease extension followed by the sale did not constitute a change in ownership for property tax purposes.

The court's decision stands in contrast to the California Court of Appeal's decision in *Shuwa Investments Corp. v. County of Los Angeles*, 1 Cal.App.4th 1635 (1991) in which it held that all three tests for applying the step-transaction doctrine were satisfied. In *Shuwa*, the court concluded that the two sellers (i.e., Bank of America and ARCO), and the single buyer (i.e., Shuwa Investment Corporation (Shuwa)) of ARCO Plaza concocted an elaborate three-step process to achieve the singular purpose of Shuwa acquiring the property, which included the execution of a letter of intent which clearly stated the desire to structure the transaction in a manner intended to avoid a "change in ownership" for property tax purposes.

The most salient factual distinctions between *Dyanlyn* and *Shuwa* may be twofold. First, when Dyanlyn executed the 15-year lease extension, there was no contractual obligation to purchase the property and the third party buyer had not been definitively identified. Second, and maybe more importantly, there was no factual evidence, documentary or otherwise, that indicated the reason Dyanlyn sought the lease extension was to avoid a change in ownership for property tax purposes.

Chris Whitney, Contributing Editor

Proposition 62—1986: In the general election on November 4, 1986, California voters approved Proposition 62, which amended the Government Code to provide that any new or higher general tax must be approved by two-thirds of a local government's or district's legislative body and by a majority of the voters. (Sec. 53720, Govt. Code, et seq.) Also, any new or higher special tax had to be approved by at least two-thirds of the voters. Finally, local governments and districts were required to stop collecting any new or higher taxes that were adopted during the so-called "window period" from August 1, 1985, to November 5, 1986, the date of adoption of Proposition 62, unless such taxes were approved by a majority of the electorate within two years of the adoption of the proposition. The California Supreme Court has held that Proposition 62 is constitutional to the extent that it requires a majority of voters to pass a new or increased general tax and a 2/3 vote of the voters to approve a special tax. (*Santa Clara County Local Transportation Authority v. Guardino*, 11 Cal4th 220 (1995), ¶ 402-790)

Proposition 218—1996: In the general election on November 5, 1996, California voters approved Proposition 218, which added provisions to the California Constitution to:

— prohibit all local governments, including charter cities, from imposing, extending, or increasing any general tax after November 5, 1996, without the approval of a majority of the local electorate and

— require that any general tax imposed, extended, or increased from January 1, 1995, through November 5, 1996, by any local government without voter approval be submitted to voters for approval by November 6, 1998, and be approved by a majority of the voters in order for the tax to continue to be imposed.

Proposition 218 also reiterated that a local government may not impose, extend, or increase any special tax until the tax is submitted to the voters and approved by a two-thirds vote. (Sec. 2, Art. XIII C, Cal. Const.)

An ordinance or resolution presented for voter approval pursuant to the requirements of Proposition 218 may propose a range of tax rates or amounts and may provide for inflation adjustments to those rates or amounts, provided that if a rate or amount is determined by using a percentage calculation, the ordinance or resolution may not provide for inflation adjustments to the percentage. A general or special tax will not be deemed to have been increased if it is imposed at a rate or amount not higher than the maximum rate approved by the electorate. (Sec. 2, Art. XIII C, Cal. Const.; Sec. 53739, Govt. Code)

Under Proposition 218, all taxes imposed by local governments are deemed to be either general taxes or special taxes, and special purpose districts or agencies, including school districts, are without power to levy general taxes. (Sec. 2, Art. XIII C, Cal. Const.)

Finally, notwithstanding any other provision of the California Constitution, there must not be any limitation on the use of the initiative power to reduce or repeal any local tax, assessment, fee, or charge. (Sec. 3, Art. XIII C, Cal. Const.) Also, neither the legislature nor any local government charter may impose a signature requirement for local initiatives that is higher than that applicable to statewide statutory initiatives.

Proposition 26—2010: In 2010, California voters approved a measure to expand the definition of a "tax" that must be approved by a two-thirds vote of the Legislature, or a vote of the electorate in the case of local taxes. (Sec. 3, Art. XIII A, Cal. Const.; Sec. 1, Art. XIII C, Cal. Const.) Proposition 26 provided that any state tax adopted since January 1, 2010, that was not adopted in compliance with this requirement was void within 12 months, unless it was reenacted in such compliance.

Under the Articles XIII A and XIII C as amended by the proposition, for supermajority requirements, a "tax" was "any levy, charge, or exaction of any kind" with a list of exceptions for each section. Both sections had exceptions for:

— charges imposed for a specific benefit conferred or privilege granted directly to the payor that is not provided to those not charged, and which does not exceed the reasonable costs to the (state or local) government of conferring the benefit or granting the privilege;

— charges imposed for a specific government service or product provided directly to the payor that is not provided to those not charged, and which does not exceed the reasonable costs to the (state or local) government of providing the service or product;

— charges imposed for the reasonable regulatory costs to a (state or local) government for issuing licenses and permits, performing investigations, inspections, and audits, enforcing agricultural marketing orders, and the administrative enforcement and adjudication thereof;

— charges imposed for entrance to or use of (state or local) government property, or the purchase, rental, or lease of (state or local) government property; and

— fines, penalties, or other charges imposed by the judicial branch of (state or local) government or a government, as a result of a violation of law.

Sec. 1, Art. XIII C also had exceptions for:

— charges imposed as a condition of property development; and

— assessments and property-related fees imposed in accordance with the provisions of Article XIII D.

In addition, for each section, the government has the burden of proving by a preponderance of the evidence that:

— a levy, charge, or other exaction is not a tax;

— the amount is no more than necessary to cover the reasonable costs of the governmental activity, and

— the manner in which those costs are allocated to a payor bear a fair or reasonable relationship to the payor's burdens on, or benefits received from, the governmental activity.

(Sec. 3, Art. XIII A, Cal. Const.; Sec. 1, Art. XIII C, Cal. Const.)

Proposition 26 was not retroactively applicable so as to require a two-thirds majority vote for a local referendum, which was approved by a simple majority of voters the same day that Proposition 26 was approved, seeking to prevent a water and sewer district from imposing base rates after service has been discontinued. Proposition 26 took effect the day after it was approved by voters, and there was neither an express retroactivity provision in the actual language of the proposition nor extrinsic sources that would have left no doubt that retroactivity was the voters' manifest intent. (*Brooktrails Township Community Services District v. Board of Supervisors of Mendocino County*, Court of Appeal of California, First District, A135900, June 26, 2013, CCH CALIFORNIA TAX REPORTS, ¶ 405-902)

¶1703 Property Subject to Tax

Law: Sec. 1, Art. XIII, Cal. Const; Secs. 201, 107, 107.9, 1150-54, 1160, 5331, 5332, 5801-10, Rev. & Tax. Code; Rule 20, 18 CCR (CCH CALIFORNIA TAX REPORTS, ¶ 20-105, 20-190, 20-260, 20-295, 20-325).

All real and tangible personal property in the state is subject to tax unless specifically exempt. (Sec. 201, Rev. & Tax. Code; Sec. 1, Art. XIII, Cal. Const.) There is no tax on intangible property. "Possessory interests" of lessees in tax-exempt public property are subject to tax if they are independent, durable, and exclusive of rights held by others in the property. (Sec. 107, Rev. & Tax. Code; Reg. 20, 18 CCR) Examples of possessory interests are leases of oil and gas properties, homesites, and boat berths.

States may not tax property interests held by the federal government, unless, in cases in which the United States is the owner of land within a state, the United States has merely proprietary interests in the land, and not exclusive jurisdiction over the land (*Coso Energy Developers v. County of Inyo* (2004) (CCH CALIFORNIA TAX REPORTS, ¶ 403-696)).

In *United States v. County of San Diego et al.* (1995) (CCH CALIFORNIA TAX REPORTS, ¶ 402-767), a federal court of appeals held that the taxpayer, a private research firm that conducted nuclear fusion research for the U.S. Department of Energy (DOE), had a taxable possessory interest in a nuclear device belonging to the DOE because the taxpayer was entitled to exclusive and independent use of the device. Moreover, the property tax assessment was properly calculated using the value of the nuclear device because tax was assessed on the possessory interest of the taxpayer rather than on the United State's ownership interest.

Certain types of property are subject to special taxes "in lieu" of property taxes and therefore are not subject to the general property tax. This applies to motor vehicles and private cars, as explained at ¶ 1903 and ¶ 1905.

Airplanes used by domestic airlines and air taxis operated in scheduled air taxi operations are assessed in proportion to the time they are in California. Aircraft owned by U.S., state, and foreign governments are exempt. (Sec. 5331, Rev. & Tax. Code; Sec. 5332, Rev. & Tax. Code) Special rules apply to the valuation of certificated aircraft, airline possessory interests, and fractionally-owned aircraft. (Sec. 107.9, Rev. & Tax. Code; Sec. 1150 et. seq., Rev. & Tax. Code; Sec. 1160 et seq., Rev. & Tax. Code)

Special rules are provided for manufactured homes. Those on a permanent foundation are taxed as real property. Others are subject either to vehicle license fees or to property taxes, depending on date of purchase and other factors. (Sec. 5801, Rev. & Tax. Code; Sec. 5810, Rev. & Tax. Code)

Floating homes are taxed as real property, with 1979 (rather than 1975) used as the valuation base for purposes of Proposition 13. (¶ 1707) A floating home does not include a vessel.

¶1704 Exemptions

Law: Secs. 3, 27, 28, Art. XIII, Cal. Const; Secs. 105, 155.20, 201-61, 436, 5331, 5332, Rev. & Tax. Code; Rules 131, 152, 203, 464, 18CCR (CCH CALIFORNIA TAX REPORTS, ¶ 20-505— 20-515).

Many categories of property and property owners are partially or fully exempt under the property tax law. There have been numerous changes in the exemptions over the years. Detailed listing and discussion are beyond the scope of this book.

Property tax is not imposed on the following categories of property:

— business inventories (including livestock held for sale) (Sec. 219, Rev. & Tax Code);

— household goods and personal effects not held or used in a trade or business (Sec. 3(m), Art. XIII, Cal. Const.; Sec. 224, Rev. & Tax. Code);

— employee-owned hand tools (up to $50,000) (Sec. 241, Rev. & Tax. Code);

— intangible property (Sec. 212, Rev. & Tax. Code);

— nonprofit cemetery property (Sec. 204, Rev. & Tax. Code);

— cargo containers (Sec. 232, Rev. & Tax. Code); and

— certain vessels and aircraft. (Sec. 209, Rev. & Tax. Code; Sec. 209.5, Rev. & Tax. Code; Sec. 217.1, Rev. & Tax. Code; Sec. 220, Rev. & Tax. Code; Sec. 220.5, Rev. & Tax. Code; Sec. 228, Rev. & Tax. Code; Sec. 5331, Rev. & Tax. Code; Sec. 5332, Rev. & Tax. Code)

In addition, a county board of supervisors may exempt from taxation certain property having a full value not exceeding:

(1) $10,000 if the costs of assessment and collection for such a property are unjustified or

(2) $50,000 for certain possessory interests.

(Sec. 155.20, Rev. & Tax. Code)

Computer programs, except for storage media, are exempt. (Sec. 152, 18 CCR) In *Hahn v. State Board of Equalization* (1999) (CCH CALIFORNIA TAX REPORTS, ¶403-042), a California court of appeal upheld a State Board of Equalization rule that basic operational computer programs (although intangible property) are not exempt from property tax when sold bundled with computer hardware but are exempt when sold separately. However, in *Cardinal Health 301, Inc. v. County of Orange* (2008) (CCH CALIFORNIA TAX REPORTS, ¶404-768), a California court of appeal noted that not all bundled software is taxable. Where there is no evidence to the contrary, assessors can value computer equipment sold or leased at a single price not segregated between taxable property and nontaxable programs. However, taxpayers have the option and the burden of presenting evidence to rebut the taxability presumption by showing that some of the bundled software at the time of purchase or lease of the computer did not constitute basic operational programs and, therefore, was not subject to tax.

Practitioner Comment: Refunds on Bundled Software May Be Available But Evidentiary Standard Uncertain.

As noted above, personal property tax refunds on "bundled" application software may be available under the *Cardinal Health* decision (2008) 167 Cal.App.4th 219. In *Cardinal Health*, the California Court of Appeal concluded that all computer software subject to property tax is "bundled," i.e., sold pre-installed on tangible equipment (e.g., a computer), but that not all "bundled" software is subject to property tax. Specifically, the court held that the value of "bundled" application software (in contrast to "bundled" basic operational software) could be excluded from the assessed value of equipment for property tax purposes.

While the evidentiary standard to support the value of the excluded software was not addressed in *Cardinal Health*, it presumably would be a "preponderance of evidence" standard. Further, California Code of Regulations, Title 18 Section 152 suggests that an itemized list of the price assigned by the manufacturer to various components of the equipment (if available) would be sufficient.

Chris Whitney, Contributing Editor

A property tax exemption is provided for $7,000 of the value of a homeowner's dwelling. (Sec. 3, Art. XIII, Cal. Const.; Sec. 218, Rev. & Tax. Code; Reg. 464, 18 CCR)

CCH Tip: Damaged/Destroyed Property

Homes destroyed or damaged in the disasters listed in Sec. 218, Rev. & Tax. Code, remain eligible for the homeowners' exemption.

Partial exemptions are also allowed for certain agricultural products, fruit and nut trees, and grapevines. (Sec. 3, Art. XIII, Cal. Const.; Sec. 202(a)(1), Rev. & Tax. Code; Sec. 211(a), Rev. & Tax. Code; Sec. 105(b), Rev. & Tax. Code; Sec. 436, Rev. & Tax. Code; Reg. 131, 18 CCR) These exemptions are in addition to constitutional exemptions for property in interstate and international commerce. (Reg. 203, 18 CCR)

In addition, California's property tax law provides full or partial exemptions for qualified property held by the following entities:

— artistic works on display in qualified galleries or museums (Sec. 217, Rev. & Tax. Code);

— religious institutions and organizations (Sec. 3, Art. XIII, Cal. Const.Sec. 214, Rev. & Tax. Code);

— governments and their agencies (Sec. 3, Art. XIII, Cal. Const.; Sec. 202(a)(4), Rev. & Tax. Code);

— Native American tribes (Sec. 237, Rev. & Tax. Code);

— educational institutions (Sec. 3(d), Art. XIII, Cal. Const.; Sec. 202(a), Rev. & Tax. Code; Sec. 203(a), Rev. & Tax. Code);

— charitable, scientific, and hospital organizations (Sec. 214, Rev. & Tax. Code);

— certain veterans and their surviving spouses (Sec. 3, Art. XIII, Cal. Const.; Secs. 205, 205.5, Rev. & Tax. Code);

— veterans organizations (Sec. 215, Rev. & Tax. Code);

— banks and insurance companies (personal property only) (Sec. 27, Art. XIII, Cal. Const.; Sec. 28, Art. XIII, Cal. Const.); and

— volunteer fire departments (Sec. 213.7, Rev. & Tax. Code).

Some exemptions require the filing of an annual return or claim. In case of any question about exemptions or filing requirements, the assessor's office should be consulted.

¶1705 Deferred Payments

Law: Sec. 8.5, Art. XIII, Cal. Const.; Secs. 3376, 3691, 20583, 20585, 20602, 20622, 20623, 20802, 20810-20812, Rev. & Tax. Code (CCH CALIFORNIA TAX REPORTS, ¶20-155, 20-315).

The Legislature can provide for property tax postponement by qualifying senior citizens or disabled persons. (Sec. 8.5, Art. XIII, Cal. Const.) The property tax postponement (PTP) law for qualifying residential dwellings has been reinstated, and the Controller can accept applications for postponement beginning July 1, 2016. In February 2009, the Controller had been prohibited from accepting any more claims. (Sec. 20623 Rev. & Tax. Code)

Postponement will not be permitted if household income exceeds $35,000. (Sec. 20585 Rev. & Tax. Code) Approved claims will be paid by electronic funds transfer directly to a county tax collector, with notice to the claimant, for property taxes owed on behalf of the qualified claimant. (Sec. 20602 Rev. & Tax. Code) A claimant must possess at least a 40% equity in the residential dwelling at issue. Claims must be filed between September 1 and April 10 of the fiscal year in which the postponement is claimed. (Sec. 20583 Rev. & Tax. Code) For purposes of the PTP law, the term "residential dwelling" no longer includes mobile homes. (Sec. 20622 Rev. & Tax. Code)

In the event of a tax-defaulted property sale, the county tax collector must include any outstanding balance of a PTP loan in the minimum bid. (Sec. 3376 Rev. & Tax. Code) In addition, counties may, prior to January 1, 2017, adopt conditions and procedures for delaying the sale of properties that it finds may be eligible to file a PTP claim and may cancel any delinquent penalties, costs, fees, and interest associated with those properties. (Sec. 3691 Rev. & Tax. Code, et. seq.)

• *County deferral program*

California counties may defer a claimant's property taxes retroactively, for property taxes due on or before February 20, 2011, and prospectively. The County Deferred Property Tax Program for Senior and Disabled Citizens allows each California county to elect to participate in the program by adopting a resolution that indicates the county's intention to participate in and administer the program. Eligible claimants in participating counties may apply for deferment between October 1 and December 10 of each year. (Sec. 20810 Rev. & Tax. Code; Sec. 20811 Rev. & Tax. Code, Sec. 20812 Rev. & Tax. Code)

A "claimant," for these purposes, is defined as an owner of a residential dwelling, as defined, who applies to a participating county for deferment of property taxes and has:

— an annual household income, as defined, that does not exceed $35,500;

— attained eligibility for full social security benefits as of the last day of the filing period for that fiscal year, or is blind or disabled, as defined, except in the case of retroactive deferment, in which the age eligibility is 62; and

— equity value of at least 20% (for these purposes, "equity value" is defined as the amount by which the fair market value of the residential dwelling exceeds the total amount of any liens or other obligations against the residential dwelling).

(Sec. 20802 Rev. & Tax. Code)

¶1706 Basis and Rate of Tax

Law: Secs. 2, 3, 8, Art. XIII, Sec. 1, Art. XIIIA, Cal. Const.; Secs. 110, 208-12, 227, 401.6, 401.17, 402.95, 607-609, 988, 995, 997, Revenue and Taxation Code; Rule 474, 18 CCR (CCH CALIFORNIA TAX REPORTS, ¶ 20-405, 20-610).

As explained at ¶1702, the overall rate of property tax is 1% of "full cash value." This may be increased by any amount necessary to pay interest and redemption charges on any indebtedness approved by the voters before July 1, 1978, or bonded indebtedness for the acquisition or improvement of real property approved on or after July 1, 1978, by two-thirds (55%, if related to school bonds) of those voting in a local election. (Sec. 1, Art. XIII A, Cal. Const.)

The value of intangible assets and rights relating to the going concern value of a business or the exclusive nature of a concession, franchise, or similar agreement must not enhance or be reflected in the value of taxable property. However, taxable property may be assessed and valued by assuming the presence of intangible assets or rights necessary to put the taxable property to beneficial or productive use. (Sec. 212, Rev. & Tax. Code; Sec. 3(n), Art. XIII, Cal. Const.) Intangible attributes of real property such as zoning, location, and other such attributes that relate directly to the real property must be reflected in the value of the real property. (Sec. 110, Rev. & Tax. Code) In a 2014 California Court of Appeal decision, it was held that a county assessor failed to attribute a portion of a hotel's income stream to the enterprise activity that was directly attributable to the value of intangible assets (the hotel's workforce, a leasehold interest in the employee parking lot, and an agreement with a golf course operator) and deduct that value prior to assessment. However, the hotel failed to provide substantial evidence that the income method used was invalid for failing to deduct the value of goodwill. (*SHC Half Moon Bay v. County of San Mateo*, Court of Appeal of California, First District, No. A137218, May 22, 2014, CCH CALIFORNIA TAX REPORTS, ¶ 406-138)

Additionally, in any case in which the cost approach method of valuation is used to value special use property, a component for entrepreneurial profit may not be added unless there is market-derived evidence that such profit exists and has not been fully offset by physical deterioration or economic obsolescence. (Sec. 401.6, Rev. & Tax. Code) Assessors must also exclude from income the benefit from federal and state low-income housing tax credits allocated by the California Tax Credit Allocation Committee when they value property under the income method of appraisal. (Sec. 402.95, Rev. & Tax. Code)

Practitioner Comment: Court of Appeal Provides Guidance on the Income Method for Determining The Value of Intangibles Exempt from Property Tax.

In *SHC Half Moon Bay v. Cnty. of San Mateo*, 226 Cal.App.4th 471 (2014) (*SHC*), the Court of Appeal, First District, held that the county assessor impermissibly taxed intangibles when applying the income method of valuation because merely deducting management and franchise fees from the hotel's projected revenue stream did not accurately exclude intangibles from the assessment. Rev. & Tax. sections 110 and 212 exempt intangible assets and rights from property taxation. The California Supreme Court provided guidance in *Elk Hills Power, LLC v. Board of Equalization*, 57 Cal.4th 593, 619 (2013) regarding which intangible assets and rights have "a quantifiable fair market value that must be deducted from an income stream analysis prior to taxation." The court explained that "intangible assets like the goodwill of a business, customer base, and favorable franchise terms or operating contracts all make a direct contribution to the going concern value of the business as reflected in an income stream analysis" and have "a quantifiable fair market value that must be deducted from an income stream analysis prior to taxation."

The *SHC* court rejected the assessor's use of the "Rushmore Approach" because it only allows return of the investment in intangibles, not a return on intangibles. The Rushmore Method allocates a hotel's value among the real, business, and personal property components by deducting management and franchise fees from the hotel's stabilized net income and determines the tangible personal property component by deducting a reserve for replacement and the actual value of the personal property in place. The court explained that only deducting the management and franchise fee paid to the hotel operator from the hotel's projected revenue stream under the income approach did not exclude certain "intangible assets such as the hotel's assembled workforce, the hotel's leasehold interest in the employee parking lot, and the hotel's agreement with the golf course operator." The county's expert conceded that these are often deducted as an intangible value of the hotel, and the county did not explain how the deduction of the management fee captured the majority of the intangible property.

The court, however, deferred to the San Mateo County Assessment Appeals Board's (Board) conclusion that the deduction did "exclude the intangible asset of goodwill" because the Board's conclusion is presumptively valid, and the court could not "conclude substantial evidence did not support the Board's finding on this issue," which is the applicable standard of review. The court did note that "[t]here may be situations where the taxpayer can establish the deduction of a management and franchise fee from a hotel's income stream does not capture the intangible asset of goodwill, but SHC, the taxpayer, has failed to do so here." Id.

On balance the decision is taxpayer favorable, particularly for those in the hospitality industry since it further underscores that intangible assets are not subject to property tax. The decision is also significant in that it rejected the "Rushmore Approach," which was gaining favor as a valuation methodology. Lastly, the decision confirms that taxpayers should be diligent in supporting their goodwill valuation.

Chris Whitney, Contributing Editor

Practitioner Comment: California Supreme Court Provides Guidance on Property Tax Valuation of Emission Reduction Credits (ERCs)

In *Elk Hills Power, LLC v. Board of Equalization*, 57 Cal.4th 593 (2013), the California Supreme Court held that the State Board of Equalization (BOE) was not permitted to include the value of intangible assets and rights in the property tax base. The decision was highly anticipated by practitioners seeking guidance regarding the taxation of intangible rights and property. Elk Hills Power, LLC (Elk Hills), is a Delaware limited liability company that owns and operates an independent electric power plant. Elk Hills purchased "emission reduction credits" (ERCs) necessary to obtain authorization to construct the plant and to operate it at certain air-pollutant emission levels. The parties agreed that the ERCs constituted intangible rights for property taxation purposes. The dispute, however, focused on whether the State Board of Equalization (BOE) improperly taxed the ERCs when it assessed the power plant for property tax purposes.

The court noted that power plants are valued using "unit taxation," which is used to capture the entire real value of the power plant when all of its component parts are considered together as a unit, rather than valuing the component parts in isolation or at scrap value. The BOE used the following two methods of unit valuation to calculate the unitary value of the plant: the replacement cost approach and the income capitalization approach. Under the replacement cost approach, the Board estimated the cost of replacing the assets of the power plant, including the estimated cost of replacing the ERCs when it valued the plant because the Board maintained ERCs are necessary to put the power plant to beneficial use. Under the income capitalization approach, the Board estimated the amount of income the property was expected to yield over its life and determined the present value of that amount. The court stated the questions to be answered were:

(1) whether the Board may include the estimated cost of replacing the ERCs in using the replacement cost method, and

(2) whether the Board was required to attribute a portion of the plant's income stream to the ERCs and deduct that value from the overall income estimate prior to taxation.

The court held that since the ERC was an intangible, it could not be included in the replacement cost computation but that the ERC's contribution to future income from the property was includable in the income based computation. Given that the court agreed that the ERC's indirect contribution to value through the income computation approach could be taken into account, it is unclear how beneficial the court's ruling will be in practice to taxpayers.

Chris Whitney, Contributing Editor

The "assessed value" of property, generally, is the full cash value as modified by Proposition 13. (¶1702) The assessed value may be retroactively reduced when a disaster occurs after the assessment date, and the base-year value of certain property damaged by a disaster may be transferred to replacement property (¶1707).

Special rules are provided for reduced valuation of several categories of property, including the following:

— certain vessels engaged in fishing or research (Sec. 227, Rev. & Tax. Code);

— "enforceably restricted" open-space land (Sec. 8, Art. XIII, Cal. Const.);

— motion pictures (Sec. 988, Rev. & Tax. Code);

— computer software programs (Sec. 995, Rev. & Tax. Code); and

— business or professional records (Sec. 997, Rev. & Tax. Code).

Effective for fiscal years 2005-2006 through 2016-2017, the value of certificated aircraft is based on the lesser of (1) the historical cost basis, or (2) prices listed in the Airliner Price Guide. (Sec. 401.17, Rev. & Tax. Code)

Practitioner Comment: Proposition 13 "Change in Ownership" Planning and Potential Legislative Response.

In *Ocean Avenue LLC v. County of Los Angeles*, 227 Cal.App.4th 344 (2d Dist. 2014) the California Court of Appeal for the Second Appellate District held in an unpublished decision that sales of interests in an entity, which owned the Fairmont Miramar Hotel in Santa Monica, to multiple, albeit related, buyers did not constitute a Proposition 13 change of ownership because no single person acquired more than 50% ownership even though 100% of the ownership interests in the entity owning the real property changed hands.

Under Proposition 13 the appraised value of real property for real property tax purposes is reassessed when real property is purchased, newly constructed, or when a change in ownership has occurred. Under existing property tax law, a "change in ownership" occurs if a legal entity or other person obtains a controlling or majority ownership interest in the legal entity. Since one individual did not acquire more than 50% ownership of Ocean Avenue LLC, the court concluded there was not a "change in ownership" that would trigger a property value reassessment.

The California Legislature repeatedly has proposed legislation to expand the circumstances under which a "change in ownership" is deemed to have occurred. For example, in the 2015 legislative session, both S.B. 259 and A.B. 1040 were introduced. These bills are substantially similar to A.B. 2372, which was introduced in the prior year and died in committee; A.B. 188, which was introduced two years before that and also died in committee; and other legislation dating back to 2010.

The S.B. 259 proposal is that a "change of ownership" in real property held by a legal entity would occur if, on or after January 1, 2015, 90% or more of the direct or indirect ownership interests in a legal entity are cumulatively transferred in one or more transactions, whether or not any one legal entity or person acquires control of the ownership interests. A.B. 1040 has not yet specified the percentage requirement.

Therefore, it is clear that the Legislature is concerned that taxpayers may rely on the *Ocean Avenue LLC* decision in attempting to plan around reassessments. Both the decision and the proposed legislation are also a reminder that large increases in property tax liabilities may result when ownership of legal entities which hold California real estate changes hands. Such property tax increases can have an adverse impact on those who are not a direct party to the underlying transaction, such as lessees under so called "triple net leases," under which property tax and other liabilities of the lessor are passed through to the lessee. Lessees may consider negotiating for contractual provisions in triple net leases to protect them from potentially significant increases in lease payments that may result from unanticipated reassessments under Proposition 13.

Chris Whitney, Contributing Editor

A 2007 amendment of a California property tax Rule 474 which provided that petroleum refinery land, improvements, and fixtures had to be valued as a unit—unlike most industrial property—was not inconsistent with constitutional and statutory provisions, but it was procedurally invalid, according to the California Supreme Court. The State Board of Equalization (BOE), in amending the rule, failed to provide an adequate assessment of the rule's economic impact, as required by the Administrative Procedures Act (APA). (*Western States Petroleum Assn. v. Board of Equalization*, California Supreme Court, S400475, August 5, 2013, CCH CALIFORNIA TAX REPORTS, ¶405-913) The rule was repealed in 2013. However, the rule was readopted in 2015 without substantive change. (*Letter to County Assessors, No. 2015/038*, California State Board of Equalization, August 14, 2015)

In *Auerbach v. Assessment Appeals Board No. 2 for the County of Los Angeles* (2008) (CCH CALIFORNIA TAX REPORTS, ¶404-780), a California court of appeal held that a property tax assessment on a business jet aircraft improperly included a theoretical sales tax on the value of the aircraft as an element of value, where the aircraft owner was eligible for a common carrier exemption from sales or use tax on the lien date.

Although Article XIIIA of the Constitution (Proposition 13) refers only to real property, the 1% rate limitation also applies to personal property. (Sec. 2, Art. XIII, Cal. Const.)

The law provides that personal property shall be treated as "secured" only if located upon real property of the same owner as of the lien date. Personal property not so located may be treated as "secured" under certain conditions. (Sec. 607, Rev. & Tax. Code; Sec. 608, Rev. & Tax. Code; Sec. 609, Rev. & Tax. Code) In order for such property to be treated as "secured" where it is not located upon real property of the same owner, the property must be located in the same county and the taxpayer must record a certificate from the assessor to the effect that the real property is sufficient to secure the payment of the tax.

¶1707 Assessment Procedure and Equalization

Law: Secs. 15, 16, 19, Art. XIII, Cal. Const.; Secs. 1, 2, Art. XIII A; Sec. 51040, Govt. Code; Secs. 51, 61-75.80, 90, 119, 170, 401-05, 441-60, 469, 480, 482, 495, 532, 721-59, 1601-45.5, 2192, 4986, 4986.2, Rev. & Tax. Code; Rules 2, 462.020, 462.180, 462.240, 18 CCR (CCH CALIFORNIA TAX REPORTS, ¶ 20-010, 20-070, 20-105, 20-405, 20-605, 20-610, 20-665, 20-710, 20-715).

California property assessment falls generally within the purview of the counties. The State Board of Equalization (BOE) assesses certain utility and other properties used owned or used by regulated railway, telegraph, or telephone companies, but the counties levy and collect the taxes on that property. In addition, the BOE performs assessment, appraisal, and collection functions for private railroad cars.

The counties are governed in their assessment responsibilities by state law. The BOE exercises oversight on county assessments through its assessment survey program and pomulgation of property tax regulations.

•*Lien date*

Property is assessed annually on its full cash value as of 12:01 a.m. on the first day of January. (Sec. 401.3, Rev. & Tax. Code; Sec. 405, Rev. & Tax. Code; Sec. 404, Rev. & Tax. Code; Sec. 2192, Rev. & Tax. Code)

•*Board of Supervisors*

The board of supervisors of each county acts as a board of equalization to equalize valuations of the county assessor. (Sec. 1601, Rev. & Tax. Code; Sec. 16, Art. XIII, Cal. Const.; Sec. 119, Rev. & Tax. Code; Sec. 1610.8, Rev. & Tax. Code) Boards of supervisors of certain counties may create assessment appeals boards to handle their equalization duties. (Sec. 16, Art. XIII, Cal. Const.; Sec. 1620, Rev. & Tax. Code) With the exception of state-assessed property, property owners may appear before the county board of equalization or assessment appeals board to protest their assessments (¶1709). The State Board of Equalization (BOE) reviews the valuation of a public utility's state-assessed property where a petition for reassessment has been made. (Sec. 741, Rev. & Tax. Code)

The law authorizes the board of supervisors of any county to provide by ordinance for the reassessment of property damaged or destroyed by a "misfortune or calamity" such as earthquake, fire, flood, or landslide. (Sec. 51, Rev. & Tax. Code; Sec. 15, Art. XIII, Cal. Const.)

The BOE assesses property, as of 12:01 a.m. on the first day of January, of certain classes of public utilities and other inter-county property, even though the property is taxed by local jurisdictions. (Sec. 19, Art. XIII, Cal. Const.) However, land and rights-of-way through which intercounty pipelines run are subject to assessment by county assessors. (Sec. 401.8, Rev. & Tax. Code)

- *Escape assessments*

The period within which an escape assessment for willful tax evasion can be made is eight years from July 1 of the assessment year in which the property escaped assessment or was underassessed. Other escape assessments generally must be made within four years after July 1 of the assessment year in which the property escaped assessment or was underassessed. However, if the escape assessment results from a failure to file a change of ownership statement or a preliminary change in ownership report, an escape assessment may be issued within eight years from July 1 of the year the property escaped assessment or was underassessed. If the escape assessment or underassessment was the result of a taxpayer's fraudulent activities or the result of the taxpayer's failure to file a statement of change of ownership or control of a corporation, partnership, or other legal entity, then an escape assessment may be made at any time for any year in which the property escaped taxation or was underassessed. (Sec. 532, Rev. & Tax. Code)

- *Cancellation of erroneous assessments*

Erroneous property tax assessments paid after the four-year statute of limitations for correction of assessments has elapsed may be canceled by the county auditor if the cancellation is initiated within 120 days of the payment of those erroneous assessments. (Sec. 4986, Rev. & Tax. Code; Sec. 4986.2, Rev. & Tax. Code)

- *Urban agriculture incentive zones*

California counties or cities and counties can establish by ordinance urban agriculture incentive zones that, among other things, will be subject to favorable property tax assessment provisions. An "urban agriculture incentive zone" is an area within a county or city and county that is comprised of individual properties designated as urban agriculture preserves for farming purposes. Following adoption of an ordinance, the county or city and county may enter into contracts with landowners to enforceably restrict the use of the land subject to the contract to uses consistent with urban agriculture. No new contracts can be entered into and no existing contract can be renewed after January 1, 2019. However, any contract entered into before that date will be valid and enforceable for the duration of the contract. (Sec. 51040, et seq., Govt. Code)

- *Transfers of base-year value*

Under certain circumstances, homeowners may be permitted to transfer the adjusted base-year value of their residences to similar properties within the county or even in other counties. These circumstances concern seniors and disabled persons, contaminated property, and damaged and destroyed property.

Although taxpayers generally must file applications for base-year value transfer within three years after the purchase or construction of the replacement property, assessors are required to consider certain transfer applications filed after expiration of the three-year period. (Sec. 69.5(f), Rev. & Tax. Code)

Seniors and disabled persons.—Homeowners who are either over the age of 55 or severely and permanently disabled may transfer the adjusted base-year value of their original residence (including an interest in a resident-owned mobilehome park) to a replacement residence (including an interest in a resident-owned mobilehome park) of equal or lesser fair market value in the same county, provided that, among other things, the purchase of the replacement principal residence is within two years of the sale of the original home. (Sec. 69.5, Rev. & Tax. Code) According to a California court of appeal, a transfer of a residence's base year value to partial interest in another property does not qualify for relief. (See *Bennion v. County of Santa Clara* (2007), CCH CALIFORNIA TAX REPORTS, ¶ 404-445)

Property tax relief also is available for moves between counties if the county where the replacement home is located has adopted an ordinance permitting the valuation transfer. (Sec. 69.5, Rev. & Tax. Code; Sec. 2, Art. XIII A, Cal. Const.) As of

September 2016, 11 California counties had property tax ordinances implementing the intercounty base year value transfer provisions for persons who are at least age 55 or are severely and permanently disabled. The counties are Alameda, El Dorado, Los Angeles, Orange, Riverside, San Bernardino, San Diego, San Mateo, Santa Clara, Tuolumne, and Ventura. (*Letter to County Assessors, No. 2016/034*, California State Board of Equalization, September 15, 2016, CCH CALIFORNIA TAX REPORTS, ¶ 406-562)

Generally, the carryover of a residence's base-year value by a person over the age of 55 or a severely and permanently disabled person is available only once. However, a person over the age of 55 who previously transferred the base-year value of a former residence to a replacement residence may utilize the base-year value transfer provisions a second time if the person subsequently becomes severely and permanently disabled. Taxpayers over the age of 55 or disabled are also allowed a base year value transfer if they would otherwise have been eligible for a base year value transfer, except for the fact that their residence was substantially damaged or destroyed by misfortune or calamity and, therefore, the value of their replacement residence exceeds the value of their original residence in its damaged condition.

Contaminated property.—An owner of qualified contaminated property may transfer the base year value of that property to replacement property located within the same county or within a different county if the other county authorizes such transfers. Alternatively, an owner of qualified property may rebuild a structure substantially destroyed or damaged by environmental remediation on qualified contaminated property without incurring a property tax reassessment for new construction. (Sec. 69.4, Rev. & Tax. Code)

The repaired or replacement structure must be similar in size, utility, and function to the original structure. To qualify for the base-year value transfer or the exemption from new construction reassessment, the fair market value of the replacement property must be equal to or less than the fair market value of the qualified contaminated property if that property were not contaminated. Additionally, the replacement property must be acquired or newly constructed within five years after ownership of the qualified contaminated property is sold or otherwise transferred. "Equal or lesser value" means the amount of the full cash value of the original property increased by 5% for each year during the five-year period in which replacement property may be purchased or constructed. To the extent that replacement property, or any portion thereof, is not similar in function, size, and utility, the property, or portion thereof, that is dissimilar will be reassessed and a new base year value assigned. (Sec. 69.4, Rev. & Tax. Code)

Damaged or destroyed property.—The base-year value of property damaged or destroyed in an area declared a disaster by the Governor may be transferred to comparable replacement property acquired or constructed within the same county or to comparable replacement property in a different county, provided the replacement property is a replacement principal residence located in a county whose board of supervisors has authorized such a transfer prior to the taxpayer's relocation. (Sec. 2, Art. XIIIA, Cal Const.; Sec. 69, Rev. & Tax. Code; Sec. 69.3, Rev. & Tax. Code) As of August 2014, there are 10 counties implementing the disaster intercounty base-year valuation transfer provision: Contra Costa, Los Angeles, Modoc, Orange, San Francisco, Santa Clara, Solano, Sonoma, Sutter, and Ventura. (*Letter to County Assessors, No. 2014/040*, California State Board of Equalization, August 28, 2014, CCH CALIFORNIA TAX REPORTS, ¶ 405-935)

The time period during which a base-year value transfer may be made for property damaged or destroyed by a disaster is:

> — five years from the date of the disaster for intracounty transfers and

> — three years from the date the replacement property is purchased or constructed for intercounty transfers.

(Sec. 69(a), Rev. & Tax. Code; Sec. 69.3, Rev. & Tax. Code)

¶1707

• *Revaluation*

Revaluation of property is required under certain circumstances: when there is new construction, a change of ownership, or property is damaged.

New construction.—New construction requiring revaluation includes site development of land, improvements erected on land, additions to existing improvements, and new fixtures (*e.g.*, store fixtures, machinery) that relate directly to the function of the structure. The value of new construction, including construction in progress, is added to the base-year value. (Sec. 69.4, Rev. & Tax. Code)

In 2010, California voters passed a constitutional proposal that, among other things, eliminated a 15-year limitation on the exclusion for unreinforced masonry buildings and provided an exclusion that parallels the exclusion that applies to other types of construction or reconstruction of seismic retrofitting components. Legislative intent, as expressed in statutes enacted in relation to the constitutional amendments, declared that anyone receiving a 15-year exclusion as of the operative date of the statute would continue to receive the exclusion after the 15-year period expired. (Sec. 2, Art. XIII A, Cal. Const.; Sec. 74.5(e), Rev. & Tax. Code)

In 2014, the California State Board of Equalization (BOE) adopted and authorized publication of Assessors' Handbook Section 410, *Assessment of Newly Constructed Property*. This section of the Handbook discusses the statutes, regulations, and various statutory exclusions that pertain to newly constructed real property.

Change of ownership.—The law provides detailed definitions of what constitutes a change of ownership that will trigger a revaluation of real property. The following is a very brief summary of transactions that are not considered to be changes of ownership:

— interspousal transfers, including those made in divorce settlements. Sale of an undivided interest results in a revaluation of the portion transferred; however, there is no revaluation if the interest transferred is less than 5% and its value is under $10,000; (Sec. 2, Art. XIIIA, Cal. Const.; Sec. 63, Rev. & Tax. Code; Reg. 462.020, 18 CCR)

— registered domestic partner transfers beginning on lien date 2006-2007 fiscal year; (Sec. 62(p), Rev. & Tax. Code)

— transfers of partnership interests, or addition or deletion of partners, unless a controlling interest is acquired; (Sec. 64, Rev. & Tax. Code; Reg. 462.180, 18 CCR)

— transfers of property among members of an affiliated group of corporations, as specifically defined; (Sec. 64, Rev. & Tax. Code)

— a transfer into a trust, if the transferor is the beneficiary or the trust is revocable; (Sec. 62(d), Rev. & Tax. Code)

— transfers of joint tenancies that do not result in changes of beneficial ownership; (Sec. 62(f), Rev. & Tax. Code)

— acquisition of property as a replacement for property that was condemned (however, where the value of the property acquired exceeds the value of the property replaced by more than 20%, the excess is revalued and added to the base-year value of the replaced property); (Sec. 63.1, Rev. & Tax. Code; Sec. 68, Rev. & Tax. Code; Sec. 1, Art. XIII A, Cal. Const.)

¶1707

— Certain transfers of residences to children (including foster children) or wards upon death of parents or guardians. To qualify, the children or wards must have (1) been disabled for at least five years prior to the transfer, (2) lived in the property at least five years, and (3) family income of $20,000 or less;. (Sec. 62(n), Rev. & Tax. Code; Reg. 462.240, 18 CCR)

— Transfers of the principal residence and up to $1 million in other property between parents and their children (including foster children) or between grandparents and their grandchildren when the parents of the children who are the blood relative of the grandparent(s) are deceased. The exclusion applies to transfers of units or lots within a cooperative housing corporation, but not to certain transfers from foster children to their biological parents; (Sec. 2, Art. XIIIA, Cal. Const.; Sec. 63.1, Rev. & Tax. Code; Reg. 462.240, 18 CCR)

— certain transfers of mobilehome parks to nonprofit entities. This also applies to transfers of rental spaces to tenants under certain conditions; (Sec. 62.1, Rev. & Tax. Code; Reg. 462.240, 18 CCR)

— acquisition by an employee benefit plan of indirect or direct control of the employer corporation; (Sec. 66, Rev. & Tax. Code; Reg. 462.240, 18 CCR)

— newly created possessory interests established by month-to-month agreements in publicly owned real property that have a full cash value of $50,000 or less; (Sec. 75.5, Rev. & Tax. Code)

— transfer of separate property inherited by a surviving domestic partner by intestate succession upon the death of a registered domestic partner; (Reg. 462.240(k), 18 CCR)

— recordation of a certificate of sale, relating to property sold subject to the right of redemption, for the period in which the right of redemption exists; (Sec. 62.11, Rev. & Tax. Code)

— qualifying transfers of a floating home marina to an entity formed by the tenants of the marina for the purpose of purchasing the marina; (Sec. 62.5, Rev. & Tax. Code) and

— transfers between cotenants effective upon the death of the transferor cotenant. (Sec. 62.3, Rev. & Tax. Code)

New owners are required to notify the assessor of a change of ownership and may be penalized for failure to do so. (Sec. 90, Rev. & Tax. Code; Sec. 480, Rev. & Tax. Code; Sec. 482, Rev. & Tax. Code)

A transferee of real property or a mobile home that is locally assessed has 90 days to file a change in ownership statement when a change in ownership occurs or if requested to do so by the local assessor. The penalty cap for nonwillful failures to file a statement is $5,000 or $20,000 if the property is not eligible for the homestead exemption. Statements sent by mail are deemed to be filed with the assessor on either the date of postmark affixed by the U.S. Postal Service or the date certified by a bona fide private courier service on the envelope containing the statement. (Sec. 482, Rev. & Tax. Code)

Corporations, partnerships, limited liability companies, or other legal entities must file a change in ownership statement within 90 days from the earlier of the date of:

(1) the change in control or ownership or

(2) a written request from the State Board of Equalization (BOE).

A required penalty for failure to file the statement can be abated by the county board of equalization or assessment appeals board if the failure was not willful. If the BOE

¶1707

mails a request to file a complete change in ownership statement to a person or legal entity based on specified erroneous information and qualifying notification of the error is made within 60 days, the penalty must be abated. (Sec. 482, Rev. & Tax. Code)

Practice Note: Life Estate Conveyance Constitutes Reassessable Change of Ownership

The California Supreme Court reversed a court of appeals decision and held that a taxpayer's acquisition of a life estate in real property upon the death of her sister constituted a change of ownership so as to trigger a property tax reassessment. During the trustee's life, she was the sole present beneficiary of the trust as to which she held the power to revoke. During her life, the trustee continued to hold the entire equitable estate personally and effectively retained full ownership of the residence, and any interest the sibling had in the residence under the terms of the trust was merely potential and could have evaporated in a moment at the trustee's whim. Upon the trustee's death, the entire equitable estate in the residence was transferred as a life estate to the sibling (with remainder interests to other siblings). In other words, upon the trustee's death, real ownership of the residence, which follows the equitable estate, transferred from the trustee to the sibling, thus constituting a change in ownership. (*Steinhart v. County of Los Angeles* (2010), CCH CALIFORNIA TAX REPORTS, ¶ 405-105)

A transfer of a floating home marina to an entity formed by the tenants of the marina for the purpose of purchasing the marina does not constitute a change in ownership requiring reassessment of the property, subject to one condition. Specifically, there will be no change in ownership provided that the tenants who were renting at least 51% of the berths in the marina prior to the transfer participate in the transaction through the ownership of an aggregate of at least 51% of the voting stock or other ownership interest in the entity that acquires the marina. (Sec. 62.5, Rev. & Tax Code)

Some real property transfers between cotenants effective upon the death of the transferor cotenant do not constitute a change in ownership that requires reassessment of the property at full cash value. Among other requirements, the cotenants must together own 100% of the property together either as joint tenants or as tenants in common and, following the transfer, the surviving cotenant must hold a 100% interest in the property. (Sec. 62.3, Rev. & Tax. Code)

Damaged property.—Detailed rules are provided for reduction in the assessed valuation where property is damaged or destroyed by a "misfortune or calamity." County boards of supervisors may enact an ordinance allowing taxpayers to apply for reassessment of any taxable property that has been damaged or destroyed by a misfortune or calamity through no fault of their own. (Sec. 170, Rev. & Tax. Code)

If an ordinance is adopted, a local assessor must determine separately the full cash value of the land, improvements, and personalty immediately before and after the damage. The assessor must separately determine the percentage reduction in value for each element of the property if the total decrease in value exceeds $10,000.

An ordinance may also allow assessor-initiated reductions in the assessed value of property when the assessor determines the property has been damaged or destroyed by a major misfortune or calamity within the preceding 12 months. After reassessment, taxes remaining due for the assessment year may be prorated, and any excess paid before the reassessment may be refunded.

If real property is damaged or destroyed by disaster, misfortune, or calamity and no ordinance providing for reassessment of the property has been adopted by the county board of supervisors, or if the taxpayer has voluntarily removed real property from land, the taxable value of the property is the sum of:

    (1) the adjusted base year value or full cash value of the land, whichever is less, and

(2) the adjusted base year value or full cash value of the improvements, whichever is less.

(Sec. 51, Rev. & Tax. Code)

Damaged or destroyed property is reassessed at current market value but retains its old base-year value if that value is lower than the reassessed value, notwithstanding the transfer of the base-year value to replacement property. Restoration or repair of the property is considered to be new construction, triggering a reassessment at that time.

In counties that have adopted an ordinance that allows assessees whose property was damaged or destroyed to apply for reassessment of the property, the assessees must file an application for reassessment within 12 months of the damage to the property. (Sec. 170, Rev. & Tax. Code)

• *Constitutionality of acquisition value assessment*

In *Nordlinger v. Hahn* (1992) (CCH CALIFORNIA TAX REPORTS, ¶402-336), the U.S. Supreme Court concluded that the acquisition value assessment method mandated by Proposition 13 does not violate the principles of the Equal Protection Clause of the Fourteenth Amendment, even though the method may result in significant assessment disparities between similar properties acquired at different times. The same conclusion was reached by a California court of appeal in *R.H. Macy v. Contra Costa County* (1990) (CCH CALIFORNIA TAX REPORTS, ¶401-862), which involved commercial property. The taxpayer's commercial premises, which were acquired before Proposition 13 was adopted, were held to have been properly assessed at full value (*i.e.*, market price) for the 1987 tax year, when the taxpayer underwent a corporate reorganization that constituted a change of ownership triggering reassessment under Proposition 13.

• *Purchase price as value*

Reg. 2, 18 CCR, provides that the value of property for revaluation purposes in the case of a change of ownership is the purchase price paid unless there is substantial and convincing evidence that the property would not have transferred for such price in an open market transaction.

• *Effective date of revaluation*

The annual lien date and valuation date for locally assessed property taxes is January 1; this date applies to taxes for the fiscal year beginning on the following July 1. (Sec. 401.3, Rev. & Tax. Code; Sec. 405, Rev. & Tax. Code; Sec. 404, Rev. & Tax. Code; Sec. 2192, Rev. & Tax. Code)

New construction or change of ownership will result in revaluation in the following month and a consequent increase in tax liability. Thus, new construction or change of ownership in July increases taxes for the fiscal year beginning in July by $^{11}/_{12}$ths of a full year's tax attributable to the increased valuation. A change in August increases the current tax by $^{10}/_{12}$ths of the tax for a full year, and so on through the fiscal year. (Sec. 75.11, Rev. & Tax. Code)

New construction or a change of ownership occurring on or after the lien date but on or before May 31 results in an increase in taxes both for the current fiscal year and for the following fiscal year. If new construction or a change of ownership occurs on or after June 1 and on or before the next lien date, the assessor will need to determine only one supplemental assessment. (Sec. 75.11, Rev. & Tax. Code)

New construction is exempt from the supplemental assessment explained above until certain events occur (sale, rental, occupancy), provided the owner gives the assessor prescribed notice and requests exemption within specified time limits. (Sec. 75.12, Rev. & Tax. Code)

• *Personal property statement*

Each taxpayer must file a personal property statement with the county assessor during any year the aggregate cost of his or her taxable personal property is $100,000 or more. Others must file a statement if requested by the assessor. The statement must include a description of all taxable property owned, claimed, possessed, controlled or managed by the individual, firm, or corporation involved. (Sec. 441, Rev. & Tax. Code; Sec. 442, Rev. & Tax. Code; Sec. 445, Rev. & Tax. Code)

The State Board of Equalization (BOE) prescribes the forms to be used for filing property statements. (Sec. 452, Rev. & Tax. Code) A taxpayer may furnish the required information as either

(1) an attachment to the property statement;

(2) an authenticated electronically filed property statement; or

(3) a property statement substantially similar to the property statement printed by the assessor that is signed by the taxpayer.

However, the attachment must be in a format specified by the assessor, and one copy of the printed property statement must be executed by the taxpayer and carry appropriate reference to the attached data. (Sec. 441.5(a), Rev. & Tax. Code) The California State Board of Equalization (BOE) has released a listing of property tax forms available for use by county assessors' offices and local appeals boards and for use by BOE staff in the implementation of various property tax programs co-administered by the BOE and county assessors. There are over 90 forms available in a PDF fillable format and 20 forms available in both PDF fillable and, for individuals with sight impairments, ADA-compliant formats. (*Letter to County Assessors, No. 2013/053*, California State Board of Equalization, November 8, 2013, CALIFORNIA TAX REPORTS, ¶ 405-984)

• *Audits*

County assessors must annually conduct a significant number of audits of the books and records of non-exempt business taxpayers with taxable property in the county. A significant number of audits means at least 75% of the fiscal year average of the total number of audits the assessor was required to conduct during the period from fiscal year 2002-2003 through fiscal year 2005-2006. Under the new process, 50% of the audits required annually must be performed on taxpayers selected from a pool of those taxpayers that have the largest assessments of trade fixtures and business tangible personal property in the county. Each taxpayer in the pool must be audited at least once every four years. The selection of businesses for the other 50% of audits performed annually must be conducted in a fair and equitable manner and may be based on evidence of underreporting. (Sec. 469, Rev. & Tax. Code)

In 2015, the California State Board of Equalization (BOE) adopted and authorized publication of Assessors' Handbook Section 506 (AH 506), *Property Tax Audits and Audit Program*. The new handbook section, which is posted on the BOE website at https://www.boe.ca.gov/proptaxes/ahcont.htm, was developed to provide guidance in developing and improving property tax audits and audit programs in county assessors' offices, according to the BOE.

¶1708 Returns and Payment

Law: Secs. 75.52, 194-4.9, 441-60, 480.8, 2512, 2605-19, 2701-05.5, 2901, 2922, Rev. & Tax. Code (CCH CALIFORNIA TAX REPORTS, ¶ 20-756).

Taxpayers may be required to file annually with the county assessor a written statement of property owned, claimed, possessed, or controlled. (Sec. 442, Rev. & Tax. Code; Sec. 445, Rev. & Tax. Code) The statement must be filed between January 1 and April 1. (Sec. 441, Rev. & Tax. Code) In cases where the cities do their own assessing, a separate statement should be filed with the city.

Owners of a cooperative housing corporation, community apartment project, condominium, planned unit development, or other residential subdivision complex with common areas and facilities in which units or lots are transferred without the use of recorded deeds might be required to file an ownership report with the local assessor by the next February 1 following the local assessor's request. If a report is not filed, the assessor will send a change in ownership statement to every occupant of each individual unit or lot with instructions for any occupant who does not have an ownership interest in the unit or lot to forward the statement to the owner or shareholder of the property. Failure to file the statement could result in penalties of up to $5,000 if the property is eligible for the homeowners' exemption or $20,000 if it is not. (Sec. 480.8, Rev. & Tax. Code)

As noted at ¶1704, owners of certain classes of exempt property must file an annual return or affidavit claiming the exemption.

A county tax collector must consolidate all of a requesting taxpayer's property tax obligations into a single tax bill. Consolidated property tax bills may be obtained only in counties in which an authorizing memorandum is recorded with the county recorder and only with respect to property listed on the secured property tax roll. (Sec. 2611.7, Rev. & Tax. Code)

Except in a few cities, the following property taxes are payable:

— **on real property:** first installment (one-half) due and payable November 1 and delinquent after December 10; second installment due and payable February 1 and delinquent after April 10.

— **on personal property:** if secured by real estate, payable (in full) with the *first* installment of real estate tax, by December 10; if unsecured, due on first day of January, delinquent after July 1, and subject to 10% penalty after August 31.

(Sec. 2605, Rev. & Tax. Code; Sec. 2606, Rev. & Tax. Code; Sec. 2617, Rev. & Tax. Code; Sec. 2618, Rev. & Tax. Code; Sec. 2701, Rev. & Tax. Code; Sec. 2702, Rev. & Tax. Code; Sec. 2704, Rev. & Tax. Code; Sec. 2705, Rev. & Tax. Code; Sec. 2901, Rev. & Tax. Code; Sec. 2922, Rev. & Tax. Code)

If the delinquency date falls on Saturday, Sunday, or a holiday, the taxes do not become delinquent until 5 p.m. or the close of business, whichever is later, on the next business day. (Sec. 2619, Rev. & Tax. Code; Sec. 2705.5, Rev. & Tax. Code) If a county board of supervisors, by adoption of an ordinance or resolution, closes the county's offices for business prior to the time of delinquency on the "next business day" or for a whole day, that day will be considered a legal holiday for purposes of establishing the delinquency date.

A few cities that do their own assessing do not use the payment dates shown above; there is no uniformity in the dates used in such cases.

A remittance made using an electronic payment option such as wire transfer, telephone credit card, or the Internet is deemed received on the date that the taxpayer completes the transaction, but only if the payment is made through the tax collector's authorized Web site or telephone number. The taxpayer must provide proof of the date of the completed transaction in the form of a confirmation number or other convincing evidence. This provision does not apply to payments made by electronic fund transfer. (Sec. 2512, Rev. & Tax. Code)

An owner of property that has sustained substantial damage as the result of a disaster in a county declared by the Governor to be in a state of disaster may apply for deferral of the first post-disaster installment of regular secured property taxes. Real property is considered substantially damaged if the damage amounts to the lesser of 10% of its fair market value or $10,000. Other property qualifies if the damage equals at least 20% of its fair market value immediately preceding the disaster causing the damage. A claim for reassessment of the disaster-damaged property must be filed, or the property must have been otherwise reassessed, in conjunction with any such application for deferral. Taxpayers that were participating in an installment payment agreement prior to the disaster may qualify to defer tax payments for one year. (Sec. 194, Rev. & Tax. Code; Sec. 194.1, Rev. & Tax. Code)

- *Payment on supplemental assessments*

Where supplemental assessments are made in cases of new construction or changes of ownership, as explained at ¶1702, a supplemental tax bill is mailed by the tax collector. The additional tax is due on the date the bill is mailed, but may be paid in two installments that become delinquent according to the month in which the bill is mailed. If the bill is mailed in the period July-October, the delinquency dates are as follows:

— first installment, December 10;

— second installment, April 10.

If the bill is mailed in the period November-June, the delinquency dates are as follows:

— first installment, last day of month following the month the bill is mailed;

— second installment, last day of the fourth calendar month following the date the first installment is delinquent. (Sec. 75.52, Rev. & Tax. Code)

¶1709 Appeals

Law: Secs. 75.31, 170, 1603, 1604, 1605, 1641.1, 5141, 5148, Rev. & Tax. Code (CCH CALIFORNIA TAX REPORTS, ¶ 20-720, 20-206).

Taxpayers wanting a reduction in assessment must file a timely written application with the county board of supervisors meeting as a county board of equalization or an assessment appeals board. Counties may also authorize the use of electronic applications. (Sec. 1603, Rev. & Tax. Code)

The filing of an appeal does not excuse a taxpayer from making timely payments. Failure to do so will result in the imposition of penalties and interest charges, regardless of the outcome of the appeal (¶1711).

The assessment reduction application must generally be filed between July 2 and September 15 in order to be timely. However, if a taxpayer does not receive a notice of assessment at least 15 calendar days prior to the deadline for filing an application for an assessment reduction, such application may be filed within 60 days of the receipt of the notice of assessment or within 60 days of the mailing of the tax bill, whichever is earlier. Furthermore, the application may be filed within 12 months following the month in which the assessee is notified of an assessment if the assessee and the assessor stipulate that there is an error in the assessment. Purchasers of real property acquired after the lien date and before the first day of the fiscal year may file for reduction by November 15. (Sec. 1603, Rev. & Tax. Code)

Practice Note: Multiple Years

An application must be filed for each year a residential assessment is contested, even if an identical appeal is still pending for a prior year (*Publication 30*, California State Board of Equalization).

An application appealing a supplemental or escape assessment must be filed within 60 days of the later of the date printed on the notice, the tax bill, or the postmark date. (Sec. 75.31, Rev. & Tax. Code)

Counties may allow a reduction application to be filed within 60 days of the mailing of the notice of the assessor's response to a request for reassessment due to a decline in value, provided the following conditions are met:

— the reassessment request was submitted to the assessor in writing on a completed form prescribed by the State Board of Equalization;

— the reassessment request was made on or before the preceding March 15;

— the assessor's response was mailed after August 31;

— the assessor did not reduce the assessment in the full amount requested;

— the assessment reduction application is filed by December 31 of the year in which the reassessment request was filed; and

— the assessment reduction application is accompanied by a copy of the assessor's response.

(Sec. 1603, Rev. & Tax. Code)

A county assessment appeals board must hear and decide a taxpayer's application for reduction of an assessment within two years of the application. If the appeals board fails to act within two years, the taxpayer's opinion of value becomes the assessed value, both for the year listed in the application and for subsequent years until the board makes a final determination on the application. The two-year limitation period may be extended if the taxpayer and the county assessment appeals board agree in writing to extend the time for the hearing or if the application is consolidated for hearing with another application for which an extension of time has been granted. The taxpayer's opinion of market value will not prevail if the taxpayer has failed to provide full and complete information as required by law or when litigation is pending directly relating to the issues involved in the application. (Sec. 1604, Rev. & Tax. Code)

Certain county boards of supervisors may adopt a resolution providing that an assessment hearing officer's decision constitutes the county board of equalization's or county assessment appeals board's decision. (Sec. 1641.1, Rev. & Tax. Code)

An appeal of a reassessment resulting from a disaster or calamity must be filed within six months of the date that the reassessment notice was mailed. (Sec. 170(c), Rev. & Tax. Code)

Special rules apply to state-assessed property.

• *Judicial appeals*

Generally, a civil action for a refund of an improper property tax payment may not be brought unless the taxpayer has filed a timely application for reduction of assessment with the county board of equalization or assessment appeals board, paid the tax (including penalties), and then filed a claim for tax refund. (Sec. 1605, Rev. & Tax. Code) However, prior administrative review has not been required under the following circumstances:

— the facts are undisputed and the property is tax exempt;

— the property is nonexistent;

— the property is outside the taxing jurisdiction;

— the taxpayer does not own the property;

— the assessment is void for failure to follow statutory procedures;

— the questions are solely those of law; or

— there is a correction of deficiencies in assessment procedures rather than individual parcel assessments.

The prior filing of a refund claim is not required with respect to refunds of state assessed taxes. (Sec. 5148, Rev. & Tax. Code)

Refund suits may be brought within six months of the date the refund claim is rejected. If a claim is not acted upon by the authorities within six months, the taxpayer may consider the claim disallowed and file suit. In that case, a taxpayer has four years from the expiration of the six months to commence a suit for refund (*Geneva Towers Limited Partnership v. City and County of San Francisco* (2000) (CCH CALIFORNIA TAX REPORTS, ¶ 403-094)). If the taxpayer designates an application for a reduction of assessment to be a claim for refund, the refund claim is deemed denied on the date the equalization board makes its final decision on the application or on the date the final installment of taxes becomes delinquent, whichever is later. (Sec. 5141, Rev. & Tax. Code)

¶1710 Collections

Law: Sec. 30, Art. XIII, Cal. Const.; Secs. 75.53, 2187, 2191.3-91.6, 2192, 2195, 2951, 3003, 3101-03, 3351, 3353, 3361, 3436, 3438, 3691, 3694, 4104, 4511, Rev. & Tax. Code (CCH CALIFORNIA TAX REPORTS, ¶ 20-756, ¶ 20-758, ¶ 20-760).

All property taxes, except for the tax on railway car companies, are collected by the county tax collector. Unpaid taxes on real property, penalties, and interest automatically become a lien on the property as of January 1 each year. (Sec. 2187, Rev. & Tax. Code; Sec. 2192, Rev. & Tax. Code) After 30 years, unless released sooner, the lien expires and the tax is conclusively presumed to have been paid. (Sec. 30, Art. XIII, Cal. Const.; Sec. 2195, Rev. & Tax. Code)

When a taxpayer defaults in paying property taxes, the property is designated "tax-defaulted" property at the end of the fiscal year as a preliminary step in the actual enforcement of the tax lien against the land. (Sec. 3351, Rev. & Tax. Code; Sec. 75.53, Rev. & Tax. Code; Sec. 3438, Rev. & Tax. Code; Sec. 3353, Rev. & Tax. Code; Sec. 3436, Rev. & Tax. Code) The tax collector may sell tax certificates giving the certificate holder the right to receive the delinquent taxes, assessments, and penalties collected in connection with certain tax-defaulted property. (Sec. 4511, Rev. & Tax. Code)

The declaration of default by the tax collector starts the running of the five-year period (three years for nonresidential commercial property and specified non-owner occupied residential property) during which the taxpayer may redeem the property by payment of taxes and interest, and at the expiration of which the tax collector may sell legal title to the property to the highest bidder. (Sec. 3691, Rev. & Tax. Code) During the redemption period, taxes continue to be assessed and the owner is liable for current, as well as delinquent, payments. (Sec. 4104, Rev. & Tax. Code) The tax collector is required to follow specific notification rules prior to declaring the property "tax defaulted" and selling the property. (Sec. 3361, Rev. & Tax. Code, et seq.) A county tax collector must receive approval from the county board of supervisors prior to selling tax-defaulted property. (Sec. 3694, Rev. & Tax. Code)

- *Unsecured property tax roll collections*

Delinquent taxes on property on the unsecured roll may be collected by the seizure and sale of the taxpayer's personal property, improvements, or possessory interests. (Sec. 2951, Rev. & Tax. Code) Alternatively, the taxes may be collected through court action (Sec. 3003, Rev. & Tax. Code), by placing a judgment lien on the owner's real property in the county through a certificate of delinquency (Sec. 2191.3, Rev. & Tax. Code, et. seq.), or by obtaining a judgment against the taxpayer by summary proceedings (Sec. 3101, Rev. & Tax. Code, et seq.).

The tax collector can utilize procedures for the collection of taxes on the unsecured roll to collect any amount assessed by the board that becomes delinquent on the secured roll. The collector must send a notice of delinquency stating the board's intent to enforce collection at least 60 days before initiating collection procedures.

¶1711 Administration—Penalties and Refunds

Law: Sec. 51298, Gov't Code; Secs. 75.52, 461-82, 501-33, 2617, 2618, 2704, 2705, 2922, 3691, 4833.1, 4985.2, 4985.3, 5096-97.2, 5367, 5902, Rev. & Tax. Code (CCH California Tax Reports, ¶20-265, ¶20-752, ¶20-770, ¶20-815).

Severe penalties may be imposed for failing to supply required information or giving false information. A taxpayer may be fined up to $1,000 and may be imprisoned for not more than six months; a corporate taxpayer is subject to an additional fine of $200 a day, up to a maximum of $20,000. In addition, civil penalties may be imposed. (Sec. 462, Rev. & Tax. Code)

A taxpayer who fails to file a required property statement is subject to a 10% penalty assessment on the unreported property. (Sec. 463, Rev. & Tax. Code; Sec. 5367, Rev. & Tax. Code) A taxpayer who willfully fails to supply information or conceals property is subject to a 25% penalty assessment. (Sec. 502, Rev. & Tax. Code; Sec. 504, Rev. & Tax. Code) These penalties may be abated upon a showing of reasonable cause. For cases involving a fraudulent act, omission, or concealment of property, the taxpayer is subject to a 75% penalty assessment. (Sec. 503, Rev. & Tax. Code)

A taxpayer who fails to file a required property statement (¶1707) is subject to a 10% penalty assessment on the unreported property. (Sec. 463, Rev. & Tax. Code; Sec. 5367, Rev. & Tax. Code) New owners who fail to file the required notification of change of ownership are subject to a penalty of $100 or 10% of the current year's tax, but not to exceed $5,000 if the property is eligible for the homeowners' exemption or $20,000 if it is not. (Sec. 482, Rev. & Tax. Code) Beginning in 2016, a county board of equalization or assessment appeals board may abate penalties for failure to timely file a specified property statement or change in ownership statement if the assessee establishes that the failure was due to reasonable cause and circumstances beyond the assessee's control and occurred notwithstanding the exercise of ordinary care in the absence of willful neglect. (Sec. 463, Rev. & Tax. Code; Sec. 482, Rev. & Tax. Code)

Life insurance companies that own real property in a separate account and fail to file the required property statement or fail to file a required statement of transfer are subject to a penalty of $1,000 in addition to any other penalty prescribed by law. (¶1707; Sec. 480.7, Rev. & Tax. Code)

A 10% penalty is imposed on delinquent payments. (Sec. 2617, Rev. & Tax. Code; Sec. 2618, Rev. & Tax. Code; Sec. 2704, Rev. & Tax. Code; Sec. 2705, Rev. & Tax. Code; Sec. 2922, Rev. & Tax. Code; Sec. 75.52, Rev. & Tax. Code) An additional 1.5% per month penalty is added for continued delinquency. (Sec. 2922, Rev. & Tax. Code) See ¶1708 for delinquency dates. Delinquency penalties may be canceled under certain conditions. (Sec. 75.52, Rev. & Tax. Code; Sec. 4985.2, Rev. & Tax. Code)

In the case of assessment corrections and cancellations, a taxpayer will be relieved of only those penalties for failure to pay tax that apply to the difference between the county board of equalization's final determination of value and the assessed value that was appealed, unless the taxpayer has paid at least 80% of the final assessed value. (Sec. 4833.1, Rev. & Tax. Code; Sec. 4985.3, Rev. & Tax. Code)

Property may be sold to satisfy liens for delinquent taxes. The law provides detailed rules for such sales, redemptions, etc.

State law provides for refunds of property taxes (including benefit assessments; see *Hanjin International Corp. v. Los Angeles County Metropolitan Transportation Authority* (2003) (CCH California Tax Reports, ¶403-498)), on order of the board of supervisors, under certain conditions. (Sec. 5096, Rev. & Tax. Code; Sec. 5097.2, Rev. & Tax. Code; Sec. 533, Rev. & Tax. Code) Generally, a claim for refund must be filed within four years from the date of payment or within one year from the date of mailing of the assessor's notice of overpayment. However, if a qualifying application has been filed for a reduction in a property tax assessment and the applicant does not state that the application is intended to constitute a claim for a refund, the applicant must request a refund within one year of the earlier of (1) the county notifying the applicant of an assessment reduction without advising the applicant to seek a refund, or (2) the expiration of the time period for the county to make a final determination. If a qualifying application has been filed for a reduction in a property tax assessment and the applicant does not state that the application is intended to constitute a claim for a refund, and the applicant is notified of both a reduction in assessment and the right to file a claim for refund, the applicant will have six months within which to file a refund claim. (Sec. 5097, Rev. & Tax. Code) As of September 30, 2016, corrections to the roll that relate to the disabled veterans' exemption may be made within eight years after the making of the assessment being corrected. (Sec. 5097.3, Rev. & Tax. Code) Refunds of city property taxes may be subject to different limitations. See also ¶1709 concerning judicial appeals.

• *Local rebate programs*

Capital investment incentive programs: The governing body of any county, city and county, or city, is authorized to adopt a local ordinance establishing a capital investment incentive program (CIIP), under which the local government may "rebate" to certain large manufacturers an amount up to the amount of California property tax revenues derived from the taxation of the assessed value in excess of $150 million ($25 million between July 10, 2014, and June 30, 2015) of any qualified manufacturing facility that a manufacturer has elected to locate in the local government's jurisdiction. California school districts are not permitted to pay a portion of their property tax revenues toward the CIIP. (Sec. 51298, Govt. Code)

Practitioner Comment: Aerospace Income Tax Credit (ATC) and Temporary Changes to the Capital Investment Incentive Program (CIIP) Are Aimed to Benefit Certain Taxpayers and Industries.

Governor Jerry Brown signed A.B. 2389 on July 10, 2014. The legislation creates the aerospace income tax credit (ATC) and temporarily expands the capital investment incentive program (CIIP). The legislation is aimed at creating and retaining aerospace industry jobs in California by providing up to $420 million in tax credits over 15 years. This program will be administered by the Governor's Office of Business and Economic Development (GO-Biz).

The ATC is an income tax credit available to "qualified taxpayers" for taxable years beginning on or after January 1, 2015, and before January 1, 2030. The credit is equal to 17.5% of qualified wages paid to qualified full-time employees during the taxable year. "Qualified taxpayer" means any taxpayer that is a major first-tier subcontractor awarded a subcontract to manufacture property for ultimate use in or as a component of a new advanced strategic aircraft for the United States Air Force. A "major first-tier subcontractor" is a subcontractor that was awarded a subcontract in an amount of at least 35 percent of the amount of the initial prime contract awarded for the manufacturing of a new advanced strategic aircraft for the United States Air Force.

The changes to the CIIP are temporarily effective between July 10, 2014 and June 30, 2015. The changes consist of a temporary increase in the amount of property tax incentives available under the CIIP, and a temporary limitation of the definition of "qualifying manufacturing facility" to those operated by taxpayers with North American Industry Classification System (NAICS) codes 3364 (Aerospace Product and Parts Manufacturing) and 3359 (Other Electrical Equipment and Component Manufacturing).

The Bill Analysis indicates that the ATC is intended to help the Lockheed Martin Aerospace Company while the changes to the CIIP were intended to benefit Tesla Motors, which was searching for a location for its so-called "Battery Gigafactory" at the time the bill was passed. Tesla subsequently selected a site in Nevada for this factory.

It is well publicized that other states have been pursuing California based companies with lucrative incentives such as the significant package Nevada offered Tesla Motors to locate its battery factory in its state. California historically did not have an incentives program until the California Competes Credit, which is administered by Go-Biz and effective beginning fiscal year 2014-2015. However, the California Competes Credit, which permits only a 6 year carryforward and is not refundable, is not as attractive as incentives available in other states.

A.B. 2389 may suggest Governor Brown and the Legislature are willing to work collaboratively with companies to develop competitive incentives packages outside the scope of the California Competes Credit. Since the Democrats currently control both the governor's mansion and the Legislature, they have an increased ability to offer incentive packages via legislative action.

Chris Whitney, Contributing Editor

To be a "qualified manufacturing facility," each of the following criteria must be met:

— the manufacturer must have made an initial investment in the facility, in real and personal property, that exceeds $150 million;

— the facility must be located within the jurisdiction of the local government authorizing the rebate;

— the facility must be operated either by a business described in Codes 3500 to 3599 of the federal Standard Industrial Classification Manual; by a business engaged in the manufacturing of parts or components related to the production of electricity using solar, wind, biomass, hydropower, or geothermal resources;

— the manufacturer must be currently engaged in commercial production, or in the perfection of a manufacturing process or product with intent to manufacture; and

— from July 10, 2014, and July 1, 2015, facilities operated by certain businesses described in specified provisions of the North American Industry Classification System Manual.

Capital investment incentive payments are issued beginning with the first fiscal year after the date a qualified facility is certified for occupancy, or in the absence of such certification, the first fiscal year after the date such a facility commences operations. Also, the manufacturer of the facility must enter into a community services agreement with the local government, under which the manufacturer agrees to pay a community services fee equal to 25% of the rebate, but not to exceed $2 million annually, and sets forth a job creation plan.

The provisions authorizing the CIIP are repealed as of January 1, 2018, although a program established prior to that date would remain in effect for the full term of that program.

• *Taxpayers' bill of rights*

A "bill of rights" for property taxpayers permits county assessors to respond to taxpayer requests for written rulings on certain property tax issues and may relieve a taxpayer from penalties and interest assessed or accrued as a direct result of the taxpayer's reasonable reliance on such a written ruling. (Sec. 5902, Rev. & Tax. Code et. seq.)

Additional protections extended to property taxpayers:

— require notice of proposed escape assessments, hearings before a county board of equalization, or judgment liens on taxpayers' unsecured property;

— extend the limitations period for certain escape assessment refund claims;

— authorize taxpayers to inspect and copy assessors' market data and assessment information; and

— provide a procedure for making stipulations with respect to property tax refund claims.

PART VIII

MISCELLANEOUS TAXES

CHAPTER 18
UNEMPLOYMENT INSURANCE TAX

¶ 1801	Unemployment Insurance Tax

¶ 1801 Unemployment Insurance Tax

California's Unemployment Insurance Tax is covered in Revenue and Taxation Code, Division 6 Withholding Tax on Wages. Comprehensive coverage of unemployment insurance is provided in Wolters Kluwer, CCH Unemployment/Social Security Reporter. For more information go to CCHGroup.com or contact an account representative at 888-CCH-REPS (888-224-7377).

CHAPTER 19

OTHER STATE TAXES

¶1901 Scope of Chapter

This chapter outlines generally and very briefly certain California state taxes and fees that have not already been covered in the text. No effort is made to explain these taxes and fees in detail or to discuss the detailed rules applicable to them. The purpose is merely to indicate in general terms the basis of each tax or fee, by whom it is administered, and where further information may be obtained if desired.

• *Enactment of taxes and fees*

Regulatory fees, such as certain environmental fees, may be enacted by a majority vote of the legislature, unlike taxes which require a two-thirds vote of either the legislature or the electorate (see *Sinclair Paint Co. v. State Board of Equalization* (1997) (CCH CALIFORNIA TAX REPORTS, ¶402-926)).

• *Taxpayers' bill of rights*

A "bill of rights" has been enacted to protect the privacy and property rights of taxpayers who are subject to the following State Board of Equalization (BOE) administered taxes and fees: motor vehicle fuel tax (Sec. 8260, Rev. & Tax. Code et. seq.), use fuel tax (Sec. 9260, Rev. & Tax. Code et seq.), underground storage tank maintenance fees (Sec. 50156, Rev. & Tax. Code et. seq.), hazardous substances tax (Sec. 43511, Rev. & Tax. Code et seq.), solid waste disposal site cleanup and maintenance fees, alcoholic beverages tax (Sec. 32460, Rev. & Tax. Code), and cigarette and tobacco products taxes (Sec. 30458, Rev. & Tax. Code). A similar "bill of rights" has been enacted for taxpayers who are subject to various state and local excise taxes and fees. All these bills of rights are substantially similar to the "bill of rights" described at ¶702, relating to personal income and corporate tax collections, except that the agency involved is the BOE, rather than the Franchise Tax Board.

¶1902 Insurance Taxes

Law: Secs.12201-84 (CCH CALIFORNIA TAX REPORTS, ¶88-001—88-050).

A gross premiums tax is imposed upon insurance companies (other than ocean marine insurers). (Sec. 12201, Rev. & Tax. Code) This tax is in lieu of all other state and local taxes and licenses, except:

— of real estate taxes;

— of retaliatory exactions imposed under Sec. 28 for Article XIII of the California Constitution;

— of ocean marine insurance tax;

— of motor vehicle license fees; and

— that each corporate or other attorney-in-fact of a reciprocal or interinsurance exchange shall be subject to all taxes imposed upon corporations or others doing business in the state, other than taxes on income derived from its principal business as attorney-in-fact.

(Sec. 12204, Rev. & Tax. Code) The rate of tax on insurers in general is 2.35% of gross premium income. The rate is $^1/2$% on premiums received under pension and profit-sharing plans that are qualified under the income tax provisions of the Internal Revenue Code. (Sec. 12202, Rev. & Tax. Code) Ocean marine insurers are taxed at the rate of 5% on their underwriting income. (Sec. 12101, Rev. & Tax. Code) Surplus line brokers and taxpayers that purchase insurance from nonadmitted insurers, with some exceptions, are taxed at the rate of 3% of gross premiums, less 3% of return premiums. (Sec. 1775.5, Ins. Code; Sec. 13210, Rev. & Tax. Code) An insurer's gross premiums tax rate will be zero for premiums received on or after July 1, 2016, and on or before June 30, 2019, if the insurer provides health insurance and has a corporate affiliate that is a licensed health care service plan or a managed care plan contracted to provide Medi-Cal services; had at least one enrollee enrolled in the health plan in the base year (not including Medicare plan enrollees, individuals who receive health care services under subcontract with another plan, or enrollees under the Federal Employees Health Benefits Act); and is subject to the managed care organization provider tax (discussed below). (Sec. 12202.2, Rev. & Tax. Code)

The administration of the gross premiums tax is divided among the Insurance Commissioner, the State Board of Equalization (BOE), the State Controller, and the Franchise Tax Board (FTB). Insurance companies other than nonadmitted insurers must file an annual tax return with the Commissioner, as shown below. A copy is transmitted to the BOE, which assesses the taxes imposed on insurers for the preceding calendar year, and notifies them of any excess or deficiency. Examination of the return by the Commissioner may result in a deficiency assessment.

Returns and annual payments are due as follows:

	Returns	*Payments*
Insurance companies generally	April 1	April 1
Ocean marine insurance	June 15	June 15
Retaliatory taxes	April 1	April 1
Surplus line brokers	March 1	March 1

(Sec. 1774, Ins. Code; Sec. 1775.5, Ins. Code; Sec. 12281, Rev. & Tax. Code; Sec. 12287, Rev. & Tax. Code; Sec. 12301, Rev. & Tax. Code; Sec. 12302, Rev. & Tax. Code)

Taxpayers that procure insurance from nonadmitted insurers must file a return with the FTB by the first day of the third month following the close of the calendar quarter during which a taxable insurance contract took effect or was renewed. (Sec. 13220, Rev. & Tax. Code)

Insurers transacting business in California whose annual tax for the preceding calendar year was $20,000 or more must prepay their tax for the current calendar year, except that no prepayments are required of ocean marine insurers tax or any retaliatory tax. (Sec. 12251, Rev. & Tax. Code) Also, insurers whose California gross premiums tax rate has been reduced to zero during the operation of the managed care organization provider tax. (Sec. 12254, Rev. & Tax. Code) Prepayments are due on or before April 1, June 1, September 1, and December 1 of the current year. (Sec. 12253, Rev. & Tax. Code) Surplus line brokers, with some exceptions, whose tax liability for the preceding calendar year was $20,000 or more, are required to make monthly installment payments. (Sec. 1775.1, Ins. Code) In addition, any insurer whose annual insurance tax exceeds $20,000 must remit all tax payments by electronic funds transfer. A penalty of 10% of the taxes due will be imposed for failure to comply with the electronic funds transfer requirement. (Sec. 1531, Ins. Code; Sec. 1775.8, Ins. Code; Sec. 12602, Rev. & Tax. Code)

¶1902

Insurance companies may qualify for a low-income housing credit or, effective for tax years beginning before 2017, a credit for qualified investments made into a community development financial institution, and effective for the 2017 tax year a college access tax credit. (Sec. 12206, Rev. & Tax. Code; Sec. 12207, Rev. & Tax. Code; Sec. 12209, Rev. & Tax. Code) These credits are the same as those allowed under the personal income tax law and are discussed at ¶138 ¶155, and ¶156, respectively. An insurer may also claim a credit equal to the amount of the gross premiums tax due from the insurer on account of pilot project insurance issued to provide low-cost insurance to qualified low-income residents of San Francisco and Los Angeles. (Sec. 12208, Rev. & Tax. Code)

Practitioner Comment: California Passes a New Managed Care Organization Tax

On March 1, 2016 California Gov. Jerry Brown signed a restructured Managed Care Organization (MCO) tax package, the day after the Legislature passed the package. Beginning on July 1, 2016, the new MCO tax is now imposed on all health plans and will levy an estimated $1.3 billion in tax on the affected health plans in 2016-2017. The new MCO tax also provides that health plans will receive certain income exclusions for Corporate Franchise Tax purposes (see ¶929) and affiliate insurers will receive a reduction of the gross premiums tax rate to zero percent (as discussed above). The tax, which is currently only applicable to fiscal years between July 1, 2016 and July 1, 2019, assesses a tax on each MCO based on the number of enrollees.

Chris Whitney, Contributing Editor

For fiscal years 2016-17, 2017-18, and 2018-19, the tax is imposed in various taxing tiers based on the type and number of enrollees in the plan, at per enrollee amounts that range from $1 to $40 for 2016-17, $1 to $42.50 for 2017-18, and $1 to $45 for 2018-19. (Sec. 14199.5, Welf. & Inst. Code)

¶1903 Motor Vehicle Taxes

Law: Secs. 5003.1-03.2., 5136, 5328, Public Utility Code; Secs. 7232-36, 10752-58, Revenue and Taxation Code; Secs. 4601-02, 6262, 9250, 9400, Vehicle Code (CCH CALIFORNIA TAX REPORTS, ¶37-101).

Motor vehicles are subject to various taxes and license and registration fees. These assessments are covered by various agencies.

Vehicle license fee: The "in lieu" tax, so called because it is a form of property tax that is imposed in lieu of local property taxation of automobiles, including automobiles awarded in a state lottery, is in effect a license fee in addition to the registration fee discussed below. The tax is imposed at 0.65% of the "market value" of the make and model involved, computed under a statutory formula. (Sec. 10752, Rev. & Tax. Code) The license fee is paid at the same time as the registration fee. The vehicle license fee is administered by the Department of Revenue.

A vehicle license transaction fee is imposed on rental car transactions. The statutory formula used to calculate the amount of the fee is based on the vehicle license fee.

Registration and weight fees: Motor vehicles are required to be registered annually. (Sec. 4601, Veh. Code; Sec. 4602, Veh. Code) The general annual state registration fee is $43, but miscellaneous additional fees may be imposed by the state and certain local jurisdictions. (Sec. 9250, Veh. Code) In addition, there are annual weight fees for the operation of certain commercial vehicles, the amount depending on the weight of the vehicle and other factors. (Sec. 9400, Veh. Code; Sec. 9400.1, Veh. Code) Trailer coaches are also subject to registration and licensing. Vehicle registration fees generally are administered by the state Department of Motor Vehicles (DMV), which operates generally under the terms of the state Vehicle Code. (http://www.dmv.ca.gov/portal/dmv/)

Motor carrier fees: For-hire motor carriers other than household goods carriers or motor carriers of property engaged in interstate or foreign transportation of property must pay an annual permit fee consisting of the following amounts: a safety fee (ranging from $60 to $1,030), a uniform business license tax fee (ranging from $60 to $2,000), and beginning January 1, 2016, a carrier inspection fee (ranging from $130 to $2,114). (Sec. 7236, Rev. & Tax. Code)

Household goods carriers: Household goods carriers must pay an annual permit fee of $500. (Sec. 5136, Pub. Util. Code) A regulatory fee is also imposed on household goods carriers owning or operating motor vehicles and transporting property for hire on the public highways. The fee is $15 plus $1/3$ of 1% of gross operating revenue, payable quarterly to the Public Utilities Commission, if the carrier is under the regulatory jurisdiction of the Commission. (Sec. 5003.1, Pub. Util. Code) However, if the carrier is not under the regulatory jurisdiction of the Commission or is transporting used office, store, and/or institution furniture or fixtures, the fee is $15 plus 0.1% of gross operating revenue. (Sec. 5003.2, Pub. Util. Code) In addition, household goods carriers are subject to a license fee of 0.1% of gross operating revenue, payable quarterly to the Commission. (Sec. 5328, Pub. Util. Code)

¶1904 Alcoholic Beverage Taxes

California's Alcoholic Beverage Tax is covered in Revenue and Taxation Code, Division 2 Other Taxes, Part 14 Alcoholic Beverage Tax. Current tax rates per gallon are:

— beer, still wines, sparkling hard cider $0.20
— champagne, sparkling wine $0.30
— distilled spirits (100 proof or less) $3.30
— Distilled spirits (more than 100 proof) $6.60

(http://www.boe.ca.gov/sptaxprog/tax_rates_stfd.htm)

Comprehensive coverage of taxation of alcohol, as well as licensing and distribution information is provided in Wolters Kluwer, CCH Liquor Control Law Reporter. For more information go to CCHGroup.com or contact an account representative at 888-CCH-REPS (888-224-7377).

¶1905 Special Taxes in Lieu of Property Tax

Law: Secs. 5701-22, 11251-406 (CCH CALIFORNIA TAX REPORTS, ¶20-125, 20-305).

A form of property tax is levied by the state upon the value of racehorses and upon the value of private cars operated on railroads within California. The railroad car tax is in lieu of local taxation of such property, and is imposed at the average rate of general property taxation for the preceding year as determined by the State Board of Equalization (BOE). Persons owning private railroad cars must make an annual report to the BOE. The tax is payable annually on or before December 10. (Sec. 11251 et seq., Rev. & Tax. Code)

Racehorses are taxed annually by the head in three classes, stallions (the rate is based on the stud fees), brood mares, and racehorses (the rate is based on the amount of winnings). (Sec. 5701 et. seq., Rev. & Tax. Code)

¶1906 Cigarette and Tobacco Products Tax

Law: Secs. 30008-30190 (CCH CALIFORNIA TAX REPORTS, ¶55-001—55-010).

A state tax is imposed on cigarettes. The tax rate applied to cigarettes is 87¢ per 20-pack. (Sec. 30101, Rev. & Tax. Code; Sec. 30123, Rev. & Tax. Code) Tobacco products are taxed at an equivalent rate, determined annually by the State Board of

Equalization (BOE). Effective July 1, 2016, through June 30, 2017, the tobacco products tax rate for taxable distributions of all tobacco products other than cigarettes is 27.30% of the wholesale cost of the tobacco products. (Sec. 30123, Rev. & Tax. Code)

Monthly reports must be filed by distributors and others by the 25th of the month for the preceding calendar month. (Sec. 30182 et. seq., Rev. & Tax Code) Distributors are allowed a stamping or metering cost allowance of .85% of the tax. (Sec. 30166, Rev. & Tax. Code) Sales to members of the armed forces in exchanges and commissaries, to state veterans' homes, and to law enforcement agencies for authorized use in a criminal investigation are exempt. (Sec. 30102 —Sec. 30105.5, Rev. & Tax. Code)

The cigarette tax may be prepaid by the use of stamps and metering machines. (Sec. 30161, Rev. & Tax. Code) Cigarette distributors that defer payment for stamps and meter register settings and that elect to remit tax on a twice-monthly basis must remit their first monthly payment by the 5th day of the month; their first monthly payment must equal the greater of one half the tax due on purchases made during the preceding month or the total tax due on purchases made between the 1st and the 15th of the preceding month. The second monthly payment must be remitted by the 25th day of the month for the remainder of the prior month's purchases. Cigarette distributors that defer payment for stamps and meter register settings and that elect to remit tax on a monthly basis must remit their monthly payment by the 25th day of each month. A distributor also can elect to pay the tax on a weekly basis. (Sec. 30168, Rev. & Tax. Code)

Persons whose estimated tax liability averages $20,000 or more per month, as determined by the California State Board of Equalization (BOE), must remit amounts due by electronic funds transfer. (Sec. 30190, Rev. & Tax. Code)

The tax is administered by the BOE.

¶1907 Other Taxes and Fees

Law: Secs. 13430-34, Business and Professions Code; Secs. 13244.5, 25299.41-99.43, Health and Safety Code; Secs. 3263, 3402, 48650-71, Public Resources Code; Sec. 4458, Public Utility Code; Secs. 7306-56, 7380-81, 8604-55, 38115, 40016, 41020, Revenue and Taxation Code (CCH CALIFORNIA TAX REPORTS, ¶31-001, 37-001, 40-001, 40-003, 80-110—80-140).

The following is a very brief statement of other taxes imposed by the state:

Motor vehicle fuel taxes: A tax is imposed upon the privilege of distributing motor fuel, and a complementary use tax applies to gasoline and other fuels. The state rate on gasoline, other than aviation gasoline, is $0.278 per gallon, effective July 1, 2016. If the federal license or use tax is reduced below specified levels, then the state rate will be increased by the amount of the federal reduction. (Sec. 7360, Rev. & Tax. Code; Sec. 8651, Rev. & Tax. Code) Returns by persons distributing motor vehicle fuel must be made monthly to the State Board of Equalization (BOE), and returns by vendors and users generally must be made quarterly to the BOE. (Sec. 7651, Rev. & Tax. Code; Sec. 8752, Rev. & Tax. Code)

A separate tax is imposed for the privilege of storage, removal, entry, or use of diesel fuel. (Sec. 60110 et. seq., Rev. & Tax. Code) Effective July 1, 2016, the state tax rate is $0.16 per gallon of diesel fuel, subject to adjustment should the federal fuel tax rate be reduced.

Some local jurisdictions also are authorized to impose a limited per gallon tax on the sale, storage, or use of motor vehicle fuel, if approved by the voters.

Aircraft fuel tax: Aviation gasoline is subject to a tax at the rate of $0.18 per gallon. (Sec. 7360, Rev. & Tax. Code) A license tax is imposed on aircraft jet fuel dealers at the rate of $0.02 per gallon. (Sec. 7392, Rev. & Tax. Code) Monthly returns are required. (Sec. 7393, Rev. & Tax. Code)

Public utilities: "Public utilities" are not specially taxed as such. However, some companies so classified are subject to special license taxes or fees. These include certain transportation companies (see also ¶1903), and operators of toll bridges, toll roads, toll ferries, street railroads, and private wharves. Information may be obtained from the Public Utilities Commission.

Oil and gas severance tax and fee: A regulatory tax and a production fee are imposed on the production of oil and sale of gas. (Sec. 3402 et. seq., Pub. Res. Code) Information may be obtained from the state Department of Conservation.

Business license taxes: License fees are imposed on many businesses, occupations, and professions. The fees range from nominal amounts to very large amounts (*e.g.*, in the case of horse racing). As there are over 100 categories of license taxes, a listing of them is beyond the scope of this book. Information may be obtained from the various state boards, commissions, etc., involved, or from the Department of Consumer Affairs in Sacramento.

Practitioner Comment: San Francisco Phasing-In Gross Receipts Tax.

Beginning in 2014, San Francisco (the City) is replacing its business tax based on payroll expense in the City (the "Payroll Expense Tax") with one measured by gross receipts attributable to the City (the "Gross Receipts Tax"). The Gross Receipts Tax phases in over a five-year period beginning 2014 and there is a corresponding phase-out of the Payroll Expense Tax over the same period. The tax is generally progressive, reported on a combined basis unlike the Payroll Expense Tax's separate filing approach, and businesses with gross receipts of less than $1 million are exempt from the Gross Receipts Tax. The nature of the taxpayer's business, which is guided by the NAICS Code classification system, determines the applicable tax rate range and methodology for determining gross receipts attributable to the City.

Gross receipts are broadly defined as "the total amounts received or accrued by a person from whatever source derived." However, some gross receipts, including "investment receipts," receipts from related parties, and certain receipts from pass-through entities, are expressly excluded from the definition of gross receipts.

Certain businesses that have their administrative offices in San Francisco will pay their business tax at a rate of 1.4% of payroll costs. The Gross Receipts Tax continues to allow the utilization of certain credits including certain Enterprise Zone credits and the "Central Market Street Limit" credits historically permitted under the payroll tax. The City also increased the annual business registration fees to as much as $35,000 for businesses with over $200 million in gross receipts.

For certain industries, particularly service related businesses, the amount of gross receipts attributable to San Francisco and therefore subject to tax is based entirely on the taxpayer's San Francisco payroll relative to total payroll. This approach runs counter to the stated policy reason behind changing the San Francisco business tax, which was to shift from a system based on payroll costs in San Francisco to one based on sales. San Francisco's Payroll Tax purportedly created a disincentive to creating new jobs in San Francisco because an employer's City tax would increase each time a new San Francisco employee was hired. Furthermore, businesses that historically have had large amounts of gross receipts, but much smaller proportionate payrolls (e.g., venture capital, private equity, internet service businesses) may see their total and proportionate share of San Francisco business tax and registrations fees increase.

The San Francisco Tax Collector is vested with significant discretion. The ordinance states that "[t]he Tax Collector may, in his or her reasonable discretion, independently establish a person's gross receipts within the City and establish or reallocate gross receipts among related entities so as to fairly reflect the gross receipts within the City of all persons." The language *fairly reflect* is somewhat similar to Section 18 of the

Uniform Division of Income for Tax Purposes Act (UDITPA), which states have increasingly relied on to adjust taxpayers' apportioned income for purposes of state corporate income tax.

Chris Whitney, Contributing Editor

Energy resources surcharge: A surcharge of, at most, $0.0003/kwh is imposed on electrical energy purchased from an electric utility. (Sec. 40016, Rev. & Tax. Code)

Timber yield tax: Forest trees on privately and publicly-owned land are subject to a severance tax at the time of harvest, at rates to be determined from time to time. (Sec. 38115, Rev. & Tax. Code) Information may be obtained from the BOE.

Emergency telephone users' surcharge: A surcharge is imposed on intrastate telephone services, to finance the state's emergency telephone system. (Sec. 41020, Rev. & Tax. Code)

Prepaid mobile telephony services (MTS) surcharge: Effective January 1, 2016, a surcharge is imposed on sellers of prepaid MTS to consumers in retail transactions. The statewide surcharge rate for calendar year 2017 is 5.9% (formerly, 9.26%). (Sec. 42010, Rev. & Tax. Code)

Practitioner Comment: Partner compensation included in San Francisco Payroll Expense Tax base.

The California Court of Appeal, First District, in *Coblentz, Patch, Duffy and Bass LLP v. City and County of San Francisco,* 233 Cal.App.4th 691 (2014), petition for review denied April 22, 2015, held that profit distributions to equity partners represent "compensation for services" and are therefore within the San Francisco Payroll Expense Tax ("Payroll Expense Tax") base. San Francisco voters passed Proposition Q during the November 2008 elections, and the proposition is effective starting in the 2009 tax year. Proposition Q clarified that the Payroll Expense Tax base of pass through entities (i.e., partnerships, Subchapter S corporations, limited liability companies, and limited liability partnerships) includes distributions to their owners to the extent the distributions are "compensation for services" and not a return on capital investment.

The taxpayer in *Coblentz* argued that the partnership's profit distributions do not constitute "compensation for services" because an equity partner is generally not entitled to "compensation for services" (other than guaranteed payments to the extent provided for in the partnership agreement), and profit distributions are not treated as "compensation for services" under federal and state tax laws for purposes of an equity partner's individual tax liability. The Court explained that the taxpayer's arguments and authorities relate to the individual partner's tax liability while the Payroll Expense Tax seeks to tax the partnership on amounts that are "compensation for services." Since the taxpayer conceded that a major source of a partnership's gross income is "compensation for services," including fees received for client services, some portion of the taxpayer's profit distributions include an equity partner's "compensation for services" as defined in Proposition Q. The Court also found unpersuasive the taxpayer's Due Process argument that Proposition Q is unconstitutionally vague on its face. Although Proposition Q did not define "compensation for services" or "return on capital investment," these terms have a common understanding or meaning.

The Court also rejected the taxpayer's Proposition 218 argument. Proposition 218 prohibits local governments from imposing taxes unless they are "submitted to the electorate and approved by a majority vote." While Proposition 218 does not define what "submitted" to the voter means, S.F. Mun. Elec. Code sections 500(8) and 501 require ballot pamphlets to "distinguish additions to or deletions from existing legislation in the printed text of the measure by underlining, bold type, strike-outs or other appropriate means." The Court explained that even though the ballot pamphlet did not emphasize the entirety of the new language introduced by Proposition Q, it did contain all of the new language proposed by Proposition Q. Thus, San Francisco complied with Proposition 218 because it held an election on Proposition Q and the ballot pamphlet contained the newly proposed language.

Lastly, the taxpayer asserted that Proposition Q violated Cal. Rev. & Tax. Code §17041.5, which prohibits any local government from imposing "any tax upon the income, or any part thereof, of any person." The taxpayer argued that Proposition Q as interpreted by San Francisco is essentially an income tax on the partnership. Citing *A.B.C. Distributing Co. v. City and County of San Francisco*, 15 Cal.3d 566 (1975), the Court explained that the California Supreme Court upheld the validity of the Payroll Expense Tax as one imposed by reason of employing labor in San Francisco. The tax is not an income tax because it is measured by wages paid to employees.

The taxpayer's petition to the California Supreme Court to review the Proposition 218, Cal. Rev. & Tax. Code §17041.5, and due process arguments was denied on April 22, 2015.

Chris Whitney, Contributing Editor

Motor oil fee: A fee is imposed on certain producers and dealers for the purchase or sale of motor oil. The maximum rate is 5¢ per gallon. (Sec. 13431, Bus. & Prof. Code)

Lubricating oil tax: Manufacturers of lubricating oil sold or transferred in California must pay a tax at the rate of $0.06 per quart. (Sec. 48650, Pub. Res. Code)

Underground storage tank fee: For calendar years 2015-2025, certain underground storage tank owners must pay a fee in the amount of 20 mills per gallon. Quarterly returns are required. (Sec. 25299.41, Hlth. & Sfty. Code; Sec. 25299.43, Hlth. & Sfty. Code)

Practitioner Comment: *Extension of Lower Tax Rate in Los Angeles for Internet Businesses.*

The Los Angeles City Council has voted to amend Section 21.41 of the Los Angeles Municipal Code to extend the tax classification of Internet businesses through 2018. Originally passed in 2010 with a five-year sunset clause, the law extends the reduced tax rate of $1.01 for every $1,000 in gross receipts. Internet companies would otherwise be taxable at the City's highest tax rate of $5.07 for every $1,000 in gross receipts. Businesses that meet the statutory definition and criteria of either an Internet-based Application Service Provider or an Internet-based Data Manipulation business are eligible for the reduced rate. New or existing businesses that may qualify should complete and mail to the City an eligibility form that is available on the Office of Finance website.

Chris Whitney, Contributing Editor

¶1908 Realty Transfer Tax

Law: Sec. 11911 (CCH California Tax Reports, ¶37-051).

Cities and counties are authorized to impose a tax on transfers of interests in real estate with a value of more than $100. The county tax is at the rate of 55¢ for each $500, and the noncharter city rate is one-half of the county rate. The tax is payable to the county recorder at the time the instrument transferring the property is recorded. (Sec. 11911, Rev. & Tax. Code)

Practitioner Comment: *Documentary Transfer Tax May Apply To Transfers of Interests in Legal Entities.*

In *926 North Ardmore Avenue, LLC v. County of Los Angeles*, Cal. App. Ct., No. B248536, September 22, 2014, the California Court of Appeal for the Second District held that the California Documentary Transfer Tax (DTT) permits a documentary transfer tax when a transfer of interest in a legal entity results in a "change of ownership" under the real estate property tax law. There is an exception, however, for certain transfers of partnership interests where the transfer does not result in a termination of the partnership.

Current California state law permits localities to impose the DTT on "realty sold" in California. While the DTT was applied to the transfer of real property itself, there has been uncertainty regarding whether the transfer of interests in an entity that holds real property maybe subject to the DTT as well. The *Ardmore* court held that "realty sold" includes transfers that result in a "change in ownership" under the real estate property tax law, which may include the transfer of interests in an entity that holds real property. The court also confirmed that the DTT exemption for a partnership interest transfer if the partnership is considered to be a continuing partnership under IRC § 708 may still apply.

While *Ardmore* is a Court of Appeal case and thus binding at the state level, its precedential authority maybe limited. In California there are general law cities and counties, which are generally bound by the DTT if they choose to impose real estate transfer taxes, and charter jurisdictions. Charter jurisdictions have the option of incorporating state model statutes or enacting their own laws, including the method and tax rates that apply to real estate transfer taxes. *Ardmore* involves a challenge regarding a charter jurisdiction, which adopted relevant portions of the DTT. It is not clear whether *Ardmore* applies to all localities that generally incorporate the model DTT, or other charter jurisdictions that have similar but not identical laws. The California Supreme Court accepted the taxpayer's petition to appeal.

Note that transfers of partnership interests that result in technical terminations of the partnership under the Internal Revenue Code generally trigger transfer tax. In addition, certain cities, mainly "charter jurisdictions," such as San Francisco and Santa Clara, have begun to assess tax under nonconforming municipal and/or county ordinances on transfers of interests in legal entities in general that result in a change in control or change in ownership for property tax reassessment purposes.

Chris Whitney, Contributing Editor

¶1909 Environmental Taxes and Fees

Law: Secs. 25205.1-05.12, 42464, Health and Safety Code; Secs. 43053-152.15, Revenue and Taxation Code (CCH California Tax Reports, ¶37-151).

California imposes a variety of fees in connection with the generation, storage, treatment, disposal, and cleanup of waste, including hazardous waste disposal fees; covered electronic waste recycling fees; facility, generator, permit, and hauler fees; fees imposed on solid waste landfill operators; tire disposal fees; various oil spill and medical waste fees; and a general "environmental fee" payable by virtually all businesses/organizations employing 50 or more persons, each employed more than 500 hours in California during the prior calendar year (see below).

• *Environmental fee*

Every corporation, limited liability company, limited partnership, limited liability partnership, general partnership, and sole proprietorship with an SIC (Standard Industrial Classification) code for any industry that uses, generates, or stores hazardous materials or conducts activities in California related to hazardous materials is subject to an annual environmental "fee," whether or not the organization is actually conducting activities related to hazardous materials. (Sec. 25205.6, Hlth. & Sfty. Code) Only those doing business as private households are excluded. The fee is based on the number of employees in California during the previous calendar year. For 2017, the fee schedule is as follows:

Number of employees	Fee
1–49	$ 0
50–74	320
75–99	562
100–249	1117
250–499	2396
500–999	4474
1,000 or more	15181

PART IX

DIRECTORY/RESOURCES

CHAPTER 20

CALIFORNIA RESOURCES

Addresses and other contact information for various state taxing agencies are listed below. In addition, the Franchise Tax Board Information Directory can be accessed online at https://www.ftb.ca.gov/forms/misc/1240.pdf, and the State Board of Equalization is available online at http://www.boe.ca.gov/info/directory.html.

Franchise Tax Board (FTB)

P.O. Box 1468
Sacramento, CA 98512-1468
Internet: http://www.ftb.ca.gov
There are 6 FTB field offices located throughout California.
Los Angeles —300 S. Spring St, Suite 5704, Los Angeles, CA 90013-1265
Oakland —1515 Clay St, Suite 305, Oakland, CA 94612-1445
Sacramento —3321 Power Inn Rd. Suite 250, Sacramento, CA 95826-3893
San Diego —7575 Metropolitan Dr, Suite 201, San Diego, CA 92108-4421
San Francisco —121 Spear St, Suite 400, San Francisco, CA 94105-1584
Santa Ana —600 W. Santa Ana Blvd, Suite 300, Santa Ana, CA 92701-4543

Members of the Board	
Chair	Betty T. Yee, Chair, State Controller
Member	Fiona Ma, CPA, Chair, State Board of Equalization
Member	Michael Cohen, Director of Finance
Executive Officer	Selvi Stanislaus
FTB on the Internet	**www.ftb.ca.gov**
Tax Practitioner Services	
✓ Hotline (not toll-free)	(916) 845-7057
✓ Hotline (Fax)	(916) 845-9300
✓ e-file	(916) 845-0353

Automated Telephone Service

FTB's automated telephone system provides services in both English and Spanish to callers with touch-tone telephones. Callers may listen to recorded answers to frequently asked questions about state income taxes, 24 hours a day, seven days a week. Callers may order personal income tax forms, verify the status of their personal income tax refund, check their balance due, and confirm recent payment amounts and dates, 24 hours a day, except 9:45 p.m. Sunday to 12:15 a.m. Monday. Callers may order business entity tax forms 6 a.m. to 10 p.m., Monday through Friday and 6 a.m. to 4:30 p.m. Saturdays.

From within the United States, call	(800) 338-0505
From outside the United States, call (not toll-free)	(916) 845-6500

General Toll-Free Telephone Service (Taxpayer Services Center)

Telephone assistance is available year-round from 8 a.m. until 5 p.m. Monday through Friday, except state holidays. We may modify these hours without notice to meet operational needs.

From within the United States, call	(800) 852-5711
From outside the United States, call (not toll-free)	(916) 845-6500

Tax Assistance for Persons with Hearing or Speech Impediments

Persons with hearing or speech impairments call:

From TTY/TDD	(800) 822-6268

Where to Call or Write

Note - If an address is not shown use:

UNIT NAME

FRANCHISE TAX BOARD

PO BOX 1468

SACRAMENTO CA 95812-1468

A

Accounting Period/Method Change 800.852.5711
    Change of Accounting Method/Period
    Franchise Tax Board
    PO Box 1998
    Rancho Cordova CA 95741-1998
Application for Revivor 916.845.7033
Audit Division
    Go to **ftb.ca.gov** and search for **management team directory**

B

Bankruptcy, Personal Income Tax 916.845.4750
    Fax 916.845.9799
        (personal income tax - chapters 7, 11, and 13)
        Bankruptcy, PIT MS A340
        Franchise Tax Board
        PO Box 2952
        Sacramento CA 95812-2952
Bankruptcy, Business Entities Tax 916.845.4750
    Fax 916.845.9799
        (Business Entities - Chapters 7 and 11)
        Bankruptcy, BE MS A345
        Franchise Tax Board
        PO Box 2952
        Sacramento CA 95812-2952
Business Entities 800.478.7194

C

City Business Tax Program - Data Exchange
    Email: LocalGovtLiaison@ftb.ca.gov
    ACD 916.845.6304
Claims for Refund 800.852.5711
Collections
    Business Entities Tax . . . .
        Collection Contact Center 888.635.0494
        or 888.635.0494
        Corporations
        Exempt Corporations
        Partnerships
        Limited Liability Corporations (LLC)
    Personal Income Tax
        Practitioner Hotline 916.845.7057
        Hotline Fax 916.845.9300
        Collection Contact Center 800.689.4776
Account Recovery and Resolution Team (ARRT) 916.845.4470
    ACD . . . . 916.845.7065 or 888.382.3707
    Fax 916.843.2425
        ARRT MS A411
        Franchise Tax Board

PO Box 2952
Sacramento CA 95812-2952 . . . . 916.845.4064
Court-Ordered Debt Collections . . . .
  Court-Ordered Debt Collections MS A113
  Franchise Tax Board
  PO Box 1328
  Rancho Cordova CA 95741-1328
Vehicle Registration Debt
  Collections (DMV) 888.355.6872
                       916.845.6872

  Vehicle Registration Collections MS A113
  Franchise Tax Board
  PO Box 419001
  Rancho Cordova CA 95741-9001
Criminal Investigation 916.845.4037

D

Data Exchange Production Services 916.845.3778
Decedent and Probate Program 916.845.3048
                Fax 916.845.0479

Decedent and Probate Program MS A454   Franchise Tax Board
                    PO Box 2952
                    Sacramento CA
                    95812-2952

Deductible Dividends, Percent of 916.845.4138
Disclosure Section 916.845.3226
Disclosure Section MS A181   Franchise Tax Board
                    PO Box 1468
                    Sacramento CA
                    95812-1468

Dishonored Checks, Status of 800.852.5711

E

Economic and Statistical Research Bureau. 916.845.3375
  Revenue Analysis Section 916.845.5125
  Statistical Research and Modeling Section 916.845.3362
  Tax Policy Section 916.845.7103
  Fax 916.845.5472
Education and Outreach 916.845.5424
e-Programs Customer Service 916.845.0353
  Email: e-file@ftb.ca.gov
  e-file 916.845.0353
  EFT 916.845.4025
  Fax 916.845.5556
     e-Programs Customer Service MS F284
     Franchise Tax Board
     PO Box 1468
     Sacramento CA 95812-1468
Equal Employment Opportunity 916.845.3651
Charities 916.845.4171
Exempt
Organizations
Unit MS F120
    Franchise
    Tax
    Board
    PO
    Box
    1286
    Rancho
    Cordova
    CA
    95812-1286

F

Federal and State Special Audit Section 916.843.2269
  Fax 916.845.2867
Federal Treasury Offset Program 916.845.4476
Filing Compliance Agreement Program . . . .
  Mail Completed FTB 5841, *Request for Filing Compliance Agreement*, to:
  (U.S. Mail)
    Filing Compliance Agreement Program MS F180
    Complex Filing Enforcement Unit
    Franchise Tax Board
    PO Box 1779
    Rancho Cordova CA 95741-1779

Corporate Officers 916.657.5448
    Secretary of State
    1500 11th Street
    Sacramento CA 95814
Settlement Bureau (fax) 916.845.4747
    Settlement Bureau MS A270
    Franchise Tax Board
    PO Box 3070
    Rancho Cordova CA 95741-3070
Small Business Liaison . . . .
Speakers' Bureau 916.845.4669
    Email: speakersbureau@ftb.ca.gov
    Requests for speakers 916.845.4669
    Speakers' Bureau MS F280
    Franchise Tax Board
    PO Box 1468
    Sacramento CA 95812-1468
Suspended Corporation 916.845.7033

T

Tax Forms
    Download forms at **ftb.ca.gov**
    Order forms by phone: 800.338.0505
    Mail: Tax Forms Request MS D120
        Franchise Tax Board
        PO Box 307
        Rancho Cordova CA 95741-0307
Tax Informant Hotline 800.540.3453
    Go to **ftb.ca.gov** and search for **fraud.**
Tax News
    Email: taxnews@ftb.ca.gov
    Tax News Editor MS F280
    Franchise Tax Board
    PO Box 1468
    Sacramento CA 95812-1468
Tax Practitioner Hotline 916.845.7057
    Fax 916.845.9300
Tax Shelter Hotline 916.845.4300
    Email: taxshelter@ftb.ca.gov
    Go to **ftb.ca.gov** and search for **Shelter Hotline.**
Taxpayers' Rights Advocate
    Advocate Hotline 800.883.5910
    Fax 916.843.6022
    Executive and Advocate Services MS A381
    Franchise Tax Board
    PO Box 157
    Rancho Cordova CA 95741-0157
Top 500
    Personal Income Tax 888.426.8555
    Business Entities Tax 888.426.8751
    Franchise Tax Board
    PO Box 3065
    Rancho Cordova CA 95741-3065
Trusts, General Information 800.852.5711

V

Voluntary Disclosure Program 916.845.4476
    Mail application to:
    (U.S. Mail)
        Voluntary Disclosure Program MS F180
        Franchise Tax Board
        PO Box 1779
        Rancho Cordova CA 95741-1779
    (private express mail carriers such as Federal Express, United Parcel Service, DHL)
        Voluntary Disclosure Program MS F180
        Franchise Tax Board
        9646 Butterfield Way
        Sacramento CA 95827
Volunteer Income Tax Assistance/Tax Counseling for the Elderly (VITA/TCE) -volunteers only
    Email: volunteercoordinator@ftb.ca.gov

W

Water's-Edge 916.845.5568
    PO Box 1779
    Rancho Cordova CA 95741-1779
Water's-Edge Elections/Termination 916.845.5568
    PO Box 1779
    Rancho Cordova CA 95741-1779
Withholding Services and Compliance
(nonresident, real estate, or backup withholding information and questions)

Email: wscs.gen@ftb.ca.gov
From within the United States 888.792.4900
From outside the United States . . : 916.845.4900
     Withholding Services and Compliance MS F182
     Franchise Tax Board
     PO Box 942867
     Sacramento CA 94267-0651
Withholding Voluntyary Compliance
     Program 888.792.4900
     Fax 916.843-0489
     Mail Completed FTB 4827, Withholding Voluntary Compliance Program Application, to:
     (U.S. Mail)
     WVCP Application
     Franchise Tax Board
     PO Box 942867
     Sacramento CA 94267-8888
     (Private express mail carriers such as Federal Express, United Parcel Service, DHL)
     Withholding Voluntary Compliance Program MS F182
     Franchise Tax Board
     9646 Butterfield Way
     Sacramento CA 95827

State Board of Equalization (SBE)

450 N Street, Room 2322, MIC 73

P.O. Box 942879

Sacramento, CA 94279-0001

Phone: (800) 400-7115 or (916) 445-6362

(800) 735-2929 (TDD phones)

(800) 735-2922 (TDD assistance/voice phones)

Internet: http://www.boe.ca.gov

Members:

— George Runner (First District)

— Finoa Ma (Second District)

— Jerome E. Horton (Third District)

— Diane L. Harkey (Fourth District)

— State Controller, Betty T. Yee

There are 21 SBE field offices for in-state accounts.

Bakersfield —1800 30th St, Suite 380, 93301-1922; (661) 395-2880

Culver City —5901 Green Valley Circle, Suite 200, PO Box 3652, 90231-3652; (310) 342-1000

El Centro —1550 W. Main St, PO Box 197, 92244-2832; (760) 352-3431

Fairfield —2480 Hilborn Rd., Suite 200, 94534; (707) 427-4800

Fresno —8050 N. Palm Ave., Suite 205, 93711-5510; (559) 440-5330

Glendale —505 North Brand Boulevard, Ste. 700, 91203-3946; (818) 543-4900

Irvine —16715 Von Karman Ave., Suite 200, 92606-2444, (949) 440-3473

Norwalk —12440 E. Imperial Hwy, Suite 201, PO Box 409, 90651-0409; (562) 466-1694

Oakland —1515 Clay St, Suite 303, 94612-1432; (510) 622-4100

Rancho Cucamonga —10760 4th Street, Ste. 200, 94612-1432; (909) 243-9650

Rancho Mirage —35-900 Bob Hope Dr, Suite 280, 92270-1768; (760) 770-4828

Redding —2881 Churn Creek Rd, Suite B, PO Box 492529, 96002-1146; (530) 224-4729

Riverside —3737 Main St, Suite 1000, 92501-3395; (951) 680-6400

Sacramento —3321 Power Inn Rd, Suite 210, 95826-3889; (916) 227-6700

Salinas —950 E. Blanco Road, Suite 20200, 93901; (831) 754-4500

San Diego —15015 Avenue of Science, Ste. 200, 92128; (858) 385-4700

San Francisco —121 Spear St., Suite 460, 94105-1584; (415) 356-6600

Santa Clarita —25360 Magic Mountain Parkway, Suite 330, 91355; (408) 277-1231

Santa Rosa —50 D St, Rm 230, PO Box 730, 95404-4791; (707) 576-2100

Ventura —4820 McGrath St, Suite 260, 93003-7778; (805) 677-2700

West Covina —1521 W. Cameron Ave, Suite 300, PO Box 1500, 91793-1500; (626) 480-7200

There are four SBE field offices for out-of-state accounts.

Sacramento, CA —3321 Power Inn Rd, Suite 130, PO Box 188268, 95826-3893; (916) 227-6600

Chicago, IL —120 N. La Salle, Suite 1600, 60602-2412; (312) 201-5300

New York, NY —485 Lexington Ave, Suite 400, 10017; (212) 697-4680

Houston, TX —1415 Louisiana St., Suite 1500, 77002-7471; (713) 739-9300

There are two non-sales tax offices.

Motor Carrier Office —1030 Riverside Parkway, Ste. 125 West Sacramento, CA 95605; (916) 373-3070

Special Taxes and Fees —450 N St. Sacramento, CA 95814; (916) 327-0859

Employment Development Department

P.O. Box 826880, UIPCD, MIC 40

Sacramento, CA 94280-0001

Phone: (888) 745-3886

(800) 547-9565 (TTY users)

Internet: http://www.edd.ca.gov

Secretary of State

1500 11th Street

Sacramento, CA 95814

Phone: (916) 653-6814

Internet: http://www.sos.ca.gov/

State Controller

P.O. Box 942850

Sacramento, CA 94250-5872

Phone: (916) 445-2636

Internet: http://www.sco.ca.gov

County property tax assessors

County assessors are the source of specific property tax information and appropriate forms. County assessor addresses and telephone numbers are as follows:

California County Assessors

ALAMEDA COUNTY ASSESSOR
1221 Oak Street, Room 145
Oakland, CA 94612-4288
(510) 272-3755
ALPINE COUNTY ASSESSOR
99 Water Street
P.O. Box 155
Markleeville, CA 96120-0155
(530) 694-2283
AMADOR COUNTY ASSESSOR
810 Court Street
Jackson, CA 95642-2132

(209) 223-6351
BUTTE COUNTY ASSESSOR
25 County Center Drive
Oroville, CA 95965-3382
(530) 538-7721
CALAVERAS COUNTY ASSESSOR
891 Mountain Ranch Road
San Andreas, CA 95249-9709
(209) 754-6356
COLUSA COUNTY ASSESSOR
547 Market Street, Suite 101
Colusa, CA 95932-2452
(530) 458-0450

CONTRA COSTA COUNTY ASSESSOR
2530 Arnold Drive, Suite 400
Martinez, CA 94553-4359
(925) 313-7500

DEL NORTE COUNTY ASSESSOR
981 H Street, Suite 120
Crescent City, CA 95531-3415
(707) 464-7200

EL DORADO COUNTY ASSESSOR
360 Fair Lane
Placerville, CA 95667-4103
(530) 621-5719

FRESNO COUNTY ASSESSOR
2281 Tulare Street, Rm. 201
P.O. Box 1146
Fresno, CA 93715-1146
(559) 488-3534

GLENN COUNTY ASSESSOR
516 West Sycamore Street, 2nd Floor
Willows, CA 95988
(530) 934-6402

HUMBOLDT COUNTY ASSESSOR
825 Fifth Street, Rm. 300
Eureka, CA 95501-1153
(707) 445-7663

IMPERIAL COUNTY ASSESSOR
940 West Main Street, Suite 115
El Centro, CA 92243-2874
(442) 265-4243

INYO COUNTY ASSESSOR
168 North Edwards Street, PO Box J
Independence, CA 93526-0609
(760) 878-0302

KERN COUNTY ASSESSOR
1115 Truxtun Avenue, 3rd Floor
Bakersfield, CA 93301-4617
(661) 868-3485

KINGS COUNTY ASSESSOR
1400 West Lacey Blvd
Hanford, CA 93230-5997
(559) 582-2486

LAKE COUNTY ASSESSOR
255 North Forbes Street
Lakeport, CA 95453-5997
(707) 263-2302

LASSEN COUNTY ASSESSOR
220 South Lassen Street, Suite 4
Susanville, CA 96130-4324
(530) 251-8241

LOS ANGELES COUNTY ASSESSOR
500 W. Temple Street, Rm. 320
Los Angeles, CA 90012-2770
(213) 974-3211

MADERA COUNTY ASSESSOR
200 West 4th St.
Madera, CA 93637-3548
(559) 675-7710

MARIN COUNTY ASSESSOR
3501 Civic Center Drive, Rm. 208
P.O. Box C
San Rafael, CA 94913-3902
(415) 499-7215

MARIPOSA COUNTY ASSESSOR
4982 Tenth Street
P.O. Box 35
Mariposa, CA 95338-0035
(209) 966-2332

MENDOCINO COUNTY ASSESSOR
501 Low Gap Road, Rm. 1020
Ukiah, CA 95482-3738
(707) 234-6800

MERCED COUNTY ASSESSOR
2222 M Street
Merced, CA 95340-3780
(209) 385-7631

MODOC COUNTY ASSESSOR
204 South Court Street, Rm. 106
Alturas, CA 96101-4064
(530) 233-6218

MONO COUNTY ASSESSOR
25 Bryant Street
P.O. Box 456
Bridgeport, CA 93517-0456
(760) 932-5510

MONTEREY COUNTY ASSESSOR
168 West Alisal Street, Floor 1
Salinas, CA 93901
(831) 755-5035

NAPA COUNTY ASSESSOR
1127 First Street, Rm. 128
Napa, CA 94559-2931
(707) 253-4467

NEVADA COUNTY ASSESSOR
950 Maidu Ave.
Nevada City, CA 95959-8600
(530) 265-1232

ORANGE COUNTY ASSESSOR
Civic Center Plaza, Building 11
25 N. Ross St., Rm. 142
Santa Ana, CA 92702-0149
(714) 834-2727

PLACER COUNTY ASSESSOR
2980 Richardson Drive
Auburn, CA 95603-2640
(530) 889-4300

PLUMAS COUNTY ASSESSOR
1 Crescent Street
Quincy, CA 95971
(530) 283-6380

RIVERSIDE COUNTY ASSESSOR
4080 Lemon Street
P.O. Box 12004
Riverside, CA 92502-2204
(951) 955-6200

SACRAMENTO COUNTY ASSESSOR
3701 Power Inn Road, Suite 3000
Sacramento, CA 95826-4329
(916) 875-0760

SAN BENITO COUNTY ASSESSOR
440 Fifth Street, Room 108
Hollister, CA 95023-3893
(831) 636-4030

SAN BERNARDINO COUNTY ASSESSOR
172 W. Third Street, 5th Floor
San Bernardino, CA 92415-0310
(909) 387-6300

SAN DIEGO COUNTY ASSESSOR
1600 Pacific Highway, Rm. 110
San Diego, CA 92101-2480
(619) 531-5507

SAN FRANCISCO COUNTY ASSESSOR
1 Dr. Carlton B. Goodlett Place, Rm 190
San Francisco, CA 94102-4698
(415) 554-5596

SAN JOAQUIN COUNTY ASSESSOR
44 N. San Joaquin St., Ste. 230
Stockton, CA 95202-3273
(209) 468-2630

SAN LUIS OBISPO COUNTY ASSESSOR
1055 Monterey Street, Suite D360
San Luis Obispo, CA 93408-2070
(805) 781-5643

SAN MATEO COUNTY ASSESSOR
555 County Center, 3rd Floor
Redwood City, CA 94063-1655
(650) 363-4988

SANTA BARBARA COUNTY ASSESSOR
105 East Anapamu Street, Rm. 204
P.O. Box 159
Santa Barbara, CA 93101-0159
(805) 568-2550

SANTA CLARA COUNTY ASSESSOR
70 West Hedding Street, East Wing
San Jose, CA 95110-1705
(408) 299-5500

SANTA CRUZ COUNTY ASSESSOR
701 Ocean Street, Rm. 130
Santa Cruz, CA 95060-4007
(831) 454-2002

SHASTA COUNTY ASSESSOR
County Courthouse
1450 Court Street, Suite 208-A
Redding, CA 96001-1667
(530) 225-3600
SIERRA COUNTY ASSESSOR
100 Courthouse Square, Room B1
P.O. Box 8
Downieville, CA 95936-0008
(530) 289-3283
SISKIYOU COUNTY ASSESSOR
311 Fourth Street, Room 108
Yreka, CA 96097-2984
(530) 842-8036
SOLANO COUNTY ASSESSOR
675 Texas Street, Suite 2700
Fairfield, CA 94533-6338
(707) 784-6210
SONOMA COUNTY ASSESSOR
585 Fiscal Drive, Rm. 104F
Santa Rosa, CA 95403-2872
(707) 565-1888
STANISLAUS COUNTY ASSESSOR
1010 10th Street, Suite 2400
Modesto, CA 95354-0847
(209) 525-6461
SUTTER COUNTY ASSESSOR
1160 Civic Center Blvd., Suite D
P.O. Box 1555
Yuba City, CA 95993-3007

(530) 822-7160
TEHAMA COUNTY ASSESSOR
444 Oak Street, Room B
Red Bluff, CA 96080-0428
(530) 527-5931
TRINITY COUNTY ASSESSOR
11 Court Street, 1st Floor
P.O. Box 1255
Weaverville, CA 96093-1255
(530) 623-1257
TULARE COUNTY ASSESSOR
221 S. Mooney Blvd, Room 102-E
Visalia, CA 93291-4593
(559) 636-5100
TUOLUMNE COUNTY ASSESSOR
2 South Green Street
Sonora, CA 95370-4618
(209) 533-5535
VENTURA COUNTY ASSESSOR
800 South Victoria Avenue
Ventura, CA 93009-1270
(805) 654-2181
YOLO COUNTY ASSESSOR
625 Court Street, Room 104
Woodland, CA 95695-3495
(530) 666-8135
YUBA COUNTY ASSESSOR
915 8th Street, Suite 101
Marysville, CA 95901-5273
(530) 749-7820

California Department of Housing and Community Development, 2020 West El Camino, CA 95833

General Information . . . . (916) 263-7400

Internet: http://www.hcd.ca.gov/

California Department of Insurance, Producer Licensing Bureau, 300 Capitol Mall, Suite 1700, Sacramento, CA 95814

General Information 800-967-9331

Internet: http://www.insurance.ca.gov/

California Department of Motor Vehicles, Office of the Director, 2415 First Avenue Mail Station F101, Sacramento, CA 95818-2606

General Information 800-777-0133

Internet: http://www.dmv.ca.gov/

California Department of Alcoholic Beverage Control, 3927 Lennane Drive, Suite 100, Sacramento, CA 95834

Headquarters 916-419-2500

Internet: http://www.abc.ca.gov/

PART X

DOING BUSINESS IN CALIFORNIA

CHAPTER 21
FEES AND TAXES

¶2101	Domestic Corporations
¶2102	Foreign Corporations

¶2101 Domestic Corporations

Law: Secs. 17941, 17946, 23151, 23153, Revenue and Taxation Code (CCH CALIFORNIA TAX REPORTS, ¶1-101).

California has several business-related enactments addressing the formation, operation, combination, and dissolution, etc. of for-profit domestic corporations and other domestic business entities. These corporate, limited liability company (LLC), and assorted partnership enactments provide significant information regarding the internal operations of a corporation, LLC, partnership, or other business entity, such as ownership rights, voting rules, director/manager obligations, and bylaw/agreement contents, etc. These enactments also address the service fees that are applicable to the various interactions between the state and the above domestic business entities. Business law resources and applicable fee information generally are found on the California Secretary of State website at http://www.sos.ca.gov/. Forms generally can be found at http://www.sos.ca.gov/business-programs/business-entities/forms/.

• *Corporate entities*

A minimum franchise tax of $800 is imposed on all corporations, including banks and financial corporations, not otherwise exempt from tax. (Sec. 23153, Rev. & Tax. Code; Sec. 23151, Rev. & Tax. Code; Sec. 17941, Rev. & Tax. Code; Sec. 17946, Rev. & Tax. Code) Corporations subject to the corporation income tax are not subject to the minimum franchise tax.

All parties desiring to incorporate a for-profit domestic corporation in California, that is, a corporation created under the laws of the state, must execute and file articles of incorporation with the Secretary of State. Among other items, such articles generally provide the name of the corporation, the number of shares that the corporation may issue, the address of the corporation's registered office in the state, and the name of its registered agent authorized to receive the service of process.

The California Secretary of State imposes and collects a service fee for this filing. The Secretary also charges other related fees for assorted corporate filing activities. Such fees are generally payable at the time that the requisite documents are filed.

• *Other business entities*

In addition to forming and operating as a domestic corporation, among other choices, a business taxpayer can choose to form and operate as either a domestic LLC or as one of the varied domestic partnership formats. The noncorporate business entity choices are briefly addressed below.

LLCs.—California's general LLC law provisions addressing domestic LLCs are found within Corporations Code, Title 2.5 Limited Liability Companies. Operative January 1, 2014, Corporations Code, Title 2.6 Revised Uniform Limited Liability Company Act will replace the current law.

All parties desiring to organize a for-profit domestic LLC in California, that is, an LLC created under the laws of the state, must execute and file articles of organization with the Secretary of State. Among other items, such articles generally provide the name of the LLC, the address of the initial designated office, the name and address of the initial agent for service of process, and the name and address of each organizer.

Partnerships.—California's general partnership law provisions addressing domestic partnerships are found within Corporations Code, Title 2 Partnerships, Chapter 5 Uniform Partnership Act of 1994.

¶2102 Foreign Corporations

Law: CCH CALIFORNIA TAX REPORTS, ¶1-110.

California has several business-related enactments addressing the qualification and operation of for-profit foreign corporations and other foreign business entities. These corporate, limited liability company (LLC), and assorted partnership enactments provide significant information regarding the internal operations of a corporation, LLC, partnership, or other business entity, such as ownership rights, voting rules, director/manager obligations, and bylaw/agreement contents, etc. These enactments also address the service fees that are applicable to the various interactions between the state and the above foreign business entities.

Business resources, fee information, and forms generally are available on the Secretary of State website (see ¶2101).

• *Corporate entities*

California's general corporation law provisions addressing foreign corporations are found within the Corporations Code, Title 1 Corporations, Division 1 General Corporation Law, Chapter 21 Foreign Corporations.

In the same manner that the incorporation of a domestic corporation and its ability to do business in California is a privilege to be conferred only by law and upon such conditions and payments as the state sees fit, the exercise of the corporate franchise in California and the transaction of business in the state by a business entity created and incorporated elsewhere is a privilege upon which conditions may be imposed and for which fees may be charged. No foreign corporation may engage in any business in California until all applicable fees have been paid, the entity has filed a statement and designation form with the Secretary of State, and the Secretary has processed the form.

After the form has been processed by the Secretary of State, the foreign corporation possesses rights, privileges, duties, and restrictions comparable to those of a domestic corporation incorporated in the state.

A party desiring to qualify a foreign corporation in California must file a statement and designation with the Secretary of State. Among other items, such an application must generally provide the name of the corporation, the place of incorporation, the address of its principal office, the number of shares that the corporation may issue, the address of the foreign corporation's registered office in the state, and the name of its registered agent authorized to receive the service of process.

A foreign corporation that transacts business in the state without filing the statement and designation is liable to the state for the years or parts thereof during which it engaged in business without a certificate of authority. The charge will be an amount equal to all fees that would have been imposed upon the corporation had it applied for and received a certificate of authority and filed all of the required reports, plus all penalties for the failure to pay the fees. The state's Attorney General will bring proceedings to recover all amounts due to the state.

- *Other business entities*

   In addition to operating as a foreign corporation, among other choices, a business taxpayer can choose to operate as either a foreign LLC or as one of the varied foreign partnership formats. The noncorporate business entity choices are briefly addressed below.

   The same type of miscellaneous fees applicable to domestic corporations also apply to foreign corporations (see ¶2101).

   LLCs.—California's general LLC law provisions addressing foreign LLCs are found within Corporations Code, Title 2.5 Limited Liability Companies. Operative January 1, 2014, Corporations Code, Title 2.6 Revised Uniform Limited Liability Company Act will replace the current law.

   All parties desiring to qualify a for-profit foreign LLC in California must present the LLC's articles of organization and execute and file an application to register with the Secretary of State. Among other items, the articles of organization generally provide the name of the LLC, the address of the initial designated office, the name and address of the initial agent for service of process, and the name and address of each organizer.

   Partnerships.—California's general partnership law provisions addressing foreign partnerships are found within Corporations Code, Title 2 Partnerships, Chapter 5 Uniform Partnership Act of 1994.

PART XI

UNCLAIMED PROPERTY

CHAPTER 22
UNCLAIMED PROPERTY

¶2201 Unclaimed Property

"Unclaimed property" generally is all property that:

— is unclaimed, abandoned, escheated, permanently escheated, or distributed to the state;

— will become unclaimed, abandoned, escheated, permanently escheated, or distributed to the state; or

— will become the possession of the state, if not claimed within the time allowed by law, even if there is no judicial determination that the property is unclaimed, abandoned, escheated, permanently escheated, or distributed to the state.

(Sec. 1300, Code of Civ. Proc.)

"Escheat" generally is the vesting in the state of property whose known owner has refused to accept it or whose owner is unknown. (Sec. 1300, Code of Civ. Proc.) Escheat is essentially a state process; procedures for federal unclaimed property are not as clearly set out as those of the states.

The California State Controller's Office periodically updates and issues the State of California Unclaimed Property Holder Handbook, Office of California State Controller. Generally, the publication discusses reporting instructions, remittance, report formats, and other considerations for holders.

• *Abandoned property—dormancy*

Generally, all tangible and intangible personal property that is held or owing in the ordinary course of a holder's business and that has remained unclaimed by the owner for more than three years either from the date of the last activity of the owner or after the property became payable or distributable, depending on the type of property, escheats to the state. (Sec. 1520, Code of Civ. Proc.) Dormancy periods for specific types of property, including properties with exceptions to the three-year rule, are as follows:

— drafts, cashier's checks, seller's checks, or certified checks, three years; (Sec. 1513(a)(4), Code of Civ. Proc.)

— demand deposits, three years; Sec. 1513(a)(1)(A), Code of Civ. Proc.

— for property distributable in the course of demutualization or related reorganization of an insurance company: (Sec. 1515.5, Code of Civ. Proc.) and

(1) the date of demutualization if the owner address is known to be incorrect,

(2) two years if notices to owner are returned uindeliverable, and

(3) three years if the notices are not returned;

— stocks, bonds, and dividends, three years; Sec. 1516, Code of Civ. Proc.

— employment benefit plan, three years; (Sec. 1521, Code of Civ. Proc.)

— escrow accounts, three years; (Sec. 1518, Code of Civ. Proc.)

— gift certificates with expiration dates that are given in exchange for money or value, three years; (Sec. 1520.5, Code of Civ. Proc.)

— interest, three years; (Sec. 1513(a)(1)(A), Code of Civ. Proc.; Sec. 1516, Code of Civ. Proc.)

— IRAs and retirement plans, three years; (Sec. 1518, Code of Civ. Proc.)

— life insurance funds, three years; (Sec. 1515, Code of Civ. Proc.)

— property held in Interest on Lawyers' Trust Accounts (IOLTA), three years; (Sec. 1564.5, Code of Civ. Proc.)

— distribution from a dissolved or liquidated business, six months; Sec. 1517, Code of Civ. Proc.

— matured time deposits (CDs), three years; (Sec. 1513(a)(1)(A), Code of Civ. Proc.)

— money orders, electronic transfers with a written instrument, seven years; (Sec. 1513(a)(5), Code of Civ. Proc.)

— ordered refunds, one year; (Sec. 1519.5, Code of Civ. Proc.)

— safe-deposit boxes, three years; (Sec. 1514, Code of Civ. Proc.)

— savings, three years; (Sec. 1513(a)(1)(A), Code of Civ. Proc.)

— traveler's checks, 15 years; (Sec. 1513(a)(3), Code of Civ. Proc.) and

— wages or salaries, one year; (Sec. 1513(a)(7), Code of Civ. Proc.)

— other tangible and intangible property, three years. (Sec. 1520, Code of Civ. Proc.)

(State of California Unclaimed Property Holder Handbook, Office of California State Controller)

Gift certificates, gift cards.—Generally, gift certificates are exempt from reporting requirements in California. However, gift certificates having an expiration date that are given in exchange for money or other things of value are presumed abandoned if left unclaimed by the owner for more than three years after they became payable or distributable. (Sec. 1520, Code of Civ. Proc.; Sec. 1520.5, Code of Civ. Proc.; Sec. 1749.5, Civ. Code) Gift cards are treated the same as gift certificates for unclaimed property purposes. (Sec. 1749.45, Civ. Code)

Practitioner Comment: Bed Bath & Beyond Inc. v. John Chiang, Superior Court of California held that merchandise return credits ("MRC") issued to California customers by Bed Bath & Beyond ("BB&B") are gift certificates exempt from California Unclaimed Property Law.

On March 4, 2016, the Superior Court of California, San Diego held that a retailer was entitled to judgment for a refund of unredeemed merchandise return credits escheated to California since store credits are considered gift certificates not subject to unclaimed property law and because the retailer did not owe money to the owner of the store credits (*Bed Bath & Beyond Inc. v. John Chiang*, Superior Court of California, County of San Diego, No. 37-2014-00012491-CU-MC-CTL, March 04, 2016).

Under the terms of BB&B's return policy, a customer returning merchandise is not entitled to a cash refund without an original receipt. As a courtesy in such instances, BB&B issues MRCs that do not expire. An MRC recipient must purchase merchandise at BB&B and present the certificate to realize the value associated with it. The court agreed with BB&B when it stated that MRCs are not a value "owed" to the customer, and are closely akin to a gift certificate. Accordingly, the court determined that MRCs are not subject to escheat.

Chris Whitney, Contributing Editor

Custodial property.—A custodial account is an account opened on behalf of someone else, such as one opened by a parent for a minor child. Custodial accounts most often arise under the Uniform Transfers to Minors Act (UTMA). A custodial account is based on a fiduciary relationship between the custodian and the beneficiary; the custodian must account for the property and turn it over to the beneficiary when he or she reaches majority. If the named custodian is a parent or other individual who opened the account for the benefit of a minor, then such property escheats pursuant to Sec. 1513, which requires property to be escheated three years from the date of last contact or date of last activity. If the holder is the named custodian on the account for the benefit of the owner, then property escheats pursuant to Sec. 1518, which requires property to be escheated three years from the date the account is payable or distributable to the beneficiary. (*Unclaimed Property Program Newsletter*,California State Controller's Office, July 1, 2013; as revised August 20, 2013, ¶ 405-924)

Practitioner Comment: U.S. Supreme Court Declines to review 9th Circuit decision upholding California's escheat regulations

On February 29, 2016, the U.S. Supreme Court denied a group of plaintiffs' petition for writ of certiorari in *Chris Lusby Taylor, et al., v. Betty Yee* (780 F.3d 928 (2015). The writ was intended to overturn the Ninth Circuit decision which held that the notice procedures for California's Abandoned Unclaimed Property system do not violate the Fifth and Fourteenth Amendments of the U.S. Constitution. The Ninth Circuit found that the Controller made the requisite "reasonable efforts" to notify property owners that the property was subject to escheat.

In a note denying the writ of certiorari, Justice Alito stated that, "The convoluted history of this case makes it a poor vehicle for reviewing the important question it presents, and therefore I concur in the denial of review. But the constitutionality of current state escheat laws is a question that may merit review in a future case."

Chris Whitney, Contributing Editor

Business-to-business exemption

California does not have a business-to-business exemption. (Sec. 1502, Code of Civ. Proc.; State of California Unclaimed Property Holder Handbook, Office of California State Controller)

• *Obligations of holder of unclaimed property*

Information reports are required of persons holding property (*e.g.*, banks and insurance companies) that has escheated to the state by reason of a presumption of abandonment, as described above. The report is made to the State Controller on Form UFS-1 and is due before November 1 for each year ending as of June 30 or earlier. The reports of life insurance companies and all insurance corporation demutualization proceeds must be filed by May 1 of each year ending as of December 31 or earlier. The report requires identification of the property and its former owner and dates when the property became payable and when the last transaction with the owner occurred. (Sec. 1530, Code of Civ. Proc.)

Aggregate reporting.—Items of value under $25 each may be reported in the aggregate. Banking and finance organizations' holder reports must include, among other items and except with respect to traveler's checks and money orders, the name, if known, and last known address of each person appearing from the records of the holder to be the owner of any property of value of at least $25. (Sec. 1530, Code of Civ. Proc.)

Negative reporting.—Organizations that neither hold nor owe unclaimed property are not required to submit a report, although it is recommended that they do so by completing and filing the UFS-1 form only. The Controller may require the filing of such a report by sending notification to the holder. (State of California Unclaimed Property Holder Handbook, Office of California State Controller)

Examination of record.—The controller may, at reasonable times and upon reasonable notice, examine the records of any person the controller has reason to believe has failed to report unclaimed property. (Sec. 1571, Code of Civ. Proc.) The controller also may bring a court action to

— enforce the duty of any person subject to the unclaimed property law to permit examination of that person's records;

— obtain a judicial determination that particular property is subject to escheat; and

— enforce the delivery of any qualifying property to the controller.

(Sec. 1572, Code of Civ. Proc.)

Electronic transactions showing account activity.—Commencing on or before January 1, 2018, unclaimed property holders must regard certain electronically initiated transactions that are reflected in the books and records of a banking or financial organization as evidence that the owner has increased or decreased the amount of the funds or deposit in an account. The electronically initiated transactions are:

— a single or recurring debit transaction authorized by the owner;

— a single or recurring credit transaction authorized by the owner;

— recurring transactions authorized by the owner that represent payroll deposits or deductions; or

— recurring transactions authorized by the owner that represent the deposit of any federal benefits, including social security benefits, veterans' benefits, and pension payments.

(Sec. 1513(c), Code of Civ. Proc.)

• *Identified unclaimed property*

In order to inform owners of identified unclaimed property, the Controller must mail, within 165 days after the final date for filing the report of escheated funds or property, a notice to each person having an address listed in the report who appears to be entitled to property with a value of $50 or more that has been escheated. If the report includes a social security number, the Controller must request that the California Franchise Tax Board (FTB) provide a current address for the apparent owner on the basis of that number. (Sec. 1531, Code of Civ. Proc.)

The Controller must mail the notice to the apparent owner for whom a current address is obtained if the address is different from the address previously reported to the Controller. If the FTB does not provide an address or a different address, then the Controller must mail the notice to the address listed in the report. The mailed notice must contain:

(1) a statement that, according to a report filed with the Controller, property is being held to which the addressee appears entitled;

(2) the name and address of the person holding the property and any necessary information regarding changes of name and address of the holder; and

(3) a statement that, if satisfactory proof of claim is not presented by the owner to the holder by the date specified in the notice, the property will be placed in the custody of the Controller and may be sold or destroyed, and all further claims concerning the property or, if sold, the net proceeds of its sale, must be directed to the Controller.

(Sec. 1531, Code of Civ. Proc.)

Practitioner Comment: A.B. 2258, passed August 29, 2016 amends Section 1513 of the Code of Civil Procedure that electronic fund transfer transactions constitute activity on the account for determining inactivity for escheat purposes.

On August 29, 2016 the Governor signed A.B. 2258, amending sections 1513 of the Code of Civil Procedure, thereby clarifying that electronic fund transfer transactions constitute activity on the account for determining inactivity for escheat purposes.

Existing law prescribes the circumstances under which property held or owing by a business escheats to the state. Existing law specifies that any demand, savings, or matured time deposit, or account subject to a negotiable order of withdrawal, made with a banking organization escheats to the state if the owner, for more than three years, has not increased or decreased the amount of the deposit. Existing law specifies that any demand, savings, or matured time deposit, or matured investment certificate, or account subject to a negotiable order of withdrawal, or other interest in a financial organization, escheats to the state when the owner, for more than three years, has not increased or decreased the amount of the funds or deposit.

This bill would require, commencing on or before January 1, 2018, for purposes of determining whether the above-described property escheats to the state, that a holder, as defined in existing law, regard specified transactions that are initiated electronically and are reflected in the books and records of a banking or financial organization as evidence of an increase or decrease in the amount of the funds or deposit in an account held by the banking or financial organization.

Chris Whitney, Contributing Editor

• *Notification program*

The Controller must establish and conduct a notification program designed to inform owners about the possible existence of unclaimed property that has been received. Upon the request of the Controller, a state or local governmental agency may furnish to the Controller from its records the address or other identification or location information that could reasonably be used to locate an owner of unclaimed property. If the address or other information requested is deemed confidential under any California laws or regulations, it shall nevertheless be furnished to the Controller. However, neither the Controller nor any officer, agent, or employee of the Controller shall use or disclose that information except as may be necessary in attempting to locate the owner of the unclaimed property. (Sec. 1531.5, Code of Civ. Proc.)

The Controller must publish a notice listing the names of the apparent owners, together with their last known address, within one year of the payment or delivery of the unclaimed property. (Sec. 1531, Code of Civ. Proc.)

The Controller may mail a separate notice to an apparent owner of a U.S. savings bond, war bond, or military award found in a safe deposit box. The notice can be sent to an apparent owner whose name:

(1) is shown on or associated with the contents of a safe deposit box and

(2) is different from the name of the reported owner.

(Sec. 1531.6, Code of Civ. Proc.)

Banking and financial organizations' notice requirements.—Generally, banks and financial organizations with records of an apparent owner for unclaimed property must make a reasonable effort to give notice to owners that their property will escheat to the state either:

(1) not less than two years nor more than two and one-half years after the date of last activity by, or communication with, the owner with respect to the account, deposit, shares, or other interest, as shown on the record of the banking or financial organization; or

(2) not less than six months nor more than 12 months before the time the item becomes reportable to the Controller.

Banks and financial organizations must provide written notice to any person opening an account informing that person that the property may be transferred to the appropriate state if no activity occurs in the account within the time specified by state law. (Sec. 1513.5(e), Code of Civ. Proc.) Similar written notice must be given by a business association to any person leasing a safe deposit box or safekeeping repository that the property, or the proceeds of the sale of the property, may be transferred to the appropriate state upon running of the time period specified by state law. (Sec. 1514(i), Code of Civ. Proc.)

If a banking or financial organization sends an escheat notice to the owner of a deposit, account, shares, or other interest that has a value greater than $2, the organization may not impose a service charge for the notice in excess of $2. Such notice is not required for deposits, accounts, shares, or other interests of less than $50 and, except as noted immediately above, no service charge may be made for those notices. (Sec. 1513.5(b), Code of Civ. Proc.)

Practitioner Comment: Court of Appeal Rejects Due Process Challenge to State Escheat Law Based Upon Two Week Notice Period

The California Court of Appeal held in an unpublished decision that California's unclaimed property law is not facially unconstitutional in *San Diego v. MJB Research LLC*, Cal. Ct. Appeal No. D055366, April 2, 2010. In *MJB*, the taxpayer filed a motion for release of funds that it claimed had been deposited in favor of its predecessor in interest with the Superior Court of San Diego in connection with eminent domain proceedings which had occurred in the 1980's. The Superior Court opposed the motion on the grounds that the funds had escheated to the court under Government Code Section 68084.1, which generally provides that money deposited with a court which remains unclaimed for three years becomes the property of the court provided that the court provides published notice. As set forth in the statute, the court had published the notice once per week for two successive weeks in a "newspaper of general circulation" in San Diego County. The court concluded that MJB failed to demonstrate that the court would in the "great majority of cases" be aware of the identity of the owner of the property in similar circumstances, a standard set forth by the California Supreme Court in *In re Guardianship of Ann S.*, 45 Cal.4th 1110 (2009) in assessing whether a statute would be sustained against a challenge on facial unconstitutionality grounds. The court thus concluded that the statute in question was not facially unconstitutional.

Chris Whitney, Contributing Editor

• *Delivery of unclaimed property*

Every person who files a report must, no sooner than seven months and no later than seven months and 15 days after the final date for filing the report, pay or deliver to the Controller all escheated property specified in the report. If a person establishes his or her right to receive any property specified in the report to the satisfaction of the holder before that property has been delivered to the Controller, or it appears that for any other reason the property may not be subject to escheat, the holder is not required to pay or deliver the property to the Controller but is instead required to file a report with the Controller that contains information regarding the property not subject to escheat. Any property not paid or delivered that is later determined by the holder to be subject to escheat is not subject to interest, as provided. (Sec. 1532, Code of Civ. Proc.)

Property reported as unclaimed must be delivered to the State Controller with the report. However, a holder of securities may register the securities in uncertificated form in the name of the Controller. Any payment of unclaimed cash in an amount of at least $20,000 must be made by electronic funds transfer. (Sec. 1532, Code of Civ. Proc.) The Controller may decline to take custody of certain tangible property. (Sec. 1533, Code of Civ. Proc.)

Practitioner Comment: 2011 UPL Amendments Seek to Ensure That Property is Returned to Rightful Owner

On September 23, 2011, the Governor signed S.B. 495, amending sections of the Code of Civil Procedure relating to unclaimed property. The legislation

— extends the period of time that property of no commercial value must be held by the Controller from 18 months to seven years;

— specifies additional circumstances under which certain funds in retirement accounts and plans become due and payable and exempts tangible or intangible property from escheating to the state if the fiduciary and owner of the property have taken specified actions regarding the property; and

— makes other technical and clarifying amendments, including property holder reporting requirements to specify that the person holding the property only need report property subject to escheat.

The UPL requires that funds held by a business association in various accounts or in safe-deposit boxes will escheat to the state after a designated period of time if the apparent owner fails to take any actions to claim that property or otherwise correspond with the holder of the property. This can happen for a variety of reasons, but most often it is due to a death, relocation, or transfer of property to an heir or relative with little or no knowledge of the account. At a certain point, usually after three years of non-activity or abandonment, the business holder reports it to the Controller and the property escheats to the state. The UPL also specifies the amount of time that the Controller must retain the property before selling or disposing of it, assuming the rightful owner cannot be located. This bill extends the amount of time that property of no commercial value is held by the Controller before disposal or liquidation. The object of the bill is to help ensure that such property is returned to the rightful owner.

Chris Whitney, Contributing Editor

Practitioner Comment: Corporation not Entitled to Immunity for Delivery of Escheated Stock to State Absent Full Compliance with Unclaimed Property Law

On July 16, 2009, the California Supreme Court held in *Azure Limited v. I-Flow Corporation*, that the immunity provided under the Unclaimed Property Law (UPL) for corporations delivering allegedly escheated stock to the state is limited to those corporations that fully comply with the UPL.

Azure Limited acquired shares of I-Flow Corporation stock. I-Flow later transferred those shares to the state as escheated property. The state sold the shares and delivered the proceeds to Azure. Azure suffered a significant loss because the sales price was lower than the price that Azure could have realized had the stock been held longer. Azure sued I-Flow for breach of fiduciary duty, alleging that I-Flow knew its location at all times and wrongly escheated its shares to the state without giving Azure notice. It sought to recover the difference between the sales proceeds and the shares' fair market value.

The trial court granted I-Flow judgment on the pleadings, finding the UPL granted absolute immunity to I-Flow. Azure appealed, and the court of appeal reversed, holding that the UPL immunized I-Flow from civil liability only when its transfer of escheated shares complied with the statute's notice requirements.

Chris Whitney, Contributing Editor

Interest, penalties, and interest amnesty.—Holders that fail to report and deliver unclaimed property, as required, are subject to annual interest payments of 12%, as well as to penalties, unless the failure is due to reasonable cause. If a holder delivers unclaimed property in a timely manner but fails to file a report that is in substantial compliance with requirements, interest payable shall not exceed $10,000. In addition, a holder is not subject to any interest payment if the failure to file a compliant report was due to reasonable cause. (Sec. 1577, Code of Civ. Proc.)

"Reasonable cause" means the exercise of ordinary business care and prudence. Specifically, interest will be waived if

(1) in the absence of willful neglect, the failure was due to circumstances beyond the holder's control or

(2) the delay or failure to file was due to erroneous information given to the holder of unclaimed property by an employee of the California Controller's office, unless the reliance was not reasonable cause for late reporting, payment or delivery.

The burden is on the property holder to establish reasonable cause. The property holder must submit a sworn affidavit to the Comptroller's office attesting to the circumstances establishing reasonable cause. (Reg. 1172.90, 2 CCR; Reg. 1172.92, 2 CCR)

Practitioner Comment: Award of Retroactive Interest Denied

In the U.S. Court of Appeals, Ninth Circuit case of *Suever v. Connell*(August 26, 2009), the court held that individuals were not entitled to retroactive interest on California unclaimed property under the Eleventh Amendment nor were they entitled to retroactive restitution in the amount of the difference between the proceeds from the sale of their unclaimed property and the current market value. The court denied the Plaintiffs' motion for a permanent injunction requiring the State to pay interest on unclaimed property at California's alternative borrowing rate. The Court also reversed the district court's rulings that the State is constitutionally required to pay interest when it returns property to owners under the Unclaimed Property Law (UPL).

Chris Whitney, Contributing Editor

• *Sale of escheated property*

No sale of escheated property may be made until 18 months after the final date for filing the report. Securities listed on an established stock exchange and other securities may be sold by the Controller no sooner than 18 months, but no later than 20 months, after the final date for filing the report. (Sec. 1563, Code of Civ. Proc.) Any property delivered to the Controller that has no apparent commercial value must be retained by the Controller for a period of not less than seven years from the date the property is delivered to the Controller. (Sec. 1501.5, Code of Civ. Proc.; Sec. 1565, Code of Civ. Proc.)

CCH Comment: Potential federal/state conflict

Escheat is an area of potential federal/state conflict. A federal statute may preempt state escheat provisions. For instance, it has been federal policy that the Employee Retirement Income Security Act of 1974 (ERISA) (particularly Sec. 514(a)) generally preempts state laws relating to employee benefit plans. Thus, funds of missing participants in a qualified employee benefit plan stay in the plan pursuant to the federal executive policy that state escheat laws are preempted by ERISA. (*Advisory Opinion 94-41A*, Department of Labor, Pension and Welfare Benefit Administration, Dec. 7, 1994) However, some states have challenged the federal position on this and similar narrowly delineated situations. Thus, practitioners are advised that a specific situation where federal and state policy cross on the issue of escheat may, at this time, be an area of unsettled law.

With respect to federal tax refunds, IRC Sec. 6408 disallows refunds if the refund would escheat to a state.

¶2201

• *Claims for recovery*

A period of five years is provided to make claims for the recovery of abandoned property. (Sec. 1351, Code of Civ. Proc.) The claim is filed with the State Controller on a form designated by that officer. The Controller must investigate the claim and render a decision within 180 days. The state officer must notify the claimant by mail. (Sec. 1540, Code of Civ. Proc.)

Only a person, other than another state, who claims to have been the owner of property paid or delivered to the Controller may file a claim to the property or to the net proceeds from its sale. The Controller will have 180 days within which to determine if the claimant is the owner. As amended, the law defines "owner" as

— the person who had legal right to the property prior to its escheat;

— his or her heir or estate representative;

— his or her guardian or conservator; or

— a public administrator acting pursuant to the Probate Code.

(Sec. 1540, Code of Civ. Proc.)

• *Claimant remedies*

Claims denied or not decided by the Controller within 180 days after the claim was filed may be appealed by filing an action naming the State Controller as defendant in the superior court of any county or city in which the California Attorney General has an office. (Sec. 1541, Code of Civ. Proc.) The action must be brought within 90 days of the Controller's decision or within 270 days after the claim is filed if the Controller fails to make a decision.

Table of Cases Cited

References are to paragraph (¶) numbers.

Table of Franchise Tax Board

Legal Rulings

References are to paragraph (¶) numbers.

Table of Franchise Tax Board

Notices

References are to paragraph (¶) numbers.

CALIFORNIA TAX FORMS AND RELATED

FEDERAL FORMS

State of California—Franchise Tax Board

The **CALIFORNIA TAX FORMS AND RELATED FEDERAL FORMS—FTB Pub. 1006** follows. The list of California Tax forms starts on page 846; the federal forms list starts on page 849.

State of California — Franchise Tax Board
FTB Pub. 1006

2016 CALIFORNIA TAX FORMS AND RELATED FEDERAL FORMS

FRANCHISE TAX BOARD (FTB) FORMS	CALIFORNIA FORM – Title or Description	RELATED FEDERAL FORM	MAY USE FEDERAL FORM See Notes
100	California Corporation Franchise or Income Tax Return	1120, 1120-F 1120-FSC, 1120-H 1120-POL, 1120-RIC 1120-REIT Sch D (1120)	No No No No No
Sch H (100)	Dividend Income Deduction	None	Not applicable
Sch P (100)	Alternative Minimum Tax and Credit Limitations — Corporations	4626	No
Sch R	Apportionment and Allocation of Income	None	Not applicable
Sch R-7	Election to File a Unitary Taxpayers' Group Return	851	No
100-ES	Corporation Estimated Tax	1120-W	No
FTB 3539	Payment for Automatic Extension for Corporations and Exempt Organizations	None	Not applicable
FTB 3805Q	Net Operating Loss (NOL) Computation and NOL and Disaster Loss Limitations — Corporations	None	Not applicable
FTB 3577	Pending Audit Tax Deposit Voucher for Corporations	None	Not applicable
FTB 3586	Payment Voucher for Corporations and Exempt Organizations e-filed Returns	None	Not applicable
FTB 3885	Corporation Depreciation and Amortization	4562	No
100S	California S Corporation Franchise or Income Tax Return	1120S	No
Sch B (100S)	S Corporation Depreciation and Amortization	4562	No
Sch C (100S)	S Corporation Tax Credits	None	Not applicable
Sch D (100S)	S Corporation Capital Gains and Losses and Built-In Gains	Sch D (1120S)	No
Sch H (100S)	S Corporation Dividend Income Deduction	None	Not applicable
Sch K-1 (100S)	Shareholder's Share of Income, Deductions, Credits, etc.	Sch K-1 (1120S)	No
Sch QS (100S)	Qualified Subchapter S Subsidiary (QSub) Information	None	Not applicable
100W	California Corporation Franchise or Income Tax Return — Water's-Edge Filers	None	Not applicable
Sch H (100W)	Dividend Income Deduction — Water's-Edge Filers	None	Not applicable
Sch P (100W)	Alternative Minimum Tax and Credit Limitations — Water's-Edge Filers	None	Not applicable
100-WE	Water's-Edge Election	None	Not applicable
FTB 1115	Request for Consent for a Water's-Edge Re-Election	None	Not applicable
FTB 1117	Request to Terminate Water's-Edge Election	None	Not applicable
FTB 2416	Schedule of Included Controlled Foreign Corporations (CFC)	None	Not applicable
FTB 2424	Water's-Edge Foreign Investment Interest Offset	None	Not applicable
100X	Amended Corporation Franchise or Income Tax Return	1120X	No
109	California Exempt Organization Business Income Tax Return	990-T	No
199	California Exempt Organization Annual Information Return	990, 990-EZ, 990-PF Sch A (990)	No No
540	California Resident Income Tax Return	1040	No
540-ES	Estimated Tax for Individuals	1040-ES	No
FTB 3519	Payment for Automatic Extension for Individuals	None	Not applicable
FTB 3885A	Depreciation and Amortization Adjustments	4562	No
Sch CA (540)	California Adjustments — Residents	None	Not applicable
Sch D (540)	California Capital Gain or Loss Adjustment	Sch D (1040)	No
Sch D-1	Sales of Business Property	4797	No
Sch G-1	Tax on Lump-Sum Distributions	4972	No
Sch P (540)	Alternative Minimum Tax and Credit Limitations — Residents	6251	No
Sch S	Other State Tax Credit	None	Not applicable
Sch W-2	Wage and Tax Statement	None	Not applicable
FTB 3525	Substitute for Form W-2, Wage and Tax Statement, or Form 1099-R, Distributions From Pensions, Annuities, Retirement or Profit-Sharing Plans, IRAs, Insurance Contracts, etc.	4852	Yes
540 2EZ	California Resident Income Tax Return	1040EZ	Not applicable
540NR	California Nonresident or Part-Year Resident Income Tax Return — (Long and Short Forms)	1040, 1040A, 1040NR, 1040NR-EZ	No No
Sch 1067A	Nonresident Group Return Schedule	None	Not applicable
Sch 1067B	Group Nonresident Return Payment Transfer Request	None	Not applicable
FTB 3864	Group Nonresident Return Election	None	Not applicable
FTB 3576	Pending Audit Tax Deposit Voucher for Individuals	None	Not applicable
Sch CA (540NR)	California Adjustments — Nonresidents or Part-Year Residents	None	Not applicable
Sch D (540NR)	California Capital Gain or Loss Adjustment	Sch D (1040)	No
Sch P (540NR)	Alternative Minimum Tax and Credit Limitations — Nonresidents or Part-Year Residents	6251	No
540X	Amended Individual Income Tax Return	1040X	No
541	California Fiduciary Income Tax Return	1041	No
Sch D (541)	Capital Gain or Loss	Sch D (1041)	No
Sch J (541)	Trust Allocation of an Accumulation Distribution	Sch J (1041)	No
Sch K-1 (541)	Beneficiary's Share of Income, Deductions, Credits, etc.	Sch K-1 (1041)	No
Sch P (541)	Alternative Minimum Tax and Credit Limitations – Fiduciaries	Sch I (1041)	No

FTB FORMS	CALIFORNIA FORM – Title or Description	RELATED FEDERAL FORM	MAY USE FEDERAL FORM See Notes
541-A	Trust Accumulation of Charitable Amounts	1041-A	No
541-B	Charitable Remainder and Pooled Income Trusts	5227	No
541-ES	Estimated Tax for Fiduciaries	1041-ES	No
541-QFT	California Income Tax Return for Qualified Funeral Trusts	1041-QFT	No
541-T	California Allocation of Estimated Tax Payments to Beneficiaries	1041-T	No
FTB 3885F (541)	Depreciation and Amortization	4562	No
565	Partnership Return of Income	1065	No
Sch D (565)	Capital Gain or Loss	Sch D (1065)	No
Sch EO (565)	Pass-Through Entity Ownership	None	No
Sch K-1 (565)	Partner's Share of Income, Deductions, Credits, etc.	Sch K-1 (1065)	No
FTB 3579	Pending Audit Tax Deposit Voucher for LPs, LLPs, and REMICs	None	Not applicable
FTB 3885P (565)	Depreciation and Amortization	4562	No
568	Limited Liability Company Return of Income	None	Not applicable
Sch D (568)	Capital Gain or Loss	Sch D (1065)	No
Sch EO (568)	Pass-Through Entity Ownership	None	No
Sch K-1 (568)	Member's Share of Income, Deductions, Credits, etc.	Sch K-1 (1065)	No
FTB 3578	Pending Audit Tax Deposit Voucher for Limited Liability Companies (LLCs)	None	Not applicable
FTB 3832	Limited Liability Company Nonresident Members' Consent	None	Not applicable
FTB 3885L (568)	Depreciation and Amortization	4562	No
570	Nonadmitted Insurance Tax Return	None	Not applicable
587	Nonresident Withholding Allocation Worksheet	None	Not applicable
588	Nonresident Withholding Waiver Request	None	Not applicable
589	Nonresident Reduced Withholding Request	8804-C	No
590	Withholding Exemption Certificate	None	Not applicable
590-P	Nonresident Withholding Exemption Certificate for Previously Reported Income	None	Not applicable
592	Resident and Nonresident Withholding Statement	1042, 8804	No
592-A	Payment Voucher for Foreign Partner or Member Withholding	8813	No
592-B	Resident and Nonresident Withholding Tax Statement	1042-S, 8805	No
592-F	Foreign Partner or Member Annual Return	1042, 8804	No
592-V	Payment Voucher for Resident and Nonresident Withholding	None	Not applicable
593	Real Estate Withholding Tax Statement	8288, 8288-A	No
593-C	Real Estate Withholding Certificate	8288-B	Not applicable
593-E	Real Estate Withholding — Computation of Estimated Gain or Loss	None	Not applicable
593-I	Real Estate Withholding Installment Sale Acknowledgement	None	Not applicable
593-V	Payment Voucher for Real Estate Withholding	None	Not applicable
FTB 3500	Exemption Application	1023, 1023-EZ, 1024	No
FTB 3500A	Submission of Exemption Request	1023, 1023-EZ, 1024	No
FTB 3502	Nonprofit Corporation Request for Pre-Dissolution Tax Abatement	None	Not applicable
FTB 3503	Natural Heritage Preservation Credit	None	Not applicable
FTB 3504	Enrolled Tribal Member Certification	None	Not applicable
FTB 3506	Child and Dependent Care Expenses Credit	2441	No
FTB 3507	Prison Inmate Labor Credit	None	Not applicable
FTB 3509	Political or Legislative Activities by Section 23701d Organizations	None	Not applicable
FTB 3510	Credit for Prior Year Alternative Minimum Tax — Individuals or Fiduciaries	8801	No
FTB 3511	Environmental Tax Credit	None	Not applicable
FTB 3514	California Earned Income Tax Credit	Sch EIC (1040A or 1040)	No
FTB 3516 (Side 1)	Request for Copy of Personal Income Tax or Fiduciary Tax Return	4506	No
FTB 3516 (Side 2)	Request for Copy of Corporation, Exempt Organization, Partnership, or Limited Liability Company Tax Return	4506	No
FTB 3519	Payment for Automatic Extension for Individuals	None	Not applicable
FTB 3520	Power of Attorney Declaration	2848, 8821	Yes
FTB 3521	Low-Income Housing Credit	8586	No
FTB 3522	LLC Tax Voucher	None	Not applicable
FTB 3523	Research Credit	6765	No
FTB 3525	Substitute for Form W-2, Wage and Tax Statement, or Form 1099-R, Distributions From Pensions, Annuities, Retirement or Profit-Sharing Plans, IRAs, Insurance Contracts, etc.	4852	Yes
FTB 3526	Investment Interest Expense Deduction	4952	No
FTB 3531	California Competes Tax Credit	None	Not applicable
FTB 3532	Head of Household Filing Status Schedule	None	No
FTB 3533	Change of Address for Individuals	8822	Yes
FTB 3533-B	Change of Address for Businesses, Exempt Organizations, Estates and Trusts	8822-B	Yes
FTB 3536	Estimated Fee for LLCs	None	Not applicable
FTB 3537	Payment for Automatic Extension for LLCs	None	Not applicable
FTB 3538	Payment for Automatic Extension for LPs, LLPs, and REMICs	None	Not applicable
FTB 3539	Payment for Automatic Extension for Corporations and Exempt Organizations	None	Not applicable
FTB 3540	Credit Carryover and Recapture Summary	None	Not applicable
FTB 3541	California Motion Picture and Television Production Credit	None	Not applicable
FTB 3544	Election to Assign Credit Within Combined Reporting Group	None	Not applicable

FTB FORMS	CALIFORNIA FORM – Title or Description	RELATED FEDERAL FORM	MAY USE FEDERAL FORM See Notes
FTB 3544A	List of Assigned Credit Received and/or Claimed by Assignee	None	Not applicable
FTB 3546	Enhanced Oil Recovery Credit	3800	No
FTB 3547	Donated Agricultural Products Transportation Credit	None	Not applicable
FTB 3548	Disabled Access Credit for Eligible Small Businesses	8826	No
FTB 3551	Sale of Credit Attributable to an Independent Film	None	Not applicable
FTB 3554	New Employment Credit	None	Not applicable
FTB 3561	Installment Agreement Financial Statement	433-D	No
FTB 3563	Payment for Automatic Extension for Fiduciaries	None	Not applicable
FTB 3567	Installment Agreement Request	9465	No
FTB 3570	Statute of Limitations Waiver	None	Not applicable
FTB 3574	Special Election for Business Trusts and Certain Foreign Single Member LLCs	None	Not applicable
FTB 3580	Application and Election to Amortize Certified Pollution Control Facility	None	Not applicable
FTB 3581	Tax Deposit Refund and Transfer Request	None	Not applicable
FTB 3582	Payment Voucher for Individual e-filed Returns	None	Not applicable
FTB 3586	Payment Voucher for Corporations and Exempt Organizations e-filed Returns	None	Not applicable
FTB 3587	Payment Voucher for LP, LLP, and REMIC e-filed Returns	None	Not applicable
FTB 3588	Payment Voucher for LLC e-filed Returns	None	Not applicable
FTB 3589	Nonprofit Organization Report of Funds Received and Used for Campaign Activity	8872	No
FTB 3592	College Access Tax Credit	None	Not applicable
FTB 3593	Extension of Time for Payment of Taxes by a Corporation Expecting a Net Operating Loss Carryback	1138	No
FTB 3596	Paid Preparer's California Earned Income Tax Credit Checklist	8867	No
FTB 3601	Transmittal of Annual 1098, 1099, 5498, W-2G Information	None	No
FTB 3604	Transmittal of Paperless Schedules K-1 (565 or 568) on CD or Portable USB/Flash Drive	None	Not applicable
FTB 3725	Assets Transferred from Corporation to Insurance Company	None	Not applicable
FTB 3726	Deferred Intercompany Stock Account (DISA) and Capital Gains Information	None	Not applicable
FTB 3800	Tax Computation for Certain Children with Unearned Income	8615	No
FTB 3801	Passive Activity Loss Limitations	8582	No
FTB 3801-CR	Passive Activity Credit Limitations	8582-CR	No
FTB 3802	Corporate Passive Activity Loss and Credit Limitations	8810	No
FTB 3803	Parents' Election to Report Child's Interest and Dividends	8814	No
FTB 3805D	Net Operating Loss (NOL) Carryover Computation and Limitation – Pierce's Disease	None	Not applicable
FTB 3805E	Installment Sale Income	6252	No
FTB 3805P	Additional Taxes on Qualified Plans (including IRAs) and Other Tax-Favored Accounts	5329	No
FTB 3805Q	Net Operating Loss (NOL) Computation and NOL and Disaster Loss Limitations — Corporations	None	Not applicable
FTB 3805V	Net Operating Loss (NOL) Computation and NOL and Disaster Loss Limitations — Individuals, Estates, and Trusts	None	Not applicable
FTB 3805Z	Enterprise Zone Deduction and Credit Summary	None	Not applicable
FTB 3806	Los Angeles Revitalization Zone Net Operating Loss (NOL) Carryover Deduction	None	Not applicable
FTB 3807	Local Agency Military Base Recovery Area Deduction and Credit Summary	None	Not applicable
FTB 3808	Manufacturing Enhancement Area Credit Summary	None	Not applicable
FTB 3809	Targeted Tax Area Deduction and Credit Summary	None	Not applicable
FTB 3811	Donated Fresh Fruits or Vegetables Credit	None	Not applicable
FTB 3834	Interest Computation Under the Look-Back Method for Completed Long-Term Contracts	8697	No
FTB 3840	California Like-Kind Exchanges	8824	Yes [3]
FTB 3843	Payment Voucher for Fiduciary e-filed Returns	None	Not applicable
FTB 5805	Underpayment of Estimated Tax by Individuals and Fiduciaries	2210	No
FTB 5805F	Underpayment of Estimated Tax by Farmers and Fishermen	2210-F	No
FTB 5806	Underpayment of Estimated Tax by Corporations	2220	No
FTB 5870A	Tax on Accumulation Distribution of Trusts	4970	No
FTB 8453	California e-file Return Authorization for Individuals	8453	No
FTB 8453-BE (PMT)	California Payment for Automatic Extension Authorization for Business Entities	None	Not applicable
FTB 8453-C	California e-file Return Authorization for Corporations	8453-C	No
FTB 8453-EO	California e-file Return Authorization for Exempt Organizations	8453-EO	No
FTB 8453-FID	California e-file Return Authorization for Fiduciaries	8453-FE	No
FTB 8453-FID (PMT)	California Payment for Automatic Extension and Estimate Payment Authorization for Fiduciaries	None	Not applicable
FTB 8453-LLC	California e-file Return Authorization for Limited Liability Companies	None	No
FTB 8453-OL	California Online e-file Return Authorization for Individuals	8453-OL	No
FTB 8453-P	California e-file Return Authorization for Partnerships	8453-PE	No
FTB 8453 (PMT)	California Payment for Automatic Extension and Estimate Payment Authorization for Individuals	None	Not applicable
FTB 8454	e-file Opt-Out Record for Individuals	None	Not applicable
FTB 8455	California e-file Payment Record for Individuals	None	Not applicable

FEDERAL FORM NUMBER	FEDERAL FORM – Title or Description	RELATED CALIFORNIA FORM (FTB FORM unless noted)	MAY USE FEDERAL FORM See Notes
FTB 8455-FID	California e-file Payment Record for Fiduciaries	None	Not applicable
FTB 8879	California e-file Signature Authorization for Individuals	8879	No
FTB 8879-FID	California e-file Signature Authorization for Fiduciaries	8879-F	No
FTB 8879 (PMT)	California Electronic Funds Withdrawal Payment and Signature Authorization for Individuals and Fiduciaries	None	Not applicable

Employment Development Department (EDD) FORMS	CALIFORNIA FORM – Title or Description	RELATED FEDERAL FORM	MAY USE FEDERAL FORM See Notes
DE 1 [2]	Commercial Employer Account Registration and Update Form	SS-4	No
DE 4	Employee's Withholding Allowance Certificate	W-4	Yes
DE 4P	Withholding Certificate for Pension or Annuity Payments	W-4P	Yes
DE 4S	Request for State Income Tax Withholding From Sick Pay	W-4S	Yes
DE 9	Quarterly Contribution Return and Report of Wages	941	No
DE 9C	Quarterly Contribution Return and Report of Wages (Continuation)	941	No

FEDERAL FORM NUMBER	FEDERAL FORM – Title or Description	RELATED CALIFORNIA FORM (FTB FORM unless noted)	MAY USE FEDERAL FORM See Notes
SS-4	Application for Employer Identification Number	DE 1 (EDD Form) [2]	No
T (Timber)	Forest Activity Schedule	None	Yes
W-2	Wage and Tax Statement	None	Yes
W-2G	Certain Gambling Winnings	None	Yes
W-3	Transmittal of Wage and Tax Statements	None	No
W-4	Employee's Withholding Allowance Certificate	DE 4 (EDD Form)	Yes
W-4P	Withholding Certificate for Pension or Annuity Payments	DE 4P (EDD Form)	Yes
W-4S	Request for Federal Income Tax Withholding From Sick Pay	DE 4S (EDD Form)	Yes
W-9	Request for Taxpayer Identification Number and Certification	None	Yes
56	Notice Concerning Fiduciary Relationship	None	Yes
433-D	Installment Agreement	FTB 3567	No
851	Affiliations Schedule	Sch R-7 (100)	No
872	Consent to Extend the Time to Assess Tax	FTB 3570	No
875	Acceptance of Examiner's Findings By a Partnership, Fiduciary, S Corporation or Interest Charge Domestic International Sales Corporation	None	Yes
907	Agreement to Extend the Time to Bring Suit	None	Yes
926	Return by a U.S. Transferor of Property to a Foreign Corporation	None	Yes
941	Employer's Quarterly Federal Tax Return	DE 9 (EDD Form)	No
966	Corporate Dissolution or Liquidation	None	Yes
970	Application to Use LIFO Inventory Method	None	Yes
982	Reduction of Tax Attributes Due to Discharge of Indebtedness (and Section 1082 Basis Adjustment)	None	Yes
990	Return of Organization Exempt from Income Tax	199	No
990 (Sch A)	Public Charity Status and Public Support	199	No
990-EZ	Short Form Return of Organization Exempt from Income Tax	199	No
990-PF	Return of Private Foundation or Section 4947(a)(1) Nonexempt Charitable Trust Treated as a Private Foundation	199	No
990-T	Exempt Organization Business Income Tax Return	109	No
1023	Application for Recognition of Exemption Under Section 501(c)(3) of the Internal Revenue Code	{ FTB 3500 / FTB 3500A	No / No
1023-EZ	Streamlined Application for Recognition of Exemption Under Section 501(c)(3) of the Internal Revenue Code	{ FTB 3500 / FTB 3500A	No / No
1024	Application for Recognition of Exemption Under Section 501(a)	{ FTB 3500 / FTB 3500A	No / No
1040	U.S. Individual Income Tax Return	540 (If SMLLC, get Form 568 Booklet.)	No
Sch A (1040)	Itemized Deductions	None	Yes
Sch B (1040)	Interest and Ordinary Dividends	None	Yes
Sch C (1040)	Profit or Loss From Business	None	Yes
Sch C-EZ (1040)	Net Profit From Business	None	Yes
Sch D (1040)	Capital Gains and Losses	{ Sch D (540) / Sch D (540NR)	No / No
Sch E (1040)	Supplemental Income and Loss	None	Yes
Sch EIC (1040A or 1040)	Earned Income Credit	FTB 3514	No
Sch F (1040)	Profit or Loss From Farming	None	Yes
Sch R (1040)	Credit for the Elderly or the Disabled	Not applicable	Not applicable
1040A	U.S. Individual Income Tax Return	540	No
1040-ES	Estimated Tax for Individuals	540-ES	No
1040EZ	Income Tax Return for Single and Joint Filers With No Dependents	540 2EZ	No
1040NR	U.S. Nonresident Alien Income Tax Return	540NR (Long)	No
1040NR-EZ	U.S. Income Tax Return for Certain Nonresident Aliens With No Dependents	540NR (Short)	No
1040-V	Payment Voucher	None	No
1040X	Amended U.S. Individual Income Tax Return	540X	No

FEDERAL FORM NUMBER	FEDERAL FORM – Title or Description	RELATED CALIFORNIA FORM (FTB FORM unless noted)	MAY USE FEDERAL FORM See Notes
1041	U.S. Income Tax Return for Estates and Trusts	541	No
Sch D (1041)	Capital Gains and Losses	Sch D (541)	No
Sch I (1041)	Alternative Minimum Tax — Estates and Trusts	Sch P (541)	No
Sch J (1041)	Accumulation Distribution for Certain Complex Trusts	Sch J (541)	No
Sch K-1 (1041)	Beneficiary's Share of Income, Deductions, Credits, etc.	Sch K-1 (541)	No
1041-A	U.S. Information Return Trust Accumulation of Charitable Amounts	541-A	No
1041-ES	Estimated Income Tax for Estates and Trusts	541-ES	No
1041-QFT	U.S. Income Tax Return for Qualified Funeral Trusts	541-QFT	No
1041-T	Allocation of Estimated Tax Payments to Beneficiaries	541-T	No
1042	Annual Withholding Tax Return for U.S. Source Income of Foreign Persons	592, 592-F	No
1042-S	Foreign Person's U.S. Source Income Subject to Withholding	592-B	No
1065	U.S. Return of Partnership Income	565	No
Sch D (1065)	Capital Gains and Losses	Sch D (565)	No
Sch K-1 (1065)	Partner's Share of Income, Deductions, Credits, etc.	Sch K-1 (565)	No
1096	Annual Summary and Transmittal of U.S. Information Returns	None	Yes
1098	Mortgage Interest Statement	None	Yes [1]
1099-A	Acquisition or Abandonment of Secured Property	None	Yes [1]
1099-B	Proceeds From Broker and Barter Exchange Transactions	None	Yes [1]
1099-C	Cancellation of Debt	None	Yes [1]
1099-DIV	Dividends and Distributions	None	Yes [1]
1099-G	Certain Government Payments	None	Yes [1]
1099-INT	Interest Income	None	Yes [1]
1099-LTC	Long-Term Care and Accelerated Death Benefits	None	Yes [1]
1099-MISC	Miscellaneous Income	None	Yes [1]
1099-OID	Original Issue Discount	None	Yes [1]
1099-PATR	Taxable Distributions Received From Cooperatives	None	Yes [1]
1099-R	Distributions From Pensions, Annuities, Retirement or Profit-Sharing Plans, IRAs, Insurance Contracts, etc.	None	Yes [1]
1099-S	Proceeds from Real Estate Transactions	None	Yes [1]
1099-SA	Distributions From an HSA, Archer MSA, or Medicare Advantage MSA	None	Yes [1]
1120	U.S. Corporation Income Tax Return	100	No
Sch D (1120)	Capital Gains and Losses	100	No
1120-F	U.S. Income Tax Return of a Foreign Corporation	100	No
1120-FSC	U.S. Income Tax Return of a Foreign Sales Corporation	100	No
1120-H	U.S. Income Tax Return for Homeowners Associations	100	No
1120-IC-DISC	Interest Charge Domestic International Sales Corporation Return	100	No
1120-POL	U.S. Income Tax Return for Certain Political Organizations	100	No
1120-REIT	U.S. Income Tax Return for Real Estate Investment Trusts	100	No
1120-RIC	U.S. Income Tax Return for Regulated Investment Companies	100	No
1120S	U.S. Income Tax Return for an S Corporation	100S	No
Sch D (1120S)	Capital Gains and Losses and Built-In Gains	Sch D (100S)	No
Sch K-1 (1120S)	Shareholder's Share of Income, Deductions, Credits, etc.	Sch K-1 (100S)	No
Sch M-3	Net Income (Loss) Reconciliation for Corporations With Total Assets of $10 Million or More	None	No
Sch UTP	Uncertain Tax Position Statement	None	Yes
1120-W	Estimated Tax for Corporations	100-ES	No
1120X	Amended U.S. Corporation Income Tax Return	100X	No
1125-A	Cost of Goods Sold	100	No
1125-E	Compensation of Officers	100	No
1128	Application to Adopt, Change, or Retain a Tax Year	None	Yes
1138	Extension of Time for Payment of Taxes by a Corporation Expecting a Net Operating Loss Carryback	FTB 3593	No

FEDERAL FORM NUMBER	FEDERAL FORM – Title or Description	RELATED CALIFORNIA FORM (FTB FORM unless noted)	MAY USE FEDERAL FORM See Notes
1310	Statement of Person Claiming Refund Due a Deceased Taxpayer	None	Yes
2106	Employee Business Expenses	None	Yes
2106-EZ	Unreimbursed Employee Business Expenses	None	Yes
2120	Multiple Support Declaration	None	Yes
2210	Underpayment of Estimated Tax by Individuals, Estates and Trusts	FTB 5805	No
2210-F	Underpayment of Estimated Tax by Farmers and Fishermen	FTB 5805F	No
2220	Underpayment of Estimated Tax by Corporations	FTB 5806	No
2350	Application for Extension of Time to File U.S. Income Tax Return	Not applicable	Not applicable
2441	Child and Dependent Care Expenses	FTB 3506	No
2678	Employer/Payer Appointment of Agent	None	Yes
2848	Power of Attorney and Declaration of Representative	FTB 3520	Yes
3115	Application for Change in Accounting Method	None	Yes
3468	Investment Credit	Not applicable	Not applicable
3800	General Business Credit	FTB 3546	No
3903	Moving Expenses	None	Yes
4137	Social Security and Medicare Tax on Unreported Tip Income	Not applicable	Not applicable
4255	Recapture of Investment Credit	Not applicable	Not applicable
4419	Application for Filing Information Returns Electronically (FIRE)	None	Yes
4461	Application for Approval of Master or Prototype or Volume Submitter Defined Contribution Plan	None	Yes
4466	Corporation Application for Quick Refund of Overpayment of Estimated Tax	Not applicable	Not applicable
4506	Request for Copy of Tax Return	FTB 3516	No
4562	Depreciation and Amortization	{ FTB 3885 / FTB 3885A / FTB 3885F (541) / FTB 3885L (568) / FTB 3885P (565)	No / No / No / No / No
4626	Alternative Minimum Tax — Corporations	Sch P (100)	No
4669	Statement of Payments Received	None	Yes
4670	Request for Relief of Payment of Certain Withholding Taxes	None	Yes
4684	Casualties and Thefts	None	Yes
4797	Sales of Business Property	Sch D-1	No
4835	Farm Rental Income and Expenses	None	Yes
4852	Substitute for Form W-2, Wage and Tax Statement, or Form 1099-R, Distributions From Pensions, Annuities, Retirement or Profit-Sharing Plans, IRAs, Insurance Contracts, Etc.	FTB 3525	Yes
4868	Application for Automatic Extension of Time to File U.S. Individual Income Tax Return	Not applicable	Not applicable
4952	Investment Interest Expense Deduction	FTB 3526	No
4970	Tax on Accumulation Distribution of Trusts	FTB 5870A	No
4972	Tax on Lump-Sum Distributions	Sch G-1	No
5227	Split-Interest Trust Information Return	541-B	No
5329	Additional Taxes on Qualified Plans (including IRAs) and Other Tax-Favored Accounts	FTB 3805P	No
5405	Repayment of the First-Time Homebuyer Credit	None	Not applicable
5471	Information Return of U.S. Persons With Respect to Certain Foreign Corporations	None	Yes
5472	Information Return of a 25% Foreign-Owned U.S. Corporation or a Foreign Corporation Engaged in a U.S. Trade or Business	None	Yes
5498	IRA Contribution Information	None	Yes [1]
5754	Statement by Person(s) Receiving Gambling Winnings	None	Yes
5884	Work Opportunity Credit	Not applicable	Not applicable
6198	At-Risk Limitations	None	Yes
6251	Alternative Minimum Tax — Individuals	{ Sch P (540) / Sch P (540NR)	No / No
6252	Installment Sale Income	FTB 3805E	No
6765	Credit for Increasing Research Activities	FTB 3523	No
7004	Application for Automatic Extension of Time To File Certain Business Income Tax, Information, and Other Returns	Not applicable	Not applicable

FEDERAL FORM NUMBER	FEDERAL FORM – Title or Description	RELATED CALIFORNIA FORM (FTB FORM unless noted)	MAY USE FEDERAL FORM See Notes
8023	Elections Under Section 338 for Corporations Making Qualified Stock Purchases	None	Yes
8275	Disclosure Statement	None	Yes
8275-R	Regulation Disclosure Statement	None	Yes
8288	U.S. Withholding Tax Return for Dispositions by Foreign Persons of U.S. Real Property Interests	593	No
8288-A	Statement of Withholding on Dispositions by Foreign Persons of U.S. Real Property Interests	593	No
8288-B	Application for Withholding Certificate for Dispositions by Foreign Persons of U.S. Real Property Interests	593-C	No
8300	Report of Cash Payments Over $10,000 Received in a Trade or Business	None	Yes
8453	U.S. Individual Income Tax Transmittal for an IRS e-file Return	FTB 8453	No
8453-C	U.S. Corporation Income Tax Declaration for an IRS e-file Return	FTB 8453-C	No
8453-EO	Exempt Organization Declaration and Signature for Electronic Filing	FTB 8453-EO	No
8453-FE	U.S. Estate or Trust Declaration for an IRS e-file Return	FTB 8453-FID	No
8453-PE	U.S. Partnership Declaration for an IRS e-file Return	FTB 8453-P	No
8453-S	U.S. S Corporation Income Tax Declaration for an IRS e-file Return	FTB 8453-C	No
8582	Passive Activity Loss Limitations	FTB 3801	No
8582-CR	Passive Activity Credit Limitations	FTB 3801-CR	No
8586	Low-Income Housing Credit	FTB 3521	No
8615	Tax for Certain Children Who Have Unearned Income	FTB 3800	No
8697	Interest Computation Under the Look-Back Method for Completed Long-Term Contracts	FTB 3834	No
8801	Credit for Prior Year Minimum Tax — Individuals, Estates and Trusts	FTB 3510	No
8804	Annual Return for Partnership Withholding Tax (Section 1446)	592, 592-A, 592-F	No
8805	Foreign Partner's Information Statement of Section 1446 Withholding Tax	592-B	No
8810	Corporate Passive Activity Loss and Credit Limitations	FTB 3802	No
8813	Partnership Withholding Tax Payment Voucher (Section 1446)	592-A	No
8814	Parent's Election To Report Child's Interest and Dividends	FTB 3803	No
8821	Tax Information Authorization	FTB 3520	Yes
8822	Change of Address	FTB 3533	Yes
8822-B	Change of Address or Responsible Party - Business	FTB 3533-B	Yes
8824	Like-Kind Exchanges	FTB 3840	Yes [3]
8825	Rental Real Estate Income and Expenses of a Partnership or an S Corporation	None	Yes
8826	Disabled Access Credit	FTB 3548	No
8827	Credit for Prior Year Minimum Tax — Corporations	Sch P (100)	No
8839	Qualified Adoption Expenses	None	Not applicable
8842	Election to Use Different Annualization Periods for Corporate Estimated Tax	None	Yes
8867	Paid Preparer's Earned Income Credit Checklist	FTB 3596	No
8869	Qualified Subchapter S Subsidiary Election	None	Yes
8872	Political Organization Report of Contributions and Expenditures	FTB 3589	No
8879	IRS e-file Signature Authorization	FTB 8879	No
8879-F	IRS e-file Signature Authorization for Form 1041	FTB 8879-FID	No
8886	Reportable Transaction Disclosure Statement	None	Yes
8918	Material Advisor Disclosure Statement	None	Yes
8940	Request for Miscellaneous Determination	None	Not applicable
9465	Installment Agreement Request	FTB 3567	No

Notes

No	California form must be used.
Yes	If there is no difference between California and federal amounts, you may use a copy of the federal form. If there is a difference between California and federal amounts, use the California form. If there is no California form, complete the federal form using California amounts and attach it to your California tax return.
Not applicable	Federal form is not applicable to California tax or California form is not applicable for federal tax.
(1)	Copies of paper information returns (1099 series, 1098, and 5498) filed with the Internal Revenue Service are not required to be filed with the Franchise Tax Board (FTB). However, if California and federal amounts differ, information returns may be attached to Form 1096 and filed with the FTB.
(2)	Form number may vary based on industry-specific registration.
(3)	FTB 3840 is required if California property is exchanged for like-kind property located out of state. If the taxpayer exchanges California property for California property, use federal Form 8824 with California amounts.

INDEX

References are to paragraph (¶) numbers.

CEA